Teresa Pica
Associate Director
Educational Linguistics/TESOL

HANDBOOK OF SECOND LANGUAGE ACQUISITION

HANDBOOK OF SECOND LANGUAGE ACQUISITION

Edited by

William C. Ritchie

Syracuse University

and

Tej K. Bhatia

Syracuse University

ACADEMIC PRESS

San Diego   New York   Boston   London   Sydney   Tokyo   Toronto

Copyright © 1996 by ACADEMIC PRESS, INC.

Academic Press, Inc.
A Division of Harcourt Brace & Company
525 B Street, Suite 1900, San Diego, California 92101-4495

United Kingdom Edition published by
Academic Press Limited
24-28 Oval Road, London NW1 7DX

Library of Congress Cataloging-in-Publication Data

Handbook of second language acquisition / edited by William C.
   Ritchie, Tej K. Bhatia
            p.   cm.
      Includes indexes.
      ISBN 0-12-589042-7
      1. Second language acquisition.   I. Ritchie, William C.
   II. Bhatia, Tej K.
   P118.2.H36   1996
   401'.93--dc20   94-44081
                                                        CIP

PRINTED IN THE UNITED STATES OF AMERICA
96   97   98   99   00   01   MM   9   8   7   6   5   4   3   2   1

To Our Parents:

To Georgia Stanchfield Metcalf
and to the memory of Gorton Ritchie
To the memory of Shri Parma Nand Bhatia
and of Shrimati Krishna Bhatia

CONTENTS

CONTRIBUTORS   xix
ACKNOWLEDGMENTS   xxi
ABBREVIATIONS   xxiii

I **Second Language Acquisition: Introduction, Foundations, and Overview**

William C. Ritchie
Tej K. Bhatia

I. Introduction   1
II. Historical Background and Theoretical Approaches   4
   A. The 1940s and 1950s   5
   B. The 1960s to the 1980s—Theoretical Approaches   6
   C. Some Integrated Models of SLA   16
   D. Summary   18
III. Current Issues in SLA Research   18
   A. Introduction: The Central Questions   18
   B. The Issues   22
   C. Summary   35
IV. The Sections and Chapters of This Volume   35
   A. Part I: Research and Theoretical Issues in Second Language
      Acquisition   35
   B. Part II: Issues of Maturation and Modularity in Second Language
      Acquisition   36
   C. Part III: Second Language Speech and the Influence of the
      First Language   38
   D. Part IV: Research Methodology and Applications   39
   E. Part V: Modality and the Linguistic Environment in Second
      Language Acquisition   39
   F. Part VI: The Neuropsychology of Second Language Acquisition
      and Use   40
   G. Part VII: Language Contact and Its Consequences   40
V. Conclusions   41
   References   42

I RESEARCH AND THEORETICAL ISSUES IN SECOND LANGUAGE ACQUISITION

2 The Logical and Developmental Problems of Second Language Acquisition
Kevin R. Gregg

I. Explanatory Goals of L2 Acquisition Theory: The Logical and
   Developmental Problems   50
II. The Logical Problem of L2 Acquisition: Explaining L2 Competence   52
   A. Why Competence?   53
   B. The Learnability Condition   54
   C. Learnability Considerations in L2 Acquisition   56
   D. The Nature of L2 Competence: Modular versus
      Nonmodular Analyses   57
III. The Developmental Problem: Explaining the Acquisition Process   66
   A. Criteria for an Acquisition Theory   66
   B. The Theoretical Framework Criterion: Interfacing with the
      Logical Problem   67
   C. The Sequence Criterion: Developmental Sequences   68
   D. The Mechanism Criterion   69
IV. Constructing an L2 Acquisition Theory: Prospects and Problems   73
   References   75

II ISSUES OF MATURATION AND MODULARITY IN SECOND LANGUAGE ACQUISITION

3 Universal Grammar and Second Language Acquisition: Current Trends and New Directions
Lydia White

I. Introduction   85
II. Principles and Parameters Theory   85
   A. Principles: C-Command   86
   B. Parameters: Verb Raising   88
III. Principles and Parameters in L2 Acquisition   90
   A. Access to UG: Competence and Acquisition of Competence   91
   B. Perspectives on Principles   94
   C. Perspectives on Parameters   96

IV. Some Current Issues   103
    A. Maturational Effects   103
    B. Near Native-Speaker Competence   105
    C. Exploring Interlanguage Competence   109
V. New Directions   112
    A. Child–Adult Differences   112
    B. Phonology   114
VI. Conclusions   115
    References   116

4 A Parameter-Setting Approach to Second Language Acquisition

Suzanne Flynn

I. Introduction   121
II. Background   123
    A. Universal Grammar and Language Acquisition:
        General Assumptions   123
III. L1 versus L2 Acquisition: The Logical Problem of L2 Acquisition
    and the Full Access Hypothesis   127
IV. Alternative Proposals   129
    A. Methodological Considerations   130
    B. The No Access Hypothesis: General Learning Strategies and
        Analogy as an Account of L2 Learning   131
    C. The Partial Access Hypothesis   133
V. Evidence against the Partial Access Hypothesis and
    for the Full Access Hypothesis   134
    A. New Parameter Settings: The CP Direction Parameter   134
    B. L1 Vacuously Applied Principles   137
    C. Error Data from Adult L2 Acquisition   140
    D. Nontransfer of Language-Specific Aspects   142
    E. Functional Categories   145
    F. Derivative Version of the Partial Access Hypothesis   149
VI. Discussion and Conclusions   150
    References   152

5 Maturation and the Issue of Universal Grammar in Second Language Acquisition

Jacquelyn Schachter

I. Background   159
II. Universal Grammar as a Knowledge Base   161

III. Biology   163
IV. A Critical Period for L1 Acquisition   164
V. A Critical Period for L2 Acquisition   166
VI. Tests of a Principle and a Parameter in Adult L2   174
VII. Child L2 versus Adult L2   179
VIII. Do Principles Mature?   183
IX. Windows of Opportunity   184
X. Conclusion   187
References   188

6 A Functional–Typological Approach to Second Language Acquisition Theory

Fred R. Eckman

I. Introduction   195
II. The Markedness Differential Hypothesis   196
A. Background   196
B. Assumptions Underlying the MDH   198
C. Supporting Evidence   199
D. Evaluation of the MDH   200
E. Problems with the MDH   202
III. The Structure Conformity Hypothesis   204
A. Background   204
B. Assumptions Underlying the SCH   205
C. Supporting Evidence   205
D. Evaluation of the SCH   207
IV. The SCH and Recent Proposals   208
V. Conclusion   209
References   209

7 Information-Processing Approaches to Research on Second Language Acquisition and Use

Barry McLaughlin
Roberto Heredia

I. What Is Information Processing?   213
II. Basic Assumptions of Information-Processing Perspective   214
A. Learning and Automaticity   214
B. Role of Practice   216
C. Restructuring   217
III. Theoretical Options   218

IV. Is Learning a Monolithic Construct? 219
V. Sources of Individual Difference 222
VI. Pedagogical Implications: Instructional Strategies 224
   References 225

8 **Variationist Linguistics and Second Language Acquisition**
Dennis Preston

  I. A Brief History of Language Variation Study 229
 II. Two Models of Variation 230
   A. The Labovian Paradigm 230
   B. The Dynamic Paradigm 240
   C. The Relationship between the Labovian and Dynamic Paradigms 245
III. Recent Trends 246
   A. Objections 246
   B. Current Work 251
   C. The Psycholinguistics of Sociolinguistics in L2 Acquisition 257
   References 263

III SECOND LANGUAGE SPEECH AND THE INFLUENCE OF THE FIRST LANGUAGE

9 **Second Language Speech**
Jonathan Leather
Allan James

  I. Introduction 269
 II. Learner Constraints on the Acquisition of L2 Speech 270
   A. Motivation 270
   B. Social Acceptance and Social Distance 271
   C. Personality Variables 272
   D. Sex 272
   E. Oral and Auditory Capacities 272
III. Perception and Production of L2 Speech Sounds 273
   A. Construction of New Perceptual Categories 273
   B. Production of New Sounds 277
   C. Developmental Interrelation of Perception and Production 281
IV. Developmental Interrelation between L1 and L2 Speech Acquisition 285
   A. Product and Process 285
   B. The Influence of L1 Structure 286

C. The Identification of L2 and L1 Elements   287
D. Processing Strategies and L1 Structural Influence   290
E. The Developmental Dimension   291
F. The Role of Universal Typological Preferences   293
G. Contextual Constraints   295
H. The Contribution of Theoretical Phonology   297
V. Conclusion   299
References   300

10 Second Language Acquisition and Linguistic Theory: The Role of Language Transfer

Susan Gass

I. Introduction   317
II. Language Transfer: An Historical Overview   318
A. Defining Language Transfer   318
B. Contrastive Analysis   319
C. Creative Construction   319
D. The Settling of the Pendulum   320
III. Language Transfer as a Cognitive Activity   321
A. The Scope of Language Transfer Phenomena   321
B. Predicting Language Transfer   324
IV. Language Transfer and UG   329
A. Principles of UG   330
B. UG Parameters   332
C. The Centrality of the NL   334
V. Language Transfer and the Competition Model   335
VI. Effects on Grammars   337
VII. Conclusion   338
References   340

IV RESEARCH METHODOLOGY AND APPLICATIONS

11 Issues in Second Language Acquisition Research: Examining Substance and Procedure

David Nunan

I. Introduction   349
II. Historical Background   349
III. Substantive Issues in L2 Acquisition Research   350
A. Creative Construction   351
B. Other Issues   351

IV. Methodological Issues in L2 Acquisition Research   359
    A. Qualitative and Quantitative Research   359
    B. Longitudinal versus Cross-Sectional Research   364
    C. Experimental versus Naturalistic Data Collection   365
    D. Elicited versus Naturalistic Data   366
    E. Role Playing   369
V. Conclusion   369
    References   371

12 The Use of Acceptability Judgments in Second Language Acquisition Research

Antonella Sorace

I. Introduction   375
II. The Nature of Linguistic Acceptability: General Issues   376
    A. Validity: What Does an Acceptability Judgment Test Measure?   376
    B. Reliability: Why Do Informants Produce Inconsistent
       Judgments?   380
    C. Acceptability Hierarchies and Universal Grammar   382
III. Linguistic Acceptability in Nonnative Languages   384
    A. Validity and Reliability of Nonnative Acceptability Judgments   385
    B. Indeterminacy in IL Grammars   386
IV. The Empirical Measurement of Linguistic Acceptability   391
    A. The Elicitation of Acceptability Judgments   391
    B. Types of Judgment Scales   393
    C. Types of Responses: Absolute versus Comparative Judgments   395
    D. Applying the Psychophysical Paradigm:
       Magnitude Estimation of Linguistic Acceptability   400
V. Conclusions   404
    References   405

V MODALITY AND THE LINGUISTIC ENVIRONMENT IN SECOND LANGUAGE ACQUISITION

13 The Role of the Linguistic Environment in Second Language Acquisition

Michael H. Long

I. Some Possible Roles for the Environment   413
II. Foreigner Talk Discourse and Positive Evidence   414
III. The Insufficiency of Comprehensible Input   421

IV. Input and Cognitive Processing   426
   A. Attention, Awareness, and Focus on Form   426
   B. Negative Evidence   430
V. Negotiation for Meaning and Acquisition   445
   A. The Role of Conversation   445
   B. The Interaction Hypothesis   451
   References   454

14 The Acquisition of English Syntax by Deaf Learners
Gerald P. Berent

I. Deafness and Language Acquisition   469
II. Deaf Learners' Knowledge of Specific English Structures   472
   A. Sentence Complexity and Parts of Speech   472
   B. The TSA Structures   473
   C. Nine Syntactic Structures in Context   480
   D. Clausal and Nonclausal Structures   482
   E. Infinitive Complement Interpretation   483
III. A Framework for Explaining Deaf Learners' Syntactic Knowledge 484
   A. Theoretical Background   484
   B. Young Hearing Children's Phrasal Structures   488
   C. Deaf Learners' Acquisition of English Syntax   489
IV. Learnability and Deaf Learners' Syntactic Knowledge   494
   A. Binding Principles and Learnability   494
   B. Movement Rules and Learnability   497
   C. *Be* as a Raising Verb   499
V. Conclusion   500
   References   502

VI THE NEUROPSYCHOLOGY OF SECOND LANGUAGE ACQUISITION AND USE

15 Neurolinguistics of Second Language Acquisition and Use
Loraine K. Obler
Sharon Hannigan

I. Introduction   509
II. The Process of L2 Acquisition   511
   A. A Critical or Sensitive Period   511
   B. Factors Involved in Successful Postpubertal L2 Acquisition 512
III. Lateral Dominance for Language in Bilinguals   513
IV. Language Breakdown   516

V. Future Directions   519
References   520

VII LANGUAGE CONTACT AND ITS CONSEQUENCES

16 The Primacy of Aspect in First and Second Language Acquisition: The Pidgin–Creole Connection

Roger W. Andersen
Yasuhiro Shirai

I. Introduction   527
II. Tense and Aspect   530
  A. Grammatical Aspect versus Inherent Lexical Aspect   530
  B. The Vendlerean Four-Way Classification   531
III. Acquisition of Tense and Aspect   533
  A. L1 Acquisition   533
  B. L2 Acquisition   543
IV. The Distributional Bias Hypothesis   548
  A. Introduction   548
  B. Distributional Bias Studies   549
V. A Prototype Account   555
  A. Prototype Theory   555
  B. Tense and Aspect Morphology as a Prototype Category   555
VI. Summary and Discussion   559
  A. Description   559
  B. Explanation   560
References   562

17 Bilingualism

Suzanne Romaine

I. Introduction   571
  A. Definitions of Bilingualism   571
  B. Relationship between Bilingualism and Other Research Fields 572
II. Bilingual Speech Communities   573
  A. The Sociolinguistic Composition of Multilingual Countries 574
  B. Domains of Language Use   576
  C. Diglossia and Bilingualism   577
  D. Language Maintenance and Shift   580
III. Bilingual Individuals   583
  A. Measuring Bilingualism   584
  B. Problems with Measuring Bilingualism   588

C. Borrowing and Interference as an Individual and Community
   Phenomenon   589
IV. Bilingualism and Education   592
   A. Bilingualism and School Achievement   592
   B. Types of Bilingual Education Programs   593
   C. Bilingual Education in an International Perspective   596
   D. Legal Implications Arising from Legislation
      on Bilingual Education   597
   E. Reactions to Bilingual Education   597
V. Attitudes toward Bilingualism   598
   A. Negative and Positive Attitudes toward Bilingualism   598
   B. Attitudes toward Code Switching   599
VI. Conclusion   600
   References   601

18 Primary Language Attrition in the Context of Bilingualism

Herbert W. Seliger

I. Defining Primary Language Attrition   605
II. Primary Language Attrition and L2 or Foreign Language Loss   607
   A. The Problem of Establishing Baseline Knowledge   607
   B. The Manner and Context of Acquisition   608
III. Primary Language Attrition and Other Forms of Language Mixing   610
IV. L1 Attrition and Linguistic Theory   614
   A. Performance or Competence   614
   B. External Sources of Evidence   616
   C. Internal Sources of Evidence   616
   D. An Example of a Universal Principle
      in Primary Language Attrition   617
   E. Redundancy Reduction as an Inevitable Process   623
V. Conclusion: Context Dependence, Bilingualism, and
   Primary Language Attrition   623
   References   625

19 Bilingual Language Mixing, Universal Grammar, and Second Language Acquisition

Tej K. Bhatia
William C. Ritchie

I. Introduction   627
II. Definitions of CM and CS, Borrowing, and
   Other Related Phenomena   629

A. Matrix and Embedded Language   631
B. Borrowing and CM and CS   632
C. CM and CS and Pidgin and Creoles   634
D. CM and CS and Diglossia   634
III. Types of CM and CS   635
IV. Constraints on CM and CS   638
A. Is CM a Random Phenomenon?   639
B. The Search for Universals   640
C. Formal Constraints on CM   640
D. Theoretical Models and Constraints on CM   645
V. Semantics of CS and CM   657
VI. Sociopsychological, Linguistic and Pragmatic Motivations
for CM and CS   659
A. Linguistic and Pragmatic Functions   659
B. Nonlinguistic (Sociopsychological) Functions   662
VII. Attitudes toward CM and CS   667
VIII. Polyglot Aphasia and CM and CS   670
IX. CM and CS and Language Acquisition   674
X. Problems   679
A. Theoretical and Analytical Problems   680
B. Methodological Problems   681
XI. Conclusions   682
References   683

GLOSSARY   689

AUTHOR INDEX   707

SUBJECT INDEX   723

CONTRIBUTORS

Numbers in parentheses indicate the pages on which the authors' contributions begin.

Roger W. Anderson (527), Department of Applied Linguistics, University of California at Los Angeles, Los Angeles, California 90024

Gerald P. Berent (469), National Technical Institute for the Deaf at Rochester Institute of Technology, Rochester, New York 14623

Tej K. Bhatia (1, 627), Linguistics/Cognitive Science Program, Syracuse University, Syracuse, New York 13244

Fred R. Eckman (195), Department of Linguistics, University of Wisconsin–Milwaukee, Milwaukee, Wisconsin 53211

Suzanne Flynn (121), Departments of Linguistics and Philosophy and Foreign Languages and Literatures, Massachusetts Institute of Technology, Cambridge, Massachusetts 02139

Susan Gass (317), English Language Center, Michigan State University, East Lansing, Michigan 48824

Kevin R. Gregg (49), St. Andrew's University, Momoyama Gakuin Daigaku, Izumi, Osaka 588, Japan

Sharon Hannigan (509), Boston University School of Medicine and The Harvard Institute for English Language Programs, Boston, Massachusetts 02116

Roberto Heredia (213), Department of Psychology, University of California, Santa Cruz, California 95060

Allan James (269), Institut für Anglistik und Amerikanistik, University of Klagenfurt, Klagenfurt, Austria

Jonathan Leather (269), Department of English, University of Amsterdam, 1012 VT Amsterdam, The Netherlands

Michael H. Long (413), Department of English as a Second Language, University of Hawaii at Manoa, Honolulu, Hawaii 96822

Barry McLaughlin (213), Department of Psychology, University of California, Santa Cruz, California 95060

David Nunan (349), Department of Applied Linguistics, University of Hong Kong

Loraine K. Obler (509), Department of Speech and Hearing, City University of New York Graduate School, New York, New York 10036

Dennis Preston (229), Department of Languages and Linguistics, Michigan State University, East Lansing, Michigan 48824

William C. Ritchie (1, 627), Linguistics/Cognitive Science Program, Syracuse University, Syracuse, New York 13244

Suzanne Romaine (571), Merton College, Oxford OX1 4JD, United Kingdom

Jacquelyn Schachter (159), Department of Linguistics, University of Oregon, Eugene, Oregon 97403

Herbert W. Seliger (605), Department of Linguistics, Queens College and Graduate School, CUNY, Flushing, New York 11366

Yasuhiro Shirai (527), Daito Bunka University, Saitama 335, Japan

Antonella Sorace (375), Department of Applied Linguistics, University of Edinburgh, Edinburgh EH8 9LN, United Kingdom

Lydia White (85), Department of Linguistics, McGill University, Montreal, Quebec H3A 1G5, Canada

ACKNOWLEDGMENTS

We have contracted many debts in developing this volume. We are grateful first and foremost to the contributors, without whom, after all, the volume would have been impossible and without whose cooperation and assistance this undertaking would have been considerably less pleasant than it was. Their patience in waiting for the final product has been nothing short of remarkable.

We gratefully acknowledge the support of the Department of Languages, Literatures, and Linguistics, the College of Arts and Sciences, and the Office of the Vice-Chancellor for Academic Affairs of Syracuse University. Ritchie is particularly grateful for a one-semester leave of absence from the University to complete the work on the volume. Our heartfelt thanks are also due to Harold Jones, the Chair of LLL, for his help in many respects—tangible and otherwise.

The volume benefited immeasurably from the advice and counsel of a number of valued colleagues in the field—most prominently Suzanne Flynn, Susan Gass, Michael Long, Barbara Lust, Teresa Pica, Dennis Preston, and Lydia White. In addition, the following have offered both moral support and valuable advice in the development of this work: Roger W. Andersen, Elizabeth Bates, Jerry Berent, Derek Bickerton, Noam Chomsky, Kevin Gregg, Jackie Schachter, Dan Slobin, and Ken Wexler.

We have been fortunate to have friends, colleagues, and teachers like Braj and Yamuna Kachru, James Gair, Suzanne Flynn, Barbara Lust, Hans Hock, Manindra K. Verma, Rajeshwari Pandharipande, and S. N. Sridhar. Their support, inspiration, and scholarship mean a great deal to us and have directly influenced this work.

We are grateful as well for the professional assistance and Job-like patience of the staff at Academic Press—particularly the Acquisitions and Production Editors for the book, Nikki Fine and Jackie Garrett, respectively.

Finally, we could not have completed the work without the constant support of our families: Laurie, Jane, and Peter; Shobha, Kanika, and Ankit. Thanks.

William C. Ritchie
Tej K. Bhatia

ABBREVIATIONS

A	Adjective	DSP	Dual Structure Principle
Adv	Adverb	EB	early bilingual
Agr	Agreement	EC	Equivalence Constraint
Agr^0	Head of Agreement Phrase	ECP	Empty Category Principle
AgrP	Agreement Phrase	EFL	English as a foreign
AH	Accessibility Hierarchy		language
ASL	American Sign Language	EL	Embedded Language
C	Complementizer *or*	ESL	English as a second
	consonant		language
C^0	Head of Complementizer	F/T	functional/typological
	Phrase	FDH	Fundamental Difference
CAH	Contrastive Analysis		Hypothesis
	Hypothesis	FHC	Functional Head Constraint
CED	Constraint on Extraction	FL	foreign language
	Domains	FMC	Free Morpheme Constraint
CM	Code mixing	FT	foreigner talk
COMP	Complementizer	FTD	foreigner talk discourse
CP	Complementizer Phrase	GB	Government Binding
CPH	Critical Period Hypothesis	GC	Government Constraint
CS	Code switching	GCP	Governing Category
D	Determiner		Parameter
D^0	Head of Determiner Phrase	GT_a	adult's (tacit) grammatical
DBH	Distributional Bias		theory
	Hypothesis	I	Inflection
DO	Direct Object	I^0	I-zero (head of an IP)
DP	Determiner Phrase	IL	interlanguage

ILG	interlanguage grammar	PET	positron emission
ILS$_u$	ultimately attained		tomography
	interlanguage system	PLD	primary linguistic data
INFL	Inflection	PNPD	punctual–nonpunctual
IO	Indirect Object		distinction
IP	Inflection Phrase	POA	Primacy of Aspect
JSL	Japanese as a second	Q	Quantifier
	language	Q^0	Head of Quantifier Phrase
L1	first language	QP	Quantifier Phrase
L2	second language	RE	reflexive external
LAD	language acquisition device	RL	reflexive long
LB	late bilingual	RP	Received Pronunciation
MDH	Markedness Differential	RS	reflexive short
	Hypothesis	S	Sentence
ML	Matrix Language	SAV	Subject–Adverb–Verb
MLAT	Modern Language Aptitude	SCH	Structural Conformity
	Test		Hypothesis
MLF	Matrix Language-Frame	SLA	second language acquisition
MLH	Matrix Language	SLM	Speech Learning Model
	Hypothesis	SMP	System Morpheme
MOP	Morpheme-Order Principle		Principle
MUP	Morphological Uniformity	SO	Subject–Object
	Principle	SOV	Subject–Object–Verb
MV	main Verb	SP	Subset Principle
N	Noun	SPD	state-process distinction
NEG	negative element	Spec	Specifier
Neg	Negative	SS	Subject–Subject
NegP	Negative Phrase	SVAO	Subject–Verb–Adverb–
NL	native language		Object
NNS	nonnative speaker	SVO	Subject–Verb–Object
NP	Noun Phrase	T	Tense
NPAH	Noun Phrase Accessibility	T/V	Tu/Vous
	Hierarchy	TL	target language
NS	native speaker	TNS	Tense
Num	Number	TP	Tense Phrase
OM	Direct Object Marker	TSA	Test of Syntactic Ability
OO	Object–Object	UEAPP	Unique External Argument
OP	Operating Principle		Proto-principle
OS	Object–Subject	UG	Universal Grammar
OV	Object–Verb	UP	Uniqueness Principle
P	Preposition	V	Verb *or* vowel

VO	Verb–Object
VOT	voice onset time
VP	Verb Phrase
X^0	X-zero (head of an XP)
XP	X Phrase
ZISA	Zweitsprachenerwerb

Italienischer und Spanischer Arbeiter (second language acquisition of Italian and Spanish workers)

CHAPTER 1

SECOND LANGUAGE ACQUISITION: INTRODUCTION, FOUNDATIONS, AND OVERVIEW

William C. Ritchie and Tej K. Bhatia

I. INTRODUCTION

The phenomena of second (third, fourth, etc.) language acquisition (SLA) and use and the interpretation of these phenomena have come to occupy an important place in the development of our understanding of the human capacity for language. By SLA we mean the acquisition of a language after the native language has already become established in the individual. The second language (L2) learner thus differs from the first language (L1) learner in two critical ways: (a) the L2 learner begins the process of acquisition at a time when he or she has matured past the age when the L1 is normally acquired, and (b) the L2 learner has a language system in place.

Because ethical considerations preclude the forced delay of L1 acquisition and the number of L2 learners in the world at any given time is considerable, SLA provides the most extensive source of evidence concerning the effects of the prior maturation of the language learner on language acquisition. In particular, the widely observed fact that adults seldom attain nativelike mastery of an L2 whereas children generally do achieve such mastery (see Larsen-Freeman & Long, 1991; and Gass & Selinker, 1994, for review) has led to the assumption in SLA research, reflected in the contributions to this volume, that the investigation of adult SLA can shed greater light on the effects of maturation than can the study of child SLA.

1

Hence, the theoretical questions in the study of SLA have centered on acquisition by adults rather than children.

The question of the influence of the L2 learner's L1 on both the course and result of SLA was long considered the most central issue in the study of SLA (if not the only one) and remains of signal importance. Though comprehensive explanations for the phenomenon of "transfer" from the L1 to the L2 (as for the apparent effects of maturation) are still in the offing, much progress has been made in the investigation of the phenomena.

Overall, advances in the theory-driven study of SLA over the last fifteen to twenty years have put SLA research in a better position than ever before to make a genuine contribution to our general understanding of language, its use, and its acquisition, making this a propitious time to analyze the direction and patterns of this research.

The **conceptual foundations** of SLA research have received increasing attention in recent years as the field takes its place as a branch of basic research in the language sciences. Debate concerning foundational questions has already led to a considerably sharpened focus in the field, and much more discussion is to be expected in the future. The present chapter as well as chapter 2 by Gregg (this volume), which form part I of this volume (Research and Theoretical Issues in the Study of Second Language Acquisition), address these issues.

The study of the cognitive capacities and abilities that underlie SLA and L2 use has recently seen major advances within a number of different **theoretical approaches** in the field, including those of generative and functional–typological (F/T) frameworks as well as information processing and variationist approaches, as represented in section II of this volume (Issues of Maturation and Modularity in Second Language Acquisition). For example, the increase in specificity and explanatory power in grammatical theory provided by Chomsky's (1981) formulation of Universal Grammar (UG) as a system of principles and parameters and the development of this proposal in the form of government-binding (GB) theory—to which we return below—has been a major source of stimulation in SLA research conducted within the generative framework over the last fifteen years. As research on SLA continues in the principles-and-parameters framework in the future under the Minimalist Program (Chomsky, 1993), we can expect it to build on the empirical results already obtained in that framework. Empirical work in the generative framework is addressed by White, Flynn, and Schachter, (chaps. 3, 4, and 5, respectively). Each of these chapters takes a different position on the question of the effects of maturation on the capacity for acquisition. Eckman (chap. 6) surveys recent work in the F/T framework, and McLaughlin and Heredia (chap. 7) examine research on SLA that adopts the information-processing approach. Finally, Preston (chap. 8) examines variationist approaches to the study of SLA.

The important issue of **the influence of the learner's L1** in SLA is addressed by Gass (chap. 10) and a survey of research on L2 speech, where L1 influence plays a major role, is given by Leather and James (chap. 9). These two chapters make up part III (Second Language Speech and the Influence of the First Language).

Similarly, the current extensive consideration of the linguistic environment in the process and result of SLA has led to a more specific understanding of those aspects of **linguistic input** that facilitate development of the L2 than had previously existed. This research has addressed such issues as the effects of modified speech, positive and negative evidence, and negotiation of meaning on the process and results of acquisition. In addition to the effects of the linguistic environment in "normal" cases of SLA, there is a growing body of research on the acquisition of what are effectively L2s in conditions of relative poverty of input—specifically, the acquisition by the deaf of spoken languages on the basis of many different kinds of input. This research provides yet another rich empirical domain in which the study of language acquisition has shown recent advances. These topics are covered in part V (Modality and the Linguistic Environment in Second Language Acquisition), which contains Long's (chap. 13) exhaustive treatment of the role of the environment in SLA and Berent's (chap. 14) review of the acquisition of English by the hearing impaired, a case of acquisition with severely limited input.

Since the last comprehensive review of work on the **neuropsychology of SLA and use** (Albert & Obler, 1978), the field has moved beyond the question of lateral dominance for the languages of a bilingual or polyglot to consideration of differential organization within the left hemisphere, among other matters. This research has benefited from the development of new brain-mapping techniques in the study of language and the brain, including measures of evoked potential and the positron emission tomography (PET) scan. This work is reported by Obler and Hannigan in chapter 15, which constitutes part VI (The Neuropsychology of Second Language Acquisition and Use).

Interesting questions related to SLA arise when one considers the consequences of **language contact;** several issues have received concerted research attention in recent years. First, studies of pidginization and creolization continue to contribute valuable empirical observations and insights to the understanding of the language acquisition phenomena. Andersen and Shirai (chap. 16) include reference to the processes of pidginization and creolization in their treatment of the acquisition of verb morphology in relation to tense and aspect. Second, grammatical competence under L1 attrition in bilinguals shows many of the same properties as grammatical competence at the stages of SLA. The study of attrition is thus of considerable interest to investigators of SLA as well, and Seliger (chap. 18) provides an overview and analysis of L1 attrition. Third, the study of bilingualism in the individual and society provides a context for research in all of these areas; Romaine (chap. 17) surveys work on bilingualism. Lastly, recent research in language mixing (code-mixing and code-switching) has revealed not only new evidence for a number of features of current grammatical theory but also provides a site for the testing of claims about L2 grammatical competence; Bhatia and Ritchie (chap. 19) investigate research in this area. These four chapters make up part VII (Language Contact and Its Consequences).

The research questions in the field have become more specific and varied, as has the **research methodology** used to explore these questions. These new, rich methods have created considerable controversy; in fact, some of the most hotly contested issues in the field concern the nature of the data used to test claims and what these data do or do not reveal about the capacities of L2 learners. The study of grammatical competence alone has engendered controversies about the effects of grammaticality judgments, elicited imitation, free production, and many other forms of data on specific claims about competence. When other areas of SLA research are considered, the issues' complexity increases considerably. In part IV (Research Methodology and Applications), Nunan (chap. 11) discusses developments in research methodology in L2 in general, and Sorace (chap. 12) covers issues in the use of acceptability judgments in L2 research. Although the treatment of research methodology in this volume is concentrated in these two chapters, such issues are addressed in other chapters as well—including the present one.

The remainder of this chapter is devoted to a treatment of the historical progression in the study of SLA and use (section II), an overview of the central issues in the study of SLA, and a discussion of the contributions to this volume, its organization, and its salient features (section IV).

II. HISTORICAL BACKGROUND AND THEORETICAL APPROACHES

Like many areas of "pure" empirical research, the study of SLA had its origins in attempts to solve practical problems. In fact, until quite recently, research in this area was widely regarded as falling entirely within applied linguistics, and many still see the primary motivation for this research as that of contributing directly to the solution of the complex and socially important problems surrounding foreign and L2 instruction. However, a large and growing body of research addresses theoretical questions independent of their practical significance, and it is this and other similarly motivated research that is the focus of this volume. As this work is broadened and deepened, we can expect it to provide an even firmer basis for the solution of practical problems; however, we will not address such problems any further in this volume.

As suggested above, many important developments have taken place in SLA research over the last fifteen to twenty years; nonetheless, much progress toward the formulation and investigation of theoretical questions in the study of SLA had already been made in the 1960s and 1970s beyond the work of the previous decades. One can divide the recent history of the study of SLA into two periods:

Bellugi-Klima, 1996; for SLA, e.g., Cazden, Cancino, 1975, and Wode, 1981). Second, the L1 order of acqui-
rphemes in English such as -ing (as in John is go-ing), t-tense morpheme -ed, and so on—found to be constant
's work (Brown, 1973)—was compared with the L2 e same types of morphemes in the SLA of English (see w; see also Nunan, chap. 11, this volume, for further e-order research).

luence that L1 acquisition research of the 1960s had on research is to be found most clearly and influentially in 7) proposed that properties of L2 learners' language that lt NSs should be considered not simply as "errors" but ive processes underlying the learner's behavior parallel in the investigation of child L1 acquisition. Selinker the L2 learner's linguistic behavior justifies the claim art by a language system, an interlanguage system (IL om both the learner's L1 and the adult native system of (1976) proposed that the IL system has a grammatical an interlanguage grammar (ILG). Adjemian claimed mar in the same sense that the adult NS has a grammar, pirical investigation the question of the exact character n, Adjemian hypothesized that ILGs are constrained by ummatical structure just as adult native grammars are. major shift in the generative research program occurred introduction of the principles-and-parameters frame-ecall that a grammatical theory is interpretable as an etic endowment, shared across the species. For empiri-zed grammatical theory must be so formulated as to s under which acquisition takes place. Any proposed be broad enough to specify the full range of possible ause any child can acquire any language) and yet must account for both the speed with which children attain e grammar and the uniformity of the resulting system

neters framework attempts to reconcile the tension be-ctiveness requirements on UG. Within this framework, tem of principles of all adult native grammars in some y in how these principles apply to a particular adult with respect to a given principle takes the form of a one of two or more values, each value determining a f the particular adult native grammar. One parameter ssed in the literature is Pollock's (1989) verb-raising es the differences in the placement of verbs in French

"early" developments from the 1940s and 1950s to later developments of the 1960s through the 1980s. It was during the latter period that the theoretical approaches to SLA represented in part II of the volume developed, and so it is appropriate to trace their histories briefly at this point.[1]

A. The 1940s and 1950s

Until the mid-1960s, organized concern for L2 phenomena was dominated by attempts to adduce implications for language teaching from the then-current behaviorist thinking in experimental psychology and American structuralist linguistics (Fries, 1945; Lado, 1957; Rivers, 1964).[2] The central task of the (descriptive) linguist at that time was to construct descriptions of natural languages where the description of a language was understood to consist of a set of inductive generalizations about the utterances in a corpus gathered from the natural speech of an adult native speaker (NS) (or speakers) of the language under investigation (Harris, 1951). Beyond considerations of accuracy of correspondence with the observed data, language descriptions were considered justified or not on the basis of whether they accorded with a general set of inductive procedures, in turn justified on the basis of their "success" in determining suitable ("compact," revealing) descriptions of previously described languages. Other than the often-voiced assumption that the observed generalizations were somehow the product of an underlying "habit structure" (e.g., Bloomfield, 1933; Harris, 1954), no attempt was made to provide specific explanations for these generalizations.[3]

With regard to the study of SLA at this time, on the basis of the observation that many features of the learner's behavior in the L2 resembled his or her L1 (e.g., "foreign accent"), it was proposed (Fries, 1945; Lado, 1957) that the comparison of a description of the learner's L1 with a description of the L2 (a "contrastive analysis") would allow accurate predictions of L1 influence in L2 behavior and, hence, provide important information for the design of language instruction. However, in addition to the empirical failures of contrastive analysis (see, e.g., Dulay & Burt, 1973, for an early critique), the fact that the linguistic descriptions involved had no genuine explanatory content rendered the value of contrastive analysis (in the form described here) of questionable value in

---

[1] The brief remarks on the history of research on SLA provided here are of necessity severely limited in scope and depth. They are restricted to the thinking about L2 phenomena in the 1950s through the 1980s that lead up to the recent work reviewed in this volume. (For further discussion of the recent history of SLA, see Newmeyer & Weinberger, 1988; Gass & Selinker, 1994.)

[2] For a history of American structuralist linguistics in relation to later developments in linguistic theory in the United States, see Newmeyer, 1986, particularly chap. 1.

[3] In fact, the goal of explanation was explicitly rejected by some. In an often-quoted statement, Martin Joos, a linguist of that time, wrote "Children want explanations and there is a child in each of us; descriptivism makes a virtue of not pampering that child" (Joos, 1958, p. 96).

providing a genuine understanding of L1 influence on L2 behavior even when its predictions appeared to be true.[4]

B. The 1960s to the 1980s—Theoretical Approaches

We turn now to the more recent work that has given the field its present character. We will first look critically at the history of a number of current approaches to the study of SLA that are, in fact, represented by the work reviewed in chapters 3 through 8 of this volume. We then look at some related work done in the 1960s and 1970s on the neuropsychological, social psychological, and research methodological issues in the study of SLA.

The Generative Approach: Universal Grammar and the Principles-and-Parameters Framework

Chomsky's (1955/1975, 1957, 1965) methodological decision to interpret a description of the form of a particular language (in his terminology, a *grammar*) as an empirical hypothesis about the NS's tacit grammatical knowledge of the language (that is, about the NS's *grammatical competence*) radically altered the relationship between research on the structure of particular languages on one hand and the study of language use on the other. Similarly, his reinterpretation of the general procedures for justifying linguistic descriptions as an empirical claim about the L1 learner's tacit knowledge of the universal principles of grammatical structure (that is, as a theory of grammars or a *grammatical theory*) changed in a fundamental way the relationship between research on the general principles of linguistic structure and the study of L1 acquisition.

Under this mentalistic conception of the goals of linguistic research, the grammar of a language—conceived of as a system of rules central to the speaker or hearer's interpretation of speech utterances in the language—became the main element in the explanation of linguistic behavior (or *performance*) in that particular language. Likewise, a grammatical theory—understood as making claims about an aspect of the human genetic endowment—became the central component in the explanation of the facts of language acquisition. In particular, a theory of the grammars of adult NSs—UG—was to become an essential element in the explanation of the facts of L1 acquisition.

As is traditional, we will use the term *grammar* in this chapter in a systematically ambiguous way to refer either to the language user's system of tacit grammatical knowledge of a particular language or to the linguist's hypothesis about

---

[4]For further discussion of the notion of contrastive analysis in this and other forms, see chaps. 6, 9, 10, and 11 of this volume. See also Gass and Selinker (1992, 1994) for additional recent discussion. It is worth noting that the explanation of specific instances of L1 influence in the perception of L2 utterances was part and parcel of the database of phonological theory in the work of the Prague School of linguistics and those influenced by it. (See, e.g., Polivanov, 1931; Trubetzkoy, 1969/1958.)

that system. Analogously, we will use to the language acquirer's system of g grammatical structure or to the lingui tematically ambiguous use of the term back at least to Chomsky (1965).[5] We a widespread practice in linguistics as volume.

Our use of the term grammatical theo be less familiar than the analogous usa terpretation of a grammatical theory as knowledge of grammatical structure j Chomsky, 1955/1975, for discussion); to distinguish between the general noti and the specific grammatical theory tha mars (i.e., UG), because the study of s acknowledge the possibility of gramma ti even remaining within the generative fr

Chomsky's proposals shifted the go lation of inductive generalizations abo equ and use to the search for theoretical ex ons them "as manifestations of entities an er phenomena], as it were" (Hempel, 19 of theory construction in the natural sc a standard features of theorizing in the n tensive idealization, and the view that but, rather, serves to adjudicate among

Early work on the process of L1 gram—particularly that conducted in and his colleagues (summarized in B in two major respects. First, the empir a comparing the processes of L1 and important, it introduced the notion learner at a given stage of acquisition from adult native behavior in the sam by a system of rules and principles (ferent in various ways from) the gram

The first kind of influence took two was compared with that of L1 Engl interrogative structures, which had b

---

[5]Chomsky (1986) proposed the term *I(nte* matical knowledge, retaining the term *gramm*

and English as shown in examples (1)–(4) below, adapted from examples (7)–(10) in White (chap. 3, this volume).

(1) a. * John *likes* **not** Mary.
     b. Jean (n')*aime* **pas** Marie.
         Jean   likes not Marie
     c. John does **not** *like* Mary.
(2) a. * *Likes* **she** John?
     b. *Aime* -t-**elle** Jean?
         likes   she Jean
     c. Does **she** *like* John?
(3) a. * John *watches* **often** television.
     b. Jean *regarde* **souvent** la télévision.
         Jean watches often   the television
     c. Mary **often** *watches* television.
     d. * Marie **souvent** *regarde* télévision.
(4) a. * My friends *like* **all** Mary.
     b. Mes amis *aiment* **tous** Marie.
         my friends like   all Marie
     c. My friends **all** *like* Mary.
     d. * Mes amis **tous** *aiment* Marie.
         my friends all   like   Marie

Note that for each *a/b* pair, in which the main verb (italicized) appears to the *left* of one of the elements in boldface (the negative element *not/pas,* the subject, a time adverb, or the quantifier *all/tous,* in [1] through [4], respectively) the French construction is well formed, whereas the corresponding English construction is not. Similarly, where the main verb appears to the *right* of the boldface element in corresponding sentences (the *c* and the *d* examples), the English form is well formed, the French is not. Pollock's hypothesis was that the position of the main verb in English is its underlying position, whereas in French the verb has been moved over the element represented in boldface. Under this hypothesis this cluster of differences between English and French is determined by a single difference in the verb morphology of English and French—a single parameter that is set in one of its values for English and in its other value for French.[6] Nonetheless, the grammars of both English and French are constrained by the principles of UG.

In the process of L1 acquisition, then, each parameter is set in a value on the basis of some specific (in fact, narrowly circumscribed) feature of the input to which the acquirer is exposed. Because the input required to fix a parameter in one of its values is limited and the consequences of setting the value of the parameter are extensive, the framework allows a solution in principle to the problem of the speed with which L1 acquisition proceeds.

[6]See chaps. 3 (White) and 14 (Berent), this volume, for further discussion and examples.

The greater restrictiveness and specificity of the principles-and-parameters framework over previous proposals regarding the form and content of UG make it a more suitable basis than previous proposals for the study of acquisition in general and SLA in particular. The major impact on research in SLA has been to allow the formulation of the central issues in terms of this highly specific and far-reaching set of proposals. Chapters 2 (Gregg), 3 (White), 4 (Flynn), and 5 (Schachter) are dedicated specifically to SLA work in the generative framework, and chapters 8 (Preston), 10 (Gass), 12 (Sorace), 13 (Long), 14 (Berent), 18 (Seliger), and 19 (Bhatia and Ritchie) provide further discussion.

The syntactic and morphological SLA research within the principles-and-parameters framework that is discussed in this volume is based on the GB theory of syntax (see, e.g., Chomsky, 1981, 1986). The influence of Chomsky's more recent work within the principles-and-parameters framework—that of the economy framework (Chomsky, 1991) and the minimalist program (Chomsky, 1993)—has yet to be felt in SLA research. However, as noted above, the research discussed here is certain to serve as the empirical basis for developments in the field as such influence grows in the future.

The Functional–Typographical Framework

Another productive program of SLA research—one based on typological studies of variation among languages in the tradition of Greenberg (1963/1966)—also took shape during the 1960s and 1970s: the F/T framework. Linguistic research within this tradition seeks universal empirical generalizations about the structure of adult native languages. Explanations of these generalizations are then sought in functional and formal features of the elements involved. An example that appears in a number of the chapters in this volume is the Noun Phrase Accessibility Hierarchy (NPAH) of Keenan & Comrie (1977, 1979), represented in terms of the various grammatical functions that noun phrases fill within sentences, as given in (5) and arranged with the high end of the hierarchy to the left and the other functions descending to the right.

(5)   Subject > Direct Object > Indirect Object > Object of a Preposition > Genitive > Object of a Comparative

The NPAH is the basis for a number of empirical generalizations about the languages of the world, one of which is stated in (6).

(6)   Within relative clauses, if a language can extract a noun phrase in a given grammatical function in the hierarchy, then it can extract a noun phrase in any grammatical function higher in the hierarchy (though not necessarily conversely).

This generalization accounts for the fact that there are languages which, for example, allow the extraction of subjects, direct objects, and indirect objects but not objects of prepositions, genitives, or objects of comparatives; an example is

Fulani, a Niger-Congo language of West Africa (see Keenan & Comrie, 1979, p. 336). This generalization also accounts for the fact that no language has been observed that allows, for example, the extraction of indirect objects but not of direct objects or subjects. The generalization (6)—in conjunction with the NPAH, given in (5)—constitutes one of a set of generalization (or laws) about the structures of languages based on the investigation of a wide range of languages within the F/T framework.

An important feature of a generalization like (6) is that it imposes an implicational hierarchy on the languages of the world with respect to the properties of the relative clause constructions found in those languages. At the top of this implicational hierarchy are languages that allow extraction from the subject position. The NPAH and the generalization (6) define a second level in this hierarchy consisting of the subset of those languages that allow extraction from the subject position and *also* allow extraction from the direct object position. The third level consists of languages (a subset of those that allow extraction from subject and direct object positions) that allow extraction from subject, direct object, and indirect object positions, and so on.

Within the F/T framework, if the presence of one property within a language (the *implicans* property) implies the presence of another (the *implicatum* property) but not conversely, the implicans is more exceptional or unusual than the implicatum and is termed the *more marked* of the two properties. In the case of the NPAH and (6), a language which allows extraction from subject and direct object position is more marked than a language that allows extraction from the subject position only and less marked than one that allows extraction from the subject, direct object, and indirect object positions, and so on. As will be seen later, one important consequence of the notion of markedness for the present discussion is that the process of acquisition (either L1 acquisition or SLA) tends to proceed from less marked to more marked structures; in this case, if the language to be learned allows extraction from subject, direct object, and indirect object positions, then early stages will tend to show extraction from subject position only, then from subject and direct object and finally from subject, direct object, and indirect object. Hence, the implicational (or markedness) hierarchy not only reflects the distribution of structures in adult native languages of the world but, in many instances, the process of acquisition as well.

A great deal has been written about the relationship between work within the F/T framework and that within the generative framework and other areas of study in linguistics and psycholinguistics (see, e.g., Hammond, Moravcsik, & Wirth, 1988; Hawkins, 1988). Though a full discussion of this problem is beyond the scope of this chapter we adopt the following view: Universal generalizations about languages—like those in (5) and (6)—have a status in linguistic research analogous to that of empirical or experimental laws in the natural sciences (Hempel, 1966; Nagel, 1961). They express regularities that have been observed in the relevant empirical domain, providing an "explanation by laws" of the particular phenomena that they describe but carrying no commitment to any specific *theoretical* explanation in terms of underlying entities and processes—in this case, in terms of cognitive structures and processes. For example, given the generalizations embodied in (5) and (6), one might attempt a theoretical explanation grounded in independently justified principles and parameters of UG.[7] Or, alternatively, one might seek an explanation for these generalizations in terms of other such aspects of the capacity for language use as processing capabilities. There is, then, a sense in which work within the F/T framework in general may be seen as "setting the task" for investigators who seek theoretical explanations in terms of theories of linguistic form or function or both.

The major question that has motivated much of the research on SLA in the F/T framework has been whether or not ILs obey the set of generalizations discovered for adult native languages. When a set of related empirical generalizations (such as those derived from the NPAH and the generalization in [6]) is shown to follow from the principles and parameters of UG, then the answer to whether ILs fall under these generalizations can contribute directly to the central question about SLA posed within the UG framework: whether UG is accessible to (adult) L2 acquirers. Similarly, to the extent that the markedness hierarchy reflects stages in the process of acquisition, work within the F/T framework contributes to an understanding of the process of SLA as well. Eckman (chap. 6) further details this work.

Information-Processing Approaches

In the late 1970s and early 1980s, some scholars (Bialystok, 1978, 1982; McLaughlin, 1978) began to apply general cognitive psychological concepts of computer-based information-processing models to the investigation of SLA. Under this approach, SLA is viewed as the development of a highly complex skill—like the attainment of other, nonlinguistic skills, such as playing chess or mathematical problem solving. Researchers thus investigate those features of SLA that may be shared with forms of skill development in these domains and others.

Whereas the two previously discussed research frameworks—UG and F/T—are concerned with the acquisition and use of specific features of linguistic structure (including the sequencing of structures in acquisition), the information-processing approach is concerned with the processes through which a given structure or complex of structures becomes established in the learner. The information-processing approach distinguishes between two types of processes: *controlled* and

---

[7] For a proposed theoretical explanation for some phenomena in Hebrew, Palestinian Arabic, and Standard Arabic relative clauses that follow from the NPAH, see Shlonsky, 1992. Specifically, both Hebrew and Palestinian allow extraction from the subject and direct object positions but neither allows it from object of a preposition. Shlonsky proposed that the preclusion of extraction from object of preposition is explained by the Empty Category Principle, a principle of UG that enters into the explanation of a wide variety of superficially disparate phenomena extending far beyond the NPAH.

automatic. Controlled processing requires attention and is sharply limited in capacity; automatic processing, which does not require attention, takes up little or no processing capacity. The learner is claimed to begin the process of acquisition of a particular aspect of the L2 by depending heavily on controlled processing of the L2; through practice, the learner's use of that aspect of the L2 becomes automatic. In the process of acquisition, learners shift from concrete, *novice* processing to more abstract, *expert* style by *restructuring* their representations of the relevant processes.

To take an example from McLaughlin and Heredia (chap. 7, this volume), it has been widely observed that L2 learners (particularly children) begin the process of SLA by storing formulaic expressions, each of which consists of a sequence of what adult NS or hearers would perceive as several morphosyntactic elements but which the learner has memorized as a single form to be produced under appropriate circumstances. For example, Huang and Hatch (1978) reported the use by a five-year-old Chinese-speaking child of the following utterances within the first 6 weeks of exposure to English, well before either yes–no questions or negative structures were productive in his speech: *Are you ready? Don't do that! Don't touch!* At some time in the process, learners switch from the storage of such expressions to the development of rules for the L2 that assign these expressions internal structure. In the example discussed above, the child began to develop the rules for negation approximately 6 weeks after first exposure with such utterances as *Ball no, Mother no, No ball,* and eventually (9th week) *This not box.* This latter pattern of acquisition has been widely observed for productive mastery of negative structures in both L1 and L2 acquisition of English by children.

Research within the UG and F/T frameworks presupposes that the learner has progressed to a stage where the acquirer's competence can be characterized as a system of rules or as susceptible to description in terms of universal generalizations. Researchers thus leave the question of the attainment of that stage unaddressed. Hence the information-processing approach examines phenomena of SLA that are for the most part complementary to those that form the subject matter for the UG and F/T frameworks. McLaughlin and Heredia (chap. 7) review this work.

Another approach to the study of language acquisition and use that is based on computer modeling has been less influential in SLA research but has received some attention. The Competition Model of Bates and MacWhinney (1981, 1989) is based on the assumption that linguistic form cannot be fruitfully investigated without reference to the function of linguistic elements. In particular, Bates and MacWhinney see sentence processing—and, more specifically, the processing of relations among elements in the sentence—as based on the identification of cues in sentences such as word order, inflections, and semantic categories. Cues of many different types may be realized in a given sentence, thus processing involves the resolution of information provided by these cues—particularly when cues are in conflict in a given sentence. Languages may differ as to which cues are more prominent in determining relations among parts of the sentence. It has been suggested that one aspect of SLA is a readjustment from one set of cues in the L1 to another in the L2. Gass (chap. 10) provides further discussion.

Variationist Approaches

A fourth approach to research on SLA—one grounded in the quantitative study of language variation—also arose during the 1970s. Under this approach, termed *variationist,* the variability of structural features in speech production is studied with the purpose of determining the linguistic, psycholinguistic, social psychological, and psychological basis for that variability. For example, Preston (chap. 8) cites the instance of the occurrence (versus deletion) of *t* and *d* in the speech of African-Americans in Detroit, Michigan. Through quantitative investigation of this structural feature, it is determined that (at least) two kinds of factors contribute to its realization in speech: (a) the linguistic (phonological or morphological) status of the *t* or *d* and (b) the social class of the speaker. This general approach was developed in the 1960s and 1970s, primarily by William Labov (Labov, 1966, 1972), for the main purpose of investigating correlations between quantitative properties of the speech of individuals on one hand and a number of other variables on the other, including various features of the situation in which the speech is produced and the socioeconomic position of the speaker within the community. This approach has also been an important source of information about (and insight into) linguistic change in progress (Labov, 1980) and has led to the development of sophisticated statistical methods for the quantitative linguistic analysis of speech production.

A second, more structural approach to variation—the *dynamic paradigm*—was originally developed in the work of Bailey (1974) and Bickerton (1971, 1975). Under this approach variation is attributed to the spread over time of structural properties of grammars through the speech community so that at any given time such a property may be evidenced in the speech of some members of the community but not in that of others and, in fact, may be found under some conditions but not others in the speech of a single individual.

A number of researchers have applied variationist approaches to SLA—most notably, Tarone (1983, 1988), Ellis (1985a, 1985b), and Preston (1989). Preston (chap. 8) surveys the results of this work and notes its contribution—actual and potential—to an understanding of the L2 learner's ability to use the L2 as well as the role of the L1 in SLA and the process of SLA as a whole.

Related Work in Neuropsychology, Social Psychology, and Research Methodology

Work on SLA during the 1960s and 1970s was not limited to the study of the SLA of linguistic structure and processing. Other work included research on the neurological basis of language in general and of the acquisition and use of L2s in particular, as well as work on affective factors (such as type of motivation and social attitudes) in relation to SLA. Finally, during this period, a number of research methodologies were developed.

In his landmark study of **the neurological basis of language,** Lenneberg (1967) argued that there is a *critical period* for language acquisition, associated with the completion of lateralization of language to the left hemisphere, claimed to occur at puberty. Though Lenneberg based his position on evidence from the study of recovery from aphasia, mentioning SLA only briefly, others soon undertook the investigation of the critical-period hypothesis with respect to age-related features of both neurological and linguistic aspects of SLA. Additional work of a variety of kinds during this period was devoted to determining the localization in the brain of the two languages of bilinguals and L2 learners. The work of the 1960s and 1970s, as well as other aspects of the neuropsychology of L2 acquisition and use, was surveyed in Albert and Obler (1978). Obler and Hannigan (chap. 15, this volume) review the work of the 1980s on these and other related topics.

Within the research literature of the 1960s and 1970s on **the role of motivation and social attitudes in SLA,** the work of Gardner and Lambert stands out. They distinguished two types of motivation for acquiring an L2—integrative and instrumental. Integratively motivated learners wish to learn an L2 in order to participate in the culture of the L2, whereas instrumental learners are concerned with more mercenary objectives such as getting a better job. Through factor analysis of the results of a number of massive studies of L2 learners conducted in Canada, the United States, and the Philippines, Gardner and Lambert (1972) found a number of relationships between characteristics of learners that they judged to measure not only motivation but positive versus negative attitudes toward NSs of the L2 (e.g., number of L2-speaking friends, family attitudes toward L2 speakers) and success in mastering features of the L2. Gardner (1985) summarized work done in the early 1980s within this research program. Though the conclusions drawn from this research vary depending upon the setting in which SLA takes place, one conclusion that this work supports is that a generally positive relationship exists between integrative motivation and positive attitudes toward L2 speakers and mastery of those aspects of the L2's structure that are relatively less susceptible to conscious manipulation (e.g., phonology).

Turning briefly to developments in **research methodology,** in a substantial number of studies conducted early in this period—particularly those involving case studies of individual child subjects—spontaneous production was used, parallel to much L1 acquisition research at that time. As the investigation of the order of acquisition and accuracy of grammatical morphemes became prominent in the field, more focused data collection instruments were devised that would be appropriate for the testing of large numbers of subjects in cross-sectional studies. A prominent example was the Bilingual Syntax Measure (Burt, Dulay, & Hernandez, 1975), based on a set of cartoons and questions to be asked of subjects by the experimenter. In work with adults, SLA researchers used not only spontaneous production (both written and spoken) but other data-elicitation techniques as well—including those used in the study of adult native grammars, such as judgments of the well-formedness and structure of utterances. Nunan (chap. 11) and Sorace (chap. 12) review these and more recent developments in SLA research methodology.

C. Some Integrated Models of SLA

As empirical results on SLA became increasingly available in the 1970s, several general models of SLA were proposed with the purpose of integrating these results. Among these were several that bear on the work examined in this volume—most prominently, Schumann's Acculturation Model and Krashen's Monitor Model.

In a series of papers Schumann (1978a, 1978b, 1978c) developed a model of SLA under which SLA—particularly for recent immigrants into a given society—is seen as one aspect of the overall process of acculturation to the society in which the L2 is spoken. Degree of success in SLA under these circumstances is thus determined by degree of success in acculturation in general, including attitudinal factors like Gardner and Lambert's integrative and instrumental motivation as discussed above. Noting that early stages of SLA resemble pidgin languages in structure, Schumann drew a parallel between SLA and the complexification of a pidgin in the process of acculturation to the surrounding society, thus relating research on SLA to that on pidgin and creole languages for the first time. In part as a consequence of Schumann's work, the relationships among pidgin and creole languages and SLA have continued to be a fruitful area of research, as evidenced by Andersen and Shirai (chap. 16, this volume).

Perhaps the most influential model of SLA has been Krashen's Monitor Model (Krashen, 1981, 1982, 1985). This model is embodied in five interrelated hypotheses. First, the Acquisition–Learning Distinction claims that the adult learner has two ways of attaining the ability to perform in an L2—tacit (or subconscious) acquisition and conscious learning. Second, the Monitor Hypothesis states that in L2 performance the subconscious knowledge of the L2 attained through acquisition initiates an utterance plan, whereas the consciously learned aspects of the L2 can serve only a self-monitoring function. The operation of this "Monitor" is claimed to depend on the conditions under which a particular use of the L2 takes place (e.g., whether the L2 user is focusing on the grammatical form as well as the semantic content of his or her utterances) and has been one attempt to account for the high degree of variability in L2 performance. Third, the Natural Order Hypothesis asserts that the acquisition process follows a specific course, as evidenced by the order of acquisition of grammatical morphemes and of negative and interrogative structures in the case of L2 English. Fourth, the Input Hypothesis claims that input to the acquirer must be "comprehensible" if acquisition is to proceed through the Natural Order. To be comprehensible in Krashen's sense, input must meet a number of conditions—most prominently, it must be meaningful and it must have a form at a stage in the Natural Order just beyond the stage at which the acquirer is functioning. And finally, the Affective Filter Hypothesis states that, if acquisition is to take place, the acquirer must be affectively open to input from the L2—in the terminology of the Model, that he or she must have a "low affective filter." This hypothesis accounts for the results of research on motivation and social attitudes as well as the role of personality and other affective factors in SLA.

Though the leading ideas of the Monitor Model continue to be highly influential in applied linguistics, the model has been severely criticized as a theory of SLA on conceptual as well as empirical grounds by, for example, McLaughlin, Gregg, and White. McLaughlin (1978) questioned the validity of the conscious–subconscious difference associated with the Acquisition–Learning Distinction, and White (1987) noted empirical problems with the Input Hypothesis. Gregg's (1984) critique was the most far-reaching, calling into question the very testability of Krashen's claims. Nonetheless, others continued to explore Krashen's ideas in a form that is more precise than that in which Krashen initially formulated them (e.g., Schwarz, 1986; Schwarz & Gubala-Ryzak, 1992; Zobl, 1995).

Several additional models of SLA and use were developed during the 1970s and 1980s that have been influential in the field. Two of these, one developed by Tarone and the other by Ellis, draw on the works of the variationists described above. Another model, called the multidimensional model, was developed through a German research project entitled *Zweitsprachenerwerb Italienischer und Spanischer Arbeiter* (ZISA—"second language acquisition of Italian and Spanish workers"). In a fifth model, proposed by Felix, the observed failure of adults to attain adult native grammars for L2s is explained as a consequence of competition between the adult's natural tacit capacity for language acquisition and his or her general problem-solving capacities. This model is also widely cited in the research literature.

Tarone (1983, 1988) proposed a characterization of L2 use that posits a continuum of styles based on attention to linguistic form with the purpose of accounting for the variability found in L2 speech. Ellis's model (1985a,b) also links variability to attention to form but with reference to Bialystok's work (1982) within a particular information-processing approach. Both of these models have been subject to some criticism (Gregg, 1990; Preston, chap. 8, this volume).

ZISA's multidimensional model (e.g., Meisel, Clahsen, & Pienemann, 1981) combines a method of establishing significant stages of acquisition with an account of variability *within* such stages based on both the motivation of individual learners studied by Gardner and Lambert and the properties of pidgin languages noted by Schumann (as discussed previously).

Felix (1987) hypothesized that the usual failure of adults to attain nativelike knowledge of an L2 is explained by the development of Piagetian formal operations at puberty and the consequent increase in abstract thought at that point. He argued that the ability of the adolescent to formulate abstract rules as part of the new stage in the development of general problem-solving capacities results in competition between these new capacities and the cognitive capacities specific to language acquisition and use. Because general problem-solving capacities are not suitable for the acquisition and use of language, Felix claimed, they can neither substitute for nor support language-specific capacities, and acquisition fails as a result.

D. Summary

By the mid-1980s, inquiry into SLA had emerged as a basic discipline with an agenda of research and methodology fully distinct from its applied sister disciplines. This agenda was (and is) theory-driven with close relationships to basic research in other domains, including research on the structure and use of language, the study of L1 acquisition, of language variation and change, and of human cognition in general. Work in neuropsychology had already contributed substantially to the understanding of the neurological basis for SLA and use, and the effect of maturation on the capacity for SLA had become well established as a central issue in the field. The stage had thus been set for the intensive study of the issues addressed in this volume.

III. CURRENT ISSUES IN SLA RESEARCH

A. Introduction: The Central Questions

We turn now to a discussion of the major current issues in the study of SLA represented by the research described in this volume. We first provide general formulations of the central questions in the investigation of SLA, with some remarks on major differences between the study of SLA and that of L1 acquisition. We then address the major empirical issues in the field.

We may describe the central facts of SLA very simply in the following way: On the basis of experience with a particular language, L (that is, linguistic input from L), a learner possessing some capacity for language acquisition develops certain cognitive abilities to use L. Given this description, we may take the central questions in the study of SLA to be the following:[8]

---

[8] The questions (7)–(10) in the text are adapted from those that Chomsky has formulated in one form or another as central to the study of language in many works from the early 1960s to the present—for older sources, see Chomsky & Miller, 1963. There are differences between the central

(7) What cognitive structures and abilities underlie the L2 learner's *use* of his or her L2?

(8) What properties of the *linguistic input* to the L2 learner are relevant to acquisition?

(9) What is the nature of the L2 learner's capacity for attaining the cognitive structures and abilities referred to in (7)? Here we may distinguish the following two subquestions:

    a. What is the nature of the L2 learner's *overall capacity* for language acquisition?

    b. How is that capacity deployed in real time to determine the *course* of SLA?

There are thus three central cognitive or behavioral problems in the study of SLA: the problems of (a) the cognitive structures and abilities that underlie L2 use, (b) the relevant linguistic input, and (c) the capacity for language acquisition. To these cognitive and behavioral questions we may add the following questions concerning the neuropsychology of SLA and use:

(10)   a. How are the L2 user's two (or more) languages represented in the brain?

      b. What changes in brain structure, if any, underlie changes in the capacity for language acquisition across the life span of the individual?

It might be thought that, because the L2 learner is older and already has a language in place, the answers to these questions for SLA will differ so fundamentally from answers to the same questions about L1 acquisition that the questions themselves may be unproductive. In the remainder of this introductory subsection we will suggest that such a conclusion would be premature. Although there is no true a priori reason to think that these questions will be less productive in the study of SLA than in the study of L1 acquisition, the special features of the L2 case are worthy of some preliminary discussion to set the stage for the more detailed treatment of the issues in subsection B.

We begin this initial discussion of (7)–(10) with consideration of question (7)—the question of **the cognitive structures and abilities that underlie L2 use.** First, because L2 users comprehend and produce (with comprehension) utterances in the L2—though often not in the same way that NSs of the L2 do—we are

---

questions for the study of SLA as presented here and the usual formulation. These questions are ordinarily formulated in relation to L1 grammatical competence and its acquisition, use, and representation in the brain; others have extended them to the study of L2 grammatical competence and its acquisition. See chap. 2 by Gregg, this volume, for detailed discussion of the conceptual issues and particularly chap. 3 (White), 4 (Flynn), and 5 (Schachter) as well as chap. 10 (Gass) and 13 (Long) for review of empirical issues. However, the questions formulated here are about the cognitive abilities and structures that underlie L2 use (of which L2 grammatical competence is an element), the acquisition of these abilities and structures, the experience or input that gives rise to them, and, finally, their representation in the brain. An early formulation of these questions for SLA in essentially the form of (7)–(10) was Ritchie (1973).

entitled to claim that they have a set of sentence structures available to them for the internal representation of L2 utterances. We have termed this set of structures an IL.

Second, to the extent that the L2 user is able to comprehend and produce utterances in the L2 that he or she has never encountered before, we can claim that he or she possesses a tacit system of rules and principles that specifies the class of available sentence structures—an ILG that embodies the L2 user's grammatical competence for the L2.

Third, L2 users exhibit not only a system of grammatical competence (an ILG) but other cognitive structures and abilities as well. These include (but are not limited to) (a) pragmatic competence (a system of assumptions about the conditions and manner of appropriate language use), (b) the ability to put grammatical competence to use in real-time comprehension and production of utterances, and (c) the ability to attend to the form of their own speech (self-monitor) and to the form of the speech of others. We may thus attribute to L2 users an IL system that includes not only an ILG but IL variants of pragmatic competence and of the others abilities referred to above.[9]

The previously mentioned high degree of variability in the performance of L2 learners (relative to L1 learners) has been attributed to both the greater richness in cognitive ability and activity in the more mature L2 learner than in the L1 learner and the relative instability of IL systems over the course of acquisition. Though such variability makes the study of IL systems difficult—and, in particular, presents certain methodological problems in the investigation of ILGs—these difficulties have not precluded systematic research on the nature of IL systems. See in particular Gregg's (chap. 2) and Preston's (chap. 8) chapters in this volume for discussion.

Regarding the nature of **linguistic input** in SLA (8), one issue that arises in the consideration of the L2 learner's experience is the possible effect of formal (classroom) instruction on the process and result of SLA. It might be thought that exposure to formal instruction would greatly influence the process and outcome of SLA. However, what careful empirical work there is on the effects of classroom instruction on SLA indicates some effect on rate of acquisition but little or none on the sequencing or result of acquisition (see Ellis, 1985b, 1990; and Larsen-Freeman & Long, 1991, for review). Though this research is clearly of some practical interest, it carries little or no theoretical significance, and the question of the specific effects of formal instruction can therefore be safely ignored in a treatment of theoretical issues.

---

[9]For a general treatment of pragmatics see Levinson (1983); for an anthology of work on L2 pragmatic competence and some general discussion of IL pragmatics as well, see Kasper and Blum-Kulka (1993). For an introductory treatment of adult L1 sentence comprehension and production, see Garrett (1990). Finally, for some general discussion of adult L1 self-monitoring see Levelt (1989). Although there is a considerable body of speculation concerning mechanisms of self-monitoring in L2 performance, there is little consensus in this area. We return briefly to this issue in the text.

In relation to question (9)a—the problem of the **overall capacity for SLA**—
we may approach a solution to this problem by discovering the major properties
of the final product of acquisition (that is, of *ultimately attained* IL systems, which
we will refer to as "ILS_us") and of the input available to the learner. We may then
regard the overall acquisitional capacity of the learner as a function that maps the
input onto an ILS_u.

An apparent problem arises in the investigation of question (9)a that does not
arise in research on the analogous question for L1 acquisition. There is, in effect,
only one case of L1 acquisition—that of a child with no previously established
language passing through the full sequence of maturational stages that contribute
to the process of acquisition. The only significant differentiating factor among
particular cases of (normal) L1 acquisition is the linguistic input the learner receives—that is, the language of the environment. On the other hand, for cases of
SLA not only may the linguistic input vary but the maturational stage of the
learner and the previously established language (and a variety of other factors)
may vary as well. Nonetheless, question (9)a is researchable as long as one understands that the overall capacity for acquisition may vary depending on the age of
the learner and that the course (and, perhaps, the result) of acquisition may vary
according to the learner's L1.

Another, related problem arises in the study of the overall capacity for SLA. As
Gregg implies, the L2 researcher cannot point to a single ultimately attained
"steady state" of acquisition (for a given input language) that is largely uniform
across a significant population of language users as can the investigator of L1
acquisition. Hence, in approaching the question of the overall capacity for language acquisition in the case of an L2, it is reasonable to consider a certain range
of stages of acquisition as possible ultimately attained IL systems—that is, as
possible ILS_us—and to investigate their properties and the relationships among
them. With this amendment, the question remains a valid one to ask about SLA.

Continuing with the discussion of the overall capacity to acquire an IL system,
let us limit ourselves to the study of the capacity to attain a certain *grammatical
competence* in the L2, ignoring for the moment the other structures and abilities
that make up an IL system. Because, in most cases, adult L2 learners attain an
ILG of some sort, we are entitled to assume that one element in the adult's capacity
for language acquisition is a *tacit grammatical theory*—a system of principles
that specifies the class of attainable ILGs for learners at that stage of maturation.
Hence, one task of SLA research—the central task in the view of many SLA
researchers—is to discover through empirical investigation what the adults' tacit
grammatical theory is. Note that this problem is fully parallel to the problem in
the study of L1 acquisition of discovering what UG is. UG is the theory of attainable adult native grammars—that is, the theory of those grammars that result when the learner receives input from a given language from birth to linguistic adulthood. Similarly, a hypothesis about the adult's tacit grammatical
theory (GT_a) will be a theory of the ILGs that can be attained by those who begin

learning a language as adults. As will be demonstrated, the investigation of the adult's tacit grammatical theory has taken the form of research on whether GT_a is the same as UG or not.

Moving on to consideration of question (9)b—how the capacity for acquisition determines the **course of acquisition**—this question will be answered by an explanation of the specific sequence of stages (that is, the specific sequence of IL systems) through which the L2 acquirer passes in arriving at whatever ultimate stage (ILS_u) he or she attains—a transition theory in the sense of Cummins (1983) (see Gregg, chap. 2, for discussion). This problem is essentially that of how one IL system is replaced by another IL system (one that falls within the overall acquisitional capacity of the learner) on the basis of input from the L2. Apparently, it is here that the influence of the learner's L1 may play a variety of roles—determining the specific character of one or more IL systems in the sequence, delaying the transition from one IL system in the sequence to the next one, and so on. Once again, although a variety of factors may determine very different courses of acquisition for SLA and L1 acquisition, there is no reason to believe that it is unproductive to ask how the capacity for acquisition is deployed in the process of acquisition.

Finally, solutions to **the neuropsychological questions** (10)a and (10)b will take the form of confirmed hypotheses about the neural substrate for SLA and use. In particular, (10)a is a question about the neurological representation of the cognitive structures and processes that constitute the L2 user's IL system and the parallel system underlying the use of the L1. Question (10)b, on the other hand, concerns maturational changes in the neural substrate for linguistic cognition that might constitute the biological basis for the difference between the child's overall capacity for language acquisition (L1 or L2) and the adult L2 learner's overall capacity for SLA.

B. The Issues

We turn now to a discussion of the central issues in the study of SLA in general as they are represented in the chapters of this volume in particular. The discussion will be organized around the questions formulated in the preceding section—(a) the nature of IL systems (questions [7] and [10]a), (b) features of linguistic input that are relevant to the attainment of IL systems (question [8]), and (c) the capacity for acquisition of IL systems (questions [9]a, [9]b, and [10]b).

The Nature of IL Systems

The discussion of the nature of IL systems will treat first the cognitive and behavioral issues and then those in the neuropsychology of L2 use. We will examine those cognitive and behavioral issues that arise with respect to all stages of acquisition here, leaving the question of changes in the course of acquisition to the section on the capacity for acquisition. We begin with questions concerning grammatical competence, then move on to consideration of performance issues and the research-methodological problems that arise as a consequence of the character of L2 performance.

Gregg argued that the grammatical competence (rather than the performance) of the L2 learner is the proper domain for a theory of SLA, and in keeping with this position, for the modularity of those mechanisms that determine the SLA of grammatical competence, countering the proposals both of general nativists and of connectionists. Although, as Gregg notes, there have been a number of references in the SLA research literature to the possibility that L2 competence (unlike L1 competence) is determined, at least in part, by principles outside the language module,[10] there are no detailed proposals in the SLA literature as to what these principles might be. We return to the issue of whether or not L2 grammatical competence falls within the principles of UG when we consider the overall capacity for SLA.[11]

Turning now to aspects of language ability other than grammatical competence in the L2 user, we stress once again the fact that adult L2 production at any given point in the acquisition process is highly variable, changing systematically in a number of ways under a variety of conditions (see Preston, chap. 8, this volume for detailed discussion). As noted earlier, one view that has played a prominent role in the study of SLA is that an important source of the variability in L2 speech is the amount of attention the speaker pays to the form of the utterances he or she is producing, shifting from a casual, relatively attention-free "vernacular" version of the L2, which more or less directly exhibits the user's tacit knowledge of the L2, to more careful production resulting from attention to form (self-monitoring) in addition to tacit knowledge. Tarone's and Ellis' approaches to variability in L2 production (Ellis, 1985a, 1985b; Tarone, 1983, 1988) characterize grammatical competence not as a single system of rules and principles but, rather, as a continuum of styles that are scaled according to amount of attention paid to speech. Preston (chap. 8, this volume), however, takes a different position. In his view, the phenomena of variability are better explained by reference to a single grammar that makes the full range of forms available to the user and a set of weighted factors that determine probabilistically which of these forms will actually be produced on a given occasion, only one of these factors being attention to form.

Information-processing approaches to the study of L2 also emphasize the role of the learner's attention to the form of his or her own speech in L2 use (that is, in

---

[10] For example, Bley-Vroman (1989) cited Andersen's (1983) proposals for a general learning mechanism as possibly providing an account of adult SLA.

[11] Note that the modularity of knowledge structures—and, in particular, the view that grammatical competence constitutes a separate "grammar module"—does not preclude the possibility that some aspects of the development of language use will show general properties of skill development of the sort investigated by researchers working within the information-processing approach to SLA.

the form of controlled processing)—particularly in the early stages of acquisition (see McLaughlin and Heredia, chap. 7, this volume for discussion).

Another factor that gives rise to the particular character of L2 performance—discussed by Gass in chapter 10—is the avoidance of certain structures in L2 production. Specifically, some work has shown that the frequency of a given structure in L2 production may be lower when the properties of that structure in the L1 of the user differ from those of the L2 structure than when those properties are similar in the L1 and the L2. These results provide indirect systematic evidence that the L2 user avoids structures that are less well established in his or her ILG than others.

The greater richness of the L2 user's cognitive abilities that underlies the variability of L2 production has implications for choice of data-elicitation methods in the study of SLA. This richness makes the SLA researcher's task of eliciting data from the L2 user more difficult than that of the L1 acquisition researcher in some respects and easier in others. In particular, if the object of inquiry is the L2 user's competence, then his or her greater capacity for self-monitoring may interfere with the tapping of tacit grammatical knowledge of the L2 in some cases—a difficulty that L1 researchers are less likely to encounter. On the other hand, in the usual case, subjects in SLA experiments are adults, and elicitation techniques used in the study of adult native grammars (in particular, acceptability judgments) can also be used in the study of L2 grammatical competence, though with certain precautions. For a discussion of SLA research-elicitation methods in general, see Nunan (chap. 11, this volume); for a detailed discussion of the use of acceptability judgments in SLA research, see Sorace (chap. 12, this volume). For remarks on related difficulties in measuring bilingualism, see Romaine (chap. 17) and in the study of code-switching and -mixing, see Bhatia and Ritchie (chap. 19). Finally, White (chap. 3) and Flynn (chap. 4) also discuss particular issues in L2 research methodology.[12]

As regards neuropsychological issues in L2 use, Obler and Hannigan (chap. 15) address the question of the neurological representation of the L2 user's two languages—question (10)a. They survey the literature on the lateral dominance pattern for the two languages, including work based on a wide variety of methods and experimental designs, reporting few noncontradictory results. Studies of further localization of the two languages within the left hemisphere by means of cortical stimulation show greater concentration of L1 than L2 function in the classic (Broca's and Wernicke's) language areas. They also review work on patterns of breakdown and recovery from aphasia, attrition (without neurological involvement), and Alzheimer's syndrome. In a separate reference to neuropsychological issues, Bhatia and Ritchie (chap. 19) discuss a case of claimed pathological code-

---

[12] Methodological issues in SLA research are currently under heated discussion. (See Tarone, Gass, & Cohen, 1994, for a rich anthology of work in this area.)

switching from the literature on polyglot aphasia, arguing that features of code-switching in the reported case do not differentiate it from normal code-switching.

Input

What features of the L2 learner's experience with the L2 are relevant to acquisition? Issues surrounding this question are at the core of the two chapters in part V. Long (chap. 13) reviews the character of input in the normal case of SLA, whereas Berent (chap. 14) surveys research on the acquisition of a spoken language (English) by the deaf—a case of acquisition under conditions of severely limited input.

In discussions of the role of input in both L1 acquisition and SLA, an important distinction exists between the evidence available to the learner that a given utterance is grammatical in the L2 (that is, *positive evidence*) and evidence from the environment that a given utterance is ungrammatical (*negative evidence*). The simple occurrence of an utterance, then, constitutes positive evidence for the acquirer—evidence that the utterance is grammatical. Correction of an utterance constitutes negative evidence—that is, evidence that the corrected utterance is ungrammatical. For the case of L1 acquisition, it was argued convincingly some time ago (e.g., Baker, 1979; Wexler & Culicover, 1980) that only positive evidence is available to the acquirer (e.g., that correction for linguistic form, if and when it occurs in the process of acquisition, is ineffectual). As will be discussed below, the *positive-evidence-only* assumption plays a central role in the justification of hypotheses about the capacity for SLA.

Long's chapter (chap. 13) provides a detailed review of the research on a variety of roles that have been hypothesized for the linguistic environment in SLA. He surveys work on the ways in which NSs modify their speech to L2 learners from NSs (that is, on 'foreigner talk') so that that input is comprehensible to the learner. Such modifications are thus claimed to serve a function parallel to that of "motherese"—the modified speech of caretakers in L1 acquisition. However, the more advanced age of the L2 learner makes it possible for him or her to direct such modifications in native-speaking interlocutors through *negotiation of meaning*. Long argues on the basis of a wide variety of empirical studies that although comprehensibility of input is necessary for SLA, it is not sufficient for full acquisition of the L2. He then examines the research literature on attention and noticing in SLA and concludes that although noticing is facilitative in SLA, it is neither necessary nor sufficient. This is also true of negative evidence (that is, correction), which might be thought a priori to play a greater role in L2 than in L1 acquisition.

Long's treatment of input is concerned with general features of the learner's experience with the L2. White, on the other hand, reviews the role of structurally specific positive and negative evidence in the resetting of the verb-raising parameter (referred to above) by native French speakers learning English.

Berent (chap. 14) examines the effects of hearing impairment in the acquisition of English by the deaf. We return to discussion of these effects in detail in our discussion of the course of SLA in the following section.

The Capacity for Acquisition

In subsection (a) we address the issue of the overall capacity of the L2 learner for language acquisition (that is, the problem of ultimate attainment in SLA)—question (9)a above. In subsection (b) we consider question (9)b—the course of acquisition.

To begin the discussion, we may characterize the process of acquisition as consisting of a sequence of IL systems: ILS_1, ILS_2, . . . , ILS_i, ILS_{i+1}, . . . , ILS_u. The final product of a particular case of SLA (ILS_u), then, is the ILS that is ultimately attained in that case. A given ILS_i in this sequence is thus replaced by a successor (ILS_{i+1}) on the basis of input from the environment, ILS_{i+1} being an ILS that is attainable given the learner's overall capacity for language acquisition. The influence of the L2 user's L1 on performance at a given stage of acquisition, which we discuss below, is to be found in features of IL systems at various stages of acquisition. Adopting the position (referred to earlier) that an account of the learner's overall capacity for language acquisition for a particular case of acquisition consists in a function that maps the input to the learner onto the final product of acquisition, a full answer to question (9)a—that of the overall capacity for acquisition—will consist of a hypothesis about the capacities that map the input into the observed ILS_u for any given case of SLA. A solution to the problem of the course of acquisition—question (9)b—will provide an account of why one finds the particular sequence of ILSs in a given case of SLA.

To make the discussion slightly more concrete, we limit ourselves for the moment to a discussion of the grammatical competence of the learner at various stages and the overall capacity for acquisition of that aspect of language ability. In the study of grammatical competence, question (9)a is termed the *logical* problem of language acquisition and question (9)b, the *developmental* problem of language acquisition. Gregg (chap. 2) provides a thorough discussion of the deeper conceptual issues surrounding the logical and developmental problems as they relate to SLA.

The Overall Capacity for SLA

As noted earlier, the central observation concerning SLA in relation to L1 acquisition is that the normal child inevitably attains adult native ability in his or her L1 (virtually by definition), whereas the adult (postpubertal) L2 learner seldom attains such ability in the L2. Much of the research on SLA is devoted directly or indirectly to establishing an explanation for this observation. The explanations that have been offered in the field at large are too numerous to survey here (see, e.g., Krashen, Scarcella, & Long, 1982; Scovel, 1988; Singleton, 1989; Long, 1990, for review and discussion). We will focus our attention on possible linguistic explanations (those that are formulable in terms of the notions of input, ILS, and overall capacity for language acquisition), ignoring nonlinguistic ones (including changes in general cognitive functioning that appear at puberty, factors of personality, social attitude, etc.). As in issues concerning the ability to use the L2, there are two aspects to the problem of the overall capacity for SLA—a cognitive or behavioral aspect (question [9]a) and a neuropsychological aspect (question [10]b).

Research on the adult's overall capacity for SLA has focused almost exclusively on the acquisition of grammatical competence—that is, in our terms, on the adult's tacit grammatical theory (GT_a), the system of principles that determines the class of attainable ILGs. In particular, the central question that has occupied researchers in the SLA of grammatical competence is whether UG (the theory of adult native grammars) is "accessible" to the adult L2 learner or not. Equivalently, we may ask whether or not GT_a is UG, or whether GT_a consists in some other system of principles. Though a number of different formulations of this question are given in this volume (see chaps. 2, 3, 4, and 5 by Gregg, White, Flynn, and Schachter, respectively), and the issues are complex, it is fruitful in our view to break the question of accessibility of UG down into two distinct questions, each of which is of sufficient independent interest to be considered in its own right:

(11)   Are (adult-attained) ILGs and IL structures constrained by the principles and parameters of UG?

(12)   Is the full range of grammars and structures specified by UG accessible or available to the (adult) L2 learner?

Note that answers to (11) and (12) are logically independent, and the various combinations of positive and negative answers to these questions define four positions on the relation between UG and the adult's tacit grammatical theory (GT_a).

Positive answers to both questions define what might be called the "GT_a = UG" position; loosely, this position is Gregg's "strong theism," White's "position (i)," and Flynn's "full-access hypothesis." [13]

A second position is defined by a positive answer to (11) and a negative answer to (12). Under this view, the class of attainable ILGs and IL structures is a proper subset of those allowed by UG; we might refer to this as the "GT_a = UG-minus" hypothesis. Loosely, Gregg's "weak theism" and White's "position (iii)" can be understood as versions of this position. Perhaps the most restrictive version of this possibility that is empirically viable is that structures attainable in the L2 are not only constrained by UG but by the narrower constraints imposed by the grammar of the learner's L1. Under this view, no structure in an IL can violate the rules and principles of the learner's L1 grammar. We will refer to this as the "GT_a = L1G" position, what Flynn refers to as the "partial-access hypothesis."

Of the two positions that follow from negative answers to question (11), we

---

[13] The GT_a = UG position may be thought of as a version of the strict continuity hypothesis under consideration in the study of L1 acquisition research extended to the case of SLA.

term the one that follows from a positive answer to (12) the "GT_a = UG-plus" position and that which follows from the negative answer to (12) the "GT_a = not-UG" hypothesis. Under the former, the class of ILGs or structures is a proper superset of those constrained by UG; under the latter, the class of ILGs or structures is in neither a subset nor a superset relation to those that fall within UG.

Schachter's position is a combination of GT_a = L1G and GT_a = not-UG. Her view is interpretable as follows: The only principles of UG that operate in SLA are those instantiated in the grammar of the learner's L1; if the learner attains structures beyond those allowed by the grammar of the L1, they are not constrained by UG. We may term this the "GT_a = L1G-plus" position.

Empirical arguments for a positive answer to (11) are to be found in the chapters by White (chap. 3), Flynn (chap. 4), and Eckman (chap. 6). White and Flynn review evidence for constraints on ILGs with respect to both principles and parameters. One type of evidence cited by White consists in the constancy throughout the SLA process of the c-command condition on anaphora. Particularly strong evidence for UG constraints on ILGs is provided by those instances in which the learner succeeds in attaining an ILG for the L2 in which a principle of UG applies that could not have the grammar of the L1 as its source. White includes discussion of such a case involving constraints on wh-movement in the ILGs of native speakers of Malagasy learning English. Flynn reviews a similar study involving *wh*-movement in NSs of Indonesian and Chinese learning English as an L2.

It follows from the claim that ILGs are constrained by parameters of UG that ILGs will exhibit the clustering of properties specific to parameter values found in adult native grammars. White and Flynn both argue on the basis of a number of empirical studies that ILGs do exhibit such clustering properties.

Work outside the UG framework also bears on question (11). Eckman (chap. 6) argues at length for the Structural Conformity Hypothesis (SCH), which claims that all ILs obey the same set of empirical generalizations that adult native languages do. Therefore, assuming that such generalizations either are or will be deducible in UG, the SCH provides important support for the view that ILGs are UG-constrained. Andersen and Shirai (chap. 16) provide additional evidence to support the view that universal principles determine the form of ILs. They argue for a particular relationship between the inherent (lexical) tense–aspect semantics of verbs and the development of tense–aspect verb morphology in L1 acquisition and SLA as well as pidgin and creole languages.

Arguments for a negative answer to question (11) are provided by Schachter (chap. 5), who cites work on the acquisition of *wh*-movement involving speakers of Indonesian, Chinese, and Korean learning English to support her case. All of these languages leave *wh*-like elements in place rather than moving them to the beginning of sentences as does English. As support of her GT_a = L1G-plus position, Schachter argues that when learners from these backgrounds attain *wh*-movement in English, they fail to incorporate UG constraints on this rule into their ILGs for English. However, White (chap. 3) summarizes a reinterpretation of Schachter's (chap. 5) results under which apparent *wh*-movement in the ILGs for these learners falls within UG constraints.

Turning now to question (12), note that a negative answer to (12) would contribute to an explanation for the general failure of adults to acquire L2s, assuming that the specific failures of adults can be explained in terms of specific differences between GT_a and UG. On the other hand, a positive answer to (12) would require an explanation of the adult's failure in terms of factors other than a "deficient" GT_a. For example, social psychological or general-cognitive factors have been cited as possible contributors to such failure (see, e.g., Larsen-Freeman & Long, 1991, chap. 6, for review).

Flynn supports her position that the answer to (12) is positive by noting that those aspects of grammatical structure that have been investigated show no evidence of "deficiency" of the sort required for a negative answer to (12). White reviews the research on near-NSs, those who are judged to be nearly indistinguishable from NSs in ability to perform in L2s in spite of having learned them as adults. The purpose of this research is to determine whether such L2 users show evidence of underlying native grammatical competence or not. Though in general the results indicate that the grammatical competence of near-NSs does not match that of NSs, the results are not unequivocal. These studies do not, for the most part, address the specifics of the structures that would directly justify a positive answer for (12); nonetheless, the results reviewed suggest such an answer.

What about the question of a possible neuropsychological basis for the usual failure of adults to attain nativelike mastery of an L2—question (10)b. Whether or not the apparent reduction in ability to acquire an L2 is to be attributed to changes in the capacity to attain grammatical competence or not, Lenneberg's (1967) claim that there is a biologically determined critical or sensitive period for language acquisition and that SLA is affected by it (10)b remains a topic of debate in SLA research, although the specifics of Lenneberg's position have been reevaluated. Obler and Hannigan (chap. 15) review some major points in this debate as it has developed over the last two decades. In addition, Schachter supports the view that there is a critical period for SLA with discussion of the research on the biological bases for critical periods in humans as well as members of other species.

The Course of Acquisition

With regard to the course of SLA, recall that we are considering the process of acquisition as a sequence of IL systems. As noted above, an answer to question (9)b will consist in what Gregg (chap. 2) and Cummins (1983) refer to as a "transition theory" for the sequence (or sequences) $ILS_1, ILS_2, \ldots, ILS_i, ILS_{i+1}, \ldots,$ ILS_u that are found to characterize the process of SLA.

An important difference in the study of the course of L2 and L1 acquisition is the significance of the ILS_1—the early IL systems in the process of SLA. Because of the fact that the L2 learner has a full-fledged processing system for another language in place at the onset of acquisition, the question of the character of early IL systems in the process of SLA is a matter of central importance. We therefore consider not only grammatical competence at early stages of SLA but the ILS_1 as a whole, though focusing primarily on the character of early ILGs.

We then take up the problem of transition to later stages of SLA, reviewing factors that have been claimed to determine the sequencing of ILSs. Subsequently, we briefly address the problem of why, as White (chap. 3, this volume) puts it, some learners "get stuck" or *fossilize* at points in the process of acquisition.

We will discuss two major issues in the study of **the early stages of SLA.** First, it has been widely observed [14] that the earliest stages of acquisition are characterized by the internalization of multiword utterances that are unanalyzed wholes from the point of view of the learner. The transition from this stage to one in which utterances are analyzed in accordance with an underlying system of rules and principles has been addressed within the information-processing approach. Second, we will address the question of the character of the early stages of SLA once a grammar has been established—particularly in relation to L1 influence or lack of it.

McLaughlin and Heredia (chap. 7) refer to the gradual process of "unpacking" of formulaic, unanalyzed utterances in earlier stages of acquisition to the later, more rule-determined representations as the result of a change in strategy for processing the L2. In fact, that this restructuring of internal representations from concrete surface elements of a task to more flexible, abstract representations in terms of task subelements is typical of shifts from novice to expert performance found in other cognitive domains.

At the stage where a rule system is in place, the central question is the role of the structure of the L1 in L2 use and, in particular, in the place of features of the L1 in the grammatical competence of the L2 user. Within Chomsky's principles-and-parameters framework, an a priori reasonable hypothesis is that in the early stages of L2 acquisition, the parameter settings of the L1 determine the grammar of the L2 user. However, there is little systematic evidence overall to support the hypothesis that L1 parameter settings fully determine the early stages of the L2. What is perhaps the best evidence in support of this claim is indirect, indicated by such effects as delays in acquisition of features of the L2 as determined by a mismatch of parameter settings between the L1 and the L2. Flynn (chap. 4) reports such an effect with respect to her complementizer phrase-direction parameter. Evidence that the L2 learner begins the process of SLA with parameters set in values other than those that determine the grammar of the L1 is reviewed by White (chap. 3) and Gass (chap. 10). This research includes, most prominently, work on the differences among languages with respect to conditions on binding represented in Wexler and Manzini's (1987) Governing Category Parameter (GCP) and their role in SLA.

---

[14] See Wong Fillmore, 1976; Vihman, 1982; and Weinert, 1995, for extensive treatment.

Research conducted outside the principles-and-parameters framework has made important contributions to the study of L1 influence in early ILSs. Gass's overview (chap. 10) reveals a number of effects of differences in morphosyntactic structure between the learner's L1 and the L2, including delay in acquisition of an L2 structure, the interpretation of an L2 structure in terms of the "closest" category in the L1, and delay in the appearance of L1 effects until a point in the development of the L2 that is clearly beyond the earliest stages. Predictions about what will be transferred are based, first, on the learner's perception of the degree of overall difference between the L1 and the L2 where perceived difference inhibits L1 influence and, second, on the basis of what aspects of the L1 the learner perceives as being universal and what aspects he or she perceives as specific to the L1.

Preston (chap. 8, this volume) points out that the statistical study of variation in L2 production can differentiate groups of learners according to their performance in relation to a number of criteria, including whether they share an L1 or not. As an example, he cites the case of a study in which factors that determine English plural marking for Chinese speakers on one hand and Czech and Slovak speakers on the other show these two groups of speakers to be from statistically distinct populations, indicating an L1 effect.

As the area of linguistic structure that was the original source of systematic speculation about L1 influence, we might expect phonology to reveal additional insights into L1 effects and it does. Leather and James (chap. 9) review the research on the influence of L1 phonology in L2 speech. Their conclusions are strikingly similar to those referred to above for morphosyntax: although there are clear L1 effects in both L2 perception and production of speech, a simple transfer theory—under which the full structure of the L1 is imposed on utterances in the L2—is inadequate. Gass's general review (chap. 10) of L1 influence also includes material on the role of the L1 in L2 phonology. Her examination of the literature includes recognition of an effect that further emphasizes the inadequacy of a simple transfer effect of the L1—that of so-called exaggeration, a form of hypercorrection in which the L2 user produces a feature of L2 phonology in a way that magnifies that feature beyond the form in which it appears in the production of NSs of the L2.

Finally, the study of the relationship between semantics and morphology in acquisition also reveals evidence of L1 influence. Andersen and Shirai noted that overgeneralization of the English progressive marker -ing to state verbs (like love, see, hate) in SLA is found in the performance of speakers from some L1 backgrounds and not from others. Andersen and Shirai attribute this phenomenon to an identification by the learner of the progressive marker with the imperfective in languages that have an overt perfective–imperfective contrast.

We turn now to the problem of **SLA beyond the earliest stages,** looking first at changes in grammatical competence—where the issues are, again, relatively clear—and then addressing briefly the issue of changes in performance over the course of acquisition as well as effects of change from one stage to the next—the question of sequencing of ILSs in the process of SLA.

Hypotheses about changes in grammatical competence in the process of SLA have taken a number of forms. We look first at *learning principles* proposed within the UG framework and—along with the study of adult native grammars, the process of L1 acquisition, and the positive-evidence-only assumption—constitute an attempt to contribute to an explanation for the *learnability* of L1s, considering possible implications for the study of SLA. We then discuss some additional generalizations concerning the sequencing of grammars in acquisition that have been proposed to explain the process of SLA.

Within the UG framework, proposed solutions to the developmental problem have depended crucially on learning principles conceived of as relationships between the grammars that form sequences in the acquisition process. It should be noted that acquisition (or learning) principles are distinct from the structural principles referred to earlier. The latter are part of UG and determine what structures are possible in human languages; the former specify relationships between grammars and determine the sequencing of grammars in the process of acquisition. We will mention two such principles—*the subset principle* (SP) and *the uniqueness principle* (UP)—as these are discussed in a number of the chapters in this volume.

The SP claims that the learner (tacitly) adopts a restrictive or conservative grammar in the early stages of acquisition—one that allows as narrow a range of structures as possible. The learner abandons this grammar for a less restrictive grammar only when examples in the input (positive evidence) require the abandonment of the earlier, more restrictive grammar. If the SP can be justified empirically, we have an account of how it is possible for acquisition to take place on the basis of positive evidence alone, because, according to the positive-evidence-only assumption referred to above, the learner can move to the next grammar in the process of acquisition only on the basis of such evidence. For more detailed discussion, see Gregg (chap. 2) and Berent (chap. 14).

The UP (or one-to-one principle) is also motivated by the fact that the acquirer is effectively exposed only to positive evidence. It states that, in the absence of direct evidence to the contrary, the acquirer will assume that there is a unique form in the language for every function. For example, if a learner overgeneralizes a rule at a particular stage of acquisition (say, produces the form *goed* in English in place of *went*), only exposure to utterances containing *went* (and no correction of the learner's utterances containing *goed*) is necessary for the acquisition of *went,* because *goed* and *went* both function as the past tense of *go.* In a case of this sort, the replacing form (here, *went*) is said to *preempt* the replaced form (*goed* in this case).

One set of questions concerning SLA within the UG framework, then, involves the operation (or nonoperation) in SLA of learning principles like the SP and UP. Though White (chap. 3) reports some work that casts doubt on the relevance of the SP as an explanatory principle even in L1 acquisition, and Gregg (chap. 2) voices concerns about the explanatory content of both of these principles, Gass (chap. 10) notes White's earlier arguments that the failure of L2 learners to attain nativelike grammars for L2s may be due to nonobservance of the principle. Berent (chap. 14) finds evidence for the operation of the SP in the acquisition of English by deaf subjects—particularly in relation to the GCP. Long (chap. 13) discusses both principles—the SP in relation to the sufficiency of positive evidence for SLA and the UP in connection with the role of negative evidence in acquisition in general. Andersen and Shirai (chap. 16) invoke both principles in their study of verb semantics and morphology, and, Seliger (chap. 18) finds a role for both in the explanation of the phenomena of L1 attrition.

Another source of claims about sequencing in the process of SLA is to be found in the notion of *markedness* within the F/T framework as discussed in section II of this chapter. Recall that if the presence of a certain structural feature in a language (the implicans) implies the presence of another (the implicatum) but not conversely, then the implicans is termed *marked* and the implicatum *unmarked.* Recall also that the example we gave earlier of markedness is embodied in (5) and (6), repeated here for convenience as (13) and (14).

(13)   Subject > Direct Object > Indirect Object > Object of a Preposition > Genitive > Object of a Comparative

(14)   Within relative clauses, if a language can extract a noun phrase in a given grammatical function in the hierarchy, then it can extract a noun phrase in any grammatical function higher in the hierarchy (though not necessarily conversely).

If we assume Eckman's (chap. 6) SCH and an additional generalization (suggested above) to the effect that acquisition proceeds from unmarked features to marked in SLA, then it is predicted that the sequence of acquisition for relative clauses in SLA will proceed from extraction of the subject only at the earliest stage to extraction of the subject and direct object at the next stage to extraction of the subject, direct object, and indirect object at the next, and so on. Eckman cites work to support this hypothesis. Long (chap. 13) uses a study of the acquisition of relativization analyzed in terms of (13) and (14) to argue for the insufficiency of comprehensible input in SLA. Berent (chap. 14) argues that a parameter that has the effect of (13) and (14) accounts for the order of acquisition of extraction in relative clauses in the acquisition of English by the deaf.

Preston's review (chap. 8) of variationist treatments of SLA includes extensive discussion of the changing pattern of variation from early stages of acquisition to later stages, providing detailed information about the nature of change in the process of SLA. Seliger (chap. 18) argues that considerations of markedness also enter into the explanation of L1 attrition. Finally, Bhatia and Ritchie (chap. 19) report work indicating that constraints on code-switching develop as the L2 learner becomes more proficient in the L2 with earlier judgments relatively unconstrained and later ones showing evidence of such constraints.

In the SLA of phonology, Eckman applies the SCH to a number of universal phonological generalizations and finds that it succeeds there as well. Leather and James (chap. 9) also report accounts of sequencing in SLA phonology in which markedness plays a role.

Andersen and Shirai (chap. 16, this volume) argue for a universal sequence of stages in the development of verb morphology in relation to verb semantics based on notions of markedness that applies across L1 acquisition, SLA, pidginization, and creolization.

Finally, considering the overall development of the cognitive abilities of the L2 learner, the information-processing approach to the study of SLA contributes to the study of SLA development in a number of respects, but two stand out. First, as McLaughlin and Heredia (chap. 7) report, any given set of structures will pass from attention-requiring controlled to attention-free automatic processing; second, restructuring of the type discussed above in relation to the earliest stages of acquisition (and, perhaps, of other sorts as well) is expected to induce an apparent reduction in the accuracy of performance as the L2 user's system of internal representations undergoes revision. Restructuring is then followed by an improvement in performance. This sequence of successful performance, followed by a slip in performance, followed in turn by improvement is termed "U-shaped behavior."

As White notes (chap. 3, this volume) an important question in the study of SLA is why most adult L2 learners do not complete the acquisition of the L2—that is, they do not attain a native IL system for the L2 with respect to some feature of the language but, rather, "get stuck" or undergo **fossilization** at a point in the process before they attain a nativelike IL system. A number of the contributions to this volume touch on this issue.

Berent's (deaf) subjects (chap. 14) provide one obvious explanation for the incompleteness of acquisition, though one that is clearly not generalizable: a severe limitation on input. An important feature of the grammatical competence that he attributes to his subjects is that it exhibits the properties of a stage of normal acquisition rather than a radically different system.

As Romaine (chap. 18) notes, the task of measuring the degree of bilingualism, dominance, and so on, is made extremely difficult by the fact that an individual may have highly developed tacit knowledge and/or skill in one aspect of language use (e.g., grammar and semantics) and have a much lower level of mastery in another area (e.g., phonology), acknowledging the widely observed fact that learner performance may be less complete in one aspect of the structure of the L2 than in others.

Finally, Preston (chap. 8) notes that some features of variation in L2 production that are not variable in the performance of NSs remain at the same level of variability throughout the course of acquisition even when the overall variation pattern of the learner has reached a point close to that of an NS, indicating a failure to attain some feature of the L2 and no likelihood of attaining it. Schachter also refers to such "fossilized variation" in support of her general claim that adult SLA is always incomplete.

C. Summary

In summary, research on SLA and use is a dynamic field characterized by discussion of a wide variety of issues, both conceptual and empirical. Conceptually, we have suggested that the questions that have dominated much research in L1 acquisition and use constitute a valid, productive basis for the investigation of L2 phenomena as well and that such problems in L1 investigation as the logical and developmental problems of language acquisition can be reasonably formulated and pursued in the study of SLA as in the study of L1 acquisition.

Empirically, the study of IL systems, linguistic input in SLA, and the capacity for SLA are all areas of active debate. The variability of IL performance and its explanation is important not only as a problem in itself but in the evaluation of methods of data elicitation as well. Also, the neural representation of the L2 user's two languages has been an important area of research. In the study of linguistic input for SLA, a central question is the place of positive and negative evidence, as is the effect of various forms of negotiation of meaning on the process and result of acquisition. And, of course, the precise effects of severe limitations on input are also a topic of discussion.

The question that has dominated the investigation of the overall capacity for SLA is that of the role of the principles and parameters of UG (or of universal typological generalizations about languages) in explaining the form of ILs and ILGs—that is, the nature of the adult's tacit grammatical theory. The key questions concerning the course of acquisition are those of the influence of the L1 and the role (if any) of learning principles such as the SP and UP. Additionally, the problem of the basis for fossilization continues to play a central role in discussion in the field. Finally, the investigation of possible neuropsychological correlates to the apparent reduction in the capacity to acquire an L2 around puberty contributes as well to our understanding of SLA phenomena.

IV. THE SECTIONS AND CHAPTERS OF THIS VOLUME

Though all of the chapters in the volume contribute in a number of ways to the discussion of the historical background and major issues in the field provided in section III of this chapter, each has its own range of topics as well; hence, we now turn to an overview of each chapter grouped by part of the volume.

A. Part I: Research and Theoretical Issues in Second Language Acquisition

Gregg's chapter, the second in part I of the volume, addresses the logical and developmental problems of SLA in depth. The logical problem of SLA is that of determining on empirical grounds what the overall capacity for the SLA of grammatical competence is; the developmental problem is that of explaining the real-time course of acquisition of grammatical competence. With respect to the logical problem, the relevance of Pinker's (1979) learnability condition for SLA is discussed. The chapter argues for the study of competence rather than other elements of linguistic ability as the basis for the development of a theory of SLA and, consequently, takes a position in favor of a modular approach to L2 ability under which grammatical competence is a separate "mental organ," distinct in character from other mental systems of principles such as those underlying visual and musical perception. The core of the treatment of the logical problem for SLA is a discussion of the implications of the two major positions regarding the accessibility of UG to the adult L2 learner that have been taken in the research literature: (a) the hypothesis the chapter refers to as the "theist" position under which UG is fully available to the adult (what we have termed the $GT_a = UG$ position) and (b) the "deist" or *deus abscondidus* hypothesis, which claims that only those features of UG that are realized in the grammar of the learner's L1 are accessible to the adult L2 learner, the $GT_a = L1G$-plus hypothesis of Schachter and others. In treating the developmental problem, the chapter adopts Atkinson's (1982) three criteria for a successful theory of acquisition in relation to a prospective theory of SLA and considers a number of kinds of empirical results—primarily from the study of L1 acquisition—that show promise as a basis for developing a theory of SLA. The chapter concludes by considering the state of the field with respect to the goal of developing such a theory.

B. Part II: Issues of Maturation and Modularity in Second Language Acquisition

The chapters in part II of this volume review the results of empirical research on the central issues in the study of adult SLA within the theoretical frameworks reviewed in part II of this chapter. The work reported in chapters 3 through 5—those by White, Flynn, and Schachter, respectively—was conducted within the generative framework. As discussed above, each of these chapters represents a somewhat different point of view regarding the question of the accessibility of UG in adult L2 learners. Eckman (chap. 6) deals with work on SLA and use that is also concerned with structural variation among languages but is, as noted above, conducted with different goals from those of the generative framework—the F/T approach to the study of linguistic phenomena in general and SLA in particular. McLaughlin and Heredia (chap. 7) review major issues in an approach to L2 phenomena that applies an information-processing framework developed in general cognitive psychology to the particular case of SLA regarded as the development of a complex skill. Their approach, unlike that of the authors of chaps. 3–5, does not assume that the process of language acquisition is determined by capacities specific to the grammar module but, rather, by principles of learning that are applied in all cases of the development of complex cognitive skills. Preston (chap. 8) outlines the variationist approach to the study of L2 phenomena—one based on statistical techniques developed in sociolinguistics to study systematic variation in the speech of individuals and communities.

White's comprehensive chapter (chap. 3) opens with an outline of the principles-and-parameters framework. The formulation of three positions regarding the accessibility of UG in adult SLA follows. These positions are formulated, first, in terms of similarities and differences in attained grammatical competence between NSs and non-NSs of a given language and, second, in terms of same or different "means of acquisition" (whether the attained competence is constrained by UG or not): (a) same competence, same means (attained native and nonnative competence are the same and both are UG-constrained); (b) different competence, different means (nonnative competence differs from native and is determined by a grammatical theory different from UG); and (c) different competence, same means (though native and nonnative competence differ, both are UG-constrained). The chapter reviews the empirical evidence bearing on each of these positions first with respect to principles of UG and then with respect to parameters. It then goes on to discuss a variety of current issues including the role of positive and negative evidence in SLA, possible maturational effects in adult L2 learners, and the competence of near-NSs. Finally, the chapter suggests some new research directions including greater attention to child SLA and to L2 phonology within the principles-and-parameters framework.

Flynn's chapter (chap. 4) begins with a discussion of the generative framework. It then argues at length for the continuity hypothesis (the "full-access" hypothesis in her terminology) and against both the $GT_a = L1G$ ("partial-access") hypothesis and a "no-access" hypothesis (Clahsen, 1988) under which adults are claimed to acquire L2s without any reference to UG at all. The empirical basis for these arguments includes Flynn's own work and that of others related to the head-direction parameter, conditions on movement rules, failure of "transfer" of certain L1 structures, and functional categories.

Chapter 5 by Schachter presents a wide range of arguments for the $GT_a = L1G$-plus hypothesis (her "incompleteness hypothesis"). This hypothesis claims that adults lose not only parameter values, except those that determine the grammar of the L1, but they also lose the principles that constrain structures not instantiated in the grammar of the L1 as well. The chapter presents general arguments based on a wide variety of considerations, including general features of adult-acquired grammars and brain development (including the critical or sensitive-period hypothesis). The specifically grammatical evidence presented here is built on Schachter's recent work on subjacency and that of Lee (1992) on the GCP.

Eckman (chap. 6) addresses research on SLA over the last fifteen to twenty years within the F/T framework. The chapter lucidly traces work within this approach that led from Eckman's own Markedness Differential Hypothesis (MDH) (Eckman, 1977), a cornerstone of much F/T work on SLA in the late 1970s and early 1980s, to the development of his SCH, and to more recent work within the framework. Recall that the SCH claims that all ILs obey universal generalizations formulated on the basis of the study of adult native languages and are therefore natural languages. Eckman summarizes the evidence in favor of the SCH.

The work reported in chapters 3–6 is concerned specifically with linguistic structure in SLA; in fact, as noted above, the White, Flynn, and Schachter chapters adopt a modular view of the mind. Departing from this view, chapter 7 by McLaughlin and Heredia takes the position that SLA constitutes the development of a complex cognitive skill which, like the attainment of other such skills, follows from general principles of cognitive functioning. The work reported in the chapter is thus concerned with features of the learning process that are not restricted to a particular cognitive domain but are, rather, claimed to be found across domains. McLaughlin and Heredia concentrate on two such features—the passage from controlled to automatic modes of processing and restructuring from relatively concrete exemplar-based internal representations to more abstract, rule-based representations.

The variationist work reviewed in Preston's insightful chapter 8 brings yet another point of view to the study of SLA. The goal of this research is to find systematic variation in the speech of language users. As noted earlier, in its original formulation and application in the study of variation in the language behavior of the individual, variationist techniques make it possible to study in detail the differences and similarities in production between L2 learners and NSs and among L2 learners. This approach also makes it possible to investigate the systematic changes that occur in the L2 learner's performance as he or she moves through the acquisition process, providing data that is crucial for a general understanding of the process of SLA and use both for those features that fall within the purview of other theoretical frameworks and those that fall outside it.

C. Part III: Second Language Speech and the Influence of the First Language

Perhaps due to the nature of recent developments in grammatical theory and in the study of L1 acquisition that have been most influential in the study of SLA, the central issues of maturation and L1 influence in theoretically grounded L2 research have been pursued primarily in terms of L2 syntax and morphology rather than L2 phonology. This relative neglect of phonology is somewhat surprising, as few L2 researchers would disagree with the position that L2 phonology is affected by both maturation and L1 influence, though the effects of maturation and L1 influence on the acquisition of syntax and morphology have sometimes been disputed (e.g., by Dulay & Burt, 1973, 1974). Nonetheless, there is a growing body of important work on L2 phonology, and that work is reviewed by Leather and James (chap. 9). As noted earlier, one of the major contributions that research on SLA has made to a general understanding of language acquisition is the fact that the learner already has a linguistic system in place. Since L1 influence is a particular concern in the study of L2 phonology, we include Gass's review of research on L1 influence (chap. 10) in this section with the Leather and James chapter.

Leather and James (chap. 9) provide a detailed and thorough review of topics in L2 phonology. Topics include the effects of motivation level, personality, social acceptance, and gender on mastery of the phonology of an L2. They also address L1 influence on phonology based on recent theoretical work, including principles-and-parameters phonology. Also included are discussions of a broad range of issues in the study of the perception and production of L2 sounds as well as topics in the interaction of L1 influence with typological universals.

After providing historical background for current work on L1 influence, Gass (chap. 10) integrates work on the form and scope of L1 influence and recent attempts to predict and explain the phenomena. It examines work on grammatical competence (both syntax and phonology) as well as pragmatics within several theoretical frameworks, including principles and parameters, F/T, and the Competition Model of Bates and MacWhinney (1981, 1989).

D. Part IV: Research Methodology and Applications

In addition to reviewing research results, several of the earlier chapters (in particular, chap. 3 by White and chap. 4 by Flynn) address issues of L2 research methodology, one of the most active areas of debate in the field. Chapters 11 by Nunan and 12 by Sorace—which make up part IV of the volume—are devoted entirely to discussions of L2 research methodology.

Nunan's chapter is a comprehensive historical survey of substantive questions in the field and the research methods employed to study those questions. In particular, he discusses the issues of qualitative versus quantitative methods, longitudinal versus cross-sectional studies, and experimental and elicited versus naturalistic data in the L2 research over the last ten to twenty years.

Though the phenomena of SLA are arguably more complex than those of L1, L2 researchers have available to them a highly productive means of eliciting data that is largely unavailable to L1 acquisition researchers—acceptability judgments. Though not without problems, the use of acceptability judgments has played a major role in the development of L2 research. Sorace (chap. 12) focuses in depth on issues in the use of judgmental data both in the investigation of L1 adult native grammars and in L2 research. In addition, she reports on her own recent, important work on the controlled use of magnitude estimation as a method of eliciting acceptability judgments for the testing of claims in L2 research.

E. Part V: Modality and the Linguistic Environment in Second Language Acquisition

As is true in the study of L1 acquisition, the nature of the learner's linguistic experience is a major issue in L2 research. Though, for obvious reasons, the study of input in normal cases of SLA occupies a central place in the field, an important contribution is also made by cases in which the quality of input is "degraded" for some reason as, for example, in instances of creolization (see chap. 16, this volume, by Andersen and Shirai). In part V of this volume, Long (chap. 13) provides a discussion of research on input in normal cases and Berent (chap. 14) reviews work on an instance of SLA (or, as Berent himself suggests, of "L1.5" acquisition) in which input is restricted—the case of acquisition of English by the deaf.

After treating research on the ways in which NSs modify their speech in addressing non-NSs to render it more comprehensible, Long's comprehensive chapter argues (*contra* Krashen) that, though necessary, comprehensible input is not sufficient for SLA. It then addresses an issue that arises more prominently in the study of SLA than in research on L1 acquisition—the question of the place of attention, noticing, and focus on form in acquisition. This is followed by a treatment of the role of negative evidence in both L1 and L2 acquisition in terms of Pinker's (1989) four criteria for the possible effectiveness of negative evidence in language acquisition, concluding that the evidence in both cases is equivocal. Long then turns to the research on the role of conversation in SLA, arguing for his interaction hypothesis.

Berent (chap. 14) begins with a thorough review of the descriptive research on the English of deaf learners. He then provides a brief outline of syntactic theory within the principles-and-parameters framework (including, specifically, the distinction between thematic and functional categories) as the basis for an insightful analysis of the data from deaf learners of English. He, in fact, proceeds to such an analysis in terms of Radford's (1990) treatment of the early L1 English of hearing children under which early grammars lack functional categories, these subsequently developing as a consequence of grammatical maturation.

F. Part VI: The Neuropsychology of Second Language Acquisition and Use

Obler and Hannigan (chap. 15) interpret the research of the last two decades in several areas related to SLA and use. After a brief history, they survey recent work on the notion of a critical or sensitive period as well as some research on exceptionally successful postpubertal acquisition that suggests that there may be a neurological basis for such success. They then review and analyze the complex evidence for representation of the L2 user's two languages in the brain and the work on language breakdown in bilinguals, concluding with proposals for future research.

G. Part VII: Language Contact and Its Consequences

The final section of the volume treats the various consequences of language contact—the result of SLA. Chapter 16 by Andersen and Shirai is a detailed discussion of the development of verb morphology as it relates to the inherent aspect of verbs. Romaine (chap. 17) surveys a wide variety of aspects of bilingualism, and Seliger (chap. 18) reviews work on L1 attrition in bilingual settings. Finally, Bhatia and Ritchie (chap. 19) review work in the study of code-switching and -mixing, including some recent research on the development of universal constraints on language mixing in the process of acquisition.

Andersen and Shirai argue convincingly for the primary-of-aspect hypothesis, which claims that the order of acquisition of verb morphology is determined in large part by the inherent lexical aspect of verbs. They base their arguments on evidence not only from the processes of L1 acquisition and SLA but from the structures of pidgins and creoles as well. They thus continue the practice, referred to in section II of this chapter, of including evidence from pidgins and creoles in the testing of hypotheses about language acquisition. Earlier accounts of primacy-of-aspect effects in L1 acquisition relied on the cognitive immaturity of the child; the fact that these effects show up in adult L2 learners calls this type of explanation into question, providing a case in which SLA evidence can be brought to bear in testing hypotheses about L1 acquisition. Andersen and Shirai also explore explanations of the primacy-of-aspect effect in terms of both frequency of occurrence of relevant input (their distributional bias hypothesis) and prototype theory.

Romaine's wide-ranging chapter (chap. 17) presents the recent trends in the extensive research on bilingualism, including discussion of the characterization of bilingualism and the study of aspects of bilingualism in a variety of disciplines (as well as the special nature of bilingual communities and individuals), bilingualism and education, and attitudes toward bilingualism. The chapter thus provides a summary of the consequences of research on the social, psychological, and educational consequences of SLA.

One important effect of SLA leading to bilingualism and beyond is the attrition of the L2 learner's L1. Seliger's chapter is a principled interpretation of work on L1 attrition in a bilingual context. He develops a variety of parallels between the dissolution of language in attrition and the process of language acquisition—both L1 and L2.

Bhatia and Ritchie address issues in the study of language mixing. The chapter includes discussion of syntactic and semantic constraints on code-switching and -mixing, as well as social psychological and other nonlinguistic motivations and attitudes. Finally, it examines some cases of claimed pathological code-switching in polyglot aphasics as well as research on the gradual appearance of universal constraints on code-switching in the process of SLA.

V. CONCLUSIONS

As the present volume attests, research on SLA has made remarkable progress over the last ten to fifteen years both in sharpening fundamental empirical questions and in addressing them with increasingly sophisticated methods. As is perhaps to be expected in the study of an empirical domain as rich as SLA, the more the field progresses, the deeper and more complex the questions become. Nonetheless, SLA research is a dynamic and growing field, and the progress made in recent years can be expected to continue in the future as these deeper questions are investigated and yet deeper ones arise.

In a field as fast-moving and diverse as the study of SLA, no single volume can be expected to cover all aspects of the field. However, we believe that the topics and their treatment in this work provide an accurate state-of-the-art of the central issues as seen by the most prominent scholars in the discipline.

REFERENCES

Adjemian, C. (1976). On the nature of interlanguage systems. *Language Learning, 26,* 297–320.

Albert, M., & Obler, L. (1978). *The bilingual brain: neuropsychological and neurolinguistic aspects of bilingualism.* New York: Academic Press.

Anderson, J. R. (1983). *The architecture of cognition.* Cambridge, MA: Harvard University Press.

Atkinson, M. (1982). *Explanations in the study of child language development.* Cambridge, UK: Cambridge University Press.

Bailey, C.-J. N. (1974). *Variation and linguistic theory.* Arlington, VA: Center for Applied Linguistics.

Baker, C. L. (1979). Syntactic theory and the projection problem. *Linguistic Inquiry, 10,* 533–582.

Bates, E., & MacWhinney, B. (1981). Second language acquisition from a functionalist perspective: Pragmatic, semantic, and perceptual strategies. In H. Winitz (Ed.), *Native language and foreign language acquisition (Annals of the New York Academy of Sciences,* no. 379) (pp. 190–214). New York: New York Academy of Sciences.

Bates, E., & MacWhinney, B. (Eds.) (1989). *The crosslinguistic study of sentence processing.* Cambridge, UK: Cambridge University Press.

Bialystok, E. (1978). A theoretical model of second language learning. *Language Learning, 28,* 69–84.

Bialystok, E. (1982). On the relationship between knowing and using linguistic forms. *Applied Linguistics, 3(3),* 181–206.

Bickerton, D. (1971). Inherent variability and variable rules. *Foundations of Language, 7,* 457–492.

Bickerton, D. (1975). *Dynamics of a creole system.* Cambridge, UK: Cambridge University Press.

Bley-Vroman, R. (1989). What is the logical problem of foreign language learning? In S. Gass & J. Schachter (Eds.), *Linguistic perspectives on second language acquisition* (pp. 41–68). Cambridge, UK: Cambridge University Press.

Bloomfield, L. (1933). *Language.* New York: Henry Holt.

Brown, R. (1973). *A first language.* Cambridge, MA: Harvard University Press.

Burt, M. K., Dulay, H., & Hernandez-Chavez, E. (1975). *Bilingual syntax measure.* New York: Harcourt Brace Jovanovich.

Cazden, C., Cancino, H., Rosansky, E., & Schumann, J. (1975). *Second language acquisition sequences in children, adolescents, and adults.* Final report submitted to the National Institute of Education. Washington, DC: Educational Resources Information Center.

Chomsky, N. (1955/1975). *The logical structure of linguistic theory.* Chicago: University of Chicago Press.

Chomsky, N. (1957). *Syntactic structures.* The Hague: Mouton.

Chomsky, N. (1964). Current issues in linguistic theory. In J. Fodor & J. Katz (Eds.), *The structure of language: Readings in the philosophy of language* (pp. 50–118). Englewood Cliffs, NJ: Prentice-Hall.

Chomsky, N. (1965). *Aspects of the theory of syntax.* Cambridge, MA: MIT Press.

Chomsky, N. (1975). *Reflections on language.* New York: Pantheon Books.

Chomsky, N. (1981). *Lectures on government and binding.* Dordrecht: Foris.

Chomsky, N. (1986). *Knowledge of language.* New York: Praeger.

Chomsky, N. (1991). Some notes on economy of derivation and representation. In R. Friedin (Ed.), *Principles and parameters in comparative grammar* (pp. 417–454). Cambridge, MA: MIT Press.

Chomsky, N. (1993). A minimalist program for linguistic theory. In K. Hale & S. Keyser (Eds.), *The view from building 20: Essays in linguistics in honor of Sylvain Bromberger* (pp. 1–52). Cambridge, MA: MIT Press.

Chomsky, N., & Miller, G. (1963). Introduction to the formal analysis of natural languages. In R. Luce, R. Bush, & E. Galanter (Eds.), *Handbook of mathematical psychology* (Vol. 2, pp. 269–321). New York: John Wiley.

Clahsen, H. (1988). Parametrized grammatical theory and language acquisition: A study of the acquisition of verb placement and inflection by children and adults. In S. Flynn & W. O'Neil (Eds.), *Linguistic Theory in Second Language Acquisition* (pp. 47–75). Dordrecht: Kluwer Academic.

Corder, S. P. (1967). The significance of learners' errors. *International Review of Applied Linguistics, 5,* 161–170.

Cummins, R. (1983). *The nature of psychological explanation.* Cambridge, MA: MIT Press.

Dulay, H., & Burt, M. K. (1973). Should we teach children syntax? *Language Learning, 23,* 245–258.

Dulay, H., & Burt, M. K. (1974). Natural sequences in child second language acquisition. *Language Learning, 24,* 37–53.

Eckman, F. (1977). Markedness and the contrastive analysis hypothesis. *Language Learning, 27,* 315–330.

Ellis, R. (1985a). Sources of variability in interlanguage. *Applied Linguistics, 6,* 118–131.

Ellis, R. (1985b). *Understanding second language acquisition.* Oxford: Oxford University Press.

Ellis, R. (1990). *Instructed second language acquisition.* Oxford: Basil Blackwell.

Felix, S. (1987). *Cognition and language growth.* Dordrecht: Foris.

Fries, C. C. (1945). *Teaching and learning English as a foreign language.* Ann Arbor: University of Michigan Press.

Gardner, R. (1985). *Social psychology and second language learning: The role of attitudes and motivation.* London: Edward Arnold.

Gardner, R., & Lambert, W. (1972). *Attitudes and motivation in second language learning.* Rowley, MA: Newbury House.

Garrett, M. (1990). Sentence processing. In D. Osherson & H. Lasnik (Eds.), *An invitation to cognitive science* (Vol. 1, *Language,* pp. 133–175). Cambridge, MA: MIT Press.

Gass, S., & Selinker, L. (Eds.) (1992). *Language transfer in language learning.* Amsterdam: John Benjamins.

Gass, S., & Selinker, L. (1994). *Second language acquisition: An introductory course.* Hillsdale: Erlbaum.

Greenberg, J. (1963/1966). Some universals of grammar with particular reference to the order of meaningful elements. In J. Greenberg (Ed.), *Universals of language* (pp. 73–113). Cambridge, MA: MIT Press.

Gregg, K. (1984). Krashen's monitor and Occam's razor. *Applied Linguistics, 5,* 79–100.

Gregg, K. (1990). The variable competence model of second language acquisition and why it isn't. *Applied Linguistics, 11,* 364–383.

Hammond, M. Moravcsik, E., & Wirth, J. (1988). *Studies in syntactic typology.* Amsterdam: John Benjamins.

Harris, Z. (1951). *Structural linguistics.* Chicago: University of Chicago Press.

Harris, Z. (1954). Distributional structure. *Word, 10,* 146–162.

Hawkins, J. (Ed.) (1988). *Explaining language universals.* Oxford: Basil Blackwell.

Hempel, C. (1966). *Philosophy of natural science.* Englewood Cliffs, NJ: Prentice-Hall.

Huang, J., & Hatch, E. (1978). A Chinese child's acquisition of English. In E. Hatch (Ed.), *Second language acquisition: A book of readings* (pp. 118–131). Rowley, MA: Newbury House.

Joos, M. (1958). *Readings in linguistics.* New York: American Council of Learned Societies.

Kasper, G., & Blum-Kulka, S. (1993). *Interlanguage pragmatics.* New York: Oxford University Press.

Keenan, E., & Comrie, B. (1977). Noun phrase accessibility and Universal Grammar. *Linguistic Inquiry, 8,* 63–99.

Keenan, E., & Comrie, B. (1979). Data on the Noun Phrase Accessibility Hierarchy. *Language, 55,* 333–351.

Klima, E., & Bellugi-Klima, U. (1966). Syntactic regularities in the speech of children. In J. Lyons & R. Wales (Ed.), *Psycholinguistics papers: The proceedings of 1966 Edinburgh Conference* (pp. 183–208). Edinburgh: Edinburgh University Press.

Krashen, S. (1981). *Second language acquisition and second language learning.* Oxford: Pergamon.

Krashen, S. (1982). *Principles and practice in second language acquisition.* Oxford: Pergamon.

Krashen, S. (1985). *The input hypothesis: Issues and implications.* London: Longman.

Krashen, S., Scarcella, R., & Long, M. (1982). Age, rate, and eventual attainment in second language acquisition. In S. Krashen, R. Scarcella, & M. Long (Eds.), *Child-adult differences in second language acquisition* (pp. 161–172). Rowley, MA: Newbury House.

Labov, W. (1966). *The social stratification of English in New York City.* Arlington, VA: Center for Applied Linguistics.

Labov, W. (1972). *Sociolinguistic patterns.* Philadelphia: University of Pennsylvania Press.

Labov, W. (1980). *Locating language in time and space.* New York: Academic Press.

Lado, R. (1957). *Linguistics across cultures.* Ann Arbor: University of Michigan Press.

Larsen-Freeman, D., & Long, M. (1991). *An introduction to second language acquisition research.* London: Longman.

Lee, D. (1992). *Universal Grammar, learnability, and the acquisition of English reflexive binding by L1 Korean speakers.* Unpublished doctoral dissertation, University of Southern California, Los Angeles.

Lenneberg, E. (1967). *Biological foundations of language.* New York: John Wiley.

Levelt, W. (1989). *Speaking: from intention to articulation.* Cambridge, MA: MIT Press.

Levinson, S. (1983). *Pragmatics.* Cambridge, UK: Cambridge University Press.

Long, M. (1990). Maturational constraints on language development. *Studies in Second Language Acquisition, 12,* 251–285.

McLaughlin, B. (1978). The Monitor Model: Some methodological considerations. *Language Learning, 28,* 309–332.

Meisel, J., Clahsen, H., & Pienemann, M. (1981). On determining developmental stages in natural second language acquisition. *Studies in Second Language Acquisition, 3,* 109–135.

Nagel, E. (1961). *The structure of science: Problems in the logic of scientific explanation.* New York: Harcourt, Brace & World.

Newmeyer, F. (1986). *Linguistic theory in America* (2nd ed.). San Diego: Academic Press.

Newmeyer, F., & Weinberger, S. (1988). The ontogenesis of the field of second language learning research. In S. Flynn & W. O'Neil (Eds.), *Linguistic theory in second language acquisition* (pp. 34–45). Dordrecht: Kluwer.

Pinker, S. (1979). Formal models of language learning. *Cognition, 7,* 217–283.

Pinker, S. (1989). *Learnability and cognition.* Cambridge, MA: MIT Press.

Polivanov, E. (1931). *La perception des sons d'une langue étrangère. Travaux du Cercle Linguistique de Prague, 4,* 75–89.

Pollock, J.-Y. (1989). Verb movement, Universal Grammar, and the structure of IP. *Linguistic Inquiry, 20,* 365–424.

Preston, D. (1989). *Sociolinguistics and second language acquisition.* Oxford: Basil Blackwell.

Radford, A. (1990). *Syntactic theory and the acquisition of English syntax: The nature of early child grammars of English.* Oxford: Basil Blackwell.

Ritchie, W. (1973). An explanatory framework for the study of adult language acquisition. In R. Shuy & C.-J. Bailey (Eds.), *Towards tomorrow's linguistics.* Washington, DC: Georgetown University School of Languages and Linguistics.

Rivers, W. (1964). *The psychologist and the foreign language teacher.* Chicago: University of Chicago Press.

Schumann, J. (1978a). The acculturation model for second language acquisition. In R. Gingras (Ed.), *Second language acquisition and foreign language teaching* (pp. 27–50). Arlington, VA: Center for Applied Linguistics.

Schumann, J. (1978b). *The pidginization process: A model for second language acquisition.* Rowley, MA: Newbury House.

Schumann, J. (1978c). The relationship of pidginization, creolization, and decreolization to second language acquisition. *Language Learning, 28,* 367–379.

Schwartz, B. (1986). The epistemological status of second language acquisition. *Second Language Research, 2,* 120–159.

Schwartz, B., & Gubala-Ryzak, M. (1992). Learnability and grammar reorganization in L2: Against negative evidence causing the unlearning of verb movement. *Second Language Research, 8,* 1–38.

Scovel, T. (1988). *A time to speak: A psycholinguistic inquiry into the critical period for human speech.* New York: Newbury House.

Selinker, L. (1972). Interlanguage. *International Review of Applied Linguistics, 10,* 209–231.

Shlonsky, U. (1992). Resumptive pronouns as a Last Resort. *Linguistic Inquiry, 23,* 443–468.

Singleton, D. (1989). *Language acquisition: The age factor.* Clevedon, UK: Multilingual Matters.

Tarone, E. (1983). On the variability of interlanguage systems. *Applied Linguistics, 4,* 142–163.

Tarone, E. (1988). *Variation in interlanguage.* London: Edward Arnold.

Tarone, E., Gass, S., & Cohen, A. (1994). *Research methodology in second-language acquisition.* Northvale, NJ: L. Erlbaum.

Trubetzkoy, N. (1969). *Principles of phonology.* (Baltaxe, C. Trans., 1969): Los Angeles: U. of California Press. (Original work published 1958).

Vihman, M. (1982). Formulas in first and second language acquisition. In L. Obler & L. Menn (Eds.), *Exceptional language and linguistics* (pp. 261–284). New York: Academic Press.

Weinert, R. (1995). The role of formulaic language in second language acquisition: A review. *Applied Linguistics, 16,* 180–205.

Wexler, K., & Culicover, P. W. (1980). *Formal Principles of Language Acquisition.* Cambridge, MA: MIT Press.

Wexler, K., & Manzini, R. (1987). Parameters and learnability in binding theory. In T. Roeper & E. Williams (Eds.), *Parameter setting* (pp. 41–76). Dordrecht: Reidel.

White, L. (1987). Against comprehensible input: The Input Hypothesis and the development of L2 competence. *Applied Linguistics, 8,* 95–110.

Wode, H. (1981). *Learning a second language: I. An integrated view of language acquisition.* Tübingen, Germany: Gunter Narr.

Wong Fillmore, L. (1976). *The second time around: Cognitive and social strategies in second language acquisition.* Unpublished doctoral dissertation, Stanford University, Palo Alto, California.

Zobl, H. (1995). Converging evidence for the 'acquisition-learning' distinction. *Applied Linguistics, 16,* 35–56.

P A R T I

RESEARCH AND THEORETICAL ISSUES IN SECOND LANGUAGE ACQUISITION

CHAPTER 2

THE LOGICAL AND DEVELOPMENTAL PROBLEMS OF SECOND LANGUAGE ACQUISITION

Kevin R. Gregg

As a scientific discipline, the study of second language (L2) acquisition is newer and less developed than the study of first language (L1) acquisition. In part this is probably because unlike L1 acquisition research, the study of L2 acquisition has grown out of practical or applied concerns, such as language teaching. Until the 1980s most work in L2 acquisition theory tended to keep one eye on the classroom; it is really not until "Government and Binding Theory" (Chomsky, 1981) began to be applied to L2 acquisition that we see a truly theory-centered approach to the question of L2 acquisition, and it becomes possible to talk meaningfully of L2 acquisition as a coherent field.[1] Unfortunately, it is also

[1] With the exception of a few articles like Ritchie (1978) and Adjémian (1976), most earlier "theoretical" work in L2 acquisition tended to be fairly superficial, if not naive, in its treatment of linguistic theory. Space considerations require that I give short shrift to these earlier approaches to L2 acquisition, such as the so-called Contrastive Analysis and Creative Construction hypotheses or Krashen's influential proposals; for discussion, see, e.g., Larsen-Freeman and Long (1991). Lado (1957) is the *locus classicus* for Contrastive Analysis; for Creative Construction see Dulay, Burt, and Krashen (1982), which can also serve as a convenient exposition of Krashen's proposals. Gregg (1984) provides reasons for excluding such proposals from discussion here.

Recently a number of writers have begun to treat L2 acquisition theory seriously within the larger context of scientific theory construction in general, and to apply to L2 acquisition some of the insights of current philosophy of science: of especial relevance are Beretta (1991), Beretta and Crookes (1993), Crookes (1993), Gregg (1993), and Long (1993).

Handbook of Second Language Acquisition

an extremely complex field, arguably more so than L1 acquisition. L2 acquisition researchers may take what comfort they can that their subjects usually answer questions and seldom wet their pants, but the number of confounding variables at work is daunting, and poses all kinds of difficulties for the would-be theoretician. In what follows I will look at the kinds of tasks the theoretician must try to accomplish, and the kinds of problems that render the tasks so difficult.

I. EXPLANATORY GOALS OF L2 ACQUISITION THEORY: THE LOGICAL AND DEVELOPMENTAL PROBLEMS

The term *the logical problem of language acquisition* was coined by David Lightfoot (Baker & McCarthy, 1981; Hornstein & Lightfoot, 1981). (For discussion of the question of a logical problem for L2 acquisition see chapters 3 by White, 4 by Flynn, and 5 by Schachter.) The problem is to explain how one comes to have the complex linguistic knowledge, or competence, one does, given the limited input one receives in the course of acquisition. This is a problem because the input vastly underdetermines the finally achieved competence.

In addition to the logical problem, there is also what Felix (1984), has termed the *developmental problem,* which "relates to the question of why natural languages are acquired the way they are, i.e., how can the regularities that have been observed in real-time acquisition processes be explained?" (p. 133). The logical problem is, How is acquisition possible? The developmental problem is, How does acquisition proceed? As Felix points out, there has been a tendency to treat the logical problem as a problem for linguistics and the developmental problem as a problem for psycholinguistics; this distinction, though, is ultimately arbitrary.

In any case these two problems can be extended to the question of L2 acquisition, although we may have to qualify our characterization of them, as we will see below. Furthermore, these two problems are both what Hempel (1965) calls "explanation-seeking why-questions," questions that can be expressed as, Why is it the case that p ? This is to say that if we are looking for a satisfactory theory of L2 acquisition, we will need to go beyond a mere description of, say, the stages of acquisition, however universal they may be and however precisely detailed. Nor can we rest content with a set of predictions, however accurate, as to the course of acquisition.

The nature and form of an explanation is an extremely complex question that has generated a good deal of controversy in the philosophy of science, and we can only touch upon it here.[2] But it is important to note that a commitment to

---

[2] See Salmon (1989) for a historical overview, and Ruben (1990) for an outline of the main questions dividing philosophers.

explaining is an essential part of the process of theory construction in general (van Fraassen, 1980), and that the presence of this commitment can be used as a criterion in assessing theoretical proposals in L2 acquisition in particular (Gregg, 1993).

But a commitment to explaining is not enough. The logical problem—explaining the nature of the human endowment that permits acquisition to take place—and the developmental problem—explaining the processes that occur and how they contribute to acquisition—are not explanatory problems of the same order. The former would seem to require what Cummins (1983) calls a *property* theory, whereas the latter requires a *transition* theory.

A transition theory asks "Why does system S change states from s-1 to s-2?" Cummins, 1983, p. 15). Why does water expand when it freezes? Why does your knee jerk when the doctor taps it? Why does opium make you sleepy? Given an event or phenomenon we want explained—an *explanandum*—a transition theory provides some other event or state or phenomenon, the *explanans*,[3] which can be seen as the cause of the explanandum phenomenon; thus a question about tides, for instance, although it can be cast as a why question in Hempel's sense (why are there tides?), is typically framed as a question about cause and effect: What causes the tides?

A property theory, on the other hand, is not in the business of providing causes and explaining effects. Rather, it is concerned with the instantiation of a property in a system; the question here is, "What is it for system S to have property P?" or "In virtue of what does S have P?" (Cummins, 1983, p. 15). Cummins distinguishes, for example, between Why did the gas get hotter?—a transition theory question, and, In virtue of what does gas have a temperature?—a property theory question. For him, the kinetic theory of gases is a property theory that answers the latter question.

Rather than describing causal agents that impinge on a system, a property theory describes the components that constitute the system, and their interrelations. This kind of description is called functional analysis. In cognitive science, functional analysis is seen as a way to avoid the homunculus problem, where a given mental competence is attributed in effect to a little person inside one's head; the problem being of course that this involves an infinite regress of homunculi inside the heads of other homunculi. We can avoid the homunculus problem if rather than homunculi of equally complex capacity we have a hierarchical organization of increasingly simple properties.[4]

The connection with L2 acquisition should be clear enough: The logical problem

---

[3] I am glossing over the question, much debated in philosophic circles, of whether an explanandum and its explanans should be seen as events, or as arguments, or as something else (see e.g., Ruben, 1990, for discussion).

[4] See Dawkins (1985, chap. 1) for a lucid exposition of this logic in relation to biological explanation.

of L2 acquisition demands at least in part a property theory, which can explain L2 knowledge by analyzing it into component parts. For instance, current linguistic theory tries to explain complex grammatical knowledge by breaking it down into interactions between less complex principles, such as move-alpha and the theta-criterion. The developmental problem, on the other hand, presumably needs to appeal to causal relations (e.g. between input and the grammatical system internalized by a learner). Thus a complete L2 acquisition theory will in fact be a complex amalgam of two different types of theory, calling upon different types of evidence and argument in their justification.

II. THE LOGICAL PROBLEM OF L2 ACQUISITION: EXPLAINING L2 COMPETENCE

L1 acquisition poses a *logical* problem because of the enormous gap between the grammatical knowledge acquired on the one hand, and the specific linguistic data the child receives on the other, such that the latter grossly underdetermines the former. This "poverty of the stimulus" argument, as it is often called, leads inevitably to the positing of innate mental structures that act on the linguistic input to produce a mental grammar. Furthermore, the highly complex and language-specific nature of linguistic knowledge suggests that these mental structures, rather than being general input-processing mechanisms, are specifically designed to act on linguistic input (for detailed arguments, see, e.g., Chomsky, 1986; J. A. Fodor, 1983). The usual term for this set of innate, language-specific mental structures is Universal Grammar (UG).

Assuming for the moment that the claim that L1 acquisition is mediated by UG is correct, the question is whether the logical problem of L2 acquisition is the same, or indeed whether there is in fact a logical problem of L2 acquisition at all. (I should make it clear that in this chapter we are dealing with the acquisition of an L2 by an adult.) If, for example, L2s were totally impossible to acquire, there would be no logical problem of acquisition; our explanandum would be the failure to acquire an L2, and a likely explanans would be biological change in the learner, such as is claimed to take place by the end of the so-called critical period. Indeed, such a situation would be confirmatory evidence for the UG position in L1 acquisition.

Of course people do acquire, or seem to acquire, L2s. On the other hand, most people do not do a very good job of it; if absolute across-the-board failure is not the case, neither is the absolute across-the-board success found that characterizes L1 acquisition. In fact it can be argued that truly nativelike competence in an L2 is never attained. But even if that turns out to be the case, it does not follow that there is no logical problem; if the learner's L2 grammar—what is known as his interlanguage (IL) grammar—is underdetermined by the input data, the problem exists however "imperfect" the acquired grammar may be. On the other hand, assume that true nativelike competence is sometimes acquired; given that most L2 learners do not achieve anywhere near the level of a native speaker (NS), it still does not go without saying that the logical problem is to be resolved in the same way in L2 as in L1 acquisition (see, e.g., Schwartz, 1986, and Gregg, 1988, for two different positions on this question). Just as there would be no logical problem if we could not learn a word of a foreign language, neither would there be a logical problem if we learned only what we were taught. All this is to say that the nature and content of L2 competence is not to be taken for granted, but rather must be examined.

A. Why Competence?

The domain of a L2 acquisition theory is not the behavior of speakers (linguistic performance), but rather the mental system (competence) underlying that behavior. (See chapters 3 by White and 4 by Flynn for competence–performance in L2 acquisition.) Nor is competence the same thing as ability, as Chomsky has often pointed out (e.g., 1980); one's ability to speak or understand can vary according to all kinds of circumstances, without one's underlying competence changing one whit. It is true that L2 learners often display a good deal of mismatch between their presumed knowledge and their use of that knowledge in performance; between what Bialystok and Sharwood Smith (1985) characterize as knowledge and control, or what Anderson (1983) calls declarative and procedural knowledge. Nor is this mismatch necessarily without theoretical interest, as it suggests that competence may not in fact be a unitary object. But the fact remains that insofar as one doesn't acquire utterances, whether or not the utterances are poorly performed should not in itself cause us to change the domain of our acquisition theory (Gregg, 1989).

Many L2 acquisition researchers are dissatisfied with the standard concept of competence, largely because they see it as unable to deal with "larger" issues of communication and use. Rejecting a "narrow," or modular, concept of grammatical competence, such researchers have rallied behind Hymes's (1972) idea of a *communicative competence,* and indeed the term has become one of the clichés of the literature (see, e.g., Angelis & Henderson, 1989; Canale & Swain, 1980). This is a pity, because the term as used in the L2 acquisition literature is largely devoid of theoretical content; it is simply another way of saying *ability to communicate.* A look at the L2 communicative competence literature will show that there has beenno proposal for a property theory of communicative competence, no attempt to formalize the properties supposedly covered by the term; which is to say that the use of the term is really a giant step backward (cf. Newmeyer, 1983; Taylor, 1988).

Another objection often raised to the concept of L2 competence is that it is unempirical, because it involves unobservable entities and phenomena (Ellis, 1986; Tarone, 1988). This objection reflects a profound misunderstanding, not only of the goals of L2 acquisition research, but also of scientific practice in general (Gregg, 1993). Any scientific discipline makes use of unobservables as a very condition of its success as a scientific discipline. Nor are unobservables licensed only if they can be "operationalized" in terms of observables. As Putnam (1988), says, "Terms referring to unobservables are *invariably* explained, in the actual history of science, with the aid of already present locutions referring to unobservables" (p. 180, italics in original) (cf. Cartwright, 1988; Chalmers, 1990; Moravcsik, 1980).

In short, although Chomsky's (1965) distinction between competence and performance certainly revolutionized linguistics, he was only applying to linguistics what is standard practice in the more advanced sciences. Where L2 acquisition researchers often go wrong is to confuse evidence for a theory (performance) with the domain of the theory (competence), thus missing the forest by a preoccupation with the trees; as Bogen and Woodward (1988, p. 305) point out, "scientific theories typically do not predict and explain facts about what we observe," but rather the unobservable phenomena underlying these facts.

B. The Learnability Condition

In assessing whether the logical problem of acquisition is the same in L2 as it is in L1 acquisition, the fundamental fact to deal with is that L1 acquisition is uniformly successful. Pinker (1979) refers to this as the Learnability Condition: "condition," in that any proposed theory of L1 acquisition must account for this fundamental fact. The Learnability Condition is thus an extremely useful constraint on the theorist, as it can be used to eliminate any proffered explanations that can be shown not to be universal.

For instance, it has been claimed that the language input of mothers and other caretakers to young children is of a special sort, being simple in structure, clear in pronunciation, related to the here-and-now, and so forth. This so-called motherese, so it is claimed, eases the learning burden on the child to the point of rendering innate language-learning mechanisms unnecessary or at least undermining the argument from the poverty of the stimulus (see, e.g., the papers in Snow & Ferguson, 1977). Putting aside the theoretical problems (see Wexler & Culicover, 1980, pp. 66–84, for discussion) and questions about the actual "simplicity" of motherese (e.g., Bard & Anderson, 1983; Newport, Gleitman, & Gleitman, 1977), the mere fact that motherese is not universal (Heath, 1983; Ochs, 1982) is enough in itself to undermine the motherese hypothesis. Similarly, no one would propose that children acquire an L1 because they receive explicit instruction. Of course the requisite instruction is in principle impossible to give, but in any case such instruction is in fact not universally given, to say the least.

But in L2 acquisition the Learnability Condition does not obtain, and this means that it is all the harder to eliminate proposed explanations. Some learners acquire an L2 and some do not; some learners receive instruction and some do not. Perhaps the only ones who acquire are those who have been instructed. No one has made such a claim, to my knowledge, but the L2 equivalent to motherese, "foreigner talk," or "teacher talk," has been made the object of an immense amount of study, based presumably on the hope that there is a causal connection between simplified L2 input and successful acquisition (see, e.g., Chaudron, 1988; papers in Day, 1986; Long, 1983). (See chapter 13 by Long for a general discussion of the role of the linguistic environment in L2 acquisition.)

Again, one of the major factors motivating a UG-type solution to the logical problem of L1 acquisition is that linguistic input to the child consists exclusively of so-called primary linguistic data (PLD), or positive evidence; that is, utterances in context. Negative evidence, such as explicit correction of deviant child utterances, is in general neither available nor used, and thus, given the Learnability Condition, it cannot be useful, let alone necessary (Pinker, 1989). But it could easily be claimed, and in fact has been claimed, that the L2 learner can get caught in situations where negative evidence is necessary to avoid or correct a faulty understanding of the L2 grammar (White, 1987). (For general discussion of the notions of positive and negative evidence see chapters 3 by White, and 13 by Long.)

In general, the fact that there is no uniformity in the level of competence attained by L2 learners—and this is true even when competence is defined in narrower, theoretically more interesting terms within a grammatical theory—leaves the field discouragingly open for a variety of explanations of a sort that can be dismissed out of hand in L1 acquisition research. (Chapter 5 by Schachter includes additional treatment of the implications of the nonuniform outcome in (adult) L2 acquisition for a theory of L2 acquisition.) If there is a critical period, for instance, perhaps that could explain failure to acquire; but then why is the failure not uniform? And of course not everyone accepts that there is a critical period (Birdsong, 1991; Flynn & Manuel, 1991; Scovel, 1988). Appeals have been made in the L2 acquisition literature to acculturation, motivation, self-image, "ego-permeability," intelligence, cognitive style, and on and on. What all these putative explanations have in common is their irrelevance to L1 acquisition.[5]

---

[5] On the other hand, L2 acquisition is spared at least one problematical debate facing L1 acquisition theorists, the debate on the role of maturation. Some theorists, such as Pinker, hold to what he calls the Continuity Assumption. They claim, based essentially on Occam's Razor, that

the most explanatory theory will posit the fewest developmental changes in the mechanisms of the virtual machine [i.e., the learner], attributing developmental changes, where neces-

C. Learnability Considerations in L2 Acquisition

Still, the fact that the Learnability Condition does not apply to L2 acquisition does not mean that the poverty of the stimulus argument is irrelevant or that the problem of learnability can be ignored. In L2 just as in L1 acquisition, the learner can be viewed as an input–output device that undergoes certain changes of state, from a point where the learner has no knowledge of the target language (TL)— but not no knowledge at all—to a point where he or she has (some) knowledge of the TL. In the case of L1 acquisition, all learners of the same language reach essentially the same end point from the same starting point; in L2 acquisition this is not the case, but for the moment that is neither here nor there—for the moment. If some L2 learners reach a terminal state that cannot be accounted for as a simple recording of input or a low-level extrapolation from input, there is at least a potential learnability problem in L2 acquisition too (White, 1985, 1989).

The learnability problem in L1 acquisition thus involves four essential components or parameters:

1. The learner's initial language-related hypotheses
2. A grammar of the TL (TL=L1)
3. Input (PLD) consisting of utterances of the TL
4. A learning mechanism to analyze and interpret input in conformity with (1)[6]

It will be seen that (1) and (2) fall within the domain of a property theory, whereas (3) and (4) are handled by a transition theory.

By manipulating the relative weights of these parameters, one can come up with quite varied theoretical stances. For instance, theoreticians divide on the question of whether (1) is language-specific, some (especially linguists) claiming that the role of (1) is essentially filled by UG, and others (largely psychologists) who see language learning as simply a form of learning. There is disagreement as to whether (1) is ready *in toto* from day 1, or whether instead it develops according

---

sary, to increases in the child's knowledge base, increasing access of computational procedures to the knowledge base, and quantitative changes in parameters like the size of working memory. (1984, pp. 6–7)

In contrast, Borer and Wexler (1987) have proposed that maturation plays a role in L1 acquisition, specifically that there will be stages in development when certain principles and parameters do not yet apply, because they have not yet been activated. If this is true, then it could mean that the grammars of very young children could be in violation of UG; they would be "wild" grammars in Goodluck's (1986) sense. This raises a potential problem of falsifiability, for the temptation is there to fob off recalcitrant data by appealing to maturation. In any case, we can assume in L2 acquisition that adults have already done whatever maturation there is, and thus we can escape at least one troublesome variable. For the role of age in L2 acquisition, see Long (1990) and Singleton (1989).

[6] See Atkinson (1992) for a detailed introduction to learnability theory in L1 acquisition. My account here differs somewhat from Atkinson's, in that I am omitting his success metric.

to a maturational schedule. If, like perhaps many psychologists (and L2 acquisition researchers!), one underestimates the complexity of (2), the burden on (1) and (4) is proportionately lightened; conversely, the more complex the grammar, the greater the need for a complex initial state. Again, if one accepts the motherese hypothesis, the role of (3) becomes relatively greater.

These same learnability parameters can be applied to L2 acquisition, although a number of important changes arise:

1. Initial state: The L2 learner has already internalized a grammar of a specific natural language; is this important? Has the adult learner, conversely, *lost* any properties of (1)? Does the learner begin the process of L2 acquisition with both UG and L1 grammar, or just the latter? Does it make a difference which L1 grammar is part of the initial state?

2. TL(=L2) grammar, or rather, the TL-related IL finally attained by the learner

3. Input: Negative evidence is available in many cases; is it necessary? Useful? Usable?

4. Learning mechanism: Does the parser vary from L1 to L2? That is, must one develop a new parser as well as a new grammar to be parsed: Do the learning mechanisms survive into adulthood? Conversely, do adults use mechanisms that children do not or cannot?

These variations can be dealt with in various ways, in various theoretical frameworks. We will now look at some of those frameworks.

D. The Nature of L2 Competence: Modular versus Nonmodular Analyses

One way to categorize L2 theories or theoretical approaches is according to where they stand on the question of modularity. It has been proposed, notably by J. A. Fodor (1983), that the mind is not a uniform system but rather contains, in addition to a largely general-purpose central processing system (responsible for such functions as memory, belief, reasoning, etc.), a set of autonomous systems or modules that function largely independent of one another. For Fodor, language is one such module, as it is for Chomsky (e.g., 1986), although the two conceptions of modularity differ in many ways. For our purposes it is enough that a modularist position sees language knowledge as a separate module from, for example, general knowledge of the world, and hence sees language acquisition as essentially different in character from the acquisition of real-world knowledge, although no doubt interacting in part with that knowledge.

Thus one question to be answered by an L2 acquisition theorist is whether L2 knowledge is modular. This is a separate question from whether the mind as a whole is modular; one could hold that the mind is indeed modular, and that L1 knowledge is a module, but that L2 knowledge is no different from real-world knowledge, and thus lies outside the language module; in other words, one could accept the role of UG in L1 acquisition but deny it in L2. Let us start by looking at positions that deny modularity across the board.

Nonmodular Approaches

In L2 acquisition research, although there has always been a good deal of resistance to modular analyses, largely motivated by a misguided concern for communicative competence, there has been little in the way of explicit nonmodular theorizing. Instead, there has been a more or less implicit denial of modularity: Learning is seen as a general process irrespective of object. That is, it is often assumed by L2 acquisition theorists that such processes as hypothesis testing, generalization, analogy, automatization, and so forth, apply equally to any learning task—linguistic or otherwise (see, e.g., McLaughlin, 1987, chap. 6, for discussion). Strictly speaking, of course, this question (parameter [4] of our learnability framework) comes under the heading of the developmental problem, and we will return to it there. As far as explicitly nonmodular concepts of the mind itself, there are perhaps two that have been touched on: O'Grady's (1987) language acquisition theory and connectionism.

O'Grady claims that "the contribution of the genetic endowment [to language acquisition] is restricted to the specification of concepts and learning strategies that are required independent of language" (1987, p. x). O'Grady himself is concerned only with L1 acquisition, but Wolfe-Quintero (1992) has attempted to apply O'Grady's theory to L2 acquisition; specifically, she sees O'Grady's Conservatism Thesis, Continuity Requirement, and Developmental Principle as playing a key role in the acquisition of L2 English. These three principles are of course intended by O'Grady to apply to all learning situations, not just language learning.

A very different antimodular approach to language learning is taken by advocates of connectionist models (e.g., Rumelhart, McClelland, & the PDP Research Group, 1986). Connectionists do away with rules, structures, and so on, and instead see learning as the relative strengthening (or spreading activation) of associations, or connections, between interconnected units or nodes. The rules or principles proposed by linguists are simply epiphenomena, in this view; they have no nonmetaphoric existence whatever, and thus play no role in language learning.

Connectionism has started to appear in the L2 acquisition literature (e.g., Gasser, 1990; Schmidt, 1988), although it is not clear to what extent the problems posed by a connectionist philosophy of the mind are appreciated by its proponents in L2 acquisition. The fact—if indeed it is a fact—that one can successfully model the acquisition of English past-tense forms with a connectionist computer program does not say anything as to whether the human mind goes about acquiring in that way; nor is a spreading activation model necessarily incompatible with a more traditional concept of mental structure (J. A. Fodor & Pylyshyn, 1988; Pinker & Prince, 1988).

Further, as Carroll and Meisel (1990) point out, connectionist accounts fail to deal with the fact that humans have knowledge that transcends the input; but that, of course, is the very heart of the logical problem. Something like spreading activation could possibly be involved in the establishing of connections between, say, irregular verbs and their past-tense endings; but we cannot appeal to a *lack* of activation for our knowledge that one sentence (e.g., *She may have been being misled*) is a possible sentence of English whereas another (e.g., *She may been have being misled*) is impossible. After all, we've probably never heard either type of sentence, and thus they are equally unlikely to have been activated. (Similarly, it is hard to see how connectionism can deal with such inferential capacities as can produce an indefinitely large number of negative beliefs, for example, that earthworms cannot tapdance, or that lipstick is not contagious (J. A. Fodor & Pylyshyn, 1988).) Given the serious shortcomings of the connectionist model, it is hard to see any good reason for taking it up in the stead of a structured system of mental representations, as assumed by almost any other view of the mind.

If in mainstream or classical cognitive science, including language acquisition, the computer has been the dominant metaphor, in connectionism the central metaphor is the brain: the densely interconnected nodes of a connectionist system resemble densely interconnected neurons, and the activation of nodes is rather like neural firing. Usually, this parallel is not pushed to a literal extreme; nodes are not neurons. But connectionism does perhaps have more appeal to those who perceive it as operating at a more "basic," less "metaphorical" level than, for example, the system of rules and representations proposed by linguists. (And in its favor, connectionism does recognize, and attempts to bypass, the homunculus problem.) In the same vein, it is sometimes suggested that explanation of language acquisition should be conducted at the neurolinguistic level, that the brain rather than the mind should be the object of inquiry (Jacobs, 1988; Jacobs & Schumann, 1992; Schumann, 1993). Such yearnings for the more basic or more inclusive are understandable, but like many other understandable yearnings, should nonetheless be resisted.

It is true, of course, that the mind is instantiated in the brain, and that any mental activity whatever must have a neurological basis. But it by no means follows from this that the neurological level is an appropriate, let alone the only proper, level at which to account for mental activity. As J. A. Fodor (1981a) points out, if there are useful generalizations that can only be made at a higher level of abstraction, that higher level is thereby justified (cf. Pylyshyn, 1984, chap. 2). As long as this is the case, there are compelling reasons to conduct inquiry into cognitive systems, including language and language acquisition, using a vocabulary appropriate to those systems.

What otherwise widely different theories such as O'Grady's "general nativism" and connectionism have in common is a reductionist animus, an attempt to account for language acquisition phenomena as nothing more than special cases of other kinds of phenomena. Although there is certainly nothing whatever misguided about attempts at theoretical reduction in general, there are excellent reasons for thinking that the reductionist project will not work in the cognitive sciences (J. A. Fodor, 1981b, 1981c). For instance, as long as linguistic theory makes productive use of terms like *empty category, bounding node, c-command,* and so forth, as long as these terms have no natural counterparts in other sciences, and as long as using these terms leads to increased understanding of linguistic phenomena, then there is no way to reduce grammar to general knowledge or language acquisition to general learning; nor is there any reason we should be unhappy about this state of affairs. Indeed, Kuhn remarks that "as a science develops, it employs in explanations an ever increasing number of irreducibly distinct forms" (1977, p. 30). If this is indeed the case, the failure of general nativist or connectionist explanations of language acquisition may in fact be a source of comfort.

Modular Approaches

By "modular approaches" to L2 acquisition, I essentially mean approaches that assume the modularity of the mind in general, and the existence of a language module (UG) specifically. In effect, the L2 acquisition modular literature centers around the question of the modularity of L2 knowledge, or in other words, the role of UG in L2 acquisition. If L2 acquisition is a process of creative construction, is UG in at the creation?

The L2 modularity literature, both polemic and empirical, can largely be seen as contributions to one of two opposing positions: (1) UG is not involved, or not directly involved, in L2 acquisition; (2) UG is a causal factor in L2 acquisition, just as, or more or less as, it is in L1 acquisition. An analogy with theology may be helpful: Position (1) sees UG roughly as the deists of the Enlightenment saw God, as a *deus abscondidus* who, once having created the universe and set things in motion, retired from active duty. UG, in other words, though essential for the development of an L1, has no role in developing an L2. Position (2) is more of a traditional not-a-sparrow-falls kind of theism; UG is immanent in language use as well as L1 acquisition, and thus also participates in L2 acquisition. (General nativists, connectionists, and so on, can be seen as various species of atheists.) There are of course variations and modifications of these two extreme positions, but we can use them to illustrate some of the explanatory problems facing a modular L2 acquisition theory. (For other discussions of possible alternative positions on the role of UG in L2 acquisition see chapters 3 by White, 4 by Flynn, and 5 by Schachter.)

Theism: L2 Acquisition Equals L1 Acquisition

The strongest form of L2 acquisition theism would be one that claimed that there is no difference between L1 acquisition and L2, at least as far as UG is concerned. That last qualification is important; there is no obligation on the strong theist (if any exist) to deny the facts of, for example, foreign accent, L1-related errors (depending on the type of error, at least), or other L1–L2 differences that do not pertain to UG. One consequence of adopting a modular view of language—whether or not one extends this view to L2 acquisition—is that the scope of the acquisition theory becomes limited, but limited in a principled (i.e., theory-determined) way.

This narrowing of the theoretical domain is a result devoutly to be wished, at least insofar as it is a theoretically motivated narrowing. This is a point that is often missed by, for instance, communicative competence advocates or by morpheme-acquisition researchers, who have found themselves in difficult situations for lack of a theoretical foundation for interpreting empirical data (Gregg, 1984; Wode, Bahns, Bedey, & Frank, 1978). But it does mean that we must be careful in assessing arguments and weighing putative evidence, to see that in fact such arguments and evidence are relevant. (See Schwartz, 1992, for detailed discussion of the evidential role of L2 developmental sequences.)

In any case, strong theism does not need to claim that L2 acquisition is exactly the same process, with exactly the same results, as L1 acquisition, and thus foreign accents, for instance, are not (or not necessarily) counterevidence to a strong theist position.[7] Theism essentially is the claim that UG operates in L2 acquisition, and strong theism would say it operates exactly as in L1 acquisition. Minimally, one would expect there never to be violations of UG in the developing grammars (not production) of L2 learners; this is another way of saying what has often been either claimed or assumed in L2 acquisition research, that the learner's version of the TL—the learner's IL—is, at every stage of development, a natural language (Adjémian, 1976). This would mean that just as there are no "wild grammars" in L1 development (Goodluck, 1986), so in L2 development: learners should not, for example, hypothesize structure-independent rules, such as a rule reversing first and last words of a sentence.

For what it's worth, it seems that indeed ILs are natural languages in this sense; but this is not that impressive a piece of evidence for strong theism in any form. For one thing, natural languages are generally[8] mutually incomprehensible;

---

[7] Of course, UG theory includes a phonological component, and thus if one could show that foreign accents, or the accents of some L2 learners, violated phonological principles of UG, then such accents would indeed be counterevidence. But the simple fact that very few L2 learners wind up sounding exactly like NSs of the L2 is not in itself a threat to strong theism.

[8] Generally, or often, or always, depending on how one draws the line between languages. If we are talking about languages as politically defined, then any two languages are virtually always mutually

nothing about UG ensures comprehensibility. Thus it would be perfectly consistent with the no-wild-grammars claim if every IL were totally incomprehensible. For instance, UG licenses both head-initial languages such as English and head-final languages such as Japanese; yet if a Japanese learner of English were to fly in the face of the English input data and produce a head-final IL English grammar, we should be hesitant, to say the least, to claim this as evidence for the equivalence of L1 and L2 acquisition processes. Wild ILs would be powerful prima facie evidence against theism, and hence grist for the deist mill, but conversely, the absence of wild ILs is not impressive support for the theist. An antitheist like Bley-Vroman (1990; see the following subsection) would reply that the learner is starting from a UG-governed L1 grammar, and that in that respect the absence of wild ILs could be credited, not to the functioning of UG in L2 acquisition, but rather simply to the effect of the L1 grammar.

Given that UG does not account for absolutely all aspects of language acquisition on the one hand, and given on the other hand that the theist must make stronger claims than mere obedience to the constraints of UG if there is to be a true clash between theist and deist positions, what we need is a way of reasonably strengthening the theist claim to enable it to make more precise and hence interesting predictions. Here is where the principles and parameters of current linguistic theory come in.

For instance, not all principles of UG are universal in the strictest sense; rather than applying to all possible languages without exception, some apply to all possible languages that meet certain conditions. (Think, for instance, of the difference in male humans between the presence of a heart and the presence of a prostate gland; both are universal, but the universality has a different status.) So, for example, the principle of Subjacency, which constrains the kinds of wh-movement permitted, is irrelevant to languages that lack wh-movement; or perhaps it would be better to say that the principle applies vacuously in such languages. In either case the question arises whether the IL grammar of a learner whose L1 lacks wh-movement will conform to the constraints of Subjacency when acquiring an L2 that has wh-movement. A theist will say yes, a deist no.

Similarly, parametric variation across languages can be used to distinguish both between theist and deist positions and between stronger and weaker forms of theism. For instance, given a binary parameter such as Pro-drop (Chomsky, 1981; Hyams, 1986) or Head-position (Flynn, 1987) or Agreement (Pollock, 1989; White, 1991a), and given an L1 and L2 with different settings for the parameter, one can make different predictions as to the acquisition of that parameter, that is

incomprehensible. If we are talking about what Chomsky calls I-language, an "element of the mind of the person who knows the language," (1986, p. 22), then there is an I-language for every speaker, and depending on the speech community of that speaker there can be hundreds of millions of mutually comprehensible languages.

as to whether the parameter will be "reset" for the L2, and if so, how. (For a review of the empirical results on the Pro-Drop [Null Subject] and Agreement [Verb Raising] Parameters in L2 acquisition see chapter 3 by White; for discussion of results on the Head-position Parameter in L2 acquisition see chapters 4 by Flynn, and 10 by Gass.)

A strong form of theism would hold that the L2 learner acquires the L2 parameter setting directly, just as a NS of the L2 does in childhood. Furthermore, because in most formulations of parameters (but see Safir, 1987; Wexler & Manzini, 1987) a given setting entails various different properties of a language, the learner should acquire all the relevant properties at the same time. A weaker position, and one that is no doubt more tenable, is that the learner may well pass through a stage where the L1 setting is applied to the L2, but will eventually attain the L2 setting. Keep in mind that in a learnability framework it is not only the input that plays a role, but also the initial state of the learner; and for an L2 learner, that initial state surely includes the L1 grammar. A radical theist would have to exclude the L1 grammar, on purely theoretical grounds, from the learnability equation, and there seems to be no good reason to do so; which is no doubt why no one actually does so.[9]

Weak theism thus would claim that UG is indeed operative in L2 acquisition but that because the L1 grammar is also part of the initial state of the learner, the take-off point for acquisition will reflect that difference. Specifically, the weak theist claims that parameters should be successfully reset, although not necessarily immediately, and nonparametric principles not instantiated in the L1 should also be acquired successfully. In either case, of course, a sufficient amount of relevant input is assumed, just as in L1 acquisition; thus weak theists would not be embarrassed by (but nor would they be committed to) acquisition sequences where the earlier stage indicates L1 "transfer."

Of course not all principles and parameters are equally useful tests of the different predictions made by theists and deists. Certain parameters might very well be resettable on the basis of simple input; the Head-position parameter may be one such example. Because the point of the UG position in the first place is that the learner's idealized grammar is underdetermined by the input, a parameter setting that could be determined by the input will not be of much help in settling the theist–deist controversy. What is needed, then, is either a principle that is not

---

[9] In addition to the range of empirical counterevidence (see White, chap. 3, this volume), there is a theoretical problem as well. It is hard to conceive of how the learner could ignore the L1 grammar when first processing L2 input, especially if, as many theists claim (e.g., Schwartz, 1986, 1987; Schwartz & Gubala-Ryzak, 1992), conscious knowledge is irrelevant to L2 acquisition. It would seem that either the learner knows that the L2 is an L2 and treats it accordingly, or else the learner does not know this, in the relevant sense of "know," in which case he or she would seem to be forced to treat the input, at first anyway, as if it were L1 input. This raises some complex problems about the ontological status of UG and of grammars. For some interesting speculations on this and related questions, see Cook (1991).

instantiated at all in the L1 but is in the L2 (such as Subjacency in Korean and English, respectively; cf. Bley-Vroman, Felix, & Ioup, 1988), or a parameter that is not only set differently in the two languages but also is set such that the L1 licenses structures forbidden by the L2 (such as Pro-drop in Spanish and English, respectively). (For discussion of empirical results on Subjacency see chapters 3 by White, 4 by Flynn, 5 by Schachter, and 10 by Gass, this volume.) Because UG principles are constraints on possible forms, in either of these two situations simple induction from examples of the L2 input will not be enough to lead to acquisition. The existence of wh-questions in English will tell the learner that wh-movement is possible, but not what kinds of wh-movement are impossible; the existence of overt subjects in English will tell the learner that overt subjects are possible, but not that they are mandatory.

This raises the question of the role of negative evidence in L2 acquisition. In L1 acquisition it is assumed that negative evidence is not necessary; indeed, it is normally not even available (Pinker, 1989). The absence of negative evidence is in fact one of the constraints on any L1 acquisition theory, and one of the motivations for positing UG. In L2 acquisition theory, the negative evidence problem is an additional source of conflict between theoretical positions. Are theists committed to claiming that negative evidence is irrelevant to L2 acquisition also? It might seem so, and certainly some theists do so claim (e.g., Schwartz & Gubala-Ryzak, 1992). However, just as one can argue in favor of UG in L2 while still accepting L1 influence, it may also be possible to claim that UG functions alike in L2 and L1 acquisition, while accepting that negative evidence may sometimes be necessary for successful acquisition. Indeed, one may even be able to allow that negative evidence is both necessary and insufficient, and that totally successful L2 acquisition may be impossible in certain circumstances. White (1987, 1989), for instance, leaves such a possibility open.

What enables White to support a (weak) theist position on UG, while entertaining the theoretical possibility of a need for negative evidence, is the distinction between principles of UG and principles of learning. White sees both kinds of principles as modular (i.e., specific to the language module, but still distinct one from the other). White's claim, essentially, is that UG as such survives intact into adulthood and hence is available to the adult L2 learner, but that the learning principles are no longer available. We will return to this question when discussing the developmental problem; before that, we turn to the position of those who claim that UG is in effect dead. (For a review of empirical results from the "weak theist" point of view, see chapter 3 by White, for a "strong theist" position see chapter 4 by Flynn.)

Deism: The Fundamental Difference Hypothesis

Theists claim that even if L2 acquisition is usually or even always incomplete, at least some L2 learners acquire nonetheless a knowledge of the L2 that transcends the input, that thus the logical problem obtains in L2 acquisition, and that UG is the solution to the problem. To this the deist replies that there are other sources of L2 knowledge besides UG, for instance, L1 knowledge; and that given the general failure of L2 acquisition, it would be more reasonable to assume that UG is not at work in L2 acquisition.

The Fundamental Difference Hypothesis, as Bley-Vroman (1990) terms his deist position, rests on the various differences between L1 acquisition and L2 acquisition, and especially on the inapplicability of the Learnability Condition to L2 acquisition. Like White, Bley-Vroman accepts the distinction between UG and language-specific learning mechanisms; but in contrast to White, he claims that neither are available to the L2 learner. In the place of UG, there is only the UG-created L1 grammar; in the place of language-specific learning mechanisms, there are only general learning mechanisms, such as those that operate in nonmodular learning tasks: hypothesis testing, inductive and deductive reasoning, analogy, and so on. The role of such mechanisms has always been minimized in L1 acquisition theory, because they are not able to produce the complex L1 knowledge that any NS has; and by the same token, an L2 theist would also wish to minimize them. But the insufficiency of general learning mechanisms is of course just what the deist wants, because it can provide an explanation for general L2 acquisition failure. Furthermore, it is well known that there is a great deal of variation across individuals in the ability to use these mechanisms; and because there is also a good deal of variation across L2 learners in terms of final state achieved—in glaring contrast to L1 acquisition—reliance on these learning mechanisms can be used to explain this variation in L2 acquisition.

On the other hand, because the L2 learner does at least have a UG-based grammar, the deist is not compelled to deny the possibility of highly complex, subtle L2 knowledge, as long as that knowledge can be attributed to the working of the L1 grammar. Superficially it might seem that the deist wants to have it both ways: if the learner succeeds it is because of UG via the L1, if the learner fails it is because UG is not available. But in fact the claims are more precise, and because both parties agree on the theory at issue, precise in the same way as theist claims are. If a given L2 instantiates a principle not instantiated in the L1, that principle will not be acquired, and if the L2 setting of a given parameter is more restrictive than the L1 setting, it will not be acquired, in the absence of negative evidence. The theist–deist contrast is blurred on the issue of negative evidence: both deists and some theists would accept the possibility of successful acquisition (in specific realms) with the aid of negative evidence.[10]

---

[10]Here again it should be stressed that the claim centers on those aspects of language acquisition in which UG is thought to be implicated. Certainly some aspects of language knowledge (e.g., some areas of lexical knowledge or pragmatic knowledge) can be and are learned with the help of explanation, such as providing a definition or a translation equivalent to a learner. No one to my knowledge is claiming that, for example, telling a learner that X means Y cannot help the learner learn that X means Y.

It is not easy to say which position is more plausible. The theist has to explain failure; it is not yet clear whether the distinction between UG and learning principles will in fact suffice for this purpose. For instance, it remains to be seen whether all instances of failure (given sufficient input, of course) can be attributed to the nonoperation of language-specific learning principles. Nor is it clear how a theist would handle, for example, the evident role played in L2 acquisition, but not at all in L1 acquisition, of attitude, motivation, and so forth, but then neither is it clear whether a theist is obligated to account for this role.

The deist, on the other hand, is most threatened by L2 acquisition success; deism has to be able to show that *all* successful examples of L2 acquisition can be accounted for either by "transfer" of L1 grammatical properties to the IL grammar, or else by the application of learning mechanisms not intended specifically for acquisition tasks. Failure certainly is the fate of most learners, but there do seem to be a few who achieve at least near-native competence.[11] (See chapter 5 by Schachter, for development of a "deist" position.)

III. THE DEVELOPMENTAL PROBLEM: EXPLAINING THE ACQUISITION PROCESS

Even assuming that the question of modularity was resolved, and that we had a complete explanatory theory of L2 knowledge—a complete property theory of L2 knowledge, in other words—we still would not have a satisfactory theory of L2 acquisition, because we would still need to explain how acquisition actually happens.

A. Criteria for an Acquisition Theory

In considering proposals that have been made in the L2 acquisition literature, it might help to measure them against the conditions Atkinson (1982) lays down for a theory of L1 acquisition. Atkinson posits two different components of an acquisition theory: a sequence of theories $T_1, T_2, \ldots T_n$, each accounting for the data in a given domain D for different times $t_1, \ldots t_n$, plus a mechanism M for getting

---

[11] One more position is worth mentioning in passing before leaving the logical problem, and that is the Competition Model of Felix (1985, 1986, chap. 3), which claims that UG is still available in L2 acquisition, but that general learning mechanisms also act on L2 input, whereas in L1 acquisition these mechanisms are not yet matured and hence offer no challenge to the dominance of UG. The incompleteness of L2 acquisition is thus to be explained as a result of the competition between two different acquisition systems. In distinction from L2 acquisition theism and deism, I suppose one could consider this a form of manichaeism.

from T_i to T_{i+1}. These two components can be seen as corresponding to the respective domains of a property theory and a transition theory.

Atkinson sets up a number of criteria that he says any theory must meet. Among them are the following three:

1. T_i must be constructed within the framework of a particular general theory. We do not want to have radically different property theories each accounting for knowledge at a different developmental stage. I will call this the Theoretical Framework Criterion.
2. The sequence $(T_1, \ldots T_n)$ must be explicable; that is, we must be able to explain why X occurs before Y and not vice versa in a developmental sequence. I will call this the Sequence Criterion.
3. There must be a detailed specification of the acquisition mechanism M. I will call this the Mechanism Criterion.

With these three criteria in mind, we can look at the attempts made up to now to deal with the developmental problem of L2 acquisition.

B. The Theoretical Framework Criterion:
Interfacing with the Logical Problem

Larsen-Freeman and Long (1991) count over forty "theories" of L2 acquisition; Long (1993) has raised the count to sixty. Either way we cannot look at them all here; fortunately, we do not have to. First of all, we can exclude from the start theories that do not attempt to deal with the logical problem; for instance, theories of acculturation (e.g., Schumann, 1978), theories of affective variables (e.g., Gardner, 1985), theories of variation (e.g., Ellis, 1985; Tarone, 1988), "discourse/functional" theories (e.g., Hatch, 1978), make no serious attempt to face the logical problem. In other words, they fail from the start to meet the Theoretical Framework Criterion, at least *insofar as our domain is L2 competence*. A theory of IL variation, for example, would meet the criterion, but because variation is not competence, the logical problem—and hence the developmental problem also—remains untouched. (But see chapter 8 by Preston for discussion of patterns of variation in performance as evidence for features of competence.) Again, a theory that establishes a positive correlation between degree of acculturation and level of L2 proficiency might be able to account for a great deal of the variation across L2 learners, and for failure to acquire, but it would have nothing to say about how competence is acquired; there is no way to directly connect the terminology of grammatical competence with the terminology of acculturation.

It is very important to understand just what is, and is not, at stake here, especially when reading other chapters in this volume. It most emphatically is *not* the case that a theory, say, that relates L2 acquisition and acculturation is (necessarily) trivial or uninteresting or otiose. It most emphatically *is* the case, however, that such a theory does not solve (or even address) the logical problem, and that that problem is central; at least central to this chapter. In other words, in order to satisfy the Theoretical Framework Criterion, we need either a linguistic theory, or else a theory of the mind that can handle language acquisition without a linguistic theory; that is, either a modular theory of language competence or a nonmodular one. This takes us back to the logical problem, so I will say no more about the Theoretical Framework Criterion here.

C. The Sequence Criterion: Developmental Sequences

The identification and description of specific developmental sequences in L2 acquisition has, of course, been a major task of L2 acquisition research, and a specific sequence—the acquisition order of grammatical morphemes in English—was for a while seemingly an obsession dominating the field. It may be a bit surprising, then, to find how seldom explanation of these sequences was attempted (see Larsen-Freeman, 1976, for one exception). Actually, there is no reason to assume that there will be anything like one single explanation for all kinds of sequences. Atkinson (1982), following Flavell (1972), suggests three kinds of explanation for a given developmental sequence: environmental (e.g., relative frequency or saliency of input), reductive (where the given items are simply the linguistic reflexes of cognates in another, more basic or general, domain), and teleological (where a different sequence would be logically impossible). Thus there can be a good deal of variation in the significance or interest of any given sequence. If, for instance, the English grammatical morpheme acquisition order is simply a consequence of differential amounts of input, it will be a lot less interesting than a sequence of, say, parameter settings, where the sequence may be explicable in terms that satisfy the Theoretical Framework Criterion. In this sense the Sequence Criterion is parasitic on the Theoretical Framework Criterion. It is also important to keep in mind, once again, the distinction between competence and performance. It is quite possible for there to be constraints on processing of input or of output, such that a predictable *production* sequence can be determined (e.g., Pienemann, 1984), without it following that the production sequence is a faithful reflection of a sequence of internal *grammars* (for discussion, see White, 1991b). As always, the learner's utterances are data, not explananda.

The Sequence Criterion is also subordinate to the Mechanism Criterion; where a successful explanation meeting the former identifies a cause, a successful explanation meeting the latter explains the effect. The difference between these two criteria reflects a distinction often made by philosophers of science, between contrastive and noncontrastive explanations (Lipton, 1991). A contrastive explanation is an answer to a question of the form, Why P rather than Q?, whereas a noncontrastive question is simply, Why P? A contrastive question will of course require a different answer depending on the focus of the contrast—the explanation of why *Fred* killed Bill is not the explanation of why Fred killed *Bill*—but will also require a different explanation from a noncontrastive question—which is why one is not satisfied with the standard explanation of why firemen wear red suspenders. This is not to say that one type of explanation is to be rejected in favor of the other; for one thing, there are cases where one is available and the other is not. If both Fred and Max have untreated tertiary syphilis, we can explain why Fred has paresis—he has untreated tertiary syphilis—but we cannot explain why Fred has it rather than Max. On the other hand, it is easy enough to explain why Max swallowed poison before jumping off the Golden Gate Bridge rather than vice versa, even if we have not got a clue as to why he did either. The problem is to recognize which kind of question one has at hand, and hence which kind of explanation one needs.

D. The Mechanism Criterion

Nonmodular Learning Mechanisms: General Learning Principles

The logical problem of language acquisition is a problem of accounting for a certain kind of knowledge; the explanation required is thus a psychological one, and it is specifically to the psychology of cognition that we must appeal. Still, Atkinson's Theoretical Framework Criterion, which requires a general theory for the domain of language competence as a framework within which to account for development, leaves some room for disagreement as to the nature of that cognitive theory.

Nonmodular explanations of L2 development appeal to learning mechanisms of the sort proposed in the mainstream cognitive psychology literature: hypothesis testing, automaticity, restructuring, inferencing, and so on. The basic idea, as McLaughlin puts it, is that "second-language learning is viewed as the acquisition of a complex cognitive *skill*" (1987, p. 133; emphasis added). (Notice that this perspective blurs the logical problem; a skill, after all, is not the same thing as knowledge.) The learning mechanisms apply in the same way as they do to the acquisition of other complex skills; thus, for example, restructuring applies both in arithmetic (e.g., learning to figure the sum of seven tens by multiplying 7×10 rather than by adding 7 ten times) and in language learning (e.g., applying a past-tense rule uniformly to verbs rather than memorizing each verb separately). (See chapter 7 by McLaughlin and Heredia, for a nonmodular approach to L2 acquisition.)

Somewhat similar are the "operating principles" (OPs) proposed (for L1 acquisition) by Slobin (e.g., 1973, 1985), or similar principles, inspired in part by

Slobin's, proposed for L2 acquisition by Andersen (e.g., 1989). These can be thought of as internalized instructions to the learner as to how to deal with input, how to store information, and how to produce linguistic output. For instance, Slobin posits such OPs as, "Pay attention to stressed syllables," or "Keep track of the frequency of occurrence of every unit and pattern that you store" (1985, p. 1251). There are three points worth making about Slobin's OPs: (1) Interestingly enough, although Slobin is concerned with determining what he calls the cognitive prerequisites for language learning, his latest list of OPs reflects, as he himself points out, a change "from general cognitive prerequisites to those that seem more adapted to the task of language acquisition in particular" (1985, p. 1243). (2) The latest list is also a good deal larger; some 40 OPs (some of them subdivided into subprinciples), some of them quite complex. (3) Some of the OPs relate to off-line processing, including reviewing the current grammar with a view to reorganizing it.

These last two points are not encouraging: the more OPs, the greater the burden on the learner, especially because (1) the OPs do not always seem that helpful— the joint effect of following three OPs is to "pay attention" to all three syllables of "banana," but not the third syllable of "banana boat"; two separate OPs each enjoin paying attention to the first syllable of "horsefeathers"—and (2) the OPs do not seem to form a natural class. It hardly seems like a principle, for instance, to pay attention to syllables that are easier to pay attention to in the first place; and such an OP seems to have little in common with one that enjoins keeping track of input frequency. (Nor would one imagine that the attention-paying function and the frequency-measuring one are carried out by the same mechanism.) And adding the possibility of off-line processing poses the threat of increasing the power of acquisition theory.

The fact that Slobin has felt it necessary to revise his OPs to a more language-specific form may indicate the difficulties of endowing a nonmodular transition theory with a sufficient degree of specificity to deal with the acquisition problem. In any case, the revised list still leaves much to be desired as far as the Theoretical Framework Criterion goes. If we wish to solve the logical problem, we need to explain *inter alia* why learners know about *un*grammaticality, and it is not clear that obedience to the OPs would be able to yield a terminal cognitive state where such knowledge was attained. For instance, I cannot see how the OPs would enable one to determine which noun phrases in a sentence are not possible referents of a given anaphor (see Bowerman, 1985, for detailed discussion).

It is also not clear to what extent either the OPs or such general mechanisms as discussed by McLaughlin could satisfy the Mechanism Criterion. It seems likely enough that hypothesis testing or restructuring or generalization do in fact take place in language acquisition; but in order for such processes to occur there need to be data to be hypothesized about or restructured or generalized from, and—if the process is to occur successfully—these data will need to be categorized in terms of the property theory. (We generalize across, for example, past-tense forms of verbs, not across utterances made by Mr. Hotchkiss in French I.) This means there needs to be some interface between the mechanism and the categories of the property theory. Most nonmodular proposals made to date stop short of that, tending as they do to either ignore or underestimate the complexity of the property theory.

Modular Learning Mechanisms

The difference between a modular and a nonmodular learning mechanism is that the former would be expected to operate only on linguistic input. Two such mechanisms have been proposed, although in fact both have nonmodular counterparts: the Subset Principle (SP) and the Uniqueness Principle (UP). Both have been discussed in the L2 acquisition literature, although the UP has only just begun to be the focus of empirical research (Trahey & White, 1993; see also Rutherford, 1989; White, 1989, chap. 6).

Briefly, the SP (Berwick, 1985) says that a learner makes the most conservative hypothesis consistent with the input, and thus avoids producing overgeneral rules that cannot be altered by positive evidence alone. Because L1 acquisition proceeds on the basis of positive evidence only, some sort of SP would seem to be necessary. White (1987, 1989) claims that it is also necessary in L2 acquisition, but unfortunately is no longer available to the learner; thus the need for negative evidence in L2. The UP (Berwick, 1985; see also Clark, 1987; and for L2, Andersen, 1983) essentially requires that the learner associate only one form with a given syntactic structure or lexical item. This is intended to allow the learner to purge his grammar of incorrect forms once the correct form is presented in the input (or presented sufficiently frequently, etc.). The standard example of the UP in action is the acquisition of the past-tense forms of irregular English verbs, where *goed* and *eated* are ostensibly preempted by (sufficient) input of *went* and *ate*.

These two principles have certain attractions in comparison with general learning principles. For one thing, given that the property theory is a highly specific one with terms limited to (specific areas of) language, there is an initial plausibility in assuming that the learning principles will be similarly limited. At least that is plausible in the absence of a compelling reductive form of linguistic theory. For that matter, in the most thoroughgoing attempt so far to create such a nonmodular acquisition theory, O'Grady (1987) acknowledges the absence of evidence supporting an overall learning strategy of conservatism.[12] And a moment's thought will suggest the pervasiveness in nonlinguistic domains of overgeneral inductions made from limited input.

Still, it is not at all clear that principles such as the SP and the UP can take on the function of learning mechanisms as such. In the case of the SP, to claim that

---

[12] Wolfe-Quintero (1992) evidently overlooks this point when claiming that such a strategy operates in L2 acquisition.

the principle actually operates in acquisition is necessarily to claim that the learner has the ability to make the computations required to establish just which of two or more choices would lead to the most conservative grammar (J. D. Fodor & Crain, 1987). This may seem unrealistic, but the alternative would seem to be that the SP is nothing but a restatement of the problem rather than a proposal for a solution: learners have to avoid overgeneralizations if they are not to receive negative evidence; they do in fact avoid overgeneralizations without the use of negative evidence; therefore they have a SP. Similarly, L2 acquisition research by White and others indicating violation of the SP probably should not yet be taken as evidence for the "nonaccessibility" or "nonfunction" of a learning principle as such, but only of the failure of L2 learners to avoid overgeneralizations. This is important evidence still, of course, but until we have an account of the computational powers of these learning principles, it does not get us closer to a true learning mechanism. To put it somewhat differently, to appeal to an unspecified SP is to run the risk of falling into the homunculus problem all over again. (For a review of empirical results bearing on the SP in L2 acquisition, see chapter 3 by White.)

With the UP, the theoretical problem is rather different; it is not the computational burden on the learning mechanism that raises doubts, but the difficulty of determining just what counts as a form or structure or semantic concept, and the difficulty of establishing clear grounds for preemption. Nor is it clear that languages in fact forbid true duplication. It is often claimed (e.g., by Clark, 1987) that such perfect synonym pairs as *almost* and *nearly* or *everyone* and *everybody* are virtually nonexistent. But if the distinctions can only be found at the level of style or register, it is not clear how useful the UP would be. Of course it could be the case that languages are in fact full of duplication, but that the learner nonetheless needs a learning principle that refuses to accept this fact in the absence of definite positive evidence. This would be a form of conservatism much like the SP. In the case of the past-tense forms (*eated* and *ate*) things seem fairly straightforward, but even here it would be nice to know what stops a learner—especially one whose L1 has two past tenses—from assuming, say, an aspectual distinction.

Although there is virtually no experimental data on the UP in L2 acquisition, there is anecdotal evidence (e.g., Bley-Vroman, 1986) that suggests that L2 learners do not necessarily honor the principle. In the course of my own, basically naturalistic, acquisition of Japanese, for example, I have (1) assumed synonymity of sometimes grossly different forms; (2) assumed nonsynonymity of forms that I am now pretty sure are in fact synonyms; (3) assumed a distinction between two forms that in fact does not exist, although another distinction does; and (4) persisted in using only one of a pair of forms despite knowing the distinction perfectly well. And I'm actually pretty good, although not brilliant, in Japanese, which suggests that my L2 acquisition experience is not particularly atypical.

But of course the question of whether or not the SP and UP in fact "operate" in L2s is secondary to our concern here, which is to try to meet the Mechanism Criterion for solving the developmental problem of L2 acquisition. If, as the evidence seems to indicate, they do not "operate" in L2 acquisition, at best we have a potential contrastive explanation of the difference between L1 and L2 acquisition. And even if it is shown conclusively that they do "operate," we manifestly do not have a noncontrastive explanation of either L1 or L2 acquisition, which is why I've put "operate" in quotes. At best, these principles are negative in their effect: they prevent overgeneralizations; they eliminate forms from the IL grammar. These may be essential functions for successful acquisition, but they do not explain the acquisition process itself. In other words, they really are not learning mechanisms of the sort we need to satisfy the Mechanism Criterion. And satisfying the Mechanism Criterion is essential if we are to solve the developmental problem of L2 acquisition.

Remember that the developmental problem requires a transition theory; that is, a theory of causal processes. Now the L2 acquisition literature is of course rife with proposals about causal processes; the problem is that, although these proposals may satisfy the Mechanism Criterion, they do not satisfy the Theoretical Framework Criterion; the mechanisms do not operate on the output of any useful property theory. Differential attention to form *may* in fact cause variation in production; integrative motivation may cause increased learning activity; acculturation may cause increased exposure to input; simplification of the input may cause an increase in the amount of usable input; and so on. All this is well and good, and indeed may be essential for a fully developed theory of L2 acquisition; but the connection with the property theory of L2 competence is indirect at best. What would seem to be needed, minimally, is a causal theory that makes use of a parser—that is, a mechanism that is specifically designed to operate on linguistic input within the framework of a property theory of that input. Although there has been a good deal of work on parsing theory in L1 acquisition, the subject has hardly been touched in L2 theory.

IV. CONSTRUCTING AN L2 ACQUISITION THEORY: PROSPECTS AND PROBLEMS

It should be clear from the preceding discussion that we do not yet have a theory of L2 acquisition. Long's (1993) 60 theories, to the extent that they can be viewed as theories and not as, say, simply intellectual stances toward the domain of L2 acquisition, are not theories *of* L2 acquisition but rather theories *in* L2 acquisition; theories of production, or variation, or interaction, and so forth. Nor are they necessarily any the worse for that limitation. After all, if we are to take the idea of modularity seriously in dealing with the logical and developmental problems—and I think there is every reason to do so—we need to face the fact that the term *language* does not refer to a natural kind. Like many other terms that stand us in good stead in daily nontechnical conversation—*vitamin, vegetable, bug*—*language* in fact covers a multitude of different phenomena. Once we step from daily conversation to scientific inquiry, we will have to either drop the term, or define it with sufficient care to avoid confusion. Unfortunately such confusion has not always been avoided in the L2 acquisition literature, but in any case it should be stressed that just as there can be no satisfactory theory of language *tout court,* neither can there be a satisfactory theory of "language" acquisition.

This does not, of course, mean that you should feel like a fool for having bought this book. Rather, it simply means that we will need a number of different, complementary theories if we are to explain the acquisition of language in the nontechnical sense. But the heart of a comprehensive L2 acquisition theory is, inevitably, a theory that deals with the logical and developmental problems of L2 acquisition; that is, a theory or set of related theories that can account for the L2 learner's competence—as defined by a rigorous linguistic theory, not as piously invoked by advocates of communicative competence—and that can also explain how that competence is achieved.

What are the prospects for producing such a theory? Current L2 acquisition research reflects an interesting imbalance between the logical and developmental problems. On the one hand, we have an increasingly well-articulated property theory of linguistic competence, that is, a theory of generative grammar; but as we have seen with the theist–deist controversy, we are still far from agreement as to how to apply this theory to the domain of L2 acquisition. On the other hand, we have a number of varyingly well-articulated transition theories, but no way of interfacing them with the property theory. This imbalance often seems to manifest itself methodologically as well: an overly jaundiced observer might feel that the literature offers a choice between carefully designed experiments yielding no theoretically significant results on the one hand, and on the other hand theoretically interesting experiments the results of which are vitiated by methodological flaws. This is a caricature of the situation, of course, and in any case the level of L2 acquisition research has risen greatly in recent years; but there is enough truth in the caricature to remind us both of the variety of backgrounds and interests represented by L2 acquisition researchers and of the serious methodological problems confronting them.

Finally, it might be worth raising explicitly a question that probably lurks somewhere in the heart of every L2 researcher, waiting for a moment of discouragement to leap into consciousness: What's the point? So let us say we get a decent answer to the logical and developmental problems: so what? After all, L2 acquisition research is often classified as part of a field called applied linguistics, and, as Long (1993) rightly stresses, success or failure in L2 acquisition itself has profound effects on the lives of millions of people. Will the theory of the acquisition of L2 competence be usefully applicable to real-life situations?

I think we need to be cautious in answering this question; at the very least, there are no good grounds for simply assuming practical applicability. The logical and developmental problems are fundamentally theoretical and not practical problems; and if an answer is to be found to them, Newmeyer and Weinberger's (1988) admonition should be heeded: progress in L2 acquisition theory, as in any other scientific discipline, comes by focusing on the explanatory problem, and not by looking over one's shoulder at the possible applications. It is at least possible that L2 acquisition theory, if attainable at all, will have only an intellectual value, and that for all the good it will do our language students we might as well have taken up Romance philology. But if, as is often claimed, language research offers the best access to knowledge of the nature of the human mind, and if, as Kean (1988, p. 70) says, "it is only through L2 research that many questions about the structure and function of mature linguistic capacity can be addressed," then that intellectual value is nothing to sneeze at.

ACKNOWLEDGMENT

My thanks to Lydia White for her comments and suggestions.

REFERENCES

Adjémian, C. (1976). On the nature of interlanguage systems. *Language Learning, 26,* 297–320.

Andersen, R. W. (1983). Transfer to somewhere. In S. Gass & L. Selinker (Eds.), *Language transfer in language learning* (pp. 177–201). Rowley, MA: Newbury House.

Andersen, R. W. (1989). The theoretical status of variation in interlanguage development. In S. Gass, C. Madden, D. Preston, & L. Selinker (Eds.), *Variation in second language acquisition: Vol. 2. Psycholinguistic issues* (pp. 46–64). Clevedon, UK: Multilingual Matters.

Anderson, J. R. (1983). *The architecture of cognition.* Cambridge, MA: Harvard University Press.

Angelis, P., & Henderson, T. (Eds.). (1989). Selected papers from the proceedings of the BAAL/AAAL joint seminar "Communicative Competence Revisited" held at the University of Warwick, 8–10 July 1988. *Applied Linguistics, 10,* 113–250.

Atkinson, M. (1982). *Explanations in the study of child language development.* Cambridge, UK: Cambridge University Press.

Atkinson, M. (1992). *Children's syntax.* Oxford: Blackwell.

Baker, C. L., & McCarthy, J. J. (1981). Preface. In C. L. Baker & J. J. McCarthy (Eds.), *The logical problem of language acquisition* (pp. xi–xii). Cambridge, MA: MIT Press.

Bard, E. G., & Anderson, A. H. (1983). The unintelligibility of speech to children. *Journal of Child Language, 10,* 265–292.

Beretta, A. (1991). Theory construction in SLA; complementarity and opposition. *Studies in Second Language Acquisition, 13,* 493–511.

Beretta, A., & Crookes, G. (1993). Cognitive and social determinants of discovery in SLA. *Applied Linguistics, 14,* 250–275.

Berwick, R. (1985). *The acquisition of syntactic knowledge.* Cambridge, MA: MIT Press.

Bialystok, E., & Sharwood Smith, M. (1985). Interlanguage is not a state of mind: An evaluation of the construct for second language acquisition. *Applied Linguistics, 6,* 101–117.

Birdsong, D. (1991). On the notion of "critical period" in UG/L2 theory: A response to Flynn and Manuel. In L. Eubank (Ed.), *Point counterpoint: Universal Grammar in the second language* (pp. 147–165). Amsterdam: John Benjamins.

Bley-Vroman, R. (1986). Hypothesis testing in second language acquisition. *Language Learning, 36,* 353–376.

Bley-Vroman, R. (1990). The logical problem of foreign language learning. *Linguistic Analysis, 20,* 3–49.

Bley-Vroman, R., Felix, S., & Ioup, G. (1988). The accessibility of Universal Grammar in adult language learning. *Second Language Research, 4,* 1–32.

Bogen, J., & Woodward. J. (1988). Saving the phenomena. *Philosophical Review, 97,* 303–352.

Borer, H., & Wexler, K. (1987). The maturation of syntax. In T. Roeper & E. Williams (Eds.), *Parameter setting* (pp. 123–172). Dordrecht: Reidel.

Bowerman, M. (1985). What shapes children's grammar? In D. I. Slobin (Ed.), *The cross-linguistic study of language acquisition* (pp. 1257–1319). Hillsdale, NJ: Erlbaum.

Canale, M., & Swain, M. (1980). Theoretical bases of communicative approaches to second language teaching and testing. *Applied Linguistics, 1,* 1–47.

Carroll, S., & Meisel, J. (1990). Universals and second language acquisition: Some comments on the state of current theory. *Studies in Second Language Acquisition, 12,* 201–208.

Cartwright, N. (1988). The truth doesn't explain much. In *How the laws of physics lie* (pp. 44–53). New York: Oxford University Press.

Chalmers, A. (1990). *Science and its fabrication.* Milton Keynes, UK: Open University Press.

Chaudron, C. (1988). *Second language classrooms: research on teaching and learning.* Cambridge: Cambridge University Press.

Chomsky, N. (1965). *Aspects of the theory of syntax.* Cambridge, MA: MIT Press.

Chomsky, N. (1980). *Rules and representations.* New York: Columbia University Press.

Chomsky, N. (1981). *Lectures on government and binding.* Dordrecht: Foris.

Chomsky, N. (1986). *Knowledge of language: its nature, origin, and use.* New York: Praeger.

Clark, E. (1987). The principle of contrast: a constraint on language acquisition. In

B. MacWhinney (Ed.), *Mechanisms of language acquisition* (pp. 1–33). Hillsdale, NJ: Erlbaum.

Cook, V. (1991). The poverty-of-the-stimulus argument and multicompetence. *Second Language Research, 7,* 103–117.

Crookes, G. (1993). Theory format and SLA theory. *Studies in Second Language Acquisition, 14,* 425–449.

Cummins, R. (1983). *The nature of psychological explanation.* Cambridge, MA: MIT Press.

Dawkins, R. (1985). *The blind watchmaker.* New York: Norton.

Day, R. (Ed.). (1986). *Talking to learn: Conversation in second language acquisition.* Rowley, MA: Newbury House.

Dulay, H., Burt, M., & Krashen, S. (1982). *Language two.* Oxford: Oxford University Press.

Ellis, R. (1985). A variable competence model of second language acquisition. *IRAL, 23,* 47–59.

Ellis, R. (1986). *Understanding second language acquisition.* Oxford: Oxford University Press.

Felix, S. W. (1984). Maturational aspects of Universal Grammar. In A. Davies, C. Criper, & A. P. R. Howatt (Eds.), *Interlanguage* (pp. 133–161). Edinburgh: Edinburgh University Press.

Felix, S. W. (1985). More evidence on competing cognitive systems. *Second Language Research, 1,* 47–52.

Felix, S. W. (1986). *Cognition and language growth.* Dordrecht: Foris.

Flavell, J. (1972). An analysis of cognitive-developmental sequences. *Genetic Psychology Monographs, 86,* 279–350.

Flynn, S. (1987). Contrast and construction in a parameter-setting model of L2 acquisition. *Language Learning, 37,* 19–62.

Flynn, S., & Manuel, S. (1991). Age-dependent effects in language acquisition: an evaluation of "critical period" hypotheses. In L. Eubank (Ed.), *Point counterpoint: Universal Grammar in the second language* (pp. 117–145). Amsterdam: John Benjamins.

Fodor, J. A. (1981a). Introduction. In *Representations* (pp. 1–31). Cambridge, MA: MIT Press.

Fodor, J. A. (1981b). Computation and reduction. In *Representations* (pp. 146–174). Cambridge, MA: MIT Press. (Originally published in *Perception and cognition,* by W. Savage, Ed., 1978, Minneapolis: University of Minnesota Press)

Fodor, J. A. (1981c). Special sciences. In *Representations* (pp. 127–145). Cambridge, MA: MIT Press. (Originally published in *Synthèse, 28,* 77–115, 1974)

Fodor, J. A. (1983). *The modularity of mind.* Cambridge, MA: MIT Press.

Fodor, J. A., & Pylyshyn, Z. W. (1988). *Connectionism and cognitive architecture: A critical analysis. Cognition, 28,* 3–71.

Fodor, J. D., & Crain, S. (1987). Simplicity and generality of rules in language acquisition. In B. MacWhinney (Ed.), *Mechanisms of language acquisition* (pp. 35–63). Hillsdale, NJ: Erlbaum.

Gardner, R. (1985). *Social psychology and second language learning: The role of attitudes and motivation.* London: Edward Arnold.

Gasser, M. (1990). Connectionism and universals of second language acquisition. *Studies in Second Language Acquisition, 12,* 179–199.

Goodluck, H. (1986). Language acquisition and linguistic theory. In P. Fletcher & M. Garman (Eds.), *Language acquisition* (2nd ed., pp. 49–68). Cambridge, UK: Cambridge University Press.

Gregg, K. R. (1984). Krashen's monitor and Occam's Razor. *Applied Linguistics, 5,* 79–100.

Gregg, K. R. (1988). Epistemology without knowledge: Schwartz on Chomsky, Fodor and Krashen. *Second Language Research, 4,* 66–80.

Gregg, K. R. (1989). Second language acquisition theory: The case for a generative perspective. In S. Gass & J. Schachter (Eds.), *Linguistic perspectives on second language acquisition* (pp. 15–40). Cambridge, UK: Cambridge University Press.

Gregg, K. R. (1993). Taking explanation seriously; or, let a couple of flowers bloom. *Applied Linguistics, 14,* 276–294.

Hatch, E. M. (1978). Discourse analysis and second language acquisition. In E. M. Hatch (Ed.), *Second language acquisition: A book of readings* (pp. 401–435). Rowley, MA: Newbury House.

Heath, S. B. (1983). *Ways with words: Language, life, and work in communities and classrooms.* Cambridge, UK: Cambridge University Press.

Hempel, C. G. (1965). *Aspects of scientific explanation and other essays in the philosophy of science.* New York: Free Press.

Hornstein, N., & Lightfoot, D. (Eds.). (1981). *Explanation in linguistics: The logical problem of language acquisition.* London: Longman.

Hyams, N. (1986). *Language acquisition and the theory of parameters.* Dordrecht: Reidel.

Hymes, D. (1972). On communicative competence. In J. B. Pride & J. Holmes (Eds.), *Sociolinguistics* (pp. 269–293). Harmondsworth: Penguin.

Jacobs, B. (1988). Neurobiological differentiation of primary and secondary language acquisition. *Studies in Second Language Acquisition, 10,* 303–337.

Jacobs, B., & Schumann, J. (1992). Language acquisition and the neurosciences: Towards a more integrative perspective. *Applied Linguistics, 13,* 282–301.

Kean, M.-L. (1988). The relation between linguistic theory and second language acquisition: A biological perspective. In J. Pankhurst, M. Sharwood Smith, & P. van Buren (Eds.), *Learnability and second languages; a book of readings* (pp. 61–70). Dordrecht: Foris.

Kuhn, T. S. (1977). Concepts of cause in the development of physics. In *The essential tension* (pp. 21–30). Chicago: University of Chicago Press.

Lado, R. (1957). *Linguistics across cultures.* Ann Arbor: University of Michigan Press.

Larsen-Freeman, D. (1976). An explanation for the morpheme acquisition order of second language learners. *Language Learning, 26,* 125–134.

Larsen-Freeman, D., & Long, M. H. (1991). *An introduction to second language acquisition research.* London: Longman.

Lipton, P. (1991). *Inference to the best explanation.* London: Routledge.

Long, M. H. (1983). Native speaker/non-native speaker conversation and the negotiation of comprehensible input. *Applied Linguistics, 4,* 126–141.

Long, M. H. (1990). Maturational constraints on language development. *Studies in Second Language Acquisition, 12,* 251–285.

Long, M. H. (1993). Assessment strategies for second language acquisition theories. *Applied Linguistics, 14,* 225–249.

McLaughlin, B. (1987). *Theories of second language learning.* London: Edward Arnold.

Moravcsik, J. M. (1980). Chomsky's radical break with modern traditions. *Behavioral and Brain Sciences, 3,* 28–29.

Newmeyer, F. J. (1983). *Grammatical theory: Its limits and possibilities.* Chicago: University of Chicago Press.

Newmeyer, F. J., & Weinberger, S. H. (1988). The ontogenesis of the field of second language learning research. In S. Flynn & W. O'Neil (Eds.), *Linguistic theory in second language acquisition* (pp. 34–45). Dordrecht: Kluwer.

Newport, E. L., Gleitman, H., & Gleitman, L. R. (1977). Mother, I'd rather do it myself: Some effects and non-effects of maternal speech style. In C. E. Snow & C. A. Ferguson (Eds.), *Talking to children: language input and acquisition* (pp. 109–149). Cambridge, UK: Cambridge University Press.

Ochs, E. (1982). Talking to children in Western Samoa. *Language in Society, 11,* 77–104.

O'Grady, W. (1987). *Principles of grammar and learning.* Chicago: University of Chicago Press.

Pienemann, M. (1984). Psycholinguistic constraints on the teachability of languages. *Studies in Second Language Acquisition, 6,* 186–214.

Pinker, S. (1979). Formal models of language learning. *Cognition, 7,* 217–283.

Pinker, S. (1984). *Language learnability and language development.* Cambridge, MA: Harvard University Press.

Pinker, S. (1989). *Learnability and cognition: The acquisition of argument structure.* Cambridge, MA: MIT Press.

Pinker, S., & Prince, A. (1988). On language and connectionism: Analysis of a parallel distributed processing model of language acquisition. *Cognition, 28,* 73–193.

Pollock, J. (1989). Verb movement, Universal Grammar, and the structure of IP. *Linguistic Inquiry, 20,* 365–424.

Putnam, H. (1988). What theories are not. In E. D. Klemke, R. Hollinger, & A. D. Kline (Eds.), *Introductory readings in the philosophy of science* (Rev. ed., pp. 178–183). Buffalo, NY: Prometheus Books. (Originally published in *Logic, methodology, and philosophy of science,* by E. Nagel, P. Suppes, & A. Tarski, Eds., 1962, Stanford, CA: Stanford University Press)

Pylyshyn, Z. W. (1984). *Computation and cognition.* (Cambridge, MA: MIT Press.

Ritchie, W. C. (1978). The right roof constraint in adult-acquired language. In W. C. Ritchie (Ed.), *Second language acquisition research: Issues and implications* (pp. 33–63). New York: Academic Press.

Ruben, D.-H. (1990). *Explaining explanation.* London: Routledge.

Rumelhart, D. E., McClelland, J. L., & the PDP Research Group. (1986). *Parallel distributed processing.* Cambridge, MA: MIT Press.

Rutherford, W. E. (1989). Preemption and the learning of L2 grammars. *Studies in Second Language Acquisition, 11,* 441–457.

Safir, K. (1987). Comments on Wexler and Manzini. In T. Roeper & E. Williams (Eds.), *Parameter setting* (pp. 77–89). Dordrecht: Reidel.

Salmon, W. C. (1989). *Four decades of scientific explanation.* Minneapolis: University of Minnesota Press.

Schmidt, R. (1988). The potential of PDP for SLA theory and research. *University of Hawaii Working Papers in ESL, 7,* 55–66.

Schumann, J. (1978). The acculturation model for second language acquisition. In R. Gingras (Ed.), *Second language acquisition and foreign language teaching* (pp. 27–50). Arlington, VA: Center for Applied Linguistics.

Schumann, J. (1993). Some problems with falsification: An illustration from SLA research. *Applied Linguistics, 14,* 295–306.

Schwartz, B. (1986). The epistemological status of second language acquisition. *Second Language Research, 2,* 120–159.

Schwartz, B. (1987). *The modular basis of second language acquisition.* Unpublished doctoral dissertation, University of Southern California, Los Angeles.

Schwartz, B. (1992). Testing between UG-based and problem-solving models of L2A: Developmental sequence data. *Language Acquisition, 2,* 1–19.

Schwartz, B., & Gubala-Ryzak, M. (1992). Learnability and grammar reorganization in L2A: Against negative evidence causing the unlearning of verb movement. *Second Language Research, 8,* 1–38.

Scovel, T. (1988). *A time to speak: A psycholinguistic inquiry into the critical period for human speech.* New York: Newbury House.

Singleton, D. (1989). *Language acquisition: the age factor.* Clevedon, UK: Multilingual Matters.

Slobin, D. I. (1973). Cognitive prerequisites for the development of grammar. In C. A. Ferguson & D. I. Slobin (Eds.), *Studies of child language development* (pp. 175–208). New York: Holt, Rinehart & Winston.

Slobin, D. I. (1985). Cross-linguistic evidence for the language-making capacity. In D. I. Slobin (Ed.), *The crosslinguistic study of language acquisition* (pp. 1157–1256). Hillsdale, NJ: Erlbaum.

Snow, C. E., & Ferguson, C. A. (Eds.). (1977). *Talking to children: Language input and acquisition.* Cambridge, UK: Cambridge University Press.

Tarone, E. (1988). *Variation in interlanguage.* London: Edward Arnold.

Taylor, D. S. (1988). The meaning and use of the term "competence" in linguistics and applied linguistics. *Applied Linguistics, 9,* 148–168.

Trahey, M., & White, L. (1993). Positive evidence and preemption in the second language classroom. *Studies in Second Language Acquisition, 15,* 181–204.

van Fraassen, B. C. (1980). *The scientific image.* Oxford: Oxford University Press.

Wexler, K., & Culicover, P. (1980). *Formal principles of language acquisition.* Cambridge, MA: MIT Press.

Wexler, K., & Mazini, R. (1987). Parameters and learnability in binding theory. In T. Roeper & E. Williams (Eds.), *Parameter setting* (pp. 41–76). Dordrecht: Reidel.

White, L. (1985). Is there a "logical problem" of second language acquisition? *TESL Canada Journal, 2*(2), 29–41.

White, L. (1987). Against comprehensible input: The input hypothesis and the development of L2 competence. *Applied Linguistics, 8,* 95–110.

White, L. (1989). *Universal Grammar and second language acquisition.* Amsterdam: John Benjamins.

White, L. (1991a). Adverb placement in second language acquisition: Some effects of positive and negative evidence in the classroom. *Second Language Research, 7,* 133–161.

White, L. (1991b). Second language competence versus second language performance: UG or processing strategies. In L. Eubank (Ed.), *Point counterpoint: Universal Grammar in the second language* (pp. 167–189). Amsterdam: John Benjamins.

Wode, H., Bahns, J., Bedey, H., & Frank, W. (1978). Developmental sequence: An alternative approach to morpheme order. *Language Learning, 28*, 175–185.

Wolfe-Quintero, K. (1992). Learnability and the acquisition of extraction in relative clauses and WH-questions. *Studies in Second Language Acquisition, 14*, 39–70.

PART II

ISSUES OF MATURATION AND MODULARITY IN SECOND LANGUAGE ACQUISITION

CHAPTER 3

UNIVERSAL GRAMMAR AND SECOND LANGUAGE ACQUISITION: CURRENT TRENDS AND NEW DIRECTIONS

Lydia White

I. INTRODUCTION

As Gregg (1989, chap. 2, this volume) reminds us, a theory of language acquisition depends on a theory of language. We cannot decide how something is acquired without having an idea of what that something is. Researchers working on Universal Grammar (UG) in second language (L2) acquisition adopt a currently well-developed theory of language, namely the principles and parameters approach, as realized in Government Binding (GB) theory and subsequently (Chomsky, 1981, 1986). This theory of grammar is itself grounded in concerns about language acquisition, especially the so-called logical problem of language acquisition, the problem being to account for the fact that one ends up knowing far more than is provided by linguistic input (Hornstein & Lightfoot, 1981). The solution offered to this problem is the postulation of a system of innate principles and parameters that form the content of UG. In this chapter, I will look at the role of UG in L2 acquisition, considering past research, present emphases, and future directions.

II. PRINCIPLES AND PARAMETERS THEORY

The principles and parameters framework has a dual aim: to characterize the native speaker's (NS) knowledge of language, or linguistic competence, and to

Handbook of Second Language Acquisition

explain how the acquisition of such competence is possible. In this approach, it is argued that much of our linguistic competence stems from innate knowledge, which takes the form of a UG. Linguists motivate UG by pointing to the end result of language acquisition, namely the adult grammar. They argue that the input alone is simply insufficient to allow the child to attain full adult competence. Our linguistic competence extends beyond the input in various ways: for instance, children and adults can understand and produce sentences that they have never heard before; they know that certain structures are not possible and that others are ambiguous, without being explicitly taught such things. Apart from dialectal differences, the competence of adult NSs of the same language is essentially identical; that is, adults achieve the same end result (a complex competence grammar), despite varying exposure to data in the course of acquisition—they may have heard different input, or the same input in different orders, or they may not have been exposed to certain kinds of input at all.

In this framework, first language (L1) acquisition is assumed to proceed on the basis of naturalistic positive evidence (utterances in the input that children are exposed to) interacting with innate principles and parameters of UG. The input data "trigger" properties of UG (Lightfoot, 1989). That is, they cause UG parameters to be set without learning having to take place. Negative evidence (information about ungrammaticality) plays a minimal role.

A. Principles: C-Command

As an example of subtle knowledge that forms part of the NS's unconscious knowledge of language, consider the notion of c-command, an abstract structural dominance relationship that plays an important role in many aspects of GB theory. C-command is defined as follows: a category α c-commands another category β if and only if the first branching node dominating α also dominates β. To see how this works, consider the tree in (1):

(1)

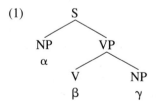

The first branching node dominating the noun phrase (NP) α is the sentence (S). This S also dominates the verb (V) β and the NP γ. Therefore, α c-commands both β and γ. β and γ, on the other hand, do not c-command α, because the first branching node dominating them is the verb phrase (VP), which does not dominate α. They do, however, c-command each other. (Chapter 5 by Schachter, this volume, includes additional discussion of the notion of C-command.)

Now let us consider some examples of c-command at work in English, by looking at the behavior of anaphoric pronouns like reflexives. A reflexive pronoun
must have a local antecedent within the same clause, as can be seen in (2), where
coreference between *Mary* and *herself* is possible in (2a) (as indicated by the
subscripts) but not in (2b) or (2c):

(2) a.   Mary$_i$ congratulated herself$_i$.
     b.   *Mary$_i$ said that Susan congratulated herself$_i$.
     c.   *Mary$_i$ told Susan to congratulate herself$_i$.

It is not sufficient for the antecedent to be within the same clause, however; it must
also bear a particular structural relationship to the reflexive. The sentences in (3)
are ungrammatical, even though there is a plausible antecedent within the same
clause. (3a) shows that the antecedent cannot follow the reflexive, and (3b) shows
that it is not sufficient for the antecedent to precede the reflexive (i.e., that *Mary*
cannot be the antecedent, although *Mary's sister* can):

(3) a.   *Herself$_i$ congratulated Mary$_i$.
     b.   *Mary$_i$'s sister congratulated herself$_i$.

In fact, the antecedent of a reflexive must c-command it. The ungrammatical cases
are the consequence of a failure of c-command, as can be seen in (4). In (4a), the
NP *Mary* c-commands *herself,* whereas in (4b) it does not.

(4) a.

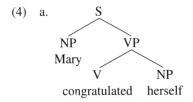

     b.

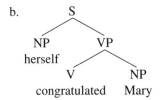

     c.

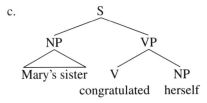

The c-command condition also allows for ambiguous sentences, as in (5). Both *John* and *Bill* c-command *himself,* as shown in (6); hence, either NP can serve as the antecedent of the reflexive.

(5)   John showed Bill a picture of himself.

(6)

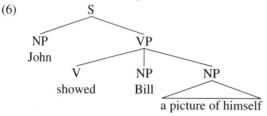

It is most unlikely that children are ever taught the c-command condition on anaphors when they acquire their L1, nor does this information seem to be inducible from the language that they hear. Yet they come to know that sentences like (2b) or (3a) are ungrammatical, whereas sentences like (5) are ambiguous. Hence, it is argued that c-command, along with many other such abstract properties, must be universal and part of the innate knowledge that children bring to the task of L1 acquisition, in other words, part of UG. L1 acquisition research suggests that children show mastery of the c-command requirement on reflexives at an early age (Wexler & Chien, 1985).

B. Parameters: Verb Raising

As well as abstract principles and structural relationships like c-command, UG also contains parameters, which are principles that differ in the way they work from language to language. The differences are accounted for by incorporating a limited number of options into UG. Parameters account for clusters of properties, which superficially seem to be unrelated. The idea is that parameters give the child advance knowledge of what the possibilities will be, that is, they limit the range of hypotheses that have to be considered. Parameter settings are fixed on the basis of input from the language being acquired.

An example is provided by certain differences between French and English (Emonds, 1978; Pollock, 1989). English and French behave differently regarding negative placement, as can be seen by comparing (7a) and (7b), question formation, as in (8a) versus (8b), adverb placement, as in (9a) and (9c) versus (9b) and (9d), and quantifier positions, as in (10a) and (10c) versus (10b) and (10d):

(7)   a. *John likes not Mary.
       b. *Jean n'aime pas Marie.*
(8)   a. *Likes she John?
       b. *Aime-t-elle-Jean?*

(9)   a. *John watches often television.
       b. *Jean regarde souvent la télévision.*
       c. Mary often watches television.
       d. **Marie souvent regarde la télévision.*
(10)   a. *My friends like all Mary.
       b. *Mes amis aiment tous Marie.*
       c. My friends all like Mary.
       d. **Mes amis tous aiment Marie.*

According to Pollock (1989), these apparently different properties can all be traced to one parametric difference between the two languages, namely whether the language allows verb raising. French has verb movement: all finite verbs must raise through Agreement (Agr) to Tense (T), in contrast to English where main verbs may not raise. This verb movement is shown in (11).[1]

(11)

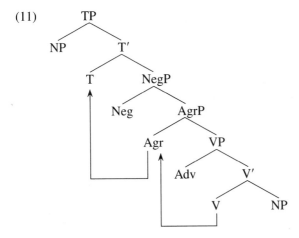

The verb-movement analysis accounts for the French–English differences in the following way. In French, the finite verb must raise to T (for reasons which I will not go into here), explaining why negative *pas* is postverbal in (7b), why questions are formed by "subject–verb inversion"[2] in (8b), and why adverbs occur to the right of the verb in (9b). Assuming that quantifiers occupy the same positions as adverbs, (10b) and (10d) are also accounted for. In English, verb-raising is prohibited, accounting for the impossibility of postverbal negation in (7a), for the lack of inversion with main verbs in (8a), and for the

---

[1] The parameter involves the "opacity" versus "transparency" of the category Agr; opaque Agr prevents verb-movement, for reasons to do with theta-role assignment (Pollock, 1989).

[2] Inversion results because the verb subsequently raises to the complementizer (C) position, which is to the left of the subject.

placement of adverbs and quantifiers immediately to the left of the verb, as in (9c) and (10c).

The parameter thus accounts for a cluster of properties; the idea is that these properties do not have to be learned separately by the L1 learner. Indeed, the child does not have to learn about verb movement at all. Rather, the possibility is built in as part of UG, and there is ample evidence from simple sentences to trigger the adoption of the appropriate setting. For example, the position of the negative *pas* in French indicates that the verb has moved, whereas the position of *not* in English indicates that it has not.[3] From such evidence, the parameter is "set" and the cluster of properties associated with ± verb movement emerges. (For additional discussion of verb raising or verb movement see chapter 14 by Berent, this volume.)

III. PRINCIPLES AND PARAMETERS IN L2 ACQUISITION

Principles and parameters theory has attracted considerable attention as a potential component in a theory of L2 acquisition (see Flynn, chap. 4, this volume, Gregg, chap. 2, this volume, and White 1989b, for detailed review). Linguistic theory, of course, says nothing directly about L2 acquisition. At a descriptive level, principles and parameters identify universal properties of grammars; at an explanatory level, these properties are assumed to be innate in the L1 learner, accounting for various aspects of acquisition. It is up to an L2 acquisition theory to offer an account of how such principles and parameters might play a role in L2 acquisition.

If the aim of an acquisition theory is (in part) to explain the acquisition of linguistic competence in an L2, it is crucial to have a theory of linguistic competence to provide a general frame of reference. Current linguistic theory offers both a highly detailed account of what linguistic competence consists of, as well as some general indication of how that competence is acquired, via the assumption of an innate UG operating at least in L1 acquisition. Less well worked out, within this framework, is a developmental theory (see Gregg, chap. 2, this volume) of how UG is implemented in developmental stages, although work on parameter resetting (Hyams, 1986), triggering (Lightfoot, 1989), and learning principles like the Subset Principle (SP) (Berwick, 1985; Wexler & Manzini, 1987) and the Uniqueness Principle (UP) (Pinker, 1984) all contribute to the developmental question. As far as L2 acquisition is concerned, an L2 acquisition theory can take as a working hypothesis that L2 learners do (or do not) still have access to abstract

---

[3] For this triggering to take place, the child has to be able to analyze the input appropriately (i.e., categories such as *verb* and *negative* must be isolated and recognized) but that is all.

principles like c-command and parameters like verb-movement, in order to establish the exact nature of L2 competence and to account for its acquisition. The L2 developmental question can also be addressed by looking at issues like parameter resetting, triggering data, learning principles, and so forth.

Not surprisingly, work in L2 acquisition done from the principles and parameters perspective has centered on the issue of the availability of UG. Arguments in favor of a role for UG in L2 acquisition hinge on the logical problem of L2 acquisition: L2 learners often end up with a highly complex unconscious mental representation of their L2 (not necessarily identical to an NS's grammar), which is underdetermined by the L2 input, suggesting that built-in knowledge must be involved (White, 1985a, 1989b). Proponents of the position that UG is available have investigated whether L2 learners in fact show evidence of observing principles of UG and whether UG parameter settings hold of the interlanguage (IL) grammar. The logical problem is addressed by investigating the nature of IL grammars: Are they constrained by UG? Are they so constrained at every stage? The developmental problem is addressed by considering whether L2 learners reset parameters (leading to different stages of development) and what kind of input or what kinds of learning principles contribute to L2 developmental stages.

Arguments against UG in L2 acquisition emphasize difficulties faced by L2 learners, and differences between L1 and L2 acquisition, both in the course of development and in the end result; it is claimed that such differences can best be explained on the assumption that UG is no longer available to adult L2 learners, and that there is a fundamental difference between L1 and L2 acquisition (Bley-Vroman, 1990; Clahsen & Muysken, 1986; Schachter, 1989, chap. 5, this volume). Proponents of this position seek to show that ILs are not constrained by UG, that learners violate UG principles, and that developmental stages cannot be accounted for in terms of parameter resetting.

A. Access to UG: Competence and Acquisition of Competence

In much of the research into UG availability, the working assumption has been that if learners can be shown to violate principles of UG, then UG cannot be available to L2 learners, whereas if they observe UG constraints, UG must be available. The question of access or no access is addressed by taking the performance of NSs of the L2 as a criterion and then comparing the performance of L2 learners with the NSs. This is done explicitly by use of NS controls or implicitly by accepting current proposals in linguistic theory. Because NSs are necessarily constrained by UG, the assumption is that if L2 learners perform similarly to NSs, they must also be constrained by UG, whereas if they perform differently, they are not. (See chapters 2 by Gregg and 4 by Flynn for competence/performance in L2 acquisition.)

Such direct comparison of L2 learners and NSs is not without problems, however. It neglects the fact that UG permits a range of grammars. As a number of researchers have reminded us over the years, the L1 or L2 learner system needs to be considered in its own right (Birdsong, 1989; Bley-Vroman, 1983; Schwartz & Sprouse, 1994; Sharwood Smith, 1992; White, 1982). Although one can take as the null hypothesis that similar linguistic behavior on the part of NSs and nonnative speakers (NNS) has the same origin (a competence grammar constrained by UG), if the behavior is not the same, one cannot automatically conclude that lack of UG is the reason. The native system is only one of a number of possible grammars permitted by UG. "Nontarget" linguistic behavior, then, has at least two potential causes: lack of UG or availability of UG but with the learner coming up with a different system from the NS.

Thus, one needs to distinguish between *what* and *how* in the acquisition of L2 competence. What is the nature of L2 competence (or mental representation)? How is that competence acquired? Of course, these questions are linked in the principles and parameters framework, in that UG both determines the nature of competence (it must be UG-constrained) and guides the L1 acquirer (certain hypotheses are never entertained). Here, I will consider three possible scenarios for L2 acquisition, which arise if one distinguishes between competence (what) and acquisition of competence (how).[4] (The range of alternative theoretical positions on the role of UG in L2 acquisition is also described in chapters 2 by Gregg, 4 by Flynn, and 5 by Schachter, this volume.)

Position 1: Same competence, same means of acquisition. NSs and NNSs have the same or similar competence, arrived at by the same means. The claim is that L2 learners (including adults) show evidence of observing principles of UG and acquire appropriate L2 parameter settings. Hence, their competence is similar to that of NSs, and this is because of the availability of UG. This position is fairly standard in the UG debate (e.g., Flynn, chap. 4, this volume). For child L2 acquisition, there appears to be a general presumption that this position is correct.

Position 2: Different competence, different means of acquisition. NSs and NNSs have different competence, arrived at by different means. This is a standard position among people who believe in the inaccessibility of UG (e.g., Schachter, chap. 5, this volume). The assumption is that if one can show that L2 learners'

---

[4]There are many more than three possibilities, if one allows for the fact that linguistic behavior (or performance) can differ from competence in a variety of ways, and that similar behavior may result from different competences. This issue is taken up in section IV, which discusses learners whose performance is near-native. In some cases, their competence may diverge from that of NSs even though their performance appears not to. In addition, there are several other possible scenarios if one also considers learning principles associated with UG, and whether or not they remain available.

linguistic performance differs from NSs in some UG domain, this reflects a difference in linguistic competence, which in turn must be due to unavailability of UG and use of alternative means of learning the L2, for example the L1 grammar and problem solving.

Position 3: Different competence, same means of acquisition. NSs and NNSs have different competence, arrived at by the same means. For adult L2 acquisition, this position is advanced more and more frequently, the claim being that IL grammars are "possible grammars" (or natural languages) in a technical sense. L2 learners, it is argued, come up with grammars that are constrained by UG but that are not necessarily the same as the L2 grammar; the IL grammar may show properties of the L1 grammar, or, more interestingly, it may be like neither the L1 nor the L2 (Broselow & Finer, 1991; du Plessis, Solin, Travis, & White, 1987; Martohardjono & Gair, 1993; Schwartz & Tomaselli, 1990; White, 1992a). For people to have different grammars arrived at by the same means is, of course, the standard situation holding true of NSs of two different languages, say French and Chinese. The NS of French has a mental representation that differs from that of the NS of Chinese; nevertheless, they have both been acquired via UG. It is also the case that in L1 acquisition the learner may have a UG-constrained grammar that differs from that of an adult NS. The difference between L1 and L2 acquisition here is that L2 learners do not necessarily converge on the same grammar, in contrast to L1 acquirers.[5]

Positions 1 and 3, then, have in common the assumption that UG constrains L2 acquisition. They differ in terms of the mental representation that the L2 learner arrives at. Indeed, the two positions are not mutually exclusive. That is, it is possible for a learner to have a mental representation that differs from a NS at certain stages but that eventually converges on a nativelike grammar. This situation is, as mentioned above, characteristic of L1 acquisition. One of the outstanding questions in current theorizing must be why some L2 learners, perhaps the majority, end up with a grammar that is different from NSs, so that Position 3 characterizes not just stages of development but their ultimate attainment.

Because of the situation described in Position 3, one cannot assume that evidence that L2 learners behave differently from NSs is automatically evidence against UG. We therefore need careful analyses of learner grammars as systems to be considered in their own right with respect to the UG question.

---

[5] A fourth possibility is that NSs and NNs have similar competence, arrived at by different means. A version of this position is advanced by Bley-Vroman (1990). On the whole, he argues that the competence of NSs and NNSs is essentially different and that different mechanisms are involved (hypothesis-testing rather than UG in the case of L2 learners). However, in certain cases, where L2 learners appear to be successful in acquiring nativelike competence, he attributes this to knowledge derived from the mother tongue, rather than directly from UG.

B. Perspectives on Principles

Evidence for Position I

An important question in investigations of UG in L2 acquisition has been whether IL grammars are constrained by UG principles. A recent example of evidence that UG is available to adult learners is provided by Thomas (1991), who investigates the L2 acquisition of various properties of reflexive binding, including the c-command constraint described in section II.A. To test whether learners were aware of the c-command constraint on antecedents of reflexives in Japanese, Thomas's study included adult learners of Japanese, at various levels of proficiency. Japanese sentences to be judged included ones quite similar to (3b), repeated below:

(3)   b.   *Mary$_i$'s sister congratulated herself$_i$.

Thomas found no significant differences between Japanese controls and learners at any level of proficiency: the majority of responses allowed only the c-commanding NP as the antecedent. This suggests that the c-command constraint is available in L2 acquisition.

A further issue is whether access to UG is mediated via the L1 grammar. In the case of c-command, it might be that the L2 learner's knowledge of c-command comes only from the L1 rather than from UG directly. In order to address the question of whether access depends on the L1 grammar, a number of researchers have isolated situations where on the basis of the way principles of UG operate in the L1, the learner could not acquire the relevant properties of the L2. If learners in such situations show evidence of observing UG principles, this suggests that UG is available in nonprimary acquisition, because access could not have been solely via the L1.

A recent study following this logic is White, Travis, and Maclachlan (1992) who present evidence that suggests that Malagasy learners of English observe constraints on wh-movement in English, even though these constraints operate very differently in the two languages. In Malagasy, extraction from complex subjects is permitted, whereas in English extraction from subjects is prohibited. In addition, object extraction and extraction from complex objects are freely allowed in English but are ungrammatical in Malagasy. Given these differences between the two languages, it is not clear how Malagasy learners should know that extractions out of subjects are not permitted, or what constraints apply to extracted objects. If UG is only accessible via the L1, once Malagasy learners acquire English wh-movement, they should not show evidence of observing the relevant constraints. Rather, one might expect them to make incorrect generalizations about wh-movement, and to violate various constraints in the process. If UG is directly accessible, on the other hand, constraints on wh-movement should be observed once wh-movement in the L2 is acquired.

Subjects for this study were low- and high-intermediate adult Malagasy learners of English. Subjects took two tests, a grammaticality judgment task and a written elicited production task. Both tasks tapped learners' knowledge of grammatical wh-question formation in English, as well as various principles of UG that constrain wh-movement. Results show that almost all the high-intermediate group and about half of the low-intermediate group perform like a native English-speaking control group: they have acquired grammatical wh-movement in English and do not violate constraints on movement; that is, they reject violations in the judgment task and do not produce violations in the production task. Those subjects in the low-intermediate group who incorrectly accept or produce violations of constraints are also inaccurate on grammatical wh-questions, suggesting that they have not yet acquired English wh-movement and thus that the relevant principles constraining movement are not yet in operation. (In other words, these learners constitute an example of Position 3, rather than Position 2.) Thus, these results suggest that the L1 is not the only source of the learners' UG-like knowledge. Rather, principles of UG remain accessible in adult L2 acquisition.

Evidence for Position 2

In contrast to the above position, other researchers argue that L2 learners do not have direct access to UG; they either have no access at all (Clahsen & Muysken, 1986) or access only via the L1 (Bley-Vroman, 1990). Thus, their grammars are different from NSs, as well as their means of acquisition. Schachter (1989, 1990, chap. 5, this volume) provides an example of this latter position. In experimental investigations of access to the Subjacency Principle (a principle constraining wh-movement) by L2 learners, she has found that NSs of languages that do not instantiate Subjacency because they lack syntactic wh-movement (i.e., Korean and Chinese) show no evidence of observing Subjacency in the L2, in contrast to learners whose L1s do instantiate Subjacency (i.e., Dutch). That is, Korean and Chinese speakers fail to recognize Subjacency violations in English, unlike Dutch speakers who are accurate at recognizing violations. Schachter concludes that UG is unavailable to adult learners because they fail to recognize violations of principles of UG unless these principles also operate in their L1. (For additional discussion of this and other empirical studies of Subjacency in L2 acquisition see chapters 4 by Flynn, 5 by Schachter, and 10 by Gass, this volume.)

Evidence for Position 3

When one compares learners' results with natives, who correctly reject the violations in question, Schachter's conclusion indeed seems reasonable. However, as discussed in section III.A, when the IL grammar appears to diverge from the grammar of NSs, it is important to explore the nature of the L2 learner's representation in more detail in order to determine whether it is or is not a natural language system. For example, as proposed by Martohardjono and Gair (1993) and by

White (1992c), it might be that Korean and Chinese-speaking learners lack wh-movement in complex sentences and use *pro* as their empty category rather than a wh-trace, as is the case in their L1s. Since *pro* is not subject to Subjacency, the violations in their grammars are more apparent than real. Their wh-questions have a different underlying structure from those of NSs of English. Thus, L2 learners have a different competence but still a UG-constrained competence. In this case, that competence is influenced by the L1 grammar, in terms of the empty categories that are permitted in the IL grammar.

C. Perspectives on Parameters

Evidence for Position 1

Much of the pioneering work on UG in L2 acquisition looked at the operation of parameters (Flynn, 1984; Liceras, 1988; White, 1985b). Position 1 is exemplified by the work of Flynn (chap. 4, this volume), who has used experimental findings on L2 acquisition of branching direction and anaphora to argue that L2 learners successfully acquire L2 parameter settings by means of UG, without going through a phase of applying the L1 settings to the L2. (She does not, however, rule out a role for the L1 but sees this as a potential source of difficulty and delay in acquiring the L2 setting when L1 and L2 do not match in their parameter settings.)

Other results that indicate successful acquisition of the L2 parameter setting without applying the L1 setting are reported by White (1992a) who shows that francophone learners of English never assume that the verb in English can raise to T (see [11]), even though this is required in French. Sentences like (7a) and (8a), repeated here, are not considered to be possible by francophone learners of English, suggesting that the parameter has been reset, in this aspect at least.

(7)   a.   *John likes not Mary.
(8)   a.   *Likes she John?

(Nevertheless, although the impossibility of verb movement to T is acquired almost immediately by L2 learners, they have considerable problems with movement to Agr.)

Evidence for Position 2

Position 2 for parameters claims that IL grammars cannot be described in terms of parameter settings, or that, at best, L2 learners will exemplify L1 settings but will be unable to reset these, because UG is no longer available. The strongest case for this position has been argued for by Clahsen and Muysken (1986), who try to show that L2 learners do not have a parameter-based grammar at all. Clahsen and Muysken argue that adult L2 learners of German have an "unnatural" grammar, allowing nonfinite verbal elements to move rightwards to the end of the sentence, whereas L1 learners have a natural grammar that moves finite elements leftwards. In particular, L2 learners lack parameters associated with word order (as well as other principles of UG) and are thus incapable of handling L2 word order in a manner that is consistent with UG. Arguments against this analysis have been advanced by du Plessis et al. (1987) and by Schwartz and Tomaselli (1990), who show that the behavior of adult learners of German is indeed UG constrained, with a number of interacting parameters being set such that these learners have an IL grammar that resembles that of neither the L1 nor the L2 (i.e., Position 3).

Evidence for Position 3

The investigation of parameters in L2 acquisition has been particularly relevant to the issue of whether access to UG is mediated via the L1. A number of researchers have reported that L1 parameter settings are adopted by L2 learners, at least in initial phases (e.g., Phinney, 1987; White, 1985b). Such results can be taken as evidence for Position 3; that is, the learner has a different competence from the NS, but it is UG-constrained. Unfortunately, these results are also consistent with Position 2; if learners acquire the L2 without UG but with the aid of their L1 grammar, then L1 parameter settings are also predicted. The difference is in the predictions made on parameter resetting: Position 2 predicts that no parameter resetting should be possible.

A number of researchers investigating parameters in L2 acquisition have argued that some L2 learners arrive at parameter settings that are those of neither the L1 nor the L2 but which do, nevertheless, represent possibilities found in natural languages (du Plessis et al., 1987; Finer & Broselow, 1986; Schwartz & Tomaselli, 1990; Thomas, 1991). These cases provide much stronger evidence that UG is still available; on a theory that denies the existence of UG in L2 acquisition, there is no reason why learners should arrive at parameter settings that are exemplified in neither language.

Some of these studies concern reflexive binding in L2 acquisition, to which we now turn. Languages differ as to whether they require a reflexive to have a local antecedent or whether they allow long-distance binding of reflexives. In languages like English, only local binding is permitted, whereas in languages like Japanese, the antecedent can also be nonlocal. In languages like Russian, a local antecedent is required in a tensed clause but not in a nonfinite clause. Thus, considering sentences like those in (2), repeated here, and looking at whether *Mary* can serve as antecedent of the reflexive, binding is only possible in (2a) in English. In contrast, Japanese also permits binding in (2b) and (2c). In Russian, binding is permitted in (2c) but not in (2b).

(2) a. $Mary_i$ congratulated $herself_i$.
   b. $Mary_i$ said that Susan congratulated $herself_i$.
   c. $Mary_i$ told Susan to congratulate $herself_i$.

Wexler and Manzini (1987) account for these differences in terms of a parameter, the Governing Category Parameter (GCP), which specifies the locality domains within which an anaphor, such as a reflexive, must be bound. A number of studies have investigated what values of the GCP are adopted by L2 learners, looking at cases where the L1 (Chinese, Japanese, or Korean) allows nonlocal binding, whereas the L2 (English) requires local binding, as well as cases where the L1 and L2 both require local binding (Spanish and English), cases where L1 and L2 both require nonlocal (Chinese and Japanese), and cases where the L1 requires local and the L2 nonlocal (English and Japanese) (Finer, 1991; Finer & Broselow, 1986; Hirakawa, 1990; Thomas, 1989, 1991). Some of the most interesting results from these studies suggest that some L2 learners adopt parameter values that do not derive from the L1 and that are not appropriate for the L2. For example, Finer and Broselow (1986), Finer (1991), and Hirakawa (1990) report that Japanese and Korean learners of English are significantly more likely to allow nonlocal binding in sentences like (2c) than in sentences like (2b). Because the tensed–nontensed distinction does not exist in the L1 and does not distinguish binding possibilities in the L2, Finer and Broselow suggest that these learners are adopting the "Russian" value of the parameter.[6] (The role of GCP in L2 acquisition is also discussed in chapters 5 by Schachter and 10 by Gass, this volume. Chapter 14 by Berent includes a treatment of the GCP in the acquisition of English by deaf learners.)

A related finding is that of Thomas (1989, 1991). She finds that her Spanish subjects, like her Chinese and Japanese subjects, accept nonlocal binding in sentences like (2b). For the Chinese and Japanese subjects, this could indicate adoption of the L1 setting, whereas for the Spanish it could not, because Spanish, like English, requires local binding.

Such results suggest that, for whatever reason, learners are sometimes able to arrive at parameter settings permitted by UG but not exemplified in the L1 or the L2. Findings like this are problematic for Position 2, because, if learners are going to depart from their L1-based grammars without access to UG, one might expect them also to allow coreference possibilities that are not found in natural languages. (See Thomas, 1991, for examples and evidence that this is not the case.)

However, the finding of UG-based settings exemplified in neither language itself raises questions. Acquisition involves an interaction of UG, the existing grammar, and the input. Thus, it makes sense if learners adopt L1 settings, based on their existing grammar, or if they adopt L2 settings, based on the L2 input interacting with UG. But where do the other possibilities come from? A possible solution in the case of the binding results is offered by Progovac and Connell (1991). In line with many current proposals, their analysis of binding assumes that governing categories are not parameterized. Rather, there are two types of anaphors,

---

[6]This is not Hirakawa's interpretation of her results. She argues that in fact the L1 setting has been adopted, because subjects also allow nonlocal binding in sentences like (2b).

namely, morphologically complex phrasal anaphors that require local binding, such as *himself, herself* in English, and morphologically simple head anaphors that allow nonlocal binding, like *zibun* ("self") in Japanese. In addition, languages vary as to whether Agr is realized. Progovac and Connell argue that head anaphors are bound to the nearest available head, namely Agr, accounting for long-distance binding over nonfinite clauses (which lack Agr) in languages like Russian. In addition, in languages without Agr, such as Chinese, they propose that reflexives have no governing category at all, hence long-distance binding is possible across any clause boundary.[7] This analysis provides a neat explanation for the behavior of L2 learners in the above studies. The Spanish learners of English, who accept long-distance binding even though this is possible in neither the L1 nor the L2, are misled into thinking that English lacks Agr because agreement in English is impoverished when compared to agreement in Spanish. This in turn leads them to treat English like Chinese, permitting nonlocal binding in general. Furthermore, the behavior of the Japanese who accept nonlocal binding only over nonfinite clauses can also be explained: because English agreement appears rich with respect to agreement in Japanese, they correctly assume that English is (+Agr) but treat English like Russian, where long-distance binding is only possible out of clauses lacking Agr.[8] Thus, the adoption of parameter settings that are exemplified in neither language is nevertheless explicable in terms of an interaction of UG and the L2 input, with the L2 input misanalyzed because of properties of the L1 grammar.

This still leaves a crucial question: why do some L2 learners get stuck (i.e., fail to converge on the L2 grammar), whereas others do not? Why, for example, do some Spanish learners of English successfully reanalyze the L2 such that they realize that English does have Agr and local binding of reflexives, whereas others fail to reanalyze? In L1 acquisition, where different intermediate grammars are also found, no one gets stuck. This is a question that clearly needs further investigation if we are to arrive at a more complete understanding of L2 acquisition.

It has been suggested in this section that some parameters are "incorrectly" set because of properties of the L2 input interacting with UG and the current grammar. Presumably, the potential for misanalysis will vary, depending on what language is the L1 and what the L2, as well as on properties of the L2 input data.

Positive and Negative Evidence and Parameter Resetting

Issues relating to L2 input have been the subject of considerable investigation by researchers interested in the role of UG in L2 acquisition. Much early work on learnability focused on the availability of a learning principle, the SP, to L2

---

[7] Progovac (1992) offers a slightly different analysis of the Chinese facts.

[8] This account of L2 learners' behavior will only work if learners also misanalyze English as having a head rather than a phrasal anaphor. Progovac and Connell (1991) argue that this is indeed the case, as does Bennett (1994).

learners, as well as the implications of the operation or nonoperation of this principle. The SP is a learning principle that has been postulated in order to guarantee acquisition without negative evidence; this principle causes learners to be conservative, preventing them from adopting overinclusive parameter settings in the absence of explicit evidence (Wexler & Manzini, 1987). Most of the evidence pointed to the unavailability of this principle in L2 acquisition (Finer & Broselow, 1986; White, 1989a), suggesting that the potential status of negative evidence in L2 acquisition might be different from its status in L1. However, recently there have been suggestions that the SP is misconceived. Hermon (1992) and McLaughlin (1995) both argue that there are in fact no cases of parameters of UG yielding languages in a subset–superset relationship, hence no potential problem of overgeneralization and no need for a SP.[9] (The SP and its putative role in L2 acquisition are also discussed in this volume, chapters 2 by Gregg, 10 by Gass, and 13 by Long. Chapter 14 by Berent includes discussion of the SP in the acquisition of English by deaf learners and chapter 18 by Seliger suggests a role for the SP in accounting for primary language attrition. Finally, chapter 16 by Andersen and Shirai applies the notion to the acquisition of verb aspect.)

Those interested in L2 learnability now focus on the nature of the triggering data in L2 acquisition. Many L2 learners are not exposed to the same kind of input as L1 learners. The positive input is often different in nature (more formal, less naturalistic, containing incorrect forms produced by others in the classroom) and negative input may also be available (in the form of correction and certain kinds of grammar teaching). The question arises as to whether the different kinds of input available in L2 acquisition are in fact appropriate for triggering principles and parameters, and whether inappropriate input places limitations on the operation of UG.

Recently, there has been increasing theoretical discussion and experimental investigation of the extent to which positive L2 evidence triggers parameter resetting, of the potential role of negative evidence, of what precise properties of L2 input serve as triggers for parameter resetting, and of the successes and failures of L2 classrooms in providing appropriate input (Felix & Weigl, 1991; Schwartz, 1993; White, 1991a; White, Spada, Lightbown, & Ranta, 1991). In a number of experimental studies, attempts have been made to control fairly precisely the kind of input available to the L2 learner and to determine whether negative evidence, explicit positive evidence, or naturalistic positive evidence can lead to parameter resetting in the L2 classroom (Trahey & White, 1993; White, 1991a, 1991b). In these studies, experimental groups get a particular kind of input, whereas control groups do not, thus allowing one to determine precisely what the effects of different kinds of L2 input are.

For example, White (1991a, 1991b) shows that francophone learners of English

---

[9] It should, however, be noted that although these researchers may have succeeded in showing that the SP is not needed in practice (because no parameters so far proposed meet the Subset Condition), they have not been able to eliminate it in principle.

incorrectly assume that English, like French, allows raising of the main verb over an adverb, one of a cluster of properties associated with the verb raising parameter proposed by Pollock (1989) (see section II.B), leading learners to accept and produce sentences like (9a) (repeated below) where the adverb intervenes between verb and object (SVAO word order):

(9) a. * John watches often television.

White argues that these learners have adopted the L1 parameter setting (permitting verb raising over an adverb) and that the errors are such that negative evidence will be required to eliminate them because SVAO order is nonoccurring in English and there appears to be nothing in the input that indicates that the order is ungrammatical; in other words, learners may require negative evidence to reset parameters in certain cases.[10]

White compares two groups of grade 5 and 6 francophone students (aged 11–12 yr) in intensive English as a Second Language (ESL) programs in Quebec, Canada. One group received two weeks of explicit instruction on adverb placement in English, including explicit positive and negative evidence on word order in English sentences containing adverbs. The second group received no instruction on adverbs; it was assumed that this group would receive positive evidence concerning adverb placement in English through naturalistic input in the classroom (but no information about ungrammaticality).[11] In essence, what White set out to investigate was whether exposure to positive evidence alone (as provided to the second group) would cause the elimination of an ungrammatical word order, or whether negative evidence (as supplied to the first group) would be necessary. Subjects were pretested immediately prior to the experimental treatment, posttested immediately afterwards, and again 5 wk later, on three different tasks. Results show that both groups started out with the L1 parameter setting, accepting and producing SVAO order in English. Only the group that received explicit instruction and negative evidence on adverb placement revealed knowledge of the impossibility of SVAO order in English.

However, the assumption that negative evidence is necessary for parameter resetting here neglects the possibility that there is positive L2 input to show that the L1 value must be incorrect (Schwartz & Gubala-Ryzak, 1992; White, 1992b). For example, input like that in (9c) (repeated here) shows that the verb has not raised past the adverb, hence that English is not like French:

(9) c. Mary often watches television.

---

[10] See Schwartz (1992, 1993) for arguments that negative evidence is too explicit to tap unconscious parameter-setting mechanisms.

[11] However, audiotapes subsequently revealed that spontaneous use of adverbs was extremely limited in these communicative classrooms. Thus, although it was originally thought that this group would be exposed to naturally occurring classroom input on adverb placement, this turned out not to be the case; rather, these subjects apparently received little or no input containing adverbs.

In another study, Trahey and White (1993) look at whether an "input flood" of positive evidence alone is sufficient to lead to parameter resetting. They show that supplying positive evidence, including sentence types like (9c), in the L2 class-room does not trigger the appropriate L2 value of the parameter. A further group of grade 5 francophone children in the intensive program were exposed to a 2-wk-long input flood of specially prepared materials containing English adverbs used naturalistically. No form-focused instruction or negative evidence on adverb placement was provided. As before, subjects were pretested immediately prior to the input flood, posttested immediately afterwards, and again 3 wk later, this time on four different tasks. All tasks reveal a dramatic increase in use of the gram-matical English order where the adverb precedes the verb (SAV) but little or no decline in use of the ungrammatical SVAO order.

The results thus suggest that positive evidence did not serve to preempt the L1 parameter setting in this case; acquiring the correct English SAV order did not lead to loss of incorrect SVAO. Such results might seem problematic for the claim that UG mediates L2 acquisition: If naturalistic positive L2 input does not trigger parameter resetting for child L2 learners, how can one really maintain the claim of the availability of UG? However, other results indicate that L2 parameter reset-ting takes place on the basis of positive evidence with very little difficulty at all, that is, the L2 input appears to play a genuinely triggering role. As mentioned in section III.C, White (1992a) shows that francophone learners of ESL do not as-sume that the verb in English can raise to T (cf. 11). That is, positive evidence, such as English do-support, appears to indicate almost immediately that sentences like (7a) and (8a) (repeated below) are not possible in English.[12]

(7) a. *John likes not Mary.
(8) a. *Likes she John?

An important issue that such studies of the effectiveness of L2 input raise is why certain types of positive L2 input should be able to trigger parameter resetting whereas others do not, or why certain parameters are triggerable whereas others are not. In some areas of L2 acquisition, there appears to be a lack of convergence on the L2 grammar, whereas in other areas L2 properties are successfully ac-quired. White (1989a, 1989b) argued that successful resetting or lack thereof would depend on the subset–superset relationships holding in the L1 and the L2. If the L1 yields a superset of sentences permitted in the L2, successful resetting would be impossible on the basis of positive evidence alone, whereas if the L2 is a superset of the L1, successful resetting should be possible. However, the results

[12]Pollock's linking of adverb placement to verb raising has been questioned (Iatridou, 1990). White's results are consistent with Iatridou's reanalysis of the parameter that leaves question formation and negative placement as part of the cluster of properties accounted for by verb raising but removes adverb placement.

described in this section suggest that success in parameter resetting is not predictable in terms of subset–superset relationships between the L1 and the L2.

IV. SOME CURRENT ISSUES

Previous research (especially on parameters) has tended to concentrate on learners still in the process of acquisition. In the ongoing debate over the availability of principles of UG in L2 acquisition, there has recently been a shift in focus from investigating properties of the developing IL grammar to the issue of ultimate attainment. If one considers people who can be said to have finished their L2 acquisition, is their L2 grammar constrained by UG or not? Is their grammar nativelike with respect to UG effects (note, as above, that it might be constrained by UG but different from the native grammar)? Does the ultimate attainment of late learners differ from that of early learners, due to maturational effects, for example?

A. Maturational Effects

Although many early studies looked at the question of whether adult learners have access to UG, few dealt specifically with maturational effects, or the question of whether there is a sudden decrease in access to UG at puberty or a gradual decline, or no decline at all. (Possible maturational effects in L2 acquisition are also discussed in this volume, chapters 5 by Schachter and 15 by Obler and Hannigan.) One pioneering study that addresses these issues is Johnson and Newport (1991).

Johnson and Newport (1991) are concerned with adult L2 acquisition, particularly with the achievements of proficient L2 users. At issue is whether principles of UG are subject to critical-period effects. Like earlier studies (Bley-Vroman, Felix, & Ioup, 1988; Schachter, 1989), they look at Subjacency.

In their first experiment, Johnson and Newport (1991) tested Chinese speakers who learned English as adults; that is, all subjects had moved to the United States after the age of 17. (They had, however, had high school instruction in English in their countries of origin.) Subjects had resided in the United States for a minimum of 5 yr and used English constantly in their day-to-day work. Subjects were deemed to have completed their acquisition of English, so that any properties of their grammars revealed in the study would reflect properties of ultimate attainment. (In other words, no further changes are presumed to be possible.)

Subjects heard sentences presented aurally (on tape), which were to be judged for grammaticality. These sentences were relevant to Subjacency and included three different kinds of Subjacency violations, together with corresponding grammatical declaratives and grammatical wh-questions. This combination gets around problems in other studies: the grammatical declaratives control for knowledge of the structures in question; the grammatical wh-questions control for knowledge of wh-movement (Schachter, 1989, has only the former; Bley-Vroman et al., 1988, have only the latter). Choice of sentences constitutes a considerable improvement over other tests investigating Subjacency. However, there are some problems: The fact that the task is aural means that problems with processing at the phonetic or phonological levels might cause difficulties unrelated to the syntax; in addition, there were a lot of sentences (180) to be judged.[13]

The results show that the Chinese subjects perform significantly below native controls on Subjacency violations, incorrectly accepting many of them. Nevertheless, they perform above chance.[14] One comparison that Johnson and Newport do not make is to compare mean number correct (i.e., accuracy) on grammatical wh-questions versus Subjacency violations. If there were no statistically significant difference between these two sentence types, it would suggest that the problem might be with wh-movement in general. In other words, these L2 speakers might have grammars without long-distance movement, using pro as their empty category (Martohardjono & Gair, 1993; White, 1992c).[15] If so, these learners have in fact got IL grammars constrained by UG but they are certainly not like English.

A second study reported in the same article looks at the maturational issue in more detail, focusing on whether there is a gradual or sudden deterioration in access to UG. Subjects were adult Chinese speakers who learned English at various ages (4–7 yr, 8–13 yr, and 14–16 yr). The same tests were taken as before and results are compared to the subjects in the previous study. Results show a continuous decline in performance on Subjacency and a correlation between performance and age of arrival in the United States. The 4–7-year-olds are not significantly different from the natives, whereas the other groups are. All three age groups perform significantly better than the adult learners. Johnson and Newport conclude that access to UG is subject to maturational effects. Although adults still show evidence of observing constraints of UG at above chance levels, their performance is significantly below that of younger learners.

[13] However, there were different versions of the test to control for potential fatigue effects; there proved to be no significant differences for version, suggesting that length of the task was not a factor.

[14] Above chance performance is due to one sentence type, namely relative clauses. It turns out that all sentences involving extractions from relative clauses violate the Empty Category Principle (ECP) as well as Subjacency (because the extraction is from a subject relative), whereas other ungrammatical sentences only violate Subjacency. This is, presumably, unintentional, because it is not discussed by Johnson and Newport. These results suggest that the ECP may still be available to adults even if Subjacency is not.

[15] Johnson and Newport present a related analysis where they look at rejections of wh-questions, both grammatical and ungrammatical, in case there is a response bias to rejection. They report that subjects show a significant difference between rejecting ungrammatical violations and rejecting grammatical wh-questions.

B. Near Native-Speaker Competence

Perhaps one of the reasons why maturational effects were found has to do with the selection of subjects in the above study. Subjects were chosen who had lived a long time in the L2 environment and who made considerable use of the L2. No attempt was made to assess their actual level of attainment. Another approach to the ultimate attainment issue has been to look at individuals who are deemed to have achieved the status of near or virtual NSs, meaning, informally, that they can (almost) pass as NSs of a language that is not in fact their mother tongue. Although such an approach seems to suggest that L2 speakers should be compared to NSs rather than being considered in their own right, it is important because one needs to know whether competent bilinguals can ever attain the kind of knowledge that is usually assumed to stem from UG. If their competence proves to be native-like, this suggests that UG must still be available and that the "failures" of many L2 learners must be attributed to other sources. If their competence does not correspond to that of NSs, one then has to pursue the question of whether it is "unnatural" (in a technical sense) (Position 2) or natural but different from that of NSs (Position 3).

A number of researchers have recently investigated the attainment of near-NSs. Results are conflicting: some report that fluent L2 speakers do not achieve native-like competence in certain areas, even if they pass as near-NSs (Coppieters, 1987; Sorace, 1993, chap. 12, this volume), whereas others report few differences between near natives and natives (Birdsong, 1992; White & Genesee, in press). Most of these studies adopt as a measure of achievement whether or not subjects pass a near-NS criterion (although how this is determined is often ad hoc and vague).

Coppieters

Coppieters (1987) investigates whether there are competence differences between NSs and near-NSs of French. Subjects (of various L1s) were identified as near native in their oral proficiency on the basis of reports from their friends and colleagues, followed by in-depth interviewing by the experimenter. All subjects had acquired French as adults, in the sense that their first communicative use of French was after the age of 18 (although many of them had studied French in high school). They had lived an average of 17 yr in France. Subjects unfortunately included a high proportion of linguists and professors of language or literature. There was also a control group of NSs of French, again including linguists and professors specializing in various modern languages. This concentration of linguists and language professors is most unfortunate as such people are trained to look at language in particular ways and one cannot be sure that unconscious linguistic competence is really being tapped.

A questionnaire was constructed, covering various aspects of French, including structures that Coppieters assumes not to stem from UG, as well as things that do.

Subjects and controls were interviewed and their intuitions and interpretations were elicited and discussed. About 40% of the test items dealt with a variety of structures where contrasting forms are found. Subjects were given sentences where they had to choose one of the contrasting items; if they chose both, they were asked whether there were meaning differences between the two, and they were asked to try and articulate the difference. About 60% of the sentences did not involve contrasts; rather, straightforward judgments of grammaticality on a number of different structures were elicited.

Results from this study reveal quantitative and qualitative differences between NSs and near-NSs. Each sentence in the questionnaire was assigned an evaluation index, corresponding to the majority of NS responses to it, to arrive at a proto-typical norm for each sentence. NSs showed considerable agreement in their re-sponses and varied far less from this norm than the near-NSs did. No near-NSs performed like NSs. Qualitatively, where differences in form reflected differences in meaning, the near-NSs had different intuitions about the meaning contrasts from the NSs. (However, these intuitions involve conscious reflecting on the sen-tences, which is not necessarily an appropriate way to tap unconscious linguistic competence.) Divergence was not uniform across the various structures tested: NSs and near NSs diverged least on formal (UG-like) properties and diverged most on semantic aspects.

Although methodologically and conceptually flawed (see Birdsong, 1992, for extensive criticism), this study is important in that it asked a significant question, which had been surprisingly neglected up till that point. Because of the flaws, however, it is not clear that the results really indicate competence differences be-tween NSs and near-NSs. Birdsong suggests that the issue is still open and seeks an answer by trying to remedy some of the problems.

Birdsong

Birdsong (1992) discusses many problems with Coppieters's study, including problems with the tasks and with subject selection. Subjects came from several different L1s, and there are too few subjects from each L1 to make generalizations. The number of sentences testing each structure in Coppieters's study is very un-even, ranging from 2 on one structure to 28 on another; this means that one has to interpret Coppieter's results on deviance from the norm with considerable caution. Birdsong also points out that the $\pm$ UG distinction is somewhat arbitrary and that results on this distinction may be an artifact of the two different procedures used in testing: all the non-UG structures were tested with the task involving contrasts; all the UG structures were tested with the outright judgment task.

Birdsong deals with the methodological problems by producing more adequate test instruments and more uniform criteria for subject selection. With these changes, he attempts to replicate Coppieters's results. In contrast to Coppieters, he finds few competence differences between NSs and near-NSs of French. Bird-song's subjects are fluent speakers of French, all with English as their L1. None of the subjects or controls are linguists or language teachers, and their backgrounds are more uniform that those of Coppieter's subjects. Subjects were chosen who had resided for at least three years in France (arriving there as adults) and who spoke French fluently, in the estimation of the experimenter.

One of the tasks was a judgment task that included a number of linguistic structures, some of which were those tested by Coppieters. Sentences were drawn from Coppieters and from the linguistic literature. In contrast to Coppieters, Birdsong finds a much lower incidence of divergence between NSs and near-NSs, even for structures where Coppieters did find such a difference. Furthermore, several of the near-NSs achieve scores comparable to the NSs. There is no clear ± UG pattern in the results.

Instead of interviewing subjects about certain sentences, Birdsong had his subjects do think-aloud protocols. These reveal no large-scale or systematic differences between the two groups. In addition, two sentence-interpretation tasks show a high degree of conformity between NSs and near-NSs. In general, Birdsong's results are very different from those of Coppieters and suggest that near-NSs are similar to, rather than different from, NSs.

White and Genesee

Another study that reports few differences between NSs and near-NSs is White and Genesee (in press). White and Genesee aim to develop criteria to classify subjects as near-NS and to compare near-NSs with NNSs with respect to the operation of principles of UG. Subjects were bilingual speakers with English as the L2; the majority had French as their mother tongue. There was also a control group of monolingual English speakers. In order to assess whether subjects were near-NS, they were interviewed and portions of each interview were submitted to two judges who rated them on general fluency, phonology, syntax, morphology, and lexicon. On the basis of these ratings, half of the subjects were classified as near-NS and half were classed as NNSs.

Subjects took a grammaticality judgment task (involving a judgment and a reaction time measure) and a written production task. Both tasks tapped subjects' knowledge of grammatical wh-question formation in English, as well as principles of UG that constrain wh-movement (ECP, Subjacency). Sentences were extensively piloted on NSs of English to ensure that judgments of grammaticality and ungrammaticality were consistent and in accordance with the predictions of UG. Surprisingly few studies on UG in L2 do this. Birdsong and Coppieters, for example, include sentences where NSs do not give consistent or clear-cut judgments, so that one wonders about the generalizability of the results beyond the particular sentences tested (see Clark, 1973).[16]

---

[16] Birdsong's sentences are drawn directly from the linguistic literature, which is somewhat problematic as linguists do not devise their sentences with psycholinguistic experiments in mind. Birdsong uses these sentences to avoid experimenter bias but runs into the problem of linguist bias instead.

White and Genesee find that the near-NSs' performance is not significantly different from the monolingual controls: they reject violations of UG in the judgment task, take no longer to make judgments than the controls, and do not produce violations in the production tasks. The NNS group differs in some respects from both near-NSs and monolinguals. Because the age at which these bilinguals started learning English varies from under 3 to over 16, age effects are also investigated and no significant effects of age of first exposure to English are found.

In conclusion, these results suggest that if consistent criteria are developed for establishing whether a bilingual is a near-NS, near-NSs can be totally nativelike in the UG domain, even if they are late learners of the L2. However, it should be noted that although this study shows that L2 learners have nativelike competence in the UG domain, one cannot determine whether the access to UG was direct or indirect. Because the L1 of the majority of the subjects was French, and because French and English are similar with respect to the operation of many of the principles investigated in this study, access might have been via the L1. In a sense, this study attempts to establish minimally whether any near NS group achieves nativelike success, regardless of whether this is due to direct access or indirect (via L1). A next step should be to look at near-NSs with very different L1s.

Sorace

A study that finds competence differences between NSs and near-NSs is Sorace (1993; chap. 12, this volume). Sorace proposes that near-NSs often have grammars that diverge from native grammars; although their performance may seem nativelike, their competence is not. Sorace distinguishes between near-native grammars that are incomplete (lacking properties of the native grammar) or divergent (containing properties that are different from the native grammar). She looks at the ultimate attainment of French and English speakers who are deemed to be near-NSs of Italian and argues that both incompleteness and divergence are to be found, and that the mother tongue plays a role in determining which kind of near-nativeness shows up.

The phenomenon studied is unaccusativity. Unaccusative verbs are verbs that, underlyingly, have one internal argument (a theme) and no external argument (see Sorace, chap. 12, this volume, for details). Unaccusatives in Italian have a number of well-known syntactic reflexes, including selection of the auxiliary *essere* 'to be' rather than *habere* 'to have' (Burzio, 1986). These reflexes are true of all unaccusative verbs in that language. French unaccusatives are much less consistent in their behavior; for example, some unaccusative verbs select *être* 'to be', whereas others take *avoir* 'to have'. In English, there are few obvious syntactic reflexes of unaccusativity.

Sorace investigates a number of properties of unaccusativity in the grammars of English-speaking and French-speaking near-NSs of Italian, who had started learning Italian after the age of 15. The criterion for selection of subjects was that they perform with nativelike fluency and accuracy (except phonology), as established in an interview with the experimenter. Acceptability judgments were elicited on sentences exemplifying properties of Italian unaccusatives. Results suggest that both groups' intuitions regarding semantic factors underlying auxiliary choice are similar to those of NSs. However, they differ from NSs on some or all of the syntactic reflexes of unaccusativity. The French-speaking learners of Italian have determinate (but sometimes nonnative) intuitions on auxiliary choice in certain constructions; that is, their acceptances or rejections may be inappropriate by native standards but they are quite consistent in their judgments. The English-speaking subjects have indeterminate intuitions; that is, their judgments suggest they are unsure about auxiliary selection in various syntactic contexts. Sorace attributes these differences to deeper properties of unaccusativity in the two L1s rather than to surface transfer. She argues that the French speakers have a grammar that is different from the Italians but not lacking anything, whereas the English-speakers actually lack something in their IL grammars.[17]

Sorace does not discuss whether the IL grammars of her learners are "possible" in the UG sense. Divergent or incomplete grammars are clearly different but may still be natural or possible, (i.e., still fall within the range of grammars permitted by UG—in other words, Position 3). In the case of Sorace's English-speaking subjects, the status of the grammar may not be possible to determine, if their grammars really are indeterminate (and this raises the question of whether UG tolerates such systems). In the case of the French speakers, whose Italian IL grammar diverges from the native Italian grammar, it appears that they do have a possible grammar. They have problems when auxiliary choice is optional. When *essere* 'to be' is obligatory, they have no problem recognizing this fact, but when it is optional, they often reject it, obligatorily choosing *habere* 'to have'. Because the latter is in fact correct (although only one of the possibilities admitted by native Italians), their divergent grammar does not appear to violate UG.

In conclusion, the results from various studies on near-native competence suggest that there may be certain areas where divergence is found and others where ultimate attainment is nativelike. This is an area that clearly needs further exploration: in what domains is divergence to be expected and why? Are divergent grammars UG-constrained or not? Is the divergence due to L1 or not?

C. Exploring Interlanguage Competence

We have already seen that an important question in the UG debate is the nature of IL competence, particularly the question of whether language learners have the

---

[17] It is not clear that this is a real distinction. A grammar lacking some property is different from a grammar with the property in question. Would one, for example, describe a grammar without syntactic wh-movement as incomplete?

same mental representation of the L2 as NSs. We have also seen that an important issue is whether their representation is UG-constrained when it is different from that of native NSs. With developments in linguistic theory, one can pursue this question at much greater depth and with a much greater degree of sophistication than formerly. Although earlier studies of UG in L2 acquisition tended to investigate whether a particular principle or parameter setting constrains the IL grammar, more recently researchers have started to explore other aspects of the IL grammar, in the framework of current GB theory. Such work focuses very much on the nature of IL competence in its own right, thus not falling into the "comparative fallacy" (Bley-Vroman, 1983).

One example is provided by the issue of functional projections and their status in the IL grammar. In current linguistic theory, a distinction is made between lexical and functional categories. Functional categories are categories like inflection (I), which may be split into T and Agr (Pollock, 1989), complementizer (C) and determiner (D). Like lexical categories (N, V, P, A), they project to the phrasal level: complementizer phrase (CP), inflection phrase (IP), determiner phrase (DP). In L1 acquisition research, there is an active debate on the status of functional categories and their projections in the early grammar. Guilfoyle and Noonan (1992) and Radford (1990) have claimed that functional projections are totally absent in the earliest stages. This explains certain properties of "early" child English, such as absence of determiners, modals, inflection, case-marking, and wh-movement. Others argue that functional categories are available in the early grammar but not always realized (e.g., Pierce, 1992). Evidence for their availability comes particularly from languages like German and French, where verb-movement possibilities depend on a ± finite distinction (a property of I). Young children observe verb placement differences depending on finiteness (though not necessarily to the extent that older children and adults do); this cannot be explained in the absence of the relevant functional projections for the verb to move to (Pierce, 1992; Whitman, Lee, & Lust, 1991).

Parallel to the L1 acquisition research on this issue has been work that explores the status of functional categories in L2 acquisition, with a similar debate about whether they are present in the earliest stages. Kaplan (1992) and Vainikka and Young-Scholten (1994) argue that functional categories are absent in the earliest adult L2 grammar, whereas Grondin and White (1995), Lakshmanan (1993), and Lakshmanan and Selinker (1994) show that they are present in early child L2 acquisition, and Schwartz and Sprouse (1994) show that they are present in early adult L2. In each case, the arguments come from detailed analysis of the L2 data, including evidence for morphological markings and evidence of syntactic movement through functional projections.

Just as the functional projection issue has been of particular interest for accounts of verb movement in L1 acquisition (the verb must move from V to I and

C), so investigating IL grammars in terms of the presence or absence of functional categories allows a much more detailed look at L2 word-order acquisition and verb movement, topics of considerable debate in the L2 literature. For example, as mentioned in section III.C, Clahsen and Muysken (1986) argue that adult L2 learners have an "unnatural" grammar, allowing nonfinite elements to move rightwards to the end of the sentence, whereas L1 learners have a natural grammar, where finite elements move leftwards. As pointed out by Schwartz and Tomaselli (1990), their analysis suffers from the lack of an I projection. Du Plessis et al. (1987) and Schwartz and Tomaselli (1990) show that the L2 data can be explained once one assumes that L2 learners (like NSs) project an IP as well as a VP, and that the position of inflected elements in the IL grammar is easily explained as movement from V to I (and in some cases C). Eubank (1992) pushes the functional category analysis further, accounting for L2 stages of German in terms of Agr and T. Similarly, White (1992a) shows that the treatment of verb placement by French learners of English is explicable if one assumes that they project both TP and AgrP.

Some of the above work explicitly aims to use L2 data to test issues in L1 acquisition theory. For example, Kaplan (1992) and Grondin (1992) both point out that status of functional projections in the L2 grammar could be used to test the claim that functional categories mature in L1 acquisition. As mentioned above, a number of researchers have argued that child L1 acquisition is characterized by an initial phase during which functional categories and their projections are absent and they have claimed that they emerge according to a maturational schedule (Radford, 1990). If functional categories show the same pattern of emergence in L1 and L2 acquisition, it is unlikely that maturation can explain any observed acquisition sequences, because L2 learners will already have gone through the relevant stages of maturation. Kaplan (1992) reports that C is late to emerge in adult L2 acquisition, as it is in child L1 acquisition, thus calling the maturational claim into question. However, both Grondin and White (1995) and Lakshmanan and Selinker (1994) report no stages of emergence for functional categories in child L2 acquisition. Their results, therefore, do not disconfirm (or confirm) the maturational claims for L1. (Functional categories are also discussed in this volume in connection with L2 acquisition in chapter 4 by Flynn and with acquisition of English by the deaf in chapter 14 by Berent.)

This kind of research illustrates how L2 data may be able to inform theories in other domains. Gass (1992) and Rutherford (1993) argue that the field of L2 acquisition is now sufficiently developed that L2 data should be used as data for linguistic theory and L1 acquisition theory. The relationship between linguistic theory and linguistic data is usually two-way: the theory makes predictions and provides insights into data, and data can be used to support or question the theory. The relationship between linguistic theory and data from other domains (such as L1 and L2 acquisition), however, has usually been unidirectional. Linguistic theory is often used to make predictions about L1 and L2 acquisition (as we have seen), and to account for observed phenomena, but L1 and L2 acquisition data do not have a clear status vis à vis linguistic theory. Gass argues that the time has come when L2 data should be used beyond L2 acquisition theory; this is another area in which the UG perspective on L2 acquisition might develop.[18]

V. NEW DIRECTIONS

So far, we have seen that work on UG in L2 acquisition has focused on whether principles and parameters are available in L2 acquisition, both during the course of learning and in ultimate attainment. It has been suggested that L2 learners often develop IL grammars that are different from the grammars of NSs but which are nevertheless constrained by UG, and that this is due, in part, to properties of the L2 input interacting with UG and the L1 grammar. Many questions remain to be answered, including the question of why some learners "fossilize" with these divergent IL grammars, whereas others successfully attain a nativelike grammar; why some parameters are successfully reset whereas others are not; why positive L2 input is only sometimes successful as a trigger for grammar change. There are also areas of L2 acquisition that have been surprisingly neglected in the UG framework. Some of these are discussed below.

A. Child–Adult Differences

The question of whether child L2 learners have access to UG received little specific attention until recently. As Johnson and Newport (1991) pointed out, it is all too easy to confound the availability of UG in L2 acquisition with the age question. Much research has compared adult L2 learners with child L1 learners and concluded that they are different, hence that L2 acquisition is different from L1, that UG is not available. Others assume without empirical investigation that child L2 learners will have access to UG. In order to determine the status of UG in child L2 acquisition, more comparisons of child and adult L2 learners are required, as well as child L1 and child L2.

Two recent studies compare child and adult learners who are still in the process of L2 acquisition, making use of data already available in the field. Hilles (1991) compares Spanish-speaking children, teenagers, and adults acquiring ESL, with respect to their performance on the Morphological Uniformity Principle (MUP),

---

[18] However, there is always the problem of whether L2 learner languages are indeed natural languages, constrained by UG. If they are not, L2 data cannot be expected to shed much light on linguistic theory or L1 acquisition.

a development that has replaced the Null Subject Parameter (Jaeggli & Safir, 1989). According to the MUP, only languages with uniform inflectional paradigms permit null subjects, where uniformity means that all forms in a morphological paradigm are morphologically complex or none are.[19] Thus, Spanish, with every form inflected, is uniform, as is Chinese, with no inflected verbs. English, on the other hand, is not uniform, because some forms are inflected and others not. The MUP has two options [+ uniform] and [− uniform]. Hilles (1991) looks at the question of whether learners of a [+ uniform] L1, such as Spanish, learning a [− uniform] L2, such as English, will show a loss of null subjects in the L2 as they realize that the L2 is not uniform. Looking at transcripts of production data from six Spanish-speaking learners of English for evidence of a correlation between the emergence of overt, nonuniform inflection and use of pronominal (as opposed to null) subjects, she argues that these properties are highly correlated in the grammars of the two child learners and one adolescent, suggesting access to the MUP, whereas there is no such correlation in the grammars of the other adolescent and the two adults, suggesting lack of access to UG. Thus, child and adult L2 acquisition differ, on this analysis, with UG only available in the former case. However, there is a problem with this reliance on correlations, or lack thereof; the MUP predicts a correlation especially in the early stages: that is, as nonuniform inflection begins to emerge, so pronominal subjects should increase and null subjects decrease. However, in the case of one of the adolescents and one of the adults, nonuniform inflection was already being used to a high degree at the beginning of the investigation. In other words, inflection is well established in the grammar rather than just emerging, so the lack of a correlation is not surprising and says nothing about the UG accessibility issue either way. The only way to use the high incidence of inflection to argue against MUP (hence UG) would be if there is a high incidence of nonuniform inflection and a continuing high incidence of null subjects. This is not the case with any of the subjects studied by Hilles.[20] (For additional discussion of null subject phenomena in L2 acquisition, see chapter 10 by Gass.)

Schwartz (1992) compares child and adult acquisition for a somewhat different reason: she points out that a comparison of child and adult L2 developmental sequences is a useful way of testing the fundamental difference hypothesis (Position 2). If child L2 learners still have access to UG (as commonly assumed) and if child and adult learners with the same L1 learning the same L2 show similar acquisition sequences, then this is problematic for theories that assume that child

[19] Uniformity is a necessary, but not sufficient, condition for null subjects.

[20] A different perspective on the issue of child access to the MUP is taken by Lakshmanan (1989), who assumes that UG is available in child L2 acquisition. She argues that the predictions of the MUP are not borne out in child L2 data and that such data can be used to cast doubt on linguistic theory, in this case the MUP, thus providing another example of how L2 data might be used beyond the L2 domain.

and adult acquisition are dissimilar. Similar acquisition sequences would thus support the claim that UG is available to adult learners. She shows that child and adult L2 developmental sequences for German word-order acquisition by Romance speakers are very similar and can be explained in terms of IL grammars that are constrained by UG.

Both the above studies make use of existing data that were not gathered to test issues relating to UG in L2 acquisition. In order to investigate the nature of child IL grammars more closely, further studies are required using tests that are designed to test specific predictions of the UG approach, perhaps modeled on some of the current research on principles and parameters in L1 acquisition.

B. Phonology

One might get the impression from reading the literature devoted to UG in L2 acquisition that UG is only concerned with syntactic principles and parameters. This, of course, is not the case. Principles and parameters are proposed for other areas of grammar as well, including phonology; it is, presumably, accidental that these have been somewhat neglected in L2 acquisition research. L2 phonology has, of course, been studied in considerable detail but phonological principles and parameters of UG and their implications for L2 acquisition have only recently received attention. This means that a whole area where the UG availability issue could be extensively tested has in fact been underused.

Archibald (1992, 1993) and Pater (1993) have investigated the effects a number of metrical parameters associated with stress assignment (Dresher & Kaye, 1990), looking at the acquisition of English word stress by NSs of languages whose settings for some of the metrical parameters differ from English. These researchers explore the effects of L1 parameter settings, and discuss what aspects of the L2 input might act as cues for resetting metrical parameters. Results suggest that some learners may arrive at parameter settings that are present in neither the L1 nor the L2, but that stress assignment in the IL grammar is always UG-constrained (i.e., neither random nor unnatural). That is, in phonology as in syntax, learners do not arrive at "impossible" systems.

Broselow and Finer (1991) investigate a phonological parameter that captures the fact that languages that allow consonant clusters to serve as syllable onsets vary as to what kinds of consonants may co-occur in the cluster. Co-occurrence possibilities are determined by a sonority hierarchy, but languages differ as to how close on the hierarchy adjacent segments must be. These differences are captured by a multivalued Minimal Sonority Distance parameter. Korean and Japanese learners of English are found to adopt a value of this parameter that is more marked than that required in their L1s but less marked than the L2.

This work is particularly interesting because it tries to look across UG domains, in order to determine the extent to which phonological principles work like syntactic ones in L2 acquisition. Broselow and Finer's results from syntax have already been discussed (section III.C); L2 learners with an L1 like Korean or Japanese appear to adopt an intermediate setting of the GCP that is neither the Japanese nor the English setting. This comparison of L2 syntactic and phonological parameters, then, suggests that different modules of UG nevertheless affect the L2 learner similarly and that the finding of same mechanisms (UG) but different competence is not confined to the syntactic domain. (Discussions of L2 speech and phonology are also found in this volume, chapters 6 by Eckman, 9 by Leather and James, and 10 by Gass.)

VI. CONCLUSIONS

Work on UG in L2 acquisition over the last 10 years or so has focused on whether principles and parameters are available in L2 acquisition, both during the course of learning and in ultimate attainment. An important issue has been whether an L2 learner's representation of language is UG-constrained when it is different from that of NSs. In this chapter, it has been suggested that L2 learners often develop IL grammars that are different from the grammars of NSs but that are nevertheless constrained by UG, and that this is due, in part, to properties of the L2 input interacting with UG and the L1 grammar. Many questions remain to be answered, including the question of why some learners "fossilize" with these divergent IL grammars, whereas others successfully attain a nativelike grammar; why some parameters are successfully reset, whereas others are not, why positive L2 input is only sometimes successful as a trigger for grammar change.

In spite of the fact that we do not yet know the answers to these questions, I should like to suggest that divergent IL grammars should not be seen as a problem for L2 acquisition theory. We should not think of L2 learners whose parameter settings or IL grammars happen not to coincide with those of the NS of the L2 as unsuccessful acquirers of their L2; instead, we should think of them as NSs of ILs. In other words, we need to explore in much more detail the nature of the linguistic systems that L2 learners arrive at, using linguistic theory to help us understand the characteristics of learner grammars, as is already happening, for example, in the recent analyses of the role and nature of functional categories in L2 acquisition (see section IV.C). Indeed, perhaps the time has come to stop asking the broad question: is UG available to L2 learners or not? This question has stimulated a great deal of fruitful research over the last decade, but it is now the turn of a somewhat more detailed focus on the precise nature of the linguistic competence of language learners, a focus that will continue to draw on current linguistic theory.

REFERENCES

Archibald, J. (1992). Transfer of L1 parameter settings: Some empirical evidence from Polish metrics. *Canadian Journal of Linguistics, 37,* 301–339.
Archibald, J. (1993). Metrical phonology and the acquisition of L2 stress. In F. Eckman (Ed.), *Confluence: Linguistics, L2 acquisition and speech pathology* (pp. 37–68). Amsterdam: John Benjamins.
Bennett, S. (1994). Interpretation of English reflexives by adolescent speakers of Serbo-Croatian. *Second Language Research, 10,* 125–156.
Berwick, R. (1985). *The acquisition of syntactic knowledge.* Cambridge, MA: MIT Press.
Birdsong, D. (1989). *Metalinguistic performance and interlinguistic competence.* New York: Springer-Verlag.
Birdsong, D. (1992). Ultimate attainment in second language acquisition. *Language, 68,* 706–755.
Bley-Vroman, R. (1983). The comparative fallacy in interlanguage studies: The case of systematicity. *Language Learning, 33,* 1–17.
Bley-Vroman, R. (1990). The logical problem of foreign language learning. *Linguistic Analysis, 20,* 3–49.
Bley-Vroman, R., Felix, S., & Ioup, G. (1988). The accessibility of universal grammar in adult language learning. *Second Language Research, 4,* 1–32.
Broselow, E., & Finer, D. (1991). Parameter setting in second language phonology and syntax. *Second Language Research, 7,* 35–59.
Burzio, L. (1986). *Italian syntax: A government-binding approach.* Dordrecht: Reidel.
Chomsky, N. (1981). *Lectures on government and binding.* Dordrecht: Foris.
Chomsky, N. (1986). *Barriers.* Cambridge, MA: MIT Press.
Clahsen, H., & Muysken, P. (1986). The availability of universal grammar to adult and child learners: A study of the acquisition of German word order. *Second Language Research, 2,* 93–119.
Clark, H. (1973). The language-as-fixed-effect fallacy: A critique of language statistics in psychological research. *Journal of Verbal Learning and Verbal Behavior, 12,* 335–339.
Coppieters, R. (1987). Competence differences between native and near-native speakers. *Language, 63,* 544–573.
Dresher, E., & Kaye, J. (1990). A computational learning model for metrical phonology. *Cognition, 34,* 137–195.
du Plessis, J., Solin, D., Travis, L., & White, L. (1987). UG or not UG, that is the question: A reply to Clahsen and Muysken. *Second Language Research, 3,* 56–75.
Emonds, J. (1978). The verbal complex V' - V in French. *Linguistic Inquiry, 9,* 151–175.
Eubank, L. (1992). Verb movement, agreement, and tense in L2 acquisition. In J. Meisel (Ed.), *Acquisition of verb placement* (pp. 225–244). Dordrecht: Kluwer.
Felix, S., & Weigl, W. (1991). Universal Grammar in the classroom: The effects of formal instruction on second language acquisition. *Second Language Research, 7,* 162–180.

Finer, D. (1991). Binding parameters in second language acquisition. In L. Eubank (Ed.), *Point counterpoint: Universal Grammar in the second language* (pp. 351–374). Amsterdam: John Benjamins.

Finer, D., & Broselow, E. (1986). Second language acquisition of reflexive-binding. In *Proceedings of NELS 16* (pp. 154–168). Amherst: University of Massachusetts, Graduate Linguistics Students Association.

Flynn, S. (1984). A universal in L2 acquisition based on a PBD typology. In F. Eckman, L. Bell, & D. Nelson (Eds.), *Universals of second language acquisition* (pp. 75–87). Rowley, MA: Newbury House.

Gass, S. (1992, April). *The need to win fields and influence disciplines.* Paper presented at the Second Language Research Forum, Michigan State University, East Lansing.

Gregg, K. (1989). Second language acquisition theory: The case for a generative perspective. In S. Gass & J. Schachter (Eds.), *Linguistic perspectives on second language acquisition* (pp. 15–40). Cambridge, UK: Cambridge University Press.

Grondin, N. (1992). *Functional projections in child second language acquisition of French.* Unpublished master's dissertation, McGill University, Montreal.

Grondin, N. & White, L. (1995). *Functional categories in child L2 acquisition of French. Language Acquisition, 4,* 4.

Guilfoyle, E., & Noonan, M. (1992). Functional categories and language acquisition. *Canadian Journal of Linguistics, 37,* 241–272.

Hermon, G. (1992). Binding theory and parameter setting. *The Linguistic Review, 9,* 145–181.

Hilles, S. (1991). Access to Universal Grammar in second language acquisition. In L. Eubank (Ed.), *Point counterpoint: Universal Grammar in the second language* (pp. 305–338). Amsterdam: John Benjamins.

Hirakawa, M. (1990). A study of the L2 acquisition of English reflexives. *Second Language Research, 6,* 60–85.

Hornstein, N., & Lightfoot, D. (Eds.). (1981). *Explanation in linguistics: The logical problem of language acquisition.* London: Longman.

Hyams, N. (1986). *Language acquisition and the theory of parameters.* Dordrecht: Reidel.

Iatridou, S. (1990). About AgrP. *Linguistic Inquiry, 21,* 551–557.

Jaeggli, O., & Safir, K. (1989). The null subject parameter and parametric theory. In O. Jaeggli & K. Safir (Eds.), *The null subject parameter* (pp. 1–44). Dordrecht: Kluwer.

Johnson, J., & Newport, E. (1991). Critical period effects on universal properties of language: The status of subjacency in the acquisition of a second language. *Cognition, 39,* 215–258.

Kaplan, T. (1992, April). *CP in Japanese as a second language.* Paper presented at the Second Language Research Forum, Michigan State University, East Lansing.

Lakshmanan, U. (1989). *Accessibility to Universal Grammar in child second language acquisition.* Unpublished doctoral dissertation, University of Michigan, Ann Arbor.

Lakshmanan, U. (1993). The boy for the cookie—some evidence for the non-violation of the case filter in child second language acquisition. *Language Acquisition, 3,* 55–91.

Lakshmanan, U., & Selinker, L. (1994). The status of CP and the tensed complementizer *that* in the developing L2 grammars of English. *Second Language Research, 10,* 25–48.

118   **Lydia White**

Liceras, J. (1988). Syntax and stylistics: More on the pro-drop parameter. In J. Pankhurst, M. Sharwood Smith, & P. Van Buren (Eds.), *Learnability and second languages: A book of readings* (pp. 71–93). Dordrecht: Foris.

Lightfoot, D. (1989). The child's trigger experience: Degree-0 learnability. *Behavioral and Brain Sciences, 12,* 321–375.

MacLaughlin, D. (1995). *Language acquisition and the subset principle. The Linguistic Review,* 12, 143–191.

Martohardjono, G., & Gair, J. (1993). Apparent UG inaccessibility in second language acquisition: Misapplied principles or principled misapplications? In F. Eckman (Ed.), *Confluence: Linguistics, L2 acquisition and speech pathology* (pp. 79–103). Amsterdam: John Benjamins.

Pater, J. (1993). Theory and methodology in the study of metrical parameter (re)setting. *McGill Working Papers in Linguistics, 9,* 211–243.

Phinney, M. (1987). The pro-drop parameter in second language acquisition. In T. Roeper & E. Williams (Eds.), *Parameter setting* (pp. 221–238). Dordrecht: Reidel.

Pierce, A. (1992). *Language acquisition and syntactic theory: A comparative analysis of French and English child grammars.* Dordrecht: Kluwer.

Pinker, S. (1984). *Language learnability and language development.* Cambridge, MA: Harvard University Press.

Pollock, J.-Y. (1989). Verb movement, Universal Grammar, and the structure of IP. *Linguistic Inquiry, 20,* 365–424.

Progovac, L. (1992). Relativized SUBJECT: Long-distance reflexives without movement. *Linguistic Inquiry, 23,* 671–680.

Progovac, L., & Connell, P. (1991). *Long-distance reflexives, Agr-subjects, and acquisition.* Paper presented at the meeting of the Formal Linguistics Society of Mid-America, University of Michigan, Ann Arbor.

Radford, A. (1990). *Syntactic theory and the acquisition of English syntax.* Oxford: Basil Blackwell.

Rutherford, W. (1993). Linguistics and SLA: The two-way street phenomenon. In F. Eckman (Ed.), *Confluence: Linguistics, L2 acquisition and speech pathology* (pp. 3–14). Amsterdam: John Benjamins.

Schachter, J. (1989). Testing a proposed universal. In S. Gass & J. Schachter (Eds.), *Linguistic perspectives on second language acquisition* (pp. 73–88). Cambridge, UK: Cambridge University Press.

Schachter, J. (1990). On the issue of completeness in second language acquisition. *Second Language Research, 6,* 93–124.

Schwartz, B. (1992). Testing between UG-based and problem-solving models of L2A: Developmental sequence data. *Language Acquisition, 2,* 1–19.

Schwartz, B. (1993). On explicit and negative evidence effecting and affecting competence and "linguistic behavior." *Studies in Second Language Acquisition, 15,* 147–163.

Schwartz, B., & Gubala-Ryzak, M. (1992). Learnability and grammar reorganization in L2A: Against negative evidence causing the unlearning of verb movement. *Second Language Research, 8,* 1–38.

Schwartz, B., & Sprouse, R. (1994). Word order and nominative case in nonnative language acquisition: A longitudinal study of (L1 Turkish) German interlanguage. In T. Hoekstra & B. Schwartz (Eds.), *Language acquisition studies in generative grammar: Pa-*

pers in honor of Kenneth Wexler from the GLOW 1991 Workshops (pp. 317–368). Amsterdam: John Benjamins.

Schwartz, B., & Tomaselli, A. (1990). Some implications from an analysis of German word order. In W. Abraham, W. Kosmeijer, & E. Reuland (Eds.), *Issues in Germanic syntax* (pp. 251–274). Berlin: de Gruyter.

Sharwood Smith, M. (1992, June). *The death of the native speaker.* Paper presented at the meeting of the European Second Language Association, Finland.

Sorace, A. (1993). Unaccusativity and auxiliary choice in non-native grammars of Italian and French: Asymmetries and predictable indeterminacy. *Journal of French Language Studies, 3,* 71–93.

Thomas, M. (1989). The interpretation of English reflexive pronouns by non-native speakers. *Studies in Second Language Acquisition, 11,* 281–303.

Thomas, M. (1991). Universal Grammar and the interpretation of reflexives in a second language. *Language, 67,* 211–239.

Trahey, M., & White, L. (1993). Positive evidence and preemption in the second language classroom. *Studies in Second Language Acquisition, 15,* 181–204.

Vainikka, A., & Young-Scholten, M. (1994). Direct access to X'-theory: Evidence from Korean and Turkish adults learning German. In T. Hoekstra & B. Schwartz (Eds.), *Language acquisition studies in generative grammar: Papers in honor of Kenneth Wexler from the GLOW 1991 Workshops* (pp. 265–316). Amsterdam: John Benjamins.

Wexler, K., & Chien, Y.-C. (1985). The development of lexical anaphors and pronouns. *Papers and Reports on Child Language Development, 24,* 138–149.

Wexler, K., & Manzini, R. (1987). Parameters and learnability in binding theory. In T. Roeper & E. Williams (Eds.), *Parameter setting* (pp. 41–76). Dordrecht: Reidel.

White, L. (1982). *Grammatical theory and language acquisition.* Dordrecht: Foris.

White, L. (1985a). Is there a logical problem of second language acquisition? *TESL Canada, 2*(2), 29–41.

White, L. (1985b). The pro-drop parameter in adult second language acquisition. *Language Learning, 35,* 47–62.

White, L. (1989a). The principle of adjacency in second language acquisition: Do L2 learners observe the subset principle? In S. Gass & J. Schachter (Eds.), *Linguistic perspectives on second language acquisition* (pp. 134–158). Cambridge, UK: Cambridge University Press.

White, L. (1989b). *Universal Grammar and second language acquisition.* Amsterdam: John Benjamins.

White, L. (1991a). Adverb placement in second language acquisition: Some effects of positive and negative evidence in the classroom. *Second Language Research, 7,* 133–161.

White, L. (1991b). The verb-movement parameter in second language acquisition. *Language Acquisition, 1,* 337–360.

White, L. (1992a). Long and short verb movement in second language acquisition. *Canadian Journal of Linguistics, 37,* 273–286.

White, L. (1992b). On triggering data in L2 acquisition: A reply to Schwartz and Gubala-Ryzak. *Second Language Research, 8,* 120–137.

White, L. (1992c). Subjacency violations and empty categories in L2 acquisition. In H.

Goodluck & M. Rochemont (Eds.), *Island constraints* (pp. 445–464). Dordrecht: Kluwer.

White, L., & Genesee, F. (in press). How native is near-native? The issue of ultimate attainment in adult second language acquisition. *Second Language Research, 12,* 2.

White, L., Spada, N., Lightbown, P. M., & Ranta, L. (1991). Input enhancement and L2 question formation. *Applied Linguistics, 12,* 416–432.

White, L., Travis, L., & Maclachlan, A. (1992). The acquisition of wh-question formation by Malagasy learners of English: Evidence for Universal Grammar. *Canadian Journal of Linguistics, 37,* 341–368.

Whitman, J., Lee, K.-O., & Lust, B. (1991). Continuity in the principles of Universal Grammar in first language acquisition: The issue of functional categories. *Proceedings of NELS* 16, 383–397.

CHAPTER 4

A PARAMETER-SETTING APPROACH TO SECOND LANGUAGE ACQUISITION

Suzanne Flynn

I. INTRODUCTION

The study of second language (L2) acquisition and that of Universal Grammar (UG) have been closely allied for over a decade.[1] During this time, important theoretical and empirical advances have occurred in both domains of research. Within L2 acquisition, one of the most promising of these has been the advancement of a *principles and parameter-setting* model in efforts to explain the L2 learning process. Development of this approach has provided the basis for an account of the role of prior language knowledge—the defining feature of the L2 acquisition process—as well as for the role of nonparametric principles universal to both first language (L1) and L2 acquisition.

In spite of such advances, however, several controversies persist with respect to the explanatory value of a UG-based approach to the study of L2 acquisition. These controversies reflect, in many instances, disagreements concerning the basic theoretical underpinnings of the endeavor, and in other cases, problems in implementing a program of research within this paradigm and in interpreting results isolated from such programs. Unfortunately, such disagreements have at times seriously undermined attempts to initiate and maintain dialogues both within and

---

[1] This claim does not refer to work developed within a generative paradigm prior to the principles and parameters era. Such work serves as a basis of development for current UG-based approaches to the study of L2 acquisition (see, for example, V. Cook, 1973, 1975; DiPietro, 1971; Dulay & Burt, 1974; Ritchie, 1978).

121

outside the field. For example, although many outside of the field of L2 research are willing to accept the importance of the study of the L1 acquisition for constraining a theory of UG, these same individuals will categorically reject, in the absence of any empirical evidence, the relevance of results from the study of the L2 acquisition process for linguistic theory. We know that such a position is problematic in that if linguistic theory is to characterize how language learning is possible in humans in general, then it must make reference to L2 learning as well. If not, it will succeed in providing only a partial explanation of the language learning process.

Within the field of L2 research, some reject such an approach because it does not provide an explanation for all aspects of language learning (see, e.g., the review in Towell & Hawkins, 1994, and references cited therein). For example, it does not provide an account of the acquisition of the language-specific morphophonetic reflexes of tense and agreement or the language-specific realization of individual lexical items.[2] At the same time, there are those critics (see review in V. J. Cook, 1988, 1993) who believe that those working within a UG-based approach to L2 acquisition *do* make the claim that UG accounts for all that is involved in the language learning process. As will be discussed below, UG is a theory of a domain-specific entity of biological endowment for language. It aims to represent in a formal manner the structures and processes that underlie a human's ability to produce and understand language. It does *not* purport to account for all that is involved in learning a new target language, although it does make the claim that it accounts for the deepest, most essential properties of language. Ultimately, any explanation of a speaker's linguistic competence must include a specification of the ways in which this domain-specific faculty interacts with other mental processes of perception, memory, and so forth. This task, however, is well beyond the scope of contemporary linguistic theory and is not the central focus of current inquiry.

There are also others who reject a UG-based approach because they interpret *any* differences that emerge between L1 and L2 acquisition to mean that the two must be fundamentally different and therefore, *cannot* be accounted for within the same theoretical framework (see, e.g., Bley-Vroman, 1989; Clahsen, 1988; Clahsen & Muysken, 1986). Again, we will consider in more detail how such a conclusion is left largely unsupported.

The views briefly outlined above are not new. Many can be understood in the context of an evolving theory of UG and the difficulties encountered in trying to isolate the latest version of a particular linguistic analysis.[3] Many others can be

---

[2] A theory of UG does, however, provide an account of the syntax of tense and agreement.

[3] This observation is particularly relevant at this time as the theory is undergoing major revision within the context of the continued development of the *Minimalist Program* for linguistics (see

understood in the context of long maintained beliefs about L2 acquisition—unfortunately, ones that are often based on anecdotal or personal experience rather than empirical fact.

Thus, the purpose of this chapter is (1) to explicate the leading ideas and premises of a UG-based approach to problems in the study of L2 acquisition—specifically a principles and parameter-setting model for L2 acquisition; (2) to review critically several widely held assumptions and beliefs about the L2 learning process; and (3) to review several central findings derived from a UG-based approach to L2 learning.

II. BACKGROUND

A. Universal Grammar and Language Acquisition: General Assumptions

Chomsky's UG is the most explicit theory of the human capacity for language and its acquisition. This theory attempts to discover and define the fundamental properties of all possible grammars and, at the same time, to determine and characterize the linguistic capacities of particular individuals (N. Chomsky, 1981a, 1981b, 1982, 1988, 1991; N. Chomsky & Lasnik, 1992).

As a theory of grammars, UG attempts to define the principles and conditions that are elements or properties of all possible natural languages not merely by accident, but by biological necessity. To attain empirical adequacy, the principles and conditions specified by UG must rule out an infinite set of abstract grammars that do not conform to these fundamental properties, which are uniformly attained in languages but underdetermined by the evidence available to the language learner.

Parameters

Within the theory, differences among languages are hypothesized to derive from certain *parameters* that are associated with *principles*. Parameters specify dimensions of structural variation across all languages. They determine those properties of language relevant to the construction of a specific grammar. They are precise mechanisms by which a particular principle interacts with specific language experience to account for the actual language acquisition process.

In particular, a finite set of parameters determines what the dimensions of linguistic variation are and, along with the values associated with these parameters, what forms this variation can take. Parameter setting has been proposed to account for the implementation of UG, which is necessary for language learning to take

---

N. Chomsky, 1992). In spite of this continuous development, however, the leading ideas of the UG theory remain.

place. Setting the value for a given parameter in one way or another will have deductive consequences for the rest of the grammar.

Complementizer Phrase Direction and the Direction Parameter

Although the specification of these parameters and where they hold in the grammar is the subject of much inquiry, it is clear that a basic distinction in the ordering of constituents, including the ordering of embedded clauses in relation to the heads of the phrases in which they occur, holds critically across languages. One proposed parameter is the head-direction parameter as defined over C(complementizer) P(phrase) and the adjunction direction that correlates with it (cf. Lust, 1992; Lust & Chien, 1984; Lust & Mangione, 1983). Head-direction in CP correlates with adjunction in that left-headed CPs in a given language correlate with right-branched adjunct phrases and right-headed CPs correlate with left-branched adjunct phrases (Lust, 1992, p. 15) as in the examples in (1) below. In this way, English is left-headed with respect to CP and consequently right-branching as defined as in (1d). Japanese, on the other hand, is right-headed with respect to CP and consequently left-branching. We will henceforth refer to the head-direction parameter as it applies specifically within the CP as the CP direction parameter.

(1) a. CP $\rightarrow$ ... C' ...
     b. i.   C' $\rightarrow$ C^0 IP (left-headed, right-branching)
         ii.   C' $\rightarrow$ IP C^0 (right-headed, left-branching)

     c. i.   CP   ii.   CP

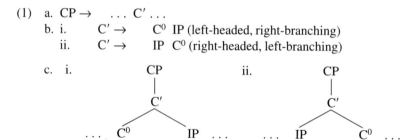

     d. " 'Principal Branching Direction' refers to the branching direction
         which holds consistently in unmarked form over major recursive
         structures of a language, where 'major recursive structures' are de-
         fined to include embeddings of sentence (CP) adjuncts under either
         NP or S 'heads.' Specifically these include relative clauses in com-
         plex NP and adverbial subordinate clauses in complex sentences."
         (from Lust, 1992, p. 15).
     e. English (right-branching) (NP, noun phrase)
         i.   Relative clause
              John read [$_{NP}$ the book [$_{CP}$ that Mary wrote]]
         ii. Adverbial adjunct clause
              Mary left [$_{CP}$ when John came]

   f. Japanese (left-branching)
      i. Relative clause
         John-*wa* [$_{NP}$[$_{CP}$ Mary-*ga*   *kaita*] *hon-o*]   *yonda*
         John-topic   Mary-nom wrote book-acc wrote
         'John read the book that Mary wrote.'
      ii. Adverbial adjunct clause
         [$_{CP}$ John-*wa*   *kitara*] Mary-*ga*   *kaetta*
         (when) John-topic came   Mary-nom left
         'When John came, Mary left.'

In short, principles (such as the principles of X-bar theory) determine what is given innately and parameters (like the head-direction parameter) determine what must be learned.

The Human Capacity for Language and the Process of L2 Acquisition

As a theory of the human capacity for language, UG is a characterization of those innate, biologically determined principles that constitute one component of the human mind—the language faculty. As such, it represents the formalization of a hypothesis about the language faculty as an identifiable system of the mind–brain as suggested in (2).

(2)   UG and the Initial State
      The initial state of the language faculty consists of a collection of sub-systems, or modules as they are called, each of which is based on cer-tain very general principles. Each of these principles admits of a very limited possibility of variation. We may think of the system as a com-plex network, associated with a switch box that contains a finite number of switches. The network is invariant, but each switch can be in one of two positions, on or off. Unless the switches are set, nothing happens. But when the switches are set in one of the permissible ways, the system functions, yielding the entire array of interpretations for linguistic ex-pressions. A slight change in switch settings can yield complex and varied phenomenal consequences as its effects filter through the net-work. . . . To acquire a language, the child's mind must determine how the switches are set. (N. Chomsky, 1988, p. 68)

In Chomsky's analogy, the principles of UG specify what is invariant (the network itself) and each parameter corresponds to a switch.

As suggested in (2), the child is innately or biologically programmed to attend to certain aspects of possible language variation in the input to which she or he is exposed. The child sets the values of these dimensions of language organization when she or he is exposed to the relevant language data, and on the basis of his or her being thus exposed, a number of different facts of the organization of a particular language can be derived deductively. As such, the principles and parameters approach to language proposes a very strong theory of L1 acquisition.

To summarize briefly, the essential claim of the theory of UG within the principles and parameters framework is that it constrains the language learner's hypotheses about which dimensions of language variation are significant in the possible grammars for a language. It constrains these hypotheses by providing a restricted range of possible values (preferably two) for a given dimension of language variation (that is, for a parameter) and it provides multiple consequences for grammar construction. It thus places heavy constraints on the hypothesis space of L1 learners.

Grammar versus Language

One important standard assumption made in UG-based approaches to acquisition studies is that the learner is acquiring a *grammar*. In current theory, a grammar is a system of universal principles with each parameter set in one or another of its values. As discussed in detail in Epstein, Flynn, and Martohardjono (1994), this means that the learner is not "learning a language." She or he is not learning some infinite set of sentences (e.g., $S_{English}$ = {Bill left; Sue leaves; A man is leaving; A tall woman has left . . .}). Rather, in theory-neutral terms, the learner is acquiring a particular system of linguistic laws (e.g., the subject precedes the verb; the verb agrees with the subject); this is a grammar (not a language) and this system of laws is what the speaker knows (Epstein et al., 1994). (See also N. Chomsky, 1955, 1964, 1982, 1986, 1988, 1991, for a discussion of the fundamental distinction between language and grammar.)

Linguistic Competence

Another important assumption that follows directly from a theory of UG concerns the notion of linguistic competence. (See chapters 2 (by Gregg) and 3 (by White), this volume, for competence–performance in L2 acquisition.) Within UG it refers to our tacit knowledge of the structure of language. It is

> the cognitive state that encompasses all those aspects of form and meaning and their relation, including underlying structures that enter into that relation, which are properly assigned to the specific subsystem of the human mind that relates representations of form and meaning. . . . I will continue to call this subsystem the language faculty. (N. Chomsky, 1980, p. 59)

The language faculty in this framework consists of those principles of UG that "are exceptionless" (N. Chomsky, 1988, p. 62) along with principles associated with parameters to be set by experience in the manner outlined above. Thus, to say that someone has the linguistic competence for English means that that person has represented internally the "exceptionless" principles of UG as well as those principles associated with parameters set in particular values in accordance with his or her experience of English, namely, the structure of English.

In contrast, to linguistic competence, "pragmatic competence underlies the ability to use such knowledge along with the conceptual system to achieve certain ends or purposes" (N. Chomsky, 1980, p. 59). Development of any theory of performance must take into account a theory of competence as well as "the structure of memory, our mode of organizing experience, and so on" (N. Chomsky 1980, p. 225).

III. L1 VERSUS L2 ACQUISITION: THE LOGICAL PROBLEM OF L2 ACQUISITION AND THE FULL ACCESS HYPOTHESIS

A theory of UG, however, makes no direct claims about L2 acquisition. As is well known, the question concerning the relevance and role of UG in L2 acquisition has been the topic of much debate.

Conceptually, it is not necessary that a theory of UG hold for the L2 acquisition process. A theory of UG could hold independently of any hypothesized role in adult L2 acquisition. For example as discussed in detail elsewhere (e.g., Eckman, 1988; Gass, 1988; Johnson & Newport, 1991; Lust, 1988; Rutherford, 1988), documenting that UG does not hold in adult L2 acquisition would suggest something about the role of UG itself as a biologically determined component of cognition. For example, it may have a once-only life—that is, it may be subject to a critical period beyond which it cannot be activated. If this scenario held, we might expect that adult L2 acquisition in contrast to child L1 acquisition would involve a large inductive component for language learning. That is, we would expect adults to approach language learning in a nonstructure-dependent way, for example, by simply translating lexical items one by one or by consulting relations of linear precedence alone in the acquisition of the L2.

Empirically, we know even in advance of detailed investigation that there are many reasons to believe that L1 and L2 acquisition are fundamentally different processes so that UG may not be involved in the L2 learning process.[4] We know, for example, that adults are more cognitively advanced than children and thus have a wider set of problem-solving skills available to them than children do. In addition, adults already know at least one language that could serve as a basis

---

[4]In this chapter we primarily focus on adult L2 learning. However, recent evidence (Epstein et al., 1993a, b, c, 1994) suggests that the child and adult L2 acquisition processes are fundamentally the same.

of translation for the learning of the new target language (TL), and in contrast to children, they can attend language classes and receive formal instruction in the TL.

From observation alone, we also know that adults often fail to achieve full native competence in their target L2s. For example, accents often persist, and some types of grammaticality judgments may be difficult for adult L2 learners to make (Coppieters, 1987; cf. Birdsong, 1992). Coupled with this observation, it also seems to be true, at least for some aspects of language, that the earlier learned the better (e.g., Oyama, 1982; Patkowski, 1982; see also Newport, 1990).

We also know that adults, in contrast to children, begin with a full-blown system of grammatical knowledge in place; that is, the learner's L1 plays a role in subsequent language learning, as will be discussed in more detail in section IV (see also discussions in Flynn, 1987, and Flynn & Martohardjono, 1993). Evidence such as this provides a good *prima facie* case for the claim that the adult–child differences do in some manner significantly alter the language learning process for the adult as is often claimed. (Chapter 10 by Gass is a general treatment of the influence of the L1 in L2 acquisition.)

On the other hand, there is sufficient reason to believe that there might be an underlying commonality to both child L1 acquisition and adult L2 acquisition. For example, current research suggests that infants and adults do not differ to the degree originally thought in terms of their attentional or computational abilities. In addition, the existence of critical periods for language as traditionally formulated has been seriously challenged (see, e.g., Flynn & Martohardjono, 1991, 1992, 1994). At the same time, we know that the human species is uniquely programmed to learn language, and we know that adults are capable of learning new languages under a wide range of learning conditions, as are children. Thus, we might expect that the language faculty involved in L1 acquisition might also be involved in adult L2 acquisition.

At the same time, we know that experience significantly underdetermines linguistic knowledge for the adult L2 learner. This knowledge far exceeds the linguistic input that the L2 learner is exposed to even in the face of intense linguistic tutoring. In addition, the L1 grammar alone will not provide the knowledge base needed to arrive at the L2 grammar. Facts such as these force us to the position that there exists a logical problem of some form for the L2 acquisition process as articulated in much other work (e.g., V. Cook, 1985; V. J. Cook, 1988; Gregg, chap. 2, this volume; Thomas, 1991; White, 1989, chap. 3, this volume).

If there is a logical problem for L2 acquisition as for L1 acquisition, we should then expect to find evidence that indicates that the L2 learner solves certain aspects of the L2 acquisition problem in a manner comparable to that of a child L1 learner. That is, we would expect that the L2 acquisition process might be constrained by a set of language principles similar to those found in L1 acquisition. For example, we might expect that the L2 learner is sensitive to the same dimensions of language organization as is the L1 learner, and that establishing these dimensions is important in terms of deriving other aspects of the new TL.

At the same time, however, L1 and L2 acquisition differ precisely because the L2 learner already holds confirmed beliefs about at least one grammar. Thus, we might predict, in contrast to child L1 acquisition, that the language-specific principles incorporated in this grammar will interact with the adult experience. For example, the L2 learner might be forced to shift hypotheses about certain dimensions of language variation when attempting to construct the grammar of the new language. If we consider the CP direction parameter discussed above, in some cases the values of the L1 and L2 with respect to the CP direction parameter will match and in other cases they will not. In the case of a mismatch (such as the case of a Japanese speaker learning English), learners will need to assign an additional new value to this parameter. In the case of a match between the L1 and L2 (as in the case of a Spanish speaker learning English), no such new assignment would be necessary. In both cases, however, the learner will need to determine anew for the target L2, the range over which the parameter holds as well as the language-specific instantiations of the parameter.

To summarize, the proposal we have briefly outlined above states that UG is fully available to the L2 learner. We will call this the *full access* hypothesis.[5] This proposal states that differences in patterns of acquisition observed between L1 and L2 acquisition and the lack of what some have termed "completeness" can be accounted for in ways other than by invoking a lack of access to UG. All principles and parameter values available to the child L1 learner are also available to the adult L2 learner. This position is exemplified in the work of Epstein, et al. (1994), Finer and Broselow (1986), Flynn (1983, 1987, 1991, 1993), Flynn and Martohardjono (1991, 1992), Lakshmanan (1992), Li (1993), Martohardjono (1991, 1993), Schwartz (1993), Thomas (1991), Uziel (1991), among many others.

IV. ALTERNATIVE PROPOSALS

The *full access* hypothesis for L2 learning is not uncontroversial. Although many might agree that there is a logical problem for L2 acquisition, these same individuals may not all agree that the solution to the problem is the same for L1 and L2 acquisition. That is, many researchers would argue that UG is either totally unavailable or only partially available to the adult L2 learner.

One alternative proposal, which we will call the *no access* hypothesis, argues that UG is totally inaccessible to the adult L2 learner. Acquisition within this

---

[5] An alternative equally appropriate name for this proposal is the *continuous access hypothesis*, in that UG never ceases to be available to the human organism for language use or language learning.

account takes place in terms of nonlinguistic problem-solving strategies such as analogizing. This position is best exemplified in the work of Bley-Vroman (1989) and Clahsen (1988).

Another position, the *partial access* hypothesis, argues that UG is available to the L2 learner inasmuch as the principles and parameters instantiated in the L1 are realized in the L2. All else must be learned in terms of general problem-solving strategies. This position is exemplified in the work of Clahsen and Muysken (1986), and Schachter (1989).

A third derivative position, outlined in White (chap. 3, this volume), argues that UG is available to the adult, although the competences arrived at by an L2 learner of a given language and a native L1 speaker of the same language may differ.

We will briefly consider each of these positions and then focus on the empirical evidence for the *full access* hypothesis referred to above. (For other discussions of possible alternative positions on the role of UG in SLA see chapters 2 by Gregg, 3 by White, and 5 by Schachter.)

To anticipate, we argue that the evidence used to support the existence of substantive fundamental differences between L1 and L2 acquisition is inconclusive at best. In addition, the need to postulate totally distinct "learning" mechanisms for adult and child language learning is not supported by existing empirical data. These alternative models ultimately fail in that they are unable to provide adequate descriptions of the grammars L2 learners internalize. In addition, these proposals implicitly assume that the L2 learner attains a natural language grammar, yet none of the alternative models demonstrate how such grammars can be acquired by utilizing the nonlinguistic principles they argue explain L2 acquisition.

A. Methodological Considerations

Before beginning a discussion of the alternative proposals, it is important to bear in mind that it is difficult to evaluate behaviors in relation, for example, to a specific parameter. No experimental task in linguistics (or in any other behavioral science) measures linguistic competence directly. Conclusions about the nature of the biologically endowed faculty for language are made by inference from some type of language behavior elicited by a certain experimental task. Acknowledging the limitations of these experimental tasks in general does not render the study of language acquisition meaningless, nor does it mean that all experimental tasks are equally valid or appropriate for testing one's hypotheses (see extended discussion of these issues in Tarone, Gass, & Cohen, in press; this volume; Flynn, 1985; Lust, Chien, & Flynn, 1986; Munnich, Flynn, & Martohardjono, 1994).

As discussed in Munnich, et al. (1994) and Lust et al. (1986), the experimental tasks used assume that the learner's developing language ability does not match a native speaker's and that the linguistic behavior elicited from each learner with each task maps the territory lying between the target language grammar and the learner's developing grammar. In this way, evaluation of the variance in the learner's behavior allows us to measure his/her development with respect to the native speaker's model.

Obviously, the choice of task depends upon the question asked. For example, if one wants to determine how a learner assigns coreference or establishes a binding domain in a sentence such as *Bill told Henry to wash himself,* then one needs to use a task that allows a learner to demonstrate his or her knowledge of coreference. For example, elicited imitation or spontaneous speech will not easily provide the necessary database (although they will provide information about a learner's construal of the coreference relationship); rather, one needs a task such as an act-out or a comprehension question or a task that elicits a type of metalinguistic judgment about a possible coreferential pairing. On the other hand, if one is interested in the degree to which a learner can produce a particular grammatical structure as an indication of the form of the mentally represented grammar, then a type of elicited imitation task would be appropriate. With this task a learner is assumed to reproduce the linguistic structure of the sentence heard; thus, the utterance elicited is argued to reflect the degree to which a learner is able to assimilate the stimulus into his or her grammar.

There is much debate in both the L1 and L2 acquisition literature surrounding the use of any of these tasks. This is positive. We need to validate empirically what each task evaluates and how each task relates to each other, given the distinct cognitive demands for each experimental task. Knowing precisely what aspect of language ability each experimental task evaluates is essential with respect to our methodology for a particular study and with respect to an interpretation of the results elicited. Ideally and ultimately, we want a certain convergence of results across distinct methodologies. We also need to continue to develop increasingly more sensitive instruments to evaluate linguistic development. (For additional discussion of research methodology in the study of L2 acquisition see this volume, chapters 3 by White, 11 by Nunan, and 12 by Sorace.)

B. The No Access Hypothesis: General Learning Strategies and Analogy as an Account of L2 Learning

Returning to our discussion of the alternative proposals, in general, hypotheses that rely upon general problem-solving strategies as pivotal in their accounts of the L2 acquisition process, are merely describing "tools" with which L2 learners construct grammars, as discussed in detail in Epstein et al. (1994). They tell us nothing about the actual content of the end state grammar represented in the learner's mind or brain, which is precisely what a theory of UG provides us with. Thus, the proposals that deny access to UG by adult L2 learners leave unaddressed the content of the grammar resulting from the process of acquisition. In addition, they seem to imply in their accounts that whatever the grammar contains, it is something attainable via the employment of learning strategies, such as analogy. "In the end, the question left unanswered by these proposals is arguably the central question in L2 theory, what exactly does (can) the L2 learner know and how does s/he acquire that knowledge?" (Epstein et al., 1994, p. 11).

In addition, those proposals that argue that L2 learning is not constrained by the language faculty fail empirically, given what we know to be true about the L2 learner's linguistic knowledge.

Bley-Vroman (1989) argues that L1 and L2 acquisition are distinct processes. Although L1 acquisition may be determined by a theory of UG, L2 acquisition is not. His proposal, *the Fundamental Difference Hypothesis* (FDH), claims that L2 learning strategies derive from Piaget's Formal Operating Principles; these include the capacity for "distributional analysis, analogy, hypothesis formation and testing" (1989, p. 54). Focusing on analogy, Bley-Vroman argues that L2 learners' core linguistic knowledge derives from their ability to analogize from the L1 to the L2. As argued in Epstein et al., 1994)

> Appealing to analogy is problematic because it fails to distinguish between what the L2 learner knows (content of a grammar) and how s/he attains this grammar (process). Furthermore, it entails a fundamental differentiation between the nature of L1 and L2 acquisition, and thereby fails to account for the significant similarities between these two types of acquisition, neither of which is explained by analogy (p. 13).

Results of much L2 acquisition research indicate that the linguistic knowledge base of adults is comparable to that for child L1 learners. For example, the following general, and very basic capacities—which are all provided by a domain-specific language faculty—characterize the linguistic knowledge base of an adult L2 learner:

1. L2 learners have the ability to distinguish between linguistic and nonlinguistic noise.

2. L2 learners have knowledge of (un)grammaticality (e.g., Birdsong, 1992; Felix, 1988; Martohardjono, 1991; Munnich, Flynn, & Martohardjono, 1991, 1994; Uziel, 1991; White, 1989, 1993). This knowledge exists independently of the surface string grammaticality properties in the L1.

3. L2 knowledge is structure dependent (Felix, 1988; Flynn, 1983; Flynn & O'Neil, 1988; Jenkins, 1988; Martohardjono, 1993; Thomas, 1991; Zobl, 1983). As in L1 acquisition, there are an infinite number of logically possible structure-independent errors that are never made by L2 learners. For example, Jenkins notes that L2 learners do not utter strings such as, "Is the dog which ____ in the corner is hungry?" they would presumably judge such strings ungrammatical. If language learners were simply choosing a structure-independent rule

that scans the string of words looking for the first occurrence of *is* on an analogy with the formation of simpler questions in English (e.g., John is here → Is John here?), we might expect utterances of the form, "Is the dog which in the corner is hungry?" from L2 learners. However, the absence of such errors strongly suggests that L2 learners have knowledge of the Head-Movement Constraint, a restriction on the movement of X^0 categories (such as that of the form of *be* in the present case) that precludes generation of the sentence (string) types in question.

To conclude our discussion of the no access hypothesis, we know of no version to date that has even descriptive power, because invariably each fails to account for or even specify knowledge of (un)grammaticality or language (as represented in a grammar). In the end, such hypotheses are often characteristically forced to attribute domain-specific knowledge (i.e., the very knowledge they presume to be unavailable in L2 acquisition) to the learner and are forced to retreat from the position that only nonlinguistic principles govern L2 acquisition (see Epstein et al., 1994, for extended discussion).

C. The Partial Access Hypothesis

Other proposals for the L2 acquisition process concern the fact that UG may play a role only to the extent that L2 properties not realized in the L1 must be learned by processes other than those that are found in L1 acquisition. For example, the partial access hypothesis claims that UG knowledge is only partially available to the L2 learner. One version argues that UG knowledge is limited to the particular way in which the L1 instantiates it (Schachter, 1989, chap. 5, this volume; for other versions, see Strozer, 1991). This means, for example, that although a child L1 learner may have available to her or him the entire range of options provided by the theory of UG, namely, all initial settings for all parameters, an L2 learner will have available only those parametric values characterizing the L1 grammar (see Epstein et al., 1994, and Flynn, 1993, for extended discussion). Thus according to Schachter (1989), if a particular value of a parameter is necessary for the acquisition of a new target L2, but this value is not realized in the learner's L1, then it will not be acquirable by the learner in his or her acquisition of the L2. This is outlined in (3) below.

(3)   Window of Opportunity Hypothesis (Schachter, 1989):
       All that remains as part of the knowledge state of an adult native speaker of a language is a language-specific instantiation of UG, that of the first language. UG in its entirety will not be available as a knowledge source for the acquisition of a second language. Only a language-specific instantiation of it will be. (Schachter, 1989, p. 13)
            If, however, it turns out that in the acquisition of the target some instantiation of principle P is necessary and P is not incorporated into

the learner's L1, the learner will have no language-internal knowledge to guide him/her in the development of P. Therefore, completeness with regard to the acquisition of the target language will not be possible. (Schachter, 1989, pp. 13–14)

According to this proposal, UG as it is available to a child L1 learner does not constrain the L2 learner's hypotheses. Grammar construction by the L2 learner is not constrained by principles and parameters of UG but rather by the principles and immutably set parameters of the particular L1 grammar. Thus, this theory predicts L2 grammar construction will differ significantly from L1 grammar construction. Furthermore, completeness in L2 acquisition is predicted to be impossible in a wide variety of cases namely, where parametric values mismatch or in the case of noninstantiation of certain principles. (Chapter 5 by Schachter, this volume, argues for what Flynn terms the partial access hypothesis.)

Although this approach might at first glance seem to provide an appealing account of L2 acquisition and might allow us to analyze observed differences between adult and child language acquisition, it fails to account for the fact that L2 learners are able to construct grammars incorporating parameter settings not instantiated in the L1. In addition, other nonparametric grammatical options not instantiated in the L1 are available to the L2 learner. We will consider some of this evidence below. Again, to anticipate our conclusion, the data falsify the above two leading predictions of the partial access hypothesis. At the same time, this falsification provides important and critical support for the full access hypothesis, namely, the continuous and complete availability of UG to the adult L2 learner.

In the next section, we summarize selected sets of results from a wide range of experimental studies that indicate that adult L2 learners, regardless of L1 background, solve problems of complex sentence formation in a manner evidenced in L1 acquisition. At the same time, results indicate a subtle interaction of the learner's L1 knowledge base in this acquisition process. The results are argued to provide essential evidence for the role of a biologically specified program for language, essentially a parameter-setting model of UG as well as providing important evidence with respect to the role of experience in the language learning process.

V. EVIDENCE AGAINST THE PARTIAL ACCESS HYPOTHESIS AND FOR THE FULL ACCESS HYPOTHESIS

A. New Parameter Settings: The CP Direction Parameter

The partial access hypothesis predicts only partial evidence of grammar construction in the manner observed in child L1 acquisition in L2 acquisition, as all that is available to the L2 learner is an L1 instantiated UG along with other un-specified nondomain-specific learning principles. Within this framework, only (1) principles that apply to the L1 nonvacuously and (2) L1 instantiated parametric values are available to the L2 learner. In this context, to construct a target L2 grammar that incorporates L1 principles applying only vacuously in the L1 and non-L1 parameter settings could be achieved in one of two ways: (1) UG constrains no aspect of the L2, or (2) UG fails to constrain those aspects of L2 acquisition where there is a mismatch between the L1 and L2 in grammatical properties. This latter claim amounts to the hypothesis that an L2 learner has a type of hybrid grammar—one part UG constrained and one part not.[6] Such a position is extremely problematic both theoretically and empirically. As suggested in our discussion above of linguistic competence, it is difficult, if not impossible, to formulate a proposal for UG in which perhaps some of the exceptionless principles obtain and some do not. Such a proposal is wholly inconsistent with the theory as currently formulated.

If on the other hand, the L2 learner has continuous access to UG and not just the L1 grammar alone, we would expect that regardless of the "match or mismatch" between L1 and L2 grammatical principles, the L2 grammars will be constrained by principles and parameters of UG. More specifically, we would expect that L2 grammars would, for example, conform to X' theory just as L1 grammars do. We would also expect that L2 learners would be able to assign a new (i.e., non-L1) parametric value to a given parameter.

Results from several empirical studies involving an investigation of Japanese speakers' acquisition of English confirm the hypothesis that L2 learners are able to assign new parametric values in the construction of the L2 grammar when there is a mismatch between the L1 and the L2 (e.g., Flynn, 1983, 1987, 1991, 1993; Flynn & Martohardjono, 1992, 1994). Importantly, these learners do so in a manner consistent with predictions made by the theory of UG. In the following, we will consider this case as well as others in which the partial access hypothesis has been empirically tested and shown not to hold in L2 acquisition.

Results of empirical studies (e.g., Flynn, 1983, 1984, 1987) investigating the role of the head-direction parameter in adult L2 acquisition indicate that, from the earliest stages of acquisition, Japanese speakers learning English as a Second Language (ESL), are able to acquire the English value of the head-direction parameter. The particular head-direction formulation examined in these studies concerns the order of the head of the CP with respect to its complement or adjunct (see discussion above in II.A). (For additional discussion of the head-direction parameter in L2 acquisition, see Chapter 10 by Gass, this volume.)

---

[6] With respect to psycholinguistic research, such as a proposal has interesting consequences regarding both language production and processing.

Results of extensive cross-linguistic L1 acquisition studies have demonstrated that young children establish the head-complement order for their L1s at early stages of acquisition (see review in Lust, 1986). It has subsequently been argued that children use this knowledge to constrain their hypotheses about other aspects of the language-particular grammar they are constructing, one such aspect being anaphora direction.

In an elicited imitation and comprehension study (Flynn, 1983, 1987), we investigated the acquisition of the English value of the head-direction parameter by 21 adult Japanese speakers learning ESL (for more detailed discussion see the original study). They were tested on structures such as those shown in (4a) and (4b).

(4)   Pre- and postposed subordinate adverbial clauses
      a. Preposed:
         When the actor finished the book, the woman called the professor.
      b. Postposed:
         The worker called the owner when the engineer finished the plans.

These structures varied in terms of the pre- and postposing of the subordinate clause in relation to the main clause. Preposed structures correspond to head-final structures (in 4a) and postposed clauses to head-initial structures (in 4b) on a formulation of head-direction consistent with CP direction.

We hypothesized that if L2 learners had access to their L1-valued parameters alone, then the Japanese speakers tested in this study would have access only to the head-final value of the head-direction parameter. If this were so, we would expect to find no evidence that these learners were able to identify and assign a new value to the head-direction parameter for the L2, English, in a manner observed for child L1 acquisition. We might even expect that those structures that followed from the L1 parameter setting would be more accessible to the Japanese learner than those that followed from the L2 parameter setting; namely, there might be a preference for preposed sentence structures rather than postposed structures.

Results of studies investigating these and other related hypotheses reveal two very important findings. First, at early stages of acquisition, Japanese learners do not find preposed sentence structures significantly easier either to imitate or comprehend. That is, they treat both of the sentence structures equivalently in production and comprehension suggesting that they "know" that English and Japanese differ in head-direction and are working out the consequences of a new parameter setting for English. The second result indicates, as shown in the graph in 5, that at the highest proficiency level tested, the Japanese speakers showed a significant preference for postposed clauses.

(5)

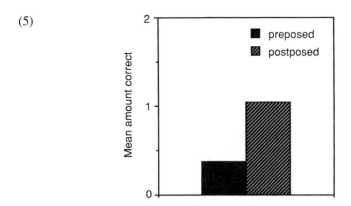

This is a finding consistent with that for L1 learners of English and one that suggests that these learners had assigned a value to the head-direction parameter in conformity with the English value. These results suggest that UG in its entirety remains available to the L2 learner. These results have been replicated with other sentence structures, namely, relative clauses (Flynn, 1989a, 1989b, 1991) and with other language groups, for example, Chinese and Spanish speakers learning ESL (e.g., Flynn & Espinal, 1985).

B. L1 Vacuously Applied Principles

As discussed in detail in Martohardjono (1993) and Epstein et al. (1994), another empirical test of the partial access hypothesis investigates nonparametric variation. For example, if in the L1, a UG principle applies vacuously to a certain construction, the partial access hypothesis predicts that the learner will not be able to apply this principle nonvacuously to the corresponding construction in the L2. Several studies have investigated this version of the partial access hypothesis by testing L2 learners' knowledge of principles constraining syntactic movement. The effects of such principles on the acquisition of wh-questions has been of particular interest to researchers because cross-linguistically there is variation in the syntax of wh-questions, some displaying overt movement of the wh-phrase, others exhibiting wh-in situ.

For example, when acquiring English, learners need to know that wh-questions are constrained by movement principles, such as Subjacency and the Constraint on Extraction Domains (CED, Huang 1982). In languages like English, which instantiate questions with overt movement of the wh-phrase, these principles have the effect of blocking wh-extractions out of certain domains like relative clauses and adjuncts, for example.

(6)   a. Indonesian
    i. *Siti makan* [*nasi goreng* [*yang di-masak   siapa*]]?
        Siti eat   rice fried   that   PASS-cook who
        * 'Who did Siti eat the fried rice that *t* cooked?'
    ii. *Surat ini datangnya* [*sesudah Siti vertemu dengan siapa*]?
        letter this arrive-poss after   Siti meet   with   who
        * 'Who did this letter arrive after Siti met with *t*?'
  b. Chinese
    iii. *ni qui xihuan* [[*piping shei de*] *shu*]
        you most like   criticize who REL book
        * 'Who do you like books that criticize *t*?
    iv. *ni* [*yinwei wo shuo-le shenme*] *er bu gaoxing?*
        you because I   said   what   then not happy
        * 'What are you unhappy because I said *t*?'

(Martohardjono, 1991)

For certain groups of L2 learners whose L1s do not involve syntactic movement in equivalent structures and hence do not instantiate movement principles, knowledge of such principles cannot be gleaned from the L1 grammar. This would be the case for Chinese or Indonesian speakers learning English. The contrast between Chinese and Indonesian and English can be seen in (6i–iv), where questioning a noun that is embedded within a relative clause or an adjunct clause results in grammatical sentences in Chinese and Indonesian, but in ungrammatical sentences in English.

Recall that the partial access hypothesis argues that knowledge of UG principles is available only in the particular form in which it is instantiated in the L1. If this view is correct, we would expect native speakers (NSs) of languages that do not instantiate overt movement in wh-questions to ignore the effects of movement constraints in English wh-questions, because in the equivalent structures in the L1 these constraints apply vacuously. Furthermore, this type of knowledge is not available in the input data; that is, L2 learners are not informed about the grammaticality status of sentences such as (6i–ii).

We now know from a set of studies testing knowledge of movement constraints on the part of adult learners of L2 English from a variety of L1 backgrounds, that these learners clearly possess and use the ability to recognize movement violations, regardless of whether overt movement is instantiated in the L1 (Martohardjono, 1991, 1992; Uziel, 1991; White & Juffs, 1992). For example, Martohardjono (1992) tested L1 speakers of Chinese and Indonesian on knowledge of ungrammaticality in English wh-questions, such as in (7):

(7)   Examples of stimulus sentences.
    a. Questioning out of relative clauses.
        i. Subject: *Which man did Tom fix the door that *t* had broken?
        ii. Object: *Which mayor did Mary read the book that praised *t*?

   b. Questioning out of adjuncts (adverbial clauses)
     i. Subject: *Which waiter did the man leave the table after *t* spilled the soup?
     ii. Object: *Which soup did the man leave the table after the waiter spilled *t*?

As shown in the table in (8), L2 learners from these L1 backgrounds are quite able to correctly identify ungrammatical wh-questions involving domains such as relative clauses and adverbial adjuncts.

(8)   Results

	Mean correct (%)	
	Relative clauses	Adjuncts
Chinese	71	88
Indonesian	87	90
English	98	100

The Indonesian subjects in this particular study provide us with a striking example of the ability to use UG knowledge independently of what the L1 grammar specifies. Namely, in addition to being able to recognize violations of movement constraints in general, they evidence a more subtle knowledge of degree of unacceptability. As is well known, movement violations range in severity depending on the particular domain of extraction. Thus, extractions out of relative clauses and adjuncts, for example, result in worse violations than extractions out of NP-complements and wh-islands, as illustrated in (9).

(9)   Knowledge of relative strength of movement constraints
   a. Weak effects:
     i. Extractions out of certain wh-islands (*whether, when*):
       ?*Which car did he wonder whether to fix _____?
     ii. Extractions out of NP complements:
       ?*Which book did John hear a rumor that you read _____?
   b. Strong effects:
     i. Extractions out of relative clauses.
       **Which book did John meet a child who read _____?
     ii. Extractions out of adjunct clauses.
       **How did you leave before fixing the car _____?

                                       (N. Chomsky, 1986)

We already know that Indonesian does not instantiate movement in wh-questions, and that therefore no movement violations occur in these structures. However, questions involving wh-islands and NP complements in this language turn out to be unacceptable or highly marginal due to other considerations. This is shown in (10).

(10)   Indonesian
    a. Wh-islands:
        * *Siti ingin tahu* [$_{CP}$ *dimana* [$_{IP}$ *Adik menyembunikan apa*]]?
        Siti want know   where   Adik ACT-hide   what?
        * 'What does Siti wonder where Adik hid?'
    b. NP complements:
        ?* *Siti dapat* [$_{NP}$ *kabar* [$_{CP}$ *bahwa saudaranya pergi kemana*]]?
        Siti receive   news   that   relative-POSS go   where?
        * 'Where did Siti receive the news that her relative went?'

In Indonesian grammar precisely the reverse situation holds for the weak and strong effects described in (9) for English. Namely, questions involving adjuncts and relative clauses, which in English constitute strong violations, are perfectly acceptable in Indonesian (as shown above in 6), whereas questions involving wh-islands and NP complements, which in English constitute only weak violations, are unacceptable in Indonesian. This, however, does not seem to affect the L2 learners' ability to differentiate correctly between the two types of violations when learning English. From the results in the table in (11), we see that their judgments of these sentences pattern in the same way as those of NSs. That is, they weakly reject NP-complements and wh-island violations, and they strongly reject extractions out of relative clauses and adjuncts (even though their L1 grammar specifies the reverse for analogous structures). Clearly this differential knowledge would not be possible if UG were not independently represented from L1 grammars. (Chapters 3 by White, 5 by Schachter, and 10 by Gass, this volume, also include discussions of conditions on wh-movement in L2 acquisition.)

(11)   Results

	Mean correct (%)	
L1	Strong	Weak
Indonesian	79.2	40.0
English	99.0	78.0

C. Error Data from Adult L2 Acquisition

A third piece of compelling evidence for the full access hypothesis emerges from error data with the same set of Japanese speakers tested above on pre- and postposed sentence structures. By testing these subjects' elicited imitation of sentences such as that exemplified in (12), we found that such sentences were extremely difficult for these learners of English. These results are shown in the figure in (13).

(12)   When the doctor received the results he called the gentleman.

(13)

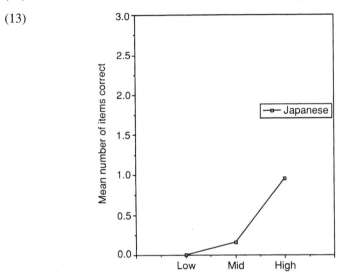

The sentence in (12) involved a preposed, left-branching adverbial adjunct clause as well as forward pronoun anaphora. Sentences with analogous structures are productively licensed in Japanese, as shown in (14). These sentences are in accord with Japanese as a head-final, or right-headed CP language.

(14)   [$_{CP}$[$_{IP}$ *Taroo-wa   nyuusi   -no   kekka-o   kiita*] *toki*]   Θ
                   Taroo-topic   entrance-exam-poss. result-acc. heard when   (he)
                   hahaoya ni denwa   sita
                   mother-dat telephone did.
       'When Taroo heard (found out) the results of the entrance exam (he) called
       his mother.'

The error rate on these sentences, illustrated in (13), is predicated by a UG parameter-setting model of grammar acquisition. As seen earlier, the Japanese speaker learning English must assign a new parameter setting for head-direction. In L1 acquisition, the setting for this parameter has been argued to involve a correlation of resultant configuration (either right or left) with directionality of anaphora. When head-complement order is principally head-initial, forward directionality of anaphora (in which the anaphor occurs after its antecedent) is productively licensed. If these learners were limited to the value of the CP parameter that determines the structure of Japanese (that is, their L1 value), then they should have no difficulty with structures like that in (12).

On the other hand, if the Japanese-based L2 acquisition of English is constrained by the same principles and range of parameter values as is child L1 acquisition of English—namely the principles and parameters of UG whether instantiated in the L1 or not—and if the L2 learner draws the same empirical consequences as the L1 learner, then the difficulty Japanese-L1 speakers have with sentences such as the one in (13) can be explained, because such sentences not only offend the head-direction parameter value for the L2 (that is, the head-initial value of English) but they also offend the empirical correlation between the head-initial value of the head-direction parameter and forward anaphora direction that follows from this parameter setting. Results such as these are left unaccounted for within a model disallowing access to principles and parameters of UG independent of the L1 grammar.

D. Nontransfer of Language-Specific Aspects

Results of a study investigating the L2 acquisition of the "control" verbs, *promise, remind,* and *tell* in English by adult Spanish speakers provide data that suggest that the L2 learner is constrained by UG rather than the L1 alone (see Flynn, Foley, & Lardiere, 1991). Consider the examples under (15) below.

(15) Infinitives and finite *that* complements
    a. English infinitives with control PRO:
        i. John promises Henry [PRO to go to the store].
        ii. John reminds Henry [PRO to go to the store].
        iii. John tells Henry [PRO to go to the store.]
    b. English finite embedded clauses:
        i. John promises Henry [that he will go to the store].
        ii. John promises Henry [that he will go to the store].
        iii. John tells Henry [that he will go to the store].
    c. Spanish infinitive with control PRO:
            Juan *le   promete* a Henry [PRO *ir   a la tienda*].
            Juan him promises to Henry   to go to the store.
            'Juan promises Henry PRO to go to the store.'
    d. Spanish finite embedded clauses:
        i. Juan *le   promete* a Henry [*que pro va   a la tienda*].
            Juan him promises to Henry that (he) (will-)go to the store.
            ('Juan promises Henry that he will go to the store.'
        ii. Juan *le   dice a* Henry [*que* pro *vaya   a la tienda*].
            Juan him tells to Henry that (he) should-go to the store.
            'Juan tells Henry to go to the store.'

iii. Juan *le   recuerda a* Henry [*que* pro *va   a la tienda*].
Juan him reminds to Henry that (he) (will-)go to the store.
'Juan reminds Henry that he will go to the store.'

In review, L1 acquisition of the control structures exemplified in 15a has been widely studied (e.g., C. Chomsky, 1969; Maratsos, 1974; McDaniels and Cairns, 1990; Sherman, 1983; Sherman & Lust, 1993; Tavakolian, 1978). Taken together the results from these and other studies indicate (1) that in comprehension, L1 learners of English interpret all control verbs as if they were object controllers, and (2) a general overall preference exists for the infinitive structures exemplified in (15a) when compared to the acquisition of their tensed counterparts illustrated in (15b), which applies to both production and comprehension studies.

Similarly, results of early L2 acquisition studies focusing on the comprehension of the structures in (16a) indicate a developmental pattern in which adult L2 learners interpreted subject control verbs as if they were object control verbs at early stages of acquisition (d'Anglejan & Tucker, 1975; Cooper, Olshtain, Tucker, & Waterbury, 1979). In addition, results of these comprehension studies found no evidence that the L2 learners attempted to translate or to map their native language structures onto those of the TL even when the L1 would have provided a correct response for the English structures tested.

Given the comparability in patterns of acquisition in comprehension between L1 and L2 learners of English, the next question asked was whether patterns of production for L1 and adult L2 learners of English would also match for control verbs. To test this, 21 adult speakers of Spanish learning ESL were tested in their production of the structures exemplified in (15a–b).[7] The Spanish speakers tested were at both an Intermediate (n = 9) and Advanced (*n* = 12) level of competence as measured by the standardized Placement Test from the University of Michigan.

Spanish clearly has both infinitives and tensed clauses, as exemplified in (15c–d). Spanish infinitivals also involve a null pronoun as in English (PRO) (15c); however, the tensed counterparts involve a pronoun form (*pro*) that differs from English as shown in (15di–iii). All three control verbs tested in this study (*promise, remind,* and *tell*) can occur in Spanish tensed clauses as in English. However, infinitives are not allowed with *tell* or *remind* in Spanish.

In this study, subjects were administered an elicited imitation task in which they were asked to repeat the sentence verbatim as given by the experimenter. The sentences administered are illustrated by (15a–b).

---

[7] Adult Japanese and Chinese speakers learning ESL were also tested on the same structures, that the Spanish speakers were tested on. We will not report on the results of these two language groups (see Flynn et al., 1991, for a complete report). We will note later in the text that the pattern of results for these two groups matches those isolated for the Spanish speakers in spite of the differences that exist in the L1s of these speakers with respect to tensed and infinitive structures and the nature of the control properties of the verbs investigated.

Results indicate as shown in the graph in 16, that Spanish speakers significantly prefer infinitives over finite *that*-clauses for the verbs tested (*promise, remind,* and *tell*) when they were administered both types of sentence structures in an elicited imitation test. Importantly, these results replicate those for L1 acquisition of English (see review in Sherman & Lust, 1993).

(16)

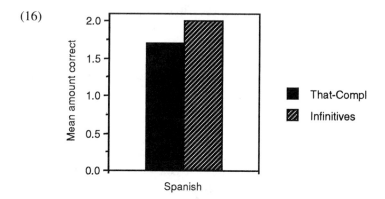

Given the results in (16), we have reasoned that if only the learner's L1 and not UG constrained L2 acquisition, we would have expected only L1 instantiated lexical properties to be available to the L2 speaker. That is, we would have expected, at the very minimum, the Spanish speakers to have found *remind* and *tell* sentences with finite *that*-clauses to be significantly easier to acquire than the infinitive structures for these verbs. However, these results indicate that this is not the case. These results along with (1) those from Japanese and Chinese speakers—which match those for the Spanish speakers—and (2) those from earlier comprehension studies that indicate that L2 learners like L1 learners interpret both *subject* and *object* control verbs as *object* control verbs have been used to argue for the role of a general principle of locality in the acquisition of ESL (see Sherman & Lust, 1993, for details of a similar proposal in L1 acquisition).

To summarize briefly, we argue that L2 learners regardless of their L1s prefer object-controlled, infinitive structures because in these structures an object antecedent minimally and unambiguously c-commands PRO (i.e., the nearest c-commanding element that appears in these structures without an intervening c-commanding element). In the infinitive structures in English, there is a control domain within which the object is the minimal c-commander of the proform, PRO. In the finite that-clauses, neither the subject nor the object minimally c-commands the subject pronoun in the subordinate clause. Both L1 and L2 learners seem to rely on this locality principle at early stages of acquisition. Within such a formulation, adults need to learn (and it appears that they do), to override this linguistic principle in order to learn the language-specific subject control properties of, for example, *promise*. Again, to emphasize for the purposes of this chapter, the important result is that the patterns of acquisition isolated for the Spanish speakers (and the Japanese and Chinese speakers) cannot be explained in terms of a model of transfer from the L1. (For discussion of object and subject control in the acquisition of English by deaf learners, see Chapter 14 by Berent, this volume.)

E. Functional Categories

A final set of data derive from an experimental study investigating the acquisition of functional categories by both child and adult speakers of Japanese learning ESL (see also Eubank, in press; Schwartz, 1993; Schwartz & Sprouse, 1991; Vainikka & Young-Scholten, 1991, 1992, 1993). These data also provide support for the full access hypothesis and not the partial access hypothesis.

We tested 33 Japanese-speaking children and 18 Japanese-speaking adults learning ESL. The Japanese children are aged 6–10. The adult speakers are graduate students at Massachusetts Institute of Technology (MIT) who were also enrolled in a low-intermediate ESL class at MIT.

We chose Japanese as our initial focus because of the status of functional categories in Japanese. They have been the subject of much debate. There are those who argue that there are no functional categories in Japanese (see Fukui, 1988, and references therein for debate), and there are those who argue that there are functional categories in Japanese (Miyagawa, 1991, 1993). One empirical prediction that follows from the partial access hypothesis is that if there are no functional categories in Japanese, then we should find no evidence of these in the early speech of these speakers.

Stimulus Sentences

The Japanese speakers in this study were tested on a wide range of complex syntactic factors. Our focus is on those structures involving functional categories, namely, the IP and CP. Examples of the stimulus sentences are shown in (17). Sentences in (17a, i–vi) (tense, modals, progressives, and negation) were designed to evaluate learner's knowledge of the IP. Sentences in (17b, vi–xi) (topicalization, relative clauses and wh-questions) were designed to evaluate speakers knowledge of the CP.

(17) Examples of stimulus sentences
    a. IP
      i. Present tense:
        The nervous professor inspects the broken television.
      ii. Past tense:
        The nervous doctor wanted a new lawyer in the office.

     iii. Modal:
          The little girl can see a tiny flower in the picture.

     iv. Progressive:
          The clever student is inspecting the expensive basket.

     v.   Negation—do support:
          The happy janitor does not want the new television.

     vi. Negation—progressive:
          The elderly grandfather is not picking the blue flower.

  b. CP

     vii. Topicalization[8] (one clause):
          Breakfast, the wealthy businessman prepares in the kitchen.

     viii. Topicalization (two clause, subject gap):
          The pencil, the talented architect says is expensive.

     ix. Topicalization (two clause, object gap):
          The photograph, the happy architect says he understands.

     x.   Relative clauses:
          The lawyer slices the vegetables that the father eats.

     xi. Wh-questions:
          Which young girl erases the tiny picture in the notebook?
          Which secret message does the young girl find in the basket?

Experimental Task

Speakers were tested with an elicited imitation test. This task was chosen as our initial diagnostic in order to elicit data comparable to the production data elicited in previous functional category studies (see, e.g., Vainikka & Young-Scholten, 1991, 1992, 1993). Speakers were given two tokens of each kind of sentence exemplified in (17). All sentences were equalized in syllable length (15) and approximately in number of words (9–11).

Results

As shown in the initial scoring of the results in the table in (18), the Japanese children and adults had little difficulty with functional categories. They were able to reproduce sentences containing X phrases (XP) in specifier (Spec) of CP positions and sentences containing X^0 in I^0 positions, thus strongly suggesting that their grammars contained the full inventory of functional categories. A closer look at the results in 18 demonstrates that overall the amount correct for these sentence structures is 59% for children and 60% for adults.

---

[8] Topicalization involves a CP on the assumption that the topic in these sentences involves movement to Specifier (Spec) of CP (cf. Lasnik & Saito, 1984).

In order for an utterance to be scored as correct, the speaker had to have uttered the stimulus sentence in its entirety with no structural or lexical changes except for the deletion of adjectives.

(18)   Results

	% Correct	
Structure	Child	Adult
Present tense	77%	78%
Past tense	66%	64%
Modal	66%	58%
Progressive	61%	72%
Negation		
Do-support	76%	64%
Progressive	69%	72%
Topicalization		
1 clause, obj gap	53%	69%
2 clause, obj gap	40%	44%
2 clause, subj gap	34%	42%
Relative clauses	56%	65%
Wh-questions		
Obj gap	58%	42%
Subj gap	48%	50%
Overall	59%	60%

Results of multifactored analysis of variance (ANOVA) indicate no significant differences in results between the child and adult L2 learners.

The figure in (19) indicates that adults and children treated the various sentence structures comparably. For example, these comparable patterns indicate that sentences involving movement to I^0 were easier than those involving movement to Spec of CP, as illustrated in 20. Another way that we can state this is that movement to Spec of CP involves long-distance movement of a maximal projection, whereas movement to I^0 involves short-distance movement of a head only. The results indicate that the former is more difficult than the latter. Note that this type of explanation is one having to do with movement, and does not reflect a lack of knowledge of Functional Categories. In addition, we can account for the higher error rates on complex as opposed to simple topicalization as a function of the number of clause boundaries crossed in the movement of the topicalized element to Spec of CP.

(19)

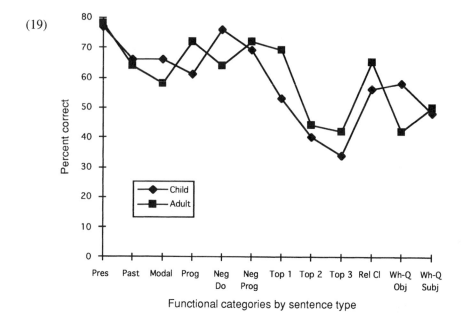

Functional categories by sentence type

(20)

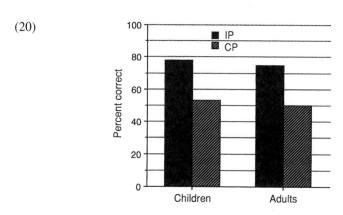

Additionally, results of the error analyses for all the stimulus sentences indicate that no greater than 15% of the errors for any one sentence type involved an error on the actual functional category under question. For example, only 15% of the errors made on topicalization involved a conversion of this structure to an un-topicalized sentence. Taken together with the results for amount correct, this sug-gests that the problems the L2 learners exhibit in their utterances of these struc-tures do not involve a grammatical deficit but some form of a production or performance deficit, independent of the grammar. Results also strongly suggest that the learners can correctly analyze the input in terms of functional categories.

Summary

Overall these results are interesting because they suggest that child L1 and adult L2 learners are similarly constrained in their acquisition. This is not a necessary result in that the child L2 learners were 10 years old or younger, whereas the adults were well beyond even the most liberal definition of adolescence (for a possible formulation of a Critical Period Hypothesis). When the two groups are equalized on ESL proficiency level, the results also suggest, against what is commonly believed, that the children did not find the task easier than the adults did. These results are interesting at another level also. If Japanese does not have functional categories, then the results suggest that the L2 learner does not attempt at early stages of acquisition to impose an L1 grammar onto the L2, as is frequently argued in many accounts of the L2 acquisition process (e.g., see White, 1989). On the other hand, even if Japanese does have functional categories, we know that it does not instantiate s-structure wh-movement (i.e., movement into Spec of CP). The results reported in this chapter indicate that although the Japanese have more difficulty on the CP structures than on the IP structures, they did not block these structures—which we might have predicted if they simply transferred from the L1. Moreover, we can explain the difficulty in at least two ways: (1) as discussed above, these structures involve long-distance movement, which is more difficult for the learners than the short-distance phrasal movement involved in IP structures, and (2) because Japanese does not instantiate s-structure wh-movement, the Japanese speakers need to assign another value to the parameter governing the spell-out of wh-movement for English. Results of other studies (e.g., Flynn, 1987; Martohard-jono, 1993) indicate that this assignment takes time in the course of acquisition. Another important fact related to the CP results is that results from the Spanish L1 group also investigated in this study (and which we do not report here) indicate a similar trend in terms of more difficulty with the CP than the IP structures, although the differences are not as great. This fact again suggests that the central problem with the CP structures is long-distance versus short-distance movement. Although this result is not conclusive in all respects, it is nonetheless strongly suggestive.

To summarize, we argue that errors in the acquisition of functional categories are characteristic of the cognitive process underlying the development of the lexicon and its integration with already existing syntactic knowledge (i.e., the computational system), rather than reflecting the development of the syntactic categories themselves. (Chapters 3 by White and 14 by Berent, this volume, include discussion of functional categories in L2 acquisition and in the acquisition of English by deaf learners, respectively.)

F. Derivative Version of the Partial Access Hypothesis

A third derivative proposal of the partial access hypothesis is outlined in White (chap. 3, this volume). This position argues that "L2 learners do not necessarily converge on the same grammar in contrast to L1 acquirers" (White, chap. 3, this volume). This formulation essentially argues that although NS and nonnative speakers (NNSs) may have different competences, they are "arrived at by the same means." It is not clear what it means to arrive at different competences by the same means. If someone "has arrived at" the competence for English then this individual has represented in his or her mind or brain all the principles of UG as well as parameters set to cohere with English input. Thus, to say that a speaker (either a NS or NNS) has the competence for English means that this speaker has the same internal representation of the grammar of English as other speakers who have a competence for English. If two speakers do not have the same competence, then each has represented a grammar for a distinctly different language; this would mean essentially that they share the same exceptionless principles of UG, but that they have parameters set in different ways to cohere with input from the distinct languages. One speaker may have, for example, the competence for English and one may have the competence for Chinese. Thus to argue that NSs and NNSs have different competences that are arrived at by the same means is to argue that one can give two individuals precisely the same set of directions to a specific location and each individual follows the directions to the letter; yet each of them arrives at a distinctly different location (S. D. Epstein, private communication). Such a proposition appears to be simply incoherent.

It is clear that during acquisition, whether L1 or L2, the developing language abilities of the learners do not always appear to converge on an adult NS. Research in both L1 and L2 acquisition can attest to this (e.g., L1: Lust, 1986; Radford, 1990; Slobin, 1973; L2: Finer & Broselow, 1986; Flynn, 1983, 1987; Martohard-jono & Gair, 1993). However, because there is a mismatch in linguistic *abilities* does not necessarily mean that there are differences in linguistic *competences*. There are many reasons for the developmental patterns observed in both L1 and L2 independent of UG. As illustrated previously in the discussion of the role of functional categories in adult L2 acquisition, the difficulty encountered with complex sentences may have to do with the number of sentence boundaries crossed in its derivation rather than with the lack of a competence for functional categories. The ability to deal, for example, with complex sentences in acquisition may reflect parsing difficulties rather than grammatical difficulties. A similar proposal is outlined above with respect to parameter setting (see also Flynn & Manuel, 1991; Lust, 1988). Thus, we argue that this derivative position is conceptually problematic and essentially proposes a position that argues for the full access hypothesis.

VI. DISCUSSION AND CONCLUSIONS

In conclusion, the empirical results we have reviewed in this chapter do not support either the no access or the partial access hypothesis. It appears that L2 learners do construct grammars of the new TLs under the constraints imposed by UG; those principles and parameters of UG carefully investigated thus far indicate that those not instantiated or applying vacuously in the L1 but operative in the L2, are in fact acquirable by the L2 learner.

We are thus forced to the conclusion that UG constrains L2 acquisition; the essential language faculty involved in L1 acquisition is also involved in adult L2 acquisition. This means that all the principles and parameters delineated by a theory of UG are available to the child and adult L2 learner. In general, such a position claims that UG rather than the learner's L1 restricts the options available to the adult L2 learner. Principles and parameters of UG constrain the language learner's hypotheses about which dimensions of language variation are significant in possible grammars for language.

The concept of parameter setting provides an important and interesting way to investigate the role of experience in the language learning process in general. For L2 acquisition, it provides a unique way to investigate not only the role of prior L1 experience but also the role of the target L2 experience and the resulting inter-actions of these two for acquisition. Prior to such study, we had little indication of the nature of the L2 learning process. Many questions remained open. For example, we did not know

1. whether the L1 returns to an initial state zero in the acquisition of a new target L2;
2. whether the additional values for a parameter atrophy and become unavail-able to the L2 learner when there was a mismatch between the L1 and L2;
3. whether it was possible to acquire a new value; and
4. whether the L2 learner initially assumes that the L2 is the L1 and tries to impose an L1 grammar on the L2 without consulting the target L2 grammar.

As a result of the past decade of research, we now have some empirical answers to these questions. As discussed above, we know that the L1 does not return to an initial state zero. At the same time, we know that additional parametric values not realized in the L1 do not atrophy and in fact appear to remain available to the L2 learner. In addition, we know that the L2 learner does not start in acquisition with the assumption that the L2 is the L1 (cf. White, 1989, chap. 3, this volume). From the earliest stages of acquisition, L2 learners are sensitive to the properties of the L2 grammar, namely, differences in parametric values. The fact that we do not see "instantaneous" learning in either L1 or L2 acquisition, even though the paramet-ric value for a principle may be instantaneously set is that the learner needs to establish and integrate the value of the parametric in the context of a language-specific grammar. This involves knowing over which structures a particular pa-rameter holds and how these structures are instantiated in a particular language. This involves learning well beyond what is provided by a theory of UG alone but which must be integrated. The results are important because they challenge many current critical period proposals (cf. Newport & Johnson, 1991). Although not denying the existence of differences between L1 and L2 acquisition, the source of the difficulty does not appear to be a lack of access to UG; rather it seems to involve problems with integration of the language faculty with other domains of cognition and problems with learning that are beyond the scope of UG (see Flynn & Manuel, 1991; Flynn & Martohardjono, 1991). Continued study will delineate precisely the nature of these differences and inform us concerning the nature of the language learning process.

ACKNOWLEDGMENT

The author wishes to thank Gita Martohardjono for important discussions and suggestions regarding the issues addressed in this paper. Many of the ideas outlined in this paper are developed in more detail in Epstein et al. (1994) and Flynn and Martohardjono (1994).

REFERENCES

Birdsong, D. (1992). Ultimate attainment in second language acquisition. *Language, 68,* 23–52.

Bley-Vroman, R. (1989). What is the logical problem of foreign language learning? In J. Schachter & S. Gass (Eds.), *Linguistic perspectives on second language acquisition* (pp. 41–68). Cambridge, UK: Cambridge University Press.

Chomsky, C. (1969). *The acquisition of syntax in children from 5 to 10.* Cambridge, MA: MIT Press.

Chomsky, N. (1955). *The logical structure of linguistic theory.* Cambridge, MA: Harvard (Revised 1956. Version published in part by Plenum Press, 1975; University of Chicago Press, 1985).

Chomsky, N. (1964). *Current issues in linguistic theory.* The Hague: Mouton.

Chomsky, N. (1980). *Rules and representations.* New York: Columbia University Press.

Chomsky, N. (1981a). *Lectures on government and binding.* Dordrecht: Foris.

Chomsky, N. (1981b). Principles and parameters in syntactic theory. In N. Hornstein & D. Lightfoot (Eds.), *Explanation in linguistics: The logical problem of language acquisition.* London: Longman.

Chomsky, N. (1982). *Some concepts and consequences of the theory of government and binding.* Cambridge, MA: MIT Press.

Chomsky, N. (1986). *Knowledge of language: Its nature, origin and use.* New York: Praeger.

Chomsky, N. (1988). *Language and problems: The Managua Lectures.* Cambridge, MA: MIT Press.

Chomsky, N. (1991). Some notes on economy of derivation and representation. In R. Freidin (Ed.), *Principles and parameters in comparative grammar.* Cambridge, MA: MIT Press.

Chomsky, N. (1992). A minimalist program for linguistic theory. *MIT Occasional Papers in Linguistics, 1.*

Chomsky, N., & Lasnik, H. (1992). *Universal Grammar.* Cambridge, MA: MIT Press.

Clahsen, H. (1988). Parameterized grammatical theory and language acquisition: A study of the acquisition of verb placement and inflection by children and adults. In S. Flynn & W. O'Neil (Eds.), *Linguistic theory in second language acquisition* (pp. 47–75). Dordrecht: Kluwer.

Clahsen, H., & Muysken, P. (1986.) The availability of universal grammar to adult and child learners. A study of the acquisition of German word order. *Second Language Research, 2,* 93–119.

Cook, V. (1973). The comparison of language development in native children and foreign adults. *International Review of Applied Linguistics, 11,* 13–28.

Cook, V. (1975). Strategies in the comprehension of relative clauses. *Language and Speech, 18,* 204–212.

Cook, V. (1985). Chomsky's universal grammar and second language acquisition. *Applied Linguistics, 6,* 2–18.

Cook, V. J. (1988). *Chomsky's Universal Grammar.* Oxford: Basil Blackwell.

Cook, V. J. (1993). *Linguistics and second language acquisition.* New York: St. Martin's Press.

Cooper, R., Olshtain, E., Tucker, R., & Waterbury, M. (1979). The acquisition of complex English structures by adult native speakers of Arabic and Hebrew. *Language Learning, 29,* 255–275.

Coppieters, R. (1987). Competence differences between native and near-native speakers. *Language, 63,* 544–573.

d'Anglejan, A., & Tucker, R. (1975). The acquisition of complex English structures by adult learners. *Language Learning, 25,* 281–296.

DiPietro, R. J. (1971). *Language structures in contrast.* Rowley, MA: Newbury House.

Dulay, H., & Burt, M. (1974). A new perspective on the creative construction process in child second language acquisition. *Language Learning, 24,* 253–278.

Eckman, F. (1988). Typological and parametric views of universals in second language acquisition. In S. Flynn & W. O'Neil (Eds.), *Linguistic theory in second language acquisition* (pp. 417–430). Dordrecht: Kluwer.

Epstein, S. D., Flynn, S., & Martohardjono, G. (1993a). The strong continuity hypothesis in adult L2 acquisition of functional categories. Paper presented at a workshop on "Recent Advances in Generative Approaches to Second Language Learning." MIT, Cambridge, MA.

Epstein, S. D., Flynn, S., & Martohardjono, G. (1993b). Evidence for functional categories in Japanese child and adult learners of English as a second language. Paper presented at Second Language Research Forum. University of Pittsburgh, Pittsburgh, PA.

Epstein, S. D., Flynn, S., & Martohardjono, G. (1993c). The full access hypothesis in SLA: Some evidence from the acquisition of functional categories. Paper presented at International Association for Applied Linguistics (AILA). Amsterdam, The Netherlands.

Epstein, S., Flynn, S., & Martohardjono, G. (1994). Explanation in SLA: Consideration of a case study of functional categories. Submitted for publication.

Eubank, L. (in press). Optionality and the "initial state" in L2 development. In T. Hoekstra & B. Schwartz (Eds.), *Language acquisition studies in generative grammar.* Amsterdam: John Benjamins.

Felix, S. (1988). UG generated knowledge in adult second language acquisition. In S. Flynn

& W. O'Neil (Eds.), *Linguistic theory in second language acquisition* (pp. 000–000). Dordrecht: Kluwer.

Finer, D., & Broselow, E. (1986). Second language acquisition of reflexive-binding. In *Proceedings of NELS 16* (pp. 154–168). Amherst: University of Massachusetts, Graduate Linguistics Students Association.

Flynn, S. (1983). *A study of the effects of principal branching direction in second language acquisition: The generalization of a parameter of Universal Grammar from first to second language acquisition.* Doctoral dissertation, Cornell University, Ithaca, NY.

Flynn, S. (1984). A universal in L2 acquisition based on a PBD typology. In F. Eckman, L. Bell, & D. Nelson (Eds.), *Universals of second language acquisition* (pp. 75–97). Rowley, MA: Newbury House.

Flynn, S. (1985). Principled theories of second language acquisition. *Studies in Second Language Acquisition, 7,* 99–107.

Flynn, S. (1987). *A parameter-setting model of second language acquisition.* Dordrecht: Reidel.

Flynn, S. (1989a). The role of the head-initial/head-final parameter in the acquisition of English relative clauses by adult Spanish and Japanese speakers. In S. Gass & J. Schachter (Eds.), *Linguistic perspectives on second language acquisition* (pp. 89–108). Cambridge, UK: Cambridge University Press.

Flynn, S. (1989b). Spanish, Japanese and Chinese speakers' acquisition of English relative clauses: New evidence for the head-direction parameter. In K. Hyltenstam & L. K. Obler (Eds.), *Bilingualism across the lifespan* (pp. 116–131). Cambridge, UK: Cambridge University Press.

Flynn, S. (1991). Government-binding: Parameter setting in second language acquisition. In C. Ferguson & T. Heubner (Eds.), *Crosscurrents in second language acquisition and linguistic theories* (pp. 143–167). Amsterdam: John Benjamins.

Flynn, S. (1993). Interactions between L2 acquisition and linguistic theory. In F. Eckman (Ed.), *Linguists, second language acquisition and speech pathology* (pp. 15–35). Amsterdam: John Benjamins.

Flynn, S., & Espinal, I. (1985). Head/initial head/final parameter in adult Chinese L2 acquisition of English. *Second Language Acquisition Research, 1,* 93–117.

Flynn, S., Foley, C., & Lardiere, D. (1991). *The Minimality principle in adult second language acquisition.* Paper presented at the Second Language Research Forum, University of Southern California, Los Angeles.

Flynn, S., & Manuel, S. (1991). Age-dependent effects in language acquisition: An evaluation of "critical period" hypotheses. In L. Eubank (Ed.), *Point-counterpoint: Universal Grammar in the second language* (pp. 117–146). Amsterdam: John Benjamins.

Flynn, S., & Martohardjono, G. (1991). *How critical is age in adult second language acquisition.* Paper presented at the annual meeting of the American Association for the Advancement of Science, Washington, DC.

Flynn, S., & Martohardjono, G. (1992). *Mapping from the initial state to the final state: The separation of universal principles and language specific properties.* Paper presented at the Conference on Syntactic Theory and First Language Acquisition: Crosslinguistic Perspective, Cornell University, Ithaca, NY.

Flynn, S., & Martohardjono, G. (1993). *Towards theory-driven language pedagogy.* Paper presented at the 22nd annual Linguistics Symposium of the University of Wisconsin-Milwaukee.

Flynn, S., & Martohardjono, G. (1994). Mapping from the initial state to the final state: The separation of universal principles and language specific properties. In B. Lust, J. Whitman, & J. Kornflit (Eds.), *Syntactic theory and first language acquisition: Crosslinguistic perspectives: Vol. 1 Phrase structure.* Hillsdale, NJ: Erlbaum.

Flynn, S., & O'Neil, W. (Eds.). (1988). *Linguistic theory in second language acquisition.* Dordrecht: Kluwer.

Fukui, N. (1988). Deriving the differences between English and Japanese: A case study in parametric syntax. *English Linguistics, 5,* 249–270.

Gass, S. (1988). Second language acquisition and linguistic theory: The role of language transfer. In S. Flynn & W. O'Neil (Eds.), *Linguistic theory in second language acquisition* (pp. 384–403). Dordrecht: Kluwer.

Huang, J. (1982). *Logical relations in Chinese and the theory of grammar.* Doctoral dissertation, MIT, Cambridge, MA.

Jenkins, L. (1988). Second language acquisition: A biolinguistic perspective. In S. Flynn & W. O'Neil (Eds.), *Linguistic theory in second language acquisition* (pp. 109–116). Dordrecht: Kluwer.

Johnson, J., & Newport, E. (1991). Critical period effects on universal properties of language: The status of subjacency in the acquisition of a second language. *Cognition, 39,* 215–258.

Lakshmanan, U. (1992, April). *The development of complementizers in child L2 grammars.* Paper presented at the Second Language Research forum, Michigan State University, East Lansing.

Lasnik, H. & Saito, M. (1984). On the nature of proper government. *Linguistic Inquiry, 15,* 235–289.

Li, X. L. (1993, January 15–16). *Adult L2 accessibility to UG: An issue revisited.* Paper presented at the MIT Workshop on Recent Advances in SLA Theory.

Lust, B. (1986). Introduction. In B. Lust (Ed.), *Studies in the acquisition of anaphora: Vol. 1. Defining the constraints* (pp. 6–103). Dordrecht: Reidel.

Lust, B. (1988). Universal grammar in second language acquisition: Promises and problems in critically relating theory and empirical studies. In S. Flynn & W. O'Neil (Eds.), *Linguistic theory in second language acquisition* (pp. 309–329). Dordrecht: Kluwer.

Lust, B. (1992). *Functional projection of CP and phrase structure parameterization: An argument for the 'strong continuity hypothesis.'* Paper presented at the Conference on Syntactic Theory and First Language Acquisition: Crosslinguistic Perspectives, Cornell University, Ithaca, NY.

Lust, B., & Chien, Y.-C. (1984). The structure of coordination in first language acquisition of Mandarin Chinese: Evidence for a universal. *Cognition, 17,* 49–83.

Lust, B., Chien, Y.-C., & Flynn, S. (1986). What children know: Methods for the study of first language acquisition. In B. Lust (Ed.) *Studies in the acquisition of anaphora. Vol II. Applying the constraints.* Pp. 271–356. Dordrecht: Kluwer.

Lust, B., & Mangione, L. (1983). The principal branching direction parameter in first language acquisition of anaphora. In P. Sells & N. Jones (Eds.), *Proceedings of NELS 13.* Amherst: University of Massachusetts.

Maratsos, M. (1974). How preschool children understand missing complement subjects. *Child Development, 45,* 700–706.

Martohardjono, G. (1991, October 23–25). *Universal aspects in the acquisition of a second language.* Paper presented at the 19th Boston University Conference on Language Development, Boston University.

Martohardjono, G. (1992, April). *Wh-movement in the acquisition of English as a Second Language.* Paper presented at the Workshop on the Acquisition of Wh-movement, University of Massachusetts at Amherst.

Martohardjono, G. (1993). *Wh-movement in the acquisition of a second language: A cross-linguistic study of three languages with and without movement.* Doctoral dissertation, Cornell University, Ithaca, NY.

Martohardjono, G., & Gair, J. (1993). Apparent UG accessibility in second language acquisition: Misapplied principles of principled misapplications? In F. Eckman (Ed.). *Confluence: Linguistics, second language acquisition, speech pathology.* Amsterdam: John Benjamins.

McDaniels, D., & Cairns, H. (1990). The processing and acquisition of control structures by young children. In L. Frazier & J. de Villiers (Eds.), *Language processing and language acquisition.* The Netherlands: Kluwer Academic Publishers.

Miyagawa, S. (1991). *Scrambling and case realization.* Cambridge, MA: MIT Press.

Miyagawa, S. (1993). Case, agr, and ga-no conversion in Japanese. In *Proceedings of 3rd Conference on Japanese/Korean Linguistics.* Stanford, CA: Stanford University, CSLI.

Munnich, E., Flynn, S., & Martohardjono, G. (1991, October). *Elicited imitation and grammaticality judgment tasks: What they measure and how they relate to each other.* Paper presented at the first biannual meeting of Applied Linguistics at Michigan State University, East Lansing.

Munnich, E., Flynn, S., & Martohardjono, G. (1994). Elicited imitation and grammaticality judgment tasks: What they measure and how they relate to each other. In A. Cohen, S. Gass, & E. Tarone (Eds.), *Research methodology in second language acquisition* (pp. 227–244). Hillsdale, NJ: Erlbaum.

Newport, E. (1990). Maturational constraints on language learning. *Cognitive Science, 14,* 11–28.

Newport, E., & Johnson, J. (1991). Critical period effects on universal properties of language: The status of subjacency in the acquisition of a second language. *Cognition, 39,* 215–258.

Oyama, S. (1982). A sensitive period for the acquisition of a nonnative phonological system. In S. Krashen, R. Scarcella, & M. Long (Eds.), *Child-adult differences in second language acquisition* (pp. 20–38). Rowley, MA: Newbury House.

Patkowski, M. (1982). The sensitive period for the acquisition of syntax. In S. Krashen, R. Scarcella, & M. Long (Eds.), *Child-adult differences in second language acquisition* (pp. 52–64). Rowley, MA: Newbury House.

Radford, A. (1990). *Syntactic theory and the acquisition of English syntax.* Oxford: Basil Blackwell.

Ritchie, W. (1978). The right roof constraint in adult-acquired language. In W. Ritchie (Ed.), *Second language acquisition.* New York: Academic Press.

Rutherford, W. (1988). Grammatical theory and L2 acquisition: A brief overview. In S. Flynn & W. O'Neil (Eds.), *Linguistic theory in second language acquisition* (pp. 404–416). Dordrecht: Kluwer.

Schachter, J. (1989). Testing a proposed universal. In S. Gass & J. Schachter (Eds.), *Linguistic perspectives on second language acquisition.* Cambridge, UK: Cambridge University Press.

Schwartz, B. (1993). *Lexical and functional categories in L2a: A principled distinction for explaining "transfer"?* Paper presented at the Conference on Recent Advances in Generative Approaches to Second Language Acquisition, MIT, Cambridge, MA.

Schwartz, B., & Sprouse, R. (1991). *Word order and nominative case in nonnative language acquisition: A longitudinal study of (L1 Turkish) German interlanguage.* Paper presented at the first biannual Conference on Applied Linguistics at Michigan State, Michigan State University, Ann Arbor.

Sherman, J. C. (1983). *The acquisition of control in complement sentences: The role of structural and lexical factors.* Doctoral dissertation, Cornell University, Ithaca, NY.

Sherman, J. C., & Lust, B. (1993). Children are in control. *Cognition, 46,* 1–51.

Slobin, D. (1973). Cognitive prerequisites for the development of grammar. In C. Ferguson & D. Slobin (Eds.), *Studies of child language development* (pp. 175–209). New York: Holt, Rinehart & Winston.

Strozer, J. (1991). Non-native language acquisition from a principles and parameters perspective. In H. Campos & F. Martinez (Eds.), *Current studies in Spanish linguistics.* Washington, DC: Georgetown University Press.

Tarone, E., Gass, S., & Cohen, A. (Eds.), (1994). *Research methodology in second language acquisition.* Hillsdale, NJ: Erlbaum.

Tavakolian, S. (1978). Children's comprehension of pronominal subjects and missing subjects in complicated sentences. In H. Goodluck & L. Solan, (Eds.), *Papers in the structure and development of child language: Occasional papers in linguistics,* (Vol. 4, pp. 145–152). Amherst: University of Massachusetts.

Thomas, M. (1991). *Universal Grammar and knowledge of reflexives in a second language.* Doctoral dissertation, Harvard University, Cambridge, MA.

Towell, R., & Hawkins, R. (Eds.). (1994). *Approaches to second language acquisition.* Clevedon, UK: Multilingual Matters.

Uziel, S. (1991). *Resetting Universal Grammar parameters: Evidence from second language acquisition of subjacency and the empty category.* Master's thesis, MIT, Cambridge, MA.

Vainikka, A., & Young-Scholten, M. (1991). Verb raising in second language acquisition: The early stages. *Theories des Lexikons, 4,* 1–48.

Vainikka, A., & Young-Scholten, M. (1992). *The development of functional projections in L2 syntax.* Paper presented at the annual winter meeting of the Linguistic Society of America, Philadelphia.

Vainikka, A., & Young-Scholten, M. (1993). *X′-theory in L2 acquisition.* Paper presented at the conference on Recent Advances in Generative Approaches to Second Language Acquisition, MIT, Cambridge, MA.

White, L. (1989). *Universal Grammar and second language acquisition.* Amsterdam: John Benjamins.

White, L. (1993). *UG effects in foreign language learners.* Paper presented at the Conference on Recent Advances in Generative Approaches to Second Language Acquisition, MIT, Cambridge, MA.

White, L., & Juffs, A. (1992). Subjacency violations and empty categories in L2 acquisition. In H. Goodluck & M. Rochement (Eds.), *Island constraints* (pp. 445–464). Dordrecht: Kluwer.

Zobl, H. (1983). Contact induced language change, learner language and the potentials of a modified contrastive analysis. In M. Bailey, M. Long, & S. Beck (Eds.), *Second language acquisition studies* (pp. 104–114). Rowley, MA: Newbury House.

CHAPTER 5

MATURATION AND THE ISSUE OF UNIVERSAL GRAMMAR IN SECOND LANGUAGE ACQUISITION

Jacquelyn Schachter

I. BACKGROUND

Let us begin with some well-known facts about child first language (L1) and adult second language (L2) acquisition, facts that theories of L1 and L2 must capture in order to be considered adequate. In general terms, what has to be explained in L1 acquisition is as follows: that all normal children manage to attain perfect knowledge of the language of the community in which they live, becoming linguistically indistinguishable from other members of the community in which they receive linguistic exposure, without training or negative data, and in spite of the fact that the knowledge they attain is underdetermined by the input to which they are exposed. Thus, even though the child's input is finite, degenerate, and noninformative in crucial respects, the child manages to arrive at full knowledge of the grammar of the language of the community in which she lives. Child L1 acquirers are, furthermore, equipotential for any natural language whatsoever; no matter what linguistic community the child is placed in, the child will acquire the language of that community and will take no lesser or longer time to do so for one language than for another. This is an unparalleled feat, and it imposes heavy requirements on a theory of child L1 acquisition that purports to be explanatorily adequate. Such a theory must provide a clear account of how a child constructs a grammar in spite of the gap between the information provided by the child's input and the full knowledge of the language the child eventually ends up with.

On the surface, it would appear that the task of the adult L2 learner is much

Handbook of Second Language Acquisition

simpler. The adult, after all, has been through the language learning experience once, already knows one language perfectly, and is cognitively mature. Nevertheless, the facts of adult L2 acquisition are not anywhere near as impressive as those of child L1 acquisition. It is true that many adults learn to communicate effectively using an L2, and some few appear to have extensive if not perfect knowledge of the grammar of the L2. Nevertheless, the overwhelming majority are not able to achieve anything like the same level of mastery as that achieved by every normal child.

There are at least four major differences between the child L1 and the adult L2 cases, each one reflecting on or highlighting the lesser achievements of adult language learners (cf. Bley-Vroman, 1989; Schachter, 1990).

The most obvious difference is that few (and possibly no) adults reach the level of tacit or unconscious knowledge of the grammar of the L2 (L2 competence) that would place them on a par with native speakers (NSs) of the L2 (cf. Schachter, 1990; Seliger, 1978); the ultimate attainment of most, if not all, adult L2 learners is a state of incompleteness with regard to the grammar of the L2. One needs to distinguish, of course, between grammatical competence (i.e., the state of subconsciously knowing the rules or representations that form the syntactic, phonological, and semantic patterns of the language) and communicative capability (i.e., the ability to communicate one's needs, desires, opinions, attitudes, and to understand those of others). Many adults become communicatively proficient in the L2 in spite of obviously defective grammatical knowledge. Many others remain frozen in a pidgin form of the target (or interlanguage, IL), barely able to communicate their most basic needs. In fact, I would venture to assert that if it were possible to quantify the L2 grammatical competence of all current L2 speakers who began L2 acquisition as adults, we would be looking at something very much resembling a bell-shaped curve, a very different picture from that of the results of child L1 learning.

The second striking difference is that adult L2 speakers typically produce a kind of variation not obviously attributable to the register variation one finds in the production of NSs. That is, long after cessation of change in the development of their L2 grammar, adults will variably produce errors and nonerrors in the same linguistic environments, a kind of variation originally called fossilization (Selinker, 1971). A perfectly fluent adult nonnative speaker (NNS) of English will produce "I see him yesterday," and shortly thereafter produce "I saw him yesterday," apparently on a random basis. This phenomenon, more properly labeled *fossilized variation,* is typically associated with morphemes that do not carry a heavy semantic load, yet it marks the adult L2 speech as distinctly nonnative and is a phenomenon not found in the speech of NSs.[1] Fossilized variation, which has

[1] This is not to say there is no variation in the speech of NS. Of course there is, and it is register and dialect bound. One might very well find a NS of English producing on one occasion "I seen him yesterday" and on another "I saw him yesterday," using each to mark appropriate registers for the social setting she finds herself in. Register differences are difficult to detect in NNSs, and fossilized variation appears to be random in nature, due possibly to the multiple processing pressures experienced by the individual L2 speech producer.

been little studied to date, may well be a processing phenomenon not directly attributable to differences in grammatical competence between NS and NNSs of a language. It is a striking difference nevertheless, and must be accounted for in the adult L2 case, if only to dispose of it as something not to be dealt with in a theory of L2 acquisition.

Nor is the adult L2 learner equipotential for language acquisition in the way the child L1 learner is. The adult's knowledge of a prior language either facilitates or inhibits acquisition of the L2, depending on the underlying similarities or dissimilarities of the languages in question. An adult speaker of English will require considerably less time and effort to achieve a given level of ability in German than in Japanese because the similarities between English and German, at all levels, are much greater than those between English and Japanese, and the adult's prior knowledge of English influences subsequent acquisition. This contributes to differences in completeness mentioned above. The closer two languages are in terms of syntax, phonology, and lexicon, the more likely it is that higher levels of completeness can be reached.

And finally, the adult learner's prior knowledge of one language has a strong effect, detectable in the adult's production of the L2, variously labeled transfer or crosslinguistic effects. A Spanish-speaking adult speaker of English is likely to produce "I can to go" because the word for *can* in Spanish is a main verb taking an infinitival complement. Although the Spanish speaker of English does not hear this form in the English input, she produces it on the basis of a misanalysis of English that is consistent with the Spanish model. The Farsi speaker of English is likely to produce a sentence of the type, "The water which I like to drink it comes from mountain springs" because in Farsi relative clauses epenthetic pronouns are standardly produced, whereas they are not in English. Other crosslinguisitic effects take place as well—as in underproduction and overproduction of various structures the learner avoids or favors (cf. Schachter, 1974; Schachter & Rutherford, 1978; Yip, 1989). (See chapter 10 by Gass, this volume, for a general discussion of L1 influence in L2 acquisition.)

These differences between child L1 and adult L2 language acquisition serve as background for the issues to be laid out below.

II. UNIVERSAL GRAMMAR AS A KNOWLEDGE BASE

The innately specified principles and parameters of Universal Grammar (UG) that are said to underlie the impressive linguistic achievements of child L1 acquirers are justified in the argumentation of L1 literature. It is hard to imagine any other way to achieve what the child standardly accomplishes, given the child's known input. The standard argumentation is as follows: Here is an abstract linguistic property (*P*) known to be a characteristic of a particular grammar (G).

Child L1 learners acquire *G,* including *P.* They could not have done so on the basis of the input they received because, without negative evidence (which children get little of and fail to attend to when offered it) they could not have incorporated *P* into *G* on the basis of input alone. (See Hornstein & Lightfoot, 1981, for several arguments of this form; see also Wanner & Gleitman, 1982.) Therefore *P* must be an innately specified property that the child already had available prior to experience. This is the proposed solution, within the principles and parameters framework, for explaining core aspects of L1 acquisition (cf. Chomsky, 1981b). And the proposed solution is convincing in many instances in the L1 literature. Because the child so clearly succeeds in spite of inadequate data, one feels compelled to accept the notion that the child can succeed because of the contribution that the child's innate knowledge, UG, makes to the child's analysis of the input and to constraints on types of knowledge representations that the child builds.

Some argue that the logical problem applies also in adult L2 acquisition (cf. White, 1985). But there is no comparable argument here. In the case of child L1 acquisition, because the child succeeds in spite of inadequate data, one feels compelled to accept the notion that the child can succeed because of the contribution UG makes to the analysis of the input and to constraints on types of knowledge representations that can be built up. There is no such compelling argument for the adult L2 learner. Granted there are the same deficiencies in the input as in the L1 case, but the adult L2 learner does not overcome them in the same way the child L1 learner does. And to the extent that she does, it can reasonably be argued that the learner's L1 knowledge, combined with knowledge gained from input, was the source, (unless it can be shown that she cannot have known it from either source.) (Chapters 2 by Gregg, 3 by White and 4 by Flynn, this volume, also include discussion of the question of a logical problem of L2 acquisition.)

Whether or not the same knowledge base, UG, can or should be said to serve as the basis for much less impressive and much more idiosyncratic achievements of adult L2 acquirers is highly questionable. The facts in the two language learning cases differ radically, and it is by no means clear that a theory (UG) developed to account for one set of facts (L1 acquisition) is the most obvious candidate theory to account for quite a different set of facts (adult L2 acquisition, in this case) (see Gregg, 1988, for further elucidation of this point).

Of course in some sense it would be simpler if it could be shown that UG serves as the basis for adult L2 acquisition as well as child L1 acquisition; a theory is strengthened if it can be shown to account for two disparate-seeming sets of facts. But this is only possible if the theory is explanatorily adequate for both sets of facts. Given the differences in the two cases outlined above, the proponent of the "UG-for-all" language learning position is in the difficult situation of trying to explain why UG does not produce the same results in the adult L2 case that it does in the child L1 case.

Because it does not, (at least) two options are open: (1) one can try to maintain the UG-for-all position and argue that differences come about as a result of procedural differences in adult and child language acquisition (and some attempts of this kind have been made; see Flynn & Martohardjono, 1992, or (2) one can reject the UG-for-all position and maintain that what remains as a knowledge base for adult L2 acquisition is simply the L1 grammar, not the L1 grammar plus UG.[2] (The range of alternative theoretical positions on the role of UG in L2 acquisition is also described in chapters 2 by Gregg, 3 by White, and 4 by Flynn, this volume.)

The purpose of this chapter is twofold. The first goal is to provide a variety of reasons why UG should not be viewed as the basis for adult L2 acquisition. It will be argued that what a mature speaker of an L1 has as a result of L1 learning is a grammar of L1 stripped of those aspects of UG not incorporated into the L1 grammar, and further, that the adult learner of an L2 does not have independent access to UG—hence that adult-formed L2 grammars are necessarily incomplete. Second, evidence is provided pointing to a maturational schedule for the development of certain principles and certain other properties of L1. Furthermore, this schedule results in sensitive periods before which *and after which* certain principles cannot be incorporated into a developing L1. If these principles and properties have not been incorporated into a learner's L1 during the sensitive period, they remain forever unavailable for incorporation into an adult learner's developing L2.

This chapter constitutes an attempt to demonstrate the viability of this position. First, I will argue that child L1 learners and adult L2 learners are so substantially different that adoption of a UG-oriented theory of child L1 acquisition to account for adult L2 acquisition is biologically, psychologically, and linguistically implausible. I will further argue that answers to many current questions in L2 acquisition research will be found in future study of middle and older child L2 acquirers, because it is from that population that answers to questions about the availability of UG in L2 acquisition will emerge. It is also from this population that the notion of multiple critical or sensitive periods for language acquisition can be developed.

III. BIOLOGY

The biological basis for the claim that UG remains available as the basis for the adult L2 acquisition case is tenuous at best. As Kean notes (1988, 1991), the brain of a child at the outset of language acquisition is distinct from the brain of that same individual when the language has been learned. Kean argues as follows:

> The brain of a child is not a miniature adult brain either in structure or function; brain systems underlying linguistic capacity and the functions [they] subserve[d]

---

[2] This is much too simple a characterization of the options. Felix (1981), for example, takes both options, maintaining a UG-for-all position while arguing that the higher cognitive processes of the adult "interfere" in some as yet unspecified way.

change through the course of development. In consequence, UG must be an emergent property of the nervous system. Under this interpretation, components of UG mature and become available to the child through the course of acquisition. The child engages with the experience provided by his/her linguistic environment under constraints imposed by the currently available functional capacity. (1988, p. 65)

We currently have insufficient data to demonstrate this on the basis of a detailed description of the biological and functional ontogeny of the language responsible areas of the neocortex, but there exist ample data from the development of other modular cognitive systems which provide the basis to argue that there are substantial changes in brain systems and their learning capacity in the course of development. (1991, p. 4)

An analogy from one of these other systems is instructive in exemplifying this issue. Hubel and Wiesel (1962, 1970), in their classic studies on the development of vision in cats, have demonstrated that the neurons of the visual cortex of cats have functional specificity (i.e., particular neurons are preset to respond to specific stimuli, e.g., a horizontal or a vertical line) during specific time periods. If kittens are placed in deprived optical environments (e.g., exposure to horizontal stripes only) during the period of the development of vision, those neurons that are present to respond to vertical lines become totally inert and the development of such specificity is interfered with. Only the class of neurons corresponding to the pattern of the rearing environment radically increases; all other optical neurons become inactive or degenerate. The development of vision in humans appears to exhibit much of the same specificity. Suppose individual parameter settings were associated with sets of specific neurons, a not unreasonable speculation given their claimed innate character; given the known behavior of neurons in the development of vision, one would then have good reason to expect that in the development of an L1 the neurons associated with a specific parameter setting would proliferate and that those neurons associated with a specific parameter setting not needed for the L1 would degenerate or become inert.

There are, of course, aspects of cognitive systems of humans and other mammals that show plasticity throughout life. In vision, for example, human subjects will adapt to the tilt induced by being required to wear prisms that shift the perceived image by 20 degress (cf. Kean, 1991). After a while, they will not notice the shift. As Kean points out, those maintaining that UG subserves adult L2 acquisition must maintain that language acquisition capability is like perceptual adaptation, plastic through life (1991, p. 7).

IV. A CRITICAL PERIOD FOR L1 ACQUISITION

The biological notions of maturation and plasticity lead directly to the thorny issue of a critical, or sensitive, period for language acquisition, for both L1 and

L2. Originally proposed by Lenneberg (1967) for L1 acquisition, the notion of a sensitive period has received considerable attention lately.[3] In Lenneberg's characterization of a critical period for language, consistent with much of the critical-period literature leading up to his proposal, the critical period was viewed as a set time frame, between ages 2–13, within which potential functional and biological linguistic development needed to be activated for normal development to occur. Otherwise the capacity for L1 learning was lost. Since then the strict boundaries have been softened both in the ethological and the psychological literature, and it is more consistent with what is known about innately determined behaviors to view them as do Oyama (1979) and Immelman and Suomi (1981), as periods of heightened sensitivity or responsiveness to specific types of environmental stimuli or input, bounded on both sides by states of lesser sensitivity. Gradual increases to such periods or declines from such periods are expected to occur, as well as variability from one individual to another.

Based on a close review of sensitive-period studies (the case of the isolated child Genie, cf. Curtiss, 1988), cases of feral children, deaf children of hearing adults with no American Sign Language (ASL), and children and adults starting to acquire ASL at different ages), Long (1990) concludes that they provide "compelling evidence of maturational constraints on first language learning. They suggest a sensitive period or periods of wide scope, affecting morphology and syntax, not just phonology" (1990, p. 259).

Focusing on the issue of modularity, Curtiss (1988), in a review of abnormal language acquisition studies (cases where learning takes place beyond the normal age range, cases where there is clear-cut damage to brain regions, and cases of language-impaired children with less clear-cut etiologies), points out that all such studies indicate that grammar acquisition involves faculty-specific mechanisms, maturationally constrained, and independent of the mechanisms governing the acquisition of pragmatic competence and lexical development. Curtiss points to an interesting group of studies looking at acquisition of ASL, all showing the same profile of impaired grammar acquisition, coupled with good vocabulary acquisition, coding of semantic relations, and discourse skills. Particularly compelling are reports of deficits in grammar acquisition in individuals who began acquisition in childhood but later than the most typically active years (cf. Newport, 1984; Woodward, 1973). As Long notes, these combine to show that when first exposure is late, ultimate attainment will be incomplete, and that not even lengthy exposure can compensate for this.

Lenneberg's proposed explanation for the critical period was that of hemispheric lateralization, which he said became complete about the age of puberty. It has since been argued that lateralization is in fact completed much earlier than puberty (Krashen, 1973), but the evidence is mixed. Satz, Bakker, Tenunissen,

---

[3] See Long (1990) for a comprehensive review and claims for multiple sensitive periods; see Flynn and Manuel (1991) for arguments against a critical period for speech and syntax.

Goebel, and Van der Vlugt (1975), in dichotic listening tests, found right ear superiority (indicating left-hemisphere dominance for language) becoming significant around 9;0, leveling off at 11;0. And as Krashen (1982) suggests, certain aspects of language may continue to undergo lateralization until puberty. Clearly, lateralization as a putative cause for the critical period needs further study.

Long (1990) reports some evidence suggestive of progressive myelination associated with the critical or sensitive period, although he is quick to point out that purported neurophysiological explanations of maturational constraints (such as lateralization and myelination) are not true explanations until it can be shown what their cognitive consequences are, and we are far from able to demonstrate such a cause-and-effect relationship between any neurophysiological process and sensitive periods for language.[4]

Furthermore, within the child L1 literature, there is considerable evidence that multiple critical periods exist (i.e., different critical periods for different components of language). Seliger (1978), who argues for multiple critical periods, describes interesting aphasia cases in which the aphasia type differs according to age group even though the lesion producing the aphasia is in the same area of the brain. For example, the same lesion in Wernicke's area produced motor aphasia in a child, conduction aphasia in youth or middle age, and jargon aphasia in later life. Seliger concludes, on the basis of various studies of age-dependent aphasia that

> there is a continuous long-term process of interhemispheric and intrahemispheric localization of function. . . . Since different aspects of language are affected at different stages in this process, it is hypothesized that there are multiple critical periods which correlate with localization and the gradual loss of plasticity. (1978, p. 18)

Long (1990) claims that the period for phonology begins to decline around age 6, and that the period for morphology and syntax lasts much longer, declining around age 15.

V. A CRITICAL PERIOD FOR L2 ACQUISITION

Against this background, one may now ask whether a critical period for L1 acquisition is synonymous with a critical period for language acquisition in general. Are human language learners like adolescent white-crowned sparrows? If after acquiring the adult song of one white-crowned dialect, they are subsequently

---

[4] Affective, input, and cognitive variables have also been proposed as causes of critical periods for language acquisition (see Felix, 1981, and Krashen, 1982, for cognitive, Brown, 1979, and Schumann, 1975, for affective and Hatch, 1977, for input variable proposals).

exposed to a second dialect, they learn some aspects of a new dialect, but not all of the grace notes and trills.[5] In fact this avian analogy seems quite apt for the adult immigrant who learns to communicate effectively in the new language but who never, even after many years, becomes nativelike in phonology, morphology, and syntax. This is a seductive analogy, but it skirts the more interesting questions that can be asked in the case of human language acquisition. What about the basic constraints on the form that rules can take—the principles underlying language? What about the parameterized possibilities for language variation *not* instantiated in the L1? Are these still available to the adult language learner subsequent to the close of the critical period for L1 acquisition?

Some have argued (cf. Flynn & Manuel, 1991; White, 1989b) that once the language learning mechanisms are actuated during the sensitive period for L1 acquisition, the innate knowledge that UG represents is available for the development of an L2 throughout the remainder of the life of an individual (perhaps akin to the perceptual plasticity that allows visual adaptation described above). Other reasons, it is argued, can be adduced to account for the lack of completion characteristic of those who have learned the L2 as adults. White points out that the adult L2 learner is faced with the same problem as the child L1 learner: The input the learner is exposed to is finite, degenerate, and underdeterminate. She argues that if adult L2 grammars are natural languages, as many have claimed, it would seem reasonable to assume that this is so because UG is still available. Felix (1985) further points out that some studies have shown similar orders of acquisition of structures (and morphemes) in the course of both child L1 and adult L2 acquisition (cf. Bailey, Madden, & Krashen, 1974; Clahsen, Meisel, & Pienemann, 1983; Felix, 1981; Schumann, 1979) and asserts that these orders of acquisition, together with White's arguments on the paucity of the data available to the learner, suggest that there is good reason to expect that UG may continue to operate even after puberty.

An alternative position is that although UG may very well guide language acquisition by the child during (a) critical, or sensitive, period(s), it is not available for adult language acquisition. Bley-Vroman (1989) and Schachter (1989, 1990) both claim that the differences between L1 and L2 achievements disprove the notion that UG in its original form is available to postpuberty language learners; if UG were available, adult L2 learners would be more proficient, and their outcomes would be uniform. It makes sense, they argue, to reason that the similarities between the grammars of child L1 learners and adult L2 learners must be due to the fact that human languages are more similar than they are different and that adults have already learned one language: They know what a language should look like, and their L1 grammars have many UG characteristics incorporated into them. Clahsen and Muysken (1986, 1989) present evidence from child L1 and

---

[5] The details of these studies can be found in Marler (1970).

adult L2 acquisition of German verb placement, verb inflection, and verb negation showing that adults and children do *not* operate in the same way in the acquisition of these structures, so that even the argument that acquisition orders of the two populations is the same is suspect.[6] The proponents of "UG for adult L2" have an uphill battle. The problem is that the differences in outcome between the child L1 and adult L2 cases are strong and unambiguous. As described earlier, L2 speakers exhibit several major characteristics that differentiate them from child L1 learners: their grammars are typically incomplete, their phonological production is almost always nonnative, they exhibit in production random error variation (fossilization), and they exhibit L1 characteristics in their L2 (transfer). Furthermore, an adult, with full knowledge of one language, will not be equipotential for L2 learning. An adult English speaker will be considerably more successful with German than with Hausa, for example.

It can be argued, and perhaps rightly, that only the first two characteristics are problems for the proponents of UG for adult L2 acquisition. The random error variation, although definitely a phenomenon to be explained, might occur only in areas of linguistic periphery not core, because, although little studied, the phenomenon looks very surfacelike. It could also be argued that some, if not all, cross-language effects and the lack of equipotentiality are due to the effects of prior knowledge rather than to the unavailability of UG. With the lack of equipotentiality issue, one could argue that what makes one L2 more difficult to learn that another is not the absence of UG but, rather, the larger number of parameters that must be reset in acquiring the one L2 as compared with acquiring the other L2. There are surely fewer parametric differences between Spanish and Italian, for example, than between Spanish, and Korean.[7]

More challenging differences are the adult's nonnative phonological production of the L2 and the incompleteness of the adult's L2 grammar—the broken English of many an adult immigrant in the United States provides eloquent testimony to the difficulty of mastering an L2 as an adult.

Using the UG framework, one can characterize the notion of incompleteness somewhat more precisely than heretofore. The principles of UG, being constraints on the forms that rules and representations may take, are said to be universal, not needing interaction with input in order to be triggered—they simply exist as part of the knowledge of prelearners, learners, and postlearners. The settings of parameters, on the other hand, must be triggered by input; at some point in the process the learner needs to pay attention to whether or not, for a specific parameter, the setting she has chosen fits with the incoming data. If so, that setting is incor-

---

[6] See Clahsen and Muysken (1989) for further discussion as well as their refutations of various attempts to reanalyze their data.

[7] But note that children too must reset parameters in every case in which they have adopted the wrong setting as the initial setting. Yet their overall learning time remains roughly the same across languages.

porated into the grammar, and the learner can move on; if not, the learner must then test another setting, and so on, until she finds one that is consistent with the data she is exposed to. So, progressively, a grammar is built, as the various parameter settings become incorporated into it.

There is, however, a big unanswered question in this characterization of the development of the grammar: What is the final knowledge of the learner? Under one view, the answer is that the final knowledge is simply the grammar of the language to which the L1 learner has been exposed, with all other possibilities stripped away. Bley-Vroman's (1989) example is as follows: Suppose some parameter, say head-direction, is to be set by experience. We can say that a grammar-specific set of rules may be developed by the individual in which the head-direction parameter setting chosen by the individual is head initial, consistent with the input. In that grammar, there is now nothing to indicate that there could have been a different head-direction parameter setting chosen, say head final, and no information about the consequences of the original choice, had it been otherwise. Given this characterization of parameter setting, the resultant grammar may not be a general schema plus information about how the parameters have been set for a particular language but rather, and more simply, a specific set of parameter settings as instantiated in a particular set of rules or representations. This view of the results of L1 acquisition fit well with Kean's biological perspective on maturation.

Not as obvious but equally pressing is a question regarding the principles of UG that has not had as much discussion as that of the setting of parameters, and that is the question of whether the principles themselves, or any subset of them, require input data in order to become incorporated into the emerging grammar of the child.[8] Otsu (1981) and Huang (1982) are exceptions. Otsu is particularly interested in the question of the course of development of a given principle of UG. And he points out that there is a class of principles whose function is dependent on other properties, innate or noninnate. Subjacency is one such principle, being one which, in standard formulations, constrains extraction rules at the level of S-structure. It is dependent upon extraction phenomena such as wh-movement, topicalization, and so forth, which exhibit dependency relations between the extracted element and its trace. If the learner has not mastered structures that exhibit such relations, Subjacency will have nothing to constrain. Otsu claims in the case he is considering (English) that "as soon as a child masters a structure that is relevant to the application of a linguistic universal, he honors that universal with

---

[8] Lust, Chien, and Flynn (1987) can be interpreted as claiming that both principles and parameters are set by experience. They note that "a finite class of core grammars may be made available by setting the principles and parameters of UG" (p. 278). They state, "We may hypothesize, in keeping with this theory, that certain grammatically determined sensitivities, principles and parameters, provide the basis for adult competence for language, and that these sensitivities are to certain dimensions of language data" (p. 279).

respect to this structure" (1981, p. 10). In other words, Subjacency does not have anything to constrain, so to speak, until some other property is mastered.

That "other property" now becomes crucial. If a language does not allow such extraction phenomena, such as a language like Korean, what is one to say about the course of development of the principle of Subjacency, and further, about the existence of the principle in the adult grammar of the language? One could argue that because the core grammar of a language *is* the set of parameters all set in some way or other, the child learner of a language like Korean is in exactly the same position as the child learner of a language like English, in which the default setting holds. Thus, just as the child learning English maintains the default setting for the S/S' parameter[9] associated with Subjacency (hearing no evidence that would lead to the rejection of that setting) so also does the child learning Korean, who also hears no evidence leading to rejection of the default setting, although for a quite different reason. Under this view, the grammars of English and Korean will be alike with regard to Subjacency, both being set for the S parameter. The adult L2 language learning consequence of this view is that the Korean learner of L2 English will have the principle available as a knowledge source for the acquisition of the L2, at the very least indirectly through the L1 grammar.

Another approach to the question, in fact, the one I wish to advocate, is to extend Otsu's notion of the dependent emergence of certain principles one step further, and to argue as follows. Certain principles of UG are triggered in L1 acquisition only if certain properties are found in the input to the child. If, in the course of development, such properties are not found in the input and incorporated into the grammar, the principles dependent on them do not subsequently form part of the adult grammars of speakers of these languages. Although they may have been available at the maturationally appropriate time, during the process of development they were not triggered and thus are not incorporated into the subsequent grammar. Subjacency is one such principle; it is triggered only if the input data provide the child with evidence that there is overt extraction in the language; if Subjacency is not triggered in this way in the course of L1 acquisition, then the principle will never be called forth and the subsequent adult grammar of the language will not contain that principle. The L2 language learning consequence of this view is that the NS of a nonextraction language will end up with no clue at all as to the existence of the principle and will not have it available as a knowledge source to constrain the acquisition of an L2 as an adult.

Given this latter approach, which might appropriately be labeled the Incompleteness Hypothesis, one could envision the possibility that there might be two answers to the original question: is UG available in mature NSs of a language?

[9]The S/S' or Bounding-Node Parameter enumerates the sets of bounding-node combinations, {NP, S, S'}, {NP, S}, {NP, S'}. Each language will be represented by one of these sets. Subjacency applies to the set of bounding nodes for a given language. English, for example, has NP and S as bounding nodes, not S'; Italian, on the other hand, has NP and S' as bounding nodes, not S (cf. Atkinson, 1992).

Assume that principle P was not logically dependent on any other property of the language, that the child was exposed to the relevant parameter-setting data regarding P at the maturationally appropriate time, and that the emerging grammar changed or developed with regard to P; it would then seem reasonable to believe that P is instantiated (in the form of an appropriate parameter setting or set of phrase structure rules, etc.) in the adult NS's language, that it must constitute part of the knowledge state of that adult speaker in order to prevent him or her from violating UG in production or in grammaticality judgments. But now assume that the child, at the maturationally appropriate time, had not incorporated into the emerging grammar the property or rule relevant for setting the parameter (or parameters) associated with P. In this case it would seem that the possibility of that principle's constituting an integral part of the knowledge of a learner at a later stage no longer exists.

These two views on the development of the innate principles and parameters of UG in L1 acquisition lead to different predictions about the form of the resultant L1 grammar. But more important for the question at hand, they also lead to different claims about the availability of UG to adult L2 language learners.

If all the principles and all parameter settings are fixed and constant over time, then they will at all times constitute part of the knowledge state of the human being, and it would seem reasonable to assume them to be available for the acquisition of an L2, whenever the acquisition process takes place, as White (1988a) and Felix (1985) have argued. If, on the other hand, some principles and parameters settings require certain types of input in order for them to be incorporated into the L1, and that input is not available at the maturationally appropriate time, then all that remains as part of the knowledge state of an adult NS of a language is a language-specific instantiation of UG that does not incorporate the aforesaid principles and parameter settings. UG as the initial state will not be available as a knowledge source for the adult acquisition of an L2. Only a language-specific instantiation of it will be. And only this language-specific instantiation of UG will be available to the learner as an internal knowledge source to guide the acquisition of the L2. Because some innate principles are instantiated in all native languages (NLs) (cf. the principle of structure dependence), this internal knowledge source will be sufficient, together with the input, to constrain much of the form of the core grammar of the L2. If, however, it turns out that in the acquisition of the target language (TL) some data associated with the triggering of principle P is necessary, and P is not incorporated into the learner's L1 (as appears to be the case with Subjacency in Korean), the learner will have neither language-internal knowledge nor initial-state knowledge to guide her in the development of P. Therefore, completeness with regard to the acquisition of the TL will not be possible. The same holds for parameter settings not instantiated in the L1.

What I should like to propose is that the Incompleteness Hypothesis is the correct hypothesis. It is consistent with the linguistic facts as we know them; it serves as a partial explanation for the lack of completeness so often found in the adult L2 case; and as the studies below demonstrate, it predicts a phenomenon that makes clear the nonequivalence of adult L1 and adult L2 underlying grammars of the same language. Therefore, and because of the Incompleteness Hypothesis, I claim (with Bley-Vroman, 1989) that what a monolingual individual retains of the principles and parameters of UG are only those principles and parameters instantiated in the individual's L1. Access to those principles that define possible rule systems will no longer be available after the core grammar of the L1 has formed, nor will those principles and parameters not triggered by input in the formation of the L1 grammar.[10] This predicts, then, that in adult L2 acquisition, the only internal knowledge source the learner will have available initially is the knowledge of the L1. This knowledge, together with the information derived from the input, constitute the database from which the learner constructs the grammar of the L2.

In the syntactic component of the grammar, two studies are of interest with regard to the incompleteness hypothesis, in that they probe certain aspects of L2 knowledge of adults that would be considered core by most definitions of that concept. Coppieters (1987) collected grammaticality judgments and semantic perceptions of 21 very proficient NNSs of French, comparing them with judgments of 20 NSs on the same items. Some of these items involved subtle semantic distinctions (such as the appropriate use of *il* and *elle* versus *ce*, the distinction between *imparfait* and *passé composé,* the distinction in meaning between pre- and postnominal adjectives; certain others involved straight grammaticality judgments on purely formal aspects of French syntax. One of these was the A-over-A constraint, prohibiting the extraction of a phrase of category A from within a larger phrase of the same category; the other involved the use of clitic pronouns and the causative construction. Coppieters found that the NNSs, six of whom were judged by NSs to be nativelike in their French production, still failed to conform to NS norms by a significant margin. The best NNSs on the grammaticality judgments still scored about three standard deviations below the NS norm. Particularly interesting for issues raised here are the judgments on the A-over-A constraint exhibited in (1a) and (1b) and on the clitic pronoun plus causative construction in (2a) and (2b).

(1)   a. *Elle en aime l'auteur* [*en = de ce livre*].
         'She likes its author.'
      b. **Elle en telephone à l'auteur.*
         'She calls up its author.'

---

[10] This of course leaves much additional language-specific knowledge available to the adult, knowledge that must have been learned from exposure to the input and that may either aid or hinder the adult in the acquisition of the target as well. The adult will, for example, have a fully formed lexicon, each item having its own subcategorization restrictions and referential range, and the adult will have a language-specific set of morphological categories that could in some cases help and in other cases hinder the acquisition of the TL.

(2) a. *On leur a tout laissé manger.*
        'We let them eat it all.'
    b. **On les a tout laissé manger.*
        'We let them eat it all.'

In pairs like (1a) and (1b), NNSs and NSs did not diverge significantly, A-over-A being a principle that is presumably instantiated in all L1 grammars. On (2a) and (2b), as Coppieters points out, whereas NSs consistently accepted (2a) and rejected (2b), only six of the 21 NNSs were able to do so (and so on with other sentence pairs of this type.)

Birdsong's (1991) replication of the Coppieters study found less dramatic results, including some individuals who were well within the NS range, but his major conclusion is the same: In terms of cumulative deviance from NS norms his L1 English speakers of L2 French as a group differ significantly from his French NSs. He also found correlational evidence favoring age of arrival in France as the best predictor of cumulative deviance. The fact that a few speakers fall within the NS range is not surprising. It is what one would expect of a normal distribution of NNSs of French, and his subjects were chosen precisely because they were highly proficient in French.

In the phonological component of the grammar, the generalization holds quite clearly that incompleteness is true of adult language learning.[11] Oyama (1979) and Patkowski (1990) have shown for studies of accentedness that the younger child is when exposed to an L2, the more likely the child is to be able to pass as an NS. Scovel (1981) shows that child perceptions of accentedness reached near-perfect classification (95% correct) by age 9 or 10, whereas even advanced adult NNSs only reached 77% accuracy; this recognition data supplements and supports the production data of others.

Many studies of child L1 acquisition have noted that intonational contours appear well before phonemic contrasts (Leopold, 1953; Peters, 1974). Ioup and Tansomboom (1987) and Li and Thompson (1978) show that the same is true for tone. Ioup and Tansomboom further point out that although children learn tone first, before segmental contrasts and before grammar, adults with nontone L1s struggle with L2 tone for long periods after they become communicatively fluent, never reaching native proficiency levels.[12]

---

[11] See Martohardjono and Flynn (1992) for some arguments to the contrary, one of which involves their distinction between competence ("initial state, what speakers start out with") and ultimate attainment ("steady state, what people end up with") and their claim that phonological competence is still available to adults (i.e., that the phonological initial state for child L1 learners is also the initial state for adult L2 learners).

[12] They further suggest that this, in general, is due to the adult preference for left-hemispheric processing of all linguistic data, whereas tone may well need to be processed initially as part of the prosodic system normally processed by the right hemisphere. In any case, it appears clear that adult learners of tone languages (whose L1s are not tone languages) are beyond the bounds of the critical period for tone and will not ever incorporate it sufficiently to become nativelike.

VI. TESTS OF A PRINCIPLE AND A PARAMETER IN ADULT L2

At this point one must choose a principle and a parameter and see what the L2 studies reveal about their acquisition. Obvious candidates are the Subjacency Principle, a universal constraint on movement, and the Governing Category Parameter (GCP), the selection of possible governors for reflexives in languages around the world. Both have been the subject of recent studies and have been extensively reported on, and both demonstrate the kinds of difficulties one runs into in trying to unravel dense issues such as these.

In her 1990 study, Schachter looked for evidence for the Subjacency Principle in the grammaticality judgments of proficient English-speaking adults whose L1s were either Dutch, Chinese, Indonesian, or Korean, as compared with those of NSs of English. Subjacency was chosen because although it is said to be a universal and innate principle of UG (van Riemsdijk & Williams, 1986), its effects vary from language to language depending on the kinds of movement the language allows. Thus it is one of those principles logically dependent upon other properties in a language.

Subjacency has been formulated as a constraint on movement rules at the level of S-structure.[13] The principle itself is that no application of a movement rule can cross more than a single barrier, barriers for English being noun phrase (NP) and S. (Chapters 3 by White, 4 by Flynn, and 10 by Gass, this volume, also include discussions of conditions on movement rules, including the Subjacency Condition.) This allows one to account for the differences in grammaticality between the sentences in (3), (4), and (5a) on the one hand and (5b) on the other, as well as in many other cases.

(3)   What does the professor expect us to know for the exam?
(4)   Who did the President say he planned to appoint as ambassador?
(5)   a. What did Susan destroy?
          What [$_s$ did Susan destroy t]
       b. *What did Susan destroy a book about?
          *What [$_s$ did Susan destroy [$_{NP}$ a book about t]

Examples (3) and (4) demonstrate that wh-words can be extracted from embedded clauses and moved to the front of the sentence in English. Example (5a) demonstrates that it can be moved from a main clause object position as well. In (5b), however, the wh-extraction has created an ungrammatical sentence. Why should this be the case? The contrast in grammaticality between (5a) and (5b) demonstrate the effect of the Subjacency Principle on extraction. In (5a), the *wh*-word must cross only one barrier (S) in order get into complementizer (COMP), but in (5b), it must cross two (NP, S) and is thus ungrammatical.

---

[13]It can also be viewed as a constraint on representations, but this makes no difference to the argumentation in this chapter.

The L1 languages Dutch, Indonesian, Chinese, Korean, were chosen because they vary in the extent to which they allow the kinds of movement to which Subjacency is said to apply. Only in Dutch is Subjacency instantiated as it is in English; Chinese and Indonesian show considerably more limited Subjacency effects, and, crucially, Korean shows no Subjacency effects at all, at the level of surface structure.

The test involved judgments of well-formedness on sentences of the types illustrated below.

(6)   a. The theory we discussed yesterday will be on the exam.
       b. *What did Susan visit the store that had in stock?

(7)   a. The judge rejected the evidence that the student committed the crime.
       b. *What did they have to accept the idea that they couldn't operate by themselves?

(8)   a. The dorm manager asked me who I wanted to have as a roommate.
       b. *Who did the Senator ask the President where he would send?

(9)   a. That oil prices will rise again this year is nearly certain.[14]
       b. *Which party did that Sam joined shock his parents?

It also included a set of nine sentences (involving one-clause, two-clause, and three-clause movement) with grammatical wh-extraction to check if the groups had knowledge of wh-extraction, such as the following:

(10) What does the professor expect us to know for the exam? (wh = object in S2)

(11) Who did Bill say liked Mary? (wh = subject in S2)

The Dutch subjects performed as the English NSs controls on differentiating the grammatical sentences and the ungrammatical Subjacency violations. The Chinese and Indonesian accepted the grammatical sentences as grammatical but showed only partial ability to reject the ungrammaticals as ungrammatical. Crucially, the Korean subjects, while accepting the grammatical sentences as grammatical, performed randomly on the ungrammaticals. This NL effect was shown, furthermore, not to be due to attribute variables such as age of first exposure to English, number of months in an English-speaking country, number of years of English study, and so forth.

Remember that the claim here is that the principle of Subjacency is incorporated into the L1 grammar of the Dutch subjects but is not incorporated into the L1 grammar of the Korean subjects. If a principle is incorporated into the L1 grammar and also into the L2 grammar of individuals, then when those individuals behave in conformance with that principle in the L2, their behavior cannot be used

---

[14] It has been noted that sentences with sentential subjects (as in [9a] and [9b] are not good detectors of Subjacency violations because the ungrammaticality of (9b) arises from two sources, violation of Subjacency and violation of the Empty Category Principle (ECP). The objection is well taken.

as evidence to decide between a claim that UG operates in L2 acquisition and a claim that it does not. For the Dutch subjects, for example, there is no principled basis for deciding that their correct rejection of English Subjacency violations was either due to their having had access to UG or to their using their L1 knowledge as a base. It is only when a principle is not incorporated into the L1 grammar that we have a useful test case to differentiate between the two claims: If the individuals behave as do native speakers of the L2, then they must have had access to UG (because this is not the kind of knowledge one could have extracted from the input). If they behave randomly, as the Korean group did in this case, then they cannot have had access to UG because their grammars are not constrained by this principle. This is why the outcome in this experiment is so important. The Korean group behaved randomly; they did not have their L1 to fall back on. We concluded that they did not have access to UG, exactly as is predicted by those who argue UG is not available as a knowledge base for adult language acquisition as an adult language learner.

Bley-Vroman, Felix, and Ioup (1988) looked as well at the operation of Subjacency (and the ECP) in adult Korean-speaking learners of English. Their subjects were also at an advanced level of proficiency and lived in the United States at the time of testing. Their task was also a written grammaticality judgment task, involving grammatical and ungrammatical wh-questions in a number of different structure types. Their findings are not consistent with mine in that they did quite well at rejecting English sentences involving Subjacency effects and quite poorly at accepting grammatical English sentences involving a variety of wh-movement possibilities. There were methodological problems involved (i.e., for the structures tested, some had three and many had only one or two exemplars, so that it is questionable whether the results can be generalized); but the conceptual problems outweigh them. For the most part, it appeared that there was little structural relationship between grammatical and ungrammatical sentences beyond the fact that all involved wh-words. With the grammatical sentences, the authors wanted to know if the subjects knew that a wide variety of wh-movement possibilities existed in English (including preposition-stranding of two types, *who* instead of *whom* as moved objects, and two cases that the authors called "factives"). With the ungrammatical sentences the authors wanted to know whether innate constraints on wh-movement applied (i.e., that wh-movement out of certain constructions was impossible). Other Subjacency studies (cf. Johnson & Newport, 1991; Otsu, 1981; Schachter, 1990) were constructed on the assumption that it was independently necessary to know if the subjects had knowledge of (1) the structures to which Subjacency applied and (2) wh-movement itself before one could interpret their Subjacency data correctly. Otherwise, the subjects' performance on Subjacency might be confounded by problems not related to Subjacency. If a set of subjects does not recognize containing relative clauses as grammatical, how is one to know that their rejection of wh-movement out of such clauses is a result of

Subjacency rather than a rejection of complexity? The Bley-Vroman et al. study prevents one from disentangling these possibilities.

Johnson and Newport (1991) focused on the role of Subjacency in proficient Chinese English speakers. Their subjects had resided in the United States for a minimum of 5 years and had substantial day-to-day exposure to English. The task was an oral, not written, grammaticality judgment task, which included grammatical declaratives with the relevant structures in them, Subjacency violations corresponding to them, and grammatical wh-questions. Their results show that the Chinese subjects performed significantly below native controls, though above chance, on Subjacency violations, a finding consistent with the finding of Schachter (1990) on Chinese subjects, also above chance and significantly below native controls. This difference between Korean and Chinese subjects cannot be precisely pinpointed but can be accounted for in a general way by the fact that although the Chinese subjects do not have wh-movement in their L1, they do have various other Subjacency effects, so that Subjacency is not totally foreign to them; the Korean subjects, in contrast, had no such subjacency effects in their L1 on which to fall back.

White and Juffs (1993) looked at Subjacency effects on (a) 16 EFL Chinese residents of Hunan and (b) 16 ESL Chinese immigrants in Canada. There were 60 wh-questions: 30 grammatical extractions and 30 ungrammatical violations. As in the Bley-Vroman et al. study, there was no test for knowledge of constructions out of which extraction is impossible. The subjects in Canada performed significantly worse than native controls on four of the six grammatical constructions (with an adjustment on one to separate out subject and object extraction), and on four of the five ungrammatical constructions. Inexplicably, the Hunan subjects did better. The same objections are applicable in this case as in the Bley-Vroman et al. case. Without clear separation of knowledge of wh-movement and of the constructions out of which the wh-word is extracted, it is impossible to tell what the subjects are responding to. Not having access to UG has to mean there was a critical period for Subjacency, which is now in the past.

An alternative approach to accounting for the Subjacency data is to argue that the L1 of the subjects in fact does not allow wh-movement and traces but rather allows base-generated sentence-initial wh-questions. This is what Martohardjono and Gair (1993) have argued is the case for Schachter's Indonesian subjects. Under this analysis, the failure of the Indonesian subjects to perform as NS of English on Subjacency violations does not constitute a violation of UG in the form of lack of knowledge of Subjacency but rather a kind of interference from the surface structure of the NL to the TL. To know that Subjacency violations are movement violations one must know (at one level or another) that movement is involved. This is a possibility that must be pursued for the Indonesian group (although this analysis is disputed by Muller-Gotama (1988)), but it in no way vitiates the findings for the other groups.

On the question of the ability to reset parameters, Lee (1992) carried out an experiment in which groups of L1 Korean speakers of L2 English were tested on their ability to reset the GCP to the English value. Korean speakers of English were chosen because of the contrast in parameter settings between Korean and English with regard to the GCP.[15] The English parameter setting (essentially the clause in which a reflexive occurs) constitutes a subset of the Korean setting such that in the sentences below, the English reflexive must refer to the subject within its own clause; in Korean, in contrast, the reflexive may refer to that NP but may also refer to the subject NP in the matrix clause.

(12)   a. Mary$_i$-nun   [John$_j$-i   caki$_{i/j}$ -lul kwasinha - n - ta
            Top   sub   self   Acc overtrust Pre Dec
            ko   maiha - ass - ta
            comp say past Dec
       b. Mary$_i$ said that John$_j$ overtrusted himself$_j$/herself$_i$.

Thus in (12b), the Korean equivalent of (12a), caki ('herself' / 'himself') may refer either to Mary or to John.

Lee administered grammaticality judgment and multiple-choice comprehension tasks to adult Korean speakers of English who varied in their age of arrival to the United States: Early Bilinguals (EB) who arrived before the age of 6, Late Bilinguals (LB) who arrived between 13 and 15, and Adults who arrived after age 20. Lee determined that the NS control group and the EBs performed similarly on detecting grammatical and ungrammatical sentences in a grammaticality judgment task involving sentences such as those in (13) below:

(13)   a. John remembered that Mary helped herself.
       b. *John remembered that Mary helped himself.

They did well on both. LBs performed well on grammatical and poorly on ungrammatical sentences. Adults, while performing more poorly on grammatical sentences than any other groups, sank precipitously on ungrammatical sentences, performing randomly on them.

Similar groupings occurred in the multiple-choice comprehension task, involving subjects answering questions such as (14):

(14)   Mary remembered that Alice had helped *herself.*
       a. Mary   b. Alice   c. either   d. neither

NSs and EBs patterned together and differently than Adults, with LBs in between. (See Figure 1). For the GCP, we have a clear indication from this experiment that

[15] The GCP (Wexler & Manzini, 1987) was proposed to capture the commonalities and variations in the binding of anaphors (including reflexives and pronouns) from language to language. Five values are specified as follows: subject, inflection (INFL), TNS, indicative TNS, root TNS. English *herself* takes subject as a governing category; Korean *caki* takes root TNS.

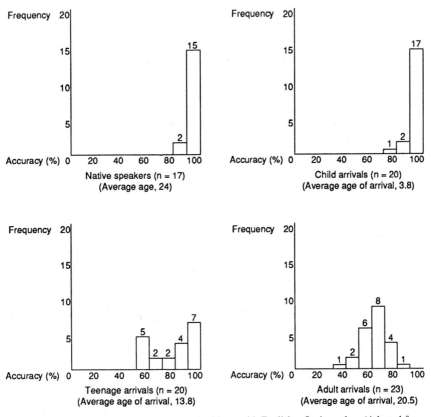

Figure I   Bar charts showing the number of subjects with English reflexive value. (Adapted from Lee, 1992, Experiment 1.)

although the EBs were able to set the GCP for English, some LBs were not, and the Adult group was totally unable to; rather, they responded randomly.

VII. CHILD L2 VERSUS ADULT L2

It is often simply assumed, both by proponents and opponents of the critical period hypothesis, that child L2 acquisition is governed by the same mechanisms as child L1 acquisition (cf. Schwartz, 1992). Certainly the evidence from children who are exposed to two languages from birth bears that out. But many children are monolingual mother-tongue learners until they reach school age or later, at which time they are first exposed to an L2. How do these learners end up in the indistinguishable from Ns category, or in the definitely nonnative category? The consensus is that the younger a child is when he or she begins the process, the more likely he or she is to end up in the former category (cf. Krashen, Long, & Scarcella, 1979). But it is within this group of learners that the issue of different critical ages for different components of grammar arises.

Particularly within a modular framework, which UG is often asserted to be (cf. Chomsky, 1981a; Fodor, 1983), it makes sense to ask for each submodule, Is there a critical period for this submodule? Thus we may profitably think in terms of the possibility of different critical periods for phonological, syntactic and morphological, and semantic components of the grammar. Two kinds of data have been amassed: ultimate achievement data and developmental sequence data. In this chapter I focus only on the former (but cf. Schwartz, 1992, and Meisel, 1991, for differing views on the latter).

The ultimate achievement data on child L2 learners normally looks at the L2 production of adults with the same L1 who vary in their ages of first exposure to the L2, comparing it with adult NSs of the L2. The NNSs will have been in the L2 environment for varying periods of time. If those first exposed to the L2 at earlier ages show nativelike linguistic behavior and those first exposed at later ages do not, this lends strong support to the critical period hypothesis, at least for the linguistic properties at issue. There are a few studies of this kind, most not carried out within a UG framework, but as a whole representing a variety of types of L2 knowledge.

Perhaps the clearest evidence in favor of a critical period for phonological production comes from Oyama's significant study (1979) on the pronunciation ability of 60 Italian immigrants whose age of arrival to the United States ranged from 6–20 and whose length of residence ranged between 5–18 yr. Oyama found age of arrival to be the significant determinant of accentedness. Child arrivals performed like NSs; those arriving after 12 did not. Oyama (1978) carried out a perception study on ability to understand masked speech and found much the same results. Oyama's study is supported by several others (cf. Asher & Garcia, 1969; Fathman, 1975; Seliger, Krashen, & Ladefoged, 1975). Patkowski's (1990) study is particularly interesting in that it indicates a marked discontinuity between the accentedness ranges of those whose age of first exposure took place between 5–15 and those whose age of first exposure took place after 15, even though both groups had about the same number of years living in the country (mean = 20.4 for prepuberty group, mean = 18.7 for postpuberty group). As Patkowski points out, the range of accent ratings (see Figure 2) for the over 15 group looks much like the bell-shaped curve one would expect of learners of anything not innately preprogrammed (reading, algebra, chess, etc.), whereas the range of the under 15 group is markedly skewed to the right. (Maturational factors in L2 acquisition of phonological structure are also dis-

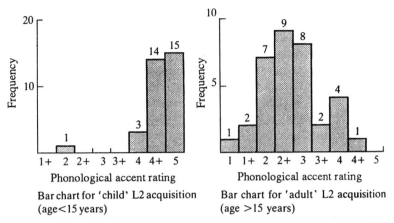

Figure 2 Phonology Ratings. (From Patkowsky, 1990. Reprinted by permission of Oxford University Press.)

cussed in chapters 9 by Leather and James and 15 by Obler and Hannigan, this volume.)

In the area of morphology and syntax very few studies have been attempted, but those that have show definite maturational effects. Patkowski (1980, p. 91) got trained NS judgments on oral production of 67 proficient NNSs and 15 NS controls. As in his pronunciation results, he found significant differences between the NNS group arriving before 15 (mean age of arrival, 8.6) and the group arriving after 15 (mean age of arrival, 27.1). The younger arriving group (see Figure 3) showed a highly skewed distribution (with mean = 4.8, mode = 5 in a range of 1–5); the curve for the older arriving group, on the other hand, exhibited the by now familiar normal distribution (mean = 3.6, SD = .6).

Of course, this study was concerned with conversational data, and it is well known that NNSs can, to some extent, avoid problem areas in free production. More telling, in some respects, are grammaticality judgments in which the strings to be judged have been chosen for specific theoretical reasons.

Johnson and Newport (1989) obtained grammaticality judgments on a range of morphological and syntactic characteristics of English from 46 NSs of Korean or Chinese whose ages of arrival ranged from 3–39 and whose lengths of residence ranged from 3–26 years at time of testing. Such phenomena as articles, wh-questions, particle movement, past tense, plural, and third-person singular were used. On every structure tested, Johnson and Newport found an advantage for early arrivals over late, with age of arrival inversely related to test scores up to puberty, but unrelated after puberty.

More critical for the question of the UG as a base for L2 acquisition is the search for evidence of constraints on grammars. With this in mind, Johnson and

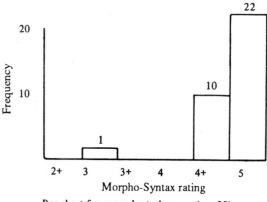

Bar chart for pre-puberty learners (*n* = 33)

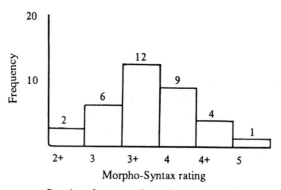

Bar chart for post-puberty learners (*n* = 34)

Figure 3 Syntax ratings. (From Patkowsky, 1980.)

Newport (1987, 1991) compared L1 Chinese speakers of L2 English with NS controls on subjacency violations (and their corresponding grammatical declaratives together with grammatical wh-questions). Again, there was a decline in correct detection of Subjacency violations associated with age of arrival (and not with length of residence after age of arrival had been partialled out). Johnson and Newport conclude over the two studies that maturation affects the learning of both language-specific and language universal structures and that Subjacency has no special status with regard to critical period effects. In the terms laid out in this article, Johnson and Newport demonstrate that Subjacency did not survive in the L1 knowledge of adult Chinese speakers of L2 English, nor were they able to access it independently.

These data force us to consider the critical age issue in a more focused way—not as one global critical period but rather as different critical periods for different components of the grammar. The phonological data are the most clear-cut. In fact, Long (1990), in his survey of relevant studies claims that age 6 marks the beginning of the end of the critical period for phonology; learners starting between 6 and 11 will typically become communicatively fluent, but a number of them will end up with measurable phonological "accents." The morphological and syntactic data are, not surprisingly, more diffuse, because with the exception of the Johnson and Newport Subjacency study and the Lee binding study, the range of phenomena tested was wide and not necessarily determined by theory. Yet even there the results are strong. In this area, Long (1990) concludes that age 15 marks the beginning of the downward slope for morphology and syntax. Whether Long has hit precisely the right ages for the beginning of declines for phonology and for morphology and syntax is not as important as the overarching claim that separate modules must be evaluated individually for critical-period effects, and that at least the phonological and syntactic modules show them.

VIII. DO PRINCIPLES MATURE?

Underlying the dispute within the UG framework over the existence of a critical period for L2 is an ongoing debate among L1 acquisition theorists on the question of the availability of the initial state, UG, to child L1 learners as they develop. Proponents of the *continuity* hypothesis claim that UG in its entirety is fixed at birth and never changes over the course of development (see Hyams, 1986; Pinker, 1984). (Chapter 4 by Flynn, this volume, argues for this position in L2 acquisition.) Thus, all principles of UG that define the domain of learning and restrict the hypotheses the child can consider will always be accessible to the child and to the adult (cf. Lust, 1988, for further discussion). Proponents of the *maturation* hypothesis hold, on the other hand, that the principles of UG (or certain other linguistic properties) are subject to an innately specified maturation schedule (cf. Borer & Wexler, 1987; Felix, 1987). They claim that these principles or properties of UG mature, like other biological properties, and become available to the learner at particular points in their linguistic development. Thus, even though exposed to the triggering data necessary to restructure her grammar, the child will not capitalize on such data until the relevant principle or linguistic ability matures. As Felix proposes:

> Although the set of universal principles is fully and exhaustively specified by the child's genetic program, each of these principles is somehow "latent" up to a

specific point in time after which it will start to operate and thus constrain the child's knowledge of what may be a humanly accessible language. (1987, p. 114)

The notion of a principle or grammatical property maturing has been pushed one step further by Borer and Wexler (1987), who argue that, in order to explain why certain constructions develop at a certain time or why certain constructions follow others, the notion of maturation is preferable both from the viewpoint of linguistic theory[16] and from general biological considerations as well. Thus they claim that there might be critical developmental points for certain pieces of grammatical properties of UG along the developmental pathway (i.e., that certain principles mature, and that there is a period before maturation during which the parameters associated with a certain principle cannot be set by the child, even though data may have been available in the input).[17] It is only subsequent to the maturation of a principle that a child can take advantage of the input to set the parameter(s). Elsewhere (Borer & Wexler, 1989) they posit proto-principles of UG and argue for the early use of a proto-theta-criterion and the later use of the adult theta-criterion, and for the early use of a unique external argument proto-principle (UEAPP) and the later use of A(rgument)-chains.

The claim that certain aspects of UG mature is consistent with what is known about innate biological systems that go through maturation. It is also compatible with observed child acquisition data, where delays in the appearance of certain constructions are frequently noted (cf. Atkinson, 1992; Goodluck, 1991). Furthermore, it may lead to explanations, rather than descriptions, of the orderings of development of linguistic structures that actually occur in child L1 linguistic development. Certainly there is currently sufficient evidence that the orderings cannot be explained by properties of the input.

IX. WINDOWS OF OPPORTUNITY

The maturation hypothesis can be viewed in two ways. One is that there is a period before which a certain principle or property is not available to the learner.

[16] From the perspective of linguistic theory development, the continuity hypothesis requires the positing of some kind of ordering mechanism (intrinsic or extrinsic) to account for developmental order; yet there is no linguistic motivation for such a mechanism.

[17] Borer and Wexler (1990) vacillate on the question of the maturation of specific principles (as opposed to certain grammatical properties). They claim at one point that no principle in the sense of a grammatical principle assumed in recent linguistic theory, matures, (e.g., no principle that acts as a grammatical filter matures). At a later point they say that "it is too early to tell whether there are cases of filterlike principles of UG (e.g., the Projection Principle, the Theta-criterion, Subjacency) which mature" (1990, p. 5). As will be seen later in this chapter, I argue for precisely this (and therefore would not be suprised to see evidence of principle violations in early grammars before the principle has matured, a claim argued for by several, cf. Felix, 1984a, 1984b; Lebeaux, 1988; Radford 1990).

And then it *is* available from a specific point onwards. This seems to be Borer and Wexler's underlying assumption, for they offer the development of secondary sexual characteristics around puberty as a physiological analogy (1987, p. 124). The other is that there is a period *before* which and there is a period *after* which the principle is not available to the learner. This is the Window of Opportunity hypothesis espoused by Schachter (1988). In this view, for certain principles and parameters that depend on interaction with the environment, the principle or parameter will mature; there will exist a sensitive period for that principle or parameter; then the sensitive period will end and that principle or parameter will no longer be available for fixing.

The Window of Opportunity hypothesis for certain principles of UG is, on the microlevel, exactly the same notion as that of a critical period for submodules of the grammar, which is, in turn, exactly the same notion as that of a critical period for language acquisition, on the macrolevel. That this should be the case should come as no surprise. It makes sense both biologically and cognitively. That it has not been proposed before is due, I believe, to the reluctance of those in the fields of L1 and L2 acquisition to take the biological notion of maturation seriously enough.

Maturational stages are periods bound *on both sides* by periods of lessened sensitivity. So far, the only researchers asking how far an individual can get *after* the normal maturational period have been those looking at language deprivation or physical impairment, and these cases fortunately occur with insufficient regularity so that the myriad specific questions necessary for development of a Window of Opportunity hypothesis can be answered. We have not thought to ask how far a normal acquirer can get after the normal maturational period has elapsed, because normal L1 learners are at that point indistinguishable from adult NSs. Yet this is precisely where we must look if we are to find evidence regarding the Window of Opportunity hypothesis. In fact, we must turn to child L2 learners who have and who have not passed through particular developmental stages in their L1. Although L1 data prove useful in determining when a window might open, it is primarily in the L2 data[18] that we will find evidence for the closing of windows.

To my knowledge, there is only one study that focuses directly on this issue: Lee (1992). The study was designed to reveal a window, if there was one, by controlling all of the following: the L1 of the subject, the subject's age of first exposure, and the subject's length of exposure to the L2. By holding the L1 and length of exposure constant and varying the age of first exposure it was reasoned that for some parameter, if any such window existed, there would be an age range during which the parameter could be reset and ages before it and ages after it

---

[18] Of course, we can continue to look at abnormal L1 studies for confirmation or disconfirmation. They present their own set of difficulties, and will always be less accessible than a researcher might want.

during which resetting of that parameter could not take place. In this study, 78 Korean–English bilinguals were tested on knowledge of the operation in English of Principle A of Binding Theory[19] (which includes knowledge of both c-command and the GCP). For additional discussion of Binding Theory and/or the GCP see chapters 3 by White and 10 by Gass for L2 acquisition, and 14 by Berent for acquisition of English by deaf learners.) The subjects were chosen so that all but the youngest group had lived in the United States approximately the same amount of time, 3 years. The youngest group were U.S. born, but not exposed to English until they began preschool at age 3. Thus they received approximately the same amount of input as the older groups. Five groups were tested, along with NS controls. The groups were broken into much finer categories than any of the previous studies. There were young children (ages 6.0–7.11), older children (ages 8.0–10.11), adolescents (11.0–13.11), teens (14.0–17.11) and adults (19.0–25.11), along with NS controls. The subjects were tested on their knowledge of Principle A in English, because it is known that the GCP setting for English is more restricted than the setting for Korean, and that in the acquisition of English the GCP would have to be reset. If the Window of Opportunity hypothesis is correct, one would expect to find one or two groups operating as if Principle A held and they had the English setting for the GCP; other groups would operate as if they did not have the English setting for the GCP. A picture identification task and a multiple-choice task were administered to elicit knowledge of c-command[20] and the GCP. In the picture-identification task, subjects heard a sentence and saw a picture and were asked if the sentence and the picture matched. There were three possibilities (exhibited by the following sentence) and a set of three pictures.

(15)   Ernie is dreaming that Mickey Mouse is pointing to himself.

One of three pictures would be paired with this sentence: one in which Mickey Mouse is pointing to himself (Reflexive Short (RS)), a second in which Mickey Mouse is pointing to Ernie (Reflexive Long (RL)), and a third in which Mickey Mouse is pointing to Popeye (Reflexive External (RE)). For cases like the RE picture–sentence pair, all subjects should reject it because reflexives cannot have sentence-external referents. Those who had maintained the Korean setting should accept both the RS pair and the RL pair. Those who had reset to the English parameter setting should accept the RS pair and reject the RL pair.

---

[19] Principle A states that an anaphor must be c-commanded by a coreferential NP with an antecedent in a governing category. NS command of c-command and the locality condition (GCP) together constitute what is considered NS competence for principle A.

[20] C-command may be defined as follows: A node A c-commands a node B if (1) A does not dominate B; (2) B does not dominate A; and (3) the first branching node dominating A also dominates B (cf. Haegeman, 1991).

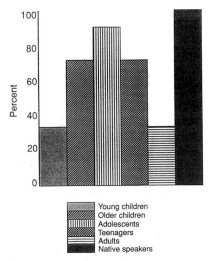

Figure 4 Bar chart showing percent of subjects with English reflexive value, by group. (Adapted from Lee, 1992, Experiment 2.)

Across both tasks (see Figure 4), the older children and adolescents showed strong evidence that they had reset the GCP, whereas the young children and adults showed that they had not been able to reset it. All groups but the young children showed evidence of knowledge of c-command. So for the GCP, there was a definite age range before which children could not set it, and a definite age range after which adults could not set it. The Window of Opportunity for setting the GCP appears to exist, and those within its frames were able to reset the parameter.[21]

X. CONCLUSION

In this chapter I have argued that a modular, principle-based approach to language acquisition, UG, although appropriate in the case of child L1 acquisition, fails to shed light on adult L2 acquisition—either in terms of a biological perspective on maturation or in terms of the known linguistic achievements of adult L2 learners.

I have further shown evidence for critical periods in both child L1 and L2 acquisition. Critical periods are seen as periods of heightened sensitivity to certain kinds of input, preceded and followed by periods of lesser sensitivity. This

[21] In the multiple-choice task, the teens performed well also, but not in the picture-identification task.

evidence for critical periods has been shown to hold for submodules within the grammar as well as for properties of languages internal to the submodules, critical periods that I have labeled Windows of Opportunity. Evidence for a critical period for phonology is already strong. Evidence for a critical period for morphology and syntax is less strong but will grow as researchers begin to turn their attention to the rich source of evidence made available in theory-oriented child L2 studies with the concept in mind. Evidence for Windows for Opportunity for aspects of language internal to the submodules is just beginning to emerge. So far we have seen evidence for a Window for the Subjacency principle and for the GCP.

If this interpretation of the available data is correct, and there is reason to believe it is, one might expect overlapping windows for those principles and parameters that mature such that the overall critical period for morphology and syntax, although extended over a considerable period of time, will be shown to consist of a progression of windows for individual principles and properties needing data in order to be triggered.

At this juncture it is not clear which principles may hold for the whole period of L1 development and which ones mature, but it is clear that those that hold universally and do not have associated parameters ought to hold for the whole developmental period (cf. structure dependency). We can be guided in the search for those that mature by looking carefully at cases of delayed L1 development (cf. Borer & Wexler, 1987, 1989, 1990) tied with child L2 development at varying ages.

REFERENCES

Asher, J., & Garcia, R. (1969). The optimal age to learn a foreign language. *Modern Language Journal, 53,* 334–341.

Atkinson, M. (1992). *Children's syntax.* Cambridge, UK: Blackwell.

Bailey, K., Madden, L., & Krashen, S. (1974). Is there a 'natural' sequence in adult second language learning? *Language Learning, 24,* 235–243.

Birdsong, D. (1991). *Ultimate attainment in second language acquisition.* Unpublished manuscript, University of Texas, Austin.

Bley-Vroman, R. Felix, S., & Toup, G. (1988). The accessibility of Universal Grammar in adult language learning. *Second Language Research, 4,* 1–32.

Bley-Vroman, R. (1989). What is the logical problem of foreign language learning? In S. Gass & J. Schachter (Eds.), *Linguistic perspectives on second language acquisition.* Cambridge, UK: Cambridge University Press.

Borer, H., & Wexler, K. (1987). The maturation of syntax. In T. Roeper & E. Williams (Eds.), *Parameter setting.* Dordrecht: Foris.

Borer, H., & Wexler, K. (1989). *The maturation of grammatical principles.* Manuscript, University of California, Irvine.

Borer, H., & Wexler, K. (1990). *A principle-based theory of the structure and growth of passive.* Manuscript, University of Massachusetts, Amherst, and MIT.

Brown, H. D. (1979). *A socioculturally determined critical period for second language acquisition.* Paper presented at the 13th annual TESOL Convention, Boston.

Chomsky, N. (1981a). *Lectures on government and binding.* Dordrecht: Foris.

Chomsky, N. (1981b). Principles and parameters in syntactic theory. In N. Hornstein & D. Lightfoot (Eds.), *Explanations in linguistics.* London: Longman.

Clahsen, H., Meisel, J., & Pienemann, M. (1983). *Deutsch alszweitsprache. Der Spracherwerb auslandischer Arbeiter.* Tubingen: Narr.

Clahsen, H., & Muysken, P. (1986). The availability of universal grammar to adult and child learners—A study of the acquisition of German word order. *Second Language Research, 2,* 92–119.

Clahsen, H., & Muysken, P. (1989). The UG paradox in L2 acquisition. *Second Language Research, 5,* 1–29.

Coppieters, R. (1987). Competence differences between native and near-native speakers. *Language, 63* (3), 544–573.

Curtiss, S. (1988). Abnormal language acquisition and the modularity of language. In F. J. Newmeyer (Ed.), *Linguistics: The Cambridge Survey: Vol. 2, Linguistic theory: Extensions and implications.* Cambridge, UK: Cambridge University Press.

Eubank, L. (Ed.). (1991). *Point counterpoint: Universal Grammar in the second language.* Amsterdam: John Benjamins.

Fathman, A. (1975). The relationship between age and second language learning ability. *Language Learning, 25,* 245–253.

Felix, S. (1981). On the (in)applicability of Piagetian thought to language learning. *Studies in Second Language Acquisition, 3,* 544–573.

Felix, S. (1984a). *Psycholinguistische Aspekte des Zweitsprachen-erwerbs.* Tubingen: Narr.

Felix, S. (1984b). *Two problems of language acquisition: On the interaction of Universal Grammar and language growth.* Manuscript, University of Passau, Passau.

Felix, S. (1985). UG-generated knowledge in adult second language acquisition. In S. Flynn & W. O'Neill (Eds.), *Linguistic theory in second language acquisition.* Dordrecht: Reidel.

Felix, S. (1987). *Cognition and language growth.* Dordrecht: Foris.

Flynn, S., & Manuel, S. (1991). Age-dependent effects in language acquisition. In L. Eubank (Ed.), *Point counterpoint. Universal Grammar in the second language.* Amsterdam: John Benjamins.

Flynn, S., & Martohardjono, G. (1992). *Evidence against a critical period hypothesis: Syntax.* Paper delivered at the annual meeting of the American Association of Applied Linguistics, Seattle, WA.

Fodor, J. A. (1983). *The modularity of mind.* Cambridge, MA: MIT Press.

Goodluck, H. (1991). *Language acquisition.* Cambridge, UK: Blackwell.

Gregg, J. (1988). Epistemology without knowledge: Schwartz on Chomsky, Fodor and Krashen. *Second Language Research, 4,* (1), 66–80.

Haegeman, L. (1991). *Introduction to government and binding theory.* Oxford: Blackwell.

Hatch, E. (1977). Optimum age or optimal learners? *Workpapers in TESL,* Department of ESL, UCLA, pp. 45–56.

Hornstein, N., & Lightfoot, D. (Eds.). (1981). *Explanation in linguistics.*

Huang, C. T. J. (1982). Move WH in a language without WH movement. *The Linguistic Review, 1,* 4.

Hubel, D. H., & Wiesel, T. N. (1962). Receptive fields, binocular interaction and functional architecture in the cat's visual cortex. *Journal of Physiology, (London), 106,* 106–154.

Hubel, D. H., & Wiesel, T. N. (1970). The period of susceptibility to the physiological effects of unilateral eye closure in kittens. *Journal of Physiology (London), 206,* 419–436.

Hyams, N. (1986). *Language acquisition and the theory of parameters.* Dordrecht: Foris.

Immelmann, K., & Suomi, S. (1981). Sensitive phases in development. In K. Immelmann, G. Barlow, L. Petrinovich, & L. Main (Eds.), *Behavioral development. The Bielefelt interdisciplinary project.* Cambridge, UK: Cambridge University Press.

Ioup, G., & Tansomboom, A. (1987). The acquisition of tone: A maturational perspective. In G. Ioup & S. Weinberger (Eds.), *Interlanguage phonology.* Rowley, MA: Newbury House.

Johnson, J., & Newport, E. (1987, October). *Summary of presentation.* Boston University Child Language Conference.

Johnson, J., & Newport, E. (1989). Critical period effects in second language learning: The influence of maturational state on the acquisition of English as a second language. *Cognitive Psychology, 21,* 60–99.

Johnson, J., & Newport, E. (1991). Critical period effects on universal properties of language: The status of subjacency in the acquisition of a second language. *Cognition, 39,* 215–258.

Kean, M.-L. (1988). The relation between linguistic theory and second language acquisition: A biological perspective. In J. Pankhurst, M. Sharwood Smith, & P. van Buren (Eds.), *Learnability and second language: A book of readings* (pp. 61–70). Dordrecht: Foris.

Kean, M.-L. (1991). *Learnability and biological reality.* Manuscript, University of California, Irvine.

Krashen, S. (1973). Lateralization, language learning, and the critical period. *Language Learning, 23,* 63–74.

Krashen, S. (1982). Accounting for child-adult differences in second language rate and attainment. In S. Krashen, R. Scarcella, & M. Long (Eds.), *Child-adult differences in second language acquisition* (pp. 202–226). Rowley, MA: Newbury House.

Krashen, S., Long, M., & Scarcella, R. (Eds.). (1979). *Child-adult differences in second language acquisition* (pp. 202–226). Rowley, MA: Newbury House.

Lebeaux, D. (1988). *Language acquisition and the form of the grammar.* Unpublished doctoral dissertation, University of Massachusetts, Amherst.

Lee, D. (1992). *Universal Grammar, learnability, and the acquisition of English reflexive binding by L1 Korean speakers.* Unpublished doctoral dissertation, University of Southern California, Los Angeles.

Lenneberg, E. (1967). *Biological foundations of language.* New York: Wiley.

Leopold, W. (1953). Patterning in children's language. *Language Learning, 5,* 1–14.

Li, C., & Thompson, S. (1978). The acquisition of tone. In V. Fromkin (Ed.), *Tone: A linguistic survey.* New York: Academic Press.

Long, M. H. (1990). Maturational constraints on language development. *Studies in Second Language Acquisition, 12,* 3.

Lust, B. (1988). Universal Grammar in second language acquisition: Promises and problems in critically related empirical studies. In S. Flynn & W. O'Neill (Eds.), *Linguistic theory in second language acquisition.* Dordrecht: Kluwer.

Lust, B., Chien, Y.-C., & Flynn, S. (1987). What children know: Methods for the study of first language acquisition. In B. Lust (Ed.), *Studies in the acquisition of anaphora* (Vol. 3, pp. 271–356). Dordrecht: Reidel.

Marler, P.-R. (1970). A comparative approach to vocal learning: Song development in white-crowned sparrows. *Journal of Comparative and Physiological Psychology Monographs, 71,* 1–25.

Martohardjono, G., & Flynn, S. (1992). *Evidence against a critical period in language acquisition: Phonology.* Paper delivered at the annual meeting of the American Association of Applied Linguistics, Seattle, WA.

Martohardjono, G., & Gair, J. (1993). Apparent UG inaccessibility in second language acquisition: Misapplied principles or principled misapplications? In F. Eckman (Ed.), Confluence: Linguistics, second language acquisition, & speech pathology, (pp. 79–103). Amsterdam: John Benjamins.

Meisel, J. (1991). Principles of Universal Grammar and strategies of language learning: Some similarities and differences between first and second language acquisition. In L. Eubank (Ed.), *Point counterpoint: Universal Grammar in second language acquisition.* Amsterdam: John Benjamins.

Muller-Gotama. F. (1988). A typology of the syntax–semantics interface. University of Southern California, unpublished paper.

Newport, E. (1984). Constraints on learning: Studies in the acquisition of ASL. *Papers and Reports on Child Language Development 23,* 1–22.

Otsu, Y. (1981). *Universal Grammar and syntactic development in children: Toward a theory of syntactic development.* Unpublished doctoral dissertation, MIT, Cambridge, MA.

Oyama, S. (1978). The sensitive period and comprehension of speech. *Working Papers on Bilingualism, 16,* 1–17.

Oyama, S. (1979). The concept of the sensitive period in development studies. *Merrill-Palmer Quarterly, 25,* 83–102.

Patkowski, M. S. (1980). The sensitive period for the acquisition of syntax in a second language. *Language Learning, 30* (2), 449–472.

Patkowski, M. S. (1990). Age and accent in a second language: A reply to James Emil Flege. *Applied Linguistics, 11* (1), 73–89.

Peters, A. (1974). The beginning of speech. *Stanford Papers and Reports on Child Language Development, 8,* 26–32.

Pinker, S. (1984). *Language learnability and language development.* Cambridge, MA: Harvard University Press.

Radford, A. (1990). The syntax of nominal arguments in early child English. *Language Acquisition, 1,* 191–224.

Riemsdijk, H. C. van, & Williams, E. (1986). *Introduction to the theory of grammar.* Cambridge, MA: MIT Press.

Satz, P., Bakker, D., Tenunissen, J., Goebel, R., & Van der Vlugt, H. (1975). Developmental parallels of the ear asymmetry: A multivariate approach. *Brain and Language, 2,* 171–185.

Schachter, J. (1974). An Error in error analysis. *Language Learning 24,* 205–213.

Schachter, J. (1988). The notion of completeness in second language acquisition. Paper presented at annual Boston University Conference on Language Development.

Schachter, J. (1989). Testing a proposed universal. In S. Gass & J. Schachter (Eds.), *Linguistic perspectives on second language acquisition.* Cambridge, UK: Cambridge University Press.

Schachter, J. (1990). On the issue of completeness in second language acquisition. *Second Language Research, 6,* 93–124.

Schachter, J., & Rutherford, W. (1978). Discourse function in language transfer. *Working Papers on Bilingualism, 19,* 1–12.

Schumann, J. (1975). Affective factors and the problem of age in second language acquisition. *Language Learning, 25,* 209–235.

Schumann, J. (1979). The acquisition of English negation by speakers of Spanish: A review of the literature. In R. Andersen (Ed.), *The acquisition and use of Spanish and English as first and second languages.* Washington, DC: TESOL.

Schwartz, B. D. (1992). Testing between UG-based and problem-solving models of L2A: Developmental sequence data. *Language Acquisition, 2, 1.*

Scovel, T. (1981). The recognition of foreign accents in English and its implications for psycholinguistic theories of language acquisition. In J. G. Savard & L. LaForge (Eds.), *Proceedings of the Fifth Congress of Associacion Internationale de Linguistique Applique.* (pp. 389–401). Laval, Canada: University of Laval Press.

Seliger, H. W. (1978). Implications of a multiple critical periods hypothesis for second language learning. In W. Ritchie (Ed.), *Second language acquisition research* (pp. 11–19). New York: Academic Press.

Seliger, H. W., Krashen, S., & Ladefoged, P. (1975). Maturational constraints in the acquisition of second language accents. *Language Sciences, 36,* 20–22.

Selinker, L. (1972). *Interlanguage. International Review of Applied Linguistics, 10,* **3,** 209–31. (Reprinted in *Contrastive analysis, error analysis, and related matters,* by B. W. Robinett & J. Schachter, Eds., 1978, Ann Arbor: University of Michigan Press).

Wanner, E., & Gleitman, L. (1982). *Language acquisition: The state of the art.* Cambridge, UK: Cambridge University Press.

Wexler, K., & Manzini, R. (1987). Parameters and learnability. In T. Roeper & E. Williams (Eds.), *Parameter setting* (pp. 41–76). Dordrecht: Reidel.

White, L. (1985). Is there a logical problem of second language acquisition? *TESOL Canada, 2,* 29–41.

White, L. (1988a). Island effects in second language acquisition. In S. Flynn & W. O'Neil, (Eds.), *Linguistic theory in second language acquisition.* Dordrecht: Kluwer.

White, L. (1988b). Universal Grammar and language transfer. In J. Pankhurst, M. Sharwood Smith, & P. van Buren, (Eds.), *Learnability and second languages: A book of readings.* Dordrecht: Foris.

White, L. (1989a). The principle of adjacency on second language acquisition. In S. Gass & J. Schachter, (Eds.), *Linguistic perspectives on second language acquisition* (pp. 134–158). Cambridge, UK: Cambridge University Press.

White, L. (1989b). *Universal Grammar and second language acquisition.* Amsterdam: John Benjamins.

White, L., & Juffs, A. (1993). UG effects in two different contexts of nonnative language acquisition. In *1993 Canadian Linguistics Association. Annual Conference Proceedings.* (Toronto Working Papers in Linguistics)

Woodward, J. (1973). Inter-rule implication in American Sign Language. *Sign Language Studies, 3,* 47–56.

Yip, V. (1989). *Aspects of Chinese/English interlanguage: syntax, semantics and learnability.* Unpublished doctoral dissertation, University of Southern California, Los Angeles.

CHAPTER 6

A FUNCTIONAL–TYPOLOGICAL APPROACH TO SECOND LANGUAGE ACQUISITION THEORY

Fred R. Eckman

I. INTRODUCTION

A functional–typological approach to second language (L2) acquisition attempts to explain facts about the acquisition of an L2 (a language acquired either by an adult, or by a child after one language is already resident) though the use of universal, linguistic generalizations that have been postulated on the basis of primary languages (L1) (languages acquired in childhood). Under this approach to universals, the linguist attempts to formulate generalizations on the basis of observations from a number of genetically unrelated and geographically nonadjacent languages. The goal of this endeavor is twofold. On the one hand, the linguist attempts to state generalizations about the occurrence, co-occurrence, or absence of the structures in any given language; and on the other hand, the linguist tries to suggest explanations for these universals. These generalizations are usually stated as implications asserting that the presence of a given structure in a language implies the presence of some other structure, but not vice versa. Several types of explanations are usually given for these universals, ranging from innateness to various functional considerations.

The functional–typological approach to L2 acquisition that will be discussed in this chapter is typified by two related hypotheses: the Markedness Differential Hypothesis (MDH) (Eckman, 1977), and the Structural Conformity Hypothesis (SCH) (Eckman, 1984; Eckman, Moravcsik, & Wirth, 1989). In what follows, the

Handbook of Second Language Acquisition

background, rationale, and development of each of these hypotheses will be discussed in detail.

The structure of this chapter is as follows. We will first consider the earlier of the two proposals, the MDH, which was proposed to account for certain problems with the Contrastive Analysis Hypothesis (CAH) (Lado, 1957). It will be argued that, although the MDH was intended to replace the CAH, the MDH is completely programmatic with the central theme of the CAH, namely, that native language (NL) interference is a factor in explaining certain errors in L2 acquisition. In fact, we will argue that it is this programmaticity with the CAH that causes problems for the MDH, leading to the formulation of the SCH. The chapter will conclude with some ideas on the current place of the functional–typological approach to L2 acquisition theory in view of some recent developments.

II. THE MARKEDNESS DIFFERENTIAL HYPOTHESIS

A. Background

The MDH was formulated as an attempt to address some of the problems with the CAH. The CAH, from its conceptualization in the 1940s (Fries, 1945), and subsequent development in the 1950s and 1960s (Lado, 1957; Moulton, 1962; Stockwell & Bowen, 1965), was the primary explanatory principle in L2 acquisition theory (Wardhaugh, 1970). This hypothesis, embodied in (1), claims that all areas of difficulty in L2 acquisition can be explained in terms of the structural differences between the NL and the target language (TL).

(1)   The Contrastive Analysis Hypothesis
        We assume that the student who comes in contact with a foreign language will find some features of it quite easy and others extremely difficult. Those elements that are similar to his native language will be simple for him, and those elements that are different will be difficult. (Lado, 1957, p. 2)

In short, the CAH holds that NL–TL differences are both necessary and sufficient to explain the difficulty that occurs in L2 learning. Under this view, all difficulty in L2 acquisition should occur only in areas of difference between the NL and TL, and thus L1 interference is paramount as an explanatory principle in L2 acquisition theory. (For a general discussion of L1 influence in L2 acquisition see chapter 10 by Gass, this volume.)

By the early 1970s, support for the CAH had begun to erode, both conceptually and empirically. On the conceptual side, the view of language that spawned the CAH, namely Structuralism, had come under severe attack from generative grammarians. Whereas the structuralists had viewed language as a set of habits, the generative grammarians characterized language as a system of rules. On the empirical side was the reporting of counterevidence to the CAH: many of the predictions of the hypothesis were simply not borne out.

Specifically, several studies showed that many areas of L2 difficulty did not result from NL–TL differences. To cite just a few examples, Sciarone (1970) reported that native speakers (NSs) of Dutch experienced difficulty with French auxiliaries, despite the fact that Dutch and French have similar auxiliary patterns. Likewise, Duškova (1969) found that many of the errors made by Czech learners of English did not result from differences between the two languages. And, on a more general level, Richards (1971) argued that many interesting L2 errors were simply not explainable through the CAH, but were apparently the result of efforts on the part of the L2 learner to work out various TL rules. This view was entirely consistent with the strong position, taking shape at this time, that L2 acquisition involved the acquisition of grammatical rules, and therefore was fundamentally the same process as L1 acquisition.

In a number of articles, Dulay and Burt (1972, 1974a, 1974b), argued that the process of L2 acquisition was guided by the learner's innate language acquisition device (LAD), which, at this time, was viewed as a task-specific, cognitive mechanism for generating and testing hypotheses about the ambient language. Dulay and Burt claimed that L2 acquisition takes place through the process of "creative construction," whereby the learner's innate language faculty is used to construct and evaluate hypotheses about the structure of the TL. L2 errors, Dulay and Burt argued, were the result of a winnowing process whereby the learner was able to cull out a set of workable L2 rules from among the various possibilities. In short, the view espoused by Dulay and Burt (1973) held that NL–TL differences are neither necessary nor sufficient to explain L2 errors, and thus the role of L1 interference in explaining errors in L2 acquisition was severely discounted.

The MDH (Eckman, 1977), when viewed in this context, was an effort to accomplish two goals. The first was to reconcile the two seemingly divergent positions, namely, the claim that L1 interference was paramount in explaining L2 difficulty (the CAH), and the position that L2 errors were the result of innate, hypothesis-testing strategies (creative construction). The second goal, which was necessary to accomplish the first, was to address some of the empirical problems of the CAH. To do this, the CAH was recast as the MDH, stated below as (2), in such a way that NL–TL differences were necessary to predict L2 difficulty, but these differences were not sufficient.

(2) MDH
     The areas of difficulty that a language learner will have can be predicted on
     the basis of a systematic comparison of the grammars of the NL, the TL,
     and the markedness relations stated in universal grammar,
     a. Those areas of the TL that differ from the NL and are more marked than
        the NL will be difficult.

b. The relative degree of difficulty of the areas of the TL that are more marked than the NL will correspond to the relative degree of markedness.

c. Those areas of the TL that are different from the NL, but are not more marked than the NL will not be difficult.

B. Assumptions Underlying the MDH

The MDH makes crucial use of the concept *markedness,* a relational term that has been viewed in different ways by different approaches, but for the purposes of the MDH, is defined as in (3).

(3)   Markedness

If the presence of a structure p in a language implies the presence of some other structure, q, but the presence of q in some language does not imply the presence of p, then structure p is marked relative to structure q, and structure q is unmarked relative to structure p.

Characterized in this way, markedness refers to the relative frequency or generality of a given structure across the world's languages.

Using these markedness relationships, the MDH makes three claims. The first is that L2 difficulty can be predicted on the basis of two considerations: (1) the differences between the NL and TL, and (2) the markedness relationships that hold within those areas of difference. Specifically, those TL structures that are both different and relatively more marked than the corresponding structures in the NL are predicted to be difficult. The second claim of the MDH is that the degree of difficulty among those TL structures that are different from those in the NL will correspond directly to the degree of markedness. And finally, the MDH predicts that those TL differences that are not more marked will not be difficult.

Consider a concrete example involving word-final consonant clusters. To establish the markedness relationships, we refer to Greenberg (1966), from which we derive the following: (1) all languages apparently allow words to end in vowels; (2) some languages allow words to end in only a single obstruent; (3) some languages that allow word-final, single obstruents also allow final, obstruent clusters consisting only of a fricative-stop sequence; and lastly, (4) some languages that have both final, single obstruents and final, fricative-stop clusters allow words ending in a stop-stop sequence. Thus, languages that have final stop-stop clusters also have final fricative-stop sequences; and languages that have final fricative-stop clusters also have words ending in a single obstruent. Consequently, final stop-stop clusters are marked relative to final fricative-stop clusters; and final fricative-stop clusters are marked relative to final, single obstruents, which, in turn, are marked relative to final vowels.

Now, if we consider an L2 situation where the TL English, which allows both types of final consonant clusters, is in contact with the NL Japanese, which allows no word-final obstruents or clusters at all, we obtain the following two predictions. First, words ending in obstruents and in obstruent clusters will be difficult for the learners in question, because all of these constructions are both different from the NL and relatively more marked than the relevant NL constructions. And second, final stop-stop clusters will be more difficult than the final fricative-stop clusters, and the final stop-stop clusters will be more difficult than the final fricative-stop sequences. (Chapter 9 by Leather and James, this volume, is a general discussion of L2 speech and phonology. Other treatments of this topic are found in chapters 3 by White and 10 by Gass.)

From this discussion, it should be clear that the MDH is programmatic with the CAH. Both hypotheses have as their goal the prediction of difficulty in L2 acquisition; and both hypotheses claim that such predictions depend, to some extent, on the differences between the NL and TL. The two hypotheses differ, however, in whether factors other than NL–TL difference must be considered. The CAH claims that such NL–TL differences are both necessary and sufficient for the prediction of L2 difficulty; the MDH claims that these differences are necessary but not sufficient. What is needed in addition, according to the MDH, is the incorporation of markedness as a measure of difficulty.

The assumption that markedness, in addition to NL–TL differences, must be considered in predicting L2 difficulty suggests a possibility for reconciling the two divergent positions on the role of L1 interference in L2 acquisition. For the CAH, such interference is paramount; for the creative construction position of Dulay and Burt, such interference is anathema; but for the MDH, both positions can be maintained to some extent. By basing predictions on NL–TL differences, the MDH allows for the influence of the L1; and by basing the notion of difficulty on markedness, which has been argued to be reflected in the order of acquisition of certain L1 sounds by Jakobson (1968), the MDH allows for some aspects of L2 acquisition to parallel L1 acquisition. More specifically, through the incorporation of markedness, the MDH can account for why some L2 errors resemble errors made during the acquisition of the TL as an L1.

Up to this point, we have considered the motivation behind the postulation of the MDH. Let us now discuss the support for this hypothesis.

C. Supporting Evidence

As stated above, the goal of the MDH is the same as that of the CAH: to explain difficulty in L2 acquisition. The MDH, however, is capable of accounting for some facts that the CAH cannot account for, namely, (1) why some NL–TL differences do not cause difficulty, and (2) why some differences are associated with degrees of difficulty and others are not. We will consider each of these questions in turn.

The MDH explains why some NL–TL differences do not cause difficulty in at least two ways. First, the hypothesis claims that simply the existence of NL–TL differences is not sufficient to cause difficulty; there must be, in addition, a markedness relationship associated with those differences. If no markedness relationship obtains, then the hypothesis predicts no systematic difficulty. And second, the MDH predicts a directionality of difficulty whereas the CAH cannot without the incorporation of additional assumptions. For example, if a language L_i differs from another language L_j in that L_i has, say, a phonological contrast that L_j lacks, the question arises as to whether one learning situation presents more of a challenge than the other. Specifically is the presence of the contrast in TL–L_i more difficult for speakers of NL–L_j than is the lack of such a contrast in TL–L_j for speakers of NL–L_i?

Because the CAH predicts difficulty on the basis of NL–TL differences, it is necessary to make additional assumptions to account for any directionality of difficulty that exists. According to the MDH, the more difficult learning situation is that in which an NL–TL difference is relatively more marked compared to the relevant NL structures. One case that is discussed in the literature involves the acquisition of a word-final voice contrast by speakers of languages that have no voice contrast word-finally (Altenberg & Vago, 1983; Eckman, 1977). Because final voice contrasts are marked relative to voice contrasts in initial or medial positions, the acquisition of a TL with a word-final voice contrast by a learner whose NL lacks this contrast is predicted to present more difficulty.

The MDH also predicts degrees of difficulty that the CAH does not predict. The above example of final, obstruent clusters is a case in point. Because the NL, Japanese, lacks both final fricative-stop and final stop-stop clusters, both are predicted by the CAH to be an area of difficulty for Japanese learners of English. However, the CAH has no natural way of determining any degree of difficulty in this case. The MDH, on the other hand, correctly predicts that stop-stop clusters will create more difficulty by virtue of their increased markedness (Eckman, 1991). A similar situation has also been exemplified for relative clauses in a number of studies in the literature (Doughty, 1991; Eckman, Nelson, & Bell, 1988; Gass, 1979; Hyltenstam, 1984; Schachter, 1974).

And finally, it should be noted that several, independent studies testing some of the claims of the MDH have been carried out with generally supportive findings (Anderson, 1987; Benson, 1986). We now turn our attention to an evaluation of the MDH.

D. Evaluation of the MDH

In this section we will consider the relative merits of the MDH as compared to the CAH. Two points involving the evaluation of any hypothesis need to be made. The first is that the empirical value of a hypothesis is determined by evaluating the hypothesis against facts. To the extent that the predictions of the hypothesis are borne out, the hypothesis is supported. The second point is that the explanatory value of a hypothesis is determined by evaluating the hypothesis against other hypotheses.

Empirically, the MDH receives support from the fact that it can account for some aspects of L2 difficulty that the CAH cannot account for, in particular, the fact that certain NL–TL differences do not cause difficulty. When we compare the MDH and the CAH directly, the MDH is a stronger hypothesis than the CAH, because the MDH is more falsifiable than is the CAH. Because the MDH links difficulty to the markedness relations that exist among NL–TL differences, any difficulty in an area of difference that does not parallel the markedness relationships will falsify the MDH, but will leave the CAH intact. Thus, there are facts that will falsify the MDH that will not falsify the CAH.

A pertinent example is the relative-clause study by Hyltenstam (1984). The TL, Swedish, differs from one of the NLs, Farsi, in that Farsi has pronominal reflexes in several relative clause types, whereas Swedish has no relative clauses with pronominal reflexes. The MDH, but not the CAH, would have been falsified if the Farsi speakers had evinced difficulty with pronominal reflexes in a way that does not correspond to the markedness relationships that exist among the different types of relative clauses (Keenan & Comrie, 1977). If, for example, the Farsi speakers had shown difficulty in the more marked relative clause types than they did in the less marked relative clauses, the MDH would have been disconfirmed. Notice, however, that these facts would not have falsified the CAH. As long as the difficulty occurs in an area of difference between the NL and TL, the CAH is supported.

There are two final points that should be highlighted in this section. The first is that the notion of markedness on which the MDH is predicated is an independently motivated, empirical construct. Whether or not a given structure is marked relative to some other structure is a matter of fact: if a cross-linguistic, implicational relationship exists between the structures in question, then one of the structures is marked relative to the other; if no such implication exists, then no markedness relationship obtains. Thus, markedness, in the sense used by the MDH, is not a matter of judgment or conjecture; it is an empirical matter.

At times this fact has been misunderstood, as discussion in some recent works has shown. For example, in his evaluation of the MDH, Ellis claims that markedness is not a well-defined construct, "Markedness, however, remains a somewhat ill-defined concept" (Ellis 1994, p. 335). To be fair to Ellis, he has a point if his claim is taken within the more general context of linguistic theory, because linguists have defined markedness in a number of ways. Depending on their framework, linguists have used markedness with a number of different meanings, including the occurrence of an actual morpheme (as in the case of the plural), the absolute frequency with which a form occurs in a given corpus, or the amount of evidence required for some principle to be learned. However, the MDH employs this term only as defined in (3) above, in which one constructions is marked relative to another if and only if there exists an asymmetrical, implicational relationship between the constructions. Consequently, contrary to the assertions by Ellis and others, there is nothing vague or ill-defined about this notion.

The second point that needs to be made in this context is that the determination of markedness, at least in the way it is defined in (3), is independent of any L2 facts. For the MDH, markedness is determined on the basis of cross-linguistic data. Thus, the MDH attempts to explain difficulty in L2 acquisition by relating this difficulty to more general phenomena, namely, the distribution of certain constructions across the world's languages.

Having discussed some of the merits of the MDH, we turn now to some of its problems.

E. Problems with the MDH

As stated above, the MDH is completely programmatic with the CAH: both hypotheses predict difficulty on the basis of NL–TL differences; the MDH bases its predictions on markedness. The type of evidence that would directly contradict the MDH is evidence in L2 acquisition of less difficulty in more marked structures, or more difficulty in less marked structures, or both. This type of evidence has not been reported in the literature.

However, there is another pattern of difficulty that is problematic for the MDH in that it is an exception to the hypothesis. This pattern involves errors that seem to reflect a markedness relationship, but the structure in which this difficulty occurs is not an area in which the NL and TL are different. Because the MDH predicts difficulty on the basis of markedness and NL–TL differences, learner difficulty in an area in which the NL and TL are not different lies outside the scope of the MDH.

This situation arises in the relative clause study by Hyltenstam (1984), referred to above. Hyltenstam reported an error pattern involving pronominal reflexes in Swedish relative clauses. Standard English does not have pronominal reflexes in relative clauses; but if it did, the pronoun "him" in (4) would be an example.

(4)   I know the boy whom you saw him yesterday.

In general, the errors on pronominal reflexes made by the Swedish learners followed the degree of markedness stated by the Accessibility Hierarchy (AH) (Keenan & Comrie, 1977). The AH is a principle that attempts to characterize the types of relative clause constructions found in the world's languages. A relative clause is an embedded sentence that is used to modify a noun phrase (NP) contained in another clause, for example, in sentence (5):

(5)   I know the girl to whom you sent a present.

The string *to whom you sent a present* is a relative clause modifying the NP *the girl.* This sentence can be thought of as being formed by combining the two sentences *I know the girl* and *You sent a present to the girl* into a sentence containing a relative clause. This process of combination "relativizes" the second occurrence of the NP, *the girl,* by replacing this NP with the relative pronoun *whom* and moving this pronoun, along with the preposition, to the front of its clause. Because, in this case, the NP that is moved functions as the indirect object of its clause, we say that the above sentence is formed by relativizing the indirect object.

The AH, shown in (6), predicts that if a language can form a relative cause by relativizing an NP from a given position (x) on the hierarchy, then that language can necessarily form relative clauses by relativizing NPs in all positions higher than x on the hierarchy, but that such a language cannot necessarily form relative clauses by relativizing an NP from positions lower than x.

(6) Accessibility Hierarchy
     Subject
     Direct object
     Indirect object
     Object of a preposition
     Genitive
     Object of a comparison

Thus, for example, any language that can form relative clauses by relativizing the indirect object NP, as in the above English example, can necessarily form relative clauses by relativizing the direct object and subject NPs. However, such a language may not necessarily be able to relativize an NP that is the object of a preposition, genitive, or object of a comparison.

Now, returning to the problem of the MDH, we consider Table I, which depicts the facts for one of Hyltenstam's (1984) Spanish-speaking subjects (subject 19, p. 49). The problem for the MDH is that some of the errors were made by speakers of Spanish and Finnish, which do not differ from Swedish with respect to pronominal reflexes in relative clauses. In other words, none of these languages allows pronominal reflexes in relative clauses.

The positions on the AH are represented in the first column. The fact that the

TABLE I

**Pronominal Reflexes Produced in Swedish
Relative Clauses by Native Speakers of Spanish**[a]

	NL Spanish	IL	TL Swedish
Subject	−	−	−
Direct object	−	−	−
Indirect object	−	+	−
Oblative	−	+	−
Genitive	−	+	−
Object of a complement	−	+	−

[a]NL, native language; IL, interlanguage; TL, target language.

NL, Spanish, has no pronominal reflexes in any position is represented by the minuses under the column marked "NL"; the fact that the TL, Swedish, also has no pronominal reflexes in any position is so indicated under the column marked "TL." The values under the IL (interlanguage) column indicate that the subject relativized four positions on the AH using pronominal reflexes. What is interesting is that the pattern represented under the IL is in conformity with the markedness relationships defined by the AH, and thus would seem to be within the domain of the MDH. The problem is that, although this error pattern follows the AH and markedness, the MDH makes no predictions in this case, because this is not an area of difference between the NL and TL. Thus, the MDH has no explanation for the error pattern produced by Hyltenstam's Spanish and Finnish subjects. (Chapter 18 by Seliger, this volume, reports the occurrence of intrusive pronominal reflexes [or "resumptive pronouns"] in attrited primary languages. Chapter 14 by Berent analyzes the acquisition of wh-questions in English by deaf learners in terms of the NP AH.)

It should be pointed out that the MDH fails to make predictions in this case because it is *too* programmatic with the CAH. Specifically, the MDH states that there must be differences before any measure of difficulty becomes relevant. Therefore, Hyltenstam's Spanish and Finnish data fall outside the scope of this hypothesis, because Spanish and Finnish do not differ from Swedish in the area of pronominal reflexes in relative clauses.

To recapitulate to this point, we have argued that both the MDH and the CAH are generally part of the same research program: both hypotheses make predictions about difficulty based on NL–TL differences, but only the MDH postulates markedness as a measure of degree of difficulty. The proposal that markedness corresponds to difficulty has received significant empirical support. Where the MDH has run into problems, however, is in situations where difficulty has occurred in areas where the NL and TL do not differ. One way to resolve this problem would be to make NL–TL differences irrelevant to the MDH. This brings us to the second hypothesis formulated within the functional–typological approach to L2 acquisition: the SCH.

III. THE STRUCTURE CONFORMITY HYPOTHESIS

A. Background

The SCH (Eckman, 1984, 1991; Eckman et al., 1989), stated in (7), asserts that the universal constraints that hold for primary languages hold also for ILs.

(7)   SCH

All universals that are true for primary languages are also true for ILs.

Although the statement of the hypothesis is neutral as to the theoretical framework within which the universals are stated, in practice, the hypothesis has been explicitly tested only with respect to functional–typological universals. In this sense, then, the SCH is in the same tradition as the MDH; but because the SCH makes no predictions based on NL–TL differences, it does not encounter the exceptions that the MDH did (see section II.E above).

B. Assumptions Underlying the SCH

The fundamental assumption underlying the SCH is the claim that ILs are linguistic systems; that is to say, Ils are languages in their own right. The idea that L2 learners internalize a system that is essentially their own version of the TL is embodied in the IL Hypothesis, put forth by Selinker (1972).

The crux of the IL Hypothesis, as Adjémian (1976) pointed out, is that ILs are systematic. Without this underlying assumption, ILs lie beyond the scope of linguistic analysis. Notice, however, that the claim that ILs are linguistic systems does not commit one to the position that that ILs are systematic in the same way that L1s are. It is logically possible for ILs to be systems, yet be systematic in a way that is different from L1s. The interest of the SCH is that it is an open and empirical question whether the structures of ILs are the same types of systems as L1s. In other words, it is an open question whether IL structures conform to the same universal constraints as do the structures of L1s. Given that we are dealing with an empirical question, the first step is to consider the evidence.

C. Supporting Evidence

There were two reported tests of the claim embodied in the SCH before the hypothesis itself actually appeared in print. The first occurred in Ritchie (1978), in which he argued that a universal principle known at that time as the Right Roof Constraint, was obeyed by the IL grammars of Japanese learners of English. The second test of the claim was reported in a study by Schmidt (1980), in which she tested various constraints on coordinate structures against L2 data.

SCH has been explicitly tested against syntactic data in Eckman et al. (1989), and against phonological data in Eckman (1991). We will consider each of these studies briefly, but because they have been published, the findings will not be discussed in detail.

To test the SCH, Eckman et al. (1989) gathered data on English interrogative structures from the ILs of fourteen, adult L2 learners. The purpose was to determine whether the IL data conformed to the following universal generalizations, taken from Greenberg (1966).

(8) a. Wh-inversion implies wh-fronting
        Inversion of statement order in interrogative-word questions, so that verb

precedes subject, occurs only in languages where the question word or phrase is normally initial.
  b. Yes–no inversion implies wh-inversion
    This same inversion (i.e., inversion of statement order so that verb precedes subject) occurs in yes–no questions only if it also occurs in interrogative word questions.

Although a number of considerations had to be taken into account in determining whether that L2 conformed to the above generalizations, the results were generally confirmatory of the SCH. With respect to the universal in (8a), all of the fourteen subjects either confirmed the universal or were consistent with it. For the universal in (8b), one subject falsified it, and the rest either confirmed it or were consistent with it.

To test the SCH in the area of phonology, L2 data on the pronunciation of a number of English consonant clusters were compared against the following phonological generalizations, taken from Greenberg (1978; Eckman, 1991).

(9) a. Fricative-stop Principle
    If a language has at least one final consonant sequence consisting of stop + stop, it also has at least one final sequence consisting of fricative + stop.
  b. Resolvability Principle
    If a language has a consonantal sequence of length m in either initial or final position, it also has at least one continuous subsequence of length $m - 1$ in this same position.

As was the case in testing the syntactic generalizations, a number of considerations had to be taken into account. Nevertheless, the results of this test turn out to be even more robust than those from the syntactic data.

Several word-initial and word-final clusters were used as instantiations of the universals in (9); data were gathered from eleven adult English as a Second Language (ESL) learners whose NLS allowed no initial or final consonant clusters. In all, these subjects provided 200 test cases for the universals, with a total of 195 (97.5%) instances of consistency or confirmation of the SCH, and only five falsifications (2.5%).

What is interesting about these results is that the language-contact situation provided for many possibilities of consonant cluster configurations in the IL. Many of these possibilities would have supported the generalizations in (9) and many others would have been counter to them. For example, the ILs could have been just like the NLs, containing no initial or final clusters whatever. Alternatively, the ILs could have been identical to the TL, containing all of the TL clusters tested. In fact, neither of these situations occurred; rather, the resultant ILs were, in the vast majority of cases, somewhere in between the NLs and TLs. The ILs could have deviated from the NL and TL in a number of logically possible ways; however, they did not. In all but five cases the clusters that were present co-occurred in an arrangement that obeyed the generalizations.

This result provides strong support for the SCH. The individual ILs reported in Eckman (1991) contain consonant-cluster patterns that are not attributable to transfer from the respective NLs, nor are they similar to the TL, English. Yet, despite the numerous possible configurations of consonant cluster types that could have resulted from these language-contact situations, many of which would be counter to the generalizations in (9), the vast majority of these structures conformed to the universals.

With these empirical results in hand, we turn now to the evaluation of the SCH relative to the MDH.

D. Evaluation of the SCH

As pointed out in section II.D above, hypotheses are evaluated empirically against facts, and theoretically against competing hypotheses. When we compare the SCH to the MDH, we find that the SCH is superior on both counts.

The SCH is superior to the MDH empirically in that it is able to account for the data from the Hyltenstam (1984) study that the MDH was unable to account for. Recall that the recalcitrant data, represented in Table I, were a pattern of errors involving pronominal reflexes in relative clauses made by Swedish L2 learners who were NSs of Spanish or Finnish. Specifically, the errors generally followed the markedness relationships derived from the AH, but these errors could not be explained by the MDH because they did not occur in an area of NL–TL difference; that is, neither the TL (Swedish) nor the NLs, (Spanish and Finnish) have pronominal reflexes in relative clauses. Because the MDH bases its predictions on NL–TL differences, it makes no predictions in this case.

The SCH, on the other hand, does not encounter this problem, because its predictions do not involve NL–TL differences whatsoever. The SCH simply asserts that ILs will adhere to the same universal constraints as L1s. Because the IL data represented in Table I are in conformity with the AH, the SCH is supported by these data. Thus, Hyltenstam's data bear on the SCH even though they do not impinge on the MDH.

This situation, it should be pointed out, is representative of the relationship between the MDH and the SCH. All of the facts that support the MDH will also support the SCH. Specifically, if the differences between the NL and TL cause more errors in more marked constructions and fewer errors in less marked constructions, then both the MDH and SCH will be supported. The MDH will be supported because the degree of difficulty reflects the degree of markedness, and the SCH will be supported because the IL will contain more marked structures only if it also contains less marked structures. Notice, however, that if the pattern of L2 errors is not in an area of NL–TL difference, then the MDH makes no prediction, as in Table I. The SCH, on the other hand, is falsified by these data if they do not conform to the markedness relationships. Thus, the SCH is vulnerable where the MDH is not, making the SCH a stronger, more easily falsifiable hypothesis.

To summarize, we have shown a progression of hypotheses, beginning with the CAH, continuing to the MDH, and ultimately leading to the SCH. What links the first hypothesis to the second is the prediction of difficulty; what differentiates them is the incorporation of markedness. What connects the second to the third is the continued use of markedness; what differentiates them is the elimination of NL–TL differences. In addition, we have also shown that in each progression, the replacement hypothesis is stronger than its predecessor because the replacement is more falsifiable. We conclude this chapter with discussion of the SCH in the context of some recent proposals.

IV. THE SCH AND RECENT PROPOSALS

Up to this point, our discussion has centered around an approach to explaining certain facts about L2 acquisition through the use of functional–typological universals. However, within current L2 acquisition research, there is another approach to explaining problems of L2 acquisition that is implemented through the theory of Universal Grammar (UG).

At the risk of oversimplifying, it is fair to say that the functional–typological approach and UG theory differ in two significant ways as to how they view linguistic universals. First, they differ in the type of generalizations stated, and second, they differ in the types of explanation given for these generalizations.

The functional–typological approach to universals is outlined in section I. To recapitulate briefly, this school of thought attempts to state empirical generalizations based on data from a number of different languages. The theory of UG (Chomsky 1981, and elsewhere) is a set of abstract and general principles that is assumed to be adequate for characterizing the core grammars of all natural languages. The central goal of the UG school is to account for the relative speed and uniformity with which children acquire their NL. To this end, UG is postulated to constitute a human's innate language faculty, and to consist of principles that form the basis for all natural-language grammars. The systematic variability found among languages is accounted for by hypothesizing that some principles of UG permit variation only along certain well-defined parameters. (See also chapters 2 through 5, Gregg, White, Flynn, and Schachter, for discussions of UG and L2 acquisition.)

Proponents from both schools of universals have made claims about L2 acquisition. The claims of the functional-typologists have already been outlined above. Proponents of the UG school have claimed that principles of UG constrain not only L1 grammars, but also L2 grammars (Flynn, 1987, 1988; White, 1985a, 1985b, 1987, 1989b). Advocates of this position, in other words, have hypothesized a version of the SCH, claiming that the grammars of ILs are constructed in conformity with the principles of UG.

This chapter is not the proper forum, nor is there adequate space, for discussing the various similarities and differences between these two approaches to universals and L2 acquisition. The point is simply that the SCH is neutral as to the framework within which the universal generalizations are stated.

V. CONCLUSION

One of the topics that has received considerable attention in L2 acquisition theory over the last decade is the role of linguistic universals in explaining facts about L2 acquisition. This chapter has traced the development of one line of thought in this area, namely, the functional–typological approach, from its original embodiment in the MDH to its subsequent formulation as the SCH.

REFERENCES

Adjémian, C. (1976). On the nature of interlanguage systems. *Language Learning, 26,* 297–320.

Altenberg, E., & Vago, R. (1983). Theoretical implications of an error analysis of second language phonology production. *Language Learning, 33,* 427–447.

Anderson, J. I. (1987). The markedness differential hypothesis and syllable structure difficulty. In G. Ioup & S. Weinberger (Eds.), *Interlanguage phonology: The acquisition of a second language sound system* (pp. 279–291). (New York: Newbury House.

Benson, B. (1986). The markedness differential hypothesis: Implications for Vietnamese speakers of English. In F. Eckman, E. Moravcsik, & J. Wirth (Eds.), *Markedness* (pp. 271–290). New York: Plenum Press.

Chomsky, N. (1981). Principles and parameters in syntactic theory. In N. Hornstein & D. Lightfoot (Eds.), *Explanation in linguistics.* London: Longman.

Doughty, C. (1991). Second language instruction does make a difference: Evidence from an empirical study of SL relativization. *Studies in Second Language Acquisition, 13,* 431–469.

Dulay, H., & Burt, M. (1972). Goofing: An indicator of children's second language learning strategies. *Language Learning, 22,* 235–252.

Dulay, H., & Burt, M. (1973). Should we teach children syntax. *Language Learning, 23,* 235–252.

Dulay, H., & Burt, M. (1974a). Errors and strategies in child second language acquisition. *TESOL Quarterly, 8,* 129–136.

Dulay, H., & Burt, M. (1974b). Natural sequences in child second-language acquisition. *Language Learning, 24,* 37–53.

Duskova, L. (1969). On sources of errors in foreign language learning. *International Review of Applied Linguistics, 7,* 11–36.

Eckman, F. (1977). Markedness and the contrastive analysis hypothesis. *Language Learning, 27,* 315–330.

Eckman, F. (1984). Universals, typologies, and interlanguage. In W. Rutherford (Ed.), *Language universals and second language acquisition* (pp. 79–105). Amsterdam: John Benjamins.

Eckman, F. (1991). The Structural Conformity Hypothesis and the acquisition of consonant clusters in the interlanguage of ESL learners. *Studies in Second Language Acquisition, 7,* 289–307.

Eckman, F., Moravcsik, E., & Wirth, J. (1989). Implicational universals and interrogative structures in the interlanguage of ESL learners. *Language Learning, 39,* 173–205.

Eckman, F., Nelson, D., & Bell, L. (1988). On the generalization of relative clause instruction in the acquisition of English as a second language. *Applied Linguistics, 9,* 1–11.

Ellis, R. (1994). "The Study of Second Language Acquisition." Oxford: Oxford University Press.

Flynn, S. (1987). *A parameter setting model of second language acquisition.* Dordrecht: Reidel.

Flynn, S. (1988). Nature of development in L2 acquisition and implications for theories of language acquisition in general. In S. Flynn & W. O'Neil (Eds.), *Linguistic theory in second language acquisition.* Dordrecht: Kluwer.

Fries, C. (1945). *Teaching and learning English as a foreign language.* Ann Arbor: University of Michigan Press.

Gass, S. (1979). Language transfer and universal grammatical relations. *Language Learning, 29,* 327–345.

Greenberg, J. (1966). Some universals of grammar with particular reference to the order of meaningful elements. In J. Greenberg (Ed.), *Universals of language* (2nd ed.). Cambridge, MA: MIT Press.

Greenberg, J. (1978). Some generalizations concerning initial and final consonant clusters. In J. Greenberg, C. A. Ferguson, & E. Moravcsik (Eds.), *Universals of human language: Vol. 2. Phonology* (pp. 243–279). Stanford, CA: Stanford University Press.

Hyltenstam, K. (1984). The use of typological markedness conditions as predictors in second language acquisition: The case of pronominal copies in relative clauses. In R. Andersen (Ed.), *Second languages: A cross-linguistic perspective.* Rowley, MA: Newbury House.

Jakobson, R. (1968). *Child language, aphasia and phonological universals.* The Hague: Mouton.

Keenan, E., & Comrie, B. (1977). Noun phrase accessibility and universal grammar. *Linguistic Inquiry, 8,* 63–100.

Lado, R. (1957). *Linguistics across cultures.* Ann Arbor: University of Michigan Press.

Moulton, W. (1962). *The sounds of English and German.* Chicago: University of Chicago Press.

Richards, J. C. (1971). A non-contrastive approach to error analysis. *English Language Teaching, 25,* 204–219.

Ritchie, W. C. (1978). The right roof constraint in an adult-acquired language. In W. C. Ritchie (Ed.), *Second language acquisition research: Issues and implications* (pp. 33–63). New York: Academic Press.

Schachter, J. (1974). An error in error analysis. *Language Learning, 24,* 205–214.

Schmidt, M. (1980). Coordinate structures and language universals in interlanguage. *Language Learning, 30,* 397–416.

Sciarone, A. G. (1970). Contrastive analysis: Possibilities and limitations. *International Review of Applied Linguistics, 8,* 115–131.

Selinker, L. (1972). Interlanguage. *International Review of Applied Linguistics, 10,* 209–231.

Stockwell, R., & Bowen, R. D. (1965). *The sounds of English and Spanish.* Chicago: University of Chicago Press.

Wardhaugh, R. (1970). The contrastive analysis hypothesis. *TESOL Quarterly, 5,* 123–130.

White, L. (1985a). The acquisition of parameterized grammars: Subjacency in second language acquisition. *Second Language Research, 1,* 1–17.

White, L. (1985b). The "Pro-drop" parameter in adult second language acquisition. *Language Learning, 35,* 47–62.

White, L. (1987). Markedness and second language acquisition: The question of transfer. *Studies in Second Language Acquisition, 9,* 261–286.

White, L. (1989a). Linguistic universals, markedness and learnability: Comparing different approaches. *Second Language Research, 5,* 127–140.

White, L. (1989b). *Universal Grammar and second language acquisition.* Amsterdam: John Benjamins.

C H A P T E R   7

INFORMATION-PROCESSING APPROACHES TO RESEARCH ON SECOND LANGUAGE ACQUISITION AND USE

Barry McLaughlin and Roberto Heredia

I. WHAT IS INFORMATION PROCESSING?

In general, the fundamental notion of the information-processing approach to psychological inquiry is that complex behavior builds on simple processes. These processes are viewed as autonomous (Massaro, 1989), and thus can be studied and described independently from the overall proposed mechanism. Processes occur in steps and therefore processing takes time. It is this reductionist view of information processing that allows us to isolate these processes from the overall psychological mechanism. That is, it allows us to break down processing into a series of stages.

This conventional view of the information-processing approach sees humans as composed of separate information-processing mechanisms. These mechanisms include perceptual systems (pattern recognition), output systems, memory systems (e.g., short-term and long-term memory), and systems for intrinsic reasoning (Norman, 1985). Although this conceptualization of information processing is well accepted, there are those who argue that this view does not consider humans as active participants or that it is too detached from the interaction of people and environment (e.g., Kolers & Roediger, 1984; Norman, 1985; however, see Eysenck & Keane, 1990). Others see this view as relying too heavily on the computer as a metaphor (e.g., Searle, 1984).

213

II. BASIC ASSUMPTIONS OF INFORMATION-PROCESSING PERSPECTIVE

The basic assumptions of the information-processing approach are listed in Table I. Because human learners are limited in their information-processing abilities, only so much attention can be given to the various components of complex tasks at one time. In order to function effectively, humans develop ways of organizing information. Some tasks require more attention; others that have been well practiced require less. The development of any complex cognitive skill involves building up a set of well-learned, efficient procedures so that more attention-demanding processes are freed up for new tasks. In this way limited resources can be spread to cover a wide range of task demands.

The notion of capacity-free (automatic) processes provides an explanation for improvement in learner performance. When one component of a task becomes automatized, attention can be devoted to other components of the task and what was previously a difficult or impossible task becomes possible. It has become common in the cognitive psychological literature to distinguish two processes in skill development. Shiffrin and Schneider called these the automatic and the controlled modes of information processing.

A. Learning and Automaticity

The first of these, *automatic processing,* involves the activation of certain nodes in memory each time the appropriate inputs are present. This activation is a learned response that has been built up through the consistent mapping of the same input to the same pattern of activation over many trials. Because an automatic process utilizes a relatively permanent set of associative connections in long-term storage, most automatic processes require an appreciable amount of

TABLE I

**Some Characteristics of
the Information-Processing Approach**

1. Humans are viewed as autonomous and active.
2. The mind is a general-purpose, symbol-processing symbol.
3. Complex behavior is composed of simpler processes. These processes are modular.
4. Component processes can be isolated and studied independently of other processes.
5. Processes take time; therefore, predictions about reaction time can be made.
6. The mind is a limited-capacity processor.

training to develop fully. Once learned, however, automatic processes occur rapidly and are difficult to suppress or alter. In short, automatic processes function rapidly and in parallel form (Shiffrin & Schneider, 1977).

The second mode of information processing, *controlled processing,* is not a learned response, but instead a temporary activation of nodes in a sequence. This activation is under the attentional control of the subject and, because attention is required, only one such sequence can normally be controlled at a time without interference. Controlled processes are thus tightly capacity-limited, and require more time for their activation. But controlled processes have the advantage of being relatively easy to set up, alter, and apply to novel situations. In short, controlled processing is flexible and functions serially (Shiffrin & Schneider, 1977).

In this framework, learning involves the transfer of information to long-term memory and is regulated by controlled processes. That is, skills are learned and routinized (i.e., become automatic) only after the earlier use of controlled processes. It is controlled processes that regulate the flow of information from short-term to long-term memory. Learning occurs over time, but once automatic processes are set up at one stage in the development of a complex information-processing skill, controlled complex cognitive skills is that they are learned and routinized (i.e., become automatic) through the initial use of controlled processes. Controlled processing requires attention and takes time, but through practice sub-skills become automatic, and controlled processes are free to be allocated to higher levels of processing. Thus controlled processing can be said to lay down the "stepping stones" for automatic processing as the learner moves to more and more difficult levels (Shiffrin & Schneider, 1977).

Complex tasks are characterized by a hierarchical structure. That is, such tasks consist of subtasks and their components. The execution of one part of the task requires the completion of various smaller components. As Levelt (1978) noted, carrying on a conversation is an example of a hierarchical task structure. The first-order goal is to express a particular intention. To do this, the speaker must decide on a topic and select a certain syntactic schema. In turn, the realization of this scheme requires subactivities, such as formulating a series of phrases to express different aspects of the intention. But to utter the phrases there is the need for lexical retrieval, the activation of articulatory patterns, utilization of appropriate syntactic rules, and so forth. Each of these component skills needs to be executed before the higher order goal can be realized, although there may be some parallel processing in real time.

Although widely cited and often used in information-processing accounts of learning, the controlled-automatic distinction is not unproblematic. As Schneider, Dumais, and Shiffrin (1984) noted, there are various ways of characterizing these operations that have been proposed by different authors. Furthermore, the empirical basis for the distinction rests mainly on performance in relatively simple tasks that combine visual and memory search (e.g., subjects are presented with a set of items and asked to say whether any members of the set appear in subsequently presented items). Several authors have questioned the claim that automatic processing is free of attentional limits in more complex tasks. Moreover, the weakness of this distinction is that it is a very descriptive approach rather than explanatory (for further details, see Cheng, 1985; Eysenck & Keane, 1990; Schmidt, 1992, for other criticisms).

Schneider (1985) distinguished two kinds of learning: *priority learning,* which attracts attention to display positions that are likely to contain targets, and *association learning,* which connects stimuli directly to responses. The mechanism underlying both kinds of learning is proportional strengthening: after each successful trial, priority and associative strength are both increased by an amount proportional to the difference between their current strength and the maximum possible strength.

B. Role of Practice

Note the importance, in this framework, of practice. Proportional strengthening occurs through practice. The development of any complex cognitive skill is thought to require building up a set of well-learned, automatic procedures so that controlled processes are freed for new learning. With enough practice, it is possible for people to carry out quite amazing feats. In one experiment, after extended practice, subjects were able to read a story aloud while writing down another story from dictation (Solomons & Stein, 1896, cited in Howard, 1983). In this case, presumably, reading had become so automatic that the subjects could devote attention to the other task.

From a practical standpoint, the necessary component is overlearning. A skill must be practiced again and again and again, until no attention is required for its performance. *Repetitio est mater studiorum*—practice, repetition, time on task— these seemed to be the critical variables for successful acquisition of complex skills, including complex cognitive skills such as second language (L2) learning.

This conceptualization, however, leaves something out of the picture, and runs contrary to the experience of researchers in the L2 field. As Patsy Lightbown argued,

> Practice does not make perfect. Even though there are acquisition sequences, acquisition is not simply linear or cumulative, and having practiced a particular form or pattern does not mean that the form or pattern is permanently established. Learners appear to forget forms and structures which they had seemed previously to master and which they had extensively practiced. (Some researchers have referred to 'U-shaped development'). (1985, p. 177)

She went on to discuss some of her own research:

> Learners were—for months at a time—presented with one or a small number of forms to learn and practice, and they learned them in absence of related contrast-

ing forms. When they did encounter new forms, it was not a matter of simply adding them on. Instead the new forms seemed to cause a restructuring of the whole system. (Lightbown, 1985, p. 177)

C. Restructuring

The notion of U-shaped performance in L2 learning has been questioned by Shirai (1990) on the grounds that statistical evidence for U-shaped behavior is lacking. Nonetheless, there are various phenomena in the L2 literature that suggest that performance declines as more complex internal representations replace less complex ones, and increases again as skill becomes expertise (McLaughlin, 1990). (For another reference to U-shaped behavior, see chapter 11, this volume, by Nunan.) An example is a common strategy adopted by young L2 learners (and, perhaps by more older L2 learners than we realize) to memorize formulas (Hakuta, 1976; Wong Fillmore, 1976). Some children are capable of amazing feats of imitation, producing multiword utterances, which, it turns out, they understand only vaguely. Such unanalyzed chunks appear to show evidence of a sophisticated knowledge of the lexicon and syntax, but it has become clear that such holistic learning is a communicative strategy that L2 learners use to generate input from native speakers (Wong Fillmore, 1976).

Subsequently, formulas are gradually "unpacked" and used as the basis for more productive speech. At this stage, the learner's speech is simpler but more differentiated syntactically. Whereas utterances were as long as six or seven words in the initial stage, they are now much shorter. The learner has at this point adopted a new strategy, one of rule analysis and consolidation. The shift from formulaic speech to rule analysis is an example of the transition from exemplar-based representations to more rule-based representations.

Representational changes of this nature are the focus of one of the major research enterprises of contemporary cognitive psychology, understanding novice–expert shifts. As the name implies, the study of the novice–expert shift is the study of the change that occurs as a beginner in some domain gains expertise. Many domains have been studied—most extensively, expertise at chess, in the physical sciences, in computer programming, and in mathematical problem solving.

For the most part, these studies show that experts restructure the elements of a learning task into abstract schemata that are not available to novices, who focus principally on the surface elements of a task. Thus experts replace complex sub-elements with schemata that allow more abstract processing. There is some evidence from L2 research that suggests that more expert language learners show greater plasticity in restructuring their internal representations of the rules governing linguistic input (Nation & McLaughlin, 1986; Nayak, Hansen, Krueger, & McLaughlin, 1990).

Thus, whereas much of what is involved in language learning may be acquired through accretion via practice whereby an increasing number of information chunks are compiled into an automated procedure, there may also be qualitative changes that occur as learners shift strategies and restructure their internal representations of the target language (TL).

In this view, practice can have two very different effects. It can lead to improvement in performance as subskills become automated, but it is also possible for increased practice to lead to restructuring and attendant decrements in performance as learners reorganize their internal representational framework (McLaughlin, 1990). It seems that the effects of practice do not accrue directly or automatically to a skilled action, but rather cumulate as learners develop more efficient procedures (Kolers & Duchnicky, 1985).

III. THEORETICAL OPTIONS

In a recent paper on language fluency, Schmidt (1992) compared several attempts to identify the psychological mechanisms underlying the cognitive learning processes involved in L2 fluency. Two of the mechanisms he discussed were the notions of automaticity and restructuring. In addition, he included the mechanisms of proceduralization, composition, generalization, discrimination, and strengthening proposed in Anderson's ACT* theory of cognition (Anderson, 1982, 1983), Bialystok's dimension of "control" (1990), and Logan's (1988) instance theory of automatization.

Anderson's ACT* theory stresses the difference between knowing concepts, propositions, and schemata (declarative knowledge) and knowing how to perceive and classify patterns and how to follow specific steps until an end goal is reached (procedural knowledge). Procedural knowledge is thought to be acquired through extensive practice and feedback and, once learned, is more easily activated in memory than declarative knowledge. This approach is in many respects similar to that based on Shiffrin and Schneider's (1977) distinction between controlled and automatic processing in that both account for the progression from a more cognitively demanding to an autonomous stage of learning.

Anderson's theory, however, is more detailed and more powerful than other accounts. The acquisition of a complex cognitive skill, such as an L2, does not merely involve the speeding up of the same procedures formed originally from declarative knowledge, but also the establishment of new procedures reorganizing previously acquired procedures. Furthermore, Anderson's is a multimechanism theory. Thus, for example, various mechanisms are postulated to contribute to the fine tuning of procedural knowledge, including generalization, discrimination, and strengthening.

Bialystok distinguished between what she calls the "analyzed factor" (1982)— or the "knowledge dimension" (1990) and the "control factor." The knowledge dimension has to do with how linguistic knowledge is represented cognitively and how representational change occurs in the course of linguistic development. In her view, there is a progressive development of knowledge from a more implicit to a more explicit and formally organized system. The control factor is involved in accessing and using information in the knowledge. It refers to the ability to select, coordinate, and integrate relevant information in real time. Where there is high control, there is skillful performance.

Hulstijn (1990) has criticized this view, arguing that development must proceed from high control to low control—i.e., from controlled to automatic processing. However, the disagreement is largely a question of terminology. For Bialystok the consequence of high levels of control is intentional processing. This is akin to intentional activity in Levelt's (1989) model of speech production, serving purposes that speakers want to realize. At the same time, control needs to be allocated where it is needed via automatic low-level components (e.g., the selection of grammatical structures, retrieval of lexical items, formulation of articulatory plans, etc.). Bialystok appears to be speaking of the first type of control, Hulstijn, the second.

Finally, Logan's (1988) instance theory views automaticity as the acquisition of domain-specific knowledge that accumulates through separate instances, each of which leaves episodic traces on memory. In contrast to the positions of Shiffrin and Schneider (1977) and Anderson (1982), which assume that automatization occurs as fewer resources are required, Logan holds that the underlying process or algorithm does not speed up because of reduction in the amount of resources required, but rather because the knowledge base changes through the accumulation of instances in memory. Thus in lexical decision tasks, reaction times decrease for specifically practiced words and nonwords, but not for new items. This is seen as evidence for Logan's position that it is experience with previous instances, rather than general procedures, that explains automatization (see also Eysenck & Keane, 1990).

Logan's position differs from a connectionist perspective in that it is not an increase in the strength of connections between generic stimuli and generic responses that produces learning, but the encoding and retrieval of separate representations of each encounter with a stimulus. Nonetheless, Logan and connectionist theorists share the view that learning does not involve the abstraction of "rules" from instances, but rather the strengthening of memory traces.

IV. IS LEARNING A MONOLITHIC CONSTRUCT?

This brings us to the question of whether learning is a unitary process, or whether it is more viable to think of learning as involving various mechanisms and processes. In a discussion of the acquisition of semantic knowledge in memory, Rumelhart and Norman (1978) distinguished three different learning processes: (1) accretion, whereby information is incremented by a new piece of data or a new set of facts; (2) tuning, whereby there is a change in the categories used for interpreting new information; and (3) restructuring, which occurs when new structures are devised for interpreting new information and imposing a new organization on that already stored. In tuning, categories or schemata are modified; in restructuring, new structures are added that allow for new interpretation of facts.

Contemporary theorists disagree on the need for more than a single learning mechanism. Logan takes the position that a single mechanism—retrieval of instances—suffices to explain how practice leads to automaticity. In this he differs from Shiffrin and Schneider (1977), who specify two kinds of learning: priority learning, which is important in focusing attention in visual search, and association learning, which connects stimuli directly to stimuli. Logan's tasks are different from Shiffrin and Schneider's, and Logan points out the two theories address different situations. Although stressing a unitary learning mechanism, Logan accepts the likelihood that humans learn in more than one way.

The most detailed and ambitious theory of general cognition is Anderson's multimechanism model. His theory applies best to the learning of general procedures where a series of steps are collapsed into one by combining adjacent procedures. The criticism of the theory is that it is too powerful, and that cooperating and competing learning mechanisms make the theory difficult to falsify (Carlson & Schneider, 1990; Schmidt, 1992).

The disagreement between contemporary learning theorists is mirrored in the literature on human memory. Recent empirical research on human memory is based on a central theoretical distinction between explicit and implicit memory retrieval tasks (Graf & Schacter, 1985). Explicit memory tasks are those tasks that require conscious recollection of studied material directly tested on episodes from recent experience (Richardson-Klavehn & Bjork, 1988). In performing these tasks subjects are instructed to remember events and presumably are aware that they are recollecting recent experiences. Free recall, recognition, and paired-associate learning are included in this category. Implicit tasks, on the other hand, refer to tests that involve no reference to an event in the subject's personal history, but are nonetheless influenced by such events (Richardson-Klavehn & Bjork, 1988). That is, the task does not require conscious recollection, but retention is measured by transfer from a prior experience relative to an appropriate baseline. Any improvement over baseline is referred to as a priming effect. Word-fragment completion tasks, lexical decision tasks, and word identification tasks are considered implicit tasks.

Differences in performance on explicit and implicit memory tasks relate to comparisons between priming effects and recall or recognition. This task incongruency is known as memory dissociation. For instance, comparison of explicit and implicit tasks has shown that amnesiac patients, whose performance in recall or recognition is gravely impaired, exhibit normal or near-normal priming effects on implicit tasks (Roediger, 1990). Other research has shown that it is possible to produce significant effects on free recall and recognition, with little or no influence on priming (Graf & Mandler, 1984; but see Hamman, 1990).

There are two contrasting explanations for memory dissociations. These are the *multimemory approach* and the *unitary-system processing approach*. The leading proponents of multimemory systems are Tulving (1986), who makes the distinction between episodic and semantic systems, and Squire (1987) and numerous other investigators who distinguish procedural and declarative systems. Tulving argues that dissociation between the implicit and explicit support his distinction between episodic and semantic memory, because research shows that it is possible to tap one particular type of memory (episodic) without being able to tap the other (semantic). Squire makes a similar argument with regard to procedural and declarative systems.

However, other researchers take a somewhat different approach (Blaxton, 1985; Jacoby, 1983; Roediger & Blaxton, 1987). They argue that differences on implicit and explicit tests should be understood in terms of a distinction between data-driven or surface processing, and conceptually driven or semantic processing, with the additional assumption that tasks may vary considerably with respect to the nature of the appropriateness of the processes involved. The underlying memory representation is a unitary system (Jacoby, 1983; Roediger & Blaxton, 1987; Weldon & Roediger, 1987). That is, it is not necessary to postulate more than one memory system to account for these dissociations.

The principle of *transfer-appropriate processing* (Morris, Bransford, & Franks, 1977) is central to this characterization of the relation between implicit and explicit memory. The argument is that performance on an implicit memory task is often more dependent on the match between perceptual conditions at study and test phases than is performance on explicit tasks. However, it is important to note that there is no necessary equivalence between data-driven and implicit and conceptually driven and explicit memory. Implicit tasks can be conceptually driven (e.g., cued recall, word-fragment identification translations), and recognition memory tests usually involve a blend of data-driven and conceptually driven processing (Durgunoglu & Roediger, 1987; Graf & Ryan, 1990; Hamman, 1990; Jacoby, 1983).

Years ago, a similar discussion took place over the question of whether it was legitimate to distinguish two types of learning—intentional and incidental. The experimental procedures by which intentional and incidental learning are distinguished typically involve the comparison of performance under instructions to learn the relevant material and no instructions to learn this material. Data from research show quantitative differences between the instructions and no-instructions groups, but all that can be concluded on the basis of such data is that learning is more difficult under disadvantageous (no-instructions) conditions. This is another instance of the importance of transfer-appropriate processing: there is no justification for the implication that two qualitatively distinct types of learning are involved (McLaughlin, 1965).

Should we then reach for Occam's razor? The most parsimonious approach is to view all learning as involving the same mechanisms. Nonetheless, strong arguments can be advanced for multiple learning mechanisms. Neurological evidence indicates that there are various kinds of memory that use different neural mechanisms and follow different rules (Bridgeman, 1988). This suggests the operation of fundamentally different learning procedures.

Most contemporary theorists, as we have seen, appear to accept a dual or multimechanism approach. The notions of automaticity and restructuring assume that learning is not a unitary process. At the very least, it seems that there is adequate evidence for the importance of data-driven and conceptually driven processes (Neisser, 1967) in the acquisition of any cognitive skill as complex as L2 learning.

V. SOURCES OF INDIVIDUAL DIFFERENCE

Why is it that people differ so greatly in their ability to learn L2s? An important source of individual differences is language learning aptitude. We conceptualize aptitude as modifiable by previous learning and experience. Novices can become experts with experience.

The classic work on aptitude is that of John B. Carroll (e.g., 1981), who argued that the variance in foreign language learning can be largely explained by means of a model that postulated several relatively independent subcomponents: phonetic coding ability, grammatical sensitivity, rote learning ability, and inductive language learning ability (see Table II). These components were arrived at by statistical analyses of correlational data involving Carroll's Modern Language Aptitude Test (MLAT) and other tests of language aptitude and classroom language performance.

Carroll (1981) has argued that the tasks contained in aptitude tests are similar to the processes described in information-processing accounts of cognitive functioning. He speculated, for example, that individual variation in the ability to recognize grammatical functions and to match functions in different sentence structures may reflect differences in the ability to operate in "executive" working memory and to store and retrieve information from short-term memory. This line of thinking anticipated recent work on expert systems and is quite consistent with this framework.

In particular, recent work on the concept of "working memory" fits in very well with the way Carroll conceptualized language learning aptitude. The concept

TABLE II

Carroll's Components of Language Learning

1. Phonetic coding ability—the ability to identify distinct sounds, to form associations between those sounds and the symbols represented by them, and to retain these associations.
2. Grammatical sensitivity—the ability to recognize the grammatical functions of words (or other linguistic entities) in sentence structure.
3. Rote learning ability for foreign language materials—the ability to learn associations between sounds and meanings rapidly and efficiently, and to retain these associations.
4. Inductive language learning ability—the ability to infer or induce the rules governing a set of language materials, given samples of language materials that permit such inferences (Carroll, 1967).

of working memory is relatively new in cognitive psychology, and refers to the immediate memory processes involved in the simultaneous storage and processing of information in real time (Harrington, 1992; Harrington & Sawyer, 1992). The term dates to Newell (1973) and is distinguished from the more traditional understanding of short-term memory as a passive storage buffer. Working memory is assumed to have processing as well as storage functions; it serves as the site for executing processes and for storing the products of these processes. For example, in processing a L2, the learner must store phonological, syntactic, semantic, and pragmatic information and must use this information in planning and executing utterances. This information can become a part of working memory via a number of routes: it may be perceptually encoded from the input of an immediate interlocutor, or it may be sufficiently activated so that it is retrieved from long-term memory, or it can be constructed as speech is planned.

Working-memory limits constrain the development of complex cognitive tasks at several stages. Assuming that the mastery of such complex tasks requires the integration of controlled and automatic processing, one would expect that more working-memory capacity is required at the attention-demanding initial phase when controlled processes predominate. Later, when subtasks that once taxed processing capacity become so automatic that they require little processing energy, working-memory load is reduced.

A second limitation of working memory on the acquisition of a complex cognitive skill occurs later as automaticity builds up and memory load is reduced. Anderson (1983) has suggested that, although initial formation of automatic processes reduces working-memory load, subsequent skill improvement actually *increases* working-memory load. The reason for this is that the size of subtasks (or what Anderson calls "composed productions") increases. Larger subtasks require more conditions to be active in working memory before they can execute. This may be an explanation for the kind of restructuring that occurs as learners impose organization on information that has been acquired.

Increased practice can lead to improvement in performance as subskills become automated, but it is also possible for increased practice to create conditions for restructuring with attendant decrements in performance as learners reorganize their internal representational framework. In the second case, performance may follow a U-shaped curve, declining as more complex internal representations replace less complex ones, and increasing again as skill becomes expertise. There are many examples of such U-shaped functions in the literature on first language (L1) and L2 learning (see McLaughlin, 1990). What we are suggesting here is that the reason for such U-shaped functions is that integrating large subtasks makes heavy demands on working memory, and hence performance is actually worse in subsequent stages than it is initially.

VI. PEDAGOGICAL IMPLICATIONS: INSTRUCTIONAL STRATEGIES

The information processing outlined in this chapter can be summarized as follows. The use of an L2 is a cognitive skill and, like other cognitive skills, involves the internalization, through practice, of various information-handling techniques to overcome capacity limitations. Skill acquisition is seen to involve the accumulation of automatic processing through initial controlled operations that require more workload and attention. Internalized rules are restructured as learners adjust their internal representations to match the target language. This restructuring process involves the use of learning, production, and communication strategies.

This does not mean that teaching should lapse into drill-and-practice exercises. The critique of the skill approach to language teaching is that such an approach leaves little room for creative construction and places too great an emphasis on the conscious learning of rules. The information-processing approach stresses that repeated performance of the components of a task through controlled processing leads to the availability of automatized routines. These routines, however, are conceptualized as higher order "plans" (McLaughlin, Rossman, & McLeod, 1983), which are flexible entities that allow for integrated execution of various complex tasks. Training should involve the frequent use of a particular sentence structure in varied lexical settings, not the frequent use of particular sentences (Levelt, 1978).

Although much research remains to be done on the role of working memory in L2 learning, we propose that individual differences in language learning aptitude are due in large measure to the joint function of availability of knowledge about the target language and the speed and efficiency of working memory—which affects the extent to which the individual succeeds in generating and altering the cognitive data required at various processing stages. That is, in L2 learning we see working memory to relate to the degree to which individuals can more flexibly and consistently reconfigure linguistic representations.

We believe that there are strategies that can be taught to increase the efficiency of working-memory processes. Indeed, within an "expert systems" framework, Faerch and Kasper (1983), McGroarty (1989), Oxford (1986), and O'Malley and Chamot (1989) have attempted to specify strategies that good language learners use and to teach them to less expert learners.

The ultimate goal of this research has been to expand and refine the repertoire of strategies of poor learners so that they may benefit from strategies used to good effect by "expert" learners. Wenden (1987) noted that intervention research in the training of cognitive strategies to learners in other skill areas has demonstrated that the continued choice and appropriate use of strategies in a variety of situations requires *metacognition*. It is not enough for learners to be trained to use a particular strategy, they must also understand the significance of the strategy and be able to monitor and evaluate its use. For example, there are various metacognitive strategies that increase the efficiency whereby information is processed (e.g., recognition, selection, generalization, and transfer) (Palincsar & Brown, 1984). We see this work on metacognitive strategies and the recent work on strategy differences that distinguish good from poor language learners (O'Malley & Chamot, 1989; Oxford, 1986; Wenden, 1987) to be important for teaching learners to be more efficient information processors. Indeed, experimental research (e.g., Chase & Ericcson, 1982) has shown that working-memory capability can be greatly expanded as a function of relevant knowledge structures and strategies.

It should be noted that by emphasizing aptitude—as reflected in working-memory processes and acquired strategies—we do not mean to denigrate the importance of attitudes and motivation in language learning. Certainly, these are important sources of individual difference in L2 learning. Aptitude, has, however, been neglected as a topic worthy of attention in L2 research, and the concept of working memory holds promise as a possible mechanism that accounts for differences in aptitude.

REFERENCES

Anderson, J. (1982). Acquisition of cognitive skill. *Psychological Review, 89,* 369–406.
Anderson, J. (1983). *The architecture of cognition.* Cambridge, MA: Harvard University Press.

Bialystok, E. (1982). On the relationship between knowing and using linguistic forms. *Applied Linguistics, 3,* 181–206.

Bialystok, E. (1990). The dangers of dichotomy: A reply to Hulstijn. *Applied Linguistics, 11,* 46–51.

Blaxton, T. A. (1985). *Investigating dissociations among memory measures: Support for a transfer appropriate processing framework.* Doctoral dissertation, Purdue University, West Lafayette, IN.

Bridgeman, B. (1988). *The biology of behavior and mind.* New York: Wiley.

Carlson, R. A., & Schneider, W. (1990). Practice effects and composition: A reply to Anderson, *Journal of Experimental Psychology: Learning, Memory, and Cognition, 15,* 531–533.

Carroll, J. B. (1967). Foreign language proficiency levels attained by language majors near graduation from college. *Foreign Language Annals, 1,* 131–151.

Carroll, J. B. (1981). Twenty-five years of research on foreign language aptitude. In K. C. Diller (Ed.), *Individual differences and universals in language learning aptitude.* Rowley, MA: Newbury House.

Chase, W. C., & Ericcson, K. A. (1982). Skill and working memory. In G. H. Bower (Ed.), *The psychology of learning and motivation* (Vol. 16). New York: Academic Press.

Cheng, P. W. (1985). Restructuring versus automaticity: Alternative accounts of skill acquisition. *Psychological Review, 92,* 214–223.

Durgunoglu, A. Y., & Roediger, H. L. (1987). Test differences in accessing bilingual memory. *Journal of Memory and Language, 26,* 377–391.

Eysenck, M. W., & Keane, M. T. (1990). *Cognitive psychology: A student's handbook.* Hillsdale, NJ: Earlbaum.

Faerch, C., & Kasper, G. (Eds.). (1983). *Strategies in interlanguage communication.* London: Longman.

Graf, P., & Mandler, G. (1984). Activation makes words more accessible, but not necessarily more retrievable. *Journal of Verbal Learning and Verbal Behavior, 23,* 553–568.

Graf, P., & Ryan, L. (1990). Transfer-appropriate processing for implicit and explicit memory. *Journal of Experimental Psychology: Learning, Memory, & Cognition, 16,* 978–992.

Graf, P., & Schacter, D. L. (1985). Implicit and explicit memory for new dissociations in normal and amnesic subjects. *Journal of Experimental Psychology: Learning, Memory, & Cognition, 11,* 501–518.

Hakuta, K. (1976). Becoming bilingual: A case study of a Japanese child learning English. *Language Learning, 26,* 321–351.

Hamman, S. B. (1990). Level-of-processing effects in conceptually driven implicit tasks. *Journal of Experimental Psychology: Learning, Memory, & Cognition, 16,* 970–977.

Harrington, M. (1992). Working memory capacity as a constraint on L2 development. In R. J. Harris (Ed.), *Cognitive processing in bilinguals.* Netherlands: Elsevier North-Holland.

Harrington, M., & Sawyer, M. (1992). L2 working memory capacity and L2 reading skill. *Studies in Second Language Acquisition, 14,* 112–121.

Howard, D. V. (1983). *Cognitive psychology: Memory, language and thought.* New York: Macmillan.

Hulstijn, J. (1990). A comparison between the information-processing and the analysis/ control approaches to language learning. *Applied Linguistics, 11,* 30–45.

Jacoby, L. L. (1983). Remembering the data: Analyzing interactive processes in reading. *Journal of Verbal Learning and Verbal Behavior, 22,* 485–508.

Kolers, P. A., & Duchnicky, R. L. (1985). Discontinuity in cognitive skill. *Journal of Experimental Psychology: Learning, Memory, & Cognition, 11,* 655–674.

Kolers, P. A., & Roediger, H. L. (1984). Procedures of mind. *Journal of Verbal Learning and Verbal Behavior, 23,* 425–449.

Levelt, W. J. M. (1978). Skill theory and language teaching. *Studies in Second Language Acquisition, 1,* 53–70.

Levelt, W. J. M. (1989). *Speaking: From intention to articulation.* Cambridge, MA: MIT University Press.

Lightbown, P. M. (1985). Great expectations: Second-language acquisition research and classroom teaching. *Applied Linguistics, 6,* 173–189.

Logan, G. D. (1988). Toward an instance theory of automatization. *Psychological Review, 95,* 492–527.

Massaro, D. W. (1989). *Experimental psychology: An information processing approach.* San Diego, CA: Harcourt Brace Jovanovich.

McGroarty, M. (1989). *The "good learner" of English in two settings.* Los Angeles: University of California, Center for Language Education and Research.

McLaughlin, B. (1965). "Intentional" and "incidental" learning under conditions of intention to learn and motivation. *Psychological Bulletin, 63,* 359–376.

McLaughlin, B. (1990). Restructuring. *Applied Linguistics, 11,* 1–16.

McLaughlin, B., Rossman, T., & McLeod, B. (1983). Second-language learning: An information-processing perspective. *Language Learning, 33,* 135–158.

Morris, C. D., Bransford, J. D., & Franks, J. J. (1977). Levels of processing versus transfer appropriate processing. *Language Learning, 16,* 519–533.

Nation, R., & McLaughlin, B. (1986). Experts and novices: An information-processing approach to the "good language learner" problem. *Applied Linguistics, 7,* 41–56.

Nayak, N., Hansen, N., Krueger, N., & McLaughlin, B. (1990). Language-learning strategies in monolingual and multilingual adults. *Language Learning, 40,* 221–244.

Neisser, U. (1967). *Cognitive psychology.* New York: Appleton-Century-Crofts.

Newell, A. (1973). Production systems: Models of control structures. In W. G. Chase (Ed.), *Visual information processing.* New York: Academic Press.

Norman, D. A. (1985). Twelve issues for cognitive science. In A. M. Aitkenhead & J. M. Slack (Eds.), *Issues in cognitive modeling* (pp. 309–336). Hillsdale, NJ: Erlbaum.

O'Malley, J. M., & Chamot, A. U. (1989). *Learning strategies in second language acquisition.* New York: Cambridge University Press.

Oxford, R. L. (1986). *Second language learning strategies: Current research and implications for practice.* Los Angeles: University of California, Center for Language Education and Research.

Palincsar, A. S., & Brown, A. L. (1984). Reciprocal teaching of comprehension-fostering and monitoring activities. *Cognition and Instruction, 1,* 117–175.

Richardson-Klavehn, A., & Bjork, R. A. (1988). Measures of memory. *Annual Review of Psychology, 39,* 475–543.

Roediger, H. L. (1990). Implicit memory: Retention without remembering. *American Psychologist, 45,* 1043–1056.

Roediger, H. L., & Blaxton, T. A. (1987). Retrieval modes produce dissociations in memory for surface information. In D. S. Gorfein & R. R. Hoffman (Eds.), *The Ebbinghaus centennial conference* (pp. 349–379). Hillsdale, NJ: Erlbaum.

Rumelhart, D. E., & Norman, D. A., (1978). Accretion, tuning, and restructuring: Three modes of learning. In J. Cotton & R. Klatzky (Eds). *Semantic factors in cognition.* Hillsdale, NJ: Erlbaum.

Schmidt, R. (1992). Psychological mechanisms underlying second language fluency. *Studies in Second Language Acquisition, 14,* 357–386.

Schneider, W. (1985). Toward a model of attention and the development of automatic processing. In M. Posner & O. Marin (Eds.), *Attention and performance XI* (pp. 475–492). Hillsdale, NJ: Erlbaum.

Schneider, W., Dumais, S., & Shiffrin, R. (1984). Automatic and controlled processing and attention. In R. Parasuraman & D. R. Davies (Eds.), *Varieties of attention.* London: Academic Press.

Searle, J. (1984). *Minds, brains, and science.* Cambridge, MA: Harvard University Press.

Shiffrin, R. M., & Schneider, W. (1977). Controlled and automatic human information processing: II. Perceptual learning, automatic attending, and a general theory. *Psychological Review, 84,* 127–190.

Shirai, Y. (1990). *U-shaped behavior in L2 acquisition.* Manuscript, University of California, Los Angeles.

Solomons, L. M., & Stein, G. (1896). Normal motor automatism. *Psychological Review, 3,* 492–512.

Squire, L. R. (1987). *Memory and brain.* New York: Oxford University Press.

Tulving, E. (1986). What kind of hypothesis is the distinction between episodic and semantic memory? *Journal of Experimental Psychology: Learning, Memory, & Cognition, 12,* 307–311.

Weldon, M. S., & Roediger, H. L. (1987). Altering retrieval demands reverses the picture superiority effect. *Memory & Cognition, 15,* 269–280.

Wenden, A. L. (1987). Metacognition: An expanded view on the cognitive abilities of L2 learners. *Language Learning, 37,* 573–598.

Wong Fillmore, L. (1976). *Cognitive and social strategies in language acquisition.* Doctoral dissertation, Stanford University, Stanford, CA.

CHAPTER 8

VARIATIONIST LINGUISTICS AND SECOND LANGUAGE ACQUISITION

Dennis Preston

The relevance of sociolinguistics to second language (L2) acquisition is two-fold. First, it is concerned with variation in language—the product, process, acquisition, and cognitive location of such variation. Those matters are the focus of this chapter. Second, it is concerned with sociological and social-psychological aspects of language. To the extent that those aspects are crucial in the account of variation in lower level structural units of language, they are included here. Similar concerns are, however, independently surveyed in other chapters of this volume, particularly from sociopolitical and affective points of view.

I. A BRIEF HISTORY OF LANGUAGE VARIATION STUDY

The earliest work on variable language focused on geographical distribution, but not for its own sake; historical linguists investigated areal diversity in order to test the major tenet of the late nineteenth-century European Neogrammarians—that sound change was without exception (e.g., Osthoff & Brugmann, 1878). If each region displayed an exceptionless application of a sound change that had operated in its territory, the interpretation of such changes as laws would be strengthened. Even though initial surveys found exceptions, suggesting that the Neogrammarian view was an exaggeration, dialect study continued to have a historical basis. Respondents were selected from older, less well-educated, rural segments of the population, and there was a focus on locating and recording

Handbook of Second Language Acquisition

older forms before they disappeared forever. Eventually, early and mid-twentieth-century dialect study, particularly in the United States, settled into a period in which its findings appeared to be of greater relevance to cultural geography or even folklore than to linguistics in general and the study of linguistic change in particular (e.g., McDavid, 1979). In early U.S. dialect studies, subgroups of the population were identified, but methods for respondent selection and categorization were inconsistent with generally accepted social science procedures (Pickford, 1956). Nevertheless, these studies have provided a wealth of information on regional language distribution, which has well served later sociolinguistic work.

That work, which began in the early 1960s, refocused the study of variation on linguistic change and on variables other than locale. Two approaches in particular—the Labovian and dynamic paradigms—have had considerable influence on L2 acquisition research and are reviewed in the next section.

II. TWO MODELS OF VARIATION

A. The Labovian Paradigm

In a series of studies in the late 1960s and early 1970s (summarized in Labov, 1972), William Labov established an approach to quantitative studies of language variation. The central claim of this approach is that the alternative forms of linguistic elements do not occur randomly. The frequency of their occurrences is predicted by (1) the shape and identity of the element itself and its linguistic context, (2) stylistic level (defined operationally), (3) social identity, and (4) historical position (assuming that one form is on the way in, the other on the way out).

The collection of "good" data is especially crucial in this paradigm, for Labov claimed there is an observer's paradox (Labov, 1972, p. 113)—the more aware respondents are that speech is being observed, the less natural their performances will be. Because self-monitored speech is less casual, that is a major drawback to a crucial assumption: less casual speech is also less systematic, and thus less revealing of a speaker's basic language system, or vernacular. That assumption suggests that sociolinguists seek a systematicity significantly different from Chomskyean competence, and I discuss below questions of Labovian and Chomskyean research programs in L2 acquisition.

Because surreptitious recording strikes most as unethical, eliciting natural samples is a serious problem, but a number of techniques have been developed to overcome the observer's paradox. In one, the familiarity of the collector was exploited. Milroy (1980) showed that a field-worker who became a member of a social network was not only allowed collection which ensured more authentic and representative data, but also was provided with insights into the norms and values of the community, which aided later interpretation.

The degree to which data-recording equipment and activities (e.g., tape record-ers, experimental settings) influence language behavior should not be minimized, but many investigators report that, after a brief period of nervousness and com-ment, instruments have little effect. Milroy went so far as to suggest that "the presence of the tape-recorder in itself . . . seemed less likely to produce a shift away from the vernacular than did conversation with a higher-status participant" (1980, p. 60).

Accidental opportunities for the collection of natural data may arise. During interviews, interaction among respondents, interaction between a respondent and another person not a part of the interview, or interaction between the field-worker and the respondent outside the interview focus or topic may occur. In all these cases, respondents often shift from a relatively formal interview style to a more relaxed one.

The formality of the interview may be reduced by topic. Such questions as, "Did you ever have a dream that really scared you?" or "Were you ever in a situation where you were in serious danger of getting killed?" (Labov, 1984, p. 33) and those that ask about childhood games (Labov, 1972, pp. 91–92) have been effective in acquiring less careful speech.

Finally, the focus of a study may be so precise that observation (not recording) may suffice. In a study of /r/-deletion in New York City department stores, Labov determined what goods were located on the fourth floor and asked a clerk for directions. Then Labov leaned forward slightly and said "Excuse me?" to elicit a more emphatic version (Labov, 1966, chap. III). Though the procedure was simple, it allowed investigation of the linguistic variable in preconsonantal ("fourth") and final ("floor") positions, in two ethnic groups, in two stylistic varieties (ordinary and emphatic), and in three different social status groups— inferred from the reputation of the stores where the survey was conducted.

His concern for the vernacular has led Labov to suggest that there is a stylistic continuum reaching from the most formal (carefully monitored, often elicited through written stimuli) to the most casual (unmonitored); it is the casual end of the continuum that exemplifies vernacular style.

Such collection procedures have, however, been criticized. The special status of an interview itself may produce suspect data. Wolfson (1976) claims that role relationships and genres determined by interviews severely limit the range of speech. A continuum based on data derived from variation in one setting may not be a good indication of general conversational styles. An additional criticism of the operational distinctions used in studying the continuum addresses the problem of reading. Romaine (1980) claims that one cannot assume that speaking and read-ing form a continuous dimension, and Milroy and Milroy (1977) note that in some speech communities skills in reading aloud might be so weak as to make the read-ing of a continuous passage require even more attention than the reading of word lists. Irvine (1979), although not specifically critical of the stylistic continuum, raises questions about types of formality and their meaning and distribution of use in different speech communities.

Early Studies

Background

To illustrate the "early Labovian" treatment of variation, the simplification of final consonant clusters in English which end in /t/ and /d/ will be used. Table I shows the percentage of such deletion under four different linguistic conditions and for four social classes of African-American speakers from Detroit.

These data show patterned variability; both linguistic facts (whether the cluster is followed by a vowel or a consonant, and whether the final member of the cluster is itself the past-tense morpheme or not) and social facts (class, i.e., socioeconomic status) have an effect on deletion. Though there has been controversy about whether or not such patterned variability occurs at other linguistic levels (e.g., Labov, 1978; Lavandera, 1977), it is agreed that such data such as those in Table I are the stuff of quantitative sociolinguistics.

Labov first attempted to deal with such facts in terms of a variable rule. Normally, linguistic rules are categorical—they work everywhere.

$$X \longrightarrow Y/ \underline{\quad} Z$$

X becomes (or 'is realized as') Y whenever Z follows. For example, in my phonological system, the following vowel-raising rule is categorical.

$$/\epsilon/ \longrightarrow [I] \ / \underline{\quad} [+\text{nas}]$$

TABLE I
t/d Deletion in Detroit African-American Speech[a]

Environments	Social Classes			
	Upper middle	Lower middle	Upper working	Lower working
Following vowel				
t/d is past morpheme (e.g., "missed in")	0.07	0.13	0.24	0.34
t/d is not past morpheme (e.g., "mist in")	0.28	0.43	0.65	0.72
Following consonant				
t/d is past morpheme (e.g., "missed by")	0.49	0.62	0.73	0.76
t/d is not past morpheme (e.g., "mist in")	0.79	0.87	0.94	0.97

[a] Adapted from Wolfram and Fasold (1974, p. 132).

/ɛ/ is realized as [I] if a nasal follows, causing "pin" and "pen" to be homophones. (I say 'ball-point' when I want something to write with rather than stick with.)

The data in Table I cannot be displayed in such a rule. If the rule is written categorically,

$$\text{/t, d/} \longrightarrow \varnothing \ / \ C \ \{\varnothing, \#\} \ \underline{\qquad} \ \#\# \ \{C, V\}$$

/t,d/ would be deleted every time it followed a consonant and appeared at the end of a word—that is, before a word boundary (##). Whether /t,d/ was or was not a separate morpheme (∅,#) and whether or not a consonant or vowel followed (C, V) have no influence on this rule, for curly brackets simply indicate that one condition or the other must be present for the rule to operate. The data in Table I show that even when all the best conditions for deletion are met (lower working class, /t,d/ is not the past-tense morpheme, and the following word begins with a consonant), the deletion percentage, although 0.97, is still not categorical.

One solution is to make such rules optional. The mechanism for this shows the product of the rule (and even constraining factors on the rule) in parentheses.

$$\text{/t, d/} \longrightarrow (\varnothing) \ / \ C \ (\#) \ \underline{\qquad} \ \#\# \ \{C, V\}$$

Here /t,d/ may be deleted word finally after a consonant, whether it /t,d/ is a separate morpheme or not (#). The product of the rule (∅ = 'nothing') and the morpheme boundary are indicated as options by enclosing them in parentheses.

This solution, however, provides no quantitative information about morpheme status, following segment, and social class. If social class constituted the only source of variation, one might be justified in claiming that variation should be represented in rules of language use or implementation only (e.g., Kiparsky, 1972). The Table I data show, however, that the variation is as much or more influenced by morpheme status and following segment as it is by social class. A variable rule allows the incorporation of such probabilistic information:

$$\text{/t, d/} \longrightarrow \langle \varnothing \rangle \ / \ C \ \left\langle \begin{matrix} \varnothing \\ \# \end{matrix} \right\rangle \ \underline{\qquad} \ \#\# \ \langle \left\langle \begin{matrix} C \\ V \end{matrix} \right\rangle$$

Angle brackets replace parentheses around both the variable output of the rule and constraints on it. To insert the probabilistic information, an alternative to Table I must be prepared in which one can see the pooled contribution of each of the elements studied (Table II).

With these figures keyed to the variable rule, one may determine the likelihood of the rule's application in a particular case. For example, if an upper middle-status speaker (.41), uses a nonpast (.71) in front of a vowel (.36), we know the various weights that influence consonant cluster simplification. Note that the social status

TABLE II

**t/d Deletion in Detroit
African-American Speech**[a]

		Combined deletions (%)
Following sound		
Consonant		.77 (1)
Vowel		.36 (4)
Morpheme status		
Nonpast		.71 (2)
Past		.42 (3)
Social status (5)	.57	
Upper middle		.41
Lower middle		.51
Upper working		.64
Lower working		.70

[a] Adapted from Wolfram and Fasold (1974, p. 132).

likelihood is associated with the overall application of the rule and that one might add the probability for the entire speech community (.57) or for a subgroup (as I have done above). Note also that the linguistic influences are usually numbered according to their relative strengths. In this case, a following consonant is the strongest promoter of cluster reduction and is assigned a 1. Finally, the exact probability for the example cited above is not an average of the probabilities for all the influencing factors. There is an interesting mathematical history to this problem in variable-rule analysis, but the details are not provided here, because later I show how a statistical package specifically developed to handle naturally occurring linguistic data (VARBRUL) provides a solution to this and other problems.[1] (See below for a detailed discussion of VARBRUL.)

Finally, it must be noted that the variable of age provides the principal variationist means for studying linguistic change: the use of apparent time. The pattern in Figure 1, taken from Trudgill's study of Norwich variation, is typical of linguistic change; the 10–19 age group has radically increased the instance of lowered and centralized /ɛ/ even in their most formal styles. It appears that RP-like [ɛ], in such words as *bell* and *tell,* is giving way to [ɜ] and even [ʌ]. Apparent time study, however, may confuse age-grading (in which linguistic forms are ap-

[1] Another numerical procedure used in early variation studies was the association of an index with different realizations of the linguistic variable. Such scores were convenient ways of representing the incidence of one or more variables from a large body of data. They did not, however, replace the necessity of treating data with more sophisticated statistical procedures. Particularly annoying was the fact that a speaker (or group of speakers) who produced 50% of the first variant and 50% of the third would have exactly the same index score as a speaker (or group of speakers) who produced 100% of the second variant.

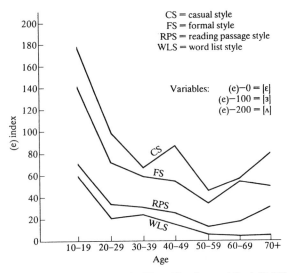

Figure I Norwich (e) by age and style. (From Chambers and Trudgill, 1980, p. 93.)

propriate to a chronological age) with language change.[2] Because change of language forms within the individual rather than change that has a lasting influence on the language itself is usually the focus in L2 acquisition, this important sociolinguistic distinction will not be of such great concern here.

The Early Labovian Paradigm in L2 Acquisition Research

The early Labovian style of quantitative variation analysis in L2 acquisition was first done by L. Dickerson (1974), and W. Dickerson (1976) more explicitly drew the parallel between stages in interlanguage (IL) development and linguistic change and noted that the use of the variable rule model was appropriate to such study. Their work showed, in particular, that two variationist rubrics could be applied to L2 acquisition data: (1) the linguistic environment is a predictor of variable occurrence, and (2) longitudinal (or apparent-time) treatment of data reveals the progress of linguistic change (in L2 acquisition, in the individual rather than in the system). Moreover, the relationship between the linguistic environment and time shows that the environments are important conditioning factors in the progress of the change itself.

[2]The older descriptive work of dialectologists is often of particular help here in determining whether or not a feature is undergoing change or represents age-grading. Labov made just such use of the Linguistic Atlas of New England in his study of Martha's Vineyard (summarized in Labov, 1972) and of the Linguistic Atlas of the Middle and South Atlantic States and other historical data in his work on New York City (Labov, 1966). Other clues to the progress of linguistic change, particularly as it is influenced by sex and social status, are comprehensively outlined in Labov (1972).

The continuous competence model (e.g., Tarone, 1982) suggests that the stylistic continuum of the language acquirer operates much like that of the native speaker (NS). The more attention the learner pays to speech, the more prestige forms are likely to occur (where prestige forms are construed to be target language [TL] forms or learners' understandings of what those forms are).

Tarone's characterization of what style is borrows heavily from the sociolinguists' operational devices used to elicit this dimension rather than from its underlying causes (e.g., degree of formality). Stylistic fluctuation, in her account, is due to the degree of monitoring or attention to form, and varying degrees of attention to form are by-products of the amount of time that various language tasks allow the language user for monitoring (e.g., writing perhaps the most, spontaneous conversation the least). According to Tarone, this variation all takes place for the early language acquirer within only one envelope or register. Only more advanced learners acquire different registers that entail such matters as genre and other complex norms of interaction and use which, in turn, contribute to the positioning of a task on the stylistic continuum.

Krashen's monitor model (e.g., Krashen, 1987) turns the stylistic continuum into a two-way distinction, suggesting that some few, easily represented rules are the result of conscious activity (learning), but that most rules, difficult to describe, are the result of nonconscious activity (acquisition). In performance, Krashen claims, learners do not have sufficient time to monitor the learned rules. NS studies, however, have been little concerned with the monitoring of learned rules. Even the most formal end of the stylistic continuum results from the application of rules that NSs lack metalinguistic awareness of. For variationists, monitoring refers to general attention to speech, not to attempts to retrieve consciously formulated rules.

It is true, however, that NSs, particularly in unfamiliar or status-ridden settings, may attempt to monitor ancient secondary-school prescriptions or other shibboleths (e.g., who versus whom), and a relatively small number of such often socially damaging stereotypes exist in every speech community. Krashen may believe that an even greater number of rules have just such status for the language learner. Because it is only dichotomous, however, the monitor theory provides no explicit account of variation within both learned and acquired sets of rules, nor does it provide a principled account of how learned items may permeate the area reserved for acquired ones.

Variable Rule Analysis

Background

The data from Table I also serve to introduce the statistical program known as VARBRUL, a more principled way of determining the probability each constraint contributes to the operation (or nonoperation) of a rule, particularly when naturally occurring language data are being studied. (See Montgomery, 1990, for an outline history of the development and modification of VARBRUL programs.)

The program calculates the probabilities for each factor and assigns a value ranging from 0.00–1.00. That range indicates the degree to which a factor promotes the operation of the tested rule (the higher the value, the greater the influence). The program was run on hypothetical raw data based on Table I, and the results are shown in Table III. In part B of Table III the columns labeled Observed and Total reconfirm the raw data figures; the column labeled Expected indicates the number of rule applications predicted by the analysis, and the column labeled Error displays the degree to which the actual data and expected number of applications correspond. Error values below 2.0 (conservatively, 1.5) are good; they indicate that the statistical model produced by VARBRUL 2 fits the raw data. In this case, the worst error score, 1.662, is acceptable.

TABLE III

VARBRUL 2 Results for t/d Deletion by African-American Speakers from Detroit[a]

A		Following vowel (V)			0.25
		Following consonant (C)			0.75
		Morpheme (M)			0.31
		Nonmorpheme (N)			0.69
		Upper middle class (UMC)			0.29
		Lower middle class (LMC)			0.42
		Upper working class (UWC)			0.60
		Lower working class (LWC)			0.69
		Input probability 0.60			

		Observed	Expected	Total	Error
B	VMUMC	7	8.09	100	0.159
	VMLMC	13	13.73	100	0.045
	VMUWC	24	24.84	100	0.038
	VMLWC	34	32.04	100	0.176
	VNUMC	28	30.61	100	0.321
	VNLMC	43	44.37	100	0.076
	VNUWC	65	62.36	100	0.297
	VNLWC	72	70.27	100	0.143
	CMUMC	49	44.39	100	0.860
	CMLMC	62	59.07	100	0.354
	CMUWC	73	74.99	100	0.211
	CMLWC	76	81.05	100	1.662
	CNUMC	79	80.01	100	0.064
	CNLMC	87	87.86	100	0.069
	CNUWC	94	93.76	100	0.010
	CNLWC	97	95.54	100	0.498
	Total chi-square			4.981	
	Average chi-square per cell			0.311	

[a] Table based on hypothetical data inferred from Table I.

The "Input probability" is the likelihood that this rule will operate in general; that is, there is a tendency for this rule to operate at 0.60 overall.

The measurement of chi-square indicates the degree to which the elements in the analysis are independent of one another. Here a total chi-square of at least 11.07 (.05 probability with five degrees of freedom) would be necessary to show that the factors were not independent. The 4.981 score ensures that three factors (morpheme status, following segment, and status) do not interact.

The average chi-square per cell indicates the degree to which the variables considered account for the variation in the data. The further from 1.0 this figure is, the surer one may be that additional variables need not be sought. The score here, 0.311, is good, indicating that following segment, morpheme status and social status account for the observed variation.

Part A of Table III is the real heart of the operation. We already know that when a consonant follows and when /t,d/ is not a separate morpheme the rule operates more frequently, and that when a vowel follows and /t,d/ is a morpheme its operation is retarded; now we have a statistically sophisticated estimate of each constraint's influence (in contrast to the pooled percentage results shown in Table II). Here is how one might use these figures to calculate the overall probability of a single occurrence for the item *mist* in the phrase *mist by the sea* (uttered by an upper middle-status speaker):

1. Enter the probability 0.60, the input probability or tendency for the rule to work overall.
2. Enter the appropriate social-class weight—0.29 for upper middle.
3. Enter 0.69, the weight contributed by the fact that /t,d/ is not the separate morpheme past tense in the item "mist."
4. Enter 0.75, the weight contributed by the following consonant in "by."

Recall that just combining the weight will not do. That is, they cannot be simply averaged. Those that retard (or promote) the operation of the rule are (blindly) in cahoots with one another, and the net effect on the probability will be even lower (or higher) than an average. Here is the formula:

$$p = \frac{p_o x \ldots x p_n}{[p_o x \ldots x p_n] + [(1 - p_o)x \ldots x(1 - p_n)]}$$

I'll do this for you for the imaginary problem we are working on.

$$p = \frac{.60x.29x.69x.75}{[.60x.29x.69x.75] + [(1 - .60)x(1 - .29)x(1 - .69)x(1 - .75)]}$$

Therefore:

$$p = \frac{.090045}{.090045 + .02201} \quad \text{or} \quad p = .8035785$$

TABLE IV

**VARBRUL 2 Results for Alberto's Use of
the "Don't" Negation Strategy[a,b]**

Subject environment		Verb environment		Complement environment	
I	0.592	can	0.783	noun	0.661
other	0.408	MV[c]	0.601	other	0.513
		like	0.540	pronoun	0.423
		have	0.136	none	0.399

[a] Adapted from Adamson and Kovac (1981, p. 288, Table 3).
[b] Input = .807; Average chi-square = .833
[c] MV, main verb.

In other words, when an African-American, middle-class Detroiter utters the phrase "mist by the sea" there is a 0.80 probability that the pronunciation will be "mis" (not "mist").

VARBRUL also performs a stepwise regression that identifies factors (technically, factor groups) that do not contribute to the variability of the rule.[3] When applied to these data, the regression analysis did not suggest doing away with any of the factors. Considering the results of both the average chi-square per cell figure and the regression analysis allows one to claim that (1) no factor that influences rule variability has been overlooked, and (2) factors that have little or no influence on variability have been excluded.

The utility of variable rules as psycholinguistic constructs has been attacked, however, and we shall return to consideration of that point and its relevance to L2 acquisition, although there is no evidence that probabilities themselves are too complex to play a role in human behavior. Studies outside linguistics have shown that probabilistic behavior occurs in individuals (Garner, 1962; Sternberg, 1963).

Variable Rule Analysis in L2 Acquisition Research

Perhaps the first published application of the VARBRUL technique to L2 acquisition data is Adamson and Kovac (1981). They treat the early development of negative strategies in the English of Alberto, a 33-year-old Spanish-speaking blue-collar worker learning English, who was extensively studied by Schumann (1978). The variable rule they treat is the alternation between NO + VERB (e.g., *I no understand*) and DON'T + VERB (*He don't like it*).[4] Table IV shows the results.

[3] There is a procedure to test the significance of even a single influencing variable within a factor group, but that sophistication is not discussed here. Young (1991) provides an account of the use of this technique.

[4] "Applications of the rule" are, in this case, instances of DON'T + VERB. The rule could just as easily have been written the other way (although it would have been developmentally silly to do so).

TABLE V
**VARBRUL 2 Results for Alberto's Use of the "Don't"
Negation Strategy (Divided by Stylistic Level)[a,b]**

Subject environment		Verb environment		Complement environment	
I	0.745	can	0.837	none	0.677
other	0.255	MV[c]	0.491	noun	0.522
		have	0.343	other	0.427
		like	0.278	pronoun	0.342

[a] Adapted from Adamson and Kovac (1981, p. 289, Table 4).
[b] Input = .807; Average chi-square = .507; Style: formal = .893; casual = .107.
[c] MV, main verb.

The subject "I" promotes the "don't" strategy as do verbs other than "have" (particularly "can"). Transitives (except for pronominal complements) also promote "don't." Note however, that the average chi-square is .833, suggesting that some other factor may be at work. In Table V, Adamson and Kovac rerun the data, separating the formal from the informal performances.[5]

The average chi-square is lowered considerably in this second run, and it is no wonder, for the range of stylistic variation (.893–.107) is the most dramatic of the data set. It is important to note, however, that the introduction of the formality distinction did not only improve the average chi-square score. Constraints in both the verb and complement environment factor groups were reordered. In the more acceptable version (Table V) both MV (main verbs) and "like" join "have" in retarding "don't." In the complement environment, an even more dramatic reordering may be observed in which intransitives ("none") move from the principal demoters of the "don't" strategy to its principal promoters.[6] In accounting for IL development by assigning influencing factors, such understandings of the data would appear to be absolutely crucial. I will return to more recent uses of VARBRUL and L2 acquisition data below.

B. The Dynamic Paradigm

Background

Bailey (1974) summarizes an alternative approach to variation and change known as wave theory. From this point of view, synchronic language variation is

[5] Informal instances were all cases gleaned from conversational interview data; formal instances were those elicited from Alberto when the interviewer provided a positive sentence and asked Alberto to construct its negative counterpart.

[6] A full interpretation of why the ordering in Table V is to be preferred to that in Table IV on linguistic grounds is given in the original (Adamson & Kovac, 1981).

Time 1   Time 2

Figure 2   The innovation and spread of a feature in wave theory. (From Wolfram and Fasold, 1974, p. 76.)

seen as a by-product of the spread of rule changes over time. Imagine a case in which an innovation (x) is introduced by one group of speakers (Figure 2). At a slightly later time, the inner circle group of Figure 2 has introduced a second innovation, while a second group (the outer circle) has just picked up the first. Because what identifies a group of speakers might be social similarity as well as geographical proximity, the diffusion of a rule occurs in social as well as geographical space and may be arrested by social or geographical barriers, as represented in Figure 3.

Waves may indicate the spread of a rule through different environments as well as the spread of an entire rule. If this picture of change is adopted, apparent variation might result from looking at the mean scores of groups of speakers who, taken individually, perform on the basis of slightly different rule configurations; that is, one speaker has already been encompassed by the wave of change as regards a particular rule and another has not.

This approach has been especially popular in the study of creole language communities. Bickerton (1975) claims that such rule spread is easy to see there, first, because change (under pressure from a standard language) is often rapid, and, second, because forms that might have gone out of use are retained even by speakers who have learned new ones, because the old forms have symbolic,

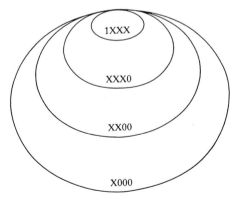

Figure 3   Interruption of spread in one direction. (From Wolfram and Fasold, 1974, p. 77.)

TABLE VI

**Distribution of "a," "doz," "Ning," and "Ving"
for 21 Guyanese Creole Speakers[a,b]**

Speaker	Ving	Ning	doz	a
1	0	0	0	X
2	0	0	0	X
3	0	0	0	X
4	0	0	X	X
5	0	0	X	X
6	0	0	X	X
7	0	0	X	X
8	0	0	X	X
9	0	0	X	X
10	0	0	X	X
11	0	X	X	X
12	0	X	X	X
13	0	X	X	X
14	0	X	X	X
15	0	X	X	X
16	X	X	X	X
17	X	X	X	X
18	X	X	X	X
19	X	X	X	X
20	X	X	X	X
21	X	X	X	X

[a] X = occurs; 0 = does not occur.
[b] Adapted from Bickerton (1975, p. 79).

speech-community membership value. Such a community ought to be an elaborate showplace for variation, but Bickerton argues that variable rules do not capture the psycholinguistic reality of its speakers. Table VI shows how individual speakers align themselves along a continuum in the use of four variable Guyanese features—*a,* a continuative-iterative marker (e.g., *mi a kom back haptanuun,* 'I'm coming back in the afternoon'; *doz,* or *das,* an iterative marker (e.g., *aagas rais das bos,* 'Rice ripens in August'; *Ning,* nominal *-ing* forms (e.g., *if yu wan niit plantin,* 'If you want neat planting'); and *Ving,* a continuative marker (e.g., *we yu livin bifo yu kom he?,* 'Where were you living before you came here?'). (See chapter 16 by Andersen and Shirai, this volume, for some additional discussion of pidgin and creole languages.)

Speakers who differ by only one rule may be combined into the same social group; therefore, the variability of their collective performances would give the impression of variation even though there was none in the individual. Bickerton argues that individuals have relatively nonvariable (though changeable) systems;

variability appears when the data from several speakers, who are at different stages in the change, are lumped together.

In Guyanese Creole, movement in Table VI from right to left reflects a historical development from deepest creole features (basilectal), through middle-level features (mesolectal), to those most like Standard English (acrolectal). Because some of the features may have the same function, co-occurrences in the same speaker indicate variability. Bickerton claims, however, that this variability is, on the one hand, short-lived and, on the other, still only apparent.

As a rule moves through a speech community in waves, two forms compete with one another, even in individual speakers, but such competition is brief—a psycholinguistic disaster. Why should a single system incorporate unnecessary features? The few speakers who show real variation belong to that middle part of an S curve (Figure 4) that is flat at both ends—they occupy its short-lived vertical dimension. The categorical state is represented in the more or less horizontal parts of the curve, occupied by those speakers who are not yet taking part in the change (at the bottom) and those who have completed it (at the top).

It is easy to see how apparent variation in a creole speech community might be exaggerated by the fact of long-term survivals that gain symbolic value. In creole, perhaps in many varieties, there can be no doubt of the existence of more than one form (with the same function) at one time and within one individual. In creoles the coexistence of groups of such forms (systems) is called the creole continuum, and societal facts explain why basilectal systems continue to exist alongside the more standardized acrolectal ones. The standard language carries with it, in addition to its representation of education and serious matters, the defect of social distance; the basilectal varieties carry with them, in spite of their associations with lack of education and backwardness, the advantage of familiar communication within closely knit communities. It is socially advantageous, then, for one speaker

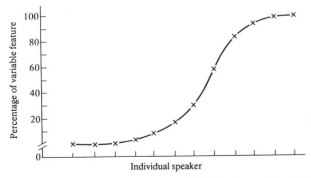

Figure 4   S-curve, displaying the smaller number of individuals who actually participate in significant variation between the 20 and 80% levels. (From Bickerton, 1975, p. 65.)

to command a number of grammars along the basilectal-to-acrolectal creole continuum. To the extent that each is a separate grammar (or lect), an individual speaker needs no variable rules; variation arises simply by shifting from one lect to another as conditions demand.

Individuals are not, however, randomly distributed along the creole continuum; Table VI is implicational. Any X (presence of a feature) implies that any feature to the right will also be an X; any 0 (absence of a feature) implies that any feature to the left will be absent. Environments as well as items may be so arrayed. In the dynamic paradigm, those environments that favor application of the rule are heavy, and those that retard it are light, or in a wave theory approach to linguistic change, heavy environments are those in which the change first appears, and light ones are those in which it operates last.

The Dynamic Paradigm and L2 Acquisition

The first application of the dynamic paradigm to L2 acquisition is very likely Gatbonton (1978). Table VII shows an implicational array of the voiced interdental /ð/ for French Canadian learners of English. The controlling environments (the preceding sound) are arranged on a scale of heaviest to lightest, but these weights are not related only to probabilistic influences of the various environments on the feature in question. The weight is an expression of the relation between one en-

TABLE VII

**Implicational Ordering of the Acquisition of English /ð/
in Five Different Environments by French Canadians[a]**

	Linguistic Environments[b]					
Heaviest . . . . Lightest						# of
Lect	V___	VCT___	VS___	VLCT___	VLS___	subjects
1	1	1	1	1	1	3
2	1,2	1	1	1	1	7
3	1,2	1,2	1	1	1	3
4	1,2	1,2	1,2	1	1	0
5	1,2	1,2	1,2	1,2	1	2
6	1,2	1,2	1,2	1,2	1,2	2
7	1,2	1,2	1,2	1,2	1,2	3
8	2	2	1,2	1,2	1,2	1
9	2	2	2	1,2	1,2	1
10	2	2	2	2	1,2	0
11	2	2	2	2	2	0

[a] Adapted from Gatbonton (1978).

[b] V, preceding vowel; VCT, preceding voiced continuant; VS, preceding voiced stop; VLCT, preceding voiceless continuant; VLS, preceding voiceless stop. 1 = categorical presence of nonnative substitute for English; 2 = categorical presence of native or nativelike English; 1,2 = variation of 1 and 2.

vironment and all the others and the lect which that unique relationship defines. Lect 1, for example, is the grammar of learners who have not even begun to vary between non-native and target-like performances of /ð/ in the most likely phonological environment for TL-like performance (i.e., after vowels). What is implicational about this arrangement is that every lighter environment also has, predictably, categorical non-TL-like performance. Conversely, speakers of lect 11 who have invariant TL-like performances in the lightest environment (i.e., the one least likely to promote such performance, here a preceding voiceless stop) predictably have it in every heavier environment. Such implicational arrays are apparently not arbitrary, for of the twenty-eight respondents sampled in Gatbonton's study, only six did not fit one of the predicted lect patterns.

The dynamic paradigm approach is perhaps even more appropriate to semanto-syntactic and morphosyntactic variation, for the emerging lects are seen as ones that reveal redefined form-function units increasingly in line with target language norms. Huebner (1983), for example, in a year-long longitudinal analysis of an adult Hmong acquirer of English, shows, among other things, how the form "is(a)" moves, in different environments, from marking asserted (or comment as opposed to topic) information to the range of functions that 'is' has in the target language.[7]

C. The Relationship between the Labovian and Dynamic Paradigms

At first, there may appear to be only trivial differences between the Labovian and dynamic paradigms. The former studies the exact degree of influence of each factor; the latter specifies the categorical states before and after variability and ignores the precise contribution of each controlling factor during variability, although the weight of each shows its relative effect. The psycholinguistic corollaries of the two modes are, however, quite distinct. The system that encloses the variety of probabilities influences within the Labovian paradigm is a unified one. That is, variability, although clearly related to change, may also be relatively stable within the single competence of a monodialectical speaker. In short, variability is inherent. In the dynamic paradigm, any inherent variability is short-lived, lasting only during the brief transition between categorical presence and absence of form–function change (in a given environment). The greater variability that appears to be present is, in fact, simply the shifting back and forth from one lect to another. In short, most variability is apparent.

The psycholinguistic ramifications of these two differing views have not been worked out in either NS or L2 acquisition contexts, and the Labovian claim that

---

[7] It is also the case that the interest in pidgin and creole languages gave rise to considerable interest in the parallel between the processes studied in those environments and those observed in L2 acquisition. Schumann (1978), already referred to, is, perhaps, the first important such study. A full review of such approaches to L2 acquisition is available in Andersen (1983).

variation is a part of linguistic competence has brought about an outcry from L2 acquisition researchers who work in the generative tradition. These facts (and other more optimistic ones) are treated in the final section.

III. RECENT TRENDS

A. Objections

If sociolinguistics had such a promising beginning in L2 acquisition research, why is it that L2 acquisition and sociolinguistics (indeed, to some extent, general linguistics and sociolinguistics) have not had a better recent friendship? I shall discuss four impediments, most already hinted at:

1. The apparent reluctance or inability of variationists to advance plausible psycholinguistic models
2. The mistaken understanding of sociolinguistic aims as sociological, social psychological, and anthropological (including ethnomethodological) ones
3. Misunderstandings of concepts, findings, and research tools developed in variation linguistics
4. The recent relative hegemony of the generative program in L2 acquisition research.

I will proceed backwards and defer comment on (1) until I have had the opportunity to say even more positive things about what the interaction has done and what potential it holds.

Variationist Linguistics and the Generative Paradigm in the Study of L2 Acquisition

I will first be concerned with the way in which sociolinguistic accounts of language are or are not compatible with those given by Universal Grammar (UG). In the long run, I believe that a more careful specification of the domain of relevance of sociolinguistic enquiry will have direct bearing on the more general question of the relationship of variationist work to linguistic (and, therefore, L2 acquisition) theory, but I begin the account of such matters squarely in the territory of the dominant paradigm.

Without detailing why things have gone this way, let me observe that grammars are now rather more negatively than positively conceived. Even the language of the enterprise suggests the general thrust—barriers, filters, control, bounding nodes. We seem to have become a good deal more concerned with mapping out the territory where human language cannot go than with where it does. Let me avoid caricature. UG is not at all uninterested in what a language does do, for some of what happens follows from the existence and settings of the various constraints of the model and from interactions or, perhaps technically better, "conspiracies" between and among them.

Consider first the relationship of an obviously hot topic to this characterization of UG. If the critical-age hypothesis turns out to hold (particularly in a strong form),[8] then other factors, namely the complex cognitive abilities of adults in general (and learners of foreign and L2s in particular) will emerge as the linguistic research areas of greatest interest in L2 acquisition. (Chapters 2 by Gregg, 3 by White, 4 by Flynn, and 5 by Schachter, this volume, address these issues.)

Lurking behind that scenario, of course, is the question of the relationship between UG and the learner, but no matter which of the logically possible forms of adult access to UG turns out to be the case, the results will not make UG a general theory of L2 acquisition.

1. If adults have no access to UG, then the same conclusions hold as those of a strong critical-age hypothesis; that is, adults learn languages through so-called nonlinguistic cognitive abilities.

2. If adults have access to the shape of UG only as it is instantiated in L1, then the same conclusions obtain for everything not "hit" in the L2 by those settings, for any resettings will have to appeal to nonlinguistic sorts of learning abilities.

3. If adults have full access to the conditions of UG (or even manipulative access through the settings of L1), it is still the chore of L2 acquisition research to explain those aspects of learners' language ability that do not fall out of the principles and parameters (a condition, by the way, as true of L1 as of L2 acquisition).

Let me be clear about what I mean by those things that do not fall out. I am not concerned with the fact that some kinds of information highlighting, staging, and referencing may not fall out (although I do not intend to demean research programs that study such facts, neither for their obviously interesting claims about how the resources provided by a language are managed nor for their more controversial claim that languages have structure because of the ends they are put to). Nor am I concerned that language-processing facts do not automatically fall out (with similar disclaimers). Nor am I in the least concerned that gender, status, age, formality, and other socially distinguishing characteristics do not fall out. What I mean to focus on is the fact that although generally autonomous or modular theories have (or are capable of developing) adequate ways of characterizing the structures of utterances as they reside in

---

[8] It is clear what some UG proponents believe about this:

For the language teacher, [the critical period] means that you simply cannot teach a language to an adult the way a child learns a language. That's why it's such a hard job. (Chomsky, 1988, p. 179)

competence, they admit to having no way of predicting one form or the other in many areas of a grammar. (For discussion of grammatical structure as an autonomous module of the mind see particularly chapter 2 by Gregg, this volume. The competence–performance (knowledge–behavior) distinction is also discussed in chapters 2 by Gregg, 3 by White, and 4 by Flynn.) That is, UG's principles and parameters cannot select the form of a number of constructions. For example, nothing predicts why standard English embedded questions like to undo auxiliary movement:[9]

1. Why did George leave?
2. *I know why did George leave.
3. I know why George left.

Although UG can precisely describe the difference between (2) and (3), it cannot use its principles or parametric settings for English to show that (3) not (2) will be the well-formed alternative.[10] (For further discussion of verb movement as referred to in footnote 10, see chapters 3 by White and 14 by Berent, this volume.)

Many 'errors' like those of (2) above appear in L2 performances. In fact, a large list of syntactic features (as well as features from other levels of the grammar) of only passing "descriptive" interest to UG (i.e., not predicted by its features) could be made from any error inventory of learner use—e.g., complement types (infinitive versus gerund) or verb valences (missing obligatory objects: "I put on the table").

Additionally, many variable data are without significance to UG. For example, once it is shown that English is a language that (under certain circumstances) can delete complementizers, then UG has done its chore.

I decided that/∅ I would go.

The fact, for example, that the complementizer is more likely to occur after main verbs that have an auxiliary than those without (Thompson and Mulac, 1991) is rightly ignored by UG. Gregg (1990, p. 374) is certainly correct when he notes that, in that territory that UG regards as linguistic competence, items are either in

---

[9] I ignore the fact that many varieties of English do not obey this rule and carefully avoid the fact that all speakers of English have this rule as a variable one, although those who believe their English is "standard" will often not admit it, even though there is ample evidence in even the written English of well-educated NSs.

[10] Briefly, the facts are these. Since WH moves to [Spec,CP], [C,C'] is an available landing site for I, but there is nothing in the parameters set for English that predicts whether I will or will not move to C. Put more specifically, there is nothing in the embedding of a question sentence that predicts I-to-C movement. Note that when C is full, as it is in embedded yes–no questions when "if" or "whether" is base-generated, one cannot get I-to-C: *I don't know if did he go. Varieties that consistently move I in embedded questions simply do not base-generate anything into C: I don't know did he go.

or out (and, quite clearly, because "that" and $\varnothing$ are options for the complementizer: they are both "in").

But from a broader psycholinguistic perspective, particularly one concerned with language change within the individual, the mechanisms that govern the choice of those forms that are unquestionably there in the linguistic competence(s) are of considerable interest, perhaps even of crucial importance in a dynamic environment when one of the forms is "doomed" (if the learner is to achieve anything like NS competence). Therefore, what L2 acquisition researchers learn from and teach those who are concerned with shoring up, tightening, and extending the agenda of UG may be limited, particularly if the goal of a relatively comprehensive L2 acquisition theory is to account for the general linguistic ability of postcritical-period L2 and foreign language acquirers. In short, L2 interests are much broader than the goals of grammatical theory. Doubtless, and to the benefit of both research efforts, some L2 acquisition researchers will want to test the tenets of UG and offer alternative representations of it in its own terms based on findings from L2 data, but if L2 researchers limit their attention to those relatively narrow boundaries, they will miss many boats. Many L2 acquisition data that have grammaticality as their central concern, quite aside from social or discoursal concerns, make that clear. In short, if a great deal of what is to be learned requires an understanding of the cognitive procedures that are involved in acquisitional territory beyond the fallout of the principles and parameters areas of the grammar, then a theory of L2 acquisition that does not include such territory will be paucal. On to the third impediment.

Misunderstandings of Variationist Linguistics in L2 Acquisition Research

No mode of enquiry has ownership rights on its concepts and procedures, so variationists can expect that what they have found out (and what they have found out about finding out) will be used by others. Unfortunately, errors in L2 acquisition characterizations of variation have developed that concern the subtypes of variation and even how variation itself is identified. Because these misunderstandings are held by leading L2 acquisition practitioners and even by inventors of overarching L2 acquisition theories, they are worth dwelling on. Ellis defined the "variable rule" as follows:

> If it is accepted that learners perform differently in different situations, but that it is possible to predict how they will behave in specific situations, then the systematicity of their behavior can be captured by means of variable rules. These are 'if . . . then' rules. They state that if x conditions apply, then y language forms will occur. (1985b, p. 9)

That is simply not so. Ellis's description is an apt characterization of a categorical (albeit context-sensitive) rule (described above), not a variable one. Although he later recognized the proportional rather than categorical nature of variable rules, one wonders how many have been confused by his earlier definition. More serious is Ellis's characterization of how systematic variability is to be discovered:

> I sometimes say /datə/ and sometimes /deitə/, sometimes /ɒfn/ and sometimes / ɒftn/, sometimes /skedjuːl/ and sometimes /ʃedjuːl/. . . . To the best of my knowledge I alternate quite haphazardly between "who" and "that" as subject relative pronouns with human references in non-restrictive relative clauses. (1985a, p. 121)

Even those who use introspection in their research limit their remarks to what they can (not what they do) say, and one should not touch what one is likely to say with a 10-foot pole. In general, intuitive assessments of performance have had value only as indicators of linguistic insecurity, marking the difference between self-assessment and actual performance, a difference that is often considerable (Labov, 1966; Trudgill, 1972).

But misunderstandings of variationist linguistics reach even further, into the methodology itself. Ellis (1987) explains how he has quantified past-tense form occurrences by nonnative speakers (NNS) of English in a variety of tasks.

> Each verb was scored as correct or deviant in contexts requiring the use of the past tense. Repetitions of any verb (common in the oral tasks, particularly in Task 3) were not counted. (Ellis, 1987, p. 7)

There are good reasons not to count some forms (e.g., categorical occurrences that exaggerate the influence of the set of factors they belong to), but not to count repetitions in general simply means that opportunities to discover the forces on variation have been ignored. If free variation exists, it is established by showing that plausible influencing factors have been subjected to a quantitative analysis and have been found to have no effect on the occurrences of the dependent variable. I am suspicious that language variation that is influenced by nothing at all is a chimera, but I would be happy to admit to such variability if I were shown that a careful search of the environment had been made and that no such influencing factors had been found. I am adamant about this, because I believe that the discovery and weighting of influencing factors is the most valuable area of interaction between variation linguistics and L2 acquisition.

In conclusion, in reference to the third of my list of impediments to cooperation, I say simply that if there is any reason to do variation analysis of L2 acquisition data, get it right. It is perhaps especially disheartening to find these same misunderstandings alive today, because they were hinted at in L2 acquisition research by a leading practitioner more than 15 years ago:

> A sociolinguist's reaction to such a definition [i.e., one which contrasts 'systematicity' with 'variability'] may be justifiably negative, since his definition of variation might well incorporate the notion of internal consistency. But I think the contrast is acceptable in second language research so long as one does not

too hastily conclude that a set of utterances shows variability simply because one cannot "find" systematicity. (H. D. Brown, 1976, p. 138)

The Mistaken Understanding of the Aims of Sociolinguistics

Impediment number two is a much more general misunderstanding of what sociolinguistics is, and (as Labov, 1972, predicted) it partly stems from the label itself. This misunderstanding limits sociolinguistic interests to what might be called socially sensitive pragmatics. The focus of such work has to do with how various linguistic tasks are appropriately done—part of the ethnography of communication. A learner of American English will want to know under what circumstances I ought to be greeted with "Hello, Dennis, you ol' sumbitch" or with "Good morning, Professor Preston." (You may take it as a rule of thumb that whether a consonant or vowel follows or precedes either greeting is not likely to have a considerable effect on my regard for one or the other.) Although I believe that studies of who says what to whom, when, where, why, and even how often are very interesting, they are not the central stuff of variationist linguistics. Even Gregg (1990), who seems to have a fair grasp of what modern variationists are about, is willing to caricature by suggesting that his (apparently conscious) decision to avoid second verb ellipsis (e.g., Tuffy thwacked Throckmorton and Spike, Beauregard) is based on a rule which he calls "Try not to sound like a twit" (p. 375). (I will try not to dwell on the fact that even one use of the word "twit" in my home speech community will mark you as one.) In many variationist studies, the list of factors that determine probabilities of occurrence includes no so-called social features (or twit-avoidance rules). Because such weighted rather than categorical factors are a part of a speaker's language ability, the study of the influence of just such factors is most typical of the variationist's concern.

I will also observe (but with lightning speed) that so-called social concerns are often much-loved, for they seem to get away from the hard stuff of linguistics. Asking a number of respondents to rate samples for their politeness, aggressiveness, or some other factor is doable almost anywhere, involves straightforward statistical analyses (if any), and, alas, seems to require little or no annoying theoretical surroundings or even training. (Often a mention of Grice, 1975, will do, although even that is often filtered through P. Brown & Levinson, 1987.) Thereby the hard stuff of phonology, morphology, syntax, and semantics is avoided; worse, the hard stuff of pragmatics, ethnography, statistics, data collection, and the like is often also not in evidence. (My sincere apologies to serious, productive researchers who till just such fields, but I suspect they are as unhappy with popularizing and simplifying caricatures of their enterprise as I am with those of mine.)

B. Current Work

Before I turn to the psycholinguistic problem, let me provide some recent examples of variationist, L2 acquisition work. I believe that such work has already

TABLE VIII

**The Influence of Perfectivity on Past-Tense Marking
in Chinese Learners of English**[a]

| | Respondent proficiency level | | | | | |
| | Lower | | | Higher | | |
Verb type[b]	p_i	%	N	p_i	%	N
Perfective	.67	42	856	.69	73	1406
Imperfective	.33	15	964	.31	38	1691
Input	.22	22	1820	.58	54	3097

[a] Adapted from Bayley (1991).
[b] P_i VARBRUL probabilistic weight. N, number.

shown that probabilistic weightings of influences on varying forms is a promising research program, perhaps even a promising way of deciding among various theoretical approaches, helping, as Bayley (1991) suggests, with the theory-pruning recommended in Beretta (1991).

Bayley (1991) examines past-tense marking by Chinese learners of English; one factor taken into consideration is perfectivity.[11] (Chapter 16 by Andersen and Shirai, this volume, is a general discussion of the semantics and morphology of verb tense and aspect in L1 acquisition, including creolization, and L2 acquisition.) Table VIII gives the VARBRUL results. Recall that the input represents the tendency for the rule to work overall (i.e., for past to be marked). The lower and higher proficiency learners represent both sides of that possibility. Overall, there is a considerable probability that a lower proficiency speaker will not mark past tense in English (.22), whereas there is some probability that a higher level proficiency speaker will (.58).

When one investigates the linguistic factor under consideration, however, although the percentages of correct forms are dramatically different for the lower and higher proficiency speakers (e.g., 15–38% correct for imperfectives), the probabilistic weights are stable (.33 and .31, respectively, in the same category). The same is true of the relationship of percentages versus weight for the perfectives.

These results imply a model in which the factor of perfectivity has a stable pattern of influence throughout the learning process. That is, perfective verbs encourage past-tense marking and imperfectives discourage it with nearly the same weight at both proficiency levels. That suggests two things. First, the path of acquisition for this feature is tied to markedness, although the category of verbal aspect studied here may be admittedly unlike those areas that are of more interest to UG. Second, and more interesting, the relatively level influence of past-tense

[11] It is a rule of thumb in both L1 and L2 acquisition studies that perfectives are typically past. Bayley (1991) reviews evidence from earlier studies.

TABLE IX

Effect of the Preceding Segment (of the Verb Stem) on Past-Tense Marking in Chinese Learners of English[a]

Preceding segment[c]	Respondent proficiency level[b]					
	Lower			Higher		
	P_i	%	N	P_i	%	N
Vowel	.47	23	128	.66	61	80
Liquid	.57	31	29	.46	45	65
Obstruent	.46	23	213	.38	36	340

[a] Adapted from Bayley (1991).
[b] The input weight and the individual N's and percentages are not all available for this table.
[c] P_i VARBRUL probabilistic weight. N, number.

marking according to perfectivity across proficiency levels suggests that no radical restructuring of the grammar as regards this feature has gone on, one of Bayley's strong claims for his findings. In other words, although the high proficiency respondents in this investigation mark more pasts, the probabilistic weight assigned to one of the factors (perfectivity) that significantly influence this marking is nearly equal to the weight assigned the same factor for lower proficiency speakers from the same group of learners.

Perhaps, therefore, we should collect evidence that shows for some factors the following:

1. All learners from the same language background make up learner communities.[12]
2. All learners from all language backgrounds belong to the same learner community.
3. Subgroups of learners even from the same language background make up distinct communities.

The implications of those three categories for transfer, universals, and some more individual notion of learning should be clear.

One does encounter just such patterns (and ones of even greater complexity), but before turning to issues of cross-linguistic patterning, I will look at a case that satisfies category (3). In Table IX Bayley (1991) provided an example from another of the factors studied, in this case the influence of the preceding segment (i.e., the verb's stem-final segment). As promised, these data reflect the conditions

[12] I have tried to suggest (e.g., Preston, 1989, p. 257) the metaphor that groups of learners belong to the same speech community when these probabilistic values are not significantly different, but that was apparently misunderstood and taken in the Bloomfieldian sense by some (e.g., Williams, 1990, p. 499).

of (3)—the higher and lower proficiency respondents do not belong to the same community of learners in spite of their shared L1. In fact, the regression test tells us that the preceding segment is not even a significant contributor to the probability of past-tense realization for the lower proficiency learners, making the difference between the two groups even more dramatic. That learning from exposure has gone on here, specifically in terms of the weights associated with the different environments, seems unquestionable. (The same order of influence of preceding segments as that seen in the higher level proficiency learners is, by the way, to be found in the performances of NSs, e.g., Guy, 1980.) This factor, unlike the one of verbal aspect, "acquires" significance in its influence on past-tense marking as learners advance in proficiency.

The implication of the contrast between the two factors is relatively clear. Some categories (L1 or universal?) that have an influence on the dependent variable appear to be a stable part of the learner's machinery. One might almost say that the successful learner learns around them but is not likely to do away with them. Other categories develop in the learner, and appear to take their shape from the surrounding evidence.

I have waffled in attributing L1 or universal influence to perfectivity in the above account, for I have not yet represented a study that separates learners from (radically) different L1s, an obvious condition for the examination of (2). The data in Table X are taken from Young's (1990) study of Czech and Slovak learners' noun plural marking in English, in which he compares those data with his earlier studies of Chinese learners. Although the Czech and Slovak learners are more proficient overall in their marking of noun plurals than the Chinese, the influence of animacy (which is a significant factor group for both L1 backgrounds) is nearly exactly the same—.34 and .36 for animates and .54 and .53 for inanimates respec-

TABLE X

The Effect of Animacy on Noun–Plural Marking in Chinese, Czech, and Slovak Learners of English[a]

| | Respondent L1[b] | | | | | |
| | Czech or Slovak | | | Chinese | | |
Animacy[c]	p_i	%	N	p_i	%	N
Animate	.34			.36		
Inanimate	.54			.53		
Total		81	560		55	299

[a] Adapted from Young (1990).

[b] The input weight and the individual N's and percentages are not all available for this table.

[c] P_i VARBRUL probabilistic weight. N, number.

TABLE XI

**The Effect of Sentence Function on Noun–Plural Marking
in Chinese, Czech, and Slovak Learners of English**[a]

| | Respondent L1[b] | | | | | |
| | Czech or Slovak | | | Chinese | | |
Function[c]	p_i	%	N	p_i	%	N
Subject	.54			.40		
Object	.57			.36		
Adverbial	.46			.68		
Complement of *be*	.32			.50		
Object of preposition	.52			not studied		

[a] Adapted from Young (1990).

[b] The input weight and the individual N's and percentages are not all available for this table.

[c] P_i VARBRUL probabilistic weight. N, number.

tively. In other words, the animacy of nouns fits the specifications outlined in (2) as a factor that has similar influence, in spite of radically different L1s.[13]

It is relatively easy, of course, to find cases where the factor group influences on respondents from different L1s do not match up. In the same study, which compares Czech and Slovak learners of English with Chinese, the data in Table XI on the influence of syntactic position on plural marking will serve. For every subcategory of this factor group, the two L1 groups are on the opposite side of the .50 watershed. That is, whatever retards noun plural marking for Czech and Slovak learners of English promotes it for Chinese learners and vice versa. Additionally, and even worse, the entire factor group is statistically insignificant for the Czech and Slovak respondents but significant for the Chinese. These are obviously two radically different learner communities as regards this factor.

Although these research samples complete the list of universal, transfer, and learning profiles outlined above, it would be possible to put variationist techniques to use at even finer levels of discrimination. Preston (1989) shows, for example, research data in which such carefully monitored performances as test-taking do and do not form a part of the well-attested stylistic continuum. Such results tend to confirm that Krashen's monitor theory is about one-half correct. When certain "simple rule" facts (e.g., third singular present marking on verbs in English) get "super-monitored" (e.g., in a grammar test), they fall in place at the top end (i.e., the heavily monitored) of the variationist's stylistic continuum. When certain

---

[13] Of course, more learners from other language groups should be investigated before any claim is made that is a universal. The point made here lies in the use of the model in investigating such relationships, not in the breadth of the claim.

"hard rule" facts (e.g., English articles) are tested, however, a variable rule analysis shows that not only do they not fall in place at the top end of the continuum but also that the statistical model cannot even understand them as a part of that continuum. That would appear to be confirmed in the more recent Johnson and Newport study (1989), in which the older subjects were most dramatically opposed to the younger subjects in precisely this grammatical domain. A monitor theory may be correct, therefore, in assuming that some sort of switched-on rule-learning program may be effective in promoting NL-like performance of some easy rules when there is time for overt extraction of that knowledge, but it is no help at all for hard rules.

Note how these findings constitute a two-way street between variation studies and L2 acquisition. The direction or slope of performances along a stylistic continuum, suggested to L2 acquisition from variation studies, gives researchers in L2 acquisition a tool to approach the question of what grammar a learner has internalized at various levels of monitoring. On the other hand, the supermonitored items that do not fit into a stylistic continuum discovered in L2 acquisition data help confirm suspicions mentioned above that some tasks (e.g., reading) may not position themselves appropriately on the stylistic continuum and may, therefore, represent questionable means of data gathering in sociolinguistics itself.

L2 acquisition is in some ways dramatically positioned, I believe, to contribute to variationist understandings of language. Its respondents are on a fast track of language change, allowing real- rather than apparent-time studies. Moreover, the variants of an item undergoing change (particularly in the early stages of acquisition) are not as likely to take on socially symbolic meanings, an influence that may confound the rate and even nature of change in monolingual settings.

From a selfish variationist perspective, then, I hope, given multivariate analyses of L2 acquisition data, that we may look forward to productive, cross-fertilizing clarification of such notions as change from above and change from below (already hinted at previously in the discussion of the stylistic continuum and Monitor Theory), hyper- (and hypo-) correction, linguistic insecurity, convergence and divergence, age-grading versus change, specific strategies in incorporating variable evidence (e.g., "fudged lects"; Chambers & Trudgill, 1980), and the more general role of markedness. Preston (1989), for example, makes the claim that marked forms develop more quickly in monitored IL performances and that unmarked ones are acquired earlier in less monitored styles—a parallel between IL development and the variationist notions of change from above and below.

Taking L2 acquisition notions first, however, I would also like to see a variationist perspective taken on such constructs as fossilization, an area that will, I expect, parallel developments on the so-called creole continuum, making those data interpretable as something other than socially motivated preservations of older forms.

I hope this discussion so far clarifies how variationist techniques can aid L2 acquisition and how L2 acquisition data can shed light on proposals from UG and other areas of linguistics by sorting out influences rather than trying to isolate them. Many a good study seems foolishly criticized by the posthoc recriminations the investigators have directed towards their own work when they note that other variables may have confounded the one they set out to study. Of course they have! Why not deal realistically with this inevitable variety, while focusing on how the factor one delights most in does (or does not) influence the data.

C. The Psycholinguistics of Sociolinguistics in L2 Acquisition

I hope this discussion will also serve to clarify the fact that the unfortunately named variable rule is not necessarily a challenge to UG models of either NL or L2 linguistic competence. On the other hand, acknowledgment of serious claims from a variationist perspective leads us to consider (1) the position in the linguistic make-up of the mechanisms that guide variation and (2) their possible contribution to questions of linguistic change in the individual (i.e., learning). Such attacks as Gregg's (1990) on variability claims and studies that assign selection devices to the domain of competence (e.g., Tarone's work) or that seriously misrepresent commonplaces in the sociolinguistic tradition (illustrated previously from Ellis's work) may be helpful in letting L2 acquisition practitioners know that variationists have not been well represented in L2 variation literature, but these attacks overlook the serious challenges to minimally elaborated psycholinguistic theories posed by careful attempts to build a variable psycholinguistic model (not necessarily a model of variable competence).

But VARBRUL (and variationist linguistics) does not come completely theory free. One must be interested in identifying and weighting the factors that promote the occurrence of one form or another in linguistic performance. One must assume that those factors are connected in some way to individual language change. If variation in a developing IL is viewed as simply a waffling back and forth between one grammar and another (for no apparent reason), then there will be little or no interest in a program that seeks the causes and mechanisms of variation itself. Perhaps for some that is simply the case.

> Every human being speaks a variety of languages. We sometimes call them different styles or different dialects, but they are really different languages, and somehow we know when to use them, one in one place and another in another place. Now each of these languages involves a different switch setting. In the case of [different languages] it is a rather dramatically different switch setting, more so than in the case of the different styles of [one language]. (Chomsky, 1988, p. 188)

This view, which assumes that there are as many grammars as there are styles (e.g., Bickerton, 1971), is rather easily cut up with Occam's razor, and I am surprised to find it still strongly asserted in 1988. More importantly, it fails in the face of more plausible variable psycholinguistic models, which, as I have suggested above, do not necessarily locate the key to variability exclusively in linguistic competence. Here is one attempt at such a model, adjusted to fit L2 acquisition.

For a two-way variable, one is equipped with a coin that is flipped before the product appears. Taking Bayley's study of past-tense marking by Chinese learners of English as our representative data, let "heads" represent the (L1-like) marking of the past tense and "tails" represent no marking. (This model does not deny the possibility that there might be cases where apparent alternatives are actually in-stantiations of different grammars, i.e., different competences. In this case, how-ever, "mark" and "don't mark" may be taken to be options in a single compe-tence, quite a different claim from one that asserts the existence of a variable competence.)

This model overlooks "dynamic" questions of two sorts. First, it ignores the issue of how two ways to do one thing arose (although some of the research samples outlined above indirectly address that question). Second, it avoids the more immediate (though not unrelated) question of the longevity of variation in the system (a problem, again, not ignored by the research efforts outlined above). The model advanced will, however, provide openings for such dynamic considerations.

The coin proposed for Bayley's respondents is fair (so far). When flipped, it is as likely to turn up heads as tails. Bayley, however, has shown that aspect, the final segment of the verb stem, respondent proficiency, verb type (e.g., strong versus weak), the following segment, and interview type all influence the proba-bility of past-tense marking.

Assuming that the reader does not have experience in petty-cash crooked gam-bling devices, let me explain that unfair coins can be (and have been) made. If I add weight to the tails side of a coin and flip it, it is more likely to come up heads; the more weight I add, the greater the probability it will come up heads. Back to Bayley's data.

The input weight (.38, higher and lower proficiency levels combined) reflects the overall performance of the dependent variable itself—in this case, the past-tense marker. It is precisely this sort of combined statistical product that fired part of Bickerton's suspicion that an individual's psycholinguistic makeup was poorly represented in such studies (1971). He is exactly right, of course, if one tries to build this .38 weight into the coin-flipping mechanism of the individual, for we have already seen that the input probability of high-proficiency learners on this past-tense marking feature is .58, whereas that for lower and intermediate profi-ciency learners is .22 (Table VIII). Even if we limit the preparation of our unfair coin to one for a high-proficiency learner (and we shall), Bickerton may still be right, for this input weight represents the overall likelihood of past-tense marking and may be just a statistical ploy (a constant or correction device) to help in the calculation of each single-factor group's influence. As far as an individual's linguistic competence is concerned, therefore, it may play no role, and that is the position taken here (although not in Preston, 1989).

The factors that constrain past-marking are treated as part of the individual's linguistic ability, and the following characterizes their influences on the coin-flip and offers suggestions for their entry-points (or abodes) in the mechanism. For the purposes of this illustration, assume that the respondent is about to blurt out, "I loved everything the linguist said." Whether "love" will be marked for past or not is the focus.

1. The importance of verbal aspect has been shown, and I will take my sample sentence to be imperfective. (After all, such admiration should be ongoing!) Because imperfectives retard past-tense attachment by a weight of .31 (Table VIII), I must activate a device that sticks an appropriate amount of weight on the heads side, giving tails (e.g., no past-tense marking) a greater likelihood of occurrence.

I must be careful about the cognitive workshop where this operation was done. In the case of an independent influence on past-tense marking by aspect, I think it is safe to assume that the options are in the learner's competence. That is, the two-sided coin is available in competence. (There are of course one-sided coins [marbles?] which, when taken from competence and readied for performance instantiation, do not need to be flipped at all.) When the fair past-tense-marking coin is engaged by the performance-readying mechanism, a weight attachment device from the temporal-aspectual ready room jumps out and sticks the weight predicted by .31 on the heads side. If nothing else influenced past-tense marking, this weight could be read as a simple probability, but there is more.

2. The salience of the difference between present and past forms is significant (Table XII). It ranges from a low of .27 for modals and weak syllabics (e.g., paint + ed) to a high of .75 for suppletives (e.g., go-went).

We shall have to add the weight contributed by a weak nonsyllabic (love) to the heads side of the coin. That is, a factor of .42 will contribute to the continuing decline of the probability for past-tense marking. It is still fairly clear, I believe, that the two-sided coin that is about to be flipped has been plucked from linguistic competence. That is, both a past-tense marker = "something" and a past-tense marker = $\varnothing$ are on the coin, and a mechanism that might be called the "salience of morpho(phono)logical alteration" has rushed in with the appropriate weight.

3. Also significant (although, as noted above, not for lower proficiency learners) is the preceding segment (Table IX). The phonemic shape of love places an obstruent [v] before the past marker, and the weight contributed by that factor is .38. Add a weight determined by that factor to (again!) the heads side of the coin.

Here, I believe, is the first significantly different operation, for the influence of this factor on performance would have occurred even if no coin (i.e., the options) had been minted in competence. (So as not to incur the wrath of phonologists, I will not suggest that the operations that are at work here have nothing to do with matters that are perhaps very much a part of linguistic competence in another component of it.) In fact, this weight reflects an operation shared with NSs for whom the variability of past-tense marking is never influenced by the first two factors considered (i.e., aspect and salience). The reason should be clear; NSs do not have past-tense-marking coins with mark and don't mark sides in their competences; therefore, such guiding factors on past-tense marking for Chinese learners of English as aspect and salience have no effect on NSs. NSs (and advanced Chinese learners of English) do have a rule, however, that influences the likelihood of consonant cluster reduction in word-final position (as elaborated earlier). In short, a consonant cluster simplifier adds the weight determined by .38 to the heads side of our increasingly unfair coin, but it is only a serendipitous fact that there is a don't flip side to the coin at all.

We see here how a carefully constructed variation study teases out and shows the independence of factors that govern (i.e., predict) performance variation, noting that two factors appear to depend on an underlying option in linguistic competence (as regards the variable feature itself), whereas another depends on a phonological operation unrelated to any option in competence. I finish this operation with two other factors provided by Bayley.

4. The following segment (which affects both high- and low-proficiency learners) is a vowel [ɛ], retrieved from the phonemic shape of the following word (everything). For the first time, we get to add weight to the tails side of the coin, making past-tense marking more likely, for a following vowel promotes the attachment (weakly, however, at .52).

This fact is like (3) and has no relation to the existence of a competence option for past-tense marking. It is interesting, however, although I will have space to make nothing more of it here, that this operation is shared by high- and low-proficiency learners (and NSs) but (3) is not. Such data require, of course, more careful consideration of the potential universal character of some phonological processes.

5. Finally, the probability of past-tense marking is slightly enhanced by the presence of other Chinese-speaking respondents (.53, Table XII). I'll assume that is the case, so, again, a little weight must be added to the tails side, making marking more likely.

At last some real *socio* sociolinguistics! Interlocutor identity is pretty clearly one of those factors that is directly related to performance on the stylistic continuum. Let's say, therefore, that some sort of carefulness device has caused us to add a weight consistent with the .53 contribution of this factor to the tails side of our coin. It is possible, by the way, that this stylistic influence might apply twice; once to the competence option of the two forms (mark and don't mark) and once to the consonant-cluster simplification strategy.

If we have prepared our crooked coin correctly, our speaker has a .34 chance of uttering *love* as *loved* in the above string. I leave the math up to you this time. Checks of actual performance of individuals and groups (where data are sufficient) have shown that such statistical modeling is accurate. That is, if our fictional respondent uttered one hundred past forms for us in exactly the environments specified above, there would be approximately 34 marked for past tense and 66 unmarked.

I believe such a model is psycholinguistically plausible, for it specifically shows how another of Bickerton's objections to inherent variability is, in fact, not an issue (1971). When respondents issue 20, 40, or 60% of one form of a variable, they are not monitoring their overall performance with some daylong tallying device. They are simply evidencing the influence of a set of probabilistic weights that come to bear on each occurrence. Because this is Bickerton's principal psychostatistical objection to the notion of variation, I assume that I may put it aside, and that a variable rule account is preferable to the claim that variation is the result of moving back and forth between alternative grammars, such movement triggered by essentially unstudiable, low-level "social" factors. In fact, as Bayley has shown, such social factors as interlocutor ethnicity are not unstudiable at all.

The attachment of weights of the sorts described above are surely not part of what has been advanced profitably in generative grammar under the label of competence, even if some of the motivating factors behind such probabilistic influences have their origins in such competence (as, for example, optimal syllable-structure rules might), and such claims as Gregg's (1990) that variation linguistics is not helpful in the L2 acquisition enterprise may be rejected.

From the outline given above, it seems clear that some variable operations are selection devices that have reference to options in competence and others are performance-oriented mechanisms that are themselves the source of the variation. Stylistic or monitoring devices are pretty clearly neither; instead, they seem to stand even further off, governing the intensity of the devices that select or produce variants. Guy said this about such factors:

> It is interesting to note that the effect of style shifting . . . is thus characterizable as a general upward or downward reweighting of the probabilities of deletion for all environments, rather than as involving different treatments for different environments. (1980, p. 34)

This more marginal role of stylistic selection is consistent with Bell (1984), who noted that the influence of such monitoring (or "stylistic") variation is always smaller than "status" variation. Preston (1991), after a review of a number of VARBRUL-style studies, added the observation that status variation (within the same speech community) is generally smaller than some linguistic factor(s) influencing the same variable.

The implication of those findings is clear. The source (and usually the guiding force) of variation is linguistic, not demographic or stylistic. When demography

TABLE XII

**The Effect of Verb Type, Aspect, Proficiency,
and Interlocutor Ethnicity on Past-Tense
Marking in Chinese Learners of English**[a,b]

Verb type	
Suppletive	.75
Weak syllabic	.27
Aspect	
Perfective	.67
Imperfective	.33
Proficiency	
High	.65
Low, intermediate	.34
Interlocutor ethnicity	
Chinese	.53
Non-Chinese	.47

[a] Adapted from Bayley (1991).
[b] The input weight and the individual N's and percentages are not available for this table.

is more significant, different speech communities (or radical change reflected in different age groups within one community) are involved. When style is more significant, some caricatured or stereotypical feature has risen to peculiar symbolic status in the community (e.g., *ain't* in American English, *você* in Brazilian Portuguese).

The IL data of Bayley's Chinese learners of English can be interpreted within such a model. As Table XII shows, the range of several linguistic factors is larger than the status (i.e., proficiency level) range, and the status range is larger than a factor that almost certainly exploits the stylistic range (i.e., interlocutor ethnicity). Not very surprisingly, I believe, the most important influencing factors on the variability of IL performance are linguistic ones. Continuing studies of such variability, coupled with attempts to relate the factors that determine variability to the components of language ability that house them, will help sort out the interactive and independent roles of underlying knowledge and other factors that result in linguistic performance.

In conclusion, and quite frankly, I think we know so little yet about language and mind that it is premature to rule out linguistic research areas on the basis of their failure to deal directly and uniquely with the ramifications of linguistic competence. Even more frankly, I do not know where the elements of a variable psycholinguistic model fit, nor do I know where the linguistic levels fit into it, but I do know that NLs as well as ILs display facts that can be captured only by a device that includes such variable weightings. Pending stupendous advances elsewhere in our general field of enquiry, the data from every subarea of investigation—L2 and L1 acquisition and use, pidgin-creole varieties, permanent and short-term language disability, alternative modes (e.g., sign), and more—will contribute to and be informed by the study of language in its broader perspective. The theories that develop from such attention need not be naively data-driven, but eventually they will want to address some of the complexities of the data, and in some areas (perhaps especially L2 acquisition) the complexities demand such attention for even early-stage, metaphoric characterizations of theory.

REFERENCES

Adamson, H. D., & Kovac, C. (1981). Variation theory and second language acquisition data: An analysis of Schumann's data. In D. Sankoff & H. Cedergren (Eds.), *Variation omnibus* (pp. 285–292). Edmonton: Linguistic Research.

Andersen, R. W. (Ed.). (1983). *Pidginization and creolization as language acquisition.* Rowley, MA: Newbury House.

Bailey, C.-J. N. (1974). *Variation and linguistic theory.* Arlington, VA: Center for Applied Linguistics.

Bayley, R. (1991, October). *Interlanguage variation and the quantitative paradigm.* A paper presented to the ALMS Conference, Michigan State University, East Lansing.

Bell, A. (1984). Language style as audience design. *Language in Society, 13,* 145–204.

Beretta, A. (1991). Theory construction in SLA. *Studies in Second Language Acquisition, 13,* 413–512.

Bickerton, D. (1971). Inherent variability and variable rules. *Foundations of Language, 7,* 457–492.

Bickerton, D. (1975). *Dynamics of a creole system.* Cambridge, UK: Cambridge University Press.

Brown, H. D. (1976). Discussion of "Systematicity and stability/instability in interlanguage systems." In H. D. Brown (Ed.), *Papers in second language acquisition* (Language Learning, Special Issue No. 4, pp. 135–140). Proceedings of the 6th annual Conference on Applied Linguistics, University of Michigan, Ann Arbor.

Brown, P., & Levinson, S. (1987). *Politeness.* Cambridge, UK: Cambridge University Press.

Chambers, J., & Trudgill, P. (1980). *Dialectology.* Cambridge, UK: Cambridge University Press.

Chomsky, N. (1988). *Language and problems of knowledge: The Managua lectures.* Cambridge, MA: MIT Press.

Dickerson, L. (1974). *Internal and external patterning of phonological variability in the speech of Japanese learners of English: toward a theory of second language acquisition.* Doctoral dissertation, University of Illinois, Urbana-Champaign.

Dickerson, W. (1976). The psycholinguistic unity of language learning and language change. *Language Learning, 26,* 215–231.

Ellis, R. (1985a). Sources of variability in interlanguage. *Applied Linguistics, 6*(2), 118–131.

Ellis, R. (1985b). *Understanding second language acquisition.* Oxford: Oxford University Press.

Ellis, R. (1987). Interlanguage variability in narrative discourse: Style shifting in the use of past tense. *Studies in Second Language Acquisition, 9,* 1–20.

Garner, W. (1962). *On certainty and structure as psychological concepts.* New York: Wiley.

Gatbonton, E. (1978). Patterned phonetic variability in second language speech: A gradual diffusion model. *Canadian Modern Language Review/La Revue Canadienne des Langues Vivantes, 34,* 335–347.

Gregg, K. (1990). The Variable Competence Model of second language acquisition and why it isn't. *Applied Linguistics, 11*(4), 364–383.

Grice, W. (1975). Logic and conversation. In P. Cole & J. Morgan (Eds.), *Syntax and semantics: 3. Speech acts* (pp. 41–58). New York: Academic Press.

Guy, G. (1980). Variation in the group and the individual: The case of final stop deletion. In W. Labov (Ed.), *Locating language in time and space* (pp. 1–36). New York: Academic Press.

Huebner, T. (1983). *A longitudinal analysis of the acquisition of English.* Ann Arbor, MI: Karoma.

Irvine, J. (1979). Formality and informality in communicative events. *American Anthropologist, 81,* 773–790.

Johnson, J. S., & Newport, E. (1989). Critical period effects in second language learning: The influence of maturational state on the acquisition of English as a second language. *Cognitive Psychology, 21,* 60–99.

Kiparsky, P. (1972). Explanation in phonology. In S. Peters (Ed.), *Goals of linguistic theory* (pp. 189–227). Englewood Cliffs, NJ: Prentice-Hall.

Krashen, S. (1987). *Principles and practice in second language acquisition.* Englewood Cliffs, NJ: Prentice-Hall.

Labov, W. (1966). *The social stratification of English in New York City.* Arlington, VA: Center for Applied Linguistics.

Labov, W. (1972). *Sociolinguistic patterns.* Philadelphia: University of Pennsylvania Press.

Labov, W. (1978). *Where does the linguistic variable stop? A response to B. Lavandera* (Sociolinguistic Working Paper No. 44. Working Papers in Sociolinguistics). Austin, TX: Southwest Educational Development Laboratory.

Labov, W. (1984). Field methods of the project on linguistic change and variation. In J. Baugh & J. Sherzer (Eds.), *Language in use: Readings in sociolinguistics* (pp. 28–53). Englewood Cliffs, NJ: Prentice-Hall.

Lavandera, B. (1977). *Where does the sociolinguistic variable stop?* (Sociolinguistic Working Paper No. 40. Working Papers in Sociolinguistics). Austin, TX: Southwest Educational Development Laboratory.

McDavid, R. I., Jr. (1979). *Dialects in culture.* University: University of Alabama Press.

Milroy, L. (1980). *Language and social networks.* Oxford: Blackwell.

Milroy, L., & Milroy, J. (1977). Speech and context in an urban setting. *Belfast Working Papers in Language and Linguistics, 2*(1).

Montgomery, M. (1990). Introduction to variable rule analysis. *Journal of English Linguistics, 22*(1), 111–118.

Osthoff, H., & Brugmann, K. (1878). *Einleitung to Morphologische Untersuchungen I.* (English translation in W. P. Lehmann, 1967, A reader in nineteenth century historical Indo-European linguistics, chap. 14. Bloomington: Indiana University Press).

Pickford, G. (1956). American linguistic geography: A sociological appraisal. *Word, 12,* 211–233.

Preston, D. (1989). *Sociolinguistics and second language acquisition.* Oxford: Blackwell.

Preston, D. (1991). Sorting out the variables in sociolinguistic theory. *American Speech, 66*(1), 33–56.

Romaine, S. (1980). A critical overview of the methodology of urban British sociolinguistics. *English World Wide, 1,* 163–198.

Schumann, J. (1978). *The pidginization process.* Rowley, MA: Newbury House.

Sternberg, S. (1963). Stochastic learning theory. In R. Luce, R. Bush, & E. Galanter (Eds.), *Handbook of mathematical psychology* (Vol. 2), New York: Wiley.

Tarone, E. (1982). Systematicity and attention in the interlanguage. *Language Learning, 32,* 69–84.

Thompson, S. A., & Mulac, A. (1991). The discourse conditions for the use of the complementizer *that* in conversational English. *Journal of Pragmatics, 15,* 237–251.

Trudgill, P. (1972). Sex, covert prestige and linguistic change in the urban English of Norwich. *Language in Society, 1*(2), 179–195.

Williams, J. (1990). Review of D. Preston, *Sociolinguistics and second language acquisition.* Oxford: Blackwell, 1989. *TESOL Quarterly, 24*(3), 497–500.

Wolfram, W., & Fasold, R. (1974). *The study of social dialects in American English.* Englewood Cliffs, NJ: Prentice-Hall.

Wolfson, N. (1976). Speech events and natural speech: Some implications for sociolinguistic methodology. *Language in Society, 5,* 189–209.

Young, R. (1990, March). *Functional interpretations of variation in interlanguage morphology.* A paper presented to the Second Language Research Forum, University of Oregon, Eugene.

Young, R. (1991). *Variation in interlanguage morphology.* New York: Peter Lang.

SECOND LANGUAGE SPEECH AND THE INFLUENCE OF THE FIRST LANGUAGE

CHAPTER 9

SECOND LANGUAGE SPEECH*

Jonathan Leather and Allan James

I. INTRODUCTION

Over the past decade there has been a considerable renewal of interest in the acquisition of second language (L2) speech with the publication of anthologies (Ioup & Weinberger, 1987; James & Leather, 1987) and a number of monographs (Flege, 1988; Grosser, 1989; Hammarberg, 1988a; James, 1988). Demographic trends have brought the sociolinguistic and psycholinguistic dimensions of multiculturalism to the attention of a wider research community. At the same time, more people in essentially monolingual societies are pursuing the learning of foreign languages (FLs), and any rationale for the training of L2 speech must make some assumptions about its acquisition (Chun, 1991; Leather, 1983a; Pennington & Richards, 1986). In the scientific domain, with a healthy cross-fertilization between linguistics and psychology, the goals of phonological theory are reaching beyond idealizations of the first language (L1) to encompass speaker–hearers' total language capabilities. All the speech sciences, moreover, have been quick to take advantage of the new information technology, making practicable the analysis of more—and hence a wider range of—data, including the speech of L2 learners. As was pointed out in the introduction of an anthology, L2 speech is now the subject of quite diverse investigations—phonetic, phonological, psychological, and so on—in which a broad range of scientific concerns often converge (Leather & James, 1987).

In this chapter we review a variety of research efforts bearing on the acquisition of L2 speech, summarizing the principal discussions and findings and attempting to identify the issues and problems that are currently being—or still remain to

* Based on Leather and James (1991). The acquisition of second-language speech. *Studies in Second Language Acquisition*, *13*, 305–341.

269

be—addressed. We consider acquisition at a number of levels, among which, in future theoretical work, we would expect to see progressively clearer interrelations. We first discuss nonlinguistic constraints on acquisition. The next section is devoted to the perception and production of L2 speech sounds and their interrelation in microlevel, sensorimotor terms. We then go on to consider the global interrelation of the L2 and L1 sound systems, and phonological universals that may bear upon it over the course of acquisition. The last section deals with the capacity of phonology to account for ever larger bodies of L2 speech data, and the implications of the latter for the evolution of phonological theory.

II. LEARNER CONSTRAINTS ON THE ACQUISITION OF L2 SPEECH

Among the constraints on the acquisition of L2 speech determined by the learner are maturational factors on one hand and individual and social constraints on the other. Due to space limitations we will restrict our discussion to individual and social factors. (See chapters 5 by Schachter and 15 by Obler and Hannigan, this volume, for general discussion of maturational effects in L2 acquisition including L2 speech and phonology.)

A number of personal and social factors constrain a learner's progress and ultimate achievement in the acquisition of L2 speech, including motivation, social acceptance and social distance, personality variables, sex, and oral and auditory capacities.

A. Motivation

It is a matter of common observation, as Strevens (1974) noted, that most people can acquire minimally adequate L2 pronunciation without systematic or formal training of any kind. Various individual and social factors, however, may motivate the individual learner to aspire to—or shun—nativelike authenticity in their L2 speech. One such factor is likely to be the relative importance to the learner of "good" pronunciation: Suter (1976; Purcell & Suter, 1980) found that the degree of concern felt by the learner about good pronunciation was a significant predictor of ultimate success (although, according to Beebe, 1982, carefulness about speech on any particular speaking occasion may not be positively correlated with pronunciation correctness). Although a survey by Willing (1988) showed widespread concern among immigrant adults to master an authentic L2 pronunciation, other sources of motivation to acquire good L2 pronunciation may be extrinsic. Spies apart, perhaps only teachers of the L2 need for professional reasons to be nativelike or near-native in their pronunciation of L2; for the majority of school and nonspecialist adult learners, a reasonable goal is to be "comfortably intelligible" (Abercrombie, 1963) and to sound socially acceptable.

However, there may be for some learners an occupation-related requirement of exceptional intelligibility: the speech of air traffic controllers and telephone operators, for example, may need for their work a more redundant variety of L2 speech, which is particularly resistant to conditions of transmission noise (see Johansson, 1980).

B. Social Acceptance and Social Distance

Motivation need not be interpreted only in practical, instrumental terms. The nonnative speaker (NNS) is met with predictable stereotype-based linguistic expectations (Cunningham-Andersson, 1990; Eisenstein, 1983). What makes a NNS sound "acceptable" to a NS would seem to depend not only on how nativelike the NNS's pronunciation is, but what variety of L2 it best approximates. Accent serves as a powerful symbol of ethnicity and "psycholinguistic distinctiveness" (Giles & Byrne, 1982). Thus, in situations where languages compete (i.e., in multilingual communities) an L2 speaker may be more favorably regarded in proportion to how his or her accent conforms to the native norms of the hearer (Brennan & Brennan, 1981; Giles, 1978). Yet the phonological variables that constitute social markers in the target variety will probably not be equally accessible to the learner (Dowd, 1984); and in some circumstances a learner who does succeed in acquiring an accent that is by some objective standard very good may elicit an unwelcoming response from NSs. Bailey (1978) explains this for the Anglo-Saxon world in terms of the "low-status of 'phoney-correctness' ": the foreign speaker's pronunciation is apparently expected to reflect his outsider role (see Clyne, 1981, *passim*), and Loveday (1981) cites Christophersen's (1973) description of the Englishman's reaction to an overperfect pronunciation in a foreign speaker as that of "a host who sees an uninvited guest making free with his possessions." Some learners, though, succeed in phonologically adjusting their speech in L2 to fulfil some of the interpersonal functions available to them in L1 (Zuengler, 1982).

A constraint on success at all levels of L2 mastery, according to Spolsky (1969), J. Schumann (1975, 1978), and Brown (1980), is the learner's attitude towards the society and culture of the people whose language is concerned. Speakers adopt various linguistic markers to identify themselves with particular sociocultural groups (Scherer, 1979), and these markers have been found in L2 as well as L1 speech: extensive studies by Berkowitz, Dowd, and Zuengler (summarized in Dowd, Zuengler, & Berkowitz, 1990) provide evidence that learners of all ages and at very different stages of proficiency make use of social as well as biological, ideological, and affective markers in their L2 pronunciations, and these markers may operate below the learner's threshold of awareness (Zuengler, 1988). If, with incomplete knowledge of the L2 marking systems, the L2 learner is to speak at all in the early stages of his acquaintance with the new culture, he must clearly risk making social self-identifications that he would not intend. (Some "mis-markings" may be the result of transfer at a sociolinguistic level from the L1; in a study by Beebe, 1980, of the English produced by adult Thais in New York City, such transfer was argued to account for the lower accuracy of subjects' initial [r] in the formal speech style.) The "social identity" constraint on L2 speech acquisition would most clearly apply under conditions where the L2 is being learned naturalistically, without systematic or formal training, among the community of its NSs (see Tahta, Wood, & Loewenthal, 1981b).

C. Personality Variables

Learners' differing L2 pronunciation achievements have been explained also in terms of their personalities. The ability to acquire accurate pronunciation has been positively correlated with psychological variables like empathy and intuition (Guiora, Brannon, & Dull, 1972; Taylor, Catford, Guiora, & Lane, 1971), self-esteem (Heyde, 1979), and flexibility of ego boundaries (Guiora et al., 1975). A study by H. H. Schumann, Holroyd, Campbell, and Ward (1978) showed that deeply hypnotized subjects performed significantly better on pronunciation tasks than less well-hypnotized subjects, and this finding was taken as evidence for a *language ego* hypothesis (see also Schiffler, 1977). Studies by Guiora and his associates investigating the effect on pronunciation of alcohol and tranquilizing drugs have provided further support for such a hypothesis (Guiora, Acton, Erard, & Strickland, 1980). Even bilingual individuals, it has been argued, have only one authentic language identity or language ego, the integrity of which, at the level of sound patterning, they must preserve (Guiora & Schonberger, 1990).

D. Sex

The gender (and presumably also sociosexual disposition) of the learner may indirectly constitute a constraint on the variety of L2 speech learned. A survey among Dutch students of English (Broeders, 1982) revealed that female learners were significantly more favorably disposed toward a "prestige" accent of L2— British "Received Pronunciation"—than male: the stronger orientation of women towards prestige speech in L1 (see, e.g., Hudson, 1980) would thus seem to carry over to the learning of other languages. This is suggested by the consistently better pronunciation evidenced by female subjects in the experiment of L. Weiss (1970). However, despite the expectations that this generates, in the data of Tahta, Wood, and Loewenthal (1981a), no variance in L2 learners' pronunciation ability was accounted for by gender.

E. Oral and Auditory Capacities

Comparatively little consideration has been given to the extent to which pronunciation mastery may be finally limited by individual and developmental variations in ability to perceive the static and changing shapes of the oral cavity, and in auditory sensitivities and organization. A learner receiving explicit training in L2 articulation must adjust the configurations and movements of his articulators according to verbally formulated instructions, and the accuracy with which he or she is able to do this will ultimately be limited by tactile and proprioceptive feedback. Even naturalistic learners who receive no formal instruction must effect some match between target sounds and articulatory configurations during the production of L2. Locke (1968, 1969) has shown that individuals differ in their capacity for accurate perception of spatial configurations within the mouth (oral stereognosis), and has offered evidence of a correlation between good oral stereognosis and the ability to learn L2 sounds. The capacity for stereognosis apparently increases with age until the midteens and remains high into adulthood (McDonald & Aungst, 1967), declining with advancing age (Canetta, 1977).

On the auditory side, Helmke and Wu (1980) have argued that standards of L2 pronunciation mastery achieved by learners may be commensurate with the suitability of the learning conditions to their individual abilities in auditory discrimination. Their learners' scores on the Goldman-Fristoe-Woodcock Auditory Discrimination Test were found to correlate significantly with their performances on two different kinds of pronunciation training (drills vs. exercises).

In another research direction, correlations have been sought between individual differences in the perceptual analysis of L2 speech and the hemispheric specialization of the brain. Wesche and Schneiderman (1982) reported indications that the more a learner's L2 processing is concentrated in the right hemisphere, the better that learner's capacity for explicit phonetic coding of the L2 in transcription tasks. Ioup and Tansomboon (1987) attributed adult learners' difficulties in mastering an L2 lexical tone system to their reliance on left-hemisphere processing, when the holistic percepts of the right hemisphere might provide better modeling of melodic patterns. However, although left- and right-hemisphere processing is evidenced through contralateral ear advantage, Schouten, van Dalen, and Klein (1985) failed to find any significant correlation between degree of ear advantage for (L1) speech and general mastery of L2 pronunciation. More generally, it has been proposed that the whole process of successful adult L2 learning presupposes a high enough degree of neurocognitive flexibility so that L2 input is not simply processed via cognitive pathways that have been established for handling L1 (Schneiderman & Desmarais, 1988).

III. Perception and Production of L2 Speech Sounds

A. Construction of New Perceptual Categories

There is abundant evidence that the beginning learner seeking to impose phonetic structure on the L2 speech to which he is exposed makes perceptual reference to the phonetic categories of his L1. Bluhme (1969) analyzed transcriptions by Australian students of the German text of *The North Wind and the Sun,* and found that these listeners had perceived short vowel phonemes correctly more often than long ones; they often understood long /e:/ and /o:/ as [i] and [u]; and they omitted most postvocalic /R/. These tendencies could be explained in terms of the phonological differences between German and Australian English. Barry (1974a, 1974b) presented German and English similar pairs like *Busch* and *bush* to German and English listeners, controlling for dialect background, and found a considerable degree of perceptual agreement among speakers of particular dialects. More detailed analyses have been made in experiments making use of synthetic stimuli. The subjects of Scholes (1967, 1968) and Schouten (1975) who listened to synthetic vowel stimuli tended to map them into the vowel systems of their respective L1s, and similar perceptual reference to L1 categories has been observed for nasals, and to some extent also liquids, semivowels, and fricatives (see the review by Repp, 1984). Strange (1992) reports that American English /w/ and /r/ may be differentiated by inexperienced Japanese listeners on the basis of their goodness-of-fit to Japanese /w/.

The largest body of research findings, however, relates to the cross-language perception and production of voice onset time (VOT), which is a sufficient acoustic cue for distinguishing between initial stop consonants in many languages. Listeners have repeatedly been found to separate a continuum of VOT-varying stimuli into categories corresponding to the stop consonant systems of their L1 (Abramson & Lisker, 1970). Adults with little or no proficiency in L2 are most sensitive to VOT differences at precisely those places on the VOT continuum where their L1 locates a phoneme boundary (and where, therefore, their identification of categories is at its least reliable). Bilingual adults appear to locate their phoneme boundaries at VOT values representing something of a compromise value between the norms of L1 and those of L2 (Williams, 1977). A shift in their phoneme boundaries with language "set" (e.g., Elman, Diehl, & Buchwald, 1977) does not necessarily mean that bilinguals are switching between two language-specific modes of perceiving speech sounds, because similar shifts have been observed for monolinguals (Bohn & Flege, in press). Child learners of an L2 seemingly progress from a phoneme boundary characteristic of L1 to one appropriate to the L2 (Williams, 1979).

The role of L1 in the perception of L2 has been observed also at the prosodic level. Studdert-Kennedy and Hadding (1973) presented to Swedish and American English listeners a short phrase resynthesized with a series of different intonation contours, and observed differences between the two L1 groups in their perceptual preferences for fundamental frequency contours appropriate to question and statement. An experimental study involving British English and European Portuguese led to the conclusion that listeners' perception of L2 intonation reflected a combination of intonation transfer (positive or negative) from L1, and universal strategies for intonation interpretation (Cruz-Ferreira, 1987). Vance (1977) synthesized 64 [jɪu] syllables differing in fundamental frequency contours and presented them to native Cantonese speakers for lexical labeling. Subjects' perceptual responses indicated that they identified them by reference to their L1 lexical tone system. And in Gandour's (1983) experiment, listeners representing four different tone–language L1s also apparently made perceptual reference to their different native tone systems in judging the similarity of stimulus pairs differing in fundamental frequency contour. Broselow, Hurtig, and Ringen (1987) showed that L1 transfer in the perception of L2 also operates across levels of linguistic structure: L1–English initial learners were better able to identify the lexical Tone 4 (falling tone) of Mandarin when it occurred in utterance-final position—and bore an acoustic resemblance to the terminal fall of English declarative intonation; they were markedly less capable of identifying it in nonfinal positions.

The nature and extent of the contribution of L1 to the perception of L2 sounds may depend on the circumstances, because listeners' perceptions are a function of their construal of the auditory task in question. Werker and Logan (1985), for example, showed that cross-language speech syllables were processed at the phonemic, phonetic, and psychoacoustic levels, depending on task conditions. In another experiment, when the primary acoustic cue to the English /l/–/r/ contrast, (the F3 pattern), was presented in isolation for auditory discrimination, Japanese adult listeners performed as accurately as native American English listeners; yet when the same acoustic cue was presented embedded in speechlike stimuli the same Japanese listeners discriminated at levels little higher than chance and much worse than an American English group (Miyawaki et al., 1975). This was taken as evidence that the effect on perception of linguistic experience is specific to a phonetic mode of listening.

Linguistic, in this context, should perhaps be broadly interpreted. The Zulu click consonants /ǀ/ (apicodental), /ǂ/ (palato-alveolar) and /ǁ/ (lateral alveolar) have no phonological function in English, nor do they expound any articulatory sequences found in running English speech. They do, however, have a place in the vocal repertoire of most or all English speakers, often serving codified communicative functions (expression of disapproval, encouragement of a horse, and so on). Best, McRoberts, and Sithole (1988) investigated the abilities of English-speaking adults and infants to discriminate these clicks in minimally paired Zulu words. Discrimination was high for adults as well as infants—a result taken to indicate that when listeners are unable to assimilate the speech sounds presented to them to any of the categories of L1, they concentrate their attention on purely auditory or articulatory properties of the stimuli. However, although Best et al. argue against the wisdom of doing so, there is some justification for including the clicks in a broad definition of linguistic experience, so that their high discrimination by adult English listeners is not surprising.

It is clear, then, that listeners may make use of the phonetic categories of their

L1 when presented with auditory stimuli for linguistic labeling and discrimination. (It would follow that the L2 perceptions of adults will differ from those of children, whose L1 is not fully established.) More specifically, the evidence suggests, L2 learners follow a hypothetical process of equivalence classification to project their L1 phonetic categories where possible upon the sounds of L2 (Flege, 1987b). Such classification occurs even when there are detectable acoustic differences between the L2 sound and its L1 "equivalent" (Flege, 1990a; Wode, 1977, 1978). Other L2 sounds that resist the learner's attempts at equivalence classification will be the subject of new phonetic category construction. MacKain, Best, and Strange (1981) found that categorical perception of the /l/–/r/ contrast was available to Japanese adults with advanced proficiency in spoken English, but not to those who lacked such proficiency, indicating that these listeners' phonetic categories for /r/ and /l/ had been developed over the period of L2 learning.

It seems likely (see, e.g., Flege, 1987b; Valdman, 1976) that the adult's L2 phonetic learning task is harder for a sound classified as equivalent to one found in L1 than for one for which a phonetic category must be constructed from scratch—because the influence of the L1 category may cause learners to develop inaccurate perceptual targets for L2. How learners' classifications of sounds as equivalent rather than new might be objectively predicted, and the degree of resemblance between an L2 sound and two or more L1 equivalence candidates quantified, remain crucial questions for research (see Flege, 1990b).[1] What is clear is that progress in L2 phonological acquisition is not simply the acquisition of successive new phonetic representations permitting an ever-better perceptual and productive approximation to nativelike norms. Experience of L2 may actually be associated with a less—rather than more—authentic production of a "similar" sound in L2: Bohn and Flege (1992), for instance, found that native Germans with relatively little experience of English produced an English [æ] vowel that was acoustically indistinguishable from the productions of native English speakers, whereas the English [æ] of other Germans with several years of exposure to English was German-accented. Bohn (1992) explains this as a function of the interrelation of similar and new vowels in the evolving vowel space encompassed by both L1 and L2.

Restructuring of acoustic-phonetic space also occurs when the learner attempts to accommodate to the acoustic-phonetic variation between individual talkers.

---

[1] Since substantive differences between some sounds of L1 and L2—whatever their phonological status—may be small, the notion "new sound" is potentially problematic. We have felt, however, that it is both possible and preferable in parts of this review to avoid making overt distinctions between phonetic and (inter-) phonological, or between different "phonetic" levels of analysis (for recent discussion of the 'levels' problem, see Ashby, 1990; Barry & Fourcin, 1990; Keating, 1989). Where the context does not disambiguate the term, we mean by a "new" sound one which in articulatory or acoustic terms plainly differs from any in L1. The methodological importance of explicit and objective criteria for deciding what sounds of L2 are "new" for the learner has been underlined by Flege (1990b).

Leather (1990), presenting data on the initial acquisition of Chinese lexical tone by nontonal speakers, underlined the need for the learner to have access to exemplars that progressively span the normal range of interspeaker variation: too much or too little variability at an early stage of learning might prevent the learner from discovering with sufficient accuracy the prototypical forms that individual exemplars expound. Thus, when two learners who had learned to perceive accurately the four citation-form tones of one speaker were exposed to new tone tokens from different speakers, they reorganized their acoustic tone spaces to try to maintain systematicity, but thereby—as a result of erroneous inferences—constructed a worse, not better, approximation to the target tone system. Logan, Lively, and Pisoni (1991), also, found that Japanese learners of English presented with natural speech English words were much more affected by talker variation than were L1–English listeners: five talkers were too few to enable these learners to develop /l/ and /r/ representations adequate for the successful categorization of the /l/s and /r/s of new talkers.

The problem of acoustic-phonetic variability in L2 speech has led to the suggestion (e.g, Jamieson & Morosan, 1986) that learners could be helped by first focusing their attention on the criterial acoustic cues to the phonetic contrast and then introducing a range of acoustic variability into the stimulus material. In such a procedure account would perhaps need to be taken of Nosofsky, Clark, and Shin's (1989) conclusion on the respective contributions of rules and exemplars to categorization, identification, and recognition: the perceiver's decision may be based on stored exemplars (specific experiences), but with attention selectively focused on those aspects of the exemplars that appear most relevant to the categorization.

B. Production of New Sounds

Articulatory Targets, Plans and Transfer

To produce a skilled motor act such as a well-learned speech event in L1, a speaker presumably makes reference to some internal representation of the intended outcome and then effects the appropriate motor commands according to known production rules (Borden, Harris, Fitch, & Yoshioka, 1981). To produce a relatively unfamiliar motor act such as a new or incompletely learned speech event in L2, the speaker presumably refers to some less well-formed perceptual target and enacts a motor program based on less well-known production rules. In order to construct the required plan, the learner must work out both the motor elements of the target production and their temporal relations (Fentress, 1984). Success in the production of L2 sounds would thus be limited, in control system terms, by inadequate knowledge of (1) the phonetic target, or (2) the means of attaining it, or both.

That the established articulatory routines of L1 may play a part in the production of the sounds of an L2 is attested by universal informal evidence of foreign accent, and has not been seriously questioned in the literature. Many accounts of developing L2 speech have attempted to explain deficiencies in L2 productions in terms of structural differences between the sound systems of L2 and L1. Based on the key construct of structuralist phonology, the segmental phoneme, a widely held view has postulated the systematic substitution of L1 sounds for elements of the L2 system (a simple and influential statement of the classic theory of phonological interference or transfer is given by Lado, 1957; see also IV.B below).

However, as Pisoni and his associates point out, it has become clear from a large volume of research over the last few decades that although the phoneme may be a useful construct in linguistic description, its status in the real-time processing of spoken language is problematic (Pisoni, Logan, & Lively, 1990; Pisoni & Luce, 1987). While studies like that of Eckman (1981)—and, for prosody Pürschel (1975), Esser (1978), and Scuffil (1982)—suggest that some aspects of the learner's phonological progress in L2 can indeed be systematically predicted from the L1 system, other research has indicated that the classic transfer hypothesis is an oversimplification, and pointed up the need for detailed phonetic investigations that are not subject to the *ab initio* data reduction of phoneme-based description. Thus, Brière (1968) trained NSs of English to produce French, Arabic, and Vietnamese sounds varying in similarity to the sounds of English, and showed that the observed patterns of L2 pronunciation learning could not be accounted for in terms only of a contrastive analysis of the phoneme inventories of L1 and L2. Rather, the relative difficulty of learning a sound could only be explained by reference to full analysis at the phonetic level. And Nemser (1971), in a study of the learning of English by NSs of Hungarian, noted a frequent association of dissimilar perceptual and productive patterns: his subjects tended to perceive the English interdentals as labial fricatives, to produce them as stops, and to imitate them as either sibilants or stops or fricatives. This dissociation of perceptual and productive patterns again argues against a simple phoneme-based model of L1–L2 transfer. That it is possible under the appropriate conditions to perceive and act upon noncontrastive acoustic–phonetic differences between L1 and L2 in the realization of similar sounds has been convincingly shown by Flege and his associates (Bohn & Flege, 1990; Flege & Hammond, 1982).

In the case of the pre-adult L2 learner, a simple transfer model is still less plausible. Mulford and Hecht (1980), concluded that while, in the context of the child bilingual, the L1 might contribute to determining the relative difficulty of acquisition of the various sounds of L2, the phonetic strategies and substitutions adopted for L2 were better predicted by those that characterize development in L1 (the developmental hypothesis). Moreover, while the L1 system is still incomplete, it may be more plausible to view the learner's progress in L2 as a progressive reorganization of the acoustic-phonetic space as a whole. Thus Chamot (1973) related the developing phonetic characteristics of the English productions of a 10-

year-old French–Spanish bilingual to both of the child's partially established sound systems, whereas Itoh and Hatch (1978) found in the early bilingual development of a 2-year-old Japanese child who begins to acquire English some evidence of a mixing of the two evolving sound systems. The cross-language VOT data of Williams (1979) are again interpretable as evidence not so much of a simple phonological transfer as of a restructuring of the acoustic-phonetic space encompassing both L1 and L2. Such a restructuring, Williams hypothesizes, may involve developing a sensitivity to *new* acoustic cues necessary for keeping separate the two phonetic systems in perception, and a realignment in production of the total phonetic space of any single acoustic-phonetic dimension. One of the consequences of such a restructuring might be L1 parameter values that deviate in the direction of the norms established for L2, and there is evidence that such effects need not be confined to preadult learners. The L1 Spanish children learning English studied by Williams (1979) produced longer VOT values for Spanish stops than monolinguals; but Caramazza, Yeni-Komshian, Zurif, and Carbone (1973) observed that (adult) L1 French speakers learning English produced longer VOT values for /p, t, k/ than French monolinguals; and long-term expatriate French–L1 and English–L2 speakers in Flege's (1987b) experiment showed accommodation to some of the acoustic-phonetic norms of English in their productions of /t/ and /u/ in French words.

Recent articulatory and acoustic studies, while acknowledging a role for L1 in the construction of target representations for the production of L2 sounds, have indicated that even if, hypothetically, L2 production plans originate in a matrix of existing L1 categories, their development may be subject to constraints imposed by the requirement of contrastiveness not only in the perceptual and articulatory modes, but across different linguistic levels as well. An explanation of the differences found in a cinefluorographic study by Zimmerman, Price, and Ayusawa (1984) between the articulations of /l/ and /r/ by an American English speaker and two NSs of Japanese with different proficiencies in English required not only acoustic–perceptual, but also orthographic factors to be taken into account. And Leather (1988) found that the shortcomings in nontonal learners' attempts to produce Chinese lexical tones reflected the lower rate of pitch change and reluctance to reach the bottom of the phonation range, which characterize their intonation in L1 (Dutch).

Feedback versus Preprogramming in Production

Speakers receive feedback on their production performance at several levels of motor organization: auditory and tactile feedback are available from air- and bone-conducted pressure changes and from the surfaces of articulators, while feedback from the joints, tendons, and muscles provides a sense (proprioception or kinaesthesia) of articulatory positions and movements (Borden, 1980; Stevens & Perkell, 1977). In addition, there are some indications of an internal feedback within the brain that provides for central monitoring of the motor commands sent to the muscles (Borden, 1979). Relatively little is known about the possible combination of two or more feedback inputs, or about the respective roles of feedback-regulated (closedloop) and centrally preprogrammed (open-loop) control in speech production.

It is quite widely believed (see, e.g., Stevens, 1977) that because speech is habitual activity, preplanning (i.e., open-loop control) mechanisms are made greater use of than peripheral feedback for the moment-to-moment control of vocal tract movements in the established adult L1. Yet open-loop control is theoretically less appropriate to the production of new sounds, because, as Kent (1976) points out, the performance accuracy of an open-loop system depends upon a known relationship between its (motor) input and (acoustic) output—a calibration that presumably can only be made with production experience. The acquisition of a new motor skill would seem to entail acting on some knowledge of results (Adams, 1971), and there is some support for the hypothesis that, as speakers gain experience of new sound productions, their articulatory activity comes to be guided less by closed-loop (i.e., feedback-regulated) and commensurately more by open-loop (centrally preprogrammed) control (Borden, 1980; MacKay, 1970; Siegel, Fehst, Garber, & Pick, 1980). The initial production of new speech patterns, whether in L1 or L2, would entail testing afferent feedback signals for the fit that they imply to some phonetic representation in auditory-perceptual space (Nooteboom, 1970; Oden & Massaro, 1978; Repp, 1977); such a representation in memory would have been previously derived from exemplars available in the community (in the case of naturalistic learning) or explicitly presented during training. Motor programs would then be progressively adjusted until a satisfactory "match" is made between feedback signals and target representation. Among speakers acquiring new phonetic contrasts, therefore, self-perception would appear to play an important role in forming associations between speech perception and speech production (Borden, 1980). Feedback may thus play a greater part relative to preplanning in the development of L1 production by children, and in the (initial) productive learning of an L2.

Three very different studies would support a production model in which, at least for many classes of speech sounds, closed-loop does progressively give way to open-loop control. First, bilingual and monolingual subjects in an experiment by MacKay (1970) read in German and English while listening to their own voice reading in the other language. Although with this distraction they spoke more slowly in both languages, the effect was greater with their L1—a result interpretable as indicating that they attended more to the articulation of L2 than of L1. Secondly, Borden and her associates (Borden, 1980; Borden et al., 1981) studied the attempts of speakers to imitate familiar and foreign syllables under conditions of reduced auditory and tactile feedback (achieved by masking noise and lingual anaesthesia). From electromyographic and acoustic analyses as well as perceptual judgments of their subjects' accuracy, they concluded that production (in skilled adults) normally operates under the control of an open-loop motor system, with fine-tuning from feedback, and subject to the availability of well-defined perceptual targets. Thirdly, a study by Manning and Hein (1981) suggested that articulations by English-speaking adults of French /y/ and /r/ were progressively more resistant to distortion under masking noise as their accuracy of production improved over a series of training sessions. However, feedback-regulated control may not extend to all production parameters because, as Flege (1988) points out, motor reactions to the afferent signals of tactile and auditory feedback may actually be too slow for effecting the necessary on-line motor adjustments (so that closed-loop control may necessarily be confined to the more slowly changing articulatory parameters such as jaw movement).

C. Developmental Interrelation of Perception and Production

The interrelation of perceptual and productive knowledge over the course of L2 speech learning has not only theoretical importance in the modeling of the speech faculty as a whole (see, e.g., Pisoni et al., 1990; Repp, 1984), but practical implications for the design of L2 pronunciation-training programs. Although there is evidence (see, e.g., Schneiderman, Bourdages, & Champagne, 1988) to support the widely held belief in some degree of positive correlation between perception and production abilities, it has often been hypothesized that in the L2 sound-learning process one of the speech modalities is dominant. The question of whether perception might *lead* production, or vice versa, was until quite recently addressed most often in the FL teaching domain, to determine where training efforts could best be concentrated in order to benefit from a hypothesized facilitating effect (i.e., positive transfer) from one modality to the other. Pimsleur (1963) found that discrimination training improved discrimination between L2 minimal phonemic pairs, and this gain in perceptual accuracy apparently carried over to production. Mueller and Niedzielski (1968) also reported positive transfer from perception to production at the segmental level. The discrimination training given by Lane and Schneider (1963), however, did not bring about better productions of, in this case, the Thai lexical tones. In Dreher and Larkins's (1972) experiment, phoneme discrimination correlated fairly highly with accuracy of production, although the directionality of any facilitation effect was not explored. Henning (1966) reported better production from learners who received only discrimination training than from other learners whose training involved only imitative production, and R. Weiss (1976) found that as good L2 vowel productions could be achieved through discrimination training as through articulatory instruction. On the other hand, Greasley's (1971) study suggested that imitation of models alone was less highly correlated than articulatory instruction with the accurate production of a sound; and Brière (1968) observed that his experimental subjects were on occasion able adequately to produce isolated L2 sounds some time before being able to discriminate between them. Catford and Pisoni (1970) trained two groups of learners in a number of new sounds by articulatory-based and auditory-based methods, and found that the articulatorily trained group performed better on all production and discrimination tests—and significantly so on all except discrimination of consonants.

Little can be concluded from these studies collectively: their divergent outcomes may perhaps be explained in terms of differing methods and, to some extent, differing interpretations of the scope of perceptual and productive knowledge (Leather, 1988). A perception–production relationship observed during or after explicit training in L2 speech may be in part a function of that training (Schneiderman et al., 1988), and not therefore simply generalizable to naturalistic learning. Nor is there any *a priori* reason to suppose that some fixed interrelation of perception and production is "hard-wired" in the speech system. Gordon and Myer (1984) interpreted their experimental results as suggesting that for place of articulation features, perceptual and productive mechanisms are independent, whereas for voicing features, there are shared or interacting perception and production mechanisms.

Unlike an infant learning an L1, the L2 learner must often attempt to produce L2 speech with little prior perceptual exposure to its sound patterning. This leads to one kind of explanation of why nativelike pronunciation of L2 is so rarely attained by adult learners: Neufeld (1977, 1978, 1980) has argued with support from the results of training studies that if L2 learners attempt productions of new sounds before they have had sufficient exposure to good exemplars, they risk misshaping the developing phonetic template that will guide their subsequent productions. Consistent with such an explanation is the superior L2 production accuracy reported for the learner groups of Postovsky (1974) and Gary (1975), whose speaking was delayed in the early stages of L2 instruction. A "perception-first" explanation would also be consistent with the performance of Lane and Schneider's (1963) learners who, when asked to persevere in imitating a model until they judged their productions to be accurate, arrived after a number of trials at pronunciations that had stabilized but in some cases did not closely approximate the exemplar. Further such evidence is perhaps to be found in the stabilization observed by Walz (1975) in learners who imitated L2 sounds from the start of their L2 curriculum, and whose productive phonetic accuracy, though it might start quite high, showed no subsequent improvement; moreover, learners in de Bot's (1981) experiment who were asked to listen critically to a playback of their (often faulty) productions actually appeared to perform worse rather than better in subsequent production attempts.

Evidence of a correlation between perceptual and productive ability—and, arguably, a perceptual etiology for L2 production deviance—is to be found in a test of an "equivalence classification" hypothesis. Flege (1987b) investigated both VOT and second format frequency in the English syllable /tu/ (two) and the French syllables /tu/ (tous) and /ty/ (tu) produced by native French speakers of English and three groups of native English speakers who were respectively monolingual, intermediate, and advanced in their command of French. The advanced L2 French speakers better approximated the acoustic-phonetic norms than the intermediate learners, though they were more successful in producing French /y/ (which has no counterpart in English) than French /u/ (which differs acoustically from English /u/).

Well-formed perceptual targets may be a necessary, but are not a sufficient condition for productive success—because the requisite motor programs must also be available. Flege and Port (1981) compared the production of stop-voicing contrasts in Arabic by Saudi Arabians and by both Americans and Saudis in American English. Despite consistently un-English patterns of VOT and closure duration, the Saudis' stops were easily perceptible by native American English-speaking listeners, with the exception of /p/. This sound, which has no counterpart in Arabic, was frequently produced with laryngeal pulsing during the closure phase. Considering its timing, however, the investigators concluded that the Saudi speakers had grasped its phonological property (i.e., of functioning analogously to /t/ and /k/ in voiced–voiceless pairs), but were unable to control adequately all the parameters for its articulation.

Other studies have suggested a production lead over perception. Gass (1984) used VOT continuum stimuli to test three times, at monthly intervals, the perceptions of subjects from five different language backgrounds following English courses in the United States. She also measured the VOT of productions in English by the same subjects at the same intervals. She found that the English stop consonant labeling functions of the L2 learners were not so clearly or sharply categorical as those of the NS American English control group, nor so monotonic. VOT values for these NNS's /p/–/b/ phoneme boundary were in many cases closer in the later tests to native values (here the results were consistent with those of Williams, 1979). Production, on the other hand, showed all along VOT values which approximate to the native norms, and which did not change in any systematic way over the 2-month period studied. This outcome was taken to indicate that production was in advance of perception (subjects' linguistic heterogeneity, however, made it difficult to draw conclusions about the possible interrelation between their productive and perceptive learning).

Production leads have also been reported for Japanese learners of the English /r/–/l/ contrast. Because Japanese has only one liquid phoneme, whereas English has two, Japanese speakers must learn to distinguish between English /l/ and /r/, and to produce an entirely new type of consonant, namely an approximant /r/. Goto (1971) compared data of several kinds on native Japanese subjects: (1) their productions of English /l/ and /r/ (rated for authenticity by NS English judges);

(2) their perception of the contrast in the utterances of English NSs and (3) in their own utterances. Goto concluded that subjects who could not perceptually differentiate /l/ from /r/ (even in their own productions) might nevertheless be capable of producing an accurate /l/–/r/ distinction.

Sheldon and Strange (1982), in a replication and extension of Goto's investigation, examined the perception and production of American English /l/ and /r/ by native Japanese adults learning English in the United States. As in Goto's study, perception by those Japanese able to produce a "good" /l/–/r/ distinction in American English was generally less accurate than their production. Also, as in the studies by Goto (1971) and Mochizuki (1981), perceptual errors were significantly correlated with position in word (hence syllable structure). But, in contrast to Goto's finding, for four out of the five speakers tested, self-perception was better than perception of others. The investigators took their findings to indicate that perceptual mastery of an L2 phonetic contrast may not necessarily precede—and may even lag behind—productive mastery. It is conceivable that subjects in both this and Goto's study made differential use of acoustic cues in their productions and perceptions of the phonetic contrast in question, but neither study directly addresses such a hypothesis.

Taken together, the findings of a variety of investigations thus do not constitute clear evidence of any constant and simple correspondence between perception and production—which should therefore not be viewed merely as two sides of the same coin.[2]

An alternative view is that the speech learning system has sufficient versatility to interrelate perceptual and productive knowledge in the most fruitful way permitted by particular—and often changing—circumstances. Leather (1987, 1988, 1990, 1991) investigated the initial learning of the lexical (syllabic) tones of standard Chinese by adult Dutch and English speakers. Computer-managed individualized training was given in tone perception, and subjects who achieved perceptual proficiency were submitted to a tone production test. Other groups of subjects were trained using a computer-managed interactive visual feedback system to produce the tones without any auditory exposure to tone exemplars, and those subjects who attained a proficiency criterion were then tested in their tone perception abilities. The results indicated that learners did not in general need to be trained in production to be able to produce, or in perception to be able to perceive, the sound patterns of the target system, because training in one modality tended to be sufficient to enable a learner to perform in the other.

A "best-fit" model of the process of L2 speech sound learning would perhaps represent the learner's primary goal as the construction of phonetic prototypes to

[2]Nor has there yet been, to our knowledge, any research taking into account the possibility (suggested by Mack, 1989) that perception–production asymmetries might have a social psychological causation—in the sense that, for example, the social cost of mispronunciation may for a particular learner exceed that of misperception.

which the processes of both perception and production may be geared. These prototypes, or parametric representations, would capture the acoustic central tendencies of "good" tokens.[3] They would serve both perceptual decisions (see Blumstein & Stevens, 1979; Klatt, 1979) and production activity (see Ladefoged, DeClerk, Lindau, & Papçun, 1972; Lindblom, Lubker, & Gay, 1979) by means of schemata (i.e., structured plans) that define the serial and hierarchical orderings of the requisite cognitive and motor events, providing algorithmically for successive decisions in perception, and the activation of articulatory plans with feedback-based adjustments in production.

The hypothetical association of independent perceptual and productive schemata with an L2 phonetic prototype may be sufficient to account for apparent divergences between a learner's perception and production of a given sound—the apparently superior productive ability, for example, of the learners observed by Sheldon and Strange (1982), whose production of a troublesome L2 contrast may reflect a background of articulatory training on purpose dissociated from the development of corresponding perceptual ability. Maintaining a separation between a phonetic prototype and the schemata that operationalize it might also satisfy one of the basic requirements—emphasized by Linell (1982)—of a phonological (in the sense of linguistically structural) unit: that it be neutral with respect to the activities of production and perception. It might, furthermore, acknowledge any heuristic biases that may be maintained in one or the other modality: Gass (1984), for instance, observed a tendency among NNSs to "overcompensate" for differences between the native language (NL) and target languages (TL), and took this to support Obler's (1982) proposal for a dual production system that would exaggerate the acoustic-phonetic divergences between the two languages.

IV. DEVELOPMENTAL INTERRELATION BETWEEN L1 AND L2 SPEECH ACQUISITION

A. Product and Process

The role of L1 in L2 speech acquisition has formed a major, if not *the* major, focus of attention almost as long as L2 speech has been studied. Polivanov (1932/1974), for example, addressed the perception of foreign sounds via the NL, and Trubetzkoy (1939/1958) characterized such perception as the "filtering" of the new sound system through the "sieve" of the NL. Indeed, it is commonplace to observe that the influence of NL on foreign language learning is most evident in speech—as opposed to, for example, grammatical or lexical structure.

However, is the influence of L1 on L2 speech acquisition present in the *process*

---

[3] For general discussions of the interrelation between prototypes, central tendencies, and exemplars, see Nosofsky (1988); and on the nature and function of prototypes in speech see Kuhl (1992).

of language development? In other words, do the same or similar kinds of mechanisms that operate in L1 ontogeny operate also in L2, and if so, how (in what form) and when (at what stage)? Moreover (or alternatively), is the influence of L1 in L2 acquisition to be found mainly in the *product* of language ontogeny, namely, in the forms produced and perceived in the L2 by the learner that are patently under the influence of phonic elements of the NL? Both these dimensions of the interrelationship between L1 and L2 speech acquisition have been explored in research on the area, although product dimension has engaged most of the research interest so far.

B. The Influence of L1 Structure

For some 20 years after the publication of Lado's (1957) seminal *Linguistics Across Cultures,* the main question addressed in L2 speech research was the influence of L1 structure on L2 speech acquisition. Contrastive analysis of the (phonetic and) phonological properties of the L1 and L2 involved in learning were assumed to be able to describe, if not predict (1) the degree of difficulty experienced by learners with elements of the FL sound system, and (2) the kinds of errors manifested in learners' renditions of the FL speech sounds. However, the "strong version" of contrastive analysis gradually gave way to a "weak version" (Wardhaugh, 1970). In phonology, because a structural description and comparison of the sound systems of L1 and L2 was shown to be inadequate for predicting all errors in L2 speech (Kohler, 1971) (i.e., the "strong" or predictive claim of contrastive analysis was untenable), the role assigned to contrastive theory became that of an adjunct to general error analysis, as one of a number of means of accounting for the origin of the L2 sound forms observed (i.e., the "weak" claim).

Much has been written on the development of contrastive analysis, including contrastive phonology, and its empirical and methodological shortcomings. The discussion need not be repeated here (for an early empirical critique, see, e.g., Whitman, 1970; for more recent discussion on the methodological weaknesses of contrastive phonology, see James, 1986a, 1988). (See also in this volume, chapter 10 by Gass for a general discussion of L1 influence in L2 acquisition including phonetic and phonological influence. See chapters 5 by Eckman and 12 by Nunan for discussion of the place of contrastive analysis in the history of the field.) Representative work in contrastive phonology includes Stockwell and Bowen (1965) on the hierarchy of difficulty in L2 sound learning, Moulton (1972) on contrastive analysis in phonemic terms, Efstathiadis (1974) in distinctive feature terms, and Eliasson (1976) and Fisiak (1975, 1976) for earlier accounts of theoretical and practical issues. Kohler (1981) offered criticism of the phonetic reality of contrastive phonological descriptions, and Eliasson (1984) provided a more recent discussion of theoretical problems in the field.

The realization through the practice of contrastive phonology that L1 "product" influence on L2 speech acquisition was far more differentiated than could be accounted for by a straight comparison of the sound structures of the languages involved led, in the course of the 1970s, to a variety of approaches to the problem. Modes of description were adopted from a number of different linguistic traditions or paradigms. In general, the conclusion was that the processing and developmental dimensions of L1 influence in L2 speech acquisition are in need of further exploration. By and large, these areas of investigation have remained dominant to the present day. Within these dimensions researchers have explored (1) the nature of the interlingual identification of phonic elements of the L2 with those of the L1; (2) the role of general learning and psychological processing strategies, such as transfer in L2 speech acquisition, and their relation to L1 structural influence; (3) the developmental dimensions of such influence, (4) the role of universal phonological-phonetic preferences in constraining L1 influence on L2 acquisition, (5) the sociolinguistic, stylistic, and discoursal dimensions of differential L1 influence, and (6) the fuller phonological implications for, and from, the influence of L1 sound structure on L2 speech acquisition—this in comparison to the more surface-level contrastive analyses that had been offered hitherto. Each of these factors and lines of research will now be considered in turn.

C. The Identification of L2 and L1 Elements

Theoretical Issues

If comparisons are made by an L2 learner—on whatever level—between elements of the L2 and L1 and are assessed for their interlingual compatibility, the units with which the learner operates are not necessarily those provided by (contrastive) phonological description. Kohler (1981), for example, pointed out that the phonological feature [± voiced] is totally inadequate for capturing the phonetic detail of the realization of /p t k/ versus /b d g/ distinctions in the L2 French of German learners. In the processing and developmental realities of L2 speech acquisition, it is likely that different properties of the L2 sound input are picked out and associated with the L1 or gauged for their similarity or difference to L1 sound elements at different stages, with reference to different units (segments, syllables) of identification. Weinreich (1953) and Haugen (1956) analyzed interlingual identification in structuralist phonemic terms to account for different types of interference found between L1s and L2s. For example, according to Haugen (1956), identification may be "divergent" (i.e., a single phoneme category of the L1 is realized as two categories in the L2); "convergent" (i.e., two categories of the L1 are realized as one in the L2); or "simple" (i.e., one and the same phoneme category is realized in both languages).

However, it soon became clear that phoneme theory was inadequate on its own for establishing the relevant elements of association, and at this point research on L1–L2 and L2–L1 identification diverged into a number of different directions of investigation. The first approach was to employ different phonological categories used as the basis for interlingual identification. The second was to incorporate the notion of the "interlingual unit of identification" in an emerging theory of interlanguage (IL) as a largely self-contained linguistic system that was conceptually, if not descriptively, independent of the L2 and the L1. The third direction pursued was to subject the sound identifications made by L2 learners to controlled experimentation and attempt to arrive at an empirically based interpretation of the categories employed. These lines of investigation will be discussed in turn.

Phonological Categories in Interlingual Identification

If a particular phonological theory was unable to offer plausible categories for the description of learner identifications, then other theories were to be explored instead. Indeed, Weinreich himself (1957) proposed using distinctive feature theory in place of phonemics to describe the bilingual's analysis and rendition of the material in the L2. Ritchie (1968) went a step further in using feature *hierarchies* to explain the differential substitution of L2 English dental fricatives by L1 speakers of Japanese and Russian. Michaels (1974) used the markedness values of features in the L2 and L1 as developed in Chomsky and Halle (1968) to explain the identification by Spanish learners of English of L2 [ŋ] as [n] and [ʃ] as [tʃ]. James (1984), with reference to L2 English and L1 Dutch, accounted for the identification of L2 [θ ð] in terms of structural properties at phonological, phonetic, and articulatory levels of association.

However, proposals to employ phonological categories as the means of identification consistently must confront the processing realities of interlingual assessments, and most phonological theories to date have offered only a processing-neutral phonetic representation to the extent that they offer phonetic representations at all. In this respect, work in experimental phonology (Ohala, 1986; Ohala & Jaeger, 1986), on the phonetics–phonology interface (Keating, 1989, 1990), and on articulatory phonology (Browman & Goldstein, 1986, 1989), which posits unitary phonetic and phonological categories at certain levels, offers potentially fruitful sources of description by which interlingual identifications in L2 speech acquisition may be more completely explained.

Units of Identification in IL Systems

A methodological and descriptive alternative to the problem of identification is to consider the units involved as part of an independent developing IL system, the elements of which are not necessarily isomorphic with the established phonological structures of the L1 and L2 in contact. Brière (1968), for example, in a study of the phonological interference realized by American English speakers in an artificially constructed TL sound system, concluded that the syllable may be a more central unit of interlingual identification than the phoneme or the (distinctive) feature. Moreover, Selinker (1972) and Tarone (1972) provided evidence from various ILs that the syllable is a unit of interlingual identification on the phonological level. With the relative demise of IL theory as such, however, the issue of the syllable (or other IL-specific units) has received little attention, although analyses of general typological constraints on developing phonological systems have continued to focus attention on the role of syllable structure in L2 speech acquisition.

Learner Interlingual Identifications in Perception

In a large number of experimental studies, Flege and his associates (e.g., Bohn & Flege, 1990, 1992; Flege, 1985, 1987a, 1987b, 1990a, 1992a; Flege & Eefting, 1987; Flege & Hillenbrand, 1984) have explored the nature of interlingual identification in L2 speech acquisition. Using data from a number of L2–L1 pairings (English–French, French–English, English–Dutch, English–German) and examining the production and perception of L2–L1 segment pairs by learners, Flege concluded that the "phonetic distance" status of the phones involved provides a reliable predictor of the TL accuracy with which phones will be realized in the L2. Whereas a "new" phone in the L2 (i.e., one not present in the L1) is shown to be masterable in acquisition, "similar" phones are consistently produced (and perceived) with nontarget values. "Identical" L2–L1 phones, on the other hand, provide little problem in acquisition. Quantitative specifications of the acoustic properties of such phones (e.g., voice-onset time for stops, formant values for vowels) form the basis for establishing these categorization types. Further support for the distinction of identical versus new and its relevancy for the acquisition of L2 speech sounds was provided by Major (1987a) in a study of the acquisition of English /ɛ/, an "identical" sound, and /æ/, a "new" sound, by Brazilian (i.e., Portuguese-speaking) learners. However, the influence of L1 structure on L2 speech acquisition may result in a situation in which the establishment of certain "new" L2 phonic categories leads to regression in the representation of already established (i.e., L1-like) ones (Nathan, 1987, 1990). It may even lead to a marginal loss of those L2 sound specifications that have a similar L1 representation (Major, 1990).

The actual unit of identification employed by the L2 learner is seen by Flege in his Speech Learning Model (SLM) as a phonetic rather than phonemic entity. Here, Flege (1992b) states that identification procedures operate on "sounds (that is, phonetically relevant phone classes)." One observes the reverse problem of description discussed earlier. A speech signal or phonetic interpretation of interlingual identifications must make a connection with a phonological interpretation of that part of an L2 speech learner's "mental grammar" as much as the latter must connect with the former as a specification of part of a learner's speech-processing arsenal. Here again those models of sound description that posit a direct link between phonological specification and sensorimotor properties of speech (see, e.g., Browman & Goldstein, 1989, for articulatory properties) may be able to provide an appropriate analytic framework for future investigation.

D. Processing Strategies and L1 Structural Influence

It has already been pointed out that in the 1960s, research into the influence of the L1 "product" in L2 speech acquisition was conducted within the framework of a contrastive phonological analysis of the L1 and L2 in question. More implicitly than explicitly, it was assumed in contrastive phonology that the process of L1 (negative) transfer or "proactive interference" in L2 learning could be modeled in terms of a behaviorist model of stimulus–response (S-R) "paired-associate learning," whereby what the FL learner had to acquire was a new set of "habit structures," namely, S-R pairings (for an early critique of the psycholinguistic inadequacies of this approach in L2 speech acquisition, see Brière, 1968). However, under the influence of the mentalism of generative grammar and Selinker's (1972) IL proposals, which give L1 influence as "transfer" a more cognitive interpretation in learning, researchers increasingly interpreted the notion of L1 structural influence as a means available to the learner for solving problems in the structuring of the L2 speech data. In this spirit, Tarone (1978), for example, listed negative transfer from the NL as one of the "processes" operative in L2 phonology, and James (1986a, 1986b, 1988) in a similar vein considered transfer as one of the "strategic solutions" open to learners of an L2 phonological structure.

Wode (1980, 1981), in looking at the acquisition of English by German speakers, observed that the substitution of an L2 phone by one of the L1 in speech learning is dependent on the existence of a critical similarity measure between properties of the L2 and L1 sounds, and that such similarity measures are, in turn, dependent on developmental factors of L2 speech acquisition. More recently, Hammarberg (1988b, 1990) showed with L2 German– L1 Swedish phone substitutions that transfer as such must be interpreted as (1) a *strategy,* "with regard to the learner's plan of action to solve a particular problem in acquiring some phonological regularity in L2"; (b) a *process,* "with regard to the event, or act of transferring something"; and (c) a *solution,* "with regard to the product . . . of the applied strategy and the occurred process" (1990, pp. 198– 199). This proposal itself is an attempt to resolve the potential confusion of a product-versus-process analysis of a phenomenon that, on the one hand, is *activated* in L2 speech acquisition and, on the other, is seen as the *result* of L1 structural influence. Wieden (1990) and Wieden and Nemser (1991), in a large-scale study of the acquisition of English sound structure by Austrian (i.e., German-speaking) learners, examined, for each segment produced, the interaction of "acquisition mode constraints," which relate to general background processes of phonic learning in the L2 and which include L1 transfer, with "operational mode constraints," which relate to the learners' actual processing of the L2 speech signal.

It seems that the tension between the role of (L1–L2) phonological "knowledge" and (L2) processing strategies has yet to be satisfactorily resolved. Weinberger (1987), in a study of Mandarin speakers' renderings of English final consonant cluster combinations, makes an appeal to the general principle of recoverability of phonological form (Kaye, 1981) to "explain" the relative occurrence of deletion versus epenthesis as a syllable-simplification strategy. Eliasson and Tubielewicz-Mattsson (1992) studied the phonological processes employed by Swedish learners of Polish in determining the underlying forms of words subject to a phonological rule of obstruent voice-assimilation. They conclude that disambiguation by the learners of identical L2 phonetic forms is brought about by a combination of knowing the L2 phonological rule in question and the application of language-independent cognitive strategies of comparison and matching.

In summary, although certain results are available, there remain many questions as to the conditions under which L1 transfer is activated in L2 speech acquisition, the role L2 phonological knowledge plays in learning, and the effects that general language-learning strategies have on the learner's moment-to-moment processing of the L2 speech input.

E. The Developmental Dimension

The degree of L1 structural influence, and with it, the role of transfer as a processing strategy, vary in the course of L2 speech acquisition. As at the syntactic or lexical level, the effects of transfer seem to be more obviously present at earlier rather than later stages of acquisition, at least as far as phone realization is concerned (for evidence that in the prosodic area such influence is present even at advanced stages of L2 learning, see Erdmann, 1973, and Grosser & Wieden, 1989, on word-stress transfer for L1 German–L2 English; Wenk, 1986, on rhythm transfer for L1 French–L2 English; and James, 1976, Cruz-Ferreira, 1987, and Grosser, 1989, on intonation transfer with reference to, respectively, L1 Swabian German–L2 English, L1 Portuguese–L2 English, and L1 Austrian German–L2 English). Concerning the realization of L2 phones, it would appear that, as acquisition proceeds, the influence of the L1 and the mechanism of transfer give way gradually to other influences that shape developing L2 speech such as the mechanisms ("developmental processes") associated with the acquisition of the NL.

Major (1986b) showed, in a study of more advanced learners' renderings of L2 English word structure (the subjects were speakers of Brazilian Portuguese), that the type of paragoge (final-vowel epenthesis) errors found indicates a predominance of developmental over transfer influences. Furthermore, Flege and Davidian (1985), in an analysis of the production of the English syllable-final stops /b d g/ by Polish, Spanish, and Mandarin learners, concluded that the many instances of final-stop devoicing and deletion observed in the data evidenced developmental processes "similar to those affecting child L1 speech production" (p. 346) rather than L1 transfer. Major (1986a) developed an Ontogeny Model to account for such a phenomenon with data from L1 English speakers acquiring L2 Spanish. He suggested that L1 influence (i.e., "transfer") in selected L2 phones manifests an absolute decrease over time, whereas "developmental processes" first increase and then correspondingly decrease over time.

Other factors relevant to the developmental dimension of L1 influence in L2 speech acquisition are the cross-linguistic similarity measures of L1 and L2 phones and sound-typological constraints on the activation of L1 transfer. Concerning the former, Wode (1980) noted with particular reference to the acquisition of English /r/ by German-speaking children that "only certain L2 elements are substituted by L1 elements, namely, those meeting specifiable similarity requirements. . . . [T]hose elements which do not . . . are acquired via developmental sequences similar to (identical with?) L1 acquisition" (p. 136). On the latter, Hecht and Mulford (1982), in a study of the English L2 of an L1 Icelandic-speaking child, concluded that L1 transfer accounts for the "order of difficulty" of fricatives and affricates, while developmental processes account for typologically "difficult" sounds like /t/ and /d/. In general, they observed that transfer processes predominate in the rendering of L2 vowels, while L1 developmental processes predominate with affricates and fricatives.

It appears, therefore, that the differential effects of L1 influence over time on L2 speech acquisition must be evaluated in the light of the competing forces of the typological (markedness) value of L2 phones as well as learner-perceived similarity between the phones of L2 and those of L1.

However, strictly contextual effects on the development of L2 segments over time have also been noted. L. Dickerson (1975) and L. Dickerson and Dickerson (1977) showed in longitudinal studies that the acquisition of selected English segments by Japanese learners correlate in a systematic way with the nature of their immediate sound environment. For instance L. Dickerson (1975) demonstrated that approximation to L2 English /z/, as measured in terms of the frequency and phonetic type of the variants produced by the learners, increases over time as a function of the context—from environment "D" (before TL [θ ð t d ts dz], through "C" (followed by silence), via "B" (followed by any consonant other than those under "D"), to "A" (followed by a vowel). The cross-sectional studies of Gatbonton (1978) and Wenk (1979, 1982) on the realization of L2 English [θ ð] by French-speaking learners similarly showed correlations between the frequency and type of variant produced and the immediate phonetic environment. They suggested, with certain reservations, that the accuracy orders observed may reflect the actual development order of the target segments over time. W. Dickerson (1976) drew attention to striking parallels in this respect with the wave model of phonological change proposed by Labov (e.g., Labov, 1973).

The correlation of the form of TL segments with environment *over time* offers a significant source of explanatory potential in the acquisition of L2 speech. Further work in this area can be expected to investigate which phonetic and phonological properties of the context and of the variants produced exactly define the conditioning observed.

F. The Role of Universal Typological Preferences

The influence exerted by the linguistic structure of an L1 on L2 speech acquisition may itself be constrained by the general phonetic and phonological properties of sounds and sound systems. Johansson (1973), in examining the Swedish pronunciation of speakers of nine different NLs, concluded that "the same vowels which appear as phonemes in children's speech and which are the most basic in the languages of the world, are also reproduced with fewest phonetic deviations" (p. 159). Other, typologically marked, vowels such as /y:/ and /y/ were ranked high on a "hierarchy of difficulty." Ferguson (1984) suggested certain "repertoire universals" of phone types that might influence the order of acquisition.

However, most researchers investigating the interplay of L1 and universal properties in L2 speech learning have concentrated on syllable structure. Tarone (1976, 1980) examined the syllable structure errors made in English by speakers of Cantonese, Portuguese, and Korean, and found little evidence that any typological preference for CV (consonant–vowel) syllables outweighed L1 transfer in determining the structures these learners produced. Further confirmation of the predominance of L1 influence over open syllable preference in L2 acquisition was provided by C. Greenberg (1983) for Turkish, Greek, and Japanese learners of English, and Sato (1984) for L1 Vietnamese and L2 English; while Hodne (1985), for L1 Polish–L2 English, and Benson (1988), for L1 Vietnamese–L2 English learners, suggested, respectively, that task stress and preceding vocalic context play a significant role in determining any universal CV preference in acquisition. Broselow (1983, 1984) examined the syllable structure errors produced by Iraqi and Egyptian Arabic speakers of English and concluded that the different way in which these speakers resolve initial consonant cluster problems in the L2 is a direct reflection of their L1 syllabification rules, with only very little evidence of considerations of typological markedness playing a role.

A comprehensive account of the influence of universal phonetic–phonological properties of the syllable in L2 speech acquisition was provided by Tropf (1983, 1987), who showed from a longitudinal study of the acquisition of L2 German syllable structure by L1 Spanish speakers that the degree of sonority of segments present in a syllable correlates well with the order of their acquisition. Thus, syllable nuclei are acquired before syllable onsets and codas, and the order of acquisition of the constituent segments in these parts of the syllable is, in turn, determined by their relative degree of sonority. However, the sonority value of a particular segment interacts with influences of the L1 in that it is only "operative" where the L1 does not, for example, possess equivalent syllable-initial or syllable-final consonant cluster types. In a study of the vowel epenthesis produced by Spanish learners of English in initial /sC/ consonant clusters, Carlisle (1992) demonstrated that comparing the realizations of a less marked cluster /sl/ with more marked clusters /sN/ and /st/ (J. Greenberg, 1966) reveals that the former combinations induce less epenthesis than the latter in L2 speech. Puppel (1990) showed with Polish learners acquiring the English vowel system that there is evidence to suggest that L2 vowel realization is determined by a pressure to "fill" the peripheral (i.e., "cardinal") points of the traditional vowel articulation trapezium.

Eckman (1977) claimed in his Markedness Differential Hypothesis (MDH) that "the areas of difficulty that a language learner will have can be predicted on the basis of a systematic comparison of the grammars of the native languages, the target language and the markedness relations stated in universal grammar" (p. 321). Drawing on, for example, the relative difficulty experienced by German speakers learning English in producing voiced obstruents in word-final position, Eckman concluded that where there are differences—distributional and substantive—between the phonemes of L1 and L2, those cases where the phone type is more "marked" (i.e., typologically less usual) than anything in the L1 (word-final contrasts, for example, being more marked than medial or initial contrasts) will be "more difficult" for the L2 learner. In further studies on the realization of English final consonant clusters by Cantonese-, Japanese-, and Korean-speaking learners, Eckman (1987, 1991) showed how the reduction of such clusters closely follows the typological markedness values posited by J. Greenberg (1966); that is, they are reduced from more marked to less marked forms (e.g., clusters with two fricatives and a stop will be shortened to clusters with a fricative and a stop rather than two fricatives).

The MDH itself, however, has been the subject of a number of critical evaluations by other researchers. Whereas Anderson (1983), in examining consonant cluster simplifications in the L2 English of L1 Arabic and Chinese speakers, found support for the idea that typological markedness is a stronger determinant of learner difficulty than L1–L2 contrast, Altenberg and Vago (1983), with an analysis of L1 Hungarian–L2 English data, pointed out that a number of cross-language phonotactic phenomena (e.g., bimorphemic final consonant clusters in English as opposed to Hungarian) are not, strictly, comparable and scalable according to the markedness criteria. They concluded that the MDH cannot, therefore, make suitable predictions for L2 speech realizations. Stockman and Pluut (1992) checked Anderson's markedness predictions regarding the realization of English syllable-final consonants by Mandarin speakers and found that the inherent phonetic (typological?) nature of the consonants involved (stops and nasals, whereby stops are somehow "easier" than nasals) appeared to offer a more consistent account of the error patterns observed. Hammarberg (1988a, 1990) showed with L1 German–L2 Swedish data that L1–L2 phonological contrast and degree of markedness operate independently as factors in L2 acquisition. He proposed that it is typological markedness relations *within* the L2 rather than across L1 and L2 that constitute the stronger predictive factor in L2 speech learning. Major (1987c) demonstrated the complex interrelationship of markedness, similarity, and transfer in the rate of acquisition of English [ɛ] and [æ] by NSs of Portuguese. (See chapter 6 by Eckman, this volume for further discussion of the MDH and its replacement, the Structural Conformity Hypothesis.)

Broselow and Finer (1991), in examining the production of the English syllable onsets /pr/, /pj/, /br/, and /bj/ by Korean and Japanese learners, found that although the clusters /br/ and /bj/ are more marked according to Selkirk's (1984) Minimal Sonority Distance principle (since the sonority values of /b/ versus /r/ and /j/ are closer than those of /p/ versus /r/ and /j/) and are more difficult to produce, the learners did not show any tendency to revert to cluster types that are even less marked than those in their L1 sound system. The conclusions so far are therefore equivocal as to the effect of cross-linguistic markedness values of phones in L2 speech acquisition.

G. Contextual Constraints

Sociolinguist Determinants

The effects of the L1 "product" in the process of L2 speech acquisition are codetermined by the use of the L2 in different registers with or without reference to an equivalent use of the L1 in similar contexts. (Chapter 8 by Preston, this volume, is a general treatment of variation in L2 performance—contextual and otherwise—and its analysis.) Studies have shown, for example, that the particular type of L1 phone transferred into the L2 reflects a particular norm realization of the L1 sound in an equivalent situation to the one in which the L2 is used. Schmidt (1977) for L1 Egyptian Arabic and L2 English, Beebe (1980) for L1 Thai and L2 English, and James (1983) for L1 Swabian German and L2 English showed that where the L1 allows register and stylistic variation between an L1 nonstandard and L1 standard variety, equivalence judgments of L2 versus L1 sounds are affected, which lead to differential L1 nonstandard versus L1 standard influence on L2 sound realization. By and large, it has been demonstrated that L1 nonstandard variety influence on the L2 is significantly filtered or constrained via the sound system of the L1 standard variety.

Stylistic Determinants

General properties of the L2 speech situation also have an influence on the type and degree of L1 transfer manifested. Nemser (1971) noted significant differences on the effect of L1 Hungarian transfer on L2 English production and perception of phones according to the formality level of the L2 task required of the learners. In a series of related studies, referred to earlier in a different context, L. Dickerson

(1975) and L. Dickerson and Dickerson (1977) reported on the systematic variability shown by Japanese learners of English in realizing, for example, target /z/ and /r/ in different L2 speech tasks (free speaking, dialogue reading, and word list reading). Gatbonton (1978) and Wenk (1979, 1982) showed that French learners' variants for English dental fricatives correlate well with the particular speech style involved in that the more formal the style (e.g., minimal pair reading as opposed to free speech), the greater the number of targetlike realizations of /θ/ and /ð/ were found. Sato (1985) noted a strong correlation of the form of word-final consonant cluster realizations in the English of a Vietnamese learner with L2 task type, whereby the proportion of targetlike realizations increased as the task shifted from free conversation to the imitation of words and phrases.

These findings raise questions as to the nature of the baseline of the L2 (and L1) data in L2 speech acquisition. Is it the case, as Tarone (1982, 1983) suggested, that the "vernacular" style of the developing IL (e.g., as opposed to the formal style) constitutes the variety least permeable to L1 influence? W. Dickerson (1987) suggested the opposite. These issues clearly remind us that the varietal status of L2 and L1 *in use* plays an important and hitherto perhaps underestimated role in determining the degree and type of L1 influence shown in a given L2 acquisition setting.

Discoursal Determinants

It is a matter of common observation that L2 speech performance covaries with the type of discourse activity engaged in. However, research into the discoursal determinants of L2 speech acquisition has not been prominent in the field to date.

Hieke (1987) shows in a story-retelling experiment run with English NSs and German L2 English learners that the latter score consistently lower on measures of casual speech absorption phenomena (here alveolar flapping and final consonant reduction). Dechert and Raupach (1987) in a quantitative analysis of the temporal variables (e.g., articulation rate, instance and length of pauses and 'runs', etc.) of German NSs' and NNSs' renderings of a cartoon story demonstrate significant differences in the pronunciation fluency of the two groups. They also highlight the importance of prosodically fixed binomials as "proceduralized units of processing" in the production of fluent (L2) speech. Treichel (1992) draws attention to the *linearization* problem in French and English speakers' L2 German production in a film-recall task. On a quantitative measure of temporal variables and intonation contouring, NNSs scored more favorably than NSs on the same task, the implication being that linearization (i.e., chunking of information in a particular serial order) is an essentially prelinguistic activity. Pennington (1990, 1992) examined the correlation of aspects of what she terms "phonological fluency" with phonological proficiency in interviews conducted with Japanese learners of English. Via correlational analysis, factor analysis, and regression analysis comparing the rate, quantity, and continuity variables (including speech rate, length of runs, etc.) in the learners' L2 speech to impressionistic ratings as to their general phonological-pronunciation level in English, it was established that there indeed seems to be a natural link between discoursal fluency and phonological proficiency in L2 speech.

The study of inter- and intradiscoursal determinants of L2 speech acquisition is only in its beginnings. However, increased attention to the macrolinguistic factors influencing L2 speech production will provide a welcome corrective to the predominantly microlevel of analysis practiced hitherto.

H. The Contribution of Theoretical Phonology

We have mentioned the different phonological categories used in contrastive analyses of L1s and L2s that were taken over from then-current phonological theories such as phonemics, distinctive feature analysis, and early generative phonology. (See chapter 3 by White, this volume, for additional discussion of phonological theory.) With the development of more recent theories, such as non-linear phonology, feature theory, lexical phonology, and also natural phonology, researchers have reassessed the predictive and explanatory value of such frameworks in the analysis of L2 speech.

Rubach (1984) employed a theory of cyclic (lexical) phonology in an analysis of L1 Polish substitutions in L2 English, with which he made the generalization that automatic, context-sensitive, postcyclic rules may cause interference, namely, (L1) phonological rules that apply across the board wherever their structural description is met. This principle encapsulates in a theoretical statement the observation that it is only the lower level (i.e., more "allophonic" or "phonetic") phonological rules of the L1 that cause transfer in L2 speech acquisition (Linell, 1979). In a similar vein, Young-Scholten (1990) showed in a study of the acquisition of pronominal clitics in German by English speakers that exceptionless postlexical rules are transferred into the L2. However, in a series of studies, Singh (1985, 1991) and Singh and Ford (1987) criticized the ability of standard generative phonology (Chomsky & Halle, 1968) and lexical phonology (e.g., Mohanan, 1982) to account for L1 interference in L2 speech by means of the notion of phonological rule. Using segmental and phonotactic interference examples from a number of different "interphonologies," Singh argued instead for the notions of well-formedness and "repair strategy" as components of a theory of generative phonotactics to explain the L1 substitutions observed.

Broselow (1983) employed the syllabification theory of Kahn (1976) to analyze the production of English syllable structures by L1 Arabic-speaking learners, as discussed earlier. Weinberger (1987), in a study of the reduction in L2 English syllable structure produced by L1 Mandarin speakers, concluded that it is the degree of phonological "recoverability" of an item in question that determines the type of syllable structure "strategy" that will be employed (e.g., vowel epenthesis vs. consonant deletion). In this he followed Kaye's (1981) theoretical treatment of recoverability, which here refers to the ability to deduce an underlying phonological representation from a given surface form. James (1988), in examining the acquisition of L2 English by L1 Dutch speakers, employed a form of metrical phonology to account for the phased emergence of prosodic structure in a tricomponential (lexical/prosodic/rhythmic) model of L2 phonological acquisition. Carlisle (1991) used a tiered syllabic phonology to express the occurrence of vowel epenthesis in initial L2 English consonant clusters as produced by L1 Spanish speakers. Mairs (1989) examined stress assignment rules employed by Spanish learners of English within the framework of metrical phonology and concluded that they were consistent with the rules of the L2, with the exception that the learners failed to apply rules of rhyme extrametricality to rhymes that were highly marked (i.e., violated syllable structure constraints) in the L1.

On the general question of the prosodic domains for postlexical rules, Vogel (1991) draws attention to the value of L2 data in revealing domains for rule application in the L1, which would otherwise be obscured, while Young-Scholten (1992) presents evidence from German learners of English that certain prosodic domains (e.g., for resyllabification) are transferred from L1 in L2 speech acquisition, but also that these domains often show an IL-specific (i.e., non-L1, non-L2) dimension.

Weinberger (1990) addressed the problem of "differential substitutions" employed by speakers of different L1s in realizing problematic L2 phonemes; for example, while L1 French speakers favor the substitutions /s/ and /z/ for L2 English /θ/ and /ð/, respectively, L1 Russian speakers favor /t/ and /d/ substitutions for the same L2 phonemes, although both French and Russian have /t d s z/. Weinberger showed that underspecification theory (Archangeli, 1984) provides the "minimal," least specified, segments of a phonological system, and it is these segments of the L1 that provide the substitutions for the L2 forms. Hancin-Bhatt and Bhatt (1992) argue for adjustments to be made in feature-geometrical representations (Clements, 1985; Sagey, 1986) to accommodate L2 evidence. With evidence from Hindi English, they argue further that implementation of phonological feature representations into a parallel distributed processing network offers a suitable test of the validity of the constructs within a computational theory of learning.

Using the framework of a principles and parameters phonology, Archibald, in a number of related studies (e.g., 1991, 1992a, 1992b, in press), investigated the degree to which metrical parameter settings (Dresher & Kaye, 1990) are transferred from L1 in L2 production and perception tasks. Examining data on English word stress patterns as realized by Polish, Hungarian, and Spanish learners, he concluded that although there is evidence of L1 parameter transfer, adults are nonetheless capable of resetting their parameters. However, in all cases, adult L2 learners do not appear to violate proposed universals of metrical phonology. On the relation of principles to parameters in L2 speech learning, Kløve (1992) shows with Cantonese learners of Norwegian that while the maximality principle of syl-

labification (Ito, 1986) is observed, the parameter of directionality of syllabification is maintained in its L1 setting. Although such approaches to L2 speech acquisition subsume a learnability perspective (Wexler & Manzini, 1987), questions
remain as to the behavioral-theoretic interpretation of such a model (James, 1990).

However, the phonological theory that has had, arguably, the greatest impact on
the study of L2 speech acquisition, at least until recently, is that of natural phonology (Dressler, 1984; Stampe, 1973). Within the terms of this theory, L2 acquisition as much as L1 acquisition is seen as the gradual suppression of "natural"
(i.e., very roughly, phonetically motivated) processes in accommodating to the
phonological structure of the TL in question. Dziubalska-Kolaczyk (1987, 1990)
treated the acquisition of L2 English by L1 Polish learners within this framework.
In Dziubalska-Kolaczyk (1987), for example, it is shown how natural phonology
offers a more explanatory account of the nasalization effects of L1 in L2 realization than a generative rule-typological approach to the same phenomenon (i.e.,
Rubach, 1984). Major (1987b) looked at the position of "natural" processes such
as those of intervocalic voicing and spirantization of stop consonants present in
the L2 English of L1 Brazilian Portuguese learners and explored the natural phonological interpretation of such phenomena in relation to the overall influences on
L2 speech acquisition of developmental processes and transfer.

Phonological theory can clearly contribute to the understanding of L2 speech
acquisition, but L2 speech acquisition can equally contribute to the understanding
of phonology, as is increasingly realized. Current theoretical concern in phonology with learning issues in acquisition (L2–L1 parameter setting, learnability),
nonsegmental issues (e.g., research on word stress, prominence and intonation and
tone in metrical and autosegmental theory), and the further refinement of feature
specification can be expected to provide more differentiated and, potentially more
explanatory frameworks for L2 speech analysis (James, 1989). However, the traffic is no longer one-way. Much revolves around the question of the appropriate
validation of phonological constructs. With the increased readiness in phonological theory construction to accept learning and learnability criteria as crucial validation measures and the readiness in L2 phonological studies to subject theoretical
constructs to empirical verification, the generation-old debate as to the position of
"internal" versus "external" evidence in phonology and the "independent motivation" of phonological primes begins to dissipate. Indeed, the relevance of phonological theory to L2 speech acquisition and that of L2 speech acquisition to
phonology has never been greater.

V. CONCLUSION

How does the learner of an L2 master its sound patterns in perception and production, at the various linguistic levels, and subject to constraints of many kinds,

over the time course of acquisition? The task is complex, and its study now characterized by a diversity of research paradigms and, often, an interdisciplinary breadth of view. Thus, rigid distinctions between (psycho-) linguistic and phonetic levels of investigation have come to seem unfruitful if not actually untenable, while the structuralists' auditory methods of data collection and analysis have been complemented by the full range of instrumental and information-processing techniques. While this methodological diversification is in principle to be welcomed, it can make the comparison and evaluation of some research findings problematic. It is clear, however, that in recent years there has been extensive theoretical reassessment. In particular, the monolithic contrastive analyses provided by classic structural phonology are no longer generally believed adequate to account for acquisition data, and have been largely superseded by models sensitive to longitudinal change as well as to those subphonemic variations that may be of developmental importance. The acquisition of L2 speech, it would now appear, is not only constrained by the established sound patterns of L1, but is at the same time subject to the processes that shaped them, although how L1 process and product, in this sense, interact in the acquisition of L2 remains very largely to be determined.

Much also remains to be understood of the domains or levels over which the acquisition of (L2) speech is distributed, and the nature and extent of the interactions between them. Although some work has been devoted to (sentence) intonation, by far the greatest proportion of research has been concerned with lower level speech phenomena (the phoneme, the distinctive feature, and so on) in comparative isolation. An adequate theory of phonological proficiency, by contrast, must also account for the higher level patternings of running speech. One impetus in this direction is a study by Pennington (1992) investigating the fluency components of L2 speech.

Finally, we have not in this review addressed the theoretical problem of what, strictly, an L2 might be. We can here do no more than underline the fact that most studies to date have investigated speakers in monolingual speech communities—which, as Hudson (1980) has emphasized, constitute only a minority in the world. New insights and fresh conceptual frameworks could result from developmental studies carried out in some of the many societies in which multilingualism has long been the norm.

REFERENCES

Abercrombie, D. (1963). *Problems and principles in language study* (2nd ed.). London: Longman.
Abramson, A., & Lisker, K. (1970). Discriminability along the voicing continuum: Cross-language tests. In B. Hála, M. Romportal & P. Janota (Eds.), *Proceedings of the 6th International Congress of Phonetic Sciences* (pp. 569–573). Prague: Academia.

Adams, J. A. (1971). A closed-loop theory of motor learning. *Journal of Motor Behaviour, 3,* 111–150.

Altenberg, E. P., & Vago, R. M. (1983). Theoretical implications of an error analysis of second language phonology production. *Language Learning, 33,* 427–447.

Anderson, J. I. (1983). The markedness differential hypothesis and syllable structure difficulty. In G. S. Nathan (Ed.), *Proceedings of the Conference on the Uses of Phonology* (pp. 85–99). Carbondale: Southern Illinois University.

Archangeli, D. (1984). *Underspecification in Yawelmani phonology and morphology.* Unpublished doctoral dissertation, MIT, Cambridge, MA.

Archibald, J. (1991). *The word tree and quantity-sensitivity in the interlanguage of adult Hungarian speakers.* Paper presented at the Boston University Conference on Language Development.

Archibald, J. (1992a). Adult abilities in L2 speech: Evidence from stress. In J. Leather & A. James (Eds.), *New Sounds 92: Proceedings of the Second Amsterdam Symposium on the Acquisition of Second-Language Speech* (pp. 1–17). Amsterdam: University of Amsterdam.

Archibald, J. (1992b). Transfer of L1 parameter settings: Some empirical evidence from Polish metrics. *Canadian Journal of Linguistics, 37,* 301–339.

Archibald, J. (in press). The learnability of English metrical parameters by Spanish speakers. *International Review of Applied Linguistics.*

Ashby, M. (1990). Prototype categories in phonetics. *Speech, Hearing and Language: Work in Progress* (University College London Department of Phonetics and Linguistics), *4,* 19–28.

Bailey, C.-J. N. (1978). Native accent and learning English as a foreign language. *International Review of Applied Linguistics, 16,* 229–240.

Barry, W. J. (1974a). Language background and perception of foreign accent. *Journal of Phonetics, 2,* 65–89.

Barry, W. J. (1974b). *Perzeption und Produktion im sub-phonemischen Bereich.* Tübingen: Niemeyer.

Barry, W. J., & Fourcin, A. J. (1990). Levels of labelling. *Speech, Hearing and Language: Work in Progress* (University College London Department of Phonetics and Linguistics), *4,* 29–44.

Beebe, L. M. (1980). Sociolinguistic variation and style shifting in second language acquisition. *Language Learning, 30,* 433–448.

Beebe, L. M. (1982, April 29). *Reservations about the Labovian paradigm of style shifting and its extension to the study of interlanguage.* Paper presented at the Los Angeles Second Language Research Forum.

Benson, B. (1988). Universal preference for the open syllable as an independent process in interlanguage phonology. *Language Learning, 38,* 221–242.

Best, C., McRoberts, G., & Sithole, N. (1988). Examination of perceptual reorganization for nonnative speech contrasts: Zulu click discrimination by English-speaking adults and infants. *Journal of Experimental Psychology: Human Perception and Performance, 14,* 345–360.

Bluhme, H. (1969). Zur Perzeption deutscher Sprachlaute durch englishsprechende Studenten. *Phonetica, 20,* 57–62.

Blumstein, S. E., & Stevens, K. N. (1979). Acoustic invariance in speech production: Evidence from measurements of the spectral characteristics of stop consonants. *Journal of the Acoustic Society of America, 66,* 1001–1017.

Bohn, O.-S. (1992). Influence of new vowels on the production of similar vowels. In J. Leather & A. James (Eds.), *New sounds 92: Proceedings of the 1992 Amsterdam Symposium on the Acquisition of Second Language Speech* (pp. 29–46). Amsterdam: University of Amsterdam.

Bohn, O-S., & Flege, J. E. (1990). Perception and production of a new vowel category by adult second language learners. In J. Leather & A. James (Eds.), *New sounds 90: Proceedings of the 1990 Amsterdam Symposium on the Acquisition of Second-Language Speech* (pp. 37–56). Amsterdam: University of Amsterdam.

Bohn, O.-S., & Flege, J. E. (1992). The production of new and similar vowels by adult German learners of English. *Studies in Second Language Acquisition, 14,* 131–158.

Bohn, O.-S., & Flege, J. E. (in press). Perceptual switching in Spanish/English bilinguals: Evidence for universal factors in stop voicing judgements. *Journal of Phonetics.*

Borden, G. J. (1979). An interpretation of research on feedback interruption in speech. *Brain and Language, 7,* 307–319.

Borden, G. J. (1980). Use of feedback in established and developing speech. In N. Lass (Ed.), *Speech and language* (Vol. 3, pp. 168–193). New York: Academic Press.

Borden, G. J., Harris, K. S., Fitch, H., & Yoshioka, H. (1981). Producing relatively unfamiliar speech gestures: A synthesis of perceptual targets and production rules. *Haskins Laboratories, Status Report on Speech Research, 66,* 85–117.

Brennan, E. M., & Brennan, J. S. (1981). Accent scaling and language attitudes: Reactions to Mexican American English speech. *Language and Speech, 24,* 207–222.

Brière, E. (1968). *A psycholinguistic study of phonological interference.* The Hague: Mouton.

Broeders, A. (1982). Engels in nederlandse oren: Uitspraakvoorkeur bij nederlandse studenten engels. In *Toegepaste Taalkunde in Artikelen* (Vol. 9, pp. 127–128). Amsterdam: Vu Boekhandel.

Broselow, E. (1983). Non-obvious transfer: On predicting epenthesis errors. In S. Gass & L. Selinker (Eds.), *Language transfer in language learning* (pp. 269–280). Rowley, MA: Newbury House.

Broselow, E. (1984). An investigation of transfer in second language phonology. *International Review of Applied Linguistics, 22,* 253–269.

Broselow, E., & Finer, D. (1991). Parameter setting in second language phonology and syntax. *Second Language Research, 7,* 35–59.

Broselow, E., Hurtig, R. R., & Ringen, C. (1987). The perception of second language prosody. In G. Ioup & S. Weinberger (Eds.), *Interlanguage phonology: The acquisition of a second language sound system* (pp. 350–361). Rowley, MA: Newbury House.

Browman, C. P., & Goldstein, L. M. (1986). Towards an articulatory phonology. *Phonology Yearbook, 3,* 219–252.

Browman, C. P., & Goldstein, L. M. (1989). Articulatory gestures as phonological units. *Phonology, 6,* 201–231.

Brown, H. D. (1980). The optimal distance model of second language acquisition. *TESOL Quarterly, 14,* 57–164.

Canetta, J. B. (1977). Decline in oral perception from 20 to 70 years. *Perceptual and Motor Skills, 45,* 1028–1030.

Caramazza, A., Yeni-Komshian, G. H., Zurif, E. B., Carbone, E. (1973). The acquisition of a new phonological contrast: The case of stop consonants in French-English bilinguals. *Journal of the Acoustical Society of America, 54,* 421–428.

Carlisle, R. S. (1991). The influence of environment on vowel epenthesis in Spanish/English interphonology. *Applied Linguistics, 12,* 76–95.

Carlisle, R. S. (1992). Markedness and variability. In J. Leather & A. James (Eds.), *New sounds 92: Proceedings of the Second Amsterdam Symposium on the Acquisition of Second-Language Speech* (pp. 64–75). Amsterdam: University of Amsterdam.

Catford, J. C., Pisoni, D. B. (1970). Auditory vs. articulatory training in exotic sounds. *Modern Language Journal, 54,* 477–481.

Chamot, A. U. (1973). Phonological problems in learning English as a third language. *International Review of Applied Linguistics, 11,* 243–250.

Chomsky, N., & Halle, M. (1968). *The sound pattern of English.* New York: Harper & Row.

Christophersen, P. (1973). *Second language learning: Myth and reality.* Harmondsworth: Penguin.

Chun, D. M. (1991). The state of the art in teaching pronunciation. *Georgetown University Round Table on Languages and Linguistics,* pp. 179–193.

Clements, G. N. (1985). On the geometry of phonological features. *Phonology Yearbook, 2,* 225–252.

Clyne, M. (Ed.). (1981). *Foreigner talk* (International Journal of the Sociology of Language 28). Mouton: The Hague.

Cruz-Ferreira, M. (1987). Non-native interpretive strategies for intonational meaning: An experimental study. In A. R. James & J. H. Leather (Eds.), *Sound patterns in second language acquisition.* Dordrecht: Foris.

Cunningham-Andersson, U. (1990). Native speaker reactions to nonnative speech. In A. James & J. Leather (Eds.), *New sounds 90: Proceedings of the 1990 Amsterdam Symposium on the Acquisition of Second Language Speech.* Amsterdam: University of Amsterdam.

de Bot, C. L. J. (1981). Visual feedback of intonation: An experimental approach. In B. Sigurd & J. Svartvik (Eds.), *Proceedings of the Sixth AILA Congress* (Vol. 1, pp. 243–245). Lund, Sweden: University of Lund.

Dechert, H., & Raupach, M. (1987). Prosodic patterns of proceduralized speech in second and first language narratives. In A. James & J. Leather (Eds.), *Sound patterns in second language acquisition* (pp. 81–102). Dordrecht: Foris.

Dickerson, L. (1975). The learner's interlanguage as a system of variable rules. *TESOL Quarterly, 9,* 401–407.

Dickerson, L., & Dickerson, W. (1977). Interlanguage phonology: Current research and future directions. In S. P. Corder & E. Roulet (Eds.), *Actes du 5ème colloque de linguistique appliquée de Neuchâtel* (pp. 18–29). Neuchâtel: Université de Neuchâtel.

Dickerson, W. (1976). The psycholinguistic unity of language learning and language change. *Language Learning, 26,* 215–231.

Dickerson, W. (1987). Explicit rules and the developing interlanguage phonology. In A.

James & J. Leather (Eds.), *Sound patterns in second language acquisition* (pp. 121–140). Dordrecht: Foris.

Dowd, J. L. (1984). *Phonological variation in L2 speech: The effects of emotional questions and field-dependence/field-independence on second language performance.* Unpublished doctoral dissertation, Columbia University Teachers College, New York.

Dowd, J., Zuengler, J., & Berkowitz, D. (1990). L2 social marking: Research issues. *Applied Linguistics, 11,* 16–29.

Dreher, B., & Larkins, J. (1972). Non-semantic auditory discrimination: Foundation for second language learning. *Modern Language Journal, 56,* 227–230.

Dresher, E., & Kaye, J. (1990). A computational learning model for metrical phonology. *Cognition, 34,* 137–195.

Dressler, W.-U. (1984). Explaining natural phonology. *Phonology Yearbook, 1,* 29–51.

Dziubalska-Kolacyzk, K. (1987). Phonological rule typology and second language acquisition. In A. James & J. Leather (Eds.), *Sound patterns in second language acquisition* (pp. 193–206). Dordrecht: Foris.

Dziubalska-Kolaczyk, K. (1990). Phonological processes vs. morphonological rules in L2 acquisition. In J. Leather & A. James (Eds.), *New sounds 90: Proceedings of the 1990 Amsterdam Symposium on the Acquisition of Second-Language Speech* (pp. 98–106). Amsterdam: University of Amsterdam.

Eckman, F. R. (1977). Markedness and the contrastive analysis hypothesis. *Language Learning, 27,* 315–330.

Eckman, F. R. (1981). On predicting phonological difficulty in second language acquisition. *Studies in Second Language Acquisition, 4,* 18–30.

Eckman, F. R. (1987). The reduction of word-final consonant clusters interlanguage. In A. James & J. Leather (Eds.), *Sound patterns in second language acquisition* (pp. 143–162). Dordrecht: Foris.

Eckman, F. R. (1991). The structural conformity hypothesis and the acquisition of consonant clusters in the interlanguage of ESL learners. *Studies in Second Language Acquisition, 13,* 23–42.

Efstathiadis, S. (1974). *Greek and English phonology: A comparative investigation.* Thessaloniki: Aristotelian University.

Eisenstein, M. (1983). Native reactions to non-native speech: A review of empirical research. *Studies in Second Language Acquisition, 5,* 160–176.

Eliasson, S. (1976). Theoretical problems in Scandinavian contrastive phonology. *Reports from the Uppsala University Department of Linguistics (RUUL), 5,* 1–46.

Eliasson, S. (1984). Toward a theory of contrastive phonology. In S. Eliasson (Ed.), *Theoretical issues in contrastive phonology* (pp. 7–26). Heidelberg: Groos.

Eliasson, S., & Tubielewicz Mattsson, D. (1992). *Cognitive processing of phonological ambiguity in second-language learning.* Paper presented at the New Sounds 92 Symposium on the Acquisition of Second-Language Speech, University of Amsterdam.

Elman, J., Diehl, R., & Buchwald, S. (1977). Perceptual switching in bilinguals. *Journal of the Acoustic Society of America, 62,* 971–974.

Erdmann, P. (1973). Patterns of stress-transfer in English and German. *International Review of Applied Linguistics, 11,* 229–241.

Esser, J. (1978). Contrastive intonation of German and English: Problems and some results. *Phonetica, 35,* 41–55.

Fentress, J. C. (1984). The development of coordination. *Journal of Motor Behavior, 16,* 99–134.

Ferguson, C. (1984). Repertoire universals, markedness, and second language acquisition. In W. Rutherford (Ed.), *Language universals and second language acquisition* (pp. 247–258). Amsterdam: John Benjamins.

Fisiak, J. (1975). The contrastive analysis of phonological systems. *Kwartalnik Neofilologiczny, 22,* 341–351.

Fisiak, J. (1976). Generative phonology and contrastive studies. *Canadian Journal of Linguistics, 21,* 171–179.

Flege, J. E. (1985). The production and perception of foreign language speech sounds. *Biocommunication Research Reports* (No. 4). Birmingham: University of Alabama. (Also published as Flege, 1988).

Flege, J. E. (1987a). A critical period for learning to pronounce foreign languages? *Applied Linguistics, 8,* 162–177.

Flege, J. E. (1987b). Effects of equivalence classification on the production of foreign language speech sounds. In A. James & J. Leather (Eds.), *Sound patterns in second language acquisition* (pp. 9–39). Dordrecht: Foris.

Flege, J. E. (1988). The production and perception of foreign language speech sounds. In H. Winitz (Ed.), *Human communication and its disorders* (pp. 224–401). Norwood, NJ: Ablex.

Flege, J. E. (1990a). English vowel production by Dutch talkers: More evidence for the "similar" vs. "new" distinction. In J. Leather & A. James (Eds.), *New sounds 90:Proceedings of the 1990 Amsterdam Symposium on the Acquisition of Second-Language Speech* (pp. 255–293). Amsterdam: University of Amsterdam.

Flege, J. E. (1990b). Contribution to the research workshop on modelling the acquisition of second-language speech. In J. Leather & A. James (Eds.), *New sounds 90: Proceedings of the 1990 Amsterdam Symposium on the Acquisition of Second Language Speech* (pp. 338–345). Amsterdam: University of Amsterdam.

Flege, J. E. (1992a). *Chinese subjects' production and perception of word-final English stops: Are they really new?* Paper presented at the New Sounds 92 Symposium on the Acquisition of Second-Language Speech, University of Amsterdam.

Flege, J. E. (1992b). The intelligibility of English vowels spoken by British and Dutch talkers. In R. D. Kent (Ed.), *Intelligibility in speech disorders* (pp. 157–232). Amsterdam: John Benjamins.

Flege, J. E., & Davidian, R. (1985). Transfer and developmental processes in adult foreign language speech production. *Journal of Applied Psycholinguistics Research, 5,* 323–347.

Flege, J. E., & Eefting, W. (1987). The production and perception of English stops by Spanish speakers of English. *Journal of Phonetics, 15,* 67–83.

Flege, J. E., & Hammond, R. M. (1982). Mimicry of non-distinctive phonetic difference between language variables. *Studies in Second Language Acquisition, 5,* 1–17.

Flege, J. E., & Hillenbrand, J. (1984). Limits on pronunciation accuracy in adult foreign language speech production. *Journal of the Acoustical Society of America, 76,* 708–721.

Flege, J. E., & Port, R. (1981). Cross-language phonetic interference from Arabic to English. *Language and Speech, 24,* 125–138.

Gandour, J. (1983). Tone perception in Far Eastern languages. *Journal of Phonetics, 11,* 149–175.

Gary, J. O. (1975). Delayed oral practice in initial stages of second language learning. In M. K. Burt & H. C. Dulay (Eds.), *New directions in second language teaching and Bilingual education.* Washington, DC: TESOL.

Gass, S. (1984). Development of speech perception and speech production abilities in adult second language learners. *Applied Psycholinguistics, 5,* 51–74.

Gatbonton, E. (1978). Patterned phonetic variability in second-language speech. *Canadian Modern Language Review, 34,* 335–347.

Giles, H. (1978). Linguistic differentiation in ethnic groups. In H. Tajfel (Ed.), *Differentiation between social groups.* London: Academic Press.

Giles, H., & Byrne, J. L. (1982). An intergroup approach to second language acquisition. *Journal of Multilingual and Multicultural Development, 3,* 17–40.

Gordon, P. C., & Myer, D. E. (1984). Perceptual-motor processing of phonetic features in speech. *Journal of Experimental Psychology: Human Perception and Performance, 10,* 153–178.

Goto, H. (1971). Auditory perception by normal Japanese subjects in the sounds "L" and "R." *Neuropsychologia, 9,* 317–323.

Greasley, V. M. (1971). *An experiment to investigate two methods of teaching French pronunciation to native American speakers of English.* Unpublished doctoral dissertation, Columbia University, New York.

Greenberg, C. (1983). Syllable structure in second language acquisition. *CUNY Forum* (City University of New York), *9,* 47–64.

Greenberg, J. (1966). Some generalizations concerning initial and final consonant clusters. *Linguistics, 18,* 5–34.

Grosser, W. (1989). Akzentuierung und Intonation im englischen Erwerb österreichischer Lerner. *Salzburger Studien zur Anglistik und Amerikanistik,* (Vol. 9). Salzburg: University of Salzburg.

Grosser, W., & Wieden, W. (1989). Principles of word-stress assignment in Austrian learners of English. In B. Kettemann et al. (Eds.), *Englisch als Zweitsprache* (pp. 89–102). Tübingen: Narr.

Guiora, A. Z., Acton, W. R., Erard, R., & Strickland, F. W. (1980). The effects of benzodiazepine (Valium) on permeability of language ego boundaries. *Language Learning, 30,* 351–364.

Guiora, A. Z., Brannon, R. C. L., & Dull, C. Y. (1972). Empathy and second language learning. *Language Learning, 2,* 111–130.

Guiora, A. Z., Paluszny, M., Beit-Hallahmi, B., Catford, J. C., Cooley, R. E., & Dull, C. Y. (1975). Language and person: Studies in language behaviour. *Language Learning, 25,* 43–61.

Guiora, A. Z., & Schonberger, R. (1990). Native pronunciation of bilinguals. In J. Leather & A. James (Eds.), *New sounds 90: Proceedings of the 1990 Amsterdam Symposium on the Acquisition of Second Language Speech.* Amsterdam: University of Amsterdam.

Hammarberg, B. (1988a). Acquisition of phonology. *Annual Review of Applied Linguistics, 9,* 23–41.

Hammarberg, B. (1988b). *Studien zur Phonologie des Zweitspracherwerbs.* Stockholm: Almqvist & Wiksell International.

Hammarberg, B. (1990). Conditions on transfer in phonology. In J. Leather & A. James (Eds.), *New sounds 90: Proceedings of the 1990 Amsterdam Symposium on the Acquisition of Second-Language Speech* (pp. 198–215). Amsterdam: University of Amsterdam.

Hancin-Bhatt, B., & Bhatt, R. (1992). On the nature of L1 filter and cross-language transfer effects. In J. Leather & A. James (Eds.), *New sounds 92: Proceedings of the Second Amsterdam Symposium on the Acquisition of Second-Language Speech* (pp. 18–28). Amsterdam: University of Amsterdam.

Haugen, E. (1956). *Bilingualism in the Americas: A bibliography and research guide.* Baltimore: American Dialect Society.

Hecht, B., & Mulford, R. (1982). The acquisition of a second language phonology: Interaction of transfer and developmental factors. *Applied Psycholinguistics, 3,* 313–328.

Helmke, B., & Wu, Y.-S. (1980). Individual differences and foreign language pronunciation achievement. *Revue de Phonétique Appliquée, 53,* 25–34.

Henning, W. A. (1966). Discrimination training and self-evaluation in the teaching of pronunciation. *International Review of Applied Linguistics, 4,* 7–17.

Heyde, A. W. (1979). *The relationship between self-esteem and the oral production of a second language.* Unpublished doctoral dissertation, University of Michigan, Ann Arbor.

Hieke, A. (1987). Absorption and fluency in native and non-native casual English speech. In A. James & J. Leather (Eds.), *Sound patterns in second language acquisition* (pp. 41–58). Dordrecht: Foris.

Hodne, B. (1985). Yet another look at interlanguage phonology: The modification of English syllable structure by native speakers of Polish. *Language Learning, 35,* 405–422.

Hudson, R. (1980). *Sociolinguistics.* Cambridge, UK: Cambridge University Press.

Ioup, G., & Tansomboon, A. (1987). The acquisition of tone: A maturational perspective. In G. Ioup & S. Weinberger (Eds.), *Interlanguage phonology: The acquisition of a second language sound system* (pp. 333–349). Rowley, MA: Newbury House.

Ioup, G., & Weinberger, S. (Eds.). (1987). *Interlanguage phonology: The acquisition of a second language sound system.* Rowley, MA: Newbury House.

Ito, J. (1986). *Syllable theory in prosodic phonology.* Unpublished doctoral dissertation, University of Massachusetts, Amherst.

Itoh, H. T., & Hatch, E. M. (1978). Second language acquisition: A case study. In E. M. Hatch (Ed.), *Second language acquisition: A book of readings* (pp. 76–88). Rowley, MA: Newbury House.

James, A. R. (1976). Dialektaler Transfer in der Prosodie. *Linguistik und Didaktik, 28,* 261–272.

James, A. R. (1983). Transferability and dialect phonology: Swabian-English. In A. James & B. Kettemann (Eds.), *Dialektphonologie und Fremdsprachenerwerb [Dialect phonology and foreign language acquisition]* (pp. 162–188). Tübingen: Narr.

James, A. R. (1984). Phonic transfer: The structural bases of interlingual assessment. In M. van den Broecke & A. Cohen (Eds.), *Proceedings of the Tenth International Congress of Phonetic Sciences* (pp. 691–695). Dordrecht: Foris.

James, A. R. (1986a). Phonic transfer and phonological explanation: Some theoretical and methodological issues. In E. Kellerman & M. Sharwood Smith (Eds.), *Crosslinguistic influence in second language acquisition* (pp. 134–149). Oxford: Pergamon.

James, A. R. (1986b). *Suprasegmental phonology and segmental form.* Tübingen: Niemeyer.

James, A. R. (1988). *The acquisition of a second language phonology.* Tübingen: Narr.

James, A. R. (1989). Linguistic theory and second language phonological learning: A perspective and some proposals. *Applied Linguistics, 10,* 367–381.

James, A. R. (1990). A parameter-setting model for second language phonological acquisition? In J. Leather & A. James (Eds.), *New sounds 90: Proceedings of the 1990 Amsterdam Symposium on the Acquisition of Second Language Speech.* Amsterdam: University of Amsterdam.

James, A. R., & Leather, J. H. (Eds.). (1987). *Sound patterns in second language acquisition.* Dordrecht: Foris.

Jamieson, D. & Morosan, P. (1986). Training non-native speech contrasts in adults: Acquisition of the English /o/—/O/ contrast by francophones. *Perception and Psychophysics, 40,* 202–215.

Johannson, F. (1973). *Immigrant Swedish phonology.* Lund: Gleerup.

Johansson, S. (1980). Another look at foreign accent and speech distortion. *Revue de Phonétique Appliquée, 53,* 35–48.

Kahn, D. (1976). *Syllable-based generalizations in English phonology.* Bloomington: Indiana University Linguistics Club.

Kaye, J. (1981). Opacity and recoverability in phonology. *Canadian Journal of Linguistics, 19,* 134–149.

Keating, P. (1989). The phonetics-phonology interface. In F. Newmeyer (Ed.), *Linguistics: The Cambridge Survey* (Vol. 1, pp. 281–302). Cambridge, UK: Cambridge University Press.

Keating, P. (1990). Phonetic representations in a generative grammar. *Journal of Phonetics, 18,* 321–334.

Kent, R. D. (1976). Models of speech production. In N. J. Lass (Ed.), *Contemporary issues in experimental phonetics* (pp. 79–104). New York: Academic Press.

Klatt, D. (1979). Speech perception: A model of acoustic-phonetic variability and lexical access. *Journal of Phonetics, 7,* 279–312.

Kløve, M. (1992). Principles and constraints on the acquisition of Norwegian phonology by Cantonese learners. In J. Leather & A. James (Eds.), *New sounds 92: Proceedings of the Second Amsterdam Symposium on the Acquisition of Second-Language Speech* (pp. 113–121). Amsterdam: University of Amsterdam.

Kohler, K. (1971). On the adequacy of phonological theories for contrastive studies. In G. Nickel (Ed.), *Papers in contrastive linguistics* (pp. 83–88). Cambridge, UK: Cambridge University Press.

Kohler, K. (1981). Contrastive phonology and the acquisition of phonetic skills. *Phonetica, 38,* 213–226.

Kuhl, P. K. (1992). Speech prototypes: studies on the nature, function, ontogeny and phylogeny of the "centers" of speech categories. In Y. Tohkura, E. Vatikiotis-Bateson, & Y. Sagisaka (Eds.), *Speech perception, production and linguistic structure* (pp. 239–264). Tokyo: Ohmsa.

Labov, W. (1973). On the mechanism of linguistic change. In W. Labov (Ed.), *Sociolinguistic patterns* (pp. 160–182). Philadelphia: University of Philadelphia Press.

Ladefoged, P., DeClerk, J., Lindau, M., & Papçun, G. (1972). An auditory-motor theory of speech production. *Working Papers in Phonetics (University of California at Los Angeles), 22*, 48–75.

Lado, R. (1957). *Linguistics across cultures.* Ann Arbor: University of Michigan Press.

Lane, H. L., & Schneider, B. (1963). Methods for self-shaping echoic behavior. *Modern Language Journal, 47*, 154–160.

Leather, J. H. (1983). Second language pronunciation learning and teaching. *Language Teaching, 16*(3), 198–219.

Leather, J. H. (1987). F0 pattern inference in the perceptual acquisition of second-language tone. In A. R. James & J. H. Leather (Eds.), *Sound patterns in second language acquisition* (pp. 59–80). Durdrecht: Foris.

Leather, J. H. (1988). *Speech pattern elements in second language acquisition.* Unpublished doctoral dissertation, University College, London.

Leather, J. H. (1990). Perceptual and productive learning of Chinese lexical tone by Dutch and English speakers. In J. Leather & A. James (Eds.), *New sounds 90: Proceedings of the 1990 Amsterdam Symposium on the Acquisition of Second Language Speech* (pp. 72–97). Amsterdam: University of Amsterdam.

Leather, J. H. (1991). Interelation of perception and production in initial learning of second-language lexical tone. In *Actes du XIIème Congrès International des Sciences Phonétiques,* (Vol. 5, pp. 138–141). Aix-en-Provence: Université de Provence.

Leather, J. H., & James, A. R. (1987). Sound patterns in second language acquisition. In A. James & J. Leather (Eds.), *Sound patterns in second language acquisition* (pp. 1–6). Dordrecht: Foris.

Lindblom, B. E. F., Lubker, J., & Gay, T. (1979). Formant frequencies of some fixed-mandible vowels and a model of speech motor programming by predicative simulation. *Journal of Phonetics, 7*, 147–161.

Linell, P. (1979). *Psychological reality in phonology.* Cambridge, UK: Cambridge University Press.

Linell, P. (1982). The concept of phonological form and the activities of speech production and perception. *Journal of Phonetics, 10*, 37–72.

Locke, J. L. (1968). Oral perception and articulation learning. *Perceptual and Motor Skills, 26*, 1259–1264.

Locke, J. L. (1969). Short-term memory, oral perception and experimental sound learning. *Journal of Speech and Hearing Research, 12*, 185–192.

Logan, J. S., Lively, S. E., & Pisoni, D. B. (1991). Training Japanese listeners to identify /r/ and /l/: A first report. *Journal of the Acoustic Society of America, 89*, 874–886.

Loveday, L. (1981). Pitch, politeness and sexual role: An exploratory investigation into the pitch correlates of English and Japanese politeness formulae. *Language and Speech, 24*, 71–89.

Mack, M. (1989). Consonant and vowel perception and production: Early English-French bilinguals and English monolinguals. *Perception and Psychophysics, 46*, 187–200.

MacKain, K. S., Best, C. T., & Strange, W. (1981). Categorical perception of /r/ and /l/ by Japanese bilinguals. *Applied Psycholinguistics, 2*, 369–390.

MacKay, D. G. (1970). How does language familiarity influence stuttering under delayed auditory feedback? *Perceptual and Motor Skills, 30*, 655–669.

Mairs, J. L. (1989). Stress assignment in interlanguage phonology: An analysis of the stress system of Spanish speakers learning English. In S. M. Gass & J. Schachter (Eds.),

Linguistic perspectives on second language acquisition (pp. 260–283). Cambridge, UK: Cambridge University Press.

Major, R. (1986a). The Ontogeny Model: Evidence from L2 acquisition of Spanish r. *Language Learning, 36,* 453–504.

Major, R. (1986b). Paragoge and degree of foreign accent in Brazilian English. *Second Language Research, 2,* 53–69.

Major, R. (1987a). A model for interlanguage phonology. In G. Ioup & S. Weinberger (Eds.), *Interlanguage phonology* (pp. 101–124). Rowley, MA: Newbury House.

Major, R. (1987b). The natural phonology of second language acquisition. In A. James & J. Leather (Eds.), *Sound patterns in second language acquisition* (pp. 207–224). Dordrecht: Foris.

Major, R. (1987c). Phonological similarity, markedness, and rate of L2 acquisition. *Studies in Second Language Acquisition, 9,* 63–82.

Major, R. (1990). L2 acquisition, L1 loss, and the critical period hypothesis. In J. Leather & A. James (Eds.), *New sounds 90: Proceedings of the 1990 Amsterdam Symposium on the Acquisition of Second-Language Speech* (pp. 207–224). Amsterdam: University of Amsterdam.

Manning, W. H., & Hein, S. L. (1981). Auditory feedback during the acquisition of new sounds. *Journal of the Acoustic Society of America, Suppl. 1, 70,* S12(A).

McDonald, E. T., & Aungst, L. F. (1967). Studies in oral sensorimotor function. In J. F. Bosma (Ed.), *Symposium on oral sensation and perception* (pp. 202–220). Springfield, IL: Thomas.

Michaels, D. (1974). Sound replacements and phonological systems. *Linguistics, 176,* 69–81.

Miyawaki, K., Strange, W., Verbrugge, R., Liberman, A., Jenkins, J. J., & Fujimura, O. (1975). An effect of linguistic experience: The discrimination of [r] and [l] by native speakers of Japanese and English. *Perception and Psychophysics, 18,* 331–340.

Mochizuki, M. (1981). The identification of /r/ and /l/ in natural and synthesized speech. *Journal of Phonetics, 9,* 283–303.

Mohanan, K. (1982). *Lexical phonology.* Bloomington: Indiana University Linguistics Club.

Moulton, W. (1972). *The sounds of English and German.* Chicago: University of Chicago Press.

Mueller, T. H., & Niedzielski, H. (1968). The influence of discrimination training on pronunciation. *Modern Language Journal, 52,* 410–416.

Mulford, R., & Hecht, B. (1980). Learning to speak without an accent: Acquisition of a second-language phonology. *Papers and Reports on Child Language Development* (Stanford, California), *18,* 61–74.

Nathan, G. (1987). On second-language acquisition of voiced stops. *Journal of Phonetics, 15,* 313–322.

Nathan, G. (1990). On the non-acquisition of an English sound system. In J. Leather & A. James (Eds.), *New sounds of 90: Proceedings of the 1990 Amsterdam Symposium on the Acquisition of Second-Language Speech* (pp. 294–299). Amsterdam: University of Amsterdam.

Nemser, W. (1971). *An experimental study of phonological interference in the English of Hungarians.* Bloomington: Indiana University Press.

Neufeld, G. G. (1977). Language learning ability in adults: A study on the acquisition of prosodic and articulatory features. *Working Papers on Bilingualism* (University of Ottawa), *12.*

Neufeld, G. G. (1978). On the acquisition of prosodic and articulatory features in adult language learning. *Canadian Modern Language Review, 34,* 168–194.

Neufeld, G. G. (1980). On the adult's ability to acquire phonology. *TESOL Quarterly, 14,* 285–298.

Nooteboom, S. G. (1970). The target theory of speech production. *IPO Annual Progress Report* (Eindhoven), *5,* 51–55.

Nosofsky, R. M. (1988). Exemplar-based accounts of relations between classification, recognition, and typicality. *Journal of Experimental Psychology: Learning, Memory and Cognition, 14,* 700–708.

Nosofsky, R. M., Clark, S. E., Shin, H.-J. (1989). Rules and exemplars in categorization, identification, and recognition. *Journal of Experimental Psychology: Learning, Memory and Cognition, 15,* 282–304.

Obler, L. (1982). The parsimonious bilingual. In L. Obler & L. Menn (Eds.), *Exceptional language and linguistics* (p. 339–346). New York: Academic Press.

Oden, G. C., & Massaro, D. W. (1978). Integration of featural information in speech perception. *Psychological Review, 85,* 172–191.

Ohala, J. J. (1986). Consumer's guide to evidence in phonology. *Phonology Yearbook, 3,* 3–26.

Ohala, J. J., & Jaeger, J. (Eds.). (1986). *Experimental phonology.* Orlando, FL: Academic Press.

Pennington, M. C. (1990). The context of L2 phonology. In H. Burmeister & P. Rounds (Eds.), *Variability in second language acquisition. Proceedings of the Tenth Meeting of the Second Language Research Forum* (Vol. 2, pp. 541–564). Eugene: University of Oregon.

Pennington, M. C. (1992). Discourse factors related to L2 phonological proficiency: An exploratory study. In J. Leather & A. James (Eds.), *New sounds 92: Proceedings of the Second Amsterdam Symposium on the Acquisition of Second-Language Speech* (pp. 137–155). Amsterdam: University of Amsterdam.

Pennington, M. C., & Richards, J. (1986). Pronunciation revisited. *TESOL Quarterly, 20,* 207–225.

Pimsleur, P. (1963). Discrimination training in the teaching of French pronunciation. *Modern Language Journal, 47,* 190–203.

Pisoni, D. B., Logan, J. S., & Lively, S. E. (1990). Perceptual learning of nonnative speech contrasts: Implications for theories of speech perception. In H. C. Nusbaum & J. Goodman (Eds.), *Development of speech perception: The transition from recognizing speech sounds to spoken words.* Cambridge, MA: MIT Press.

Pisoni, D. B., & Luce, P. (1987). Acoustic-phonetic representations in word recognition. *Cognition, 25,* 21–52.

Polivanov, E. (1974). The subjective nature of the perception of sounds. In A. Leontev (Ed.), *E. D. Polivanov: Selected writings* (D. Armstrong, Trans., pp. 223–237). The Hague: Mouton. (Original work published in 1932)

Postovsky, V. A. (1974). Effects of delay in oral practice at the beginning of second language learning. *Modern Language Journal, 58,* 229–239.

Puppel, S. (1990). Some preliminary observations of Polish and English vowel spaces in contact. In J. Fisiak (Ed.), *Further insights into contrastive linguistics* (pp. 241–253). Amsterdam: John Benjamins.

Purcell, E. T., & Suter, R. W. (1980). Predictors of pronunciation accuracy: A re-examination. *Language Learning, 30,* 271–288.

Pürschel, H. (1975). *Pauze und Kadenz: Interferenzerscheinungen bei der englischen Intonation deutscher Sprecher.* (Linguistische Arbeiten 27). Tübingen: Niemeyer.

Repp, B. (1977). Dichotic competition of speech sounds: The role of acoustic stimulus structure. *Journal of Experimental Psychology: Human Perception and Performance, 3,* 37–50.

Repp, B. (1984). Categorical perception: Issues, methods, findings. In N. J. Lass (Ed.), *Speech and Language: Advances in Basic Research and Practice* (Vol. 10). New York: Academic Press.

Ritchie, W. (1968). On the explanation of phonic interference. *Language Learning, 18,* 183–197.

Rubach, J. (1984). Rule typology and phonological interference. In S. Eliasson (Ed.), *Theoretical issues in contrastive phonology* (pp. 37–50). Heidelberg: Groos.

Sagey, E. (1986). *The representation of features and relations in nonlinear phonology.* Unpublished doctoral dissertation, MIT, Cambridge, MA.

Sato, C. (1984). Phonological processes in second language acquisition: Another look at interlanguage syllable structure. *Language Learning, 34,* 43–57.

Sato, C. (1985). Task variation in interlanguage phonology. In S. Gass & C. Madden (Eds.), *Input in second language acquisition* (pp. 181–196). Rowley, MA: Newbury House.

Scherer, K. R. (1979). Personality markers in speech. In K. R. Scherer & H. Giles (Eds.), *Social markers in speech* (pp. 147–209). Cambridge, UK: Cambridge University Press.

Schiffler, L. (1977). Lernpsychologische Überlegungen zur Korrekturphonetik im Fremdsprachenanfangsunterricht. *Der fremdsprachliche Unterricht, 41,* 20–47.

Schmidt, R. (1977). Sociolinguistic variation and language transfer in phonology. *Working Papers on Bilingualism, 12,* 79–95.

Schneiderman, E. I., Bourdages, J., & Champagne, C. (1988). Second-language accent: The relationship between discrimination and perception in acquisition. *Language Learning, 38,* 1–19.

Schneiderman, E. I., & Desmarais, C. (1988). The talented language learner: Some preliminary findings. *Second Language Research, 4,* 91–109.

Scholes, R. J. (1967). Phoneme categorization of synthetic vocalic stimuli by speakers of Japanese, Spanish, Persian and American English. *Language and Speech, 10,* 46–68.

Scholes, R. J. (1968). Phonemic interference as a perceptual phenomenon. *Language and Speech, 11,* 86–103.

Schouten, M. E. H. (1975). *Native language interference in the perception of second language vowels.* Doctoral dissertation, University of Utrecht.

Schouten, M. E. H., van Dalen, T. E., Klein, A. J. J. (1985). Ear advantage and second language proficiency. *Journal of Phonetics, 13,* 53–60.

Schumann, H. H., Holroyd, J., Campbell, R. N., & Ward, F.A. (1978). Improvement of foreign language pronunciation under hypnosis: A preliminary study. *Language Learning, 28,* 143–148.

Schumann, J. (1975). Affective factors and the problem of age in second language acquisition. *Language Learning, 25,* 209–235.

Schumann, J. (1978). The acculturation model for L2 acquisition. In R. C. Gringas (Ed.), *Second language acquisition and foreign language teaching.* Arlington, VA: Center for Applied Linguistics.

Scuffil, M. (1982). *Experiments in comparative intonation: A case study of English and German.* Tübingen: Niemeyer.

Selinker, L. (1972). Interlanguage. *International Review of Applied Linguistics, 10,* 209–231.

Selkirk, E. (1984). On the major class features and syllable theory. In M. Aronoff & R. Oehrle (Eds.), *Language sound structure* (pp. 107–136). Cambridge, MA: MIT Press.

Sheldon, A., & Strange, W. (1982). The acquisition of /r/ and /l/ by Japanese learners of English: Evidence that speech production can precede speech perception. *Applied Psycholinguistics, 3,* 243–261.

Siegel, G., Fehst, C., Garber, S., & Pick, H. (1980). Delayed auditory feedback with children. *Journal of Speech and Hearing Research, 23,* 803–813.

Singh, R. (1985). Prosodic adaptation in interphonology. *Lingua, 67,* 269–282.

Singh, R. (1991). Interference and contemporary phonological theory. *Language Learning, 41,* 157–175.

Singh, R., & Ford, A. (1987). Interphonology and phonological theory. In A. James & J. Leather (Eds.), *Sound patterns in second language acquisition* (pp. 163–172). Dordrecht: Foris.

Spolsky, B. (1969). Attitudinal aspects of second language learning. *Language Learning, 20,* 271–287.

Stampe, D. (1973). *A dissertation on natural phonology.* Bloomington: Indiana University Linguistics Club.

Stevens, K. N. (1977). Discussion contribution. In M. Sawashima & F. S. Cooper (Eds., *Dynamic aspects of speech production.* Tokyo: University of Tokyo Press.

Stevens, K. N., & Perkell, J. S. (1977). Speech physiology and phonetic features. In M. Sawashima & F. S. Cooper (Eds.), *Dynamic aspects of speech production* (pp. 323–341). Tokyo: University of Tokyo Press.

Stockman, I. J., & Pluut, E. (1992). Segment composition as a factor in the syllabification errors of second-language speakers. *Language Learning, 42,* 21–45.

Stockwell, R., & Bowen, J. (1965). *The sounds of English and Spanish.* Chicago: University of Chicago Press.

Strange, W. (1992). Learning non-native phoneme contrasts: Interactions among subject, stimulus and task variables. In Y. Tohkura, E. Vatikiotis-Bateson, & Y. Sagisaka (Eds.), *Speech perception, production and linguistic structure* (pp. 197–219). Tokyo: Ohmsa.

Strevens, P. (1974). A rationale for teaching pronunciation: The rival virtues of innocence and sophistication. *English Language Teaching Journal, 28,* 182–189.

Studdert-Kennedy, M., & Hadding, K. (1973). Auditory and linguistic processes in the perception of intonation contours. *Language and Speech, 16,* 293–313.

Suter, R. W. (1976). Predictors of pronunciation accuracy in second language learning. *Language Learning, 26,* 233–253.

Tahta, S., Wood, M., & Loewenthal, K. (1981a). Foreign accents: Factors relating to transfer of accent from the first language to a second language. *Language and Speech, 24,* 265–272.

Tahta, S., Wood, M., & Loewenthal, K. (1981b). Age changes in the ability to replicate foreign pronunciation and intonation. *Language and Speech, 24,* 363–372.

Tarone, E. (1972). A suggested unit for interlingual identification in pronunciation. *TESOL Quarterly, 6,* 325–331.

Tarone, E. (1976). Some influences on interlanguage phonology. *Working Papers on Bilingualism, 8,* 87–111.

Tarone, E. (1978). The phonology of interlanguage. In J. Richards (Ed.), *Understanding second and foreign language learning* (pp. 15–33). Rowley, MA: Newbury House.

Tarone, E. (1980). Some influences on the syllable structure of interlanguage phonology. *International Review of Applied Linguistics, 16,* 143–163.

Tarone, E. (1982). Systematicity and attention in interlanguage. *Language Learning, 32,* 69–84.

Tarone, E. (1983). On the variability of interlanguage systems. *Applied Linguistics, 4,* 142–163.

Taylor, L. L., Catford, J. C., Guiora, A. Z., & Lane, H. L. (1971). Psychological variables and the ability to pronounce a second language. *Language and Speech, 14,* 146–157.

Treichel, B. (1992). The linearization problem in L2 speech production. In J. Leather & A. James (Eds.), *New sounds 92: Proceedings of the Second Amsterdam Symposium on the Acquisition of Second-Language Speech* (pp. 156–173). Amsterdam: University of Amsterdam.

Tropf, H. (1983). *Variation in der Phonologie des ungesteuerten Zweitspracherwerbs* (Bd. 1, Bd. 2). Unpublished doctoral dissertation, University of Heidelberg.

Tropf, H. (1987). Sonority as a variability factor in second language phonology. In A. James & J. Leather (Eds.), *Sound patterns in second language acquisition* (pp. 173–191). Dordrecht: Foris.

Trubetzkoy, N. (1958). *Grundzüge der Phonologie* (Travaux du cercle linguistique de Prague 7). Göttingen: Vandenhoek & Ruprecht. (Original work published 1939)

Valdman, A. (1976). *Introduction to French phonology and morphology.* Rowley, MA: Newbury House.

Vance, T. J. (1977). Tonal distinctions in Cantonese. *Phonetica, 34,* 93–107.

Vogel, I. (1991). Prosodic phonology: Second language acquisition data as evidence in theoretical phonology. In T. Huebner & C. Ferguson (Eds.), *Crosscurrents in second language acquisition and linguistic theories* (pp. 47–65). Amsterdam: John Benjamins.

Walz, J. (1975). *A longitudinal study of the acquisition of French pronunciation.* Unpublished doctoral dissertation, Indiana University, Bloomington.

Wardhaugh, R. (1970). The contrastive analysis hypothesis. *TESOL Quarterly, 4,* 123–130.

Weinberger, S. (1987). The influence of linguistic context on syllable simplification. In G. Ioup & S. Weinberger (Eds.), *Interlanguage phonology* (pp. 401–417). Rowley, MA: Newbury House.

Weinberger, S. (1990). Minimal segments in L2 phonology. In J. Leather & A. James (Eds.), *New sounds 90: Proceedings of the 1990 Amsterdam Symposium on the Ac-*

quisition of Second-Language Speech (pp. 137–179). Amsterdam: University of Amsterdam.

Weinreich, U. (1953). *Languages in contact.* The Hague: Mouton.

Weinreich, U. (1957). On the description of phonic interference. *Word, 13,* 1–11.

Weiss, L. (1970). *Auditory discrimination and pronunciation of French vowel phonemes.* Unpublished doctoral dissertation, Stanford University, Stanford, CA. (Summarized in *Dissertation Abstracts International, 31,* 4051-A)

Weiss, R. (1976). The role of perception in teaching the German vowels to American students. In G. Nickel (Ed.), *Proceedings of the Fourth International Congress of Applied Linguistics,* (Vol. 3). Stuttgart: Universität Stuttgart.

Wenk, B. (1979). Articulatory setting and de-fossilization. *Interlanguage Studies Bulletin, 4,* 202–220.

Wenk, B. (1982). Articulatory setting and the acquisition of second language phonology. *Revue de Phonétique Appliquée, 65,* 51–65.

Wenk, B. (1986). Crosslinguistic influence in second language phonology: Speech rhythms. In E. Kellerman & M. Sharwood Smith (Eds.), *Crosslinguistic influence in second language acquisition* (pp. 120–133). Oxford: Pergamon.

Werker, J. F., & Logan, J. S. (1985). Cross-language evidence for three factors in speech perception. *Perception and Psychophysics, 37,* 35–44.

Wesche, M. B., & Schneiderman, E. I. (1982). Language lateralization in adult bilinguals. *Studies in Second Language Acquisition, 4,* 153–169.

Wexler, K., & Manzini, R. (1987). Parameters and learnability in binding theory. In T. Roeper & E. Williams (Eds.), *Parameter setting.* Dordrecht: Reidel.

Whitman, R. (1970). Contrastive analysis: Problems and procedures. *Language Learning, 20,* 191–197.

Wieden, W. (1990). Some remarks on developing phonological representations. In J. Leather & A. James (Eds.), *New sounds of 90: Proceedings of the 1990 Amsterdam Symposium on the Acquisition of Second-Language Speech* (pp. 189–197). Amsterdam: University of Amsterdam.

Wieden, W., & Nemser, W. (1991). *The pronunciation of English in Austria.* Tübingen: Narr.

Williams, L. (1977). The perception of stop consonant voicing by Spanish-English bilinguals. *Perception and Psychophysics, 21,* 289–297.

Williams, L. (1979). The modification of speech perception and production in second language learning. *Perception and Psychophysics, 26,* 95–104.

Willing, K. (1988). *Learning strategies in adult migrant education.* Adelaide: NCRC.

Wode, H. (1977). The L2 acquisition of /r/. *Phonetica, 34,* 200–217.

Wode, H. (1978). The beginnings of non-school-room L2 phonological acquisition. *International Review of Applied Linguistics, 16,* 109–125.

Wode, H. (1980). Phonology in L2 acquisition. In S. Felix (Ed.), *Second language development* (pp. 123–136). Tübingen: Narr.

Wode, H. (1981). *Learning a second language.* Tübingen: Narr.

Young-Scholten, M. (1990). Interlanguage and postlexical transfer. In J. Leather & A. James (Eds.), *New sounds 90: Proceedings of the 1990 Amsterdam Symposium on the Acquisition of Second-Language Speech* (pp. 107–129). Amsterdam: University of Amsterdam.

Young-Scholten, M. (1992). Acquiring a new domain of resyllabification. In J. Leather & A. James (Eds.), *New sounds 92: Proceedings of the Second Amsterdam Symposium on the Acquisition of Second-Language Speech* (pp. 200–217). Amsterdam: University of Amsterdam.

Zimmerman, G. N., Price, P. J., & Ayusawa, T. (1984). The production of /r/ and /l/ by Japanese speakers differing in experience with English. *Journal of Phonetics, 12,* 187–193.

Zuengler, J. (1982). Applying accommodation theory to variable performance data. *Studies in Second Language Acquisition, 4,* 181–192.

Zuengler, J. (1988). Identity markers and L2 pronunciation. *Studies in Second Language Acquisition, 10,* 33–50.

CHAPTER 10

SECOND LANGUAGE ACQUISITION AND LINGUISTIC THEORY: THE ROLE OF LANGUAGE TRANSFER*

Susan Gass

I. INTRODUCTION

The role of the native language (NL) in a second language (L2) context has been debated for over 2000 years. However, most of the early debate did not concern learning per se, but was centered around the value (or lack thereof) of using the NL in the classroom (cf. Kelly, 1976, for exemplification). Throughout the debate, the phenomenon itself was not in dispute: rather, the issues centered around the appropriate role of the NL in a pedagogical setting.

With the development of L2 acquisition as an autonomous and independent discipline, the issues and questions surrounding the use of NL information have changed. Within the past 40–50 years we have witnessed great flux in research directions, traditions, and assumptions. Four phases of research can be discerned. In the first, the primary importance of the NL was assumed (e.g., Lado, 1957); in the second (e.g., Dulay & Burt, 1974a), the influence of the NL in the acquisition of an L2 was minimized; in the third phase, research turned to qualitative aspects of NL influence; in the fourth phase (i.e., current research) the influence of the NL is driven by current theoretical issues of language and language acquisition. In the first two phases (from the 1950s to the 1970s) the traditions were diametrically opposed, with later research being a reaction to earlier research. In both cases, extreme positions were taken in that the NL was seen as having either a major or a minimal role in the learning of an L2. From the late 1970s to the present day,

* Portions of this article are reprinted by permission of Kluwer Academic Publishers.

317

researchers have assumed neither that learners "tended to transfer" everything nor that nothing (or little) is transferred but rather have sought to understand the constraints that govern which aspects of an NL are transferred and the underlying principles that determine the transferability of NL information.

In this chapter, I review some of the issues surrounding NL influence.[1] In the final part of the chapter, I will make a connection between specific linguistic theories, in particular Universal Grammar (UG) and the Competition Model, and language transfer.

II. LANGUAGE TRANSFER: AN HISTORICAL OVERVIEW

A. Defining Language Transfer

Providing a simple definition of *transfer* is by no means an easy task, because definitions often depend on the theoretical framework within which they are discussed. For example, within a behaviorist framework, such as the one in which Lado (1957) and Fries (1945) were operating, transfer was seen as the imposition of NL[2] information (in the form of direct reflexes) on an L2 utterance or sentence. More generally, what is meant is the use of prior linguistic information in a non-NL context. What constitutes prior linguistic information is not without controversy. Early studies on transfer took a narrow view, considering language transfer solely as the physical carryover of NL surface forms to an L2 context (generally with lexical, morphological, or both modifications). For example, if an Italian speaker learning English produces *"I want that you come,"* *Voglio che tu venga,* one would argue that this utterance represents Italian surface structure and that this is a matter of transfer. The recognition of the fact that there was more to NL influences than overt manifestations of an NL form, in part, prompted Corder (1983, 1992) to call for the abolishment of the term *transfer* in favor of what he viewed a more neutral term, *mother tongue* influence. The same recognition caused others such as Kellerman and Sharwood Smith (1986) and Odlin (1989) to adopt the term cross-linguistic influence or cross-linguistic generalization (Zobl, 1984).

---

[1] Parts of this chapter originally appeared in *Linguistic Theory in Second Language Acquisition,* edited by Suzanne Flynn and Wayne O'Neil and published by Kluwer Academic Publishers in Dordrecht, Germany. I am grateful to Kluwer Publishers for allowing me to update and reprint portions of the original article.

[2] In most of the literature, the words *transfer* and *native language influences* are used interchangeably. This is of course a misnomer, as is the name of the discipline L2 acquisition, because one is often dealing with influences from any prior languages known. Thus, NL influences, loosely speaking, can refer to influence from any known language, much as L2 acquisition often refers to the acquisition of a second, third, fourth, and so forth, language.

More recently scholars such as Schachter (1983, 1992) have defined transfer in much broader terms, incorporating all prior linguistic knowledge including the "imperfect" knowledge a learner may have of the L2. For example, suppose a learner constructs a hypothesis about a structure, one that is neither nativelike nor targetlike. Then, suppose that this hypothesis influences subsequent hypotheses this learner may come up with. One could not claim that this is NL influence because the influence does not come from the NL. In a similar vein, one would want to claim that the influence comes from prior linguistic knowledge, and one would therefore want to incorporate this sort of influence into a general model of linguistic influences on L2 learning.

B. Contrastive Analysis

Contrastive analysis was used as a means of comparing languages. It grew out of pedagogical concerns in which the basis of language instruction was the difference between the NL and the target language (TL). Because one needed to have a means of determining language differences, one made a systematic comparison of a learner's NL and TL and NL culture and TL culture. Out of this approach and following these assumptions sprung numerous contrastive analyses, the goal being to predict learner difficulty by finding language differences.[3] (See chapters 6 by Eckman and 11 by Nunan, this volume, for further discussions of the place of contrastive analysis in the history of L2 research.)

C. Creative Construction

In the early 1970s, there was a strong reaction to the contrastive analysis hypothesis as an hypothesis capable of even accounting for L2 data never mind explaining them. A number of reasons were responsible for this reaction. First, many errors that learners made were not attributable to the NL. As Kellerman says, these were the gate-crashers of a theory (1984, p. 99). As evidence, researchers pointed to the fact that there were many similarities between the learner grammars produced by speakers of different NLs. Second, there were predicted areas of transfer, as determined by contrastive analyses, that did not occur. The theoretical underpinnings of the shift away from a contrastive analysis approach was its association with the dominant linguistic and psychological position of the time: behaviorism. These empirical and theoretical factors were influential

---

[3] Although most contrastive analyses in North America had as their goal the betterment of pedagogical materials, in Europe there existed a strong trend of contrastive linguistics that had as its goal a better understanding of the nature of language. These studies were ultimately not concerned with pedagogy but rather dealt with the comparison of two language structures for theoretical purposes only (cf. Fisiak, 1980, 1991).

in causing researchers to rethink the phenomenon of NL influences and, as a result, to downplay the role of transfer. Language transfer became an "embarrassment" because there was no way of incorporating it within existing theoretical models. In terms of accountability, it was possible not to have to account for transfer, because many of the errors previously attributed to the first language (L1) could be accounted for differently, for example, by "developmental" factors. Researchers turned their attention to similarities in the acquisition process among all language learners regardless of NL background. As attention was focused on similarities in language learning, there was a concomitant disinterest in the phenomenon of language transfer and the dissimilarities among language learners (e.g., Richards, 1971).

With the influence of child language research and the potential similarity between L1 and L2 acquisition, the study of L2 acquisition began to take on a character of its own, with its own research issues and polemics, and was no longer exclusively related to issues in pedagogy, as had previously been the case.

Central in this reaction to contrastive analysis was the work of Dulay and Burt (1974a, 1974b), who were influenced by work in L1 acquisition, most notably that of Brown (1973). They proposed what they called the Creative Construction Hypothesis, claiming that the guiding force in L2 acquisition are universal innate principles and *not* the NL. Within their framework, it is the L2 system and not the NL system that guides the process of acquisition. Their major source of evidence came from the order of acquisition of a set of grammatical morphemes in English. The order of acquisition was similar in two groups of language learners of unrelated language backgrounds (Chinese and Spanish). There was no other way of explaining the similarities between Chinese and Spanish learners other than universal principles. It was, therefore, argued that the NL had little effect on the process of acquisition.

The work by Dulay and Burt focused on the acquisition of an L2 by children. Additional work by Bailey, Madden, and Krashen (1974) furthered this work with adults, also suggesting a similar acquisition order for speakers of different language backgrounds and a reduction in the importance of NL effects. (The creative construction hypothesis is also discussed in Chapter 11, this volume, by Nunan.)

D. The Settling of the Pendulum

In the past 10–15 years there has been a resurgence of interest in the phenomenon of language transfer, not as a mechanical transference of L1 structures but as a cognitive mechanism that underlies L2 acquisition.[4] In other words, L1 struc-

---

[4]Evidence of the shift of interest is the appearance of publications devoted solely to the phenomenon of language transfer (e.g., Gass & Selinker, 1983, 1992; Kellerman & Sharwood Smith, 1986; Odlin, 1989; Ringbom, 1987) and a conference held at the University of Michigan in 1981 which had as its title *Language Transfer in Language Learning.*

tures are not simply preserved in an unanalyzed manner, but reflect active selection and attention on the part of the learner. In the attempt to come to an understanding of the processes involved in acquiring an L2, it became evident that we must consider generalizations and approximations of TL structures. However, it also became clear that an explanatory account of L2 acquisition could not be given on the basis of the TL alone; additional factors (among which is the NL) shape the progress of development. In the late 1970s and early 1980s an attempt to unify these positions was evident in work by Andersen (1983), Eckman (1977, 1984), Flynn (1983, 1985, 1986), Gass (1979, 1980), Wode (1977, 1984), Zobl (1980a, 1980b, 1982), among others. (See chapters 3 by White, 4 by Flynn, 5 by Schachter, and 6 by Eckman, this volume, for unified views of L1 and developmental influences.)

III. LANGUAGE TRANSFER AS A COGNITIVE ACTIVITY

During the late 1970s and the early 1980s transfer began to be examined from an increasing number of perspectives. An important finding was that L1 influences occur not only as *direct* linguistic reflexes, but they also indirectly reflect underlying organizational principles of language. This body of research implicitly and explicitly redefined language transfer by claiming that the notion of language transfer involved the use of NL (or other language—see also section VI) information in the acquisition of an L2 (or additional language). A broader definition of this sort allows for observed phenomena such as (1) delayed rule restructuring, (2) transfer of typological organization, (3) different paths of acquisition, (4) avoidance, (5) overproduction of certain elements, (6) additional attention paid to the TL resulting in more rapid learning, or (7) differential effects of socially prestigious forms. These phenomena were difficult to detect within the framework of early transfer studies.

A. The Scope of Language Transfer Phenomena

Zobl (1980a, 1980b, 1982) viewed transfer and developmental influences not as two opposing processes, but as interacting ones. He argued that the effect of the L1 can be manifest in (1) a prolongation or delay in the restructuring of a language learner's rule, or (2) in the number of rules traversed on the path from the acquisition of one form to another. Thus, the L1 inserts variation into a developmental sequence.

With regard to the first type of L1 effect, he presents data suggesting that if there is a natural developmental stage that corresponds to a pattern in a learner's NL, the learner will use that pattern longer than if it were not in her or his NL. For example, Spanish speakers often use preverbal negation in English as in (1), an example from Schumann (1976).

(1)   I no use television.

As this structure is similar to the negative in Spanish, in which the negative *no* precedes the verb, its occurrence can reasonably be attributed to transfer. However, we also find that preverbal negation is typical even of speakers of languages that do not have preverbal negation. Comparing Japanese speakers to Spanish speakers, Schumann (1982) claims that *no* + VERB forms in Spanish–English learner languages will be more pervasive and enduring. Similarly, Gilbert and Orlovic (1975, cited in Andersen, 1983) present an example from Gastarbeiter Deutsch: Turkish, Yugoslav, Portuguese, Italian, Greek, and Spanish speakers learning German use no articles in their L2 German. For those learners whose NL has articles (Portuguese, Italian, Greek, and Spanish) there is a shorter period in which articles do not appear in their speech and more rapid acquisition of the article *die,* which serves a generalized function.

As an example of the second type of L1 effect, Zobl (1982) presents data on the acquisition of articles by a Chinese child (from Huang, 1971) whose NL does not have the formal category of articles and by a Spanish child (from Hernandez-Chavez, 1977) whose NL does have articles. The Chinese child initially used a deictic determiner to approximate English article usage. For the Spanish child the deictic determiner did not occur as a stage of acquisition preceding the use of English articles. Thus, with respect to the acquisition of determiners, the route of acquisition differs for the children of different language backgrounds.

Wode (1977, 1984) claims that the acquisition of prerequisite structures must occur before transfer can take place. A crucial prerequisite is a certain amount of similarity between L1 and L2 structures. In other words, L1 rules can have an effect only after L2 developmental prerequisites have been met. (Unfortunately, Wode does not provide an operational definition for similarity.) He presents evidence from German children learning English. Initially, these children negate utterances with *no* as in (2a) and (b).

(2)   a. no sleep
      b. no bread

At a later stage the children produce utterances such as that in (c).

      c. that's no right.

In (a) and (b) there is no similarity between the learner's forms and the L1, whereas in (c), there is (NEG placement with respect to the copula). It is at this stage that these children begin to produce utterances such as those in (d) and (e), which are L1-influenced, as exemplified by the postverbal negation.

      d. Everybody catch no the fish.
      e. John go not to the school.

In other words, the NEG marker that these learners use (*no* in [d] and *not* in [e])
is placed immediately after the verb as in German main clauses.

Work by Hyltenstam (1977) coupled with a reanalysis of his work by Hammerberg (1979) suggests that there are developmental paths of negation through
which learners progress. An early stage is one in which preverbal negation occurs
similar to what was given in (2a) and (2b). However, progress along that path is
impeded when the L1 has preverbal negation.

Similarly, in a study comparing a Japanese, a German, and a Finnish child's
acquisition of interrogative structures, Keller-Cohen (1979) found that the lack of
congruence between L1 and L2 structures resulted in the slower development of
the productive use of yes–no questions in English on the part of the Finnish and
Japanese children in comparison with the German child. According to Keller-
Cohen's description, both languages have *wh*-words, there is movement in both,
interrogative elements are in utterance initial position, and both have rising intonation. Japanese and English differ along many dimensions: in Japanese there is
no movement, an interrogative particle is used, *wh*-words are generally not in
initial position, and there is rising intonation. Finnish, on the other hand, has inversion in yes–no questions, but not in *wh*-questions. Furthermore, there is no
rising intonation. In Keller-Cohen's study the German child was the most advanced. This, she claims, was due to the syntactic and prosodic congruence between the L1 and the L2. It is the congruence that allows the learner to notice
relevant L2 features (cf. Gass, 1988).

Yet another perspective on the role of the L1 comes from Schachter's (1974)
examination of the production of English relative clauses by Persian, Arabic, Chinese, and Japanese students. She found that Chinese and Japanese learners produced far fewer relative clauses than did the Persian and Arabic students. She
hypothesized that the major syntactic difference between Chinese and Japanese
on the one hand and English on the other (i.e., postnominal vs. prenominal relative
clauses), a difference that does not exist among Arabic and Persian and English
(all with postnominal relative clauses), resulted in slow progress for the Chinese
and Japanese learners, which was manifest not in errors, but in lack of use or, as
Schachter claims, *avoidance* of a structure. Her results concerning the effect of
the direction of modification on acquisition are compatible with those of Flynn
(1983), who found that the match or mismatch of the L1 branching direction affected both production and comprehension of an L2.

In examining compositions of Chinese and Japanese students whose NLs are
topic-prominent, Schachter and Rutherford (1978) noted an overproduction of
particular TL forms: extraposition sentences and existential sentences with *there*.
The form was being used to carry the weight of a particular discourse function,
even though the TL makes use of other forms for that same function. They hypothesized that overproduction of this sort is a type of language transfer: that of
L1 function to L2 form.

Ard and Homburg (1983, 1992) proposed that transfer be viewed in its original psychological sense as a facilitation of learning. In investigating the responses of native speakers (NSs) of Spanish and Arabic to a vocabulary question on the standardized Michigan Test, they found differences between two groups that could be related only indirectly to the structure of the languages in question. Test items in which no relevant English words resembled Spanish words were more accurately identified by Spanish speakers than by Arabic speakers, suggesting that general similarities between languages will influence language development even in the absence of specific overt similarity. It may be that a large number of similarities frees learners from focusing on those aspects, in turn allowing them to concentrate on other aspects of the grammar (cf. Corder, 1981, p. 102).

Another departure from traditional notions of language transfer came from Schachter (1983, 1992), who claimed that language transfer is not a process at all, but rather a constraint on the acquisition process. A learner's previous knowledge constrains the hypotheses that he or she can make about the L2. For example, an NS of Spanish learning English maintains the hypothesis in English that modals are main verbs (as they are in Spanish), and produces utterances as in (3a) and (3b), which reflect that hypothesis.

(3) a. The poor people there can to do anything.
     b. He can't to eat.

Previous knowledge includes not only knowledge of the NL or other languages known, but is cumulative in that whatever is acquired of the TL is also part of one's previous knowledge and is thus available for use in further L2 learning. In addition to the knowledge of the L2 already obtained (regardless of completeness or accuracy) learners' expectations about the TL are also included in this category of prior knowledge.

B. Predicting Language Transfer

A theory of language transfer requires that we have some ability to predict where the phenomena in question will and will not occur. In this regard contrastive analysis alone falls short; it simply is not predictive. Thus, a major question in language transfer research is: What is transferred? (cf. Selinker, 1969). What linguistic elements are selected by the learner as transferable? And, importantly, if we are to come up with a coherent theory of transfer, what explanation can be given to account for the differential transferability of linguistic elements?

Kellerman (1979, 1983), reacting to earlier approaches in L2 acquisition studies that attempted to deny the importance of language transfer primarily on the basis of its behaviorist associations, argued that transfer is indeed an active mental activity. Constraints on language transfer transcend the linguistic similarity or dissimilarity of the NL and TL, encompassing as a major variable the learner's decision-making processes relating to the potential transferability of linguistic elements. Of course, the similarity or dissimilarity dimension has major import in these decision-making processes.

In Kellerman's framework there are two major factors that interact in the determination of transferable elements. One is the learner's perception of L1–L2 distance, and the second is the degree of markedness of an L1 structure. There are parts of one's language that NSs consider irregular, infrequent, or semantically opaque. In Kellerman's terms, these items are highly marked and are less transferable than frequent and regular forms. The former he refers to as *language specific,* whereas the latter are *language neutral.* Language-specific elements are those that a learner views as unique to his or her language, whereas language-neutral elements are those that the learner believes to be common to at least the NL and TL.

To give examples at the extreme ends of what is actually represented as a continuum, consider the following two examples:

(4)   He hit the roof.

This has an idiomatic meaning, whereas (5) does not:

(5)   He hit the roof (with a bat).

Sentence (4) is one that is most likely viewed as language specific and not transferable to the L2, whereas sentence (5) is most likely considered language neutral and would be transferable to the L2. It is important to note that language neutrality and language specificity are relative notions, expressible in terms of a continuum that interacts with a continuum of perceived language distance. For example, Dušková (1984) has found that in the area of bound morphology, Czech speakers learning Russian (two closely related languages) find more elements transferable than Czech speakers who are learning English. Czech learners of Russian produce forms as in (6a), (b), and (c), where the morphological endings of the NL are transferred to the L2 (Russian):

		Czech (NS)	Russian (NS)	Russian learner (Czech NS)	
(6)	a.	*ucitele*	*ucitelja*	*ucitele*	"teachers"
	b.	*delnice*	*rabotnicy*	*rabotnice*	"workwomen"
	c.	*umrel*	*on umer* + ∅	*on umrel*	"he died"

Kellerman refers to the perception of the distance between the L1 and the L2 as a learner's *psychotypology,* which develops on the basis of many factors, not the least of which is actual linguistic typology. Transferability in Kellerman's framework is a relative notion depending on the perceived distance between the L1 and the L2 and the structural organization of the learner's L1. The notion of perceived distance changes continually as the learner acquires more of the L2.

Jordens (1977) has shown that advanced Dutch learners of German are more likely to accept as grammatical the German equivalent of (7a) than of (b):

(7)   a. It is awkward to carry this suitcase.
      b. This suitcase is awkward to carry.

This occurs despite the fact that the translation equivalents are acceptable in both German and Dutch. Jordens claims that the former is semantically more transparent than the latter and is less marked, hence its greater availability for transfer.

In a similar vein, Gass (1979) observed that language transfer was promoted in cases where the resultant learner language form was more easily interpretable than the actual syntactic form of the TL. For example, learners tended to transfer pronominal copies into relative clauses. Including the anaphoric pronoun increases the potential recoverability of the antecedent of the anaphor.

Kellerman's notions have been further discussed in work by van Helmond and van Vugt (1984). They investigated the transferability of nominal compounds of NSs of Dutch learning German and English, finding that neither the learner's perceptions of language distance nor the organizational structure imposed by the learner on the L1 are valid predictors of the transferability of nominal compounds. They argue that Kellerman's framework cannot account empirically for transfer data, and that there is a lack of theoretical precision in the terminology that prevents the validation of predictive statements.

A different perspective on what is and what is not transferable comes from Rutherford (1983), who examined the interlanguages (IL) of Mandarin, Japanese, Korean, Spanish and Arabic speakers learning English, focusing in particular on language typology. He discussed three kinds of typological organization: (1) topic-prominent versus subject-prominent language, (2) pragmatic word order versus grammatical word order, and (3) canonical arrangements. He found that topic versus subject prominence and pragmatic versus grammatical word order figure in language transfer but not the canonical arrangements of the primes of subject, verb, and object. That is, NL orderings of canonical elements do not appear with any frequency or regularity in learner grammars. Rutherford argues that the differentiation between the transferability of typological types is due to a difference between the importance of sentence-level versus discourse phenomena. The two typologies that were transferred, topic-prominence and pragmatic word-order, are discourse phenomena, whereas the ordering of subjects and verbs is a sentence-level phenomenon. Based on these observations, Rutherford further speculated that it is discourse and not syntax that guides the overall development of an L2. On the surface Rutherford's data seem to contradict Kellerman's claims that if two languages are very different, learners will find little available in the way of correspondence; perception of L1–L2 distance will then be great, leading to a lesser likelihood of transfer. However, Rutherford (1983) attempts to put his results within Kellerman's framework by suggesting that learners may perceive discourse-related information as being less marked, or more universal, than syntax-related information and hence more available for transfer. Another way of accounting for the apparent contradiction is to consider that there must be a certain level of awareness on the part of the learner before such notions as L1–L2 distance are even appropriate (Gass, 1988; Schmidt, 1990). Ordering of elements within a sentence is something of which at least tutored, if not untutored, learners are conscious. Textbooks generally deal with sentences and arrangements of elements within the sentence and only infrequently deal with such concepts as emphasis and topic. This may contribute to the learner's awareness of the former concepts, but not the latter. Being aware of canonical organization, the learner will immediately notice that the TL and the NL are different and, as a consequence, will be unlikely to transfer.

Although most of this literature was carried out in the area of syntax, phonology was not ignored. (In this volume, chapter 9 by Leather and James is a general discussion of L2 phonetics and phonology; chapters 3 by White, 5 by Schachter, and 6 by Eckman also include material on L2 phonology.) Flege (1980) argues that production in an L2 involves two aspects: (1) phonological reorganization and (2) modification of automatic articulatory movements and patterns of phonetic implementation. In this study Flege investigates the acquisition of a stop-voicing contrast by Arabic speakers learning English. An interesting finding is that phonetic learning involves both the creation of new forms and the superimposition of TL forms on the pronunciation of an L2. The hypothesis discussed above with regard to syntax, that developmental factors interact with NL information in the acquisition of an L2, is supported by Flege (1980) and Flege and Davidian (1984). In the latter study the authors discuss the production of Consonant–Vowel–Consonant (CVC) English words by English speakers and three groups of nonnative speakers (NNSs) (Chinese, Polish, and Spanish). They found that processes known to occur in child language acquisition (final-stop devoicing and final-stop deletion) also occur in nonnative speech. Furthermore, transfer effects in the form of utilizing an NL form in place of a TL form were also observed. Unlike the suggestion by Zobl (1980a, 1980b, 1982) regarding the interaction of developmental and transfer processes (see section III.A), Flege and Davidian claim that the two are independent with both occurring in the same speaker. What was not examined in their study, however, was the prolongation effect that Zobl discussed. When the result of developmental and transfer effects coincide, does a learner use that particular form for a longer period of time than when only one process is operative?

A number of studies in L2 phonetic learning have pointed to an exaggeration effect. Flege (1980) found that an Arabic speaker produced a larger duration contrast in both word-final and word-initial position with [p] and [b] (a nonexistent contrast in Arabic) than is found in English. Fourakis and Iverson (1985) similarly noted that NSs of Arabic learning English produced sounds that went in a direction away from the TL. This exaggeration effect, or maximization of a difference was also discussed in Gass (1984a) with regard to an Italian speaker's voice onset time (VOT) in the production of English [b]. The learner overcompensated for the difference between English and Italian, resulting in a phonetic sound that maximized the difference between the two languages. This result, although similar to that in Flege (1980) and Fourakis and Iverson (1985), differs in that the phonetic contrast under investigation is present in some form in the NL. What the learner must do in this case is fix new boundaries on the VOT continuum. Therefore, in both the acquisition of a new contrast as well as in the acquisition of a different degree within an existing contrast, overcompensation, or exaggeration, is evident. Similar phenomena have been discussed in related areas. Gass and Ard (1984) deal with the same issue in L2 acquisition with regard to syntax and semantics; Macken and Barton (1977) and Simon (1978, cited in Flege, 1980) discuss the concept for the acquisition of a primary language, and Obler (1982) relates it to child bilingual acquisition. What this suggests is that learners first identify *that* there is something to learn and then work out the details, which in many cases involves the maximization of the features of the new element and contrast. In other words, learners move from a Gestalt approach to an analytic one. Whether this is true for all learners or whether, as in child language acquisition (Peters, 1977, 1983), some learners approach the task holistically, whereas others approach it analytically, is a matter of future empirical investigation.

Another area of transfer studies deals with speech perception. There are two issues that will be raised here because they are the ones that most directly relate to NL influences: (1) What is the relationship between perception and production? and (2) Does the NL affect the perception of sounds in the TL, and if so, how?

The first question was investigated by Sheldon and Strange (1982), who considered the acquisition of the /r–l/ contrast by Japanese learners of English from the perspective of production and perception. They conclude that contrary to what is generally believed, accurate perception does not necessarily precede accurate production (see Brière, 1966, and Gass, 1984a, for a similar conclusion).

With regard to the second question, Gass (1984a) investigated the relationship between L1 and L2 perception, finding NL effects in terms of perception of a phoneme boundary. On the other hand, a fundamental difference in the way perception takes place in an L1 and an L2 was noted. These results differ from those reported for syntax. At this juncture I make what I hope is a useful distinction— that of transfer based on the actual form of a learner's grammar and the behavior that *results* from that knowledge. The former reflects the traditional view expressed by the contrastive analysis hypothesis, the second reflects recent research. Thus, I would like to distinguish between (1) overt structures that are influenced by a learner's NL and (2) behaviors, such as avoidance, delayed restructuring, more effective learning in non-NL-related domains, and so forth.

Within the area of phonology, similar questions have been raised. Eckman (1981) has sought explicitly to investigate the question of the independent nature of ILs. To what extent are IL phonological processes determined by the phonology of the NL and the TL? He found evidence for both NL and TL effects in the L2 data he examined as well as for phonological processes that are not motivated by either language system.

Broselow (1983, 1992) considered L2 English epenthesis data from NSs of two Arabic dialects. She argued that what appears on the surface to be counterevidence to the influence of the NL on IL forms can best be viewed as an example of a productive NL phonological rule of epenthesis. An important aspect of her work as it relates to linguistic theory is the use she makes of L2 data in the validation of linguistic theories. Specifically, she argued that a generative framework based on segments is not empirically adequate. Rather, she argued for a syllable-based analysis of the data showing that the relevant construct for learners is the notion of possible syllable structure. Learners are sensitive to constraints on syllable structure and use epenthesis to break up what would be impermissible NL syllables. Beebe (1980) argued that the high degree of accuracy of initial /R/ by Thai learners of English is influenced by the fact that initial /R/ has a "highly conscious, learned social meaning" (p. 442).

What seems to emerge from the literature reviewed here is that there are constraints on the notion of transfer. The variables that enter into "decisions" about transfer on the part of the learner involve unpredictable combinations of many aspects of the learner's experience, including other languages known, success with the TL, and importance attached to social factors. What is needed at this point is greater precision of the concepts that have been claimed to constrain the hypotheses a learner can come up with. Without such precision our theories will be vacuous and the argumentation circular (cf. van Helmond & van Vugt, 1984).

IV. LANGUAGE TRANSFER AND UG

Much of the work I have reviewed thus far was carried out outside the confines of a particular linguistic theory. Research in the past decade has taken a decidedly different turn with a focus on the role of the NL as it relates to UG. In the early 1980s many scholars attempted to investigate UG as an explanatory framework for L2 acquisition (e.g., Adjémian, 1983; Flynn, 1983, 1986; Liceras, 1983; Ritchie, 1978, 1983; van Buren & Sharwood Smith, 1985; White, 1985a, 1985b). (In this volume, chapters 2 by Gregg, 3 by White, 4 by Flynn, and 5 by Schachter discuss transfer within a UG framework.) In this section I will consider how the issue of language transfer has been reconfigured within the confines of UG. In so doing, I will consider UG principles and UG parameters.

When a learner begins the study of an L2, a question of theoretical importance is: What is the starting point? The major question underlying this issue is the accessibility to UG of L2 learners. Two main possibilities have been articulated in the literature:

1. Learners have access to UG either (a) fully, in the way that children do, or (b) partially, in the sense that other factors (e.g., the NL) may interact with UG and prevent full access to UG.
2. Learners have no access to UG.

Examining each of these possibilities in turn, the first (UG access) suggests that UG is the starting point for L2 grammar formation. In the strong version of UG access, UG constrains grammar formation through the entire process of L2 acquisition; in the weak version, UG is the starting point, but the NL is an important part of the picture, effectively blocking full operation of UG. The second possibility suggests that the NL is the starting point and provides the basis on which L2s develop.

A. Principles of UG

Principles are inviolable and therefore available to all humans when learning a (first) language. Flynn argued for the fundamental similarity of L1 and L2, in that both are constrained by principles of UG. However, the evidence for the availability of principles to L2 learners is mixed.

Otsu and Naoi (1986, reported by White, 1989) in an investigation of the principle of Structure Dependence, which claims that linguistic rules operate on structural units, examined data from Japanese learners (ages 14–15) of English. Under consideration was L2 question formation with subjects containing relative clauses. In Japanese, questions are formed by the addition of a particle with no change in word order. Thus, from the NL there is no direct information as to how question formation of this type is done in English. In general, subjects adhered to the constraints of structure dependency, although, as White points out, given the age of the subjects, the results may not have direct bearing on adult L2 acquisition. The purpose of this research was to determine access to a principle that is not manifested in the NL. However, White correctly suggests that this principle may indeed be present in the NL via other structures. If this is the case, then it is not clear whether UG is directly available to L2 learners or whether it is available through the NL.

Schachter's research (1989, 1990) supports the view that UG principles are available only through the L1. She chose to investigate Subjacency (a constraint on syntactic movement) in the English NSs of Chinese, Dutch, Indonesian, and Korean. Indonesian allows *wh*-movement after the *wh*-word had been promoted to subject position within its own clause; thus, there is limited exposure to *wh*-

movement. Korean is a language without *wh*-movement because the *wh*-word remains *in situ*. Thus, NSs of Korean come to the English language-learning situation with no prior exposure to Subjacency. Chinese is like Korean in that there is no *wh*-movement. However, Chinese speakers have been exposed to Subjacency through other movement operations, although not in *wh*-movement. Dutch, on the other hand, is much like English in both movement and Subjacency. In testing these learners' knowledge of English Subjacency violations, Schachter used a test of grammaticality judgments. The Dutch learners performed similarly to NSs of English; Korean learners in general did not recognize Subjacency violations. Chinese and Indonesian learners fell in between the other two groups, doing better than the Koreans, but not as well as the Dutch learners. Thus, the results of Schachter's tests provide evidence that NL knowledge "has a significant effect on knowledge of one principle of Universal Grammar in post-puberty-acquired second language grammars" (1990, p. 116).

Yet another study that investigated Subjacency violations is that of Bley-Vroman, Felix, and Ioup (1988), in this case with Korean learners of English, and again using grammaticality judgments. The learners identified Subjacency violations at better than chance levels making it difficult to claim that learners do not have access to UG. One possibility, supported by subsequent research (Schachter and Yip, 1990) is that processing difficulty is indeed an important factor when ascribing an explanation to results. That is, the effects seen may have been due more to processing than to UG. This is further supported by comments by Bley-Vroman et al. (1988) when they questioned the learners' poor performance. Although learners did better than chance, they did not recognize Subjacency violations all of the time. A theory of UG is not a statistical theory, but an absolute theory, so that if learners recognize Subjacency violations some of the time, they should recognize them all of the time. (Additional discussion of these results and others on Subjacency in L2 acquisition are found in this volume, chapters 3 by White, 4 by Flynn, and 5 by Schachter.)

The Subset Principle (SP) has been the object of recent research that considers the accessibility to UG principles by L2 learners (Broselow & Finer, 1991; Eckman, 1994; Finer, 1991; Finer & Broselow, 1986; Hirakawa, 1990; Lakshmanan & Teranishi, 1994; Thomas, 1989, 1991). Given the inadequacy of positive evidence, the SP has been claimed to be necessary for the appropriate resetting of a variety of UG parameters (e.g., Governing Category Parameter [GCP], proper antecedent parameter, adjacency parameter). The SP constrains the choices of possible grammars that a learner can make. The basic claim is that learners (first or second) will initially choose a grammar generating the smallest language given the available evidence because one can move from the grammar for a subset language to that for a superset language through positive evidence. In the absence of negative evidence, it should not be possible to move from a grammar generating a superset language to one generating a subset language. Although it is not possible to review in detail all of the literature dealing with this principle, the general conclusion is that L2 learners do not use the SP as a guiding force in L2 grammar formation (cf. Hirakawa, 1990; Thomas, 1989; although see Berent, 1994, for alternative explanations of L2 data). (The SP in L2 acquisition is also discussed in this volume: chapters 2 by Gregg, 3 by White; chapters 14 by Berent and 18 by Seliger relate the SP to the acquisition of English by deaf learners and to L1 attrition, respectively. For a discussion of positive and negative evidence, see chapter 13 by Long.)

With specific reference to issues of NL, in an investigation of the GCP (a parameter that deals with the interpretation of reflexives), Lakshmanan and Teranishi (1994) found that some of their Japanese learners of English were correctly able to set their parameters to the English value (the subset), whereas others appeared to have transferred the Japanese value. Assuming that those who eventually succeeded in adopting the English value had at one time adopted the Japanese value, the question to be asked is, How did they move from a superset grammar to a subset grammar? Such movement (from a superset to a subset grammar) is not allowed if the SP is operative. Lakshmanan and Teranishi showed the importance of considering facts of both the NL and UG. In Japanese there are two forms of the reflexive, the common (and morphologically simple) *zibun* and the less common, morphologically complex *zibun-zisin* 'self-self', *kare-zisin* 'he-self', and *kanoji-zisin* 'she-self', *karera-zisin* 'they-self', and so forth. The morphologically simple form has a superset value, whereas the morphologically complex forms have a subset value. What Lakshmanan and Teranishi propose is that the learners make the association between the morphologically complex 'herself,' 'himself,' and so forth, and the morphologically complex Japanese forms, thereby assuming the subset value of English along with the associated subset value of Japanese. This is possible only at a sufficient point of English language knowledge, a point in which learners recognize the morphological complexity of herself, themselves, and so on. (For additional discussion of the interpretation of reflexives or the GCP see chapter 3 by White, and chapter 14 by Berent for acquisition of English by deaf learners.)

The general picture with regard to principles is that they are not available to L2 learners in an unadulterated form. The NL continues to exert major force, at times interacting with UG principles.

B. UG Parameters

The issue of the starting point is even more relevant to the question of parameters than to the issue of principles. Unlike principles, parameters are multivalued (usually only two values), often with "settings" or parametric values differing between the NL and the L2. To determine the role of the NL and its interaction with UG, one must consider not only the starting point, but also the end point. One possibility is that a learner begins with the L1 and initially adopts the L1 value for all parameters. There are two possibilities for the end point: (1) appropriate L2 values are learnable through the positive evidence of the L2, guided by knowledge of UG; (2) appropriate L2 values are not learnable unless they are available through surface facts of the L2. A second possibility is that a learner begins with UG and acquires the L2 much as a child does. In this case, there should be no effect of the L1 parameter value. As with the discussion of principles, the results are not totally satisfactory. In general, it does appear that the NL parametric values cannot be ignored and that access to UG, if it exists, is mediated by the NL. Below we consider one parameter with binary values and one with multivalues.

A number of studies have been conducted on the prodrop parameter, a parameter with two values that incorporates a clustering of properties (Hilles, 1986; Lakshmanan, 1991; Phinney, 1987; White, 1985b). There are varying positions that come out of this research. White argues that what is involved in L2 acquisition is resetting the parameters. However, she finds that not all aspects of what is traditionally subsumed under the rubric of prodrop parameters are learned at once. One could argue on this basis (as does Bley-Vroman, 1989, 1990) that this suggests that there are no parameters in L2 acquisition to be set. Furthermore, Meisel (1983) has shown that prodrop by Romance speakers in L2 German is not uniform across all persons, with it occurring more in third person than first. This cannot be accounted for solely on the basis of parameter setting. Phinney's results are particularly interesting because she compared Spanish speakers learning English and English speakers learning Spanish, finding that the former group had not reset their parameters to the English value, but the learners of Spanish had. If the L1 is the starting point, as it appears to be, and assuming some access to UG, why are the two groups asymmetrical? Asymmetry of this sort suggests that in addition to NL information, TL information and universal information, one must also consider issues of markedness. The results of Lakshmanan's study contradict the hypothesis of access to UG because in her data there appeared to be no clusterings of properties as would be predicted by a theory of UG. However, it is to be noted that Lakshmanan's data are based on child L2 learners, so we are left with the question of whether or not access is available to all L2 learners, both child and adult, or whether these two processes are fundamentally different. (For further discussion of the prodrop parameter in L2 acquisition, see this volume, chapter 3 by White.)

Not all parameters are binary. As discussed previously, the GCP, which deals with the interpretation of reflexives, is an example of a multivalued parameter. The earliest study on this topic was one by Finer and Broselow (1986) investigating the acquisition of English reflexives by Korean speakers, as in the following:

(8)   a. Mr. Fat believes that Mr. Thin will paint himself.
      b. Mr. Fat asked Mr. Thin to paint himself.

Learners did not transfer the NL parameter setting and at the same time did not adopt the English value. Rather, the learners adopted a value somewhere between the English and the Korean setting. These results were further supported by Thomas (1989), Broselow and Finer (1991), and Finer (1991). On the other hand, Hirakawa (1990) found that learners did adopt the Korean setting as a starting point. As mentioned earlier, the study by Lakshmanan and Teranishi (1994) suggests that even where it appears that the NL setting has not been adopted, closer scrutiny might reveal that unpredicted interlingual identifications are the source of the parameter setting.

C. The Centrality of the NL

Bley-Vroman (1989, 1990) and Schachter (1988) present another view of the role of UG and the NL in L2 learning. They both argue that child language and adult L2 acquisition are fundamentally different processes. With regard to the role the NL plays, Bley-Vroman is more specific. He claims that neither principles nor parameters are available to adults, but that the NL replaces principles of UG. (For further discussion of a closely related position, see chapter 5, this volume, by Schachter.) Adult language learning is guided by general problem-solving abilities rather than by domain-specific learning procedures (cf. also Clahsen, 1984; Clahsen & Muysken, 1986, 1989; Felix, 1985). Language-specific and language-universal features of the NL are gleaned by means of general problem-solving abilities, thus allowing for the kinds of decision-making abilities noted by Kellerman.

Bley-Vroman's view is an important challenge to current thinking and forces us to consider how we deal with counter-evidence to the kinds of clusterings predicted by a theory of parameter setting. For example, one can view parameter setting as an on–off phenomenon. In such a case one would predict that all aspects of a proposed setting should appear at once and are at least accessible in an experimental setting. On the other hand, it can be viewed as having a domino effect (cf. Macedo & d'Introno's 1988 discussion of a disjunctive–conjunctive framework). In this case, incomplete clusterings are not counterexamples and may be more appropriately considered as part of grammars in transition, or nonconformity grammars (Sharwood Smith, 1988). With this analysis, it is only a question of when subjects were sampled. At a later point in time one would predict that complete clusterings would be apparent; however, there are at least two alternatives. First, if we take the view that having learned one aspect of the grammar, a learner is then free to focus on other aspects, it may be that clustering of the domino type is only a result of time and attention and not due to any inherent relatedness of elements. A second alternative is that parameters are not a relevant construct in the domain of L2 acquisition. How one teases apart these possibilities is not obvious at present. However, it clearly must become part of the development of argumentation in our field.

V. LANGUAGE TRANSFER AND THE COMPETITION MODEL

Another framework within which transfer assumes a central role is the Competition Model. The basis for the Competition Model comes from work by Bates and MacWhinney (1981a, 1981b; Bates, McNew, MacWhinney, Devescovi, & Smith, 1982). Their model was developed to account for the ways monolingual speakers interpret sentences. A fundamental difference between this model and a UG model is that whereas the latter separates the form of language from its function, the Competition Model is based on the assumption that form and function cannot be separated. As in other psycholinguistic approaches to L2 acquisition, the Competition Model is concerned with how language is used (i.e., performance), as opposed to being concerned with a determination of the underlying structure of language (i.e., competence).

A major concept inherent in the Competition Model is that speakers must have a way to determine relationships among elements in a sentence. Language processing involves competition among various cues, each of which contributes to a different resolution in sentence interpretation. Although the range of cues is universal (that is, the limits on the kinds of cues one uses are universally imposed), there is language-specific instantiation of cues and language-specific strength assigned to cues. Bates et al. (1982) showed that there are different aspects of language to which NSs show a greater or lesser sensitivity. For example, Italian uses semantics as a basis for sentence interpretation, and English relies on syntax to determine grammatical relationships. For L2 acquisition, the question is, How does one "adjust" one's internal speech-processing mechanisms from NL-appropriate ones to ones appropriate for the TL? Does one use the same cues as are used in the NL, and are those cues "weighted" in the same way as they are in the NL?

In sentence interpretation, the initial hypothesis is consistent with interpretation in the NL. However, there may be universal tendencies towards the heavy use of particular cues.

A number of studies have been conducted using this paradigm. One of the findings is that a meaning-based comprehension strategy takes precedence over a grammar-based one. For example, English speakers learning Italian (Gass, 1987) and English speakers learning Japanese (a language which relies on the pragmatics of the situation for sentence interpretation) (Harrington, 1987; Kilborn and Ito, 1989; Sasaki, 1991) readily drop their strong use of word-order cues and adopt meaning-based cues as a major cue in interpreting Italian and Japanese sentences. On the other hand, Italian speakers learning English and Japanese speakers learning English maintain their NL meaning-based cues as primary, not readily adopting word order as a major interpretation cue.

Although the tendency of learners to adopt a meaning-based strategy as opposed to a grammar-based one is strong, there is also evidence that learners first look for correspondences in their NL as their initial hypothesis. Only when that appears to fail (i.e., when learners become aware of the apparent incongruity between L1 and L2 strategies) do they adopt what might be viewed as a universal prepotency: that of using meaning to interpret sentences.

Particularly relevant to this area of research is the finding that English learners of Japanese make use of rigid word order as a cue (in this case the subject-object-verb [SOV] word order of Japanese) even before they figure out how rigid Japanese word order is. In other words, English NSs assume rigid word order as the first hypothesis. Their first task is to figure out what that word order is. Once they figure out that Japanese has SOV order, they *rigidly* apply the new word order. This is supported by data from learners of English who were asked to differentiate between sentences such as (9) and (10) in terms of identifying the appropriate subject of the second verb (Gass, 1986).

(9) The man told the boy to go.
(10) The man promised the boy to go.

The data showed that learners first learned that English is a rigid word-order language before learning what the appropriate word order is.

In sum, the research conducted within the Competition Model suggests that learners are indeed faced with conflicts between NL and TL cues and cue strengths. The resolution of these conflicts is such that learners first resort to their NL interpretation strategies and upon recognition of the incongruity between TL and NL systems, resort to a universal selection of meaning-based cues as opposed to word order (or syntax-based) cues. What then is involved in L2 processing, at least with regard to comprehension, is a readjustment of which cues will be relevant to interpretation and a determination of the relative strength of those cues. What is not known is how learners recognize which NL cues lead to the wrong interpretation and which cues lead to the correct interpretation. In fact, Bates and MacWhinney (1981b) noted that an L2 learner, even after 25 years of living in the TL country, still did not respond to sentence interpretation tasks in the same way as NSs of the TL.

VI. EFFECTS ON GRAMMARS

Since the days of Contrastive Analysis, it has always been clear that the NL acts in consort with other language factors. For example, Selinker and Lakshmanan (1992) integrated the NL with learning plateaus, or fossilization. They established the Multiple Effects Principle:

When two or more SLA factors work in tandem, there is a greater chance of stabilization of interlanguage forms leading to possible fossilization. (p. 198)

They go on to discuss possible L2 acquisition (SLA) factors claiming that language transfer is either a *privileged* or a *necessary* cofactor in this process. An example of multiple effects is the well-known phenomenon of adverb placement or violations of adjacency, where, for example, learners of English whose NL allows the interruption of verb and direct object sequences are frequently known to produce utterances such as

(11) I like very much ice cream.

Selinker and Lakshmanan argue that there are at least three factors that can be identified: (1) language transfer, (2) nonoperation of the SP, and (3) inappropriate interpretation of TL facts. Importantly, for our purposes, the presence of language transfer is crucial in the prediction of plateaus as a result of multiple effects. (Chapter 3, this volume, by White also includes discussion of the L2 English structure in which an adverbial intervenes between a verb and its direct object.)

One final point to mention is one alluded to in footnote 2 of this chapter. When speaking of NL influences, we are using the term *native language* loosely. A more apt term is cross-linguistic influence (see section II.A) or even language transfer, because other languages may influence what happens in the learning of a second, third, and so on language. As an example, Zobl (1992) compares learners who only know their NL (unilinguals) with those who know their NL and other language(s) (multilinguals). He notes that adults create what he calls wider grammars than the L2 input would warrant. What is meant by this? He means simply that transfer from the NL leads learners to produce sentences that are possible in their L1 but not in their L2. If we can agree that adult L2 learners formulate what he calls wider grammars than the input data would warrant due to the well-established phenomenon of language transfer, then we can also see that the more languages that an individual has to draw on, the greater the possibilities will be that their grammars will be even wider.

There are two pieces of evidence that Zobl uses to differentiate multilingual from unilingual L2 learners. One is anecdotal, the other empirical. First, the anecdotal: Zobl refers to reports that multilinguals generally pick up languages with greater ease than do unilinguals. Assuming that this is true, how can this be accounted for? One way is to claim that multilinguals are less conservative in their learning procedures and hence progress at a faster pace. That is, the hypotheses they formulate on the basis of the input are likely to be more liberal and based upon more slender evidence.

Zobl's empirical evidence for his claim comes from multilinguals' and unilinguals' performance on a cloze test and on a grammaticality judgment test. The results were not as clear-cut as Zobl would have liked; however, they do lend some support to the notion that unilinguals and multilinguals formulate different hypotheses on the basis of what is presumably the same input, thereby supporting the notion that prior linguistic knowledge (broadly speaking) is crucial in the formation of L2 grammars. His data support the view that multilinguals recognize the ungrammaticality of sentences less frequently than the unilinguals (in this case violations of adjacency). That is, their grammars appear to be less conservative than the unilinguals' grammars. These findings are important for understanding how L2 grammars come to be, but also for understanding what is necessary to destabilize incorrect forms. In other words, what type of evidence is necessary for a learner to recognize that these are indeed ungrammatical sentences in English? It is clear that both groups of Zobl's learners need negative evidence, but there will be differences between the two groups in how they will respond to the input. That is (and this may depend on the languages the learners know), there may be more converging information that leads multilinguals to believe that ungrammatical adjacency violations are grammatical than there is for unilinguals. It would therefore take at least more frequent and direct negative evidence to disabuse multilinguals of their faulty hypotheses.

VII. CONCLUSION

In this chapter I have dealt with the role of the NL within the framework of theoretical models. The question arises: What new insight do recent linguistic approaches and, in particular, theoretical paradigms provide regarding the old concept of transfer? That is, is current research anything more than chewed over Contrastive Analysis?

White (1992) provided detail on this issue. She noted four areas that make current views of the phenomenon of transfer truly different from earlier conceptualizations, particularly those embodied in the framework of Contrastive Analysis. I deal with three of these areas here: (1) levels of representation, (2) clustering of properties, and (3) learnability.

The first way in which UG accounts for the role of the NL relates to levels of representation in linguistic theory. Within a theory of UG, our knowledge of syntax is best represented by positing different levels of grammatical structure. If sentences have multiple levels of representation, one can imagine that transfer can occur not just on the basis of surface facts, but also on the basis of underlying structures.

The second point of difference is in the area of clustering. Within a theory that claims that learning involves setting or resetting of parameters, there are properties that cluster together within a parameter. One is concerned with how multiple properties of language do or do not behave in a like fashion. Furthermore, there is evidence that mixed values are adopted for multivalued parameters and continuous linguistic features (see Gass, 1984b, for examples.) Within earlier approaches to transfer (particularly a contrastive analysis approach), there was no way to show how related structures were linked in the mind of L2 learners. The picture, however, may be more complex, because the research agenda is to determine whether learners relate structures that are said to be related by the theoretical model on which the descriptions are based. In fact, Gass and Ard (1984) and Eckman (1992) argued that not all language universals will equally affect the formation of L2 grammars. Gass and Ard argued that one must look at the underlying source of the universal and understand why structures are related to determine whether they will or will not affect L2 acquisition, whereas Eckman made the claim that universals must involve the "same" structure (e.g., relative clauses, question formation) before they will have an effect on the development of L2 grammars. Nonetheless, a model that involves structural relatedness clearly represents an innovative approach to language transfer.

The third issue is the central one when dealing with UG—that of learnability. White reminds us that a UG perspective on L2 acquisition is heavily dependent on arguments from learnability. In particular, the issue of positive evidence is central because learners construct grammars on the basis of the input (the positive evidence to which the learner is exposed), the NL, and knowledge of UG. As was discussed earlier, the nature of the input necessary for the learner is different depending on the superset and subset relationship of the two languages in question. Where positive evidence is readily available, allowing a learner to reset a parameter, little transfer is predicted. When, on the other hand, positive evidence will not suffice to provide learners with sufficient information about the L2, possibly necessitating negative evidence, transfer is predicted. Transfer, as it was earlier conceptualized, has clearly not dealt with the learnability and types of evidence issues with which UG is centrally concerned.

Despite its somewhat unusual history, the NL has always dominated any research paradigm in L2 acquisition. Whether the basis of a total theory of L2 acquisition (Contrastive Analysis) or the object of rejection (Creative Construction), researchers in the field of L2 acquisition have always had to come to grips with the specter of the NL. In recent years and in future research, the main task facing those interested in the NL is the determination of how the NL interacts with the

TL input, how it interacts with UG or other models of universals, and to what extent it guides learners in the development of L2 grammars.

REFERENCES

Adjémian, C. (1983). The transferability of lexical properties. In S. Gass & L. Selinker (Eds.), *Language transfer in language learning*. Rowley, MA: Newbury House.

Andersen, R. (1983). Transfer to somewhere. In S. Gass & L. Selinker (Eds.), *Language transfer in language learning*. Rowley, MA: Newbury House.

Ard, J., & Homburg, T. (1983). Verification of language transfer. In S. Gass & L. Selinker (Eds.), *Language transfer in language learning*. Rowley, MA: Newbury House.

Ard, J., & Homburg, T. (1992). Verification of language transfer. In S. Gass & L. Selinker (Eds.), *Language transfer in language learning*. Amsterdam: John Benjamins.

Bailey, N., Madden, C., & Krashen, S. (1974). Is there a 'natural sequence' in adult second language learning? *Language Learning, 24,* 235–243.

Bates, E., & MacWhinney, B. (1981a). Functionalist approaches to grammar. In E. Wanner & L. Gleitman (Eds.), *Language acquisition: The state of the art.* New York: Cambridge University Press.

Bates, E., & MacWhinney, B. (1981b). Second language acquisition from a functionalist perspective: Pragmatics, semantics and perceptual strategies. In H. Winitz (Ed.), *Annals of New York Academy of Sciences Conference on Native Language and Foreign Language Acquisition.* New York: New York Academy of Sciences.

Bates, E., McNew, S., MacWhinney, B., Devescovi, A., & Smith, S. (1982). Functional constraints on sentence-processing: A cross-linguistic study. *Cognition, 11,* 245–299.

Beebe, L. (1980). Sociolinguistic variation and style shifting in second language acquisition. *Language Learning, 30,* 433–448.

Berent, G. (1994). The subset principle in second language acquisition. In E. Tarone, S. Gass, & A. Cohen (Eds.), *Research methodology in second language acquisition.* Hillsdale, NJ: Erlbaum.

Bley-Vroman, R. (1989). What is the logical problem of foreign language learning. In S. Gass & J. Schachter (Eds.), *Linguistic perspectives on second language acquisition.* Cambridge, UK: Cambridge University Press.

Bley-Vroman, R. (1990). The logical problem of foreign language learning. *Linguistic Analysis, 20*(1–2), 3–49.

Bley-Vroman, R., Felix, S., & Ioup, G. (1988). The accessibility of Universal Grammar in adult language learning. *Second Language Research, 4,* 1–32.

Brière, E. (1966). An investigation of phonological interference. *Language, 42,* 768–798.

Broselow, E. (1983). Non-obvious transfer: On predicting epenthesis errors. In S. Gass & L. Selinker (Eds.), *Language transfer in language learning*. Rowley, MA: Newbury House.

Broselow, E. (1992). Non-obvious transfer: On predicting epenthesis errors. In S. Gass & L. Selinker (Eds.), *Language transfer in language learning*. Amsterdam: John Benjamins.

Broselow, E., & Finer, D. (1991). Parameter setting in second language phonology and syntax. *Second Language Research, 7,* 35–59.

Brown, R. (1973). *A First Language*. Cambridge, MA: Harvard University Press.

Clahsen, H. (1984). The acquisition of German word order: A test case for cognitive approaches to L2 development. In R. Andersen (Ed.), *Second languages: A cross-linguistic perspective*. Rowley, MA: Newbury House.

Clahsen, H., & Muysken, P. (1986). The availability of Universal Grammar to adult and child learners: A study of the acquisition of German word order. *Second Language Research, 2*, 93–119.

Clahsen, H., & Muysken, P. (1989). The UG paradox in L2 acquisition. *Second Language Research, 5*, 1–29.

Corder, S. P. (1981). *Error analysis and interlanguage*. Oxford: Oxford University Press.

Corder, S. P. (1983). A role for the mother tongue. In S. Gass & L. Selinker (Eds.), *Language transfer in language learning*. Rowley, MA: Newbury House.

Corder, S. P. (1992). A role for the mother tongue. In S. Gass & L. Selinker (Eds.), *Language transfer in language learning*. Amsterdam: John Benjamins.

Dulay, H., & Burt, M. (1974a). Natural sequences in child second language acquisition. *Language Learning, 24*, 37–53.

Dulay, H., & Burt, M. (1974b). A new perspective on the creative construction processes in child second language acquisition. *Language Learning, 24*, 253–278.

Duškova, L. (1984). Similarity—an aid or hindrance in foreign language learning? *Folia Linguistica, 18*, 103–115.

Eckman, F. (1977). Markedness and the contrastive analysis hypothesis. *Language Learning, 27*(2), 315–330.

Eckman, F. (1981). On the naturalness of interlanguage phonological rules. *Language Learning, 31*, 195–216.

Eckman, F. (1984). Universals, typologies and interlanguage. In W. Rutherford (Ed.), *Language universals and second language acquisition*. Amsterdam: John Benjamins.

Eckman, F. (1992, April). *Second languages or second-language acquisition? A linguistic approach*. Paper presented at the Second Language Research Forum, Michigan State University, East Lansing.

Eckman, F. (1994). Local and long-distance anaphora in second language acquisition. In E. Tarone, S. Gass, & A. Cohen (Eds.), *Research methodology in second language acquisition*. Hillsdale, NJ: Erlbaum.

Felix, S. (1985). More evidence on competing cognitive systems. *Second Language Research, 1*, 47–72.

Finer, D. (1991). Binding parameters in second language acquisition. In L. Eubank (Ed.), *Point/counterpoint: Universal Grammar in the second language*. Amsterdam: John Benjamins.

Finer, D., & Broselow, E. (1986). Second language acquisition of reflexive binding. *Proceedings of the North Eastern Linguistic Society, 16*, 154–168.

Fisiak, J. (Ed.). (1980). *Theoretical issues in contrastive linguistics*. Amsterdam: John Benjamins.

Fisiak, J. (1991). *Contrastive linguistics and language acquisition*. Paper presented at the Regional Language Center (RELC) Conference: Language Acquisition and the Second/Foreign Language Classroom, Singapore.

Flege, J. (1980). Phonetic approximation in second language acquisition. *Language Learning, 30*, 117–134.

Flege, J., & Davidian, R. (1984). Transfer and developmental processes in adult foreign language speech production. *Applied Psycholinguistics, 5*(4), 323–347.

Flynn, S. (1983). *A study of the effects of principal branching direction in second language acquisition: The generalization of a parameter of universal grammar from first to second language acquisition.* Doctoral thesis, Cornell University, Ithaca, NY.

Flynn, S. (1985). Principled theories of L2 acquisition. *Studies in Second Language Acquisition, 7*(1), 99–107.

Flynn, S. (1986). Acquisition of pronoun anaphora: Resetting the parameter. In B. Lust (Ed.), *Studies in the acquisition of anaphora: Defining the parameters.* Dordrecht: Reidel.

Fourakis, M., & Iverson, G. (1985). On the acquisition of second language timing patterns. *Language Learning, 35,* 431–442.

Fries, C. (1945). *Teaching and learning English as a foreign language.* Ann Arbor: University of Michigan Press.

Gass, S. (1979). Language transfer and universal grammatical relations. *Language Learning, 29*(2), 327–344.

Gass, S. (1980). An investigation of syntactic transfer in adult second language learners. In R. Scarcella & S. Krashen (Eds.), *Research in second language acquisition.* Rowley, MA: Newbury House.

Gass, S. (1984a). Development of speech perception and speech production abilities in adult second language learners. *Applied Psycholinguistics, 5*(1), 51–74.

Gass, S. (1984b). A review of interlanguage syntax: Language transfer and language universals. *Language Learning, 34*(2), 115–132.

Gass, S. (1986). An interactionist approach to L2 sentence interpretation. *Studies in Second Language Acquisition, 8*(1), 19–37.

Gass, S. (1987). The resolution of conflicts among competing systems: A bidirectional perspective. *Applied Psycholinguistics, 8*(4), 329–350.

Gass, S. (1988). Integrating research areas: A framework for second language studies. *Applied Linguistics, 9*(1), 198–217.

Gass, S., & Ard, J. (1984). Second language acquisition and the ontology of language universals. In W. Rutherford (Ed.), *Language universals and second language acquisition.* Amsterdam: John Benjamins.

Gass, S., & Selinker, L. (Eds.). (1983). *Language transfer in language learning.* Rowley, MA: Newbury House.

Gass, S., & Selinker, L. (Eds.). (1992). *Language transfer in language learning.* Amsterdam: John Benjamins.

Gilbert, G., & Orlovic, M. (1975). Pidgin German spoken by foreign workers in West Germany: The definite article. Paper presented at the International Congress on Pidgins and Creoles, January. Hawaii: Honolulu.

Hammerberg, B. (1979). On intralingual, interlingual and developmental solutions in interlanguage. In K. Hyltenstam & B. Linnarud (Eds.), *Interlanguage.* Stockholm: Almqvist & Wiksell.

Harrington, M. (1987). Processing transfer: Language-specific strategies as a source of interlanguage variation. *Applied Psycholinguistics, 8,* 351–378.

Hernandez-Chavez, E. (1977) *The acquisition of grammatical structures by a Mexican-American child.* Doctoral thesis, University of California, Berkeley.

Hilles, S. (1986). Interlanguage and the pro-drop parameter. *Second Language Research, 2,* 33–52.

Hirakawa, M. (1990). A study of the L2 acquisition of English reflexives. *Second Language Research, 6,* 60–85.

Huang, J. (1971). *A Chinese child's acquisition of English syntax.* Master's thesis, University of California at Los Angeles.

Hyltenstam, K. (1977). Implicational patterns in interlanguage syntax variation. *Language Learning, 27,* 383–411.

Jordens, P. (1977). Rules, grammatical intuitions and strategies in foreign language learning. *Interlanguage Studies Bulletin, 2,* 5–76.

Keller-Cohen, D. (1979). Systematicity and variation in the non-native child's acquisition of conversational skills. *Language Learning, 29,* 27–44.

Kellerman, E. (1979). Transfer and non-transfer: Where we are now. *Studies in Second Language Acquisition, 2,* 37–57.

Kellerman, E. (1983). Now you see it, now you don't. In S. Gass & L. Selinker (Eds.), *Language transfer in language learning.* Rowley, MA: Newbury House.

Kellerman, E. (1984). The empirical evidence for the influence of the L1 in interlanguage. In A. Davis, C. Criper, & A. Howatt (Eds.), *Interlanguage.* Edinburgh: University of Edinburgh Press.

Kellerman, E., & Sharwood Smith, M. (Eds.). (1986). *Crosslinguistic influence in second language acquisition.* Oxford: Pergamon Press.

Kelly, L. (1976). *25 centuries of language teaching.* Rowley, MA: Newbury House.

Kilborn, K., & Ito, T. (1989). Sentence processing strategies in adult bilinguals. In B. MacWhinney & E. Bates (Eds.), *The linguistic study of sentence processing.* Cambridge, UK: Cambridge University Press.

Lado, R. (1957). *Linguistics across cultures.* Ann Arbor: University of Michigan Press.

Lakshmanan, U. (1991). Morphological uniformity and null subjects in child second language acquisition. In E. Eubank (Ed.), *Point/counterpoint: Universal Grammar in the second language.* Amsterdam: John Benjamins.

Lakshmanan, U., & Teranishi, K. (1994). Preferences vs. grammaticality judgments: Some methodological issues concerning the Governing Category Parameter. In E. Tarone, S. Gass, & A. Cohen (Eds.), *Research methodology in second language acquisition.* Hillsdale, NJ: Erlbaum.

Liceras, J. (1983). *Markedness, contrastive analysis and the acquisition of Spanish syntax by English speakers.* Doctoral thesis, University of Toronto.

Macedo, D., & D'Introno, F. (1988). Pidginization as language acquisition. In S. Flynn & W. O'Neil (Eds.), *Linguistic theory in second language acquisition.* Dordrecht: Kluwer.

Macken, M., & Barton, D. (1977). A longitudinal study of the acquisition of the voicing contrast in American English word initial stops, as measured by VOT. *Papers and Reports on Child Language Development, 14,* 74–121.

Meisel, J. (1983). Strategies of second language acquisition: More than one kind of simplification. In R. Andersen (Ed.), *Pidginization and creolization as language acquisition.* Rowley, MA: Newbury House.

Obler, L. (1982). The parsimonious bilingual. In L. Obler & L. Menn (Eds.), *Exceptional language and linguistics.* New York: Academic Press.

Odlin, T. (1989). *Language transfer: Cross-linguistic influence in language learning.* Cambridge, UK: Cambridge University Press.

Otsu, Y., & Naoi, K. (1986). Structure-dependence in L2 acquisition. In Japanese Association of College English Teachers, Tokyo: Keio University.

Peters, A. (1977). Language learning strategies. *Language, 53*(3), 560–573.

Peters, A. (1983). *The units of language acquisition.* Cambridge, UK: Cambridge University Press.

Phinney, M. (1987). The pro-drop parameter in second language acquisition. In T. Roeper & E. Williams (Eds.), *Parameter setting.* Dordrecht: Reidel.

Richards, J. (1971). A non-contrastive approach to error analysis. *English Language Teaching Journal, 25*(3), 204–219.

Ringbom, H. (1987). *The role of the first language in foreign language learning.* Clevedon, UK: Multilingual Matters.

Ritchie, W. (1978). The right roof constraint in adult-acquired language. In W. Ritchie (Ed.), *Second language acquisition research: Issues and implications.* New York: Academic Press.

Ritchie, W. (1983). Universal Grammar and second language acquisition. In D. Rogers & J. Sloboda (Eds.), *The acquisition of symbolic skills.* New York: Plenum Press.

Rutherford, W. (1983). Language typology and language transfer. In S. Gass & L. Selinker (Eds.), *Language transfer in language learning.* Rowley, MA: Newbury House.

Sasaki, Y. (1991). English and Japanese comprehension strategies: An analysis based on the competition model. *Applied Psycholinguistics, 12*(1), 47–73.

Schachter, J. (1974). An error in error analysis. *Language Learning, 24,* 205–214.

Schachter, J. (1983). A new account of language transfer. In S. Gass & L. Selinker (Eds.), *Language transfer in language learning.* Rowley, MA: Newbury House.

Schachter, J. (1988). Second language acquisition and its relationship to Universal Grammar. *Applied Linguistics, 9,* 219–235.

Schachter, J. (1989). Testing a proposed universal. In S. Gass & J. Schachter (Eds.), *Linguistic perspectives on second language acquisition.* Cambridge, UK: Cambridge University Press.

Schachter, J. (1990). On the issue of completeness in second language acquisition. *Second Language Research, 6,* 93–124.

Schachter, J. (1992). A new account of language transfer. In S. Gass & L. Selinker (Eds.), *Language transfer.* Amsterdam: John Benjamins.

Schachter, J., & Rutherford, W. (1978). Discourse function and language transfer. *Working Papers in Bilingualism, 19,* 1–12.

Schachter, J., & Yip, V. (1990). Grammaticality judgments: Why does anyone object to subject extraction? *Studies in Second Language Acquisition, 12*(4), 379–392.

Schmidt, R. (1990). The role of consciousness in second language learning. *Applied Linguistics, 11,* 127–158.

Schumann, J. (1976). Second language acquisition: The pidginization hypothesis. *Language Learning, 26,* 391–408.

Schumann, J. (1982). Simplification, transfer and relexification as aspects of pidginization and early second language acquisition. *Language Learning, 32,* 337–366.

Selinker, L. (1969). Language transfer. *General Linguistics, 9,* 67–92.

Selinker, L., & Lakshmanan, U. (1992). Language transfer and fossilization: The 'multiple effects principle.' In S. Gass & L. Selinker (Eds.), *Language transfer in language learning.* Amsterdam: John Benjamins.

Sharwood Smith, M. (1988). On the role of linguistic theory in explanations of second language developmental grammars. In S. Flynn & W. O'Neil (Eds.), *Linguistic theory in second language acquisition.* Amsterdam: John Benjamins.

Sheldon, A., & Strange, W. (1982). The acquisition of /r/ and /l/ by Japanese learners of English: Evidence that the speech production can precede speech perception. *Applied Linguistics, 3,* 243–261.

Simon, C. (1978). Stop voicing in English and French monolinguals: Some developmental issues and experimental results. Paper presented at NICHD Conference on Child Phonology, May. MD: Bethesda.

Thomas, M. (1989). The interpretation of English reflexive pronouns by non-native speakers. *Studies in Second Language Acquisition, 11,* 219–235.

Thomas, M. (1991). Universal Grammar and the interpretation of reflexives in a second language. *Language, 67,* 211–239.

van Buren, P., & Sharwood Smith, M. (1985). The acquisition of preposition stranding by second language learners and parametric variation. *Second Language Research, 1*(1), 18–46.

van Helmond, K., & van Vugt, M. (1984). On the transferability of nominal compounds. *Interlanguage Studies Bulletin, 8*(2), 5–34.

White, L. (1985a). The acquisition of parameterized grammars: Subjacency in second language acquisition. *Second Language Research, 1*(1), 1–17.

White, L. (1985b). The 'pro-drop' parameter in adult second language acquisition. *Language Learning, 35*(1), 47–61.

White, L. (1989). *Universal Grammar and second language acquisition.* Amsterdam: John Benjamins.

White, L. (1992). Universal Grammar: Is it just a new name for old problems? In S. Gass & L. Selinker (Eds.), *Language transfer in language learning.* Amsterdam: John Benjamins.

Wode, H. (1977). On the systematicity of L1 transfer in L2 acquisition. In C. Henning (Ed.), *Second Language Research Forum.* Los Angeles: University of California.

Wode, H. (1984). Some theoretical implications of L2 acquisition research and the grammar of interlanguages. In A. Davies, C. Criper, & A. Howatt (Eds.), *Interlanguage.* Edinburgh: University of Edinburgh.

Zobl, H. (1980a). Developmental and transfer errors: Their common bases and (possibly) differential effects on subsequent learning. *TESOL Quarterly, 14,* 469–482.

Zobl, H. (1980b). The formal and developmental selectivity of L1 influence on L2 acquisition. *Language Learning, 30,* 43–58.

Zobl, H. (1982). A direction for contrastive analysis: The comparative study of developmental sequences. *TESOL Quarterly, 16,* 169–183.

Zobl, H. (1984). Aspects of reference and the pronominal syntax preference in the speech of young child L2 learners. In R. Andersen (Ed.), *Second languages: A cross-linguistic perspective.* Rowley, MA: Newbury House.

Zobl, H. (1992). Prior linguistic knowledge and the conservation of the learning procedure: Grammaticality judgments of unilingual and multilingual learners. In S. Gass & L. Selinker (Eds.), *Language transfer in language learning.* Amsterdam: John Benjamins.

PART IV

RESEARCH METHODOLOGY AND APPLICATIONS

CHAPTER 11

ISSUES IN SECOND LANGUAGE ACQUISITION RESEARCH: EXAMINING SUBSTANCE AND PROCEDURE

David Nunan

I. INTRODUCTION

This chapter addresses substantive and methodological issues in second language (L2) research. It is intended as an introductory state-of-the-art survey, not only for students and researchers whose primary focus is language acquisition, but also for those whose primary interest is in areas other than L2 acquisition.

The chapter begins by tracing the historical background to research in L2 acquisition. This is followed by a critical review of selected studies in the field. Although the primary focus is on methodological issues, it will become apparent that one cannot easily separate research methodology from substantive issues. This is because the questions being addressed by the researcher should determine how data are to be collected and analyzed. (For additional discussion in this volume of issues in research methodology in the study of L2 acquisition, see chapters 4 by Flynn and 12 by Sorace.)

II. HISTORICAL BACKGROUND

L2 acquisition research is concerned with investigating the processes and stages that learners undergo in acquiring L2s and subsequent languages. The research

349

Handbook of Second Language Acquisition

can be concerned with acquisition in naturalistic environments (that is, where the learner is attempting to acquire the language without formal instruction), acquisition in tutored environments, and acquisition in mixed environments. The ultimate aim of the research is to relate the processes of acquisition with products or outcomes, that is, with what learners are able to do at different stages in their progress towards native or near-native mastery. (See chapter 2 by Gregg, this volume, for another discussion of the aims of L2 acquisition research.)

The field of L2 acquisition was largely created from a line of inquiry known as contrastive analysis. The central question investigated by contrastive analysis was, What is the role of the first language (L1) in the acquisition of an L2 or subsequent language? (Chapters 6 by Eckman and 10 by Gass, this volume, also discuss the place of contrastive analysis in the history of L2 acquisition.)

In the early stages of the development of L2 acquisition as a field of research, it was believed that the development of an L2 was strongly influenced by the learner's L1. This belief was enshrined in the "contrastive hypothesis." This hypothesis predicts that where L1 and L2 rules are in conflict, then errors are likely to occur, these errors being the result of interference between the L1 and L2. According to this hypothesis, Spanish L1 learners will tend, when learning English, to place the adjective after the noun, rather than before it, as this is the way it is done in Spanish. Such an error is the result of *negative transfer* of the L1 rule to the L2. When the rules are similar for both languages, *positive transfer* will occur and language learning will be facilitated. Where a target language (TL) feature does not exist in the L1, learning will also be impeded. Such is the case for English L1 learners trying to master the use of nominal classifiers in certain Asian languages such as Thai. (For a general discussion of the contrastive hypothesis, see Nunan, 1991a.)

The names most closely associated with contrastive analysis are Charles Fries and Robert Lado. Fries's motive was basically pedagogical in nature. He was concerned with the development of teaching materials and believed that

> the most efficient materials are those that are based upon a scientific description
> of the language to be learned, carefully compared with a parallel description of
> the native language of the learner. (Fries, 1945, p. 9)

Lado (1957) carried Fries's early work even further, and materials were developed for a range of languages that were based on a detailed contrastive analysis of the L1 and TL.

III. SUBSTANTIVE ISSUES IN L2 ACQUISITION RESEARCH

In this section I shall focus on some key substantive issues that have preoccupied L2 acquisition researchers along with some of the methods used in investigating those questions. The discussion begins with a review of a series of studies that questioned the assumptions of the contrastive analysts. This is then followed by a review of some key questions in L2 acquisition.

A. Creative Construction

During the early 1970s, some empirical investigations, known as the morpheme-order studies, were carried out that had the effect of calling into question the contrastive hypothesis. (The creative construction hypothesis is also discussed in chapter 10, this volume, by Gass.) These studies appeared to indicate that learners from widely divergent L1 backgrounds, learning English as a Second Language (ESL), appeared to acquire grammatical morphemes in virtually the same order (Dulay & Burt, 1973, 1974a, 1974b). The researchers concluded that a universal order of acquisition existed, and that this was based on an innate learning process in which the role of the L1 was minimal. In particular, it was argued that:

1. There appear to be innate, subconscious processes that guide L2 acquisition.
2. Exposure to natural communication in the TL is necessary for the subconscious processes to work well. The richer the learner's exposure to the TL the more rapid and comprehensive learning is likely to be.
3. The learner needs to comprehend the content of natural communication in the new language.
4. A silent phase at the beginning of language learning (when the learner does not produce the new language) is observed in most learners who then exhibit fewer interlingual errors and better pronunciation when they do begin production.
5. The learner's motives, emotions, and attitudes screen what is presented in the language classroom, or outside it.
6. The influence of the learner's L1 is negligible on grammar (for detailed treatment, see Dulay, Burt, & Krashen, 1982).

Methodologically, these studies received a great deal of criticism, and there were other studies published simultaneously and later that accorded a much greater role to L1 interference (see, for example, Odlin, 1989). Some of these studies are set out in Table I, which is taken from Ellis (1985).

It is now generally accepted that the L1 has a greater influence on the acquisition of an L2 than was allowed for by the morpheme-order studies (see, for example, Odlin, 1989). For an interesting and readable reevaluation of contrastive analysis and a detailed discussion of language transfer, see Selinker (1992).

B. Other Issues

In the rest of this section, I wish to review some of the questions that have preoccupied L2 acquisition researchers since the emergence of the morpheme-

TABLE I

**Percentage of Interference Errors Reported by
Various Studies of L2 English Acquisition**

Study	Interference errors (%)	Type of learner
Grauberg (1971)	36	L1 German, adult, advanced
George (1972)	~33	Mixed L1s, adult, graduate
Dulay and Burt (1973)	3	L1 Spanish, children, mixed level
Tran-Chi-Chau (1975)	51	L1 Chinese, adult, mixed level
Mukattash (1977)	23	L1 Arabic, adult
Flick (1980)	31	L1 Spanish, adult, mixed level
Lott (1983)	~50	L1 Italian, adult, university

order studies in the 1970s and the methods that have been used in the investigation of these questions.

Is There a Distinction between Conscious Learning and Subconscious Acquisition?

In some ways, the most controversial of the claims growing out of the morpheme-order studies is related to the proposed distinction between learning—a conscious process—and acquisition—a subconscious process. Krashen (1981, 1982), whose name is most closely associated with this distinction, based his claim on the observation that consciously learned grammar does not appear directly in the communicative repertoire of the learner but acts only as a self-monitor. Krashen claims that this lack of relationship between learning and use can be accounted for in terms of two separate mental systems.

> Learning does not "turn into" acquisition. The idea that we first learn a new rule (consciously), and eventually, through practice, acquire it (subconsciously), is widespread and may seem to some people intuitively obvious. (Krashen, 1982, p. 83)

This supposed distinction between learning and acquisition has been widely criticized since it first appeared (see, for example, Gregg, 1984). Although it retains a certain attraction for some practitioners, it no longer generates much excitement amongst researchers.

Rather than being directly investigated, the conscious learning–subconscious acquisition distinction, was inferred from investigations into L2 development. Researchers collected samples of learner language and compared the morphosyntactic structures that learners used with the frequency and order in which structures were presented in the instructional context. It was the observed mismatch between instruction and use that led certain researchers to propose the learning–acquisition distinction. However, most of the learner data were collected through elicitation devices of one sort or another, and this led to criticisms that observed acquisition orders might be artifacts of the elicitation devices themselves. (This issue is dealt with in greater detail later in the chapter with reference to one of the most widely used elicitation instruments, the Bilingual Syntax Measure.)

Is Learning an L2 like Learning an L1?

Another question that preoccupied researchers for a time related to the issue of whether or not psycholinguistic mechanisms in L2 acquisition were basically the same as or different from those in L1 acquisition (see, for example, Ervin-Tripp, 1974). In relation to the acquisition of grammatical morphemes, Dulay and Burt (1974a, 1974b) began with the premise that L1 and L2 acquisition in children were the same process, and that the kinds of errors made by an L2 learner would be the same as those made by an L1 learner of the same language. (See also chapters 2–5 by Gregg, White, Flynn, and Schachter, this volume, for discussions of this issue.) However, as a result of their research, they concluded:

> We can no longer hypothesize similarities between L2 and L1 acquisition as we did at the outset of our investigations. Although both the L2 and L1 learner reconstruct the language they are learning, it is intuitive to expect that the manner in which they do so will differ. Children learning a second language are usually older than L1 learners; they are further along in their cognitive development, and they have experienced a language once before. These factors should combine to make the specific strategies of the creative construction process in L2 acquisition somewhat different for those of the creative construction process in L1 acquisition. (Dulay & Burt, 1974b, p. 225)

Turning from syntax to discourse, Nunan (1984), investigated the discourse-processing operations of L1 and L2 learners. He looked in particular at the perception of semantic and discoursal relationships in written texts, and found a high level of agreement between L1 and L2 readers. Although the L2 readers had greater overall difficulty with the texts than the L1 readers, in relative terms, those relationships that L1 readers found difficult were also found to be problematic for L2 readers, and those that the L1 readers found easy, were also found to be easy by the L2 readers.

Similarities and differences between L1 and L2 acquisition have most often been inferred from comparative studies into language processing and production by L1 and L2 users. Such studies are generally experimental or quasi-experimental in nature, and also usually employ some sort of elicitation device. For example, the study by Nunan (1984) elicited data from L1 and L2 readers through a modified cloze procedure. The problem with elicitation devices, and particularly with forced production tasks, is that one can never be entirely certain that the results obtained have not been determined, at least in part, by the elicitation devices and instruments themselves (for a discussion, see Nunan, 1992).

What Is the Role of Chronological Age in the Acquisition of an L2?

The effect of age on acquisition has been extensively documented, although research to date has not conclusively settled the issue of age one way or another (Scovel, 1988). As Ellis (1985), points out, it is necessary to distinguish between the effect of age on the route of acquisition and the rate and ultimate attainment. Ellis concludes from his review of the available literature that although age does not alter the route of acquisition, it does have a marked effect on the rate and ultimate success. However, the results are by no means straightforward. For example, in terms of rate, adults appear to do better than children (6–10 years), and teenagers (12–15 years) appear to outperform both adults and children. Ellis concludes the following:

1. Starting age does not affect the route of SLA. Although there may be differences in the acquisitional order, these are not the result of age.
2. Starting age affects the rate of learning. Where grammar and vocabulary are concerned, adolescent learners do better than either children or adults, when the length of exposure is held constant. Where pronunciation is concerned, there is no appreciable difference.
3. Both number of years of exposure and starting age affect the level of success. The number of years' exposure contributes greatly to the overall communicative fluency of the learners, but starting age determines the levels of accuracy achieved, particularly in pronunciation. (Ellis, 1985, p. 106)

These age-related differences have been explained in terms of a biological mechanism known as the *critical period*. This construct refers to a limited period of time in the development of an organism during which a particular behavior can be acquired. Psycholinguists have looked for evidence of the critical period in both L1 and L2 acquisition. It has been argued (see, for example, Penfield & Roberts, 1959), that the optimum age for acquiring another language is in the first 10 years of life because it is then that the brain retains its maximum 'plasticity' or flexibility (the plasticity metaphor, seems a favored one among investigators of the critical period). It is suggested that at around puberty, the brain loses its plasticity, the two hemispheres of the brain become much more independent of one another, and the language function is largely established in the left hemisphere. The critical period hypothesis argues that after these neurological changes have taken place, acquiring another language becomes increasingly difficult. (The effect of maturation or age in L2 acquisition is discussed at length in chapters 5 by Schachter and 15 by Obler and Hannigan, this volume.)

The hypothesis, however, is not without its critics. As Ellis (1985) points out, it is only partially correct to suggest that acquisition is easier for younger children. In fact, pronunciation is the only area where the younger the start the better, and the hypothesis is at a loss to explain *why* the loss of plasticity only affects pronunciation.

Evidence relating to brain plasticity and the differential functions of the two hemispheres of the brain have come, not from research into language acquisition, but from clinic work on both children and adults who have suffered physical injury, or who have brain or speech disorders of one sort or another. Investigations into the effect of age on acquisition have come from experiments and quasi-experiments. Such experiments typically take subjects from two contrasting age groups, such as children versus adolescents, or children versus adults, teach some aspect of the TL, such as a grammatical form or phonological feature, and then test the subjects to determine whether one group has learned more effectively than the other. For example, Asher and Price (1967) compared the efforts of a group of preadolescents to learn Russian with a group of college students, and found that the adults outperformed the children. One of the major shortcomings of these experiments is that they are generally extremely selective, looking at a small subset of the features of one aspect of the TL. They also tend to be carried out over relatively short periods of time. For instance, the conclusions of Asher and Price (1967) are derived from a mere 25 minutes of instruction.

Why Do Some Learners Fail to Acquire an L2 Successfully?

One of the challenges for L2 acquisition is to explain not just success with L2 and foreign languages but also failure. Most researchers pursuing this line of inquiry have looked at affective factors such as aptitude, motivation, social and psychological distance, and anxiety on acquisition. The name most closely associated with this work is Schumann (see, for example, 1978a, 1978b, 1978c), who concluded that fossilization, or failure to acquire occurred when the learner found him or herself alienated from the TL and culture. Using a case study approach, Schumann documented the progress of a number of L2 learners over a period of time. He found that one learner in particular failed to develop his grammatical competence, despite explicit instruction. In accounting for this failure, Schumann found that his subject did not identify with or particularly want to fit into the target society or culture. He also used the data to support his "pidginization hypothesis," which sees fossilization within the individual as analogous to the development of pidgins and creoles amongst groups. (Chapter 7, this volume, by McLaughlin and Heredia also refers to U-shaped behavior.)

Schumann's work has received a good deal of criticism. Larsen-Freeman and Long (1991, p. 260) point out that although the model "has served to turn what have otherwise often been rather vague notions about the role of social and psychological factors in SLA into coherent predictions," it has three major problems. In the first place, the underlying constructs are unoperationalizable. Second, there is a great deal of inconsistency in the findings from other studies (see, for example, Stauble, 1980, 1981). Finally, according to Larsen-Freeman and Long, there are problems in the ways in which the relationships between psychological and group sociological factors are conceptualized.

The principal method for investigating the question of fossilization or failure to learn another language has been the case study. The most widely cited investigation in the area (Schumann, 1978a,b,c) has already been discussed. Another inter-esting case study is Schmidt (1983). Case studies have been widely employed in L2 research. They are also controversial. The most problematic aspect of the case study concerns external validity, that is, establishing the domain or population to which a study's findings can be generalized. This problem has been a major stum-bling block for the case study researcher because of the obvious difficulty of mak-ing generalizations based on a single individual or group and applying those gen-eralizations to a broader population (Yin, 1984).

How Can We Account for Variation (a) between Learners (b) within Learners?

Variation is a key concept in all kinds of research. In fact, the bulk of research is aimed at identifying relationships among phenomena that vary, and ultimately to trace the cause of such variation. A necessary step in the research process is to decide which observed variations are random, and which are systematic. In lin-guistics, when researchers observe systematic variations in language use, they want to identify the linguistic and situational variables to which the linguistic variations can be attributed. These variables might include the following:

1. The linguistic environment itself—We know, for example, that certain pho-nemes vary according to the phonological company they keep.
2. Sociolinguistic factors—Our language will vary according to the interlocu-tors' gender, social class, race, and so on.
3. The type of speech event—A formal interview will generate different lan-guage from an informal party.
4. The developmental stage of the learner—In L2 acquisition, certain gram-matical items, which appear to have been mastered at a particular stage will be "destabilized" at a later stage by the acquisition of other closely related items.
5. Factors associated with the data collection procedures themselves—The means whereby the research elicits the data from subjects can itself partly determine the type of language that is produced.

The pioneer in this work is Labov (1970, 1972) who was particularly interested in the notion of speech *styles*. Labov demonstrated that all speakers possess sev-eral styles, determined by social context, and that these can be ranged on a con-tinuum from unmonitored speech use to closely monitored speech. He coined the famous Observer's Paradox, which has it that the only way to obtain samples of unmonitored data is through systematic observation, but that such observation precludes the use of unmonitored speech.

In L2 acquisition research, the researcher wants to know which variations (par-ticularly deviations from the target norms) are random, and which provide evi-dence that the learners are constructing their own interim grammars of the TL. The most comprehensive treatment of variation in interlanguage (IL) is Tarone

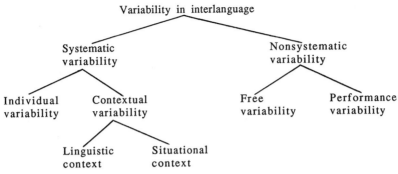

Figure 1   Variability in learner language.

(1988), who synthesized the research findings, and concluded with a call for the development of an adequate theoretical model, for the accumulation of more empirical data, and for the more careful design of studies into IL variation. (See also chapter 8 by Preston, this volume, on the analysis of variation in L2 performance.)

Ellis (1985, p. 76) argued that there are two types of variability, systematic, and nonsystematic variability, the difference lying in the fact that systematic variability can be predicted and explained. It is further subdivided into individual and contextual variability. Individual variability, as the name suggests, can be attributed to such individual learner factors as motivation, whereas contextual variability is determined either by the linguistic or situational context in which the language occurs. The relationship between these concepts is captured in Figure 1.

As with the other questions covered in the chapter, variability has been investigated in various ways. One of the more common procedures has been through the use of elicitation. For example, Labov (1970), who wanted to test the relationship between speech styles and context, created situations with varying degrees of formality. He then elicited samples of language in these different contexts and examined the effect of formality on the linguistic features of interest. Similar means have been employed to investigate the effect of linguistic environment on the variability of specific phonological and morphosyntactic features, such as the presence or absence of the copula *be*. The use of elicitation has already been critiqued, and will be dealt with again later in the chapter, so I shall not repeat the criticisms at this point.

Thus far, I have reviewed research that is not specifically referenced against the context of the classroom. Turning to such research—that is, research investigating acquisition in tutored environments—the following question emerges.

What Modes of Classroom Organization, Task Types, and Input Facilitate L2 Development?

A growing body of research, under the general rubric of "process-oriented" or "task-based" research addresses this question (or rather the various questions implicit in the question). The bulk of this research has focused on the activities or procedures that learners carry out in relation to the input data. Given the amount of work that has been carried out, this review must necessarily be selective. For a more detailed coverage of the research, see Larsen-Freeman and Long (1991). (Chapter 13 by Long, this volume, is a general discussion of the role of the linguistic environment in L2 acquisition.)

In the first of a series of investigations into learner–learner interaction, Long (1981) found that two-way tasks (in which all students in a group discussion had unique information to contribute) stimulated significantly more modified interactions than one-way tasks (that is, in which one member of the group possessed all the relevant information). Similarly, Doughty and Pica (1986) found that required information exchange tasks generated significantly more modified interaction than tasks in which the exchange of information was optional. (The term *modified interaction* refers to those instances during an interaction when the speaker alters the form in which his or her language is encoded in order to make it more comprehensible. Such modification may be prompted by lack of comprehension on the part of the listener.)

These investigations of modified interaction were theoretically motivated by Krashen's (1981, 1982) hypothesis that comprehensible input was a necessary and sufficient condition for L2 acquisition—in other words, that acquisition would occur when learners understood messages in the TL. Long (1985) advanced the following argument in favor of tasks that promote conversational adjustments or interactional modifications on the part of the learners taking part in the task:

> Step 1: Show that (a) linguistic/conversational adjustments promote (b) comprehensible input.
> Step 2: Show that (b) comprehensible input promotes (c) acquisition.
> Step 3: Deduce that (a) linguistic/conversational adjustments promote (c) acquisition. Satisfactory evidence of the a → b → c relationships would allow the linguistic environment to be posited as an indirect causal variable in SLA. (The relationship would be indirect because of the intervening "comprehension" variable.) (Long, 1985, p. 378)

More recently, attention has focused on the question of the types of language and discourse patterns stimulated by different task types. Berwick (1988) investigated the different types of language stimulated by transactional and interpersonal tasks. (A transactional task is one in which communication occurs principally to bring about the exchange of goods and services, whereas an interpersonal task is one in which communication occurs largely for social purposes.) He found that the different functional purposes stimulated different morphosyntactic realizations.

In a similarly motivated study, Nunan (1991a) investigated the different interactional patterns stimulated by open and closed tasks. An open task is one in which there is no single correct answer, whereas a closed task is one in which there is a single correct answer, or a restricted number of correct answers. It was found that the different task types stimulated very different interactional patterns, and that this needed to be taken into consideration by curriculum developers and discourse analysts (Nunan, 1993). In addition to the fact that the different task types stimulated different interactional patterns, the research also indicated that some task types might be more appropriate than others for learners at particular levels of proficiency. In the Nunan (1991a) study, it was found that with lower intermediate to intermediate learners, the relatively closed tasks stimulate more modified interaction than relatively more open tasks. This is not to say that such students should engage in closed tasks to the exclusion of open tasks. The important thing is that program planners and teachers should select a mix of tasks to reflect the pedagogic goals of the curriculum. This work underlines the importance of developing a reasonable working relationship between L2 acquisition researchers and curriculum specialists. At the very least, they should be aware of each other's concerns.

Most of the investigations into the relationship between L2 development and pedagogical factors such as task types, input, and modes of interaction have been carried out through experiments and quasi-experiments. For example Doughty and Pica (1986) carried out an experiment in which they systematically varied the modes of interaction and the task type, and documented the effects on learner output. Such experiments have been criticized by Ellis (1990) among others, who argued that the necessarily selective and atomistic nature of the experimental method can only ever provide partial and selective understanding of the nature of language learning.

IV. METHODOLOGICAL ISSUES IN L2 ACQUISITION RESEARCH

Historically, two competing conceptions of the nature and purpose of the research enterprise have driven work in L2 acquisition. The first of these is that external truths exist somewhere in the ether, and the function of research is to uncover these truths. The second view is that "truth" is a negotiable commodity contingent upon the historical context within which phenomena are observed and interpreted (Nunan, 1992). These days, philosophers of science seem inclined to the view that "standards are subject to change in the light of practice [which] would seem to indicate that the search for a substantive, ahistorical methodology is futile" (Chalmers, 1990, p. 21).

A. Qualitative and Quantitative Research

Within the research literature, there is a traditional distinction between qualitative and quantitative research. Qualitative research is generally of a nonexperimental kind, and yields nonnumerical data. Quantitative research is often experimental, or quasi-experimental in nature, and yields numerical data, that is, data that can be counted. It is sometimes suggested that qualitative data has to do with meanings, whereas quantitative data has to do with numbers (Dey, 1993). In recent years, it has become fashionable to argue (1) that the distinction is an oversimplification (see, for example, Grotjahn, 1987), and (2) that the choice of research methodology ought to be driven by the question one wishes to have answered, not by adherence to one research paradigm rather than another.

In Reichardt and Cook (1979), we find an implicit rejection of the notion that qualitative and quantitative methods exist on a continuum. They argue that underneath each paradigm are very different conceptions of the world. In other words, although it might be the case that the question should drive the methodology, the worldview of the researcher will lead him or her to question whether certain questions are worth asking in the first place.

Larsen-Freeman and Long (1991) rejected Reichardt and Cook's position, arguing that the supposed paradigm attributes are not logically linked to one another. They preferred to draw a distinction, not between paradigms, but between methods of data collection.

> The distinction we have chosen to exemplify is the one between longitudinal and cross-sectional studies. A longitudinal approach (often called a case study in the SLA field) typically involves observing the development of linguistic performance, usually the spontaneous speech of one subject, when the speech are collected at period intervals over a span of time. In a cross-sectional approach, the linguistic performance of a larger number of subjects is studied, and the performance data are usually collected at only one session. Furthermore, the data are usually elicited by asking subjects to perform some verbal task such as having subjects describe a picture. (Larsen-Freeman & Long, 1991, p. 11)

Grotjahn (1987), argued that the qualitative–quantitative distinction is simplistic. He emphasized that, in classifying research, one needs to consider at least three things: (1) how the data were collected (through an experiment or quasi-experiment or nonexperimentally); (2) what kind of data are yielded by the data collection procedure (qualitative or quantitative); and (3) how the data were ana-

TABLE II

Classroom-Based Studies: Design and Method

Design	Experiment	2
	Nonexperiment	13
Method	Observation	7
	Transcript	5
	Elicitation	3
	Diary	1
	Introspection	1

TABLE III
Laboratory, Simulated, and Naturalistic Studies: Design and Method

Design	Experiment	13
	Nonexperiment	15
Method	Elicitation	21
	Interview	5
	Transcript	2
	Questionnaire	2
	Diary	1
	Case study	1

lyzed (statistically or interpretively). It is an oversimplification to assume that there are only two types of research as follows:

1. Experimental research yielding quantitative data that are analyzed statistically
2. Naturalistic research yielding qualitative data that are analyzed interpretively.

Using Grotjahn's scheme, in 1991, in a critical review of L2 acquisition research in tutored environments, I analyzed 50 widely reported studies that made claims of relevance for pedagogy (see Nunan, 1991b). The studies were initially classified according to whether they were classroom-based, nonclassroom-based, or mixed. Tables II, III, and IV, set out the design and method of data collection for the three types of study.

In terms of the environment in which the data were collected, I distinguished between classroom-based, nonclassroom-based, and mixed studies. Classroom-based studies were those in which the researchers collected their data exclusively from classroom contexts. Nonclassroom-based studies were those in which the data were collected exclusively outside the classroom in the laboratory, or in simulated or naturalistic settings; mixed studies were those in which some data were collected in classrooms, and some were collected outside the classroom.

TABLE IV
Mixed Studies: Design and Method

Design	Experiment	3
	Nonexperiment	4
Method	Observation	3
	Transcript	2
	Diary	2
	Elicitation	1
	Interview	1
	Introspection	1
	Case study	1

In relation to research design, a principal distinction was drawn between studies based on some form of experimentation, and those in which the data were collected nonexperimentally. In a true experiment, one or more variables are manipulated, whereas the others are held constant. True experiments derive their rationale from the logic of inferential statistics, and require two particular conditions to be fulfilled. These are (1) the existence of an experimental as well as at least one control group and (2) the random assignment of subjects to groups.

Data collection methods included elicitation, interviews, transcript, questionnaire, diary, case study, and introspection. Elicitation referred to a range of procedures for collecting speech samples and other data from subjects, usually through devices such as pictures and realia or standardized tests. Interviews involved the collection of data by one person from another through person-to-person encounters. Transcripts were written records of oral discourse. Questionnaires were defined as instruments in which prespecified information was collected from informants through either written or oral responses. The term *diary* was used as a form of shorthand to refer to written, discursive accounts of teaching or learning containing free-form accounts of the learning and teaching process. Case studies investigated the way in which a single instance or phenomenon (usually a single individual or limited number of individuals) functions in context. Finally, introspection was defined as the process of observing and reflecting on one's thoughts, feelings, motives, reasoning processes, and mental states with a view to determining the ways in which these processes and states determine or influence behavior.

From Tables II, III, and IV, it can be seen that there are 18 studies that are based on some form of experiment, and 32 based on the collection of data through nonexperimental means.

The researchers carrying out these studies used a range of linguistic, statistical, and interpretive techniques for analyzing their data. These techniques are set out in Tables V, VI and VII.

TABLE V

Classroom-Based Studies:
Type of Analysis

Linguistic:	Functions	5
	Complexity	4
	Morphosyntax	3
	Suprasegmentals	1
	Lexis	1
Statistical:	Correlation	2
	Chi-square	2
	t-test	1
	U test	1
Interpretive:		9

TABLE VI

Laboratory, Simulated, and Naturalistic Studies: Type of Analysis

Linguistic:	Morphosyntax	9
	Functions	8
	Complexity	2
	Quantity	2
Statistical:	Correlation	7
	Chi-square	5
	t-test	6
	Factor analysis	2
	F ratio	2
	Cronbach's alpha	2
	ANOVA[a]	2
	ANCOVA[b]	1
Interpretive:		6

[a] ANOVA, analysis of variance.
[b] ANCOVA, analysis of covariance.

Teleni and Baldauf (1988) classify statistical tests in applied linguistics as either basic, intermediate, or advanced. Basic techniques include descriptive statistics, Pearson product–moment coefficient, chi-square, independent t-test, dependent t-test and one-way ANOVA (analysis of variance). If this scheme is applied to the studies analyzed here, it can be seen that the great majority of studies (29 out of 39) employ basic statistical tools. Although there is nothing wrong with this, it may indicate a need for the application of more sophisticated techniques for data analysis. More serious were basic flaws in the research designs of experimental studies and those employing statistical analysis, as well as the manner in which they are reported. Critical data, such as the number of subjects and whether or not they were randomized are frequently either not reported or buried away in the body of the report. Assumptions underlying the statistical procedures employed were also violated in some of the studies reviewed. The most frequent problem, in studies involving the comparison of group means through t-tests, or ANOVA, was

TABLE VII

Mixed Studies: Type of Analysis

Linguistic:	Functions	6
	Morphosyntax	2
Statistical:	Chi-square	3
	t-test	2
	Correlation	1
Interpretive:		3

the fact that n sizes were often far too small for the analysis to be valid. (Similar criticisms have been made by Chaudron, 1988.)

B. Longitudinal versus Cross-Sectional Research

The distinction between longitudinal and cross-sectional approaches has created controversy in the literature. If one wishes to obtain evidence on the development of language over time, it would seem logical to track the development of language from a group of learners over the chosen period of time. However, there are practical reasons why this is not always a viable option. In the first place, few researchers have the time or funding to follow the development of language over several years, or even several months. An alternative is to adopt a cross-sectional approach in which samples of language data are obtained at one point in time from learners who are at different developmental stages. The assumption is that these various still shots, taken at one point in time can be put together to give us a moving development picture of language development over time.

A number of researchers have been particularly critical of the assumption that cross-sectional data will provide an accurate picture of the ontogenesis of language Thus, Ellis (1985), in critiquing the cross-sectional approach employed in the Morpheme Order Studies, argued that

> there is not a sufficient theoretical base for assuming that the accuracy with which learners use morphemes corresponds to the order in which they are acquired. The case studies have shown that learners may begin by using a grammatical form correctly, only to regress at a later stage, which makes a mockery of attempts to equate accuracy and acquisition. (Ellis, 1985, p. 69)

The instability of a learner's IL is a major problem for L2 acquisition researchers employing a cross-sectional approach to data collection. Indeed, it is a problem for language testers, or anyone else wishing to extrapolate from data collected at a single point in time. As Ellis points out, accuracy orders for many grammatical forms can move up and down over time. This has led Kellerman to refer to the learner's L2 development as being "U-shaped." If, on a graph, we plot a learner's accuracy order for a given feature, we are likely to find a lower order at time 2 than time 1, and a higher order at time 3 than at time 1 or 2. A line joining these points describes a "U." This instability reflects the fact that TL items are not discrete entities, but are in interaction with other closely related features. Thus a learner who has a relatively high accuracy order for, say, the simple present-tense form in English, may find that accuracy temporarily destabilized by the appearance within his or her repertoire of the present continuous tense. (Concerning U-shaped behavior, see also chapter 7, this volume, by McLaughlin and Heredia.) The dilemma for the researcher employing a cross-sectional approach in which data are collected at a single point in time is in knowing the status of the particular features under investigation at the point in time at which the data are collected.

C. Experimental versus Naturalistic Data Collection

The controversy over the employment of experimental or naturalistic research designs, which I have already commented on, is evident in L2 acquisition research as in other areas of the behavioral sciences. Some researchers (see, for example, van Lier, 1989) argue that naturalistic inquiry is a valid tradition in its own right. Others see naturalistic inquiry as acceptable as a preliminary activity, useful for identifying possible variables for more "rigorous" attention through experimental research. Proponents of naturalistic inquiry argue that the relationship between context and social behavior has been clearly established. They further argue that language, as a dimension of social behavior, must be studied in the contexts in which it naturally occurs, and that this precludes the artificial context of the formal experiment.

One of the most widely used research methods in L2 acquisition is the case study. The method has a long history in the social and behavioral sciences, and is widely employed in other areas of applied linguistics, including L1 acquisition and language disability. In the L1 field, ground-breaking work by researchers such as Brown (1973) and Halliday (1975) gave a lead to researchers investigating L2 acquisition:

> The most common type of CS [case study] involves the detailed description and analysis of an individual subject, from whom observations, interviews, and (family) histories provide the database. . . . CSM [case study methodology] is particularly characteristic of some areas of psychological research, such as clinical psychology, which studies and aims to treat abnormal (e.g., anti-social) behaviour. In principle, though, CSM may involve more than one subject (e.g., a series of CSs, cf. Meisel, Clahsen, & Pienemann, 1981). It may be based on particular groups (e.g., group dynamics within a classroom); organizations (e.g., a summer intensive language learning program at a university); or events (e.g., a Japanese language tutorial . . . where one could examine the amount of time a teacher speaks in either Japanese or English for class management purposes). (Duff 1990, p. 35)

One of the problems here is in deciding when a particular investigation is in fact a case study and when it is not:

> While it would seem reasonably clear that the study of an individual language learner is a case, and that the same can be said for the study of an individual classroom, what about an investigation of a whole school, or a complete school district? . . . Adelman et al. . . . . suggest that it is the study of an 'instance in action'. In other words, one selects an instance from the class of objects and phenomena one is investigating (for example 'a second language learner' or 'a science classroom') and investigates the way this instance functions in context. (Nunan, 1992, pp. 74–75)

Smith, cited in Stake (1988), argued that the term *bounded system* defines the method for him.

The crux of the definition is having some conception of the unity or totality of a system with some kind of outlines or boundaries. For instance, take a child with learning disabilities as the bounded system. You have an individual pupil, in a particular circumstance, with a particular problem. What the research looks for are the systematic connections among the observable behaviors, speculations, causes, and treatments. What the study covers depends partly on what you are trying to do. The unity of the system depends partly on what you want to find out. (p. 255)

Case studies in L2 acquisition range from the extremely circumscribed to the highly comprehensive. An example of the former is Sato (1985), who investigated the IL phonology of a single L2 subject. Sato focused on a single phonological feature, word-final consonants and consonant clusters, and investigated targetlike and nontargetlike production of this item in three contexts: free conversation, oral reading of continuous text, and elicited imitation of words and short phrases.

An example of a comprehensive case study is the investigation by Schmidt (1983) of the development of communicative competence of a single English as a Second Language (ESL) learner over a 3-year period. Schmidt sought to explore the relationships between social and interactional variables in the acquisition of communicative competence, and he took as his point of departure the earlier work of Schumann (1978a,b,c). One of his aims was to broaden the research agenda beyond its (then) preoccupation with morphosyntactic development, and he therefore utilized Canale and Swain's (1980) four-component model of communicative competence. This model specifies grammatical, sociolinguistic, discourse, and strategic competence as the basic elements constituting a user's overall competence. Schmidt's subject was a Japanese L1 speaker who was living and working in Hawaii as an artist. Schmidt presented evidence to suggest that Wes, his subject, was an individual with low social and psychological distance from the target culture. He was therefore, in a sense, the opposite to Schumann's subject. Schmidt drew on a range of data, including taped monologues and dialogues, fieldnotes, tables of morphosyntactic items, and interviews. Schmidt demonstrated that despite Wes's low psychological and social distance his grammatical competence shows little evidence of development over the 3 years that Schmidt collected his data. It therefore calls into question Schumann's acculturation hypothesis. However, if the focus is broadened to encompass discourse, strategic, and sociolinguistic competence, there is evidence of considerable development.

D. Elicited versus Naturalistic Data

It can be seen in the study reported in Nunan (1991b) that by far the most popular means of collecting data were through some form of elicitation, with just one half of the studies using some form of elicitation procedure to obtain their data. I counted as elicitation any studies that obtain their data by means of a stimulus, such as a picture, diagram, standardized test, and so on. Such devices have been common in L2 acquisition research since the original morpheme-order studies that employed the Bilingual Syntax Measure for the purposes of data collection. It is critically important, when evaluating research utilizing such devices, to consider the extent to which the results obtained might be an artifact of the research tools themselves (Nunan, 1987, discusses the dangers of deriving implications for L2 acquisition from standardized test data).

Particular caution needs to be exercised when looking at research making claims about acquisition orders based on elicited data, as Ellis (1985), amongst others, has pointed out. Eisenstein, Bailey, and Madden (1982) also observed:

> It is evident that serious questions must be raised about data from production tasks. When a particular structure does not appear, several alternatives are possible: the structure may simply not be present in the grammar of the learner, or the learner may have some knowledge of the structure but lack the confidence to use it and may be exhibiting an avoidance strategy. A third possibility is that the learner knows the structure but has not used it as a matter of chance. When a structure is used correctly in a form that has high frequency in the language, it could be part of an unanalyzed chunk which does not reflect the learner's creative use of grammar. (p. 388)

One of the reasons for the employment of elicitation devices, rather than relying on naturalistic data, is that the linguistic features of interest to the researcher may simply not be very frequent in naturally occurring data. Imagine, for example, that the researcher is interested in studying the development of the speech acts of "requesting" or "apologizing" among L2 learners. One may spend an enormous amount of time recording naturalistic samples of language and not find a single instance of these speech acts in the data.

Originally, Dulay and Burt had planned to use a naturalistic, case study approach in their investigation of morpheme orders. The original plan was to study about three Chinese and three Spanish L1 children at weekly intervals over a 1-year period. However, they were concerned that this would create a sampling problem for them. Added to this was the fact that they were involved at the time in a project that gave them access to nearly 1,000 L2 children. They therefore decided to develop an elicitation device, the Bilingual Syntax Measure, which allowed them to collect small samples of "relevant" data from a large number of subjects, rather than large samples of possibly "irrelevant" data from a small number of subjects.

In addition to standardized tests and elicitation instruments such as the Bilingual Syntax Measure, researchers have employed surveys, interviews, and questionnaires in their quest for relevant data. However, these also have pitfalls and dangers for the naive researcher. In particular, one needs to treat with caution the claim that interviews are direct measures of a learner's proficiency, and that they yield naturalistic samples of IL speech. The following extracts serve to remind us that the interview is a unequal encounter in which the power is very much with the interviewer, and that this inequity is reflected in the discourse itself. The extracts can be safely left to speak for themselves.

(1) (From an oral proficiency interview)

Interviewer: Where is your mother? What does your mother do?
Subject: She's dead.
I: Ah-she's dead. Very good.
I: What's your father's name?
S: [no response]
I: What does your father do?
    Where does he work? Where does your father work?
    Come on girl, talk! talk! Don't be afraid. Where does your father work?
S: [no response]
I: What does your mother do? Where is your mother? What does your mother do?
S: [no response]
I: What do you do at home? Do you help your mother? What do you do?
S: [no response]
I: (into the microphone) Doesn't talk. (van Lier, 1989, pp. 499–504)

(2) (From an interview aimed at eliciting data on the subject's syntactic development)

Interviewer: In Colombia do the lobsters have claws?
Subject: Claws?
I: Claws. Do they have . . . the lobsters, do they have claws (form my hands into claws)?
S: Octopus?
I: No. The lobsters. Do the lobsters have hands?
S: Huh?
I: I don't know how to say it. I know . . . I am a lobster. This is my . . . I am a lobster. This is my claw (hands formed like claws).
S: Hm. Hm.
I: Do lobsters in Colombus have claws? Like this, you know? They pinch people.
S: Lobster?
I: On Sunday do you catch many lobsters?
S: Eh, huh?
I: Yeah, do you get many?
S: Eh. Dictionary?
I: Oh, do you want to go get your dictionary?
S: No. No necessary.

I: How many, how many do you get? How many do you catch?
S: Catch?
(Butterworth, 1972, cited in Hatch, Wagner Gough, & Peck, 1985, p. 55)

E. Role Playing

Confronted with the frustrations of obtaining relevant data, and not finding enough of the "right stuff," researchers have also looked to role plays. In an investigation into the sociocultural competence of L2 speakers, Cohen and Olshtain (1981), used a procedure in which subjects were presented with role cards such as the following:

Instructions

You will be asked to read eight brief situations calling for an apology. In each case, the person who you owe the apology to will speak first. I will role play this person. Respond as much as possible as you would in an actual situation. Your response will be tape-recorded. Indicate when you've finished reading.

Sample Situations

You're at a meeting and you say something that one of the participants interprets as a personal insult to him.
He: "I feel that your last remark was directed at me and I take offense."
You:

You completely forget a crucial meeting at the office with your boss. An hour later you call him to apologize. The problem is that this is the second time you've forgotten such a meeting. Your boss gets on the phone and asks you:
Boss: "What happened to you?"
You:

Although this is a carefully conducted study, it is not beyond criticism. In studies such as this, in which role plays are employed, one is always left wondering whether the data themselves are an artifact of the elicitation procedure. In the case of Cohen and Olshtain's study, one is left wondering whether the subjects would really have acted in the way they did in the role play if the situation had been genuine.

V. CONCLUSION

In this chapter, I have reviewed what I see as some of the current substantive and methodological issues in L2 acquisition research. In many ways, the core issues associated with the selection of appropriate methods of collecting, analyzing, and interpreting L2 acquisition data come down to the selection of an appropriate metaphor to represent the acquisition process. The value of metaphors is that they mesh with the way we conceptualize experience:

> Our ordinary conceptual system, in terms of which we both think and act, is fundamentally metaphorical in nature. . . . New metaphors have the power to create a new reality. . . . New metaphors, by virtue of their entailments, pick out a range of experiences by highlighting, downplaying, and hiding. The metaphor, then, characterizes a similarity between the entire range of highlighted experiences and some other range of experiences. (Lakoff & Johnson, 1980, p. 3)

In relation to language teaching, for example:

> A new metaphor is a theory, a speculation. It leads to questions of the kind: What might we do to make the language classroom more, or less, like the analogy? How might we restructure our perception of classroom factors in order to characterize it more or less comprehensively in terms of a given scale or opposition? Or what metaphorical terms might we utilize to draw attention to generalizable features which might otherwise go unobserved? (Bowers, 1986, p. 8)

Much of the research to date has assumed that L2 acquisition is a linear process in which learners acquire one linguistic item perfectly, an item at a time. This is what I have called the "building block" metaphor. The learner puts down one linguistic block at a time, until the imposing edifice called an L2 is complete.

However, I would argue that the metaphor is all wrong. Learners do not acquire one thing perfectly one at a time. Rather, they learn lots of things imperfectly all at once, they forget things, and their IL is destabilized when a newly acquired item collides with a preexisting item. We need a newer, a more aptly organic metaphor to represent the acquisition process. I believe that the notion of a garden can provide us with such a metaphor. In a garden, numerous things grow simultaneously, albeit at different rates. Some things are trampled on, other are encouraged through the appropriate administration of fertilizer, some are adversely affected by shade, and others are adversely affected by sun.

This organic metaphor is also implicit in the work of Rutherford on pedagogic grammar (1987):

> Given all that we presently know about language, how it is learned, and how it is taught, the 'grammatical' part of a 'grammatical syllabus' does not entail specification of the language content at all; rather, it specifies how that language content (chosen in accordance with a variety of other non-linguistic criteria) is to be exploited. . . . [Learning activities should reflect the fact that language acquisition] is not a linear progression, but a cyclic one, or even a metaphoric one. That is, the learner is constantly engaged in reanalyzing data, reformulating hypotheses, recasting generalizations, etc. (Rutherford, 1987, p. 159)

I believe that the challenge for the future lies in the evolution of research methods that are in harmony with emerging conceptualizations of language and learning. It is also of crucial importance, as I have tried to demonstrate in this chapter, that there be harmony between the substantive and methodological aspects of the research. If the data and analysis are appropriate to the questions driving the research, then debates as to which particular research tradition the research belongs become relatively unimportant.

REFERENCES

Asher, J., & Price, B. (1967). The learning strategy of total physical response: Some age differences. *Child Development, 38,* 1219–1227.

Berwick, R. (1988). *The effect of task variation in teacher-led groups on repair of English as a foreign language.* Unpublished doctoral dissertation, University of British Columbia, Vancouver.

Bowers, R. (1986). *That's all very well in practice, but how will it work in theory?* Paper presented at the Colloquium on Theory and Practice, University of Reading, Centre for Applied Language Studies.

Brown, R. (1973). *A first language: The early stages.* London: Allen & Unwin.

Butterworth, G. (1972). *A Spanish-speaking adolescent's acquisition of English syntax.* Unpublished MA-TESL thesis, University of California, Los Angeles.

Canale, M., & Swain, M. (1980). Theoretical bases of communicative approaches to second language teaching and testing. *Applied Linguistics, 1,* 1–47.

Chalmers, A. (1990). *Science and its fabrication.* Milton Keynes, England: Open University Press.

Chaudron, C. (1988). *Second language classrooms: Research on teaching and learning.* Cambridge, UK: Cambridge University Press.

Cohen, A., & Olshtain, E. (1981). Developing a measure of sociocultural competence: The case of apology. *Language Learning, 31*(1), 113–134.

Dey, I. (1993). *Qualitative data analysis: A user-friendly guide for social scientists.* London: Routledge.

Doughty, C., & Pica, T. (1986). "Information gap" tasks: Do they facilitate second language acquisition? *TESOL Quarterly, 20,* 305–325.

Duff, P. (1990). *Developments in the case study approach to SLA research.* Paper presented at the First Conference on Second Language Acquisition and Teaching, International University of Japan, Tokyo.

Dulay, H., & Burt, M. (1973). Should we teach children syntax? *Language Learning, 23,* 235–252.

Dulay, H., & Burt, M. (1974a). Natural sequences in child second language acquisition. *Language Learning, 24,* 37–53.

Dulay, H., & Burt, M. (1974b). A new perspective on the creative construction process in child second language acquisition. *Language Learning, 24,* 253–278.

Dulay, H., Burt, M., & Krashen, S. (1982). *Language two.* Oxford: Pergamon Press.

Eisenstein, M., Bailey, N., & Madden, C. (1982). It takes two: Contrasting tasks and contrasting structures. *TESOL Quarterly, 16*, 381–393.

Ellis, R. (1985). *Understanding second language acquisition.* Oxford: Oxford University Press.

Ellis, R. (1990). Researching classroom language learning. In C. Brumfit & R. Mitchell (Eds.), *Research in the language classroom* (pp. 54–70). London: Modern English Publications.

Ervin-Tripp, S. (1974). Is second language learning like the first? *TESOL Quarterly, 8*, 111–127.

Flick, W. (1980). Error types in adult English as a second language. In B. Ketterman & R. St. Clair (Eds.), *New approaches to language acquisition.* Heidelberg: Julius Groos.

Fries, C. (1945). *Teaching and learning English as a foreign language.* Ann Arbor: University of Michigan Press.

George, H. (1972). *Common errors in language learning.* Rowley, MA: Newbury House.

Grauberg, W. (1971). An error analysis in the German of first-year university students. In G. Perren & J. Trim (Eds.), *Application of linguistics.* Cambridge, UK: Cambridge University Press.

Gregg, K. (1984). Krashen's monitor and Occam's razor. *Applied Linguistics, 5*, 79–100.

Grotjahn, R. (1987). On the methodological basis of introspective methods. In C. Færch & G. Kasper (Eds.), *Introspection in second language research.* Clevedon, UK: Multilingual Matters.

Halliday, M. A. K. (1975). *Learning how to mean: Explorations in the development of language.* London: Edward Arnold.

Hatch, E., Wagner Gough, J., & Peck, S. (1985). What case studies reveal about system, sequence, and variation in second language acquisition. In M. Celce-Murcia (Ed.), *Beyond basics: Issues and research in TESOL.* Rowley, MA: Newbury House.

Krashen, S. (1981). *Second language acquisition and second language learning.* Oxford: Pergamon.

Krashen, S. (1982). *Principles and practice in second language acquisition.* Oxford: Pergamon.

Labov, W. (1970). The study of language in its social context. *Studium Generale, 23*, 30–87.

Labov, W. (1972). *Sociolinguistic patterns.* Oxford: Blackwell.

Lado, R. (1957). *Linguistics across cultures.* Ann Arbor: University of Michigan Press.

Lakoff, G., & Johnson, M. (1980). *Metaphors we live by.* Chicago: University of Chicago Press.

Larsen-Freeman, D., & Long, M. H. (1991). *An introduction to second language acquisition research.* London: Longman.

Long, M. H. (1981). Input, interaction and second language acquisition. *Annals of the New York Academy of Sciences, 379*, 259–278.

Long, M. H. (1985). Input and second language acquisition theory. In S. Gass & C. Madden (Eds.), *Input in second language acquisition* (pp. 377–393). Rowley, MA: Newbury House.

Lott, D. (1983). Analysing and counteracting interference errors. *ELT Journal, 37*(3), 256–261.

Meisel, J., Clahsen, H., & Pienemann, M. (1981). On determining developmental stages in natural second language acquisition. *Studies in Second Language Acquisition, 3*(1), 109–135.

Mukattash, L. (1977). *Problematic areas in English syntax for Jordanian students.* Jordan: University of Amman.

Nunan, D. (1984). *Discourse processing by first language, second phase, and second language learners.* Unpublished doctoral dissertation, Flinders University of South Australia.

Nunan, D. (Ed.). (1987). *Applying second language acquisition research.* Adelaide: National Curriculum Resource Centre.

Nunan, D. (1991a). *Language teaching methodology.* London: Prentice-Hall.

Nunan, D. (1991b). Methodological issues in classroom research. *Studies in Second Language Acquisition, 13,* (2), 1991.

Nunan, D. (1992). *Research methods in language learning.* New York: Cambridge University Press.

Nunan, D. (1993). *Introducing discourse analysis.* London: Penguin.

Odlin, T. (1989). *Language transfer.* Cambridge, UK: Cambridge University Press.

Penfield, W., & Roberts, L. (1959). *Speech and brain mechanisms.* New York: Atheneum Press.

Reichardt, C., & Cook, T. (1979). Beyond qualitative versus quantitative methods. In T. Cook & C. Reichardt (Eds.), *Qualitative and quantitative methods in evaluation research.* Beverly Hills, CA: Sage.

Rutherford, W. (1987). *Second language grammar: Teaching and learning.* London: Longman.

Sato, C. (1985). Task variation in interlanguage phonology. In S. Gass & C. Madden (Eds.) *Input in second language acquisition* (pp. 181–196). Rowley, MA: Newbury House.

Schmidt, R. (1983). Interaction, acculturation and the acquisition of communicative competence: A case study of an adult. In N. Wolfson & E. Judd (Eds.) *Sociolinguistics and language acquisition* (pp. 137–174). Rowley, MA: Newbury House.

Schumann, J. (1978a). The acculturation model for second language acquisition. In R. Gingras (Ed.), *Second language acquisition and foreign language teaching.* Arlington, VA: Center for Applied Linguistics.

Schumann, J. (1978b). *The pidginization process: A model for second language acquisition.* Rowley, MA: Newbury House.

Schumann, J. (1978c). Social and psychological factors in second language acquisition. In J. Richards (Ed.), *Understanding second and foreign language learning.* Rowley, MA: Newbury House.

Scovel, T. (1988). *A time to speak: A psycholinguistic inquiry into the critical period for human speech.* New York: Newbury House.

Selinker, L. (1992). *Interlanguage revisited.* London: Longman.

Stake, R. (1988). Case study methods in educational research: Seeking sweet water. In R. M. Jaeger (Ed.), *Complementary methods for research in education.* Washington, DC: American Educational Research Association.

Stauble, A. (1980). Acculturation and second language acquisition. In R. Scarcella & S. Krashen (Eds.), *Research in second language acquisition* (pp. 43–50). Rowley, MA: Newbury House.

Stauble, A. (1981). *A comparative study of a Spanish-English and Japanese-English second language continuum: Verb phrase morphology.* Unpublished doctoral dissertation, University of California, Los Angeles.

Tarone, E. (1988). *Variation in interlanguage.* London: Edward Arnold.

Teleni, V., & Baldauf, R. B. (1988). *Statistical techniques used in three applied linguistics journals: Language Learning, Applied Linguistics and TESOL Quarterly 1980–1986: Implications for readers and researchers.* Unpublished manuscript, James Cook University of Northern Queensland.

Tran-Chi-Chau. (1975). Error analysis, contrastive analysis and students' perception: A study of difficulty in second language learning. *International Review of Applied Linguistics, 13,* 119–143.

van Lier, L. (1989). Reeling, writhing, drawling, stretching, and fainting in coils: Oral proficiency interviews as conversation. *TESOL Quarterly, 23,* (3), 489–508.

Yin, R. (1984). *Case study research.* Beverly Hills, CA: Sage.

CHAPTER 12

THE USE OF ACCEPTABILITY JUDGMENTS IN SECOND LANGUAGE ACQUISITION RESEARCH

Antonella Sorace

I. INTRODUCTION

It is a widespread practice of both linguists and second language (L2) acquisition researchers to rely on grammaticality judgments to support their theoretical claims. In both cases, the object of investigation is linguistic competence: the steady state of knowledge of the native speaker (NS), on the one hand, and the evolving interlanguage (IL) knowledge of the nonnative speaker (NNS), on the other. (See chapters 2 by Gregg, 3 by White, and 4 by Flynn, this volume, for competence–performance in L2 acquisition.) However, there has been a growing awareness of the fact that very little is known about the psychological nature of linguistic intuitions. My aim in this chapter is to assert the case that a clearer understanding of the cognitive factors involved in the internal origin of linguistic intuitions and in their overt expression as judgments is essential for a more effective and informative exploitation of intuitional data in linguistic research. (For additional treatment of aspects of research methodology in the study of L2 acquisition, see chapters 4 by Flynn and 11 by Nunan, this volume.) This chapter will have the following structure: first, it will deal with the general nature of linguistic acceptability; second, it will focus on a number of questions arising specifically from the investigation of nonnative acceptability; finally, it will address issues related to the empirical measurement of linguistic acceptability in L2 research.

Handbook of Second Language Acquisition

II. THE NATURE OF LINGUISTIC ACCEPTABILITY: GENERAL ISSUES

Criticisms of acceptability judgments as linguistic evidence have been mainly concerned with two issues. The first—and most crucial—is the *validity* of judgments, which has to do with the relationship between judgments and the state of knowledge they are supposed to reflect (i.e., grammatical competence). The second issue is the *reliability* of judgments, which is related to the degree of consistency among the judgments produced by different informants (intersubject consistency), or by the same informant (intrasubject consistency) in different replications of the test.

A. Validity: What Does an Acceptability Judgment Test Measure?

Two arguments have been raised against the supposed validity of linguistic intuitions as indicators of competence. The most fundamental one is that the capacity to have relevant intuitions may not be a reflection of grammatical competence: it may derive from a separate faculty characterized by a set of properties *sui generis* that are not shared by other kinds of linguistic behavior (Bever, 1970, 1974; Gleitman & Gleitman, 1979; Snow & Meijer, 1977). It is obvious that if linguistic intuitions turned out to be totally (or even largely, if unpredictably) independent of the speaker's internalized grammar, then it would make no sense to use them as basic data for the purpose of constructing models of grammar. Although the psychological laws of the intuitional process are poorly understood, it is indisputable that the use of acceptability judgments and introspective reports has led to the establishment of a substantial number of significant generalizations about syntactic processes (see Newmeyer, 1983, on this point). These results would hardly be explainable if no more than a chance relationship was assumed between grammatical knowledge and expressed linguistic intuitions. Moreover, acceptability judgments and linguistic performance have often been shown to be highly correlated (Greenbaum & Quirk, 1970; Quirk & Svartvik, 1966): This suggests that NSs tend to rely on the same grammar for both the sentences they accept and those they are able to produce. There are therefore sufficient grounds to disregard the claim that there is no orderly relationship between linguistic competence and intuitional processes, and between intuitional processes and performance.

The second argument is that even if linguistic intuitions are directly related to grammatical competence, they may be affected by other factors that are extralinguistic in nature and cannot be easily isolated. A sentence may be judged acceptable or unacceptable for reasons that have little to do with its status in the competence of speakers—in other words, speakers may direct their attention towards aspects of the sentence irrelevant to the purpose of the experiment and judge something different from what they were expected to judge (Botha, 1973; Levelt, 1974).

Grammatical Competence and Extralinguistic Factors

The problem of the influence of extragrammatical factors on linguistic intuitions arises because the speaker's internalized grammar is not the only system activated in the intuitional process. The interaction of the grammar with other cognitive and pragmatic systems is explainable within a modular conception of language, according to which the grammar is only one of a number of human cognitive systems, each governed by its own principles and each contributing to the superficial complexity of language (Newmeyer, 1983; White, 1982). (Chapter 2 by Gregg, this volume, includes discussion of the language faculty as a distinct module of the mind.) Botha (1973) reserves the term *spurious* for intuitions determined or affected by extragrammatical factors, as opposed to *genuine* intuitions, which originate from the informant's internalized grammar. A variety of factors may be at the source of spurious intuitions. To mention the most relevant:

1. Parsing strategies (Bever, 1970, 1974; Snow, 1974). Difficulty of parsing may be responsible for the rejection of perfectly grammatical sentences (as in the famous garden path example "The horse raced past the barn fell," which tends to be judged as ungrammatical by most informants because of the tendency to take the first noun phrase–verb–noun phrase [NP V NP] sequence as the main clause); conversely, ease of parsing may lead to the acceptance of sentences that are predicted to be ungrammatical on theoretical grounds (Cowart, 1989; Schachter & Yip, 1990).

2. Context and mode of presentation (Greenbaum, 1977; Levelt, 1971, 1974; Snow, 1974). A sentence of dubious grammaticality is more likely to be judged as ungrammatical if placed after a set of clearly grammatical sentences, or as grammatical if following a set of clearly ungrammatical sentences. This suggests that judgments in isolation are very different from judgments by contrast (as will be pointed out in section IV). In general terms, people are usually better at producing *relative* rather than *absolute* judgments (see Nunnally, 1967, p. 44). This seems to be true of acceptability judgments, even when they involve rating isolated sentences. When a given form has close variants, informants may match the variants mentally before making a judgment (Greenbaum, 1988), or try to find a context in which the sentence could make sense (see Levelt, Haans, & Meijers, 1977, who suggest that acceptability judgments tend to be faster and more positive for high imagery, or concrete materials than for low imagery, or abstract materials). If so, then inconsistencies in absolute acceptability ratings may be due to differing abilities of individuals to retrieve a matching variant, or to construct adequate mental contexts.

3. Pragmatic considerations. When faced with syntactic ambiguity, informants tend to prefer the reading that (a) represents the most frequent interpretation, and (b) requires fewer assumptions about previous discourse (Altmann & Steedman, 1988; Hawkins, 1982). The importance of context for certain kinds of construc-

tions is often underestimated. Some decontextualized sentences may be judged in arbitrarily different ways, depending on the context provided by the informant in order to interpret them.[1]

4. Mental or introspective state. Speakers have been found to have different intuitions on the same sentences, depending on whether they were facing a mirror. The theory here distinguished subjective and objective self-awareness (Carroll, Bever, & Pollack, 1981). These states were experimentally manipulated by the presence or absence of a mirror in front of the informants. Objective self-awareness (brought about by the presence of the mirror) was conducive to attention of semantic properties, whereas subjective self-awareness (in the absence of the mirror) enhanced attention to syntactic properties.

5. Linguistic training (Botha, 1973; Levelt, 1974). When linguists use themselves as main (or only) informants (producing "the theory and the data at the same time," as Labov, 1972, puts it) there cannot be any guarantee that their judgments are not biased by theoretical expectations. Furthermore, linguistically naive NSs have been found to be different in their acceptability judgments from linguistically sophisticated NSs (Gleitman & Gleitman, 1979; Snow & Meijer, 1977; Spencer, 1973), although it is difficult to pinpoint the exact nature of such difference: Naive informants appear to be more normative and more confident (Ross, 1979), or less consistent (Bradac, Martin, Elliott, & Tardy, 1980; Snow & Meijer, 1977).

The validity problem that underlies intuitional data can therefore be summarized as follows: Linguistic intuitions reflect grammatical competence, but they are also open to the influence of other cognitive or contextual factors. The extragrammatical factors can be controlled for, at least to a certain extent, by carefully selecting the test sentences, the test design, and the informants. Ultimately, however, one can never be absolutely sure that intuitions are derived *exclusively* from grammatical competence.

Acceptability versus Grammaticality

The argument we have developed so far leads to the conclusion that the terms *acceptabiity* and *grammaticality,* although often confused, correspond to two distinct points of view on the status of sentences. From the point of view of the linguist, sentences may or may not be *grammatical* with respect to a particular formal representation of competence (i.e., a linguistic theory). The term *grammaticality,* however, is inappropriate to describe the feelings (naive) informants

---

[1] The modular view of language within cognition holds that grammar and discourse context are two distinct but interacting domains (see Newmeyer, 1983, p. 57 on this issue). According to this view, "the grammaticality of a sentence is most profitably regarded as independent of its discourse context." The problem with using contextualized sentences in experiments on linguistic acceptability is that very little is known of the modes of interaction of grammatical knowledge and contextual variables, and it is therefore difficult to evaluate which of the two factors is at the source of judgments.

have about the well-formedness of sentences: to them sentences are only *acceptable* with respect to the various variables (grammatical competence, metalinguistic knowledge, pragmatic appropriateness, etc.) that, as we have just seen, may determine their judgments. Thus, if speakers are asked to judge whether a sentence is grammatical without any indication of what grammaticality means, they will attribute different meanings to the term (interpretable, contextualizable, possible in a given dialect, correct with respect to prescribed rules, etc.). There often is a conflict between grammaticality, as predicted by linguistic theory, and acceptability and intelligibility: Sentences that are grammatical may be judged as unacceptable, and vice versa (Cowart, 1989).

Which Knowledge Is at the Source of Acceptability Judgments?

Even if it is assumed, for the sake of simplicity, that all extralinguistic factors can be isolated, a decision about the nature of the rules underlying genuine intuitions is not a straightforward task. In producing acceptability judgments speakers may unconsciously shift towards the norm they believe they should follow, and away from the norm actually governing their internalized grammar (Coppieters, 1987; Greenbaum & Quirk, 1970). It is important to distinguish among different *attitudes to usage* that speakers may have. According to Greenbaum and Quirk, three potentially different but often interacting factors can be reflected by speakers' judgments: (1) beliefs about the forms they habitually use, (2) beliefs about the forms that ought to be used, and (3) willingness to tolerate usage in others that corresponds neither to their own habitual forms nor to prescriptive forms.

Speakers' conscious beliefs about language may lead them to formulate *adaptive rules* that, under certain circumstances, modify the output of their mentally represented grammars, often in order to avoid the production of stigmatized forms (Pateman, 1985). Adaptive rules are cognitively different from "tacit" rules belonging to the internalized competence: they are social or cultural in character and usually more accessible to introspection than internalized rules. Adaptive rules may therefore be more readily available to informants as a basis for acceptability judgments.

Intuitions and Judgments

It may also be appropriate to distinguish between *intuitions* and *judgments,* although the terms are often used interchangeably. Linguistic intuitions ("non-reasoned feelings," Botha, 1973) are not easily accessible, either to the speaker's conscious mind or to the researcher: They can be portrayed as the result of a computational process that is said to take place in the speaker's mentally represented grammar and below the level of conscious awareness. Intuitions are registered and reported by the speaker in the form of judgments, which are linguistic *descriptions* and may therefore be inaccurate. This applies in particular to judgment tests requiring complex verbalizations of rules or other forms of metalinguistic statements.

"Correctness" of Intuitions

If judgments are to be regarded as empirical facts, then it should be possible to verify their correctness: This would imply measuring the disparity between the informants' judgments and the objective physical states of affairs about which judgments are made, or, in other words, having at one's disposal an assessment procedure independent of the reports of the speakers whose judgments are being assessed. For the correctness of judgments to be empirically assessable, it should be possible to measure intuitions of degree of grammaticality against some independently established grammaticality scale. But because intuitions are used as primary data for the construction of models of grammar, obviously there cannot be such a grammaticality scale independent of intuitions. The implicit practice is to assume that informants have *final epistemic authority* on their intuitions, in the same way as they have final epistemic authority on their sensations (which cannot be disproved, because mental states like sensations are in principle uncheckable).

This is an interesting paradox for linguistic research. To the extent that acceptability is a function of grammatical competence, and on the assumption that grammatical competence derives from a mental faculty characterized by physical and biological properties, linguistic perceptions should be subject to the same psychophysical laws as other perceptions: It would then be possible to measure the disparity between acceptability judgments on given aspects of the grammar and the objective representation of those aspects in the mind. In practice, however, there are no ways of measuring the mental representation of linguistic knowledge other than asking informants to provide acceptability judgments. This crucial issue has important implications for the empirical measurement of linguistic acceptability, as will be seen in section IV.

B. Reliability: Why Do Informants Produce Inconsistent Judgments?

It is well known that there are areas of grammar on the acceptability of which NSs do not agree, or do not have any clear intuitions. Early theories of transformational grammar implicitly recognized the existence—if not the extent—of this problem, although their solution was based on the concept of definite grammaticality: "In many intermediate cases we shall be prepared to let the grammar itself decide, when a grammar is set up in the simplest way so that it includes the clear cases and excludes the clear non-cases" (Chomsky, 1957, p. 14).

Intersubject Inconsistency

The easiest—and least satisfactory—solution to the question of intersubject inconsistency is to ascribe conflicting intuitions (assuming that they are genuine) to idiolectal or dialectal differences. In other words, speakers may disagree in their intuitions because they do not share the same grammar. According to this position, there cannot exist any built-in variation in the grammar.

Another common solution is to minimize the inconsistencies of NSs' intuitions. Newmeyer (1983) draws a distinction between *superficial* and *genuine* disagreement about sentence grammaticality. Superficial disagreement does not concern the actual grammaticality status of a given sentence but rather its analysis: whether, for example, some fundamental characteristics of a sentence should be explained by a grammatical principle or by an extragrammatical one. Genuine disagreement, on the other hand, arises from conflicting intuitions about the grammaticality of the sentence. In Newmeyer's view, the vast majority of alleged NSs' disagreements on data are "essentially theoretical disagreements that are only superficial disagreements about the acceptability of sentences" (Newmeyer, 1983, p. 66).

Intermediate Grammaticality

Cases of genuine disagreement, however, are far from uncommon. The alternative way of accounting for intersubject disagreement is to assume that native language (NL) grammars are *indeterminate,* and that such indeterminacy is a characteristic of natural human languages. In this perspective, linguistic structures are not simply grammatical or ungrammatical: they may be grammatical to a degree. From the point of view of the informant, structures may have varying degrees of acceptability, which may determine different degrees of consistency in her judgments. Conceptually, indeterminacy may be defined as indefiniteness of status in the speaker's grammatical competence. Operationally, indeterminacy may be defined as variability in the speaker's acceptability judgments. Such variability may manifest itself in inconsistency of judgments (both within and between speakers), or in an inability to distinguish acceptable from unacceptable sentences. The question that arises here is whether indeterminacy is random and unpredictable, or whether it is lawful and predictable.

"Fuzzy" Grammars and Acceptability Hierarchies

Outside the generativist framework, models of grammars have been elaborated on the basis of grammaticality as a *relative* property of sentences. Lakoff (1973) and Mohan (1977) maintain that there exists an ordinal scale of acceptability within a speech community such that all speakers are likely to argue on the rank order of acceptability values in a given set of sentences, although they may disagree on the absolute rating of individual sentences. The pattern of individual rating judgments, therefore, should not be random but should reveal an implicational scale, the basis of which is a shared ordinal scale. In other words, it would be inconsistent for a speaker to rank sentence A as more acceptable than sentence B but then accept B and reject A.[2]

[2]Mohan (1977) raises the interesting issue of the predicting power of Lakoff's fuzzy grammar model, (i.e., the fact that it can only make the weak claim that members of a speech community will share the same ordinal scale for an acceptability hierarchy, but not the stronger claim that they will agree on the ordering of the differences between items on the hierarchy).

Along the same lines, Ross (1979) suggests that a language (L) may be seen as consisting of an indefinite number of acceptability hierarchies, each leading away from the core to the periphery of L, and governed by implicational laws such that (1) acceptance of a sentence at distance x from the core implies acceptance of any more central sentences along the same hierarchy (i.e., between x and the core), and (b) speakers may disagree on the absolute acceptability values of individual sentences because they may have different acceptability thresholds on the same hierarchy.

C. Acceptability Hierarchies and Universal Grammar

The concept of acceptability hierarchy relies on the distinction between a *core* and a *periphery*. While early generative grammar could not admit this distinction without violating some of its basic assumptions, recent developments within a principles and parameters framework do make frequent reference to it, thus allowing for the existence of language indeterminacy—at least in principle—in a more satisfactory way. However, the research to date has done very little to substantiate the notion of periphery, or to investigate the modes of its interaction with the core. Furthermore, statements concerned with the periphery seem to contain a fundamental ambiguity with respect to the nature of the relationship between core and periphery: at times, this is seen as a *discontinuous* relationship, whereas at other times it is regarded as a *continuous* relationship.

It is recognized, for example, that the periphery may contain "borrowings, historical residues, inventions and so on" (Chomsky, 1981, p. 8), and that

> we would expect phenomena belonging to the periphery to be supported by specific evidence of sufficient 'density', to be variable among languages and dialects, and so forth. . . . What we "know innately" are the principles of the various subsystems of [the initial state] S_0 and the manner of their interaction, and the parameters associated with these principles. What we learn are the values of the parameters and the elements of the periphery (along with the lexicon, to which similar considerations apply). (Chomsky, 1986, pp. 147, 150)

These statements suggest that acquiring the periphery of any language may require substantially different evidence from that necessary to acquire the core, and thus they implicitly subscribe to the discontinuity assumption.

Elsewhere, however, it is said that "the distinction between core and periphery leaves us with three notions of markedness: core versus periphery, internal to the core, and internal to the periphery." (Chomsky, 1986, p. 147). This statement, unlike the previous ones, contains implicit support for the continuity assumption. If the periphery is contiguous with the core, then it is possible to see both as the extremes of the same scale of markedness. The continuity assumption has the advantage of providing constraints on theories of the core: in Fodor's view,

> If two or more alternative formulations of the principles appear to be equally
> compatible with the facts of the core, we can select between them on the basis of
> which most appropriately ranks other phenomena as more and less peripheral.
> (Fodor, 1989, p. 131)

The continuity assumption has another fortunate consequence: it allows us to say that indeterminacy of linguistic intuitions is naturally compatible with Universal Grammar (UG), and offers an explanation for acceptability hierarchies. With Pateman (1985), we can distinguish among the following:

1. Cases in which UG rigidly specifies the form of grammar independently of any evidence in the input. Principles such as structure dependency are well known to constrain linguistic development in such a way that, regardless of the amount and type of evidence they are exposed to, children never make errors that contain violations of these principles.
2. Cases in which UG offers a preference structure for an array of input data subsuming marked and unmarked structures as alternative analyses of the data; the acquisition of marked structures requires positive evidence. (For discussion of positive and negative evidence and their functions in language acquisition see in particular chapters 2 by Gregg and 13 by Long, this volume.) This claim does not imply that alternative solutions may not be entertained by the learners. For example, although there is a tendency towards regularization (that is, towards unmarked structures), irregular (marked) forms are nonetheless eventually incorporated in the grammar and passed on to the next generation of speakers.
3. Cases in which UG offers a small, unordered set of structures as analyses for given input patterns, presumably because of some (still largely unknown) relaxation of UG constraints (Chomsky, 1981).

The type of structures described in (3) properly belongs to the periphery, and allows for unpredictable elements of variation to enter linguistic reproduction. Regardless of whether the introduction of innovative change happens abruptly and discontinuously with respect to previous stages of the evolution of a language (see Lightfoot, 1983, 1991), or whether it implies a gradual and cumulative process (Traugott & Heine, 1991), one can say that

> there will always have to be at least one initiating change motivated externally in
> terms of changes in the community that provides the data to which the learner is
> exposed. . . . These changes may be determined either by variation in adults, or
> at least postmaturational usage, or by population shifts and other kinds of so-
> cially motivated factors. (Vincent, 1989, in Lightfoot, 1989)

Consistent with this view, language change can be regarded as a process that starts by creating indeterminacy at the periphery of acceptability hierarchies, which then gradually extends towards the core. Such indeterminacy steadily increases, affecting the frequency and consistency of appearance of certain forms in the input, and therefore the triggering experience of children in the course of language acquisition. This process would reach a point when, in the course of generations, abrupt reanalysis of learners' grammars becomes necessary because the affected forms are in disharmony with other structural properties of the language, and a grammar containing such forms is unlearnable (Kroch, 1989, in Lightfoot, 1989, Lightfoot, 1991).[3]

Thus, it is not implausible that UG and cognitive resources nonspecific to language have a combined influence on the periphery, although the modes of their combination are still largely unexplored. This means that cultural norms, speech adaptations, individual beliefs, and conscious rationalizations about language would find a more fertile ground at the periphery than at the core, and this accounts for the fact that the maximum amount of variation and inconsistency is usually found in this area.

III. LINGUISTIC ACCEPTABILITY IN NONNATIVE LANGUAGES

The single most important notion underlying the field of L2 acquisition research is that of IL. Clearly inspired by generative linguistics, the Interlanguage Hypothesis (whose original formulations are found in Corder, 1974, 1981; Selinker, 1972) assumes that L2 learners have a mentally represented grammar at every stage of the acquisition process. IL grammars can be studied in their own right (as any fully developed natural language) and not necessarily in terms of a comparison with the TL. The state of learners' IL competence can be formally characterized by a grammar that can (minimally) meet the level of descriptive adequacy, when it correctly accounts for the data produced by learners, or the higher level of explanatory adequacy, when it explains how the learners came to acquire that competence. Most early research on L2 acquisition was devoted to the former aim (for example, Cazden, Cancino, Rosansky, & Schumann, 1975; Dulay & Burt, 1973; Wode, 1978), whereas recent theories developed within the principles and parameters framework address the latter (see White, 1989, this volume; Gregg, this volume; see also the papers in Eubank, 1991; Flynn & O'Neill, 1988; Pankhurst, van Buren, & Sharwood Smith, 1988, among others).

If learners are assumed to have IL internalized grammars, then learners' lin-

---

[3]Critics of the generativist position on the nature of language change, such as Kroch (1989), seem nevertheless to agree with it when they claim that

> change is more often gradual than abrupt . . . and one generation is more likely to differ from its predecessor in the frequency with which its speakers use certain forms than in whether those forms are possible at all. *Only when the frequency of a form drops below a minimum threshold do learners reanalyze their grammatical systems so as to exclude it* [italics added].

guistic intuitions become the primary indicators of IL competence. The problem then arises of whether it is appropriate to treat native and nonnative competences as identical objects of investigation. It is easy to get the impression, in reading the L2 acquisition literature, that principles and methodologies have been borrowed from linguistic theory without questioning their validity and their applicability to the study of IL grammars. Given the fundamental difference between native and nonnative grammars—that the former are, at least in their core, fully developed, steady states of linguistic competence, whereas the latter are unstable, transitional states of knowledge—it is even more surprising that very few studies (among which are found Birdsong, 1989, 1992; Chaudron, 1983; Sorace, 1988, 1990) have so far attempted a more precise definition of nonnative linguistic intuitions, or of the elicitation procedures employed in the collection of intuitional data from L2 learners.

A. Validity and Reliability of Nonnative Acceptability Judgments

Like the acceptability judgments of NSs, the judgments expressed by NNSs are generally assumed to be related both to (1) the transitional state of their IL knowledge, and to (2) their actual intuitions. The same arguments underlying the question of the validity of native acceptability judgments apply to nonnative judgments. Thus, it seems reasonable to claim that IL judgments at least partly reflect IL knowledge: The more extraneous variables are controlled for, the clearer this reflection is (see the arguments outlined in section II.A).

It can be a more complex task, however, to decide about the kind of *norm* consulted by learners in the process of producing a judgment, particularly in a learning environment that fosters the development of metalinguistic knowledge: It is difficult to tell whether subjects reveal what they think or what they think they should think. The elicitation of immediate judgment responses under well-defined time constraints may provide a partial solution to this problem, as I will show later.

A further difference between native and nonnative intuitions concerns the correctness issue. We saw earlier that native acceptability judgments present a paradox: on the one hand, they result from grammatical competence, but on the other hand they cannot be compared to objective states of grammatical competence because competence eludes direct measurement. Nonnative acceptability judgments can, at first glance, be compared with the standard represented by native judgments; this is indeed common practice in most experimental studies in L2 research, where a control group of NSs serves as the basis for comparison. However, there are two considerations to bear in mind. First, native judgments themselves can be indeterminate, particularly when the objects of investigation are highly marked or very subtle syntactic properties: native judgments may therefore provide a point of reference only in the most uncontroversial cases. Second, the ultimate purpose of testing nonnative linguistic intuitions is to construct a model of the nonnative grammar of a particular learner, or group of learners at a particular level of proficiency: unless such nonnative grammar is seen as an imperfect realization on the native grammar, the learners' judgments themselves should provide the primary criterion for deciding which structures are or are not part of it. The evaluation of the distance between native and nonnative grammars becomes an irrelevant criterion.

B. Indeterminacy in IL Grammars

The crucial feature that characterizes IL grammars and distinguishes them from native grammars is the pervasiveness of indeterminacy. In many cases, the indefiniteness of Il competence leads to the learner's ability to express a clear-cut judgment of acceptability.

At the most basic level, constructions are indeterminate because the learners do not have any knowledge of them. IL indeterminacy due to ignorance was for a long time the only kind of indeterminacy recognized by L2 acquisition researchers (typical of this early attitude is the study by Schachter, Tyson, & Diffley, 1976). This kind of indeterminacy characterizes nonnative grammars throughout the acquisition process, although it is more conspicuous at the initial and intermediate stages of IL development.

At more advanced stages, constructions may *become* indeterminate (after a period of relative stability) because of the increased amount and sophistication of the learner's knowledge. One of the factors contributing to this kind of IL indeterminacy is the permeability of IL grammars, their "openness" to the influence of other linguistic systems. It has been debated whether permeability is a competence phenomenon, or if it is restricted to the performance level (Adjémian, 1976; Liceras, 1983); or whether permeability is peculiar to IL but does not affect NL grammars (Arditty & Perdue, 1982). If permeability is a crucial, though not unique, property of IL *competence* then it generates indeterminacy by creating the conditions for the coexistence of more than one rule for the same aspect of grammar. The coexisting rules may belong to different linguistic systems known to the learner, or to successive stages of IL development, or both. The result is variability or indecisiveness in learners' intuitions. (See chapter 8 by Preston, this volume, for discussion of the study of variation in L2 performance.)

As Klein (1986) suggests, IL grammars may be regarded as "test grammars" in which a rule is associated, at a given time (T), with both a degree of confirmation (indicating the confidence with which the learner knows a particular structure) and a degree of criticalness (representing the stability of that rule)—that is, whether that rule is undergoing a process of change at that time. The relation between confirmation and criticalness is not necessarily linear although, as Klein points out, weakly confirmed rules are more likely to become critical. Naturally, the criticalness of rules may increase only if IL grammars are permeable to new input. The ever-changing nature of ILs necessarily brings about diachronic variability, and therefore makes rules critical. Rules cease to be critical when IL grammars are no longer permeable (i.e., when a rule has been acquired or when a rule has become fossilized). Both weak confirmation and criticalness contribute— as separate dimensions—to IL indeterminacy. We shall return to this point in section IV.C.

IL Indeterminacy from a UG Perspective

An important cause of indeterminacy can be identified in the fact that the UG-driven specification of core properties is narrower in scope and strength than in native grammars. This underspecification may be due to the reduced availability of UG as a cognitive module, or to inadequate exposure to input, or—in most cases—both.[4] The result is a wider periphery and consequently more room for permeability and variation. Let us examine the latter point in more detail.

The typical L2 acquisition situation allows either (or both) of the following conflicted conditions to obtain:

1. Incompatibility between the parameter settings of the learner's NL and those instantiated by the L2. Depending on the nature of the evidence available and on the specific markedness relationship between the NL and the TL,[5] L2

[4]Much of L2 acquisition research conducted in the past 5 years has been concerned with the availability of UG issue (see chapters 3 by White, 2 by Gregg, 4 by Flynn, and 5 by Schachter, this volume). The aim of such research is to achieve an explanation of how adult learners attain competence in an L2, and current linguistic theory offers a natural framework for this purpose. Arguments in favor of a role for UG in L2 acquisition center around the logical problem of L2 acquisition (i.e., the fact that learners who achieve a reasonable degree of success in the L2 have necessarily "gone beyond" the input they were exposed to). Open questions are whether UG principles are available in toto, or whether they are available only through the specific instantiations exhibited by the L1; whether IL grammars are "natural grammars" (i.e., constrained by UG) at every stage of development; and what kind of input contributes to L2 developmental stages. A substantial number of researchers, on the other hand, do not believe in the availability of UG, and emphasize the fundamental differences between L1 and L2 acquisition, the difficulties faced by L2 learners, and the impossibility of complete acquisition by adult learners (see in particular Schachter, chap. 5, this volume).

[5]Early work on L2 learnability focused on the availability of the Subset Principle (SP) to L2 learners (see White, 1989, chap. 3, this volume for a comprehensive review). The SP is a learning principle (available to the L1 acquirer) that guarantees acquisition without negative evidence: the principle is an in-built instruction to the learner to be conservative, preventing him or her from adopting overinclusive parameter settings in the absence of explicit evidence. The findings on L2 acquisition indicate that the SP is not available to L2 learners; this, together with the natural tendency of learners to transfer the parameter settings instantiated by their L1s, explains the learning asymmetries that have been observed between learners whose L1 is a superset of the L2 and learners whose L1 is a subset of the L2. Only in the former case does the learner have a potential problem of overgeneralization. Recent developments in linguistic theory, however, suggest that parametric variation may be the result of variation in the properties of lexical items rather than in the principles of UG (Ouhalla, 1991; Wexler & Manzini, 1987). A further refinement of this lexical parameterization hypothesis identifies the site of variation in the properties of the functional categories rather than in the major lexical categories (functional parameterization hypothesis). The implication for L2 acquisition is that parameter resetting may be an impossibility for the L2 learner because functional categories may be acquired by the child as a result of a genetically determined schedule (Tsimpli & Roussou, 1991).

parameters may have to be reset, or simply left unset (see Flynn, 1987, this volume; Schachter, 1989, chap. 5, this volume, on these issues; White, 1988, 1989; chap. 3, this volume). The quantity, quality, or both of the input available may be insufficient for the L2 parameters to be (re)set and for significant projections to take place. Alternatively, learners may simply *fail to notice* the linguistic relevance of the input to which they are exposed (Sorace, 1993a).

2. Competition between UG and problem-solving cognitive resources generally available to adult learners (Felix, 1985), which may suggest solutions to input configurations not definable in terms of UG constraints (often called "unnatural" or "wild" rules).

These conflicts may account for the fact that acceptability hierarchies for an L2 never become fully determinate: only a reduced portion of the L2 core is unambiguously specified by UG, but a relatively larger portion is the site of long-lasting or even permanent parametric variation. Furthermore, an ample periphery remains open to the influence of different kinds of factors, both grammatical and extra-grammatical in nature. If so, this would partly explain why variable or inconsistent intuitions are found in NNSs even at very advanced stages of language proficiency. To the extent that ILs are natural languages, falling within the range of possible grammars allowed by UG, learners' intuitions will vary around a limited number of alternatives ('possible' alternatives); to the extent that ILs are also determined by problem-solving strategies, learners' intuitions will take more idiosyncratic and largely unpredictable forms.

Where the input presents limitations in terms of quality and variety, as in conventional instructional settings, the scope of action of the language-specific faculty is further restricted by the lack of triggering evidence. Consequently, alternative structural solutions are likely to be provided either by the L1 or by cognitive resources not specific to language. These solutions in turn determine (1) greater intersubject variability, because different learners may come up with idiosyncratic hypotheses, and (2) greater intrasubject variation, because individual learners may formulate alternative hypotheses, the competition among which cannot be solved by positive confirmation or disconfirmation, as would happen in naturalistic acquisition.[6] (For a general discussion of language attrition (referred to in ftn. 6), see chapter 18, this volume, by Seliger.)

[6]Indeterminacy induced by input restrictions has even more obvious consequences in situations of language attrition, where it is the L1 that is removed from its natural context. The absence of L1-input, coupled with the overwhelming presence of L2-input, leads to a progressive "disintegration" of the core through a process of constant erosion that undermines the determinacy of its structures. This is what Py (1986) defines as the process of 'positive retroaction' ("*rétroaction positive*"), which accompanies the growing indeterminacy of norms, due to the increasing permeability of the core to L2-inspired deviations. Because of the reduced availability of UG constraints, there is seldom simple replacement of L1-core features with L2-core features; more often there is no replacement at all, with resulting indeterminacy, variation, and increased openness to change.

Near-Native Indeterminacy

Does IL indeterminacy invariably decrease over time, and eventually disappear? A positive answer to both questions would imply that it is possible for the adult learner to construct nativelike mental representations of grammatical knowledge for core aspects of the target language (TL)—or, in other words, that non-primary language acquisition can be "complete."

This question is closely related to the ongoing debate on the availability of UG as a constraint on IL and the learnability of specific grammatical aspects of an L2: If IL development was constrained by UG in its entirety, there would be no cognitive obstacle to complete success in the L2 acquisition enterprise. The existing empirical findings, however, do not allow unequivocal interpretations. On the one hand, they show that IL grammars are underdetermined by the input, because L2 learners can and do acquire knowledge of subtle and complex linguistic properties that (1) are not instantiated by their L1, and (2) cannot be the focus of formal instruction. On the other hand, they provide indisputable evidence suggesting that many L2 learners fail to acquire grammatical properties that are not instantiated in their L1, or fail to reset parameters after the initial, inappropriate adoption of the L1 setting (see White, 1989, for a comprehensive account of the research to date). (See also chapters 2–5 by Gregg, White, Flynn, and Schachter, this volume.) Experimental evidence and intuitive observation at the present stage seem to be consistent in suggesting that—whatever the reason—reaching nativelike competence with respect to *the whole* of the L2 grammar is in practice an impossibility for the adult learner.

Most studies, however, do not address the question of ultimate attainment directly, because they are not concerned with learners at the most advanced stage of IL development. Yet the "ultimate attainment" issue can only be properly addressed by looking at the competence of learners who have supposedly reached that stage. One of the few exceptions is Coppieters's (1987) study, which aimed at investigating competence differences between the intuitions of NSs and those of near-NSs of French about some highly productive aspects of grammar, such as the contrast imperfect and present perfect, the distinction between the third-person pronouns *il/elle,* and *ce,* and that between preposed and postposed uses of adjectives. The most striking result of this study was the extent of the gap between native and near-native intuitions: while NSs seemed to share a "native majority norm," with respect to which they showed minimal variation, all near-NSs deviate from the native norm in statistically significant ways (the closest nonnative value to the majority norm was three standard deviations from it), and revealed extensive variation. Furthermore, the *interpretation* that near-NSs produced of the grammatical forms in question was on several occasions remarkably different from the interpretation offered by NSs, even when their actual rating judgments were the same. This suggests, according to Coppieters, that the two groups of informants may have developed "significantly different grammatical systems for French," despite the fact that they are virtually indistinguishable in production. Finally, near-NSs often lacked any clear intuitions on some of the grammatical rules investigated (in particular, the distinction perfect and imperfect) and their preference for either form was unsystematic. These results, however, have been challenged by Birdsong (1992), who replicated Coppieters's original study and found that although near-NSs differ significantly from natives *as a group,* the majority of individual subjects perform well within the NS range.

The variety of near-native knowledge patterns revealed by these studies suggests that the concept of near-nativeness may be more complex than it appears. The term *near-native* itself seems to contain an implicit statement on the question of ultimate attainment, because it implies that the near-native grammar is *almost*—but not quite—the same as the native grammar. Accordingly, the sense in which near-nativeness is usually understood is that of *incompleteness,* indicating the absence in the near-native grammar of a property required by the native grammar.

There is, however, another possible meaning of near-nativeness: the near-native grammar could be not so much incomplete as *divergent,* containing representations of L2 properties that are *different* from the native representations. Such a distinction between states of nonnative knowledge might be expected to affect the near-NS's grammaticality judgments. The incomplete grammar, lacking a given L2 property (P), would lead to random, inconsistent, in short *indeterminate* judgments about P, whereas the divergent grammar, because it incorporates an alternative representation of P, would lead to *determinate* judgments that are consistently different from native judgments. Both the incomplete and the divergent near-native grammars could produce seemingly native-like performance, presumably because performance is based on a more restricted range of structures than the IL competence would generate. Sorace (1993a) found both patterns of judgments in her study on unaccusativity and auxiliary selection in English and French near-native grammars of Italian. The English near-NSs exhibited incompleteness in their judgments on certain complex syntactic phenomena related to unaccusativity, such as the obligatoriness of the *avere* → *essere* ("to have" → "to be") auxiliary change with clitic-climbing or the optionality of such change under restructuring. In contrast, the French near-NSs exhibited divergent judgments on the same properties (i.e. they had a determinate representation of these phenomena that does not coincide with the native representation).

Finally, it is worth noticing that near-native grammars may also be indeterminate in the same sense as native grammars (i.e. because of the intermediate grammaticality of certain constructions). This is the natural consequence of near-NSs' success in acquiring acceptability hierarchies that are similar to those of NSs. Given that, as we saw earlier, this type of indeterminacy leads to inconsistent and variable judgments, it may be empirically difficult to decide whether inconsistency in near-native judgments is due to incompleteness or to intermediate grammaticality.

IV. THE EMPIRICAL MEASUREMENT OF LINGUISTIC ACCEPTABILITY

A. The Elicitation of Acceptability Judgments

Given the complexity of the intuitional process, eliciting acceptability judgments is a much more problematic task than is usually assumed. Minimally, the following conditions have to be met:

1. In order to obtain valid data, the effect of the informant's internalized grammatical competence has to be disentangled from extragrammatical factors that may interfere with it.
2. In order to obtain reliable data, the experiment should be replicated with the same subjects in the same experimental conditions.
3. In order to obtain indicators of the status of acceptability hierarchies in the informant's competence, it is crucial to capture both determinacy and indeterminacy—and particularly degrees of indeterminacy—in linguistic intuitions.
4. In order to provide an account of variability in judgments that can be legitimately generalized, it is necessary to find statistically valid ways of making comparisons on measurements of linguistic acceptability.

All the four conditions above are conspicuously overlooked in linguistic research. The linguistic intuition, although still the most often consulted behavior in the linguistic literature, has not given rise to quantitative models comparable to those adopted in other experimental fields. The elicitation of acceptability judgments continues to take the form of an informal consultation of colleagues (often of the same theoretical persuasion), who are asked to say whether they like a sentence or not. And while notations of varying acceptability like "**", "*", "??" and "?" now abound in the syntax literature, they make very little advance on an either–or scale because they provide an ordinal scale of acceptability. Such notations indicate that a sentence classified "?" is more acceptable than a sentence classified "??", but provide no information about the difference in acceptability between the two sentences: whether this difference is of the same size, or smaller, or larger, than the difference between sentences classified "*" and "**" and—more crucially—whether larger or smaller differences reflect important or trivial factors at the level of linguistic competence.

Moreover, restricting the measurement of intuitions to an ordinal scale prevents our doing any interesting analysis of the results: Biological and physical laws, inferential statistics, and even the most useful accounts of the variability of behavior all demand at least an interval scale, one in which successive points are separated by equal intervals and the measurement can be subjected to arithmetic operations.

These problems affect both studies of native judgments and studies of nonnative judgments, but given the inherent instability and indeterminacy of IL grammars, they require more urgent attention in L2 acquisition research. Is it possible to turn the elicitation of linguistic intuitions into a properly designed experiment?

The next sections will examine the characteristics of the most common elicitation techniques used in linguistic research and will discuss their shortcomings. Although the main focus will be on NNS judgments, most of the arguments that will be made apply to NS judgments as well. An alternative will then be suggested that borrows from the domain of psychophysics: magnitude estimation. It will be shown that the magnitude scaling of acceptability judgments is, in principle, feasible and allows us to approach variability of judgments directly.

Reliability Criteria

We saw earlier how the reliability question concerns the consistency of judgments, both within- and between-individual informants. There are two basic possibilities:

1. Inconsistency may be an artifact of the experiment (because of an inadequate test design, poor test items, etc). In this case, inconsistency may disappear if informants are given a properly designed test.
2. Inconsistency may be an effect of the inherent indeterminacy of the grammatical construction investigated. In this case, successive replications of the test would continue to produce inconsistent results.

Only the latter type of inconsistency is relevant here. However, we saw earlier that a structure may be indeterminate in the speaker's intuitions for a variety of reasons, which can be subsumed under the two basic notions of (1) developing knowledge, and (2) intermediate grammaticality. The former of course tends to characterize NNS judgments, whereas the latter may affect both NS and NNS judgments. Replication of the test, as the reliability criterion most often recommended, is not always applicable to nonnative intuitions, particularly if they present developmental indeterminacy. Greenbaum (1977), for example, proposes four reliability criteria for NS's intuitions, three of which are concerned with intrasubject consistency and one with intersubject consistency. Let us examine them briefly:

1. Replication of the same test with different subjects belonging to the same speech community. This leaves us the problem of defining the same speech community. Although in the case of NSs this usually means other NSs of the same language, it is more problematic to identify the speech community that NNSs would belong to. However, it is often assumed that learners at the same proficiency level, or from the same language background, share common characteristics and can therefore be regarded as members of the same group.

2. Replication of the same test with the same subjects after a lapse of time. What needs to be defined in this case is the optimal length of time between two successive administrations of the test. The interval cannot be too short if one wants to avoid producing a learning effect in the subjects. When working with L2 learners, the interval cannot be too long because IL grammars are in constant evolution. If learners are continuously exposed to the L2, even a short interval between two testing sessions may produce different results.

3. Replication of the same test with the same subjects, using different but equivalent materials. Different lexical versions of the same sentence type should be built into experiments as a matter of course, but inconsistent responses to lexical versions may then indicate either unreliable subjects, or the effect of irrelevant syntactic or lexical differences among sentences. Equivalence among lexicalizations cannot be taken for granted (except perhaps for the most common constructions), because sentences regarded as theoretically identical by the researcher may turn out to be different in the informants' perception (see an example in Bradac et al., 1980): Appropriate statistical tests should be applied to control for the intrusion of irrelevant lexical differences. In the case of nonnative informants, particularly at low-proficiency levels, there is the additional problem that lexicalizations may be judged differently because of ignorance, either of the lexicon, or of other irrelevant syntactic aspects of the sentences.

4. Replication of the test with the same subjects and the same test materials but using different kinds of measurements. The obvious question in this case is whether different measurements actually elicit the same aspects of informants' judgments or, in other words, whether they are equally valid.

We will now turn our attention to question (4) in some detail. The discussion in the following sections will focus on general principles and methods for the scaling of stimuli, particularly on (1) the type of scales for responses, and (2) the types of responses required of informants.

B. Types of Judgment Scales

There are four basic types of scales on which subjects are asked to respond in experiments concerned with the measurement of stimuli:

1. Category scales, where the relation among items can be represented as $x \neq y$
2. Ordinal scales, where the relation among items can be represented as $x > y$
3. Interval scales, where the relation among items can be represented as $x - y = z$
4. Ratio scales, where the relation among items can be represented as $x/y = z$

Category (or nominal) scales partition a given dimension into a set of mutually exclusive subclasses. The assignment of items to any one subclass involves the relations of *equivalence* and *difference;* all items assigned to the same subclass must be equivalent with respect to the property that defines that subclass and different with respect to items assigned to other subclasses. A category scale of acceptability would have a number of mutually exclusive subcategories defined, for example, as right or wrong. The labels that define the various subcategories may be interchanged, provided that this is done consistently: this operation does not affect the essential information in the scale.

Ordinal scales imply that the items in one category are not only different from the items in other categories but also stand in some relation to them. Thus, if responses are expressed on an ordinal scale, items assigned to a category are *greater* (i.e., more preferred, more difficult, higher, etc.) than sentences assigned to another category. An ordinal scale of acceptability would be one that requires informants to rank a set of sentences from most to least acceptable: such a scale would convey the information that sentence *x* is more (or less) acceptable than sentence *y* but it would not provide the interval between *x* and *y*. Nunnally (1967) mentions three other kinds of methods based on ordinal estimation: *paired comparisons,* in which subjects are required to rank stimuli two at a time in all possible pairs; *constant stimuli,* in which a standard stimulus is paired with each member of a constant set of stimuli; *successive categories,* in which subjects are required to sort a collection of stimuli into a number of distinct categories, which are ordered with respect to a given attribute.

Interval scales have all the properties of ordinal scales but in addition they specify the *distance* between any two points on the scale. An interval scale of acceptability, for example, would therefore provide not only the information that a given sentence is more acceptable than another, but also—and crucially—*how much* more acceptable it is. Interval scales are characterized by a common and constant unit of measurement that attributes a number to all pairs of items on the scale. The unit of measurement and the zero point are arbitrary. One method of interval estimation mentioned by Nunnally (1967) consists of giving subjects two stimuli of unequal intensity and asking them to select a third stimulus that is halfway between the two in terms of a specified attribute.

The application of interval scales to nonmetric continua often relies on the assumption that the informant's response of yes to any one item is exactly equivalent to other affirmative responses to other items. Creating an interval scale for acceptability, for example, would imply that the response "acceptable" to a sentence is exactly equivalent to the "acceptable" response to any other sentence.

Finally, ratio scales have all the characteristics of interval scale but in addition have a true zero point at their origin. The ratio of any two points on such scales is independent of the unit of measurement. On a ratio scale all four of these relations are possible to attain: (1) equivalence, (2) greater than, (3) known ratio between two intervals, and (4) known ratio of any of two values on the scale (Siegel &

Castellan, 1988, p. 31). Real ratio scales are difficult to find, or to create, outside the physical sciences.

Admissible Operations with Different Measurement Scales

The four types of measurement scales that we have just discussed differ in terms of the type of statistical manipulation of data that they allow. Measurement can be regarded as the process of assigning numbers to observations in order to represent quantities of attributes, so that it is possible to perform mathematical and statistical operations on them. The type relations that characterize the assignment of items to points on a scale define and limit the type of operations that can be applied on the data. The permissible operations must be the ones of the numerical structure to which the particular scale is isomorphic (Siegel & Castellan, 1988, p. 32). This requirement separates nominal and ordinal scales, on the one hand, and interval and ratio scales on the other. Only interval and ration scales are isomorphic to the structure of arithmetic: more precisely, it is the *differences* between values in an interval scale that are in such an isomorphic relation, whereas in a ratio scale it is the numerical values themselves. It follows that only interval and ratio scales permit the application of parametric statistical tests on the data, because these tests require the operations of arithmetic (i.e., means and standard deviations) on the original scores. Nominal and ordinal data do not satisfy the parametric assumptions because the intervals between successive classes are not equal; therefore the arithmetic operations implied by parametric statistics do not have substantial meaning when they are performed on such data.

C. Types of Responses: Absolute versus Comparative Judgments

The second important distinction that we need to consider is whether informants are required to produce an *absolute* judgment on each sentence separately, or to make *relative* judgments among different sentences. The first type of test involves a *rating* response, and the second type involves a *ranking* response. This distinction is clearly related to the choice of a particular type of measurement scale, as will be seen later. These two fundamental types of responses, and the corresponding scales of measurement, present different properties and, when applied to acceptability judgments, may yield qualitatively and quantitatively different patterns of results.

Absolute Judgments

The most common measurement technique used in linguistic research is one or another form of *category scaling* in which informants rate a sentence or express an absolute judgment by choosing one of a fixed number of options. Typically, informants are presented with a binary choice: correct versus incorrect, or good versus bad, or acceptable versus unacceptable, and so on. Alternatively, judgments can be expressed by choosing among categories on a scale that has more than two points.

In general terms, this kind of measurement has a number of serious weaknesses. Category scales compress the informants' judgments into a limited number of options, so that sentences more or less alike are placed into the same category. The resolution of the categories, that is, the proportion between the true range of stimuli and the fixed range points on the category scale, is usually poor, and at its worst in binary scales. Inevitably, the more limited the resolution of the scale, the more constrained the informants' responses are, and the more likely the researcher is to get uninformative data at best, and invalid responses at worst.

But category scales present another major defect, arising specifically from the nature of the internalized competence that they are supposed to test. As we saw earlier, NSs may not be able to express absolute judgments on the indeterminate areas of their NL. Given the pervasiveness of indeterminacy in IL grammars, it is apparent that rating scales, especially in binary form, are even more inadequate for the investigation of nonnative competence. Let us examine in some detail why judgments obtained by means of a dichotomous scale may provide inaccurate or deceptive information about the learner's state of competence.

Consider the case in which learners are asked to produce an absolute judgment (correct vs. incorrect) on a construction that is not—or no longer—determinate in their IL grammar. Any sentence exemplifying that construction will be marked as either correct or incorrect without having such a status in the IL grammar: the learner's choice will be random. If there are different tokens of the same test sentence type, judgments may or may not be inconsistent. If they are not, the researcher is left with the deceptive impression that the construction is determinate in the informant's mental grammar, whereas in actual fact such consistency is the spurious result of guessing. If judgments are inconsistent, there cannot be any unambiguous interpretation of such inconsistency: no way of deciding whether it can be traced back to random choice, for example, because the learner has no representation of the structure in question, or whether it is due to intermediate or advanced indeterminacy (which, as was seen earlier, may be caused by the temporary coexistence of old and new rules in the learner's IL grammar). The validity of judgments obtained through binary rating scales is therefore questionable.

Three-Point Scales and the Certainty Dimension

The fundamental inadequacy of binary rating scales is not much improved if binary scales are replaced by three-point scales. The addition of a third category labeled "not sure" or "in between" to a dichotomous scale would seem at first sight to solve the problem of learners' random choice and consequent uninterpretability of the consistency factors. It might be argued, in fact, that because of the presence of such a category, informants would not be forced to produce an either–or judgment: they would be free to express their uncertainty by channeling their responses to the neutral category. In practice, however, the likelihood of obtaining invalid results is still quite high.

The first problem lies in the definition of the middle category, which can be chosen either because of a state of psychological uncertainty of the informant, or because of a state of intermediate grammaticality of the structure in question. In theory, it is possible for a sentence to be judged completely acceptable but with less than full confidence or, conversely, a sentence may be judged as being of intermediate grammaticality with complete confidence. Although in practice acceptability and certainty tend to be related, in the sense that informants choose the extremes of a scale with more confidence than when they choose intermediate points, this possibility cannot be ruled out, essentially because *certainty* and *acceptability* are two quite distinct and independent dimensions. This is suggested by a number of studies where the two factors were subjected to separate analyses. A study by Yule, Yanz, and Tsuda (1985) explored the relationship between correctness in answering and accuracy in judging the correctness of the chosen answer; the results reveal that subjects were more sure of their correct answers than of their wrong answers, but two other combinations emerged: nonconfident correct answering, and very confident wrong answering. Sorace (1985), refining a procedure originally suggested by Kohn (1982), was able to calculate separate scores for consistency and certainty in IL judgments, and concluded that the two values do *not* follow parallel developmental curves: learners are more confident at the initial stages of the acquisition process, regardless of the consistency of their responses, but their certainty decreases dramatically at intermediate stages, while the consistency of their judgment improves.

Decisions about how to label the middle category are therefore not trivial, because they may bias responses in either direction: if the category is labeled "not sure" or "don't know," informants may feel more inclined to interpret it as an admission of uncertainty or ignorance, whereas if it is named "in-between," they might use it only if they feel that, for some reason, a particular sentence is neither acceptable nor unacceptable. In practice, however, there is no guarantee that a label like "in between" may not be interpreted in the same way as "not sure": This suggests that intermediate categories on a rating scale are always difficult to interpret correctly, both from the point of view of the informant and from that of the experimenter. Furthermore, NSs and NNSs may have different preferences and biases, because NNSs are more likely to feel uncertain about, or to lack knowledge of, particular constructions; they are also less likely, at least up to an advanced proficiency level, to have the degree of linguistic sophistication necessary to consistently judge a construction as having intermediate grammaticality. Finally, personality factors may override genuine acceptability judgments: some learners may feel reluctant to choose the middle category (regardless of the label attached to it) because of a fear or revealing their uncertainty; other learners may be inclined to choose it most of the time in order not to commit themselves to a definite judgment. This tendency could be defined as the "may-be-saying factor" in analogy with the well-known "yea-saying factor" in acceptability judgments (i.e., a tendency to accept sentences regardless of their particular structure) (Mohan, 1977).

A possible solution may consist of including a *separate* scale for certainty, so that informants are asked to express both their acceptability judgments and the degree of confidence with which their judgments are produced. This would be conceptually justified, because, as we saw earlier, learners' perception of their own knowledge may be very different from their actual knowledge (see Klein's, 1986, distinction between confirmation and criticalness of rules). The difficulty in this case lies in ensuring (through clear instructions and examples) that acceptability and certainty are perceived as distinct by the informants: giving certainty judgments involves providing a kind of "meta-evaluation" about one's own judgments of acceptability, which may be a very demanding task to some informants.

Finally, scales including more than three points are statistically more reliable, and have a better resolution. Depending on how they are used, these scales may yield ordinal information (see Nunnally, 1967, on the method of "equal-appearing-intervals") but they do not solve the problem of how to interpret intermediate points. Subjects may find it difficult to maintain a stable and consistent criterion in their use of middle categories, unless these are clearly labeled and the labels are defined unambiguously. If they are, however, the experimenter imposes an additional constraint on the informants' responses. For category scales, the alternatives seem to be only two: either predetermining the range and type of judgments, or leaving the informants free to interpret categories in their own way, with the obvious risk of obtaining substantially different interpretations.

To conclude, category acceptability scales are oblivious to the true range of stimuli and the subjective range of judgments (Lodge, 1981). They are insensitive to indeterminacy or uncertainty in judgments, or they conflate the two dimensions. They deny access to powerful statistical treatments (analysis of variance—ANOVA—regression, etc.) because they are based on a nominal (or at best ordinal) level of measurement, which involves an arbitrary number of categories and the arbitrary assignment of numbers to categories. In short, category scales may result in (1) misclassification of sentences and (2) loss of information.

Relative Judgments

Ranking measurements are essentially comparative and require the expression of *relative* (not absolute) judgments. With ranking scales, sentences are typically presented in groups of two or more, and the informant responds to the "more" or "less" of acceptability. It is a fact that people are better at making relative judgments than at expressing absolute judgments (see Nunnally, 1967, on this

point). This is probably because most judgments in life are inherently comparative; even when giving absolute judgments, subjects tend to relate their responses
to (1) stimuli of the same kind that they have experienced in the past, and (2) the
range of stimuli in the set presented.

As seen earlier, the most straightforward way of obtaining relative judgments is
to present informants with a set of sentences and ask them to rank them from "most
acceptable" to "least acceptable" (or vice versa). The reliability of ranking tests
involving more than three sentences is not clear, although experiments with NSs
have used sets of 6 (Snow & Meijer, 1977) or even 11 sentences (Mohan, 1977).

An alternative method is that of *successive categories,* in which subjects are
instructed to sort a collection of sentences—each individually printed on a separate card—into a number of distinct piles or categories, which are ordered with
respect to their degree of acceptability. Unlike the procedure of ranking sets of
sentences, this leaves informants free to manipulate the sentences and to move
them around while distributing them into piles, without being tied to the original
order of presentation. Variants of this method have been used in research on the
structure of the mental lexicon (Miller, 1969) and in research on NL transfer in
L2 acquisition (Kellerman, 1978).

All these methods allow for the possibility of tied ranks if two or more sentences have the same degree of acceptability and, depending on whether they are
timed or not, leave ample margin for correcting one's initial response.

Ranking scales present the following advantages over rating scales:

1. The resolution of this type of scales is less constraining, because the only
   limit to the number of response categories that informants can use is given
   by the number of sentences: in principle, each sentence can be assigned to a
   separate category.
2. They have greater psychometric plausibility, because they explicitly ask for
   relative judgments.
3. They are more suitable to the purpose of capturing indeterminacy in acceptability, because informants are not forced to produce categorical judgments
   on sentences that are indeterminate in their competence.

However, most ranking methods (including those mentioned so far) generate
ordinal measurements, and are therefore vulnerable to the same kind of statistical
criticism as rating scales. Unless the experimenter instructs the subjects to mark
the distance between successive categories, the result will be a simple rank-order.
Although there are ways of obtaining interval responses from methods of successive categories (see Lodge, 1981, for a discussion; Nunnally, 1967), these imply
assigning numbers to categories in a post-hoc fashion and in an essentially arbitrary way.

Is there an alternative to nominal or ordinal scales of acceptability? Can acceptability be measured on an interval scale?

D. Applying the Psychophysical Paradigm: Magnitude Estimation of Linguistic Acceptability

> [Refusing to use linguistic intuitions as data] would eliminate linguistics as a discipline, just as surely as a refusal to consider what a subject senses or perceives would destroy psychophysics. . . . In both cases, [i.e., linguistics and psychophysics] we are trying (though in very different ways) to find a basis for intuitive judgments. In both cases, furthermore, the difficulty of obtaining reliable and relevant reports is quite apparent. (Chomsky, 1961, p. 225)

The analogy between linguistics and psychophysics is not new, but it has not been systematically investigated. The following sections will explore this analogy in some detail. The question that will be addressed is, Can acceptability judgments be treated in the same way as judgments in a psychophysical experiment?

The primary aim of psychophysical investigations is to discover and describe the relationship between the objectively determined physical dimensions of stimuli and the subjective estimates of the magnitudes of those dimensions: psychophysical methods are essentially concerned with measuring the discrepancy between the informants' judgments and the objective physical states of affairs about which judgments are made. As we saw earlier, there is no such a thing as an objective measurement of linguistic acceptability in the mental representation of knowledge: there are linguistic theories, which make certain linguistic predictions about the possible outcome of an acceptability judgment test. It follows that the correctness of an acceptability judgment cannot be ascertained, because this would involve specifying the linguistic analog to the light meters or meter sticks that are used in assessing the correctness of subjective judgments in a psychophysical experiment.

In this respect, linguistic acceptability is more similar to other sociopsychological dimensions, like prestige of occupation, seriousness of crime, and so on, which lack objective metrics, than it is to physical dimensions like brightness, weight, and length. Does this fundamental difference preclude the extension of the psychophysical paradigm and methodology to nonmetric continua? The answer is negative: it has been shown by numerous studies (see Lodge, 1981, for a review) that social opinions *can* be subjected to the same quantitative methods and analyses as psychophysical judgments and sensations. In particular, it has been demonstrated that the *magnitude scaling* approach can be successfully employed to validate social scales, thus providing a quantitative and powerful measurement of social opinions. This suggests that scales obtained though judgments on sociopsychological variables obey the same laws as judgments obtained through judgments on sensory variables.

Magnitude Estimation

The simplest form of magnitude estimation requires the informant to associate a numerical judgment with a physical stimulus. It is therefore a form of cross-modality matching (S. S. Stevens, 1971). Other versions of the method involve matching a different physical continuum to the one the stimuli belong to: so, for example, the relative brightness of different lights is estimated by the force of hand-grip on a handle (itself measurable by the experimenter in dyne/cm^2). The number continuum is often regarded as the most convenient to use because it is known to the informants and thus does not need to be introduced to them.

In numerical estimation, informants are presented with a series of stimuli of unequal magnitudes, one at a time in random order, and are asked to assign a number (the modulus) to the perceived magnitude of the first stimulus (the standard), and then successive numbers to the perceived magnitude of stimuli in proportion to the modulus. Prototypical instructions read:

> You will be presented with a series of stimuli in irregular order. Your task is to tell how bright/loud/long they seem by assigning numbers to them. Call the first stimulus any number that seems appropriate to you. Then assign successive numbers in such a way that they reflect your subjective impression. For example, if a stimulus seems 20 times as bright/loud/long, assign a number 20 times as large as the first. If it seems one-fifth as bright/loud/long, assign a number one-fifth as large, and so forth. Use fractions, whole numbers, or decimals, but make each assignment proportional to the brightness/loudness/length as you perceive it. (S. S. Stevens, 1971, p. 428)

Experiments using numerical estimation have repeatedly shown the following:

1. Informants are capable of using numbers to make proportional judgments of stimulation levels for virtually any sensory attribute.
2. When the numerical estimates of the perceived strength of sensory stimuli are log-transformed, averaged, and plotted directly against the objectively measured physical values of the stimuli on log–log coordinates, the points typically fall along a straight line.[7] The law underlying this linear relationship between objective measurements and subjective perceptions can be summarized as follows: *equal stimulus ratios produce equal subjective ratios,* or, put in a different way, subjective judgments are approximately proportional to physical values.[8]

---

[7] The geometric mean is the standard measure of central tendency with magnitude data. It is the arithmetic mean computed on variables that have been transformed into logs. The geometric mean is little affected by the steep peakedness characteristic of magnitude response data (cf. Lodge, 1981, pp. 46–47). The general formula for the geometric mean is:

$$\text{Geometric mean} = \sqrt[n]{x_1, x_2, x_3 \ldots x_n}$$

[8] This generalization is known as the Power Law, which may be represented as

$$\Psi = R = kS^b,$$

where Ψ is the subjective magnitude, R, is the magnitude of the response, S, is the magnitude of the stimulus, b is the exponent that characterizes the relationship, and k is a constant of proportionality that depends on the unit used (Lodge, 1981, p. 13; S. S. Stevens, 1966, p. 530).

By reflecting ratios between judgments of stimuli, magnitude estimation provides more than interval measurement, because ratios depend not only on the intervals between measured points but also on the distance of each from the origin. Similar results have been obtained where magnitude estimation was applied to linguistic perception of stimuli for which some objective interval scale is available: similarity of syllables from different languages (Takefuta, Guberina, Pizzamiglio, & Black, 1986), speech rate (Green, 1987), vowel roughness (Toner & Emanuel, 1989), quality of synthesized speech (Pavlovic, Rossi, & Espesser, 1990), speech intelligibility (Fucci, Ellis, & Petrosino, 1990).

Extending Magnitude Estimation to Linguistic Acceptability

We saw earlier that the main difference between physical and nonphysical continua is that the latter lack objective metric properties. Estimates of loudness can be plotted in a graph on the y-axis against objectively measured decibels of sound pressure on the x-axis, and the relationship between the two can be appraised. But in the case of nonmetric dimensions, such as linguistic acceptability, what is to be placed on the x-axis?

The solution suggested by Lodge (1981) relies on the *cross-modality matching paradigm* developed by J. C. Stevens, Mack, and Stevens (1960). To quote Lodge:

> If the power law is valid and if the exponents derived from magnitude estimation are truly characteristic, then any *two* quantitative response measures with established exponents could be used to judge a sensory continuum and the validity of the derived ratio scale confirmed by obtaining a close match between the theoretical and empirically obtained ratios *between the two response measures.* (Lodge, 1981, p. 28)

The extension of magnitude estimation to socio-psychological variables is governed by the principle that "the empirically obtained ratio between response modalities when matched to social stimuli should *approximate* the ratio established for the same two response modalities when matched to physical stimuli" (Lodge, 1981, p. 31). This involves the comparison between the exponents obtained from the estimates of sociopsychological stimuli through two response modalities and the exponents obtained from the same informants when they match the same two response modalities to metric stimuli. The application of magnitude estimation to judgments of linguistic acceptability thus implies three stages:

1. In the first stage (*calibration task*), informants are given instruction and practice in making proportional judgments of metric stimuli by using two quantitative response modalities (i.e., line length estimation and numerical estimation), each used to estimate the stimuli properly belonging to the other. This stage gives the informants the opportunity to receive some training in using the concept of proportionality. It also provides the experimenter with a way of determining whether such a concept has been understood and accurately applied. When the

geometric means of the two sets of judgments are plotted against each other, the result should be a straight line;

2. In the second stage, informants use the same two response modalities to judge the linguistic acceptability of sentences. The assumption here is that informants transfer the skills developed for the metric continua to the acceptability continuum. This assumption, of course, can be verified only indirectly. If subjects are able to estimate the relative magnitude of sentence acceptability as they could with interval continua, then the plot of the two magnitude estimates of linguistic acceptability would again cluster around a straight regression line.

3. In the third stage, the slope of the regression line obtained in the calibration session and that of the regression line obtained in the estimation of linguistic acceptability are compared: in order to validate the magnitude scaling of acceptability, the two slopes should not be statistically different from one another (see Lodge, 1981, for a complete account of the experimental and statistical techniques required by the validation procedure).

Preliminary applications of the validation procedure to native judgmental data (Bard, Robertson, & Sorace, 1994) have indicated that magnitude estimation can be applied to linguistic acceptability in much the same way as to other nonmetric continua. Research on magnitude estimation of linguistic acceptability with both native and nonnative judgments has been carried out by the present author (Sorace, 1990, 1992, 1993a, 1993b) and has shown that judgments elicited via this method can be made and analyzed in finer detail than has heretofore been possible. This research has also produced some interesting differences between judgments obtained via magnitude estimation and judgments obtained via untimed test: Such differences were particularly noticeable in nonnative judgments. Given that magnitude estimation, in its canonical form, is a timed procedure that encourages informants to respond before they can consult metalinguistic rules, it is plausible to assume that the technique may tap "tacit," rather than metalinguistic, knowledge.

To conclude, the available findings have so far indicated that linguistic acceptability can be judged via magnitude estimation with greater delicacy than other methods allow. Magnitude estimation is a method that requires relative or comparative judgments. Unlike other ranking procedures, however, it offers the following advantages:

1. It produces at least interval scales, which can be legitimately subjected to parametric statistics for the ANOVA.
2. It places no constraints on the number and range of responses available to informants, who are thus able to express precise judgments without compressing them into a predetermined scale.
3. It thus allows us not only to capture variability and indeterminacy in judgments, but also to discover the differences among degrees of acceptability of sentences falling on an acceptability hierarchy.

V. CONCLUSIONS

This chapter has illustrated some of the conceptual issues underlying the use of acceptability judgments in linguistic research. It was argued that natural language grammars are characterized by *indeterminacy,* which corresponds to the unclarity of the grammaticality status of certain constructions in the speaker's internalized competence, and can be operationally defined as variability in the speaker's acceptability judgments on these constructions. The internalized grammatical knowledge of NSs may be regarded as consisting of an indefinite number of *acceptability hierarchies,* ranging from a determinate core to an indeterminate periphery. The notion of acceptability hierarchy was found to be compatible with recent theoretical arguments put forward within generative grammar in favor of continuity between a UG-specified core and a UG-underspecified periphery.

Furthermore, it was claimed that the IL grammars constructed by adult L2 learners are affected by indeterminacy to a much greater extent than native grammars because of their inherent instability. IL indeterminacy does not necessarily decrease or disappear at higher levels of proficiency. Even the competence of near-NSs may be characterized by *incompleteness* with regard to certain constructions, manifested in variable or inconsistent acceptability judgments. If near-NSs come to attain acceptability hierarchies similar to those acquired by NSs, then their intuitions on peripheral constructions will also be indeterminate (and their judgments will be variable), because of the intermediate grammaticality of these constructions, rather than because of incomplete knowledge representations.

Methodologically, the elicitation of acceptability data requires more careful handling than has generally been assumed. The most commonly used elicitation methods in linguistic research are of limited value because they produce categorical or ordinal scales of measurement, which are inadequate to capture indeterminacy and preclude the application of parametric statistical analyses. In exploring the parallel between acceptability judgments and psychophysical judgments, the question was raised as to whether magnitude estimation can be applied to the investigation of linguistic acceptability. Under the assumption that linguistic acceptability is a continuous nonmetric dimension, and that acceptability judgments are subjected to the same laws as any other human judgment, it was suggested that the answer is definitely positive and that the use of magnitude estimation may provide the researcher with a fine-grained picture of linguistic competence.

A great deal more research is needed on the nature of linguistic acceptability in general, and on linguistic acceptability in an L2 in particular. Chomsky (1986) argued:

> In actual practice, linguistics as a discipline is characterized by attention to certain kinds of evidence that are, for the moment, readily accessible and informative: largely, the judgments of native speakers. Each such judgment is, in fact, the

result of an experiment, one that is poorly designed but rich in the evidence it provides. . . . the judgments of native speakers will always provide relevant evidence for the study of language . . . although one would hope that such evidence will eventually lose its uniquely privileged status. (Chomsky, 1986, pp. 36–37)

In this chapter I hope to have shown that acceptability judgments need not be elicited only in "poorly designed" experiments. Furthermore, although I agree with Chomsky that linguists and L2 acquisition researchers would do well to make use of other sources of evidence, I have argued that when elicited in appropriately designed studies, acceptability judgments can provide evidence about internal grammars that is far richer even than commonly supposed. I hope that future studies of the sort reported here will make it possible to investigate a wide range of grammatical phenomena in both native and nonnative grammars and perhaps even to justify the "uniquely privileged status" of acceptability judgments for some time to come.

REFERENCES

Adjémian, C. (1976). On the nature of interlanguage systems. *Language Learning, 26,* 297–320.

Altmann, G. T. M., & Steedman, M. (1988). Interaction with context during human sentence processing. *Cognition, 30,* 191–238.

Arditty, J., & Perdue, C. (1982). Variabilité et connaissance en langue étrangère. *Encrages: Numero Special de Linguistique Appliquée,* pp. 32–43.

Bard, E. G., Robertson, D., & Sorace, A. (in press). Magnitude estimation of linguistic acceptability. *Language.*

Bever, T. G. (1970). The cognitive bases for linguistic structures. In R. Hayes (Ed.), *Cognition and the development of language* (pp. 279–362). New York: Wiley.

Bever, T. G. (1974). The ascent of the specious, or there's a lot we don't know about mirrors. In D. Cohen (Ed.), *Explaining linguistic phenomena* (pp. 173–200). New York: Wiley.

Birdsong, D. (1989). *Metalinguistic performance and interlinguistic competence.* Berlin & New York: Springer-Verlag.

Birdsong, D. (1992). Ultimate attainment in second language acquisition. *Language, 68,* 706–755.

Botha, R. P. (1973). *The justification of linguistic hypotheses.* The Hague: Mouton.

Bradac, J. J., Martin, L. W., Elliott, N. D., & Tardy, C. H. (1980). On the neglected side of linguistic science: multivariate studies of sentence judgment. *Linguistics, 18,* 967–995.

Carroll, J. M., Bever, T. G., & Pollack, C. R. (1981). The non-uniqueness of linguistic intuitions. *Language, 57,* 368–383.

Cazdeh, C. H., Cancino, H., Rosansky, E., & Schumann, J. (1975). *Second language acquisition sequences in children, adolescents and adults.* Washington, DC: U.S. Department of Health, Education and Welfare.

Chaudron, C. (1983). Research on metalinguistic judgments: A review of theory, methods and results. *Language Learning, 33,* 343–377.

Chomsky, N. (1957). *Syntactic structures.* The Hague: Mouton.

Chomsky, N. (1961). Some methodological remarks on generative grammar. *Word, 17,* 219–239.

Chomsky, N. (1981). *Lectures on government and binding.* Dordrecht: Foris.

Chomsky, N. (1986). *Knowledge of language: Its nature, origins, and use,* New York: Praeger.

Coppieters, R. (1987). Competence differences between native and fluent nonnative speakers. *Language, 63,* 544–573.

Corder, S. P. (1974). The significance of learners' errors. In J. Richards (Ed.), *Error analysis* (pp. 19–27). London: Longman.

Corder, S. P. (1981). *Error analysis and interlanguage.* Oxford: Oxford University Press.

Cowart, W. (1989). *Illicit acceptability in picture NPs* (pp. 27–40). Papers from the 25th Annual Regional Meeting, Chicago Linguistics Society.

Dulay, H., & Burt, M. (1973). Should we teach children syntax? *Language Learning, 23,* 245–258.

Eubank, L. (Ed.). (1991). *Point counterpoint, Universal Grammar in the second language.* Amsterdam: John Benjamins.

Felix, S. W. (1985). More evidence on competing cognitive systems. *Second Language Research, 1,* 47–72.

Flynn, S. (1987). *A parameter-setting model of second language acquisition.* Dordrecht: Reidel.

Flynn, S., & O'Neill, W. (Eds.). (1988). *Linguistic theory and second language acquisition.* Dordrecht: Reidel.

Fodor, J. D. (1989). Learning the periphery. In R. J. Matthews & W. Demopoulos (Eds.), *Learnability and linguistic theory* (pp. 129–154). Dordrecht: Kluwer.

Fucci, D., Ellis, L., & Petrosino, L. (1990). Speech clarity/intelligibility: Test-retest reliability of magnitude estimation scaling. *Perceptual and Motor Skills, 70,* 232–234.

Gleitman, H., & Gleitman, L. (1979). Language use and language judgment. In C. J. Fillmore, W. Kempler, & W. S.-Y. Wang (Eds.), *Individual differences in language ability and language behavior* (pp. 103–126). New York: Academic Press.

Green, K. (1987). The perception of speaking rate using visual information from a talker's face. *Perception and Psychophysics, 42,* 587–593.

Greenbaum, S. (Ed.). (1977). *Acceptability in language.* The Hague: Mouton.

Greenbaum, S. (1988). *Good English and the grammarian.* London: Longman.

Greenbaum, S., & Quirk, R. (1970). *Elicitation experiments in English: Linguistic studies in use and attitude.* London: Longman.

Hawkins, J. A. (1982). *Constraints on modelling real-time language processes: Assessing the contribution of linguistics.* Paper presented at the Conference on Constraints on Modelling Real-Time Processes, St. Maximin, France.

Kellerman, E. (1978). Giving learners a break: Native language intuitions as a source of predictions about transferability. *Working Papers on Bilingualism, 15,* 59–92.

Klein, W. (1986). *Second language acquisition.* Cambridge, UK: Cambridge University Press.

Kohn, K. (1982). Beyond output: The analysis of interlanguage development. *Studies in Second Language Acquisition, 4,* 137–152.

Kroch, A. (1989). Language learning and language change. Response to Lightfoot (1989).

Labov, W. (1972). *Sociolinguistic patterns.* Philadelphia: University of Pennsylvania Press.

Lakoff, G. (1973). *Fuzzy grammar and the performance/competence terminology game* (pp. 271–291). Papers from the 9th Regional Meeting of the Chicago Linguistic Society.

Levelt, W. J. M. (1971). Some psychological aspects of linguistic data. *Linguistische Berichte, 17,* 18–30.

Levelt, W. J. M. (1974). *Formal grammars in linguistics and psycholinguistics: Vol. 3. Psycholinguistic applications.* The Hague: Mouton.

Levelt, W. J. M., Haans, J. A. W. M., & Meijers, A. J. A. (1977). Grammaticality, paraphrase, and imagery. In S. Greenbaum (Ed.), *Acceptability in language.* The Hague: Mouton.

Liceras, J. (1983). *Markedness, contrastive analysis, and the acquisition of Spanish syntax by English speakers.* Doctoral thesis, University of Toronto.

Lightfoot, D. (1983). *The language lottery: Towards a biology of grammars.* Cambridge, MA: MIT Press.

Lightfoot, D. (1989). The child's trigger experience: Degree-0 learnability. *Behavioral and Brain Sciences, 12,* 321–375.

Lightfoot, D. (1991). *How to set parameters: Arguments from language change.* Cambridge, MA: MIT Press.

Lodge, M. (1981). *Magnitude scaling. Quantitative measurement of opinions. Sage University Paper series on quantitative applications in the social sciences* (Series No. 07-025). Beverly Hills, CA & London: Sage.

Miller, G. (1969). A psychological method to investigate verbal concepts. *Journal of Mathematical Psychology, 6,* 169–191.

Mohan, B. A. (1977). Acceptability testing and fuzzy grammars. In S. Greenbaum (Ed.), *Acceptability in language.* The Hague: Mouton.

Newmeyer, F. J. (1983). *Grammatical theory: Its limits and its possibilities.* Chicago: University of Chicago Press.

Nunnally, J. C. (1967). *Psychometric theory.* New York: McGraw-Hill.

Ouhalla, J. (1991). *Functional categories and parametric variation.* London: Routledge.

Pankhurst, J., van Buren, P., & Sharwood Smith, M. (Eds.). (1988). *Learnability and second languages.* Dordrecht: Foris.

Pateman, T. (1985). From nativism to sociolinguistics: Integrating a theory of language growth with a theory of speech practices. *Journal for the Theory of Social Behaviour, 15,* 38–59.

Pavlovic, C., Rossi, M., & Espesser, R. (1990). Use of magnitude estimation technique for assessing the performance of text-to-speech synthesis systems. *Journal of the Acoustical Society of America, 87,* 373–382.

Py, B. (1986). Native language attrition amongst migrant workers: Towards an extension of the concept of interlanguage. In E. Kellerman & M. Sharwood Smith (Eds.), *Crosslinguistic influence in second language acquisition.* Oxford: Pergamon.

Quirk, R., & Svartvik, J. (1966). *Investigating linguistic acceptability.* The Hague: Mouton.

Ross, J. R. (1979). Where's English? In C. J. Fillmore, W. Kempler, & W. S.-Y. Wang (Eds.), *Individual differences in language ability and language behavior* (pp. 127–165). New York: Academic Press.

Schachter, J. (1989). Testing a proposed universal. In S. Gass & J. Schachter (Eds.), *Linguistic perspectives on second language acquisition.* Cambridge, UK: Cambridge University Press.

Schachter, J., Tyson, A., & Diffley, F. (1976). Learners' intuitions of grammaticality. *Language Learning, 26,* 67–76.

Schachter, J., & Yip, V. (1990). Grammaticality judgments: Does anyone object to subject extractions? *Studies in Second Language Acquisition, 12,* 379–392.

Selinker, L. (1972). Interlanguage. *International Review of Applied Linguistics, 10,* 209–231.

Siegel, S., & Castellan, N. J. (1988). *Nonparametric statistics for the behavioral sciences.* New York: McGraw-Hill.

Snow, C. (1974). Linguists as behavioural scientists: Towards a methodology for testing linguistic intuitions. In A. Kraak (Ed.), *Linguistics in the Netherlands 1972–1973.* Assen: Van Gorcum.

Snow, C., & Meijer, G. (1977). On the secondary nature of syntactic intuitions. In S. Greenbaum (Ed.), *Acceptability in language.* The Hague: Mouton.

Sorace, A. (1985). *Certainty and consistency in interlanguage intuitional data.* Unpublished manuscript, University of Southern California, Los Angeles.

Sorace, A. (1988). Linguistic intuitions in interlanguage development: The problem of indeterminacy. In J. Pankhurst, M. Sharwood Smith, & P. van Buren (Eds.), *Learnability and second languages. A book of readings.* Dordrecht: Foris.

Sorace, A. (1990). Indeterminacy in first and second languages: Theoretical and methodological issues. In J. de Jong & D. Stevenson (Eds.), *Individualizing the assessment of language abilities.* Clevedon, UK: Multilingual Matters.

Sorace, A. (1992). *Lexical conditions on syntactic knowledge: Auxiliary selection and native and non-native grammars of Italian.* Doctoral dissertation, University of Edinburgh.

Sorace, A. (1993a). Incomplete vs divergent representations of unaccusativity in non-native grammars of Italian. *Second Language Research, 9,* 22–47.

Sorace, A. (1993b). Unaccusativity and auxiliary selection in non-native grammars of Italian and French: Asymmetries and predictable indeterminacy. *Journal of French Language Studies, 3,* 71–93.

Spencer, N. J. (1973). Differences between linguists and nonlinguists in intuitions of grammaticality-acceptability. *Journal of Psycholinguistic Research, 2,* 83–98.

Stevens, J. C., Mack, J. D., & Stevens, S. S. (1960). Growth of sensation on seven continua as measured by force of handgrip. *Journal of Experimental Psychology, 59,* 60–67.

Stevens, S. S. (1966). A metric for the social consensus. *Science, 151,* 530–541.

Stevens, S. S. (1971). Issues in psychophysical measurement. *Psychological Review, 78,* 426–450.

Takefuta, Y., Guberina, P., Pizzamiglio, L., & Black, J. (1986). Cross-lingual measurement of interconsonantal differences. *Journal of Psycholinguistioc Research, 15,* 489–507.

Toner, M., & Emanuel, F. (1989). Direct magnitude estimation and equal appearing scaling of vowel roughness. *Journal of Speech and Hearing Research, 32,* 78–82.

Traugott, E. C., & Heine, B. (Eds.). (1991). *Approaches to grammaticalization.* Amsterdam: John Benjamins.

Tsimpli, M.-I., & Roussou, A. (1991). Parameter-resetting in SLA? *University College London Working Papers in Linguistics, 3,* 149–169.

Vincent, N. (1989). Observing obsolescence. In Lightfoot (1989).

Wexler, K., & Manzini, M. R. (1987). Parameters and learnability in binding theory. In T. Roeper & E. Williams (Eds.), *Parameter setting.* Dordrecht: Reidel.

White, L. (1982). *Grammatical theory and language acquisition.* Dordrecht: Foris.

White, L. (1988). Island effects in second language acquisition. In S. Flynn & W. O'Neil (Eds.), *Linguistic theory in second language acquisition.* Dordrecht: Kluwer.

White, L. (1989). *Universal Grammar and second language acquisition.* Amsterdam: John Benjamins.

Wode, H. (1978). Developmental sequences in naturalistic L2 acquisition. In E. M. Hatch (Ed.), *Second language acquisition.* Rowley, MA: Newbury House.

Yule, G., Yanz, J. L., & Tsuda, A. (1985). Investigating aspects of the language learner's confidence: An application of the theory of signal detection. *Language Learning, 35,* 473–488.

PART V

Modality and the Linguistic Environment in Second Language Acquisition

CHAPTER 13

THE ROLE OF THE LINGUISTIC ENVIRONMENT IN SECOND LANGUAGE ACQUISITION

Michael H. Long

I. SOME POSSIBLE ROLES FOR THE ENVIRONMENT

The linguistic environment for second language (L2) acquisition may be thought of in many ways, but perhaps most fundamentally in terms of the positive and negative evidence speakers and writers provide learners about the target language (TL). As positive evidence, in the process of communicating they offer models of what is grammatical and acceptable (not necessarily the same) in the L2, but also instances of ungrammatical language use at a time when learners do not know which is which. Under certain conditions they adapt their speech or writing in ways that make those models comprehensible to the learner and thereby usable for acquisition. As negative evidence, they provide direct or indirect information about what is ungrammatical. This may be explicit (e.g., grammatical explanation or overt error correction) or implicit (e.g., failure to understand, incidental error correction in a response, such as a confirmation check, which reformulates the learner's previous utterance without interrupting the flow of conversation—in which case, the negative feedback simultaneously provides additional positive evidence—and perhaps also the absence of items in the input). In addition, conversational partners may be important as facilitators and shapers of learner output and as participants in a process whereby nonnative speakers (NNSs) learn at least part of a new grammar by doing conversation. (Chapters 2 by Gregg and 3 by White, this volume, also discuss positive and negative evidence in L2 acquisition.)

413

Each of these possible roles of the environment is the subject of some debate in L2 acquisition, as in first language (L1) acquisition. From an innatist perspective, the adequacy of TL performance as positive evidence for L1 or L2 acquisition is questionable given its alleged degeneracy and underspecification of the full complexity of native competence. The existence of negative evidence or, if it exists, the need to posit any major role for it in acquisition is denied on the basis of adult learners' supposed continuing (complete or partial) access to innate knowledge of universals and of constraints on the ways languages may vary. This knowledge, it is claimed, obviates the need for negative evidence and interactionally triggered retreats from overgeneralizations, and rigorous proof criteria are specified to be met by those who persist in invoking negative evidence in their theories. The need for learner output in development, and hence for conversational support, is also denied by some on the basis of individuals who have supposedly learned a language without speaking, whereas others maintain that production facilitates development, and still others that it is essential.

Few aspects of human development have turned out to be explicable solely as a function of either innate or environmental variables acting separately. Most involve both, the interaction of the two, and changes in the relative importance of each and of their interaction over developmental time (Bornstein & Bruner, 1989). A reasonable working hypothesis for L2 acquisition, therefore, would be that neither the environment nor innate knowledge alone suffice. The following review focuses on L2 (and some L1) acquisition research findings. In an updated version of the so-called Interaction Hypothesis (Long, 1981a, 1983c), it is proposed that environmental contributions to acquisition are mediated by selective attention and the learner's developing L2 processing capacity, and that these resources are brought together most usefully, although not exclusively, during *negotiation for meaning*. Negative feedback obtained during negotiation work or elsewhere may be facilitative of L2 development, at least for vocabulary, morphology, and language-specific syntax, and essential for learning certain specifiable L1–L2 contrasts.

II. FOREIGNER TALK DISCOURSE AND POSITIVE EVIDENCE

Because language acquisition entails not just linguistic input but *comprehensible* linguistic input, the relationship often goes unnoticed until abnormal cases are encountered of beginners trying to learn from (to them) incomprehensible language samples originally intended for mature speakers. Such efforts invariably result in failure in both L1 and L2 acquisition (Long, 1981a). The importance for L2 acquisition of input comprehensibility has been one of the incentives for many studies of how comprehensibility is achieved. The principal research foci in that work have been the ways native speakers (NSs) modify their speech to NNSs, or *foreigner talk,* the conditions under which they do so, and the NNS's active role in the process of negotiation for meaning. They have been by no means the only objects of such research, however.

Research on input for L2 acquisition began in the 1970s, nearly a decade after the initial studies of "motherese" in L1 acquisition but with a broader focus than the L1 work. The earliest L2 studies were sociolinguistically oriented and sought to describe what Ferguson (1971) termed one of the "conventionalized varieties of 'simplified' speech available to a speech community," (i.e., the way NSs addressed NNSs, or *foreigner talk,* FT). Other research was motivated by a search for characteristics of "simple codes" of various kinds, including foreigner talk, child language, pidgins, early L2, telegraphese, and lecture notes, and for common processes in their creation (Bickerton, 1979; Corder, 1977; Ferguson, 1977; Janda, 1985; Meisel, 1977; Schumann, 1978; Tweissi, 1990; Zwicky & Zwicky, 1980, 1981). The third and largest body of work, and the one most comparable with the L1 acquisition research, sought to identify differences between language used with native and nonnative interlocutors, both children and adults, and to determine whether the adjustments to NNSs were necessary for or facilitative of L2 comprehension or acquisition.

Although the sociolinguistic studies focused on the NS, part of whose communicative repertoire is the ability to modify language appropriately for different interlocutors, the psycholinguistic work targeted the hearer, specifically the status of modified language as *input* to the learner, and what the characteristics of that input might suggest about the power and internal structure of the putative language acquisition device. In the case of older learners, interest was further motivated by the fact that, whereas child L1 and L2 acquisition are almost always successful, adult efforts at either typically end in partial failure. Because the differential outcome is often attributed to the deterioration or categorical loss of some as yet poorly understood language-specific biology after the closure of one or more sensitive periods, any potentially facilitative qualities of input modifications would be even more important for adults than for the language-learning child.

Ferguson's classic early work (1971, 1975; Ferguson & DeBose, 1976) identified three main "simplifying" processes in the production of FT: omission, expansion, and replacement or rearrangement, as well as some "nonsimplifying" tendencies: elaboration, regularization, and attitude expression. Omission includes nonsuppliance of articles, copulas, conjunctions, subject pronouns, and inflectional morphology (*Man eat fish, get sick*). Expansion refers to the addition of such features as unanalyzed tags (*yes, no, Ok*) to questions (*Have baby, yes?*), and the insertion of subject pronoun *you* in imperatives (*You eat now!*). Replacement and rearrangement is illustrated by NS use of uninverted questions (*You see man?*), formation of negatives with *no* plus the negated item (*No have work*), conversion of possessive adjective-plus-noun to noun-plus-object pronoun constructions (*my father* to *father me*), and replacement of subject with object pronouns (*me have*). The FT the three processes produce is reminiscent of Tarzan comic strips (Hinnenkamp, 1982) and strikingly different from the (usually) well-formed speech to language-learning children documented by L1 acquisition studies.

Ferguson's results were potentially suspect because they had been obtained using an artificial elicitation procedure in which Stanford University students rewrote sentences as they imagined they would say them to a group of illiterate, non-European aliens who spoke no English. They were confirmed, however, by observational studies of FT across a variety of languages and settings—in Australian factories (Clyne, 1968, 1977, 1978), on German streets (Heidelberger Forschungsprojekt, 1978; Meisel, 1977), through Dutch municipal government office windows (Snow, van Eeden, & Muysken, 1981), in a U.S. department store (Ramamurti, 1977)—and in the speech not only of adults, but also of young children addressing nonnative age peers (Andersen, 1975; Katz, 1977; Wong-Fillmore, 1976). The ungrammaticality was not an artifact of written elicitation studies, in other words. Some language teachers were also occasionally observed to use ungrammatical speech (De Bot & Janssen-Van Dieten, 1984, cited in Issidorides & Hulstijn, 1992; Hakansson, 1986; Hatch, Shapira, & Wagner-Gough, 1978; Ishiguro, 1986; Kleifgen, 1985; Van Helvert, 1985, cited in Issidorides & Hulstijn, 1992). Issidorides and Hulstijn (1992, p. 148) also report that a Dutch L2 textbook (De Praatkist, 1982) for immigrant elementary school children presents dialogs in three versions, the first of which uses simplified, often ungrammatical, sentences.

Validated though they were by the naturalistic observations, the reports of deviant speech were soon far outnumbered by the findings of some 60 descriptive and quasi-experimental laboratory and classroom studies of NS–NNS conversation, the majority in university settings (for review, see Larsen-Freeman & Long, 1991). The laboratory studies showed that, like caretaker talk, most speech to NNSs (and all of it in many corpora) was a modified but well-formed version of the TL. The classroom studies revealed the same patterns, although instructional FT also includes some features of L1 teacher talk, such as framing moves and the frequent use of known information or display questions (for review, see Chaudron, 1988). Arthur, Weiner, Culver, Young, and Thomas (1980) proposed a distinction between FT, a separate, reduced code marked by nonstandard rules, and Foreigner Register, the variety of speech to NNSs that remained grammatical vis-à-vis the standard variety, but differed, like any register, in terms of the frequency of certain linguistic elements.

Most speech adjustments to NNSs are quantitative, not categorical, and result in *grammatical* input. Although there is considerable individual variation and more than a little inconsistency across studies, FT in and out of classrooms tends to be well formed (Freed, 1978; Henzl, 1979), delivered more slowly than speech to NSs (Derwing, 1990; Hakansson, 1986; Ishiguro, 1986), with clearer articulation and fewer sandhi processes, such as contraction, in both the oral mode (Henrichsen, 1984) and in NS to NSS signing (Swisher, 1984). Again, with considerable variability, grammatical FT often employs shorter, syntactically or propositionally less complex utterances (Arthur et al., 1980; Early, 1985; Freed, 1978; Gaies, 1977; Ishiguro, 1986; Scarcella & Higa, 1981; Shortreed, 1993), and a narrower range of higher frequency vocabulary items (Arthur et al., 1980; Tweissi, 1990).

FT is not always linguistically simpler, however (Long, 1980) and can occasionally even be more complex (Pica, Young, & Doughty, 1987; Ross, Long, & Yano, 1991; Tweissi, 1990). In such cases, comprehensibility is maintained by accompanying interactional adjustments and by the tendency for FT to be a more "regular" and more redundant version of the TL than that intended for NSs (Long, Ghambiar, Ghambiar, & Nishimura, 1982; Tweissi, 1990; Wesche & Ready, 1985). Examples of regularity and redundancy include the more frequent use of canonical word orders, retention of more optionally deleted constituents (such as subject pronouns in prodrop languages, and of full noun phrases (NPs) instead of anaphoric referents), and more complete overt marking of grammatical and semantic relations (such as Japanese particles indicating topic, subject, object, directionals and locatives). Such features are often absent in NS–NS conversation if made redundant by context. These and other changes are widely observed in adult speech to NNSs, and also in the speech of young children addressing NNS age peers (Andersen, 1975; Cathcart-Strong, 1986; Hirvonen, 1988; Katz, 1977; Peck, 1978; Wong-Fillmore, 1976).

What NSs react to when adjusting their speech to NNSs has been the subject of some research. Individual NSs incorporate specific features of their interlocutors' nonnative varieties (Clyne, 1978; Hatch et al., 1978), but a simple matching hypothesis is untenable. As Meisel (1977) points out, although both NNSs' developing grammars (always) and NSs' FT (less often) exhibit simplification processes resulting in omission and other kinds of ungrammaticality, interlanguages (ILs) are marked by certain other kinds of processes and "errors," such as overgeneralization (children*s*, the boy go*ed*) not found in FT. Laboratory studies suggest that NSs react to a combination of factors when they make linguistic or conversational adjustments. They initially adapt to the comprehensibility of the NNS's speech (e.g., its degree of accentedness) (Varonis & Gass, 1982), although age, physical appearance, and L2 proficiency, occasionally also play a role. As a conversation or lesson progresses, however, modifications become less a function of NNS comprehensibility, and other factors come into play. Adjustments become more extensive and more varied for NNSs of lower proficiency (Gaies, 1977; Lynch, 1987; Snow et al., 1981), and increasingly reflect the NS's perception of the NNS's comprehension (Long, 1983a; Warren-Leubecker & Bohannon, 1982).

The trigger for *ungrammatical* FT, a categorical change on the NS's part, is less clear. Valdman (1981) suggested that ungrammaticality maintains distance between NSs and subordinate NNSs while allowing the NNSs to participate in the dominant group's world. After reviewing 40 studies, Long (1981c) suggested four relevant factors: (1) zero or very low NNS proficiency in the language of communication, (2) (perceived or genuine) higher NS social status, (3) prior FT experience, but only with NNSs of low L2 proficiency, and (4) the spontaneity of the conversation. Considerable variation was evident at the level of the individual speaker, however, and at least one study provided counterevidence to each condition (a picture made cloudier since 1981). The best generalization still seems to be that factors (1), (2), and (4) are usually necessary for ungrammatical FT to occur, but that no single condition is sufficient.

In addition to studying linguistic input to NNSs, researchers broadened their focus in the late-1970s to include the structure of NS–NNS conversation in which it occurred, or FT discourse (FTD) (Hatch et al., 1978; Long, 1980, 1981a). When interlocutor, task, and setting variables were controlled, few statistically significant differences other than shorter utterance length distinguished the linguistic characteristics of speech to NSs and NNSs. The *interactional* structure of conversations with NS and NNS interlocutors differed significantly, however. This was especially true on so-called two-way tasks, the completion of which required participants to exchange information held uniquely by them at the outset. Conversely, one-way tasks, such as storytelling and giving instructions, where only the NS held unknown information, tended not to produce statistically significant modifications of either input or interactional features, even when the NS was aware of the NNS's limited linguistic ability. It appears that the informational structure of two-way tasks obliges NSs and NNSs to negotiate for meaning, and through the negotiation process, to make what they say comprehensible to their interlocutors. *Negotiation for meaning* is the process in which, in an effort to communicate, learners and competent speakers provide and interpret signals of their own and their interlocutor's perceived comprehension, thus provoking adjustments to linguistic form, conversational structure, message content, or all three, until an acceptable level of understanding is achieved.

The devices employed in the negotiation process—repetitions, confirmations, reformulations, comprehension checks, confirmation checks, clarification requests, etc.—are used both strategically, to avoid conversational trouble, and tactically, to repair communication breakdowns when they occur (Long, 1983c; Varonis and Gass, 1985a, 1985b). All have been found to occur more frequently in NS–NNS than in NS–NS conversation (Early, 1985; R. Ellis, 1985; Long, 1980, 1981b, 1983c; Mannon, 1986; Pica & Doughty, 1985; Tweissi, 1990; Wesche & Ready, 1985), on two-way rather than one-way tasks (Doughty & Pica, 1986; Long, 1980; Pica, 1987), on unfamiliar tasks or with unfamiliar interlocutors (Gass & Varonis, 1985), in mixed rather than same L1 dyads (Varonis & Gass, 1985a), with mixed rather than same proficiency interlocutors (Porter, 1983), and in mixed rather than same gender dyads (Gass & Varonis, 1986; Pica, Holliday, Lewis, & Morgenthaler, 1989; for review, see Long, 1989, 1990; Long & Porter, 1985; Pica, 1992).

Interactional adjustments can affect input in various ways. Thus, partial repetition can reduce mean utterance length, a here-and-now orientation can increase the proportion of verbal elements marked temporally for present, and semantic repetition, or paraphrase, can include lexical switches, as illustrated (using constructed examples for comparative purposes) in (1b):

(1) a. (NS–NS conversation)
        Do you like the city?

                                                                I love it.

     b. (NS–NNS conversation)
        Do you like the city?

                                                                Huh?

        Do you like Los Angeles?

                                                                Yes, very nice.

They can also operate quite independently, however, as shown in (1c), where exact self-repetition succeeds in getting the message across to the NNS without the linguistic input itself having changed at all.

     c. Do you like the city?

                                                                Huh?

        Do you like the city?

                                                                Yes, very nice.

Similarly, (1b) and (1c) also differ from (1a) in their interactional structure, due to the NS's use of semantic and exact self-repetition, respectively, but from an input perspective, exhibit identical utterance structure.

Various other interactional modifications are commonly observed. Conversational topics tend to be treated simply and briefly in FTD, as measured by "information bits" (Arthur et al., 1980) or the ratio of topic-initiating to topic-continuing moves (Gaies, 1981; Long, 1981b). Possibly for cultural reasons, the kinds of topics nominated (e.g., personal or impersonal) can also differ from those preferred in NS–NS conversation, with topic sequences less predictable in FTD, and topic shifts more abrupt (Scarcella, 1983). As in caretaker–child conversation, and despite the absence of cognitive limitations in the adult, a slight here-and-now orientation is often observable in FTD in and out of classrooms, as measured by the relative frequencies of verbs marked temporally for present and nonpresent (Gaies, 1981; Long, 1980; Long & Sato, 1983). Unless the task dictates otherwise, NSs attempts to relinquish topic control in various ways. "Or choice" questions (Hatch, 1978), as in (2), make NNSs' participation easier by containing potential answers in the form of a list of responses from which they can choose:

(2) Well what are you doing in the
United States? . . . Are you just
studying? Or do you have a job? Or—

> No, I have job.

Acceptance of unintentional NNS topic-switches also facilitates NNS participation. If the task allows, skillful NNs may treat an inappropriate response as a topic nomination, as in (3), simultaneously repairing the discourse and allowing the NNS to determine topic:

(3) Are you going to visit San
Francisco? Or Las Vegas?

> Yes, I went to
> Disneyland and to
> Knott's Berry Farm.

Oh Yeah?

High frequencies of NS questions of various kinds are one of the most salient characteristics of FTD, probably reflecting NSs' attempts to encourage NNSs to talk. Uninverted (intonation) and yes–no questions are favored with lower proficiency NNSs, presumably because, unlike wh-questions, they maintain canonical word order and contain all the propositional information needed for a minimally adequate response, which may take the form of a simple confirmation or denial. They are especially frequent in topic-initiating moves, and are also widely used as confirmation checks, comprehension checks, and clarification requests. NSs sometimes help out by providing anticipated answers to their own questions, as in (4):

(4) Right. *When* do you take the break? At 10:30?

Additional adjustments are apparently designed to increase topic saliency. These include use of a slower rate of delivery, left-dislocation, stress on key information-bearing words, and pauses before or after them, as in (5):

(5) Did you . . . *like* San Diego? . . . San Diego . . . did you like it?

Also serving to make topics salient is "decomposition" (Long, 1980), as shown in (6):

(6) a. When do you go to the, uh, Santa Monica?
. . . You say you go fishing in Santa
Monica, right?

> Yeah.

When?

b. Uh, what does your father do in, uh,
you're from Kyoto, right?

> Yeah.

> Yeah. What does your father do in
> Kyoto?

Decomposition occurs when a topic nomination in the form of a wh-question is repaired, either after it fails to elicit a response (6a) or to preempt failure (6b), by breaking it down into two parts. First, repetition of the (sub)topic in isolation is used to establish what is being talked about, the repetition usually taking the form of a yes–no or uninverted (intonation) question, often with a tag (*right?*) added. After the NNS confirms that the topic has been understood, the comment, in the form of a question about the topic, is restated. Decomposition occurs more frequently in NS–NNS conversation (Tweissi, 1990), and like most interactional adjustments, can be used, as in (6a) and (6b), preemptively and reactively.

Although the underlying simplification and elaboration processes in adjustments to NNSs may be universal, coding devices for interactional modifications, such as retention of redundant morphological marking and changes among question forms, can vary cross-linguistically (see Tweissi, 1990), and the use of at least some interactional modifications may be culture-specific. Shortreed (1993), for example, reports less NS self-repetition in NS–NNS dyads than in NS–NS controls in a laboratory study of Japanese FTD, a finding he attributes to the previously documented higher frequency of back-channeling and redundancy in spoken Japanese than English conversation. Indeed, it is possible that input or interactional modifications differ across classes, genders, and cultures, just as speech adjustments for children reportedly do. This is a crucial issue for future research and implies systematic extension of the database to include populations rarely, if ever, sampled in work to date, such as informants with no previous contact with NNSs or from cultures with different norms concerning appropriate ways of communicating with children or outsiders. The absence of adjustments in any successful L2 acquisition context would eliminate input or interactional modifications or both as necessary for acquisition, although leaving their facilitative status an open question.

III. THE INSUFFICIENCY OF COMPREHENSIBLE INPUT

The importance of input interpretability for L2 acquisition has motivated a number of studies of the effect of input and interactional adjustments on the comprehensibility of spoken and written discourse. When exclusively linguistic adjustments for NNSs are made to lectures or reading passages intended for NSs, the typical result is *simplification,* with shorter, syntactically less complex utterances or sentences, use of a narrower range of verb tenses, fewer modifiers, and frequently some loss of semantic content. Extreme simplification can result in ungrammaticality. Interactional modifications, on the other hand, produce longer texts, in which mean utterance or sentence length and syntactic complexity are maintained or even increased. Interactional adjustments compensate for linguistic complexity by *elaboration* (i.e., adding redundancy to discourse through the use of repetition, paraphrases and appositionals) and by making semantic structure more explicit, as shown in (7):

(7)   a. NS baseline version
         Because he had to work at night to support his family, Paco often fell asleep in class.
      b. Simplified version
         Paco had to make money for his family. Paco worked at night. He often went to sleep in class.
      c. Elaborated version
         Paco had to work at night to earn money to support his family, so he often fell asleep in class next day during his teacher's lesson.

It has been shown that linguistic adjustments that result in ungrammaticality do not necessarily enhance comprehension. Issidorides (1988) compared the comprehensibility to zero beginners and low-proficiency listeners of three versions of a set of sentences: (1) nonsimplified (e.g., The apple is on the table), pronounced with normal intonation, (2) nonsimplified, pronounced with a flat, monotonous intonation (i.e., with equal pitch on all syllables), and (3) simplified (e.g., Apple on table), with semantically redundant function words omitted, but uttered with normal intonation. The nonsimplified sentences uttered with normal intonation proved to be no more difficult for subjects to understand than the ungrammatical simplified ones, whereas the prosodically monotonous versions seriously affected comprehension by the beginners. Similarly, Issidorides and Hulstijn (1992) found that normal grammatical Dutch sentence patterns involving some obligatory inversion rules were no more difficult for learners of Dutch than "simplified" ungrammatical versions that preserved canonical word order and omitted verb inflection, provided they did not convey extremely implausible meanings.

Modifications that preserve grammaticality generally do facilitate message comprehension. Yano et al. (1994) reviewed 15 investigations of the absolute or comparative effectiveness of simplification and elaboration on SL comprehension. Generalizations were difficult because of differences across studies with respect to modality, approach to modification, specific examples of each type of modification employed, and how and when comprehension was assessed. Six generalizations were possible, nevertheless, and have been strengthened by subsequent findings.

1. Comprehension is usually increased by linguistic simplification, although simple sentences alone do not always help and can even hinder.
2. Simplification and elaboration often co-occur, but when their effects can be distinguished, simplification is not consistently superior to elaboration, and some studies find elaboration more effective.

3. Comprehension is consistently improved by (a) interactional modifications, and (b) by a combination of simplification and elaboration.

4. Modifications are more useful to NNSs of lower L2 proficiency.

5. Apart from rate of delivery, isolated input or interactional adjustments, such as shorter sentence length or greater topic saliency, are insufficient to improve the comprehensibility of whole texts.

6. NNSs' perceived comprehension is greater when speech has been modified for them.

In sum, input must be comprehensible for acquisition to occur, and there is some evidence that global linguistic and conversational adjustments to NNSs improve comprehensibility.

Although *necessary* for L1 or L2 acquisition, however, there is abundant evidence that comprehensible input alone is *insufficient,* particularly with adults and if nativelike proficiency is the goal. An important source of data on this issue are the evaluations of L2 achievement by pupils in Canadian French immersion programs, reviewed by Swain (1981, 1991, and elsewhere). Studies have shown that students attain levels in French far superior to those typically achieved in foreign language programs, indeed levels good enough for immersion students' abilities routinely to be compared with those of monolingual French-speaking age peers (e.g., Barik & Swain, 1976), something inconceivable with most foreign language learners. When this is done, immersion students are found to perform comparably with NSs on tests of listening and reading comprehension, but not on production measures, such as a cloze test (Hart & Lapkin, 1989). Even after daily school instruction through the medium of the L2 for nearly 7 years in one program (Swain, 1985), 9 years in another (Lapkin, Swain, & Cummins, 1983, cited in Swain, 1985, p. 245), or continued L2 exposure at university (Vignola & Wesche, 1991, cited in Wesche, 1994), immersion students continue to make a wide range of grammatical errors in such domains as verb tenses, prepositional usage, and gender-marking on articles, and to lack some basic vocabulary items (Harley & Swain, 1978, 1984; Lapkin, Hart, & Swain, 1991). In general, productive skills "remain far from native-like" (Swain, 1991, p. 98). A similar plateauing effect in some verb tense and gender marking morphology across grades 1–4 by children in the Culver City Spanish immersion program was reported by Plann (1976, 1977).

Premature stabilization with non-TL rules is also observed in adults who should have acquired nativelike abilities if prolonged exposure to comprehensible input was necessary *and* sufficient for development. Cases abound of learners who have lived in an L2 environment for many years, some of whom communicate successfully through the L2, many of whom face constant communication difficulties (suggesting that communicative need alone is not enough to drive IL development, either), and all of whom retain numerous deviant forms in their speech. Schmidt (1983), for example, provided a detailed longitudinal case study of Wes, an adult

Japanese naturalistic acquirer of English in Honolulu. Wes could communicate well enough to satisfy his basic needs in English (e.g, to order food in restaurants), often quite appropriately from a sociolinguistic standpoint, through the skillful use of formulaic utterances. He had little morphology, however, and showed little progress in learning any over a 5-year period during which he lived in an almost entirely English-speaking world both at home and at work, and despite having a close to optimal sociopsychological and affective profile.

Further evidence of the insufficiency of comprehensible input is found in the observation that, even when errors are not involved, many quite advanced learners also never incorporate into their ILs lexical items, grammatical constructions, and distinctions that are successfully learned, often quite early, by child NSs. To illustrate, graduating high school French immersion students were found to lack basic vocabulary knowledge and to perceive this (Harley & King, 1989; Harley & Swain, 1984; Hart & Lapkin, 1989). Similarly, after lengthy L2 exposure, 38 Italian adults learning English naturalistically while living and working in Scotland developed less sophisticated relativization abilities than 48 instructed high school English as a Foreign Language (EFL) students in Italy with far less exposure (Pavesi, 1986). Fewer of the adults could form relative clauses to 80% criterion out of the lowest five categories in the noun phrase accessibility hierarchy (E. Kennan & Comrie, 1977), despite functioning in English at home and at work for an average of 6 years (range 3 months to 25 years), although it should be remembered that relative clauses are widely reported to be infrequent in most face-to-face conversation. (For additional discussion of the noun phrase accessibility hierarchy in L2 acquisition, see chapters 4 by Flynn and 6 by Eckman, this volume. In addition, chapter 6 includes a fulsome treatment of the hierarchy with examples. Chapters 14 by Berent and 18 by Seliger treat the role of the hierarchy in the acquisition of English by deaf learners and in L1 attrition, respectively.) Few of the naturalistic acquirers (mostly restaurant waiters) were able to relativize out of NP positions (genitive and object of a comparative) at the more marked end of the implicational hierarchy at all.

In addition to the empirical evidence, there are learnability arguments against the sufficiency of comprehensible input. White (1987, 1989) and others have argued for a need for negative evidence if SL acquirers are to attain nativelike proficiency in cases where learner hypotheses or the structure of the L1 leads to L2 overgeneralizations from which it is impossible to recover on the basis of positive evidence alone. French, for example, allows placement of adverbs between verb and direct object, as in *Je bois* toujours *du café* (* 'I drink *every day* coffee'), whereas English does not. The English speaker learning French should have no problem with the contrast because it involves adding an option that will be learnable from examples in the input (positive evidence). The problem is for French speakers learning English. The structure of French will lead them to produce verb-adverb-direct object strings, and there will be nothing in the input (no ungrammatical utterances with asterisks) to tell them they are wrong. A subset of cases like these, including the present example, are especially problematic, and the prognosis for recovery particularly poor, White argued, because the ungrammatical utterances are perfectly comprehensible, and so will not cause a communication breakdown that might alert the NNS that something was amiss. It could be argued, contra White, that some learners might notice the absence of such utterances in the English input (indirect negative evidence). However, as attested by the persistence of adverb placement errors in the speech of many very advanced ESL speakers, such contrasts do provide fertile ground for premature IL stabilization. (On negative evidence in L2 acquisition, see also Bley-Vroman, 1986; Rutherford, 1987; Rutherford & Sharwood-Smith, 1988; Schachter, 1983, 1986, 1991; and for a seminal review, Birdsong, 1989.) (The Subset Principle (SP) and its putative role in L2 acquisition are also discussed in chapters 2 by Gregg, 3 by White, and 10 by Gass, this volume. Chapter 14 by Berent includes discussion of the SP in the acquisition of English by deaf learners and chapter 18 by Seliger suggests a role for this principle in accounting for L1 attrition. Finally, chapter 16 by Andersen and Shirai applies the notion to the acquisition of verb aspect.)

Environmental support in the form of comprehensible input is necessary for language learning, but insufficient for learning certain specifiable aspects of an L2. Paradoxically, comprehensible input may actually inhibit learning on occasion, because it is often possible to understand a message without understanding all the structures and lexical items in the language encoding it, and without being aware of not understanding them all. Linguistic redundancy, contextual information, and knowledge of the world can all compensate for the unknown elements. Learners may not notice new forms precisely because, at a global level, a message is comprehensible, with the result that their focal attention is directed elsewhere. Because overt NS correction of NNS errors is as rare in noninstructional NS–NNS conversation (Chun, Day, Chenoweth, & Luppescu, 1982) as it is in caretaker–child communication (Brown & Hanlon, 1970; Hirsh-Pasek, Treiman, & Schneiderman, 1984), a failure to comprehend may sometimes be needed if IL development is to proceed (White, 1987). Communicative trouble can lead learners to recognize that a linguistic problem exists, switch their attentional focus from message to form, identify the problem, and notice the needed item in the input. In other words, although some learners may stabilize prematurely because they receive little comprehensible input despite lengthy L2 exposure, as Terrell (1990) claims, the far from nativelike proficiency of so many learners, such as Wes and the Canadian French immersion students, who clearly encounter plenty of usable data, suggests that success or failure to learn can rarely if ever be attributed to the environment alone. Part of the explanation lies inside the learner, most importantly in the areas of attention, awareness, and cognitive processing.

IV. INPUT AND COGNITIVE PROCESSING

A. Attention, Awareness, and Focus on Form

Attention is widely claimed to be both necessary and sufficient for extracting items from a stimulus array (e.g., linguistic input) and storing them in long-term memory (one step in several needed to convert input to intake), with each instance an item is encountered and attended to leading to storage in memory, although not necessarily to efficient retrieval, in some theories, (e.g., Logan's Instance Theory) (Logan, 1988; Robinson & Ha, 1993). It has been claimed that learners' focus of attention and noticing of mismatches between the input and their output determines whether or not they progress (Schmidt & Frota, 1986), and that *noticing,* or conscious perception (for which attention is a prerequisite), is necessary and sufficient for converting input into intake, at least for low-level grammatical items, such as plural or third-person singular *s* (Schmidt, 1990a, 1993, 1994).

Schmidt's claim about the necessity of noticing does not refer to higher level understanding or awareness of language:

> I use *noticing* to mean registering the simple occurrence of some event, whereas *understanding* implies recognition of a general principle, rule, or pattern. For example, a second language learner might simply notice that a native speaker used a particular form of address on a particular occasion, or at a deeper level the learner might understand the significance of such a form, realizing that the form used was appropriate because of status differences between speaker and hearer. Noticing is crucially related to the question of what linguistic material is stored in memory. . . . understanding relates to questions concerning how that material is organized into a linguistic system. (Schmidt, 1990a, p. 218)

In preference to a single global construct, Tomlin and Villa argue for the greater explanatory power of three theoretically and empirically distinguishable components of attention: alertness, orientation, and detection. In their view:

> Schmidt's idea of noticing can be recast as detection within selective attention. Acquisition requires detection, but such detection does not require awareness. Awareness plays a potential support role for detection, helping set up the circumstances for detection but it does not directly lead to detection itself. (Tomlin and Villa, 1993, p. 14)

Any claim for the necessity of noticing for L2 acquisition in the higher level sense of understanding, or conscious awareness, would be problematic. Some linguistic knowledge, such as several rules for English articles, and subtle aspects of the use of the T/V distinction to mark power and solidarity in Romance and other languages, is too abstract, complex, or semantically opaque to be understood by linguistically naive learners. Some, such as gender-marking in French (Sokolik & Smith, 1992) and English dative alternation (Wolfe-Quintero, 1992) involve too many irregularities and fuzzy categories, and some, such as subject-auxiliary inversion after preposed negative adverbials (*Seldom have I seen . . .*) and uses of *whom,* are too rare or perceptually nonsalient. Noticing in this second sense might be sufficient, but it could not be necessary for all aspects of an L2. The fact that untutored, linguistically naive learners often *are* successful with such patterns suggests, therefore, that they usually learn them on the basis of lower level conscious perception (what Gass, 1988, calls *apperceived input*) or implicitly (i.e., without conscious analysis or understanding) and that the product is tacit knowledge, (i.e., neither understanding nor awareness).

Based on reviews of the relevant L1 literature and some L2 work, Schmidt (1990a, 1990b) argues that forms that are not noticed in the first, lower level sense (i.e., not consciously perceived), do not contribute to learning. That is, there is no such thing as *subliminal* language learning. He accepts that *implicit* language learning probably occurs (i.e., learning by noticing forms without understanding the rule or principle involved) but thinks that understanding those rules is highly facilitative in cases where straightforward ones can be formulated. (For further discussion and similar views on the importance of attention, noticing, and "mental effort" in L2 acquisition see Gass, 1988; Hulstijn, 1989; Schmidt, 1993, 1994; and Watanabe, 1992.)

On this account, failure to learn is due either to insufficient exposure or to failure to notice the items in question, even if exposure occurred and the learner was attending. (A learner could attend carefully to a lecture in an L2 and still fail to notice a particular linguistic item in it.) This is the opposite position to that taken by Krashen (e.g., 1985, 1989), VanPatten (1988), and others, who have denied there is any evidence of beneficial effects of a focus on form, at least in the early stages of language learning. Krashen has claimed that adults can best learn an L2 like children learn an L1, subconsciously (i.e., incidentally, without intention, while doing something else) and implicitly (via subconscious abstraction of patterns from input data), while attending to something else (meaning). Attention to (and understanding or awareness of) linguistic forms is supposedly neither necessary nor beneficial.

While adults may learn much of a new language incidentally, a pure "L1 = L2" position is difficult to sustain for complete L2 acquisition. First, as noted earlier, there is empirical evidence of premature stabilization by learners with access to plenty of comprehensible input over long periods of time (e.g., Pavesi, 1986; Schmidt, 1983; Swain, 1991). Second, some L2 rules cannot be learned incidentally by exposure to positive evidence, because there simply is no positive evidence for them—just an absence of evidence for a transferred L1 rule. Examples include the previously mentioned constraints on the placement of English adverbs for French speakers (White, 1991), and the relinquishing of typologically more marked options for relative clause formation in the L1 when the L2 allows relative clauses only in a more restricted set of positions (Schachter, 1990). Such rules and constraints can only be acquired if their operation is noticed, either unaided, which is unlikely, or because the absence or impermissability of an L1 construction in the L2 is brought to learners' attention by negative evidence. This can take several forms, including grammar rules, overt feedback on error, recasts, or communication breakdowns followed by repair sequences containing positive evidence of permissable alternatives.

Some support for Schmidt's position lies in Bardovi-Harlig's (1987) finding that the typologically marked preposition-stranding construction in English is acquired earlier than unmarked pied-piping, even by learners whose L1 only allows pied-piping. Bardovi-Harlig suggests that the frequency of preposition-stranding in English makes it salient and draws learners' attention to it. Also consistent are the results of experimental studies comparing learning of new L2 vocabulary and morpho-syntax by learners whose attention is partly manipulated by the researcher onto or away from the target items. In general (but not always), superior learning is seen in subjects whose attention researchers attempt to focus on the items during performance of a task using such devices as prior instructions to attend to both form and meaning (Hulstijn, 1989), showing them rules applied to examples in order to structure the input (N. Ellis, 1993), multiple-choice margin glosses (Hulstijn, 1992; Watanabe, 1992), highlighting and capitalization (Doughty, 1991), and other forms of what is referred to as "input enhancement" (Sharwood-Smith, 1991, 1993). Finally, especially relevant is a study by Alanen (1992) which, although failing to find an advantage for input enhancement, nevertheless produced strongly supportive evidence for the claimed importance of noticing. Alanen compared the learning through reading of locative suffixes and a phonological phenomenon, consonant gradation, in Finnish by 36 English speakers under one of four conditions: input enhancement (italicization), rule, rule and enhance, and control. Subjects described their thoughts as they went along in a taped think-aloud procedure. Across all four groups, the think-aloud protocols showed that subjects' performance on subsequent unexpected tests of the target items was greatly influenced by attentional focus and reported noticing during the two learning tasks, with learners who reported that they paid attention to the target forms generally having acquired them, regardless of the treatment they had received, and no learners having acquired the targets without having noticed them.

Further evidence of the suggested interaction of input and focused attention is to be found in the results of the mostly quasi-experimental classroom studies comparing groups of learners left to acquire structures incidentally with groups for whom the target structures are made more salient (enhanced) in some way (e.g., by error correction, highlighting, rule statements, seeding the input with high frequencies of the item—input-flooding—or the use of tasks with structures that encourage orientation to language in context) (Day & Shapson, 1991; Doughty, 1991; Harley, 1989; Lightbown & Spada, 1990; Manheimer, 1993; Rankin, 1990; Spada, 1987; Spada & Lightbown, 1993; Tomasello & Herron, 1989, White,

1991; White, Spada, Lightbown, & Ranta, 1991; and for review, Long, to appear). The latter groups generally learn faster (but not always—for discussion, see Mellow, 1992) and probably reach higher levels of ultimate L2 attainment provided the structures targeted are processable, and so learnable, at the time form-focused instruction occurs. Although other factors (motivation, literacy, social class, etc.) may sometimes work in favor of instructed learners, the differences may at least partly be because the attention-focusing devices increase the saliency of otherwise problematic items and cause learners to *focus on form* (Long, 1988, 1991) (i.e., to attend to language as object during a generally meaning-oriented activity). Focus on form differs from *focus on forms,* which abounds in L2 classrooms and involves a predominant, often exclusive, orientation to a series of isolated linguistic forms presented one after the other, as in a structural syllabus, with meaning and communication relegated to the sidelines. *Focus on form* involves learners' orientation being drawn to language as object, but in context. In other words, it is a claim that learners need to attend to a task if acquisition is to occur, but that their orientation can best be to both form and meaning, not to either form or meaning alone.

The continuing studies of the effect of instruction and of improvements on pure incidental L2 learning suggest a further role of the environment: that the process whereby NS and NNS negotiate to establish and maintain communication serves to promote noticing. A NS's clarification request, for example, may simultaneously provide a nativelike model of all or part of the message a NNS has just attempted to encode, perhaps making a specific linguistic item salient to the NNS in the process, as with the auxiliary in this example from NS–NNS conversation on a two-way Spot the Difference task (from Long, in press):

(8)   NNS: Uh, yes, . . . a
                                                 woman drinking
                                                 (and bottle) wine, uh,
                                                 bottle
                                                 and man drinking (a)
                                                 beer

NS: Yes and she's drinking a
glass or a bottle of wine?

                                                 NNS: No, uh, she? She's
                                                 drinking in (no) glass.

Negative feedback of this type (i.e., in the form of implicit correction immediately following an ungrammatical learner utterance) is potentially of special utility because it occurs at a moment in conversation when the NNS is likely to be attending to see if a message got across, and to assess its effect on the interlocutor. Furthermore, given that the NNS already knows the intended meaning, the feedback occurs when attentional space is available for the NNS to orient to the form of the response, prosodic and nonverbal cues functioning to signal that it is indeed a repair of some kind rather than an utterance with entirely new semantic content.

If a complete L2 cannot be acquired purely by incidental learning, the opposite claim, that noticing is necessary for all language learning, is also not without problems. It is unlikely that negative feedback very often materializes with non-salient critical items highlighted at a developmental time when the feedback is usable, or that when it does, noticing always occurs. (Example 8 provides no direct evidence of noticing, of course.) The claim here, then, is that negative feedback is generally facilitative of L2 acquisition, and necessary for the acquisition of speci-fiable L2 structures (such as the English adverb-placement example for French speakers) for which positive evidence will be insufficient. A mechanism is posited whereby, while correct form–meaning associations are strengthened both by posi-tive evidence *and* that negative feedback that contains positive evidence, incorrect associations are weakened and in some cases ultimately relinquished altogether as a result both of negative evidence *and* prolonged absence of support in the input. This last might be a process not unlike subtractive bilingualism, in which, as a new language is acquired, an earlier acquired one is gradually forgotten and even lost altogether if it is neither encountered nor used for long periods.

B. Negative Evidence

Simply claiming that negative feedback or some other kind of negative evidence takes care of noticing nonsalient or nonoccurring forms in the input can constitute just as miraculous a solution to the problems of underdetermination and overge-neralization as positing innate linguistic knowledge. Those who rely on negative evidence are justifiably called upon to do more than assert their remedy. For Pinker (1989) in L1 acquisition, and Beck and Eubank (1991) in L2, among oth-ers, it must be shown that negative evidence (1) exists, (2) exists in usable form, (3) is used, and (4) is necessary. As the research has been more intensive and the argumentation more explicit in L1 acquisition to date (see, e.g., Bohannon, MacWhinney, & Snow, 1990; Gordon, 1990; Grimshaw & Pinker, 1989), the is-sues raised and empirical findings in that debate will be briefly reviewed first so that they can serve both as a framework for discussing the more recent and sparser L2 research, and as an indication of some of the work that is still needed.

Negative Evidence in L1 Acquisition

Demonstrating the *existence* of negative evidence involves showing that some-thing in the learner's linguistic, conversational, or physical environment reliably provides the information necessary to alert the learner to the existence of error. Clear evidence might take the form of a consistent, categorical difference in the behavior of interlocutors following grammatical and ungrammatical utterances by the learner, such as topic-continuing moves and smiles after grammatical speech, and puzzled looks and clarification requests after errors. Repeated unexpected outcomes, communication breakdowns, negative affective reactions, and interlocutor repetitions with questioning intonation or abnormal stress might also satisfy the test. In a language teaching classroom setting, consistent overt error correction could be expected.

L1 researchers who have sought such evidence in caretaker–child conversation have reported mixed findings. Brown and Hanlon (1980) found no difference in the ratio of sequiturs and nonsequiturs (indicating lack of comprehension) or in affective contingent approval in parental responses following their children's grammatical and ungrammatical utterances. Hirsh-Pasek et al. (1984) also reported no difference in the expression of approval. They found parents of 2-year-olds showed a small difference in the proportion of their children's grammatical and ungrammatical utterances they repeated (including expanded)—12% and 21%, respectively—but there was no difference in the same measure for parental responses to children aged 3–5. Demetras, Post, and Snow (1986) found slightly more parental exact repetitions and topic continuations following four 2-year-olds' grammatical utterances, and slightly more clarification requests following their ungrammatical ones, but no relationship between grammaticality and several other measures. A clearer differentiation was observed with 2-year-olds by Penner (1987), however, who found that mothers and fathers repeated their children's grammatical utterances more than their ungrammatical ones and recast their ungrammatical utterances roughly twice as often as their grammatical ones. Bohannon and Stanowicz (1988) reported similar findings, and showed that about 90% of exact repetitions followed children's grammatical utterances; about 70% of recasts and expansions followed their ungrammatical ones; a third of ungrammatical utterances elicited parental recasts and expansions (two-thirds did not); and children were eight times more likely to repeat recasts of their ungrammatical utterances than exact imitations of their grammatical ones. Farrar (1992) found corrective recasts followed 22% of children's ungrammatical utterances, and that children imitated the corrected morpheme two or three times as often after corrective recasts than after any other kind of parental response providing positive evidence. Furrow, Baillie, McLaren, and Moore (1993) reported more strict repetitions, move-ons, and no responses after children's grammatical utterances in three mother–child dyads, and more clarification questions and expansions or recasts after ungrammatical utterances. They also demonstrated that a portion of such differential responding was to the grammaticality of child speech, independent of its ambiguity. The direction rather than the degree of differential treatment of grammatical and ungrammatical speech across these latter studies is more significant, because researchers sometimes used different operational definitions of error or some parental response categories, or both.

Skeptics, like Grimshaw and Pinker (1989) and Gordon (1990), reject these findings as evidence against the need to posit a strong innate endowment, and are at most willing to countenance a possible facilitating role for conversational assistance in language acquisition. They point out that not all language learning occurs at age two, that none of the differences in responses to grammatical and ungrammatical speech are categorical, and that there is no evidence that children can register relative frequency data concerning the (apparent) acceptability of what they say in order to interpret such information over time.

Addressing the frequency issue, Bohannon et al. (1990) deny that differences in responses to grammatical and ungrammatical speech need to be categorical, citing evidence to the effect that corrective feedback on less than 25% of trials is sufficient to produce accurate concept learning. The important factor, they write, is not that each trial receives clear feedback, but that the preponderance of the evidence over time clearly indicates the correct learning target. Farrar (1992) notes that both his 22% recast rate after ungrammatical utterances and the 33% recast and expansion rate of Bohannon and Stanowicz (1988) would meet this criterion, especially when it is considered that additional ungrammatical utterances elicit other types of negative feedback, such as clarification requests. Bohannon et al. (1990) further suggest that something like Wexler and Culicover's (1980) uniqueness principle, Clark's (1987) principle of contrast, or MacWhinney's (1987, and elsewhere) competition principle operates in conjunction with negative evidence. With some differences among them, the principles assume that there is only one means of expressing a given meaning, or one form for one function. Thus, when a learner's version of the TL contains two or more forms for the same function, the learner assumes only one is correct. Under MacWhinney's formulation, if competition between forms is a zero-sum game, with gains for one meaning losses for the other(s), subsequently encountered positive instances of the correct form (which will usually be much more frequent or even the only version) in the input, will not only serve to strengthen that form, but also to weaken the competing one(s). In this sense, interlocutor responses to ungrammatical speech are not the only source of negative evidence: "each piece of positive evidence for Form A is equivalent to a piece of negative evidence for Form B" (Bohannon et al., 1990, p. 223). (For applications of the uniqueness principle to L1 acquisition and to L1 attrition, see, respectively, chapters 16 by Andersen and Shirai and 18 by Seliger, this volume.)

To demonstrate not only that negative evidence exists, but is *usable,* and thereby to meet Pinker's second requirement, it must be shown that learners notice the feedback, and perceive it for what it is. The problem here is that much negative evidence takes the form of partial repetitions, and such repetitions also serve as expressions of agreement, confirmations that a message has been understood, and other functions in the same conversation. The fact that an utterance is intended as a correction, therefore, does not necessarily mean that a learner will perceive it that way. From a learner's perspective, interlocutors might be repeating part of an utterance quizzically because they did not catch all of it, because the meaning was clear but surprising, because there is another way of saying the same thing, because they disagree, because something was linguistically awry, or for multiple reasons, as shown in the following (constructed) L2 example concerning adverb placement:

(9)   NNS: When I was a child
                                                 in France I drank
                                                 every day wine with
                                                 my meals.

NS: (astonished) Really? You
drank wine *every day?*

                                                 NNS: Sure. Wine with
                                                 water.

Even if a learner correctly perceives an utterance as a correction, there is still the problem for any kind of cognitive comparison or hypothesis-testing theory (e.g., Bohannon & Stanowicz, 1989; Nelson, 1987) of whether a learner can hold both the original errorful utterance and the interlocutor's response in memory long enough to compare them, and if that is (sometimes) possible, the additional question of whether the identity of the error will be clear. Was pronunciation the problem, for example, or were one or more parts of the lexis or grammar wrong? Because *use* entails *usability,* we will move directly to Pinker's third criterion.

Critics claim it is also difficult to show that learners *use* any negative evidence that is available. First, the literature contains amusing anecdotes of children who seem oblivious to repeated explicit correction, and it is claimed that correction can only be recognized as such, and so even potentially be used, when children attain metalinguistic awareness (Birdson, 1989). Second, when child speech development does appear to benefit from corrections, recasts, or some other intervention, Grimshaw and Pinker (1989) argue, this does not constitute unambiguous evidence of the effect of the negative feedback, because the utterances containing the correction simultaneously provide positive evidence of the item concerned.

Neither of these arguments withstand scrutiny, however. The anecdotes, first of all, are of questionable relevance. Quite apart from the fact that they are of uncertain frequency, they presumably show nothing more or less than that processing constraints will always limit the evidence, positive or negative, from which a child or adult learner can benefit. Input must be within a reasonably close developmental distance from an L1 or L2 learner's current proficiency level if it is to be comprehensible, and therefore usable (Meisel, Clahsen, & Pienemann, 1981; Pienemann, 1989). Children imitate emergent structures more frequently than already acquired or wholly unfamiliar ones (Bloom, Hood, & Lightbown, 1974). Examples of particular children being unable to use particular pieces of negative evidence, in other words, do not show that those or other children cannot or do not use negative evidence.

The second suggestion, that negative evidence really works (only) as positive evidence, is also dubious. If the data showed only that children who received negative feedback, such as recasts and expansions, on particular structures outperformed children who received less positive evidence on those structures, more general exposure to the same structures or more positive evidence on different structures (e.g., Malouf & Dodd, 1972; Nelson et al., 1973; Nelson, 1977; Nelson, Denninger, Bonvillian, Kaplan, & Baker, 1984), the results would indeed be susceptible to the alternative interpretation that the negative feedback provided in the various treatment conditions worked by offering additional models of the target structures (i.e., positive evidence). What has been demonstrated, however, is more than that. Controlled comparisons have shown that, in otherwise natural conversation, recasts, (i.e., adult responses that add morphosyntactic or semantic information to some component of a child's preceding utterance without changing its essential meaning) are more successful than (1) equal numbers of noncontingent models of control structures for the same children or than (2) models of the same structures in comparable children (Baker & Nelson, 1984; Farrar, 1990; Nelson, 1988, 1991; Nelson et al., 1984). In other words, children who receive additional positive evidence, either in the general input or as models, are outperformed by comparable children who receive equivalent amounts of data in the form of negative evidence, specifically negative feedback, following their ungrammatical speech.

Recasts are utterances that rephrase a child's utterance by changing one or more sentence components (subject, verb, or object) while still referring to its central meanings. Following a child's utterance, "Jimmy eat all the bread," a simple recast, in which one component is changed, might be "That's right, Jimmy ate all the bread." Following "Jimmy watch TV," a complex recast, in which two or more components are changed, might be "Yes, Jimmy's watching television, isn't he?" In two experimental intervention studies with eight children ranging in age from 2.6 to 3.10 and in mean length utterances (MLU) from 3.07 to 4.81, adult recasts of the children's utterances that contained the target structures were found to speed up productive use of passives, relative clauses, and previously nonused auxiliaries, to do so more than models of the same items, and to do so more when the child's rather than the experimenter's utterances were recast. The children whose use of the structures was stimulated were also younger than those who usually attempt them (Baker & Nelson, 1984). The advantage for recasts over models (which also improved performance), and for recasts of the children's over the researchers' utterances, Nelson points out, suggests that it is the opportunity for cognitive comparison by the child of his or her own utterance with the semantically related adult version, and not just hearing new forms in the input, which is useful.

Four properties are confounded in recasts: (1) reformulation, (2) expansion, (3) semantic contingency, and (4) position (following the child's utterance), and could each or in combination account for the relationship. Farrar (1990) noted, however, that the four properties occur in unique combinations in other parental moves in caretaker–child discourse; recasts (all four), expansions (2, 3, and 4), topic continuations (3 and 4), and topic changes (4 only). In an ex post facto correlational design, Farrar compared the relative utility of each move containing a specific morpheme in promoting use of that morpheme in 12 mother–child pairs recorded twice over a 6-month period. After any effects of the other moves on those morpheme's development were partialed out, recasts (the only moves to involve reformulation of the child's utterance) were found to be strongly related to the development of two bound morphemes, plural *s* and present progressive -*ing*. Expansions and topic continuations were similarly positively associated with regular past tense and copulas. Topic changes were not positively associated with development. With the exception of a presumably spurious correlation between recasts of copulas and use of third-person singular *s,* there were also no effects for particular or general response types on any of the other morphemes, suggesting very specific relationships between input and acquisition not easily accounted for by the general provision of positive evidence.

One possible reason for the effectiveness of recasts is that children imitate them two or three times as often as other parental responses (Bohannon & Stanowicz, 1988, 1989; Farrar, 1992). This is true provided they are not too far removed from the child's initial attempt, as is usually the case. Adults recast child utterances with one error more often than those with multiple errors, and recasts with one added or corrected morpheme are in turn more likely to be imitated by the child than recasts with two or more such morphemes, which are often ignored (Bohannon & Stanowicz, 1989; Farrar, 1992; Nelson et al., 1984). Recasts that involve only one change presumably make comparison of the original and corrected utterance easier for the child. Imitation has independently been claimed to play various useful roles in language development (Speidel & Nelson, 1989). Importantly, Farrar found that children were more likely to imitate corrective recasts than noncorrective recasts, exact repetitions, topic continuations, or topic changes, despite the fact that exact repetitions tend to be syntactically simpler. Farrar noted (1990, p. 65) that this suggests they respond to the negative evidence, not simply to a recast's imitative quality. Corrective recasts appear to be more salient to children; they attend to, notice, and imitate them more than other response types containing identical linguistic information, satisfying Pinker's third condition. Although immediate learner incorporation of new grammatical items speaks only to short-term effects (Birdsong, 1989), earlier findings (Baker & Nelson, 1984; Farrar, 1990; Nelson, 1991; Nelson et al., 1984) suggest that the relationship between recasts and subsequent development is lasting.

Pinker's fourth and final requirement is to show that negative evidence is *necessary.* At first sight, this looks well motivated, given the well-known resilience of language acquisition in the face of variable input and variable provision of conversational support by individual caretakers across families of different social classes (Lieven, 1978), as well as for male and female children and firstborn and later children. More critically, some ethnographic studies have described communities in which certain styles of adult–child conversation believed to be advantageous for language development are supposedly culturally inappropriate, and so not used, with no obvious harm to child language development (Heath, 1983; Ochs, 1982; Ochs & Schieffelin, 1984). If valid, such findings would automatically reduce negative evidence from a necessary to, at most, a facilitative role.

The argument is again controversial, however. Just as anecdotes describing instances of nonuse of parental corrections show neither that such results are general nor that the children concerned do not benefit from negative evidence on other occasions, so reports of community members not utilizing certain styles of caretaker talk have to be viewed in context. In some cases (e.g., Western Samoa), elder siblings, not adults, are reported to be the principal caretakers, making reports of what does not occur in adult–child conversation less relevant than descriptions of older–younger child talk. Furthermore, as pointed out when these studies first began to appear, although some communities apparently eschewed use of simple codes with children, there was sometimes evidence that caregivers did make interactional modifications of the kind now under discussion, and it was these, not simple input, that were relevant to acquisition (Long, 1981a). In the Western Samoan case, for example, although excerpts from mother–child conversation reported by Ochs (1982) did not show use of simplified speech to children, they did show examples of repetition and other potentially facilitative response types. This has since proven to be the case with the language socialization practices of other culturally very different peoples, such as the Kaluli of Papua New Guinea (Ochs & Schieffelin, 1984; Schieffelin, 1979, 1987). Some of those groups also employ highly conventionalized, quasi-instructional speech events with language-learning children, such as the Kaluli *elema* (roughly, Say it like that), a form of elicited imitation (Schieffelin, 1979, 1987), and in Malaita in the western Solomon Islands, the Kwara'ae *fa'amanata'anga* (teaching of knowledge and abstract skills) for teaching children reasoning skills and cultural values (Watson-Gegeo & Gegeo, 1990).

In the case of the African-American community described by Heath (1983), Bohannon et al. (1990) noted that the reported opinion of a single community member that repeating children's utterances is pointless is not the same as showing that members of the community share this view or that their behavior with children bear it out if they do. Nor would the unavailability of a particular form of feedback to some children render it useless to children who receive it or show that no form of feedback is necessary. Snow (1989) has also argued that the language acquisition process has redundancy built into it such that the absence of one environmental factor of relevance can be compensated for by another, and Bohannon et al. (1990) suggested that even if the community described by Heath really does not repeat what its children say, it can be expected to ensure that they are clear and comprehensible in other ways.

Empirical support for a role for negative evidence in L1 acquisition is far from sufficient (cf. Moerk, 1991). Positive correlations between various types of semantically contingent parental responding moves, such as expansions and extensions, and language development have been few and somewhat erratic both within and across studies (Barnes, Gutfreund, Satterly, & Wells, 1983; Gleitman, Newport, & Gleitman, 1984; Hoff-Ginsberg, 1986; Scarborough & Wyckoff, 1986), and there are still relatively few data of the kind reported by Nelson (1977), Baker and Nelson (1984), and Farrar (1990), showing specific effects of recasts over time on the items they targeted. Also, if it is really true that children never make errors on some items, as innatists often assert, then as Farrar (1992) noted, negative evidence could not be involved there, at least. That would be consistent with claims for innate knowledge of constraints on language, or else with a radically different view from Chomsky's of the language-learning process or of end-state grammatical knowledge. Finally, and perhaps most seriously, recast items are often language-specific and not of the order of complexity or abstractness of most supposed principles of Universal Grammar (UG). Hence, although negative feedback is of potentially great interest as a mechanism by which some aspects of languages may be learned, research must focus on some of the tougher areas of syntax and pragmatics before it is likely to interest skeptics in the innatist camp.

Negative Evidence in L2 Acquisition

Thus far, the discussion has primarily concerned L1 acquisition, where it has been argued that various forms of implicit correction, and recasts in particular, play an important facilitative role in development. The L2 picture is less clear, as researchers have for the most part restricted the scope of their studies to overt oral error correction during classroom lessons or written feedback on student writing (for review, see Chaudron, 1987, 1988). Although important in helping to determine the effects of formal instruction on IL development, neither case speaks to the ability of learners to perceive and utilize implicit corrective feedback during spontaneous communicative language use. Further, L2 researchers who have sought evidence of learners modifying their output as a result of feedback on error have tended to limit their focus to the short-term, usually immediate, effects, perhaps because L2 acquisition among instructed adult subjects progresses rapidly in the early stages and because of the difficulty of controlling for outside exposure in longitudinal studies, even in foreign language environments.

Where usability and use are concerned, some studies show that metalinguistically mature adult classroom learners, who might be expected to be on the lookout for form-focusing devices, whether proactive or reactive, often do not perceive them as such when working with an NS on a problem-solving task (Hawkins,

1985) or even during classroom lessons with a primary focus on language as object (Slimani, 1992). Most researchers report students not only noticing corrections, however, but benefiting from them—in the short term, at least (Chaudron, 1988). Salica (1981) found that adult ESL students responded correctly to 64% of teacher corrective feedback moves, and Wren (1982) that an advanced adult ESL student was able to self-correct 14% of her errors, but 83% of them after teacher treatment during individual tutorial sessions with the researcher. In a study of French immersion classrooms, Chaudron (1977) showed that, as compared with simple repetition of the correct model, teacher feedback in the form of a reduced version of the student's utterance to help locate the error increased the rate of correct student responses to error treatment by about 15%, that adding emphasis (questioning tone or stress) increased correct responses by about 20%, and that a combination of reduction and emphasis was most effective of all. Research on ESL by francophone adolescents in Quebec (Lightbown & Spada, 1990; Spada & Lightbown, 1993; White, 1991; White et al., 1991) has shown at least a temporary advantage for intact groups of students whose attention is drawn to a targeted construction by form-focused activities or error correction over groups experiencing the same amount of natural classroom exposure. In some cases, however, the advantage may be due in part to the rarity of the forms concerned (e.g., frequency adverbs), in incidental classroom input, a fact that may also account for its failure to survive intervals of noninstructional focus before delayed posttests in some studies.

Nonclassroom studies are more revealing because spontaneous conversation with no metalinguistic focus *before* negative evidence is provided is the norm for most L2 learners and the only experience available to many. NSs were found very rarely to attempt overt correction of NNS errors in 23 informal 20-minute conversations outside classrooms (Chun et al., 1982), where it would usually be sociolinguistically inappropriate and also difficult, because interlocutors are focused on communication. Using the same database, Brock, Crookes, Day, and Long (1986) found no differential effect for implicit and explicit feedback on error, and minimal evidence of NNSs incorporating such feedback in their next utterance following the NS feedback move. Inside classrooms, the fast pace of typical language lessons means that teachers understandably fail to notice many errors, ignore others if they are not the current pedagogic focus, and (paralleling the L1 acquisition findings) often "correct" those to which they do respond inconsistently and also ambiguously (e.g., by using exact repetition of the target utterance both when confirming a correct student utterance and correcting an incorrect one) (Allwright, 1975; Fanselow, 1977; Long, 1977). Crookes and Rulon (1988) studied incorporation of corrective feedback as a function of the type of task upon which 16 NS–NNS dyads were engaged. They found that two collaborative problem-solving tasks generated four or five times more corrective utterances after NNS errors and more negotiation for meaning than free conversation by the same pairs. Use of corrective feedback was only higher on one of the two tasks than in free conversation, however, apparently that involving most new vocabulary for the learners and hence more opportunities for incorporation of new words.

In a small-scale study extending Farrar's (1992) analysis to L2 acquisition, Richardson (1993) examined 15-minute free conversations by three adult NS–NNS dyads. Classifying NS responses to learners' grammatical and ungrammatical utterances containing any of seven classes of target grammatical morphemes into Farrar's four categories—corrective recasts, noncorrective recasts, topic continuations, and topic changes—she then looked at NNS reactions to each type of response. Paralleling the L1 acquisition findings, NNSs were found to be (here, 1.6 to 4.5 times) more likely to imitate the correct grammatical morpheme after a corrective recast (negative feedback) than after any of the other three responding moves (positive evidence). It was generally the more easily remediable ungrammatical utterances that the NSs recast; only 13% of corrective recasts were responses to NNS utterances with multiple errors, and there were only two cases where a NNS imitated recasts containing two corrections. In other words, again as in L1 acquisition, NSs provided fewer recasts with multiple corrections, and NNSs were less likely to use them when they occurred. The higher NNS tendency to imitate corrective recasts could have been due to the negative feedback they provided or because they contained a partial imitation of what the NNS had said. These two factors were distinguishable by comparing NNS imitations of corrective recasts and noncorrective recasts, because the latter also contained an imitative component but provided positive evidence of the target morphemes. Richardson found that the NNSs imitated 42% of corrective recasts compared with 26% of noncorrective recasts, suggesting that they were indeed responding at least in part to the negative evidence in corrective recasts rather than to their imitative component. In sum, although based on a very small sample and corpus, Richardson's study provides preliminary evidence to satisfy Pinker's third criterion: i.e., evidence consistent with the claim that negative feedback in L2 acquisition is usable and is used, although as yet with unknown impact on long-term acquisition.

Similar findings have been obtained by Oliver (in press). As part of a larger study, Oliver analyzed child NS reactions to their NNS interlocutors' ungrammatical turns, and the child NNSs' use of the NS feedback, in 8 (8–13-year-old) dyads performing two picture-description tasks. With regard to NS reactions to NNS error, of 283 error turns in the corpus, 39% were ignored by the NSs, and 61% received implicit negative feedback of some kind, either recasts (22%) or negotiation, such as clarification requests and confirmation checks (39%). Oliver found three relationships between NNS error type and NS response: (1) Errors involving incorrect or omitted auxiliary, copula, pronoun, word order, word choice, word, or subject tended to elicit NS negotiation. Singular/plural and subject–verb agreement errors were more often recast. There were no clear differences in NS reactions to article, tense, and obvious pronunciation errors. (2) Semantically ambiguous (opaque) utterances were more likely to be recast (cf. Furrow et al., 1993). (3) The 'opaque-negotiate' and 'transparent-recast' pattern was clearer when single- and multiple-error turns were distinguished: 78% of negotiations and 31% of recasts were in response to turns containing two or more errors; 22% of negotiations and 69% of recasts were in response to single-error turns (cf. Richardson, 1993). With reference to NNS use of the feedback, Oliver found the NNSs incorporated 10% of all recasts, and over one-third when given an opportunity to do so and when incorporation was appropriate. Oliver showed that incorporation by the NNS was impossible 16% of the time because NSs continued their turn rapidly immediately following an utterance containing a recast, and inappropriate 55% of the time, e.g. because the recasts occurred in the form of yes/no questions. Examining non-use of information in recasts in this way constitutes an important methodological advance for L1 and L2 research, for it suggests that learners may well use substantially more of the negative feedback they receive than is revealed by immediate incorporation, the measure employed in most L1 and L2 studies. Neither Richardson's nor Oliver's studies provide unambiguous evidence of use (as opposed to usability), of course, since longitudinal studies or use of pre- and posttests in cross-sectional designs would be required for that.

The relative utility of models and what might best be called "pseudo-recasts" has been investigated in two innovative classroom studies by Herron and Tomasello of what they call the Garden Path technique. Herron and Tomasello (1988) found that adult learners of French as an L2 who were shown examples of a structure or lexical item so that they formed a correct generalization based on a pattern in the L2 data, and who were then induced to make errors by being shown another example to which the rule should logically have applied but did not, and who then had their overgeneralization errors explicitly corrected, learned better than comparable subjects who were given a series of correct examples of the structure. Tomasello and Herron (1989) replicated this finding with induced errors attributable to L1 transfer (i.e., interlingual errors), as opposed to intralingual errors in the earlier study. Herron and Tomasello claim that their results are explained by Nelson's (1981, 1987) rare event cognitive comparison theory of language acquisition, which holds that recasts are especially useful for children to compare their own speech against native models because they occur immediately after the child's incorrect utterance, in the same discourse context, and with the same semantic context.

This claim was criticized by Beck and Eubank (1991) on the grounds that neither Tomasello and Herron (1989) nor Nelson had provided data to satisfy Pinker's four tests for the functioning of negative evidence in language development, particularly for the claim that negative evidence is a requirement for language acquisition, and because of alleged methodological inadequacies in the transfer study. Tomasello and Herron (1991) responded that their studies concern negative feedback, not negative evidence in a strict Learnability Theory sense, and mostly structures that involve lexical choice and article use (i.e., items considered part of the semantic–pragmatic aspect of language), which lie outside Chomskyan UG or "core grammar." They further specified that their claim is for the beneficial effect of negative feedback, not its necessity.

Although Tomasello and Herron indeed failed to address several issues required of an argument for a role for negative evidence, this is less important in light of the more recent child language data summarized above, which should satisfy Pinker's (and Beck and Eubank's) concerns about its availability, perception, and usability. What neither Tomasello and Herron nor Beck and Eubank discuss, on the other hand, is the external validity of the Garden Path findings. Tomasello and Herron (1989, p. 392) point out that the conditions that Nelson (1987) argues make negative feedback, particularly recasts, so important in L1 acquisition hold in the Garden Path technique, too: (a) occurrence "immediately after a child's incorrect formulation, (b) in the same discourse context, and (c) with an attempt to match the child's intended meaning." After citing unpublished data showing that provision of recasts in their L1 form does not seem to work in the classroom, however, they go on to assert the relevance of Nelson's (1987) cognitive comparison theory in explaining their results.

Tomasello and Herron's position deserves closer examination. In spontaneous noninstructional talk:

> (A) recast occurs when, in reply to the preceding utterance of the child, the mother maintains reference to the same meaning but syntactically changes one or more of those sentence components: subject, verb, or object. (Baker & Nelson, 1984, p. 5)

In the Garden Path technique, however, the "recasts" (1) are not triggered by an error occurring as part of learners' attempts to communicate, (2) are provided to metalinguistically aware subjects, (3) occur when the attention of both parties is already focused on an isolated target form for the explicit purpose of language learning, not in spontaneous conversation when the interlocutors are primarily focused on meaning, (4) are delivered in the form of explicit correction (the correct forms being written on the blackboard above the students' incorrect ones and commented upon by the teacher), not incidentally, and (5) are accompanied by opportunities for unhurried visual inspection and cognitive comparison. Although Farrar (1992) showed that it was reformulation, not expansion, semantic contingency, or discourse position, that distinguished recasts from other less beneficial forms of maternal feedback to children, that does not mean that the message-initiation quality of the learner's triggering utterance outside classrooms is irrelevant. All four types of feedback compared by Farrar shared that feature. Nor does the Garden Path research address the issue of the saliency of recasts to learners in noninstructional talk (the only L2 experience for the majority of L2 learners). Do adult L2 learners benefit incidentally from recasts or other forms of implicit, "off-record" negative evidence when they encounter them in spontaneous conversation unaccompanied by metalinguistic explanation or opportunities for unhurried visual comparison?

In a study designed partly to answer that question, but which maintained sufficient control to permit a possible causal interpretation, Mito (1993) randomly assigned 27 adult NSs of English enrolled in a second semester course in Japanese as an L2 (JSL) to form five groups. Subjects were pretested on two Japanese target items, a locative construction and adjective ordering, using one of two equivalent versions of an oral picture-description task, and were found not to know either. In a within-subjects, repeated measures design, the 18 subjects in the four treatment groups then played one of two variants of each of two communication games (involving manipulation of objects by researcher and subject separated by a screen), each game designed to elicit one of the target constructions, during which they received either six models (on a prerecorded audiotape) or six recasts (live) of the structure from the researcher, before doing a second version of the picture-description task as a posttest. Training exemplars (modeled or recast) of the target structures and pre- and posttest items were different. Structures (locatives and adjective ordering) and treatments (models and recasts) were crossed, such that each subject received models of one structure and recasts of the other. Structures, treatments, and pre- and posttest forms were counterbalanced. The nine subjects in the control group did the same tests and practiced writing *kanji* for a period equivalent to the other four groups' treatment sessions. All sessions, including testing, were conducted individually, lasted 30 minutes, and were audio-recorded. Transcripts were checked to ensure that equivalent numbers of models and recasts had been delivered to each subject. The posttest showed no learning of either structure in the modeling condition or by the control group, whereas there was a small but statistically significant improvement on adjective ordering and locative structures by 6 of the 18 subjects in the recast condition. Mito cautions that the learnability of the two structures for students of her subjects' Japanese proficiency was assessed impressionistically on the basis of pilot-testing of the procedure and examination of students' textbooks, not empirically established developmental sequence research in JSL (which is minimal), and that this may have obfuscated the effects of one or both treatments. (Even in the recast condition, the structures were apparently too difficult for most subjects, 12 failing to learn either.) Also, some subjects spontaneously echoed some of the recasts, thereby obtaining additional output opportunities that may have favored the recast condition. With these caveats in mind, Mito's results are consistent with those from the L1 acquisition literature in suggesting the usability of negative evidence in general and recasts in particular by adult L2 learners, and the superiority of recasts to models. Further research of this sort is clearly needed.

Another limitation of the Tomasello and Herron studies concerns the indeterminate nature of the learning achieved by the treatment groups. Carroll, Roberge, and Swain (1992) pointed out that the targeted forms were absolute exceptions to taught rules, exceptions all learners need to memorize. It is not clear whether the Garden Path technique was being used to teach rules or restrictions on rules, or simply to draw learners' attention to the exceptions, about which information would in any case be independently available as positive evidence in the input. Accordingly, Carroll et al. (1992) conducted a study of the effect of explicit corrective feedback on the learning of French morphological generalizations by adult speakers of English. Thirty-nine intermediate and 40 advanced learners were randomly assigned to one of two groups. After a nine-item training session, subjects were shown flashcards on which were written French sentences containing a verb, and related sentences in which they had to supply the missing noun form derivable from that verb. The nominal form required either a short or long form of the stem plus either -*age* (39 cases), -*ment* (38 cases), or some other suffix (13 cases), choice among which in French is grammatically conditioned (simplifying a little) by whether or not a verb is of the -*er* or -*ir* class and is transitive or reflexive. Subjects in the treatment group received correction on any errors they made in the first 45 instances, which also included four completely exceptional items of the kind targeted in the Tomasello and Herron studies, but no correction in the second 45, during which items turning on the -*er*/-*ir* distinction were first introduced. Control group subjects received the same 90 items, but with no correction at all. The inclusion of the four exceptional items during the first (feedback) phase further allowed the researchers to compare the effects of correction of absolute exceptions with correction of items based on one (-*er*) verb class on items based on another (-*ir*) class (i.e., on learners' ability, if any, to generalize the effects of feedback. Carroll et al. tested subjects immediately and 1 week later using the 45 items from the feedback phase. Experimental subjects outperformed controls, showing the beneficial effects of correction, with advanced learners retaining more information than intermediates after a week. They had failed to induce morphological generalizations, however, seeming instead to have used correction to learn individual lexical items.

The troubling implications of these findings for any inductive language learning theory, in which negative feedback would have to play a role, were somewhat ameliorated by the results of further research showing that adults could learn from negative feedback and also *generalize* the knowledge to new cases. Using similar materials and procedures in another tightly controlled laboratory study, Carroll and Swain (1993) examined the effects of negative feedback on 100 adult Spanish speakers' learning of the English dative alternation in such sentence pairs as *Mary found a job for Antonio* and *Mary found Antonio a job*. There were four treatment groups: Explicit hypothesis rejection (subjects told they were wrong and given an explicit rule statement every time they made an error), Explicit utterance rejection (subjects simply told they were wrong every time they made an error), Modeling/

Implicit negative feedback (subjects given a reformulated correct response every time they made an error, but no rule statement), and Indirect metalinguistic feedback (subjects asked if they were sure their response was correct every time they made an error, but given neither a model nor a rule. All four treatment groups generally outperformed the (no feedback) control group on both treatment verbs and new verbs on an immediate posttest and on a delayed posttest a week later. The Explicit hypothesis rejection group did best, often outperforming the other treatment groups, as well, followed by the Modeling/Implicit negative feedback group. Carroll and Swain warn that the Explicit hypothesis rejection group had more time on task (looking at the cards) than other groups because the metalinguistic explanation often took longer, and that all treatment groups may have looked at the stimuli on the cards longer than the control group for the same reason. Furthermore, although the results of this study at least leave open the possibility that adults can learn abstract linguistic generalizations from either direct or indirect feedback, the controlled circumstances under which they did so made induction a simpler task than that facing learners in the real world. The laboratory subjects (1) did not have to provide the meaning and syntactic form of sentences, which were both done for them, and so could attend to language as object; (2) knew all their utterances were categorically either correct or incorrect, and (3) knew they would receive, and received, feedback always and only following an error.

In sum, various forms of negative evidence, particularly overt corrective feedback following learner error, are well documented in instructed L2 acquisition. However, the status of negative feedback in natural NS–NNS conversation, where a metalinguistic focus is lacking and where attempts at overt error correction rarely occur, is the theoretically and practically more interesting question. Two small studies (Oliver, in press; Richardson, 1993) show the existence and usability of negative evidence in spontaneous NS–NNS conversation, with patterns and proportions both of differential NS responses to grammatical and ungrammatical learner utterances, and of learners' differential reactions to corrective recasts and other response types, approximating those in caretaker talk. The usability of L2 corrective feedback, demonstrated by evidence that learners perceive the feedback for what it is, is seen in NNSs in the Oliver study incorporating between 10% and over 30% of recasts, depending on the analysis used, and in NNSs in the Richardson study imitating roughly 40% of corrective recasts compared with roughly 25% of noncorrective recasts, and being roughly two to four times more likely to produce a correct target morpheme after corrective recasts than after other NS responses. Evidence of use is proving no easier to come by than in L1 acquisition. There is the difficulty of (1) preempting a metalinguistic focus, and (2) allowing sufficient input and time for specific learning effects to become apparent, while (3) maintaining control of the linguistic environment in an experimental study, compounded by (4) the problem of matching target structures to one another and to adult learners' current proficiency and processing abilities. Some limited evidence exists of use, however, and of the relative efficacy of recasts over models (Carroll & Swain, 1993; Mito, 1993), and further studies of the issue are currently in progress. A facilitative role for negative feedback in L2 acquisition seems probable, and, as White (1989, 1991) has claimed, its necessity for learning some L2 structures is arguable on logical learnability grounds.

V. NEGOTIATION FOR MEANING AND ACQUISITION

A. The Role of Conversation

In a pioneering exploration of the issue in the L2 acquisition literature, Hatch (1978) urged L2 acquisition researchers to consider the proposition then emerging from L1 work (Atkinson, 1979; Ervin-Tripp, 1976; Keenan, 1974; Macnamara, 1972; Scollon, 1973) that, rather than grammatical knowledge developing in order to be put to use in conversations at some later date, "language learning evolves *out of* learning how to carry on conversations" (Hatch, 1978, p. 404). (Most language teaching syllabi and "methods" assume the reverse.) Hatch (1983) cautioned, however, that some aspects of conversation might actually inhibit learning. For example, "(M)istakes in the marking of verbs . . . would not be caught by when? questions. Such question corrections would more likely elicit a time adverb rather than a verb correction for morphology" (Hatch, 1983, p. 432).

Sato (1986, 1988, 1990) examined these ideas as part of a larger longitudinal study of naturalistic L2 acquisition motivated by Givón's claims concerning the shift from presyntactic to grammaticized speech in language change (e.g., Givón, 1979). Sato's data consisted in part of spontaneous conversations between NSs and two Vietnamese brothers whose English development she observed each week for a year. In the area of emergent syntax, Sato found some examples comparable to those in L1 acquisition (Ochs, Schieffelin, & Platt, 1979) of collaborative complex propositions across utterances and speakers, as with the precursors to adverbial and relative clauses in (10) and (11):

(10)   Than: vɪtnam dei   (bli) kɔ :
               '[In] Vietnam they (play) cards'
        NS: They what?
        Than: pleị   kɔ :
               'play cards'
        NS: They play cards?
        Than: yæ   wɛn wɛn krismɛs
               'Yeah, when [it's] Christmas

                                                    (Sato, 1988, p. 380)

(11)   Tai: hi lɒk   əm   əm-
              'He's looking, um'
        Than: æt mæn
              'At [the] man
        Tai: æt mæn hi hi smoᵂkiŋ
              'At the man [who is] smoking'

                                                              (Sato, 1988, p. 380)

Such cases were rare during the first year, however, perhaps due to the limited
overall proficiency of the children, who were near beginners when the study
began.

When it came to inflectional morphology, Hatch's caution proved well founded.
Sato showed how the brothers initially used conversational scaffolding, specifically their interlocutors' prior establishment of reference to a past event to compensate for their lack of overt inflectional past time marking. Even severe communication breakdowns failed to elicit learner attempts at the missing verbal
morphology:

(12)   NS: Oh, Mary said that you went to,
                                                um—went to a game by the Fever?
        Tai: noʉ tan   hi go yɛt.
              no-Thanh-he-go-yet.

                                                You didn't go yet? To the Fever?
        Tai: wat?
              What?

                                                Did you go to see the Fever play
                                                soccer?
        Tai: yɛs.
              Yes.

                                                When was that?
        Tai: nat nat naʉ
              not-not-now

                                                Oh, uh—later? Oh, I see. Who else
                                                is going?
        Tai: tan hi go   ɪn də pɪʉ
              Than-he-go-in-the [pɾʉ]

                                                              (Sato, 1986, p. 36)

Later, like adult learners of German (Meisel, 1987), the brothers moved to alternative surrogate systems of their own, such as the use of temporal adverbials
('Yesterday, I go . . .') and order of mention, but neither boy progressed very far
with past time inflectional morphology during the first year of the study.

In an explicit discussion of the issue, Sato (1986) proposed that conversation is *selectively facilitative* of grammatical development, depending on the structures involved. The beneficial effects of conversational scaffolding and situational knowledge on communication makes overt past time marking on verbs expendable in most contexts, which may hinder acquisition by lessening the need to encode the function morphologically in speech. (Although it is true that not needing to produce an item may not impede acquisition, or encoding of the item in the underlying grammar, failure to perceive a gap, or mismatch between output and input is arguably less likely to promote IL change, at least, than awareness of a communication breakdown.) There is some limited evidence that conversation nourishes emergent L2 syntax, on the other hand (Sato, 1988), most of the few attempts at complex syntactic constructions produced during the children's first year of English occur in a conversational context. Studies of collaborative syntax across utterances and speakers in talk between NSs and adult beginners and NSs and more proficient learners remain serious lacunae in the L2 database. A valuable contribution in this area, however, is Bygate's (1988) study of the ways pairs of adult classroom learners working on problem-solving tasks used intraturn repairs and cooperative dialogue to build syntactically more complex freestanding utterances out of various kinds of shorter, syntactically dependent "satellite units."

The claim that conversation facilitates the emergence of at least some types of grammatical devices is essentially one about learner production. So, too, is a second claimed role for conversation in acquisition, the "Comprehensible Output Hypothesis" (Swain, 1985). Swain suggested that the failure of French immersion students to reach nativelike levels might partly be due to the lack of much genuine opportunity for them to participate in classroom conversation in more than a response mode. Although their receptive skills can reach nativelike standards this way, the ability to decode input using semantic and pragmatic knowledge may inhibit syntacticization (see also Skehan, 1992). Production, on the other hand, can push learners to analyze input grammatically, with accuracy also increased by the negative feedback that verbal hypothesis testing elicits. As suggested by Schachter (1983, 1984, 1986), confirmation checks, comprehension checks, clarification requests, and other triggers of negotiation work can sensitive learners to a need for greater comprehensibility on their part. They can aid acquisition by pushing learners to increase control over forms they have already internalized (Nobuyoshi & Ellis, 1993).

As Krashen (1985, pp. 35–36, 65–67) pointed out, a claim that production is necessary for acquisition is problematic in light of the exceptional cases of individuals who have supposedly learned languages with minimal or no opportunity to speak (Fourcin, 1975; Lenneberg, 1962). (Such cases are not only exceptional, but somewhat poorly documented, it should be noted.) Similarly, R. Ellis (1992) concluded from a review of classroom studies that there was no clear evidence of a positive effect for "controlled" production practice, at least. Ellis noted, however, that such practice might at least raise learners' consciousness of the target items or of language form in general, possibly leading to a delayed benefit. In sum, a more defensible view is that spoken production is probably useful, as Swain suggests, because it elicits negative input and encourages analysis and grammaticization, but that it is facilitative, not necessary.

There has been a considerable amount of research on "pushed output" in NS–NNS conversation. An early study that sought evidence of modification and incorporation of feedback produced very few examples in a corpus of 23 informal NS–NNS conversations (Brock et al., 1986). The null finding may have been due to looking for incorporation only in NNS utterances immediately following correct NS models, and also to use of informal phatic conversation as the database. Free conversation is notoriously poor as a context for driving IL development for a number of reasons, because the lack of any fixed topics or outcomes permits rapid, superficial treatment of topics and the dropping of any that cause linguistic trouble (Long, 1983c). In contrast, tasks that orient participants to shared goals and involve them in some work or activity produce more negotiation work (Pica, Kanagy, & Falodun, 1993), as do unfamiliar tasks that involve participants in the discourse (Gass & Varonis, 1984; Plough & Gass, 1993) and tasks performed by mixed proficiency dyads in which the lower and higher proficiency NNSs are in the sender and receiver (of information) roles, respectively (Yule & Macdonald, 1990). When working cooperatively on certain kinds of problem-solving tasks (e.g., two-way tasks that are closed—known by participants to have only one or a small number of correct solutions) (Long, 1989, 1990), participants' conversational feet are held to the fire. The nature of the task causes topics and subtopics to be recycled until solutions are reached, producing more negotiation work (Paul, 1991) and as shown by a tendency for some (but not all) two-way tasks to engender a higher ratio of topic-continuing to topic-initiating moves than free conversation, for NSs to provide NNSs significantly more feedback while working on such tasks than in free conversation, and for NNSs to incorporate more of the feedback on some two-way tasks (Crookes & Rulon, 1988).

Pica (1992) provided a detailed review of research in these areas. She concluded that studies such as those by Gass and Varonis (1989), Pica (1987), and Pica et al. (1989) demonstrate a clear contribution of negotiation work to learner reformulations and "pushed output," as Swain proposed, and also suggest the importance of negotiation for revealing relevant information about segmentation possibilities in the L2, and hence about L2 grammatical structure. Both NSs and NNSs modify their output in response to signals of incomprehension or miscommunication, using semantic, morphological, and syntactic changes achieved through repetition, rephrasing, segmentation, and movement—the NSs revealing TL form–meaning relationships in the process.

Pica cautions, however, that it would be a mistake to assume that all negotiation work achieves the desired IL modifications or that learners always take up the opportunities negative feedback provides. To begin with, some interactional modifications are inherently less likely to trigger modifications than others. A confirmation check allows NSSs simply to confirm or deny, and so is less likely to lead them to reformulate their own or others' utterances than a clarification request, as shown in (13) and (14), respectively:

(13)   NNS: I many fren.
                                            NS: [CC] You have many friends?
        NNS: Yes.
(14)   NNS: . . . you have a three which is . . .
        white square of which appears sharp
                                            NS: [CR] Huh?
        NNS: . . . you have a three houses . . .
        one is no- no- not- *one* is
        not square, but with a little bit—a small house.
                                                                    (Pica et al., 1989)

Moreover, although modifications in the desired direction are often visible, as in (8), above, some negative input, including recasts, is simply ambiguous. For example, intonation and contextual cues may be required, but may be unavailable or too subtle for the NNS to determine whether a NS response is a model of the correct way or just a different way of saying the same thing. And the grammatical information in some feedback is either not noticed or ignored or, at least, is not immediately utilized or perhaps utilizable, as in (15):

(15)   NNS: Uh, how—how do you feel Taiwan?
                                            NS: How did I like it?
        NNS: Yeah, how do you like it?
                                                            (Brock et al., 1986, p. 235)

Finally, Pica (1992, p. 227) pointed out, even modifications of NNS output, as in (8), which involve incorporation of forms in the NS feedback that triggered the modification, cannot necessarily be taken as evidence of sustained IL change. Longitudinal data, at least over several sessions, are needed to make that assessment.

Moving from output and production to input and comprehension, conversation appears to facilitate acquisition in three other ways, with talk that involves participants in negotiation for meaning being especially beneficial. A third contribution is its role in improving comprehension. Because, as described in section III, studies show that adjustments that occur when meaning is negotiated improve input comprehensibility, and because comprehensible input is necessary, although insufficient, for acquisition, there is clear evidence of an indirect causal relationship between conversation and acquisition, as proposed by Long (1983b).

A possible fourth role is a direct one between interactional modifications and acquisition, but evidence for this is still scarce. Acquisition takes time, and it is difficult to control for outside exposure during an experimental study that lasts long enough. There have been some efforts at short-term cross-sectional studies, however. Using a pretest–posttest control group design, Loschky (1989, 1994) randomly assigned 41 English-speaking college students learning Japanese to three groups, one of which received unmodified input, one premodified input, and one negotiated input, in the form of spoken descriptions of pictured objects that the listeners had to identify by circling or numbering. The input contained examples of two target Japanese locative structures and new vocabulary items. An immediate posttest consisting of two vocabulary recognition tests and a sentence-verification task showed significantly greater comprehension for the negotiated input, but not the premodified input, group over the control group in both lexis and morpho-syntax. Aural recognition and sentence-verification tasks a day later failed to find any greater retention of the target structures or vocabulary by those learners, however, although there were significant pretest–posttest gains across all three groups, perhaps due to the task focus on form–meaning relationships.

In a study of the effects of input modification and opportunity to negotiate for meaning on both comprehensibility and IL change, Gass and Varonis (1994) compared the performance of 16 adult NS–NNS dyads under various conditions on two closed, two-way, object-location tasks. The researchers looked at (1) the immediate comprehensibility for NNSs of prescripted modified and unmodified NS input, with or without the opportunity for NS–NNS negotiation of that input, and (b) the effect of having heard modified or unmodified input on task 1, with or without the opportunity to negotiate, on the accuracy of NNS descriptions on task 2, as measured by NS comprehension of those descriptions. As reflected in their ability to locate unseen objects accurately, on task 1 NNSs understood modified input statistically significantly better than unmodified input, and (consistent with Pica, Doughty, & Young, 1986, and Loschky, 1989, 1994) negotiated input statistically significantly better than unnegotiated (modified or unmodified) input. On task 2, half the NS listeners were allowed to interact with their NNS partners, and half were not. This was not found to affect their success in placing the 20 objects accurately. Of most interest, it was found that on task 2 those NNSs who had been allowed to interact with their NS partners during task 1 were now statistically significantly more accurate in their descriptions than those who had not been allowed to interact on task 1, as measured by the NSs' success in placing the 20 objects on the new board scene.

A qualitative analysis of the transcripts revealed that the advantage for NNSs able to negotiate on task 1 lay not in their ability to clarify unknown vocabulary items and learn them, but in the opportunity the negotiation provided for them to acquire various descriptive devices the NSs used to explain the items, such as *eat(s) nuts* to indicate a squirrel. NNSs who had heard unmodified input on task 1 also picked up descriptive devices used by the NSs, but tended to use them inappropriately on task 2, as if they had acquired the form but not the function. Thus, Gass and Varonis pointed out, although there were immediate effects on comprehension on task 1 for both input modification and interaction, on task 2 there was an effect for *preceding* interaction (task 1), but neither current interaction (task 2) nor input modification. Gass and Varonis argued that the advantage of the negotiation work is that it focuses learners' attention on linguistic form, in this case, on ways of describing objects. This allows them to notice mismatches between their output and NS input, especially when communication breakdowns are repaired. This, in turn, can trigger IL restructuring, the effects of which may be visible immediately or later.

A fifth, indirect contribution of conversation is that the need to communicate may raise learners' awareness of language, as R. Ellis (1992) suggests, with a resulting increase in attention to form and a heightened proclivity to notice mismatches between input and output. In this regard, it is noteworthy that two studies of the relative utility of models and recasts have favored recasts in L1 (Baker & Nelson, 1984) and in L2 (Mito, 1993) acquisition. A possible interpretation of these results is that some items that researchers consider unprocessable, and so unlearnable, at a given stage of development may actually be processable but not normally noticed. Both Baker and Nelson and Mito found at least some child or adult learners acquiring one construction through recasts that comparable learners did not acquire from models, while failing to acquire a second matched structure from models which the second group did acquire from recasts.

Finally, although often analyzed separately and shown to occur independently in FTD (Long, 1980, 1983b), there is also an important connection between modifications to input and to the interactional structure of conversation. Braidi (1992) points out that the comprehensibility brought about by interactional modifications allows the input itself to remain relatively more complex—ultimately not modified at all—thereby allowing learners access to new target forms, and eventually to the full target code. Linguistic modifications that simplify the input, conversely, achieve comprehensibility partly by removing unknown forms, thereby improving comprehension at the expense of acquisition potential. Linguistic modifications can simultaneously dilute the semantic content, too (Long & Ross, 1993), which would suggest that interactional modifications are additionally valuable for the semantic richness they preserve. The semantic transparency achieved by interactional modifications as speakers negotiate for meaning is important, therefore, not just because it makes input comprehensible, but because it makes *complex* input comprehensible. Both comprehensibility and complexity are necessary for acquisition.

B. The Interaction Hypothesis

Based on the arguments and literature reviewed above, I would like to suggest that *negotiation for meaning,* and especially negotiation work that triggers *interactional* adjustments by the NS or more competent interlocutor, facilitates acquisition because it connects input, internal learner capacities, particularly selective attention, and output in productive ways.

Negotiation for meaning by definition involves denser than usual frequencies of semantically contingent speech of various kinds (i.e., utterances by a competent speaker, such as repetitions, extensions, reformulations, rephrasings, expansions and recasts), which immediately follow learner utterances and maintain reference to their meaning (for review, see Snow, 1988). Such semantically related talk is important for acquisition for a number of reasons. The frequencies of target forms in the reformulations tends to be higher, as negotiation involves recycling related items while a problem is resolved, which should increase their saliency and the likelihood of their being noticed by the learner. Many of the input modifications described in section II, such as stress of key words, partial repetition, lexical switches and decomposition, involved in some reformulations can also serve to make target forms salient independent of increased frequency in the input, for example, by moving them to initial or final position in an utterance and through the addition of stress and pauses before and after key forms, once more increasing the likelihood of their being noticed. The reformulations also often involve rearrangements of adjacent utterances that both reveal how their constituents should be segmented, and weave rich semantic nets that illustrate the communicative value of TL forms (Widdowson, 1978, pp. 10–12) in ways that isolated linguistic models can do less well if at all. In general, the increased comprehensibility that negotiation brings helps reveal the meaning of new forms and so makes the forms themselves acquirable. Any tentative adjustments to the IL grammar can be tested very quickly if they are reflected in the learner's modified output and in turn elicit feedback.

The reformulations occur when the child or adult L1 or L2 learner is more likely to be alert, in Tomlin and Villa's (1993) analysis of attention, because he or she is already participating in the talk, has just spoken, has said something with enough propositional content for the caretaker or NS to say something relevant in reply, knows what he or she intended to say, and is interested in seeing the effect his or her utterance produces in the interlocutor. (Many other conversational moves lack some or all of these qualities.) At that moment, when the intended message is clear to the learner and his or her attention is focused on the other speaker, the fact that the semantic content is already at least partially clear also means that more processing resources can be oriented, if necessary, to the form of what the interlocutor says next. In the majority of cases, where only slight meaning changes are required in the reformulation, most of the learner's attention is free to work on those changes, and at least some of them and the new input they involve are more likely to be within the processable range for the learner and so detectable. Greater linguistic complexity may be manageable because it is compensated for by interactional modifications and the greater than usual semantic transparency in such negotiation work. Although there is no guarantee that the spare attentional resources will be allocated to form, of course, the chances that the learner will detect the changes, understand them, and incorporate them is likely to be higher than when both form and meaning are opaque.

These qualities of negotiation work, in other words, may function to focus the learner on form in a similar way that input enhancement appears to do in the classroom and laboratory studies discussed briefly in section IV. Heightened attention makes detection both of new forms and of mismatches between input and output more likely, and such mismatches may also provide at least some of the information a learner needs about what is *not* permissible in a language. More such incorporations and changes can be predicted, therefore, in learners who receive higher quantities of semantically contingent speech through negotiation for meaning.

As should be obvious, the above updated version of the Interaction Hypothesis (Long, 1981a, 1983c) involves a mix of well and less well-established L1 and L2 acquisition research findings, some rather high inference interpretation, and some speculation. It is certainly not intended, of course, as anything like a complete theory of language learning. Many aspects of the proposal have barely begun to be investigated in adult L2 acquisition and pose potential problems. For instance, does negotiated input really preserve needed structural data, and if so, do learners notice them more readily than in other input? Does the negative input provided in negotiation work contain sufficient information on what is ungrammatical in an L2, as well as what is possible? Can learners hold their own and others' utterances in memory long enough to perform the cognitive comparison of an original and reformulated version of an input string, or of input and output, required if the linguistic reformulations often present in semantically contingent speech, such as recasts, are to serve the purpose claimed for them? Does semantically contingent speech facilitate adult L2 acquisition as it appears to do for child L1 acquisition? Do adults perceive negative input for what it is and respond differentially to recasts and other reacting moves in the way children have been found to, or do alternate sociolinguistic norms operate to prevent this? What L2 abilities can be derived from "static" written input and the relatively "nonnegotiable" conversation of some classroom language lessons—the only learning opportunities available to many learners? Are attentional resources freed up by semantic transparency oriented to form in the input? Are observed short-term benefits of negotiated interaction, such as incorporations of corrective feedback, indicative of genuine long-term IL development? L2 acquisition research on the environment has come a long way, but a great deal of systematic work clearly remains.

In a salutory warning to students of the linguistic environment for language learning, Durkin (1987) noted the dangers inherent in seeking, and especially in finding, real or potential environmental contributions. There is a tendency in such work, Durkin points out, to focus on the associations between grammatical input and development and to ignore or downplay the numerous environmental features that apparently make no difference whatsoever. There is also a tendency to forget the resilience of human language learning capacities in the face of quite extreme environmental impoverishment. As Shatz (1982) pointed out, care must certainly be exercised not to attribute exclusive causative status to qualities of input to the learner or to qualities of the learner's conversational experience. The learner's current knowledge of the L2 and built-in acquisition processes clearly exert a major influence on learning. The search is for those features of input and the linguistic environment that best interact with learner-internal factors to facilitate subsequent language development. Moreover, although some experimental results suggest that recasts can be sufficient to induce acquisition of new structures, there is no evidence that they are necessary for acquisition. In fact, if production is not necessary, recasts logically cannot be.

It may be that many children or adult L2 acquirers never receive recasts of various structures, for example, yet acquire them, or rarely receive the kind of interactional experience that recasts occur in at all, yet again acquire language in other ways. What is of interest to L2 acquisition theorists and L2 educators alike, however, is the preliminary evidence of a facilitating effect on comprehension and acquisition of semantically contingent speech and negotiation for meaning. For theorists, it suggests some of the variables—semantic transparency, feedback, and attention, for example—that play a central role in learning. For educators, with the caveat that we are dealing with a claim, not established wisdom, it suggests the importance of classroom activities that engage those attributes. In this last regard, tasks that stimulate negotiation for meaning may turn out to be one among several useful language-learning activities in or out of classrooms, for they may be one of the easiest ways to facilitate a learner's focus on form without losing sight of a lesson's (or conversation's) predominant focus on meaning. In so many learning situations, including task-based, content-based, bilingual, and immersion programs, it is this twin focus on language learning and learning through language that is sought by learners and society alike.

ACKNOWLEDGMENTS

I thank Kevin Durkin, Kevin Gregg, Charlie Sato, and Dick Schmidt for helpful comments on an earlier version of this paper.

REFERENCES

Alanen, R. (1992). *Input enhancement and rule presentation in second language acquisition.* Masters in ESL thesis, University of Hawaii at Manoa, Honolulu.
Allwright, R. L. (1975). Problems in the study of the language teacher's treatment of learner

error. In M. K. Burt & H. C. Dulay (Eds.), *On TESOL '75* (pp. 96–109). Washington, DC: TESOL.

Andersen, E. (1975). *Learning how to speak with style.* Unpublished doctoral dissertation, Stanford University, Palo Alto, CA.

Arthur, B., Weiner, R., Culver, J., Young M., & Thomas, D. (1980). The register of impersonal discourse to foreigners: Verbal adjustments to foreign accent. In D. Larsen-Freeman (Ed.), *Discourse analysis in second language acquisition research* (pp. 111–124). Rowley, MA: Newbury House.

Atkinson, M. (1979). Prerequisites for reference. In E. Ochs & B. B. Schieffelin (Eds.), *Developmental pragmatics* (pp. 229–249). New York: Academic Press.

Baker, N. D., & Nelson, K. E. (1984). Recasting and related conversational techniques for triggering syntactic advances by young children. *First Language, 5,* 3–22.

Bardovi-Harlig, K. (1987). Markedness and salience in second language acquisition. *Language Learning, 37*(3), 385–407.

Barik, H. C., & Swain, M. (1976). A Canadian experiment in bilingual education: The Peel study. *Foreign Language Annals, 9,* 465–479.

Barnes, S., Gutfreund, M., Satterly, D., & Wells, G. (1983). Characteristics of adult speech which predict children's language development. *Journal of Child Language, 10,* 65–84.

Beck, M.-L., & Eubank, L. (1991). Acquisition theory and experimental design: A critique of Tomasello and Herron. *Studies in Second Language Acquisition, 13*(1), 73–76.

Bickerton, D. (1979). Beginnings. In K. C. Hill (Ed.), *The genesis of language* (pp. 1–22). Ann Arbor, MI: Karoma.

Birdsong, D. (1989). *Metalinguistic performance and interlinguistic competence.* Berlin: Springer-Verlag.

Bley-Vroman, R. (1986). Hypothesis-testing in second language acquisition theory. *Language Learning, 36*(3), 353–376.

Bloom, L., Hood, L., & Lightbown, P. M. (1974). Imitation in language development: If, when and why. *Cognitive Psychology, 6,* 380–420.

Bohannon, J. N., III, MacWhinney, B., & Snow, C. (1990). No negative evidence revisited: Beyond learnability or who has to prove what to whom. *Developmental Psychology, 26,* 221–226.

Bohannon, J. N., III, & Stanowicz, L. (1988). The issue of negative evidence: Adult responses to children's language errors. *Developmental Psychology, 24*(5), 684–689.

Bohannon, J. N., III, & Stanowicz, L. (1989). Bidirectional effects of repetition in conversation: A synthesis within a cognitive model. In G. Speidel & K. E. Nelson (Eds.), *The many faces of imitation in language learning* (pp. 121–150). New York: Springer-Verlag.

Bornstein, M. H., & Bruner, J. S. (Eds.). (1989). *Interaction in human development.* Hillsdale, NJ: Erlbaum.

Braidi, S. (1992). Issues in input: An integrative framework for analyzing second language input. In D. Staub & C. Delk (Eds.), *Proceedings of the Twelfth Second Language Research Forum* (pp. 335–336). East Lansing: Michigan State University, Department of English.

Brock, C., Crookes, G., Day, R. R., & Long, M. H. (1986). The differential effects of corrective feedback in native speaker/non-native speaker conversation. In R. R. Day

(Ed.), *"Talking to learn": Conversation in second language acquisition* (pp. 327–351). Cambridge, MS: Newbury House.

Brown, R., & Hanlon, C. (1970). Derivational complexity and order of acquisition in child speech. In J. Hayes (Ed.), *Cognition and the development of language*. New York: Wiley.

Bygate, M. (1988). Units of oral expression and language learning in small group interactions. *Applied Linguistics, 9*(1), 59–82.

Carroll, S., Roberge, Y., & Swain, M. (1992). The role of feedback in second language acquisition: Error correction and morphological generalizations. *Applied Psycholinguistics, 13*(2), 173–198.

Carroll, S., & Swain, M. (1993). Explicit and implicit negative feedback. An empirical study of the learning of linguistic generalizations. *Studies in Second Language Acquisition, 15*(3), 357–386.

Cathcart-Strong, R. (1986). Input generation by young second language learners. *TESOL Quarterly, 20*(3), 515–530.

Chaudron, C. (1977). A descriptive model of discourse in the corrective treatment of learners' errors. *Language Learning, 27*(1), 29–46.

Chaudron, C. (1987). The role of error correction in second language teaching. In B. K. Das (Ed.), *Patterns of classroom interaction in Southeast Asia* (pp. 17–50). Singapore: SEAMEO Regional Language Centre.

Chaudron, C. (1988). *Second language classrooms. Research on teaching and learning.* Cambridge, UK: Cambridge University Press.

Chun, A., Day, R. R., Chenoweth, A., & Luppescu, S. (1982). Errors, interaction, and correction: A study of native-nonnative conversations. *TESOL Quarterly, 16,* 537–547.

Clark, E. V. (1987). The principle of contrast. In B. MacWhinney (Ed.), *Mechanisms of language acquisition* (pp. 1–33). Hillsdale, NJ: Erlbaum.

Clyne, M. (1968). Zum Pidgin-Deutch der Gastarbeiter. *Zeitschrift für Mundartforschung, 35,* 130–139.

Clyne, M. (1977). Multilingualism and pidginization in Australian industry. *Ethnic Studies, 1,* 40–55.

Clyne, M. (1978). Some remarks on foreigner talk. In N. Dittmar, H. Haberland, T. Skutnabb-Kangas, & U. Teleman (Eds.), *Papers from the First Scandinavian-German Symposium on the Language of Immigrant Workers and their Children* (pp. 155–169). Roskilde, Denmark: Roskilde Universiteits Center.

Corder, S. P. (1977). 'Simple codes' and the source of the second language learner's initial heuristic hypothesis. *Studies in Second Language Acquisition, 1*(1), 1–10.

Crookes, G., & Rulon, K. A. (1988). Topic and feedback in native speaker/non-native speaker conversation. *TESOL Quarterly, 22*(4), 675–681.

Day, E. M., & Shapson, S. M. (1991). Integrating formal and functional approaches to language teaching in French immersion: An experimental study. *Language Learning, 41*(1), 25–58.

De Bot, K., & Janssen-Van Dieten, A. M. (1984). Het onderwijs Nederlands aan Turkse en Marokkaanse leerlingen: Een poging tot evaluatie. [The instruction of Dutch to Turkish and Moroccan pupils: An evaluation attempt.] *Levende Talen, 395,* 520–525.

Demetras, M. J., Post, K. N., & Snow, C. E. (1986). Feedback to first language learners:

The role of repetitions and clarification questions. *Journal of Child Language, 13,* 275–292.

De Praatkist (1982). Een intercultureel pakket voor het leven van mondeling Nederlands. [The speaking Kir: An intellectual course for the acquisition of oral Dutch. Den Bosch, Netherlands: Malmberg.

Derwing, T. (1990). Speech rate is no simple matter: Rate adjustment and NS–NNS communicative success. *Studies in Second Language Acquisition, 12,* 303–313.

Doughty, C. (1991). Second language instruction does make a difference. Evidence from an empirical study of SL relativization. *Studies in Second Language Acquisition, 13*(4), 431–469.

Doughty, C., & Pica, T. (1986). "Information gap" tasks: An aid to second language acquisition? *TESOL Quarterly, 20*(2), 305–325.

Durkin, K. (1987). Minds and language: Social cognition, social interaction and the acquisition of language. *Mind and Language, 2*(2), 105–140.

Early, M. (1985). *Input and interaction in content classrooms: Foreigner talk and teacher talk in classroom discourse.* Unpublished doctoral dissertation, University of California, Los Angeles.

Ellis, N. (1993). Rules and instances in foreign language learning: Interactions of explicit and implicit knowledge. *European Journal of Cognitive Psychology, 5,* 217–238.

Ellis, R. (1985). Teacher-pupil interaction in second language development. In S. M. Gass & C. Madden (Eds.), *Input in second language acquisition* (pp. 69–85). Rowley, MA: Newbury House.

Ellis, R. (1992). The role of practice in classroom learning. In *Second Language acquisition and language pedagogy* (pp. 101–120). Clevedon, UK: Multilingual Matters.

Ervin-Tripp, S. (1976). Speech acts and social learning. In K. H. Basso & H. A. Selby (Eds.), *Meaning in anthropology.* Albuquerque: University of New Mexico Press.

Fanselow, J. (1977). Beyond Rashomon—conceptualizing and describing the teaching act. *TESOL Quarterly, 11*(1), 17–39.

Farrar, M. J. (1990). Discourse and the acquisition of grammatical morphemes. *Journal of Child Language, 17,* 607–624.

Farrar, M. J. (1992). Negative evidence and grammatical morpheme acquisition. *Developmental Psychology, 28*(1), 90–98.

Ferguson, C. (1971). Absence of copula and the notion of simplicity: A study of normal speech, baby talk, foreigner talk and pidgins. In D. Hymes (Ed.), *Pidginization and creolization of languages* (pp. 141–150). Cambridge, UK: Cambridge University Press.

Ferguson, C. (1975). Towards a characterization of English foreigner talk. *Anthropological Linguistics, 17*(1), 1–14.

Ferguson, C. (1977). Baby talk as a simplified register. In C. E. Snow & C. A. Ferguson (Eds.), *Talking to children: Language input and acquisition* (pp. 209–235). Cambridge, UK: Cambridge University Press.

Ferguson, C., & DeBose, C. (1976). Simplified registers, broken languages and pidginization. In A. Valdman (Ed.), *Pidgin and creole linguistics* (pp. 99–125). Bloomington: Indiana University Press.

Fourcin, A. (1975). Language development in the absence of expressive speech. In E. Lenneberg & E. Lenneberg (Eds.), *Foundations of language development* (pp. 263–268). New York: Academic Press.

Freed, B. (1978). *Foreigner talk: A study of speech adjustments made by native speakers of English in conversations with non-native speakers.* Unpublished doctoral dissertation, University of Pennsylvania, Philadelphia.

Furrow, D., Baillie, C., Mclaren, J., & Moore, C. (1993). Differential responding to two- and three-year-olds' utterances: The roles of grammaticality and ambiguity. *Journal of Child Language, 20,* 363–375.

Gaies, S. (1977). The nature of linguistic input in formal second language learning: Linguistic and communicative strategies in ESL teachers' classroom language. In H. D. Brown, C. A. Yorio, & R. H. Crymes (Eds.), *On TESOL '77* (pp. 204–212). Washington, DC: TESOL.

Gaies, S. (1981). Learner feedback and its effect in communication tasks: A pilot study. *Studies in Second Language Acquisition, 4*(1), 46–59.

Gass, S. M. (1988). Integrating research areas: A framework for second language studies. *Applied Linguistics, 9,* 198–217.

Gass, S. M., & Varonis, E. M. (1984). The effect of familiarity on the comprehensibility of non-native speech. *Language Learning, 34*(1), 65–89.

Gass, S. M., & Varonis, E. M. (1985). Variation in native speaker speech modification to non-native speakers. *Studies in Second Language Acquisition, 7*(1), 37–58.

Gass, S. M., & Varonis, E. M. (1986). Sex differences in non-native speaker/non-native speaker interactions. In R. R. Day (Ed.), *"Talking to learn": Conversation in second language acquisition* (pp. 327–351). Rowley, MA: Newbury House.

Gass, S. M., & Varonis, E. M. (1989). Incorporated repairs in nonnative discourse. In M. Eisenstein (Ed.), *The dynamic interlanguage: Empirical studies in second language variation* (pp. 71–86). New York: Plenum Press.

Gass, S. M., & Varonis, E. M. (1994). Input, interaction, and second language production. *Studies in Second Language Acquisition, 16*(3), 283–302.

Givon, T. (1979). *On understanding grammar.* New York: Academic Press.

Gleitman, L. R., Newport, E. L., & Gleitman, H. (1984). The current status of the motherese hypothesis. *Journal of Child Language, 11*(1), 43–79.

Gordon, P. (1990). Learnability and feedback. *Developmental Psychology, 26*(2), 217–220.

Grimshaw, J., Pinker, S. (1989). Positive and negative evidence in language acquisition. *Behavioral and Brain Sciences, 12,* 341–342.

Hakansson, G. (1986). Quantitative aspects of teacher talk. In G. Kasper (Ed.), *Learning, teaching and communicating in the F. L. classroom* (pp. 83–98). Aarhus: Aarhus University Press.

Harley, B. (1989). Functional grammar in French immersion: A classroom experiment. *Applied Linguistics, 10*(3), 331–359.

Harley, B., & King, M. L. (1989). Verb lexis in the written compositions of young L2 learners. *Studies in Second Language Acquisition, 11*(4), 415–439.

Harley, B., & Swain, M. (1978). An analysis of the verb system by young learners of French. *Interlanguage Studies Bulletin, 3*(1), 35–79.

Harley, B., & Swain, M. (1984). The interlanguage of immersion students and its implications for second language teaching. In A. Davies, C. Criper, & A. Howatt (Eds.), *Interlanguage.* Edinburgh: Edinburgh University Press.

Hart, D. J., & Lapkin, S. (1989). *French immersion at the secondary/postsecondary interface: Final Report on Phase 2* [Mimeo]. Toronto: Modern Language Centre, Ontario Institute for Studies in Education.

Hatch, E. M. (1978). Discourse analysis and second language acquisition. In E. Hatch (Ed.), *Second language acquisition: A book of readings* (pp. 401–435). Rowley, MA: Newbury House.

Hatch, E. M. (1983). Input/interaction and language development. In *Psycholinguistics: A second language perspective* (pp. 152–187). Rowley, MA: Newbury House.

Hatch, E. M., Shapira, R., & Wagner-Gough, J. (1978). 'Foreigner-talk' discourse. *ITL Review of Applied Linguistics, 39/40,* 39–59.

Hawkins, B. (1985). Is an 'appropriate response' always so appropriate? In S. M. Gass & C. Madden (Eds.), *Input and second language acquisition* (pp. 162–180). Rowley, MA: Newbury House.

Heath, S. B. (1983). *Ways with words.* Cambridge, UK: Cambridge University Press.

Heidelberger Forschungsprojekt. (1978). The acquisition of German syntax by foreign migrant workers. In D. Sankoff (Ed.), *Linguistic variation: Model and methods* (pp. 1–22). New York: Academic Press.

Henrichsen, L. (1984). Sandhi-variation: A filter of input for learners of ESL. *Language Learning, 34*(1), 103–126.

Henzl, V. M. (1979). Foreigner talk in the classroom. *International Review of Applied Linguistics, 17,* 159–167.

Herron, C., & Tomasello, M. (1988). Learning grammatical structures in a foreign language: Modelling versus feedback. *The French Review, 61,* 910–923.

Hinnenkamp, V. (1982). *Foreigner talk und Tarzanisch.* Hamburg: H. Buske.

Hirsh-Pasek, K., Treiman, R., & Schneiderman, M. (1984). Brown and Hanlon revisited: Mothers' sensitivity to ungrammatical forms. *Journal of Child Language, 11*(1), 81–88.

Hirvonen, T. (1988). Monolingual and bilingual children's foreigner talk conversations. In A. Holmen, E. Hansen, J. Gimbel, & J. N. Jorgensen (Eds.), *Bilingualism and the individual.* Clevedon, UK: Multilingual Matters.

Hoff-Ginsberg, E. (1986). Some contributions of mothers' speech to their children's syntactic growth. *Journal of Child Language, 12*(2), 367–385.

Hulstijn, J. H. (1989). Implicit and incidental second language learning: Experiments in the processing of natural and partly artificial input. In H. W. Dechert, & M. Raupach (Eds.), *Interlingual processing* (pp. 50–73). Tubingen: Narr.

Hulstijn, J. H. (1992). Retention of inferred and given word meanings: Experiments in incidental vocabulary learning. In P. Arnaud & H. Bejoint (Eds.), *Vocabulary and applied linguistics* (pp. 113–125). London: Macmillan.

Ishiguro, T. (1986). *Simplification and elaboration in foreign language teacher talk and its source.* Unpublished doctoral dissertation, Stanford University, Palo Alto, CA.

Issidorides, D. C. (1988). The discovery of a miniature linguistic system: Function words and comprehension of an unfamiliar language. *Journal of Psycholinguistic Research, 17*(4), 317–339.

Issidorides, D. C., & Hulstijn, J. (1992). Comprehension of grammatically modified and non-modified sentences by second language learners. *Applied Psycholinguistics, 13*(2), 147–161.

Janda, R. (1985). Note-taking as a simplified register. *Discourse Processes, 8,* 437–454.

Katz, J. (1977). Foreigner talk input in child second language acquisition: Its form and function over time. In *Proceedings of the First Second Language Research Forum.* Los Angeles: University of California.

Keenan, E., & Comrie, B. (1977). Noun phrase accessibility and universal grammar. *Linguistic Inquiry, 8,* 63–99.

Keenana, E. O. (1974). Conversational competence in children. *Journal of Child Language, 1,* 163–183.

Kleifgen, J. A. (1985). Skilled variation in a kindergarten teacher's use of foreigner talk. In S. M. Gass & C. Madden (Eds.), *Input in second language acquisition* (pp. 59–68). Rowley, MA: Newbury House.

Krashen, S. D. (1985). *The input hypothesis.* London: Longman.

Krashen, S. D. (1989). We acquire vocabulary and spelling by reading: Additional evidence for the Input Hypothesis. *Modern Language Journal, 73,* 440–464.

Lapkin, S., Hart, D., & Swain, M. (1991). Early and middle French immersion programs: French language outcomes. *Canadian Modern Language Review, 48*(1), 11–40.

Lapkin, S., Swain, M., & Cummins, J. (1983). Final Report on the Development of French Language Evaluation Units for Saskatchewan. Toronto: Ontario Institute for Studies in Education.

Larsen-Freeman, D., & Long, M. H. (1991). *An introduction to research on second language acquisition.* London: Longman.

Lenneberg, E. (1962). Understanding language without ability to speak: A case report. *Journal of Abnormal and Social Psychology, 65,* 419–425.

Lieven, E. (1978). Conversations between mothers and young children: Individual differences and their possible implications for the study of language learning. In N. Waterson & C. E. Snow (Eds.), *The development of communication: Social and pragmatic factors in language acquisition.* London: Wiley.

Lightbown, P. M., & Spada, N. (1990). Focus-on-form and corrective feedback in communicative language teaching: Effects on second language learning. *Studies in Second Language Acquisition, 12*(4), 429–448.

Logan, G. (1988). Towards an instance theory of automatization. *Psychological Review, 95*(4), 492–527.

Long, M. H. (1977). Teacher feedback on learner error: Mapping cognitions. In H. D. Brown, C. A. Yorio, & R. H. Crymes (Eds.), *On TESOL '77* (pp. 278–293). Washington, DC: TESOL.

Long, M. H. (1980). *Input, interaction, and second language acquisition.* Unpublished doctoral dissertation, University of California, Los Angeles.

Long, M. H. (1981a). Input, interaction, and second language acquisition. *Annals of the New York Academy of Sciences, 379,* 259–278.

Long, M. H. (1981b). Questions in foreigner talk discourse. *Language Learning, 31*(1), 135–157.

Long, M. H. (1981c). *Variation in linguistic input for second language acquisition.* Paper presented at the First European-North American Workshop on SLA, Lake Arrowhead, CA.

Long, M. H. (1983a). Does second language instruction make a difference? A review of research. *TESOL Quarterly, 17*(3), 359–382.

Long, M. H. (1983b). Linguistic and conversational adjustments to non-native speakers. *Studies in Second Language Acquisition, 5*(2), 177–194.

Long, M. H. (1983c). Native speaker/non-native speaker conversation and the negotiation of comprehensible input. *Applied Linguistics, 4*(2), 126–141.

Long, M. H. (1988). Instructed interlanguage development. In L. M. Beebe (Ed.), *Issues in second language acquisition. Multiple perspectives* (pp. 115–141). Cambridge, MA: Newbury House.

Long, M. H. (1989). Task, group, and task-group interactions. *University of Hawaii Working Papers in ESL, 8*(2), 1–26.

Long, M. H. (1990). Task, group, and task-group interactions. In S. Anivan (Ed.), *Language teaching methodology for the nineties* (pp. 31–50). Singapore: RELC/Singapore University Press.

Long, M. H. (1991). Focus on form: A design feature in language teaching methodology. In K. de Bot, R. Ginsberg, & C. Kramsch (Eds.), *Foreign language research in cross-cultural perspective* (pp. 39–52). Amsterdam: John Benjamins.

Long, M. H. (in press). *Task-based language teaching.* Oxford: Basil Blackwell.

Long, M. H., Ghambiar, S., Ghambiar, V., & Nishimura, M. (1982, March 15–20). *Regularization in foreigner talk and interlanguage.* Paper presented at the 17th annual TESOL Convention, Toronto, Canada.

Long, M. H., & Porter, P. A. (1985). Group work, interlanguage talk, and second language acquisition. *TESOL Quarterly, 19,* 207–227.

Long, M. H., & Ross, S. (1993). Modifications that preserve language and meaning. In M. Tickoo (Ed.), *Simplification. Theory, research and practice* (pp. 29–52). Singapore: RLC/Singapore University Press.

Long, M. H., & Sato, C. J. (1983). Classroom foreigner talk discourse: Forms and functions of teachers' questions. In H. W. Seliger & M. H. Long (Eds.), *Classroom-oriented research in second language acquisition* (pp. 268–285). Rowley, MA: Newbury House.

Loschky, L. C. (1989). *The effects of negotiated interaction and premodified input on second language comprehension and retention* (Occas. Pap. No. 16). Honolulu: University of Hawaii at Manoa, ESL Department.

Loschky, L. C. (1994). Comprehensible input and second language acquisition: What is the relationship? *Studies in Second Language Acquisition, 16*(3), 303–323.

Lynch, T. (1987). *Modifications to foreign listeners: The stories teachers tell.* Washington, DC: Center for Applied Linguistics. (ERIC Document No. ED 274 255).

Macnamara, J. (1972). Cognitive basis of language learning in infants. *Psychological Review, 79,* 1–14.

MacWhinney, B. (1987). The competition model. In B. MacWhinney (Ed.), *Mechanisms of language acquisition* (pp. 249–308). Hillsdale, NJ: Erlbaum.

Malouf, R. E., & Dodd, D. H. (1972). Role of exposure, imitation, and expansion of an artificial grammatical rule. *Developmental Psychology, 7*(2), 195–203.

Manheimer, R. D. (1993). Close the task, improve the discourse. *Estudios de Linguistica Aplicada, 17,* 18–40.

Mannon, T. M. (1986). *Teacher talk: A comparison of a teacher's speech to native and non-native speakers.* Unpublished masters in TESL thesis, University of California, Los Angeles.

Meisel, J. M. (1977). Linguistic simplification: A study of immigrant workers' speech and foreigner talk. In S. P. Corder & E. Roulet (Eds.), *The notions of simplification, interlanguages and pidgins, and their relation to second language pedagogy* (pp. 88–113). Geneva: Droz.

Meisel, J. M. (1987). Reference to past events and actions in the development of natural second language acquisition. In C. Pfaff, (Ed.), *First and second language acquisition processes* (pp. 206–224). Cambridge, MA: Newbury House.

Meisel, J. M., Clahsen, H., & Pienemann, M. (1981). On determining developmental stages in natural second language acquisition. *Studies in Second Language Acquisition, 3*(2), 109–135.

Mellow, D. (1992). *Towards a theory of second language transition: Implications from constrained studies of instruction and attrition.* Paper presented at the Second Language Research Forum, Michigan State University, East Lansing.

Mito, K. (1993). *The effects of modelling and recasting on the acquisition of L2 grammar rules.* Honolulu: University of Hawaii at Manoa, Department of ESL.

Moerk, E. L. (1991). Positive evidence for negative evidence. *First Language, 11*(3), 219–251.

Nelson, K. E. (1977). Facilitating children's syntax acquisition. *Developmental Psychology, 13,* 101–107.

Nelson, K. E. (1981). Toward a rare event cognitive comparison theory of syntax acquisition. In P. S. Dale & D. Ingram (Eds.), *Child language: An international perspective* (pp. 229–240). Baltimore: University Park Press.

Nelson, K. E. (1987). Some observations from the perspective of the rare event cognitive comparison theory of language acquisition. In K. E. Nelson (Ed.), *Children's language* (Vol. 6, pp. 289–331). Hillsdale, NJ: Erlbaum.

Nelson, K. E. (1988). Strategies for first language teaching. In R. Scheifelbusch & M. Rice (Eds.), *The teachability of language* (pp. 263–310). Baltimore: Dan Brooks.

Nelson, K. E. (1991). On differentiated language-learning models and differentiated interventions. In N. A. Krasnegor, D. M. Rumbaugh, R. L. Schiefelbusch, & M. Studdert-Kennedy (Eds.), *Biological and behavioral determinants of language development* (pp. 399–428). Hillsdale, NJ: Erlbaum.

Nelson, K. E., Carskaddon, G., & Bonvillian, J. D. (1973). Syntax acquisition: Impact of experimental variation in adult verbal interaction with the child. *Child Development, 44,* 497–504.

Nelson, K. E., Denninger, M. M., Bonvillian, J. D., Kaplan, B. J., & Baker, N. D. (1984). Maternal input adjustments as related to children's linguistic advances and language acquisition theories. In A. D. Pellegrini & T. D. Yawkey (Eds.), *The development of oral and written language: Readings in developmental and applied linguistics* (pp. 31–56). New York: Ablex.

Nobuyoshi, J., & Ellis, R. (1993). Focused communication tasks and second language acquisition. *English Language Teaching Journal, 47*(3), 203–210.

Ochs, E. (1982). Talking to children in Western Samoa. *Language in Society, 11*(1), 77–104.

Ochs, E., & Schieffelin, B. B. (1984). Language acquisition and socialization: Three Developmental stories and their implications. In R. Shweder & R. LeVine, (Eds.), *Culture and its acquisition.* New York: Academic Press.

Ochs, E., Schieffelin, B. B., & Platt, M. (1979). Propositions across utterances and speakers. In E. Ochs & B. Schieffelin (Eds.), *Developmental pragmatics* (pp. 251–268). New York: Academic Press.

Oliver, R. (in press). Negative feedback in child NS/NNS conversation. *Studies in Second Language Acquisition, 17.*

Paul, M. (1991). *Negotiating open and closed tasks.* (Term paper, ESL 650, Second language acquisition). Honolulu: University of Hawaii at Manoa.

Pavesi, M. (1986). Markedness, discoursal modes. and relative clause formation in a formal and an informal context. *Studies in Second Language Acquisition, 8*(1), 38–55.

Peck, S. (1978). Child-child discourse in second language acquisition. In E. M. Hatch (Ed.), *Second language acquisition: A book of readings* (pp. 383–400). Rowley, MA: Newbury House.

Penner, S. G. (1987). Children's responses to grammatical and ungrammatical child utterances. *Child Development, 58,* 376–384.

Pica, T. (1987). Interlanguage adjustments as an outcome of NS-NNS negotiated interaction. *Language Learning 38*(1), 45–73.

Pica, T. (1992). The textual outcomes of native speaker/non-native speaker negotiation. What do they reveal about second language learning? In C. Kramsch & S. McConnell-Ginet (Eds.), *Text in context: Crossdisciplinary perspectives on language study* (pp. 198–237). Lexington, MA: D. C. Heath.

Pica, T., & Doughty, C. (1985). Input and interaction in the communicative language classroom: A comparison of teacher-fronted and group activities. In S. M. Gass & C. Madden (Eds.), *Input in second language acquisition* (pp. 115–132). Rowley, MA: Newbury House.

Pica, T., Doughty, C., & Young, R. (1986). Making input comprehensible: Do interactional modifications help? *ITL Review of Applied Linguistics, 72,* 1–25.

Pica, T. Holliday, L., Lewis, N., & Morgenthaler, L. (1989). Comprehensible output as an outcome of linguistic demands on the learner. *Studies in Second Language Acquisition, 11*(1), 63–90.

Pica, T., Kanagy, R., & Falodun, J. (1993). Choosing and using communication tasks for second language instruction and research. In G. Crookes & S. M. Gass (Eds.), *Tasks and language learning. Integrating theory and practice* (pp. 9–34). Clevedon, UK: Multilingual Matters.

Pica, T., Young, R., & Doughty, C. (1987). The impact of interaction on comprehension. *TESOL Quarterly, 21*(4), 737–758.

Pienemann, M. (1989). Is language teachable? Psycholinguistic experiments and hypotheses. *Applied Linguistics, 10*(1), 52–79.

Pinker, S. (1989). Resolving a learnability paradox in the acquisition of the verb lexicon. In M. L. Rice & R. L. Schiefelbusch (Eds.), *The teachability of language.* Baltimore: Paul H. Brookes.

Plann, S. (1976). *The Spanish immersion program: Towards native-like proficiency or a classroom dialect?* Masters in TESL thesis, University of California, Los Angeles.

Plann, S. (1977). Acquiring a second language in an immersion situation. In H. D. Brown, C. Yorio, & R. Crymes, (Eds.), *On TESOL '77* (pp. 213–223). Washington, DC: TESOL.

Plough, I., & Gass, S. M. (1993). Interlocutor and task familiarity: Effects on interactional structure. In G. Crookes & S. M. Gass (Eds.), *Tasks and language learning. Integrating theory and practice* (pp. 35–56). Clevedon, UK: Multilingual Matters.

Porter, P. (1983). *Variations in the conversations of adult learners of English as a function of the proficiency level of participants.* Unpublished doctoral dissertation, Stanford University, Palo Alto, CA.

Ramamurti, R. (1977). *How do Americans talk to me?* (Term paper). Philadelphia: University of Pennsylvania, Folklore Department.

Rankin, J. (1990). *A case for close-mindedness: Complexity, accuracy and attention in closed and open tasks* (Term paper, ESL 730, Task-based language teaching). Honolulu: University of Hawaii at Manoa.

Richardson, M. A. (1993). *Negative evidence and grammatical morpheme acquisition: Implications for SLA.* Perth: University of Western Australia, Graduate School of Education.

Robinson, P. J., & Ha, M. A. (1993). Instance theory and second language rule learning under explicit conditions. *Studies in Second Language Acquisition, 15*(4), 412–438.

Rutherford, W. (1987). *Second language grammar: Learning and teaching.* New York: Longman.

Rutherford, W., & Sharwood-Smith, M. (Eds.). (1988). *Grammar and second language teaching: A book of readings.* New York: Newbury House.

Salica, C. (1981). *Testing a model of corrective discourse.* Unpublished masters in TESL thesis, University of California, Los Angeles.

Sato, C. J. (1986). Conversation and interlanguage development: Rethinking the connection. In R. R. Day (Ed.), *"Talking to learn": Conversation and second language acquisition* (pp. 23–45). Cambridge, MA: Newbury House.

Sato, C. J. (1988). Origins of complex syntax in interlanguage development. *Studies in Second Language Acquisition, 10*(3), 371–395.

Sato, C. J. (1990). *The syntax of conversation in interlanguage development.* Tubingen: Narr.

Scarborough, H., & Wyckoff, J. (1986). Mother, I'd still rather do it myself: Some further non-effects of 'motherese.' *Journal of Child Language, 13*(2), 431–438.

Scarcella, R. (1983). Discourse accent in second language performance. In S. M. Gass & L. Selinker (Eds.), *Language transfer in language learning* (pp. 306–326). Rowley, MA: Newbury House.

Scarcella, R., & Higa, C. (1981). Input, negotiation, and age differences in second language acquisition. *Language Learning, 31*(2), 409–437.

Schachter, J. (1983). Nutritional needs of language learners. In M. A. Clarke & J. Handscombe (Eds.), *On TESOL '82: Pacific perspectives on language learning and teaching* (pp. 175–189). Washington, DC: TESOL.

Schachter, J. (1984). A universal input condition. In W. Rutherford (Ed.), *Universals and second language acquisition* (pp. 167–183). Amsterdam: John Benjamins.

Schachter, J. (1986). Three approaches to the study of input. *Language Learning, 36*(2), 211–225.

Schachter, J. (1990). The issue of completeness in second language acquisition. *Second Language Research, 6*(2), 93–124.

Schachter, J. (1991). Corrective feedback in historical perspective. *Second Language Research, 7*(2), 89–102.

Schieffelin, B. B. (1979). Getting it together: An ethnographic approach to the study of the development of communicative competence. In E. Ochs & B. B. Schieffelin (Eds.), *Developmental pragmatics* (pp. 73–108). New York: Academic Press.

Schieffelin, B. B. (1987). *How Kalului children learn what to say, what to do, and how to feel.* Cambridge, UK: Cambridge University Press.

Schmidt, R. W. (1983). Interaction, acculturation, and the acquisition of communicative competence. In N. Wolfson & J. Manes (Eds.), *Sociolinguistics and second language acquisition* (pp. 137–174). Rowley, MA: Newbury House.

Schmidt, R. W. (1990a). Consciousness, learning and interlanguage pragmatics. *University of Hawaii Working Papers in ESL, 9*(1), 213–243.

Schmidt, R. W. (1990b). The role of consciousness in second language learning. *Applied Linguistics, 11*(2), 129–158.

Schmidt, R. W. (1993). Awareness and second language acquisition. *Annual Review of Applied Linguistics 1992, 13*, 206–226.

Schmidt, R. W. (1994). Implicit learning and the cognitive unconscious. In N. Ellis (Ed.), Implicit and explicit learning of languages (pp. 165–209). London: Academic Press.

Schmidt, R. W., & Frota, S. (1986). Developing basic conversational ability in a second language: A case study of an adult learner of Portuguese. In R. R. Day (Ed.), *"Talking to learn": Conversation in second language acquisition* (pp. 237–326). Rowley, MA: Newbury House.

Schumann, J. H. (1978). *The pidginization process: A model for second language acquisition.* Rowley, MA: Newbury House.

Scollon, R. (1973). A real early stage: An unzippered condensation of a dissertation on child language. *University of Hawaii Working Papers in Linguistics, 5*(6), 67–81.

Sharwood-Smith, M. (1991). Speaking to many minds: On the relevance of different types of language information for the L2 learner. *Second Language Research, 7*(2), 118–132.

Sharwood-Smith, M. (1993). Input enhancement in instructed SLA: Theoretical bases. *Studies in Second Language Acquisition, 15*(2), 165–179.

Shatz, M. (1982). Influences of mother and mind on the development of communication competence: A status report. In M. Permlutter, (Ed.), *Minnesota Symposia on Child Psychology* (Vol. 17). Hillsdale, NJ: Erlbaum.

Shortreed, I. M. (1993). Variation in foreigner talk input: The effects of task and proficiency. In G. Crookes & S. M. Gass (Eds.), *Tasks and language learning. Integrating theory and practice* (pp. 96–122). Clevedon, UK: Multilingual Matters.

Skehan, P. (1992). *Second language acquisition strategies and task-based learning.* London: Thames Valley University.

Slimani, A. (1992). Evaluation of classroom interaction. In J. C. Alderson & A. Beretta (Eds.), *Evaluating second language education* (pp. 197–220). Cambridge, UK: Cambridge University Press.

Snow, C. E. (1988). Conversations with children. In P. Fletcher & M. Garman (Eds.), *Language acquisition* (2nd ed., pp. 69–89). Cambridge, UK: Cambridge University Press.

Snow, C. E. (1989). Understanding social interaction and language acquisition: Sentences are not enough. In M. Bornstein & J. Bruner (Eds.), *Interaction in human development* (pp. 83–104). Hillsdale, NJ: Erlbaum.

Snow, C. E., van Eeden, R., & Muysken, P. (1981). The interactional origins of foreigner talk: Municipal employees and foreign workers. *International Journal of the Sociology of Language, 28,* 81–92.

Sokolik, M. E., & Smith, M. E. (1992). Assignment of gender to French nouns in primary and secondary language: A connectionist model. *Second Language Research, 8*(1), 39–58.

Spada, N. (1987). Relationships between instructional differences and learning outcomes: A process-product study of communicative language teaching. *Applied Linguistics, 8*(1), 137–161.

Spada, N., & Lightbown, P. M. (1993). Instruction and the development of questions in L2 classrooms. *Studies in Second Language Acquisition, 15*(2), 205–224.

Speidel, G. E., & Nelson, K. E. (Eds.). (1989). *The many faces of imitation in language development.* New York: Springer-Verlag.

Swain, M. (1981). Target language use in the wider environment as a factor in its acquisition. In R. W. Andersen (Ed.), *New dimensions in second language acquisition research* (pp. 109–122). Rowley, MA: Newbury House.

Swain, M. (1985). Communicative competence: Some roles of comprehensible input and comprehensible output in its development. In S. M. Gass & C. Madden (Eds.), *Input in second language acquisition* (pp. 235–253). Rowley, MA: Newbury House.

Swain, M. (1991). French immersion and its offshoots: Getting two for one. In B. F. Freed, (Ed.), *Foreign language acquisition research and the classroom* (pp. 91–103). Lexington, MA: D. C. Heath.

Swisher, M. V. (1984). Signed input of hearing mothers to deaf children. *Language Learning, 34*(2), 69–85.

Terrell, T. D. (1990). Foreigner talk as comprehensible input. In J. E. Alatis (Ed.), *GURT '90. Linguistics, language teaching and language acquisition: The interdependence of theory, practice and research* (pp. 193–206). Washington, DC: Georgetown University Press.

Tomasello, M., & Herron, C. (1988). Down the garden path: Inducing and correcting overgeneralization errors in the foreign language classroom. *Applied Psycholinguistics, 9*(3), 237–246.

Tomasello, M., & Herron, C. (1989). Feedback for language transfer errors: The garden path technique. *Studies in Second Language Acquisition, 11*(4), 385–395.

Tomasello, M., & Herron, C. (1991). Experiments in the real world: A reply to Beck and Eubank. *Studies in Second Language Acquisition, 11*(3), 385–395.

Tomlin, R. S., & Villa, V. (1993). *Attention in cognitive science and SLA.* (Tech. Rep. No. 93-12). Eugene: University of Oregon, Institute of Cognitive and Decision Sciences.

Tweissi, A. I. (1990). 'Foreigner talk' in Arabic: Evidence for the universality of language simplification. In M. Eid & J. McCarthy (Eds.), *Perspectives on Arabic linguistics II. Current issues in linguistic theory* (Vol. 72, pp. 296–326). Amsterdam: John Benjamins.

Valdman, A. (1981). Sociolinguistic aspects of foreigner talk. *International Journal of the Sociology of Language, 28,* 41–52.

Van Helvert, K. (1985). *Nederlands van en tegen Turkse kinderen* [Dutch spoken by and addressed to Turkish children]. Unpublished doctoral dissertation, University of Nijmegen.

VanPatten, B. (1988). How juries get hung: Problems with the evidence for a focus on form in teaching. *Language Learning, 38*(2), 243–260.

Varonis, E. M., & Gass, S. M. (1982). The comprehensibility of non-native speech. *Studies in Second Language Acquisition, 4*(1), 41–52.

Varonis, E. M., & Gass, S. M. (1985a). Miscommunication in native/nonnative conversation. *Language in Society, 14*(3), 327–343.

Varonis, E. M., & Gass, S. M. (1985b). Non-native/non-native conversations: A model for negotiation of meaning. *Applied Linguistics, 6*(1), 71–90.

Vignola, M.-J., & Wesche, M. (1991). Le savoir-écrire en langue maternelle et en langue seconde chez les diplomes d'immersion française. *Etudes de Linguistique Appliquee, 82,* 94–115.

Warren-Leubecker, A., & Bohannon, J. N., III. (1982). The effects of expectation and feedback on speech to foreigners. *Journal of Psycholinguistic Research, 11*(3), 207–215.

Watanabe, Y. (1992). *Effects of increased processing on incidental learning of foreign language vocabulary.* Masters in ESL thesis, University of Hawaii at Manoa, Honolulu.

Watson-Gegeo, K. A., & Gegeo, D. W. (1990). Shaping the mind and straightening out conflicts: The discourse of Kwara'ae family counseling. In K. A. Watson-Gegeo & G. M. White (Eds.), *Disentangling: Conflict discourse in Pacific societies* (pp. 161–213). Stanford, CA: Stanford University Press.

Wesche, M. B. (1994). Input, interaction and acquisition: The linguistic environment of the language learner. In B. Richards & C. Gallaway (Eds.), *Input and interaction in language acquisition* (pp. 219–249). Cambridge, UK: Cambridge University Press.

Wesche, M. B., & Ready, D. (1985). Foreigner talk in university classrooms. In S. M. Gass & C. Madden (Eds.), *Input in second language acquisition* (pp. 329–344). Rowley, MA: Newbury House.

Wexler, K., & Culicover, P. (1980). *Formal principles of language acquisition.* Cambridge, MA: MIT Press.

White, L. (1987). Against comprehensible input: The Input Hypothesis and the development of L2 competence. *Applied Linguistics, 8,* 95–110.

White, L. (1989). The adjacency condition on case assignment: Do learners observe the Subset Principle? In S. N. Gass & J. Schachter (Eds.), *Linguistic perspectives on second language acquisition* (pp. 134–158). Cambridge: Cambridge University Press.

White, L. (1991). Adverb placement in second language acquisition: Some effects of positive and negative evidence in the classroom. *Second Language Research, 7*(2), 133–161.

White, L., Spada, N., Lightbown, P. M., & Ranta, L. (1991). Input enhancement and question formation. *Applied Linguistics, 12,* 416–432.

Widdowson, H. G. (1978). *Teaching language as communication.* Oxford: Oxford University Press.

Wolfe-Quintero, K. (1992). *The representation and acquisition of the lexical structure of English dative verbs: Experimental studies of native English speakers and Japanese and Chinese adult learners of English.* Unpublished doctoral dissertation, University of Hawaii, Honolulu.

Wong-Fillmore, L. (1976). *The second time around: Cognitive and social strategies in second language acquisition.* Unpublished doctoral dissertation, Stanford University, Palo Alto, CA.

Wren, D. (1982). A case study of the treatment of oral errors. *Selected Papers in TESOL, 1,* 90–103.

Yano, Y. Long, M. H., & Ross, S. (1994). The effects of simplified and elaborated texts on foreign language reading comprehension. *Language Learning, 44*(2), 189–219.

Yule, G., & Macdonald, D. (1990). Resolving referential conflicts in L2 interaction: The effect of proficiency and interactive role. *Language Learning, 40*(4), 539–556.

Zwicky, A. M., & Zwicky, A. D. (1980). America's National Dish: The style of restaurant menus. *American Speech, 55*(2), 83–92.

Zwicky, A. M., & Zwicky, A. D. (1981). Telegraphic registers in written English. In D. Sankoff & H. Cedergren (Eds.), *Variation omnibus* (pp. 535–544). New York: Linguistic Research.

CHAPTER 14

THE ACQUISITION OF ENGLISH SYNTAX BY DEAF LEARNERS

Gerald P. Berent

I. DEAFNESS AND LANGUAGE ACQUISITION

Deafness has dramatic consequences for the learning of a spoken language. Unlike the majority of hearing children who acquire spoken languages relatively unconsciously and effortlessly, a deaf child acquiring a spoken language is confronted with the arduous task of trying to perceive speech sounds that cannot be heard or which, depending on the degree of hearing loss, might be heard partially and with distortion. Although some speech sounds are visible on the lips, speechreading (lipreading) does not serve as a satisfactory substitute for spoken language input: similar sounds such as the labials /p/, /b/, and /m/ are not distinguishable from one another on the lips; natural communication does not always guarantee that the speaker's face is visible to the deaf language learner; and the nuances of stress and intonation are not visually perceptible. Printed language also does not serve as a satisfactory substitute for spoken language input because the ability to read a language, which takes several years to develop, presupposes knowledge of that language, and because natural, spontaneous communication in a language simply does not occur through reading and writing. By the time a deaf child develops the ability to read, the effects of restricted spoken language input have already had a profound impact on the learning of the target language (TL).

In contrast to the formidable task of acquiring a spoken language, a deaf child

Handbook of Second Language Acquisition

acquires a sign language, which is a visual-gestural as opposed to an oral-aural language, as unconsciously and effortlessly as a hearing child acquires a spoken language. Despite the difference in modality, sign languages are fully grammaticized languages that display the same kinds of grammatical characteristics found in spoken languages. In their overview of the acquisition of American Sign Language (ASL), Newport and Meier (1985) demonstrate that the stages of acquisition of ASL by deaf children parallel the stages of spoken language acquisition by hearing children with respect to virtually every milestone of language development—first words or signs, acquisition of morphology, emergence of syntax, and so forth.[1] For the 5–10% of American deaf children born to deaf parents, ASL is generally the first language of exposure. However, the 90–95% of deaf children born to hearing parents are typically not exposed to ASL during early childhood (Meier & Newport, 1990), though many learn ASL from other deaf children once they begin school.

Along with parents' hearing status and language background, the variables influencing deaf children's early language input and their language development are numerous and complex. Depending on the educational philosophy that the parents embrace, a deaf child in an English-speaking environment may receive language input consisting of oral English, some form of manually coded (signed) English, or ASL (Quigley & Paul, 1987). For the reasons noted above, the quantity and quality of exclusively oral language input will be quite low in comparison to signed input. Other factors influencing the deaf child's language development include the age of onset of deafness, the severity of the hearing loss, the parents' sensitivity to the communication needs of the child, the parents' competence in using a particular sign system (if any), the degree to which parents oversimplify the language input to their child (indefinitely), and the quality of parent–child interactions generally (Marschark, 1993).[2]

Degree of hearing loss is an important determinant of the extent to which spoken language input is accessible. Typically, hearing loss is measured in decibels (dB) as the average loss across speech frequencies at 500, 1000, and 2000 hertz. Conventionally, five categories of hearing loss are recognized: *slight* (27–40 dB), *mild* (41–54 dB), *moderate* (55–69 dB), *severe* (70–89 dB), and *profound* (90 dB and greater). Although definitions of deafness vary, Quigley and Paul (1987) consider a person "deaf" once vision, rather than audition, becomes the major

---

[1] One possible difference between sign language and spoken language acquisition occurs in the early stages of vocabulary acquisition, where first signs seem to appear earlier than first words. See Meier and Newport (1990) for a discussion.

[2] Further details on the acquisitional, sociolinguistic, educational, psychological, cultural, and political issues affecting deaf individuals' language development can be found in Bochner (1982), Bochner and Albertini (1988), Davis and Silverman (1978), Kretschmer and Kretschmer (1978, 1986), Luterman (1986), Quigley and Kretschmer (1982), Quigley and Paul (1984), Strong (1988), Swisher (1989), Van Cleve (1987), and Wilbur (1987).

link to receptive language development. This shift seems to occur at around the level of a 90-dB loss. However, the most serious consequences of deafness for the acquisition of a spoken language tend to be observed in persons who are either severely or profoundly deaf; therefore, the terms "deaf" and "deafness" in this chapter will include both severe and profound deafness. These terms will also imply *prelingual deafness,* or deafness occurring before the age of 2 or 3, because deafness occurring before age 2 or 3 has more extreme consequences on the acquisition of a spoken language than deafness occurring after this period. The phrases "acquisition of a spoken language" and "acquisition of English" are used in this chapter to refer to learners' explicit or implicit knowledge of English as it is used or understood in any modality, including speaking, signing, writing, or reading.

Given the foregoing discussion, it should be apparent that, except in the case of deaf children of deaf parents who are native users of ASL, it is difficult to ascertain what a deaf child's first language (L1) is or whether that child actually has an L1. Unless deaf children exposed to English are able to compensate in certain ways for the severe reduction in English language input, they could be considered to have no actual L1 or only a partial L1 relative to the TL, depending on the degree of hearing loss and all of the other complex factors noted above.[3] Because such children's formal exposure to English would generally only begin with schooling, well after the critical age of 2–3, English could legitimately be considered a second language (L2) for them, just as English would be considered the L2 for a hearing child with an intact L1 (e.g., Spanish) whose exposure to English began with schooling. Indeed, the English instruction provided to deaf children, adolescents, and adults is often essentially no different from the kinds of instruction employed in teaching English as a Second Language (ESL). Because many deaf learners can be viewed as having a partial L1 English as they continue to study the standard, target L2 English, Berent (1988) described the English learning environment of deaf students as "L1.5 acquisition," splitting the difference between L1 and L2. Although English language acquisition by deaf persons has been explored in the literature from a variety of perspectives, much of the existing work in this area has been largely descriptive and often atheoretical. This chapter reviews crucial segments of the existing research on the acquisition of English by deaf learners and offers a new theory-based approach to understanding the impact of deafness on spoken language acquisition based on recent theoretical developments in linguistics.

---

[3] Some deaf learners of English actually do compensate quite successfully for the severe restriction to their spoken language input, attaining English language abilities essentially no different from most hearing learners of English. It may be that early intervention with such learners has been swift and aggressive. Although an examination of the reasons for this successful attainment of English language skills is difficult to carry out retrospectively, more research involving these kinds of learners is needed.

II. DEAF LEARNERS' KNOWLEDGE OF SPECIFIC ENGLISH STRUCTURES

A. Sentence Complexity and Parts of Speech

Cooper and Rosenstein (1966) provided a concise review of American research conducted between 1916 and 1964 on deaf learners' English language abilities. Most of the studies they reviewed reported the results of analyses of deaf students' written language samples. These studies revealed that, in comparison with hearing students, deaf students' written samples were "found to contain shorter and simpler sentences, to display a somewhat different distribution of the parts of speech, to appear more rigid and more stereotyped, and to exhibit numerous errors or departures from standard English usage" (p. 66).

In studying students' written compositions, Heider and Heider (1940) found that, in addition to writing shorter sentences than hearing students aged 8–14, deaf students aged 11–17 used more simple sentences (e.g., *The girl ate an apple.*) and fewer compound sentences (e.g., *The girl ate an apple, and the boy ate a pear.*) and complex sentences (e.g., *The girl ate an apple when she came home.*). Myklebust (1964) compared the written compositions of deaf and hearing students aged 7–15 years and, like Heider and Heider, observed a greater use of shorter simple sentences by the deaf students. In particular, he noted that deaf students overused "carrier phrases," or strings of sentences that vary only in the choice of a noun (e.g., *I see a boy. I see a dog. I see a baby.*). This overuse of carrier phrases—75% of the students used them at age 7—virtually disappeared by age 15.

Myklebust (1964) also analyzed the parts of speech used in deaf and hearing students' written compositions. He found that the deaf students used more nouns but fewer verbs than the hearing students did. Regarding articles, whereas the deaf students used virtually no articles at age 7, from age 9 they surpassed the hearing students in the use of articles. Myklebust attributed the deaf students' patterns of article usage to the fact that their higher percentage of nouns required a higher percentage of accompanying articles and to the fact that deaf students were often drilled in article-plus-noun combinations in school. With regard to pronouns, at ages 7–9, the deaf students used virtually no pronouns. After that age usage increased, but some deaf students produced no pronouns at all through age 15. The use of prepositions among the deaf students increased gradually from none at age 7 to a level equivalent to that of the hearing students by age 15. Unlike the hearing students, the deaf students used few adjectives until age 11. Again, there were some deaf students at all age levels who used no adjectives in their compositions. The difference between deaf and hearing students in the use of adverbs was striking. The hearing students' use of adverbs increased steadily across age levels. In contrast, the deaf students used no adverbs until age 13 and then used very few. The hearing students began using conjunctions at age 9, whereas the deaf students began using them at age 11. Some deaf students, even at age 15, used no conjunctions at all.

Goda (1964) analyzed the occurrence of the parts of speech in the *spoken* language of deaf and hearing adolescents aged 12–18. He found that 75% of speech produced by the deaf students consisted of nouns and verbs as compared to 60% for the hearing students. Although the deaf and hearing students produced about the same percentage of nouns, the deaf students produced a greater percentage of verbs. Furthermore, only 17% of the deaf students' speech consisted of function words (e.g., articles, prepositions, conjunctions, and auxiliary verbs like *have, do, can,* etc.) as compared to the hearing students' 27%. Goda attributed the greater variety in the syntax of the hearing students to their use of more function words and also to their use of more adjectives. Whereas the hearing students "expanded utterances" through the use of 26 different function words, the deaf students used only three words to expand utterances: *and, because,* and *while.*

Brannon (1968) conducted a study in which he compared the spoken English produced from picture prompts by deaf students aged 8 to 18 and hearing junior high school students. The parts of speech evaluated included the following: nouns, verbs, adjectives, adverbs, personal pronouns, relative pronouns, articles, indefinite pronouns (e.g., *someone*), auxiliary verbs, quantifiers (e.g., *every*), prepositions, conjunctions, and interjections. Relative to the hearing students, the deaf students used fewer adverbs, auxiliary verbs, personal pronouns, prepositions, and quantifiers. They used no indefinite pronouns, and they overused nouns and articles. Brannon concluded that hearing loss in early life interferes with the learning of function words more than with the learning of content words (nouns, verbs, adjectives, adverbs), with the exception of adverbs.

In summary, the articles reviewed in Cooper and Rosenstein (1966) as well as Heider and Heider (1940), Myklebust (1964), Goda (1964), and Brannon (1968) revealed, with some degree of variation, that many prelingually deaf individuals' English language abilities are characterized by the production of short, simple sentences, by the overuse of nouns and articles, and by a considerable restriction in the use of most function words and adverbs.[4]

B. The TSA Structures

A comprehensive project for assessing the development of English syntax in deaf children and adolescents in the context of transformational generative grammar (Chomsky, 1957, 1965) was conducted in the 1970s using the Test of

---

[4]MacGinitie (1964) observed much higher performance, relative to the results of the studies which analyzed written and oral production, when deaf students aged 10–15 were required to supply English parts of speech in a sentence-completion task. He maintained that "although deaf children are likely to omit certain classes of words in free composition, they appear to be more capable of using these same word classes in contexts that call for them" (p. 147). He cautioned, however, that his materials were drawn from second-grade readers and that his subjects were drawn from a single school.

Syntactic Ability (TSA). The TSA was standardized for diagnostic use by Quigley, Steinkamp, Power, and Jones (1978). The TSA project has been described and the results summarized in numerous publications including Quigley and King (1980, 1982); Quigley, Power, and Steinkamp (1977); and Quigley, Wilbur, Power, Montanelli, and Steinkamp (1976). The TSA consists of 22 different subtests employing sentence-completion and sentence-correction formats that were designed to assess deaf learners' comprehension and production of a large sample of English syntactic structures. The TSA project tested 450 deaf students between the ages of 10 and 18 along with 60 hearing students aged 8–10. Some of the major findings of the project are reported below, along with the results of other relevant studies. Because the hearing students outperformed the deaf students on all TSA structures, only the performance of the deaf students will be discussed.

Pronominalization

The results of the TSA pronominalization subtests are reported in Wilbur, Montanelli, and Quigley (1976). These subtests explored students' abilities to supply the following pronominal forms in appropriate sentence environments: personal pronouns (e.g., *you*), possessive adjectives (e.g., *your*), possessive pronouns (e.g., *yours*), reflexives (e.g., *yourself*), and relative pronouns (e.g., *who*). Accordingly, the tests revealed knowledge of case forms (e.g., subject *we* vs. object *us*) and the features of person (e.g., first person *I* vs. second person *you*), number (e.g., singular *it* vs. plural *they*), and gender (e.g., masculine *him* vs. feminine *her*).

The deaf students improved on each pronoun tested with increasing age. As an example, knowledge of the appropriate use of *them* increased from 31% correct at age 10 to 84% correct at age 18. Of the various pronominal forms, relative pronouns caused the greatest difficulty. Since performance on the pronominalization subtests was distinguished by many interactions among the categories of case, person, number, and gender as well as student age, Wilbur et al. (1976) concluded that "the pronoun system is mastered pronoun by pronoun rather than by categories" (p. 137).

Verb Processes

The TSA subtests on verb processes assessed students' abilities to judge the grammaticality of English sentences containing verbs inflected for tense (present, past), aspect (simple, progressive, perfect), and voice (active, passive). Tense, aspect, and voice combine in various ways. Thus, *is kicking* in (1a) below is present progressive, *has opened* in (1b) is present perfect, and *was kicked* in (1c) is past passive.

(1) a. The boy *is kicking* the ball.
     b. The man *has opened* the door.
     c. The ball *was kicked* by the boy.

Quigley, Montanelli, and Wilbur (1976) reported that deaf students had great difficulty with all of the verb forms in (1). However, they were overall relatively more successful in judging the grammaticality of present progressive verbs, less successful in judging present perfect verbs, and still less successful in judging passive verbs. The grammaticality of sentences with a missing auxiliary verb (e.g., *The door opened by the man.*) was the most difficult to judge. Slightly less difficult were sentences with missing verb endings (e.g., *The boy has kick the ball.*), and slightly less difficult than those were passive sentences with a missing *by* (e.g., *The ball was kicked the boy.*). Quigley, Montanelli, and Wilbur (1976) also noted that deaf students show confusion between the verbs *be* and *have,* often substituting a form of *have* for a form of *be,* and that they sometimes fail to use a verb in a sentence, especially in environments where *be* is possible. Given the low percentages on the verb processes subtests, Quigley, Montanelli, and Wilbur (1976) concluded that deaf students have considerable difficulty with the verb system of English.

In an analysis of spoken language samples, Pressnell (1973) also found verb structures to be of considerable difficulty for deaf learners of English aged 5–13 years. In terms of relative performance, her subjects were much more successful in using simple uninflected verbs (e.g., *see* in *I see you*) than in using present progressive verbs (e.g., *is walking*). This pattern reflects the opposite order of acquisition found in hearing children. Pressnell speculated that this result might be a consequence of classroom instruction, because many deaf schools taught verb tenses in the order simple present, past, future, and then present progressive. Her subjects also had considerable difficulty with third-person singular verbs (e.g., *plays*), past tense (e.g., *played, saw*), and various forms of *be.* The deaf children's performance on modal verbs and the auxiliary verb *do* was variable. They were more successful on *can, will, may,* and *do* than on the past forms *could, would, might,* and *did,* and least successful on *must* and *shall.* Performance was quite low on perfect progressive forms (e.g., *have been studying*) and modal perfect forms (e.g., *may have eaten*). There was only one instance of the use of a passive verb in the entire sample.

Power and Quigley (1973) specifically explored deaf learners' knowledge of passive sentences. Deaf students aged 9 to 18 performed two tasks, a "comprehension" task in which they acted out written sentences by manipulating toys, and a "production" task in which they completed sentences associated with pictures. The structures targeted on both tasks were reversible passive sentences as in (2a), nonreversible passive sentences as in (2b), and Agent-deleted passive sentences as in (2c).

(2) a. The girl was pushed by the boy.
     b. The car was washed by the boy.
     c. The girl was pushed.

In an active sentence (e.g., *The boy pushed the girl.*) the subject (*the boy*) is usually the *Agent,* or the one who performs an action, and the object (*the girl*) is the *Patient,* or the one who receives the action. In a passive sentence the normal subject-verb-object (SVO) relationship of an active sentence is reversed: the object (Patient) becomes the subject, and the subject (Agent) becomes the object of za *by*-phrase. In a reversible passive sentence like (2a), unlike a nonreversible passive, switching the subject and the object of the *by*-phrase results in a sentence with a plausible meaning. Switching the subject and *by*-phrase Agent in a nonreversible passive results in an anomalous sentence (compare [2b] with the nonsensical sentence, *The boy was washed by the car.*). Previous research had shown that hearing children do not fully master passive sentences until age 8 or 9 and that nonreversible passives were easier to comprehend than reversible passives (Slobin, 1966).

The results of Power and Quigley (1973) revealed that the students were quite unsuccessful at comprehending and producing passive sentences, but that they were overall more successful on nonreversible passives than on reversible passives, as hearing children are, and least successful on Agent-deleted passives. Power and Quigley concluded that the deaf students tended to interpret passive sentences like active ones by applying the S (Agent) VO (Patient) word order to passive sentences. Their greater success on nonreversible passives derives from the likelihood that the nonsensical meaning resulting from reversing a nonreversible passive would force the students into a correct interpretation. As for Agent-deleted passives, Power and Quigley noted that deaf students generally rely more on the *by*-phrase to mark a passive sentence than on the passive form of the verb; therefore, a missing *by*-phrase hindered interpretation more than the inability to process passive morphology.

Complementation

The TSA complementation subtest assessed students' abilities to judge the grammaticality of English sentences containing infinitive complements like those italicized in (3) and gerund complements like those italicized in (4).

(3) a. Cats like *to sleep.*
     b. The policeman told me where *to stop.*
(4) a. *Playing* is fun.
     b. The baby pigs love *eating.*

Quigley, Wilbur, and Montanelli (1976) reported that complementation structures were among the most difficult of the TSA structures for deaf students. At age 10 they scored 50% correct on the complementation subtest and at age 18 only 63% correct. In judging the grammaticality of sentences containing complements, the students were slightly more successful overall with gerund complements than with infinitive complements. As part of their analysis, Quigley, Wilbur, and Montanelli (1976) examined students' written language samples, which were gathered using an elicitation procedure established for deaf students in Stuckless and Marks (1966). They found that the students attempted more complement structures with increasing age. Despite the fact that the students were more successful on gerund complements than on infinitive complements on the TSA complementation subtest, they produced very few gerund complements in their writing samples, producing mostly infinitive complements instead. A common error type, especially among the younger students, was the omission of *to* from an infinitive (as in *I wanted Bill go*).

Question Formation

The question-formation subtests of the TSA assessed students' knowledge of yes–no questions as in (5), tag questions as in (6), and wh-questions as in (7).

(5) a. Was the girl crying?
     b. Will mother buy the bed tomorrow?
     c. Do you want to go?
(6) a. Tom bought a car, didn't he?
     b. The children didn't walk to school, did they?
     c. Susan can ride the bicycle, can't she?
(7) a. What will Jim eat?
     b. When did you plant the flowers?
     c. Which dog sleeps in the house?

Collectively, the subtests assessed students' abilities to choose correct answers to specific question types. They also assessed knowledge of Subject-Auxiliary Inversion, whereby an auxiliary verb (e.g., *was* in [5a] or *will* in [7a]) is moved to the left of the subject to form a question from a statement, and *do*-support, whereby the appropriate form of *do* appears to the left of the subject in forming certain questions as in (5c) and (7b). As seen in (6), these processes are also involved in forming tag questions. The subtests also assessed knowledge of wh-movement (Chomsky, 1977), whereby a wh-word moves to the left of both the subject and any auxiliary verb in wh-questions.

As reported in Quigley, Wilbur, and Montanelli (1974), the younger deaf students performed only at chance levels on the question-formation subtests, indicating poorly established knowledge of English question formation. With respect to relative orders among question types, the deaf subjects were most successful overall on yes–no questions, less successful on wh-questions, and least successful on tag questions. That tag questions were the most difficult is not surprising, because these involve not only *do*-support in the tag but also reversing the polarity of the tag (i.e., if the statement is positive the tag is negative, and vice versa). Of the other two types, both involve *do*-support or Subject-Auxiliary Inversion, but wh-questions additionally involve wh-movement, presumably accounting for their greater difficulty. (For a discussion of yes–no questions and wh-questions in L2 acquisition, see chapter 6 by Eckman.)

Conjunction

The conjunction subtests of the TSA assessed students' abilities to produce conjoined sentences and phrases using the conjunction *and,* as well as their abilities to judge the grammaticality of structures requiring *and* and to correct ungrammatical structures. Target grammatical structures included conjoined sentences as in (8), conjoined subject noun phrases (NPs) as in (9), conjoined object NPs as in (10), and conjoined verb phrases (VPs) as in (11).

(8)   The lady picked the flowers and the man cut the grass.
(9)   A man and a woman danced.
(10) A lady bought a coat and a hat.
(11) Mary bought a fish and cooked it.

Other target structures included ungrammatical formations that have been observed in the written productions of some deaf learners. These were what Wilbur, Quigley, and Montanelli (1975) referred to as and-deletion structures like (12), Object–Object (OO) deletion structures like (13), and Object–Subject (OS) deletion structures like (14).

(12) A boy a girl went home.
(13) John threw the ball and Mary dropped.
(14) The boy saw the turtles and ate the fish.

In (12), a required *and* is missing. In OO deletion the missing object of the second conjunct (i.e., conjoined clause) is identical to the object of the first conjunct (*the ball* in [13]) and would normally be represented by a pronoun. Thus, the second conjunct in (13) should be *Mary dropped it,* where *it* is coreferential (identical in reference) with *the ball.* Normally, the second conjunct if (14) would be interpreted to mean *the boy ate the fish.* However, the context of their productions (e.g., picture stimuli) made it apparent that some deaf learners were interpreting structures like (14) to mean *the turtles ate the fish.* That is, the object of the first conjunct was equivalent to the subject of the second conjunct, which is missing, hence OS deletion.

Results of the conjunction subtests revealed that the deaf students improved with age in their ability to judge the grammaticality of sentences containing conjoined structures like those in (8)–(11) above. Their acceptance of ungrammatical *and*-deletion sentences like (12) decreased with age. The production of conjoined structures (from sentence-combining stimuli) was more difficult for the deaf students than judging grammaticality. In producing sentences from stimuli in which two sentences contained identical objects (e.g., *John threw the ball. Mary dropped the ball.*), deaf students produced the correct target sentence (e.g., *John threw the ball and Mary dropped it.*) 25% of the time at age 10 and 68% of the time at age 18. From such stimuli, the students produced ungrammatical OO deletion sentences like (13) 6% of the time at age 10 and only 1% of the time at age 18. In producing sentences from stimuli in which the object of the first sentence was identical to the subject of the second (e.g., *The boy saw the turtles. The turtles ate the fish.*), the deaf students produced the correct target sentence (e.g., *The boy saw the turtles and they ate the fish.*) 44% of the time at age 10 with an increase to only 45% of the time at age 18. From such stimuli, there was actually an increase in the production of ungrammatical OS deletion sentences like (14) from 12% at age 10 to 32% at age 18.

As reported in de Villiers (1988), Gross and de Villiers (1983) obtained considerably different results from Wilbur, Quigley, and Montanelli (1975). Gross and de Villiers used a pragmatically based procedure for eliciting sentences containing conjoined subject and object NPs and conjoined VPs like those in (9)–(11) from deaf students between the ages of 7 and 13. The procedure involved pictures that provided clear pragmatic contexts for the (oral) production of specific structures. In most cases, the students produced conjoined structures that were appropriate to the pragmatic contexts provided. None of the students produced *and*-deletion sentences, and only one student produced an OO deletion sentence. De Villiers attributed the discrepant results between the two studies possibly to the differences in subject sampling and also to the different tasks used. In Wilbur, Quigley, and Montanelli (1975), the task stimuli consisted of two written conjoined sentences with no pragmatic context; in Gross and de Villiers, the stimuli were visual rather than verbal, and a clear pragmatic context was provided. It is possible, then, that deaf learners' knowledge of conjoined structures is not as insufficient as indicated in Wilbur, Quigley, and Montanelli (1975).

Relativization

The TSA relativization subtests assessed students' abilities to process and comprehend English sentences containing relative clauses like those in (15) and (16).

(15) a. The woman *who sold the bicycle to Tom* had a car.
      b. The men *who Bill chased* had a blue car.
(16) a. I saw the men *who stole the dog.*
      b. I caught the boy *who Tom chased.*

In (15), the italicized relative clause identifies the subject of the main clause, whereas in (16) the relative clause identifies the object of the main clause. In (15a) and (16a), *who* functions as the subject of the relative clause, whereas in (15b) and (16b) *who* functions as the object of the relative clause. Thus, on the basis of both the function of the head NP and the function of the relative pronoun, the relative clause in (15a) is a Subject–Subject (SS) relative, the one in (15b) a Subject–Object (SO) relative, the one in (16a) an OS relative, and the one in (16b) an OO relative.

Quigley, Smith, and Wilbur (1974) reported that deaf students improved with age in their ability to interpret the meanings of sentences containing relative clauses. In terms of types of relative clause sentences, the students were most successful in interpreting OO relatives, less successful with OS relatives, still less successful with SS relatives, and least successful with SO relatives. In interpreting the appropriate forms of relative clause sentences, the deaf students in all age groups often accepted both OS deletion and OO deletion sentences as grammatical equivalents to relative clause sentences. For example, prompted by sentence-combining stimuli, they preferred sentences like (13) and (14) over the properly formed relative clause sentences (17) and (18), respectively.

(17)   John threw the ball which Mary dropped.
(18)   The boy saw the turtles which ate the fish.

Correct acceptance of relative clause sentences over OO deletion sentences ranged from 44% at age 10 to only 49% at age 18, and correct acceptance of relative clause sentences over OS deletion sentences ranged from 47% at age 10 to only 56% at age 18.

Using pragmatically based elicitation procedures, de Villiers (1988) obtained very different results from those of Quigley, Smith, and Wilbur (1974). De Villiers's deaf subjects, aged 11–18, produced relative clause sentences that were distributed across all four types. In this case, students were most successful in producing SS relatives. The other relative clause types proved more difficult for the subjects. After SS relatives, OS relatives were the most frequent. The students produced both SO and OO relatives with very low frequency. Again, de Villiers attributed these different results possibly to the different populations sampled in the two studies and to the fact that his task provided a clear pragmatic context for the production of the target structures. (Discussions of relativization in L2 acquisition appear in chapters 4 by Flynn, 5 by Schachter, and 6 by Eckman. Chapter 18 by Seliger includes treatment of relativization in L1 attrition.)

C. Nine Syntactic Structures in Context

Wilbur, Goodhart, and Montandon (1983) investigated nine structures that were not investigated in the TSA project (section II.B). Their subjects were deaf students between the ages of 7 and 23. Wilbur, Goodhart, and Montandon (1983) used a comic book format with multiple-choice items to provide a pragmatic context for assessing the deaf students' knowledge of why-questions as in (19a), conditionals as in (19b), nonlocative prepositions as in (19c), indefinite pronouns as in (19d), quantifiers as in (19e), modal verbs as in (19f), elliptical constructions as in (19g), reciprocal pronouns as in (19h), and comparative constructions as in (19i), where relevant constituents are italicized.

(19) a. *Why* is Mary crying?
   b. *If* it rains tomorrow, we will go to the library.
   c. The present is *for* Mary.
   d. John saw *something* behind the tree.
   e. *All* the men left the room.
   f. Mary *might* come to the party.
   g. Yes, it *is.*
   h. John and Mary like *each other.*
   i. John is *taller than* Bill.

The deaf students were divided into eight groups according to reading level. Results of the study revealed that performance on the nine target structures, though quite low at reading level 1, generally improved as reading level increased. The overall order of difficulty among the nine structures is the order shown in (19), where performance ranged from 77% correct overall on why-questions to 58% correct on comparative constructions. Within each structure there was great variation in performance on the substructures comprising that structure, suggesting that forms belonging to a given syntactic structure, which often vary semantically among themselves, are learned item by item. For example, overall performance on the quantifier substructures was as follows: *some* (81%), *no* (72%), *all* (67%), *any* (57%), *each* (45%), *every* (34%).

Noting how different indefinite pronouns and quantifiers vary greatly from one another in semantic complexity, Wilbur and Goodhart (1985) elaborated the results on indefinite pronouns and quantifiers obtained in Wilbur et al. (1983). They established theoretical predictions of difficulty orders based on the semantic complexity of individual lexical items. For example, they predicted that positive *some* should be acquired before negative *no* and that the explicit negative *no* should be acquired before the implicit negative *any*. They found that such predictions indeed accounted for deaf students' performance but that developmental predictions based on hearing children's acquisition of indefinite pronouns and quantifiers did not account for the deaf students' performance very well. They argued that theoretical predictions of complexity might be more accurate for deaf learners of English than for hearing learners, because hearing learners are affected to a greater extent by overriding factors such as frequency of exposure to certain forms and pragmatic factors. That is, deaf learners' performance appears to be associated more clearly with the intrinsic complexity of structures.

D. Clausal and Nonclausal Structures

Berent (1988) assessed deaf college students' knowledge of nine English syntactic structures using a revised multiple-choice version of the Test of Ability to Subordinate (Davidson, 1978). The conceptual framework of the study included assumptions of Chomsky (1977, 1971), in which Empty Categories are postulated as placeholders of moved constituents and of "invisible" subjects of certain kinds of verbs. The nine structures tested included three phrasal structures—prenominal adjectives, adverbs, and prepositional phrases—and six clausal structures—infinitive clauses, participial clauses, gerund clauses, adverbial clauses, noun clauses, and relative clauses. Examples of the three phrasal structures are shown in (20), and examples of the six clausal structures are shown in (21) according to their underlying theoretical representations.

(20)   a. John took *our new* chairs.
       b. They *usually* meet on Monday.
       c. She talks to her students *in a loud voice.*
(21)   a. We allowed Mary [PRO *to leave school*].
       b. [PRO slowly *pouring the milk*], I filled my cup.
       c. They are responsible *for* [PRO *cleaning the house*].
       d. [*When* [*we came home from work*]], it was cold in the house.
       e. We think [*that* [*she will go away*]].
       f. Football is a sport [*which* [*many people watch* [t]]].

In (21), the clausal portions of the italicized target structures are enclosed by the outermost brackets. In (21a–c), the empty category PRO represents the subject of the infinitive clause, the participial clause, and the gerund clause, respectively. In each instance, PRO receives its reference from another NP in the sentence, usually but not always the closest one (see section II.E). Thus, in (21a), PRO is interpreted as *Mary;* in (21b), PRO is interpreted as *I;* and in (21c), PRO is interpreted as *they.* All major constituents of the adverbial when-clause in (21d) and the noun clause in (21e) are represented explicitly (i.e., there are no empty categories). In the relative clause in (21f), however, the relative pronoun *which* has moved, via wh-movement, to the front of the clause from its object position after *watch,* leaving the Empty Category [t], called a trace, as a placeholder (see section III.A)

Results of Berent (1988) revealed that the deaf students with higher general English language proficiency as measured by the Michigan Test of English Language Proficiency (1977) also performed higher on the specific structures targeted on the Revised Test of Ability to Subordinate than students with lower general English proficiency. On the phrasal structures, the students' overall order of success was prepositional phrases (PPs), prenominal adjectives, and adverbs (Adv). The overall success order on the clausal structures was adverbial clauses, noun clauses, infinitive clauses, gerund clauses, relative clauses, and participial clauses. Berent explained that the deaf students were most successful on those clausal structures in which major constituents were represented explicitly in noun-verb-noun (NVN) sequences maintaining SVO grammatical relations and least successful on those structures with empty categories in which the explicit representation of SVO relations was disturbed. Of the three "PRO structures," there was higher performance on infinitive clauses because they disturb the explicit representation of NVN word order the least. For example, compare the NVNVN sequence of (21a), *we-allow-Mary-leave-school,* with the VNNVN sequence of (21b), *pour-milk-I-fill-cup.* In a follow-up study, Berent (1993) found that deaf college students continued to improve on the targeted structures over time.

E. Infinitive Complement Interpretation

Berent (1983) explored deaf college students' abilities to interpret the logical subjects of English infinitive complements. The target structures of the study included sentences like the following, in which the infinitive complements are bracketed:

(22)   a. George asked *Tom* [PRO to buy a newspaper].
       b. Larry told *John* [what [PRO to do]].
       c. *Tom* asked Bill [what [PRO to buy]].
       d. *Mike* was reminded by George [PRO to study the lesson].

In accordance with Chomsky (1980), the antecedent of the PRO subject of an infinitive clause is generally the nearest noun phrase in configurations like those in (22). The antecedent is said to control PRO. Thus, as indicated by the italics, *Tom* controls PRO in (22a) and it is, accordingly, *Tom,* rather than *George,* who is to buy a newspaper. Similarly, *John* controls PRO in (22b). Both *Tom* and *John* are objects of their main clause verbs, and (22a,b) thus reflect the general case of object control. However, some verbs (e.g., *ask* when it is followed by a wh-word) are exceptions to the object control principle and are marked specifically as subject control verbs. In (22c), it is the subject *Tom,* rather than the object *Bill,* that controls PRO; it is *Tom* who will buy something. With a passive verb as in (22d), the normal object control property is reversed, so (22d) reflects subject control.

Berent (1983) found that deaf college students, just like young children learning English as an L1 and adult learners of ESL, correctly applied object control in interpreting sentences like (22a,b) but overextended object control to subject control sentences like (22c,d). That is, many of the students interpreted sentences like (22c) incorrectly as if *Bill* would buy something and (22d) as if *George* was to study the lesson. Performance on subject control sentences did, however, improve as general English proficiency level increased.

Actually, performance on the subject control sentences was variable. For example, students overall were more successful in interpreting a passive sentence like (22d) than (22c), which is structurally no different from (22b). Thus, contrary to the claim in Pinhas and Lust (1987), Berent's subjects showed knowledge of the configurational property on which Chomsky's (1980) theory of control was based. That is, they realized that an embedded *by*-phrase in a passive sentence is not the "nearest" NP according to Chomsky's formulation of nearness. Thus it was the exceptional subject control feature associated with *ask* followed by a *wh*-word and with certain other verbs that caused the most difficulty. (For discussion of subject versus object control in L2 acquisition, see chapter 4 by Flynn.)

III. A FRAMEWORK FOR EXPLAINING DEAF LEARNERS' SYNTACTIC KNOWLEDGE

This section outlines a theoretical framework within which language acquisition data have begun to be explored and offers possible explanations within that framework for many aspects of deaf learners' syntactic knowledge, which were described in the studies reviewed in section II.

A. Theoretical Background

Thematic and Functional Phrasal Categories

Following Chomsky (1986a), all phrases, including NPs, VPs, adjective phrases (APs), PPs, and so forth, have the same structure as shown in (23).

(23)

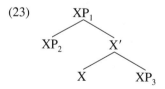

The symbol XP in (23) stands for a phrase of any of the categories NP, VP, and so on. Where XP_1 is a phrase of a particular category, XP_2 is the Specifier, or Spec, of XP_1, X is the Head of XP_1, and XP_3 is the Complement of X. For example, if XP_1 represents the NP *Mary's interest in linguistics* (NP_1 in [24]), where $XP_1 = NP_1$, *interest* (= N) is the Head of NP_1, *Mary's* (itself an NP), is the Specifier of NP_1, and *in linguistics,* a PP, is the Complement of N. Thus, the structure of the NP *Mary's interest in linguistics* is as shown in (24).

(24)

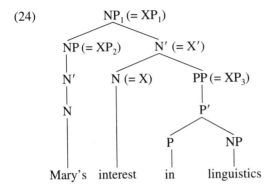

In addition to lexical categories (e.g., N, V, A, P), Chomsky recognized two nonlexical categories, complementizer (C), which is the Head of a complementizer phrase (CP), and Inflection (I), which is the head of an inflectional phrase (IP). The lexical categories are associated with thematic relations like Agent, Patient, and so forth, and, following Abney (1987), may be referred to as thematic categories. The nonlexical categories comprise a small class of elements with special functions of relating thematic categories to one another, which may be referred to as functional categories.

The structure of a clause or CP is shown in (25) below.

(25)

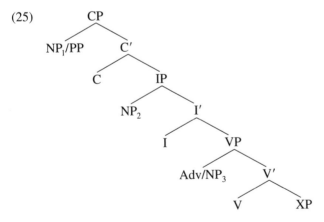

NP$_1$/PP is the Spec of CP, C is the Head of CP, and IP is the Complement of C. Within IP, the Spec position, NP$_2$, is the position of the NP subject of a clause. The category I is the Head of IP, and VP is the Complement of I. Within VP, the Spec of VP (Adv/NP$_3$) is a position for certain adverbs and—on some analyses (see below)—the subject NP of the clause; V is the Head, and XP represents the Complement, which may be an NP object, a PP, or another CP.

Complementizers like *that* (as in, *They said that it was raining.*) or *for* (as in, *It is important for you to study.*) appear under C. The category I carries features associated with present or past tense that are passed on to the verb of a tensed clause (e.g., *The children walk.* vs. *The children walked.*) It also contains an agreement (Agr) element that passes on features of person and number to the verb to establish Subject–Verb Agreement (e.g., *The child sleeps.* vs. *The children sleep.*) and which assigns nominative (i.e., subject) Case to the subject NP of a tensed clause (e.g., *She eats potatoes* vs. **Her eats potatoes.*) Modal verbs, the auxiliary verb *do,* and the *to* sign of an infinitive (as in, *They want to leave.*) also appear under I.

The functional categories are also positions to which other constituents move in the course of certain derivations. Specifically, in question formation, a modal or the auxiliary verb *do* moves from I to C in (25). This movement is the formal equivalent of do-support and Subject-Auxiliary Inversion (cf. section II.B). Additionally, in the formation of a wh-question, a wh-word moves up to Spec of CP ('NP$_1$/PP' in [25]) by wh-movement, leaving a trace [t] in its original position (cf. section IV.B). Thus, no constituent moves out of IP in a statement like (26a) and the Head of CP (that is, C) is empty (as represented by the symbol $\varnothing$); in a yes–no question like (26b) and a wh-question like (26c), *does* moves out of IP to C; and in (26c), *what* moves out of IP to Spec of CP, leaving its trace in the direct object position after *eat.*

(26) a. $[_{CP} [_{C'} [_C \varnothing]] [_{IP}$ Mary eats potatoes]].
      b. $[_{CP} [_{C'} [_C$ Does]] $[_{IP}$ Mary eat potatoes]]?
      c. $[_{CP} [_{NP}$ What] $[_{C'} [_C$ does] $[_{IP}$ Mary eat [t]]]]?

With the exception of modals and auxiliary *do,* a verb otherwise appears under V as the Head of VP in (25). Pollock (1989) argued that the verb *be* and the auxiliary verb *have* move up to I from their initial position under V.[5] Because, as noted, certain adverbs appear in Spec of VP, this verb movement accounts for word-order differences distinguishing *be* and *have* from other, main verbs. For example, in (27a), *always* appears before *eats,* showing that *eats* has not moved out of VP (cf. **John eats always apples.*); but in (27b,c), *always* appears after *is* and *have,* showing that these verbs have indeed moved out of VP.

(27) a. $[_{CP} [_{IP}$ John] $[_{VP} [_{Adv}$ always] eats apples]]].
      b. $[_{CP} [_{IP}$ John $[_I$ is] $[_{VP} [_{Adv}$ always] eating apples]]].
      c. $[_{CP} [_{IP}$ John $[_I$ has] $[_{VP} [_{Adv}$ always] eaten apples]]].

---

[5] Pollock (1989) argued that IP really consists of two separate phrasal categories, a tense phrase (TP) headed by tense (T) and an agreement phrase (AgrP) headed by Agr. Under this proposal, *be* and *have* actually move from V to Agr to T. For the current discussion it suffices to discuss verb movement with reference to (25) in the context of Chomsky (1986a).

In questions, *be* and auxiliary *have* move further up to C, just as auxiliary *do* and modals do, as evidenced by Subject-Auxiliary Inversion in *Is John eating applies?* or *What is John eating?* and in *Has John eaten apples?* or *What has John eaten?* (Functional categories are also discussed (in connection with L2 acquisition) in chapters 3 by White and 4 by Flynn. For additional discussion of verb movement (or verb raising) see chapter 3 by White.)

The Determiner Phrase

In the context of Chomsky (1986a), Abney (1987) proposed a modification to the conventional analysis of noun phrases that establishes a close parallelism between the structure of noun phrases and the structure of clauses. Abney noted that in certain languages (e.g., Hungarian and Turkish) noun phrases incorporate an agreement element similar to the agreement element Agr responsible for Subject–Verb Agreement and nominative Case assignment in clauses (Section III.A). Abney argued that, just as the functional constituent I has a small class of lexical items associated with it—namely, the modals—the noun phrase has a small class of lexical items with special functions associated with it, namely, determiners, which include articles, demonstrative pronouns (e.g., *this, that*), and so forth. Therefore, Abney proposed that a noun phrase is not simply an NP, but rather that it is a determiner phrase (DP), as shown in (28), with an optional Spec (in [28], another DP), a determiner (D) Head, and an NP Complement.[6] He regarded D in a noun phrase as the functional equivalent of Agr in I in a clause.

(28)

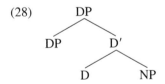

Following Abney's (1987) "DP-analysis," noun phrases have structures like the following.

(29) a. [DP [D' [D those] [NP books]]]
    b. [DP [DP John] [D' [D 's] [NP books]]]
    c. [DP [D' [D we] [NP linguists]]]
    d. [DP [D we]]

[6] Abney (1987) used the term *noun phrase* in the traditional, pretheoretic sense of a phrase in which the most prominent element is a noun and that functions as a subject, object, and so on, within a clause. He used the labels NP, DP, and so on, in making specific theoretical proposals about noun phrases. This terminological distinction is followed also in this and subsequent sections of this chapter.

In (29a), the determiner *those* takes the NP *books* as its Complement. Abney argued that in a noun phrase like *John's books,* as in (29b), *John,* itself a DP, occupies the Spec position of DP, and the possessive suffix *-'s* is actually a determiner that assigns possessive Case to *John* just as Agr assigns nominative Case to the subject noun phrase of a clause. Abney argued also that pronouns occupy the D position as *we* does in (29c) and (29d). Thus, a pronoun by itself as in (29d) is simply the D head of a DP without an NP Complement.

Conventionally, a quantifier (Q) like *every* as in *every student* was analyzed as occurring within a quantifier phrase (QP) embedded within an NP, and an adjective (A) like *new* as in *new students* was analyzed as occurring within an adjective phrase (AP) also embedded within an NP (Jackendoff, 1977). However, as part of the DP-analysis, Abney (1987) argued further that QP is the Complement of D, AP is the Complement of Q, and NP is the Complement of A. This structure is illustrated in (30), minus the Spec positions.

(30)

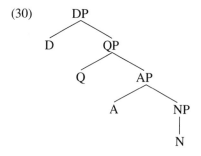

In conformity with this structure, *the many new proposals* would be represented as in (31), where *the* is a D, *many* is a Q, *new* is an A, and *proposals* is an N.

(31) $[_{DP} [_D$ the] $[_{QP} [_Q$ many] $[_{AP} [_A$ new] $[_{NP} [_N$ proposals]]]]]

B. Young Hearing Children's Phrasal Structures

Within the theoretical context of Chomsky (1986a), Radford (1988) explored the English syntactic development of young hearing children in the age range of 19–25 months, during the early patterned speech stage of language development. Radford provided evidence, based on speech samples of over 100 children and from other sources, that young hearing children's early clauses are characterized by the lack of the functional constituents CP and IP; in his terms, early child clauses lack a C-system and an I-system. Radford's evidence for the lack of a C-system is based on the observation that child clauses at the early patterned speech stage lack Complementizers, have no Subject-Auxiliary Inversion, and exhibit no wh-movement. As noted in section III.A, the first two processes involve the movement of constituents to C, and the third involves movement to Spec of C. Radford's evidence for the lack of an I-system is based on the observation that child clauses lack the *to* of the infinitive, lack modals, lack verbs marked for tense and agreement, and lack mastery of nominative Case assigned to the subject NP. As noted, all of these clausal phenomena involve IP.

In a second study, Radford (1990) argued that children in the early patterned speech stage also lack the D-system elaborated in Abney's (1987) DP-analysis (section III.A). For example, at this stage children omit articles, which are Ds, and they omit the possessive marker -*'s,* which Abney analyzed as the functional constituent D as in (29b) above. Furthermore, they do not use personal pronouns, analyzed as Ds as in (29c,d), using nouns in pronominal contexts instead. From this and other evidence, Radford concluded that young children use NPs where adults require DPs. Radford (1990) concluded, more generally, that early child structures are characterized by the presence of the thematic categories N, V, A, and P and by the lack of all the functional categories D, C, and I.

Radford's position has been modified somewhat in Radford (1994), where he argued that certain functional categories are not actually absent from child grammars but that they are "immature" or "underspecified" with respect to certain features associated with these categories in adult grammars. Specifically, Radford argued that an underspecified Agr constituent explains the absence of tensed clauses in early grammars as well as other characteristics of children's clauses. Others (e.g., Déprez & Pierce, 1993) have offered similar arguments. Pending further research, and as the debate continues over whether certain categories in emerging grammars are immature or absent, the strong claim is maintained in section III.C that functional categories, and even some thematic categories, are absent from deaf learners' early grammars.

C. Deaf Learners' Acquisition of English Syntax

Comparative studies of deaf and hearing learners' English syntactic development have generally revealed that deaf and hearing learners acquire English syntax in a similar fashion but that deaf learners do so at a much slower rate (Quigley & King, 1980). If hearing children acquire thematic categories before functional categories as concluded in Radford (1988, 1990), then deaf learners would also be expected to do so if acquisition is similar in both groups. Moreover, if deaf learners generally acquire English syntax at a much slower rate than hearing learners, then evidence of the earlier acquisition of thematic categories and later acquisition of functional categories should remain apparent in many deaf learners for a much longer period of time. Given the discussions in sections III.A and III.B, many of the acquisitional facts summarized in section II do suggest that deaf learners' acquisition of English syntax follows a developmental pattern in which thematic categories are acquired before functional categories and that, for many deaf learners, the functional categories resist acquisition indefinitely.

One difficulty in making this determination is the fact that there is a lot of "noise" in the data on deaf learners' knowledge of English. In the case of hearing children in the early patterned speech stage, the data consist of straightforward utterances that imply either the acquisition or nonacquisition of specific forms. In the case of deaf learners, the data have been culled from numerous sources that used many different assessment and analysis procedures and that targeted a wide range of age groups with diverse learner characteristics. What is more, English has generally been taught to deaf students as a system of rules to be learned consciously in the way that English is often taught to speakers of other languages. Thus, deaf learners have English skills that reflect the combination of naturally acquired structures guided by principles of Universal Grammar (UG) and consciously learned, or attempted, structures taught in the classroom. This situation might make the task of establishing deaf learners' acquisitional stages a difficult one. However, as will be seen, the cumulative deaf learner data lend themselves to interpretation within the theoretical framework elaborated in section III.A; they are consistent with assumptions of UG; and they are compatible with the learnability predictions to be discussed in section IV. Therefore, the data appear to constitute a fair approximation of the course of deaf learners' acquisition of English syntax.

Deaf Learners' Clause Structure

The data summarized in sections I and II suggest that, starting with the earliest easily documentable stage of English acquisition (i.e., the early school years), many deaf learners use short, simple sentences consisting largely of nouns and verbs but lacking most of the other parts of speech. Furthermore, a preference for NVN sequences reflecting SVO grammatical relations persists for years. With reference to (25) (section III.A), it would seem that, at this stage, deaf learner grammars might contain an IP constituent, in which the sentential subject appears under NP_2, the verb under V, and a noun phrase object in the XP position, but that they probably do not contain a CP constituent.

The evidence for the absence of CP derives, for instance, from the fact that deaf learners have great difficulty in forming questions in English. As noted, yes–no questions involve the movement of a modal or other auxiliary verb into C, the head of CP, effecting Subject-Auxiliary Inversion. Additionally, wh-questions require wh-movement, which moves a wh-word from its original position into the Spec of CP position, NP_1/PP in (25).[7] There are, in fact, several other CP structures of which deaf learners generally have limited knowledge. A relative clause is a CP that is embedded within a noun phrase and which involves wh-movement

---

[7] It was noted in section II.C that why-questions were less difficult than the other structures assessed in Wilbur et al. (1983). High performance on these wh-questions no doubt stems from the fact that knowledge of why-questions was verified by a student's ability to recognize simply that a because-clause was an appropriate response to a why-question.

to the Spec of CP just as wh-questions do. A participial clause is also a CP which describes a noun phrase. Furthermore, verbal complements (e.g., noun clauses, infinitive clauses, gerund clauses) are CPs appearing in the XP position in (25).

Though the use of NVN sequences by deaf learners should imply the presence of IP in their grammars, other data in fact suggest the absence of I. For example, deaf learners have difficulty marking verbs for tense and agreement, which are features transferred onto verbs via I. They also often omit the *to* of the infinitive and have difficulty with modals and auxiliary *do,* all of which originate under I. With respect to *be* and auxiliary *have,* following Pollock (1989), these verbs raise from V to I (see fn. 5), where they acquire their tense and agreement features. Assuming the lack of I, all *be* and *have* structures requiring the presence of I— namely, passive, progressive, and perfect verb forms—should cause deaf learners difficulty, which they do. The frequent omission of the verb *be* from a sentence is also explained if I is absent. Furthermore, difficulty with elliptical constructions (e.g., [19g], section II.C) also suggests the absence of I. In an elliptical construction the auxiliary verb that represents the deleted information understood from context appears under I.

The absence of I explains an interesting detail pertaining to *be/have* confusion noted in section II.B, namely, that *have* is often substituted for *be* by deaf learners. Pollock (1989) argued that *be* and auxiliary *have* raise to I, but that the main verb *have* does not, as evidenced by differences in adverb placement. Compare the position of *always* in *John has always eaten apples* (= [27c], section III.A), which contains auxiliary *have,* and in *John always has money,* which contains the main verb *have* (cf. **John has always money.*). This difference demonstrates that the main verb *have* remains under V. Thus, the main verb *have* should be easier to acquire than *be,* hence the frequent substitution of *have* for more difficult *be* rather than vice versa.

If there is evidence that deaf learners' earlier grammars of English do not contain CP and also do not contain I, how does one account for the presence of sentential subjects, which are generally regarded as appearing in the Spec of IP position, namely, NP_2 in (25)? There is a straightforward answer to this question which is motivated not only by the deaf learner data but also on theoretical grounds. Based on the facts of various languages, some linguists have proposed that the subject of a clause actually originates in the Spec of VP position (Adv/ NP_3 in [25]). For example, Kuroda (1988) argued that in both English and Japanese a subject noun phrase originates in the Spec of VP and that in English, but not in Japanese, the subject must subsequently move up to the Spec of IP position in order to bring about certain Agreement phenomena and to facilitate wh-movement, which Japanese in fact does not permit. Because, early on, deaf learners show limited knowledge of verb agreement and tense marking as well as wh-movement, it can be proposed that, at early stages, deaf learners' clauses are VPs alone and that IP and CP are absent. Accordingly, at these stages deaf learners' clausal subjects appear in the Spec of VP position. This proposal is consistent with the view that thematic categories like VP are acquired before functional categories like IP and CP.

Deaf Learners' Noun Phrase Structure

This discussion can be extended to the data pertaining to deaf learner's knowledge of noun phrase structure. It was noted in section II that, early on, deaf learners use many nouns but no articles and no pronouns. Given Abney's (1987) DP-analysis (section III.A), in which both articles and pronouns are determiners appearing under D in (28), it would seem that deaf learners' early noun phrases are NPs rather than DPs. That is, deaf learners, like hearing children in the early patterned speech stage, have the thematic category N but not the functional category D. It was noted that, after deaf learners begin to use articles, they soon start overusing them. This overuse was attributed to the emphasis on article-plus-noun combinations in classroom instruction for deaf children (Myklebust, 1964). Furthermore, deaf learners often use articles incorrectly or omit them where they are required. Wilbur (1977) noted that it is this incorrect article usage along with incorrect pronoun usage that gives many deaf students' written compositions their characteristic "stilted effect." Clearly, the use of a class of words, when they are used incorrectly, implies only the metalinguistic awareness of that class of words rather than the successful acquisition of the category to which those words belong. Thus, deaf learners' early noun phrases appear to be NPs and not DPs.

The data from section II shed light on deaf learners' acquisition of other constituents associated with noun phrases. For example, it was noted that deaf learners have considerable difficulty with quantifiers and indefinite pronouns, both of which theoretically involve a QP (May, 1985). As indicated in (30) in section III.A, Abney (1987) proposed that QP lies along the path from DP to NP as the Complement of D. Given deaf learners' difficulty with structures associated with QP, it would appear that, along with the functional category D, deaf learners' early grammars also lack the category Q. A similar argument can be made with respect to the AP constituent. It was noted that many deaf learners of English use few or no adjectives early on. This would imply the absence of the category A, as well, from their early grammars.

Even after adjectives appear, it was noted that comparative constructions cause deaf learners great difficulty (section II.C). This fact is not surprising because, as elaborated in Abney (1987), various comparative constructions involve all three later acquired constituents, D, Q, and A. Similarly, adverbs, which appear late in deaf learners' grammars and cause persistent difficulty, are also associated with many different constituents. For example, in addition to various positions within clauses, following Abney, adverbs can appear in the Spec positions of QP and AP [not shown in (30)]. For example, in *exceedingly many very beautiful paintings, exceedingly* is in the Spec of QP position, and *very* is in the Spec of AP position.

As long as QP and AP are not acquired, adverbs associated with them would not be acquired. From all the evidence, then, deaf learners' early noun phrases appear to be NPs, rather than DPs, QPs, or APs. It seems, therefore, that it is more than the functional categories that resist acquisition. The other categories through which noun phrases are expanded also show later acquisition.

Related to the acquisition of noun phrases is the acquisition of prepositional phrases, which, following Abney (1987), consist of a P head and a DP Complement. If deaf learners' early noun phrases are NPs rather than DPs, then their early PPs must consist of a P head and an NP Complement. Abney argued that prepositions actually have the characteristics of both functional and thematic categories. They are functional in that they relate thematic constituents to one another, but many prepositions have semantic content like other thematic constituents (e.g., *beside, on top of*). The deaf learner data indicate low use of prepositions in early stages but a steady developmental increase in use and in accuracy with age. Deaf learners' early difficulty with prepositions might be attributed to their functional side. Their thematic side is perhaps what makes them more acquirable than conjunctions (see below).

Deaf Learners' Conjoined Structures

Myklebust's (1964) data revealed that deaf learners began using conjunctions later than prepositions and that the acquisition of conjunctions did not show the steady development that prepositions did. This pattern is to be expected if, as claimed by Abney (1987), conjunctions comprise a functional, rather than a thematic category. That is, although prepositions have both a thematic and a functional character, conjunctions have primarily a functional character and should resist acquisition more so than prepositions.

Actually, prepositions and conjunctions overlap in certain respects, as seen, for example, in the use of *after* both as a preposition (*after lunch*) and as a subordinating conjunction (*after we eat lunch*). Subordinate clauses are in fact frequently interpreted in linguistic analyses as consisting of a P head (the subordinating conjunction) and a clausal Complement (e.g., Reinhart, 1981). Some conjunctions and prepositions with different syntactic requirements have similar meanings. Compare, for example, *and* and *along with* as in *John and Bill eat apples* and *John along with Bill eats apples* (cf. **John along with Bill eat apples*). Given such similarities, it is possible that deaf learners at certain stages would treat prepositions and conjunctions alike. If conjunctions resist acquisition more than prepositions, one possibility is that deaf learners treat conjunctions as prepositions. In this case, not only a subordinate clause but also the second of two conjoined main clauses might actually be a PP in deaf learners' grammars.

Under such a proposal OO deletion and OS deletion sentences (section II.B) would have a principled explanation. It was noted that deaf learners often prefer such sentences over properly formed relative clause sentences. Both relative clauses and PPs can occur inside noun phrases as modifiers of the Head noun. If deaf learners perceive conjunctions as prepositions, then what appears to be a conjoined independent clause might in fact be a modifying PP clause occurring inside a noun phrase. For example, (13) and (14) in section II.B might be represented roughly as in (32a) and (32b), respectively.

(32) a. John threw [$_{NP}$ the ball [$_{PP}$ and [$_{VP}$ Mary dropped *e*]]].
      b. The boy saw [$_{NP}$ the turtles [$_{PP}$ and [$_{VP}$ *e* ate the fish]]].

The constituent *e,* a gap, is an empty pronominal category that appears in many languages as an option of UG (Chomsky, 1986b). Because it was proposed that deaf learners' grammars lack the functional category D (section III.C), the presence of an empty pronominal in such structures would be a natural mechanism for reducing redundancy where lexical pronouns were not an option. In (32), *e* receives its reference locally inside the NP, in (32a) from *the ball,* and in (32b) from *the turtles.* This analysis explains the structure of OO and OS deletion sentences and the interpretations assigned to them. Apparently, deaf learners' preference for explicit NVN sequences (section II.D) is overridden at early stages by the consequences of the absence of the functional category D.

IV. LEARNABILTY AND DEAF LEARNERS' SYNTACTIC KNOWLEDGE

After many years of exposure to English, many deaf learners still show only relative degrees of success in mastering English syntax. Furthermore, success orders among groups of structures seem to indicate that certain structures are more learnable than others. For example, as noted in section II.D, deaf learners were quite successful on adverbial clauses but quite unsuccessful on relative clauses. Berent and Samar (1990) pointed out that, in terms of markedness, many of the details of deaf learners' English knowledge reported in the literature (e.g., Quigley & King, 1980) suggest greater knowledge of the unmarked properties of English and less knowledge of the marked properties of English. This section reviews the few studies that have explored deaf learners' relative knowledge of particular English structures specifically in the context of Learnability Theory.

A. Binding Principles and Learnability

Berent and Samar (1990) explored deaf learners' knowledge of certain kinds of English pronouns in the context of Wexler and Manzini's (1987) parametric theory of learnability. Following Chomsky (1981, 1986b), principles of UG have parameters associated with them, which have different values from language to language. In acquiring a language, a learner is assumed to arrive at the correct value of a particular parameter after sufficient exposure to positive language evidence (i.e., grammatical sentences). One parameter of UG proposed by Wexler and Manzini is the Governing Category Parameter (GCP), which is associated with Chomsky's (1981) Binding Principles. The Binding Principles stipulate conditions on the interpretation of pronouns and other nominal expressions. (Chapters 2–4 by Gregg, White, and Flynn discuss L2 acquisition as parameter (re)setting.) (The role of the Governing Category Parameter and Binding Principles (or Conditions) in L2 acquisition is discussed in chapters 3 by White, 5 by Schachter and 10 by Gass.)

The GCP can be illustrated using sentence (33).

(33)   [$_3$ Bill wants [$_2$ John to discuss [$_1$ *Tom*'s criticism of *himself*]]]

Following Chomsky's (1981) Binding Principle A, a reflexive pronoun like *himself* must have an antecedent inside a certain domain called a governing category. Potential governing categories are bracketed in (33). In English, the governing category is the smallest possible one, the innermost bracketing labeled 1 (*Tom's criticism of himself*). As indicated by the italics, *Tom* is the only possible antecedent for *himself* inside governing category 1. Other languages, however, can have larger governing categories. If, for example, a language has governing category 2 (*John to discuss Tom's criticism of himself*), then in an analogous sentence in that language, either *Tom* or *John* (but not *Bill*) could be the antecedent of *himself.* As indicated by the numbering, the two possible interpretations are equivalent to two different sentences. So, if a language had governing category 3 (i.e., the whole sentence), any of the names in (33) could be the antecedent of *himself* and the sentence would really represent three sentences of the language.

As demonstrated by Wexler and Manzini (1987), the language resulting from having the GCP set at value 1 in (33) is a subset of language resulting from having the parameter set at value 2, which is a subset of the language resulting from having the parameter set at value 3. That is, the language based on value 2 contains all of the grammatical sentences resulting from value 1, plus additional sentences, and the language based on value 3 contains all of the grammatical sentences resulting from value 2, plus additional sentences.

From the learnability standpoint, Wexler and Manzini (1987) argued that GCP value 1, which defines the smallest language with respect to Binding Principle A, is the unmarked or default value. Value 2, which defines a larger language, is more marked than value 1, and value 3, which defines the largest language, is the most marked GCP value. This markedness hierarchy derives from the Subset Principle (SP), a general learning principle which Berwick (1985) claimed guides many aspects of language acquisition. As interpreted by Wexler and Manzini, the SP stipulates that the language learner acquires the smallest language compatible with the available language input, but only for parameters with values that yield languages that are subsets of one another, as in the case of the GCP. Because learners of English will never encounter evidence that *John* or *Bill* is the antecedent of *himself* in (33), the SP guarantees that they would never select GCP value 2 or 3 for English reflexive pronouns. If a learner did select one of those values, there would never be a way to retreat to the correct value 1 defining a smaller language, because all new positive evidence would be consistent with the larger, incorrect language because it contains all potential sentences of the smaller language. (The Subset Principle and its putative role in L2 acquisition are discussed in chapters 2 by Gregg, 3 by White, 10 by Gass, and 13 by Long. Chapter 18 by Seliger suggests a role for this principle in accounting for the form of L1 attrition. Finally, chapter 16 by Andersen and Shirai applies the notion to the acquisition of verb aspect.)

Because deaf learners experience a severe restriction in spoken language input, they might have access to the minimal positive evidence required to set an unmarked parameter value but insufficient access to the considerable positive evidence required to set a marked parameter value. With respect to (33), from the developmental perspective, GCP value 1 would be predicted to be the "easiest" value to acquire and value 3 the "hardest" value to acquire.[8]

Interestingly, with respect to personal pronouns like *him* in (34), Chomsky's (1981) Binding Principle B stipulates, roughly, that a personal pronoun cannot have an antecedent inside its governing category but may have an antecedent outside the governing category.

(34)   [$_1$ *Bill* wants [$_2$ *John* to discuss [$_3$ Tom's criticism of *him*]]]

English also has the smallest possible governing category for personal pronouns, the one labeled 3 in (34). In this case, the learnability implication is the opposite of that for reflexive pronouns. With governing category 3, (34) represents three different sentences, one in which *John* is the antecedent of *him,* one in which *Bill* is the antecedent of *him,* and one in which *him* can refer to someone outside the sentence, which is always an option with personal pronouns. Furthermore, with the larger governing category 2, there are actually fewer possible sentences—in this case, two—than with governing category 3: one in which *Bill* is the antecedent of *him* and one in which *him* has an external referent. Finally, with the largest governing category labeled 1, (34) represents only one sentence, where *him* can only have an external referent.

From the learnability standpoint, Wexler and Manzini (1987) argued that, with

---

[8]The SP, as articulated by Wexler and Manzini (1987), says nothing about acquisition orders or success orders. However, Wexler (1993) argued that the SP in fact does predict acquisition orders and that a child learning a language with a more marked parameter value might exhibit an interim grammar with a less marked value. The data on deaf learners reported here supports such developmental predictions of the SP.

respect to personal pronouns and Binding Principle B, GCP value 3 in (34), the English value, now defines the largest language and is accordingly the most marked value, the hardest for a language learner to acquire. Value 2 defines a smaller language and, being less marked, should be easier to acquire. Value 1 defines the smallest language and, being the least marked, should be the easiest to acquire.

In assessing deaf college students' knowledge of the antecedent restrictions associated with sentences like (33) and (34), Berent and Samar (1990) verified the SP's learnability (and developmental) predictions for the GCP and thereby provided evidence in support of the psychological reality of the SP as a determinant of language learning. Specifically, deaf college students with fairly low overall general English skills showed knowledge of the correct and easiest-to-learn value 1 in (33) for English reflexive pronouns, but at the same time they showed a lack of knowledge of the correct, but hardest-to-learn value 3 in (34) for English personal pronouns. In fact, they showed knowledge of the incorrect, but easiest-to-learn, value 1, an option in some languages but not in English. Thus, the severe restriction in spoken language input experienced by many deaf learners appears to result in the acquisition of "smaller languages."[9]

B. Movement Rules and Learnability

Relative Clause Learnability

Berent (1994a) extended the learnability perspective of Wexler and Manzini (1987) and Berent and Samar (1990) to deaf learners' knowledge of English relative clauses. He explored deaf college students' knowledge of a variety of relative clause structures including those in (35), in which a wh-word moves to Spec of CP, leaving its trace [t] in the position marking its true grammatical relation within the clause (see sections II.B and III.A).

(35)   a. Louise likes the teacher [who [[t] explained the answer to the visitor]].
       b. Vicky shot the burglar [who [the captain caught [t] in the house]].
       c. Kathy misses the teenager [who [the baby poured the milk on [t]]].

Languages differ as to which positions in a clause may be "relativized" (Keenan & Comrie, 1977). There are some languages that can relativize only the subject position as in (35a), others that relativize both the subject position as in (35a) and the direct object position as in (35b), and still others, like English, that can relativize those positions and the object of a preposition as in (35c). (For additional

---

[9]Using the methodology employed in Berent and Samar (1990), Berent, Samar, Gass, and Plough (1994) assessed the GCP values of hearing adult learners of ESL. They obtained results similar to those reported in Berent and Samar (1990). Specifically, the adult L2 learners displayed greater knowledge of the unmarked GCP value for English reflexive pronouns, but the L2 learners at lower levels of ESL proficiency displayed less knowledge of the marked GCP value for English personal pronouns.

discussion of the noun phrase accessibility hierarchy in L2 acquisition, see chapters 4 by Flynn, 6 by Eckman, and 13 by Long. In addition, chapter 6 includes a general treatment of the hierarchy with examples. Chapter 18 by Seliger treats the role of the hierarchy in L1 attrition.)

Reinterpreting relativizable positions in terms of how far a wh-word moves to Spec of CP in various languages, Berent (1994a) proposed a Relative Clause Parameter with easier and harder-to-learn values similar to Wexler and Manzini's (1987) GCP (section IV.A). Languages that form only subject relatives have the value defining the smallest language, the easiest-to-learn value in accordance with the SP. Languages that form both subject and direct object relatives have a value defining a larger language, and languages that form subject, direct object, and object of preposition relatives have the value defining the largest language, the hardest-to-learn value.

In accordance with the SP and the learnability predictions for values of the Relative Clause Parameter, Berent (1994a) hypothesized that deaf college students would exhibit greater knowledge of relative clause sentences like (35a), less knowledge of sentences like (35b), and still less knowledge of sentences like (35c). The students performed as predicted. Along with the results of Berent and Samar (1990), these results provided further support for the psychological reality of the SP.

Wh-question Learnability

Support for the learnability predictions of the SP was also provided in Berent (in press), a study of deaf college students' knowledge of English wh-questions (cf. section II.B and see [26c], section III.A). As with relative clauses, wh-questions involve the movement of a wh-word to Spec of CP via wh-movement with a trace marking the position of the grammatical relation assigned to the wh-word. Berent assessed students' knowledge of structures like (36), in which various constituents within the matrix (i.e., main) clause are questioned, and (37), in which various constituents within the embedded (i.e., subordinate) clause are questioned.

(36) a. Who [[t] gave the bomb to the soldier]?
      b. Who [did [the wife leave [t] on the road]]?
      c. Who [did [the boy pour the milk on [t]]]?
(37) a. Who [did [Mary say [[t] gave the bomb to the soldier]]]?
      b. Who [did [Judy dream [the wife left [t] on the road]]]?
      c. Who [does [Kathy think [the boy poured the milk on [t]]]]?

In (36a,b,c), *who* has moved to Spec of CP from the subject, direct object, and prepositional object position, respectively, of a matrix clause. In (37a,b,c), *who* has moved to Spec of CP from the subject, direct object, and prepositional object position, respectively, of embedded clauses that are Complements to the matrix verbs *say, dream,* and *think,* respectively.

English permits question formation via wh-movement from all of the positions illustrated in (36) and (37). Other languages permit question formation via wh-movement only from matrix positions as in (36), and still other languages do not permit question formation via wh-movement at all. With respect to these language types, the number of positions that can be questioned via wh-movement appears to be parameterized in a fashion similar to the GCP (section IV.A) and the Relative Clause Parameter (section IV.B). From the learnability perspective, Berent (in press) proposed a wh-question parameter of which no wh-movement is predicted to be the easiest value to learn; wh-movement from a matrix clause is predicted to be a harder value to learn, and wh-movement from either a matrix clause or an embedded clause is predicted to be the hardest value to learn (cf. Roeper & de Villiers, 1992).

The results of Berent (in press) supported these learnability predictions. Deaf college students with relatively low general English proficiency showed evidence of the easiest-to-learn parameter value, exhibiting little knowledge of wh-movement, although students at higher levels of general English proficiency exhibited varying degrees of success on the target sentences, approximating the harder parameter values. Again, even after years of exposure to English input, many deaf learners acquire smaller languages from the learnability perspective.[10]

C. *Be* as a Raising Verb

There are other kinds of movement besides wh-movement. For example, passive sentences (section II.B) involve the movement of a noun phrase in object position to an empty subject position. Recently, Samar and Berent (1993) demonstrated that, even at relatively high levels of general English proficiency, deaf college students continue to experience difficulty with certain subtle kinds of syntactic movement, which are apparently difficult to learn despite a greater ability to compensate for restricted spoken language input.

It was proposed by Burzio (1986), Stowell (1983), and others that English sentences containing the verb *be* involve the movement of a noun phrase from a lower position within the sentence to an empty subject position, just as passive sentences do. This movement is in addition to the movement of *be* itself from V to I, following Pollock's (1989) analysis (section III.A). According to these proposals, a sentence like (38b) is derived from an underlying structure like (38a), where the dash

---

[10]With respect to L2 acquisition by hearing learners, White (1989) and others have argued that L2 acquisition orders in many cases do not follow the learnability predictions derived from the SP, in other words, that unmarked values are not necessarily acquired before marked values. However, Berent (1994b) and MacLaughlin (1995) demonstrated that several of the UG parameters that White (1989) and others have investigated in this regard do not have values ordered as proper subsets of one another. Therefore, the SP does not apply to such parameters and makes no predictions for acquisition orders in these cases.

represents the empty subject position and [t] is the trace of *a book,* which has moved into the empty subject position in (38b).

(38) a. [___ [is [*a book* on the table]]].
      b. [*A book* [is [[t] on the table]]].

In a psycholinguistic reaction time experiment employing hearing college students, Samar and Berent (1991) provided evidence in support of the psychological reality of the movement analysis of *be* sentences and against the traditional analysis of *be* sentences, which does not posit an empty subject position and hence no movement.

In a follow-up study, Samar and Berent (1993) applied the same techniques as in Samar and Berent (1991) to determine whether there was evidence that *be* sentences involved movement in the "mental grammars" of deaf college students as there was for hearing college students. Deaf students with relatively low general English language proficiency showed no consistent knowledge of any of the movement structures targeted. In contrast, the deaf students with high general English language proficiency did show evidence of movement in their representations of passive sentences and other movement sentences but did not show any evidence in their mental grammars of movement in *be* sentences. Samar and Berent (1993) concluded that the restriction of spoken language input resulting from deafness can impede acquisition of certain exceptional properties of verbs even when general English language proficiency is otherwise quite high, and even where students show knowledge of other movement structures.

V. CONCLUSION

Like young hearing children in the early patterned speech stage of English language acquisition (section III.B), deaf learners of English appear to lack a C system, an I system, and a D system in early documentable stages of English acquisition (section III.C). For many deaf learners this situation persists for years, as evidenced by the nonacquisition or partial acquisition of many of the structures implying the presence of the functional categories C, I, and D. However, deaf learners' early low use of English adjectives and their difficulty with quantifiers, among other structures, suggest that their acquisition of English syntax is not explained exclusively by the dichotomy between thematic and functional categories. Adjectives, for example, comprise one of the thematic categories.

Section IV addressed how the SP can be invoked to explain some acquisitional phenomena associated with deaf learners of English: pronoun interpretation, relative clauses, *wh*-questions, and so on. From the learnability perspective, deaf learners appear to learn smaller spoken languages. Strong support for the SP based on deaf learner data is consistent with Wilbur and Goodhart's (1985) assessment, with respect to the semantic complexity of indefinite pronouns and quantifiers (section II.C), that deaf learners' knowledge of English is associated more clearly with the intrinsic complexity of structures because they are less influenced than hearing learners by pragmatic and other extrinsic factors. To the extent that this assessment is valid and to the extent that the SP predicts language acquisition generally, deaf learner data would be expected to support the learnability implications of the SP more unambiguously than hearing learner data.

There is another respect in which many deaf learners appear to learn smaller languages relative to the target, standard language. It was proposed in section III.C that deaf learners' early clauses are VPs. With reference to (25) in section III.A, the VP constituent is contained within IP, which is contained within CP. A language in which clauses are VPs is smaller than a language in which clauses are IPs or CPs because it lacks sentences with wh-movement structures, Subject–Verb Agreement morphology, and so on. It was noted in section II.B that deaf learners were relatively more successful on yes–no questions than on wh-questions. Because modals and *do* appear under I in (25), and under the assumption that the subject of a clause originates as an NP in the Spec of VP position, a yes–no question could be formed at an intermediate stage of acquisition exclusively within IP. That is, Subject–Auxiliary Inversion and *do*-support would not require the C constituent at that stage. On the other hand, wh-questions would imply the presence in the grammar of both IP and CP, because two functional positions are required, I for the auxiliary and C for the wh-word. Thus, with respect to the successful acquisition of English phrase structure, there is evidence that deaf learners' clauses grow, bottom up, from VP to IP to CP, each successive stage leading to a larger language.

With respect to English noun phrase structure, the assertion in section III.C that deaf learners' early noun phrases are NPs rather than DPs also indicates the learning of smaller languages initially. With reference to (30) in section III.A, NP is contained within AP, which is contained within QP, which is contained within DP. Bottom-up acquisition of noun phrase structure would mean that deaf learners' noun phrases grow from NP to AP to QP to DP. There does seem to be evidence in support of this development inasmuch as nouns appear earlier than adjectives, and quantifiers remain troublesome, as do articles and pronouns. However, teasing out the details of noun phrase development would require finer analysis of some sort.

The general conclusion of this chapter is that, under conditions of severely restricted spoken language input, deaf learners tend to learn smaller languages. However, it must be emphasized that deaf learners of English represent a broad range of English language abilities and that many deaf learners attain English language knowledge substantially no different from hearing learners' knowledge (see footnote 3). That is, some deaf learners of English compensate for the severe restriction of available spoken language input and more successfully "digest" the input required to learn larger languages. How they compensate in this way is not clear. The effects of early intervention, educational approach, and language teaching methodology have been difficult to assess. There is a great need for more research in all areas pertaining to language and deafness to better understand the mechanisms of spoken language acquisition by deaf persons and also to find better methods for facilitating the learning of English in educational settings.[11]

ACKNOWLEDGMENTS

This research was conducted at the National Technical Institute for the Deaf, a college of Rochester Institute of Technology, in the course of an agreement with the U.S. Department of Education. I am indebted to Vince Samar for valuable comments during the development of this chapter and to Stephanie Polowe and Erik Drasgow for their feedback on an earlier draft.

REFERENCES

Abney, S. P. (1987). *The English noun phrase in its sentential aspect.* Unpublished doctoral dissertation, MIT, Cambridge, MA.
Berent, G. P. (1983). Control judgments by deaf adults and by second language learners. *Language Learning, 33,* 37–53.
Berent, G. P. (1988). An assessment of syntactic capabilities. In M. Strong (Ed.), *Language learning and deafness* (pp. 133–161). Cambridge, UK: Cambridge University Press.
Berent, G. P. (1993). Improvements in the English syntax of deaf college students. *American Annals of the Deaf, 138,* 55–61.
Berent, G. P. (1994a). *Noun phrase accessibility and relative clause learnability.* Manuscript submitted for publication.
Berent, G. P. (1994b). The subset principle in second-language acquisition. In E. E. Tarone, S. M. Gass, & A. D. Cohen (Eds.), *Research methodology in second-language acquisition* (pp. 17–39). Hillsdale, NJ: Erlbaum.
Berent, G. P. (in press). Learnability constraints on deaf learners' acquisition of English *wh*-questions. *Journal of Speech and Hearing Research.*

[11] One recent promising method for facilitating deaf children's English language learning is reported in Kelly et al. (1994). Kelly et al. report on the use of interactive personal captioning technology with severely and profoundly deaf children aged 8–12 as a means of enhancing written English language skills. The participating students provided English captions to ASL videotapes over a 36-week period. They showed significant increases in their use of function words relative to content words, in the use of gerunds and participles, in the correct use of verbal morphology, and in their English grammatical knowledge generally.

Berent, G. P., & Samar, V. J. (1990). The psychological reality of the subset principle: Evidence from the governing categories of prelingually deaf adults. *Language 66,* 714–741.

Berent, G. P., Samar, V. J., Gass, S. M., & Plough, I. C. (1994, October). *Second language acquisition of English anaphors and pronominals: Adult learner evidence for the subset principle.* Paper presented at the Second Language Research Forum, Montreal, Canada.

Berwick, R. C. (1985). *The acquisition of syntactic knowledge.* Cambridge, MA: MIT Press.

Bochner, J. H. (1982). English in the deaf population. In D. G. Sims, G. G. Walter, & R. L. Whitehead (Eds.), *Deafness and communication: Assessment and training* (pp. 107–123). Baltimore: Williams & Wilkins.

Bochner, J. H., & Albertini, J. A. (1988). Language varieties in the deaf population and their acquisition by children and adults. In M. Strong (Ed.), *Language learning and deafness* (pp. 3–48). Cambridge, UK: Cambridge University Press.

Brannon, J. B. (1968). Linguistic word classes in the spoken language of normal, hard-of-hearing, and deaf children. *Journal of Speech and Hearing Research, 11,* 279–287.

Burzio, L. (1986). *Italian syntax: A government-binding approach.* Dordrecht: Reidel.

Chomsky, N. (1957). *Syntactic structures.* The Hague: Mouton.

Chomsky, N. (1965). *Aspects of the theory of syntax.* Cambridge, MA: MIT Press.

Chomsky, N. (1977). On wh-movement. In P. W. Culicover, T. Wasow, & A. Akmajian (Eds.), *Formal syntax* (pp. 71–132). New York: Academic Press.

Chomsky, N. (1980). On binding. *Linguistic Inquiry, 11,* 1–46.

Chomsky, N. (1981). *Lectures on government and binding.* Dordrecht: Foris.

Chomsky, N. (1986a). *Barriers.* Cambridge, MA: MIT Press.

Chomsky, N. (1986b). *Knowledge of language: Its nature, origin, and use.* New York: Praeger.

Cooper, R. L., & Rosenstein, J. (1966). Language acquisition of deaf children. *The Volta Review, 68,* 58–67.

Davidson, D. M. (1978). *Test of ability to subordinate.* New York: Language Innovations.

Davis, H., & Silverman, S. R. (1978). *Hearing and deafness* (4th ed.). New York: Holt, Rinehart, & Winston.

Déprez, V., & Pierce, A. (1993). Negation and functional projections in early grammar. *Linguistic Inquiry, 24,* 25–67.

de Villiers, P. A. (1988). Assessing English syntax in hearing-impaired children: Eliciting production in pragmatically-motivated situations. In R. R. Kretschmer & L. W. Kretschmer (Eds.), *Communication assessment of hearing-impaired children: From conversation to the classroom* (pp. 41–71). (Monograph supplement of *The Journal of the Academy of Rehabilitative Audiology, 21*)

Goda, S. (1964). Spoken syntax of normal, deaf, and retarded adolescents. *Journal of Verbal Learning and Verbal Behavior, 3,* 401–405.

Gross, D., & de Villiers, P. A. (1983). Acquisition of coordinate sentences in oral deaf children. *Proceedings of the Wisconsin Symposium on Research in Child Language Disorders, 5,* 21–34.

Heider, F. K., & Heider, G. M. (1940). A comparison of sentence structure of deaf and hearing children. *Psychological Monographs, 52,* 42–103.

Jackendoff, R. (1977). *X-bar syntax: A study of phrase structure* (Linguistic Inquiry Monograph No. 2). Cambridge, MA: MIT Press.

Keenan, E. L., & Comrie, B. (1977). Noun phrase accessibility and universal grammar. *Linguistic Inquiry, 8,* 63–99.

Kelly, R. R., Samar, V. J., Loeterman, M., Berent, G. P., Parasnis, I., Kirchner, C. J., Fischer, S., Brown, P., & Murphy, C. (1994). CC school project: Personal captioning technology applied to the language learning environment of deaf children. *Technology and Disability, 3,* 26–38.

Kretschmer, R. R., & Kretschmer, L. W. (1978). *Language development and intervention with the hearing impaired.* Baltimore: University Park Press.

Kretschmer, R. R., & Kretschmer, L. W. (1986). Language in perspective. In D. M. Luterman (Ed.), *Deafness in perspective* (pp. 131–166). San Diego: College-Hill Press.

Kuroda, S.-Y. (1988). Whether we agree or not: A comparative syntax of English and Japanese. *Lingvisticae Investigationes, 12,* 1–47.

Luterman, D. M. (Ed.). (1986). *Deafness in perspective.* San Diego, CA: College Hill Press.

MacGinitie, W. H. (1964). Ability of deaf children to use different word classes. *Journal of Speech and Hearing Research, 7,* 141–150.

MacLaughlin, D. (1995). Language acquisition and the subset principle. *The Linguistic Review, 12,* 143–191.

Marschark, M. (1993). *Psychological development of deaf children.* New York: Oxford University Press.

May, R. (1985). *Logical form: Its structure and derivation.* Cambridge, MA: MIT Press.

Meier, R. P., & Newport, E. L. (1990). Out of the hands of babes: On a possible sign advantage in language acquisition. *Language, 66,* 1–23.

Michigan Test of English Language Proficiency. (1977). Ann Arbor: University of Michigan, English Language Institute.

Myklebust, H. R. (1964). *The psychology of deafness: Sensory deprivation, learning, and adjustment* (2nd ed.). New York: Grune & Stratton.

Newport, E. L., & Meier, R. P. (1985). The acquisition of American Sign Language. In D. I. Slobin (Ed.), *The crosslinguistic study of language acquisition: Vol. 1. The data* (pp. 881–938). Hillsdale, NJ: Erlbaum.

Pinhas, J., & Lust, B. (1987). Principles of pronoun anaphora in the acquisition of oral language by the hearing-impaired. In B. Lust (Ed.), *Studies in the acquisition of anaphora: Vol. 2. Applying the constraints* (pp. 189–224). Dordrecht: Reidel.

Pollock, J.-Y. (1989). Verb movement, universal grammar, and the structure of IP. *Linguistic Inquiry, 20,* 365–424.

Power, D. J., & Quigley, S. P. (1973). Deaf children's acquisition of the passive voice. *Journal of Speech and Hearing Research, 16,* 5–11.

Pressnell, L. M. (1973). Hearing-impaired children's comprehension and production of syntax in oral language. *Journal of Speech and Hearing Research, 16,* 12–21.

Quigley, S. P., & King, C. M. (1980). Syntactic performance of hearing impaired and normal hearing individuals. *Applied Psycholinguistics, 1,* 329–356.

Quigley, S. P., & King, C. M. (1982). The language development of deaf children and youth. In S. Rosenberg (Ed.), *Handbook of applied psycholinguistics* (pp. 429–475). Hillsdale, NJ: Erlbaum.

Quigley, S. P., & Kretschmer, R. E. (1982). *The education of deaf children: Issues, theory, and practice.* Baltimore: University Park Press.

Quigley, S. P., Montanelli, D. S., & Wilbur, R. B. (1976). Some aspects of the verb system in the language of deaf students. *Journal of Speech and Hearing Research, 19,* 536–550.

Quigley, S. P., & Paul, P. V. (1984). *Language and deafness.* San Diego, CA: College-Hill Press.

Quigley, S. P., & Paul, P. V. (1987). Deafness and language development. In S. Rosenberg (Ed.), *Advances in applied psycholinguistics: Vol. 1. Disorders of first language development* (pp. 180–219). Cambridge, UK: Cambridge University Press.

Quigley, S. P., Power, D. J., & Steinkamp, M. W. (1977). The language structure of deaf children. *The Volta Review, 79,* 73–84.

Quigley, S. P., Smith, N. L., & Wilbur, R. B. (1974). Comprehension of relativized sentences by deaf students. *Journal of Speech and Hearing Research, 17,* 325–341.

Quigley, S. P., Steinkamp, M., Power, D. J., & Jones, B. (1978). *Test of syntactic abilities.* Beaverton, OR: Dormac.

Quigley, S. P., Wilbur, R. B., & Montanelli, D. S. (1974). Question formation in the language of deaf students. *Journal of Speech and Hearing Research, 17,* 699–713.

Quigley, S. P., Wilbur, R. B., & Montanelli, D. S. (1976). Complement structures in the language of deaf students. *Journal of Speech and Hearing Research, 19,* 448–457.

Quigley, S. P., Wilbur, R. B., Power, D. J., Montanelli, D. S., & Steinkamp, M. W. (1976). *Syntactic structures in the language of deaf children.* Urbana, IL: Institute for Child Behavior and Development.

Radford, A. (1988). Small children's small clauses. *Transactions of the Philological Society, 86,* 1–43.

Radford, A. (1990). The syntax of nominal arguments in early child English. *Language Acquisition, 1,* 195–223.

Radford, A. (1994). Tense and agreement variability in child grammars of English. In B. Lust, M. Suner, & J. Whitman (Eds.), *Syntactic theory and first language acquisition: Cross-linguistic perspectives: Vol. 1. Heads, projections, and learnability* (pp. 135–157). Hillsdale, NJ: Erlbaum.

Reinhart, T. (1981). Definite NP anaphora and c-command domains. *Linguistic Inquiry, 12,* 605–636.

Roeper, T., & de Villiers, J. (1992). Ordered decisions in the acquisition of wh-questions. In J. Weissenborn, H. Goodluck, & T. Roeper (Eds.), *Theoretical issues in language acquisition* (pp. 191–236). Hillsdale, NJ: Erlbaum.

Samar, V. J., & Berent, G. P. (1991). BE is a raising verb: Psycholinguistic evidence. *Journal of Psycholinguistic Research, 20,* 419–443.

Samar, V. J., & Berent, G. P. (1993). Is *be* a raising verb in the mental English grammars of congenitally deaf adults? In A. Crochetiere, J.-C. Boulanger, & C. Ouellon (Eds.), *Actes du XVe Congres International des Linguistes (Proceedings of the 15th International Congress of Linguists), 3,* 529–532. Sainte-Foy, Quebec, Canada: Presses de l'Université Laval.

Slobin, D. I. (1966). Grammatical transformations and sentence comprehension in childhood and adulthood. *Journal of Verbal Learning and Verbal Behavior, 5,* 219–227.

Stowell, T. (1983). Subjects across categories. *Linguistic Review, 2,* 285–312.

Strong, M. (Ed.). (1988). *Language learning and deafness.* Cambridge, UK: Cambridge University Press.

Stuckless, E. R., & Marks, C. H. (1966). *Assessment of the written language of deaf students.* Pittsburgh: University of Pittsburgh, School of Education.

Swisher, M. V. (1989). The language learning situation of deaf students. *TESOL Quarterly, 23,* 239–257.

Van Cleve, J. V. (Ed.). (1987). *Gallaudet encyclopedia of deaf people and deafness.* New York: McGraw-Hill.

Wexler, K. (1993). The subset principle is an intensional principle. In E. Reuland & W. Abraham (Eds.), *Knowledge and language: Vol. 1. From Orwell's problem to Plato's problem* (pp. 217–239). Dordrecht: Kluwer.

Wexler, K., & Manzini, M. R. (1987). Parameters and learnability in binding theory. In T. Roeper & E. Williams (Eds.), *Parameter setting* (pp. 41–76). Dordrecht: Reidel.

White, L. (1989). *Universal grammar and second language acquisition.* Amsterdam: John Benjamins.

Wilbur, R. B. (1977). An explanation of deaf children's difficulty with certain syntactic structures of English. *The Volta Review, 79,* 85–92.

Wilbur, R. B. (1987). *American sign language: Linguistic and applied dimensions* (2nd ed.). Boston: College Hill Press.

Wilbur, R. B., & Goodhart, W. C. (1985). Comprehension of indefinite pronouns and quantifiers by hearing-impaired students. *Applied Psycholinguistics, 6,* 417–434.

Wilbur, R., Goodhart, W., & Montandon, E. (1983). Comprehension of nine syntactic structures by hearing-impaired students. *The Volta Review, 85,* 328–345.

Wilbur, R. B., Montanelli, D. S., & Quigley, S. P. (1976). Pronominalization in the language of deaf students. *Journal of Speech and Hearing Research, 19,* 120–140.

Wilbur, R. B., Quigley, S. P., & Montanelli, D. S. (1975). Conjoined structures in the language of deaf students. *Journal of Speech and Hearing Research, 18,* 319–335.

THE NEUROPSYCHOLOGY OF SECOND LANGUAGE ACQUISITION AND USE

C H A P T E R 1 5

NEUROLINGUISTICS OF SECOND LANGUAGE ACQUISITION AND USE

Loraine K. Obler and Sharon Hannigan

I. INTRODUCTION

For the first half of the past century, neurologists' and psychologists' interests in bilingualism were substantially independent. (See chapters 17–19 by Romaine, Seliger, and Bhatia and Ritchie, this volume, for discussion of various aspects of bilingualism.) For European neurologists the focus developed from observing language breakdown in bilingual and multilingual aphasics—individuals with language disturbance resulting from brain damage. In a series of small group studies over the last decade of the nineteenth century and the first half of this century, they argued either that Pitres (1895) was right in positing that the language used most frequently preceding the aphasia-producing incident would return first, or that Ribot (1881) was right in positing that what is first learned is most likely to remain after breakdown. (Note that Ribot himself did not talk explicitly about bilingualism.) Only in 1977 did Paradis, a linguist, break through these discussions. By limiting his attention to which language returned first, he developed a more refined notion of possible patterns of recovery and breakdown in aphasia, with their implications for gross brain organization of language premorbidly.

In the mid-1960s (with the publication of Gloning & Gloning, 1965) a second theme emerged in the neurology literature. It centered on whether, in fact, polyglot aphasics evidence more crossed aphasia (aphasia in right-handers resulting from a lesion to the right rather than the left hemisphere) than did monolinguals. At

509

issue was the question of the basic lateral organization of responsibility for languages within the brain of the bilingual.

By contrast, psychologists, after Ribot, were concerned primarily with issues of "intelligence" as it relates to bilingualism. By the mid-1950s, Ervin and Osgood (1954) developed the theoretical constructs of *compound, coordinate,* and *subordinate* bilingualism, and Weinreich (1953) contributed a comprehensive discussion of such phenomena as interference, switching, and transfer in second language (L2) acquisition and use, along with descriptive taxonomies of factors likely to account for the wide range of bilingual proficiency observed. With the emergence of the field of L2 acquisition in the 1960s, a few new concepts were introduced, such as interlanguage (IL), from which arose the notions of acquisition orders and developmental sequences (see Larsen-Freeman & Long, 1991, pp. 88–96).

The 1950s also marked a period of substantial growth for the discipline of neuropsychology. This was largely due to the development of noninvasive techniques for the study of the lateral organization of language representation (and other abilities). Of these the most noteworthy are tachistoscopic and dichotic presentation of stimuli, procedures that were employed to investigate the organization of languages in bilinguals through the 1960s, 1970s, and to some extent in the 1980s. These techniques, which have been virtually supplanted by more sophisticated technologies, represent the first integration of neurolinguistic and psychological approaches to the study of L2 acquisition and bilingualism.

In 1967, the Critical Period Hypothesis (CPH) suggesting biological constraints for primary language (L1) acquisition was proposed by Lenneberg in his benchmark publication, *Biological Foundations of Language.* Although L2 acquisition was clearly not a part of his central thesis, he did make glancing reference to it— evidently for the sole pupose of strengthening his core argument. However modest, Lenneberg's mention of foreign language acquisition sparked considerable debate within linguistic circles with regard to a critical period for L2 acquisition which, in its revised form (the Sensitive Period Hypothesis), has ensued throughout the 1980s and into the 1990s. Only recently have researchers begun to find ways to test and find some support for this hypothesis.

Throughout the 1960s and 1970s, psychologists and English as a Second Language (ESL) practitioners studied factors underlying successful L2 acquisition. With the entry of neurolinguists into this field in the 1980s, neurolinguistic studies of talent in L2 acquisition have been reported, and theoretical understandings of brain areas that might plausibly be involved in L2 acquisition and maintenance have been developed (primarily in Lamendella, 1977, and more recently, Jacobs, 1988, and Schumann, 1990).

In this chapter, we endeavor to present the major developments in the neurolinguistics of L2 acquisition of the past two decades (for a review of earlier literature in this area, see Albert & Obler, 1978). As is the case with most comprehensive reviews, the selection of a primary structuring device (chronology, theory, research methods, etc.) has proven difficult given the multiplicity of pertinent perspectives, levels, and disciplines.

In this chapter our structure follows that of the human life span, with first a focus on L2 acquisition in childhood and then postchildhood acquisition. Central to a developmental framework are the issues of the Critical and Sensitive Period hypotheses and talented L2 acquisition from the neurolinguistic perspective. Subsequently, we turn to neurolinguistic knowledge of L2 proficiency and use, with particular attention paid to the concept of lateral organization of language. Here we also present relatively new evidence for the organization of L1 faculties exclusively within the left hemisphere (the so-called within-hemisphere hypothesis), as well as language-specific effects on the organization of two or more languages. Finally, we discuss the literature on language breakdown in aphasia and frank dementia, along with language attrition in normals, for the purpose of understanding what this research tells us, by implication, about L2 acquisition.

For the purposes of this chapter our definition of bilingualism will be broad: reasonable proficiency in two or more languages, at least in the oral–aural modalities. L2 acquisition, for our purpose, will be any process en route to such bilingualism.

II. THE PROCESS OF L2 ACQUISITION

A. A Critical or Sensitive Period

Recall that Lenneberg (1967) never explicitly developed the CPH to deal with L2 acquisition, although he did mention the possibility. In the earlier literature debating the existence of the CPH for L2 acquirers, the question centered on what age delimited such a period. Scovel (1969, 1988) posited puberty for pronunciation, as Lenneberg had; Krashen (1973) reviewed the scant literature on the laterality studies in bilingual children and brought the critical age down to 5. Although Scovel focused primarily on phonology, the debate continued with researchers like Snow and Hoefnagel-Hohle (1978) arguing that adults could learn language as well as children when given similar opportunities.

Eventually, researchers realized that the question could not be phrased, Are children or adults better acquirers of an L2? Instead, one had to distinguish whether by "better" one refers to the *rate* of acquisition or rather, to the *ultimate levels of proficiency.* Krashen, Long, and Scarcella (1979) noted on the basis of the literature they reviewed that older learners acquire L2s faster, but in the long run younger learners become more proficient. Oyama (1976) demonstrated that earlier age of acquisition correlated with less accent in childhood; Patkowski (1980) reported greater ability to acquire morphosyntax prepuberty. By this time, however, authors such as Seliger (1978) had already proposed multiple critical periods, thus raising the possibility that different maturational constraints operated on different skills. In the 1980s the notion of a critical period was further relaxed to sensitive periods (Lamendella, 1977, had considered a single sensitive period, in place of a critical period). In his review and structuring of the literature, Long (1990) integrated these notions into a theory of multiple sensitive periods for different aspects of L1 as well as L2 acquisition. He reviews the classes of explanations that have been postulated to account for age-related differences in L2 acquisition (social, psychological, affective factors, input factors, cognitive factors, neurological, and neurophysiological factors) concluding that all, as currently construed, are susceptible to criticism. He expects, and we concur, that an explanation via neurological constraints on development with cognitive consequences that constrain L2 acquisition will prove most tenable.

Johnson and Newport (1989) offer further evidence that sensitive periods appear to exist for the linguistic demands of morphology and syntax. When they asked subjects who had either arrived in the United States by age 15 or a second group who had arrived later to perform grammaticality judgment tasks, they found a linear relationship between age of arrival in the early arrival group, but none in the group who arrived after puberty. Note that this understanding of the term *critical period* (in a footnote they note that *critical period* and *sensitive period* are virtually coterminus for them) is markedly different from that of Long (1990), who refers to sensitive periods that govern first-language or second-language development. During these sensitive periods, he maintains, acquisition of linguistic abilities succeeds; after them, it is "irregular" and "incomplete" (p. 251). For Johnson and Newport, it would appear that the age effects occur during the critical or sensitive period and once it has ended, acquisition of morphology and syntax appear to be randomly successful. (See chapter 5 by Schachter, this volume, for additional discussion of the critical period hypothesis.)

B. Factors Involved in Successful Postpubertal L2 Acquisition

In the 1970s and early 1980s the focus of study on factors explaining L2 acquisition regularly took into account a set of variables in the language-learning situation and, most crucially, in the motivation of the learner. By the late 1980s, research assuming there were neuropsychological underpinnings for talented L2 acquisition began to appear. After years of factor-analytic studies suggesting motivation was important in successful adult L2 acquisition, Schumann (1990) studied the neuroanatomical structures and neurophysiological processes that may underlie how affect interacts with cognition in L2 acquisition. In addition, we may briefly refer to the neuropsychological study of Novoa, Fein, and Obler (1988) suggesting that talented L2 acquirers possess an exceptionally good verbal memory and a cognitive style whereby subjects are able to focus on form perhaps better than meaning, (but certainly in conjunction with meaning). That article also argued in favor of Geschwind and Galaburda's neuroimmunoendocrinological theory, with particular respect to talents. In that theory Geschwind and Galaburda (1985a, 1985b, 1985c) argued that hormonal influence in the developing fetal brain can bring about unusual cell migrations yielding brain bases for special talents, as well as disabilities such as dyslexia. Schneiderman and Desmarais (1988) discuss cognitive flexibility and those aspects of the Geschwind and Galaburda Hypothesis that predict some cognitive deficits in conjunction with skills such as ability in L2 acquisition.

III. LATERAL DOMINANCE FOR LANGUAGE IN BILINGUALS

In the 1970s there was a proliferation of literature on lateral dominance in bilingualism with a range of positions apparently supported. A series of studies reported greater bilateral organization for bilinguals than monolinguals, whereas another series of studies reported no differences between the two groups. Studies looking only at bilinguals indicated either no differences in lateral dominance for the two languages, or more right-hemisphere involvement in the L2 than in the L1 (see Vaid, 1983, for a review). It became increasingly clear that substantial methodological issues can subtly influence the outcome of noninvasive studies of lateral dominance. As a result, reviews of these issues as they pertain to the literature on lateral dominance in bilingualism were published (Obler, Zatorre, Galloway, & Vaid, 1982; Zatorre, 1989). This pattern of findings has continued, with a series of papers evidencing no differences between the two languages (Galloway & Scarcella, 1982; Soares, 1982, 1984; Walters & Zatorre, 1978) or between bilinguals and monolinguals (Soares, 1982, 1984).

Likewise, the bulk of the literature of crossed aphasia suggests no differences or minimal ones between bilinguals and monolinguals. Early studies (Albert & Obler, 1978; Gloning & Gloning, 1965) suggested that there was a higher incidence of crossed aphasia in bilingual subjects than in monolinguals. Crossed aphasia (i.e., aphasia in a right-handed individual resulting from *right*-hemisphere brain damage) suggests right-hemisphere participation in language. Thus, if there is higher incidence among bilinguals and polyglots, this means they have more right-hemisphere involvement in language processing than monolinguals do. However, after a thorough review of pertinent records, April and Han (1980) found no increased incidence of crossed aphasia in a Chinese–English bilingual population. Chary (1986) reported virtually equal incidence of crossed aphasia among bilingual speakers of South Indian languages and monolingual speakers of these languages. Karanth and Rangamani (1988), by contrast, found a relatively high incidence of crossed aphasia among their multilingual aphasic speakers of

South Indian languages as compared to their monolingual speakers; however, they interpret this in light of the cultural taboos on left-handedness, whereby the monolingual population evidences only 2.5% of left-handedness. Such a taboo could result in more apparent crossed aphasia than is warranted in terms of cerebral organization, although of course this should hold true equally for monolinguals and multilinguals.

Some modern techniques employ instruments to measure laterality in bilinguals. Genesee et al. (1978) used evoked potential measures of left- and right-hemispheric activity to study French–English bilinguals. On observing N^1 peak differences among their subjects, they asserted that those who had learned their L2 earlier used more "left-hemisphere strategies", whereas those who had learned their L2 during adolescence used more "right-hemisphere strategies", despite the fact that both groups were balanced bilinguals when proficiency was tested.

A similar population was studied by Vaid (1987), with contradictory results, however. Her late bilinguals (LBs) (those who learned their L2 between the ages of 10 and 14), showed a more pronounced left-hemisphere effect than did either early bilinguals (EBs) (who learned their L2 before age 4) or monolinguals. Albanese (1985) studied French–English speakers via a dichotic measure and reported more right-hemisphere participation in the later stages of L2 acquisition. Moreover, Gordon and Zatorre (1981) reported no differences between a group of Latinos who had acquired their L2 (English) around age 9 and another who had acquired theirs at approximately 13.5. Of course age of acquisition can be confounded with proficiency. Gordon and Zatorre report no correlation between proficiency and degree of lateralization; however, as we mentioned above, Albanese did. Sussman, Franklin, and Simon (1982) found EBs (those who acquire their L2s before age 6) to show left-hemisphere dominance for both languages on the finger tapping interference task, unlike LBs (those who acquired their L2 after age 6) who only demonstrated left-hemisphere dominance for their L1 and showed more bilateral organization for their L2.

The findings of this set of articles discussing age of acquisition differences are clearly contradictory. Authors such as Obler et al. (1982), Zatorre (1989), and Paradis (1990a) suggest that such conflicting findings may be due to methodological limitations on the study of laterality and that the question of lateral organization for language should be put aside until more reliable methods are available.

As to the stage hypothesis, more right-hemispheric participation is seen in the earlier stages of L2 acquisition, and the strongest support for this, it would seem, is provided by Silverberg, Bentin, Gaziel, Obler, and Albert (1979). Other authors, however, have found no evidence for it (e.g., Galloway & Scarcella, 1982), or even contradictory evidence (Albanese, 1985). Vaid (1983) extracted an understanding from this literature, essentially arguing that right-hemisphere involvement is "more likely the later the second language is acquired relative to the first"

(p. 336). She stated further that the manner of L2 acquisition may also influence cerebral processing patterns, with the right hemisphere implicated in learning situations that are more informal, or natural, in nature.

Since 1978, researchers have gone beyond simple questions of lateral dominance for languages to explore possibly differential organization within the left hemisphere. The original article in this small series is that of Ojemann and Whitaker (1978) in which they performed cortical stimulation on two bilingual epileptics and determined that the "primary" language was likely to be more interrupted in a smaller, core, peri-Sylvian region than was the "second" language. A case studied by Fedio and colleagues (1992) via cortical stimulation provided similar data, with the classic left-hemisphere brain areas for language involved in both languages, whereas L2s appeared to be more broadly mediated by adjacent regions in addition. Rapport, Tan, and Whitaker (1983), however, reported what would appear to be contradictory results from two of the three patients they studied via cortical stimulation. Although one, Case 2, showed more diffuse organization in the less dominant language, English, Case 1 showed more diffuse organization, it would appear, in the L1, Cantonese—although this was not the dominant language. Case 5 presented confounding data in that no Broca's area could be identified with cortical stimulation of the left hemisphere (despite the patient being strongly right-handed). Furthermore, in this patient, stimulation in regions around the language area could result in naming either in English or Cantonese, but not both.

Complementary evidence can be seen from sodium amytal testing, a technique in which this anesthetic is injected into an artery and travels to one or the other cortical hemisphere. Although standardly used to test the lateral dominance for language before surgery, in fact, one may observe the progression and recovery of two or more languages over the course of a 15-min period as the anesthetic subsides. In the case reported by Fedio et al. (1992), data consistent with their cortical stimulation findings were evident: the L1 (Spanish) recovered after one minute, whereas the L2 (English) recovered after 2.5 minutes. This finding would appear to be in frank contrast with that reported by Berthier, Starkstein, Lylyk, and Leiguarda (1990), whose Spanish–English subject began speaking in the L2, English, first, despite having been addressed in Spanish. Even among the four Rapport et al. (1983) patients such conflicting patterns can be seen. In Cases 1 and 3 the dominant, but not the first-learned language, returned first; in Case 2 the dominant language returned last of the three tested, the mother tongue returned second, and English, a much-used language that the patient did not call his dominant language, returned first. Similarly, in Case 4 neither the dominant nor the mother tongue returned first (note that in this patient, unlike any of the others reported on, amytal injection to the right hemisphere also resulted in some linguistic errors, and they were in the mother tongue, Hokkien).

The absence of any detectable pattern(s) in language recovery under sodium amytal is suggestive of great individual variability of language acquisition and/or processing. However, one must note that all patients tested with cortical stimulation or sodium amytal are severely epileptic, and therefore do not have "normal" brains.

The newest technique to have been used to study language organization for a bilingual within the left hemisphere is the use of positron emission tomography (PET), a technique that permits observation of on-line changes in brain activity while language processing is taking place. When Fedio and colleagues (1992) studied their Spanish–English speaker using PET scanning, they found more widespread brain activation during the patient's repetition and sentence construction in the L2, English, as compared to the first, Spanish. Different areas were involved in repeating Spanish and English sentences (left supramarginal gyrus for Spanish, left mesial temporal areas for English), which the authors take to suggest that more memory is involved in L2 repetition, whereas exclusively semantic processing is the focus of "primary" language processing. These data suggest differential processing in the accomplished bilingual, with little indication of the acquisition processes that lead up to such a state. With longitudinal PET studies, in principle, one could observe the extent to which such a picture represented a stage towards more overlapping organization, or, rather, a permanent solution on the part of the brain for keeping the bilingual processing as independent as necessary.

IV. LANGUAGE BREAKDOWN

For the first 80 years of discussions of language breakdown, the focus was on aphasic patients, individuals in whom frank brain damage of the language areas of the brain had resulted in difficulty in speaking or comprehending (or writing or reading) one or more languages. From this literature we learned the variety of recovery patterns (Obler & Albert, 1977; Paradis, 1977) that can obtain when a bilingual polyglot becomes aphasic. For a long while the debate continued as to whether it was the first-learned language or the language being used around the time of the accident that was likely to return first in cases of differential recovery. Statistical analysis of the data on 109 patients (Obler & Albert, 1977) suggested that use is the more crucial factor, predicting with significantly greater than chance accuracy which language will return first in cases of differential recovery, whereas the first-learned language recovers first or disproportionately better than the second-learned one only with chance frequency. However, Obler and Mahecha (1991), after incorporating additional cases, did not find L1 use and practice crucial for access to it in polyglot aphasics. Added support for the assertion that "practice" or use enhances access can be found in the smaller literature on therapy in aphasic patients, as well as the recent literature on language attrition in non-aphasic, nondemented older adults.

Speech-language pathologists give speech-language therapy to bilingual patients often in the language of the environment, rather than in the language the patient might choose for his or her own pragmatic reasons. Although the earliest (semi-) experimental article (Fredman, 1975) appeared to suggest that aphasics' recovery in the language of therapy was no greater than that in which therapy was not given, more recent articles have suggested that the language of therapy is crucial, perhaps especially for productive language (Junque, Vendrell, Vendrell-Brucet, & Tobena, 1989; Watamori & Sasanuma, 1976). Watamori and Sasanuma (1976, 1978), after having detailed the recovery patterns of two English–Japanese aphasics (one a fluent, Wernicke's aphasic, and the second a nonfluent, Broca's aphasic) found that the treated language showed considerably more overall improvement than did the untreated language in both patients. Junque and colleagues (1989) studied naming performance in thirty Catalan–Spanish bilinguals, demonstrating more improvement in the treated language (Catalan) than in the untreated one. Both of these studies are methodologically more refined than the Fredman one in that, rather than questionnaire data to family members, pre- and posttreatment language testing was conducted in all languages.

Of course aphasia therapy is different in many ways from language acquisition (either L1 or L2). Indeed there is controversy in the speech-language pathology literature as to the extent to which, when therapy works, it reflects a patient's relearning or reaccessing of language made unavailable. However, apart from one presentation (Roberts, 1992) suggesting better results from therapy in the untreated language (English) as compared to the treated language (French—which calls into question the practices of the particular speech-language pathologist!), we must conclude that some of the standard armamentarium of L2 teachers, such as drill in and/or explanation about patterns in a specific language, are useful in rehabilitation after brain damage.

One of the explanations for differential language recovery has been that brain-damaged patients have fewer overall cognitive resources available than normals and thus, although they may have been proficiently bilingual premorbidly, postmorbidly only one language can be accessed at a time. A series of papers have, indeed, evidenced a form of differential recovery that Paradis has labeled "alternate antagonism" (Nilipour & Ashayeri, 1989; Paradis & Goldblum, 1989; Paradis, Goldblum, & Abidi, 1982). In each instance, their patients were able to speak a given language A, on one day (or for several days) and then another language B, for a brief period, then reverting to language A's being available but not B. Green (1986) has developed a theory of limited resources to account for such phenomena.

By contrast, recent literature on language attrition in neurologically normal bilinguals indicates that routine use is crucial for the continued ease of access to L1 and/or L2. Bahrick's classic 1984 paper demonstrated that for a period of 2–5 years after completing study of an L2 (Spanish), subjects lost some of their abilities—regardless of the proficiency they had achieved. This pattern of attrition was then seen to plateau for approximately 25 years, after which a mild decline was again evidenced. Neisser (1984) suggested that this second decline may be related to the advancing age of subjects. He also provided an alternative interpretation of Bahrick's (1984) data, positing that a critical threshold could be achieved in proficiency beyond which attrition would be retarded.

Although the data to determine whether Neisser or Bahrick is correct with regard to the question of a critical threshold are not in, the studies of Olshtain (1989) and Cohen (1989) suggest that preliterate children appear to be more susceptible to attrition than literate ones. As the preliterate children were younger than the literate ones in their studies, we cannot know whether the threshold achieved was one of proficiency per se, or some special "attrition retardant" associated with knowledge of the written modality.

Weltens, Van Els, and Schils (1989) also provided some support for the proficiency threshold argument, demonstrating that the French spoken by highly proficient Dutch secondary school students evidenced little attrition in the 2-year interval following their discontinuation of language study. They narrowed Bahrick's estimation of a 5-year decline to 2 years for these students, as they saw no additional performance decline between years 2 and 4 postlearning.

Clyne (1981) had originally suggested that even (neurologically) normal elderly individuals might revert to their L1 after years in a country of immigration. In a follow-up study (De Bot & Clyne, 1989), no decline in proficiency in either Dutch or English was seen over a period of 16 years, prompting Clyne to modify his original "language reversion" hypothesis. Thus, one may reasonably conclude that continued neural activation of a language through using it is necessary for continued ease of access. The extent to which the peak proficiency achieved may retard attrition when a language is not continually used remains unresolved. (See chapter 18 by Seliger, this volume, for additional discussion of language attrition.)

It is worth noting that the aphasia data over the years have provided substantial indication that production abilities and receptive abilities in a language can be dissociated for bilinguals and polyglots, as for monolinguals. Throughout the differential-impairment-in-bilingual-aphasia literature, cases of production more impaired than comprehension, or the converse, are seen in parallel to Broca's aphasia and Wernicke's aphasia long reported for monolinguals. The written modality, also, may be independently impaired or spared. The implications for L2 acquisition are that the different abilities must be independently learned or acquired, as they can break down independently as well. The better aphasia therapy study (Watamori & Sasanuma, 1978) evidenced differential abilities across modalities, as do the cases of alternate antagonism (e.g., Nilipour & Ashayeri, 1989; Paradis et al., 1982).

In recent years discussion of a so-called language switch has declined, although discussion of a "language choice" phenomenon has increased. The putative language switch, Paradis (1980, 1990b) demonstrated, had been reported to be impaired after lesions to so many points in the brain that it was virtually unlocalizable. However, curiously enough, some patients with substantial brain damage evidenced no problems with it, as in the case of a patient with Alzheimer's dementia in the mid-to-late stage tested by one of the authors (LKO), who chose to speak German or English with his interlocutors fully appropriately depending on their native language. Other patients with Alzheimer's dementia, however, have been reported to have impaired language choice. In this instance, (unlike the aphasic patients for whom, as were mentioned above, it is *not* the L1 that is most often likely to be reverted to), the errors in the demented patients seem to be in the direction of inappropriately choosing the L1 in a situation in which no one speaks it (of course this could be due to where these patients are studied; there are few enough such patients studied today, and they are all in the land to which they immigrated). Hyltenstam and Stroud (e.g., 1989) initiated this research; Dronkers, Koss, Friedland, and Wertz (1986) reported on one such case, and De Santi, Obler, Sabo-Abramson, and Goldberger (1989) reported on four such cases in English–Yiddish speakers. Pragmatic aspects of language choice, of course, are rarely, if ever, taught in L2 language courses; rather, they are acquired. The fact that pragmatics appropriate for language choice can break down with brain damage, particularly with the frontal and diffuse brain damage characteristic of Alzheimer's dementia, suggests that it may indeed be acquired in classroom situations as well as in more standard immersion contexts. (Chapter 19 by Bhatia and Ritchie, this volume, includes discussion of language switching in both normals and aphasics.)

V. FUTURE DIRECTIONS

Current research in the neurolinguistics of bilingualism and L2 acquisition seems to be moving away from descriptions of the breakdown in individual aphasics with differential impairment or recovery, and away from questions of lateral dominance in the bilingual. Rather, L2 acquisition theorists are likely to continue to refine and, hopefully, test notions of multiple critical periods for acquiring L2 skills, along with immersing themselves in studies of neuroanatomy and neurophysiology as these may provide motivation for testing the neurobiology of L2 acquisition. From the side of the neurolinguists, more research on the longitudinal details of attrition in patients with Alzheimer's dementia should provide evidence for neurocognitive aspects of L2 maintenance or loss, as should study of the subtle processes of aging as they interact with acquisition, maintenance, and loss. Neuropsychological abilities linked to talent will also continue to be studied, we project, in order to tease out factors predictive of L2 acquisition skills. Finally, additional research on L2 processing as studied through dynamic instruments such as PET scans should prove extremely useful (particularly if they could be carried out longitudinally) in documenting the range of activities that the brain undertakes while acquiring an L2.

REFERENCES

Albanese, J. F. (1985). Language lateralization in English–French bilinguals. *Brain and Language, 24,* 284–296.

Albert, M. L., & Obler, L. K. (1978). *The bilingual brain: Neuropsychological and neurolinguistic aspects of bilingualism.* New York: Academic Press.

April, R., & Han, M. (1980). Crossed aphasia in a right-handed bilingual aphasic man. *Archives of Neurology (Chicago), 37,* 341–346.

Bahrick, H. P. (1984). Semantic memory content in permastore: Fifty years of memory for Spanish learned in school. *Journal of Experimental Psychology: General, 113,* 1–29.

Berthier, M. L., Starkstein, S. E., Lylyk, P., & Leiguarda, R. (1990). Differential recovery of languages in a bilingual patient: A case study using selective amytal test. *Brain and Language, 38,* 449–453.

Chary, P. (1986). Aphasia in a multilingual society: A preliminary study. In J. Vaid (Ed.), *Language processing in bilinguals: Psycholinguistic and neuropsychological perspectives* (pp. 183–197). Hillsdale, NJ: Erlbaum.

Clyne, M. (1981). Second language attrition and first language reversion among elderly bilinguals in Australia. In W. Meid & K. Heller (Eds.), *Sprachkontakt als Ursache von Veränderungen der Sprach- und Bewußtseinsstrukturen* (pp. 26–39). Innsbruck: Universität.

Cohen, A. D. (1989). Attrition in the productive lexicon of two Portuguese third language speakers. *Studies in Second Language Acquisition, 11,* 135–149.

De Bot, K., & Clyne, M. (1989). Language reversion revisited. *Studies in Second Language Acquisition, 11,* 167–177.

De Santi, S., Obler, L., Sabo-Abramson, H., & Goldberger, J. (1989). Discourse abilities and deficits in multilingual dementia. In Y. Joanette & H. Brownell (Eds.), *Discourse abilities in brain damage: Theoretical and empirical perspectives.* (pp. 224–235). New York: Springer.

Dronkers, N., Koss, E., Friedland, R., & Wertz, R. (1986). *"Differential" language impairment and language mixing in a polyglot with probable Alzheimer's disease.* Paper presented at the European International Neuropsychological Society meeting.

Ervin, S., & Osgood, C. (1954). Second language learning and bilingualism. In C. Osgood & T. Sebeok (Eds.), *Psycholinguistics: A survey of theory and research problems* (pp. 139–146). Baltimore: Waverly Press.

Fedio, P., August, A., Myatt, C., Kertzman, C., Miletich, R., Snyder, P., Sato, S., & Kafta, C. (1992, February). *Functional localization of languages in a bilingual patient with intracarotid amytal, subdural electrical stimulation, and positron emission tomography.* Paper presented at International Neuropsychological Society, San Diego, CA.

Fredman, M. (1975). The effect of therapy given in Hebrew on the home language of the bilingual or polyglot adult aphasic in Israel. *British Journal of Disorders of Communication, 10,* 61–69.

Galloway, L. M., & Scarcella, R. (1982). Cerebral organization in adult second language acquisition: Is the right hemisphere more involved? *Brain and Language, 15,* 210–233.

Genessee, F., Hamers, J., Lambert, W., Mononen, L., Seitz, M., & Starck, R. (1978). Language processing in bilinguals. *Brain and Language, 5,* 1–12.

Geschwind, N., & Galaburda, A. M. (1985a). Cerebral lateralization: Biological mechanisms, associations, and pathology: 1. A hypothesis and a program for research. *Archives of Neurology (Chicago), 42,* 428–459.

Geschwind, N., & Galaburda, A. M. (1985b). Cerebral lateralization: Biological mechanisms, associations, and pathology: 2. A hypothesis and a program for research. *Archives of Neurology (Chicago), 42,* 521–552.

Geschwind, N., & Galaburda, A. M. (1985c). Cerebral lateralization: Biological mechanisms, associations, and pathology: 2. A hypothesis and a program for research. *Archives of Neurology (Chicago), 42,* 634–654.

Gloning, I., & Gloning, K. (1965). Aphasien bei polyglotten. *Wiener Zeitschrift für Nervenheilkunde, 22,* 362–397.

Gordon, D. P., & Zatorre, R. J. (1981). A right ear advantage for dichotic listening in bilingual children. *Brain and Language, 13,* 389–396.

Green, D. W. (1986). Control, activation, and resource: A framework and a model for the control of speech in bilinguals. *Brain and Language, 27,* 210–233.

Hyltenstam, K., & Stroud, C. (1989). Bilingualism in Alzheimer's disease: Two case studies. In K. Hyltenstam, & L. K. Obler, (Eds.), *Bilingualism across the lifespan: Aspects of acquisition, maturity and loss.* Cambridge, UK: Cambridge University Press.

Jacobs, B. (1988). Neurobiological differentiation of primary and secondary language acquisition. *Studies in Second Language Acquisition, 10,* 303–337.

Johnson, J. S., & Newport, E. L. (1989). Critical period effects in second language learning: The influence of maturational state on the acquisition of English as a second language. *Cognitive Psychology, 21,* 60–99.

Junque, C., Vendrell, P., Vendrell-Brucet, J., & Tobena, A. (1989). Differential recovery in naming in bilingual aphasics. *Brain and Language, 36,* 16–22.

Karanth, P., & Rangamani, G. N. (1988). Crossed aphasia in multilinguals. *Brain and Language, 34,* 169–180.

Krashen, S. D. (1973). Lateralization, language learning, and the critical period: Some new evidence. *Language Learning, 23,* 63–74.

Krashen, S. D., Long, M., & Scarcella, R. (1979). Age, rate, and eventual attainment in second language acquisition. *TESOL Quarterly, 13,* 573–582.

Lamendella, J. T. (1977). General principles of neurofunctional organization and their manifestation in primary and nonprimary language acquisition. *Language Learning, 27,* 155–196.

Larsen-Freeman, D., & Long, M. H. (1991). *An introduction to second language acquisition.* New York: Longman.

Lenneberg, E. (1967). *Biological foundations of language.* New York: Wiley.

Long, M. H. (1990). Maturational constraints on language development. *Studies in Second Language Acquisition, 12,* 251–285.

Neisser, U. (1984). Interpreting Harry Bahrick's discovery: What confers immunity against forgetting? *Journal of Experimental Psychology: General, 113,* 32–35.

Nilipour, R., & Ashayeri, H. (1989). Alternating antagonism between two languages with successive recovery of a third in a trilingual aphasic patient. *Brain and Language, 36,* 23–38.

Novoa, L., Fein, D., & Obler, L. (1988). Talent in foreign languages: A case study. In L. Obler & D. Fein (Eds.), *The exceptional brain: Neuropsychology of talent and special abilities,* (pp. 294–302). New York: Guilford Press.

Obler, L. K., & Albert, M. L. (1977). Influence of aging on recovery from aphasia in polyglots. *Brain and Language, 4,* 460–463.

Obler, L. K., & Mahecha, N. R. (1991). First language loss in bilinguals and polyglot aphasics. In H. W. Seliger & R. M. Vago (Eds.), *First language attrition.* New York: Cambridge University Press.

Obler, L. K., Zatorre, R. J., Galloway, L., & Vaid, J. (1982). Cerebral lateralization in bilinguals: Methodological issues. *Brain and Language, 15,* 40–54.

Ojemann, G. A., & Whitaker, H. A. (1978). The bilingual brain. *Archives of Neurology (Chicago), 35,* 409–412.

Olshtain, E. (1989). Is second language attrition the reversal of second language acquisition? *Studies in Second Language Acquisition, 11,* 151–165.

Oyama, S. C. (1976). A sensitive period for the acquisition of a phonological system. *Journal of Psycholinguistic Research, 5,* 261–283.

Paradis, M. (1977). Bilingualism and aphasia. In H. Whitaker & H. A. Whitaker (Eds.), *Studies in neurolinguistics* (Vol. 3, pp. 65–121). New York: Academic Press.

Paradis, M. (1980). The language switch in bilinguals: Psycholinguistic and neurolinguistic perspectives. *Zeitschrift für Dialektologie und Linguistik Beihefte, 32,* 501–506.

Paradis, M. (1990a). Bilingual and polyglot aphasia. In F. Boller & J. Grafman (Eds.), *Handbook of neuropsychology* (Vol. 2, pp. 117–140). New York: Elsevier.

Paradis, M. (1990b). Differential recovery of languages in a bilingual patient following selective amytal injection: A comment on Berthier et al. *Brain and Language, 39,* 469–470.

Paradis, M., & Goldblum, M. (1989). Selective crossed aphasia in a trilingual aphasic patient followed by reciprocal antagonism. *Brain and Language, 36,* 62–75.

Paradis, M., Goldblum, M., & Abidi, R. (1982). Alternate antagonism with paradoxical translation behavior in two bilingual aphasic patients. *Brain and Language, 15,* 55–69.

Patkowski, M. (1980). The sensitive period for the acquisition of syntax in a second language. *Language Learning, 30,* 449–472.

Pitres, A. (1895). Etude sur l'aphasie. *Revue de Medecine (Paris), 15,* 873–899.

Rapport, R. L., Tan, C. T., & Whitaker, H. A. (1983). Language function and dysfunction among Chinese- and English-speaking polyglots: Cortical stimulation, Wada testing, and clinical studies. *Brain and Language, 18,* 342–366.

Ribot, T. (1881). *Les maladies de la mémoire.* Paris: Lib. Baillière et Cie.

Roberts, P. (1992, October). *Therapy and spontaneous recovery in a bilingual aphasic.* Presented at Academy of Aphasia, Toronto.

Schneiderman, E. I., & Desmarais, C. (1988). A Neuropsychological substrate for talent in second-language acquisition. In L. K. Obler & D. Fein (Eds.), *The exceptional brain: Neuropsychology of special talents and abilities* (pp. 103–126). New York: Guilford Press.

Schumann, J. H. (1990). The role of the amygdala as a mediator of affect and cognition in second language acquisition. In J. Alatis (Ed.), *Georgetown University round table on language and linguistics* (pp. 169–176). Washington, DC: Georgetown University Press.

Scovel, T. (1969). Foreign accents, language acquisition, and cerebral dominance. *Language Learning, 19,* 245–253.

Scovel, T. (1988). *A time to speak: A psycholinguistic inquiry into the critical period for human speech.* New York: Newbury House.

Seliger, H. (1978). Implications of a multiple critical period hypothesis for second language learning. In W. Ritchie (Ed.), *Second language acquisition research* (pp. 11–19). New York: Academic Press.

Silverberg, R., Bentin, S., Gaziel, T., Obler, L., & Albert, M. (1979). Shift of visual field preference for English words in native Hebrew speakers. *Brain and Language, 8,* 184–190.

Snow, C. E., & Hoefnagel-Hohle, M. (1978). The critical period for language acquisition: Evidence from second language learning. *Child Development, 49,* 1114–1128.

Soares, C. (1982). Converging evidence for left hemisphere language lateralization in bilinguals. *Neuropsychologia, 20,* 653–659.

Soares, C. (1984). Left-hemisphere language lateralization in bilinguals: Use of the concurrent activities paradigm. *Brain and Language, 23,* 86–96.

Sussman, H. M., Franklin, P., & Simon, T. (1982). Bilingual speech: Bilateral control? *Brain and Language, 15,* 125–142.

Vaid, J. (1983). Bilingualism and brain lateralization. In S. Segalowitz (Ed.), *Language functions and brain organization* (pp. 315–339). New York: Academic Press.

Vaid, J. (1987). Visual field asymmetries for rhyme and syntactic category judgments in monolinguals and fluent early and late bilinguals. *Brain and Language, 30,* 263–277.

Walters, J., & Zatorre, R. J. (1978). Laterality differences for word identification in bilinguals. *Brain and Language, 6,* 158–167.

Watamori, T. S., & Sasanuma, S. (1976). The recovery process of a bilingual aphasic. *Journal of Communication Disorders, 9,* 157–166.

Watamori, T. S., & Sasanuma, S. (1978). The recovery process of two English-Japanese Bilingual Aphasics. *Brain and Language, 6,* 127–140.

Weinreich, U. (1953). *Languages in contact, findings and problems* (Publ. No. 1). New York: Linguistic Circle of New York.

Weltens, B., Van Els, T. J. M., & Schils, E. (1989). The long-term retention of French by Dutch students. *Studies in Second Language Acquisition, 11,* 205–216.

Zatorre, R. J. (1989). On the representation of multiple languages in the brain: Old problems and new directions. *Brain and Language, 36,* 127–147.

LANGUAGE CONTACT AND ITS CONSEQUENCES

CHAPTER 16

THE PRIMACY OF ASPECT IN FIRST AND SECOND LANGUAGE ACQUISITION: THE PIDGIN–CREOLE CONNECTION

Roger W. Andersen and Yasuhiro Shirai

I. INTRODUCTION

Since the early 1970s, with studies such as Bronckart and Sinclair (1973), Brown (1973), and Antinucci and Miller (1976), there has been considerable interest in the acquisition of verb morphology, with a strong emphasis on the acquisition of tense and aspect. During this same period, Bickerton (1974) proposed that creole languages around the world exhibit striking evidence of linguistic universals in the area of tense and aspect:

> I am therefore claiming that what distinguishes a creole language from a pidgin on the one hand and a developed standard language on the other is simply that *a creole is much closer than either to linguistic universals, in particular to natural semantax*" (italics in original). (From reprinted 1974 paper, in Day, 1980, p. 5.)

Creole languages arise in contexts where people who speak different languages are brought together out of economic necessity, colonialization, slavery, and so forth. When the slaves far outnumbered the masters, attempts to learn the masters' language as a common language resulted in a minimal second language (L2) called a *pidgin,* which barely resembled the masters' language as they spoke it. The slaves had little access to their masters' language and most learned the pidgin from each other, moving it even further away from the target—the master's language. When the children of the pidgin speakers grew up in such a community

527

they created a new natural native language (NL) from this pidgin. This new language is called a creole language.

Bickerton (1981), who expanded this proposal considerably, devotes an entire chapter to the connection between creole universals and language acquisition. As he states in his introduction:

> In Chapter 3, which will deal with "normal" language acquisition in noncreole societies, I shall show that some of the things which children seem to acquire effortlessly, as well as some which they get consistently wrong—both equally puzzling to previous accounts of "language learning"—follow naturally from the theory which was developed to account for creole origins: that all members of our species are born with a bioprogram for language which can function even in the absence of adequate input. (p. xiii)

In his extensive discussion of tense–aspect (pp. 26–30 for pidgins, pp. 58–59 and pp. 72–98 for creoles, pp. 146–181 for normal acquisition) he argues that "normal" language acquisition operates differently from creolization (the process of creation of a creole language) because the child is presented with a viable learnable system—his parents' or caretakers' language. The first-generation creole speakers, in contrast, cannot acquire the tense-aspect of their parents' or caretakers' language—the pidgin—because it does not have a coherent consistent system. The children must therefore create the tense–aspect from scratch, relying on the innate bioprogram that is the focus of Bickerton's book.

In spite of these differences between natural language acquisition and the creation of a creole language, Bickerton argued that independent research on L1 acquisition provides evidence that children follow the two bioprogram universals specific to tense–aspect: the state–process distinction and the punctual–nonpunctual distinction. The state–process distinction hypothesis states that children do not attach progressive or "nonpunctual" markers[1] to stative verbs in initial stages of acquisition. The punctual–nonpunctual distinction hypothesis states that children mark the distinction between an event with no duration and a durative event or situation (including habitual and iterative). Nonpunctual means durative.[2]

This review will not evaluate Bickerton's claims. There are adequate sources on this topic already available. For example, Bickerton (1984a) is a thorough restatement of his bioprogram proposal with extensive discussion by a large number of linguists, psychologists, and researchers from related disciplines. Romaine (1988) devoted two extensive chapters to "Language acquisition and the study of pidgins

---

[1] By *nonpunctual* markers Bickerton means imperfective markers—linguistic forms that explicitly encode meanings of duration, progressivity, iteration, and so on.

[2] As is discussed later, Bickerton's terminology has often been confusing, especially because *punctual* and *stative* are usually used to refer to inherent semantic aspect, whereas Bickerton frequently uses *punctual* and *nonpunctual* to also refer to grammatical aspect (*perfective* and *imperfective,* respectively, in Comrie, 1976).

and creoles" (Chap. 6, pp. 204–255) and "Language universals and pidgins and creoles" (Chap. 7, pp. 256–310). Newmeyer (1988) contains an extensive dialogue between Bickerton and Peter Muysken, a frequent critic of Bickerton's proposals (pp. 268–306). And the journal *First Language* contains an extensive discussion of the issues by Cziko (1989a, pp. 1–31, 1989b, pp. 51–56), Bickerton (1989, pp. 33–37), Kuczaj (1989, pp. 39–44), and Weist (1989, pp. 45–49).[3] In addition, Andersen (1981, 1983) provided a thorough discussion of the relationship between creolization and pidginization on the one hand, and language acquisition, on the other.

The purpose of this review is to assess the state of our understanding of both L1 and L2 acquisition of tense and aspect. Such a review is important independent of Bickerton's proposals. But Bickerton's strong proposals and the ensuing controversies in this area provide additional motivation for such a review. What is at stake is the degree to which there is evidence across the various language acquisition studies on tense and aspect for a common path of development independent of language-specific features, what the nature of that evidence is, and what explanations have been offered to account for such evidence. The most striking explanations proposed are in the area of "linguistic and cognitive universals," including Bickerton's bioprogram. We will also review evidence within the literature on L2 acquisition, which was not available when Bickerton (1981) was written.

In the search for universals in language acquisition research, it is important to distinguish (1) the description of potential cases of universals from (2) explanations for these putative universals. In this chapter we first attempt to describe the phenomenon and show that numerous studies attest to its existence. Then we discuss explanations that have been offered to account for the described phenomenon.

It has been consistently observed that L1 and L2 learners, in the early stages of acquiring verbal morphology, use tense–aspect markers selectively according to the inherent lexical aspect[4] of the verb to which the tense–aspect marker is attached or with which it is associated (Andersen, 1989, 1991). For example, in L1 acquisition of English, children initially use past marking on accomplishment and achievement verbs much more frequently than on activity and stative verbs, while attaching the progressive *-ing* to activity verbs more frequently than to accomplishment and achievement verbs. This phenomenon of limiting a tense–aspect marker to a restricted class of verbs, according to the inherent aspect of the verb, is known as the Primacy of Aspect (POA). In spite of the relatively large number

---

[3] This discussion is flawed, however, by pervasive terminological confusion, relating partly to Bickerton's confusing use of *nonpunctual* to refer to both inherent semantic aspect and grammatical aspect and partly by other writers' rather idiosyncratic use and interpretation of terms.

[4] Terminology will be explained in section II. Here it is sufficient to note that verbs fall into one of four categories according to their inherent aspect: states, activities, accomplishments, or achievements. The terms are Vendler's (1967) and the distinctions date back to Aristotle.

of studies on POA, there is considerable disagreement concerning the phenomenon, both at the level of description and at the level of explanation (see, especially, Weist, Wysocka, Witkowska-Stadnik, Buczowska, & Konieczna, 1984, and the ensuing debate in the *Journal of Child Language*—Rispoli & Bloom, 1985; Smith & Weist, 1987; Bloom & Harner, 1989).

II. TENSE AND ASPECT

Both tense and aspect are terms that refer to the notion of temporality. In this study, we are only interested in how the learners use verbal morphology to code tense or aspect. Although in both L1 and L2 acquisition the learner can also use other devices to code temporality (e.g., adverbials), we restrict temporality here to explicit morphological encoding of tense and aspect. Tense locates a situation in relation to some other time (such as the time of utterance); therefore, it is a category that signifies temporal deixis. On the other hand, aspect is not concerned with relating a situation with some other time (i.e., it is nondeictic), but rather characterizes "different ways of viewing the internal temporal constituency of a situation" (Comrie, 1976, p. 3). For example, the difference between *he is eating* and *he was eating* is that of tense, because the contrast of *is* and *was* signifies the difference between the two in relation to the speech time. The difference between *he ate bread* and *he was eating bread,* however, is that of aspect, because the difference is about how the action of eating is viewed by the speaker; the former views the situation in its entirety (external view), whereas the latter views the situation as consisting of phases (internal view) (see Comrie, 1976).

A. Grammatical Aspect versus Inherent Lexical Aspect

There are two types of aspect: grammatical aspect and inherent lexical aspect. Grammatical aspect (which Smith, 1983, called viewpoint aspect) refers to aspectual distinctions that are marked explicitly by linguistic devices, usually auxiliaries and inflections. The progressive aspect in English, and the perfective–imperfective aspect in languages such as Spanish, Russian, and Greek are examples of grammatical aspect.

Inherent lexical aspect, also referred to as situation aspect (Smith, 1983) or Aktionsart, refers to the characteristics of what is inherent in the lexical items that describe the situation. For example, *know* is inherently stative, whereas *jump* is inherently punctual (i.e., momentary and having no duration). Not all agree that Aktionsart is the same as inherent lexical aspect (e.g., Comrie, 1976; Matthews, 1990). In this study, however, we will use the terms interchangeably. It should also be pointed out that Smith's (1983) term *situation aspect* includes not only Aktionsart (lexical aspect) but also all other nonmorphosyntactic aspectual information in a sentence, such as temporal adverbials. For this reason, we prefer the term *inherent lexical aspect.*

It is very important to distinguish between grammatical and inherent lexical aspect, especially because some disagreements and misunderstandings have stemmed from terminological, and therefore, conceptual, confusions. For example, Bloom, Lifter, and Hafitz (1980), in their discussion of "aspect before tense," were not explicit about the grammatical-inherent lexical aspect distinction, possibly leading to their disagreement with Weist (see Weist et al., 1984). As will be argued, what is important in the early stages of the acquisition of verbal morphology is not grammatical aspect, but inherent aspect.

It must be noted that both grammatical and inherent lexical aspects are linguistic properties, and, as Smith (1983) pointed out, should not be confused with "the properties of an actual situation" (p. 480). In viewing an actual situation, which is "out there" in the real world (or in the conceptual world in the speaker's mind), the speaker has to make choices on how to describe the situation. In describing the situation, there are two levels of aspectual choice—that of inherent lexical aspect (situation aspect) and that of grammatical aspect (viewpoint aspect), both of which are basically linguistic choices. The point here is that actual situations are distinct from language; they serve as bases for linguistic choice by the speaker.

It is especially important to make a distinction between the level of situational properties and the level of inherent aspect, because in experimental studies, researchers can manipulate situational properties (such as duration of events; see, for example, Bronckart & Sinclair, 1973), in which subjects describe situations using their linguistic choices (i.e., inherent and grammatical aspect). However, in the case of studies using naturalistic data, the level of situational properties is not easily distinguishable from the level of inherent aspect, because the researcher does not have access to actual situational properties (to be discussed in more detail in section IV).

B. The Vendlerean Four-Way Classification

Vendler (1967) proposed a four-way classification of the inherent semantics of verbs (i.e., inherent lexical aspect): achievement, accomplishment, activity, state. The roots of this classification date back to Aristotle, and it has been elaborated on since by philosophers such as Ryle (1949) and Kenny (1963). Later, Dowty (1979) and Mourelatos (1981) developed the classification schema further.

The four-way distinction, which is based on temporal properties of verbs, can be captured in the following way, following Andersen (1991):

1. Punctual event (achievement)—that which takes place instantaneously, and is reducible to a single point in time (e.g., *recognize, die, reach the summit,* etc.).

2. Telic event (accomplishment)—that which has some duration, but has a single clear inherent end point (e.g., *run a mile, make a chair, build a house, write a letter*, etc.).

3. Activity—that which has duration, but with an arbitrary end point, and is homogeneous in its structure. For example, in *John is running*, at every moment, the fact of his running has the same quality of "running." (e.g., *run, sing, play, dance*, etc.).

4. State—that which has no dynamics, and continues without additional effort or energy being applied (e.g., *see, love, hate, want*, etc.).

Although accomplishments have some duration, achievements and accomplishments both share the feature of having a clear end point. An achievement is different from the other categories in that it is not durative; a state is different from the other three categories in that it is not dynamic (Comrie, 1976).

In this chapter we will use *accomplishment* and *achievement* to refer to inherent aspectual categories. *Telic* and *punctual* will be used as parameters—telic denoting "having an inherent endpoint," and punctual denoting "having no duration." Therefore, accomplishment and achievement are both telic, but only achievement is punctual. Table I, taken from Andersen (1991), shows how these features map onto the four categories.

Many operational tests have been proposed to classify verbs into the four inherent aspectual categories, although not without controversy regarding the validity of the categories and the tests (see Brinton, 1988; Dowty, 1979). Dowty (1979) has the most comprehensive treatment of the tests for classification, listing 11 tests (p. 60).

The four-way classification is arguably a linguistic universal, and has been applied to many languages, such as Japanese (W. M. Jacobsen, 1982), Tagalog and Lakhota (Foley & Van Valin, 1984), Polish (Weist et al., 1984), and Georgian (Holisky, 1981). (See Smith & Weist, 1987, for a more comprehensive list.) It is also claimed to be a cognitive universal; as Smith and Weist (1987, p. 388) put it, "[i]t depends ultimately on the perceptual and cognitive distinctions that human beings make." *Cognitive universal* is based on the assumption that only

TABLE I

Semantic Features for the Four Categories of Inherent Lexical Aspect[a]

Semantic features	Lexical aspectual classes		Accomplishments (Telic events)	Achievements (Punctual events)
	States	Activities		
Punctual	−	−	−	+
Telic	−	−	+	+
Dynamic	−	+	+	+

[a]From Andersen, 1991.

cognitively important distinctions receive linguistic encoding as linguistic universals (i.e., if linguistically significant, then cognitively significant, the reverse does not necessarily hold.) Moreover, the distinction in question here is based on the ontological distinction of event, process, and state (see, for example, Mourelatos, 1981).

III. ACQUISITION OF TENSE AND ASPECT

A. L1 Acquisition

As noted, the POA phenomenon has been observed repeatedly in L1 acquisition. Table II summarizes the studies that report findings relevant to POA in L1 acquisition. Although not all the studies in Table II investigated the acquisition of tense–aspect marking as a specific goal of the study, almost all of them support the POA observation as summarized below. In this section, we will report on the most important studies in this area to clarify the issues, discuss some possible counterexamples to the general claim of POA, and point out some methodological problems. Because this discussion includes both descriptive and explanatory issues, we will try to make clear which is at issue at each point in the discussion.

Evidence for the Primacy of Aspect

The descriptive claims of the POA hypothesis can be summarized as follows:

1. Children first use past marking (e.g., English) or perfective marking (Chinese, Spanish, etc.) on achievement and accomplishment verbs, eventually extending its use to activity and stative verbs. This roughly corresponds to Bickerton's (1981) punctual–non-punctual distinction (PNPD).[5]
2. In languages that encode the perfective–imperfective distinction, imperfective past appears later than perfective past, and imperfective past marking begins with stative verbs and activity verbs, then extending to accomplishment and achievement verbs.
3. In languages that have progressive aspect, progressive marking begins with activity verbs, then extends to accomplishment or achievement verbs.
4. Progressive markings are not incorrectly overextended to stative verbs. This corresponds to Bickerton's (1981) state–process distinction (SPD).

Not all studies consistent with POA report their results in such detail. For example, some studies report that past marking is only given to actions with clear

---

[5] Although Bickerton's (1981) PNPD in his discussion of pidgin and creole languages actually corresponds to a perfective–imperfective distinction, that is, a feature of grammatical aspect, the way he discusses PNPD in L1 acquisition studies roughly corresponds to (1).

TABLE II

The Primacy of Aspect in First Language Acquisition

	N	Age[a]	Type of data[b]
Chinese			
Erbaugh (1978)	4	2;0 to 3;0	sp.
Li (1989)	135	3;11 to 6;4	exp.
English			
Antinucci and Miller (1976)	1	1;9–2;2	sp.
Bloom et al. (1980)	4	1;10–2;6	sp., long.
Brown (1973)	3	1;6–3;8	sp., long.
Harner (1981)	100	3;0 to 7;11	exp.
Kuczaj (1976, 1978)	1	2;4–5;0	sp., long.
	14	2;0 to 5;1	sp.
McShane and Whittaker (1988)	45	3;0 to 5;9	exp.
Osser and Dillon (1969)	35	2;6 to 5;11	exp.
Shirai (1994), Shirai and Anderson (in press)	3	1;6–4;10	sp., long.
Smith (1980)	17	2;5 to 5;8	sp.
	28	4;7 to 6;6	exp.
Finnish			
Toivainen (1980)	25	1;0–4;4	sp., long.
French			
Bronckart and Sinclair (1973)	74	2;11 to 8;7	exp.
Champaud (1993)	1	1;9–2;5	sp., long.
German			
Behrens (1993)	4	1;9–4;0	sp., long.
Greek			
Stephany (1981)	4	1;8	sp.
Hebrew			
Berman (1983)	hundreds	one-word stage to 4+	sp.
Italian			
Antinucci and Miller (1976)	7	1;6–2;6	sp., long.
Japanese			
Cziko and Koda (1987)	1	1;0–4;11	sp., long.
Rispoli (1981)	1	1;6–2;1	sp., long.
Shirai (1993)	1	0;11–2;2	sp., long.
Polish			
Weist (1983)	20	2;6 & 3;6,	exp. (comprehension)
Weist et al. (1984)	6	1;7–2;5	sp., long.
	18	2;6 & 3;6	exp.
Portuguese (Brazilian)			
de Lemos (1981a, 1981b)	3	1;0–2;5	sp., long.
Simoes and Stoel-Gammon (1979)	4	1;8–3;0	sp., long.
Spanish			
Eisenberg (1982)	2	1;4–2;4 & 1;10–3;0	sp., long.
T. Jacobsen (1986)	1	2;3–3;5	sp., long.
Turkish			
Aksu-Koc (1988)	3	1;9–2;6	sp., long.
	60	3;0 to 6;4	exp.

[a] Age—ages of children studied. 1;9–2;6 indicates the child(ren) was/were studied over time, whereas 3;0 to 6;4 indicates the study included a number of children ranging from 3;0 to 6;4.

[b] Type of data—sp., spontaneous interaction; exp., experimental elicitation; long., longitudinal study.

end results (e.g., Antinucci & Miller, 1976). Such findings, however, can be interpreted to be consistent with the claims that are generalized from other studies. We will summarize and discuss several important studies below.

Bronckart and Sinclair (1973), investigating the use of inflectional morphology by 74 French-speaking children (ages 2;11–8;7) by using experimental elicitation of data, showed that the children tended to use present forms for inherently durative verbs, and past forms (*passé composé*) for achievement and accomplishment verbs (i.e., actions with clear end results). Moreover, the children tended to use past forms more often for events of shorter duration. This tendency diminished as the children grew older, thus approximating adult use. Imperfective past (*imparfait*) was seldom used by the children.

Antinucci and Miller (1976) found a similar tendency in longitudinal studies based on the conversational data of one English- and seven Italian-speaking children. Both Antinucci and Miller and Bronckart and Sinclair, whose studies were conducted within the Piagetian framework, attributed the nonnormative use of past marking by children to a cognitive deficit, suggesting that children did not have the concept of tense (i.e., the concept of temporal deixis). Thus, they claimed, the children used morphology to encode something more relevant to them, which were those events that had clear end results.

Bickerton (1981), on the other hand, interpreted the studies by Bronckart and Sinclair and Antinucci and Miller as evidence for his Language Bioprogram Hypothesis. Based on his pidgin–creole studies, which are not without controversy,[6] he claimed that children are genetically equipped with the ability to make distinctions such as punctual versus nonpunctual, state versus process, and specific versus nonspecific. For Bickerton, the above two studies were good examples of the punctual–nonpunctual distinction that children make.

Bloom et al. (1980) investigated the development of verbal morphology by English-speaking children using longitudinal data, and found results similar to Bronckart and Sinclair's and Antinucci and Miller's: children used past marking more often on accomplishment or achievement verbs. They also reported that the -*ing* form (progressive) appeared mainly with activity verbs. However, Bloom et al. emphasized the aspectual contours of the actions rather than the end state of the actions, thus de-emphasizing the cognitive-deficit explanation given by earlier studies (Antinucci & Miller, 1976; Bronckart & Sinclair, 1973).

In their discussion section entitled "aspect before tense," Bloom et al. do not make a clear distinction between lexical aspect and grammatical aspect, thus implying that both grammatical and lexical aspects are important in tense marking. They emphasize the principle of 'aspect before tense' on two grounds. First, they

---

[6] See, for example, Aitchison (1983), Goodman (1985), Muysken (1988), and the synthesis in Romaine's (1988) chap. 7 on the bioprogram (especially pp. 264–295, which deal with tense, mood, and aspect).

cite an adult grammar model by Woisetschlaeger (1976) and Jakobson (1957), whose observation that aspect marking is closer to the stem than tense marking (in languages of the world) supports the principle of aspect before tense. (This observation corresponds to Bybee's, 1985, Relevance Principle.) Second, they cite Radulovič's (1975) study in which Serbo-Croatian-speaking children acquired a perfective–imperfective distinction (grammatical aspect) before they acquired tense. In fact, Bloom et al. (1980) claimed that "[w]here tense and aspect are coded differently, . . . the expectation is that aspect would be learned before tense" (p. 407).

The claim that *grammatical* aspect is acquired before tense is suspect. As Andersen (1989) pointed out, although children as young as 1½ years old provide evidence for the POA hypothesis, in languages with a perfective–imperfective distinction such as Spanish and Portuguese, clear evidence for use of the imperfective does not emerge until around age 3. The strong correlation between perfective aspect and accomplishment and achievement verbs (to be discussed in section V) may make it look like children are marking grammatical aspect of perfectivity, when, in fact, the children are being guided by inherent aspect of punctuality and achievementhood.

Weist et al. (1984) took issue with Bronckart and Sinclair (1973), Antinucci and Miller (1976), and Bloom et al. (1980), labeling the claims made in these studies "the Defective Tense Hypothesis." By using experimental and naturalistic data on the acquisition of Polish, Weist et al. claimed that children marked both tense and aspect (both of which are grammaticalized in Polish) at early stages, thus providing counterexamples to the "aspect before tense" hypothesis. (The study does not show, however, how grammatical aspect and tense marking appeared in even earlier stages, i.e., prior to age 1;7.) As Andersen (1989) points out, Weist et al. were criticizing what can be called the Absolute Defective Tense Hypothesis, which is a strong, all-or-nothing version of the hypothesis. According to the absolute version, only [+ telic] verbs (i.e., accomplishments and achievements) receive past-tense inflection; a tense distinction will be redundant and only accompany an aspectual distinction; only references to immediate past situations will be made (Weist et al., 1984, p. 348). Weist et al.'s claim is correct if they were criticizing this absolute version of the Defective Tense Hypothesis. However, a less stringent version of POA still holds true; namely, past inflections are predominantly attached on achievement and accomplishment verbs in the early stages, and imperfective past marking, which emerges later, is used predominantly with state–activity verbs in the beginning. Andersen (1989) called this version the Relative Defective Tense Hypothesis. It makes an observational descriptive claim about inherent-lexical-aspect and grammatical tense–aspect marking pairings and does not include the cognitive deficiency explanatory claim that Weist et al. argue so cogently against. Andersen (1989) and Bloom and Harner (1989) both independently reanalyzed tables given in Weist et al. (1984), and showed how past marking is indeed governed by inherent lexical aspect in Weist et al.'s data, which supports the POA hypothesis and the Relative Defective Tense Hypothesis.

At this juncture, it should be noted that some treat Weist et al. (1984) as if it is the last word on this issue; namely, inherent aspect (i.e., semantics of the verb) does not have any influence on the development of tense–aspect morphology. For example, Borer and Wexler (1992) claim, by extensively citing Weist et al., that "[t]he study clearly shows . . . that there is no correlation between the semantic class of the verb and the difficulties in its acquisition" (p. 177). As discussed above, however, the inherent semantics of verbs do indeed appear to affect the acquisition of tense–aspect inflections in Weist et al.'s data.

In sum, the review presented showed that although there are differences in emphasis from study to study, the claim that children at first use tense–aspect morphology to mark inherent aspect is supported by many studies. It was also pointed out that the claim of POA is not absolute, but relative. In the following section, we discuss possible counterexamples to the POA hypothesis.

Problematic Cases

What are the possible counterexamples to POA? Here we review two studies on acquisition of Spanish, one potential counterexample on Japanese, two confirmatory Japanese studies, and a major study on acquisition of Mandarin Chinese. L1 acquisition data on Spanish seem to be problematic for POA claims. T. Jacobsen (1986) reported that in her Spanish L1 acquisition study, the past participle was not used for achievements, although other aspects reported in her study are totally consistent with POA claims (Andersen, 1989). These results could be interpreted in the following manner: the children gave each of the two different past forms in Spanish (perfective past and past participle) a distinct function: the perfective past (i.e., preterit) for achievements, and the past participle for entry into states that continue in the present. It is understandable that children would give different functions to different forms, regardless of adult use, because the functional distinction between past perfective and past participle is subtle (see the One to One Principle, Andersen, 1984; the Uniqueness Principle, Pinker, 1984; The Principle of Contrast, E. V. Clark, 1987). (For applications of the uniqueness principle to L2 acquisition and to L1 attrition, see respectively, chapters 13 by Long and 18 by Seliger, this volume.) The past participle, however, such as *sentado* 'seated,' used with this meaning of "entry into states that continue in the present" is apparently the same meaning given to the form by adults, albeit with a *have* auxiliary (*me he sentado* 'I've sat down'). Moreover, a number of Jacobsen's examples are unclear. For example, a child (at 2;3) is reported by T. Jacobsen (1986, p. 105) as having said, *me sentado,* with apparently this same meaning. Because the *he* auxiliary would phonetically be [e] and thus indistinguishable from the [e] of *me,* we cannot be sure that the child used the past participle by itself. There are clearer examples, however, of the past participle used without the obligatory *have* auxiliary, *ha, he,* and so forth.

E. V. Clark (1985) reviewed studies on the acquisition of verb morphology in Romance languages (French, Italian, Portuguese) and arrived at similar conclusions; children used past markers to refer to results, not to code pastness, which is consistent with POA. On the other hand, Clark, citing Eisenberg (1982), treated Spanish as an important exception to studies on other Romance languages, thus presenting a potential counterexample to the POA hypothesis. Gonzales (1989; summarized in Andersen, 1993), however, reanalyzed Eisenberg's data using the Vendlerean classification, and showed that her study was actually consistent with the POA Hypothesis. It therefore appears that Spanish L1 acquisition data do not pose a serious problem for the POA Hypothesis.

Cziko and Koda (1987) reported more problematic results in their study of Japanese L1 acquisition. In analyzing longitudinal data provided by Noji (1976), they attempted to test Bickerton's two hypotheses: the PNPD and the SPD. First, they found no relationship between past-tense use and punctuality.[7] Second, although they claimed that the SPD is supported by their data (i.e., the progressive marker is not extended to stative verbs), there were some methodological problems in their study (see Youseff, 1988, 1990). This study might, therefore, constitute counterevidence to the POA claims (1) and (4) (section III.A of this chapter). Rispoli (1981), however, provided important longitudinal data of another Japanese child, and our reanalysis of the data in that study seems to support general claim (1). In the earliest samples (1;6 and 1;8), verbs used with the past marker *-ta* are almost exclusively accomplishment or achievement verbs, with one exception of *hiita* 'played [an instrument],' which can probably be classified as an activity. In later samples (1;10 to 2;0), the past marking extends to more activity and state verbs. In addition, Shirai (1993) analyzed the same data that Cziko and Koda (1987) used, and obtained results consistent with the POA claims; namely, past marking initially developed with achievement verbs, and progressive/continuative marking (*-tei*) with activity verbs. Clearly, more studies are needed in the acquisition of Japanese as an L1 in order to resolve the apparent contradictions in these studies.

Li's (1989) study on child Mandarin appears to be the most problematic for the POA hypothesis. This study is very important in that it specifically tested Bickerton's two hypotheses, PNPD and SPD, by using three experiments. It therefore merits an extensive review here. Based on the results of three experimental studies (comprehension, production, imitation), Li argued that no support was found for

[7]It is not unanimously agreed that a Japanese inflection *-ta* is a past-tense marker. Some have claimed it is a perfective–completive aspectual marker; others suggest that *-ta* functions as both a tense and an aspect marker. For more discussion on the issue, see Matsumoto (1985) and Soga (1983).

PNPD and SPD, but that support was found for Slobin's (1985) result–process distinction as a cognitive universal. However, a closer examination of his study is necessary before any conclusions can be drawn. In particular, the results of the study, which were interpreted by Li as evidence against Bickerton's claim, must be reinterpreted within the present framework of POA.

Li (1989) argued that the lack of distinction between the three levels of aspect (situational characteristics, grammatical aspect, and inherent lexical aspect) creates confusion. In particular, he criticized Bickerton (1981) for a lack of distinction in this regard. Although Li did not point this out, if analyzed using the three levels, Bickerton's (1981) punctual–nonpunctual hypothesis primarily pertains to grammatical aspect, not inherent lexical aspect. Bickerton's (1981) "punctual aspect" is basically perfective aspect, and his "nonpunctual aspect" is imperfective aspect. This distinction is clear in his discussion of pidgin and creole languages, in view of the fact that he includes iterative–habitual and progressive as nonpunctual. However, this distinction is not very clear in his discussion of L1 acquisition, as pointed out earlier; he uses the terms *punctual verbs* and *activity* (or nonpunctual) *verbs* (p. 174), to refer to Aktionsart (i.e., inherent aspect) distinctions. To make matters worse, the "test for inherent punctuality" (p. 173) that Bickerton cited (without citing any source) is, as Weist (1989) has pointed out, a test for telic–atelic distinctions; that is, "If you stop halfway through *Ving,* have you *Ved?*" (Bickerton, 1981, p. 173). Furthermore, in his review of L1 acquisition studies, Bickerton (1981) discussed situational characteristics, claiming that the duration of a situation was a determining factor for the use of verbal morphology at the early stages. Li (1989) criticized Bickerton, stating that it was impossible to determine at what level (among three: situation, Aktionsart, grammatical aspect) the bioprogram works, if Bickerton was talking about PNPD at all three levels to begin with.

There appear to be two problems involved in the confusion. First, it appears that Li (1989) was not aware that Bickerton's punctuality was actually telicity when translated into inherent aspect. Second, Bickerton was somewhat arbitrary in discussing how the bioprogram worked for the PNPD. In his discussion of Bronckart and Sinclair (1973), Bickerton concluded that the bioprogram works at the level of situation when the child is young; the PNPD is sensitive to the pure length of the situation. However, when the child is older, Bickerton claimed, the PNPD works at the level of inherent aspect. Bickerton (1981) stated that "as they [the children] grow older, the criterion of durativity is replaced by another which is also related to the PNPD. For the punctual–nonpunctual opposition must also be marked in the semantic features of individual verbs" (p. 170). Bickerton (1989, p. 35), however, claimed that "nonpunctuality marking is determined by situations, not by verb classes." It appears that he has changed his position on this point.

Bickerton's (1981) state–process distinction, on the other hand, appears to be an Aktionsart distinction, as he emphasizes that state verbs cannot be combined with nonpunctual markers (i.e., imperfective markers) in creole grammar (see also Cziko, 1989b). The SPD is, therefore, not very problematic in terms of interpretation.

When interpreted in the context of this chapter, Bickerton (1981) was arguing that (1) the state–process distinction (i.e., state vs. activity/accomplishment/ achievement) is innate; (2) the perfective–imperfective distinction of grammatical aspect is innate; (3) the telic–atelic distinction (i.e., accomplishment and achievement vs. state and activity) is innate; and (4) the punctual–durative distinction (i.e., achievement vs. accomplishment/activity/state) is innate, although the level at which (2), (3), and (4) work differ depending on the age of the child. These are basically consistent with POA except for the claim of the perfective–imperfective distinction being innate, which is not included in the POA hypothesis. This agreement with POA, of course, is at the level of description; POA, as presented in this chapter, makes no claim as to its innateness, which is at the level of explanation.

Generally speaking, Li's study is consistent with the POA claims in this study. Li's main point is that the result–process distinction is innate, a claim he makes based on his experiments. Resultative verbs, in the child language context at least, are closely associated with telicity (having a clear end point, whether as an achievement or an accomplishment verb), and process verbs, in his terms, are activity verbs, in our terminology. Slobin's (1985) Result/Process hypothesis, which Li provides support for, is very much in line with POA. However, there are two very important points revealed by Li's study, which are possibly genuine challenges to POA.

First, in the comprehension study, Li (1989) used achievement verbs that described unitary punctual actions that had no observable results (*jump, kick,* and *turn a somersault*), and the finding was that, when combined with the Mandarin perfective marker -*le,* achievement verbs did not result in significantly higher comprehension by children than activity verbs. Moreover, achievement verbs were better understood with -*zai* (progressive marker) than -*le* (perfective marker). This contradicts one of the predictions of the POA Hypothesis (i.e., claim 1): strong associations between the perfective marker and punctual verbs.

A second important finding in Li (1989) was the incorrect overextension of the progressive marker -*zai* to stative verbs in the production study. The stative verbs that received progressive marking were Chinese posture verbs such as *sit, stand, kneel.* (As Li observed, posture verbs in Chinese do not receive progressive markers, unlike in English.) This contradicted one of the predictions of the POA Hypothesis (i.e., claim 4); that is, that there will be no overextension of progressive markers to stative verbs.

It is possible, as Matthews (1990) has pointed out, that the methodology (use of a picture story) created difficulty for the children. If natural production data had been used in Li's study, there might not have been any overextension of the progressive marker to stative verbs. In the case of natural production data, children can restrict their production within their linguistic capacity, whereas in experimental production, they have to perform beyond their limitations, in which case there may be some ungrammatical linguistic behavior that may not be observed in spontaneous production. As Bickerton's bioprogram prediction (no overextension of the progressive marker to stative verbs) rests on spontaneous data in Brown (1973), this methodological factor pointed out by Matthews should be taken into account. Nevertheless, further study is necessary to investigate whether overextension of -zai to stative verbs is prevalent in child Mandarin, including further research using naturalistic production data (see Shirai, 1994, for further discussion).

In sum, Li's study presents two important challenges to the POA hypothesis for further investigation: (1) it is not the temporal contour of the situation (i.e., punctuality) that is important, but the result that arises out of a situation that is important for past–perfective marking; and (2) overextension of progressive markers to stative verbs may not be nonexistent. Otherwise, Li (1989) reported results consistent with POA.

One methodological problem on Li's study needs to be pointed out. In his production task (study 2), he used only repeated punctual actions (*jumping, blinking*) as punctual situations to be described. Because they are essentially iterative, they are qualitatively different from unitary (i.e., nonrepeated, noniterative) punctual events. His conclusion that the children "associate punctual verbs and stative verbs more with imperfective aspect than with perfective aspect" (Li, 1989, p. 121) is, therefore, misleading. However, this problem only concerns his production task; his claims based on other aspects of the study remain sound.

Methodological Problems

One major problem for POA studies is that different researchers use different methodologies based on different frameworks. First of all, some researchers use Vendler's categories (e.g., Weist et al., 1984), whereas others use their own four-way classification of verb semantics (i.e., lexical aspect). A three-way classification is often used, too, without distinguishing between accomplishment and achievement verbs (e.g., Cziko & Koda, 1987; Stephany, 1981).

To further complicate matters, different terminologies are used to refer to the same concepts, and the same terminologies are used to refer to different concepts. For example, Bickerton (1981) uses the term *punctual* in a sense different from Comrie (1976) and others that rely on the Vendlerean classification, as pointed out earlier. To attempt to clarify some of the terminological confusion, we have summarized some of the different terminologies used in acquisition studies in Table III.

The confusion among the three levels (situational properties, inherent aspect, and grammatical aspect) is, in a sense, inevitable, because there is a strong association among the levels. For example, if a situation is punctual (i.e., occurs instantly), it is most probably described by a verb phrase in which inherent aspect is punctual and

TABLE III

Terminology Used in Studies on Aspect

Study	Grammatical aspect (Viewpoint aspect)		Inherent lexical aspect/Aktionsart (Situation aspect/verb semantics)			
Andersen (1991)	perfective	imperfective	punctual event	telic event	activity	state
Weist et al. (1984)	perfective	imperfective	achievement	accomplishment	activity	state
Li (1989)	perfective	imperfective	punctual	telic	process	state
Bickerton (1981)	punctual	nonpunctual	punctual			nonpunctual
Cziko (1989a)	perfective	imperfective	perfective			imperfective
Smith (1980)	perfective	imperfective	perfective			imperfective
Ontological distinctions						
Lyons (1977)	event	process–state	event		process	state
Mourelatos (1981)	event	process–state	event		process	state

the grammatical aspectual marking used, if the situation is not iterative or habitual, is perfective (or punctual aspect in Bickerton's terminology). (Andersen & Shirai (1994) elaborate further on this.) As has been pointed out by Lyons (1977) and Mourelatos (1981), among others, both the perfective–imperfective distinction and the Vendlerean lexical aspect may rely on the ontological distinction (which is on the situation level) of state/process/event. (Lyons, 1977, and Mourelatos, 1981, however are in disagreement in that Lyons classifies accomplishment—telic event—as process, whereas Mourelatos categorizes it as event.)

Another problem with POA studies is the reliability of the classification systems. Most studies in L1 acquisition do not report operational tests, except for Shirai (1993, 1994), Shirai and Andersen (in press), and Weist et al. (1984), and we can only blindly believe in the researchers' classificational accuracy in such cases. It must be admitted here that the reliability of the classification system used is also seldom reported, the known exceptions being Cziko and Koda (1987), Shirai (1994), and Shirai and Andersen (in press) which report intrarater reliability. However, classification is no easy matter.

Different tasks used in the studies also create interpretation problems. Researchers have used various tasks, such as comprehension, imitation, and production, and these task differences must be taken into account in interpretation of the studies. Even among production data, there are differences. First, there is a difference between spontaneous speech and experimentally elicited speech. Generally speaking, spontaneous speech is easier for the children. That is, they can function within the limit of their cognitive and linguistic potential. They can perform as they wish, avoiding anything (both in terms of linguistic structure and content) for which they are not ready. Experimental elicitation, on the other hand, often forces children to use their full potential because the children have to perform as required by the task, which may require them to go beyond their linguistic competence.

One of the strongest features of Weist et al. (1984) is, in fact, their innovative combination of tasks. Their most important claim, that very young Polish-speaking children do indeed have access to both grammatical aspect and tense, rests on nicely designed situations in which the researcher leads the child through talk about events that they both experienced together in a recent and a more remote past. The adult who is talking to the child gets him or her to talk about detail that the child is indeed capable of referring to linguistically, but probably only under these specific conditions. Weist et al. make an important distinction between what the child normally says versus what he or she is capable of saying. (See also, in this regard, the discussion in the next paragraph.)

Second, elicited speech can also vary due to subtle differences in methodology. For example, as McShane and Whittaker (1988) pointed out, with most experimental studies addressing the issue of POA, "toys and props remained visible to the child" (p. 55) when he or she was describing what happened, and this may have been the reason for the child's using present tense. In their own study, McShane and Whittaker had the toys and props removed from sight, and relatively speaking, their subjects were very successful in producing past forms. Given these variations due to elicitation measures, we should always be aware of these differences in interpreting data, a task that is by no means easy.

In sum, differences in terminology and methodology in obtaining language data from children make it very difficult to interpret and compare studies, often resulting in confusion and disagreements.

B. L2 Acquisition

The phenomenon of POA has also been observed in L2 acquisition studies. Table IV summarizes the studies relevant to POA in L2 acquisition. Most of the studies report on adult L2 learners (except for Andersen, 1986a, 1986b, 1986c, 1991, Economides, 1985, and H. Taylor, 1987, who studied children), and naturalistic (i.e., noninstructed) L2 acquisition (except for Bardovi-Harlig, 1992, Shirai, 1995, and Ramsay, 1989a, who investigated classroom L2 acquisition, and Nixon, 1986, and Shirai & McGhee, 1988, whose subjects had studied English extensively before coming to the United States, and had been in the United States for only a short period at the time of the study). The results generally support POA except for one major difference regarding the use of progressive on stative verbs.

Most of the relevant studies have English or Spanish as the L2. The English data generally show (although with some variations) that (1) past morphology is strongly associated with achievement or accomplishment verbs or both (Cushing, 1987; Economides, 1985; Flashner, 1982; Robison, 1990; Rothstein, 1985; Shirai & McGhee, 1988; H. Taylor, 1987), and (2) -ing is strongly associated with durative (i.e., state, activity, accomplishment) verbs, with activity verbs receiving more -ing marking (Cushing, 1987; Economides, 1985; Kumpf, 1982; Rothstein, 1985; H. Taylor, 1987). A number of these studies use the term "perfective" to

TABLE IV

Studies on Primacy of Aspect in L2 Acquisition

	N	Learner characteristics	L1
English			
Rothstein (1985)	1	3 years in U.S.	Hebrew
Kumpf (1984b)	1	28 years in U.S.	Japanese
Shirai and McGhee (1988)	1	6 months in U.S.	Japanese
Mishina (1993)	3	1.5 to 15+ years in U.S.	Japanese
Nixon (1986)	1	1–6 months in U.S.	Mandarin
Yoshitomi (1992)	1	7 years in U.S.	Mandarin
Bayley (1991, 1994)	20	mixed	Mandarin
Huang (1993)	5	5 months to 8 years in U.S.	Mandarin
Flashner (1982)	3	2, 3, and 4 years in U.S.	Russian
Cushing (1987)	1	1.5 years in U.S.	Serahuli
Kumpf (1982)	1	30+ years in U.S.	Spanish
Robison (1990)	1	less than 3 years in U.S.	Spanish
Robison (1993)	26	1st year university students in Puerto Rico	Spanish
H. Taylor (1987)	1	1–10 months in U.S.	Spanish
Economides (1985)	1	12+ months in U.S.	Vietnamese
Bardovi-Harlig (1992)	135	Foreign students in U.S.	mixed
Japanese			
Shirai (1995)	3	7 months in Japan	Chinese
Spanish			
Andersen (1986a, 1991)	2	8 to 14 years old	English
Ramsay (1989a, 1990)	30	Classroom L2 acquisition	English

refer to the use of English past marking on event verbs (i.e., achievements or accomplishments) and "imperfective" to refer to use of -*ing* on activity verbs, in some studies, or the base verb for durative Aktionsart, in others. We maintain this use of these terms in our discussion, but enclose the terms in quotation marks to distinguish them from the usual use of perfective and imperfective for grammatical aspectual marking, as in the Mandarin case discussed above. In still another study, Nixon's (1986) Chinese subject expressed "perfective aspect" mostly by using "have + verb (base form)" instead of using past morphology.

In the studies in Table IV, the results regarding the use of -*ing* are important because they are different from what is found in L1 acquisition in that progressive markers are sometimes overextended to stative verbs in some of the L2 studies.[8] This is probably because the learner has an L1 on which to map L2 forms. Flashner (1982, reported also in Wenzell, 1989) attributes her subjects' use of past morphology for 'perfective' contexts and the base form for 'imperfective' contexts to transfer from Russian, the subjects' L1. Many of the L1s of the subjects in the

---

[8]Besides the studies listed in Table IV, Bickerton (1984b) also discusses, anecdotally, a case of a Hindi speaker showing overextension of -*ing* to state verbs.

above studies have imperfective aspect, which is strongly associated with durativity (Comrie, 1976; Weist et al., 1984). It is plausible that these learners associate the -ing marker with imperfective aspect in their L1, as progressive is part of imperfectivity (Comrie, 1976).

Although the notion of L1 transfer as an account of overextension of -ing seems plausible, transfer alone cannot explain it. There may be an interaction between universal factors and L1 factors. As has been suggested in L2 acquisition research, universal factors (i.e., markedness, prototype) and the learner's L1 interact and subtly influence L2 development. See, for example, Eckman (1977) and Major (1987) for phonology, Andersen (1983) for morphology, Hatch (1983a) for phonology and morphology, Zobl (1980) and Gass (1984) for syntax, and Tanaka (1983) and Shirai (1989) for semantics. For a study specifically dealing with tense–aspect, see Gass and Ard (1984). (See chapter 10 by Gass for a general discussion of L1 influence in L2 acquisition.)

As other aspects of L2 acquisition of verbal morphology (especially past morphology) are consistent with findings in L1 acquisition studies, it may be reasonable to assume that universal factors are at work in the case of progressive morphology, too. The issue of "how much" each factor contributes to language development is a difficult question to tackle; it requires careful reanalysis of the data, comparing the L1s of the learners, considering whether they have imperfective or progressive morphemes or both, and what the functions of the morphemes are. Gass and Ard (1984) is a study in this direction, comparing the acceptability judgments of progressive sentences by Japanese and Spanish learners of English. Although the study is consistent with POA claims here in that "action in progress" (i.e., progressive form attached to activity verbs) is acquired easily, the results show how difficult it is to interpret such data (Kumpf, 1984a).

One possible counterexample to the general trend of POA seen in L2 acquisition is reported by Kumpf (1984b). Her subject, Tamiko, a Japanese speaker, tended to use base forms for completed actions in the foreground, whereas frequently using past-tense markers for stative verbs, activity verbs being marked with -ing in the background (see Hopper & Thompson, 1980, for the notions of 'foreground' and 'background'). Further research, such as more studies on Japanese subjects, is clearly necessary before we treat this example as an idiosyncratic variation. For example, Shirai and McGhee (1988) studied a Japanese subject, and reported more frequent use of past marking on nonstative verbs, which is consistent with POA.

An apparent counterexample to POA is Meisel (1987). Based on his study on German as L2, he claimed that:

> [L]earners do not systematically use an aspectual system. It may well be that this is a very marginal phenomenon, occurring only occasionally, which has received too much attention by researchers who base their expectations on findings in L1 studies or on creole studies." (p. 220)

TABLE V

Level-1 Past-Tense Marking[a]

State	31.6% (live)
Activity	35.1% (work 47.3%; take care of 26.3%, stay 31.6%)
Achievement	63.2% (tell 68.4%; die 57.9%)

[a] Adapted from Bardovi-Harlig, 1992.

Meisel (1987) failed to cite any L2 study in this area despite his criticism that "Anyone who wants to claim that an aspectual system is characteristic of certain phases of L2 acquisition . . . will have to give solid empirical evidence" (p. 220). However, his study had a very different framework, and does not constitute a problem for the claim of POA. POA only concerns the acquisition of verbal morphology, whereas Meisel's focus was on how past time reference is encoded in interlanguage (IL), including other devices such as adverbials, discourse organization, and so forth (function-to-form analysis, see Long & Sato, 1983).

Echoing the caution by Meisel (1987), Bardovi-Harlig (1992) concluded that her study does not constitute support for the POA hypothesis. She states, "The learners in this study also marked tense fairly consistently across aspectual classes" (p. 274). However, a reanalysis of her data clearly shows that her data follow the prediction of POA. For the sake of simplicity let us discuss the level-1 (elementary) learners in her study. Tables V and VI show that the general trend is that L2 learners fail to supply past marking in obligatory context much more frequently for state and activity verbs than for achievement verbs. Specifically, Table V shows that correct suppliances of past forms on achievement verbs are much more frequent than those on activity and state verbs. Furthermore, Table VI shows that even when incorrect markings of pastness (i.e., past progressive, past perfect, and past perfect progressive) are included, the trend remains the same, although in a less dramatic way.

It should also be noted that Bardovi-Harlig's data elicitation procedure is quite different from other studies reviewed here. It consists of responses to a cloze test in which careful monitoring is possible. In addition, her subjects are enrolled in an ESL program at an American university and are therefore exposed to formal instruction. This shows that POA is very broad in its application; that is, not only

TABLE VI

Level-1 Past-Tense Marking[a]

State	42.1% (live)
Activity	43.9% (work 57.9%, take care of 36.9%, stay 36.9%)
Achievement	63.2% (tell 68.4%; die 57.9%)

[a] Adapted from Bardovi-Harlig, 1992. Including past prog., past perf, past perf. prog

is it observed in the naturalistic data of naturalistic L2 acquisition but also in the paper-and-pencil test data of ESL learners with formal grammar instruction.[9]

The acquisition of Spanish as an L2 has been a good testing ground for POA, and the studies of Spanish L2 acquisition provide some of the clearest cases of the general claims of POA (1) and (2) (i.e., the correlation of past perfective morphology with accomplishment and achievement verbs, and past imperfective forms with state–activity verbs). Andersen's quasi-longitudinal study (1986a, 1986b, 1986c, 1991, based on the same data) clearly shows that past perfective appeared first, and the order of emergence was "achievement → accomplishment → activity → state," and the slower development of imperfective past followed the course of "state → activity → accomplishment → achievement." Ramsay's (1989a, 1989b, 1990) cross-sectional studies of classroom Spanish learners also show the same tendency as Andersen's, clearly following the general developmental pattern as predicted by POA.

What are the implications of L2 acquisition research for the POA phenomena in general? Earlier studies in POA on L1 acquisition (Antinucci & Miller, 1976; Bronckart & Sinclair, 1973; Smith, 1980) attributed POA to a cognitive deficit, suggesting that children did not have the concept of deictic past. However, as Andersen (1989) points out, this "cognitive deficit" cannot be the sole reason for POA, because adult learners, who clearly have a concept of deictic past, also show the same tendency as children acquiring an L1 at least with respect to the acquisition of past–perfective morphology.

The overextension of the progressive forms is also noteworthy. The absence of overextension in L1 acquisition, and its presence in L2 acquisition, suggest that the universal capacity that may be available to children is no longer available for adults, or at least it is weakened or mediated by the L1 tense–aspect system. (Chapter 5 by Schachter, this volume, is a general discussion of the linguistic consequences of maturation in L2 acquisition.) This suggests that L1 acquisition data—or, better, combined L1 and L2 acquisition data—are more suitable for investigating the effect of universal factors, because one of the strong intervening variables (L1 transfer) can be controlled.

Another interesting point is that POA is observed for classroom learners (Bardovi-Harlig, 1992; Ramsay, 1989a) as well as for L1 and naturalistic L2 learners. In fact, the Japanese subject in Shirai and McGhee (1988) clearly knew the past tense and its marker in English through his strong background in grammar. However, in actual performance, he did not have ready access to this knowledge. It is also noteworthy that two types of special populations—deaf speakers (Herman, 1990) and patients with Alzheimer's disease (Matthews, 1989)—are reported to

---

[9]Recent studies by Bardovi-Harlig and her colleagues, which were not available at the time of writing this paper, support the POA hypothesis (Bardovi-Harlig & Reynolds, 1995; Bardovi-Harlig & Bergström, in press). See also Robison's (1995) large-scale cross-sectional study which supports the hypothesis.

have shown the POA phenomenon. All of these cases might suggest the existence of strong cognitive or linguistic universals or both at work in acquisition and use of verbal morphology. However, an alternative explanation is also possible, to which we now turn.

IV. The Distributional Bias Hypothesis

A. Introduction

Regarding explanations for POA, Andersen (1986c, 1988, 1993) has suggested that there is a distributional bias in the linguistic input (i.e., native speakers' (NS) speech) addressed to language acquirers. The claim is that if NSs use verbal morphology in such a biased way as to be consistent with POA (in English, for example, more -*ing* forms with activity verbs and more past forms with achievement and accomplishment verbs), it would not be surprising that children and L2 learners would start using verbal morphology in a way that would be consistent with POA.

Andersen (1988) phrased the Distributional Bias Hypothesis in these terms:

> [T]here are . . . properties of the input that promote the incorporation of an inappropriate form:meaning relationship into the interlanguage. That is, the learner misperceives the meaning and distribution of a particular form that he discovers in the input, following the Distributional Bias Principle:
>
> > If both X and Y can occur in the same environments A and B, but a bias in the distribution of X and Y makes it appear that X only occurs in environment A and Y only occurs in environment B, when you acquire X and Y, restrict X to environment A and Y to environment B. (p. 123)

For the POA issue, a statistical tendency for past or perfective forms to occur primarily on achievement and accomplishment verbs and for progressive forms to occur primarily on activities could cause the learner to perceive these associations as absolute and only use past or perfective forms on achievement and accomplishment verbs and only use progressive forms on activity verbs.

The fact that there is a distributional bias in native speech has been observed by a number of linguists. Although not necessarily concerning the distribution of inherent aspect, Comrie (1976) states:

> The most typical usage of verbs in the present tense are those decoding actions in progress and states, . . . whereas in the past the most typical usages of verbs, especially nonstative verbs, are those with perfective meaning. (p. 72)

Bybee (1985), more clearly, observes:

> Inherent aspectual meaning determines the frequency with which different lexical stems are paired with different aspectual inflections. This is evident in early child language, where perfective inflection is first used on telic, punctual verbs,

while progressive or imperfective inflection is first used only on activity verbs (Bloom et al., 1980). *This skewing is also reflected in frequency counts of adult language* (italics added). (p. 77)

It should also be noted that Comrie (1976) and Bybee (1985) do not cite any study that has quantitatively established the skewing.

In spite of these observations, however, the skewing in the native speech has not been viewed as a possible source of POA in language acquisition by previous acquisition researchers (e.g., Bardovi-Harlig, 1992; Bloom et al., 1980; Weist et al., 1984). As Andersen (1993) puts it, "Most of the [acquisition] studies reviewed in Andersen (1989) appear to assume that, except for any language-specific restrictions, there is an equal distribution of verbal inflections across the various semantic classes in native speech." In fact, it appears that these researchers are not aware of the strong distributional bias in native speech (but see Weist, 1989, p. 48). For example, in their response to Smith and Weist (1987), Bloom and Harner (1989) reanalyzed the data in Weist et al. (1984) and showed that there is a statistically significant relationship between past-tense forms and inherent aspect in Weist et al.'s data on Polish children's speech. (Weist et al., 1984, argued against Bloom et al.'s, 1980, "aspect before tense" hypothesis.) It should be noted, however, that the same "statistically significant" relationship might be found in adult–adult Polish speech as well as in motherese addressed to these children. If the correlation is seen in adult Polish speech, it could be that children show the same correlation simply because this is how the language is spoken. Moreover, even if such a correlation is not statistically significant, there may be a significant correlation in the mother's speech addressed to Polish children, in which case it can be argued that the source of the biased distribution in the child's speech is simply bias in Polish motherese.

The idea of explaining language acquisition by the frequency of particular linguistic items in the input is not new. Indeed, there have been extensive attempts to explain the order of acquisition (especially grammatical morphemes) by a frequency factor in the input addressed to the learner, both in L1 and L2 acquisition research (i.e., studies on "caretaker speech and motherese" and "foreigner talk") (see, for example, Snow & Ferguson, 1977). However, there has not been much attempt made in the area of POA to investigate the relationship between input and acquisition.

B. Distributional Bias Studies

Distributional Bias in Input to Learners

There have been only a few studies on NS input in relation to POA. These studies, however, all support the Distributional Bias Hypothesis (henceforth, DBH). In the following sections, we first review studies on the speech addressed to L1 and L2 learners, and then studies on more varied types of native speaker discourse. Table VII summarizes the distributional bias studies.

TABLE VII

Distributional Bias Studies

	Language	Type of discourse
Child-directed speech (L1 acquisition)		
Brown (1973)	American English	natural interaction
Stephany (1981)	Greek	natural interaction
Ramsay (1989b)	British English	natural interaction
Shirai (1991)	American English	natural interaction
Foreigner talk		
Shirai (1990)	American English	play activity (Peck, 1977)
Native speaker's discourse (spoken)		
Stephany (1981)	Greek	natural dialogues with an adult
Andersen (1986b,c)	Spanish	conversation
Ramsay (1989b)	Spanish	oral narrative for children
	Spanish	oral narrative (elicited data)
Gonzales (1990)	Spanish	interview
Yap (1990)	American English	interview
Leone (1990)	Italian	interview
Takashima and Kamibayashi (1990)	Japanese	interview
Takahashi (1990)	Japanese	oral narrative (elicited data)
Native speaker's discourse (written)		
Ramsay (1989b)	English	narrative for children
	Spanish	narrative for adults

Brown (1973) was probably the first to point out the relationship between children's use of progressive and past markers and the distributional bias in the input. He observed that children never incorrectly used the progressive marker on involuntary state verbs, and checked the speech by Eve's mother during the period before Eve started to use -*ing* frequently, finding no progressive marking on involuntary state verbs. Brown (1973) also pointed out that past marking started with

> a small set of verbs which name events of such brief duration that the event is almost certain to have ended before one can speak. These are: *fell, dropped, slipped, crashed, broke.* It is reasonable to guess that these forms may have been always or almost always in the past in the mother's speech. (p. 334)

He did not, however, provide quantitative data on this point, nor did he attribute the lack of overextension to the distributional bias in motherese.

Stephany (1981) studied both children's speech (Greek) and mothers' speech directed to children, and found a strong relationship between the two. First, at the level of grammatical aspect, she observed that "the distribution [in mothers' speech] of the perfective and imperfective aspect closely resembles the one in the children's data" (p. 52). Ninety-six percent of past forms were found to be perfective in the mothers' speech, and 100% in the children's speech. Second, analysis based on her own three semantic verb classes (i.e., the level of inherent lexical aspect) also showed a strong correlation between mothers' speech and children's speech. She stated that "a surprising conformity of the distribution of semantic verb classes . . . can be seen between child speech and child-directed mother's speech" (p. 53). For example, "with stative verbs, 93% of the occurring verb forms are indicative present imperfective forms in both kinds of data" (p. 53). Regarding past forms in mother's speech, the stative verb was used only once for indicative past, whereas resultative-dynamic verbs (which correspond to accomplishment and achievement verbs) were used 158 times, and nonresultative dynamic verbs (activity verbs) were used 94 times. (The figures in this sentence are calculated based on the percentages given in Table 5 in Stephany, 1981, p. 52.) This dramatic distributional bias may well favor children's development of the tense–aspect system in the direction predicted by the POA hypothesis.

Ramsay (1989b) also looked at motherese (British English) in Fletcher (1985). She found three stative verbs and eight achievement verbs in simple past forms, and three activity verbs and two accomplishment verbs in present progressive forms in the motherese data. Although her data support the DBH, the number of tokens is too small to be conclusive.

In a study of input to L2 learners, Shirai (1990) investigated input to Spanish-speaking children acquiring ESL in play situations with native English-speaking friends (child–child interaction, using data from Peck, 1977), and found that there was a strong correlation between (1) activity verbs and present progressive, and (2) accomplishment and achievement verbs and past morphology.

Shirai (1991) investigated the motherese addressed to three children acquiring English, using data from the CHILDES database (MacWhinney & Snow, 1990). The results showed that there is a strong relationship between morphology and inherent aspect in the mothers' speech to their children. Seventy-five percent, 80%, and 70% of the past inflections used by each of the three mothers were attached to accomplishment and achievement verbs, whereas 56%, 53%, and 61% of progressive inflections were attached to activity verbs.

In sum, it could be suggested (though tentatively, considering the number of relevant studies) that the above examples of native speech directed to L1 and L2 learners are biased in such a way that the distribution favors the course of acquisition predicted by the POA hypothesis. The next question is whether or not this distributional bias is unique to speech addressed to learners.

Distributional Bias in Adult–Adult NS Speech

Stephany (1981) provides the best attempt to answer the above question. She collected not only mothers' speech directed to children, but also speech to adults by these same mothers. The findings are that (1) a much higher percentage of dynamic verbs (activity, accomplishment, or achievement) in subjunctive forms were found in child-directed speech than in adult-directed speech, and (2) the distribution of semantic classes of verbs is similar in both adult-directed and child-

TABLE VIII

**The Frequency of Indicative Verbs by
Semantic Class in Mothers' Speech**[a]

Stephany's classification The Vendlerean system	Stative State	Nonresultative dynamic Activity	Resultative dynamic Achievement/ Accomplishment
Child-directed speech			
Present imperfective	129	300	158
Past perfective	0	85	158
Past imperfective	1	9	0
Adult-directed speech			
Present imperfective	234	365	242
Past perfective	19	132	200
Past imperfective	23	62	28

[a] Adapted from Stephany, 1981.

directed speech, although the distribution is less dramatic in the adult-directed speech than in the child-directed speech. Stephany attributes the first finding to the context of motherese; in Greek, the subjunctive is used to direct the addressee's behavior, and is thus naturally more predominant in mothers' speech to children. The second finding, which is more relevant to the POA hypothesis, has interesting implications. The frequency of past perfective and imperfective and present imperfective, calculated based on the percentages given in Tables 5 and 6 in Stephany (1981), is summarized in Table VIII.

It is interesting to note that even in the adult-directed speech, there are tendencies that are consistent with the DBH; a strong association is seen between past perfective and dynamic verbs, particularly accomplishment and achievement verbs. However, it is also clear that this correlation is even more dramatic in child-directed speech. Indeed, with the kind of exclusive mapping of perfective past on dynamic verbs found in Stephany's child-directed speech sample, a child can easily be misled into thinking that only resultative-dynamic (and less prominently, nonresultative dynamic) verbs are used in the past tense. As Stephany notes, "in talking to the very young child, mothers restrict the number of grammatical categories used as well as the frequency of certain of these categories" (1981, p. 55).

More recently, Ramsay (1989b) and R. Andersen's students (Gonzales, 1990; Leone, 1990; Shirai, 1990; Takahashi, 1990; Takashima & Kamibayashi, 1990; Yap, 1990) analyzed various types of NS's discourse in several languages. Ramsay studied (1) an English narrative written for children, (2) a Spanish oral narrative, (3) a Spanish narrative (novel), and (4) a Spanish oral narrative elicited experimentally. The results were consistent with the DBH. Andersen's students, whose findings are summarized and discussed in Andersen (1993), also basically found support for the DBH. However, these results were not as unproblematic as other studies reviewed so far; some studies lend stronger support for DBH than others.

One factor that appears to be important in explaining why some of the studies by Andersen's students provide only a partial support for DBH is the frequent reference to past habitual situations in their data. Andersen (1993) observed that some deviations from the DBH prediction can be accounted for by this factor. The greater number of achievement verbs in imperfective forms, and stative and activity verbs for past and perfective forms in Gonzales (1990) and Yap (1990) is attributed to past habitual reference. It is interesting to note that Ramsay's (1989b) analysis, which fits the DBH better, counts habitual aspect separately. It may be possible to hypothesize that the frequency of past habitual events is the key factor in determining whether a particular discourse fits the DBH.

Returning to the question of whether NS–NS discourse fits the DBH, or whether only the speech addressed to learners fits the DBH, it appears that learner-directed speech is more consistent with the DBH than is NS–NS discourse. As can be seen from Stephany's (1981) controlled study, child-directed speech is more consistent with the DBH than is adult-directed speech. However, it is not clear whether the topic of the conversation or the simplified nature of the learner-directed speech is the key determining factor. In other words, the question is whether the semantically restricted use of verbal morphology to L1 and L2 learners is due to speech modification (simplified input) or due to the context or topic (simple input, i.e., it is not "simplified"). It has been observed in the study of motherese and foreigner talk that NSs modify their speech to learners, especially by avoiding difficult structures (Hatch, 1983a). It is possible, then, as Hatch (1983b) suggests, that NSs restrict the use of polysemous words (such as *line, break*) to prototypes (parallel line, break the glass) when talking to foreigners with limited English competence. Andersen (1990) also suggested the possibility that NSs tend to restrict the use of progressive (as a polysemous category) in speech to L2 learners. These possibilities point to a "simplified input" account of strong distributional bias in the input to the learner. On the other hand, it is also possible that the restricted use of verbal morphology is due to the context or topic. Thus far, the kind of input (addressed to learners) that has been studied in relation to a distributional bias is limited in terms of content and topic: play situations (Shirai, 1990) and caretaker–child interactions (Ramsay, 1989b; Shirai, 1991; Stephany, 1981). Therefore, it is not clear whether the strong distributional bias observed in these cases is due to speech modification, to topic of the speech, or to both. It may be that both factors (the topic factor and the speech modification factor) are probably interdependent, and indeed it is difficult to separate the two, because speech modification also involves limitation of the topic. For example, mothers may unconsciously avoid topics that involve past habitual references because they feel they are cognitively and linguistically too complex.

Although it is not clear whether the reason for the conformity with the DBH is due to topic or to the restricted nature of foreigner talk or motherese or to both, at least it appears that learners, in general, receive input consistent with the DBH. If this indeed is the case, it may not be necessary to posit an innateness account to explain the phenomenon of POA, as does Bickerton (1981, 1984a, 1984b, 1988).

Andersen (1993) suggests an interpretation for these findings. He suggests that both adult NSs and L1 and L2 learners follow two general principles in matching verb inflections with particular verbs: the Relevance Principle and the Congruence Principle. Learners, unlike adult NSs, are also subject to the One to One Principle.

According to the Relevance Principle (Bybee, 1985; Slobin, 1985) a grammatical morpheme, such as a verb inflection, will be placed closer to the verb stem the more relevant the meaning of the morpheme is to the meaning of the verb. Because aspectual meanings are more relevant to the meaning of a verb than tense or agreement inflections, learners and fluent NSs alike will choose inflections in terms of their relevance to the inherent aspect of the verb. The Congruence Principle is a corollary of the Relevance Principle. Andersen (1993, pp. 328–329) states this as:

> [A] grammatical morpheme is used by learners according to how congruent the meaning of the morpheme is with the meaning of the lexical item to which it is attached. Progressive morphemes are especially [congruent with] . . . activities, which have inherent duration like the duration conveyed by the morpheme itself, and past and perfective inflections are especially [congruent with . . . achievements and accomplishments]. "Past" can be conceptualized as referring to an event that is finished, over with, as can "perfective," and both apply most logically to [achievements and accomplishments], which by their very nature are finished and over with once they have occurred. Present morphology typically refers to situations that are continually true and present inflections are logically more [congruent with] . . . states (as well as, perhaps, activities) than to [achievements and accomplishments], since states continue to exist and are timeless. Thus, the first inflections that children use are those that are most relevant to the meaning of the verb (the Relevance Principle) and of these inflections, it is the inflection whose meaning is most congruent with the meaning of the verb stem that will be attached to a particular verb (the Congruence Principle). (pp. 328–329)

Language learners, however, have an additional restriction imposed on them in at least early stages of acquisition. The One to One Principle (Andersen, 1984) guides the learner to assume that each grammatical morpheme he discovers has one and only one meaning, function, and distribution. Thus, learners will assign a more conservative form–meaning relation to a morpheme than fully proficient NS adults. The principle causes learners to follow a much more conservative and absolute version of the POA hypothesis than adult NSs. Learners thus initially apply the Relevance Principle and the Congruence Principle such that an inflection is used *only* with verb types whose semantic aspect is congruent with the aspect of the inflection, whereas for adult NSs this is only a strong tendency.

We must assume from the DBH studies that learners find reinforcement for this absolute version of POA in the native speech they are exposed to. They apparently disregard or do not even notice the counterexamples present in the NS speech. A high-frequency preference is interpreted as an absolute one-to-one form–meaning correspondence.

These proposals thus call into question a purely innatist explanation for the POA observations. More research is clearly needed on this question. In the next section, we present one possible scenario for the acquisition of tense–aspect marking using the framework of prototype theory.

V. A PROTOTYPE ACCOUNT

A. Prototype Theory

Linguistics and philosophy, which have been the bases for the study of tense and aspect, have generally assumed a classical theory of categorization. The assumption is that it is possible to define a category by a set of necessary and sufficient conditions. However, there has been a challenge to this position. Unlike the classical theory, the assumption of "prototype categories" (e.g., A. Clark, 1989; Lakoff, 1987; Rosch, 1973; Ross, 1973; J. R. Taylor, 1989) suggests that human categorization is not clear-cut, but fuzzy in nature. According to the theory of prototype category, there are good members (prototypes) and marginal members of a category, the goodness being gradient and determined by the commonality with the central members (prototype) of the category.[10] This theory has been applied to linguistics and language acquisition studies (see J. R. Taylor, 1989, for a review). When applied to acquisition studies, the claim is that in learning a category, the learner acquires prototypical (central) members first, then gradually extends the scope to less prototypical members (J. R. Taylor, 1989).

B. Tense and Aspect Morphology as a Prototype Category

Although mainstream linguistics still assumes classical categories in language, there are many studies suggesting linguistic categories as prototype categories

---

[10]For a debate over the validity of prototype categories, see Osherson and Smith (1981) and Armstrong, Gleitman, and Gleitman (1983), who criticize the prototype category, and Lakoff's (1987, chap. 9) rebuttal.

(see J. R. Taylor, 1989). It is, therefore, possible to regard tense–aspect morphology as a prototype category consisting of good members and marginal members. If we limit ourselves to English,[11] for purposes of illustration, two categories are relevant: past tense and progressive aspect. J. R. Taylor (1989, pp. 149–154) discussed the internal structure of the past tense as a morphosyntactic category. He argued that the prototypical member of past tense is "deictic past," whereas the less prototypical members of past tense are "unreality and counterfactuality" (e.g., *If I had enough time* . . .) and "pragmatic softener" (e.g., *Could you do me a favor?*). J. R. Taylor (1989) further suggested that in view of the fact that children's "[e]arliest uses [of past tense] are restricted to items like *fall, drop, slip, crash, break,* which designate punctual events [achievements]" (p. 243), the central meaning of past tense may be "completion in the immediate past of a punctual event [achievement], the consequences of which are perceptually salient at the moment of speaking" (p. 243). This is closely associated with achievement and accomplishment verbs. Sachs (1983) proposed a similar idea as to the development of past reference, stating that immediate past is the prototype ("original meaning" in her terminology), and extension is more distant past.

Interestingly, the category perfective is argued to have a prototype similar to that of past. Based on his cross-linguistic survey, Dahl (1985) described the prototypical case of perfective as follows:

> [It] will typically denote a single event, seen as an unanalyzed whole, with a well-defined result or end-state, located in the past. More often than not, the event will be punctual, or at least, it will be seen as a single transition from one state to its opposite, the duration of which can be disregarded. (p. 78)

It appears that his description also fits the description of the prototype past. This convergence of the prototype past and the prototype perfective is interesting in view of the similar behavior children show crosslinguistically with respect to acquisition of past and perfective. (See also Bybee & Dahl, 1989, who show how, historically, perfectives often develop into past forms.)

One important implication of Dahl's definition may be his reference to "single event" as part of the prototype. Although J. R. Taylor (1989) does not mention it, we argue that an iterative or habitual meaning may need separate consideration. First, in the literature on verb semantics classification (e.g., Dowty, 1979; Robison, 1990), iterative and habitual senses are often treated as special cases. For example, "finish/stop + VP" is a test to be used to distinguish achievement verbs from accomplishment verbs, as in (1):

(1)   *John stopped noticing the painting. (Dowty, 1979, p. 59)

[11] If we extended our discussion to languages like Spanish and Portuguese, which distinguish perfective from imperfective in the past, we would probably take a unitary punctual event as the prototypical perfective and a static description as the prototypical imperfective.

This sentence is ungrammatical in an ordinary reading, but acceptable if John somehow noticed the painting every morning, and after a while stopped noticing it. Second, as discussed in VB, past habitual situations appear to have a special status in the frequency analysis of verb semantics classification (Andersen, 1993). It is also noteworthy that many creole languages have a morphological distinction between unitary achievements and repeated achievements (Bickerton, 1981). It appears, then, that a habitual or iterative meaning should be regarded as a less prototypical use of past tense. (Here, *iterative* is used for repeated actions on a single occasion [Brinton, 1988], and *habitual* for repeated situations over an extended period of time.)

Based on the above considerations, we hypothesize the following as a possible internal structure of the category past tense, from prototype to marginal members:

Deictic past (achievement → accomplishment → activity→ state → habitual or iterative past) → counterfactual or pragmatic softener

It is unlikely that this sequence is strictly linear. It is more likely hierarchical. For example, once accomplishments are included, the door is opened for various sorts of durative situations. Habitual and iterative pasts are types of extensions of durativity. It is logical that they may begin to develop gradually even while accomplishments are still being added to potential past-marked verbs.

It may sound circular to argue that the prototype is acquired first, on the one hand, and that the prototype can be determined based on the order of acquisition, on the other. In fact, this is one of the weaknesses of prototype theory. At this point, there is no established and reliable measure to determine the internal structure of a prototype category. It is usually determined based on the researcher's intuition, or based on psycholinguistic experiments or elicitation (Tanaka, 1990). Another problem in using acquisition data for determining a prototype is that it is not clear whether children's acquisition reflects what is represented in adult competencies of the language. It is quite possible that the adult's prototype is different from what children acquire as a prototype.

Although progressive aspect has been the object of many studies, it is rarely treated as a prototype category. We would argue that the "process" meaning of the progressive is more basic than other meanings. There is considerable disagreement among linguists as to what constitutes the meaning of progressive (see Brinton, 1988). However, we are not aware of any that go against this claim. Sag (1973) distinguishes three senses of progressive aspect: process, futurate, and habitual. The following are examples adapted from Sag (1973, p. 85):

(2) At the moment, we're singing.   (process)
(3) We're leaving tomorrow.   (futurate)
(4) Nowadays we're singing the song every day. (habitual)

Action in process or progress seems to be the prototype of progressive aspect. Matthews (1990) explicitly discussed progressive aspect as a prototype category within a cognitive linguistics framework, and makes a case for "dynamicity" as its prototype. His use of "dynamicity" corresponds to the process meaning in the present context. Gass and Ard (1984) also treat the progressive category as having internal structure, and claim that "ongoing witnessed activity which persists for an extended period of time" (p. 50) is basic and prototypical. Bybee and Dahl (1989) stated that "the prototypical use . . . would emphasize the subject's ongoing activity" (p. 81). Andersen (1990) states that "the prototypical use of the Progressive appears to be to express the sense of an action in progress" (p. 22).

As in the case of past tense, the iterative meaning of the progressive should be treated separately. Some achievement verbs, if used with the progressive, cannot indicate "action in progress" without an iterative meaning. Thus, *he's coughing* means that he is coughing repeatedly.

Moreover, Brown (1973, p. 319) pointed out that although the base form of verbs is highly frequent in children's speech, and present tense often refers to recurrent, habitual actions, habitual meanings emerge relatively late. These all point to the marked nature of iterative or habitual meaning. Of the two, however, the iterative progressive is treated as closer to the prototype because it also has the "action in progress" meaning, the only difference being the ongoing action is 'repeated' actions (e.g., *jumping, kicking*).

We hypothesize the following as a possible internal structure of the category progressive aspect, from prototype to marginal members: [12]

process (activity → accomplishment) → iterative→ habitual or futurate → stative progressive

Within the process meaning, prototypical cases are activity and accomplishment verbs, which mostly take the process meaning when progressive aspect is applied (e.g., *he is running*—activity; *he is making a chair*—accomplishment). Achievement verbs are not included in the process category because when used with progressive, they have an iterative, futurate,[13] or habitual meaning. Stative verbs are usually not congruent with progressive aspect, as in *she is knowing the answer.* Therefore, stative progressive is treated as the most marginal member of the category, although the progressive is often used in NS discourse with statives (see Sag, 1973, and Smith, 1983, for a discussion of stative progressive, and Yap, 1990, summarized in Andersen, 1993, for frequency data). The treatment of stative as a marginal member is motivated also by the observation in L1 acquisition that there is practically no overextension of the progressive marker to stative verbs (e.g.,

---

[12] Gass and Ard (1984) have the following hierarchy of prototypicality: process → futurate → stative progressive, which is in agreement with ours.

[13] *Futurate* here includes the meaning of "process leading up to the endpoint" (e.g., *He is reaching the summit.*).

Brown, 1973; Kuczaj, 1978) in spite of the fact that progressive does apply to stative verbs in adult speech.

VI. SUMMARY AND DISCUSSION

We summarize first in terms of descriptive findings and then explanations that have been offered to account for the descriptive findings.

A. Description

The Primacy of Aspect Hypothesis

We have concluded that the POA hypothesis is strongly confirmed for both L1 and L2 acquisition, with a few disconfirmatory findings. The POA hypothesis is composed of four elements: (1) Learners will initially restrict past or perfective marking to achievement and accomplishment verbs (those with an inherent end point) and later gradually extend the marking to activities and then states, with states being the last category to be marked consistently; (2) in languages with an imperfective marker, imperfective past appears much later than perfective past and then is initially restricted to states and activity verbs, then extended to accomplishments, and finally to achievements; (3) progressive marking is initially restricted to activity verbs and then extended to accomplishments and achievements; (4) progressive marking is not incorrectly overextended to states.

The L1 acquisition research basically confirms all four components of the POA hypothesis. Some of the Japanese studies appear to disconfirm the first part of the hypothesis, but subsequent reinterpretation of the data in that study led to confirmation. Apparent disconfirmatory evidence from Spanish was also found to be consistent with the POA when interpreted in terms of the Vender and Mourelatos categories. The two disconfirmatory findings of Li (1989) on Mandarin still need to be taken seriously. Li argues that the important distinction the children encode is the result or process distinction, not inherent aspect. However, this may be a question of different methodology.

L2 acquisition studies also confirm the POA hypothesis, except for the last component: L2 learners do overextend the progressive marking to states. This may be the result of transfer from the learner's L1 of a more general imperfective notion to the progressive marker.

The Distributional Bias Hypothesis

Most studies appear to assume that the descriptive findings that confirm the POA hypothesis are due to the acquisition process. That is, learners are predisposed to discover explicit encoding for an event, process, or state distinction or some subset of it (or, following Li, a result and process distinction). Learners thus reinterpret morphological forms in the input in terms of these categories. We have tried to show, however, that NSs exhibit, in quantitative terms, the same tendencies. We have called these observations the DBH: NSs will exhibit the same distributions of morphological markings on selected verbs (according to their inherent semantics) that are found in learners.

Adult NSs in speech to other adult NSs exhibit a distributional bias in the use of these verb inflections in the same direction predicted by the POA hypothesis. NSs' speech to nonnative speakers or to young L1 learners exhibits a distributional bias that matches the POA predictions much more closely than in speech to other adult NSs. But even in the more extreme cases of distributional bias in speech by NSs to learners, where the bias is even closer to the distribution found in early stages of learner speech, the bias still is a strong tendency rather than the close to absolute conformity to the POA found in early learner speech.

B. Explanation

The Defective Tense Hypothesis

We have shown that the absolute version of the Defective Tense Hypothesis, as stated by Weist et al. (1984), is strongly disconfirmed. Weist et al. disconfirmed it with their innovative approach to their study. In addition, because the Absolute Defective Tense Hypothesis attributes the POA distribution to a cognitive inability of a young child to conceive of a notion of "past event or situation," the finding that the POA holds also for L2 acquisition clearly shows that the POA phenomenon could not be due to any such cognitive limitation, because adult L2 learners cannot be assumed to be subject to such a limitation.

A Prototype Account for the POA Findings

We have argued that tense and aspect morphemes are prototype categories and that learners (both L1 and L2 learners) initially discover the least marked member of each category (one unitary achievement or accomplishment for past or perfective) and only later and gradually add progressively more marked members to their pool of "past" and "perfective" marked verbs. What is still needed, however, are independent criteria for determining the prototypical member of each category and the hierarchical relationship of more marked members within the category. In addition, more attention needs to be paid to the means by which the learner discovers one particular morphological marking and assigns a prototypical meaning to it, but not some other marking present in the input.

The Role of the Distributional Bias in the Input

In the preceding section we discussed the observational findings concerning the DBH. These findings appear to weaken the case for an innatist account such as

Bickerton's bioprogram. *If* NSs exhibit a distributional bias in their use of tense–aspect morphemes similar to the more absolute distribution found in early learner speech, then it may be that learners are simply inferring from the input they are exposed to a more absolute one-to-one version of the biased distribution found in native speech.

Distributional Bias in the Input versus the Bioprogram

This then takes us back to the bioprogram proposal. Bickerton's argument is based on the scenario we must imagine existed when the first generation of creole speakers *created* their NL (the creole) as they attempted to acquire the pidgin, as spoken by their parents and other community members. The pidgin, however, as Bickerton (1981) has argued did not provide the young children with a consistent model in the same way that speakers of English, Japanese, Mandarin, and Spanish provide their children with a consistent model from speaker to speaker. The first creole speakers then had to invent their own grammatical markers. In the case of tense–aspect marking, the result is remarkably consistent across diverse creole languages: [14] creole languages have an explicit progressive or imperfective marker and encode perfective or nonprogressive simply with the absence of explicit progressive or imperfective marking (a "zero" marker). Bickerton claims that this is evidence that young children will mark the "punctual–nonpunctual" (i.e., perfective–imperfective) distinction when the input they receive is inadequate for acquiring an existing tense–aspect system.

As Matthews (1993) has shown, this creole progressive and imperfective marker is typically derived from a locative marker (e.g., English *there* becomes aspect marker *de/da/a* in various English creoles). Thus, according to Matthews' argument, through metaphorical extension, children convert the meaning "location" to "state" and then to the grammatical aspectual category "progressive" and then expand it to "imperfective." The fact that creole languages tend to mark only one side of the opposition (the imperfective side) and children acquiring their NL from adequate input soon mark both sides (e.g., past and progressive or perfective and progressive, depending on the language) suggests that this natural (thus innate?) predisposition to mark a process–result or durative–punctual distinction interacts with the types of model provided by the caretaker or NS.

Thus, although the DBH findings weaken an absolute bioprogram argument, they are not inconsistent with Bickerton's proposals. Matthews (1993) observed that marking the process, progressive, imperfective side of the opposition in creoles is consistent with Dahl's (1985) finding that languages consistently use inflectional or derivational marking for perfective but periphrastic marking (such as a free preverbal *da* in creoles derived from *there*) for progressive. The progressive

---

[14] We will restrict ourselves to the marker of grammatical aspect found in creole languages and not deal with tense and mood marking or the various controversies surrounding claims and counterclaims in this debate.

marking can then later be expanded to become an imperfective. Matthews argued that creole languages *canNOT* develop a perfective marker initially because perfective markers must be inflectional or derivational and creoles, by being isolating languages, do not have inflectional or derivational machinery. Although Matthews was proposing that Bickerton does not need a special Bioprogram to account for creoles, he is nevertheless making Bickerton's argument more plausible: the first-generation creole speakers do depend on an innate "nonpunctual [durative] versus punctual" distinction in the absence of adequate input and create a marked progressive–imperfective category, much in the same way that young children acquiring from adequate input treat a past or perfective marker as marking *only* punctual or a progressive marker as marking only durative. Thus, as unrelated as the creation of a creole may seem to acquisition of a well-known noncreole language under conditions of adequate input, the creole case appears to confirm the POA hypothesis. More work is needed on how a POA principle interacts with a distributional bias in the input. Apparently the input to children helps them confirm what the POA principle independently motivates them to discover in the input.

ACKNOWLEDGMENTS

Both authors contributed equally to this chapter. The order of authors' names is strictly alphabetical. We gratefully acknowledge grants to Andersen from the National Science Foundation (BNS-8812750) and to Shirai from a Grant-Aid for Scientific Research from the Japanese Ministry of Education (No. 05881078), which contributed to the writing of this chapter. We thank Foong Ha Yap for her helpful comments and suggestions.

REFERENCES

Aitchison, J. (1983). On roots of language. *Language & Communication, 3,* 83–97.

Aksu-Koc, A. (1988). *The acquisition of aspect and modality: The case of past reference in Turkish.* Cambridge, UK: Cambridge University Press.

Andersen, R. W. (1981). Two perspectives on pidginization as second language acquisition. In R. W. Andersen (Ed.), *New dimensions in second language acquisition research* (pp. 165–195). Rowley, MA: Newbury House.

Andersen, R. R. (Ed.). (1983). *Pidginization and creolization as language acquisition.* Rowley, MA: Newbury House.

Andersen, R. W. (1984). The One to One Principle of interlanguage construction. *Language Learning, 34,* 77–95.

Andersen, R. W. (1986a). El desarrollo de la morfología verbal en el español como segundo idioma. In J. M. Meisel (Ed.), *Adquisición de lenguaje/Aquisição da linguagem.* Frankfurt: Vervuert.

Andersen, R. W. (1986b). *Interpreting data: Second language acquisition of verbal aspect.* Unpublished manuscript, University of California, Los Angeles.

Andersen, R. W. (1986c). *The need for native language comparison data in interpreting second language data.* Unpublished manuscript, Forum lecture, 1986 TESOL Summer Institute, University of Hawaii, Honolulu.

Andersen, R. W. (1988). Models, processes, principles, and strategies: Second language acquisition in and out of the classroom. *IDEAL, 3,* 111–138. (Reprinted in *Second language acquisition—Foreign language learning,* pp. 45–68, by B. VanPatten & J. F. Lee, Eds., 1990, Clevedon, UK & Philadelphia: Multilingual Matters.

Andersen, R. W. (1989). *The acquisition of verb morphology.* Los Angeles: University of California. Published in Spanish as: La adquisición de la morfología verbal. *Lingüística, 1,* (1989).

Andersen, R. W. (1990). Verbal virtuosity and speakers' purposes. In H. Burmeister & P. L. Rounds (Eds.), *Variability in second language acquisition: Proceedings of the Tenth Meeting of the Second Language Research Forum* (Vol. 2, pp. 1–24). Eugene: University of Oregon, Department of Linguistics.

Andersen, R. W. (1991). Developmental sequences: The emergence of aspect marking in second language acquisition. In T. Huebner & C. A. Ferguson (Eds.), *Crosscurrents in second language acquisition and linguistic theories* (pp. 305–324). Amsterdam: John Benjamins.

Andersen, R. W. (1993). Four operating principles and input distribution as explanations for underdeveloped and mature morphological systems. In K. Hyltenstam & A. Viborg (Eds.), *Progression and regression in language* (pp. 309–339). Cambridge, UK: Cambridge University Press.

Andersen, R. W., & Shirai, Y. (1994). Discourse motivations for some cognitive acquisition principles. *Studies in Second Language Acquisition, 16,* 133–156.

Antinucci, F., & Miller, R. (1976). How children talk about what happened. *Journal of Child Language, 3,* 169–189.

Armstrong, S. L., Gleitman, L., & Gleitman, H. (1983). What some concepts might not be. *Cognition, 13,* 263–308.

Bardovi-Harlig, K. (1992). The relationship of form and meaning: A cross-sectional study of tense and aspect in the interlanguage of learners of English as a second language. *Applied Psycholinguistics, 13,* 253–278.

Bardovi-Harlig, K. & Bergström, A. (in press). The acquisition of tense and aspect in SLA and FLL: A study of learner narratives in English (SL) and French (FL). *Canadian Modern Language Review.*

Bardovi-Harlig, K. & Reynolds, D. W. (1995). The role of lexical aspect in the acquisition of tense and aspect. *TESOL Quarterly, 29,* 107–131.

Bayley, R. (1991). *Variation in interlanguage tense marking.* Paper presented at the annual meeting of the Linguistic Society of America, Chicago.

Bayley, R. (1994). Interlanguage variation and the quantitative paradigm: Past tense marking in Chinese-English. In E. E. Tarone, S. M. Gass, and A. D. Cohen (Eds.), *Research methodology in second-language acquisition* (pp. 157–181). Hillsdale, NJ: Erlbaum.

Behrens, H. (1993). *Temporal reference in German child language: Form and function of early verb use.* Dissertation, University of Amsterdam, Amsterdam, The Netherlands.

Berman, R. A. (1983). Establishing a schema: Children's construals of verb-tense marking. *Language Sciences, 5,* 61–78.

Bickerton, D. (1974). Creolization, linguistic universals, natural semantax and the brain. *University of Hawaii Working Papers in Linguistics, 6*(3), 124–141. (Reprinted in *Issues in English creoles: Papers from the 1975 Hawaii conference,* pp. 1–18, by R. R. Day, Ed., 1980, Heidelberg: Julius Groos Verlag).

Bickerton, D. (1981). *Roots of language.* Ann Arbor, MI: Karoma.

Bickerton, D. (1984a). The language bioprogram hypothesis. *Behavioral and Brain Sciences, 7,* 173–188.

Bickerton, D. (1984b). The language bioprogram hypothesis and second language acquisition. In W. E. Rutherford (Ed.), *Language universals and second language acquisition* (pp. 141–161). Amsterdam: John Benjamins.

Bickerton, D. (1988). Creole languages and the bioprogram. In F. J. Newmeyer (Ed.), *Linguistics: The Cambridge Survey* (Vol. 2, pp. 268–284). Cambridge, UK: Cambridge University Press.

Bickerton, D. (1989). The child, the bioprogram and the input data: A commentary on Cziko, *First Language, 9,* 33–37.

Bloom, L., & Harner, L. (1989). On the developmental contour of child language: A reply to Smith and Weist. *Journal of Child Language, 16,* 207–216.

Bloom, L., Lifter, K., & Hafitz, J. (1980). Semantics of verbs and the development of verb inflection in child language. *Language, 56,* 386–412.

Borer, H., & Wexler, K. (1992). Bi-unique relations and the maturation of grammatical principles. *Natural Language and Linguistic Theory, 10,* 147–189.

Brinton, L. J. (1988). *The development of English aspectual systems: Aspectualizers and post-verbal particles.* Cambridge, UK: Cambridge University Press.

Bronckart, J. P., & Sinclair, H. (1973). Time, tense, and aspect. *Cognition, 2,* 107–130.

Brown, R. (1973). *A first language: The early stages.* Cambridge, MA: Harvard University Press.

Bybee, J. L. (1985). *Morphology: A study of the relation between meaning and form.* Amsterdam & Philadelphia: John Benjamins.

Bybee, J. L., & Dahl, O. (1989). The creation of tense and aspect systems in the languages of the world. *Studies in Language, 13,* 51–103.

Champaud, (1993). *Tense forms and functions in French speaking children: The early stages in a cross-linguistic perspective.* Paper presented at the 6th International Congress for the Study of Child Language, Trieste, Italy.

Clark, A. (1989). *Microcognition: Philosophy, cognitive science, and parallel distributed processing.* Cambridge, MA: MIT Press.

Clark, E. V. (1985). The acquisition of Romance, with special reference to French. In D. Slobin (Ed.), *The crosslinguistic study of language acquisition* (Vol. 1, pp. 687–782). Hillsdale, NJ: Erlbaum.

Clark, E. V. (1987). The principle of contrast: A constraint on language acquisition. In B. MacWhinney (Ed.), *Mechanisms of language acquisition* (pp. 1–33). Hillsdale, NJ: Erlbaum.

Comrie, B. (1976). *Aspect.* Cambridge, UK: Cambridge University Press.

Cushing, S. T. (1987). *Use of verb morphology in the English interlanguage of a native speaker of Serahuli.* Unpublished paper, Applied Linguistics, University of California, Los Angeles.

Cziko, G. A. (1989a). A review of the state-process and punctual-nonpunctual distinctions in children's acquisition of verbs. *First Language, 9,* 1–31.

Cziko, G. A. (1989b). Of verbs, universals and language acquisition research: A reply to Bickerton, Kuczaj and Weist. *First Language, 9,* 51–56.

Cziko, G. A., & Koda, K. (1987). A Japanese child's use of stative and punctual verbs. *Journal of Child Language, 14,* 99–111.

Dahl, O. (1985). *Tense and aspect systems.* Oxford: Basil Blackwell.

Day, R. R. (Ed.). (1980). *Issues in English creoles: Papers from the 1975 Hawaii conference.* Heidelberg: Julius Groos Verlag.

de Lemos, C. (1981a). Interactional processes in child's construction of language. In W. Deutsch (Ed.), *The child's construction of language* (pp. 57–76). London: Academic Press.

de Lemos, C. (1981b). *Ser and Estar in Brazilian Portuguese, with particular reference to child language acquisition.* Tübingen: Narr.

Dowty, D. R. (1979). *Word meaning and Montague grammar: The semantics of verbs and times in generative semantics and in Montague's PTQ.* Dordrecht: Reidel.

Eckman, F. R. (1977). Markedness and the contrastive analysis hypothesis. *Language Learning, 27,* 315–330.

Economides, P. J. (1985). *The expression of tense and aspect in the English interlanguage of a Vietnamese child.* Unpublished master's thesis, University of California, Los Angeles.

Eisenberg, A. (1982). *Language acquisition in cultural perspective: Talk in three Mexican homes.* Unpublished doctoral dissertation, University of California, Berkeley.

Erbaugh, M. (1978). Acquisition of temporal and aspectual distinction in Mandarin. *Papers and Reports on Child Language Development* (Department of Linguistics, Stanford University), *15,* 30–37.

Flashner, V. (1982). *The English interlanguage of three native speakers of Russian: Two perspectives.* Unpublished master's thesis, University of California, Los Angeles.

Fletcher, P. (1985). *A child's learning of English.* New York: Basil Blackwell.

Foley, W. A., & Van Valin, R. D. (1984). *Functional syntax and universal grammar.* Cambridge, UK: Cambridge University Press.

Gass, S. M. (1984). A review of interlanguage syntax: Language transfer and language universals. *Language Learning, 34,* 115–132.

Gass, S. M., & Ard, J. (1984). Second language acquisition and the ontology of language universals. In W. E. Rutherford (Ed.), *Language universals and second language acquisition* (pp. 33–67). Amsterdam: John Benjamins.

Gonzales, P. A. (1989). *The emergence of verbal morphology in early child language: A reanalysis of Eisenberg 1982.* Unpublished paper, Applied Linguistics, University of California, Los Angeles.

Gonzales, P. A. (1990). *The imperfect/past progressive distinction in Spanish discourse: An aspectual analysis.* Unpublished master's thesis, University of California, Los Angeles.

Goodman, M. (1985). Review of roots of language. *International Journal of American Linguistics, 51,* 109–137.

Harner, L. (1981). Children talk about the time and aspect of actions, *Child Development, 52,* 498–506.

Hatch, E. M. (1983a). *Psycholinguistics: A second language perspective.* Rowley, MA: Newbury House.

Hatch, E. M. (1983b). Simplified input and second language acquisition. In R. W. Andersen (Ed.), *Pidginization and creolization as language acquisition* (pp. 64–86). Rowley, MA: Newbury House.

Herman, R. (1990). How do deaf speakers talk about time? *Clinical Linguistics & Phonetics, 4,* 197–207.

Holisky, D. A. (1981). Aspect theory and Georgian aspect. In P. J. Tedeschi & A. Zaenen (Eds.), *Syntax and semantics: Vol. 14. Tense and aspect* (pp. 127–144). New York: Academic Press.

Hopper, P. J., & Thompson, S. A. (1980). Transitivity in grammar and discourse. *Language, 56,* 251–299.

Huang, C. (1993). *Distributional biases of verb morphology in native and non-native English discourse.* Unpublished master's thesis, University of California, Los Angeles.

Jacobsen, T. (1986). ¿Aspecto antes que tiempo? Una mirada a la adquisición temprana del español. In J. M. Meisel (Ed.), *Adquisición de lenguage. Aquisição da linguagem* (pp. 97–210). Frankfurt: Vervuert.

Jacobsen, W. M. (1982). Vendler's verb classes and the aspectual character of Japanese te iru. In *Proceedings of the Eighth Annual Meeting of the Berkeley Linguistics Society* (pp. 373–383). Berkeley, CA: Berkeley Linguistics Society.

Jakobson, R. (1957). *Shifters, verbal categories, and the Russian verb.* Cambridge, MA: Harvard University, Russian Language Project, Department of Slavic Languages and Literature.

Kenny, A. (1963). *Action, emotion and will.* New York: Springer.

Kuczaj, S. A. (1976). *-ing, -s, and -ed: A study of the acquisition of certain verb inflections.* Unpublished doctoral dissertation, University of Minnesota, Minneapolis.

Kuczaj, S. A. (1978). Why do children fail to overgeneralize the progressive inflection? *Journal of Child Language, 5,* 167–171.

Kuczaj, S. A. (1989). On the search for universals of language acquisition: A commentary on Cziko. *First Language, 9,* 39–44.

Kumpf, L. (1982). *Tense, aspect, and modality in interlanguage: A discourse-functional perspective.* Paper presented at the 1982 TESOL convention, Honolulu, Hawaii.

Kumpf, L. (1984a). Comments on the paper by Gass and Art. In W. E. Rutherford (Ed.), *Language universals and second language acquisition* (pp. 69–72). Amsterdam: John Benjamins.

Kumpf, L. (1984b). Temporal systems and universality in interlanguage: A case study. In F. R. Eckman, L. H. Bell, & D. Nelson (Eds.), *Universals of second language acquisition* (pp. 132–143). Rowley, MA: Newbury House.

Lakoff, G. (1987). *Women, fire, and dangerous things: What categories reveal about the mind.* Chicago: Chicago University Press.

Leone, P. (1990). *Tense and aspect in Italian: A bias in the distribution of verbal inherent semantics and verbal morphology.* Unpublished paper, University of California, Applied Linguistics, Los Angeles.

Li, P. (1989). *Aspect and aktionsart in child Mandarin.* Doctoral dissertation, University of Leiden, Leiden, The Netherlands.

Long, M. H., & Sato, C. J. (1983). Classroom foreigner talk discourse: Forms and functions of teacher's questions. In H. W. Seliger & M. H. Long (Eds.), *Classroom oriented research in second language acquisition* (pp. 268–286). Rowley, MA: Newbury House.

Lyons, J. (1977). *Semantics* (Vol. 2). Cambridge, UK: Cambridge University Press.

MacWhinney, B., & Snow, C. E. (1990). The child language data exchange system: An update. *Journal of Child Language, 17,* 457–472.

Major, R. C. (1987). A model for interlanguage phonology. In G. Ioup & S. H. Weinberger (Eds.), *Interlanguage phonology: The acquisition of a second language sound system* (pp. 101–124). Cambridge, MA: Newbury House.

Matsumoto, K. (1985). *A study of tense and aspect in Japanese.* Unpublished doctoral dissertation, University of Southern California, Los Angeles.

Matthews, S. J. (1989). *Where was I . . . ?: Tracking tense and aspect in Alzheimer's disease.* Unpublished manuscript, University of Southern California, Los Angeles.

Matthews, S. J. (1990). *A cognitive approach to the typology of verbal aspect.* Unpublished doctoral dissertation, University of Southern California, Los Angeles.

Matthews, S. J. (1993). Creole aspect and morphological typology. In F. Byrne & J. Holm (Eds.), *Atlantic meets Pacific: A global view of pidginization and creolization* (pp. 233–241). Amsterdam & Philadelphia: John Benjamins.

McShane, J., & Whittaker, S. (1988). The encoding of tense and aspect by three- to five-year-old children. *Journal of Experimental Child Psychology, 45,* 52–70.

Meisel, J. M. (1987). Reference to past events and actions in the development of natural second language acquisition. In C. W. Pfaff (Ed.), *First and second language acquisition* (pp. 206–224). New York: Newbury House.

Mishina, S. (1993). *Second language acquisition of verb morphology by three Japanese speakers.* Unpublished paper, Applied Linguistics, University of California, Los Angeles.

Mourelatos, A. P. (1981). Events, processes, and states. In P. J. Tedeschi & A. Zaenen (Eds.), *Syntax and semantics: Vol. 14. Tense and aspect* (pp. 191–212). New York: Academic Press.

Muysken, P. (1988). Are creoles a special type of language? In F. J. Newmeyer (Ed.), *Linguistics: The Cambridge Survey* (Vol. 2, pp. 285–301). Cambridge, UK: Cambridge University Press.

Newmeyer, F. J. (Ed.). (1988). *Linguistics: The Cambridge Survey* (Vol. 2). Cambridge, UK: Cambridge University Press.

Nixon, N. (1986). *Tense/aspect in the English interlanguage of a native Mandarin speaker.* Unpublished master's thesis, University of California, Los Angeles.

Noji, J. (1976). *Yojiki no gengo seikatsu no jittai [The language development of a child]* (Vols. 1–4). Hiroshima: Bunka Hyoron.

Osherson, D., & Smith, E. (1981). On the adequacy of prototype theory as a theory of concepts. *Cognition, 9,* 35–58.

Osser, H., & Dillon, P. L., Jr. (1969). *The child's acquisition of the present progressive inflection.* Paper presented at the Western Psychological Association Convention, Vancouver, B.C., Canada.

Peck, S. (1977). *Play in child second language acquisition.* Unpublished master's thesis, University of California, Los Angeles.

Pinker, S. (1984). *Language learnability and syntactic development.* Cambridge, MA: MIT Press.

Radulovič, L. (1975). *Acquisition of language: Studies of Dubrovnik children.* Unpublished doctoral dissertation, University of California, Berkeley.

Ramsay, V. (1989a). The acquisition of the perfective/imperfective aspectual distinction by classroom learners. In R. Carlson, S. DeLancy, S. Gildea, D. Payne, & A. Saxena (Eds.), *Proceedings of the Fourth Meeting of the Pacific Linguistics Conference* (pp. 374–404). Eugene: University of Oregon, Department of Linguistics.

Ramsay, V. (1989b). *On the debate over the acquisition of aspect before tense: Setting the record straight.* Paper presented at the annual Conference of the American Association for Applied Linguistics, Washington, DC.

Ramsay, V. (1990). *Developmental stages in the acquisition of the perfective and the imperfective aspects by classroom L2 learners of Spanish.* Unpublished doctoral dissertation, University of Oregon, Corvallis.

Rispoli, M. J. V. (1981). *The emergence of verb and adjective tense-aspect inflections in Japanese.* Unpublished master's thesis, University of Pennsylvania, Philadelphia.

Rispoli, M. J. V., & Bloom, L. (1985). Incomplete and continuing: Theoretical issues in the acquisition of tense and aspect. *Journal of Child Language, 12,* 471–474.

Robison, R. E. (1990). The primacy of aspect: Aspectual marking in English interlanguage. *Studies in Second Language Acquisition, 12,* 315–330.

Robison, R. E. (1993). *Aspectual marking in English interlanguage. A cross-sectional study.* Unpublished doctoral dissertation, University of California, Los Angeles.

Robison, R. E. (1995). The aspect hypothesis revisited: A cross-sectional study of tense and aspect marking in interlanguage. *Applied Linguistics, 16,* 344–370.

Romaine, S. (1988). *Pidgin and Creole languages.* London: Longman.

Rosch, E. H. (1973). On the internal structure of perceptual and semantic categories. In T. E. Moore (Ed.), *Cognitive development and the acquisition of language* (pp. 111–144). New York: Academic Press.

Ross, J. R. (1973). A fake NP squish. In C. J. N. Bailey & R. Shuy (Eds.), *New ways of analyzing variation in English* (pp. 96–140). Washington, DC: Georgetown University Press.

Rothstein, G. (1985). *The expression of temporality in the English interlanguage of a native Hebrew speaker.* Unpublished master's thesis, University of California, Los Angeles.

Ryle, G. (1949). *The concept of mind.* London: Barnes & Noble.

Sachs, J. (1983). Talking about the there and then: The emergence of displaced reference in parent-child discourse. In K. E. Nelson (Ed.), *Children's language* (Vol. 4, pp. 1–28). Hillsdale, NJ: Erlbaum.

Sag, I. (1973). On the state of progress on progressives and statives. In C. J. N. Bailey & R. Shuy (Eds.), *New ways of analyzing variation in English* (pp. 83–95). Washington, DC: Georgetown University Press.

Shirai, Y. (1989). *The acquisition of the basic verb PUT: Prototype and transfer.* Unpublished master's thesis, University of California, Los Angeles.

Shirai, Y. (1990). *The Defective Tense Hypothesis: Is there a distributional bias in the input?* Unpublished paper, Applied Linguistics, University of California, Los Angeles.

Shirai, Y. (1991). *Primacy of aspect in language acquisition: Simplified input and prototype.* Unpublished doctoral dissertation, University of California, Los Angeles.

Shirai, Y. (1993). Inherent aspect and acquisition of tense/aspect morphology in Japanese. In H. Nakajima & Y. Otsu (Eds.), *Argument structure: Its syntax and acquisition* (pp. 185–211). Tokyo: Kaitakusha.

Shirai, Y. (1994). On the overgeneralization of progressive marking on stative verbs: Bioprogram or input? *First Language, 14,* 67–82.

Shirai, Y. (1995). Tense–aspect marking by L2 learners of Japanese. In D. MacLaughlin and S. McEwen (Eds.), *Proceedings of the 19th Annual Boston University Conference on Language Development* (pp. 575–586). Somerville, MA: Cascadilla Press.

Shirai, Y. & Andersen, R. W. (in press). The acquisition of tense/aspect morphology: A prototype account. *Language.*

Shirai, Y., & McGhee, R. (1988). *An interlanguage analysis of a Japanese ESL learner.* Unpublished paper, Applied Linguistics, University of California, Los Angeles.

Simoes, M. C., & Stoel-Gammon, C. (1979). The acquisition of inflections in Portuguese: A study of the development of person markers on verbs. *Journal of Child Language, 6,* 53–67.

Slobin, D. I. (1985). Crosslinguistic evidence for the Language-Making Capacity. In D. I. Slobin (Ed.), *The crosslinguistic study of language acquisition: Vol. 2. Theoretical issues* (pp. 1157–1249). Hillsdale, NJ: Erlbaum.

Smith, C. S. (1980). The acquisition of time talk: Relations between child and adult grammars. *Journal of Child Language, 7,* 263–278.

Smith, C. S. (1983). A theory of aspectual choice. *Language, 59,* 479–501.

Smith, C. S., & Weist, R. M. (1987). On the temporal contour of child language: A reply to Rispoli and Bloom. *Journal of Child Language, 14,* 387–392.

Snow, C. E., & Ferguson, C. A. (Eds.). (1977). *Talking to children: Language input and acquisition.* Cambridge, UK: Cambridge University Press.

Soga, M. (1983). *Tense and aspect in modern colloquial Japanese.* Vancouver: University of British Columbia Press.

Stephany, U. (1981). Verbal grammar in modern Greek early child language. In P. S. Dale & D. Ingram (Eds.), *Child language: An international perspective* (pp. 45–57). Baltimore: University Park Press.

Takahashi, K. (1990). *A study of tense/aspect marking in Japanese narrative.* Unpublished paper, University of California, Applied Linguistics, Los Angeles.

Takashima, H., & Kamibayashi, K. (1990). *Superman and PTA: Is there a distributional bias in Japanese?* Unpublished paper, University of California, Applied Linguistics, Los Angeles.

Tanaka, S. (1983). *Language transfer as a constraint on lexico-semantic development in adults learning a second language in acquisition-poor environments.* Unpublished doctoral dissertation, Columbia University, Teachers College, New York.

Tanaka, S. (1990). *Ninchi imiron: Eigo doshi no tagi no kozo* [Cognitive Semantics: The structure of polysemy of English verbs]. Tokyo: Sanyusha.

Taylor, H. (1987). *Tense/aspect: A longitudinal study of a native Spanish speaker.* Unpublished paper, Applied Linguistics, University of California, Los Angeles.

Taylor, J. R. (1989). *Linguistic categorization: Prototypes in linguistic theory.* Oxford: Oxford University Press.

Toivainen, J. (1980). *Inflectional affixes used by Finnish-speaking children aged 1–3 years.* Helsinki: Suomalaisen Kirjallisuuden Seura.

Vendler, Z. (1967). *Linguistics in philosophy.* Ithaca, NY: Cornell University Press.

Weist, R. M. (1983). Prefix versus suffix information processing in the comprehension of tense and aspect. *Journal of Child Language, 10,* 85–96.

Weist, R. M. (1989). Aspects of the roots of language: Commentary on Cziko. *First Language, 9,* 45–49.

Weist, R. M., Wysocka, H., Witkowska-Stadnik, K., Buczowska, E., & Konieczna, E. (1984). The defective tense hypothesis: On the emergence of tense and aspect in child Polish. *Journal of Child Language, 11,* 347–374.

Wenzell, V. E. (1989). Transfer of aspect in the English oral narratives of native Russian speaker. In H. W. Dechert & M. Raupach (Eds.), *Transfer in language production* (pp. 71–97). Norwood, NJ: Ablex.

Woisetschlaeger, E. (1976). *A semantic theory of English auxiliary system.* Bloomington: Indiana University Linguistics Club.

Yap, F.-H. (1990). *Semantic categories in an adult speech sample: A case against distributional bias?* Unpublished paper, Applied Linguistics, University of California, Los Angeles.

Yoshitomi, A. (1992). *Primacy of aspect: Another support for the hypothesis based on an interlanguage analysis of a Chinese speaker's ESL.* Unpublished qualifying paper, University of California, Los Angeles.

Youseff, V. (1988). The language bioprogram hypothesis revisited. *Journal of Child Language, 15,* 451–458.

Youseff, V. (1990). On the confirmation of bioprograms. *Journal of Child Language, 17,* 233–235.

Zobl, H. (1980). Developmental and transfer errors: Their common bases and (possibly) differential effects on subsequent learning. *TESOL Quarterly, 14,* 469–479.

CHAPTER 17

BILINGUALISM

Suzanne Romaine

I. INTRODUCTION

Modern linguistic theory generally takes the monolingual individual as its starting point in dealing with basic analytical problems such as the construction of
grammars and the nature of competence. From this perspective bilingualism has
in the past often been regarded as inherently problematic both for speech communities and the individual. In some quarters these negative views persist today
(see section V). However, there are a number of books that attempt to offer a
more balanced view of the issues (see, e.g., Appel & Muysken, 1987; Baetens-
Beardsmore, 1982, 1986; Grosjean, 1982; Hakuta, 1986; Hoffman, 1991; Romaine, 1989).

A. Definitions of Bilingualism

Bilingualism has often been defined and described in terms of categories,
scales, and dichotomies, such as ideal versus partial bilingual, coordinate versus
compound bilingual, and so on. These notions are generally related to such factors
as proficiency, function, and others. At one end of the spectrum of definitions of
bilingualism would be one that, like Bloomfield's (1933, p. 56), would specify
"native-like control of two languages" as the criterion for bilingualism. By contrast, Haugen (1953, p. 7) draws attention to the other end, when he observes that
bilingualism begins when the speaker of one language can produce complete
meaningful utterances in the other languages. Diebold (1964), however, gives
what might be called a minimal definition of bilingualism when he uses the term

Handbook of Second Language Acquisition

incipient bilingualism to characterize the initial stages of contact between two languages. In doing so, he leaves open the question of the absolute minimal proficiency required in order to be bilingual and allows for the fact that a person may be bilingual to some degree, yet not be able to produce complete meaningful utterances. A person might, for example, have no productive control over a language, but be able to understand utterances in it. In such instances linguists generally speak of "passive" in "receptive" bilingualism.

Although allowing for passive bilingualism, Diebold's definition does have the disadvantage that practically everyone in the United States, Britain, or Canada, and no doubt most other countries, would have to be classified as incipient bilinguals because probably everyone knows a few words in another language. The concept of bilingualism has, if anything, become increasingly broader with increasing attention being paid to second language (L2) acquisition (see chapter on L2 acquisition). As Hakuta (1986, p. 4) noted, Haugen's broad definition incorporates a developmental perspective that brings the entire process of L2 acquisition within the scope of the study of bilingualism.

Mackey (1968, p. 555) concluded that in order to study bilingualism we are forced to consider it as something entirely relative because the point at which the speaker of an L2 becomes bilingual is either arbitrary of impossible to determine. He therefore considers bilingualism as simply the alternate use of two or more languages. Following him, I have also used the term *bilingualism* in this chapter to include multilingualism.

B. Relationship between Bilingualism and Other Research Fields

In a discipline as large and specialized as modern linguistics, it is perhaps inevitable that the study of various aspects of bilingualism has been parceled out among various subdisciplines and related fields of research. Thus, historical linguists, for example, have been interested in bilingualism only insofar as it could be used as an explanation for certain changes in a language (i.e., contact-induced phenomena). The study of the acquisition of proficiency in another language is generally regarded as the province of a separate subdiscipline called L2 acquisition. However, it has an obvious overlap with the study of bilingualism if in dealing with the bilingual individual, one investigates the circumstances surrounding the creation of bilingualism and its maintenance and attrition.

Linguists are also giving increasing attention to the systematic study of language contact, and some have used the term *contact linguistics* in a wide sense to refer to both the process and outcome of any situation in which languages are in contact. Linguists who study language contact often seek to describe changes at the level of linguistic systems in isolation and abstraction from speakers. Sometimes they tend to treat the outcome of bilingual interaction in static rather than in dynamic terms, and lose sight of the fact that the bilingual individual is the ultimate locus of contact, as Weinreich (1968) pointed out many years ago (see section III).

When we look at related disciplines that have an interest in aspects of language, we can see that they too tend to focus on some aspects of bilingualism and neglect others. Psychologists, for instance, have investigated the effects of bilingualism on mental processes (see chap. 15, this volume, on the neuropsychology of bilingualism), whereas sociologists have treated bilingualism as an element in culture conflict and have looked at some of the consequences of linguistic heterogeneity as a societal phenomenon (see section II). Educationists have been concerned with bilingualism in connection with public policy. Basic questions about the relationship between bilingualism and intelligence, whether certain types of bilingualism are good or bad, and the circumstances under which they arise, also impinge on education (see section IV). Within the field of international studies, bilingualism is seen as an essential element in cross-cultural communication.

In each of these disciplines, however, bilingualism is too often seen as incidental and has been treated as a special case or as a deviation from the norm. Each discipline on its own therefore seems to add in a rather piecemeal fashion to our understanding of bilingualism with its complex psychological, linguistic, and social interrelationships.

Mackey (1968, p. 554) also pointed out that bilingualism is not a phenomenon of language but of its use, and he advocates a perspective in which the various interests mentioned above complement one another. From this vantage point, the study of bilingualism could also be said to fall within the field of sociolinguistics in so far as the latter is a subdiscipline that is concerned with the ways in which language is used in society. Even monolingual communities are not homogeneous because there are usually regional, social, and stylistic varieties within what is thought of as "one language."

II. BILINGUAL SPEECH COMMUNITIES

From a global societal perspective, of course, most of the world's speech communities use more than one language and are therefore multilingual rather than homogeneous. Grosjean (1982, p. vii) estimated that about half the world's population is bilingual and that bilingualism is present in practically every country of the world. Mackey (1967, p. 11) observed that "bilingualism, far from being exceptional, is a problem which affects the majority of the world's population." It is thus monolingualism that represents a special case.

Although there are no really precise figures on the number or distribution of speakers of two or more languages, it would appear that there are about thirty times as many languages as there are countries. The way in which language resources are organized and allocated in bilingual societies has implications for a wide range of activities.

A. The Sociolinguistic Composition of Multilingual Countries

Most of the studies of societal bilingualism have taken the nation-state as their reference point, and have relied on census data and various typologies to determine the linguistic composition of these units. However, it must be remembered that large-scale surveys and census statistics will yield quite a different perspective on questions of language use than detailed ethnographic case studies.

There are also many problems in doing research on multilingualism using census statistics (see, e.g., de Vries, 1985; Lieberson, 1969). The kinds of questions that can be asked about bilingualism are usually restricted by a variety of constraints. A census operates under limitations of time and money, and thus many facets of bilingualism, such as extent of interference, code-switching, and so on, cannot be investigated in any detail. On the other hand, a census can yield data on bilingualism for a population of much larger size than any individual linguist or team could hope to survey in a lifetime. In cases of de jure bilingualism, for instance, where certain laws dictate the use of two or more languages, knowledge about the demographic concentration of particular ethnic minorities is necessary for the implementation of language legislation. In Canada, for example, it is required in order that so-called bilingual districts are provided with services of the federal government in both French and English.

One major problem in such surveys is the fact that self-reports are subject to variance in relation to factors such as prestige, ethnicity, political affiliation, and so on. (see section III). Even where these factors are not present to a great degree, a respondent and census taker may not share the same ideas about what terms such as, *mother tongue, home language, first language* mean, especially because linguists themselves do not agree on bilingualism's definition. Usually censuses do not recognize that an individual might have more than one "mother tongue," or that the language learned first might not be the language best mastered. For example, until 1941 the Canadian censuses defined mother tongue as the language first learned by the respondent and still spoken. From 1941 through 1976, however, it was taken to mean the language first learned and still understood, following the definition of mother tongue given in the Official Language Act of 1969 (see de Vries, 1985, p. 358). This makes longitudinal comparison of statistics difficult.

There is even a more fundamental problem that is often ignored: namely, what is the difference between a language and a dialect? As a rule, censuses are interested in languages, not dialects. From a linguistic point of view, however, the term *language* is a relatively nontechnical one. Although two varieties may have very few linguistic differences and often are mutually intelligible, such as Norwegian and Swedish, their speakers regard them as separate languages for a variety of social, historical, and political reasons. Many speakers of Marathi regard Konkani as a variety of Marathi. Kloss (1969, p. 302) observed that in the state of Madras, speakers of Sourashtra petitioned the government for primary schools conducted in the medium of their own language. They were, however, refused on the grounds that Sourashtra was only a dialect. Interestingly, this variety is listed among the languages of India in the 1950 census, but in 1960 it is classified as a dialect of Gujerati.

The status of speakers represented in census statistics is not always clear. If we look, for instance, at the Irish census returns over the past century, we can see that although Irish retreated dramatically from the midnineteenth century onwards, in 1971 it seems to have a great upsurge, with 26% of the population claiming to speak it. This indicates a gain of nearly a quarter of a million speakers in a decade. The figures represent the number of children and adults who are recorded by heads of households as being able to speak Irish. At the time of the 1971 census a research team was investigating attitudes toward Irish and they decided to look into the census returns, because it was a matter of common knowledge that there were not 816,000 speakers of Irish. They found that the 26% represented those who were strongly supportive of the language. The real figure for L1 speakers of Irish as a proportion of the total population is around 2%. A further 7.4% are L2 speakers. The latter, however, are an unrepresentative, though influential, sector of educated Irish society. Outside native Irish-speaking districts, fluent Irish is a fairly reliable indicator of middle-class status, whereas the working class remains ignorant of the language. The new bilinguals constitute a network, not a community, and only a small number of them might be expected to pass the language on to the next generation. More recent statistics suggest that the latter group may number as few as 8,000 (see Hindley, 1990).

In addition, degree of bilingualism is usually left unspecified in census questions. The question used in Canada for years was simply, Can you speak French and English? In the Philippines census of 1960, a conversational criterion was stipulated: Any person who can carry on a simple conversation in Tagalog, English, or Spanish on ordinary topics is considered "able" (to speak) for the purpose of this census (Lieberson, 1969, p. 289). In others cases, such as the Israeli census of 1948, respondents were asked to say only which languages they used rather than which ones they knew. Lieberson (1969, p. 292) pointed out that the frequency with which respondents claimed to use Hebrew was probably exaggerated due to national pride during the early years of new nationhood. The question of whether a person uses a language also has to be viewed in context, because different languages and varieties are used for different things. Detailed information of this kind usually emerges from a different kind of study.

B. Domains of Language Use

In their research in the Puerto Rican community in New York City, Fishman, Cooper, and Ma (1971) arrived at a list of five domains in which either Spanish or English was used consistently. A *domain* is an abstraction that refers to a sphere of activity representing a combination of specific times, settings, and role relationships. The domains were established on the basis of observation and interviews and comprised family, friendship, religion, employment, and education. These served as anchor points for distinct value systems embodied in the use of Spanish as opposed to English. The team conducted further studies to support their claim that each of these domains carried different expectations for using Spanish or English.

They constructed hypothetical conversations that differed in terms of their interlocutors, place, and topic. The way in which these variables were manipulated determined the extent to which the domain configuration was likely to be perceived as congruent or incongruent. For example, a highly congruent configuration would be with a priest, in church, about how to be a good Christian. A highly incongruent one would be a discussion with one's employer at the beach about how to be a good son or daughter.

Students were asked to imagine themselves in hypothetical situations where two of the three components of the conversational context were given. For example, they might be asked to imagine they were talking to someone at their place of work about how to do a job most efficiently. They were then asked to whom they would most likely be talking and in what language. The students tended to provide congruent answers for any given domain, and their choice of language was consistent. The most likely place for Spanish was the family domain, followed by friendship, religion, employment, and education.

In each domain there may be pressures of various kinds (e.g., economic, administrative, cultural, political, religious, etc.) that influence the bilingual towards use of one language rather than the other (see Mackey, 1968, pp. 563–564). Often knowledge and use of one language is an economic necessity. Such is the case for many speakers of a minority language, such as Gujerati in Britain, or French in provinces of Canada where francophones are in a minority. The administrative policies of some countries may require civil servants to have knowledge of an L2. For example, in Ireland, the knowledge of Irish is required. In some countries it is expected that educated persons will have knowledge of another language. This is probably true for most of the European countries, and was even more dramatically so earlier in places such as pre-Revolutionary Russia, where French was the language of "polite," cultured individuals. Languages such as Greek and Latin have also had great prestige as L2s of the educated. A bilingual may also learn one of the languages for religious reasons. Many minority Muslim children in Britain receive religious training in Arabic. Due to competing pressures, it is not possible to predict with absolute certainty which language an individual will use in a particular situation.

C. Diglossia and Bilingualism

Ferguson (1959/1972, p. 232) originally used the term *diglossia* to refer to a specific relationship between two or more varieties of the same language in use in a speech community in different functions. As examples, he cites Haitian Creole (L) and French (H) in Haiti, Swiss German (L) and (Standard) High German in Switzerland, Classical Arabic (H) and colloquial Arabic (L) in Egypt. The superposed variety is referred to as "high" (H) and the other variety as low (L). The most important hallmark of diglossia is the functional specialization of H and L. In one set of situations only H is appropriate, whereas in another, only L. Although there may not be a universal set of unvarying functions, some of the typical situations in which the two varieties are used are indicated in Table I. There is only slight overlap between the two sets. For instance, in all the defining speech communities it is typical to read aloud from a newspaper in H and discuss its contents in L.

Ferguson notes nine separate areas in which H and L may differ: namely, function, prestige, literary heritage, acquisition, standardization, stability, grammar, lexicon, and phonology. As Fishman (1980, pp. 6–7) puts it, this is a societal arrangement in which individual bilingualism is not only widespread, but institutionally buttressed. The separate locations in which L and H are acquired immediately provide them with separate institutional support systems. L is typically acquired at home as a mother tongue and continues to be used throughout life. Its use is also extended to other familial and familiar interactions. H, on the other hand, is learned later through socialization and never at home. H is related to and

TABLE I

Some Situations for High and Low Varieties in Diglossia

	High	Low
Sermon in church	+	
Instructions to servants, waiters, and so on		+
Personal letter	+	
Speech in parliament, political speech	+	
University lecture	+	
Conversation with family or friends		+
News broadcast	+	
Radio soap opera		+
Newspaper editorial, news story	+	
Poetry	+	
Folk literature		+

supported by institutions outside the home. Diglossic societies are marked not only by these compartmentalization restrictions, but also by access restriction. That is, entry to formal institutions such as school and government requires knowledge of H.

The extent to which these functions are compartmentalized is illustrated in the importance attached by community members to using the right variety in the appropriate context. An outsider who learns to speak L and then uses it in a formal speech will be ridiculed. The speakers regard H as superior to L in a number of respects. In some cases it is the only recognized "real" version of the language to the extent that speakers claim they do not speak L. In some cases the alleged superiority is avowed for religious or literary reasons. For example, the fact that classical Arabic is the language of the Koran, endows it with special significance. In other cases a long literary tradition backs the H variety (e.g., Sanskrit). There is also a strong tradition of formal grammatical study and standardization associated with H.

Since Ferguson's initial characterization of diglossia, there have been a number of revisions to the model. Fishman (1980, p. 4), for example, recognized several different kinds of linguistic relationships between the H and L varieties. Some examples are given below of four possible configurations between H and L:

1. H as classical, L as vernacular, where the two are genetically related (e.g., classical and vernacular Arabic, Sanskrit, and Hindi).
2. H as classical, L as vernacular, where the two are not genetically related (e.g., textual Hebrew and Yiddish).
3. H as written and formal-spoken and L as vernacular, where the two are not genetically related to one another (e.g., Spanish and Guaraní in Paraguay).
4. H as written and formal-spoken and L as vernacular, where the two are genetically related to one another (e.g., Urdu and spoken Panjabi).

In cases like (4), some have used the term *digraphia*. There may or may not be a genetic relationship between the varieties. In Ferguson's original characterization of diglossia, it was assumed that the varieties involved belonged to "one language," and that only two varieties could participate in such a relationship.

There are also cases in which societies have two H varieties in conjunction with a single L, or so-called triglossia. In Tunisia, for example, Classical and Tunisian Arabic are in diglossic distribution, but French is also used, so three varieties are in functional distribution. More formal speaking situations are split between French and Classical Arabic. This has also been referred to as "broad diglossia" by Fasold (1984), who would allow any formal variety in use in a speech community to be the H variety. In cases like Tanzania, the same variety, Swahili, may act as both H to local L varieties and the L to a superposed language such as English. Platt (1977) has also extended the notion of diglossia in his use of the term *polyglossia* to refer to cases like Singapore and Malaysia, where several codes exist in a particular arrangement according to domains. Platt takes into account the prestige accorded to varieties so that in the case of Malaysia, for example, Mandarin Chinese serves as a "dummy H" because it is seen as prestigious, even though it is not used extensively in any domain. Other varieties in use include Bahasa Malaysia (the H variety of Malay), an L variety of Malay and English.

In all these cases the linguistic repertoire of the speech communities in such that it defies reduction to a binary opposition between H and L, where these are confined to varieties of the same language. Fishman (1980, p. 4) cited the Old Order Amish as a case in point, where the H varieties are High German (as exemplified in the Luther Bible) and English, and Pennsylvania German are the L varieties.

Ferguson (1959/1972, p. 240) also said that diglossia is stable. It tends to persist at least several centuries, and some diglossic situations, such as in the Arabic-speaking world, seem to go as far back as our recorded history of the language. In some cases the communicative tensions may be resolved in the creation of an intermediate variety between H and L. Diglossia is likely to come into being under certain conditions. One of these occurs when there is a sizable body of literature in a language closely related to (or even identical with) the natural language of the community, and this literature embodies some of the fundamental values of the group. Another precondition for diglossia obtains when literacy in the community is limited to a small elite.

Fishman (1967) pointed out that the relationship between individual bilingualism and societal diglossia is not a necessary or causal one. Either phenomenon can occur without the other one. Both are relative notions. According to Fishman (1980, p. 3), diglossia differs from bilingualism in that diglossia represents an enduring societal arrangement. Although many would disagree with this, it is useful to look at Fishman's (1967) schematization of the relationships between diglossia and bilingualism, as shown in Table II.

Because I have already discussed diglossia with bilingualism, I will not say more about it here. The second case, diglossia without bilingualism, was characterized by Fishman (1980, p. 7) as an instance of political or governmental diglossia in which two or more different monolingual entities are brought together under

TABLE II

The Relationships between Diglossia and Bilingualism

	Diglossia	Bilingualism
1. Both diglossia and bilingualism	+	+
2. Diglossia without bilingualism	+	−
3. Bilingualism without diglossia	−	+
4. Neither diglossia nor bilingualism	−	−

one political roof. Various modern states such as Canada, Belgium, and Switzerland fall into this category. There is institutional protection for more than one language at the federal level, although in individual territories there is widespread monolingualism. Fishman observed that both diglossia with and without bilingualism tend to be relatively stable, long-term arrangements. Stability, however, is a subjective notion. There are many bilingual situations that do not last for more than three generations. In some cases indigenous languages can be swamped by intrusive ones. This is what has happened to the Aboriginal languages of Australia and the Celtic languages of the British Isles. In other cases, immigrant languages have disappeared as their speakers have adopted the language of the new environment. This is the case for many speakers of South Asian languages, like Gujerati and Bengali, in Britain.

In cases such as these of bilingualism without diglossia, the two languages compete for use in the same domains. Speakers are unable to establish the compartmentalization necessary for survival of the L variety. In such cases Fishman (1980, p. 9) predicted that language shift is inevitable.

Fishman recognized, however, that there is much in modern life that militates against strict compartmentalization of H and L varieties. There has been an increase in open networks, social mobility, more fluid role relationships, and urbanization. All of these factors tend to diminish compartmentalization of the two varieties.

D. Language Maintenance and Shift

A number of researchers have commented on the extreme instability of bilingualism in the United States. Hakuta (1986, p. 166), for instance, has observed that probably no other country has been host to more bilingual people. However, each new wave of immigrants has seen the decline of their language by dint of pressure from English. Lieberson, Dalto, and Johnston (1975) say that in 1940, 53% of second-generation white Americans reported English as their mother tongue. In the previous generation, however, only 25% had English as their mother tongue. Thus, this probably represents a substantial shift within one generation. Some groups, however, such as Spanish speakers, have shown an increase in numbers in recent years because they have renewed themselves via new immigration. The United State is now the fifth largest Hispanic country in the world.

In Australia the decline of non-English languages has been similarly dramatic. Only 4.2% of the Australian-born population regularly uses a language other than English. This figure includes Aboriginal languages too. Different languages are concentrated in different states; however, Australia has no single minority language of the significance of Spanish in the United States (see the chapters in Romaine, 1991).

There are many reasons for language shift and language death. Most studies of language shift have looked at a community's transition to the new language (see

Fishman, 1964, for an overview of the field of language maintenance and shift, and Fishman, 1991). The classic pattern is that a community that was once monolingual becomes transitionally bilingual as a stage on the way to the eventual extinction of its original language. Thus, language shift involves bilingualism (often with diglossia) as a stage on the way to monolingualism in a new language. Bilingualism of course need not imply that one of the languages is going to be lost. Although the existence of bilingualism, diglossia, and code-switching have been often cited as factors leading to language death, in some cases code-switching and diglossia are positive forces in maintaining bilingualism. Swiss German and Faroese may never emerge from diglossia, but are probably in no danger of death.

Another type of study focuses more specifically on what happens to the language that is undergoing attrition and may die out as a consequence of language shift. The study of language death has emerged as a field in its own right in the last few decades (see Dorian, 1981, 1989, for a collection of representative studies). (Chapters 18 by Seliger, this volume, is a discussion of primary language attrition.)

Among the external factors cited as significant in various studies of language maintenance, shift, and death are numerical strength of the group in relation to other minorities and majorities, social class, religious and educational background, settlement patterns, ties with the homeland, degree of similarity between the minority and majority language, extent of exogamous marriage, attitudes of majority and minority, government policy towards language and education of minorities, and patterns of language use. I will take a few brief examples of how each of these factors can be implicated in, but does not entirely determine, the fate of a minority language (see also Fishman, 1991).

The number of speakers of a language per se tells us little of the ability of a group to maintain its language. *Who* speaks a language is more important than how many speak it. Nevertheless, a large minority group is often in a better position by dint of numerical strength to make itself prominent and to mobilize itself in support of its language. When large groups concentrate in particular geographical areas, they are often better able to preserve their languages (e.g., the American Chinese in New York and San Francisco). Conversely, when Norwegian Americans left their rural communities to work in urban areas, this led to language loss (see Haugen, 1953). In rural communities, however, Haugen (1989) observed that the Norwegian language and a strong degree of religious cohesion were instruments of union and a barrier against rival English-speaking Protestant sects.

Migration to urban areas has also led to the decline of many languages in Papua New Guinea. Even though towns like Lae will often have settlement areas that continue old village networks and receive new influxes of *wantoks* ('one language'—a term used to refer to a clansman), conversations with out-group members will be in Tok Pisin, a variety of pidgin English spoken by more than a million people and now undergoing creolization, particularly in the domain of work and business. Even though local vernacular languages like Buang are still used in the towns in social interaction with other Buangs, town Buang has more borrowings from Tok Pisin. Hooley (1987, p. 282) found that meetings of the Buang Taxi Truck Company in Lae are conducted in Tok Pisin, even when all those present are Buangs. However, even where out-migration from the villages has not been prevalent, Tok Pisin poses a threat to the maintenance of vernacular languages.

None of the Celtic languages has secured a major urban area that is predominantly monolingual. The Isle of Lewis is the major stronghold for Scottish Gaelic with over 85% of the population speaking the language. However, Stornoway, its capital, is in no sense a Gaelic town. In effect, this means that Gaelic does not claim a town of even 12,000, and thus, the language is largely rural rather than urban in its spread. The same is true of Welsh, Irish, and Breton. These languages also show an uneven social distribution. On the Isle of Harris, for example, agricultural workers and manual laborers provide the numerical stronghold for Scottish Gaelic, whereas English monolingualism is associated with the white-collar and professional classes (MacKinnon, 1977).

It is thus not enough to ask questions about the number of speakers that provides a threshold for a stable speech community; nor is it sufficient to look at spatial distribution, geographic location, migration, and so on. There are always difficulties in using statistical data on language ability as a surrogate measure of strength or vitality in the absence of information about opportunities for language use. Ambrose and Williams (1981) make this clear when they show that Welsh is not "safe" even in places where over 80% of the people speak it. Conversely, it is not lost where only 10% do so. Areas of Wales differ dramatically in terms of their proportions of Welsh speakers, and there are significant dichotomies between urban and rural. Gwynedd, which is symbolically the center of Welshness, has maintained a stable population since 1891, but in-migration has significantly altered its composition. By 1971 only 13 out of 150 community divisions had a level of 90% Welsh speakers. Previously this level of intensity was reported for 100 of Gwynedd's divisions.

Where a mixed language community exists, the loss rate is highest. The implications can be seen at the level of family structure. In mixed marriages there is usually a shift to the majority language, and this is an important factor in understanding what is happening in Wales. The incidence of language-group exogamy has increased to the point where there are almost as many marriages where only one spouse speaks Welsh as there are those where both speak Welsh. This has happened through the out-migration of Welsh speakers and the influx of English monolinguals into Wales. This tendency is out of proportion to the distribution of Welsh speakers in the overall population. This means that the family is no longer able to reproduce the language.

The inability of minorities to maintain the home as an intact domain for the use of their language has often been decisive in language shift. However, this is generally symptomatic of a more far-reaching disruption of domain distribution and pattern of transmission. In the case of Wales, an original pattern of diglossia without bilingualism, in which the governing elite belonged to one group and the masses to the another, was altered when Welsh acquired a public domain. It became the language of the Methodist church and acquired institutional status. Literacy also helped strengthen its position. Now, however, English speakers are an increased presence everywhere. All Welsh speakers are bilingual; furthermore, it is a bilingualism in which few English people participate. The losses are almost invariably in one direction and there is a group of new L2 speakers. Even though Welsh has been introduced in public domains where it used to be excluded (e.g., public administration and education, in social interactions, and elsewhere), its previous dominance has been weakened. There are also few employment contexts in which it is relevant.

The nature and extent of ties with the homeland for immigrant minorities can affect language maintenance. Is there a "myth of return" or even a mandate to return? Are there new waves of immigration that add to already existing communities? Refugees often reject the language of the oppressive regime they fled from and try to assimilate to the new culture as quickly as possible. Recent Russian-Jewish refugees in Australia employ Russian as a means of communication, but not as a language of symbolic identification. Hebrew fulfills the latter function. Similarly, in the German Jewish community in Australia, loyalty to the language of the grandparents has been transferred to the symbolic ethnic language, Hebrew, among the third generation. Other refugee groups, such as Poles and Hungarians, are divided as to how much support from the home country they will accept (e.g., materials for schools, etc).

Almost none of the factor cited in connection with language shift or death is on its own a reliable predictor of the outcome of any particular situation of language contact. Spolsky (1978, p. 70), for instance, proposed an accessibility index, which correlates with the extent of shift from Navajo to English in the southwestern United States. The less accessible a place is, the more likely Navajo is to be retained. The degree of isolation of a community is an important factor in language shift the world over, but it can work to maintain as well as to undermine a language. It may favor maintenance if the group members do not have to interact with members of the dominant language group, but it can also favor shift if, for example, the group is an immigrant community that has lost ties with the mother country. In Australia, Kalumburu, which is an extremely isolated settlement, has undergone language shift. The Arrernte language, however, has managed to hold its own in Alice Springs, which is a major English-speaking center.

III. BILINGUAL INDIVIDUALS

It is not possible to make a neat separation between bilingualism as a societal and individual phenomenon, particularly in the treatment of certain aspects of bilingual behavior, like borrowing and interference. The connection between individual and societal bilingualism also becomes evident when we consider some of the reasons why certain individuals are or become bilingual. Usually the more powerful groups in any society are able to force their language upon the less powerful. If we take Finland as an example, we find that the Sami (Lapps), Romanies, and Swedes have to learn Finnish, but the Finns do not have to learn any of these languages. Or similarly in Britain, the British child does not have to learn Panjabi or Welsh, but both these groups are expected to learn English.

A. Measuring Bilingualism

Much of the early literature on bilingualism in the 1950s and 1960s is concerned with the problem of how to measure bilingualism objectively in quantitative terms (see, e.g., the chapters in Kelly, 1969). This has led to a concentration of study on aspects of language that are more easily measured than others (e.g., size of vocabulary, control of inflectional morphology, etc.). Ideas about bilingualism have as a result often been adversely influenced by the use of terms like *the ideal bilingual, full bilingualism,* or *balanced bilingualism,* because they imply that there are other kinds of bilingualism that are not ideal, full, or balanced (see section IV).

Degree of Bilingualism

A bilingual's competence may encompass a range of skills, some of which may not be equally developed, in a number of languages and varieties. The fact that speakers select different languages or varieties for use in different situations shows that not all languages or varieties are equal or regarded as equally appropriate or adequate for use in all speech events. Because the bilingual's skill may not be the same for both languages at all linguistic levels, proficiency needs to be assessed in a variety of areas, such as those in Table III, in two languages, A and B. Within this model bilingualism is treated as a series of continua that may vary for each individual.

TABLE III

Measuring Degree of Bilingualism

	Levels								
	Phonological/Grammatical		Lexical		Semantic		Stylistic		Graphic
	A	B	A	B	A	B	A	B	A	B
Skills									
Listening									
Reading									
Speaking									
Writing									

A few examples will suffice to show some of the possibilities for these two sets of related variables. At the phonological-graphical level, we could take the case of the Panjabi speaker in Britain, who understands spoken Panjabi, but is unable to read the Gurmukhi script in which it is written. Listening and speaking skills might rate high for such a bilingual, but writing and reading would not. Also included under this level would be pronunciation. The bilingual's level of phonological ability might differ in the two languages. It might also be that an L2 has been learned only for the purpose of reading, in which case speaking and listening skills for that language would be poor. An interesting case is that of the novelist Joseph Conrad, who had excellent command of written English, but apparently always spoke it with a strong Polish accent.

In principle, there is no necessary connection between ability in one level and another. For example, a bilingual might have good pronunciation, but weak grammatical knowledge in one of the languages or vice versa. Or a bilingual might have excellent skills in all the formal linguistic aspects of production and perception in both written and spoken media, but be unable to control the stylistic range. However, in practice, there are some interdependencies. It is highly unlikely, for instance, that one would develop speaking without any listening skills. This schema, nevertheless, allows for a wide difference in ability under each level and skill category. A person who would otherwise be thought of as monolingual, but who has some familiarity with Arabic script without any accompanying ability to understand what was written in it, could be thought of as bilingual in English and Arabic. There may also be some biological constraints that affect, for instance, the degree of phonological ability in an L2 after a certain age. (See chapters 5 by Schachter and 15 by Obler and Hannigan, this volume, for discussion of maturational effects in L2 acquisition.)

Given the recent emphasis on the notion of communicative competence within sociolinguistics, this should be added as another type of skill. Because communicative competence has to do with both rules of grammar (understood here in the widest sense as embracing phonology, grammar, lexicon, and semantics) and rules for their use in socially appropriate circumstances, it is possible that a bilingual will be lacking in some aspects of communicative competence for one of the languages. Although appropriate use of the stylistic level would be part of good control of communicative competence, it would not be sufficient. A speaker might know how to vary his speech in culturally appropriate ways to make requests, but might not know the times and places at which it was appropriate to make a request.

It might also happen that a bilingual has excellent communicative competence, but weak productive control of one language This rather interesting linguistic profile has been characterized most fully by Dorian (1982) in her work in Gaelic–English bilingual communities along the east coast of Sutherland in Scotland. There she found some speakers who had minimal control of Scottish Gaelic, but whose receptive competence was outstanding. It included a knowledge of the sociolinguistic norms that operated within the community, as evidenced by their ability to understand everything, appreciate jokes, interject a proverb or other piece of formulaic speech at the appropriate place in a conversation. Their weak productive skills often went unnoticed by more proficient speakers in the community because they were able to behave as if they were ordinary members of the bilingual speech community by participating so fully in its interactional norms.

Dorian (1982, p. 26) refers to these speakers as "semi-speakers," whom she defines as "individuals who have failed to develop full fluency and normal adult proficiency in East Sutherland Gelic, as measured by their deviations from the fluent-speaker norms within the community." Communicative competence is less easily measurable by means of the kinds of formal testing procedures to be discussed next, which usually focus on rules of grammar in isolation from their use in context.

Dominance

A variety of tests have been used by psychologists to assess the relative dominance of one language over another in particular areas. One outcome has been greater precision in defining different types and degrees of bilingualism in relation to different configurations of dominance. However, this has been accomplished at the expense of the more qualitative differences in language proficiency that are harder to measure.

Macnamara (1967, 1969) grouped the kinds of tests used to measure bilingual ability into four categories: rating scales, fluency tests, flexibility tests, and dominance tests. Rating scales include various instruments such as interviews, language usage scales, and self-rating scales. In self-rating the individual would be asked to assess his ability in a language in relation to various skills. A balance score would be computed by subtracting the values obtained for one language from those of the other. If the difference is close to zero or zero, the bilingual is considered to be equally fluent in both languages, or a balanced bilingual. Baetens-Beardsmore (1986, p. 9) has used the term *equilingual* to refer to this kind of bilingual profile. Similarly, Halliday, McIntosh, and Strevens (1970) have used the term *ambilingual* to refer to a person who is capable of functioning equally well in either of the languages in all domains of activity and without any traces of one language in his use of the other.

Some practical examples will illustrate some of the problems with this method of measuring degree of bilingualism. Let's say, for example, that a Panjabi–English bilingual is asked to rate her ability in both languages in terms of this sort of matrix. She rates her Panjabi skills as consistently higher (on a scale of 0–4, where 0 = no knowledge and 4 = excellent knowledge) than English, except for reading and writing. She gives herself 4 on speaking and listening for all levels for Panjabi, but 0 for reading and writing. Her English scores range from 2–4 across the skills and levels averaging out at 3. The problem can already be seen. If we average her self-ratings in Panjabi across levels and skills we would obtain

2, given the total lack of reading and writing ability. If we then subtract this from the English score of 3, the result is 1. This of course indicates a degree of imbalance, but it does not tell us anything about the nature of the imbalance, and that much of it may result from lack of literacy in Panjabi. Thus, an extreme imbalance of skills within one of the languages may affect the balance of scores across two languages.

One of the most recent large surveys to rely on self-rating scales of various kinds was done by the Linguistic Minorities Project (1985) in England. They asked respondents to rate their productive and receptive skills in the spoken and written medium for each language they claimed to know. They found that the four different abilities for each language were quite strongly correlated with each other, though the correlation between oral and written skills was sometimes weaker (1985, p. 186).

The reliability of self-assessment is affected by many variables, such as the attitudes that the person has towards a particular language and the relative status of the languages in a particular context. If one of the languages has higher prestige, informants may claim greater knowledge of it (and conversely, lesser knowledge of the nonprestige language) than they actually have.

Different cultures may embody different notions of what it means to be a competent member of a particular language community. Speakers who know a nonstandard form of a language may not regard it as a "real" language, particularly when they have been schooled in the standard variety. Because literacy may play an important part in definitions of proficiency, a person who knows a language but cannot read and write it, may say that he or she doesn't know that language very well.

Fluency

Fluency has generally been given a great deal of weight in measurements of proficiency. A variety of fluency tests have been used to assess dominance, (e.g., picture naming, word completion, oral reading, and following instructions). Lambert (1955) developed a task in which subjects had to respond to instructions in both languages. Their response time was taken as an indication of whether they were balanced or dominant in one language. It was assumed that a balanced bilingual should take more or less the same time to respond to instructions in both languages.

Another frequently used set of tasks focuses on synonyms, associations, and word frequency estimations. Lambert, Havelka, and Gardner (1959) gave bilinguals nonsense words such as *dansonodent* and asked them to identify as many English and French words as possible. If the person detected as many English as French words in a given amount of time, he or she was considered a balanced bilingual. Another type of test relies on an ambiguous stimulus such as *pipe,* which could be a French or an English word, given to a bilingual in a reading list.

If the person pronounces it as in French, he or she is taken to be dominant in English. These two tests happen not to pose too many problems when the languages are as similar as French and English. When the languages concerned are more divergent with respect to their graphological conventions and phonotactic patterns, there is more difficulty. There may well be no ambiguous stimuli, or one of the languages may be written in an entirely different script, like Russian. Moreover, the bilingual may not be able to read in one of the languages.

Synonym tests rely on the assumption that a bilingual will have a larger and stronger network of semantic associations in the dominant language. In one kind of task, subjects are asked to name as many words that are synonymous with a given stimulus. Languages, however, differ in the number of synonyms that exist in a semantic field. English happens to be a particularly rich language due to the borrowing of Latinate and French vocabulary. This gives rise to semantically related items, such as *commence, start, begin,* and so on, which are stylistically differentiated. There is also the difficulty that a person may be able to use synonyms in context, but may not be able to recall them in a list fashion.

Lambert et al. (1959) found that rating scales, fluency, and flexibility, and dominance tests yielded measures of bilingualism that could be intercorrelated. Thus, they concluded that although these tests appeared to be assessing distinct skills, they were measuring a single factor. This indicates that competence is not divisible into isolated components.

B. Problems with Measuring Bilingualism

It is obvious that there are other problems with each of the tests I have discussed. Although self-ratings have often been found to be highly related to independent assessments of language skills and tests of language proficiency, they sometimes are not, for various reasons I have noted.

Jakobovits (1969) has questioned whether it is valid to measure dominance by taking the difference between two language scores, especially in tests involving speed of response. Various nonlinguistic factors may lead a subject to respond more slowly in one or the other language (see the discussion of domain congruence in II). There is no real basis for the assumption that reaction speed will be the same cross-linguistically. Tests that rely heavily on performance measures, where limitations of memory and time can affect the results, should not be regarded as adequate estimates of competence. These tests also do not take into account the contexts in which language is used. Cooper (1971) found that Spanish–English bilinguals had different scores on word naming tasks depending on whether the domain was family, neighborhood, school, or whatever. In some domains they would have been rated as balanced bilinguals, whereas in others they would not.

Many of these measures become problematic when applied in educational settings to bilingual children (see section IV). For instance, when the so-called cognitive aspects of language are tested in terms of being able to produce synonyms or create neologisms, the child who cannot is branded as "lacking in the cognitive aspects of language development." Then it becomes easy to believe that abstract and usually quantitative measures, such as size of vocabulary or response time, must express something more real and fundamental than the data themselves. Once such features as the mastery of complex syntax, accurate spelling, or punctuation become established measures of language proficiency, it is hardly questioned what is actually meant by language ability and what role these features play in it.

There are a variety of other problems with both the notions of balance and dominance and the tests that are used to measure them. Fishman (1971, p. 560), for example, has cautioned against the notion of balanced bilingualism in more general terms. He says that bilinguals are rarely equally fluent in both languages about all possible topics. This reflects the fact that the allocation of functions of the languages in society is normally imbalanced and in complementary distribution. Any society that produced functionally balanced bilinguals who used both languages equally well in all contexts would soon cease to be bilingual because no society needs two languages for the same set of functions. Because of the inherent connection between proficiency and function, it is doubtful whether bilingualism per se can be measured apart from the situation in which it functions for a particular individual.

The search for the true balanced bilingual depicted in some of the literature on bilingualism is elusive. The notion of balanced bilingualism is an ideal one, which is largely an artifact of a theoretical perspective that takes the monolingual as its point of reference. It can also be seen that, given the relative nature of dominance, such notions as mother tongue, native language, and native speaker become problematic, too.

C. Borrowing and Interference as an Individual and Community Phenomenon

Interference is one of the most commonly described and hotly debated phenomena of bilingualism. The reason for much of the debate about it has to do with its definition and identification and the extent to which it is distinct from other phenomena of language contact, such as borrowing, transfer, convergence, and code-switching. (See chapter 19 by Bhatia and Ritchie, this volume, for a general discussion of code-switching and code-mixing.) Here I will attempt to illustrate some of the various phenomena that have been talked about under the heading of borrowing, interference, and transfer in order to clarify some of the terminology.

Part of the problem in discussing these concepts lies in the fact that they must be dealt with at the level of the individual as well as the community. What has been called "interference" is ultimately a product of the bilingual individual's use of more than one language in everyday interaction. At the level of the individual, interference may be sporadic and idiosyncratic. However, over time the effects of interference in a bilingual speech community can be cumulative and lead to new norms, which are different from those observed by monolinguals who use the languages elsewhere. For instance, in some parts of Ireland certain Gaelic features persist in the speech of English monolinguals long after a period of active bilingualism has disappeared from the community. Some monolingual speakers use syntactic constructions that are traceable to Gaelie (e.g., *I'm after eating my dinner.* = 'I have already eaten my dinner.').

In the simplest terms *interference* refers to the influence of one language on another. It arises from mismatches in structures between two languages in contact. What is referred to as a foreign accent, for instance, is an obvious reflection of cross-linguistic influence at the level of pronunciation. For example, when the substitution of /s/ for /z/ by Norwegian–English bilinguals in the United States is explained by the fact that there is no contrast between /s/ and /z/ in Norwegian (see Weinreich, 1968, pp. 14–28, for a detailed analysis of what happens when the phonological systems of the bilingual individual are in contact). Similarly, the Japanese–English bilingual who says [gurando] for English [graund] 'ground' is making the English word conform to the syllable structure patterns of Japanese, which allows no consonant clusters.

Interference can in principle arise at any level of grammar, including morphology, syntax, semantics, prosody, as well as in the area of communicative competence. When German–English bilinguals borrow the word *breakfast* it is assigned to the class of neuter gender words probably because in German *Frühstück* is neuter. One of the most obvious effects of cross-linguistic influence at the syntactic level is reflected in word-order divergence. For example, Dutch–French bilinguals in Belgium may place adjectives before the nouns they modify instead of after them. This occurs as a result of the fact that in Dutch adjectives precede nouns. Not saying the right thing at the right time or in the right way may result from the application of the communicative norms from one language to a setting in which the other language is used, Take, for instance, the differences in offering routines in Swedish and English. The meaning of the Swedish term *varsågod* (literally 'be so kind') includes not only "please" but conveys much more. A Swedish host would say *varsågod* when offering a guest a seat, food, or drink, as well as when asking someone to do a favor. I have observed many Swedish–English bilinguals when speaking English say "please" when putting a plate in front of a guest. In English, however, the appropriate behavior would be either to say nothing or something like, "hope you enjoy it," or "please go ahead."

Within the field of L2 acquisition these mismatches between two languages are referred to as transfer. (See chapter 10 by Gass, this volume.) Sharwood-Smith and Kellerman (1986, p. 1) suggested that the more neutral term *crosslinguistic influence* should be adopted to take into account all such cases where one language influences another. This seems a sensible idea, considering that the field of bilingualism is already pervaded with terms that have negative implications (see I and IV). It can be used as a general term, though as I will indicate below, it is also useful to have other additional terms with more specific reference to aspects of the mechanism involved in certain kinds of cross-linguistic influence, like calquing, loan blend, and so on.

What happens to lexical items has been central to discussions of interference, transfer, and borrowing. It is usually in this context that the term *borrowing* is used. However, it is not possible to talk about cross-linguistic influence at the lexical level without also taking into account the fact that in order to be used, words must interact with phonology, syntax, morphology, and semantics.

One of the earliest attempts to categorize types of lexical influence (based on degree or manner of integration) can be found in Haugen (1950). At the phonological level a word may be unassimilated, in which case there is no adaptation to the phonology of the recipient language, or it may be partially or wholly assimilated. Similarly, at the morphological and syntactic levels, there may be assimilation of various degrees or no assimilation. Borrowed items tend to have an uncertain linguistic status for some time after they are first adopted. Before a particular loan has met with more general social acceptance, each individual may adapt to it varying degrees. Moreover, the same individual may not use the same phonological form for the same *loanword* from one occurrence to the next (see, e.g., Poplack, Sankoff, & Miller, 1988).

Words that are adapted phonologically and morphologically are referred to by Haugen as loanwords (e.g., *pizza, czar,* etc. in English). However, these are of a different character from those that are only partially assimilated. The former are used by monolinguals who may or may not be aware of their foreign origin, unless they happen to know the history of the language. In other words, they are probably not even perceived as foreign by the majority of speakers.

Another type of borrowing is called a *loanblend.* In such cases one part of a word is borrowed and the other belongs to the original language (e.g., in the German spoken in Australia, *Gumbaum* 'gumtree,' *Redbrickhaus* 'red brick house,' and *Grüngrocer* 'greengrocer.' In each of these cases part of the compound is borrowed from English, while the other is German. Loanwords and loanblends are particularly common in cases of so-called immigrant bilingualism for obvious reasons. When moving to a new setting, speakers will encounter a variety of things that are specific to the new environment or culture and will adopt readily available words from the local language to describe them. There are no equivalents in German, for example, to refer to gum trees and various types of brick and weatherboard houses found in Australia.

Another type of borrowing is called a *loanshift*. This consists of taking a word in the base language and extending its meaning so that it corresponds to that of a word in the other language. This type of loanshift has also been called (semantic) extension. For example, Portuguese–English bilinguals in the United States have taken the Portuguese word *grossería* 'rude remark' and have extended it to refer to a 'grocery store' instead of borrowing the English term. In this case the phonetic similarity between the Portuguese and English terms motivates the shift.

Another type of borrowing is referred to as *loan translation* or *calque*. The English term *skyscraper* has been adopted into many languages via loan translation. Compare the French, *gratteciel* ['scrape' + 'sky']; Spanish, *rascacielos* ['scrape' + 'skies']; and German, *Wolkenkratzer* ['cloud' + 'scrape']. In each case the adopting language has analyzed the component morphemes of the English term and replaced them with ones of equivalent meaning. Often bilinguals may borrow whole idioms or phrases from the other language in this way.

IV. BILINGUALISM AND EDUCATION

A. Bilingualism and School Achievement

Bilingualism has often, and still is, cited as an explanation for the failure of certain groups of children. It has been argued that it is counterproductive to the child's welfare to develop and maintain proficiency in more than one language. A great deal of the early literature appeared to indicate that bilingualism exerted a negative influence on children's development and intelligence. This has been used to support a policy of monolingual instruction in the majority language, in particular for children of minority language background.

Many people now recognize that these ideas are based on questionable assumptions about language proficiency, how it is measured, and how bilingualism affects academic development. For instance, scores for verbal IQ will be lower for bilinguals tested in their nondominant language and should therefore be discounted when trying to determine whether to send children to special programs. Moreover, there are a variety of other factors that influence children's development in school, such as lack of exposure to the school language, linguistic and cultural mismatch between home and school, inferior quality of education provided to some students, socioeconomic status, disrupted patterns of intergenerational cultural transmission as a result of minority–majority status relations, attitudes towards bilingualism, and so on. As one of society's main socializing instruments, the school plays a powerful role in exerting social control over its pupils. It endorses mainstream, and largely middle-class values. Children who do not come to school with the kind of cultural background supported in the schools are likely to experience conflict (see Romaine, 1984, chap. 6). This is true even of working-class children belonging to the dominant culture, but even more so for children of ethnic minority background. In the United States, grade 12 Hispanic students are about $3\frac{1}{2}$ years behind national norms in academic achievement. The children's degree of bilingualism in English and Spanish is only one of many variables affecting their performance.

B. Types of Bilingual Education Programs

The term *bilingual education* can mean different things in different contexts. If we take a commonsense approach and define it as a program where two languages are used equally as media of instruction, many so-called bilingual education programs would not count as such. Moreover, the "same" educational policy can lead to different outcomes, depending on differences in the input variables. One can compare, for example, the relatively poor academic performance of Finns in Sweden, where they are a stigmatized minority group with their favorable achievement in Australia, where they are regarded as a high-status minority. There have also been results from some of the Canadian French–English immersion programs of bilingual education that support the view that bilingualism fosters intellectual development and academic achievement.

Submersion

The traditional policy, either implicitly assumed or explicitly stated, that most nations have pursued with regard to various minority groups who speak a different language has been eradication of the native language and culture and assimilation into the majority one. It was not too long ago that minority children in countries like Australia, the United States, Britain, and the Scandinavian countries were subject to physical violence in school for speaking their home language. Skutnabb-Kangas (1984, p. 309), for example, reports the experiences suffered by Finnish schoolchildren in the Tornedal area of Sweden. Some had to carry heavy logs on their shoulders or wear a stiff collar because they had spoken Finnish. In other areas of Sweden, like Norrbotten, there were workhouses, which poor children attended and earned their keep by doing most of the daily domestic work. When one of the children spoke Finnish, they were all lined up and had their ears boxed one by one.

Often the education of minority children entailed removing them from their parents and their own cultural group. The Statutes of Iona in Scotland, which date from 1609, is one early instance of legislation designed to promote linguistic and cultural assimilation. The Statutes had the expressed purpose of separating Highland children from their native Gaelic culture and language and educating them in English in the Lowlands, where they would learn not only the dominant language, but would do so in an environment where their own culture was seen as barbaric (Romaine & Dorian, 1981). It required every gentleman or yeoman to send his eldest son (or daughter) to Lowland schools to be brought up there until they were sufficiently competent in written and spoken English.

In many parts of the world today children are not taught enough of their own language and culture to be able to appreciate it. They are made to feel ashamed of their parents and origin. Although this is not usually done by physical punishment or by telling the children that their parents are primitive and uncivilized, the school is organized in such as way so as to convey the same message by educating them in a language that is not their own. An example would be the Romanies in Finland, whose children are placed in ordinary Finnish schools without any consideration for the Romany language or culture. There is no attempt to provide any mother tongue teaching or extra teaching in Finnish as an L2. This is the most common experience for immigrant children. An educational program of this type is often called "submersion" because the children's native language (NL) is suppressed or ignored and the children have to sink or swim in a completely different language environment. The aim of such a program is assimilation, and the result is often "subtractive bilingualism." That is, the outcome is generally loss rather than retention of the child's L1.

Immersion

A similar type of instructional program goes by the name of "immersion." Despite their superficial similarity, submersion and immersion programs are different and they lead to different results. The educational aim of immersion is enrichment of language skills and the desired outcome is "additive bilingualism." An example would be the immersion programs in French and English in Canada, where speakers of one language opt for education in the medium of the other in order to add another language to their skills. The child's NL is intact and develops, even though the child has not had the same amount of instruction as its monolingual peers in majority language schools. It adds an L2 without threatening the first.

Transitional Bilingualism

A less direct and extreme educational policy that nevertheless has assimilation as its goal is transitional bilingualism. A good example here is the provision made in the United States under the Bilingual Education Act for the education of children who have limited proficiency in English. Its aim is to provide instruction in the mother tongue only as an aid to allow the children to proceed into ordinary mainstream classes in the majority language. Fishman (1980) has been in general critical about the way in which countries like the United States have used the terms bilingualism and biculturalism in connection with its educational programs supported by this legislation. Neither the institutional stability nor the functional compartmentalization required is recognized in order for it to be pursued seriously. As implemented under this legislative provision, bilingual education is transitional and peripheral in relation to the mainstream culture. The actual number of children in the United States who presently receive bilingual education represents only a quarter of the population for whom it is intended. Most of these schools do not attempt to maintain the NL of the children and over half do not provide any content area instruction in the NL.

In both submersion and transitional programs subtractive bilingualism is often the result. An L2 gradually undermines proficiency in the first. This has been called subtractive or disruptive bilingualism on the grounds that the development of the child's L1 has been disrupted and is incomplete. Many researchers, particularly in Scandinavia, have claimed that the development of the children in both languages is fragmentary and incomplete. They have been referred to as "semilingual."

This is, however, a term which must be used with considerable caution (see Martin-Jones & Romaine, 1985). It relies on an idealized notion of balanced bilingualism as an implicit synonym for "good" or "complete" bilingualism and uses it as a yardstick against which other kinds of bilingualism can be measured and stigmatized as inadequate or underdeveloped. The term *balanced bilingual* also reveals a static conception of language. Where languages are in contact, there is usually considerable intergenerational variation in patterns of language use and often quite rapid change in communicative repertoires. There is no general agreement among child language researchers about the "normal" course of development among monolingual, let alone, bilingual children. Most of the studies of both groups focus on the middle-class child.

Silva-Corvalán (1983, p. 11) notes that if we assumed that complete acquisition included knowledge of the monolingual standard variety, then the Spanish of second- and third-generation bilinguals in California would have to be considered an incompletely acquired variety, in spite of the fact that these speakers are able to communicate fluently in Spanish in all the domains where they are expected to use the language. One could not test the competence of these speakers by measuring their control over the categories and rules of the monolingual code, some of which do not exist in their own speech. A realistic assessment of bilinguals must be based firmly on a knowledge of developmental norms for the two languages, and typical patterns of interference as well as socialization practices. Because bilingualism always develops in a particular social context, socioeconomic class is a crucial intervening variable. Yet it is often ignored in discussions of the possible connections between bilingualism and school achievement.

Often children are caught in a vicious circle. Because the school fails to support the home language, skills in it are often poor. At the same time they do not progress in the new language at school, and are labeled semilingual. Often it is argued that bilingualism impedes development in the L2. Thus, the failure of the school to let children develop further in their mother tongue is often used to legitimize further oppression of it.

Language Shelter

In other kinds of programs children are taught through the medium of their L1 with a goal of maintenance and further development of the language and culture in interaction with the majority. This type of program has been called a "language shelter." The Swedish school system in Finland is a good example. A Swedish-speaking child in Finland can attend a Swedish day nursery and continue education in Swedish through university level. At the same time the children receive instruction in Finnish as an L2 at school. The negative results for bilingualism, (e.g., lower IQ, poorer achievement in language tests, etc.) have been obtained largely in connection with subtractive bilingualism in submersion type programs, whereas positive results have emerged in connection with Canadian immersion programs. One guiding principle does emerge from this consideration of different policies and their probable outcomes. In order to achieve high(er) levels of bilingualism, it is better to support via instruction the language that is less likely to develop for other reasons (see Skutnabb-Kangas, 1984, p. 130).

C. Bilingual Education in an International Perspective

In practice, the situation in individual countries is complex and often several different options are available for different kinds of children, depending on a variety of circumstances, which vary from place to place. For example, in Germany, there are also assimilationist programs in addition to segregationist ones. In the United States some children have received assimilationist treatment (with or without special instruction in ESL), whereas others have had the opportunity to participate in bilingual programs along with majority children who were being exposed to the L1 of the minority group in an enrichment scheme. In Canada, where the immersion type is popular, there are also language heritage programs for certain minority language groups in certain provinces, which provide language classes in ethnic minority languages such as Ukrainian. In the Netherlands, one regional language variety, Frisian, has official language status and is a mandatory school subject in the province of Friesland. However, for children speaking non-indigenous minority languages like Turkish, Dutch immersion is the most frequent program given. The different treatment given to Frisian in the Elementary Education Act by comparison with that given to other indigenous varieties of Dutch and nonindigenous minority languages is based on political rather than linguistic or educational criteria.

After the U.S. federal government had passed the Bilingual Education Act of 1968, over $7 million were appropriated for 1969–1970 to support educational programs that were aimed at the special educational needs of children of "limited English-speaking ability in schools having a high concentration of such children from families with incomes below $3,000." The budget for bilingual education increased steadily until 1980, when it peaked at $191.5 million. The money was intended to support initiatives in bilingual education that would later be financed through state and local funds. In the first few years the emphasis was on elementary education.

D. Legal Implications Arising from Legislation on Bilingual Education

Although the Bilingual Education Act provided opportunities for schools to set up bilingual education programs, it did not place individual schools under any legal obligation to do so. Litigation brought to the courts on behalf of various groups of minority students led in some cases to court-mandated bilingual education programs. The most famous precedent-setting case was that of *Lau v. Nichols*. In this instance a class action suit was brought against the San Francisco Unified School District by Chinese public school students in 1970. It was argued that no special programs were available to meet the linguistic needs of these students. As a consequence, they were prevented from deriving benefit from instruction in English and were not receiving equal treatment.

The plaintiffs made their appeal not on linguistic grounds, but on the basis of the Civil Rights Act of 1964, which states that "no person in the United States shall, on the ground of race, color or national origin, be excluded from participation in, be denied the benefits of, or be subject to discrimination under any program or activity receiving Federal financial assistance" (Teitelbaum & Hiller, 1977, p. 6). In their case against the school board, the plaintiffs requested a program of bilingual education. Although the case was lost, the Supreme Court overturned the decision of the federal district court in 1974. It was concluded that: "the Chinese-speaking minority receives fewer benefits than the English-speaking majority from respondents' school system which denies them a meaningful opportunity to participate in the educational program—all earmarks of discrimination banned by the regulations" (Teitelbaum & Hiller, 1977, p. 8). This was a landmark decision because it meant that for the first time in the United States the language rights of non-English speakers were recognized as a civil right.

The actual number of children in the United States who presently receive bilingual education represents only a quarter of the population for whom it is intended. Most of these schools do not attempt to maintain the NL of the children and over half do not provide any content area instruction in the NL.

E. Reactions to Bilingual Education

In some respects it is ironic that one of the reasons why bilingual education has been viewed so negatively by many people in the United States is due to the fear that it aims to maintain languages, and by implication cultures, other than English. Often the most outspoken opponents are those of immigrant background for whom no provision was made, and who were eager to assimilate as quickly as possible to the mainstream American way of life.

The antipathy to multiculturalism and multilingualism runs deep in the American ethos. One of its more recent manifestations can be found in the English Language Act passed in California and other states, which makes English the official language for public use. This came about through the efforts of the organization called U.S. English, founded by former Senator Hayakawa to lobby for a constitutional amendment that would make English the official language of the United States. The organization also seeks to repeal laws mandating multilingual ballots and voting materials, to restrict government funding to short-term transitional programs, and to control immigration so that it does not reinforce trends toward language segregation. It welcomes members "who agree that English is and must remain the only language of the people of the United States."

V. ATTITUDES TOWARD BILINGUALISM

A. Negative and Positive Attitudes toward Bilingualism

It can be seen from the reactions toward bilingual education in the United States that negative attitudes still prevail. In many cases bilingualism is viewed negatively and with suspicion. Members of the bilingual community often share the negative attitudes of monolinguals, often to the point where they discourage their children from using the language of the home, when this is different from the one used in society at large.

It is true of most multilingual societies that the differential power of particular social groups is reflected in language variation and attitudes toward this variability. The study of language attitudes is important because attitudes represent an index of intergroup relations, and they play an important role in mediating and determining them. In cases where increased institutional support is given to the language of lesser prestige, more positive attitudes toward it may begin to be expressed overtly. This has been true for Welsh in parts of Wales and for French in Canada.

Identification with a language and positive attitudes toward it do not necessarily guarantee its maintenance. This has been true in Ireland, where the necessity of using English has overpowered antipathy toward English and English speakers. The adoption of English by the Irish is a case of language shift not accompanied by favorable attitudes toward English (see Macnamara, 1973). In instances such as these, an instrumental rather than integrative orientation is more important in determining the speakers' choice. The distinction between integrative and instrumental attitudes has been discussed by Gardner and Lambert (1972) as an important factor in predicting the success of L2 learning. They found that when speakers wanted to learn a language for integrative reasons (e.g., because they wanted to interact with speakers of that language and share in their culture), they were more successful than if their motives were more instrumental (i.e. motivated by factors such as the utility of the language).

The attitudes of the majority towards the minority can also play a decisive role. Different cultures have different ideas about the integrity of their own group in relation to outsiders. If speakers of the minority language manage to find an ecological niche in the majority community that is conducive to language maintenance, they may have a better chance of survival. Hamp (1980), for example, explains the success of Albanian enclaves in Italy (and conversely, their failure in Greece) in securing safe places for their language by noting the differences in cultural ideology between Italy and Greece. In Italy, a localist attitude prevails, with each region valuing its own local dialect, while in Greece, a more exclusionist policy is pursued.

However, there are often considerable differences of opinion within the "same" community. Other surveys have used questionnaires to tap other aspects of attitudes toward bilingualism. Dorian (1981), for example, investigated the reasons that Scottish Gaelic speakers had for valuing their knowledge of the language and the extent to which these differed from those professed by English monolinguals living in their midst. She found that 100% of the bilinguals selected the statement that Gaelic was a beautiful language as well as an important one. In fact, both bilinguals and monolinguals seemed to feel the appeal of Gaelic as a language rather than as a means to anything else.

B. Attitudes toward Code Switching

Gumperz (1982, pp. 62–63) reported a range of differing attitudes toward code-switching cross-culturally. Some characterize it as an extreme form of mixing attributable to lack of education, bad manners, or improper control of the two languages. Others see it as a legitimate form of informal talk. Some communities have no readily available terms or labels to describe switching, whereas others do. These very often reveal the stereotypical reactions of community members. In Texas and the American Southwest, where code-switching takes place among Mexican Americans, the derogatory term "Tex-Mex" is used. In parts of French-speaking Canada the term *joual* has similar connotations.

In the Panjabi-speaking community in Britain many people label mixed varieties with the stereotype *tuṭi fuṭi* (i.e., 'broken up') Panjabi, and do not consider it to be "real," pure Panjabi. In communities like these there is almost an inherent conflict between the desire to adopt English loanwords as prestige markers and their condemnation as foreign elements destroying the purity of the borrowing language. The ambiguity felt by Norwegian Americans is described by Haugen (1977, p. 332):

> Even though they admired the book norms exhibited by clergymen, they did not approve people from their own group who tried to speak a 'pure' Norwegian like that of the ministers. On the other hand, they poked fun at those who adopted excessive numbers of English words, calling them 'yankeefied' and holding them to be 'proud', 'trying to be big shots' and the like. Most people steered a middle course between these extremes, and while professing a low opinion of their own dialects, an attitude reflecting their low status in the homeland, they went right on using them into the second and third generation. In doing so they created quite unconsciously a communicative norm which anyone who has known their society will immediately recognize as genuine.

It would seem then that in the majority of communities where it has been studied, some social stigma has been attached to this mode of speaking by both community as well as out-group members (e.g., educators). Haugen (1977, p. 94), for example, reports that a visitor from Norway made the following comment on the Norwegian spoken by immigrants in the United States: "Strictly speaking, it is no language whatever, but a gruesome mixture of Norwegian and English, and often one does not know whether to take it humorously or seriously."

Gumperz (1982) notes, however, that when political ideology changes, attitudes toward code-switching may change too. In California and elsewhere in the southwestern United States, *pocho* and *calo* served as pejorative terms for the Spanish of local Chicanos. However, with a rise in ethnic consciousness, these speech styles and code-switching have become stylistic of Chicano ethnicity. *Pocho* and *calo* are now increasingly used in modern Chicano literature.

VI. CONCLUSION

Bilingualism is not a unitary phenomenon. It is shaped in different ways depending on a variety of social and other factors, which must be taken into account when trying to assess the skills of bilingual speakers. Therefore, the study of the behavior of bilingual groups and individuals requires us to go beyond many of the concepts and analytical techniques presently used within linguistic theory, which are designed for the description of monolingual competence.

Notions like interference, which are commonly used in discussions of bilingualism, depend on the assumption that we know what the individual codes are, which is not always the case. When speakers of different languages are in contact, the codes they use may not be stable. Because new and different norms develop in such situations, there are problems in talking about proficiency because competence may span several codes, which are unequally developed. It is possible for a bilingual to be fluent in both languages taken together without being able to function like a monolingual in either one on its own. This means that the bilingual's system will be different in some respects from the monolingual's.

The idea that monolingualism is a normal and desirable state of affairs, whereas multilingualism is divisive, is still with us. There is, however, no reason to believe that bilingualism is an inherently problematic mode of organization, either for a society, or an individual, or human cognitive systems. As far as societal multilingualism is concerned, the co-existence of more than one language is not in itself a cause of intergroup conflict. Although the media often suggest otherwise, conflicts involving language are not really about language, but about fundamental inequalities between groups who happen to speak different languages.

REFERENCES

Ambrose, J. E., & Williams, C. (1981). On the spatial definition of minority: Scale as an influence on the geolinguistic analysis of Welsh. In E. Haugen, J. D. McClure, & D. S. Thomson (Eds.), *Minority languages today* (pp. 53–71). Edinburgh: Edinburgh University Press.

Appel, R., & Muysken, P. (1987). *Language contact and bilingualism.* London: Edward Arnold.

Baetens-Beardsmore, H. (1982). *Bilingualism. Basic principles.* Clevedon, UK: Tieto Ltd.

Baetens-Beardsmore, H. (1986). *Bilingualism. Basic Principles* (2nd ed.). Clevedon, UK: Tieto Ltd.

Bloomfield, L. (1933). *Language.* New York: Holt.

Cooper, R. (1971). Degree of bilingualism. In J. Fishman, R. L. Cooper, & R. Ma (Eds.), *Bilingualism in the barrio.* Bloomington: Indiana University Press.

de Vries, J. (1985). Some methodological aspects of self-report questions on language and ethnicity. *Journal of Multilingual and Multicultural Development, 6,* 347–369.

Diebold, A. R. (1964). Incipient bilingualism. In D. Hymes, (Ed.), *Language in culture and society* (pp. 495–511). New York: Harper & Row.

Dorian, N. C. (1981). *Language death. The life cycle of a Scottish Gaelic dialect.* Philadelphia: University of Pennsylvania Press.

Dorian, N. C. (1982). Defining the speech community to include its working margins. In S. Romaine (Ed.), *Sociolinguistic variation in speech communities* (pp. 25–33). London: Edward Arnold.

Dorian, N. C. (Ed.). (1989). *Investigating obsolescence: Studies in language contraction and death.* Cambridge, UK: Cambridge University Press.

Fasold, R. (1984). *The sociolinguistics of society.* Oxford: Blackwell.

Ferguson, C. F. (1959). Diglossia. *Word, 15,* 325–340. (Reprinted in *Language and social context,* pp. 232–252, by P. Gigliolo, Ed., 1972, Harmondsworth: Penguin.)

Fishman, J. (1964). Language maintenance and language shift as a field of inquiry; a definition of the field and suggestions for its further development. *Linguistics, 9,* 32–70.

Fishman, J. (1967). Bilingualism with and without diglossia; diglossia with and without bilingualism. *Journal of Social Issues, 32,* 29–38.

Fishman, J. (Ed.). (1971). *Advances in the sociology of language.* The Hague: Mouton.

Fishman, J. (1980). Bilingualism and biculturalism as individual and societal phenomena. *Journal of Multilingual and Multicultural Development, 1,* 3–17.

Fishman, J., Cooper, R. L., & Ma, R. (Eds.). (1971). *Bilingualism in the barrio.* Bloomington: Indiana University Press.

Fishman, J. (1991). *Reversing language shift.* Clevedon, UK: Multilingual Matters.

Gardner, R., & Lambert, W. E. (1972). *Attitudes and motivation in second language learning.* Rowley, MA: Newbury House.

Grosjean, F. (1982). *Life with two languages. An introduction to bilingualism.* Cambridge, MA: Harvard University Press.

Gumperz, J. J. (1982). *Discourse strategies.* Cambridge, UK: Cambridge University Press.

Hakuta, K. (1986). *Mirror of language. The debate on bilingualism.* New York: Basic Books.

Halliday, M. A. K., McIntosh, A., & Strevens, P. (1970). The users and uses of language. In J. Fishman (Ed.), *Readings in the sociology of language* (pp. 139–169). The Hague: Mouton.

Hamp, E. (1980). Problems of multilingualism in small linguistic communities. In J. E. Alatis (Ed.), *International dimensions of bilingual education* (pp. 155–165). Washington, DC: Georgetown University Press.

Haugen, E. (1950). The analysis of linguistic borrowings. *Language, 26,* 210–231.

Haugen, E. (1953). *The Norwegian language in America: A study in bilingual behavior.* Philadelphia: University of Pennsylvania Press. (Reprinted in 1969, Bloomington: Indiana University Press)

Haugen, E. (1977). Norm and deviation in bilingual communities. In P. Hornby, (Ed.), *Bilingualism. Psychological, social and educational implications.* New York: Academic Press.

Haugen, E. (1989). The rise and fall of an immigrant language: Norwegian in America. In N. C. Dorian (Ed.), *Investigating obsolescence: Studies in language contraction and death.* Cambridge, UK: Cambridge University Press.

Hindley, R. (1990). *The death of the Irish language. A qualified obituary.* London: Routledge.

Hoffman, C. (1991). *An introduction to bilingualism.* London: Longman.

Hooley, B. A. (1987). Death or life: The prognosis for central Buang. In D. C. Laycock, & W. Winter (Eds.), *A world of language: Papers presented to Professor S. A. Wurm on his 65th birthday* (Pacific Linguistics C-100, pp. 275–285). Canberra: Australian National University.

Jakobovits, L. (1969). Commentary on 'How can one measure the extent of a person's bilingual proficiency?' In L. G. Kelly (Ed.), *Description and measurement of bilingualism* (pp. 98–102). Toronto: University of Toronto Press.

Kelly, L. G. (Ed.). (1969). *Description and measurement of bilingualism.* Toronto: University of Toronto Press.

Kloss, H. (1969). Commentary on How can we describe and measure the incidence and distribution of bilingualism? In L. G. Kelly (Ed.), *Description and measurement of bilingualism* (pp. 296–315). Toronto: University of Toronto Press.

Lambert, W. E. (1955). Measurement of the linguistic dominance of bilinguals. *Journal of Abnormal and Social Psychology, 50,* 197–200.

Lambert, W. E., Havelka, J., & Gardner, R. (1959). Linguistic manifestations of bilingualism. *American Journal of Psychology, 72,* 77–82.

Lieberson, S. (1969). How can we describe and measure the incidence and distribution of bilingualism. In L. G. Kelly (Ed.), *Description and measurement of bilingualism* (pp. 286–295). Toronto: University of Toronto Press.

Lieberson, S., Dalto, G., & Johnston, E. (1975). The course of mother tongue diversity in nations. *American Journal of Sociology, 81,* 34–61.

Linguistic Minorities Project. (1985). *The other languages of England.* London: Routledge, Kegan & Paul.

Mackey, W. F. (1967). *Bilingualism as a world problem [Le bilinguisme: Phenomène mondial].* Montreal: Harvest House.

Mackey, W. F. (1968). The description of bilingualism. In J. Fishman (Ed.), *Readings in the sociology of language* (pp. 554–584). The Hague: Mouton.

MacKinnon, K. (1977). *Language, education and social processes in a Gaelic community.* London: Routledge & Kegan Paul.

Macnamara, J. (1967). The bilingual's linguistic performance: A psychological overview. *Journal of Social Issues, 23,* 59–77.

Macnamara, J. (1969). How can one measure the extent of one person's bilingual proficiency? In L. Kelly (Ed.), *Description and measurement of bilingualism* (pp. 80–98). Toronto: University of Toronto Press.

Macnamara, J. (1973). Attitudes and learning a second language. In R. W. Shuy, & R. W. Fasold (Eds.), *Language attitudes: Current trends and prospects.* Washington, D.C.: Georgetown University Press.

Martin-Jones, M., & Romaine, S. (1985). Semilingualism: A half-baked theory of communicative competence. *Applied Linguistics. 6,* 105–117.

Platt, J. (1977). A model for polyglossia and multilingualism (with special reference to Singapore and Malaysia). *Language in Society, 6,* 361–379.

Poplack, S., Sankoff, D., & Miller, C. (1988). The social correlates and linguistic consequences of lexical borrowing and assimilation. *Linguistics, 26,* 47–104.

Romaine, S. (1984). *The language of children and adolescents. The acquisition of communicative competence.* Oxford: Blackwell.

Romaine, S. (1989). *Bilingualism.* Oxford: Blackwell. [second edition. 1995].

Romaine, S. (Ed.). (1991). *Language in Australia.* Cambridge, UK: Cambridge University Press.

Romaine, S., & Dorian, N. C. (1981). Scotland as a linguistic area. *Scottish Literary Journal, Language Supplement, 14,* 1–24.

Sharwood-Smith, M., & Kellerman, E. (1986). Crosslinguistic influence in second language acquisition: An introduction. In E. Kellerman & M. Sharwood-Smith, (Eds.), *Crosslinguistic influence and second language acquisition* (pp. 1–9). Oxford: Pergamon Press.

Silva-Corvalán, C. (1983). Convergent and autonomous adaptations in the Spanish of

Mexican American bilinguals. Paper given at a Conference on El Español en Los Estados Unidos IV, Hunter College, University of New York.

Skutnabb-Kangas, T. (1984). *Bilingualism or not: The education of minorities.* Clevedon, UK: Multilingual Matters.

Spolsky, B. (1978). *Educational linguistics: An introduction.* Rowley, MA: Newbury House.

Teitelbaum, H. and Hiller, R. J. (1977). "The legal perspective." *Bilingual education: Current perspectives.* Vol. 3. Arlington, VA: Center for Applied Linguistics.

Weinreich, U. (1968). *Languages in contact.* The Hague: Mouton.

C H A P T E R 1 8

PRIMARY LANGUAGE ATTRITION
IN THE CONTEXT OF BILINGUALISM

Herbert W. Seliger

The easiest thing for me when I speak is just
to open both faucets and whatever comes
out, comes out.
—An adult bilingual speaking about the attrition of her first language

I. DEFINING PRIMARY LANGUAGE ATTRITION

This chapter addresses a phenomenon of human language as common and universal as bilingualism: the loss[1] of aspects of a previously fully acquired primary[2]
language resulting from the acquisition of another language. Primary language

---

[1] The terminology used to describe this new area of linguistic research is still evolving. The terms
loss and *attrition* are used here to convey the perception rather than necessarily the linguistic facts of
the phenomena discussed. See also footnote 2 regarding the term *attriter.*

[2] I have chosen to use the designation *primary language* rather than first language to mitigate but
not eliminate confusion in bilingual contexts since *first* may imply sequence of acquisition. *Primary*
will refer to that language in which the speaker is most competent and which was acquired naturalistically before the onset of the critical period. The term also refers to what is commonly called the "first
language" or the "mother tongue" but is used here to take into account a language acquired later in
childhood that became the dominant, primary, or even the only language of the speaker. Section II of
this chapter will deal with the contrast between primary language attrition and L2 and FL loss.

Handbook of Second Language Acquisition

attrition is the temporary or permanent loss of language ability as reflected in a speaker's performance or in his or her inability to make grammaticality judgments that would be consistent with native speaker (NS) monolinguals at the same age and stage of language development. (See chapter 17 by Romaine, this volume, for a general treatment of bilingualism.)

Perhaps the earliest recorded instance of language attrition is found in the book of Exodus (4 : 10). We are told that Moses fled Egypt to the land of Midian where he remained for forty years. When told by God that he must return to Egypt to lead the children of Israel to freedom, he replies that he is "heavy of mouth and heavy of tongue." One medieval biblical commentator stated that Moses is referring to the fact that, having been away from Egypt for 40 years and having become fluent in the language of the Midianites, he no longer fluently spoke his first language, the language of the Egyptian court.

The fact of bilingualism itself does not determine whether primary language attrition will be manifested. Unlike first language (L1) acquisition in which stages of acquisition appear at predicted developmental stages, there is no deterministic aspect of primary language attrition. It is not an automatic consequence of acquiring another language nor is it an automatic consequence of bilingualism for those who have been exposed to the same second language (L2) within the same social context for the same amount of time. We do not know at this point in the research on primary language attrition whether there are predictable developmental stages such as those found for L1 acquisition.

Primary language attrition may reveal itself at both competence and performance levels of language in any of the following ways: dysfluency and the inability to retrieve lexicon, the inability to pronounce the L1 with an NS pronunciation, the production of syntax that would not be acceptable to NSs and the inability to make judgments of grammaticality in the same way that NS monolinguals would. Some aspects of primary language attrition may be relegated to levels of language performance, whereas others may indicate that competence or abstract levels of language knowledge are affected, as revealed by a bilingual's inability to make grammaticality judgments or to perform tasks such as paradigmatic conjugations or declensions easily done by NS monolinguals (Vago, 1991). This dysfunction can express itself as (1) the ability to recall a meaning shared by both the L1 and the L2 but only being able to retrieve the L2 lexical item (Olshtain & Barzilay, 1991); (2) rule reordering or simplification in the morphophonemics of the L1 (Silva-Corvalan, 1991), or the inability to inflect in accordance with previously acquired morphology, or not being aware that incorrectly inflected morphology is deviant where previously the speaker inflected in accordance with the L1 grammar (Huffines, 1991); (3) the acceptance of syntactically deviant sentences and the "correction" of syntactically grammatical sentences (Seliger, 1989, 1991).

II. PRIMARY LANGUAGE ATTRITION AND L2 OR FOREIGN LANGUAGE LOSS

A distinction should be made between the attrition of an acquired primary language in the context of bilingualism and the loss of an L2 or a foreign language (FL) that has been incompletely acquired in an educational context. The differences in the manner of acquisition results in qualitative differences in the kinds of loss and concomitant differences in the kinds of research questions and methods used to investigate questions of language loss under these different circumstances.

In recent years, there have been a number of studies and collections that deal primarily with the loss of L2s and FLs rather than primary language attrition (Bahrick, 1984; Cohen & Weltens, 1989; Lambert, & Freed, 1982; Weltens, de Bot, & van Els, 1986). From an educational perspective, the maintenance of school-taught languages has great importance. However, the theoretical and research methodological problems in studying L2 and FL loss are enormous. It is not within the scope of this chapter to give an in-depth review of L2 and FL loss, and the reader is referred to the several collections noted above. Rather, this section will discuss several important differences between the two kinds of language loss and the problems engendered in the study of L2 or FL loss.

A. The Problem of Establishing Baseline Knowledge

In order to study any change in language development, whether it is acquisition or loss, it is necessary to establish a consistent baseline to which any change can be compared. In the case of language attrition, this means that research must be able to establish universal assumptions about the degree of knowledge that existed before change. Data used to establish loss or attrition must be based on the comparison of what is deviant to populations of normal monolinguals at the same age and stage of language development as the subjects who are undergoing language attrition. Because studies in L1 acquisition have established that speakers of a specific language follow generalizable stages of development, it may be assumed that monolingual control groups can provide a valid and accurate representation of the state of the bilingual's grammar before the onset of bilingualism. There are no established universal or generalizable stages for the acquisition of L2s or FL and therefore, control groups of other L2 learners would not be a valid manner of establishing antecedent states of knowledge. They only possible recourse for the reliable study of L2 or FL loss would be the longitudinal study of data and protocol records for an individual L2 learner over a long period of time.[3]

---

[3] It is not clear how much time would be needed in order to establish first, that a stable grammar has been acquired in the L2 or FL and second, that attrition or loss has begun. Olshtain (1986) con-

B. The Manner and Context of Acquisition

In comparing loss in primary language and L2 or FL, it is important to consider differences in interactions between the contexts in which language acquisition takes place and the manner in which it takes place. What may, on the surface, appear to be the same language performance may in fact be languagelike behavior or memorized prefabricated routines that are learned differently from the manner in which language is naturally acquired. Differences in manner of acquisition imply different modes of memory storage and that retrieval (absent, changed, ungrammatical) was once not deviant in the same speaker. In order to discuss loss, the antecedent conditions and states of acquisition become crucial. This has been a serious problem in the study of polyglot aphasia, in which it is difficult to establish the degree of language knowledge of other than a L1 before loss.

Similar problems exist in establishing the specific state of language knowledge of an FL or L2 when the informant has been removed for several years from the FL or L2 learning environment. A classical example of this is the study of Bahrick (1984), in which details of FL loss are established on the basis of self-reports by informants, the contents of school curricula, and grade-point averages from school records for subjects who studied the language up to 50 years previous to the research. It is obvious that this kind of data cannot give a consistent or reliable picture of the states of knowledge of the language of informants. Receiving high grades in an FL course could mean good test-taking skills rather than a measure of true language competence. In addition, language teaching methodologies, if they are used consistently, have changed significantly over the past several years so that different skills and abilities have been emphasized and evaluated.

A more serious problem exists in establishing what can be considered stable rules in the interlanguage (IL) grammars of L2 and FL learners. The loss of unstable rules or rules that are used presystematically is different from the loss of rules that have been acquired in childhood. The performance data gathered from L2 learners may consist of permanently fixed rules, fossilization errors, and rules in a state of flux undergoing change. By its very nature, an IL grammar is unstable, and any sampling for the purposes of establishing later loss must be founded on the questionable premise that a form was a stable component in the grammar to begin with.

These problems might be overcome by identifying a subset of the L2 or FL grammar in which an individual subject has demonstrated stability over time thus

---

ducted a study of Israeli children who had spent 1–8 years in an English-speaking environment and had returned to the primary language environment, Israel, when they were studied for the affects of L2 loss. Because they acquired the L2 as children and in a naturalistic manner, these subjects could be considered to have acquired another primary language depending on the age of acquisition and amount of time spent in an exclusively English-speaking environment. In this study, there were no protocols of the children's language abilities before their return to Israel.

permitting a preattrition norm for that individual subject. It is improbable that norms can be identified for a whole population of FL learners as claimed by Bahrick (1984), because each follows his or her own internal syllabus and is affected by innumerable internal and external variables. It has been demonstrated by Coppieters (1987) that even bilinguals who pass as near-NSs of the same L2 have different underlying representations of the same rules that are also different from those of NSs. It is also safe to assume that in the attrition of L2s or FLs, the near-NS will be affected differently from the NS because he has different underlying representations of that language.

In the study of primary language attrition, baseline norms of states of language knowledge can be established by referring and qualitatively different kinds of loss or attrition (Coppieters, 1987).

Primary or L1 acquisition takes place under naturalistic conditions, is not instructed, and is restricted by both cognitive development and Universal Grammar (UG) or innate mechanisms that guide and constrain what is acquired and how. Research in L1 acquisition has demonstrated that because of the degenerate nature of language data available to the child, the underdeterminate nature of this data, and the unavailability or ineffectiveness of negative evidence, the child would not be able to develop a grammar based on information available from the external input alone.

L2 and FL acquisition takes place at different developmental stages and under different conditions than primary or L1. Felix (1981) suggested that different cognitive processes are involved in classroom language learning and that although primary language acquisition is independent of cognitive function, FL learning is more affected by Piagetian stages of development. Felix (1981) also demonstrated that because students in FL classes have to learn language for which they are not prepared linguistically, they utilize learning such strategies as memorization, which are different from those used by the child in acquiring the primary language. Bley-Vroman (1990) has proposed that adult L2 learning is qualitatively different from child primary language acquisition because of the inaccessibility of the UG. Adults utilize problem solving and other general learning strategies. (For arguments in favor of a similar position, see chapter 5 by Schachter, this volume.)

Because the processes of learning or acquisition in different contexts result in different types and manners of acquisition, it is reasonable to assume that the acquired knowledge is stored and retrieved differently. It is also reasonable to hypothesize that these different kinds of learning and storage will result in qualitatively different kinds of loss or attrition. The forgetting of memorized vocabulary lists, formal grammar rules, or dialogues investigated by Bahrick (1984) is quite different from the inability to retrieve words that were part of the speaker's active primary language lexicon since early childhood or the acceptance of a grammatically deviant utterance that would have been rejected before the onset of bilingualism.

III. PRIMARY LANGUAGE ATTRITION AND OTHER FORMS OF LANGUAGE MIXING

In its initial stages, primary language attrition may resemble forms of language mixing, such as that which occurs in normal bilingualism. It is therefore important to distinguish between the former and the latter. In the case of code-mixing or code-switching, it is generally agreed that the bilingual speaker has not lost control of either of the languages being mixed (Pfaff, 1979). Code-mixing can be cued by external factors such as the social or cultural context in which the languages are being used. Paradoxically, not mixing languages appropriately under certain social circumstances would be considered deviant and perhaps evidence for primary language attrition. The inability to mix languages according to accepted norms would indicate that the bilingual cannot retrieve elements of one of the languages when communicating with another bilingual. (Chapter 19 by Bhatia and Ritchie, this volume, discusses code-switching in general.)

Viewed externally, the language behavior of an attriter might resemble normal code-mixing and to the observer might not indicate that there is anything amiss linguistically, because all of the speakers in the situation are switching back and forth between the two languages. The difference is that the code-mixing bilingual can switch to either language with approximately equal facility without any disruption in fluency or grammatical accuracy. In addition, code-switching maintains the grammaticality or linguistic autonomy of the switched elements so that phrases in L1 observe the grammatical constraints of L1, and those of L2 maintain the grammatical constraints of L2.

Sociolinguistically, true code-switching by bilinguals results from a sensitivity to the interlocutor and the topic. The underlying motivation is that switching in and out of the two languages shared by the bilinguals makes the communication more effective. Pfaff (1979) states that code-mixing is used to indicate solidarity as well as neutrality. It is clear from the literature on code-mixing that switching back and forth between the two languages is affected by sociolinguistic rules of appropriateness.

This is not the case with primary language attrition. It is clear that although primary language attrition surface performance may resemble code-mixing in some its manifestations, it can be distinguished from it on the basis of when and how it is used in a social context. Bilinguals exhibiting primary language attrition will use mixed forms in situations that are not sociolinguistically appropriate, where the audience does not speak the L2. This is especially evident where the attrition manifests itself in syntax, morphological neologisms, and calquing of language material from various levels from L2 into L1.

One area that can be examined in terms of differences between primary language attrition and code-mixing is with regard to the kinds of mixing found. Much of the literature on code-mixing is concerned with explaining how the bilingual maintains the autonomy of each respective language system (Sridhar & Sridhar, 1980). If autonomy were not maintained within a bilingual setting, the languages of the bilingual would eventually be melded into a single system, as is the case with primary language attrition. Some cross-linguistic borrowing will occur in any situation of language contact; however, in the case of primary language attrition, the mixing leads to the nonobservance of language-specific constraints of the borrowing language (L1). An unusual case is the following collected from a Hebrew L1–English L2 college student who had lived in the United States for several years:

(1) *ze lo ma   sheanahnu midabrim   al*
     this not what that we   (are) talking about
     That's not what we are talking about.

In this unusual case, the speaker has stranded the preposition of the end of the sentence. Although this is common and acceptable in English, it is not acceptable in Hebrew, which is a nonstranding language and in which prepositions are always bound. This is not the type of borrowing that would be expected in normal code-mixing.

In example (2), taken from the production of a Hebrew L1–English L2 bilingual, the borrowed element is no longer perceived as foreign.

(2) *hidrapti et hakours.*
     I dropped the course.

In this example, the lexeme "drop" from L2 is assimilated into the morphological and phonological systems of the L1, Hebrew. Hebrew verbs are built primarily around roots consisting of three discontinuous consonants that are then fitted with the particular prefixes and infixes specific to one of the four verb paradigms or conjugations. (See Aronson-Berman, 1978, for a full discussion of verb morphology in Hebrew.) In this case, the speaker has taken the English (L2) drop, created a discontinuous root, [d-r-p], and embedded it into the Hebrew *hifil* conjugation, which as a causative and transitive meaning. In cases where an item from L2 is borrowed into L1, its form is merged and changed in some way to fit the borrowing device. In this example, it appears that the surface phonetic characteristics of drop make it amenable to conform to the phonological features of this verb conjugation. Here, the verb affixes for the *hifil* would be [hiC-CaC—ti], where C refers to a consonant in the discontinuous root of the verb. Although sentence (2) would be comprehensible to bilinguals who had been exposed to the same languages, the sentence would not make any sense to a Hebrew monolingual. (Chapters 17 by Romaine and 19 by Bhatia and Ritchie, this volume, include discussion concerning borrowing and code-switching.)

It can be argued that as more and more elements of the type shown in sentences (1) and (2) are introduced into the language of bilinguals who share the same languages, there occurs a loss of sensitivity for the ungrammaticality of the borrowing that does not observe the constraints of L1. That is, code-mixing is a precursor stage for primary language attrition and for eventual death of the L1 within the bilingual community. Kuhberg (1992) argues that code-switching is "developmentally systematic, clearly reflecting deterioration" (p. 149). However, at this stage in our research it is difficult to show clear systematicity in many aspects of language attrition in the same manner that such systematicity appears to have been demonstrated with normal or appropriate code-switching.

Pfaff (1979) presents these Spanish–*English* examples that could be either primary language attrition or code-mixing as a precursor stage for primary language attrition:

(3) *Ella va a ir bien* train*iada.*
     She's going to go well-trained.
(4) *No puedo* taip*ar muy bien.*
     I can't type very well.

Examples (3) and (4) resemble the type of borrowing found in (2) because the borrowed material is embedded into the morphology of the L1. Again, it is unlikely that monolingual Spanish speakers would comprehend these borrowings.

Consider now the following example of Hebrew–*English* mixing.

(5) *ex hi   yixola li-* carry *et ze?*
     how she can   to carry   that
     How can she carry that?

This primary language attrition example appears to be the result of a lexical retrieval problem because there is really no motivation for code-switching other than the speaker not being able to recall the verb form for carry in Hebrew, his L1. What is interesting here is that the English verb form is attached to the infinitival prefix without any change in its phonetic shape to make it conform to the host language.

Kuhberg (1992) presents examples in which the mixing is bidirectional between L1 (Turkish) and L2 (German). In the case of his study of two Turkish children who had learned German as an L2 and then returned to Turkey and began to lose German, it is not clear how firmly established German (L2) was or even whether German might have become the dominant language while the children had attended school in Germany. What is interesting in his data of lexical and morphological mixing is that at initial stages, the mixing can go in either direction, apparently depending upon pragmatic criteria such as functionality or frequency:

(6) *ge-*koy*en*—past participle of put—The verb stem is Turkish but the participial suffix is German.
(7) *schuh-*lar-*i*—'the shoes'—noun stem is German but the case and plural markers are Turkish.

(Kuhberg, 1992, p. 140)

To summarize this section, although there are similarities between primary language attrition and code-mixing, they can be distinguished by the fact that code-mixing, as a normal aspect of bilingualism, is motivated by the features of the external sociolinguistic context that triggers the switching. Within such a context, switching or mixing is considered not only appropriate but obligatory. In addition, code-mixing observes the linguistic constraints of each of the grammars being used and does not occur across certain linguistic boundaries. On the other hand, primary language attrition is motivated by *internal factors* such as on-line retrieval or lacunae in the competence or knowledge base of the language. (See discussion below.) Primary language attrition may occur within the same contexts as bilingual code-mixing but it also occurs within contexts in which the interlocutors do not know the L2. Code-mixing can be considered a precursor condition for primary language attrition when mixing begins to occur in contexts that are not motivated by external factors such as interlocutor, topic, or cultural environment. In addition, primary language attrition does not observe the linguistic constraints of the host language (L1), leading to the creation of utterances that are not grammatical with L1.

In the ultimate case of primary language attrition, the speaker would return to a state of monolingualism but with the L2 completely replacing the first. This is often the case with immigrant children who lose the mother tongue or L1, to the extent that so little remains that nonnative speakers (NNSs) of the L1 may surpass the abilities of the former bilingual. To a different and less extreme extent, primary language attrition occurs among adult immigrants as well, depending on such factors as the degree of acculturation and assimilation, the level of literacy in L1, and the functions served by the different languages in the bilingual's repertoire, as well as such group factors as the size of the L1 group, the relationship of inferiority or superiority to the other language group, the degree of cohesion within the L1 group, and the degree of vitality within L1 language and cultural institutions, such as literature, theater, and religion.

Primary language attrition at the individual speaker level is a precursor condition for language death at the societal level. At this point in time, insufficient research exists as to the permanency of primary language attrition in individual bilinguals.[4] In the case of primary language attrition as a social phenomenon, it is clear that once a community of speakers begins to replace elements of an L1 with those of another, language death may result and the effect can be the permanent extinction of a language.

The progression of primary language attrition, although evident in individual

---

[4]Questions that remain to be investigated are whether attrited language is permanently lost, whether it must be reacquired as if it were never learned, or whether some residue of language ability remains that would enable the attriter to reacquire more efficiently. For example, given research on the effects of the critical period for L2 acquisition, would a speaker who had acquired and lost an L1 be able to reacquire that language as an adult but with none of the deficits normally associated with the critical period. (See Johnson & Newport, 1991, for a recent review of these issues.)

speakers of a language, is traceable through successive generations when many individuals within a language community experience primary language attrition and the language community remains within the contact situation (Dorian, 1982; Dressler, 1991; Larmouth, 1974). When primary language attrition occurs among a majority of individual speakers of a language, the L1 is passed on to the next generation of speakers in its changed or attrited form resulting in its gradual disappearance.[5] It might also result in the creation of a creole that combines elements of both languages, or the creation of an overseas dialect of a language not always easily comprehended by monolingual NSs of the language in the home country. (See chapter 16 by Andersen and Shirai, this volume, on creole languages.) This is precisely what happens with immigrant speech communities or "enclave speech communities" (Maher, 1991) in which the speakers of a particular language are surrounded by and dominated by speakers of another language with whom they come into regular contact. This has been the primary language attrition effect on immigrant speakers of Finnish, where studies of successive generations have shown the gradual restructuring of the language (Karttunen, 1977; Larmouth, 1974). Unfortunately, primary language attrition sometimes leaves the bilingual with two languages that are incompletely controlled so that the speaker does not feel completely at home in either language—a situation that might be referred to as *semilingualism*.

IV. L1 ATTRITION AND LINGUISTIC THEORY

A. Performance or Competence

The language attriter[6] often substitutes material from the L2 for missing information in the L1, either because of on-line retrieval problems or problems in the underlying grammar of the language. Primary language attrition might occur in the same contexts but not be within the control or awareness of the speaker. Even when we can distinguish between primary language attrition and normal code-mixing, it is not always easy to distinguish between primary language attrition due to on-line retrieval problems or problems of control (Sharwood-Smith, 1991)

[5] As an example of how quickly the process of primary language attrition progresses, Schmidt (1991) states that of an estimated 200 languages spoken on the Australian continent, approximately only 50 will survive to the year 2000. One recent estimate states that approximately 1,000 of the world's 6,000 languages are in the process of dying "the helpless victims of cultural engulfment." (Murphy, 1992)

[6] The author realizes that the term *language attriter* is awkward. However, I feel that it is to be preferred to other alternatives such as "language loser" (Sharwood-Smith, 1991) especially because, as the following discussion will show, language attrition is, in fact, a creative and often additive process. In addition, the term "loser" has come to have a derogatory sense in colloquial American English.

and language attrition due to a deterioration of the knowledge base or competence of the first or primary language.

The Logical Problem of Primary Language Attrition

Given that primary or L1 attrition is part of the continuum of L1 acquisition and bilingualism, it is reasonable to expect that factors that affect L1 and L2 acquisition would also affect primary language attrition. An important difference is that with L1 and L2 acquisition there is a *convergence* in the direction of a putative model grammar to which the acquirer, child or adult, is exposed. It is assumed that the model grammar aspired to is realized in the data of language users in the environment of the language learner. Child interim grammars of L1 and the ILs of L2 learners are all assumed to develop in the direction of the model. Of course, the L2 grammars of adult learners rarely, if ever, achieve NS status (Birdsong, 1992; Coppieters, 1987; Johnson & Newport, 1991). On the other hand, primary language attrition may be assumed to be *divergent* in the sense that there is no model to be aspired to and there is no L1 language data in the environment of the attriter that can be used as the basis for building this divergent grammar.

Sources of Evidence for Primary Language Attrition

This raises the important question of what might be the sources of "evidence" (data) that the attriter might use to construct (or reconstruct) the changing L1 grammar. Keep in mind that a fully developed grammar of L1 already exists in the mind of the speaker at the onset of bilingualism and L2 acquisition. The questions that must be explained in the case of both L1 acquisition and primary language attrition are (1) how are generalizations and overgeneralizations first learned and then unlearned as the grammar changes? and (2) what conditions and what kinds of language data are necessary to trigger these change? In the case of L1 acquisition, a theory must explain how the child unlearns incorrect hypotheses about the language given the lack of any data that can be regarded as corrective or for that matter correct, because one of the well-known characteristics of L1 data is its degeneracy.[7] (See chapters 2–5 by Gregg, White, Flynn, and Schachter, this volume, for discussion of a logical problem of L2 acquisition.) The L1 data to which the L1 acquirer is exposed have been described as being both degenerate and insufficient to determine the system of knowledge ultimately acquired. In short, the evidence or data to which L1 acquirers are exposed and upon which they must base their grammars are lacking. This, of course, has been the foundation for claiming that innate capabilities in the form of UG are what enable the miracle of L1 acquisition to take place.

---

[7] This has become known as the "logical problem of language acquisition." Recently, this question has been applied to L2 acquisition as well and would appear to have important implications for explanations of primary language attrition. See White (1989, 1990) and Bley-Vroman (1990) for a discussion of these issues with regard to L2 acquisition.

B. External Sources of Evidence

Interestingly, explaining the development of primary language attrition is even more problematical. In cases other than language pathology, we do not expect an established L1 to deteriorate or diverge away from the grammar that has been fully acquired. In terms of degeneracy and underdetermination, we have a different problem than that which confronts theorists in L1 acquisition. The data for the individual language attriter to base changes on are limited either to written form, language found in foreign TV and movies, and perhaps even formal language instruction in the L1.[8] The only remaining external source of data for a diverging L1 grammar would be other speakers who are also bilingual in the same languages. Seliger (1977) did find that adult Hebrew L1–English L2 speakers who worked together and produced similar errors in Hebrew idioms, did respond in a similar fashion in terms of the acceptance of ungrammatical sentences. But, we know little about how other attrited speakers affect changes in the L1 grammar. Our only proof that this happens is implied by the situation in communities where language change and death take place over the course of several generations. However, this does not change the fact that primary language attrition does happen to individual bilinguals who are not exposed to social situations in which the external input could be regarded as the impetus for the changes that take place. Given the fact that external sources of L1 data are very limited and are underdetermined in the sense that they cannot explain the changes that take place in primary language attrition, we are left to consider possible *internal* sources for the process.[9]

C. Internal Sources of Evidence

Although we refer to the loss of language abilities as attrition, in fact, it can be shown that what takes place in the changes in the L1 grammar is the replacement or displacement of one set of language rules with another. We are, therefore, left to consider possible *internal* sources of evidence that can bring about primary language attrition. There are only two that can be considered sources of data or evidence for the construction of a grammar of L1, because access to L1 data by

[8] The description of the context for primary language attrition here assumes that the language attriter lives in a society where the L1 is not spoken and where access to L1 data is limited to reading, perhaps imported television programs (as would be the case of an American immigrant living abroad), and American movies Often, if there is a sufficient number of L1 speakers, educational programs might be organized to maintain L1 language skills. This is the case of Japanese and Israelis living in New York and Americans living in Israel. In the case of Israeli children living in New York City, these language programs have not prevented primary language attrition.

[9] By *underdetermined,* we mean that the kind of L1 data to which the bilingual may have access is probably highly grammatical, as in the case of written language or language instruction, and therefore cannot explain how what was grammatical in the grammar of the speaker becomes ungrammatical.

nonbilingual NSs has been cut off. One source of change is the other grammar that exists in the mind of the bilingual, the grammar of the L2 and the other source is what remains of UG abilities. Given these two sources of evidence, one could predict that changes that take place in the L1 grammar as a result of attrition will reflect (1) transfer from the L2 and (2) a preference to transfer those elements in L2 that are more in agreement with core universals and therefore less marked, that is, elements not belonging to what has been called the periphery (Chomsky, 1986).

The process can be described in terms of the following stages of progression:

Stage I   The bilingual is able to maintain autonomy for each of the languages in his or her repertoire. As was discussed above, in the case of language mixing, constraints indigenous to each language are maintained.

Stage II   Because of the inaccessibility of L1 data, the L2 grammar becomes the source of evidence affecting grammaticality abilities in L1. Because it appears, by the very existence of language attrition, that languages need continued access to data sources to support a grammar at a particular state of development and because L1 data are no longer available, L2 becomes an indirect data source for L1.

Stage III   Where similar rules exist in both L1 and L2, rules are fused in the direction of that which is less marked. Grammars strive for a reduction of redundancy in rules especially in the case where two separate language grammars have to be maintained.

We will now examine two examples of the above stages from the language attrition data of an English L1–Hebrew L2 bilingual child. In all of these examples, we shall see that the tendency is on the part of the bilingual to conflate or fuse the grammars in order to reduce the redundancy of rules leading to a more parsimonious grammar but at the same time leading to one that diverges from the original source grammar of L1.

D. An Example of a Universal Principle in Primary Language Attrition

The question that must be addressed in L1 attrition is not the fact of attrition itself but rather whether there are any principles that might predict those elements that are replaced or changed in L1 as a result of contact with another language. When two languages come into contact within the same psycholinguistic environment, the speaker is forced to contend with a problem of the possible duplication of rules and functions in the two languages and the need to simplify this cognitive burden in some way. That is, attrition within L1s is not random forgetting but guided by a principle of arriving at the most parsimonious grammar that can service both languages. What appears to take place, as will be shown in the examples below, is that the bilingual creates a new rule for L1 in those areas of the grammar where the L2 rule is simpler or less marked in some way. The L2 rule is then assimilated into L1 and replaces the existing but more complex L1 rule.

As we shall see, although the overall process of attrition is motivated by the reduction of redundancy of underlying or abstract language structures, it appears to be guided by principles similar to those that determine the learnability of structures in L1 acquisition, such as the Uniqueness Principle (UP) and the Subset Principle (SP). (The Subset Principle and its putative role in L2 acquisition are discussed in this volume, chapters 2 by Gregg, 3 by White, 10 by Gass, and 13 by Long. Chapter 14 by Berent includes discussion of the Subset Principle in the acquisition of English by deaf learners. Finally, chapter 16 by Andersen and Shirai applies the notion to the acquisition of verb aspect.) The process is facilitated by the fact that the bilingual speaker has come to view the separate and previously autonomous language systems as a single large system with some interchangeable and therefore replaceable parts. As summarized by White (1989), the UP states that for any semantic concept, there will be only one syntactic or morphological realization. In bilingualism, a semantic concept may be realized in two different grammars. In the case of primary language attrition, this could mean that if the two languages of the bilingual have a semantic concept or function in common but which is expressed in two different ways by the abstract rules of the respective grammars, only one of those realizations that are available to the speaker of the data will survive. A modified version of the SP provides that given two possible grammatical versions of the same concept, that which is most restrictive and present in the input will be preferred. In adapting this to primary language attrition, we might state that when the input data in the L2 contains a comparable grammatical form that is *more universal* and *less marked* than the competing grammar in the primary language, that form in the L2 input will be preferred. In other words, the reduction of redundancies between the combined L1 and L2 grammars may be seen as guided by these principles. In cases to be examined in morphology and syntax, less marked, more inclusive grammars from L2 replace more marked forms in L1.

In order to show how the Redundancy Reduction Principle works we will look at an example in morphology and one in syntax.[10] All data are taken from studies conducted by the author with an English L1–Hebrew L2 bilingual child who immigrated to Israel at age six and was a monolingual at the time of exposure to the L2. Data were collected at ages 9 and 10 through both the recording of utterances in discourse and metalinguistic testing based on errors that appeared in the naturalistic data.

Redundancy Reduction: Morphology

In this first example of the attrition of English in the context of English L1–Hebrew L2 bilingualism, changes in the status at the syntactic level affect changes

---

[10] For fuller discussions of the research that these examples are taken from, the reader is referred to Seliger (1989, 1991).

at the morphological level, leading to the creation of a new category of morpheme in L1 and the reduction of seeming redundancy between L1 and L2 structures.

The following sentence demonstrates the characteristics of Hebrew relative clause sentences critical to our discussion:

(6)   *hayeled šehakelev nasax oto boxe.*
       the boy *that*-the-dog bit *him* (is) crying"

1. The relative marker *še* that is used to introduce the relative clause regardless of the type of relativization. It does not function as a relative pronoun as 'that' would in English but rather signals the subordinate status of the clause or sentence to which it is attached.

2. Pronominal referents are always copied in the relative clause except with the subject position where a pronominal copy is optional.

3. Pronominal objects of prepositions are bound to prepositions. Prepositions are never stranded.

4. Elements are not fronted or moved for the purposes of relativization as in English. Word order may be changed for purposes of topicalization or emphasis.

Hebrew relatives also differ from English by the fact that there is no set of relative pronouns and that one bound morpheme, *še,* which is roughly equivalent to English 'that,' functions as an all-purpose complementizer to introduce relative clauses as well as other kinds of subordinate structures.

On the basis of the informant's free discourse, metalinguistic tests were developed that tested whether deviances found in this data were errors of on-line retrieval or changes that had taken place in the underlying competence level knowledge of the language. If errors were produced in naturalistic speech, it could not be determined whether there errors were the result of problems in the knowledge of the language or errors caused by problems of on-line retrieval or performance factors. In addition, the same tests were administered to a control group of monolingual English-speaking children of the same approximate age as the informant before immigrating to Israel and becoming bilingual.

In addition to asking the informant and the group of monolingual children to accept or reject the grammaticality of the sentences on the metalinguistic test, they were asked to make them better if they rejected a sentence. Thus, when the stimulus sentence was as in (7a), the informant rejected it:

(7)   a. There is the man who I talked to you about him.

In order to know why the informant rejected it, the speaker was asked if she could make it better. Whereupon, she replied as follows:

(7)   b. There is the man that I talked to you about him.

The monolingual control group responded:

(7)   c. There is the man who I talked to you about.

It is clear that in this kind of procedure, we are not concerned with the problem of on-line retrieval because the informants are responding to sentences that are supplied to them. Any changes that reoccur in subsequent test sentences can reliably be said to emanate from underlying competence.

In this type of sentence in which different kinds of relatives were tested (subject, object, indirect object, possessive, etc.) and pronominal copy was retained, the bilingual consistently ignored the pronominal copy and changed the relative pronoun to 'that.' These two changes, the simplification of the set of relatives from *who, which, whose* and *that* to '**that**' and nondeletion of the referent pronoun, change the status of the subordinate clause (*[that] I talked to you about*) to an independent clause (. . . *[that] I talked to you about him*), thus changing what was a relative pronoun, *that,* to a complementizer:

(8)   I knew that he was going home.

This is similar to the function of *še* in Hebrew as seen in example (6) above. That is, the retention of the referent pronoun in the relative clause as in Hebrew allows for the change in status or function from that of a relative pronoun to a morpheme that functions both as a relativizer and a complementizer. (For applications of the UP to L2 acquisition and to L1 attrition, see, respectively, chapters 13 by Long and 16 by Andersen and Shirai, this volume.)

The resulting rule for relativization in English has resulted from the attrition process because it functions for both languages. In addition, the new rule allows the same clause structure used for relatives with the included pronoun copy to be used for conjoined sentences. In this situation, in which the bilingual's L1 is gradually eroding or where there is competition for cognitive processing space or difficulty with on-line retrieval, the assimilation of Hebrew (L2) rules for relativization into English (L1) results in the following:

1. The embedding of relative clauses is still in the same position, after the head NP.
2. The simpler sentence structure rules for relative clause in Hebrew eliminates the need for a maintaining rules associated with fronting, stranding, and pronoun deletion associated with English wh-movement.
3. The set of relative pronouns can be replaced by an all-purpose morpheme, '*that*' or *še,* which can serve as either a relativizer or a complementizer.

Redundancy Reduction: Syntax

A dilemma is faced by the bilingual when both languages at his or her disposal contain syntactic rules that convey the same semantic information but are expressed through different linguistic mechanisms. As discussed above (section D), proposals in learnability theory that attempt to explain how L1 acquisition handles such problems in the data through the UP and the SP may be applicable as explanations for the gradual dissolution of a language as well.

The way this problem is solved in language attrition provides interesting insights into the way languages in contact might resolve these conflicts. In order for such questions to be resolved at the linguistic level, there must exist some implicit hierarchy of possible solutions that provides a decision-making mechanism within either a superordinate grammar composed of the common elements (universal?) of the two grammars or a conflated grammar, which is simply the melding of the grammars of L1 and L2.

If markedness is used as the criterion for predicting what is replaced and what is maintained in the L1 grammar, then markedness would also have to be conceived of in a cross-linguistic sense, and again the concept of a superordinate grammar consisting of language-shared rather than language-specific elements might be relevant.

One area of primary language attrition where this has been examined is with double object or direct–indirect object (DO, IO) sentences, also known as datives. Both English and Hebrew have rules for forming such sentences. English dative sentences and dative alternation are strictly governed by syntax with constraints relevant to potential alternation imposed by the lexical characteristics of the verb (V). Hebrew, on the other hand, provides case markings in some instances (definite DO), and the IO is always bound to its preposition, (PP) but allows flexible word ordering for the DD and IO. Given this and given accepted definitions of markedness, which version of dative syntax would be considered more marked and a candidate for replacement and possible attrition?

Hebrew and English have different ways with which to express dative arguments. In English we have two possible ways of expressing such relationships.[11]

(9) I gave John the book.
(10) I gave the book to John.
(11) *I gave to John the book.

The two sentences, (9) and (10), may be regarded as paraphrastic. The English verb, *to give,* allows either of these two constructions (NP, noun phrase): NP V NP_{DO} PP as in (10) or NP V NP_{IO} NP_{DO} as in (9).

However, dative alternation in English is dependent on lexical features or "arguments" that accompany each verb so that some verbs will only be grammatical if in the form of (10) but not of (9). For example, the verb *to donate* cannot freely substitute for *give* in (9) but it can in (10). Part of the NS's knowledge of English consists of the lexical information that tells him which verbs and verb meanings allow for dative alternation and which do not. No class of verbs in English will allow for the order of constituents in (11); but as will be shown below, the order in (11) is acceptable in Hebrew.

---

[11] The discussion of datives in both English and Hebrew is necessarily simplified because of the limitations of space. The reader is referred to Mazurkewich and White (1984) and Aronson-Berman (1978) for fuller discussions of English and Hebrew, respectively.

Hebrew dative does not contain an alternation rule similar to English. DOs and IOs may alternate in position after the V with the restrictions noted below. As was noted in example (1), PPs are bound to their objects, move with them, and may not be stranded. *(OM, direct object marker)*.

(11) *Dan šalax et hasefer lemoše.*
      Dan sent (OM) the book to Moshe.
(12) *Dan šalax lemoše et hasefer.*
      Dan sent to Moshe (OM) the book.
(13) *Dan šalax lo et hasefer.*
      Dan sent to-him (OM) the book.
(14) **Dan šalax et hasefer lo.*
      Dan sent (OM) the book to him.

From this sample of IO sentences, it can be seen that (1) DO and IO constituents may alternate in position after the V unless the IO, which is bound to its PP, is pronominalized, in which case, the IO may not be in the final sentence position. As noted above, unlike English, PPs must always accompany their objects and may not be stranded.

Attrition of Dative Rules

The same informant described above produced free discourse sentences such as the following:

(15) I'm gonna tell you a different things that everyone likes it.
(16) I told it to the girl thats [*sic*] was sitting next to me.
(17) The school gives the girl that she has the birthday a present.

Subsequent metalinguistic testing on a 32-item test investigated both the informant's responses and those of the control group of monolingual NSs ages 5–7 and 8–9. As noted in section D, these ages were chosen as representative of the linguistic knowledge of the informant at the time of immigration and immersion into the L2 environment, whereas the older group represented what the informant might have known had she remained a monolingual. The test examined different aspects of the dative including word order in which the PP was placed before the DO:

(18) *Dick handed to Sally the book.

The use of the double object construction appeared where it would be considered unacceptable in English because of constraints on the verb:

(19) David made Susan the choice.
(20) Ariella answered the teacher the question.
(21) Harry made Tom the decision.

An analysis of the performance of both groups revealed that the informant tended to accept both ungrammatical and grammatical sentences, especially those that tested the placement of the PP as in (18) above, whereas the control group over-whelmingly rejected these sentences.[12]

E. Redundancy Reduction as an Inevitable Process

The same basic elements that have been discussed can be found in the examples of redundancy reduction: the recognition that different forms in the two different languages of the bilingual share a common meaning of semantic function. Once access to supportive language data or evidence for the L1 is severely restricted, and code-switching or mixing becomes prevalent, the speaker views the two systems as one and the L2 as providing a valid source of evidence for the L1 system. Once the two languages acquire this kind of isomorphism, the sense of grammaticality for a specific language (L1) is impaired and the bilingual finds himself with an inventory of redundant forms from both L1 and L2 conveying the same information. This inventory must be pruned so that the combined system will be more parsimonious and cognitively less demanding.

The criteria used for this pruning appears to be some form of markedness. In the examples cited here and elsewhere in the literature on primary language attrition, those forms that are less marked in L2 are more likely to replace more marked forms in L1, whereas the less marked forms in L1 appear to be more resistant to attrition. In the examples above, the triggers for attrition would appear to be the more unmarked pronominal copy in the relative clause in Hebrew, which in turn leads to the simplification of the relative clause marker from a system of several different relative pronouns requiring piping or stranding to a single morpheme, 'that,' which becomes an analog for a morpheme with a similar function and meaning in the L2, Hebrew, *še*.

V. CONCLUSION: CONTEXT DEPENDENCE, BILINGUALISM, AND PRIMARY LANGUAGE ATTRITION

It has been suggested by Karmiloff-Smith (1986) and Coppieters (1987) that the child differs from the adult in that the child progresses from a system of redundant unanalyzed linguistic units that are paired to particular functions, whereas in the adult grammar, linguistic form is independent of function or context. The child may have many different forms that are stored independently and paired to specific contexts. Only later as the child begins to analyze language and unconsciously understands that the same forms carry similar meanings does he begin to eliminate some of these linguistic units leading to a more complex, more abstract, but less redundant system.

---

[12]For a full discussion and analysis of these data, see Seliger (1991).

Similarly, in the context of bilingualism, having two languages means being able to manage two systems with similar linguistic rules or forms (e.g., paraphrasing using different optional word orders, relativizing, expressing the dative or aspect, having morphemes such as prepositions, plurality, etc.) that are assigned to different linguistic contexts (L1 or L2) depending on external sociolinguistic factors such as topic and interlocutor. Language attrition progresses through stages in which the separate contexts become confused and finally unified into one system when code mixing progresses to the point where it is used inappropriately, indicating that the two languages are being used interchangeably and not triggered by factors in the external sociolinguistic context.

In a paradoxical sense, it might be claimed that given the predominance of L2 data in the linguistic environment, the bilingual appears to undergo a process of "linguistic maturation" moving from a *context-dependent,* redundant system of multiple forms and rules for what are perceived by the bilingual as the same function to a system in which he views the comparable forms from L1 and L2 as *context-independent,* that is, independent of L1 and L2 (Table I). Once this stage

TABLE I
Context-Dependence, Bilingualism, and Language Attrition

Stage	Language relationships	Description
1	[(L1 (L2))]	L2 acquisition
2	[(L1) + (L2)]	Bilingualism
3	[(L1 + L2)]	Precursor stage for L1 attrition
4	[(L2 (L1))]	L1 attrition
5	[$L2_{L1}$]	Language death

Stage 1: L2 acquisition

The L1 is dominant as indicated by the direction of language transfer from L1 to L2. L2 is viewed as a subset of L1.

Stage 2: Bilingualism

Both languages are maintained separately or autonomously and used in appropriate sociolinguistic contexts. Code-mixing and switching are appropriate.

Stage 3: Precursor stage for L1 attrition

The two systems are perceived as a single combined unified system. Language mixing is done inappropriately. Uniqueness and Subset principles are activated to deal with redundancies within the combined grammars.

Stage 4: L2 attrition

The L2 becomes dominant. Transfer is in the direction of L2 into L1. L1 may now be viewed as a subset of L2.

Stage 5: Language death

The L2 becomes either the only language, as in the case of children completely losing the L1, or the L1 remains as a residue in the dialects of second- or third-generation immigrant populations (Dorian, 1982; Dressler, 1991; Karttunen, 1977; Silva-Corvalan, 1991).

is reached in binguality, the speaker is able to prune away those aspects of the unified system considered to be redundant. As was noted above, one determinant of this process appears to be a tendency to prefer less marked or simpler forms.

REFERENCES

Aronson-Berman, R. (1978). *Modern Hebrew structure.* Tel Aviv: University Publishing Projects.

Bahrick, H. P. (1984). Fifty years of second language attrition: Implications for programmatic research. *Modern Language Journal, 68*(ii), 105–118.

Birdsong, D. (1992). Ultimate attainment in second language acquisition. *Language, 68,* 706–755.

Bley-Vroman, R. (1990). The logical problem of foreign language learning. *Linguistic Analysis, 20*(1–2, 3–49.

Chomsky, N. (1986). *Knowledge of language: Its nature, origin and use.* New York: Praeger.

Cohen, A. D., & Weltens, B. (Eds.). (1989). Language attrition. *Studies in Second Language Acquisition, 11*(2) (issue devoted entirely to second or foreign language attrition).

Coppieters, R. (1987). Competence differences between native and non-native speakers. *Language, 63,* 544–573.

Dorian, N. C. (1982). Language loss and maintenance in language contact situations. In R. D. Lambert & B. F. Freed (Eds.), *The loss of language skills* (pp. 44–59). Rowley, MA: Newbury House.

Dressler, W. U. (1991). The sociolinguistic and patholinguistic attrition of Breton phonology, morphology and morphonology. In H. W. Seliger, & R. M. Vago (Eds.), *First language attrition* (pp. 99–112). Cambridge, UK: Cambridge University Press.

Felix, S. (1981). The effect of formal instruction on second language acquisition. *Language Learning, 31*(1), 87–112.

Huffines, M. L. (1991). Pennsylvania German: Convergence and change as strategies of discourse. In H. W. Seliger and R. M. Vago (Eds.), *First Language Attrition.* pp. 125–138. Cambridge, UK: Cambridge University Press.

Johnson, J., & Newport, E. (1991). Critical period effects on universal properties of language. *Cognition, 39,* 215–258.

Karmiloff-Smith, A. (1986). From meta-processes to conscious access: Evidence from children's metalinguistic and repair data. *Cognition,* 23, 95–147.

Karttunen, F. (1977). Finnish in America: A case study of monogenerational language change. In B. G. Blount, & M. Sanches (Eds.), *Sociocultural dimensions of language change.* New York: Academic Press.

Kuhberg, H. (1992). Longitudinal L2-attrition versus L2-acquisition, in three Turkish children—empirical findings. *Second Language Research, 8*(2), 138–154.

Lambert, R. D., & Freed, B. (Eds.). (1982). *The loss of language skills.* Rowley, MA: Newbury House.

Larmouth, D. W. (1974). Differential interference in American Finnish cases. *Language, 50,* 356–366.

Maher, J. (1991). A crosslinguistic study of language contact and language attrition. In H. W. Seliger, & R. M. Vago (Eds.), *First language attrition,* (pp. 67–84). Cambridge, UK: Cambridge University Press.

Mazurkewich, I., & White, L. (1984). The acquisition of the dative alternation: Unlearning overgeneralizations. *Cognition, 16,* 261–283.

Murphy, C. (1992, August). Notes: Huiswants es. *The Atlantic, 270*(2), 18–22.

Olshtain, E. (1986). The attrition of English as a second language with speakers of Hebrew. In B. Weltens, K. de Bot, & T. van Els (Eds.), *Language attrition in progress* (pp. 187–204). Dordrecht: Foris.

Olshtain, E. and Barzilay, M. (1991). Lexical retrieval difficulties in adult language attrition. In H. W. Seliger, & R. M. Vago (Eds.) *First Language Attrition,* pp. 139–150. Cambridge: Cambridge University Press.

Pfaff, C. (1979). Constraints on language mixing: Intersentential code-switching and borrowing in Spanish. *Language, 55,* 291–318.

Schmidt, A. (1991). Language attrition in Boumaa Fijian and Dyirbal. In H. W. Seliger, & R. M. Vago (Eds.), *First language attrition* (pp. 113–124). Cambridge, UK: Cambridge University Press.

Seliger, H. W. (1977). Biological analogs for language contact situations. *International Review of Applied Linguistics,* No. 2.

Seliger, H. W. (1989). Deterioration and creativity in childhood bilingualism. In *Bilingualism across the agespan* (pp. 173–184). Cambridge, UK: Cambridge University Press.

Seliger, H. W. (1991). Language attrition, reduced redundancy and creativity. In H. W. Seliger, & R. M. Vago, (Eds.), *First language attrition* (pp. 227–240). Cambridge, UK: Cambridge University Press.

Sharwood-Smith, M. (1991). First language attrition and the parameter setting model. In H. W. Seliger, & R. M. Vago (Eds.), *First language attrition* (pp. 17–30). Cambridge, UK: Cambridge University Press.

Silva-Corvalan, C. (1991). Spanish learning attrition in a contact situation with Spanish. In H. W. Seliger, & R. M. Vago (Eds.), *First language attrition* (pp. 151–171). Cambridge, UK: Cambridge University Press.

Sridhar, S. N., & Sridhar, K. K. (1980). The syntax and psycholinguistics of bilingual code-switching. *Canadian Journal of Psychology, 34*(4), 407–416.

Vago, R. M. (1991). Paradigmatic regularity in first language attrition. In H. W. Seliger, & R. M. Vago (Eds.), *First language attrition* (pp. 241–251). Cambridge, UK: Cambridge University Press.

Weltens, B., de Bot, K., & van Els, T. (Eds.). (1986). *Language attrition in progress.* Dordrecht: Foris.

White, L. (1989). *Universal Grammar and second language acquisition.* Philadelphia: John Benjamins.

White, L. (1990). Another look at the logical problem of foreign language learning. *Linguistic Analysis, 20*(1–2), 50–63.

BILINGUAL LANGUAGE MIXING, UNIVERSAL GRAMMAR, AND SECOND LANGUAGE ACQUISITION

Tej K. Bhatia and William C. Ritchie

I. INTRODUCTION

Following Chomsky (1986) we break down the central questions in the study of language to the following four: What constitutes the knowledge of a particular language? How is this knowledge put to use in the production and recognition of speech? How is it acquired? How is it represented in the brain? Though these are generally conceived of as questions about monolinguals, we ask them with respect to bilinguals as well: How are the bilingual's two (or more) systems of linguistic knowledge organized in relation to each other? How does possession of two systems of linguistic knowledge affect the mental processes that underlie speech recognition and production? How do the two systems interact at various stages in the attainment of bilinguality? and, How are the two systems represented in the brain as indicated by the ways in which various forms of brain damage affect linguistic performance in the two languages? In addition to these questions, research on bilingualism must address the problems of the effects of bilingualism on cognitive functioning and of the social determinants of various forms of bilingual linguistic behavior. In spite of a view of bilingualism as somehow deviant or pathological— held by many early researchers—investigation of these questions has proceeded intensively (particularly since the 1960s), and some degree of understanding has been achieved, although much remains to be done. (For a general discussion of bilingualism see chapter 17 by Romaine, this volume.)

Handbook of Second Language Acquisition

All of these issues come together in the study of the way in which bilinguals mix and integrate their two linguistic systems in their day-to-day verbal interaction. In many bi- or multilingual communities, this is not a peripheral, idiosyncratic, or "strange" phenomenon. On the contrary, it is such a common and natural part of linguistic behavior that speakers in such communities are largely unaware of mixing and do not react to it unless they are consciously made aware of it by listeners; nor is their fluency hampered in any way, nor is there any evidence that suggests that the speaker is not understood by his or her bilingual listeners. In addition, whether bilingualism is grounded in a widely spoken European language on one hand or in one of the aboriginal languages of Australia and New Guinea on the other, one conclusion that seems to be inescapable is that language mixing is widespread if not universal among bilinguals. Although no systematic quantitative studies of language mixing have been carried out, McConvell (1988) estimated, based on a study of Gurindji–English bilinguals, that such verbal behavior constitutes a major portion of a bilingual's everyday discourse. According to McConvell's estimate, roughly one-third of discourse in Gurindji (an aboriginal language of Australia) is mixed.

Code-mixing (CM) has been the subject of investigation by linguists and non-linguists, including sociologists, anthropologists, psychologists, speech therapists, and computer scientists, for a number of reasons. First, it appears to hold a key to the understanding of bilingual language processing and the treatment of certain speech disorders. Second, it sheds light on the deeper principles of human communication, namely creativity and optimization as well as complex social and psychological motivations in verbal communication. And third, it is of increasing interest to linguistic theory.

This chapter presents a state-of-the-art view of research on CM and code-switching (CS). Section II draws a distinction among several phenomena related to language mixing in general, thereby isolating CM and CS for further discussion. Section III draws further distinctions among types of CM and CS. Sections IV and V discuss formal and semantic constraints on CM, and sections VI and VII cover sociopsychological and attitudinal aspects of CM and CS. Section VIII looks critically at work on bilingual aphasia; section IX reviews recent research on language mixing at different stages of second language (L2) acquisition and presents a model based on that research. Finally, section X deals with some residual problems, and section XI is a conclusion.

Kamwangamalu (1989) listed more than 200 studies on CM involving a wide variety of language pairs published from 1970 to 1988. In fact, the body of research on this topic is increasing at a rapid rate. Only those works have been selected for review here that are important according to one or more of the following criteria: historicity, theoretical frameworks, and impact on subsequent research. The restrictions on the scope of the chapter are as follows: A full discussion of speech processing in bilinguals is beyond the scope of this chapter. No attempt is made to give an array of definitions of bilingualism or bilinguals. Unless specified otherwise, the chapter deals with the speech of the balanced or fluent bilingual. Furthermore, it should be stressed that the question of multiple mixing is not addressed here (see Bhatia, 1988, for details). The data are drawn from a wide variety of cross-linguistic research including our own research on this topic.

II. Definitions of CM and CS, Borrowing, and Other Related Phenomena

We begin our discussion of CM and CS with the examples in (1) and (2).

(1) *Spanish*–English (Valdés-Fallis, 1978, p. 1).
   a. *No, yo sí brincaba en el trampoline* when I was a senior.
      'No, I did jump on the trampoline when I was a senior.'
   b. *La consulta era* eight dollars.
      'The office visit was eight dollars.'
   c. Well, I keep starting some. *Como por un mes todos los días escribo y ya dejo.*
      'Well, I keep starting some. For about a month I write everything and then I stop.'

(2) *Hindi*–English
   a. Train *mẽ* seat *mil jaae to* . . .
      'If one gets a seat in the train, then . . .'
   b. Third class *kaa Dibbaa* . . .
                of compartment
      'a third-class compartment' (lit.: compartment of third class)
   c. *buund* -ify *kar-naa* 'to liquefy'
      'liquid-ify do-to'

As indicated by these examples, CS can be either intrasentential as in examples (1a–b) and (2a–c) or intersentential as in example (1c). In this chapter we will use the term CM for the intrasentential case and the term CS for the intersentential case. Therefore, the two terms will be applied in the following fashion:

(3) a. CM refers to the mixing of various linguistic units (morphemes, words, modifiers, phrases, clauses, and sentences) primarily from two participating grammatical systems within a sentence. In other words, CM is intrasentential and is constrained by grammatical principles and may be motivated by sociopsychological motivations.
   b. CS refers to the mixing of various linguistic units (words, phrases, clauses, and sentences) primarily from two participating grammatical systems across sentence boundaries within a speech event. In other words, CS is intersentential and may be subject to some discourse principles. It is motivated by social and psychological motivations.

The distinction between CS and CM is controversial, with some scholars doubting the usefulness of the distinction (Hatch, 1976, p. 202), and others finding it important and useful (Bokamba, 1988; Kachru, 1978; McLaughlin, 1984; and many others). In an actual discourse, the interaction between CS and CM often becomes so complex and fused that it is quite difficult to draw a clear line between them, as is shown by this discourse from Hindi–English CM and CS.

(4)   *Hindi*–English
         baabaa, you have become a dirty boy. *itne baRe ho gaye, par itnii tamiiz nahĩ aayii ki* drawing room *mẽ* Papa *ke* friends *baiThe hãĩ aur aap apne* boots *liye cale aaye. jaao xud* polish *karo.* This is your punishment.
                                                  (cited from Bhatia, 1982, p. 243)
         'Baba, you have become a dirty boy. You have become so grown up but you have not learned any manners. In the drawing room, Papa's friends are sitting and you have come with your shoes on. Go, polish your shoes. This is your punishment.'

The forms from Hindi in the above passage are italicized. The important features of this passage, spoken by a mother who is upset with her son's manners are as follows: first, entire sentences ('you have become a dirty boy,' 'this is your punishment'), phrases ('drawing room'), and single lexical items ('Papa, friends, boots') have been mixed in with what is essentially a Hindi discourse. Second, with the exception of the first and last sentences, the forms from English exemplify CM (rather than CS). The passage also illustrates an extremely productive device, hybridization, according to which so-called complex verbs are derived by combining an English noun, verb, or adjective with the Hindi verb *karnaa* 'to do' or *honaa* 'to be.' In this example, the conjunct verb, *polish karo* '(do) polish(ing),' is derived by combining the English noun/verb *polish* with a form of *karnaa*—in this case the imperative *karo.* Because this takes place within a sentence boundary it is, again, a case of CM in our terminology. Third, the first and the last sentences are from English. Because the onset site of the last full English sentence is a sentence boundary, it is a case of CS. The first sentence can also be treated as an example of CS, if one considers the address element *baabaa* separate from the remainder of the sentence. Thus, in this discourse, a number of sentences containing CM are sandwiched between two CS sentences.

Besides the extensive intermixing of CS and CM, there are a number of other reasons for the lack of consensus among researchers as to the distinction between CM and CS. Some researchers (Gumperz and others) adopt a functionalist approach to the study of CM and CS in which sociopsychological factors are the primary basis for analysis. For these researchers, the distinction between CS and CM is neutralized because this distinction is sometimes blurred at the sentence level as is evident by the opening sentence of (4) and also at the discourse level.

Other differences among researchers appear to be purely terminological. For instance, Pfaff (1979, p. 295) employs the term *mixing* as a neutral cover term for both CM and borrowing, whereas Beardsome (1991, p. 49) rejected the use of the term CM "since it appears to be the least favored designation and the most unclear for referring to any form of non-monoglot norm-based speech patterns." Yet others use the term CM to refer to other related phenomena, such as borrowing, interference, transfer, or switching (McLaughlin, 1984, pp. 96–97). Hatch (1976, p. 202) maintained that there is no sharp distinction between intersentential CS and intrasentential CM, and other scholars rejected the distinction on functional grounds and treat them both as "situational shifting" (Gumperz, 1982, p. 70; Pakir, 1989; Tay, 1989).

This chapter makes a distinction between CM and CS on one hand and other related phenomena (such as borrowing, etc.) on the other for the reason that CM and CS appear to differ systematically from these other phenomena in ways to be examined. This approach is consistent with the works of scholars such as Kachru (1978, 1982) and Bokamba (1988, 1989) and many others who stress the need for such a distinction on the same grounds. We turn now to a discussion of these issues.

A. Matrix and Embedded Language

A distinction that is important in any discussion of CM and CS and related phenomena is that between the matrix (host, base) language and the embedded (guest) language in a particular case of language alternation. The matrix language is the language that gives the sentence its basic character, and the embedded language is the language that contributes the "imported" material. In example (1b) the matrix language is Spanish, the embedded language English; in example (2a) and the middle two sentences of example (4), the matrix language is Hindi and the embedded language is English.

Though many researchers adopt this distinction, the distinction is still problematic for some. A number of criteria have been proposed to identify the matrix language in code-mixed or code-switched discourse. These criteria can be classified into the following groups: structural language of INFL (i.e., "Inflection," the element that functions as head of the sentence) in the Government and Binding framework by Klavans, 1985; Treffers-Daller, 1991; overall structural properties of the sentence such as Topic-Comment structure, Nishimura 1989; sociolinguistic and psycholinguistic (e.g., language proficiency or the mother tongue and intuitions of the bilingual employing CM and CS); and frequency, Kamwangamalu and Lee (1991). These criteria are important for defining the matrix language but are not sufficient to account for the notion at hand. In our opinion any characterization of the matrix language has to adopt a multifactorial approach drawing from the three categories identified above. (See section X.A and Myers-Scotton, 1993, pp. 66–70, for further details).

B. Borrowing and CM and CS

One of the theoretical assumptions that underlies most (if not all) studies of CM and CS is the distinction between borrowing on one hand and CM and CS on the other. Borrowed or loan words have the following characteristics that separate them from code-mixed or code-switched elements. First, they primarily serve the linguistic function of filling a gap in the lexicon of the matrix language, or they are prompted by nonlinguistic factors such as modernization or both, whereas CM and CS are motivated by sociopsychological factors, such as social identity (see section VI). Second, borrowed items are restricted to specific lexical items of the matrix language, whereas such a restriction is not applicable in CM and CS with lexical items from both matrix and embedded language being freely chosen. Romaine (1989, p. 63) points out that most scholars accept the view that lexical items are most easily borrowed (with nouns more easily borrowed than verbs), followed by derivational morphological material, followed by inflectional material with syntactic structures the least likely to be borrowed. Third, borrowed items are assimilated into the matrix language by regular phonological and morphological processes of either the matrix or the embedded language. In contrast, CM and CS material is generally unassimilated to the phonological and morphological processes of the matrix language. Fourth, borrowed material is part of the lexicon of monolingual as well as bilingual members of the community, whereas CM and CS is limited to bilinguals in the speech community.

It is worth mentioning that there is some disagreement among scholars about the phonological and morphological assimilation of loan words. For instance, Sobin (1976, p. 42) claims that some phonologically adapted items must be considered switches rather than borrowings for speakers of Spanish in Texas. Elías-Olivarés (1976, p. 187) contends that nouns of a dominant embedded language in business and other functional domains (English, in this case) often remain morphologically and syntactically unintegrated into the matrix nondominant language (Spanish) and yet must be treated as part of the Spanish lexicon of some Chicanos. It seems that prestige together with functional domains allow the borrowed lexicon to remain unassimilated into the matrix language.

As regards the criterion of morphological integration, not all scholars recognize it as a reliable basis for distinguishing between borrowing and CM and CS. Myers-Scotton (1988) rejects both morphological and syntactic integration as a reliable yardstick for distinguishing between CS and borrowing. Pfaff (1979, p. 298) refers to differing degrees of morphological integration for various syntactic categories, particularly verbs. Verbs need to be morphologically integrated in terms of tense and aspect, whereas other categories such as adjectives or nouns do not have to undergo such a rigorous process of adaptation to attain borrowed status. Sankoff, Poplack, and Vanniarajan (1986) argue that any nonnative lexical item must be treated as borrowed, if it is adapted morphologically and syntactically with respect to only one of the two languages (see also Sankoff et al., 1986, for the concept of base language). However, if the syntactic and morphological systems of the two languages coexist and their nonassimilative tendency is noticeable within the sentence, then CM or CS has occurred. That means that the presence of the morphological and syntactic systems of the two participating languages with respect to the use of nonnative lexicon constitute an important distinguishing factor between CM or CS and borrowing.

Yet another dimension is added to the problem by the concept of *nonce borrowing*. Poplack, Wheeler, and Westwood (1989) distinguished between the well-established notion of borrowing discussed above and a notion of nonce borrowing. They state that the entire nominal lexicon of English is subjected to nonce borrowing by Finnish–English bilinguals. Thus, borrowing represents a continuum as shown in the Figure 1. Nonce borrowing involves syntactic, morphological and possibly phonological integration into the matrix language of an element of the donor language. This seems to suggest that as far as the question of CM and CS

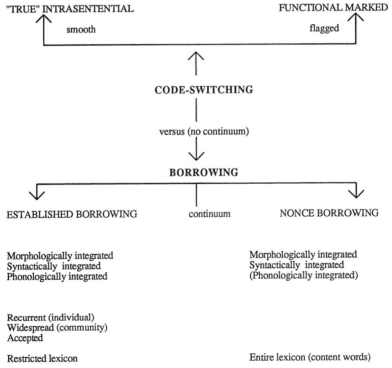

Figure I   Characterization of CS and CM and borrowing (from Poplack, Wheeler, and Westwood, 1989).

is concerned one has to go beyond the degree to which a particular lexical item is integrated and take into account certain performance factors (hesitancy) as well as sociopsychological motivations.

C. CM and CS and Pidgin and Creoles

A pidgin language is a mixed language, usually with material from both a world or prestige language such as English or French and a more local, low-prestige language. Pidgins have very restricted functional domains primarily having to do with business. They are not native languages (NL) for anyone. Their lexicon is very limited (1000–2000 words) and grammar is "simplified." Furthermore, the mixture of the two languages involved is uneven, tilted more in favor of the prestige language. CM and CS, on the other hand, is employed by children and in that respect is considered to be virtually the mother tongue of code-mixers. As we will show in the following section, CM and CS also involve a complex grammar (see section on constraints on CM) and performs a wide variety of sociopsychological functions that cannot be fulfilled by means of the employment of the two "pure" linguistic systems that serve as the source languages for CM and CS (see section V).

A creole language is the result of a pidgin language becoming the mother tongue of the children of the community in which the pidgin is used. In addition to the difference in the input languages between creole and code-switched or code-mixed languages, the developmental phase of creole languages is different. As shown in the tree diagram, creole languages undergo either the process of decreolization (that is, elaboration toward the prestige language) or intense creolization (hypercreolization). In that respect then creolization marks language shift or even language death. However, CM and CS does not affect bilingualism in an adverse fashion (i.e., it does not lead to monolingualism). (Chapter 16 by Anderson and Shirai, this volume, also includes discussion of pidgin and creole languages.)

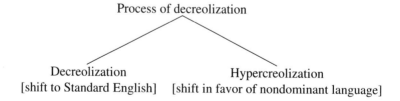

Process of decreolization

Decreolization   Hypercreolization
[shift to Standard English]   [shift in favor of nondominant language]

D. CM and CS and Diglossia

CM also differs from diglossia. Ferguson (1959/1972, p. 232) applies this term to the relationship between two or more varieties of a language when they are used in different functions in a speech community. Such a situation reflects an underlying bilingualism or bidialectalism, although the speech community in which the two varieties coexist considers itself to be monolingual. One of the varieties in a diglossic situation, termed the *high variety* (H), carries greater prestige than the other, *low variety* (L). For instance, in the Arabic-speaking speech community, Classical Arabic represents the H variety and colloquial Arabic, the L variety. The most important feature of diglossic societies is the complementary function that the two varieties perform (i.e., where the H variety is appropriate, the L variety is not and vice versa) (see Table I, chapter 17 by Romaine, this volume).

The main difference between diglossia and CM and CS is that in diglossia the two varieties are always kept separate and are never mixed, whereas in CM and CS the languages are constantly subject to mixing. Therefore, the question of the interdependence and interaction of the two linguistic varieties never arises in diglossic societies, whereas interdependence and interaction is a hallmark of societies in which CM and CS is practiced. Furthermore, the complementarity of the domains of the varieties in a diglossic society is determined by a stable and normative grammatical tradition in the speech community. CM and CS speech fills a different functional domain (see section VI for further details) and continues to be innovative in this respect. The functional domain is determined on descriptive rather than on prescriptive grounds.

III. TYPES OF CM AND CS

As pointed out earlier, we use the sentence as a syntactic determinant of distinguishing between CM and CS. Those researchers who do not subscribe to the terms CM and CS, nevertheless, consider intrasentential and intersentential mixing as two distinct types of the general process of mixing or switching.

Poplack (1980) and others, for instance, distinguished between CS and CM and note an additional phenomenon—"tag-switching." Tags are identified as expressions such as "you know," "I mean," "It's cool," "Is it?", "Isn't it?", "man" and their translational equivalents. They often perform the function of a sentence filler in addition to performing the usual tag functions such as seeking confirmation about the information known to the speaker and small talk. Tag-switching is exemplified by sentences like the following:

(5)   *Chinese Tag*–English
       I don't want . . . he is not there already *la* . . . not there *la*, no, that I meet him . . . I ask him about the car . . . he wants one thousand, man. I said I pay him eight, *la* . . . I told Bernard like that . . . I told him, I pay you more a bit *la*. He wants one thousand no less *la*.

(6) English Tag–*Punjabi* (Romaine, 1989, p. 112)
I mean, unconsciously, subconsciously, *kari jaande āā,* you know, *par* I wish, you know, *ke māi* pure *punjabi bol sakāā.*
'I mean, unconsciously, subconsciously, we keep doing it, you know, but I wish, you know, that I could speak pure Punjabi.'

Bilinguals often insert a tag from one language in a sentence that is otherwise entirely in an other language, as in examples (5) and (6). Even though a tag in a different language from the rest of the sentence in which it occurs is ostensibly a case of CM, tags exhibit the flexibility of code-switched items because they occur at phrase or clause boundaries and present minimal syntactic disruption when embedded within a sentence. A tag is usually a phrase, clause, or particle. It is questionable whether tag-switching should be considered a type of CM or CS because such a classification is functional in nature. As we will show in section VI, one can enumerate a number of other functions of CM and CS, such as quotatives, reiteration, and message qualification. If one has to posit tag-switching as a type of CM or CS, then one is compelled to consider the other functional-types, too. There is no compelling reason to assign a special status to tags.

Although we have drawn the distinction between CS and CM in section II, we should stress that CM or "intrasentential" mixing has been argued to involve the highest level of skills and competence on the part of bilinguals and, therefore, some linguists (e.g., Poplack) have treated it as a defining criterion for a true bilingual. This marks a point of departure from Weinreich, who considered intersentential switching as the mark of the ideal bilingual. Weinreich's (1953, p. 73) characterization of bilinguals excluded those who engage in intrasentential mixing by stating that "the ideal bilingual switches from one language to the other according to appropriate changes in the speech situation (interlocutors, topic, etc.) but not in an unchanged speech situation, and *certainly not within a sentence*" [emphasis ours].

From the discussion so far, it is clear that one can classify CM and CS on the basis of the following three or four criteria: (1) structural types (intersentential vs. intrasentential mixing of languages—that is, CS vs. CM), (2) degree of bilingualism of the language user (appropriate vs. odd mixing; smooth vs. flagged mixing—see Figure 1), and (3) social attitudes toward CM and CS (CM and CS seen as "good" vs. "bad"). In addition, instances of CM and CS can also be classified on functional grounds. Depending upon the type of function it performs, one can arrive at a further subclassification of CM and CS.

Myers-Scotton (1989) considered the distinction between CM and CS to be poorly motivated from a functional point of view and classifies CM and CS on functional grounds. She claimed that both intra- and intersentential switching can occur as part of the same conversation, with both serving the same social function. She argued that the points of individual switches do not carry any special social message, but the overall pattern of the use of a given language pair expresses social meaning. Treating CM and CS under her markedness hypothesis, she viewed all CM and CS as "a message about the balance of rights and obligations which the speaker expects or desires (or both) for the current talk exchanges" (Myers-Scotton, 1989, p. 339). In her view CM and CS, thus, can be classified in terms of four functional types:

1. Sequential unmarked CM and CS occurs when situational factors change and, therefore, change the unmarked balance of rights and balances for a specific exchange. This can best be characterized as what Blom and Gumperz (1972) referred to as "transactional switching" (also referred as situational switching). This type of switching is controlled by the various manifestations of a speech event such as topic and participant (see, for example, Ervin-Tripp, 1964; Weinreich, 1953). Blom and Gumperz showed the sequential arrangement of language exchange when residents in Hemnesberger in rural Norway come to the post office. At the counter the greetings and inquiries about the family members are carried out in the local dialect, whereas the business is conducted in the Standard Norwegian.

2. The unmarked type is used between in-group members who are peers and share the dual identities that the switched language symbolizes. However, no situational change occurs at all. This type of CM and CS is illustrated below:

(7) Two Tanzanian graduate students at an American university are chatting about shipping things home when their studies are over. Swahili is the matrix language.
Student (*Swahili*–English): carpet *ni matatizo. Inabidi u-li*-ship. *huwezi kulipeleka kwenye ndege kwa sababu ya urefu wake. . . . Sisi tunayotaka kununua ni ki*-cloth.
'A carpet is problems. You have to ship it. You can't carry it on the plane because of its length. . . . What we want to buy is cloth.' (Myers-Scotton, 1989, p. 337)

Notice that the Swahili words for the English words are accessible to the speaker. Also, English is mixed intrasententially without any apparent change in the speech event.

3. The marked type is motivated either by considerations of solidarity or power. Marked choices are flagged and are punctuated by hesitation. The following example illustrates the case of two polarized marked choices (e.g., Kikuyu for solidarity and English for power).

(8) Four young office workers from an government office are talking about setting up a group emergency fund in Nairobi. Out of the four participants, one is a Kalenjin, one is a Kisii, and the other two are Kikuyu. Swahili–English has been the unmarked choice until Kikuyus switch to Kikuyu to make a negative comment in Kikuyu about what has been just said. The choice of

Hakuta, 1986, p. 14). Furthermore, it unveiled a complex aspect of CM that has occupied many CM and CS researchers since then. Let us now turn our attention to some constraints on CM that have been posited in the linguistic literature.

B. The Search for Universals

Some of the earliest restrictions on CM were proposed primarily as language-specific constraints. Proposals such as the size-of-constituent constraint of Gumperz and Hernández-Chávez (1975) and Poplack (1980) and conjunction or complementizer constraints (Gumperz, 1977; Kachru, 1978) made no explicit claims either about their cross-linguistic applicability or their universality.

The constraint on the size of constituents was motivated by the observation that the higher the level or size of the constituent the more was its probability of mixing. Essentially, this constraint states that mixing applies at the phrasal level and constituents smaller than a phrase are not subject to mixing. As examples (1a–b) and (2a–c) indicated, mixing of terminal constituents (e.g., Adj, N, V) and inflections is fully acceptable; in fact, such CM is widely found. We will return to the conjunction or complementizer constraints shortly during our discussion of a more recently proposed principle, the Functional Head Constraint (FHC).

C. Formal Constraints on CM

The following constraints were proposed as general syntactic constraints on CM and they are among the most widely cited constraints in the literature.

The Free Morpheme Constraint

> A switch may not occur between a bound morpheme and a lexical form unless the latter has been phonologically integrated into the language of the bound morpheme. (Sankoff & Poplack, 1981, pp. 5–6)

The free morpheme constraint (FMC) has some parallels with the size-of-constituent constraint. What such constraints do at the syntactic level, the FMC performs at the word level. It is intended to account for the ill-formedness of expressions such as *run-*eando* 'running.' The Spanish-bound morpheme -*eando* violates the restriction against the mixing of a bound morpheme and a free morpheme from two different languages. However, languages with agglutinative elements (such as Bantu and Arabic) and nonagglutinative languages (such as Hindi) both violate this constraint, as shown by the following sentences.

(9)   *Nairobi Swahili*–English (Scotton, 1983)
       *vile   vitu   zake zi-me-*spoil-*iw-a*
       those things her   they-perf-spoil-pass
       'Those things of hers were spoiled.'

(10) *Arabic*–English (El-Noory, 1985)
    *?ana ba-*cope   *ma?a l-lahja.*
    I   pres-cope with the-dialect
    'I cope with the dialect.'

In (9) not only one but four different bound morphemes are affixed to the English verbal stem, *spoil*. These morphemes are the following: the subject prefix *zi-;* the perfective tense marker *-me;* the passive marker *-iw* and *-a.* In the Arabic example, the present tense marker bound morpheme occurs with the verb *cope.* Myers-Scotton (1993) proposed the violations of the FMC are limited to agglutinative languages like Swahili. However, example (2c) shows that switches in a nonagglutinative language (Hindi) also violate the FMC.

The Equivalence Constraint

> Code-switches will tend to occur at points in discourse where the juxtaposition of L1 and L2 elements does not violate a syntactic rule of either language (i.e., at points around which the surface structures of the two languages map on to each other). (Poplack, 1980, p. 586; Sankoff & Poplack, 1981, p. 5)

The Equivalence Constraint (EC) implies that CM can take place only at those positions that are common to both languages and dissimilar points will not yield mixing. For instance, Spanish and English differ from each other in terms of the placement of adjectives within a noun phrase (i.e., in Spanish the adjective is positioned after the noun). However, they share similar behavior with reference to the placement of noun and determiner (i.e., the determiner precedes the noun). The EC predicts that mixing will be permissible between N and determiner, whereas it will be blocked between N and adjective. Thus, the EC will make the right prediction that the following phrases will be ill-formed in *Spanish*–English mixing: **El viejo* man; ***the old *hombre;* ***the *viejo hombre.* However, noun phrases such as *el* old man and the *hombre viejo* will be grammatical.

Now, let us consider the examples of Hindi–English mixing. The phrase structure rule of the noun phrase (NP) of English and Hindi are identical, (i.e., NP → (Det) (Adj) N). This will predict that the mixing between *Hindi* and English at the NP level should be free.

(11) (a)   the old   man   (12) (a) *vo buuRaa aadmii*
     (b) *the *buuRaa* man   (b) *vo* old   *aadmii*
     (c) *the *buuRaa aadmii*   (c) *vo* old   man
                                                'that old man'

The comparison of (11a–c) and (12a–c) shows that although (12b and 12c) allow mixing with English in the adjectival and nominal positions, the English translational equivalent of (12) does not permit Hindi mixing in these two positions. The underlying source of the ungrammaticality of (11b and 11c) is apparently that Hindi lacks articles. Berk-Seligson (1986, p. 328) found a similar situation in Hebrew–Spanish CM. Hebrew lacks the indefinite article. To fill the gap created by the absence of English articles in Hindi, the Hindi-speaking bilingual will employ one of the following two strategies: Either the demonstrative pronoun *vo* 'that' is used instead of the article, or the definite article is dropped as in the code-mixed phrase old *aadmii*. The result thus produced is well formed. The presence of the English article with a Hindi adjective and a noun is totally unacceptable. Romaine (1989, p. 118) pointed out that one of the shortcomings of the EC is that it overlooks the absence of a neat mapping of grammatical categories cross-linguistically. The mismatch of categories is responsible for the ungrammaticality of mixed utterances in spite of the fact that code-mixed sentences may otherwise meet the EC.

In addition, some categories perform more than one function depending upon their placement in a sentence. Consider for example the case of auxiliaries in English. They mark tense–aspect when they occur in the body of the sentence and, when placed sentence initially, they function as the marker of yes–no questions as well. Hindi and English fall under the EC with reference to yes–no question formation in the sense that a yes–no marker is placed sentence initially in yes–no questions in both languages. However, mixing is not permitted at the site of the question-marking element. Consider the following sentences, mixed and unmixed:

(13) (a)   Will Ram play?   (14) (a) *kyaa*   Ram *khel-egaa?*
                                             yes–no mkr Ram *play*-fut.
                                             'Will Ram play?'
      (b) **-*egaa* Ram play?   (b) *will   Ram *khel-egaa?*
      (c) *kyaa*   Ram play?   (c) *what   Ram *khel-egaa?*

The English auxiliary *will* has two possible translational equivalents in Hindi: either the future marker -*egaa* or the Hindi wh-word *kyaa,* the latter of which performs a dual function. When *kyaa* appears within a sentence, it functions like a wh-word parallel to English *what*; when it appears sentence initially, on the other hand, it serves as a yes–no marker. Comparison of (13a) and (14a) reveals that English and Hindi fall under the EC in that there is placement of a yes–no marker sentence initially in both languages, and the EC therefore predicts that sentence-initial position should serve as a potential site for CM. However, the ill-formedness of (13b) and (13c) reveals that mixing from Hindi is not allowed in an English sentence in that position. The same is true of the mixing of English into a Hindi sentence as shown by (14a) and (14b). (It should be noted that the Hindi equivalent of the English auxiliary, which is a bound morpheme, certainly increases the degree of the ungrammaticality of [13b].)

Even if the EC is met in a language pair, the positions of numerals, function words, and negative markers in either language are usually not among the potential sites for mixing. This point will be further detailed in our discussion of a more recently proposed condition on CM—the FHC.

The EC, to some extent, subsumes other constraints that are based on word-order typology. Poplack and Sankoff (1988) attempted to predict possible sites of mixing on the basis of different word-order language types. For example, both language typology and the EC predict that given a CM–CS pair consisting of a subject-object-verb (SOV) (e.g., Hindi, Punjabi) and a subject, verb, object (SVO) language (English), then the mixing will be blocked between the verb and the object. Also, because SOV languages have postpositions and SVO languages are prepositional in nature, there should be no mixing at the level of prepositional or postpositional phrase. Romaine (1989), however, cited some counter-examples to these predictions, drawn from the speech samples of *Punjabi*–English bilinguals.

(15) *Punjabi*–English (Romaine, 1989, p. 124)
    parents *te* depend *hondaa*   *ai.*
            on   be-present is (aux.)
    'It depends on the parents.'

(16) *Punjabi*–English (Romaine, 1989, p. 129)
    ke asii language *nūū*   improve *kar lããge.*
    that we language (obj. mk) improve do take-will
    'That we will improve (the) language.'

Nartey (1982) gives numerous counter-examples to the EC in CM between English and Adanme, a Western Kwa language spoken in southern Ghana.

Furthermore, the EC fails to subsume the Clitic Pronoun Constraint, as stated next.

The Clitic Pronoun Constraint

Clitic pronoun objects are realized in the same language as the verb to which they are cliticized, and in the position required by the syntactic rule of that language. (Pfaff, 1979, p. 303)

Because both English and Spanish are SVO, one would predict by the EC that mixing will be possible in the verb and the object position and even the subject position. The clitic pronoun constraint rules out sentences such as the following:

(17) English–*Spanish*
    * She sees *lo.*
            him
    'She sees him.'

Let us now turn our attention to another proposed constraint—the Dual Structure Principle (DSP) of Sridhar and Sridhar (1980).

The Dual Structure Principle

The internal structure of the guest [embedded] constituent need not conform to the constituent structure rules of the host [matrix] language, so long as its placement in the host language obeys the rules of the host language. (Sridhar & Sridhar, 1980, p. 412)

The DSP was formulated to account for examples like the following from Kannada–English CM.

(18)   *Kannada*–English
       nanna abhipraayadalli his visiting her at home *sariyalla*
       my   opinion-in   his visiting her at home proper-not
       'In my opinion, his visiting her at home is not proper.'

The Kannada phrase corresponding to the English phrase 'his visiting her at home' is given in (18a).

(18a)   *avanu avaḷannu mane-yalli nooḍuvudu*
        he   her   home-in   visiting
        'his visiting her at home'

The English phrase differs radically in structure from its corresponding Kannada phrase in the following four important respects: (1) the English subject is coded with possessive ending, whereas the Kannada subject is in the nominative case; (2) English follows the OV order, whereas Kannada has the VO order; (3) the locative of a preposition in English and a postposition in Kannada; and (4) the adverbial phrase (*at home*) follows the object in English, whereas it precedes in Kannada. However, the fact that the position of the English phrase in the matrix Kannada sentence (18) corresponds to that of (18a) in an unmixed version of (18) is sufficient to make (18) well formed.

The DSP incorrectly predicts, for example, the grammaticality of the sentences that result from substituting the English verb phrases *depend on the parents* and *improve the language* in (19) and (20), respectively. (For additional arguments, see Pandharipande, 1990).

(19)   *Punjabi*–English
       *depend on the parents *hondaa*   *ai.* (Romaine, 1989, p. 124)
                                be-present is (aux.)
       'It depends on the parents.'

(20)   *Punjabi*–English
       **ke*   *asii* improve the language *kar lāāge.*
         that we   do take-will
       'That we will improve (the) language.'

We turn now to Pfaff's Adjectival (Noun) Phrase Constraint (Pfaff 1979).

The Adjectival (Noun) Phrase Constraint

Adjective/noun mixes must match the surface word order of both the language of the adjective and the language of the head. (Pfaff 1979, p. 306)

This constraint, subsumed by the EC, was formulated to account for the grammaticality values of sentences such as the following:

(21)   English–*Spanish*
        *I want a motorcycle *verde.*
        'I want a green motorcycle.'

Finally, to complete this list of constraints, we consider Joshi's Closed Class Constraint.

The Closed Class Constraint

> Closed Class items (e.g., determiners, quantifiers, prepositions, possessive, Aux, Tense, helping verbs, etc.) cannot be switched. (Joshi, 1985, p. 194)

Although it is observationally accurate for a wide range of cases, the Closed Class Constraint (like the other constraints addressed in this section) carries less explanatory power than the constraints to be discussed in the next subsection. (See, in particular, the discussion of the FHC below.)

The constraints discussed so far are inadequate, and as we have seen, they fail to make correct cross-linguistic predictions. The underlying problems are several but most importantly (1) most of them are sensitive to surface and linear word order of the language pairs, and (2) some of them fail to make use of the hierarchical notion of linguistic structures, although others are rooted in the classification of the lexicon. In spite of their shortcomings, they have certainly made important gains in dispelling the conception that CM is a "strange" and "irregular" phenomenon.

D. Theoretical Models and Constraints on CM

In the light of this progress, the real challenge is not whether or not CM is subject to constraints but how best to capture those constraints and how to make deeper claims about human language in general and bilinguals' mixing competence and their language acquisition in particular. In what follows we will consider four such attempts, which are largely driven by deeper theoretical considerations and, thus, have serious implications for the study of Universal Grammar (UG) and language acquisition as well as linguistic performance.

Woolford's Model

Using Spanish and English as the two languages involved in CM, Woolford (1983) proposed a model, outlined in Figure 2, to show how two monolingual grammars cooperate to generate code-mixed sentences. Under the proposed model, the grammars of the two languages are not altered in any way; no hybrid rules of any sort are created. The intersecting portion of the two grammars represents those phrase structure rules that are common to both languages and, thus, permits

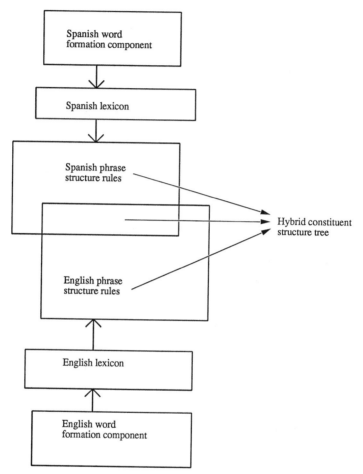

Figure 2 Woolford's model of code-mixing. [From Woolford (1983). Reprinted by permission of The MIT Press, Cambridge, MA.]

mixing rather freely from the two languages. The nonshared portion generates a hybrid constituent structure tree drawing from the phrase structure rules of either language. Bhatia (1989) questioned the adequacy of the proposed model in the light of the treatment of a set of three syntactic phenomena from Filmi English— namely verb formation, adjectival agreement, and the phenomenon that he calls "head deletion." In the interest of brevity we will outline only the verb-formation phenomenon, for the other two, see Bhatia (1989) for details.

Bhatia's study of CM between English and Hindi draws its data from a popular Indian film magazine, *Stardust,* which has both national and international editions. The noteworthy aspect of CM in this publication is that it involves a very productive process of verb formation that exhibits a special process of deriving infinitival verb forms from Hindi nouns and verbs, which comes neither from English nor from Hindi. The process is outlined in (22).

(22) *Verb Formation*	*Conjunct verb derived from Noun*	*Simple verb*
a. Hindi stem	*mask* [N 'joke']	*manaa* [V 'cause someone to agree']
b. stem-formation	*mask*+o	*manaa*+o
c. English derivational suffix *-fy* attachment	*mask*+o+fy	Not applicable

This process of stem formation determines the following hierarchical structures:

(23) a.   b.

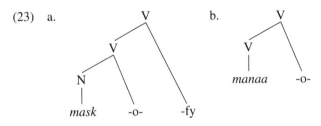

The following sentences exemplify such verbs.

(24) you *mask-o*   -fi   -ed/**mask*-ifi-ed him
       joke -stem-forming vowel -denominal suffix -past
       'You joked with him.' or 'You flattered him.'

(25) He was *gheraa -o*   -ed   /* *gheraa* -ed by more girls
       encircle-stem vowel-past (i.e., encircled/*encircle-past)
       than he could handle.
       'He was encircled by more girls than he could handle.'

(26) I *manaa*   -o   -ed /* *manaa*   -ed her.
       cause x to agree-stem vowel-past./* cause x to agree-past
       'I consoled her.'

These data exhibit two major features that bear on Woolford's model. First, the morphological rule of stem formation is part of neither the grammar of English nor the grammar of Hindi but is unique to Filmi English. Second, although the suffix *-fy* may appear to be the English causative suffix *-ify* (as in *pur-ify* 'make pure,' *solid-ify* 'make solid,' etc.) it carries no causative content in Filmi English but rather serves merely to change a noun into a verb; note that the word *maskofy* does not mean 'make into a joke' but simply '(to) joke/flatter' (see Bhatia, 1989).

Thus, the following conception of grammar of CM proposed by Woolford (1983) and Pfaff (1979) is too narrow.

> The grammars of the two languages are not altered in any way; no hybrid rules of any sort are created. The two grammars operate during code-switching just as they do during monolingual speech, except that each grammar generates only part of the sentence. (Woolford, 1983, p. 522)

> This finding that no separate new system is created is to be expected, since speakers are competent in two related languages which often have a high degree of similarity. (Pfaff, 1979, p. 315).

The Government Constraint

Di Sciullo, Muysken, and Singh (1986) attempt to capture the constraints on CM, in terms of the Government Constraint—formulated in terms of GB Theory—given below:

(27)   a. X governs Y if the first node dominating X also dominates Y, where X is a major category, N, V, A, P, and no maximal boundary intervenes between X and Y.
   b. If Lq carrier has [language] index q, then Y_{maxq}.
   c. In a maximal projection Y_{max}, the Lq carrier is the lexical element which asymmetrically c-commands the other lexical elements or terminal phrase nodes dominated by Y_{max}.
   d. At least the Lq carrier of a governed category must have the same Lq index as its governor.

Because under Di Sciullo et al.'s definition of government, only N, V, A, and P are potential governors, the constraint claims that in the structure (28) the Lq carrier of the governed category Y_{max} (that is, Zq) must have the same Lq index as Xq, where Xq is N, V, A, or P.

(28)

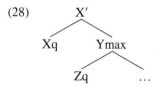

The Government Constraint is noteworthy on two grounds: First, the assignment of language indices results from the process of lexical insertion and not from the Phrase Structure (PS) rules as proposed by Woolford (1983); second, the phenomenon of syntactic integration is explained by an underlying principle that is valid not just for CM or for a single language but for linguistic structure in general and for all languages. It predicts that because a verb governs its complement clauses, direct and indirect objects and complement pre- and postpositional phrases, they must be in the same language as the verb and similarly for the other major categories. The Government Constraint can capture some previously proposed constraints such as those of Kachru (1978) and Singh (1981), predicting that the complementizer of a complement clause will be in the same language as the matrix verb, as shown in examples (29) and (30).

(29)   English–*Hindi*
     I told him that *ram bahut bimaar hai.*
                  Ram very sick   is
     'I told him that Ram was very sick.'
(30)   *I told him *ki   ram bahut bimaar hai.*
                 that Ram very sick   is
     'I told him that Ram was very sick.'

However, in other cases the Government Constraint makes false predictions. *Punjabi*–English mixed sentences such as (15) and (16) constitute counterexamples to the claims made by the Government Constraint because the postpositions *te* and *nũũ* in those examples govern the mixed nouns parents and language, respectively. Furthermore, Bentahila and Davies (1983; French and Arabic), Romaine (1989), Bhatia (1989, p. 274) and Belazi, Rubin, and Toribio (1994), drawing from a wide array of language pairs, argued convincingly against the constraint.

We referred to the class of Hindi "complex" verbs in section II. We return to a more detailed treatment of the construction. Kachru (1978, p. 36) observed how Hindi and other South Asian languages participate in language mixing within the complex verb construction. A new mixed verb consists of a preverbal element in a language other than Hindi followed by one of the two Hindi verbs *karnaa* 'to do' or *honaa* 'to be' (less frequently, *denaa* 'to give' or *lenaa* 'to take'); the preverbal element can be a noun, adjective, or pronoun of Hindi or another language such as Sanskrit, Persian, or English. This is a very productive process of coining new verbs and is one of the important areal features of South Asian languages (Masica, 1976).

Consider now some further examples of complex verb formation in Hindi:

(31)

Preverbal element	*Verb*	*Complex verb*
kaam 'work'	*karnaa* 'to do'	*kaam karnaa* 'to work'
apnaa 'self' (reflexive pro.)	*karnaa* 'to do'	*apnaa karnaa* 'to make one's own/adopt'
acchaa 'good'	*honaa* 'to be'	*acchaa honaa* 'to recover'

The general distributional constraint on language mixing in complex verbs is as follows: mixing is permitted only in the preverbal position and is blocked in the verb position.

(32)	*Preverbal element*	*Verb*	*Complex verb*
	try [English]	*karnaa* 'to do' [Hindi]	try *karnaa* 'to try'
	try [English]	do/be [English]	*try do/try be 'to try'
	koshish [Hindi]	*karnaa* [Hindi]	*koshish karnaa* 'to try'
	koshish	do [English]	**koshish* do 'try'

In addition to simple pre-verbs, one can generate complex verbs, such as *attention pay karnaa* 'to pay attention,' *exam pass karnaa* 'to pass an exam' by adding Hindi verb *karnaa* to English phrases such as *pay attention, pass exam*. The new verbs cannot be treated as instances of the borrowing of frozen constructions because they are adapted to the structure of the Hindi language. Note the word order changes that occur in the English phrase before it becomes the part of the Hindi verbal system. If English word order is maintained the resultant verb phrases *pay attention karnaa* and *pass exam karnaa* will yield ill-formed output (for more details, see Romaine, 1989, pp. 120–123).

The overall syntactic frame of the Hindi complex verb can be summarized below:

(33)	*Noun*	*Preverbal element*	*+Verb*
	NP [English/Hindi]	N, Adj [English/Hindi]	+*karnaa/honaa/lenaa/ denaa* [Hindi]
		verb [English]/[*Hindi]	*to do/to be/etc. [English]
		pronoun [Hindi]/*[English]	

Returning to the Government Constraint, Di Sciullo et al. (1986, p. 18) considered these complex verbs found in Hindi and many South Asian languages as evidence of an "interesting confirmation" of their position. Consider the following Hindi examples presented by Di Sciullo et al. (1986, p. 18) with their proposed structure (Di Sciullo et al., 1986, p. 12) added:

(34) English–*Hindi*
mãĩ [VP[V'   *yah* [V' [X prove] [V *kar*]]*saktaa*] *hũũ*.
                                *$\varnothing$
      I   this   prove   do   can   am
      'I can prove this.'

In Di Sciullo et al.'s view, then, the complex verb *prove kar* constitutes a "small V" with the Hindi verb *kar* as head and *prove* as a complement of indeterminate category. First, although Di Sciullo et al. claimed that "the English verb is nativized (though, not in the phonological sense) by the addition of the Hindi dummy verb *karnaa* 'to do'," (p. 18), in this structure the Hindi verb *kar* governs the English form *prove* (under their definition of Government—[27a]) so that this sentence constitutes a counterexample to the Government Constraint, whatever Di

Sciullo et al. may intend by the term *nativization* in this context. We return to the complex verb construction below in relation to our discussion of a more recent proposal—the FHC—which, along with certain assumptions regarding the insertion of dummy elements and economy of derivation, provides an insightful explanation of the properties of conjunct verbs in general.

Considering Di Sciullo et al.'s discussion of complex verbs in Hindi further, suppose, in the spirit of their proposal regarding these verbal structures, that we assume a notion of "nativization" under which an English verb may be nativized in Hindi by the addition of an appropriate form of the Hindi verbal element *karnaa* and, in addition, that it follows from this notion of nativization that a nativized verb will take on all of the syntactic properties of its translational equivalent in Hindi. We will argue below in our discussion of (36) that mixed English-, Persian-, or Sanskrit–Hindi complex verbs in general (and the mixed English–Hindi conjunct verb *try karnaa* 'to try' in particular) differ from their unmixed Hindi translational equivalents (in this case *koshish karnaa* 'to try') with respect to the types of object complements they take, and thus constitute counterexamples to such a notion of nativization. So even if one accepts the nativization argument at face value, the verb *try karnaa* 'to try' will be nativized with respect to word order and agreement but it will not be nativized in terms of subcategorization.

The FHC

To remedy the inadequacy of the Government Constraint and other constraints such as the FMC, Belazi et al. (1994) proposed the FHC, as stated below:

(35) The language feature of the complement f-selected by a functional head, like all other relevant features, must match the corresponding feature of that functional head.

Based on X-bar syntax, the FHC is grounded in the system of syntactic categories of Chomsky (1986) as modified by Abney (1987) to distinguish between categories that are functional: [+F], including complement, I(nflection), D(eterminer), K(=case), and Deg(ree) and, under more recent proposals, Agr(reement), Neg(ative), Modal, and Num(ber) (see Ritter, 1991, for the technical details on Num) and those that are thematic ([−F], including N, V, A, P(reposition), Adv, Q(uantifier). Abney argues for a special relation between a functional head and its complement—f-selection—parallel with selection in the case of a relationship between a thematic head and its complement—more specifically, a head and the head of its complement. F-selection then dictates that certain features of a functional head and the corresponding features of its complement must match (e.g., the finiteness of a C^0 and the I^0 of its complement IP. The FHC extends the scope of f-selection to language indexing, that is, the language feature of a functional head must match the language feature of its complement in the same way a functional head must match other features of its complement. Constraints on language switching are thus understood to be local and hierarchical, limited to heads and their complements (or internal domains)—more specifically to a head and the head of its complement. This view comports well with Chomsky's (1993) Minimalist Program, which placed severe restrictions on the range of possible syntactic relations, one of which is that of selection or head–head. By extending the scope of the relationship between a functional head and its complement to include language switching, the FHC attempts to explain CM as one consequence of a more general, independently motivated relationship; hence, this proposal is explanatory in a sense that earlier, more descriptive formulations are not.

Now let us examine the claims of the FHC in the context of the Hindi complex verbal phenomenon. Because the verbal element has to be from Hindi, it will predict that the Hindi verb has to be the functional head. Because the complement (the preverbal element) of the functional head has to be in the same language as the language of the functional head, that will be very restrictive on one hand and will make wrong claims on the other. If it is argued that the preverbal element represents lexical head, that means mixing between at the preverbal site should be free. However, this is not the case. Hence, the FHC will either overgenerate or will be too restrictive for Hindi complex verbs.

Furthermore, the NP complement of the VP is subject to the selectional restriction of the language of the preverbal element. Consider the following data.

(36)   *Hindi*–English
    a. *khaanaa*/food   try *kiijiye.*
       food   try do—imp.
       'Please try (the) food.'
    b. *khaanaa/food   *koshish*   *kiijiye.*
       food   try   do—imp.
       'Please try (the) food.'

The English-based complex verb *try karnaa* 'to try' show similar behavior with the Hindi-based complex verb *koshish karnaa* 'to try' in this selection of the infinitival complement. However, the former can select a nominal NP either from Hindi or English as is evident from the grammaticality of (36a), but the latter verb (i.e., the Hindi-based complex verb, *koshish karnaa* 'to try') cannot take the nominal complement that explains the ill-formedness of (36b).

The FHC can account for a number of cases where CM is claimed not to be permissible by the Government Constraint but is nonetheless well formed. For example, according to Belazi et al., in both production and judgment data collected from educated Tunisian Arabic–French and Spanish–English bilinguals, no instances were found where a C^0 was not in the language of its complement (Kachru, 1978, and Di Sciullo et al., 1986, notwithstanding—see above). In fact, they showed that in production such bilinguals avoided (by restarts) those instances in which the language of the complement clause turned out to be different from the language of C^0. The Government Constraint fails to account for the following sentences fromtheir *Spanish*–English data where the complementizer is in the language of the complement clause and not in the language of the verb that governs it.

(37) a. (Belazi et al.'s [10a])
The professor [VP   said [CP *que* [IP *el estudiante había recibido una A*]]].
The professor   said   that   the student   had   received an A
'The professor said that the student had received an A.'
b. (Belazi et al.'s [10c])
*The professor [VP said [CP that [IP *el estudiante había recibido una A*]]].
the professor   said   that   the student   had   received an A
'The professor said that the student had received an A.'

The FHC will predict (correctly, given Belazi et al.'s data) the grammaticality of (37a) and the ungrammaticality of (37b) because it prohibits mixing between the functional head C^0 and its complement IP. Similarly, it rules out mixing between Det (D^0) and N, as in

(38) English–*Spanish*
*He is a *demonio*.
'He is a devil.'

Belazi et al. (1994) note that Ritter (1991), Pollock (1989), and Rivero (1994) have identified Num (quantifiers, numbers), Neg, and Modals, respectively as functional heads. They predict that the complements of these functional heads will not serve as sites for mixing. Their predictions are borne out by the following data:

(39) French–*Arabic*
a. *ktib*   dix   livres
wrote-he ten   books
'He wrote ten books.'
b. **ktib*   *ʕasra* livres
wrote-he ten   books
'He wrote ten books.'
(40) French–*Arabic*
a. *Je   ne   *hib-ha* pas.
I   neg.   like-it   neg
'I don't like it.'
b. **Ana ma*   l'aime-s
I   neg.   like-it   neg
'I don't like it.'
(41) French–*Arabic*
a. *Je serai   *sae:fir-t fi-l-ʕasra*.
I   will-be   went-I   at-the-ten
'I will have gone by ten o'clock.'

   b. *N-ku:n   parti à dix heures.
       I-will-be gone at ten hours
       'I will have gone by ten o'clock.'

Example (39b) is ungrammatical because the Num and its C NP are from two
different languages, whereas (39a) is grammatical because the language both of
the Num and of its complement NP is French. Sentences (40a–b) and (41a–b) are
ill formed because mixing is not permitted between Neg and its complement VP
and between modal auxiliary and VP, respectively. The FHC can thus also provide
a principled explanation of several independent constraints posited earlier (nu-
meral constraint, complement constraint, etc.).

   In contrast to the restriction against mixing between the functional head and its
complement, the mixing between a lexical head and its complement occurs quite
freely. The Government Constraint, which blocks mixing between a V and its
complement and between a pre- and postposition and its complement NP, is permitted by the FHC, and Belazi et al.'s data support this prediction as well.

   In addition, the FHC is the basis for an insightful account of the syntax of the
complex verb constructions in South Asian languages referred to by Di Sciullo
et al. (1986) as the "nativization" of verbs as discussed above. Consider the two
sets of examples below.

(42)   Hindi–English
   a. mãĩ   yah dikhaa saktaa hũũ.
       I   this show can   am
       'I can show (prove) this.'
   b. *mãĩ yah prove   saktaa hũũ   (Di Sciullo et al., 1986)
(43)   Hindi–English
   a. *mãĩ yah dikhaa kar saktaa hũũ.
       I   this show do can   am
       'I can show (prove) this.'
   b. mãĩ yah prove   kar saktaa hũũ.   (Di Sciullo et al., 1986)

In each of these four examples the (functional) modal element saktaa f-selects the
position immediately preceding it which, by the FHC, must therefore be in the
same language as saktaa. This prediction is borne out as shown by the grammaticality of (42a) and the ungrammaticality of (42b). Hindi includes a rule that inserts
kar (which is not a functional head) in derivations that contain such verbs (as in
[42b]), so that the FHC is circumvented, hence allowing such sentences to surface.
In accordance with the notions of economy of derivation and representation discussed in Chomsky (1993), this rule does not apply when the verb is in the language of the f-selecting element, hence the ungrammaticality of (43a).

   This case is typical of a wide range of other instances of f-selected mixed verbs in
Hindi–English sentences as well as those in many other language-mixing combinations including the following (matrix language given first): Punjabi–English

(Romaine, 1989), Tamil–English (Annamalai, 1978), Spanish–English (Pfaff, 1976), Philippine Creole Spanish–Tagalog/English (Molony, 1977), Japanese–English (Stanlaw, 1982), Turkish–Dutch (Boeschoten & Verhoeven, 1985), Warlpiri–English (Bavin & Shopen, 1985), and Navajo–English (Canfield, 1980). (See Bhatia & Ritchie, in press, for details.)

Although the FHC is quite successful in accounting for a wide range of data on language mixing, it does face some challenges on universal and cross-linguistic grounds.

Myers-Scotton's Matrix Language-Frame Model

In a recently published work, Myers-Scotton (1993) proposed a comprehensive hypothesis about CM. Unlike the proposals considered to this point in the discussion of constraints on CM (which are grounded in the theory of linguistic competence or knowledge), Myers-Scotton's Matrix Language-Frame (MLF) model is based on some results in research on linguistic performance—in particular, research on sentence production. As such it merits acknowledgment as an effort to go beyond description to provide a genuine explanation of the phenomena of CM within an independently motivated account of linguistic performance (for other work in the same vein, see de Bot, 1992, and Azuma, 1993).

Myers-Scotton presupposes a three-way distinction among constituents in code-mixed utterances: (1) Matrix Language (ML) Islands—constituents made up only of morphemes from the matrix language, (2) Embedded Language (EL) Islands—constituents made up only of EL morphemes, and (3) ML + EL constituents, which are mixed. Her model also presupposes the distinction between system morphemes and content morphemes. The former include quantifiers, specifiers, and inflectional morphology; prototypical content morphemes are verbs, nouns, prepositions, and descriptive adjectives.

The MLF model consists of four major hypotheses. First, the ML Hypothesis (44a) is concerned with the form of ML + EL constituents. The MLH has two general test implications—the Morpheme–Order Principle and the System Morpheme Principle as stated in (44b) and (44c), respectively.

(44) a. *The MLH*
        As an early step in constructing ML + EL constituents, the ML provides the morphosyntactic frame of ML + EL constituents. (Myers-Scotton, 1993, p. 82)
      b. *The Morpheme-Order Principle* (MOP)
        Morpheme order [in ML + EL constituents] must not violate ML morpheme order. (Myers-Scotton, 1993, p. 7)
      c. *The System Morpheme Principle* (SMP)
        All syntactically relevant system morphemes must come from the ML. (Myers-Scotton, 1993, p. 7)

In support of the MOP and SMP, Myers-Scotton provides production data from a wide variety of CM language combinations in the form of both occurrence of utterances that comply with these principles and nonoccurrence of utterances that violate them.

Myers-Scotton offers three additional hypotheses, one (the Blocking Hypothesis) is designed to strengthen the SMP and the other two (the EL Island Trigger Hypothesis and the EL Implicational Hierarchy Hypothesis) to account for the occurrence of EL islands. Statements of these hypotheses are given in (45), (46), and (47), respectively.

(45)   *The Blocking Hypothesis*
       "In ML + EL constituents, a blocking filter blocks any EL content morpheme which is not congruent with the ML with respect to three levels of abstraction regarding subcategorization" (Myers-Scotton, 1993, p. 120).

(46)   *The EL Island Trigger Hypothesis*
       "Whenever an EL morpheme appears which is not permitted under either the ML Hypothesis or the Blocking Hypothesis, the constituent containing it must be completed as an obligatory EL island" (Myers-Scotton, 1993, p. 7).

(47)   *The EL Implicational Hierarchy Hypothesis*
       "Optional EL Islands occur; generally they are only those constituents which are either formulaic or idiomatic or peripheral to the main grammatical arguments of the sentence" (Myers-Scotton, 1993, p. 7).

With respect to the Blocking Hypothesis, an EL content morpheme is not congruent with the ML when (1) it represents a given grammatical category that is realized by a system morpheme in the ML; (2) it differs from an ML content morpheme counterpart in terms of thematic role assignment; or (3) it differs from its ML counterpart with respect to discourse or pragmatic functions.

A thorough discussion of the rich and far-reaching implications of Myers-Scotton's Model is far beyond the scope of this chapter. Nonetheless, Myers-Scotton's major proposal—that the phenomena of CM are to be explained in terms of a model of linguistic production—is of particular interest, and we turn to that claim now.

The MLF model is grounded in a model of speech production in which the calculation of the morphological-syntactic "frame" of a sentence (including Myers-Scotton's system morphemes and word-order restrictions) is distinct from that of lexical retrieval (see Garrett, 1988, 1990; Levelt, 1989, for reviews). The ML Hypothesis, then, claims that it is the grammar of the ML that functions in the calculation of the frame for an utterance. The EL then may or may not contribute to lexical retrieval; if it does, the result is a code-mixed utterance.

Setting aside the question of the detailed justification of the MLH, we consider the question of whether this hypothesis (or any hypothesis based on a production model) is sufficient as an explanation of CM. If there is one class of CM phenomena that can be shown to receive an explanation in terms of independently justified constraints on the structural descriptions available to the language user (that is, in terms of constraints on competence) but defies explanation in terms of an independently justified account of sentence production, then the sufficiency of a production model is disconfirmed. The analysis of code-mixed verbs in Hindi given above involving the FHC and the rule of "*kar*-insertion" ('do' insertion) appears to constitute a relevant case. Because the FHC and the possibility of the rules like *kar*-insertion are both well grounded in the theory of grammatical competence, the sufficiency of the MLH can be established only by the discovery of a superior explanation of these phenomena in terms of an independently motivated theory of sentence production. Though this is surely not impossible, it seems unlikely.

V. SEMANTICS OF CS AND CM

The semantics of CM is one of the more neglected areas of CM research. (Pfaff (1976, pp. 254–255) reported that there exists a verb construction similar to the Hindi complex verb construction in Californian Spanish. In this construction, the verb *hacer* 'to do' is followed by an English infinitive construction as in (48).

(48)   *Spanish*–English
       su hija   hace   teach *alla en* San Jose
       his daughter do-3rd Sg Pres teach there in San Jose
       'His daughter teaches there in San Jose.'

This construction can be used with the English verb + particle (e.g., *beat up*) construction as well as simple verbs. Pfaff claims that there is no parallel structure of this type either in Spanish or in English. This suggests that CM is setting the stage for semantic restructuring. The following discussion will further clarify the point that we are making here.

Romaine (1989, p. 143) claimed in her examination of the English-based Punjabi complex verb phenomenon that one can find evidence of 'covert semantic restructuring.' Observe the case of causatives in Hindi. Hindi and other South Asian causatives are derived by the morphological process of suffixation. By adding the suffixes *-aa-* and *-waa-*, the first and the second causative verbs are formed as in: *paR* 'to study/read,' *paRaa* 'to teach it' (lit. 'cause to study') and *paRwaa* 'cause x to cause y to study/read'. We claim that mixing with English has resulted in the introduction of a new class of transitive and causative verbs of a mixed type (i.e. *study karnaa* 'to research (on a topic),' *teach karnaa* 'to teach,' *study karwaanaa* 'to guide research,' *teach karwaanaa* 'to guide teaching.' The verb *study* *karnaa* 'to research' is not just a paraphrase or translational equivalent of Hindi *paR* 'to study/read'; the English-based verb expresses the meaning 'to research or study a topic from the viewpoint of research' and the causative counterparts (i.e., *study karwaanaa* 'to guide research' and, *teach karwaanaa* 'to guide teach' highlight the 'facilitative'—help the causee to do a particular act), while the Hindi causative mark 'compulsive' meanings.

Let us consider some other examples of semantic restructuring. Hindi has two expressions with the meaning 'to travel': *yatraa karnaa* and *safar karnaa*. The former is Sanskrit-based and the latter is Persian-based. The former connotes leisurely travel with religious overtones, whereas the latter marks any ordinary travel. The English-based *tour karnaa* has added yet a new semantic dimension, which expresses the concept of business travel, which is contrary to what the verb *tour* conveys in English.

Semantic restructuring of this sort has syntactic consequences that are often overlooked in the literature on CM. Consider, for example the case of the complex verbs, *koshish karnaa,* and *try karnaa* 'to try,' which differ from each other in terms of subcategorization restrictions. The former does not take an NP complement, whereas the latter (i.e., the English-based complex verb) can take such a complement NP (see [36]). That leads us to conclude that in fact the complex verb *try karnaa* 'to try' is semantically ambiguous (i.e., expresses the meaning of 'to taste' as well as 'to attempt'). The Hindi equivalent, *koshish karnaa* 'to try,' expresses the latter meaning and not the former.

The example of the complex verbs meaning 'to try' indicates that any attempt to capture constraints on code-mixing without paying satisfactory attention to semantics is likely to land researchers in the confusion land of the complex phenomena of CM. Consider the following example. Hindi can derive a complex verb by employing an adjective as a preverbal element (i.e., from the Hindi adjective, *acchaa* 'good,' one can derive the complex verb, *acchaa karnaa* 'to make someone healthy/recover'). On the other hand, direct substitution of the English adjective in this construction is ill formed: **good karnaa*. This result may lead one to the conclusion that English cannot participate in adjective-based complex verb constructions in Hindi. However, such a conclusion fails to take semantic considerations into account. The semantic requirement of the Hindi complex verb is not met by the positive adjective in English but by its comparative degree counterpart (i.e., *better*). Thus, the gap represented by the ill-formedness of **good karnaa* 'to make someone healthy' can be better explained on semantic than on syntactic grounds. The failure to look into semantic considerations has contributed to some extent, in our view, to the problem of positing constraints on CM. Therefore, on methodological grounds, we propose the following principle:

(49) Semantic Congruence Principle
      Despite being disparate on lexical grounds (e.g., not a direct translational equivalent or membership in a different lexical category), a constituent can

be a candidate for mixing provided it meets the semantic equivalence requirements of the element it replaces in the sentence.

VI. SOCIOPSYCHOLOGICAL, LINGUISTIC AND PRAGMATIC MOTIVATIONS FOR CM AND CS

The search for new approaches to CM and CS continues in the 1990s. Although Treffers-Daller (1991, p. 249) argued in favor of "a division of labor between grammatical and sociolinguistic constraints on" CM, Bentahila and Davies (1992) drew attention to the neglect of social and psychological factors that prompt CM among bilinguals in the first place. In the view of the latter researchers, such neglect is in part responsible for the failure in the search for universal constraints on CM. The challenge that research on the topic has to meet in the 1990s is to separate systematic limitations on CM that are prompted by syntactic and morphological constraints from those that are motivated or triggered by nonlinguistic factors, such as social and psychological motivations for CM and CS, and then develop a unified and integrated approach. This will in turn provide researchers with a holistic view of the what, how, and why aspects of CM.

Gumperz (1982) and others provided a functional typology of CM and CS by identifying the following functions of mixing on a cross-linguistic basis.

A. Linguistic and Pragmatic Functions

Quotations

Direct quotation or reported speech trigger CS or CM among bilinguals cross-linguistically. This function has been attested by a wide variety of empirical studies. The following examples illustrate this function.

(50) *Spanish*–English (Gumperz, 1982, p. 76)
From a conversation between two Chicano professionals. While referring to her baby-sitter, the speaker says the following:
She doesn't speak English, so, *dice que la reganan: "Si se les va olvidar el idioma a las criaturas."*
'She does not speak English. So, she says they would scold her: "The children are surely going to forget their language.'

Addressee Specification

Another function of mixing or switching is to direct the message to one of the several possible addressees. Consider the following interaction in a typical multilingual, educated Kashmiri family:

(51)   English–*Kashmiri*–**Hindi** (Kachru, 1990, p. 63)
       A: Hello, how are you kaul Sahib?
       B: *vaaray mahraj*
           'Well, sir.'
       A: *valiv bihiv*
           'Come in, sit down.'
       B: [to the servant] **zaraa caay laanaa bhaaii.** [to the visitor] I will be back
           in a minute.
           'Bring some tea, brother [mode of address]. I will be back in a minute.'

In the above discourse, three languages—Kashmiri, Hindi, and English have been
switched. The greetings are exchanged in Kashmiri. The visitor is addressed either
in Kashmiri or in English. The use of the Hindi language is specific to the servant.

Consider the exchange among four graduate students in Singapore given in
(52). The background of the participants is as follows: A is a computer science
graduate who has just found a job and a speaker of Teochew, one of the seven
mutually unintelligible "dialects" of Chinese spoken in Singapore; B is an accountancy graduate, is looking for a job and speaks Hokkien, another of the Chinese varieties of Singapore; and D is an arts graduate and speaks Teochew and
Hokkien. Also present but not included at this point in the conversation is C, an
accountancy graduate, who has been working for a week and speaks Cantonese,
another of the varieties of Chinese spoken in Singapore. All four participants
speak English in addition to one or more varieties of Chinese. Now observe the
following piece of conversation among them.

(52)   English–*Hokkien*–**Teochew** (Tay, 1989, p. 416)
       D to B: Everyday, you know *kào taim*
                'Everyday, you know at nine o'clock'
       D to A: **lì khi á**
                'You go.'

In the above conversation, D addresses B in Hokkien but speaks to A in Teochew.

Interjections

Another function of language mixing or switching is to mark an interjection or
sentence filler. Bilinguals in Singapore are well known to exploit this function by
mixing a number of particles, as in (53). Interlocutors, A, C, and D are as described for (52) above.

(53)   English–*Hokkien* (Tay, 1989, p. 416)
       D: Do what?
       A: System analyst *la*
           'System analyst, what else?'
       C: *hà*
           'Is that so?'
       A: Programmer *la*.

Reiteration

Reiteration or paraphrasing marks another function of mixing. The message expressed in one language is either repeated in the other language literally or with some modification to signify emphasis or clarification. The following examples illustrate the emphatic and clarificatory role of mixing, respectively.

(54)   English–*Spanish*: Chicano professionals (Gumperz, 1982, p. 78)
    A: The three old ones spoke nothing but Spanish. *No hablaban ingles.*
      'The three old ones spoke nothing but Spanish. They did not speak English.'
(55)   English–*Hindi*: Father calling his small son while walking through a train compartment. (Gumperz, 1982, p. 78)
    Father: Keep straight. [louder] *siidhe jaao.*
      'Keep straight. Go straight.'

Message Qualification

Frequently, mixing takes the form of qualifying a complement or argument as exemplified by the disjunctive argument and the adverbial phrase in the following sentences, respectively.

(56)   Slovenian–*German* (Gumperz, 1982, p. 60)
    Uzeymas ti kafe? *Oder te?*
    'Will you take coffee? or tea?'
(57)   *Hindi*–English (Gumperz, 1982, p. 79)
    A: *binaa* wait *kiye aap aa gaye.*
      'Without waiting you came?'
    B: *nahīī,* I came to the bus stop *nau biis pacciis par.*
      'No, I came to the bus stop at about nine twenty five.'

The five functions described above primarily perform what might be characterized as 'Pragmatic' or 'Stylistic' functions. To this list one can add other functions of a linguistic nature such as contrast.

Topic-Comment and Relative Clauses

Related with the function of message qualification is yet another function—the Topic-Comment function. Nishimura's study (1989) devoted to Japanese–English CM revealed that the topic is introduced in Japanese (formally marked with *wa*) and the comment is used in English, as shown in the following example:

(58)   *Japanese*–English (Nishimura, 1989, p. 370)
    kore wa   she is at home
    this   topic
    'As for this (daughter; referring to a photograph of her daughter), she is at home.'

A similar situation can be witnessed with respect to English–Hindi relative clauses. Hindi has three different types of relative clauses (see Bhatia, 1974; Lust, Bhatia, Gair, Sharma, & Khare, 1988). The English relativized head NP can be mixed with Hindi as in (59).

(59)   English–*Hindi*
       The boy who is going *meraa dost   hai.*
                            my   friend is
       'The boy who is going is my friend.'

In CM English–Hindi, the English sequence *the boy* is understood to be a topicalized NP with two associated Comments—the English 'who is going' and the Hindi *meraa dost hai.*

Other linguistic factors such as the language of the preceding or following code trigger mixing. (See Clyne, 1980, and the section on Repair Strategies below for further details.) Some social routines such as greetings and thanking also trigger CS or CM. For instance, two Spanish speakers may carry out an exchange only in Spanish and, at the end, one speaker thanks the other in English. The response of the second speaker will be in English.

B. Nonlinguistic (Sociopsychological) Functions

Turning now to some nonlinguistic (i.e., sociopsychological) functions, the following two functions have been widely attested in the linguistic literature.

Personalization versus Objectivization

This distinction, according to Gumperz, suggests the degree of speaker involvement or distance from a message, whether the statement reflects personal opinion or knowledge or echoes an authoritative source. Observe the following exchange in an Austrian village setting. The discussion concerns the origin of a certain type of wheat. The participant A makes a statement in Slovenian and B disputes A's statement. In this situation A responds in German in order to give authority to his position.

(60)   Slovenian-*German* (Gumperz, 1982, p. 80)
       A: vigǝlǝ ma yǝ sa amricɔ.
          'Wigele got them from America.'
       B: kanada pridǝ.
             'It comes from Canada.'
       A: *kanada mus i sɔgn nit.*
          'I would not say Canada.'

Similarly, in (61) the speaker's personal involvement and the statement of objective fact is the underlying reason for switching between English and Hindi in the speech of participant B. Both participants are young men.

(61)   *Hindi*–English (Gumperz, 1982, p. 80)
    A: *vaishna aaii?*
       'Did Vaishna come?'
    B: She was supposed to see me at nine-thirty at Karol Bagh.
    A: Karol Bagh?
    B: *aur mãi nau baje ghar se niklaa.*
       'And, I left the house at nine.'

The failure to respond to a question in Hindi on the part of B is motivated by the fact that in a society where socialization between the sexes is not as free as it is in the West, a Hindi response from the participant B to A's initial question would run the risk of indicating personal involvement with Vaishna (the name of a girl). The reply in English indicates personal distance and reports the appointment as an objective fact. However, because the last statement does not focus on Vaishna, the speaker switches to Hindi in order to highlight his personal involvement and implying that he is willing to take the blame for not leaving his house sufficiently early to keep his appointment with Vaishna.

'We' versus 'They' Code

Related with the Personalization versus Objectivization function described above, is another function: Solidarity (use of the 'we' code) versus power (use of the 'they' code). When the solidarity versus power (intimacy versus distancing) function interacts with functions such as that of addressee specification, it can result in negative consequences as shown by the example (8), repeated below as (62) for convenience, in which four young office workers in the same government ministry in Nairobi are chatting.

(62)   Kikuyu–*Swahili*–**English** (Myers-Scotton, 1989, p. 338)
    Kikuyu II: Andu amwe nimendaga kwaria maundu maria matari na ma
            namo.
            'Some people like talking about what they're not sure of.'
    Kikuyu I: Wira wa muigi wa kigina ni kuiga mbeca. No tigucaria mbeca.
            'The work of the treasurer is only to keep money, not to hunt
            for money.'
    Kisii: *Ubaya wenu ya kikuyu ni ku-***assume** *kila mtu anaelewa kikuyu.*
            'The bad thing about Kikuyus is assuming that everyone under-
            stands Kikuyu.'
    Kalenjin: *Si mtumie lugha ambayo kila mtu hapa atasikia?* **We are sup-**
            posed to solve this issue.
            'Shouldn't we use the language which everyone here under-
            stands.' (said with some force): We are supposed to solve this
            issue.'

Two are Kikuyu, one is Kisii, and one is a Kalenjin. Swahili–English has been the unmarked choice up to the switch to Kikuyu. The conversation about setting up a group emergency fund has been proceeding, when Kikuyus switch to Kikuyu to make a negative comment on what has been said, a marked choice communicating solidarity between the two Kikuyus, but distancing them from the others. At this point, the Kisii complains in Swahili and English and the Kalenjin makes a switch from Swahili to a sentence entirely in English, a marked choice, to return the discussion to a more businesslike plane.

Now, compare this situation with the situation described in exchange (52) involving four graduates in Singapore. In the case of Singapore, although addressee specification in Teochew led to the exclusion of two participants, particularly C who spoke Cantonese and who neither shared nor switched to either Hokkien or Teochew during the entire speech event. Because such an exclusion was underlyingly motivated only by the group addressee specification and not by group solidarity, the excluded participants demonstrated linguistic accommodation on their parts and acted as if they understood everything that had been going on.

Since the "We" code is used for intimacy and the "They" code for distancing, the They code is also seen as a neutral code. In situations dealing with taboo subjects the They code takes precedence over the We code in order to reduce the strength of the taboo effect, as demonstrated by example (61).

Discourse Allocation and Mixing

Mixing or switching is also subject to consideration of the discourse domain (topics, etc.), which is in part responsible for rendering the two functions described above as We versus They and Personalization and Objectivization. In bi- and multilingual societies, languages often do not overlap each other's discourse domain. On the contrary, the pie of discourse domains is cut up by the various languages used in such societies into mutually exclusive pieces. Consequently, some languages are viewed as more suited to particular settings or topics than others. For example, in the Hindi-speaking areas of multilingual India, the discussion of topics pertaining to science and technology invites mixing with English, whereas discussion of topics such as romance call for mixing with Persian. Bhatia (1992, p. 201) showed that within the discourse domain of advertising, language mixing reflects a very complex dynamic. A case in point is the use of multiple mixing (with Hindi, English, Sanskrit, and Persian) in Hindi advertising. Table I summarizes the determinants of language mixing in the advertising discourse.

Language Dominance and Speaker

We should mention in passing that considerations such as a speaker's language proficiency and language dominance also determine the incidence and the nature

TABLE I

Determinants of Language Mixing in Advertising

Language	Audience	Appeal	Value or aim	Product or discourse domain
English	Male or Female	Outworldly (modern, innovative)	Modern, Western, scientific	Fashion, science
Hindi	Female	Emotional	Utility, pragmatic	Domestic
Sanskrit	Male or Female	Deep-rooted cultural	Reliability	Fabrics
Persian	Male	Luxury (royal)	Utility (physical)	Cigarettes, sports, fashion

of CM. For instance, balanced, educated bilinguals tend to code-mix with a prestige language more than balanced but uneducated bilinguals.

Repair Strategies

In the process of integrating the structure of the two (or more) languages, bilinguals embark on some problematic areas that are likely to cause them to fall short of their target. A number of factors contribute to this situation. The 'trigger phenomenon' noted by Clyne (1980), the failure of the Equivalence Constraint, and false starts are such factors. Naturally then, bilinguals have to rely on linguistic-accommodative and repair strategies in order to achieve linguistic integration. The use of Punjabi postpositions rather than English prepositions in examples (15) and (16) and the dropping of or substitution of English articles in example (12) can be viewed as a strategy to repair structural conflict between the language pairs. Omission, insertion, and repetition are other notable repair strategies.

Romaine (1989) gives an example of the omission of the English dummy subject in the mixing between English and Punjabi.

(63)   *Punjabi*-English (Romaine, 1989, p. 127)
        te   depend *kardaa ai.*
        and depend do-pres is (aux)
        '(That) depends.'

English is not a prodrop language, whereas Punjabi is. Although an English sentence requires a dummy subject such as 'it' or 'that' to be grammatical (utterances such as: *and depends/*and depends on,* are ungrammatical in English), the insertion of the English dummy subject will be ungrammatical in Punjabi.

(63a)   *Punjabi*–English (Romaine, 1989, p. 127)
        te it/that depend *kardaa ai.*
        and it/that depend do-pres is (aux)
        '(That) depends.'

Similarly, any attempt to substitute a Punjabi subject for the English dummy subject will alter the meaning of the sentence. Therefore, a Punjabi bilingual drops the subject in sentences such as (63).

Clyne (1987, p. 753) gave an example of subject pronoun insertion in Dutch–English CM, even where it violates a Dutch word order constraint.

(64)   *Dutch*–English (Clyne, 1987, p. 753)
        en   dan je   realize *dat* this *dat farmleven.* . . .
        and then you realize that this that farm-life
        'And then you realize that this, that farm life . . .'

The Dutch word order will permit the placement of the verb before *je*. Also, observe the example of repetitions:

(65) *German*–English (Clyne, 1987, p. 753)
      das ist ein foto, *gemacht   an   de der*   beach.
      that is   a   photo made   on   the the   beach
           can be, *kann* be,   *kann sein* in Mount Martha.
           can be can   be   can to-be in Mount Martha
      'This is a photo taken on the beach. Could be in Mount Martha.'

This multiple repetition of the verb with a modal auxiliary seems to be the result of the trigger phenomenon (triggered by the English word *beach*). The speaker attempts to resolve the problem arising from the triggering of *can be*. Finally, the speaker finds a common ground in colloquial German, which permits the verb after the auxiliary, the rule that also satisfies the word order of English. Standard German requires the sentence to end with the verb, *sein* 'be.'

In short, the determinants of CM and CS are summarized in Table II. In addition, individual and sociolinguistic attitudes also determine the incidence and the nature of CM and CS. The next section will focus on linguistic attitudes and CM.

VII. ATTITUDES TOWARD CM AND CS

The innovative multifunctions performed by CM in bilingual communication will lead one to assume, on a commonsense basis, that CM will be valued and admired immensely both by bilinguals and society. Ironically, just the reverse turns out to be true. CM invites, at least overtly, a near universal negative evaluation. Grosjean (1982, pp. 146–148) provided a cross-linguistic array of negative attitudes toward CM. A cursory examination of such attitudes reveals that CM is considered a linguistic system that lacks 'grammar/rules.' Puritans and self-appointed guardians of language decry CM as a sign of the linguistic death of the two participating languages and call for action to maintain the purity of the linguistic systems in question. The following remarks of Haugen (1969) are instructive in this regard. Commenting on the linguistic behavior or reporting of Norwegian-American prescriptivists, he notes,

> Reports are sometimes heard of individuals who 'speak no language whatever' and confuse the two to such an extent that it is impossible to tell which language they speak. No such cases have occurred in the writer's experience, in spite of the many years of listening to American-Norwegian speech. (Haugen 1969, p. 70)

What is even more remarkable is that with the exception of a handful of linguistically aware bilinguals, the vast majority of bilinguals themselves hold a negative view of code-mixed speech. They consider CM as a sign of laziness, an inadvertent speech act, impurity, linguistic decadence, and potential danger to

TABLE II

Determinants of Code-Mixing and Code-Switching

Linguistic or pragmatic	Speaker	Domain	Socio-psychological (affective features)
Innate or Universal	language proficiency, social roles	Topics, settings, or situations (including formal versus informal)	Addressee specification
Grammar consideration			'We' versus 'They' code
Stylistic (repetition, clarification, contrast, quotation, paraphrase, message qualification)			'personalization' versus 'objectivization'
Topic-comment			'Intimate' versus 'neutral' code
Interjections or fillers			
Language trigger or repair			
Social routines			

their own linguistic performance. Usually, they apologize for their "inappropriate" verbal behavior. Gumperz noted that when bilinguals are made aware of their mixed speech, they blame "the lapse of attention" for their "poor" linguistic performance and promise improvement by eliminating CM. So natural is CM among bilinguals that one witnesses the return of the mixed system either immediately or very shortly after such expressions of guilt. No hesitation or pauses in sentence rhythm or pitch level are witnessed and the speakers maintain an even and fluent mode of communication.

The above discussion provides evidence of a discrepancy between overt (conscious) and covert (unconscious) attitudes toward CM. If Hindi–English bilinguals do not report having positive attitudes towards CM, then how can one explain such speakers' return to CM in spite of the pledge to avoid it altogether? They must find this form of language use appropriate for their communicative needs at the unconscious level; otherwise they would tend to avoid it, as promised. This leads us to postulate four relations that can in turn determine the rate of the incidence and the nature of CM among members of bilingual speech communities. Positive attitude in Table III is indicated by the plus symbol [+], whereas the negative attitude is signified by the minus symbol [−]. As pointed out earlier, differing attitudes toward CM and CS play an important role in the rate of the incidence and the nature of CM in different bilingual communities. For instance, Puerto Rican bilinguals in New York City unconsciously have positive attitudes toward bilingualism and CM, consequently, they tend to code mix and switch 97% of the time and this CM and CS is smooth as observed by Poplack (1985). English–Hindi mixing in India and Punjabi–English mixing in Great Britain follow this pattern. When such mixing becomes the mark of cultural or social identity, the speech community begins to view mixing positively at both the unconscious and the conscious level. This may further promote the incidence of CM and CS both

TABLE III
Attitudes and Code Mixing Continuum

Speech community	Covert attitude (unconscious)	Overt attitude (conscious)	Frequency of mixing
Arabic–French–English (Lebanon)	+	+	very high
Puerto Rican community in NY; Punjabi–English in UK; Hindi–English in India	+	−	high
English–French Ottawa–Hull community	−	+	middle
Flemish–French bilinguals in Brussels	−	−	low

quantitatively and qualitatively. As a case in point, extensive Arabic–French–English CM and CS occurs in Lebanon, where trilingual mixing is viewed as a distinctive feature of Lebanese culture (see Grosjean, 1982, p. 149).

The third type of attitude toward mixing can be exemplified by the Ottawa–Hull speech community (Poplack et al., 1989). In Hull the English–French mixing is one-third to one-fourth as frequent as in Ottawa. The metalinguistic commentary offered by bilinguals and accompanied by flagged mixing provide evidence that bilinguals view mixing covertly in negative terms although consideration of linguistic accommodation at the conscious level leads to flagged mixing (see Poplack et al., 1989).

The last type of bilingual, who considers bilingualism negatively on both conscious and unconscious grounds, is exemplified in the speech patterns of Flemish and French bilinguals in Brussels. Because of the long history of linguistic rivalry and conflict in Belgium, one witnesses Flemish and French trenched in their own language while talking with each other and no attempt is made in favor of CS or CM of the two linguistic systems (see Grosjean, 1982). (Chapter 17 by Romaine, this volume, includes additional discussion of attitudes toward language mixing.)

VIII. POLYGLOT APHASIA AND CM AND CS

Although most bilinguals and bilingual groups have a fairly positive attitude toward CM and CS, either at the conscious or unconscious level, in actual practice such groups constitute a minority view because of the long history of prescriptivism at the global level (see Grosjean, 1989). The negative view of CM and CS is nearly universal. Bilinguals and monolinguals largely fail to appreciate the positive functions of CM and in turn take a puritan view of this linguistic phenomenon. The chunking of linguistic elements from two languages is considered as constituting the disintegration of the participating linguistic systems at both the level of comprehension and production. Therefore, such verbal behavior is seen as evidence of language disturbance even among normal bilinguals. Consequently, it is not surprising that CM among bilingual aphasic patients invites a more rigid and adverse reaction on the part of language therapists and educationists than CM in normal bilinguals. (For a general discussion of the neuropsychology of L2 acquisition and use, see Chapter 15 by Obler and Hannigan.)

Paradis (1977) identified six modes of language recovery among bilingual and multilingual aphasics. Of these six types, the recovery of particular interest for the purpose of this chapter is the 'mixed' recovery in which two or more languages are recovered in some combination. Albert and Obler (1978) claimed that language mixing is found only in 7% of polyglot aphasics most of whom are sensory aphasics. One possibility is that language mixing among aphasics is not rare, but is viewed as "jargon" and therefore has gone unreported. (Perecman, 1989,

p. 241). Our own investigation of the transcripts of the Hindi agrammatic aphasic patient (Bhatnagar, 1990; supplement to Chapter 13) shows a high incidence of overt mixing with English and "spontaneous translation" from English that has gone unobserved in the neurolinguistic literature. In defense of Bhatnagar we hasten to add that mixing was by no means the main objective of his investigation, so our statement should be taken in the spirit of the underreporting of language mixing among polyglot aphasics. In fact, it appears that bilingual polyglot aphasia is extremely complex and multifaceted (see Vaid & Hall, 1991).

An early reference to language mixing disorder was by Bastian (1875), who reports that a German–English bilingual aphasic with a right hemiplegia began to mix English and German in his speech. Since then bilingual aphasics have received considerable attention in the literature. An examination of the aphasic literature reveals many types of possible disorders and symptoms (Table IV) associated with bilingual aphasic patients.

TABLE IV

Disorders and Symptoms in Bilingual Aphasic Patients

Disorder or symptoms	Studies
1. Lexical level mixing from two or more than two languages in the same utterance	Gloning and Gloning (1965, cases 2–4); Herschmann and Poetzl (1920); Kauders (1929); Mosner and Pilsch (1971); Poetzl (1925); Stengel and Zelmanowitz (1933).
2. Morpheme-level mixing	Herschmann and Poetzl (1920); Kauders (1929); Perecman (1980); Schulze (1968); Stengel and Zelmanowitz (1933).
3. Syllable-mixing in a word	Gloning and Gloning (1965, cases 2 and 4); Kauders (1929).
4. Substitution of phonetically similar words from an unsolicited language	Herschmann and Poetzl (1920).
5. Segmental and suprasegmental mixing—imposition of an intonation pattern of one language over the vocabulary of the other.	Stengel and Zelmanowitz (1933).
6. Segmental and syntactic mixing—imposition of a syntactic pattern of one language over the vocabulary of the other.	L'Hermitte, Hécaen, Dubois, Culioli, and Tabouret-Keller (1966).
7. Naming ability impaired: production of the correct name of an object in an unsolicited language even when it is impossible for the same patient to name the object correctly in the solicited language	Gloning and Gloning (1965, case 2); Kauders (1929); L'Hermitte et al. (1966, case 4); Stengel and Zelmanowitz (1933); Weisenberg and McBride (1935, case 4).
8. Language switching: Responding in a language different from the one in which the patient is addressed.	Gloning and Gloning (1965, cases 1–2); Hoff and Poetzl (1932); Kauders (1929); Pick (1909).

Out of the possible set of eight types of symptoms identified in Table IV, only the last two appear to be central to the linguistic deficiency of bilingual aphasics. From the discussion in the earlier sections, it becomes quite clear that the first six types, which are formal in nature, are quite widespread among normal bilinguals. As advances were made in empirical research on language mixing, it quickly became clear that some types of mixing, namely mixing at the syllabic and morphemic levels, which were earlier considered abnormal for the normal bilinguals, turned out to be attested widely cross-linguistically among normal bilinguals. A case in point is the refutation of the FMC. The lesson we learn from this is that mixing-related deficiency symptoms identified by the neurolinguistic research calls for its reexamination in the light of our present understanding of the phenomenon of CM and CS. Likewise, the cross-linguistic findings discussed earlier make it clear that none of the six formal types of mixing reflect any abnormality of verbal behavior, because such mixing is quite prevalent among normal bilinguals.

Perecman (1984) examines the incidence of language mixing in a case of polyglot aphasia. The patient in question, H.B., was an 80-year-old male who was born in Cameroon, West Africa. He learned German as a NL from his parents, French as an L2, and English as a third language when he settled in the United States in 1923 at the age of 18. In 1980, he developed aphasia at the age of 75 as the result of a car accident. (For details concerning the nature of the brain injury, see Perecman, 1984, p. 50.)

Using a microgenetic model of language processing (Brown, 1977, 1979), Perecman identified the following two symptoms of polyglot aphasia. First, according to Perecman, the patient suffered from language mixing, particularly 'utterance level mixing,' which in Perecman's view reflects a linguistic deficit; second, the patient exhibited "spontaneous translation," which indicates a prelinguistic processing deficit. From an examination of the patient's transcript presented by Perecman, it becomes clear that her use of "spontaneous translation" is synonymous with what is termed CS in the linguistic literature in addition to its traditional predominant meaning.

Commenting on the two symptoms, Grosjean (1985) argued that both language mixing and spontaneous translation are also found in normal polyglots, therefore, they should not necessarily be treated as a sign of linguistic deficit (Hyltenstam & Stroud (1989) observed the incidence of CS among bilingual Alzheimer's dementia patients and reached a similar conclusion). In a reply to Grosjean (1985), Perecman (1985, p. 356) corrected her earlier assumption that utterance-level mixing is not seen in normal bilinguals. However, she disputed Grosjean's claim that spontaneous translation is evidence of "a deliberate" communicative strategy (Perecman, 1985, p. 357). Referring to the verbal behavior of the patient H.B., Perecman asked why H.B. would choose to "translate" from German to English (as is evident by the English phrase in (66) below), when addressing a native

German speaker (i.e., the German–English bilingual interviewer). She goes on to claim that such mixing as shown in example (66) is devoid of any communicative content and, on the contrary, is distracting:

(66) H.B.:
> *Verstehen sie Deutsch. Verstehen* do you understand German. *Verstehen*
> understand you German understand do you understand German understand
>
> *sie Deutsch. aber nur ein bisschen.*
> you German but   only a   bit
> 'Do you know German? Do you understand German? But only a little.'

As shown in the section dealing with the sociopsychological function of CM (section VI), it is quite clear that paraphrasing, elaboration, and emphasis do induce CM and CS. Therefore, it is not surprising that the patient employs CM and CS in such a setting, particularly if the patient expects a monolingual interviewer and instead is pleasantly surprised to find a bilingual, and that, too, in a language of his ethnic origin. Furthermore, it is noteworthy that such language mixing is not restricted to the patient. At one point the interviewer uses the same type of mixing as well.

In order to strengthen her claim, Perecman goes on to claim that interactions of the following type are not motivated by any communicative strategy either. On the contrary, it is counterproductive.

(67)   (Perecman, 1984, p. 52; Example 23)
> Interviewer: *wie steht es jetzt/ist es* . . .
> H.B.: *à la/ à la/ à la/* I say/*il est il est un peu/voulez voulez un peu.*

Though the "content" of the patient's utterance is clearly disturbed, the patient's switch to French from the Interviewer's German greeting (apparently counterproductive on the surface) cannot in itself be considered pathological. In our opinion there are at least two possible reasons that might prompt this switch.

First, the switch to French is indicative of the change in the situation. Compare the H.B. and the Kashmiri guest. The guest does not answer the host's English greeting (i.e., 'How are you, Kaul Sahib?') in English; instead, the guest employs Kashmiri in his response.

Second, switches like the one to French are sometimes motivated either by playfulness or other creative desires on the part of the speaker. Whether it was some linguistic deficiency or a creative desire that motivated H.B. to switch to French in the example in question cannot be determined conclusively on the basis of the data and the analysis presented by Perecman.

Other possible interpretation of the data cannot be ruled out either. Therefore, Perecman's argument is not convincing. However, from another set of data dealing with the phenomenon of naming, it seems to us that H.B. had trouble with "naming" in the language requested (see Perecman, 1984). From the above discussion and further evidence from Perecman's work, naming seems to be a symptom of language deficit among bilingual aphasics in general and H.B. in particular. The remaining symptoms identified do not necessarily reflect linguistic deficit.

IX. CM AND CS AND LANGUAGE ACQUISITION

In their attempts to capture universals of language mixing, recent theoretical studies (such as those discussed earlier in section IV) are based on the view that language mixing is constrained by general principles of grammatical competence such as the Government Constraint or the FHC. These constraints are interpreted by their proponents as being subsumed by UG.

Rubin and Toribio (in press) propose that language matching is an instance of Chomsky's (1993) general notion of feature-checking. For instance, in Rubin and Toribio's view, the FHC has a natural place in Chomsky's Minimalist Program because f-selection dictates that functional heads must be matched by the corresponding features of their complements and one such feature to be matched is the feature of language index. Therefore, Rubin and Toribio argued, Abney's (1987) notion of f-selection can easily be expanded to include language matching. The following Spanish–English sentences exemplify the language-matching feature requirement:

(68)   *Spanish*–English
   a.   *Los estudiantes habían resuelto* a major mathematical problem.
        the   students   had   resolved
        'The students have resolved a major mathematical problem.'
   b.   **Los estudiantes habían* resolved a major mathematical problem.
        the   students   had
        'The students have resolved a major mathematical problem.'

Under the FHC, the functional head Aux—realized in these sentences as the perfect auxiliary form *habían* 'had'—carries the language feature value [+Spanish] among other feature values. Since Aux f-selects its complement, the head of its complement (*resuelto* 'resolved') is predicted by the FHC to be [+Spanish] (and only [+Spanish]) as well. As the grammaticality values of (68a) and (68b) indicate, this prediction is borne out.

Because the FHC is viewed as a part of UG, the question arises as to what its role in language acquisition might be. In particular, in view of the centrality of the general question of UG accessibility in adult L2 learners, the question arises whether or not the FHC plays a role in the adult's acquisition of an L2 and of the ability to code-mix between his or her two languages. Toribio and Rubin set out to explore this question by way of testing the following two competing hypotheses:

1. The Null Hypothesis—If the FHC is not accessible to adult L2 learners, their CM and CS behavior will be random with respect to the operation of the FHC.
2. The FHC Availability Hypothesis—If the FHC is available to adult learners as a part of the UG, learners' verbal behavior will be parallel to that of balanced bilinguals.

Using a methodology similar to that employed extensively by Lust and others in the study of L1 acquisition, Toribio, Lantolf, Roebuck, and Perrone (1993) asked beginning, intermediate, and advanced learners of Spanish to imitate Spanish–English code-mixed utterances that were both "legal" and "illegal" with respect to the FHC. Analysis of the results obtained from this elicited imitation task revealed that the beginning students showed a wide range of random processing errors, leading to the conclusion that they had general difficulty with the task. Intermediate learners could repeat well formed as well as ill formed sentences with great fluency, indicating they had not yet acquired the tacit linguistic knowledge to differentiate the sentences that were well formed with respect to the FHC from those that were not. The advanced students either showed symptoms of disfluency or "corrected" the token sentence in their repetitions when the sentence violated the FHC and repeated it without change when it obeyed the FHC. These findings lead Toribio et al. (1993) to suggest that the beginning and intermediate adult learners had not acquired the necessary aspects of the system of the L2 to allow them to separate the ungrammatical code-mixed sentences from the grammatical ones. According to their analysis of the data, the beginning and intermediate students reinterpreted the Spanish segment of the sentence into their L1—English—and therefore judged their grammaticality in terms of English. Their failure to distinguish between grammatical and ungrammatical code-mixed utterances on independent grounds (i.e., a system of knowledge distinct from the L1—that is, UG) points to the fact that these subjects did not show the effects of UG. However, the advanced subjects showed the emergence of the universal principle to some degree, the FHC.

A pilot study conducted by the present authors also supports Toribio et al.'s view that the principles of UG are accessible to adult learners. Four unmixed grammatical Hindi sentences plus 10 grammatical and 14 ungrammatical English–Hindi code-mixed sentences were given to six intermediate and four advanced adult English learners of Hindi. They were asked to give grammaticality judgments on the sentences. The ungrammatical sentences violated the dependency between C^0 and IP, between Agr^0 and VP, between Agr^0 and Neg, between D^0 and NP, and between Q^0 and NP in English–Hindi code-mixing. In addition, sentences with mixed complex verbs (with *karnaa* 'to do'—see section IV) were also given.

Our results reveal that some intermediate learners clearly showed a tendency for translation and structural reinterpretation. Mixed sentences of the following type were judged grammatical by four (two-thirds) of the intermediate learners,

(69)   *Hindi*–English
        *us ne   book him *dii.*
        he   erg. book him gave
        'He gave him a book.'

Two, (one-third) of the intermediate subjects judged the violation between the
functional head Agr^0 and Neg^0 in (70) as correct.

(70)   *Hindi*–English
        *ve books to buy not *caahte.*
        they books to buy neg want
        'They do not want to buy books.'

Apparently, the subjects who judged the above two sentences as correct, reinterpreted the sentences taking the following steps: (1) the sentences yield well-
formed interpretive meaning in English; (2) the chunking of phrases such as the
infinitive phrase conforms to the structural rules of English; and (3) the placement
of the syntactic English chunks conforms to the Hindi SOV word order.

The responses of the four advanced subjects, who correctly judged sentences
such as (70) as ill formed, indicate that the FHC is accessible to them. This claim
is further strengthened by the fact that none of the advanced students judged sentences permitting mixing between the functional head Agr^0 and Neg^0 as well
formed. Two-thirds of the intermediate students exhibited the same pattern.

In order to test further whether the FHC or the Government Constraint is part
of the grammatical knowledge of the code-mixers, the following six types of complement clauses with Hindi–English *that* complementizer were presented to the
subjects.

1. Hindi matrix verb with English complementizer *that* and English complement clause (in accordance with the FHC and in violation of the Government
Constraint).

(71)   *us ne*   [*kahaa* [that [he will go there]]].
        he agent said
        'He said that he will go there.'

2. Hindi matrix verb, Hindi complementizer *ki* 'that' and English complement
clause (in accordance with the Government Constraint and in violation of the
FHC).

(72)   *us ne*   [*kahaa* [*ki* [he will go there]]].
        he agent said   that
        'He said that he will go there.'

3. Hindi matrix verb, English complementizer *that,* and Hindi complement
clause (in violation of both the Government Constraint and the FHC).

(73) *us ne*   [*kahaa* [that [*vo vahāā jaay-egaa*]]].
      he agent said   that he there go-will
      'He said that he will go there.'

   4. English matrix verb, Hindi complementizer *ki,* and Hindi complement clause (in accordance with the FHC and in violation of the Government Constraint).

(74) he [said [*ki* [*vo vahāā jaay-egaa.*]]]
                  that he there go-will
      'He said that he will go there.'

   5. English matrix verb, English complementizer *that,* and Hindi complement clause (in accordance with the Government Constraint and in violation of the FHC).

(75) he [said [that [*vo vahāā jaay-egaa*]]].
                    he there go-will
      'He said that he will go there.'

   6. English matrix verb, Hindi complementizer *ki,* and English complement clause (in violation of both the Government Constraint and the FHC).

(76) he [said [*ki* [he will go there.]]]
                 that
      'He said that he will go there.'

No intermediate or advanced student judged the structures (3; example 73) and (6; example 76) as well formed. Nor did any intermediate or advanced learner rate structures (2; example 72) and (5; example 75) as incorrect, therefore indicating a strong preference for the Government Constraint over the FHC. As regards structures following the FHC (i.e., example [71] and 4; example [74]), they were judged by four of the intermediate subjects as well formed; the remaining two judged them ill formed. There was a split among advanced students on the acceptability of such structures. The results from one of the advanced students practically spelled out the Government Constraint, thus, emphatically rejecting the FHC. From the above discussion it becomes clear that the principles of UG either in the form of the Government Constraint or in that of the FHC are accessible to intermediate and advanced English-speaking learners of Hindi.

   The fact that adult learners do not treat all functional heads uniformly—some functional heads such as Agr, Num (quantifiers, numbers), and Modals do not permit switching between the functional head and its complement, whereas C^0 does permit switching between it and its complement clause—can also be witnessed in the verbal behavior of Hindi–English balanced bilinguals. A case in point is the data dealing with the *that* complementizer supporting either the Government Constraint or the FHC, thus providing evidence for systematic variation involving *that*-type complementizers in the verbal behavior of Hindi–English balanced bilinguals. A remarkably similar pattern is witnessed in the verbal behavior of intermediate and advanced students.

This circumstance calls for a distinction between strong and weak functional heads. The strong functional heads do not permit mixing between the functional head and its complement argument, whereas as the weak functional heads allow for variable mixing. Functional heads such as Agr, Num (quantifiers, numbers), and Modals fall in the former category, whereas the *that* complementizers fall in the latter.

There is cross-linguistic support from the performance of fluent bilinguals for the view that C^0 is a weak f-selector. Although Belazi et al. (1994) report that they found no cases of violation of the FHC with respect to C^0 in their Spanish–English and Arabic–French subjects, in a review of the CM literature covering Spanish–English, Swahili–English, Yoruba–English, Chewa–English, Egyptian Arabic–English, and Lingala–French CM, Myers-Scotton (1993) concludes that there is considerable variability in language of C^0, though there is a strong tendency for embedded-language C^0 to be avoided whether the f-selected complement is in the embedded language or the matrix language.

There is another motivation for creating a distinction between strong and weak f-selectors. As we demonstrated in Table II, CM performs some stylistic functions such as quotation, repetition, clarification, contrast, paraphrase. Consider, for example, the interaction of the quotative function and the language index of the complement clause. Even if the FHC is operative in the speech of a bilingual, the language index of the complement clause will not be dependent upon the language feature of its complement functional head. Consider, for example, (77).

(77) *Hindi–*English

a. *us ne   kahaa ki   I will go there.*
   he erg. said   that
   'He said, "I will go there." '

b. *us ne   kahaa that I will go there.*
   he erg. said
   'He said that I (i.e., the speaker) will go there."

In (77a) the Hindi complementizer *ki* 'that' is followed by an English complement clause that represents quotative material—that is, the element *I will go there* is interpreted as a direct quote. In (77b) the Hindi matrix verb and English C^0 with the English complement clause represents an indirect quote. Although Hindi, traditionally, never exhibited a distinction between direct and indirect speech, mixed sentences such as are exemplified in (77a–b) are capable of drawing a clear line of demarcation between the direct and indirect speech and the language of the C^0, and its complement clause plays an important role in establishing that distinction. If the language of the C^0 and the language of the complement clause is the same, the indirect speech reading predominates.

Even if the FHC holds in the speech variety of the bilingual who uses (77a) in the quotative sense, the complement clause will fail to bear the language feature of the functional head—that is, Hindi in this case. The quotative function of the complement clause can be fulfilled only if the complement clause has a Hindi C^0. For this reason, the language index of the C^0 does not be need to be adjusted. Perhaps we should mention that, to carry the quotative reading, the exact words of the person quoted do not have to be repeated; it is sufficient to use the language of a speaker to whom the quote is attributed. For example, (77a) reveals the identity of the person quoted as belonging primarily to the English-speaking group.

The question arises as to how to deal with cases such as (77) within the framework of the FHC. Either such instances will have to be ruled out on methodological grounds or the notion of f-selection needs to be expanded to override the language-matching requirement of the functional head.

On the basis of our research findings and those of Rubin and Toribio (in press), we propose the following stages that bilinguals go through in the process of acquiring the mixed linguistic system:

1. Stage I: During this stage the process of borrowing takes place but the borrowed as well as the native lexicon is treated as one lexical storage.

2. Stage II: The two lexicons are firmly grounded and the process of translation or reinterpretation from the L1 becomes a part of language processing.

3. Stage III: The third stage can be characterized as the period of duality. The functional domains of the two participating linguistic systems begin to separate. The process of domain allocation goes hand-in-hand with the process of reinterpretation and translation, which is complex and bidirectional in nature.

4. Stage IV: Emergence of UG constraints: General principles such as the Government Constraint and the FHC take effect.

We claim that bilingual children and adult learners will pass through these stages with some degree of uniformity. The Spanish–English and our Hindi–English language development data lend support to the stages posited above. The evidence of these stages can also be found in the language development of a bilingual child.

X. PROBLEMS

In this section we will briefly review the issues and problems that the CM research has encountered in the past two decades. Some of the problems can be attributed to the theoretical assumptions and analytical frameworks, the methodological procedures, and the level at which researchers attempt to seek explanations of CM phenomena. These problems have affected the research findings on one hand and the direction of research on the other.

A. Theoretical and Analytical Problems

As the discussion in section IV demonstrates, with the change in researchers' conception of bilingual verbal behavior came some significant changes in our understanding of the grammar of CM. It is clear that CM involves the integration and the interdependence of a language pair; however, the level at which such integration takes place either implicitly or explicitly lacks consensus. Most of the studies assume, at least for quite some time, that such an integration takes place at the level of the sentence and phrase, and not at the level of lower constituents, particularly inflections. That is the reason that models of CM still shy away from the question of morphological mixing. For a long time mixing at the morphological level in particular was seen as 'random' (Valdés-Fallis, 1978, p. 16). The interface of levels (semantic, syntactic, morphological, and phonological or phonetic) still awaits research on CM. Consider, for instance, the question of the language of C^0 and its complement clause. As we have shown above, it is not a syntactic matter alone, it depends upon considerations such as direct versus indirect speech. In addition, phonetic factors also play an important role in CM and CS. For example, we conjecture that pauses play an important role in determining whether or not Hindi–English balanced bilinguals follow the FHC. We predict that the speakers whose grammars obey the FHC will pause before C^0, and the speakers whose grammars obey the Government Constraint will pause after the C^0. Any deviancy from these patterns will interfere seriously with the processing of the sentence and will be considered in some cases as an indicator of performance factors, which will be dealt with briefly in the next section.

We pointed out in section II the lack of consensus concerning the distinction between borrowing and CM. Related to that issue is the question of the matrix language of CM discourse. Sankoff et al. (1986) proposed the concept of base language in the context of borrowing. Nishimura (1985, 1986, 1989) extended the notion of base language to CM. For example, in earlier studies Nishimura (1985, 1986) employed word order as evidence for establishing the base language. Japanese is an SOV language and English is a SVO language. In Japanese–English mixed sentences, she argued that the base language is Japanese no matter how many English items appeared in the mixed sentence so long as the word order of the sentence remained SOV. Nishimura (1989) argued that a certain class of English–Japanese utterances are understood by their users to have a Japanese-based topic-comment structure, although they are predominantly English with respect to lexicon, as in (78).

(78)   *Japanese*–English
        she *wa*   took her a month to come home *yo*
            topic   Tag
        'Talking about her, it took her a month to come home, you know.'

If one posits the base language for (78) on the basis of the topic-comment nature of the sentence, this conflicts with the word order of the sentence which is SVO, which will lead one to claim the base language of the sentence to be English. The question then arises in such cases as to whether one has to impose qualitative (primacy) or quantitative conditions on the determinants (such as word order and topic-comment structure) of the base or matrix language of a sentence. Notice also that the question of sentence tags is still unresolved. The question is how much evidence is needed and what is the nature of the argument in order to establish conclusively the identity of the base or matrix language of a particular code-mixed sentence. Furthermore, theoretical studies add to yet a new list of determinants of language identification in CM.

Finally, CM and CS and language acquisition research seem to be on divergent paths. While language acquisition research is quite open to the role of universal grammar in the process of language acquisition, CM research (with some notable exceptions discussed in section VIII) seems to be resistant to admitting the role of universal grammar in the grammar of CM. The predominant tendency exhibited by the research of the grammar of CM is to analyze its grammar primarily in terms of the grammars on the language pair in spite of the mounting evidence that the emergence of the third grammatical system cannot be easily ruled out (see Bhatia, 1989, Bokamba, 1989, and others).

B. Methodological Problems

Of course, CM research is not free from methodological issues or shortcomings. One such issue is where to draw a line between performance and competence-based data. According to Beardsome (1991, p. 44) the whole issue of bilingualism is a performance question, thus implying the irrelevance of the strict dichotomy between competence and performance. For others, though, the issue cannot be settled easily even at the level of borrowing and CM (Poplack and Sankoff, 1988). Some researchers (notably, Bokamba) go so far as to propose that the attempt to discover such constraints be abandoned. Bokamba and others (Myers-Scotton, 1989; Pakir, 1989; Tay, 1989) argue that the distinction between intersentential and intrasentential code alternation and attempts at capturing formal constraints on CM are of considerably less consequence than functional constraints. There-fore, a new functional approach is more suited to the phenomenon of CM and CS.

In our view, there are a number of reasons why the search for formal universal constraints has not been met with the success that it might have. The reasons for this are outlined as follows. First, mixed speech data fails to take into account the semantic equivalence criterion discussed in section V. A monolingual sentence is subjected to the substitution of a lexical item and the mixed sentence thus achieved is subjected to grammaticality judgments without giving any serious thought to the semantics of the mixed output. A case in point is provided by sentences such as (36). If one overlooks the semantics of mixed sentences, it will result in different claims about the formal nature of Hindi–English mixing in particular and of mixing in general. Two, the question of language proficiency, educational background, and variation witnessed in the participating languages is often slighted. It appears, for example, that Hindi–English mixing is subject to linguistic variation with respect to the Government Constraint and the FHC. Three, the distinction between the competence and the performance type of naturalistic data is not rigorously drawn. In other words, one cannot take naturalistic data at its face value. The following example will further clarify the point that we are making and at the same time highlight the difficulty of arriving at universal constraints.

(79)   *Hindi*–English
    a. he said *ki*   I will go there.
              that
     'He said, "I will go there." '
    b. *us ne*   *kahaa* that *vo vahãã jaayegaa.*
      he erg. said   that he there go-will

It is not difficult to find sentences such as (79) in the verbal behavior of Hindi–English balanced bilinguals. Usually in such sentences the C^0 element will be preceded as well as followed by a pause and the final output will still be considered well formed. On the basis of such data one can reject the existence of both the Government Constraint and the FHC; however, such a claim would be misleading because when C is sandwiched between the pauses such data is contaminated on performance grounds. The pauses reflect the sorting-out state of the speaker. For this reason the C^0 becomes homophonous with the phrase *yaanii ki* 'in other words' and, thus, the sentence ceases to have a C^0 element in it.

In short, the theoretical, analytical, and methodological problems of the type discussed above have blurred our previous attempts to arrive at universals of language mixing.

XI. CONCLUSIONS

Language mixing reflects a natural and universal aspect of bilingual verbal behavior. Jakobson claims that bilingualism poses a special challenge to linguistic theory. This claim is particularly true of language mixing. Although remarkable progress has been registered in our understanding of language mixing over the past two decades, many challenges still need to be met. The long history of prescriptivism and foreign language teaching have resulted in the severe negative societal evaluation of this speech form, which is ironically capable of unlocking new dimensions of human linguistic creativity, therefore, its value in linguistics— ranging from theoretical linguistics to neuro- and educational-linguistics—can hardly be underestimated. Furthermore, a phenomenon that was and in some circles is still seen as ad hoc, random, and inconsequential seems to have a natural role in Chomsky's Minimalist Program. Language matching is similar to Chomsky's CASE checking, which is central to studies of language contact in general and language mixing in particular.

REFERENCES

Abney, S. P. (1987). *The English noun phrase in its sentential aspect.* Unpublished doctoral dissertation, MIT, Cambridge, MA.

Albert, M., & Obler, L. (1978). *The bilingual brain.* New York: Academic Press.

Annamalai, E. (1978). The anglicized Indian languages: A case of code-mixing. *International Journal of Dravidian Linguistics, 7,* 239–247.

Azuma, S. (1993). The frame-content hypothesis in speech production: Evidence from intrasentential code switching. *Linguistics, 31,* 1071–1093.

Bastian, C. (1875). *On paralysis from brain disease in its common forms.* New York: Appleton.

Bavin, E., & Shopen, T. (1985). Warlpiri and English: Languages in contact. In M. Clyne (Ed.), *Australia: Meeting place of languages* (pp. 81–94). Canberra: Australian National University.

Beardsome, H. B. (1991). *Bilingualism: Basic principles* (2nd ed.). Philadelphia: Multilingual Matters.

Belazi, H. M., Rubin, E. J., & Toribio, A. J. (1994). Code switching and X-bar theory: The functional head constraint. *Linguistic Inquiry, 25*(2), 221–237.

Bentahila, A., & Davies, E. E. (1983). The syntax of Arabic-French code-switching. *Lingua, 59,* 301–330.

Bentahila, A., & Davies, E. E. (1992). Code-switching and language dominance. In R. J. Harris (Ed.), *Cognitive processing in bilinguals* (pp. 443–458). Amsterdam: Elsevier.

Berk-Seligson, S. (1986). Linguistic constraints on intersentential code-switching: A study of Spanish-Hebrew bilingualism. *Language in Society, 15,* 313–348.

Bhatia, T. K. (1974). *Testing four hypotheses about relative clause formation and the applicability of Ross' constraints in Hindi.* Unpublished paper, University of Illinois, Urbana.

Bhatia, T. K. (1982). Englishes and vernaculars of India: Contact and change. *Applied Linguistics, 3*(3), 235–245.

Bhatia, T. K. (1988). English in advertising: Multiple mixing and media. *World Englishes, 6*(1), 33–48.

Bhatia, T. K. (1989). Bilingual's linguistic creativity and syntactic theory: Evidence for emerging grammar. *World Englishes, 8*(3), 265–276.

Bhatia, T. K. (1992). Discourse functions and pragmatics of mixing: Advertising across cultures. *World Englishes, 11*(2/3), 195–215.

Bhatia, T. K., & Ritchie, W. C. (Eds.). (1989). *Code-mixing: English across languages. Special issue of World Englishes* (Vol. 8, No. 3). New York: Pergamon Press.

Bhatia, T. K., & Ritchie, W. C. (in press). Functional head constraint: Language mixing in Universal Grammar. Manuscript submitted for publication.

Bhatnagar, S. C. (1990). Supplement to Chapter 13. In L. Menn & L. K. Obler (Eds.), *Agrammatic aphasia: A cross-language narrative sourcebook* (pp. 1761–1773). Amsterdam: John Benjamins.

Blom, J. P., & Gumperz, J. J. (1972). Social meaning in structure: Code-switching in Norway. In J. J. Gumperz & D. Hymes (Eds.), *Directions in sociolinguistics* (pp. 407–434). New York: Holt, Rinehart, & Winston.

Boeschoten, H. E., & Verhoeven, L. (1985). Integration niedeländischer lexicalischer elemente ins Turkische: Sprachmischung bei immigranten der ersten und zweiten generation. *Linguistiche Berichte, 98,* 347–364.

Bokamba, E. (1988). Code-mixing, language variation and linguistic theory: Evidence from Bantu languages. *Lingua, 76,* 21–62.

Bokamba, E. (1989). Are there syntactic constraints on code-mixing? In T. K. Bhatia & W. C. Ritchie (Eds.), *Code-mixing: English across languages* (pp. 277–292). New York: Pergamon Press.

Brown, J. W. (1977). *Mind, brain and consciousness.* New York: Academic Press.

Brown, J. W. (1979). The neurological basis of language processing. In H. Steklis & M. Raleigh (Eds.), *Neurobiology of social communication in Primates: An evolutionary perspective* (pp. 133–195). New York: Academic Press.

Canfield, K. (1980). A note on Navajo-English code-mixing. *Anthropological Linguistics, 22,* 218–220.

Chomsky, N. (1986). *Knowledge of language.* New York: Praeger.

Chomsky, N. (1991). Some notes on economy of derivation and representation. In R. Freidin (Ed.), *Principles and parameters in comparative grammar* (pp. 417–454). Cambridge, MA: MIT Press.

Chomsky, N. (1993). A minimalist program for linguistic theory. In K. Hale & S. J. Keyser (Eds.), *The view from Building 20: Essays in linguistics in honor of Sylvain Broberger* (pp. 1–52). Cambridge, MA: MIT Press.

Clyne, M. G. (1980). Trigger and language processing. *Canadian Journal of Psychology, 34*(4), 400–406.

Clyne, M. G. (1987). Constraints on code-switching: How universal are they? *Linguistics, 25,* 739–764.

de Bot, K. (1992). A bilingual production model: Levelt's 'speaking' model adapted. *Applied Linguistics, 13,* 1–24.

Di Sciullo, A., Muysken, P. & Singh, R. (1986). Government and code-mixing. *Journal of Linguistics, 22,* 1–24.

Elías-Olivarés, L. (1976). *Ways of speaking in a Chicano community: A sociolinguistic approach.* Unpublished doctoral dissertation, University of Texas, Austin.

El-Noory, A. (1985, March 21–23). *Code-switching and the search for universals: A study of (Egyptian) Arabic/English bilingualism.* Paper presented at the 16th annual Conference on African Linguistics, Yale University, New Haven, CT.

Ervin-Tripp, S. (1964). Language and TAT content in bilinguals. *Journal of Abnormal and Social Psychology, 68,* 500–507.

Ferguson, C. (1959). Diglossia. *Word, 15,* 325–340. (Reprinted in *Language and social context,* pp. 232–252, by P. Gigliolo, Ed., 1972. Harmondsworth: Penguin).

Garrett, M. (1988). Process in sentence production. In F. Newmeyer (Ed.), *The Cambridge Linguistics Survey* (Vol. 3, pp. 69–96). Cambridge, UK: Cambridge University Press.

Garrett, M. (1990). Sentence processing. In D. Osherson & H. Lasnik (Eds.), *An invitation to cognitive sciences* (Vol. 1, No. 1, pp. 133–175). Cambridge, MA: MIT Press.

Gloning, I., & Gloning, K. (1965). Ashasien bei pologlotten: Beitrag zur dynamik des sprachabbaus sowie zur localizations frage dieser storungen. *Wiener Zeitschrift fuer Nervenheilkunde und Deren Grenzgebiete, 22*, 362–397.

Grosjean, F. (1982). *Life with two languages.* Cambridge, MA: Harvard University Press.

Grosjean, F. (1985). Polyglot aphasics and language mixing: A comment on Perecman (1984). *Brain and Language, 26*, 349–355.

Grosjean, F. (1989). Neurolinguists, beware! The bilingual is not two monolinguals in one person. *Brain and Language, 36*, 3–15.

Gumperz, J. J. (1977). The sociolinguistic significance of conversational code-switching. *RELC Journal, 8*, 1–34.

Gumperz, J. J. (1982). Conversational code-switching. *Discourse strategies* (pp. 233–274). Cambridge, UK: Cambridge University Press.

Gumperz, J. J., & Hernández-Chávez, E. (1975). Cognitive aspects of bilingual communication. In E. Hernández-Chávez, A. Cohen, & R. L. Whitehead (Eds.), *El lenguaje de los Chicanos* (pp. 154–164). Arlington, VA: Center for Applied Linguistics.

Hakuta, K. (1986). *Mirror of language: The debate on bilingualism.* New York: Basic Books.

Hatch, E. (1976). Studies in language switching and mixing. In W. C. McCormack & S. A. Wurm (Eds.), *Language and man: Anthropological issues* (pp. 201–214). The Hague: Mouton.

Haugen, E. (1969). *The Norwegian language in America.* Cambridge, MA: Harvard University Press.

Herschmann H., & Poetzl, O. (1920). Bemerkungen ueber die aphasie der polyglotten. *Neurologisches Zentralblatt, 39*, 114–120.

Hoff, H., & Poetzl, O. (1932). Uber die aphasie eines zweisprachigen linkshaenders. *Wiener Medizinische Wochenschrift, 82*, 369–373.

Hyltenstam, K., & Stroud, C. (1989). Bilingualism in Alzheimer's dementia: Two case studies. In K. Hyltenstam & L. K Obler (Eds.), *Bilingualism across the lifespan* (pp. 202–226). Cambridge, UK: Cambridge University Press.

Joshi, A. (1985). Processing of sentences with intrasentential code switching. In D. Dowty, L. Kartunnen, & A. M. Zwicky (Eds.), *Natural language parsing: Psychological, computational and theoretical perspectives* (pp. 190–205). Cambridge, UK: Cambridge University Press.

Kachru, B. B. (1978). Toward structuring code-mixing: An Indian perspective. *International Journal of the Sociology of Language, 16*, 28–46.

Kachru, B. B. (1982). The bilingual's linguistic repertoire. In B. Harford & A. Valdman (Eds.), *Issues in International bilingual education: The role of the vernacular* (pp. 25–52). New York: Plenum Press.

Kachru, B. B. (1990). *The alchemy of English: The spread, functions, and models of nonnative Englishes.* Urbana: University of Illinois Press.

Kamwangamalu, N. M. (1989). A selected bibliography of studies on code-mixing and code-switching (1970–1988). In T. K. Bhatia & W. C. Ritchie (Eds.), *Code mixing: English across languages* (pp. 433–439). New York: Pergamon Press.

Kamwangamalu, N. M., & Lee, C. L. (1991). "Mixers" and "Mixing": English across cultures. *World Englishes, 10*, 247–261.

Kauders, O. (1929). Uber polyglotte reaktionen bei einer sensorischen aphasie. *Zeitschrift fuer die Gesamte Neurologie und Psychiatrie, 122,* 651–666.

Klavans, J. L. (1985). The syntax of code-switching: Spanish and English. In L. D. King & C. A. Maley (Ed.), *Selected papers from the XIIIth Linguistic Symposium on Romance Languages* (pp. 213–231). Amsterdam: John Benjamins.

Labov, W. (1971). The notion of "system" in creole languages. In D. Hymes (Ed.), *Pidginization and creolization of languages* (pp. 447–472). Cambridge, UK: Cambridge University Press.

Lance, D. (1975). Spanish-English code-switching. In E. Hernández-Chavez, A. D. Cohen, & A. F. Beltramo (Eds.), *El lenguaje de los Chicanos: Regional and social characteristics used by Mexican Americans* (pp. 138–153). Arlington, VA: Center for Applied Linguistics.

Levelt, W. J. M. (1989). *Speaking from intention to articulation.* Cambridge, MA: MIT Press.

L'Hermitte, R., Hécaen, H., Dubois, J., Culioli, A., & Tabouret-Keller, A. (1966). Le problème de l'aphasie des polyglottes: Remarques sur quelques observations. *Neuropsychologia, 4,* 315–329.

Lust, B., Bhatia, T. K., Gair, J., Sharma, V., & Khare, J. (1988). A parameter setting paradox: Children's acquisition of Hindi anaphora. *Cornell Working Papers in Linguistics, 8,* 107–132.

Masica, C. P. (1976). *Defining linguistic area: South Asia.* Chicago: University of Chicago Press.

McLaughlin, B. (1984). *Second-language acquisition in childhood: Vol. 1. Preschool children.* Hillsdale, NJ: Erlbuam.

McConvell, P. (1988). MIX-IM-UP: Aboriginal code-switching, old and new. In M. Heller (Ed.), *Code-switching: Anthropological and sociolinguistic perspective* (pp. 97–151). Mouton: de Gruyter.

Molony, C. H. (1977). Recent relexification processes in Philippine Creole Spanish. In B. G. Blount & M. Sanches (Eds.), *Sociocultural dimensions of language change* (pp. 131–159). New York: Academic Press.

Mosner, A., & Pilsch, H. (1971). Phonematisch-syntaktisch aphasie: Ein sonderfall motorischer aphasie bei einer zweisprachigen patientin. *Folia Linguistica, 5,* 394–409.

Myers-Scotton, C. M. (1988). Code-switching and types of multilingual communities. In P. Lowenberg (Ed.), *Language spread and language policy* (pp. 61–82). Washington, DC: Georgetown University Press.

Myers-Scotton, C. M. (1989). Code-switching with English: Types of switching, types of communities. In T. K. Bhatia & W. C. Ritchie (Eds.), *Code-mixing: English across languages* (pp. 333–346). New York: Pergamon Press.

Myers-Scotton, C. M. (1993). *Duelling languages: Grammatical structure in code-switching.* Oxford: Clarendon Press.

Nartey, J. (1982). Code-switching, interference or faddism: Language use among educated Ghanians. *Anthropological Linguistics, 24,* 183–192.

Nishimura, M. (1985). *Intrasentential code-switching in Japanese-English.* Unpublished doctoral dissertation, University of Pennsylvania, Philadelphia.

Nishimura, M. (1986). Intrasentential code-switching: The case of language assignment. In J. Vaid (Ed.), *Language processing in bilinguals: Psycholinguistic and neuropsychological perspectives,* (pp. 123–143). Hillsdale, NJ: Erlbaum.

Nishimura, M. (1989). The topic-comment structure in Japanese-English code-switching. In T. K. Bhatia & W. C. Ritchie (Eds.), *Code-mixing: English across languages* (pp. 365–377). New York: Pergamon Press.

Pakir, A. (1989). Linguistic alternants and code selection in Baba Malay. In T. K. Bhatia & W. C. Ritchie (Eds.), *Code-mixing: English across languages* (pp. 379–388). New York: Pergamon Press.

Pandharipande, R. (1990). Formal and functional constraints on code-mixing. In R. Jacobson (Ed.), *Codeswitching as worldwide phenomenon* (pp. 33–39). New York: Peter Lang.

Paradis, M. (1977). Bilingualism and aphasia. In H. Whitaker & H. Whitaker (Eds.), *Studies in neurolinguistics* (pp. 65–121). New York: Academic Press.

Perecman, E. (1980). *Semantic jargon over time.* Paper presented at the International Neuropsychological Society meeting, San Francisco.

Perecman, E. (1984). Spontaneous translation and language mixing in a polyglot aphasic. *Brain and Language, 23,* 43–63.

Perecman, E. (1985). Language mixing in polyglot aphasia: Conscious or preconscious necessity? A reply to Grosjean. *Brain and Language, 26,* 356–359.

Perecman, E. (1989). Language processing in the bilingual. In K. Hyltenstam & L. K. Obler (Eds.), *Bilingualism across the lifespan* (pp. 227–244). Cambridge, UK: Cambridge University Press.

Pfaff, C. (1976). Functional and structural constraints on syntactic variation in code-switching. In S. B. Steever, C. A. Walker, & S. S. Mufwene (Eds.), *Papers from the parasession on diachronic syntax* (pp. 248–259). Chicago: Chicago Linguistics Society.

Pfaff, C. (1979). Constraints on language mixing: Intrasentential code-switching and borrowing in Spanish/English. *Language, 55,* 291–318.

Pick, A. (1909). Forgesetzte beitrage zur pathologie des sensorischen aphasie. *Archiv fuer Pschiatrie and Nervenkrankheiten, 37,* 216–241.

Poetzl, O. (1925). Uber die parietal bedingte aphasie und ihren einfluss auf die sprechen mehrerer sprachen. *Zeischrift fuer die Gesamte Neurologie und Pschiatrie, 96,* 100–124.

Pollock, J. (1989). Verb movement, universal grammar, and the structure of IP. *Linguistic Inquiry, 20,* 365–424.

Poplack, S. (1980). Sometimes I'll start a sentence in Spanish and termino en Español: Toward a typology of code-switching. In J. Amestae & L. Elías-Olivares (Eds.), *Spanish in the United States: Sociolinguistic aspects* (pp. 230–263). Cambridge, UK: Cambridge University Press.

Poplack, S. (1985). Contrasting patterns of code-switching in two communities. In E. Wande et al. (Eds.), *Aspects of multilingualism* (pp. 51–77). Uppsala: Borgström.

Poplack, S., & Sankoff, D. (1988). Code-switching. In U. Ammon, N. Dittmar, & K. J. Mattheier (Eds.), *Sociolinguistics: An international handbook of language and society* (pp. 1174–1180). Berlin: de Gruyter.

Poplack, S., Wheeler, S., & Westwood, A. (1989). Distinguishing language contact phenomena: Evidence from Finnish-English bilingualism. In T. K. Bhatia & W. C. Ritchie (Eds.), *Code-mixing: English across languages* (pp. 389–406). New York: Pergamon Press.

Ritter, E. (1991). Two functional categories in noun phrases: Evidence from Modern Hebrew. In S. D. Rothstein (Ed.), *Perspectives on phrase structure: Heads and licensing* (Syntax and Semantics, 25, pp. 37–62). San Diego, CA: Academic Press.

Rivero, M. (1994). Clause structure and V-movement in the languages of the Balkans. *Natural Language and Linguistic Theory, 12:1,* 63–120.

Romaine, S. (1989). *Bilingualism.* Oxford: Basil Blackwell.

Rubin, E. J., & Toribio, A. J. (in press). Feature checking and the syntax of language contact. In J. Amaste, G. Goodall, M. Montalbetti, & M. Phinney (Eds.), *Selected papers from the XXII Linguistic Symposium on Romance languages.* Amsterdam: John Benjamins.

Sankoff, D., & Poplack, S. (1981). A formal grammar of code-switching. *Papers in Linguistics: An International Journal of Human Communication, 14,* 3–46.

Sankoff, D., Poplack, S., & Vanniarajan, S. (1986). *The case of nonce loan in Tamil* (Tech. Rep. No. 1348). Montreal: University of Montreal, Centre de recherche de mathématiques appliquées.

Schulze, H. A. F. (1968). Unterschiedliche ruchbildung einer sensorischen und einer ideokinetischen motorischen aphasie bei einem polyglotten. *Psychiatrie, Neurologie und Medizinische Psychologie, 20,* 441–445.

Scotton, C. M. (1983). *Roots in Swahili?: A locative copula becomes a stative marker.* Paper read at the Linguistic Society of America annual meeting, Minneapolis, MN.

Singh, R. (1981). Grammatical constraints on code-switching. *Recherches Linguistics à Montréal, 17,* 155–163.

Sobin, N. (1976). Texas Spanish and lexical borrowing. *Papers in Linguistics, 9,* 15–47.

Sridhar, S. N., & Sridhar, K. (1980). The syntax and psycholinguistics of bilingual code-mixing. *Canadian Journal of Psychology, 34*(4), 407–416.

Stanlaw, J. (1982). English in Japanese communicative strategies. In B. B. Kachru (Ed.), *The other tongue: English across cultures* (pp. 168–197). Urbana: University of Illinois Press.

Stengel, E., & Zelmanowitz, J. (1933). Uber polygotte motorische aphasie. *Zeitschrift fuer die Gesamte Neurologie und Pschiatrie, 149,* 291–301.

Tay, M. W. J. (1989). Code switching and code mixing as a communicative strategy in multilingual discourse. In T. K. Bhatia & W. C. Ritchie (Eds.), *Code mixing: English across languages* (pp. 407–417). New York: Pergamon Press.

Toribio, A. J., Lantolf, J., Roebuck, R., & Perrone, A. (1993). Syntactic constraints on code-switching: Evidence of abstract knowledge in second language acquisition. Unpublished manuscript, Cornell University. Ithaca, NY.

Treffers-Daller, J. (1991). *French-Dutch language mixture in Brussels.* Unpublished doctoral dissertation, University of Amsterdam, Amsterdam.

Vaid, J., & Hall, D. G. (1991). Neuropsychological perspectives on bilingualism: Right, left and center. In A. G. Reynolds (Ed.), *Bilingualism, multiculturalism, and second language learning* (pp. 81–112). Hillsdale, NJ: Erlbaum.

Valdés-Fallis, G. (1978). Code switching and the classroom teacher. *Language in Education: Theory and Practice* (Vol. 4). Arlington, VA: Center for Applied Linguistics.

Weinreich, U. (1953). *Languages in contact.* The Hague: Mouton. (Reprint, 9th ed., 1979)

Weisenberg, T., & McBride, K. (1935). *Aphasia: A clinical and psychological study.* New York: Hafner.

Woolford, E. (1983). Bilingual code-switching and syntactic theory. *Linguistic Inquiry, 14,* 520–536.

GLOSSARY

A-over-A constraint Syntax. A principle proposed as part of Universal Grammar that precludes moving an element of any category A out of a larger structure of category A. Example: This principle is claimed to allow the extraction of the Prepositional Phrase clitic *en* 'of-it' from a Noun Phrase when it is the Complement of a Verb but not from a Prepositional Phrase in the same position. Example: *Elle en aime l'auteur* lit. 'She of-it likes the author' id. 'She likes its author.' but **Elle en aime téléphone á l'auteur* lit. 'She of-it telephones to the author' id. 'She calls up its author.'

ACT* Theory A format for the formulation of computer simulations of human cognitive functions.

Adjunct Syntax. A constituent that is relatively loosely associated with other elements in the larger constituent in which it occurs. Example: The Adjunct *this afternoon* in *John watched the game this afternoon* is more loosely associated with the Verb *watch* than is the phrase *the game,* the Complement (q.v.) of *watch.*

Adverbial Clause Syntax. A clause that is associated with (that "modifies" in the traditional sense) a verbal element or full (main) clause. Example: The clause *before he left* is an Adverbial Clause in *John turned out the lights before he left* and in *Before he left, John turned out the lights.*

Affricate Phonology/Phonetics. A sound produced by stoppage of the vocal tract with a slow release of that stoppage. Example: The initial and final sounds in *judge,* and *church* are affricates.

Agreement Syntax. In general terms, a relationship between two elements in a sentence such as Subject–Verb, Modifier–Head, etc., whereby the lexical or syntactic properties of one of the elements requires a particular form for the other. Example: *that book* but *these books.* Within the Government-Binding theory of syntax, Agr(eement) is an element of the category I(nflection), which, among other things, determines agreement between the Subject of a sentence and the form of its Verb.

Agreement Parameter Syntax. Also referred to as the Verb Raising or Verb Movement Parameter. A parameter with the values strong Agr (e.g., French) and weak Agr (e.g., English). Strong Agr results in main verbs being raised, for example, past the negative element as in French *Jean (n')aime pas Marie;* weak Agr precludes Verb Raising as in the ill-formed English sentence *John likes not Mary.*

Analogy A proposed mechanism for language acquisition and use under which learners "analogize" from utterances they have encountered like *John ate a sandwich, John cut a sandwich* and *John ate an apple* to the new utterance *John cut an apple.*

Anaphora Syntax/Semantics. A relationship between one expression (e.g., a full Noun Phrase) and another one (e.g., a pronoun) such that the two are understood to refer to the same person or thing. Given appropriate structural circumstances, the Noun Phrase may either precede the pronoun (Forward Anaphora: *John turned the light out before he left.*) or follow the pronoun (Backward Anaphora: *Before he left, John turned out the light.*)

Aphasia Neurological damage that results in a language impairment.

Aptitude, Language Learning The ability to acquire a second language.

Aspect Syntax/Semantics. A mode of time reference in which a situation is viewed with respect to its internal temporal parts rather than as a whole.

Attrition Loss of language through nonuse, either within an individual or a society.

Automatic Processing Within the Information Processing approach to the study of cognition, a form of processing in which certain nodes in memory are activated each time the appropriate inputs are present. Although such processes require extensive training, they proceed rapidly once learned and are, in fact, difficult to suppress.

B

Binding Theory Syntax/Semantics. A system of principles that determine the relationships between pronomial or anaphoric elements and their antecedents in terms of the formal notion "governing category" which varies systematically among languages in accordance with the Governing Category Parameter (q.v.). Example: It follows from Principle A of the Binding Theory and the English value of the Governing Category Parameter that *John believes in himself* is well-formed but *John believes that himself is talented* is not.

Bounding Node Syntax. The node dominating a constituent which restricts movement in accordance with Subjacency (q.v.) for a given language.

Bounding Node Parameter Syntax. The parameter of Universal Grammar that determines the range of possible bounding nodes in the languages of the world.

Broca's Area An area in the inferior frontal gyrus of the frontal left lobe of the human brain which mediates the motor programming of speech.

C

C-command Syntax. A particular relationship between two elements in a sentence—if A is dominated by a node which dominates B, then A c-commands B.

Cloze Test An experimental procedure in which the subject is required to fill in the missing words in a text.

Code-mixing/-switching The mixture of two languages or dialects in a single utterance or discourse.

Communicative Competence A person's ability to use a language, including knowledge of whether a given utterance is formally possible, the feasibility of its implementations, its appropriateness in a given context, whether it is actually used, and what its use entails.

Competence The system of tacit or subconscious knowledge underlying the exercise of a cognitive skill as opposed to the real-time behavior (Performance, q.v.) that results from the exercise of that skill. *Linguistic* competence is the system(s) of knowledge underlying language use; *grammatical* competence is the system of knowledge that determines the formal features of sentences in a given language; *pragmatic* competence determines perceptions of appropriateness of language use in context.

Competition Model A model of sentence perception and production in which various formal and semantic features of utterances are understood to "compete" in determining their interpretation.

Complement (Comp) of a Phrase Syntax. In the Government-Binding theory of syntax, a constituent closely associated with the Head of the phrase in which it occurs. Example: In the Verb Phrase of the sentence *John watched the game this afternoon,* the Noun Phrase *the game* is the Complement of the Verb Phrase *watch the game,* whereas the phrase *this afternoon* is an Adjunct (q.v.).

Complementizer (C) Syntax. An element that functions as the Head of a Complementizer Phrase (CP). Example: The element *that* is a Complementizer in the sentence *John knows that Mary left.* Other Complementizers in English are *whether* and *if.*

Complementizer Phrase (CP) Syntax. A phrase with a Complementizer as Head and an Inflection Phrase (IP) as its Complement. Example: In the sentence *John knows that Mary left,* the constituent *that Mary left* is a Complementizer Phrase.

Complementizer Phrase (CP-) Direction Parameter Syntax. A proposed parameter of Universal Grammar that determines the order of elements within a CP. It is intended to account for the difference in preferred placement of sentence Adjuncts like the Adverbial Clause *before he left* in *John turned out the lights before he left.* For English, sentences in which the Adverbial Clause is ordered after the main clause are more preferred than those in which they precede the main clause (as in *Before he left, John turned out the light.*); for Japanese the converse is true.

Consonant Cluster Phonology/Phonetics. A sequence of two or more consonants.

Constraint on Extraction Domain (CDE) Syntax. A proposed constraint on syntactic movement that allows the movement of an element out of a Complement (q.v.) but not out of an Adjunct (q.v.). Examples: *Which lights did John turn out __ before he left the office?* but **Which office did John turn out the lights before he left __ ?*

Continuity Hypothesis The hypothesis that the full set of grammatical principles of Universal Grammar are present in the mind at birth. This view is opposed to the maturational hypothesis, which claims that the principles of Universal Grammar grow or mature in the mind as the child matures.

Contrastive Analysis A procedure whereby the structures of two languages are compared with the purpose of determining what difficulties a native speaker of one of the languages will have in acquiring the other one.

Contrastive Analysis Hypothesis The hypothesis that the major (or only) source of difficulty in acquiring a second language consists in differences between the two languages. A strong form of this hypothesis is that a Contrastive Analysis (q.v.) will fully predict the outcome of acquisition of one language by a speaker of another (Contrastive Analysis *a priori*); a weaker version claims that a Contrastive Analysis will provide a basis for explaining the result of acquisition (Contrastive Analysis *a posteriori*).

Control Verb Syntax. A verb that induces the occurrence of the anaphoric pronoun PRO (q.v.) in its Complement and, therefore, the operation of the principle of Control, which determines the reference of PRO. Whether Control determines the coreference of PRO with the Subject of the verb or the Direct Object of the verb is a lexical property of the verb itself. Examples: The verbs *prefer* and *persuade* are Control verbs. The sentence *John prefers [[PRO to turn the light out]]* shows Subject Control since PRO is coreferential with the Subject of *prefer,* that is *John,* whereas the sentence *John persuaded Mary [[PRO to leave]]* shows Object Control—PRO is coreferential with *Mary,* the Direct Object of *persuade.*

Controlled Processing Within Information Processing approaches to the study of cognition, a type of cognitive processing which, unlike Automatic Processing (q.v.), requires the subject's attention and, hence, is tightly capacity-limited.

Coordinate Structure Syntax. A structure consisting of two or more constituents joined together at the same structural level. Example: *John turned the lights out and Mary left,* where the clauses *John turned out the lights* and *Mary left* are at the same level of structure.

Copula Syntax/Semantics. A verbal form that joins two elements in such a way as to equate them semantically. Examples: *Mary is a doctor, John seems happy.*

Coreference Semantics. A semantic relation between two elements—usually a full Noun Phrase and a pronoun—such that they designate the same entity. Example: The elements *John* and *he* are coreferential in the sentence *John turned out the lights before he left,* whereas *John* and *he* are not coreferential in *He turned out the lights before John left.*

Creative Construction Hypothesis The hypothesis that second language acquisition proceeds "from scratch" without significant influence from the native language.

Creole Language A language that is the result of first language acquisition on the basis of input from a Pidgin Language (q.v.).

Creolization The process(es) involved in the development of a Creole Language from a Pidgin Language.

Critical Period Hypothesis In specific relation to the study of language acquisition, the hypothesis that there is a period in the maturation of the human organism during which full acquisition of a language is possible but before which and after which it is not. The hypothesized period is generally assumed to last until puberty. One version of this claim is that the acquisition of all aspects of linguistic structure are affected simultaneously—the Global Critical Period Hypothesis; another position—the Multiple Critical Periods Hypothesis—claims that there are a number of critical periods differentially affecting various aspects of the capacity for acquisition.

Cross-sectional Study With respect to the study of language acquisition, a research study in which a large number of subjects at different stages of acquisition are studied to determine the character of performance at each stage.

D

D-structure Syntax. The level of representation of the syntactic structure of a sentence at which Movements (q.v.) have not applied and where the grammatical functions and the structure in terms of which thematic roles are assigned are directly represented.

Dental Phonology/Phonetics. A sound made with the tongue placed behind or between the teeth.

Determiner (D) Syntax. A class of elements that includes *the, a/an, this, that.*

Determiner Phrase (DP) Syntax. A phrase Headed by a Determiner.

Developmental Problem of Language Acquisition The problem of explaining why the process of the acquisition of a language takes the form (e.g., exhibits the stages) that it does.

Direct Object Syntax. A Noun Phrase that functions as the Complement of a Verb Phrase. Examples: The Noun Phrase *the game* in *John watched the game this afternoon* is the Direct Object of the sentence.

Distinctive Feature Theory Phonology/Phonetics. A system of phonology in which each sound is represented as a complex of phonetic properties which serve to distinguish sounds as well as to group them into classes.

***Do*-support** Syntax. A phenomenon in the syntactic structure of English in which the semantically empty verb *do* carries the verb inflections in a sentence. Examples: ***Did** John turn out the lights?, John **did** not turn out the lights, Mary turned out the lights and John **did,** too.*

Dual Structure Constraint A proposed condition on code-switching that allows a constituent in the Embedded Language (q.v.) to occur so long as its position accords with the rules of the Matrix Language (q.v.) in which the constituent is included.

Dynamic Paradigm A type of analysis of variation in second language performance data that takes the structure of each stage of acquisition as the consequence of competition between elements already present in the learner's Interlanguage (q.v.) on one hand and newly acquired elements on the other.

E

Ego-permeability The tendency among some second language learners to be affectively "open" to input from the second language.

Embedded Language In an instance of code-switching, the language of the switched element. Opposed to Matrix Language (q.v.).

Empty Category Syntax. Within the Government-Binding theory of syntax, one of the set of phonetically null elements PRO, *pro,* NP-trace, and *WH*-trace. (See separate entries for explanation and examples.)

Empty Category Principle Syntax. Within the Government-Binding theory of syntax, a condition which stipulates that a Trace (q.v.) can occur only if it is in a particular relationship with its antecedent or with a Thematic Category (q.v.).

Epenthesis Phonology/Phonetics. The insertion of a sound into a form under specific phonetic conditions.

Equivalence Constraint In code-switching, a proposed constraint that claims that elements in the Embedded Language (q.v.) will tend to occur where the rules of neither the Embedded nor the Matrix Language (q.v.) are violated.

Error A systematic feature of a second language learner's performance in his/her Target Language (q.v.) that is distinct from that of a native speaker of the same language.

Error Analysis A technique for investigating second language performance under which the subject's errors are identified and an attempt is made to explain them.

Extraction Syntax. Movement (q.v.).

F

F-selection Syntax. The relationship between a Functional Category (q.v.) and its Complement (q.v.).

Finite Verb Syntax/Semantics. A verb that indicates occurrence of the situation described in the sentence at some definite time. Distinct from a Nonfinite or Infinitive verb. Examples: Finite—*John works, John worked.* Nonfinite—*John will try to work, John's working is welcome.*

First Language Influence Any feature of second language performance that is related to the subject's Native Language (q.v.).

Foreigner Talk The simplified form of speech often used in communication with nonnative speakers.

Fossilization In the study of second language acquisition, the point at which the learner of a second language has ceased to advance in mastery of the second language.

Free Morpheme Constraint In code-switching, a proposed constraint that claims that a switch cannot occur within a word.

Fricative Phonology/Phonetics. A sound made with restricted but continuous airflow through the vocal tract. Examples: The initial sounds in *fin, thin, sin,* and *zip* are all fricatives.

Full Access Hypothesis The hypothesis that adult second language learners have full access to the principles and parameters of Universal Grammar.

Functional (Nonlexical) Category Syntax. In the Government-Binding theory of syntax, one of the categories that do not enter into the assignment of thematic or semantic roles. These include Complementizer, Inflection, Determiner, and their projections. Distinct from Thematic Categories (q.v.).

Functional Head Constraint In code-switching, a proposed constraint that claims that a switch cannot occur between a Functional Category (q.v.) and its Complement (q.v.).

Fundamental Difference Hypothesis The hypothesis that there is a fundamental difference between first language acquisition and second language acquisition.

G

Governing Category Syntax. Within the Government-Binding theory of syntax, the domain in which the Principles of Binding Theory apply in a particular language. These determine the possibilities of Anaphoric (q.v.) relationships among expressions in a sentence. Example: A Reflexive (q.v.) must be in the same Governing Category as its antecedent. In English, the Governing Category of an element is the minimal constituent that includes the prospective antecedent, the element in question, and a Subject. Hence, the sentence *John has persuaded himself that Mary is talented* . is well-formed but **John has persuaded Mary that himself is talented* . is not.

Governing Category Parameter Syntax. In the Government-Binding theory of syntax, a Parameter (q.v.) of Universal Grammar that determines the range of possible Governing Categories (q.v.) in the languages of the world.

Government-Binding Theory Syntax. A theory of syntactic structure in the generative framework first presented in Chomsky's *Lectures on Government and Binding* (Foris, 1981) and developed in subsequent works by Chomsky and his colleagues.

Grammatical Competence See Competence.

Government Constraint In code-switching, a proposed constraint that claims that a switch may not occur between a governor and the lexical element that asymmetrically c-commands the other lexical elements in the maximal projection governed by that governor.

Grammaticality Judgment A judgment made about the well-formedness of an utterance in either spoken or written form.

H

Head Direction Parameter Syntax. A parameter of Universal Grammar that determines the range of possible

basic word orders in the phrases of the languages of the world. See also Head Position Parameter and Head-initial/Head-final Language.

Head Movement Syntax. In the Government-Binding theory of syntax, a rule that moves the Head of a Phrase to another position in a sentence.

Head Movement Constraint Syntax. A principle of Universal Grammar that restricts the Movement of a Head to the Head position of the phrase immediately above it.

Head of a Phrase Syntax. The category that is the main element in a phrase, that is obligatory and that determines the overall character of the phrase.

Head Position Parameter Syntax. A Parameter of Universal Grammar that determines the range of possible orders of Head and Complement in the languages of the world. See Head-initial/Head-final Language.

Head-initial/Head-final Language Syntax. A Head-initial language is one in which the Head precedes the Complement in all phrases; a Head-final language is one in which the Head follows the Complement in all phrases. Example: English is a Head-initial language and Japanese is a Head-final language.

I

Imperfective Syntax/Semantics. A type of time reference in which explicit reference is made to the internal temporal constituency of the situation as opposed to the situation as a whole. Example: In the sentence *Mary was sleeping when John called.* the first clause refers to an internal portion of Mary's sleeping whereas the second clause views John's calling as a whole event. The first clause is thus Imperfective in Aspect (q.v.).

Indirect Object Syntax. A grammatical function which, in the usual instance, designates a receiver of some sort. Example: The Noun Phrase *John* is the Indirect Object of the sentence *Mary gave John the book.*

Infinitive Syntax/Semantics. A form of a verb that refers to the situation described in the sentence independent of any particular time. Distinct from a Finite verb. Examples: Infinitive—*John will try **to work.*** Finite—*John **works**, John **worked.***

Inflection (general) Morphology. A morphological element that indicates a grammatical category or relationship within a sentence such as a plural or case element in a Noun or a tense or agreement element in a Verb.

Inflection (I, INFL) Syntax. Within the Government-Binding theory of syntax, the functional category that subsumes the Tense and Agr elements (q.v.).

Inflection Phrase (IP) Syntax. The phrase headed by INFL; equivalent to S(entence) in early versions of Government-Binding theory.

Information Processing Approach An approach to the study of complex cognitive skills that views such skills as composed of isolable, simple, autonomous processes that occur in real time.

Initial State In a highly idealized view of language acquisition, the learner's cognitive state prior to any linguistic experience, at which point all of the potential terminal states of the acquisition process are represented. In the case of first language acquisition, the Initial State is characterized by Universal Grammar (q.v.) and the terminal state by the grammar of a particular language.

Input The linguistic stimuli to which the language learner is exposed.

Interference First language influence that leads to errored performance in a second language.

Interlanguage The language system of a second language learner at any stage in the process of second language acquisition.

Inversion Syntax. A Movement (q.v.) in the grammar of English that raises an auxiliary verb over its Subject. Example: In the sentence *Will John win the prize?* the auxiliary verb *will* has been moved over the Subject *John* as a consequence of an application of Inversion.

L

Lateralization The localization of a particular brain function in one side of the brain or the other.

Learnability The property of the grammars of natural languages such that they are attained under specific conditions. The consideration of alternative ways in which this attainment might be explained.

Lect A regionally or socially determined speech variety usually considered in relation to other varieties which form a continuum of shared and distinct characteristics.

Lexicon The language user's mental dictionary.

Locality Principle Syntax. In the Government-Binding theory of syntax, any one of a number of principles that restrict the application of a syntactic operation to a particular structural domain.

Logical Problem of Language Acquisition The problem of how it is that adults have attained a highly complex grammar for a language on the basis of linguistic experience that underdetermines that grammar.

Longitudinal Study With respect to the study of language acquisition, a research study in which one or more subjects are investigated through several stages of the acquisition process.

M

Markedness The relatively complex or exceptional character of a given property of some language. Relatively common properties of languages are termed Unmarked and exceptional properties are termed Marked.

Markedness Differential Hypothesis The hypothesis that properties of a given Target Language that are Marked relative to corresponding properties of the learner's Native Language will be difficult for the learner to attain.

Matrix Language In Code-switching (q.v.), the language which provides the overall structure of an utterance containing a switched element or elements. Opposed to Embedded Language (q.v.).

Maturation Hypothesis The hypothesis that the principles of Universal Grammar grow or mature in the mind as the child matures. Opposed to the Continuity Hypothesis, which claims that the full set of grammatical principles of Universal Grammar are present in the mind at birth.

Modal Auxiliary Syntax/Semantics. A verbal form that indicates the speaker's view of the necessity, possibility, or desirability, of the situation referred to by the utterance. Examples: *John **may** (**can, might, could**) win the prize.*

Modularity/Module Modularity is a claimed property of the human mind that imputes to it an organization consisting of distinct Modules of representations and principles, each of which contributes to the overall cognitive processing capacity of the organism. One such Module is claimed to consist in the language user's grammar of his/her language.

Morpheme Order The order of acquisition of a set of grammatical (that is, functional) morphemes.

Morphological Uniformity Principle Syntax. A possible property of the verbal paradigms in a language such that it either has an inflectional element in every form or no such element in any form. Italian, with an inflectional element in every verb form, is Morphologically Uniform as is Chinese, the verbs of which lack any inflectional elements. Neither English nor French is Morphologically Uniform, since they each show inflectional elements in some forms of their verb paradigms but not in others.

Motherese The form of language used by caretakers to their children.

Movement Syntax. In the Government-Binding theory of syntax, a rule that enters into the relationship between D-structure (q.v.) and S-structure (q.v.) that moves an element from one position in a sentence structure to another leaving a Trace *t* (q.v.) in its D-structure position. Examples: NP-Movement enters into the mapping of the (schematic) D-structure *e was seen John by Alice* to give the (schematic) S-structure *John was seen t by Alice.* *Wh*-movement enters into the mapping of the (schematic) D-structure *John might see who* to give the (schematic) S-structure *who John might see t.*

N

Negation Syntax. The form that a sentence takes in expressing the denial or contradiction of some or all of the meaning of another sentence. Example: The sentence *John will not win the prize.* is the Negation of the sentence *John will win the prize.*

Negative Evidence Evidence available to the language learner from the environment that a particular utterance is unacceptable in the language he/she is learning. Negative evidence may be either direct or indirect. Direct negative evidence includes correction from the environment whereas indirect negative evidence takes the form of the absence of a particular structure from the linguistic input to the learner.

Negotiation of Meaning A joint attempt within a conversation between a native speaker and an nonnative speaker of a given language to correct a misunderstanding.

No Access Hypothesis The hypothesis that the adult second language learner has no access to the principles and parameters of Universal Grammar.

Noun Phrase (NP) Syntax. A phrase of which a Noun is the Head.

Noun Phrase Accessibility Hierarchy Syntax. A set of cross-linguistic generalizations concerning the movability of a Noun Phrase within a Relative Clause as determined by the grammatical function of the Noun Phrase. With respect to this generalization, grammatical functions form an implicational hierarchy of accessibility to movement from Subject down to Object of Comparative. For a given language, movability from a position in the hierarchy implies movability from any higher position.

Null Subject Parameter Syntax. Within the Government-Binding theory of syntax, a Parameter of

Universal Grammar which determines, among other aspects of the syntactic structure of a language, whether or not a sentence in that language may be grammatical without an overt Subject. Example: Spanish is a Null Subject language, allowing sentences lacking overt Subjects like *Habla inglés* 'He/She speaks English.' whereas English is not a Null Subject language since strings like *Speaks English.* are ungrammatical.

O

Observer's Paradox In the study of spontaneous speech, the contradiction between the need to observe such speech and the fact that, under most conditions, the very presence of an observer will influence the character of that speech.

Obstruent Phonology/Phonetics. A sound, the production of which requires substantial restriction of the vocal tract. The obstruents include Stop, Fricative, and Affricate sounds.

Operating Principle A generalization about the process of first language acquisition stated as a principle to be followed in arriving at the end product of acquisition. Example: The Operating Principle "Pay attention to the ends of words." is adduced to account for the fact that children attain suffixes before they attain prefixes.

Overgeneralization In language acquisition, the extension by a learner of a rule in the Target Language to cases where it does not apply in the adult native grammar of the language. Example: Extension of the regular past tense suffix in English to irregular verbs—*John **runned** down the street* for *John **ran** down the street.*

P

Parameter Within the principles and parameters approach to the study of grammatical structure, a point in Universal Grammar where variation among languages is possible. Each value of a Parameter determines a systematic cluster of (typological) differences among languages. Under this view of Universal Grammar, a major part of the language learner's (tacit) task is to determine on the basis of Input (q.v.) which of the values of the Parameters of Universal Grammar are valid for the language of the environment. Example: See 'Head-Position Parameter' and 'Head-initial/Head-final Language.'

Partial Access Hypothesis The hypothesis that the adult language learner has partial access to the principles and parameters of Universal Grammar through the grammar of his/her first language.

Past Tense Syntax/Semantics. A form of time reference in which an event or situation is regarded as a whole and as having occurred at some point before the time of speaking.

Perfective Syntax/Semantics. A type

of time reference in which explicit reference is made to the situation as a whole rather than to the internal temporal constituency of the situation. Example: In the sentence *Mary was sleeping when John called.* the first clause refers to an internal portion of Mary's sleeping whereas the second clause views John's calling as a whole event. The second clause is thus Perfective in Aspect (q.v.).

Performance The deployment of linguistic knowledge (i.e., of linguistic Competence, q.v.) in real time; linguistic behavior (as opposed to linguistic knowledge).

PET Scan Positron Emission Tomography, a technique for mapping brain anatomy and physiology.

Pidgin Language A language, usually functioning as a lingua franca, that arises as the product of contact between peoples who previously had no language in common and that has a simplified structure and no native speakers.

Pidginization The process whereby a pidgin language is created.

Plural Syntax/Semantics. The form of a Noun that is interpreted as designating more than one.

Positive Evidence Evidence available to the language learner from the environment that a particular utterance is acceptable in the language he/she is learning. The usual form of positive evidence for the grammaticality of a given utterance is its occurrence in the environment.

Poverty of the Stimulus Argument The argument that the linguistic knowledge acquired by a learner of a language is underdetermined by his/her experience with the language.

Preposition (P) Syntax. A syntactic category. Examples: The words *in, on,* and *into* in the following sentences are Prepositions. *John put the car in the garage. John sat on the table. John threw the paper into the wastebasket.*

Prepositional Phrase (PP) Syntax. A phrase of which a Preposition is the Head. Examples: *in the garage, on the table, into the wastebasket.*

Prescriptive Grammar A set of rules that prescribe what language behavior should be. Opposed to descriptive grammar, the purpose of which is to describe and explain what language behavior actually is.

Primary Language A first language that has been acquired at the normal time of acquisition (beginning at age two years) under normal circumstances; native language.

Principle Branching Direction (PBD) Syntax. The position of the recursive elements in the phrases of a language. If the recursive elements are to the left of the phrase Head, the language is a left-branching language (e.g., Japanese); if to the right of the Head, a right-branching language (e.g., English).

Principles and Parameters Approach An approach to the explanation of grammatical form and language acquisition under which Universal Grammar (q.v.) is conceived of as a system of principles—each of which is true of the grammars of all human languages—with some principles allowing for some variation among the grammars of particular languages. These points of variation are termed Parameters, each of which may take one of two or more values. Acquisition of a particular language then consists in the setting (or, in the case of second language acquisition, resetting) of each Parameter of Universal Grammar in one of its values.

PRO Syntax. The Empty Category (q.v.) that serves as the Subject of a nonfinite Verb form. Examples: *John wants [PRO to win the prize]. [PRO winning the prize] was John's goal.*

pro Syntax. The Empty Category (q.v.) that serves as the phonetically null Subject of finite Verbs in a language that allows such Subjects. Example: The element *pro* is the phonetically null Subject of the Spanish sentence *Hablamos inglés.* 'We speak English.'

Pro-drop Language Syntax. A language that, like Spanish and unlike English, allows finite sentences that contain phonetically null Subjects.

Proficiency Level of mastery of a language.

Projection Syntax. Within X-bar Theory (q.v.), the phrases that are associated with a given Head. Example: In an NP, the N' level and the full NP itself are projections of the Head N.

Projection Principle Syntax. The principle that, at D-structure (q.v.), S-structure (q.v.), and Logical Form,

all Projections (q.v.) of a given Head are maintained.

Prosody Phonology/Phonetics. The pattern of relative pitch, loudness, rhythm, and tempo of elements in a linguistic expression.

R

Received Pronunciation Phonology/Phonetics. Standard British English pronunciation.

Recoverability Principle Syntax. The principle that the content of a phonetically null element in a sentence is determinable from the sentence structure in which the element appears.

Reflexive Syntax. An anaphoric element (see Anaphora) that must have an antecedent in the same clause. Example: The form *himself* in the sentence *John convinced himself [that he was talented].* is a Reflexive; it cannot occur in a clause in which there is no antecedent for it, as in the sentence **John convinced Mary [that himself was talented].*

Register A "situational dialect" or style.

Relative Clause Syntax. A construction in which a sentence modifies a Noun. Example: The element *who John saw* is a relative clause in the sentence *The man who John saw is my uncle.*

Relativization Syntax. The operations which determine the form of Relative Clauses (q.v.) in a language. Example: Relativization in English consists in the *Wh*-movement of an element of the Relative

Clause and the interpretation of the moved element as coreferential (see Coreference) with the Head Noun of the Noun Phrase (q.v.).

Resolvability Principle   Phonology/Phonetics. The principle that if a given language has a consonant sequence of length m in either initial or final position, then it has at least one continuous subsequence of length $m - 1$ in this same position.

Restructuring   Reorganization of the learner's linguistic knowledge in the process of language acquisition.

S

S-structure   Syntax. Within the Government-Binding theory of syntax, the structure of a sentence that results from the application of overt Movements (q.v.) to the D-structure of the sentence.

Specifier (Spec) of a Phrase   Syntax. Within the X-bar Theory (q.v.) of phrase structure, the element in a given phrase that is external to the Head-Complement structure.

Spirantization (of Stops)   Phonology/Phonetics. The weakening of a Stop (q.v.) sound to its corresponding Fricative (q.v.).

Stative Verb   Syntax/Semantics. A verb that designates a state of affairs rather than an action. Examples: The verb *know* designates a state (and is therefore a stative verb) whereas the verb *jump* designates an action.

Stop   Phonology/Phonetics. A consonant sound produced by completely closing the vocal tract in the oral cavity.

Structural Conformity Hypothesis   The hypothesis that all universal generalizations that are true of Primary Languages (q.v.) are also true of Interlanguages (q.v.).

Structure Dependence   Syntax. The condition on Movements (q.v.) that they apply to a word sequence only in terms of the phrase structure of that sequence. Also, the principle that language learners assign structure to the utterances in the language they are learning.

Subjacency   Syntax. A condition on Movements (q.v.) that restricts the structural distance over which an element can be moved. More specifically, an element cannot be moved past more than one Bounding Node (q.v.) where Bounding Nodes vary across languages in accordance with the Bounding Node Parameter (q.v.).

Subset Principle   A condition on the sequence of grammars that characterizes the process of language acquisition such that early grammars in the process generate languages that are subsets of those generated by later grammars in the process. The Subset Principle is motivated by the observation that the evidence that is effective for the child in first language acquisition is essentially limited to Positive Evidence (q.v.)

Syllable Onset   Phonology/Phonetics. The beginning of a syllable.

T

Target Language   The language that a given learner is acquiring.

Teacher Talk   A Register (q.v.) that is used by teachers in communicating with language learners. In the usual case this Register is simplified.

Tense (general semantic category) Syntax/Semantics. A form of time reference in which an event or situation is referred to as a whole and as occurring in relation to some other time, usually the time of speaking.

Tense (T, Tns) (formal, theory-internal category)   Syntax. In the Government-Binding theory of syntax, either an element of I(nfl) or a separate category that carries the semantic interpretation of semantic Tense (q.v.).

Thematic (Lexical) Category   Syntax. A category that enters into the assignment of Thematic Roles (q.v.)—Verb, Noun, Adjective, and Preposition.

Thematic (Semantic) Role   Syntax/ Semantics. The role that the referent of a Noun Phrase plays in the event or situation designated by a sentence. Example: In the sentence *Mary threw the ball to John.* Mary is the Agent of the action designated by the Verb, the ball is the Patient or Theme and John is the Goal of the action.

Third Person Singular (in English) Morphology. The English suffix *-s* that represents the agreement of the Verb with a third person singular Subject in the present Tense. Example: *John likes rutabaga.*

Topic-Comment Structure   Syntax. A sentence structure in which the major syntactic division in the sentence is between a topic and a comment on that topic rather than between a Subject and a predicate. Example: In the sentence *Beans, he hates.* the element *beans* is the Topic and *he hates* is the Comment.

Topic-prominent Language   Syntax. tax. A language in which the normal or canonical sentence structure is a Topic-comment structure rather than a Subject-predicate structure. Examples: Chinese and Japanese are Topic-prominent Languages whereas English is a Subject-predicate or Subject-prominent language.

Topicalization   Syntax. A Movement (q.v.) or other operation or structure that determines a Topic-Comment Structure (q.v.). Example: In English, the Movement that places the element *beans* in initial position in the sentence *Beans, he hates.*

Trace   Syntax. An Empty Category (q.v.) that is "left behind" when a Movement (q.v.) applies to a structure. Example: The element *t* in the S-structure representations of sentence structures that have undergone NP-Movement (*John was seen t by Alice.*) or *Wh*-Movement (*who might John see t.*) are Traces.

Transfer   The influence of the Native Language of a language learner on his/her performance in the second language. Positive Transfer, which consists in characteristics of the two languages that are similar, is claimed to facilitate performance in the second language whereas Negative Transfer, respects in which the two languages differ, is claimed to interfere with performance.

Trigger Within the Principles and Parameter Approach, an aspect of the Input to the language learner that induces the setting of a Parameter in one of its values.

U

U-shaped performance A feature of the learning process whereby, in language acquisition, the learner apparently performs in accordance with the structure of the Target Language but after which performance is disrupted temporarily with a subsequent return to targetlike performance.

Ultimate Attainment The point in the process of language acquisition at which it ceases.

Uniqueness Principle (UP) A principle that the language learner is claimed to apply in the process of language acquisition that says that each meaning is represented by a single form in the language being acquired. Also termed the One-to-One Principle.

Universal Grammar The system of principles and Parameters (q.v.) that constitute the innate human capacity for language acquisition.

V

Variability/Variation Features of linguistic structure that change (systematically or not) in the perfor-

mance of speakers of a language under particular linguistic and social circumstances.

Verb Movement (Verb Raising) Syntax. Within the Government-Binding theory of syntax, the Movement (q.v.) of a Verb from its D-structure position in the Verb Phrase to be adjoined to the Functional Category Agr(eement) or T(ense). Some languages (e.g., French) require Verb Movement, others (English) exclude it.

Verb Movement Parameter Syntax. The Parameter that accounts for the difference between, for example, French and English that determines whether a language exhibits Verb Movement or not.

Voice Onset Time (VOT) Phonology/Phonetics. The time between the release of a Voiceless Stop and the onset of Voicing of the following Vowel.

Voicing Phonology/Phonetics. In the production of speech sounds, the presence (or absence) of vibration of the vocal folds. Examples: The sounds canonically represented by the letters *f* and *s* by the English writing system are Voiceless (lack vocal fold vibration) whereas those canonically represented by *v* and *z* are Voiced (exhibit vibration).

W

Wernicke's Area of the Brain An area in the posterior part of the superior temporal gyrus that is involved in auditory association and reception of speech which allows for oral comprehension.

***Wh*-in situ** Syntax. A structure in which an interrogative word remains in its D-structure position [i.e., does not undergo *Wh*-movement (q.v.)].

***Wh*-island** Syntax. A structure in which a Complementizer Phrase containing a *Wh*-phrase in its Specifier position. Movement (q.v.) out of such a structure is precluded. Example: *What does John wonder [how Mary fixed t t]* . from the D-structure *John wonders [Mary fixed what how]*. is excluded because it moves the element *what* out of a Complementizer Phrase with a *Wh*-phrase (*how* in *[how Mary found t t]*) in the Specifier position.

***Wh*-movement (-extraction)** Syntax. The Movement (q.v.) of a *Wh*-phrase to a position at the beginning of a clause.

***Wh*-question** Syntax. A question that includes a *Wh*-phrase in it. Example: *Who did John see?*

X

X-bar Theory Syntax. In the Government-Binding theory of syntax, a theory of phrase structure that claims that all phrases in all languages consist most centrally of a Head element around which the phrase is built, a closely related element (the Complement of the phrase), and a more loosely associated element, the Specifier.

AUTHOR INDEX

A

Abercrombie, D., 270
Abidi, R., 518
Abney, S., 485, 487–490, 492, 493, 651, 674
Abramson, A., 274
Acton, W., 272
Adams, J., 280
Adamson, H., 239, 240
Adjemian, C., 8, 49, 61, 205, 329, 386
Aitchison, J., 535
Aksu-Koc, A., 534
Alanen, R., 428
Albanese, J., 514
Albert, M., 3, 15, 510, 513, 514, 516, 670
Albertini, J., 470
Allwright, R., 438
Altenberg, E., 200, 294
Altmann, G., 377
Ambrose, J., 582
Andersen, E., 416, 417
Andersen, R., 53, 70, 242, 252, 321, 322, 432,
    529, 531–534, 536–538, 542–550, 552,
    554, 557, 558, 614, 620, 634
Andersen, A., 54

Anderson, J., 3, 16, 23, 28, 31, 33, 34, 40, 41,
    71, 100, 200, 218, 219, 220, 223, 224, 294
Angelis, P., 53
Annamalai, E., 655
Antinucci, F., 512, 534–536, 547
Appel, R., 571
April, R., 513
Archangeli, D., 298
Archibald, J., 114, 298
Ard, J., 323, 328, 339, 545, 558
Arditty, J., 386
Aronson-Berman, R., 611, 621
Arthur, B., 416, 417, 419
Ashayeri, H., 517, 518
Asher, J., 180, 355
Atkinson, M., 36, 56, 66–69, 170, 184, 445
Aungst, L., 272
Ayusawa, T., 279
Azuma, S., 683

B

Baetens-Beardsmore, H., 571, 586
Bahns, J., 61

Bahrick, H., 517, 518, 607, 609
Bailey, C-J., 14, 240, 271
Bailey, K., 167
Bailey, N., 320, 367
Baillie, C., 431
Baker, C., 25, 50
Baker, N., 434, 435, 437, 441, 451
Bakker, D., 165
Baldauf, R., 363
Bard, E., 54, 403
Bardovi-Harlig, K., 428, 543, 544, 546, 547
Barik, H., 423
Barnes, S., 437
Barry, W., 274, 276
Barton, D., 328
Barzilay, M., 606
Bastian, C., 671
Bates, E., 13, 39, 335, 336
Bavin, E., 655
Bayley, R., 252, 253, 258, 261, 262, 544
Beardsome, H., 631, 681
Beck, M., 430, 440, 441
Bedey, H., 61
Beebe, L., 270, 272, 295, 329
Behrens, H., 534
Belazi, H., 649, 651–654, 678
Bell, L., 200
Bellugi-Klima, U., 8
Bennett, S., 99
Benson, B., 200, 293
Bentahila, A., 649, 659
Bentin, S., 514
Berent, G. P., 3, 9, 25, 32, 33, 34, 40, 90, 98, 100,
     111, 145, 149, 186, 204, 332, 424, 471, 482,
     483, 484, 494, 497, 498, 499, 500, 618
Bergström, A., 547
Berk-Seligson, S., 642
Berkowitz, D., 271
Berman, R., 534
Berretta, A., 49, 252
Berthier, M., 515
Berwick, R., 71, 90, 358, 495
Best, C., 275, 276
Bever, T., 376, 377, 378
Bhatia, T., 4, 10, 19, 24, 33, 41, 509, 519, 590, 610,
     611, 629, 630, 646, 647, 649, 655, 662, 664
Bhatnagar, S., 671
Bhatt, R., 298
Bialystok, E., 12, 17, 53, 90, 218, 219
Bickerton, D., 14, 241–243, 257, 258, 261, 415,

527–529, 533, 535, 538–542, 544, 554,
     557, 561, 562
Birdsong, D., 55, 92, 105–107, 128, 132, 173,
     385, 390, 425, 433, 615
Bjork, R., 220
Black, J., 402
Blaxton, T., 221
Bley-Vroman, R., 23, 62, 64, 65, 72, 91, 92, 95,
     103, 104, 110, 122, 130, 132, 160, 167,
     169, 176, 177, 321, 333, 425, 609, 615
Bloom, L., 433, 530, 531, 534–536, 549
Bloom, J., 637
Bloomfield, L., 5, 253, 571
Bluhme, H., 274
Blum-Kulka, S., 20
Blumstein, S., 285
Bochner, J., 470
Boeshoten, H., 655
Bogen, J., 54
Bohannon, J., 417, 430–436
Bohn, O., 276, 278, 289
Bokamba, E., 630, 631, 681
Bonvillian, J., 434
Borden, G., 277, 279, 280
Borer, H., 56, 56, 183, 184, 188, 537
Bornstein, M., 414
Botha, R., 376–379
Bourdages, J., 281
Bowen, R., 196
Bowen, J., 286
Bowerman, M., 70
Bowers, R., 370
Bradac, J., 378, 393
Braidi, S., 451
Brannon, J., 473
Brannon, R., 272
Bransford, J., 221
Brennan, E., 271
Brennan, J., 271
Bridgeman, B., 222
Brière, E., 278, 288, 290, 328
Brinton, L., 532, 557
Brock, C., 438, 448, 449
Broeders, A., 272
Bronckart, J., 527, 531, 534–536, 539, 547
Broselow, E., 93, 97, 98, 100, 114, 115, 129,
     150, 275, 293, 297, 329, 331, 333, 334
Browman, C., 288, 290
Brown, H., 166, 251, 271
Brown, J., 672

Brown, P., 251
Brown, R., 7, 8, 320, 365, 425, 431, 527, 534,
    541, 550, 558, 559
Brugmann, K., 263
Bruner, J., 414
Buchwald, S., 274
Buczowska, E., 530
Burt, M. K., 5, 15, 38, 121, 197, 317, 320,
    351–353, 367, 384
Burzio, L., 108, 499
Butterworth, G., 369
Bybee, J., 536, 548, 549, 554, 557, 558
Bygate, M., 447
Byrne, J., 271

C

Cairns, H., 143
Campbell, R., 272
Canale, M., 53, 366
Cancino, E., 8
Cancino, H., 384
Canetta, J., 273
Canfield, K., 655
Caramazza, A., 279
Carbone, E., 279
Carlisle, R., 294, 298
Carlson, R., 220
Carroll, S., 59, 443–445
Carroll, J., 222, 223, 378
Cartwright, N., 54
Castellan, N., 395
Catford, J., 272, 282
Cathcart-Strong, R., 417
Cazden, C., 8, 384
Chalmers, A., 54, 256, 359
Chamot, A., 225, 278
Champagne, C., 281
Champaud, C., 534
Chary, P., 513
Chase, W., 225
Chaudron, C., 55, 364, 385, 416, 438
Cheng, P., 216
Chenoweth, A., 425
Chien, Y-C., 87, 124, 130, 169
Chomsky, C., 143
Chomsky, N., 2, 6, 7, 8, 10, 18, 30, 52–54, 57,
    62, 85, 123, 125–127, 139, 162, 180, 208,
    247, 257, 288, 297, 380, 382, 383, 400,

    404, 405, 437, 473, 477, 482–487, 488,
    494–496, 617, 651, 652, 654, 674
Christophersen, P., 271
Chun, A., 425, 438
Chun, D., 269
Clahsen, H., 37, 91, 95, 96, 111, 122, 130, 167,
    168, 334, 365, 433
Clark, A., 555
Clark, E., 71, 72, 432, 537, 538
Clark, H., 107
Clark, S., 277
Clyne, M., 271, 416, 417, 518, 662, 664, 667
Coder, S., 318
Cohen, A., 24, 130, 369, 518, 607
Comrie, B., 10, 11, 201, 202, 424, 498, 528,
    530, 532, 541, 545, 548, 549
Connell, P., 98, 99
Cook, T., 360
Cook, V., 63, 121, 122, 128
Cooper, R., 143, 472, 576, 588
Coppieters, R., 105, 106, 107, 128, 172, 173,
    379, 389, 390, 609, 615, 623
Corder, S. P., 8, 324, 384, 415
Cowart, W., 377, 379
Crain, S., 72
Crookes, G., 49, 438, 448
Cruz-Ferreira, M., 275, 291
Culicover, P. W., 25, 54, 432
Culver, J., 416
Cummins, J., 423
Cummins, R., 22, 29, 51
Cunningham-Andersson, U., 271
Curtiss, S., 165
Cushing, S., 543, 544
Cziko, G., 529, 534, 538, 540–542

D

d'Anglejan, A., 143
d'Introno, F., 334
Dahl, O., 556, 558, 561
Dalto, G., 580
Davidian, R., 291, 327
Davidson, D., 482
Davies, E., 649, 659
Davis, H., 470
Dawkins, R., 51
Day, E., 428
Day, R., 55, 425, 438

de Bose, C., 415
de Bot, C., 282, 518
de Bot, K., 416, 607, 655
de Lemos, C., 534
de Praatkist, 416
de Santi, S., 519
de Villiers, J., 499
de Villiers, P., 479, 480
de Vries, J., 574
Dechert, H., 296
DeClerk, J., 285
Demetras, M., 431
Denninger, M., 434
Déprez, V., 489
Derwing, T., 417
Desmarais, C., 273, 513
Devescovi, A., 335
Dey, I., 360
Di Sciullo, P., 648, 650–652, 654
Dickerson, W., 235, 292, 296
Dickerson, L., 235, 292, 295, 296
Diebold, A., 571, 572
Diehl, R., 274
Diffey, F., 386
Dillon, P., 534
Dodd, D., 434
Dorian, N., 581, 585, 586, 593, 599, 614, 624
Doughty, C., 200, 358, 359, 417, 418, 428, 450
Dowd, J., 271
Dowty, D., 531, 532, 556
Dreher, B., 281
Dresher, E., 114, 298
Dressler, W., 299, 614, 624
du Plessis, J., 93, 97, 111
Dubois, J., 671
Duchnicky, R., 218
Duff, P., 365
Dulay, H., 5, 15, 38, 121, 197, 317, 320, 351–353, 367, 384
Dull, C., 272
Dumais, S., 215
Durgunoglu, A., 221
Durkin, K., 453
Duskova, L., 197, 325
Dziubalska-Kolaczyk, K., 299

E

Early, M., 417, 418
Eckman, F., 2, 12, 28, 33, 34, 36, 37, 115, 127,
195, 197, 200, 204–207, 278, 286, 294,
295, 319, 321, 327, 328, 331, 339, 350,
424, 478, 498, 545
Economides, P., 543, 544
Eefting, W., 289
Efstathiadis, S., 286
Eisenberg, A., 534, 538
Eisenstein, M., 271, 367
El-Noory, A., 641
Elías-Olivarés, L., 632
Eliasson, S., 286, 291
Elliot, N., 378
Ellis, L., 402
Ellis, N., 428
Ellis, R., 14, 17, 20, 23, 54, 67, 201, 249, 250,
257, 351, 354, 357, 359, 364, 367, 418,
447, 451
Elman, J., 274
Emanuel, F., 402
Emonds, J., 87
Epstein, S., 126, 127, 129, 131–133, 150, 152
Erard, R., 272
Erbaugh, M., 534
Erdmann, P., 291
Ericcson, K., 225
Ervin, S., 510
Ervin-Tripp, S., 445, 637
Espesser, R., 402
Espinal, I. 137
Esser, J., 278
Eubank, L., 111, 145, 384, 430, 440, 441
Eysenck, M, 213, 216, 219

F

Faerch, C., 225
Falodun, J., 448
Fanselow, J., 438
Farrar, M., 431, 432, 434, 435, 437, 439, 441
Fasold, R., 232, 241, 578
Fathman, A., 180
Fedio, P., 515, 516
Fehst, C., 280
Fein, D., 512
Felix, S., 17, 18, 50, 64, 66, 100, 103, 132, 163, 166,
167, 171, 176, 183, 184, 331, 334, 388, 609
Fentress, J., 277
Ferguson, C., 54, 293, 415, 416, 417, 577, 634
Finer, D., 93, 97, 98, 100, 114, 115, 129, 150,
331, 333, 334

Fishman, J., 576–578, 581, 590, 594
Fisiak, J., 286, 319
Fitch, H., 277
Flashner, V., 543, 544
Flavell, J., 68
Flege, J., 269, 276, 278, 279, 281, 283, 289, 291, 327, 328
Fletcher, P., 551
Flick, W., 352
Flynn, S., 2, 10, 19, 24, 27, 28, 30, 36–38, 50, 55, 60, 62–64, 90–92, 95, 96, 111, 126, 128, 129, 130–138, 142, 143, 149, 150, 152, 162, 167, 169, 173, 174, 183, 208, 209, 247, 248, 318, 321, 329–331, 349, 353, 375, 384, 387–389, 424, 480, 487, 495, 498, 615
Fodor, J., 52, 57, 59, 60, 72, 180, 383
Foley, W., 532
Foley, C., 142
Ford, A., 297
Fourakis, M., 327, 328
Fourcin, A., 276, 447
Frank, W., 61
Franklin, P., 514
Franks, J., 221
Fredman, M., 517
Freed, B., 416, 417, 607
Friedland, R., 519
Fries, C., 5, 318, 350
Frota, S., 426
Fucci, D., 402
Fukui, N., 145
Furrow, D., 431, 440

G

Gaies, S., 417, 419
Gair, J., 93, 95, 104, 150, 177, 662
Galaburda, A., 513
Galloway, L., 513, 514
Gandour, J., 275
Garber, S., 280
Garcia, R., 180
Gardner, R., 15, 16, 17, 67, 587, 598
Garner, W., 239
Garrett, M., 656
Gary, J., 282
Gass, S., 1, 2, 3, 5, 6, 14, 19, 24, 30, 31, 33, 39, 63, 64, 95, 98, 100, 111–113, 115, 127, 128, 130, 135, 140, 161, 174, 186, 196,
199, 200, 283, 285, 286, 320, 321, 326, 327, 328, 335, 336, 339, 350, 351, 417–419, 427, 448, 450, 451, 495, 498, 545, 591, 618
Gasser, M., 58,
Gatbonton, E., 244, 292, 296
Gay, T., 285
Gaziel, T., 514
Gegeo, D., 436
Genesee, F., 105, 107, 514
George, H., 352
Geshwind, N., 513
Ghambiar, S., 417
Ghambiar, V., 417
Gilbert, G., 322
Giles, H., 271
Givon, T., 445
Gleitman, H., 54, 376, 378, 437, 555
Gleitman, L., 54, 162, 376, 378, 437, 555
Gloning, I., 509, 513, 671
Gloning, K., 509, 513, 671
Goda, S., 473
Goebel, R., 166
Goldberger, J., 519
Goldblum, M., 517
Goldstein, L., 288, 290
Gonzales, P., 538, 552, 553
Goodhart, W., 480, 481, 501
Goodluck, H., 61, 184
Goodman, M., 535
Gordon, D., 514
Gordon, P., 282, 430, 431
Goto, H., 283, 284
Graf, P., 220, 221
Grauberg, W., 352
Greasley, V., 281
Green, D., 517
Green, K., 402
Greenbaum, S., 376–379
Greenberg, C., 293
Greenberg, J., 10, 199, 205, 206, 294
Gregg, K., 2, 10, 17, 19, 20–23, 25–27, 29, 32, 35, 49, 53, 54, 61, 85, 90–92, 126, 128, 130, 162, 163, 208, 247, 248, 251, 257, 261, 329, 332, 350, 352, 353, 375, 377, 383, 384, 387, 389, 413, 495, 496, 615, 618
Grice, W., 251
Grimshaw, J., 430, 431, 433
Grondin, N., 110, 111
Grosjean, F., 571, 573, 667, 670, 672
Gross, D., 479

Grosser, W., 269, 291
Grotjahn, R., 360, 361
Gubala-Ryzak, M., 17, 63, 64, 101
Guberina, P., 402
Guilfoyle, E., 110
Guiora, A., 272
Gumperz, J., 599, 600, 630, 631, 637, 639, 640, 659, 661–663
Gutfreund, M., 437
Guy, G., 254, 261

H

Ha, M., 426
Haans, J., 377
Hadding, K., 274
Haegeman, L., 186
Hafiz, J., 531
Hakansson, G., 416, 417
Hakuta, K., 217, 571, 572, 580, 640
Hall, D., 671
Halle, M., 288, 297
Halliday, M., 365, 586
Hamman, S., 221
Hammerbarg, B., 269, 294,
Hammerberg, B., 323
Hammond, M., 11
Hammond, R., 278
Hamp, E., 599
Han, M., 513
Hancin-Bhatt, B., 298
Hanlon, C., 425, 431
Hannigan, S., 3, 15, 24, 29, 103, 181, 270, 354, 385, 670
Hansen, N., 217
Harley, B., 423, 424, 428
Harner, L., 530, 534, 536, 549
Harrington, M., 223
Harris, K., 277
Harris, Z., 5
Hart, D., 423, 424
Hatch, E., 13, 67, 166, 279, 369, 416–419, 445, 545, 553, 631
Haugen, E., 287, 571, 581, 591, 600, 667
Havelka, J., 587
Hawkins, B., 437
Hawkins, J., 11, 377
Hawkins, R., 122
Heath, S., 54, 436

Hécaen, H., 671
Hecht, B., 278, 292
Heidelberger Forschungsprojekt, 416
Heider, F., 472, 473
Heider, G., 472, 473
Heike, A., 296
Hein, S., 281
Heine, B., 383
Hempel, C., 7, 11, 50
Henderson, T., 53
Henning, W., 281
Henrichsen, L., 417
Henzl, V., 416
Heredia, R., 2, 13, 24, 30, 34, 36, 38, 69, 355, 364
Herman, R., 547
Hermon, G., 100
Hernández-Chávez, E., 15, 322, 640
Herron, C., 428, 440–442
Herschmann, H., 671
Higa, C., 417
Hillenbrand, J., 289
Hiller, R., 597
Hilles, S., 112
Hindley, R., 575
Hinnenkamp, V., 416
Hirakawa, M., 98, 331, 332, 334
Hirsh-Pasek, K., 425, 431
Hirvonen, T., 417
Hodne, B., 293
Hoefnagel-Hohle, M., 511
Hoff-Ginsberg, E., 437
Hoffman, C., 571
Holisky, D., 532
Holliday, L., 419
Homburg, T., 323
Hood, L., 433
Hooley, B., 582
Hopper, P., 566
Hornstein, N., 50, 85, 162
Howard, D., 216
Huang, C., 164, 544
Huang, J., 13, 137
Hubel, D., 164
Hudson, R., 272, 300
Huffines, M., 606
Hulstijn, J., 219, 416, 422, 427, 428
Hurtig, R., 275
Hyams, N., 62, 90, 183
Hyltenstam, K., 200–204, 207, 323, 519, 672
Hymes, D., 53

I

Iatridou, S., 102
Immelman, K., 165
Ioup, G., 64, 103, 173, 176, 269, 273, 331
Irvine, J., 231
Ishiguro, T., 416, 417
Issidorides, D., 416, 422
Itoh, H., 279, 299
Iverson, G., 327, 328

J

Jackendoff, R., 488
Jacobs, B., 59, 510
Jacobsen, T., 534, 537
Jacobsen, W., 532
Jacoby, L., 221
Jaeger, J., 288
Jaeggli, O., 113
Jakobovits, L., 588
Jakobson, R., 199, 536
James, A., 3, 31, 34, 38, 39, 115, 181, 199,
    269, 286, 288, 290, 291, 295, 298, 299,
    327
Jamieson, D., 277
Janda, R., 415
Janssen-Van Dieten, A., 416
Jenkins, L., 132
Johansson, S., 271, 293
Johnson, E., 580
Johnson, J., 103, 104, 112, 127, 151, 176, 177,
    181, 182, 256, 512, 613, 615
Johnson, M., 370
Jones, B., 474
Joos, M., 5
Jordens, P., 325, 326
Joshi, A., 645
Juffs, A, 138, 177
Junque, C., 517

K

Kachru, B., 630, 631, 640, 649, 652
Kachru, Y., 649
Kahn, D., 297
Kamibayashi, K., 550, 552
Kamwangamalu, N., 628, 631

Kanagy, R., 448
Kaplan, B., 434
Kaplan, T., 110, 111
Karanth, P., 513
Karmiloff-Smith, A., 623
Karttunen, F., 614, 624
Kasper, G., 20, 225
Katz, J., 416, 417
Kauders, O., 671
Kaye, J., 114, 291, 298
Kean, M-L., 75, 163, 164, 169
Keane, M., 213, 216, 219
Keating, P., 276, 288
Keenan, E., 10, 11, 201, 202, 424, 445, 498
Keller-Cohen, D., 323
Kellerman, E., 318, 320, 324, 325, 326, 334,
    364, 399, 591
Kelly, L., 317, 584
Kenny, A., 531
Kent, R., 280
Khare, J., 662
King, M., 424
King, C., 474, 489, 494
Kiparsky, P., 233
Klatt, D., 285
Klavans, J., 631
Kleifgen, J., 416
Klein, A., 273
Klein, W., 386, 398
Klima, E., 8
Kloss, H., 375
Kløve, M., 298
Koda, K., 534, 538, 541, 542
Kohler, K., 286, 287
Kohn, K., 397
Kolers, P., 213, 218
Konieczna, E., 530
Koss, E., 519
Kovac, C., 239, 240
Krashen, S., 8, 16, 17, 26, 40, 49, 165, 166, 167,
    180, 236, 255, 320, 351, 352, 358, 427,
    447, 511
Kretschmer, L., 470
Kretschmer, R., 470
Kroch, A., 384
Krueger, N., 217
Kuczaj, S., 529, 534, 559
Kuhberg, H., 612
Kuhl, P., 285
Kuhn, T. S., 60

Kumpf, L., 543, 544, 545
Kuroda, S-Y., 491

L

L'Hermitte, R., 671
Labov, W., 14, 230, 231, 232, 235, 250, 251, 292, 356, 357, 378, 639
Ladefoged, P., 180, 285
Lado, R., 5, 196, 278, 286, 317, 318, 350
Lakoff, G., 370, 381, 555
Lakshmanan, U., 110, 111, 113, 129, 331– 334, 337
Lambert, W., 15, 16, 17, 587, 588, 598, 607
Lamendella, J., 510, 512
Lance, D., 639
Lane, H., 272, 281, 282
Lapkin, S., 423, 424
Lardiere, D., 142
Larkins, J., 281
Larmouth, D., 614
Larsen-Freeman, D., 1, 3, 20, 29, 49, 67, 68, 355, 358, 360, 416, 510
Lasnik, H., 123, 146
Lavandera, B., 232
Lavinson, S., 20, 251
Leather, J., 3, 31, 34, 38, 39, 115, 181, 199, 269, 276, 279, 282, 284, 327
Lebeaux, D., 184
Lee, C., 631
Lee, D., 37, 178, 183, 185, 187
Lee, K-O., 110
Leiguarda, R., 515
Lenneberg, E., 15, 29, 165, 447, 510, 511
Leone, P., 550, 552
Leopold, W., 173
Levelt, W., 20, 215, 219, 224, 376–378, 656
Li, C., 173
Li, P., 534, 538–542
Liceras, J., 329, 386
Lieberson, S., 574, 575, 580
Lieven, E., 436
Lifter, K., 531
Lightbown, P., 100, 216, 217, 428, 429, 433, 438
Lightfoot, D., 50, 85, 86, 90, 162, 383, 384
Lindau, M., 285
Lindblom, B., 285
Linell, P., 285, 297
Lipton, P., 68

Lisker, K., 274
Lively, S., 277, 278
Locke, J., 273
Lodge, M., 398–403
Loewenthal, K., 272
Logan, G., 218–220
Logan, J., 275, 277, 278
Long, M., 1, 3, 10, 19, 20, 25, 29, 33, 40, 49, 55, 56, 67, 73, 100, 165, 166, 180, 183, 355, 358, 360, 383, 414, 416, 417–419, 429, 436, 438, 448, 449, 451, 453, 495, 498, 510 512, 537, 546, 618, 620
Loschky, L., 450
Lott, D., 352
Loveday, L., 271
Lubker, J., 285
Luce, P., 278
Luppescu, S., 425
Lust, B., 110, 124, 127, 130, 136, 143, 144, 150, 169, 183, 484, 662
Luterman, D., 470
Lylyk, P., 515
Lynch, T., 417
Lyons, J., 542

M

Ma, R., 576
Macdonald, D., 448
Macedo, D., 334
MacGinitie, W., 473
Mack, J., 402
Mack., M., 284
MacKain, K., 276
MacKay, D., 280
Macken, M., 328
Mackey, W., 572, 573, 576
MacKinnon, K., 582
Maclachlan, A., 94
MacLaughlin, D., 499
Macnamara, J., 445, 586, 598
MacWhinney, B., 13, 39, 335, 336, 430, 551
Madden, C., 320, 367
Madden, L., 167
Mahar, J., 614
Mahecha, N., 516
Mairs, J., 298
Major, R., 289, 291, 292, 295, 299, 545
Malouf, R., 434
Mandler, G., 221

Mangione, L., 124
Manheimer, R., 428
Manning, W., 281
Mannon, T., 418
Manuel, S., 55, 150, 152, 167
Manzini, R., 30, 63, 90, 98, 100, 178, 299, 387, 494–498
Maratsos, M., 143
Marks, C., 477
Marler, P.-R., 167
Marschark, M., 470
Martin, L., 378
Martin-Jones, M., 595
Martohardjono, G., 93, 95, 104, 128, 129, 130, 132, 135, 137, 138, 149, 150, 152, 163, 173, 177
Masica, C., 649
Massaro, D., 213, 280
Matthews, S., 530, 540, 547, 560–562
May, R., 492
Mazurkewich, I., 621
McBride, L., 671
McCarthy, J., 50
McClelland, J., 58
McConvell, P., 628
McDaniels, D., 143
McDavid, R., 230
McDonald, E., 273
McGhee, R., 543–545, 547
McGroarty, M., 225
McIntosh, A., 586
McLaren, J., 431
McLaughlin, B., 2, 3, 12, 13, 17, 24, 30, 36, 38, 58, 69, 70, 100, 217, 218, 222, 224, 355, 364, 630, 631
McLeod, B., 224
McNew, S., 335
McRoberts, G., 275
McShane, J., 534, 543
Meier, R., 470
Meijer, G., 376, 378, 399
Meijers, A., 377
Meisel, J., 17, 59, 167, 180, 333, 365, 415, 416, 417, 433, 446, 545, 546
Mellow, D., 429
Michaels, D., 288
Miller, C., 591
Miller, G., 18, 399
Miller, R., 527, 534, 535, 536, 547
Milroy, J., 231
Milroy, L., 230, 231

Mishina, S., 544
Mito, K., 442, 445, 451
Miyagawa, S., 145
Miyawaki, K., 275
Mochizuki, M., 284
Moerk, E., 437
Mohan, B., 381, 398, 399
Mohanan, K., 297
Molony, C., 655
Montandon, E., 480
Montanelli, D., 474, 475, 476, 477, 478, 479
Montgomery, M., 236
Moore, C., 431
Moravcsik, E., 11, 195
Moravcsik, J., 54
Morgenthaler, L., 419
Morosan, P., 277
Morris, C., 221
Mosner, A., 671
Moulton, W., 196, 286
Mourelatos, A., 531, 533, 542
Mueller, T., 281
Mukattash, L., 352
Mulac, A., 248
Mulford, R., 278, 292
Muller-Gotama, F., 177
Munnich, E., 130, 132
Murphy, C., 614
Muysken, P., 91, 95, 96, 111, 122, 130, 167, 168, 334, 416, 529, 535
Myer, D., 282
Myers-Scotton, C., 631, 632, 636, 637, 638, 641, 655, 656, 663, 678, 681
Myklebust, H., 472, 473, 492, 493

N

Nagel, E., 11
Naoi, K., 330
Nathan, G., 289
Nation, R., 217
Nayak, N., 217
Neisser, U., 222, 518
Nelson, D., 200
Nelson, K., 433, 434, 437, 440, 441, 451
Nemser, W., 278, 290, 295
Neufeld, G., 282
Newell, A., 223
Newmeyer, F., 5, 54, 75, 376, 377, 381, 529
Newport, E., L., 54, 103, 104, 112, 127, 128,

Newport, E., L., (*continued*)
    151, 165, 176, 177, 181, 182, 183, 256,
    437, 470, 512, 613, 615
Niedzielski, H., 281
Nilipour, R., 517, 518
Ninio, A., 53
Nishimura, M., 417, 631, 662, 680
Nixon, N., 543, 544
Nobuyoshi, J., 447
Noji, J., 538
Noonan, D., 110
Nooteboom, S., 280
Norman, D., 213, 220
Nosofsky, R., 277, 285
Novoa, L., 512
Nunan, D., 4, 8, 16, 24, 39, 131, 217, 286, 319,
    320, 350, 353, 358, 359, 361, 365, 366,
    367, 375
Nunnally, J., 377, 394, 398, 399

O

O'Grady, W., 58, 60, 71
O'Malley, J., 225
O'Neil, W., 132, 318, 384
Obler, L., 3, 15, 24, 29, 40, 103, 181, 270, 285,
    328, 354, 510, 512, 513, 514, 516, 519,
    585, 670
Ochs, E., 54, 436, 445
Oden, G., 280
Odlin, T., 318, 320, 351
Ohala, J., 288
Ojemann, G., 515
Oliver, R., 444
Olshtain, E., 143, 369, 518, 606, 607
Orlovic, M., 322
Osgood, C., 510
Osherson, D., 555
Osser, H., 534
Osthoff, H., 263
Otsu, Y., 169, 170, 176, 330
Ouhalla, J., 387
Oxford, R., 225
Oyama, S., 128, 165, 173, 180, 511

P

Pakir, A., 631, 681
Pandharipande, R., 644

Pankhurst, J., 384
Papcun, G., 285
Paradis, M., 509, 514, 516–518, 670
Pateman, T., 379, 383
Pater, J., 114
Patkowski, M., 128, 173, 180, 182, 511
Paul, M., 448
Paul, P., 470
Pavesi, M., 427
Pavlovic, C., 402
PDP Research Group, 58
Peck, S., 369, 417, 550, 551
Penfield, W., 354
Penner, S., 431
Pennington, M., 269, 296, 300
Perdue, C., 386
Perecman, E., 671, 672, 673
Perkell, J., 279
Peters, A., 173, 328
Petrosino, L., 402
Pfaff, C., 610, 612, 632, 643, 644, 648, 655, 657
Phinney, M., 97, 333
Piaget, J., 18, 132, 535
Pica, T., 358, 359, 417, 418, 419, 448, 449, 450
Pick, H., 280
Pickford, D., 230
Pienemann, M., 17, 68, 167, 365, 433
Pierce, A., 110, 489
Pilsch, H., 671
Pimsleur, P., 281
Pinhas, J., 484
Pinker, S., 36, 40, 54, 55, 59, 64, 90, 183, 430,
    431, 433, 440, 441, 537
Pisoni, D., 277, 278, 281, 282
Pitres, A., 509
Pizzamiglio, L., 402
Platt, J., 578
Platt, M., 445
Plough, I., 498
Plough, J., 448
Pluut, E., 294
Poetzl, O., 671
Polivanov, E., 6, 285
Pollack, C., 378
Pollock, J.-Y., 8, 87, 88, 89, 101, 102, 110, 485,
    486, 491, 499, 653
Poplack, S., 591, 632, 635, 640, 641, 643, 669,
    670, 681
Port, R., 283
Porter, P., 418, 419

Post, K., 431
Postovsky, V., 282
Power, D., 474, 475
Pressnell, L., 475
Preston, D., 2, 10, 14, 17, 20, 23, 31, 34, 36, 38,
    67, 253, 255, 256, 259, 261, 295, 357, 386
Price, B., 355
Price, P., 279
Prince, A., 59
Progovac, L., 98, 99
Puppel, S., 294
Purcell, E., 270
Pürschel, H., 278
Putnam, H., 54
Pylyshyn, Z., W., 59

Q

Quigley, S., 470, 473, 475–480, 489, 494
Qurik, R., 376, 379

R

Radford, A., 40, 110, 111, 150, 184, 488, 489
Radulovič, L., 536
Ramamurti, R., 416
Ramsay, V., 543, 544, 547, 550–553
Rangamani, G., 513
Rankin, J., 428
Ranta, L., 100, 429
Rapport, R., 515
Raupach, M., 296
Ready, D., 417, 418
Reichardt, C., 360
Reinhart, T., 493
Repp, B., 274, 280, 281
Reynolds, D., 547
Ribot, T., 509, 510
Richards, J., 269, 320
Richardson, M., 439, 440, 444
Richardson-Klavehn, A., 220
Ringbom, H., 320
Ringen, C., 275
Rispoli, M., 530, 534
Ritchie, W., 4, 10, 19, 24, 33, 41, 121, 205, 280,
    329, 509, 519, 538, 590, 610, 611, 655
Ritter, E., 651, 653
Rivero, M., 653

Rivers, W., 5
Roberge, Y., 443
Roberts, L., 354
Roberts, P., 517
Robertson, D., 403
Robinson, P., 426
Robinson, R., 543, 544, 547, 555
Roediger, H., 213, 221
Roeper, T., 499
Romaine, S., 3, 24, 34, 41, 231, 528, 571, 592,
    593, 595, 606, 611, 627, 632, 642–644,
    649, 650, 655, 657, 666, 670
Rosansky, E., 8, 384
Rosch, E., 555
Rosenstein, J., 472
Ross, J., 378, 382, 555
Ross, S., 417, 451
Rossi, M., 402
Rossman, T., 224
Rothstein, G., 543, 544
Roussou, A., 387
Rubach, J., 297, 299
Ruben, D-H., 50, 51
Rubin, E., 649, 674, 679
Rulon, K., 448
Rumelhart, D. E., 58, 220
Rutherford, W., 71, 111, 127, 161, 323, 326,
    370, 425
Ryan, L., 221
Ryle, G., 531

S

Sabo-Abramson, H., 519
Sachs, J., 556
Safir, K., 63, 113
Sag, I., 557, 558
Saito, M., 146
Salica, C., 438
Salmon, W. C., 50
Samar, V., 494, 498, 499, 500
Sankoff, D., 591, 632, 633, 640, 641, 643, 680,
    681
Sasanuma, S., 517, 518
Sato, C., 293, 296, 366, 419, 445, 446, 447, 546
Satterly, D., 437
Satz, P., 165
Sawyer, M., 223
Scarborough, H., 437

Scarcella, R., 514
Scarcella, S., 26, 180, 417, 419, 511
Schachter, J., 2, 4, 10, 19, 27, 28, 29, 34, 36, 37, 38, 50, 60, 64, 66, 86, 91, 92, 95, 98, 103, 130, 133, 134, 140, 160, 161, 167, 176, 177, 185, 200, 208, 247, 270, 319, 321, 323, 324, 327, 329, 330, 331, 334, 353, 377, 386–389, 425, 427, 447, 480, 495, 512, 585, 609, 615
Schacter, D., 220
Scherer, K., 271
Schieffelin, B., 436, 445
Schiffler, L., 272
Schils, E., 518
Schmidt, M., 205
Schmidt, R., 58, 216, 220, 295, 327, 356, 366, 423, 426, 427
Schneider, B., 281, 282
Schneider, W., 214–216, 218–220
Schneiderman, E., 273, 281, 282, 513
Schneiderman, M., 425
Scholes, R., 274
Schonberger, R., 272
Schouten, M., 273, 274
Schulze, H., 671
Schumann, J., 8, 16, 17, 59, 67, 166, 167, 271, 322, 355, 356, 366, 384, 415, 510
Schwartz, B., 17, 53, 61–64, 92, 93, 97, 100, 101, 110, 111, 113, 129, 145, 179, 180, 512
Sciarone, A., 197
Scollon, R., 445
Scotton, C., 640
Scovel, T., 24, 55, 173, 354, 511
Scuffil, M., 278
Searle, J., 213
Seliger, H., 3, 10, 33, 41, 160, 166, 180, 204, 332, 388, 424, 480, 496, 498, 512, 537, 581, 606, 616, 623
Selinker, L., 1–6, 8, 110, 111, 205, 289, 290, 320, 324, 337, 351, 384
Selkirk, E., 295
Shapira, R., 416
Shapson, S., 428
Sharma, V., 662
Sharwood-Smith, M., 92, 318, 320, 329, 334, 384, 425, 428, 591, 614
Shatz, M., 454
Sheldon, A., 284, 328
Sherman, J., 143, 144
Shiffrin, R., 214, 215, 218–220

Shin, H.-J., 277
Shirai, Y., 3, 16, 28, 31, 33, 34, 40, 41, 100, 217, 242, 252, 425, 432, 534, 538, 541–545, 547, 550–553, 614, 620, 634
Shlonsky, U., 12
Shopen, T., 655
Shortreed, I., 417, 421
Siegel, S., 395
Siegel, G., 280
Silva-Corvalán, C., 595, 606, 624
Silverberg, R., 514
Silverman, S., 470
Simoes, M., 534
Simon, C., 328
Simon, T., 514
Sinclair, H., 527, 531, 534–536, 539, 547
Singh, R., 297, 648, 649
Singleton, D., 26, 56
Sithole, N., 275
Skehan, P., 447
Skutnabb-Kangas, T., 593, 596
Slimani, A., 438
Slobin, D., 69, 70, 150, 476, 539, 540, 554
Smith, C., 530–532, 534, 542, 547, 549, 558
Smith, E., 555
Smith, M., 426
Smith, N., 480
Smith, S., 53, 335
Snow, C., 54, 376–378, 399, 416, 417, 430, 431, 436, 452, 511, 549, 551
Soares, C., 513
Sokolik, M., 426
Solin, D., 93
Solomons, L., 216
Sorace, A., 4, 10, 16, 24, 39, 105, 108, 109, 131, 349, 385, 388, 390, 397, 403
Spada, N., 100, 428, 429, 438
Speidel, G., 435
Spencer, N., 378
Spolsky, B., 271, 583
Sprouse, R., 92, 110, 145
Squire, L., 221
Sridhar, K., 611, 643
Sridhar, S., 611, 643
Stake, R., 365
Stampe, D., 299
Stanlaw, J., 655
Stanowicz, L., 431, 432, 433, 435
Starkstein, S., 515
Stauble, A., 355

Steedman, M., 377
Stein, G., 216
Steinkamp, M., 474
Stengel, E., 671
Stephany, U., 534, 541, 550–553
Sternberg, S., 239
Stevens, J., 402
Stevens, K., 285
Stevens, P., 279, 280
Stevens, S., 401, 402
Stockman, I., 294
Stockwell, R., 196, 286
Stoel-Gammon, C., 534
Stowell, T., 499
Strange, W., 274, 276, 284, 328
Strevens, P., 270
Strickland, F., 272
Strong, M., 470
Stroud, C., 519, 672
Strozer, J., 133
Stuckless, E., 477
Studdert-Kennedy, M., 274
Suomi, S., 165
Sussman, H., 514
Suter, R., 270
Svartvik, J., 376
Swain, M., 53, 366, 423, 424, 427, 443–
    445, 447
Swisher, M., 417, 470

T

Tabouret-Keller, A., 671
Tahta, S., 272
Takahashi, K., 550, 552
Takashima, H., 550, 552
Takefuta, Y., 402
Tan, C., 515
Tanaka, S., 545, 557
Tansomboom, A., 173, 273
Tardy, C., 378
Tarone, E., 14, 17, 23, 24, 67, 130, 236, 289,
    290, 293, 296, 356
Tavakolian, S., 143
Tay, M., 631, 681
Taylor, D., 54
Taylor, H., 543, 544
Taylor, J., 555, 556
Taylor, L., 272

Teitelbaum, H., 597
Teleni, V., 363
Tenunissen, J., 165
Teranishi, K., 331–334
Terrell, T., 425
Thomas, D., 416
Thomas, M., 94, 97, 98, 128, 129, 132, 331,
    332, 334
Thompson, S., 173, 248, 545
Tobena, A., 517
Toivainen, J., 534
Tomaselli, A., 93, 97, 111
Tomasello, M., 428, 440–442
Tomlin, R., 426, 452
Toner, M., 402
Toribio, A., 649, 674, 676, 679
Towell, R., 122
Trahey, M., 71, 102
Tran-Chi-Chau, 352
Traugott, E., 383
Travis, L., 93, 94
Treffers-Daller, J., 631, 659
Treichel, B., 296
Treiman, R., 425
Tropf, H., 293
Trubetzkoy, N., 6, 285
Trudgill, P., 234, 250, 256
Tsimpli, I., 387
Tsuda, A., 397
Tubielewicz, Mattsson, D., 291
Tucker, A., 143
Tulving, E., 221
Tweissi, A., 415, 417, 417, 418, 421
Tyson, A., 386

U

Uziel, S., 129, 132, 138

V

Vago, R., 200, 294, 606
Vaid, J., 513, 514, 671
Vainikka, A., 110, 145, 146
Valdés-Fallis, G., 629, 680
Valdman, A., 276, 418
van Buren, P., 329, 384
van Cleve, J., 470

van Dalen, T., 273
van der Vlugt, H., 166
van Eeden, R., 416
van Els, T., 518, 607
van Fraassen, B.,C., 51
van Helmond, K., 326, 329
van Helvert, K., 416
van Lier, L., 365
van Patten, B., 427
van Riemsdijk, H., 174
van Valin, R., 532
van Vugt, M., 326, 329
Vance, T., 275
Vanniarajan, S., 632
Varonis, E., 417–419, 448, 450, 451
Vendler, Z., 529, 531
Vendrell, P., 517
Vendrell-Brucet, J., 517
Verhoeven, L., 655
Vihman, M., 30
Villa, V., 426, 452
Vincent, N., 383
Vogel, I., 298

W

Wagner Gough, J., 369, 416
Walters, J., 513
Walz, J., 282
Wanner, E., 162
Ward, F., 272
Wardhaugh, R., 196, 286
Warren-Leubecker, A., 417
Watamori, T., 517, 518
Watanabe, Y., 427, 428
Waterbury, N., 143
Watson-Gegeo, K., 436
Weigl, W., 100
Weinberger, S., 5, 75, 269, 291, 297, 298
Weiner, R., 416
Weinert, R., 30
Weinreich, U., 287, 288, 510, 573, 590
Weisenberg, T., 671
Weiss, L., 272
Weiss, R., 281
Weist, R., 529–536, 537, 539, 541, 542, 544,
    545, 549, 560
Weldon, M., 221
Wells, G., 437
Weltens, B., 518, 607

Wenden, A., 225
Wenk, B., 291, 292, 296
Wenzell, V., 544
Werker, J., 275
Wertz, R., 519
Wesche, M., 273, 417, 418
Westwood, A., 633
Wexler, K., 25, 30, 54, 56, 63, 87, 90, 98, 100, 178,
    183–185, 188, 299, 387, 494–498, 537
Wheeler, S., 633
Whitaker, H., 515
White, L., 2, 4, 9, 10, 17, 19, 27, 28, 32, 34, 38,
    39, 50, 53, 55, 56, 60, 64, 65, 71, 72, 75,
    90–97, 100–102, 105, 107, 110, 111, 126,
    128, 130, 132, 138, 140, 149, 150, 151,
    162, 163, 167, 171, 174, 177, 186, 208,
    209, 247, 248, 297, 321, 327, 329, 330–
    333, 337- 339, 353, 375, 377, 384, 387–
    389, 413, 424, 425, 427–429, 438, 445,
    487, 495, 496, 499, 615, 618, 621
Whitman, J., 110
Whitman, R., 286
Whittaker, S., 534, 543
Widdowson, H., 452
Wieden, W., 290, 291
Wiesel, T., 164
Wilbur, R., 470, 473, 475–481, 492, 501
Williams, C., 582
Williams, E., 174
Williams, J., 253,
Williams, L., 274, 279, 283
Willing, K., 270
Wirth, J., 11, 195
Witkowska-Stadnik, K., 530
Wode, H., 8, 61, 276, 290, 292, 321, 322, 384
Woisetschlaeger, E., 536
Wolf-Quintero, K., 58, 71, 426
Wolfram, W., 232, 241
Wolfson, N., 231
Wong-Fillmore, L., 30, 217, 416, 417
Wood, M., 272
Woodward, J., 54, 165
Woolford, E., 645, 648
Wyckoff, J., 437
Wysocko, H., 530

Y

Yano, Y., 417, 422
Yanz, J., 397

Yap, F-H., 550, 552, 553, 558
Yeni-Komshian, G., 279
Yin, R., 356
Yip, V., 161, 331, 377
Yoshioka, H., 277
Yoshitomi, A., 544
Young, M., 416
Young, R., 239, 254, 417, 450
Young-Scholten, M., 110, 145, 146, 297, 298
Youseff, V., 538
Yule, G., 397, 448

Z

Zatorre, R., 513, 514
Zelmanowitz, J., 671
Zimmerman, G., 279
Zobl, H., 17, 132, 318, 322, 327, 337, 338, 545
Zuengler, J., 271, 321
Zurif, E., 279
Zwicky, A. D., 415
Zwicky, A. M., 415

SUBJECT INDEX

A

A-over-A constraint, 172, 173
Acceptability
  core vs. periphery of language, 382, 385–389
  cross-modality matching Paradigm, 402–404
  extending magnitude estimation, 402–403
    in L2, 404–405
    in linguistics, 404–405
  hierarchy, 381–383
    and fuzzy grammars, 381–382
    and Universal Grammar, 382–383
  judgments, 39
    four conditions for elicitation of, 391–392
    nonnative, 385
  magnitude estimation of, 400–403
  nonnative, 375
    competency, 384–385
  phonological
    accent, 183, 271
    accent ratings, 180, 181
  ratings and mental contexts, 377
  role of determinacy and indeterminacy, 391, 403, 404
Accessibility
  noun phrase accessibility hierarchy, 202–203, 207
Acculturation
  hypothesis, 366
  model, 16
Acoustic–phonetic, norms approximation by

French advanced learners of English, 283
Acoustic–phonetic divergence, between native language and target language, 285
Acquisition
  and affective variables, 67
  and age, 56
  and attention, 70, 73
  and conservative strategy, 71
  and developmental problem, 90
  and fatigue effect, 104
  and focus, 40
  and fossilization stage, 30, 34, 35
  and language contact, 40
  and memorization, 69
  and nonmodular approaches, 58–60
  and pidgin and creole languages, 527–530
  and variation, 67
  beyond early stages, 31
  by normal vs. deaf children, 40
  child–adult differences, 112–115
  cognitive factors, 29
  developmental problem, 49, 50, 66, 73, 74, 75
  domain specific knowledge, 219
  environment, naturalistic, 388
  first and second language, 90–93
  incomplete, 168
  L1 and L2, 90
  means, native vs. nonnative, 92, 93
  mechanism, 66
  modular approaches, 60, 71–73, 187

Acquisition (*continued*)
  neuropsychological factors, 29, 40
  of morphology, 527–530, 535, 537, 538, 545,
      546, 548
    and markedness, 545
    and transfer, 545, 547
    morpheme order, 68
    prototype theory, 555–559
  of semantics, 31, 33, 34
    relations, 165
  of syntax, 31, 34, 38, 39
    child L2 vs. adult L2, 181
    conjoined structure by deaf learners, 494
    relative clauses by deaf learners, 490
    order, 353, 510
  principle-based approach, 187
  process, 36, 38, 50, 66
    role of indeterminacy, 386, 403, 404
    role of environment, 55
  smaller languages by deaf learners, 497
  social psychological factors, 29, 39, 41
  stages of, 24
  theory
    beyond, L2, 112
    conceptual foundations, 2
    conceptual problems, 176
    criteria, 66, 67
    developmental problem, 26, 32, 35
    developmental sequence, 68
    domain, 73
    Mechanism Criterion, 67–70, 72
    problems, 73–75
    prospects, 73–75
    Sequence Criterion, 67-68
    Theoretical Framework Criterion, 67–70, 73
    transition to later stages, 30
  vs. learning 16
Adaptation (speech) and periphery of language,
    384
Adequacy, descriptive and explanatory, 384
Adjectival phrase, 492–493
Adjectives, deletion of, 147
Adjuncts, 137
Adult grammars, range of, 8
Adult learner, 2–30, 39
Adverb placement, 87, 101, 102, 337
Adverbial
  adjunct clause, 124–125, 138, 139, 140, 141
  subordinate pre- and postposed, 136–137
Affective Filter Hypothesis, 17
Aggressiveness, 251

Agreement (Agr), 96, 99, 110, 486, 487, 488
Agreement Parameter, 62–63
Alzheimer's syndrome, 24
Ambiguity, 377
American Sign Language (ASL), 470
Amnesiac patients, 221
Analogy, 131, 133
Anaphor, 70
Anaphora, 28, 96, 98, 99
  direction of, 136, 141, 142
Anaphoric pronoun, 87, 141
ANOVA, 363 398, 403
Aphasia, 15, 24, 166, 511
  age-dependent, 166
  Broca's, 517, 518
  jargon, 166
  language recovery patterns among bilinguals,
      516–519
  motor, 166
  polyglot, 25, 41, 509, 608, 671–674
    and cognitive deficit theory, 517
    pre- and posttreatment language testing,
        517
  Wernicke's, 517–518
Applied linguistics, 4
Approaches, L2 acquisition study, 4
  Functional–Typological, 195–196, 204
  modular principle-based, 187
Aptitude, 222–225, 355
  and classroom language, 222
  differences, 222, 225, 355
  tests, 222
Arabic, 12, 576, 577, 578
  religious domain, 576
Argument chains, 184
Articles, 181
  difficulties of deaf learners, 492
Articulatory phonology, 288
Articulatory parameters, 281
Aspect
  grammatical vs. lexical, 530
  in Tagalog, Lakhota, Georgian, 532
  lexical
    classification and semantics, 531–533
  perfective vs. imperfective
    in Spanish, Greek, and Russian, 530, 537
  progressive
    in English, 530
  types, 72
Association learning, 216

Attention, 23, 425–448
  attention and storage in long-term memory, 426
  input enhancement device, 428
  noticing input–output mismatch, 426, 447
  prestige forms, 236
  selective, 414
  three components 426
Attitudes, 15, 27, 41, 351, 355
  and code-mixing continuum, 669
Attrition, 3, 4, 388
  disfluency, 606
  L1, 614–615, 624
  L2, 624
  L2 or foreign language, 607
  language
    among bilinguals, 24, 41
    creation of creoles, 614
    developmental stages or other reasons, 606
    intergenerational restructuring, 614
    lexical retrieval failure, 606
    semilingualism, 614
  monolingual control group, 607
  primary language, 607
    and language mixing, 610–613
    different types of, 609
    establishing baseline norms, 608–609
    external sources of, 616
    internal sources of, 616–617
    process, 617
    sources of, 615–617
    the logical problem, 615
    three stages of, 617
    various manifestations, 606
    vs. manner, context of normal language acquisition, 608–609
  temporary or permanent, 606
Auditory Discrimination Test, 273
Automatic processing, 13, 34
Automatization, instance theory of, 216
Avoidance, 24
  of English relative clauses by Chinese adult learners, 323
  strategy, 367
Awareness, 425

B

Bahasa Malaysia, 579
Barriers, social and geographical, 241

Beliefs, negative, 59
Bilingual aphasia; *see* Aphasia, polyglot
Bilingual
  brain
    epileptic, differential organization, 515
    peri-Sylvanian region, 515
  community, 41, 572–573
    Puerto Ricans in New York City, 576
  countries, profiles of, 574–575
  education
    immersion programs, 594
    international perspective, 596–597
    language shelter programs, 596
    legal implications, 597
    reactions to, 597–598
    submersion programs, 593–594
    transitional programs, 594–595
  fluency, 587–588
  language
    assessment, culture, other variables, 587
    domain dominance, 586–587
    phonological ability, 585
    language processing, 516, 519
    semantic association, 588
  situation
    assessment problem, 574–575
    in Ireland, Israel, India, Canada, Spain, Philippines, 574–575
  verbal behavior; *see* Code switching
Bilingual Education Act, United States, 594–596
Bilingual Syntax Measure, 15, 353, 367
Bilingualism, 4, 24, 40, 41, 509, 571–601
  attitudes toward, 598–599
  borrowing, 584, 588–592
  brain damage, 509
  children's development, 592–593
  consequences of; *see* Language maintenance and shift
  Civil Rights Act, 597
  definition of, 511, 571–572
  deviant or pathological view of, 627
  difficulties of measuring, 24, 34
  domains of language use, 576–577
  dominance, 34
  English Language Act, 598
  individual
    degree of, 584–586
    measurement of, 584–588
  intelligence, 510
  interference, 510, 584, 588–592

Bilingualism, (*continued*)
  intergenerational communication, 592
  IQ testing, 592, 596
  lack of conservativism, 338
  language choice criteria, 576–577
  language attrition, 41, 605–624
    stages, 623–624
  Lau vs. Nichols, 597
  measurement problems, 588–589
    children's, 589
  minority languages, 576–577, 580–583
  Reduction Redundancy Principle, 618–623
  school achievement, 592–593
  scope of, 572–573
  subtractive, 594
  theoretical and analytical problems, 571
  transfer, 588–592
  types of, 571–572
    compound, coordinate, and subordinate, 510
  US English campaign, 598
Bilinguals, 3–4, 40, 107, 186
  early, 178
  late, 178
Binding, critical period, 183
Biological basis, of language, 22
Bioprogram
  distributional bias in, 561–562
  language learning, 528, 535, 539
  tense–aspect sub systems, 528, 535–539
Borrowing, 633
  as a periphery of language, 382
Bounded system, 365
  learning disabilities, 366
Bounding node, 60, 246
Bounding Node Parameter, 170
Brain
  Broca's area, 24
  child vs. adult, 163
  damage
    break down of language, 24, 40
    language acquisition, 165
    loss of pragmatic language choice, 519
    speech disorder, 355
  development
    role of home influence, 513
  general purpose central processing system, 57
  hemisphere, 3, 19, 24
    differential organization of language in
      bilinguals, 515

  hemispheric specialization
    lateralization, 165, 166
    L2 perception, 273
    processing, 173
  injury; *see* Brain, damage
  interconnected neurons, 59
  lateralization, 354
    dichotic listening, 166
    in monolingual vs. bilinguals, 513, 519
    in monolingual vs. crossed aphasic bilin-
      guals, 513
    measuring instruments, 514
    methodological problem, 514
  mapping techniques
    cortical stimulation, 515
    dichotic listening, 510
    noninvasive techniques, 510
    positron emission tomography (PET) scan,
      3, 516, 519
    sodium amytal testing, 515
    tachistoscopic listening, 510
  modules, 57
  neural firing, 59
  neurological changes with age, 354
  nonmodular approaches, 58
  plasticity, 164
    differential functions of two brains, 354–
      355
    gradual loss of, 166
    human cognitive systems, 164
    in restructuring, 217
    L2 learning, 354
    loss and L2 pronunciation, 354
    perceptual, 167
  right hemispheric involvement
    in bilinguals, 513, 514
  vs. mind 59
  Wernicke's area, 24
Branching Direction Principle, 124

C

C-command, 28, 60, 86, 87, 90, 94, 144, 186–
  87
Calque, 592
Canada, 15
Canadian French Immersion programs, 423, 425
Capacity
  behavioral, 27

cognitive, 27
for language, 21, 26, 27, 35, 36
inferential, 59
linguistic, 75
neuropsychological, 27

Capacity-free processing; *see* Automatic processing
Caretaker and child interaction, 435
Case assignment, 487
Case studies, 365–66
Categories, absolute vs. fuzzy, 555
Child, 2
grammar construction, 159
innate knowledge; *see* Universal Grammar
knowledge representation, 162
L1 and L2 acquisition, 334
L1, ordering constraint, 184
L2 acquisition, 159, 188
language acquisition
community language, 159
role of frequency and consistency, 384
language capacity, 159
vs. adult language acquisition, four differences, 160–161

Child–adult language acquisition; *see* L1 and L2 acquisition
Children
deaf, 165
feral, 165
head-complement order, 136
imitation, effectiveness of recasting among children, 435
language-impaired, 165
modeling and recasting advantage, 434

Chinese, 13, 28, 31, 93, 95, 96, 98, 103, 104, 137–139, 143–145, 150, 174, 175–177, 181–182, 252, 254–255, 320, 367
Clarification by L1 speaker, 431
Classroom studies, 365, 428–429
Clitic climbing in native and nonnative French, 390
Cloze tests, modified, 353
Clusters, 198, 206
Code mixing, 4, 24, 25, 41; *see also* Code switching; Language mixing
and discourse allocation, 664–665
and *do*-insertion, 651–655, 657
and dummy verbs, 649–650
and language dominance, 664–666

and methodological problems, 681–682
and other related phenomena, 628–635
borrowing, 632–634
code switching, 629–631
diglossia, 634–635
pidgin and creoles, 634
and polyglot aphasia, 671–674
and relativization, 661–662
and repair strategy, 662, 666–667
and sociopsychological motivations of, 662–664
and stem formation, 647
and theoretical and analytical problems, 680–681
and topic-comment structures, 661–662
and Universal Grammar, 645, 674, 675
attitudes toward, 667–672
constraints, 638–657
Adjectival Noun Phrase, 644–645
approaches to, 638–639
Blocking Hypothesis, 656
Clitic Pronoun, 643
Closed Class, 645
Dual Structure Principle, 643–644
Embedded Language Implicational Hierarchy Hypothesis, 656
Embedded Language Island, 656
Equivalence, 641–643
formal, 640–645
Free Morpheme, 640–641, 673
Functional Head Constraint, 640, 651–655, 674–682
Government Constraint, 648–654, 677–682
in agglutinative languages, 640
in Bantu languages, 640
matrix vs. embedded language, 631
Matrix Language-Frame Model, 655–657
Matrix Language Hypothesis, 655
Morpheme Order Principle, 655
random or systematic, 639–640
Semantic Congruence Principle, 658–659
semantics, 657–659
syntactic, 41
System Morpheme Principle 655
theoretically driven, 645–657
Trigger Hypothesis, 656
universal vs. language specific, 41, 640
Woolford's Model, 645–648
determinants of, 659–668

Code mixing, (*continued*)
  disorders; *see* Aphasia, polyglot
  types of, 635–638
    exploratory, 638
    sequential unmarked, 637
    unmarked vs. marked, 637–638
Code switching, 4, 24, 25, 41, 599–600
  and language proficiency, 33
  pathological, 24, 670–671
Cognition,
  Anderson's ACT* theory, 218
  meta-, 225
Cognitive
  capabilities, 2,4, 18, 19, 34, 36
  Comparison Theory, 441
  domains, 30, 38, 152
  functioning principles, 38
  pathways and L2 processing, 273
  processing, 425
  psychology, 36, 217
  structures, 19, 38
Community, norms and values, 230
Comparative construction
  difficulties of deaf learners, 492
Comparison,
  object of, 203
Competence, 52
  acquisition of, 90
  communicative, 53, 58
    four-component model, 366
  differential, 37, 105
  discourse, 366
  grammatical and extralinguistic factors, 375–377, 391
  grammatical, 3, 4, 6, 20–39, 50, 366–367
    and other mental systems, 36
    as a separate mental organ, 36
    as an unobservable phenomena, 54
  initial state, 173
  interlanguage, 386
  lexical, 65
  linguistic, 126, 130, 375
    and other mental processes, 122
  model of variable, 257
  modular conception, 53
  multiple grammar, 257
  native vs. nonnative, 92, 93, 106
  native and near native, 66, 105–106
  pragmatic, 20, 39, 65, 127

  sociolinguistic, 366
  strategic, 366
  ultimate attainment of, 173
  variable, 257, 258
  vs. performance, 248
  vs. performance in L2, 126
Competition Model, 13, 39, 66
  main concept, 335
  vs. Universal Grammar model, 335
Complement, 485–488, 493
Complement Phrase, 110, 248
Complementizer, 174
Complementizer Phrase, 110, 485–490
Complementizer Phrase Direction Parameter, 134–136
Complementizer Phrase Parameter, 124, 129, 135, 141, 146, 149
Complementizer system, 488, 500
  lack in early young hearing children, 488
Comprehensible Output Hypothesis, 447
Comprehension, 20
  strategies, grammar vs. meaning-based, 335–336
Comprehension Model, 20
Computer sciences, 217
Computer modeling, 13
Congruence Principle, 554–555
Conjunction
  as prepositions in deaf learners, 493
  difficulties of deaf learners, 493
Connectionist Hypothesis, 23
Consistency
  inter-subject, 392
  intra-subject, 392
Consonant cluster simplification strategy, 260
  social class determinants of, 232, 233
Context, linguistic and its effect on L2 acquisition, 292
Continuative marker, 242
Continuity Hypothesis, 183
  for L1, 183
  for L2, 183
Continuity Assumption Hypothesis, 55
Continuous Access Hypothesis, 129
Contraction, 417
Contrast Principle, 537
Contrastive Analysis, 5–6, 49, 286, 337, 338, 350, 351
  and its multiple manifestations, 319

shortcomings, 278, 286, 319–320
strong and weak versions, 286
Contrastive Analysis Hypothesis, 196- 208
problems of, 201
Contrastive phonology, 286–287, 290, 297
Control, 218, 246
Controlled processing, 12, 24
information transfer, 215
long-term memory, 215
Convergence, 256
Conversation
as a grammar development facilitator, 447
conversation as a complex task, 215
development of past tense morphology, 446–447
hierarchical structure, 215
input modification, 445–454
English (L2) learners of Japanese, 450
learner production of, 447
topic initiation in, 448
topic continuation in, 448
Coordinate structures, 205
Core vs. periphery of language, 382, 385–389
discontinuous relation, 382
Coreference, 131
Coreferential pairing, 131
Creative Construction Hypothesis, 49, 320, 339
Creative Construction process, 353
Creole languages, 527
continuum, 256
tense-aspect acquisition of, 528
Creolization, 3, 34, 40
processes
decreolization and hypercreolization, 634
sequencing, 34
Critical period, 15, 55, 247
and affective variables, 166
and brain plasticity, 354
and hemispheric lateralization, 165, 166
and input variables, 166
and level of proficiency, 511
and Universal Grammar, 167
cognitive variables, 166
for L1 acquisition, 164–166
for L2 acquisition, 166–173
for morphology and syntax, 183, 188
for phonology, 180, 183, 188
for Subjacency, 177, 183
for tone acquisition, 173

global, 183
one or multiple, 165, 166, 180, 183, 187, 512
postpubertal, 26, 40
progressive myelination, 166
variability, 165
Critical Period Hypothesis, 15, 18, 29, 35–40, 128, 149, 354, 605
criticism of, 354
Cross-modality matching paradigm, 402
Crossed aphasia
monolinguals vs. bilinguals, 509
over reporting of, 514
Crossed aphasic
Chinese–English bilinguals, 513
South Indian, 513
Cultural norms
and periphery of language, 384
Curriculum development
and tasks type, 359
Czech, 31, 197, 254–255
Case study, 361, 362, 365

D

Data
correlational, 222
cross-sectional and experimental data, 360
elicited vs. naturalistic, 366
qualitative, 360
quantitative, 360
natural speech, 5
relevant vs. irrelevant, 367
representative data, 230–231
types, 39
Data collection method, 360, 361–369
diagrams, 367
dialogues, 366
diary, 360–362
elicitation techniques, 39, 360, 361, 362, 366, 367
elicited imitation, 366
experimental vs. naturalistic, 365
field notes, 366
free conversation, 366
interview, 361–362, 367
introspective, 360–362
monologues, 366
observation, 360

Data collection method, (*continued*)
  oral reading, 366
  pictures, 367
  questionnaire/survey 361, 367
  role play, 369
  standardized tests, 361–362, 367
  transcript, 360–362
Data interpretation
  interpretive, 361
  statistical, 361
Database, CHILDES, 551
Dative construction, in English and Hebrew, 621–622
Deaf learners, 33, 34, 40
  acquisition of English, 145, 149
  Determiner, Quantifier categories, 492, 500, 501
  early grammar of English, 491
  failure with relative clauses, 494
  knowledge of antecedent restrictions, 497
  noise problem, 490
  success with English adverbial clauses, 494
  syntactic knowledge, 484–494
Deaf speech
  be as raising verb, 499–500
  be/have verb in, 491
  clause structure, 490
  function words in, 473
  stilted effect, 492
Declarative, 182
Defective Tense Hypothesis, 536, 560
Deism Hypothesis, 62, 64, 66
Delayed L1, 188
Deletion vs. epenthesis of sound segments by Mandarin Chinese learners of English, 291
Dementia, 511
  Alzheimer's, 519
  and code mixing, 672
Determiner acquisition, two different paths by Chinese and Spanish children, 167
Determiner Phrase, 110, 487–488, 492–494, 501
Determiner Phrase Analysis, 487, 492
Determiner system, 489,500
  in children, 489
Developmental stages and Universal Grammar, 89
Developmental problem of language acquisition, 26, 32, 35

Dialect learning, 166
Dialectal studies, 229
Dialectology, 230
Diary
  definition of, 362
Diglossia
  definitions of, 577
  language domains of, 577–580
  revised model, 580
  typology of, 579
Diglossic societies, language use in, 577–580
Digraphia, 578
Discourse styles, linearization problem of German L2 recall, 296
Discrimination tests, 282
Distinctive feature theory, 297
Distributional Bias Hypothesis
  in adult–adult native speech, 551–555
  in Input vs. the Bioprogram Hypothesis, 561–562
Distributional Bias studies, 550
Do-support, 147, 486, 487, 501
  in English, 102
Dummy verbs, 649–650
Dutch, 95, 174–176, 197, 279, 288
Dutch simplified, 422
Dynamic paradigm, 14

E

Elaboration, as a nonsimplifying process, 415
Emotion, learner's, 351, 362
Empirical observation, 7–8
Empty category, 60, 96, 103, 107
Empty Category Principle, 12, 175–176, 482, 486, 500
English, 7–9, 14, 16, 25, 28, 31–33, 40, 58, 62, 64, 68, 71, 87–89, 95–99, 101–102, 106–115, 124, 129, 133–150, 161, 168–186, 197–198, 202, 204–207, 243–248, 252, 255, 274, 279, 288, 335–336, 350, 424
  as a second language, 101, 112, 135–137, 143–145, 206, 351 546–547, 551
  proficiency, 149
  programs 101, 112
  Chinese learners of, 252, 254, 255
  dative construction, 443
  do-support, 102
  German accented, 276

nonnative speakers, 250
pied-piping, 428
pronominal, 494
question formation, 133, 139
Received Pronunciation, 234, 272
right-branching, 124
variation
    in Afro-American, 232, 239
    in Norwich, 234

English, acquisition of
by deaf learners, 186
discourse, story-telling experiment, 296
morphology, third person singular, 181
phonology
    bimorphemic final clusters by L1 Hun-
        garian speakers, 294
    by adult Thai speakers, 272
    consonant cluster simplification by L1 Ara-
        bic, Chinese speakers, 294, 297
    dental and fricatives, 296
    epenthesis and syllable structure, 329
    final clusters by Chinese, Japanese, Korean
        adult learners, 291, 294
    fricatives and affricates acquisition by Ice-
        landic children, 292
    /l/-/r/ contrast by adult Japanese subjects,
        275–279
    /r/ by German children, 292
    /r/ by Thai learners, influence of learned
        social meaning, 329
    segments by Japanese adult learners, 292
    sound structure by German-speaking Aus-
        trian subjects, 290
    spoken and written acquisition by deaf
        learners, 472–473, 489
    syllable final consonant, acquisition by L1
        Mandarin Chinese speakers, 294
    syllable-final stop production by Polish,
        Spanish, and Mandarin Chinese adult
        learners, 291
    syllable onset acquisition by L1 Korean
        and Japanese speakers, 295
    word stress, 114
        by adult Polish, Hungarian and Spanish
            learners, 298
syntax
    adverb placement by French learners, 424,
        427, 430
    articles, 256
    by deaf vs. hearing children, 475, 489, 500

    by deaf learner, the Subset Principle, 332
    interrogative structures, Japanese, German,
        Finnish children differential, 323, 330
    modals by Spanish learners, 324
    PRO structures by deaf children, 482–483
    pronominal clitics by L1 German, 297
    reflexive acquisition by Korean speakers,
        333
    relative clauses, Chinese, Japanese, Persian,
        Arabic adult students, 323
    transfer from Italian, 318
Environment, Critical Period, 165
Equivalence judgments, 295
Equivalence Classification Hypothesis, 283
Error Analysis 237
Errors, 8, 61, 148, 196–197, 207- 208, 248,
    417, 432–437
absence of, 133
and developmental factors, 320
and shortcomings of Contrastive Analysis,
    197
by children, 383
by adults, 160
by advanced Brazilian Portuguese learners of
    English, 291
developmental vs. transfer, 291–292
English syllabic structure
    and lack of typological considerations, 293
    by Cantonese Chinese, Portuguese, Korean
        speakers, 293
    by Iraqi, Egyptian Arabic speakers, 293–
        295
    by Turkish, Greek, and Japanese speakers,
        293
grammatical
    by immersion students, 423
in L2 acquisition, 196–197
    of English, 352
    markedness and NL–TL differences, 200–
        202, 207–208
in L2 and L1, 199
negative evidence for, 430–437
random by adult, 168
single vs. multiple, 440
structure-independent, 132
type, nonnative, 439–440
Ethical consideration, 1
Evidence
external vs. internal in phonology acquisition,
    299

Evidence (*continued*)
  for grammar rules, 428, 431
  positive, in foreigner talk discourse, 414, 424
Experimental methods
  and logic of inferential statistics, 362
  atomistic nature, 359
Experimental phonology, 288
Experimental studies, 134
  conceptual and methodological flaws, 106
  experimenter bias, 107
  linguistic bias, 107
  test instruments, 106, 107
Experimental task, 256
  assumptions of, 130–131
  Cloze test, 338
  comprehension, 136
  debates, 131
  dialogue reading, 296
  elicitation, 480
  elicited imitation, 131, 136, 143, 144–146
  film recall, 296
  free speaking, 296
  free speech, 296
  grammaticality judgments, 172, 177–178,
    331, 338
  L2-L1 pairing, 289
  lexical decision, 220
  limitations of, 130
  minimal pair reading, 296
  multiple choice comprehension, 178, 186–187
  oral, 177
  picture identification, 186–187, 479
  semantic perception, 172
  specific parameter evaluation, 130
  spontaneous speech, 131
  transcription, 273
  word fragment completion, 220
  word identification, 220
  word list reading, 296
  written, 177
Expert systems, 222
Explanandum phenomenon, 51
Explanans phenomenon, 51
Explanation
  by laws, 11
  contrastive vs. noncontrastive, 68, 73
  in natural phonology, influence of L1 on L2
    speech acquisition, 299
  innate and functional, 195

nature of, 5–6, 11
theoretical, 7–12
Explanatory goals, 50

F

Factor analysis, 296
Falsifiability problem, 56
Farsi, 161, 201
Feedback
  corrective, 25, 31
    and negative children performance, 434–
      437
    in classroom setting, 438–439, 454
    in learning French morphological general-
      izations, 443
    to English as a second language learners,
      438
    to francophone adolescents in Quebec, 438
  indirect metalinguistic, 444
Final stop devoicing
  deletion in children and adult learning, 327
  devoicing in children and adult learning, 327
Final epistemic authority, 380
Finite
  embedded clauses, 142
  that complements, 142
Finnish, 203, 204, 207
Fluency, psychological mechanism, 218
Foreign accent, 5, 61, 278
Foreign language learning, Piagetian stages of
  development, 609
Foreign syllable, 280
Foreigner talk, 25, 55, 415, 549, 554
  by children to nonnative peers, 416
  complexity, 417
  discourse, 418–421
    high frequency of native speaker questions,
      420
    interactional modification, 419
    meaning negotiation processes, 418
    topic saliency strategies, 420–421
  elaboration processes, 415
  grammaticality, 416
  in Austrian factories, 416
  in Dutch government office, 416
  in Dutch L2 elementary books, 416
  in meaning negotiation, 418

in US department stores, 416
Interlanguage, 417
linguistic input to nonnative speakers, 418
negative placement in, 415
observational studies, 417
omission processes, 415
on German streets, 416
phonetic and phonological correlates, 416–417
nonsimplifying processes, 415
selection of frequent words, 417
ungrammaticality, 417–418
universal formal and discourse features, 421

Formal Operating Principle, 132
Formality, effects of, 357
Formulaic expressions, 13, 30, 424
Formulas, 217
Fossilization
in L2 learning, 355
interlanguage grammars, 112, 115, 387
problem of external validity, 356
France, 105
French, 9, 25, 71, 87–89, 93, 96, 101–102,
    106–111, 172–173, 279, 296, 389, 424
auxiliaries, 197
causative construction, 172
clitic pronoun, 172
Immersion Program, its failure, 447
in Canada, 576
unaccusatives, 108

French–English fluency test, 587
Frequency, 352
acceptability, 384
role in speech acquisition (L2), 292

Functional–typological approach, 2,3, 13, 39
Fudge lects, 256
Fulani, 11
Full Access Hypothesis, 27, 37, 129, 130, 134,
    140
Functional
analysis, 51
specificity in vision and language, 164

Functional categories, 40, 110–111, 387, 485,
    492–493, 500
adult acquisition of, 145–149
child acquisition of, 145, 149, 489
in L1 and L2, 111, 115

Fundamental Difference Hypothesis, 65, 132

G

Garden Path Technique, 440–443
Gender, 39, 247
Generative framework, 2, 11, 36–37, 121
Generative grammarians, 196
Genie, the isolated child, 165
Genitive, 203
Geometric mean, 401
German, 17, 96–97, 110–111, 161–162, 296–
    298
child vs. adult L2 acquisition of, 168
verb inflection acquisition, 168
verb negation acquisition, 168
verb placement acquisition, 168
word order acquisition by Romance speakers,
    114
vs. Australian phonological differences, 274

Gestalt approach, 328
Governing Category Parameter, 30, 98, 115,
    174–178, 186–188, 331–333, 495–499
English acquisition by Japanese learners, 332
value for hearing and deaf learners, 497, 501

Government and Binding theory, 85–86, 110
Grammar
adult, 110
complex initial stage, 57
deficit, 147
early child, 110
in transition, 334
interaction with cognitive and pragmatic sys-
    tem, 377
interlanguage, 53
internal sequence, 68
L1 and problem solving, 93
language specific, 57
models of, 376
monolingualism vs. bilingualism approach, 571
native and nonnative, 385
natural, 111
older child, 110
range of, first vs. second language, 92
restructuring, 253
unnatural, 96, 111
vs. language, 126
wild, 61

Grammatical knowledge; see Competence,
    grammatical

Grammatical
  functions, 10
  knowledge, end-state, 437
  structures, 219
  theory 6,7, 21, 27
    and natural sciences, 7, 11
Grammaticality judgments,
  need for quantitative models, 391
  variability, 391, 403
Guarani, 578
Guyanese Creole continuum, 242–243
  acrolect, 243
  basilect , 243
  mesolect, 243
  S-curve, 243

H

Habit structure, 5
Handedness dominance, French–English bilinguals, 514
Hausa, 168
Head of phrase, 485, 487
Head Direction Parameter, 37, 124–125, 135–
  137, 141–142, 169
  head-complement order, 136
  head-final language, 141
  head-final value, 136
  head-initial language, 141
Head Movement Constraint, 133
Head Position Parameter, 62- 63
Hearing impairment 25
Hearing loss
  and input, 470–471
  and speech frequencies, 470
Hebrew, 12, 578
Hierarchy
  adjacent segment, 114
  implicational, 11, 33
  internal structure of past tense, 557
  internal structure of progressive aspect, 558
  noun phrase, 498
  of difficulties
    English fricatives and affricates acquisition
      by Icelandic children, 292
    Germans learning English voicing, 294
    nasal vs. oral segments, 294
Historical residues as a periphery of language,
  382

History of second language acquisition, 2, 6–18
Hmong, 245
Human capacity, 1, 3, 18
  for language acquisition, 123
Hypothesis
  Critical Period or Sensitive Period, 510–512
  formation, 132
  functional parameterization, 387
  Primacy of Aspect, 533–538, 559
  strong innate, 431
  testing, 132

I

I-language, 62
Identity and language, 272
Immersion programs vs. nonimmersion foreign
    language program, 423
Immigrant languages, 580–583
Impaired grammar acquisition, 165
Implicans property, 11, 33
Implicatum property, 11, 33
Impossible systems in phonology and syntax, 114
Incomplete grammars, 109
Incompleteness Hypothesis, 37, 170–173
  for phonology, 173
  for syntax, 172
Indefinite pronoun, difficulties of deaf learners,
  492
Indeterminacy
  and language change, 383
  and inconsistency of grammaticality, 390
  due to language attrition, 388
  in near native speakers, 389–390, 404
  in native and nonnative grammars, 385
  in native and near native grammars, 390, 404,
    405
  of norms, 388
Individual variation; *see* Variability types
Indonesian, 28, 138–140, 174–177
Infant/child learner, 128, 132, 133, 134
Infinitives, 142–144
Inflection, 13, 631
  categories, 110
  nonuniform, 113
Inflection-system, 488, 500–501
  lack in child clauses, 489
  presence vs. absence in deaf learners, 491
Inflectional Phrase, 110, 149, 485–491

Informants and inconsistent judgment, 380
Information process, autonomous, 213
Information processing
  approach, 2, 3, 17, 36
  assumptions, 214
  break down, 213
  computer as a metaphor, 213
  mechanism
    intrinsic reasoning, 213
    long-term memory systems, 213
    memory systems, 213
    output system, 213
    pattern recognition, 213
    perceptual systems, 213
    psychological, 213
    short-term memory systems, 213
  reductionist view, 213

Innate language learning mechanism, 54
Innovations
  as a periphery of language, 382

Input, 25, 32–35, 40–41,48, 50, 52, 57, 59, 68,
    73, 85, 86, 101, 112, 148, 339–340, 358–
    359, 383–388, 413–468
  and accessibility to Universal Grammar prin-
    ciples, 171
  and Critical Period, 165, 187
  and influence of interactional adjustments,
    419
  and learners' attention, 426, 452
  and learners' failures, 388
  and parameter trigger, 168–172
  and role of instruction, 388
  and undermining of Interlanguage, 389
  apperceived, 427
  as a modified language, 415, 452–454
  cognitive processing, 426
  comprehensibility, 358, 433
    effect of output, 421, 449
    insufficiency of, 421, 452–454
    negotiation of meaning, 449
  covert, 426
  enhancement techniques, 428
  flood, 102
  L2, processing via cognitive pathways, 273
  L2, processing, 291
  L2, grammatical change, 112, 115
  L2, handling via L1, 273
  lack and bioprogramming, 528
  ordering constraint, 184
  overwhelming disintegration of norms, 388

patterns, 383
poverty, 3, 19, 20, 24, 33
  American Sign Language (ASL), 165
  and deaf learners, 497, 500
  and isolated child, 165
  deaf reading acquisition, 469
  language and vision, 164
probability, 238
processing L2, 63
processing mechanism, 52
prolonged, 423–425,
quality, variety of limitations, 389
restructuring, 217
role in L1 , L2 production, 282
role of Distributional Bias hypothesis, 548-
    551, 560–561
saliency, 68–70, 73
simplified 553; *see* Speech modification
to child language, 159, 162
Universal Grammar trigger, 86, 100
usable, 73
vs. comprehensible input, 414
weight, 258

Input Hypothesis, 16–17
Insecurity, 256
Instructional strategies, 224–225
  communication strategies, 224
  drill practice exercises, 224
  expert system approach, 225
  high order plans, 224
  metacognitive, 225
  production strategies, 224
  restructuring processes, 224
  training in sentence structure, 224
  varied lexical settings, 224
  working memory efficiency, 225

Integrated Model, 16
Interactional modification
  cross-cultural variability, 421
  elaboration, 421–422
  preservation of grammaticality, 422
  relationship with learner capacities and pro-
    duction, 452
  tag question, 421
  topic selection and continuation moves, 419
  ungrammaticality as a comprehension en-
    hancer, 422
  uninverted question, 421

Interactional Hypothesis, 414, 451–454
  revised, 453

Interference
    among Dutch–French bilinguals, 590
    among Japanese–English bilinguals, 590
    among Swedish–English bilinguals, 590
    between native L1, target language L2 , 336
Interlanguage, 61–62, 90, 93–97, 160, 203–
        209, 256–257, 356, 364, 370, 375, 384–
        389, 510
    and Universal Grammar constraints on, 389
    competence, 109, 110
    development
        effects of formal instruction, 437
        prolonged exposure, 423
        role of meaning negotiation in conversa-
            tion, 448–454
        role of vernacular styles, 296
        ultimate attainment question, 389–390
    grammar, 8, 20, 27–29, 35, 38, 94, 109–115,
        384–385, 608, 615
        as test grammars, 386
        early, 30
        indeterminacy in, 386–388, 392
        influence of nonlinguistic factors, 386
        of Mandrin, Japanese, Korean, Spanish,
            and Arabic learners of English, 326
        measurement and need for certainty dimen-
            sion, 396–397
        measurement need for three point scale,
            396–397
        measurement shortcomings of binary scal-
            ing, 396
    naturalistic samples of, 368
    performance, 262
    permeability and variation, 386–387
    phonological processes, F1 and F2 influence,
        329
    premature stabilization, 425
    stabilization, 337
    stages of, 386
    system, 8, 20–29, 35
        sequence of, 32
    theory, 288–289, 296
    types of variability, 357
    units of, 288–289
    Universal Grammar perspective on indetermi-
        nacy in, 387–388
    validity, 385
Interlanguage Hypothesis, 205
Interlanguage-specific units, 289
Interlingual identification, different types of in-
        terference, 287

Interphonologies, 297
Interrogatives, 7, 13, 16
Intervocalic voicing, 299
Intonation
    synthesized, 274
    contours and phonemic contrast in child L1, 173
Intralingual compatibility, 287
Intralingual identification
    and assessment, 288
    distinctive feature theory, 288
    distinctive feature hierarchy, 288
    phonological categories, 288
    units, phonetic vs. phonemic, 289
Introspection, definition, 362
Intuitions
    context/mode of presentation, 377
    correctness of, 380
    determinants of spurious, 377
    difference between Native and Near Non-
        native speakers of French, 389
    difference between native and nonnative
        speakers, 389
    genuine vs. spurious, 377
    indeterminacy of, 382–383
    native and nonnative paradox, 385
    parsing strategies, 377
    process, the psychological laws of, 376
    reliability criteria, 392–393
    vs. judgments, 379
Irish, 575
Irregularization
    inter-generation transmission, 383
Issues
    conceptual, 19, 35
    empirical, 19, 35
    in second language acquisition, 18–35
    methodological, 24, 35
Italian, 17, 108–109 168–170, 180, 319, 335–
        336
    unaccusatives, 108

J

Japanese, 62, 72, 94–99, 114–115, 124, 129,
        135, 140–145, 161, 198, 205, 296, 336, 417
    left-branching, 125, 129
    locative structures, 450
    particles, 417
    two reflexive forms, 332
    vs. English noun phrases, 491

Judgments
  absolute
    rating response, 395
    shortcomings of category scaling, 395–396
  acceptability, magnitude scaling of, 392
  comparative, 395
  grammaticality, 3, 4
    and linguistic training, 376
    in English and French near native grammars of Italian, 390
    in isolation vs. contrast, 377
    indeterminacy of natural language grammars, 381
    indeterminate vs. determinate, 390
    of naive native speakers and trained linguists, 378
    relative vs. absolute, 377
    reliability of, 376
    subjective vs. objective self-awareness, 378
    superficial vs. genuine, 381
    validity of, 376–378
  inconsistency
    notion of intermediate grammaticality, 392
    notion of developing knowledge, 392
    two possibilities, 392
  response, absolute vs. comparative, 395
  scales, four types of, 393–395
  socio-psychological and sensory variables, 400

K

Knowing
  concepts and propositions, 218
Knowledge
  analyzed factor vs. control factor, 218
  declarative, 218
  of L1–L2 phonological processing strategies, 291
  procedural, 218
Korean, 28, 64, 95–99, 114–115, 168–181, 186, 334

L

Language
  acquisition
    by aphasia therapy, 517
    by deaf substitution, 469
    by recasting, 433–434
    of mixed system, stages of, 679

  and vision, 164
  attrition
    in Alzheimer's dementia, 518–519
    among normal bilinguals, 517
    and age, 518
    stages and bilingualism, 623–624
  change, gradual or abrupt, 384
  contact, 3, 5, 206–207
  death 624; *see* Language maintenance and shift
  definition of, 605–606
  development stages and constraints of Universal Grammar, 387–388
  disability case studies, 365
  Indeterminacy Principle, 381–382
  lateral organization of, 511
  learning
    deafness, 469
    implicit, 427
    subliminal, 427
  maintenance and shift, 580–583
  mixing; *see also* Code mixing; Code switching
    and attrition of Dative rules, 622–623
    and language attrition stages, 623–624
    and linguistic conflict resolution, 621
    and markedness of L1 and L2, 618
    and reformulation of L1 rules, 618
    in topic-comment structures, 631, 680
  language pairs
    Arabic–English, 641
    Arabic–French, 652–653
    Dutch–English, 666
    English–Hokkien, 660
    English–Hokkien–Toechew, 660
    Gurindji–English discourse in Australia and New Guinea, 628
    Hindi–English, 629–630, 642, 649, 654, 661, 662, 663, 676, 678, 682
    Hindi–English–Kashmiri, 660
    Japanese–English, 655, 661, 680
    Kikuyu–Swahili–English, 663
    Navajo–English, 655
    Philippine Creole Spanish–Tagalog/English, 655
    Punjabi–English, 643, 655, 666
    Slovenian–German, 661–662, 667
    Spanish–English, 629, 643–645, 652–655, 659, 661, 674
    Spanish–Hebrew, 642
    Swahili–English, 640

Language (*continued*)
  Tamil–English, 655
  Turkish–Dutch, 655
  Warlpiri–English, 655
  loss of L1 constraints, 611
  morphology redundancy reduction, 618–620
  normal vs. attritional, 613
  Redundancy Reduction Principle, 618–623
  stages of language attrition, 624
  Subset Principle, 618, 620
  syntactic redundancy reduction, 618, 620–623
  Uniqueness Principle, 618, 620
  modular conception of, 64, 377
  mutual intelligibility criterion, 575
  neurolinguistic level, 59
  neurological basis, 15
  ontogeny, 286
  other cognitive systems, 59
  processing in bilinguals, 516
  production and processing, 135, 136
  recovery; *see* Language restoration; Aphasia
  restoration in bilingual aphasics
    different patterns, 509, 515–519
    language reversion hypothesis, 518
    alternate antagonism, 517
  role of written modality, 518
  situation
    in Australia, 583
    in Britain, 576, 581–582
    in New Guinea, 581–582
    in pre-Revolutionary Russia, 576
  socialization practices
    in different culture, 436
    of Kaluli of Papua New Guinea, 436
  teaching, 5
  universals
    and primary languages, 204
    functional–typological, 205, 208
    interlanguages, 204
    phonetic, 206
    phonological, 205
    yes–no inversion and *wh*-inversion, 206
  variation, 123–126
  vs. dialect, 574

L1 (First Language)
  acquisition, 195, 208
    benefits of correction, recast and other
      negative feedback, 433, 449
    beyond phonological theory, 269

Critical Period, 166–173
functional categories, 110
operating principles of, 69
parsing theory, 73
Primacy of Aspect, 529–530, 533–537, 539–540
Primacy of Aspect in Chinese, Greek, German, French, Finnish, Hebrew, Italian, Japanese, Polish, Portuguese, Spanish, and Turkish, 534–552
process, role of redundancy, 436
role of highly conventionalized and quasi-instructional speech events, 436
tense before aspect, 535–536, 549
Uniqueness Principle, 432
Western Samoan case, 436
attrition, 425
case studies, 365
influence on L2, 3, 6, 26, 30, 31, 38, 39, 62, 161, 168, 175, 177
  accessibility of Universal Grammar, 331–333
  degree of, 317, 351
  developmental factors, 291–293
  differential and markedness, 292–295
  discourse, 287
  during early stages, 149
  foreign language learning, 285–286
  grammar vs. meaning-based processing, 336
  history of research, 317–318
  interference, 196, 199, 351
  intonation, 274–275
  learning fossilization, 337
  mental lexicon, 399
  Ontogeny Model, 292
  overt structural, 328
  perceived equivalent, 276
  phonetic structures, 273, 285
  phonological-nasalization effects, 299
  resultant behavior, 328
  sociolinguistic determinants of, 295
  sounds and function of tasks, 275
  speech acquisition
    developmental interrelation, 285
    limitations of phonological theories, 297
    syllabification theory, 297
    typological considerations, 293–295
  starting and end points of, 333

stylistic determinants of, 295–296
  translation, 143
language-specific and universal features, 334
learning, role of simplified code, 416
learning, U-shaped performance, 224
lexical influence on L2, stages of, 291
other terms, 574
parameter transfer influence on L2, 298
phonetic influence on L2, 279
phonological-nasalization effects of L2, gen-
    erative rule-typological approach, 299
processing influence on L2, 287
production, open-loop control, 280, 281
prosodic influence on L2, stages of, 291
prosodic influence on L2 domains, 298
role in L2 acquisition, 128, 149, 350
sociolinguistic influence on L2, 287
speech, ear advantage, 273
standard vs. nonstandard influence on L2, 295
structural influence on L2,
    degree of, 291
    new L2 phonic categories, 287–289
    processing strategies, 290–291
stylistic influence on L2, 287
syntactic influence on L2
    stages of, 291
transfer and its resurgence, 320
word stress influence on L2
    stages of, 291

L1 and L2 (First language and Second language)
acquisition
    differences, 1, 122, 126, 129, 132–134,
        168, 172
    parallelism in the emergence of syntax, 446
    role of correction , recasting, 437
    similarities, 127–129, 134, 197, 167, 172,
        320
    suppression of natural processes, 299
    tense-aspect, 530
contrast, 414
core features, 388
distance perception by Czech learner of En-
    glish and Russian, 325
phonological knowledge and L2 processing
    strategies, 291
other language influence, 337
production
    differences, 282
    motor acts, 277
    role of input, 282

speech sounds
  global relation, 270
  phonological universals, 270
L2 (Second language)
  acquisition, 208
    adult learning and neurocognitive flexi-
        bility, 27
    age, 165, 181, 185, 187, 247, 354
      and Critical Period, 511
      and language change, 234–235
      grading, 256
    alternative models of, 130
    analogizing, 130
    and acculturation, 55, 67
    and adult nonlinguistic cognitive ability,
        247
    and affective factors, 229
    and attention, 40
    and attitudes, 66
    and automatic processing, 214
    and code mixing, 41, 627–682
    and cognitive style, 55
    and curriculum development, 359
    and ego-permeability, 55
    and four roles of conversations, 449–450
    and grammar teaching, 100
    and incomprehensible input, 414
    and intelligence, 55
    and markedness, 11, 33, 427
    and maturation factors, 180, 270
    and motivation, 55, 66
    and neuroanatomical and neurophysical
        processes, 512
    and no access hypothesis, 131–133
    and noticing, 40
    and self-image, 55
    and social constraints, 270, 272
    and social concerns, 249, 251
    and sociopolitical factors, 229
    and translation, 143
    and variable rule, 239
    and variational linguistics, 246–249
    and Universal Grammar, 246
    Anderson's ACT* theory, 218
    anxiety, learner's, 355
    Arabic sounds produced by English speak-
        ers, 278
    as complex cognitive skill, 69
    attention or subconscious learning, 427
    bell-shaped model, 160

L2 (Second language) (*continued*)
    branching direction, 96
    by children, 354
    by teenagers, 354
    by the deaf, 111
    capability and cognition deficit, 513; *see*
        Capacity
    capacity, phonetic coding, 273
    child vs. adult, 179–183
    childhood, postchildhood, 511
    choice between Universal Grammar and
        problem solving resources, 388
    complete vs. incomplete, 389–390,404
    continuous competence model, 236
    cyclic process, 370
    data, VARBRUL, 239–240
    data, variationist analysis, 250, 251
    degree of formality, 236
    disagreement on role of attention, 427
    discourse concerns, 249
    domain-specific knowledge, 133
    early stages, 30–32, 135
    effects of instruction, 428–429
    emergence of syntax from conversation,
        445–451
    environment
        classroom, 100, 357
        formal, 349
        mixed, 349, 361
        naturalistic, 349
        nonclassroom, 361
        tutored, 357
    experimental studies and their short-
        comings, 355
    fossilization stage, 99
    fossilized variation by adults, 160
    full access hypothesis, 127, 129–130, 134,
        140
    goals, explanation of success and failure, 355
    impossibility of parameter setting, 387
    individual constraints on, 270
    Information-Processing, 213
    input interpretability, 421
    insufficiency of comprehensible input,
        421–425
    Interactional Hypothesis, 414
    learner's role, 425
    lexical Chinese tone by nontonal speakers,
        277, 284
    lexical tones, left-hemispheric processing,
        273

    logical problem, 128, 162
    methodology, 130–131
        need for native and nonnative judgments,
            392
    Monitor Model, 236
    morphology, 31, 33–34, 38
        by adults, 160, 167
        by child vs. adult, 181
    morphosyntax, 511
    motivation factor, 512
    melodic pattern modeling and right-
        hemispheric processing, 273
    nonlinear process, 370
    nonlinguistic problem-solving strategy of,
        130–131
    nonlinguistic principles of, 130, 133
    of fuzzy categories, 427
    of irregularities, 427
    of multiculturalism, 269
    of power and solidarity of Romance lan-
        guage, 426
    of Primacy of Aspect, 543–555
    of spontaneous conversations, 445
    operating principles, 70
    partial access hypothesis, 133–137
    phonological and syntactic principles, 115
    phonological structure, 180, 290
    phonology, 31, 34, 37, 38, 39, 114, 180, 511
        by adults, 167, 168
        child vs. adult accent, 181
        restructuring of acoustic–phonetic cate-
            gories, 276
        role of new contrast, 276, 279
        tone, 173
    postpuberty, 512
    pragmatics, 39
    prescriptivist models, 236
    Primacy of Aspect, 543–555
    problem solving vs. domain specific learn-
        ing, 334
    processes, 350
    progress, individual constraints, 270
    progress, social constraints, 270
    rate and course, 20, 22, 29
    rate vs. level of proficiency, 511
    register variation,160
    replacement of Universal Grammar by first
        language by adults, 334
    resetting parameters, 333
    role of age, 354
    role of conversation, 445–451

role of Critical Period, 354
role of experience, 134, 354
role of linguistic environment, 413
role of mental effort, 427
role of noticing, 427
role of social distance, 366
role of starting age, 354
semantic load by adults, 160
shift from presyntactic to grammaticized
    speech, 445
shortcomings of the variationist linguistics,
    246
socially sensitive pragmatics, 251
socio and psycholinguistic dimensions, 269
sociolinguistics, 229
Speech Acts, 367
stages and Interlanguage grammars, 384
stylistic continuum, 236
substantive issue, 350–359
syntax by adults, 167
theory of a comprehensive grammar, 249
ultimate level of proficiency, 511
Universal Grammar vs. Functional–
    Typological, 208–209
variable psycholinguistic model, 257–258
variation model, 229, 235, 256
weighing of influencing factors, 250, 262
word-final voice, 200
children learning
    restructuring, 217
    transition from exemplar-based to rule-
        based, 217
    unanalyzed chunk, 217
    unpacking of formulas, 217
children learners, phonemic boundaries of L1,
    274
communicative competence, 366
competence, 67, 74
competence adult, 132
comprehension, 422
difficulties, 199–202
    Markedness Differential Hypothesis, 202
discourse processing 353
domain, 335
English
    articles, 426
    by deaf adults, over time, 483
    by Japanese child during earlier bilingual
        stage, 279
    clausal and nonclausal acquisition by deaf
        adults, 483–483

comparative construction by deaf children,
    481
complementation by deaf children, 474–
    476
conditionals by deaf children, 481
conjunction deletion in conjunctive clauses
    by deaf children, 479
conjunction structures by deaf children,
    478–479
conjunction and pragmatic context in deaf
    children, 479
dative alternation, 426
deletion in relative clauses by deaf chil-
    dren, 480
dental fricative substitution by L1 Japanese
    and Russian speaker, 288
do-support by deaf children, 477–478
elliptical construction by deaf children,
    481
identical sounds by Portuguese-speaking
    Brazilian adult learners, 289
indefinite pronouns by deaf children, 481
infinitive complements by deaf adults,
    483–484
modal verbs by deaf children, 481
new sounds by Portuguese-speaking Bra-
    zilian adult learners, 289
nonlocative preposition by deaf children,
    481
Object–Object deletion by deaf children,
    478–479
Object–Object relative clauses by deaf
    children, 480
passives by deaf children, 475–476
pronominalization by deaf children, 474
prosodic structure by L1 Dutch learners,
    298
quantifiers by deaf children, 481
question formation by deaf children, 477–
    478
reciprocal pronouns by deaf children, 481
relative clauses by deaf children, 479–480
sounds, by Hungarian speakers, 278, 295
Subject–Aux inversion after preposed
    negative adverbial, 427
Subject–Object relative clauses by deaf
    children, 480
Subject–Subject relative clauses by deaf
    children, 479–480
syntactic structures, order of difficulties by
    deaf children, 474–484

L2 (Second language) (*continued*)
    tag question formation by deaf children,
        477–478
    variation, by deaf learners, 473
    verb structures in context by deaf children,
        480–481
    verb structures by deaf children, 474–476
    wh-movement in deaf children, 477–478
    why question by deaf children, 481
    French
      gender-marking, 426
      sounds, by English speakers, 278
    goals, the choice of methodology, 360
    learner capacity,
      analogy, 132
      hypothesis formation, 132
      hypothesis testing, 132
    learners
      accessibility of
        strong version of Universal Grammar,
          330
        Universal Grammar via L1 or other
          structures, 330
        weak version of Universal Grammar, 330
      grammar construction tools, 131, 134
      multilingual vs. monolingual, 337
      nonaccessibility of Universal Grammar, 330
      white-crowned sparrows, 165
    learning
      ability
        inductive, 223
        grammatical sensitivity, 223
        phonetic coding, 223
        rote learning, 223
      assumptions and beliefs, 123, 129
      beyond Universal Grammar, 152
      classroom setting, 431
      context, 608
      exceptional, 447
      focus on form vs. focus on forms, 429
      incidental vs. salient, 428
      individual differences, 222–224, 276
      noticing, 426, 428
      phonetic exaggeration effect, 327–328
      proactive interference, 290
      process of positive retroaction, 388
      restructuring, 217
      role of experience, 219, 222
      role of experience, plasticity in restructur-
        ing, 217

    silent phase, 351
    single, dual or multiple process, 219–222
    social and psychological distancing, 355
    subcomponent model, 222
    subcomponent storage, 223
    U-shaped
      behavior, 355, 364
      performance, 216, 217, 224
    methodology; *see also* Data; Experimental
      task
      classroom-based, 360
      data analysis and new information tech-
        nology, 269
      elicitation and measurement of linguistic
        acceptability, 375, 390–405
      future challenge, 371
      issues, 359–370
      laboratory, 360, 363
      measurement of linguistic acceptability,
        375, 404–405
      mixed, 360, 363
      naturalistic, 360, 363
      problems, 681–682
      process-oriented vs. task-based, 357
      simulated, 360, 363
      some wrong assumptions, 370
      statistical studies, shortcomings 363
    new sound production, relative role of closed
      and open-loop control, 280–281
    Norwegian, syllable directionality parameter
      setting by Mandarin speakers, 298–299
    parameter setting, 388–389
      impossibility, 387
    perception
      by British English and European Portu-
        guese learners, 274
      hemispheric specialization, 273
    performance, *see* Learning; Variability
    processing
      capacity, 414
      role of variation, 229
      strategies, L1- phonological knowledge,
        291
    production
      accuracy and superiority of perception-first
        strategy, 282
      air- and bone-conducted pressure changes,
        279
      auditory, tactile feedback, 279–280
      deviance, 282

internal feedback within brain, 279, 281
regulation, closed-loop, 280–281
role of feedback, preprogramming, 279–281
role of kinaesthesia or proprioception, 279
role of variation, 229
pronunciation
affective constraints, 271
and alcohol, tranquilizing drugs, 270
auditory capacity, 272
biological constraints, 271
by bilinguals, 272
by hypnotized subjects, 272
changing oral capacity with age, 273
comfortably intelligible, 270
contralateral ear advantage, 273
desire for social acceptability, 270
difference and personality constraints, 272
evaluation in Anglo-Saxon world, 271
exceptional intelligibility, 270
for professional purposes, 270
for social distancing, 271
gender constraint, 272
group identity, 271
hypothetical equivalence projection of L1 phonetic categories, 276
ideological constraints, 271
incompleteness, 271
mastery and learners' attitude toward target culture, 271
motivation constraint, 270–271
oral capacity, 272
prestige accent by females, 272
reaction to overperfect, 271
socially motivated factors, 383
sociocultural competence, 369
stereognosis, 273
training programs
articulatory training, 281
articulatory-based vs. auditory-based approach, 282
computer-managed interactive visual feedback, 284
design, 273, 281
imitation models, 273, 281
segmental level, 281
sound
by bilingual child, 278
evolution of phonological theory, 270
learning, best-fit model, 284

nonlinguistic constraints on, 270
perception, 270
production, 270
systematic variability, 296
Vietnamese produced by English speakers, 278
speech
acoustic-phonetic reorganization, 278–279
acoustic-phonetic problem, 277
and impact of natural phonology, 299
conditions for transfer (L1) activation, 291
development factors, 290
domains or levels, 300
learnability, 299
learners' categorization, 277
natural phonology explanation of L1 influence on, 299
nonsegmental issues, 299
product vs. process analysis by learners, 290
role of syllable structure, 289
role of typological constraints, 289, 293
typological factors, 293–295
L2-L1 pairing, English-German, 289
L2-L1 pairing, French-English, 289
L2-L1 pairing, English-French, 289
L2-L1 pairing, English-Dutch, 289
L2-L1 perception, L2-L1 segment pairing, 289
L2-L1 production, L2-L1 segment pairing, 289
Languages
head-final, 62
head-initial, 62
mutual incomprehensibility of, 61
Pro-drop, 62
Latin, its religious domain, 576
Learnability, 339
and Binding principles of deaf learners, 494
and L2 speech, 299
by deaf learners' syntactic knowledge, 494–500
condition, 36, 54–56
parameters, 57, 63
theory, 63
different accounts, 56
negative evidence vs. negative feedback, 440–445
Universal Grammar constraint on, 389
Learner
analysis of input, 56
as an 'input-output' device, 56

Learner (*continued*)
  behavior, 5
  deaf, 3, 5, 40, 98, 100, 204, 469–508
  good vs. bad, 225
  idealized grammar, 63
  innate language acquisition device, 197
  learner-learner interaction, 358
  L2 and Universal Grammar modules, 115
  naturalistic, 273
  novice vs. expert, 222
  perception, 31
  performance, tasks type, 359
  post-, 168
  pre-,168
  prelingually deaf, 473
  procedures and input data, 358
  proficiency level, 94
  reconstruction, 370

Learning
  aptitude, 222
  asymmetries, 387
  automaticity, 214
  bilingual, 454
  communities, two radically different, 254–255
  computational theory, 298
  Connectionist Model, 58–60, 219
  conscious vs. subconscious, 352
  Conservative Thesis, 58
  content-based, 454
  Continuity Requirement, 58
  cross linguistic patterning, 253
  Developmental Principle, 58
  difference between monolingual vs multilin-
      gual, 338
  domain specific vs. problem solving, 334
  holistic, 217
  immersion, 454
  innate, 351
  language, and matching ability between
      grammatical functions and sentence
      structures, 222
  mechanism, 57–58, 65
    accretion, 220
    automaticity, 69, 218–222
    composition, 218
    computational burden, 72
    controlled processing, 214, 219
    cooperative and competitive, 220
    discrimination, 218
    generalization, 218

  hypothesis testing, 69
  inferencing, 69
  intentional and incidental, 221
  modular, 71–73
  naturalistic, 280
  nonmodular, 69–71
  proceduralization, 218
  restructuring, 69, 218, 220, 222, 224
  strengthening, 218
  three different processes, 220
  tuning, 220
  principles, 32, 38, 64, 70, 90, 92
    domain-specific, 133
    language specific, 65, 66
    nonaccessibility of, 72
    nondomain-specific, 135
    production vs. perceptive, 283
  situations, 58
  strategies, 58
    cognitive, 291
    L2, 132
    effects of, 291
  task-based, 454
  theory, disagreements, 220
  vs. acquisition, 352
Learnability and parametric value, 496–497,
    500
Left hemispheric dominance, 166
Lesion, Wernicke's area, 166
Levels of unitary phonological and phonetic
    categories, 288
Lexical
  categories, 110, 485
  item retrieval, 219
  parameterization, 387
  tone, 4, 275
Lexicon 172
Licensed structures, 64
Linguistic
  acceptability, 375
    accommodation, 379
    adaptive rules, 379
    attitudes toward usage, 379
    issues, 376
    source of, 379
    speakers' beliefs about frequent usage, 379
    speakers' beliefs about norms, 379
    uniquely privileged status, 405
    vs. grammaticality, 378–379
  adaptation 413,

change in progress, 235
environment in L1 , L2, some debate, 3, 5,
    414
goals, 6
hypothesis, 7
input, 3, 5, 21
insecurity, 250
intuitions
    cognitive factors, 375
    role of extralinguistic factors, 377
perception, use of magnitude estimation tech-
    niques, 402
performance, 6
variability, difference in grammaticality
    judgments, 380–381
Linguistic Atlas of New England, 235
Linguistic Minorities Project, 586
Linguistics, 269
and psychophysics, 400
Lip reading, 469
Literacy, 429
Loan
shift, 592
translation; see Calque
Loanblend, 591
Local binding, 97, 98, 99
Locality principle, 144
Logan's Instance Theory, 426
Logical problem of language acquisition, 35–
    36, 50–85
its interface with acquisition theory, 67
Long distance movement, 104
Long distance binding, 97, 99
Longitudinal study
Japanese naturalistic learner of English L2,
    424
of speech acquisition (L2), 292
syllabic structure of L2 German by L1 Span-
    ish learners, 293

M

Mandarin tones, 275
Magnitude estimation, 392
experimental techniques, 400–402
Malagasy, 28, 94, 95
Mandarin Chinese, 579
Marathi vs. Konkani, 575

Marked structures,
inter-generation transmission, 383
Markedness, 333, 382–383
as a measure of difficulty, 199–200
as a measure of empirical matter, 201
core vs. periphery of language, 382
degree of, 202, 207
differential influence of, L1, 292
hierarchy of difficulties, 293
    English acquisition by deaf learners, 495–
        497
hypothesis
    acquisition stages, 11, 33, 34
    attrition stages, 33
in phonology, 199
multiple definitions of, 201
perfectivity, 252
relationship between Native language and
    Target language, 387
relative frequency, 198
sequencing, 33–34
Markedness Differential Hypothesis, 37, 195,
    196, 197, 198, 199, 200, 203, 204, 205,
    207, 208 294, 295
as an empirical question, 201
evaluation, 200–202
L2 speech, 294
power, 200, 202
problems, 202–204,
Martha's Vineyard, 235
Maturation, 2, 38, 40, 55, 56, 75; see also Criti-
    cal Period; Puberty
as a base for L2 acquisition, 181
biological perspective, 169
constraints and neurophysical explanation,
    166
constraints on L1 acquisition, 165
effects, 2, 4, 103
L2 acquisition, 270
learning of language specific and universal
    structures, 182
modularity of, 36
of Universal Grammar and biological matura-
    tion, 183
schedule, 57,163, 171, 183
stages, 1, 21
two views, 184
Maturation Hypothesis, 183
Meaning

Meaning (*continued*
  negotiation, 3, 5, 25, 35
  modifications by native speakers, 451–452
  processes, 418, 452
  pushed output, 448
  semantically contingent speech, 452–453
Measurement of response, four scales, 393–395
Memory, 57,122, 219, 280
  dissociations
    multimemory approach, 221
    unitary system processing approach, 221
  explicit, 220
  implicit, 220
  long-term, 213, 223
  neurological evidence, 222
  passive storage buffer, 223
  recall, 221
  search, 215
  semantic knowledge in, 220
  short-term, 213, 222–223
  storage, 608
  systems
    episodic and semantic, 221
    procedural and declarative, 221
    surface and semantic processing, 221
    transfer-appropriate processing principle, 221–222
  working, 222–225
Mental
  representations, 59
  states, 362
  structures 52, 59
Mentalistic approach, 6
Methodological
  effectiveness of negative evidence in L2 learning, 437
  problems, testing, 176
  problems, 74
Methodology; *see also* Data; Data collection method; Experimental task
  analysis
    correlational, 296
    interpretive, 362
    linguistic
      functions, 362
      lexical, 362
      morphosyntactic, 362–363
      suprasegmental, 362
    statistical, 362
      ANOVA, 363

Chi-square, 362–363
    correlation, 362–363
    Cronbach's alpha, 363
    F ratio, 363
    Factorial analysis, 363
    product-moment coefficient, 363
    test, 362–363
    U-test, 362
  approach
    control group and subjects 106–108
    cross-sectional approach and its criticism, 364
    longitudinal vs.cross-sectional approach, 39, 364
    qualitative and quantitative approaches, a continuum, 360
    qualitative vs. quantitative, 39
  determinants of kind and process of norms, 385
  Distributional Bias Hypothesis, 548, 550–551
  for native and nonnative grammars, 385, 405
  four reliability criteria judgments, 392–393
  four types of judgment scales, 393–395
  four conditions for elicitation of acceptability judgments, 391–392
  instruments, 131
  interpretation of results, 131
  interviewing techniques, 231
  issues, 24
    quantitative vs. qualitative research, 359–364
    research, 4, 6, 14–15, 24, 39, 349
  magnitude estimation of linguistic acceptability, 400–403
  obtaining relative judgments
    from ranking test, 399
    from successive categories, 399
  problem of eliciting
    acceptability judgments, 391
    norms in nonnative grammars, 385, 405
    with elicitation devices, 353, 357
  research design, 360–361
  stylistic continuum, 231
  variationist misunderstanding, 250
Metrical phonology
  acquisition of prosodic structure, 298
  universals of, 298
Michigan Test of English Language Proficiency, 482

Mind, 126
learners', 131
Connectionist computer program, 58, 59
Minimal Sonority Distance Parameter, 114
Minimal Sonority Distance Principle, 295
Minimalist Program, 2, 4, 10, 122, 674
Modality and linguistic environment, 39
Modals, 146, 147, 259
Modern Language Aptitude Test (MLAT), Carroll's, 222
Modified speech, 3, 5, 358
Modular framework,
of Universal Grammar, 180
Modularity, 2–5, 36
grammar module, 23, 36
Monitor Hypothesis, 16, 20
criticism of, 17, 23–24
Monitor Model, 16, 255–256
Monolingual societies
learning of foreign languages, 269
Morpheme, 201
third-person singular in L1, 435
Morpheme order
acquisition of, 8–9, 15–16
order studies, 35 1–352, 364, 367
Morphological categories, 172
Morphological Uniformity Principle, 112–113
Morphology, 251
critical period for, 166
L1 acquisition, 435
multiword utterance, 217
Morphosyntactic
rating
post-puberty learners, 182
pre-puberty learners, 182
structures, 352, 362–363
Morphosyntax, 31
Motherese, 25, 54, 56, 415, 549–551, 553
semantic class in, 552
universality of, 54
Motherese Hypothesis, 54
Motivation, 41, 429
instrumental 15–16
integrative 15–16
level, 39
Motives, learner's, 351, 357, 362
Motor 261, 280–281
adjustment, on-line, 281

new motor skill, acquisition, 280
programs, 280
Movement
Constraint on Extraction Domain, 137, 139, 141
constraints and effects, 139
extraction
constraint, in L1 and L2, 169–170
from complex objects, 94
from complex subjects, 94
from embedded clauses, 174
from relative clauses, 202
of finite elements, 111
long-distance, 147, 149
particle, 181
short distance, 147, 149
syntactic, 137–139
syntactic violations, 138
universal constraint, 174
Verb to Inflection, 111
Multilingual societies
future of L2 speech acquisition, 300
Multilingualism; *see* Bilingualism; Bilingual
Multiple Effect Principle, 337

N

Native
and nonnative conversation
in classroom studies, 416
inpushed output, 448
and near nativeness
difference and divergence, 106–110, 390
qualitative and quantitative differences, 106–107, 390, 404
language-target language (NL-TL), difference, 196–200, 203–204
like mastery, 1, 3, 29
speech for nonnative speakers; *see* Foreigner talk
Native Hypothesis, 23
Native language
interference; *see* L1 interference/influence
vs. Target language
differences, 319
markedness relationship, 387
wider conception, 337
Native speaker

Native speaker (*continued*)
  adjustment: *see* Foreigner talk; Interactional
    adjustment
  adjustment and the matching hypothesis, 417
  control group, 178
  correction of nonnative speakers, 425
    degree of adjustment and proficiency of
      nonnative speaker, 417
Natural Order Hypothesis, 16
Negation, 88–89, 101, 146–147, 168, 239
  acquisition of, 13, 16
  complement environment, 240
  development stages, 323
  placement, 87, 89, 102
  preverbal placement by Spanish learner of
    English, 322
  subject environment, 240
  verb environment, 240
Negative evidence, 3, 25, 35, 37, 40, 55, 57, 64,
    65, 86, 99, 100, 101, 162, 338, 339, 383
  adult–child conversation style, 436
  as positive evidence, 434
  cultural appropriateness, 436
  existence of, 430–432
  in L1 learning, 430–437, 441
  in L2 learning, 437–445
    direct vs. indirect, 413–14, 424–425, 428,
      430–445
  in native and nonnative conversations, 444
  necessity of, 435–437
  off record, 442
  overt correction in L2, 444
  problems with its usable existence, 432–433
  solution to overgeneralization and underdeter-
    mination, 430
Negative feedback, 432–445, 449
  effects on adult Spanish learners of English
    (L2), 443–444
  from meaning negotiation, 414, 429–430
  in native-nonnative speakers conversations, 447
  Interlanguage development, 449
Neogrammarian, 229
Neurocognitive flexibility
  and L2 adult learning, 273
Neuropsychology
  and bilingualism, 510
  of language acquisition, 3, 5, 22, 24
New York City, 235
No Access Hypothesis, 37, 131–133

Nominals, 242
Nonlocal binding, 98–99
Nonnative pronunciation
  its acceptability by native speakers, 271
  stereotypes, 271
Nonparametric principles in L1 and L2 acquisi-
    tion, 121
Nonparametric grammatical options. 134
Nontransferability
  phonological, 327
  of ordering subject-verb, 326–327
  of sentence-level phenomenon. 326
Norm, in nonnative grammars 385, 405
Norwegian, 581
Norwegian vs. Swedish, 575
Noun phrase, 174, 202–203
Noun Phrase Accessibility Hierarchy 10–12, 33,
    202–204, 207
  in L2, 424
Noun Phrase Complements, 139–140
Null Subject, 63
Null Subject Parameter, 113

O

Object, Direct, 203
Object, Indirect, 203
Object deletion, obligatory, 248
Object–Object, Subject–Object deletion in deaf
    learners, 493
Observer's paradox, 230–231, 356
Obstruent, 198, 253
  voice-assimilation, 291
One to One Principle, 537, 554
Order
  by learners of unrelated languages, 320
  of acquisition, English as L2, 244
  of segment acquisition and sonority, 293
Ordinal estimation
  constant stimuli, 394
  paired comparison, 394
  successive categories, 394
Organization of language in bilinguals, 510
Overcompensation, 285
  phonetic, 327–328
  semantics, 328
  syntax, 328
Overgeneralization, 31–32, 71, 417
  in L2, 387

Overproduction, 323
Overt correction, 413

P

Parameter, for individual parameters; *see* listing
  for particular parameter
  associated with principle, 123
  binary, 62, 333
  child's knowledge, 87
  interaction, 97
  metrical, 114
  mixed value, 339
  multivalued, 333, 339
  operation 96, 104
  phonological, 114
  relative weight of, 56
  structural variation among languages, 123,
    125–126
Parameter setting, 9, 30, 62, 87, 96–99, 110,
  332, 339, 495, 497
  as a starting point, 334
  asymmetrical, 333
  clustering properties, 334
  default, 170
  domino effect, 334
  in L1, 101, 114
  in L1 and non-L1, 135–136, 142
  in phonological acquisition, 299
  incompatibility between native and nonnative,
    387–388
  language specific instantiations, 129
  metrical, 298
  model, 123, 126, 134, 150
  neither L1 nor L2, 334
  new, 134, 141
  operation, some current issues, 103
  resetting, 63, 89–90, 96–100
    by adult L2 learners, 178
    by children, 168, 185
    by children L2 learners, 102
    in adults, 298
    subset–superset relationship, 103
  role of neuron, 164
  trigger, 89–90, 100, 102
  Universal Grammar Principles, 169, 185
Parameter value, 133–134, 150 332
  clustering of properties, 333
  mismatch or noninstantiation, 134
  new, 135–136, 150

Parametric difference, English and French, 88
Partial Access Hypothesis, 27, 37, 130, 133–
  134, 137–138
  evidence against 134–138
Past tense
  marking
    age, 262
    ethnicity, 262
    in Chinese learners of English, 252–253,
      258, 260, 262
    influencing factors, 259, 262
    learners' proficiency, 252, 254, 258- 262
    perfectivity influence on, 252, 259–260
    preceding segment influence on, 253, 260
    verb type, 262
  morpheme, 232–233
  probability of its occurrence, 259
Perception, 39, 122
  and production
    asymmetries, socio-psychological causa-
      tion, 284
    knowledge, innateness, 282
    knowledge, developmental interrelation,
      281–285
    mechanisms, autonomy vs. dependence of
      282
  categories, new construction of, 273–277
  short vs. long vowels by Austrian students of
    German, 274
  target, 281
  vs. production, 328
Perfectivity
  as a protocategory, 556
  markedness, 252
  vs. imperfective contrast, 31
Performance, 54
  in phonology, 34, 38
  in second language, 23–24, 31
  slip 34
  U-shaped behavior 34
  variation, 216, 260–261
Periphery of language
  borrowings, 382
  historical residues, 382
  influence of
    nonlinguistic cognitive factors, 384
    Universal Grammar factors, 384
  innovations, 382
Persian; *see* Farsi

Personality, 27, 39
    and acceptability judgments, 397–398
Philippines, 15
Phoneme, shortcomings, 278
Phonetic distance as predictor of target language
    accuracy, 289
Phonetic–phonology interface, 288
Phonological
    categories, 297
    change and speech acquisition (L2), 292
    effects of developments on, 327
    processes, Swedish learners of Polish, 291
    strategies, syllable simplification, 291
    theory, 287
Phonology, 206, 251
    Critical Period, 166
    lexical, 297
    natural, 297
    nonlinear, 297
Physical sciences, 217
Piagetian formal operations, 18
Pidgin and Creoles, 242, 263, 415
    as minimal L2, 527
Pidginization, 3, 5, 34
    hypothesis in L2 learning, 355
    sequencing, 34
Plural marking, 255
    and retardation, 255
    animacy influence on, 254
    effects of sentence function on, 255
    in Chinese, Czech and Slovak learners of En-
        glish, 254–255
Plurals, 181, 201
Politeness, 251
Polyglossia, 578–579
Portuguese, 295
    Brazilian, 262
Positive evidence, 3, 25, 32–37, 55, 71 86, 99–
        102, 338, 339, 383
    in L2, 413–414, 427, 430, 439, 443
Possible grammars, 123
Postmaturation usage, 383
Postposed sentence structures, 136, 140
Postpuberty, 26, 35, 40
Postvocalic r, omission by Austrian students of
        German, 274
Poverty of stimulus, 52, 56
Power law, 401

Practice
    in L2 acquisition, 216
    role of, 216
Pragmatics, 251
Predictions, influence of L1, 5–6, 31
Preposed sentence structures, 136, 140
Preposition
    difficulties of deaf learners, 493
    Object of, 203
    stranding, two types of, 176
    stranding in English, 428
Primacy of Aspect
    in Alzheimer's patients 547–548
Primacy of Aspect Hypothesis, 41, 543–555
    counter evidence, 537–548
    Distributional Bias Hypothesis, 548–555,
        559–560
    methodological problems, 541–543
Primacy of Aspect Parameter
    a Prototype account, 555–560
Priming effect, 220–221
Principle
    violation, in early grammars, 184
Principle A of the Binding Theory, 186, 495
Principle B of the Binding Theory, 497
Principles; see listing for particular principle
Principles and parameters
    and innateness in L1, 85, 89, 114
    and language development, 383
    framework, 2–39, 161
    in adult L2, 174–179
    model of L2 acquisition, 123
    of subsystems of a language, 382
    setting, 121
Priority learning, 216
PRO, 96, 103 144
PRO structures, 482–483
Probability, 23
    of deletion, 238–239
Problem, 217, 447
    developmental 35
    logical 35
    solving 217, 447
    solving capacity 18
Procedural knowledge, 53
Processing
    and accessibility of Universal Grammar,
        331

cues, 335
  Italian vs. English speakers, 335
  parallel, 215
  syntactic vs. semantic cues, 335
Pro-drop languages, 417
Pro-drop Parameter, 62–64, 333
  setting by Romance speakers of L2 German,
    333
Production, 20, 23, 38–39
  accuracy, acoustic studies, 280–281
  accuracy, electromyographic studies, 280–
    281
  accuracy, perceptual studies, 281
  and ordering of cognitive and motor events,
    285
  feedback adjustment, 285
  lead, for Japanese learners of English /r/-/l/
    contrast 283, 284
  model, 20, 280–281
  sequence, 68
  tests, 282
  theory, 73
Proficiency
  level
    acceptability judgments, 386, 397
    native, 172–173
    meaning negotiation, 448
Projection
  functional, 110
  inflection, 111
  phrasal, 110
Projection Principle, 184
Pronominal subjects, 113
Pronouns
  personal and Binding Principle B, 497
  reflexive and Binding Principle A, 495
  resumptive, 204
Pronunciation training, 273, 281, 284
Property theory 51–52, 56, 66–67, 71–74
  interphase, 71
Prosodic
  domains for postlexical rules, 298
  system, 173
Proto-theta criterion, 184
Pseudo-recasting, 440
Psychology, 269
  learner's, 325
Psychophysics, 392

Puberty, 165, 181, 185, 354
Punjabi, 78

Q

Quantifier, 488
  difficulties of deaf learners, 492
  Phrase, 492–493
  position, 87
Question formation, 87, 339

R

r-deletion in New York City, 231
Reading by German and English
  by monolinguals and bilinguals, 280
Real world knowledge 57–58
Reasoning, 57
  processing, 362
Recall
  impaired, 221
  recognition, 221
Recasting
  beneficial and nonbeneficial aspects, 441–
    443
  children productive use of, 434
  four properties, 434–435
  of correct grammatical morpheme, 439
  role of semantics in, 434, 441
  usability, by adult English learners of Japa-
    nese as a second language, 442
Recoverability Principle, 291, 297
Redundant system
  context dependent, 624
  context independent, 624
Redundancy and elaboration, 422
Reflexives, 87, 97–99, 178, 201–207, 333
  and Binding Principle A, 495–497
  external, 186
  long, 186
  short, 186
Regression, 398
  analysis, 296
Regularization
  as a nonsimplifying processes, 415
  in inter-generation transmission, 383

Relations
  difference, 394
  equivalence, 394
Relative Clause Parameter in deaf adults, 498–
  499
Relative clauses, 11, 33, 124, 137–140, 145–
  147, 201, 207, 339, 424, 493–494, 500
  and learnability by deaf learners, 497–498,
    500
  and Noun Phrase Accessibility Hierarchy, 202
  in the world's languages, 202
  in Farsi, 161
Relative Defective Tense Hypothesis, 536–537
Relativization process, 203
Relevance Principle, 536–537, 554–555
Repair strategies, 418, 447
  in language mixing, 662, 666–682
  prosodic, nonverbal and verbal cues, 429–
    430
Repetition, 216
  topic continuation, 435
Resolvability Principle, 206
Restructuring, and plasticity, 217
Right Roof Constraint, 205
Romance philology, 75
Rule
  categorical, 232–233, 249
  optional, 233
  quantitative information, 233
  reversing, 61
  spread over time, 241
  systematicity in variable, 249–250
  unnatural or wild, 388
  variability, 232–233, 238, 249
  variability factors, 239–240
Russian, 97–99

S

S/S' Parameter; see Bounding Node Parameter
S-structure, 169, 174
Salience, morphophonological, 259
Sandhi processes, 417
Sanskrit, 578
Scale
  category, 393–395
  different and their admissible operations, 395
  interval, 393–395
  isomorphic and nonisomorphic, 395
  nonmetric continuum, 394
  ordinal, 393–395
  ranking vs. nonrating scale, 399
  ratio, four relations, 393–395
Schools, 365, 370
Schumann's Model and its three shortcomings,
  355; see also Acculturation, model
Segmental contrast, 173
Self-assessment, 250
Self-monitoring, 24, 352
Self-repetition, role of semantics in, 419
Semantics, 251
  categories, 13
  concepts, 72
Semantic Congruence Principle, 658–659
semilingualism, 595
Semimotor properties of speech, 289
Sensitive period; see Critical period
Sentence function
  adverbial, 255
  complement of be, 255
  object of preposition, 255
  object, 255
  subject, 255
Sentential subject, 175
Sign language
  acquisition, 470
  as a visual-gestural language, 470
  issues in, 470–471
  vs. spoken language, 470–471
Simplification
  adjustment for nonnative speakers, 421
  by elaboration, 422
Simplified codes, 415
Situational shifting, 631
Slovak, 31, 254–255
Social
  acceptance, 39
  class, 429
    and variable rules, 232–233, 237
  cost of mispronunciation, 284
Sound change, 229
SOV word order, 335
Spanish, 17, 64, 98–99, 112–113, 137, 142–
  144, 161, 168, 203–207, 239, 288, 298,
  320, 333, 350, 367, 578
  immersion program, Culver City, 423
  infinitival complement, 161
  infinitives, 143

Speakers' beliefs
  adaptive rules, 379
  and periphery of language, 384
Specifier [Spec], 248, 485–493, 497–499
  of CP, 145–147, 149
Speech
  act acquisition in L2, 367
  developmental processes, 291
  disability and cell migration, 513
  events, instructional, 436
  intelligibility, 402
  language pathology and bilingualism, 517
  language therapy
    language recovery patterns among bilin-
      guals, 517
    practices for bilingual patients, 517
  rate, 402
  synthesized, 402
Speech Learning Model, 289
Speech Production Model, Levelt's, 219
Spirantization of stop consonants, 299
Spoken language, 470
Standardized Michigan Test
  Spanish and Arabic group performance,
    324
Standardized Placement Test, 143, 362
Statistical
  analyses, 222, 238–240, 251
  analysis, VARBRUL, 234, 236, 237, 252–
    257, 261
  index in early variation studies, 234
  procedures, 363
  regresional analysis, 239
  studies, 31
  techniques, 37
Status, 247
  variation, 261
Stimulus-response pairing, 290
Stop-voicing contrast in Arabic by Saudi Arabi-
    ans and Americans, 283
Story
  dictation, 216
  reading, 216
  telling, 216
Strong Theism Hypothesis, 27, 36
Structural Conformity Hypothesis, 28, 195, 204,
    208–209, 295
  evaluation, 207–208
  in phonology, 206

recent Universal Grammar proposals, 208–209
  supporting evidence, 205–207
  underlying assumptions, 205
Structural phonology, 278,
  inadequacy of, 300
Structural order
  in L1 and L2 acquisition, 167
Structuralism, 196
  vs. Generativism, 196–197
Style shifting, weight of influencing factors,
    261–262
Stylistic
  continuum, 236, 255–256
  variation, 261
Subcategorization restrictions, 172
Subjacency, 37, 62–64, 137, 331
  constraint in English by Chinese, Dutch, In-
    donesian, and Koreans, 330–331
Subjacency Principle, 95–96, 103–104, 107,
    169–177, 184, 188
  violation, 103, 104, 175, 176, 177, 182, 331
Subject, 203
  Verb Agreement, 487, 501
  Verb Inversion, 88, 486, 487, 488, 490, 491,
    501
Subjective judgments, assessment of their cor-
    rectness, 400
Subset Principle 32, 71–72, 89, 99–100, 331–
    332, 387, 425, 495–501
Substitution
  as a process, 290
  as a solution, 290
  as a strategy, 290
  differential problem, 298
  of L2 English-L1 Polish phone, 297
  of L2 German-L1 Swedish phone, 290, 294
Subsystems of a language, dialects, 382
Success matrix, 56
Super motoring, 355
Superior learning
  and attention saliency, 428
  and comparison of incidental vs. salient learn-
    ing, 428–429
Suprasegmental, 362
Swahili, 578
Swedish, 201–207
  vowel acquisition by non-Swedish children,
    293

Syllable, 70
  centrality to interlingual unit identification, 288
  codas, acquisition of, 293
  nuclei, acquisition of, 293
  onset, 114,
    acquisition of, 293
  similarity, 402
  synthesized, perception by Cantonese Chinese
    subjects, 275
Syntax, 251
  critical period, 166
System
  episodic and semantic, 221
  procedural and declarative, 221

T

t/d deletion in Detroit African-American En-
    glish, 232–234
Target language, 128, 171, 218, 245, 333–340
  accuracy, determinants of 289
  distancing between L1 and L2, 350, 364
  grammar, 56
  segments over time in L2, 292
Task
  closed, 358–359
  complex and hierarchical structure, 215
  impersonal, 358
  judgment, 107
  naming and cortical stimulation, 515
  open, 358–359
  oral picture, 442
  production, 107
  repetition in bilinguals, 516
  simple, 215
  transactional, 358
  types and discourse pattern, 358
Teacher talk, 55
Teaching of English as a Second Language
    (ESL), 471, 497
Telegraphese, 415
Tense, 145, 178
  agreement difficulties of deaf learners, 491
  and aspect, 28, 41
  distinction, 528–533, 539
    in creolization, 252
    in L1 and L2 acquisition, 252
  perfect vs. imperfect distinction, 528, 533- 540
    by Serbo-Croatian children, 536

  morphology, 252
    as a Prototype category, 555–559
  morphophonetic reflexes of, 122, 146
  past, 181
Test of Syntactic Ability, 474–480
  revised, 482
Tests, listening and reading comprehension, 423
Tex–Mex, 599
Theism Hypothesis, 61, 64
Thematic categories, 40, 485, 492, 493, 500
  in deaf learner's early grammar, 489, 492,
    500, 501
Theoretical approach, 2–8
  acculturation, 67
  affective variables, 67
  discourse/functional, 67
  functional-typological, 10–13, 37, 39
  general nativism, 60
  information-processing, 12–14, 17, 23, 30–
    36
  neuropsychological, 14, 35, 40
  principles and parameters, 8–10, 37–39
  social psychological, 14
  variationist, 14, 38, 67
Theory
  neuroimmunoendocrinological, 513
  of grammars (adults), 6
  pruning, 255
Theta Principle, 184
Time
  exposure to L2, 185
  on task, 216
Tok Pisin, 581–582
Topic-comment, 245, 553
Topicalization, 145–147, 169
Transfer, 63, 66, 168, 207, 255
  and avoidance, 321
  and bilingualism, 624
  and clustering of properties 338–339
  and differential effects of socially prestigious
    forms, 321
  and interchangability of terms, 318
  and learnability, 338–339
  and markedness, 287
  and overgeneralization, 321
  appropriate processing principle and memory,
    221–222
  any known language influence, 318
  as a strategic solution, by L2 learners, 290

as an acquisition constraint, 324
behavioristic view, 318
by L1 Austrian German-L2 English, 291
by L1 German-L2 English, 291
by preadult learners, 278
definitions of, 318
delayed restructuring, 321
developmental processes, interaction, 321
different paths, 321
direct reflexes, 318
discourse phenomenon, 326
imperfect knowledge or learner's hypothesis,
    319
intonation, 274, 291
    by L1 French-L2 English, 291
    by L1 Portuguese-L2 English, 291
    by L1 Swabian German-L2 English, 291,
        295
L1, 145, 318, 440
levels of representation of, 338–339
mentalistic vs. behavioristic studies of, 290
narrow and wider views of, 318–321
negative, 350
norms, 295
Ontogeny Model, 292
operational mode constraints, 290
parameter, 298
phonetic and phonological, 273–274, 278,
    287
phonological, 297
positive, 350
positive or negative, 274, 281, 290
pragmatic word order, 326
predictions of, 324–329
prior linguistic information, 318
pronominal copies into relative clauses, 326
scope of, 321
stages of linguistic, 291
three categories of, 253
topic-prominence, 326
typological organization of, 321
Universal Grammar, 274–275, 329–330
unmarked syntactic
    by Dutch learners of German, 325–326
variability, 321

Transferability
    degree of markedness of L1 structure, 325
    determinants of, 325
    L1 information, 318
    L1–L2 distinction, 325

nominal compounds by Dutch learning Ger-
    man and English, 326
phonological 327
Transition theory, 51, 56, 74

U

Ultimate L2 attainment, 429
Uniqueness Principle, 32, 71–72, 89, 432, 537
United States, 15, 103–104
Universal Grammar, 2–28, 32–37, 52–56, 60–
    65, 121, 130–135, 142, 338–339, 400, 490
    access, 90, 92, 95, 98, 112, 113, 387, 547
        continuous access, to L2 learners, 129
        full access, to adult L2 learners, 247
        to L2, 129–134, 140, 145, 150
            to child, 183
                to L2 learners, 164–171, 176, 183
                via L1, 94, 115
        no access, 92–97, 113–115, 167, 176–177
            to L2 learners, 129, 131–133, 152
        partial access
            deviate version of, 149–150
            to L2 learners, 129, 133–138, 145, 150
    adequacy
        for L1 learning, 187
        for L2 learning, 162, 187
    aims, 85–86
    and acceptability hierarchies, 383
    and Complementizer deletion variable data,
        248
    and comprehensibility among natural lan-
        guages, 62
    and external argument proto-principles, 184
    and language mixing, 609, 615, 618
    and maturation effects, 103–104
    and negative feedback, 437
    and nervous system, 164
    and other approaches to L2 acquisition, 122
    and recasting, 437
    and social factors, 247
    approach to L2 acquisition, 123
    as an initial stage, 171
    beyond, 249
    biological basis of, 163
    cognitive basis of, 532
    constraints, 29, 37, 90, 93, 94, 95
        on divergent grammars, 109
        on Interlanguages, 204

Universal Grammar, (*continued*)
  on L2 acquisition, 151
    reduced access to, 388
  core, 404
  domains, 114–115
  dominance, 66
  filter-like principles, 184
  for all, 162
  for primary languages, 204
  form and content, 10
  formal properties of, 106
  in adulthood, 64
  in L1 acquisition, 187
  in L1 and L2 acquisition, 209
  in L2 acquisition, 85, 114, 115, 162, 187
  in L2 and age, 112
  initial state, 125, 150
  language-specific instantiation, 133, 171
  marked relations stated in, 197
  modular theories of, 247
  parameter setting
    for L1, 247
    role of neurons, 164
    shortcomings, 248
  parameters of, 86, 89, 115
  principles and parameters, 247
  scope of, 8
  theoretical approaches for L2, 163
  underspecified periphery of, 404
  universality of, 62
  violation of, 56, 61, 90, 108
  vs. variable rules, 257
Universals, repertoire, 293
Unmarked structures, inter-generation transmission, 383
Urdu, 578
Utterance
  planning and execution, 223

V

Variability
  among L2 learners, 356
  among native speakers, 389
  among near native speakers, 389
  and domain of competence, 257
  and shifting, 245
  contextual, 357
  copula *be*, 357
    due to Universal Grammar nonspecification, 387
  free, 357
  individual,357
  internal consistency of, 250
  L2 learning,
    data collection factors, 356
    developmental stages of learners, 356
    random vs. system, 356
    role of linguistic variable, 356
    sociolinguistic factors, 356
    speech styles, 356
    speech event factor, 356
  learners, 356
  linguistic context, 357
  maximal, factors of, 384
  performance, 357
  periphery of language, 383
  range of forms, 23
  situational context , 357
  social motivations in preserving linguistic, 256
  speech production, 14, 20, 31, 36, 38
  types of, 357
  vs. systematicity, 250
Variable
  input, 435
  L1 or universal categories influence on, 254
  linguistic, 235
    and probablistic weightings of influences, 252
    and relationship to competence and performance, 261
    and stereotypes, 262
  output, 233
  performance among deaf learners, 484
  rule, 232, 244
  analysis, 256
    and alternative grammars, 261
    and psychological reality, 242, 261
  vs. nonvariable systems, 242
Variance analysis; *see also* Methodology
  multifactored analysis, 147
Variation, *see also;* Variability
  and age grading, 234
  and language change, 256
  and linguistic context, 230
  and social identity, 230
  and stylistic level, 230
  approaches, 2–5, 14, 33, 37, 230, 245
    dynamic paradigm, 14

misrepresentation of, 257
nonparametric, 137
others, 14, 17
parametric, 62
quantitative, 14
typology, 10
cognitive location, 229
dynamic model, 230, 240–245
fossilized, 34
historical, 229–230
intrasubject, 388
Labovian model, 230–240
longevity of, 258
nonrandom and its determinants, 230
parameter resetting, 167–168
psycholinguistic model, 259–262
quantitative studies, 230
random error, 168
sites of, 387
synchronic, 240
techniques, 38
finer discrimination, 255
theory, 73
wave theory, 241
Variationist linguistics, 250
Verb, 168
control, 142, 143, 144
ellipsis, 251
irregular, 59, 71, 72
morphology, 40
past tense, 58–59, 69, 72
Relevance Principle, 536, 537, 554, 555
third person singular present English marking, 255
movement, 110
and finiteness, 110
Movement Parameter, 90, 96, 101, 102
object control, 144
raising 63, 87–89, 101, 102
semantic classification in creole languages,
557
stative, 31
subject control, 144
Vietnam, 296
Visual
cortex and functional specificity of neurons,
164
search, 215
Vocabulary, 59

Voice onset time
by Italian learner of English, 327–328
closure duration, 283
continuum, 328
crosslinguistic perception, 274, 279
crosslinguistic production, 274
for stops, 289
in bilinguals, 279
production in English, 283
second formant frequency in English and
French, 283
Voicing
acquisition by L2 French learners of German,
287
shared perception, production mechanisms,
282
Vowel, 198, 253, 260
formant values, 289
raising, 232
roughness, 402
synthesized and mapping L1 categories on,
274
/w/ , /r/ distinction by Japanese learners of
American English, 274

W

Weak syllable, 259
Weak Theism Hypothesis, 27
Weights, influencing factors, 252–254
Wh-in situ, 137, 331
Wh-inversion and wh-fronting, 205
Wh-island, 139
violations, 140
Wh-movement, 28, 62, 64, 94–96, 104, 107,
109, 111, 137–139, 169, 174–177, 248,
330, 331, 491, 498, 499, 500
an alternative approach, 177
in L2 acquisition, 140
Wh-question, 95, 103–104 137–139, 145–149,
182, 204–205
and auxiliary movement, 248
by deaf adults, 498–499
in embedded clauses, 248
repair and decomposition, 421
Wh-trace, 96
Window of Opportunity Hypothesis,133, 184–
187

Within-Hemisphere Hypothesis, 511
Word order, 13, 335–336
   L2, 111
   SAV, 102
   SVAO, 101, 102

X

X-bar syntax, 651

Y

Yes–no question, 501
Yiddish, 578

Z

Zulu click sound, perception by English adults
   and infants, 275

ISBN 0-12-589042-7

9 780125 890427